Twentieth Century Music

TWENTIETH CENTURY MUSIC

by Richard Burbank

Introduction by Nicolas Slonimsky

THAMES AND HUDSON

TWENTIETH CENTURY MUSIC

First published in Great Britain in 1984
by Thames and Hudson Ltd, London

Printed in the United States of America

Contents

Author's Preface ix

Introduction by Nicolas Slonimsky xi

1900-1909 1

1910-1919 46

1920-1929 93

1930-1939 140

1940-1949 196

1950-1959 251

1960-1969 314

1970-1979 371

Bibliography 425

Index 429

Author's Preface

This chronology traces evolutionary changes that have taken place in twentieth century music by enumerating 80 years of facts, thoughts and ideas about music. The book reports and describes musical events that have occurred between January, 1900 and December, 1979. It includes events in opera, dance, instrumental and vocal music, births, deaths, debuts and related events, thoughts, ideas, declarations and statements on music by people who have written music, thought about music, and by people whose life and work has affected music in some way.

Events in the first three categories largely report first performances and often give the conductor, cast, choreographer, dancers, orchestra or ensemble, place of performance and, in many cases, a brief description of the work. The instrumental and vocal category includes symphonic, chamber and keyboard music, songs, electronic music, and non-operatic vocal music, both sacred and secular — in short, any kind of piece that could not clearly be logged as opera or dance. Review quotes, whether objective or biased, have been attached to some entries specifically for the purpose of illustration and comment. I do not necessarily agree with the comments of any critic represented in this book. The births, deaths and debuts sections include birth announcements, obituaries and debuts of many famous musicians. The obituaries are designed to summarize a musician's work and, with important figures, assess the impact of his or her life and work on the world of music. The related events sections include everything else that is not a premiere, birth, death or debut — for example, developments in the recording industry, political events affecting music and anecdotal material.

In certain cases, a first performance occurred as a private performance not open to the public. In such cases, mention of this fact is made. The text is written in the present tense to create a sense of vividness — enabling the reader to become an observer of the panorama of musical events. An effort has been made to list the place of premiere in terms of its geographical name at the time of the work's premiere. Thus musical events that took place in Saint Petersburg in 1913 would be listed as having taken place in Petrograd if it was 1920 or in Leningrad if it was 1926. Russian dates are given in Western, new-style calendar form. The illustrations in the book are included as supplementary reference material to the text. Many of them are archival photographs that are, in and of themselves, of historical importance.

In beginning this book in 1979 I was overwhelmed by the amount of available information and yet the scarcity of unusual and obscure information. I chronicled premieres of works that were noteworthy in terms of their intrinsic importance to the world of music or to the careers of their composers — and works that were important because of the effect the music may have had on a contemporary audience.

This book may be read in a number of ways. The reader interested in a specific event or piece of information may consult the index to look it up by date and category. In this way, for example, the reader can trace the careers of individual composers and performers or follow events in some aspect of the music business. The reader interested in a specific year or decade may consult that part of the book and read one or more sections at a time to trace events in one or more areas for that time period. The reader interested in comparing developments in more than one category may flip back and forth between years and categories to see how events may or may not have paralleled each other. I also hope the reader will find this book enjoyable casual reading. I was surprised, for example, after finishing the text, to discover that nothing of extraordinary musical importance graced the world on my birthday.

It would be impossible to thank everyone who made valuable suggestions throughout the research and writing of this book. To Nicolas Slonimsky, a wizard of music, I owe my inspiration and greatest thanks. It was he who first encouraged me to undertake this project and to see it through. It was he who consistently commented on my research and offered clues, suggestions and corrections. It was his sense of humor that helped make the project great fun. I once mentioned to him, in a letter, that I had contemplated monastic life. He answered: "So you contemplated becoming a monk. But there is no fun in monastic life in the present world. It must have been great fun in the Middle Ages when one could believe in hard-core miracles, epiphanies and visions, and when everybody spoke Latin. My favorite TV commercial is the one in which that fat monk (who also played cholesterol) works on his illuminated manuscript, and then a xerox man comes in and does a hundred copies in seconds. The monk lifts his gaze to the sky, and says 'A miracle!' Nowadays people join idiotic cults, they speak Californian dialect instead of Latin, and they are 'into' ESP, astrology, psychic precognition and other spiritualistic junk."

Two other gentlemen — Mr. Harvey J. Satty and Mr. Gunther E. Theurer — were especially helpful in terms of their criticism, suggestions and general concern. Mr. Satty's help on aspects of the text and Mr. Theurer's help on aspects of photo research and arrangement were invaluable. To them: Thank you. Other individuals who have helped in various ways and tolerated my outbursts during the past four years are Robert Jolley, Barbara Leighton, William Levi, Irv Lerner, Clark Maurer, Ira Sitomer and Robert Zack.

Judith Linn, Grace Ferrara, Susan Cohan, Mimi Clifford Bassow, Henry Grant, Howard Epstein, Rachel Ginsburg and many others at Facts On File Publications were a constant source of help in virtually every aspect of the book. Three people, in particular, helped make the book a reality: Eleanora Schoenebaum, Philip Saltz and Edward Knappman. Eleanora, my editor, challenged my ideas, Phil tested my methods and Ed gave me the opportunity to do the book. Without these three operating on my work this book would not have gone to press.

The staff of the Music Division of the Library for the Performing Arts at Lincoln Center (New York Public Library) was also enormously helpful. Their clipping file is an invaluable source of obscure information. The file contains materials on virtually every important figure in twentieth century music and provides an exceptional research bank for anyone interested in music.

Wayne D. Shirley of the Music Division of the Library of Congress was generous in commenting on various aspects of the text and illustrations. The biographical composer files of the American Music Center were also very useful and I thank Ms. Margarite Jory for her permission to use them.

I would also like to thank the many foreign consulates and musical organizations around the world that supplied huge amounts of printed matter and other materials (including photographs) relating to twentieth century musical life in their countries. These people include: Line Bellache (Services Culturels, Ambassade de France); Andreas te Boekhorst (Consulaat-General der Nederlanden); Roger Duce (National Library of Scotland); Ritva-Liisa Elomaa (Consulate General of Finland); Sylvia Gardner (Austrian Press and Information Office); Nancy Gilbert (Boston Symphony Orchestra); Mrs. B.H. Goodfriend (Acoustical Society of America); Nicholas and Richard Gordon (Music Mountain, Connecticut); James Gregory (The New-York Historical Society); F. Hertogh-Zaat (Instituut voor sonologie); Marc Honegger (Institut de Musicologie, Strasbourg); Stanislas Jares and Jaroslav Seda (CTK Praha); Kevin Kopps (New York Philharmonic); Dr. Jan Ledec (Czechoslovak Music Service); Nicholas Lorimer (New Zealand Consulate General); Dr. Mircea Maciu (Editura stintifica si enciclopedica, Rumania); Jan Nordlander (Swedish Consulate General Information Service); D. Porte (Institut Jaques-Dalcroze Geneve); Mrs. Hella Roth (Inter Nationes); Elsa Rothe (Danish Information Office); Dr. Boris Schwarz (Copland School, Queens College of the City University of New York); Lynette Shaw (Australian Information Service); and Hans Steinbeck (Swiss Music Archives).

Richard Burbank
New York City

August 14, 1983.

Introduction

The 20th century marked a revolution in the style and technique of musical composition greater than in any century before. This revolution can be summarized in three main points: emancipation of dissonance, departure from tonality and development of asymmetrical meters and rhythms.

Until the very end of the 19th century, the unbreakable rule of composition was that each separate, individual section, each movement and certainly the complete work itself had to terminate on a perfect triad — a major triad in most cases, a minor triad in certain cases. Major triads were in the majority and minor triads in the minority.

In classical music, if this term is applied to all music before 1900, the terminal point had to be on the tonic of the original key or on the tonic of a relative key. So firm was this unspoken rule that Richard Strauss made a joke of it in one of his songs, which ended in a tonality other than the initial key. He provided an alternate ending to the piece, in the initial key, with a sly footnote: "This ending is to be used for all performances given before 1900."

Instances could be found in old music when a composition would end on the dominant seventh chord, a marked dissonance that could not be tolerated in its naked state. But in such cases there was always a sequel, which provided a proper resolution into the tonic triad. A bold Russian innovator, Vladimir Rebikov, defied the musical establishment by ending his little opera *The Christmas Tree* on the augmented triad, technically a discord, although it consists of two concords — to wit, major thirds. Then on the threshold of the 20th century, the musical ground began to shift. First these shifts appeared in spontaneously generated popular music; ragtime players would add a major sixth to the obligatory major triad for a concluding concord. Acousticians philosophized that this major sixth above the concluding major triad, usually occurring in the treble, was not a dissonance at all but actually a 27th overtone of the fundamental tonic. This explanation begs the question. Our tuning does not follow the pure series of overtones, and the extra high note would be off the overtone series by a substantial microtonal interval.

Another few years elapsed, and the instinctive, untutored and unprejudiced pianists of the ragtime era began adding the major seventh to the final chord, invariably in the major mode. Now, a major seventh is a striking dissonance, so what is it doing masquerading as a member of the concluding harmony? Well, the major seventh, when sufficiently distanced from the fundamental tone, is its 15th overtone! Since it is theoretically a part of the overtone series, it is as good a consonance as any. Later a major ninth was added, always in the high treble, to the terminal major triad; it forms an even closer member of the overtone series than the added sixth or the seventh: It is the ninth overtone of the fundamental tone! The natural corollary was to add both the 9th overtone and the 27th overtone and arrange them in a euphonious chord forma-

tion. Counting for convenience' sake from the fundamental low C (C, G, E, A, D), this typical terminal chord was used by ragtime players and by their successors, jazz and rock musicians.

Among so-called classical composers who knew what they were doing, such terminal dissonances came into vogue simultaneously with the instinctual and academically untutored jazz players. The pioneer in this revolution was Claude Debussy. He was apt to write these taunting and provocative formations on the white keys of the piano keyboard. He also began adding notes to the common dominant seventh chords.

Then came Alexander Scriabin. He knew little of Debussy and even less of American ragtime music. He was not interested in acoustics or in the science of overtones. Rather, he was fascinated by expanding the realm of chords built on perfect and augmented fourths as some sort of ethereal suspensions over the major dominant chord. These enhanced dominant seventh chords could be traced to Richard Wagner's chromatic harmonies, but Scriabin liked to attribute a mystical origin to them. In his poetic piano piece entitled *Desir*, he uses a chord combining an augmented fourth with two perfect fourths (C, F-sharp, B, E). From there it is only a small step to his "mystic chord," which he set as a sort of extraterrestrial basic chord for his "Poem of Fire," *Prometheus*. Scriabin's mystic chord is (starting on C) C, F-sharp, B-flat, E, A, D. To make this chord understandable, it suffices to lead the F-sharp up a semitone to G and the A up a semitone to B-flat, thus forming an old familiar dominant seventh chord, very Wagnerian-sounding indeed.

But what is that F-sharp doing in Scriabin's mystic chord in the first place? Why it is the 45th overtone of the bass note C, brought down from its ethereal heights to the middle of the piano keyboard. Interestingly enough, jazz players are also apt to add an F-sharp high in the treble, over the deep fundamental tone on C, a fascinating development proving that art (Debussy, Scriabin) follows life (ragtime, jazz). Yet the perfect fourth never appears in the treble of any of these dissonant chords that offended the delicate ears of music critics and academic musicians at the turn of the century. No F ever, no matter how high in the stratospheric treble over the fundamental C! Not in Debussy, not in any of his followers, not in any written or unwritten ragtime or jazz pieces.

In 1937 I proposed the term *pandiatonicism* to describe such enhanced diatonic harmonies and their constituent melodies. The term took root and is now duly enshrined in all music dictionaries and even in the *Encyclopaedia Britannica*. This type of harmony is found in the works of Debussy, Igor Stravinsky and many other composers. Pandiatonic chords are built on perfect fifths, augmented fourths, perfect fourths, sevenths, and also major and minor thirds. A typical pandiatonic chord, containing all seven notes of the scale (usually the major scale) is C, G,

D, F, B, E, A. The presence of F lends the chord a *feeling* of the dominant seventh on the organ point of C.

Polytonality (or more strictly, bitonality, for it is rare that more than two different tonalities appear in a harmonic complex) is a natural development in the process of emancipation of dissonance. Fantastic paradoxes and fascinating musical oxymorons result from the most common bitonal combination, that of two major triads placed at a distance of an augmented fourth. The priority of such a combined bitonal form, C major versus F-sharp major, is usually credited to Igor Stravinsky and is in fact often called the "Petroushka chord," because Stravinsky used it, vertically and horizontally, in the music of his famous ballet. But approximation and eventual coalescence of these two opposed tonalities were a fact of musical life long before Stravinsky. C major and F-sharp major lie on the opposite points of the circle of scales, and they are also mutually exclusive in their initial hexachords. The close approximation and the tangential encounter of these two tonalities are found in a number of works by Franz Liszt, Wagner, Nikolai Rimsky-Korsakov and Modest Mussorgsky. But it was Stravinsky who resolutely put them together, both harmonically and melodically, and in so doing asserted the resulting bitonality.

In medieval universities music was a part of the faculty of sciences, and early musicians were concerned primarily with the mathematical foundation of intervals, melodies and chords. The reading of medieval theoretical manuscripts, in their vulgar Latin (vulgar not in the sense of baseness, but in the sense of academic language), provides a lot of innocent merriment. Why is the octave a perfect interval? Because Abraham was circumcised on the eighth (octavo) day. Why is triple time the best of time, as it was regarded in the Middle Ages? Because of the Trinity. Why was the tritone banished from use? Because it was *diabolus in musica*, the work of Satan. In Bach's time a student would be punished by a painful strike with a rattan stick across the knuckles for writing a tritone. In free composition the tritone served to depict all kinds of deviltry. When the malevolent giant Fafner in Wagner's *Ring* becomes a dragon, he does so with the aid of a diabolical tritone in the bassoon. The irony of fate: The tritone became the cornerstone of polytonality and atonality, accepting the function of a dominant in classical harmony.

The inevitable product of chromatic harmony as practiced by Wagner and Liszt was the decay of governing tonality. Attempts had been made by many composers to salvage the modulatory principles of tonality (Rimsky-Korsakov once used a triple sharp in order to justify the spelling rules of tonal transition), but in vain. The first symptom of this decay was the disappearance of the key signature, that guardian of classical music. No more Symphony in D or Prelude in E-flat! The music staff was denuded of the familiar ladders of sharps and flats. The absence of these accidentals did not mean, of course, that everybody began writing music in C major, but it was a sign that it was no longer necessary to indicate a key if tonalities were to switch in every bar.

I propose a designation of euphonious dissonances for tonal combinations that exclude major sevenths, minor ninths and minor seconds — the intervals that have a high degree of tonal interference. By this definition chords formed of whole tones employing tritones, minor sevenths, major thirds and major ninths are euphonious dissonances, while chords containing major sevenths, minor ninths and minor seconds are noneuphonious dissonances. The major dominant seventh chords (e.g., C, G, E, B-flat, D) so beloved by Wagner and, after Wagner, by Debussy are euphonious dissonances. The great advantage of euphonious dissonances is that they can be moved in parallel motion, ignoring the resulting consecutive fifths. Noneuphonious dissonances — such as minor seconds, major sevenths and minor ninths — are usable in pandiatonic structures, but they are inexorably confined to a single tonal matrix and cannot be used in parallel motion. In *Le Sacre du printemps*, Stravinsky makes use of noneuphonious dissonances in scale passages set at a distance of minor ninths, pitting a C major scale against C-sharp major.

The name of Stravinsky is often associated with that of Picasso, who abolished the ideal of prettiness, symmetry and optical perspective in his paintings. He would be apt to add an extra eye to a human face just as Stravinsky would add a jarring, noneuphoniously dissonant note to an otherwise peaceful tonal passage. There is a parallel to these artistic events in social life. Crinolines (strict triads) disappeared after Queen Victoria died; corsets (diminished seventh chords) fell into desuetude with the outbreak of World War I; the bra (whole-tone scales) in women and necktie in men followed into oblivion in the wake of World War II.

According to Isaac Newton's third law, every action is followed by an equal and opposite reaction. When musical action reached its greatest accumulation of tonal masses, producing a maximum of decibels, so that the human ear seemed to have reached its limit of tolerance, the wave reversed itself. Composers voluntarily reduced their symphonic and operatic apparatus to a workable minimum. No more super-Wagnerian masses of instruments. No more five-act operas. No more horses on the stage, and no more huge mixed choruses. The new economy took the form of neoclassicism. Suddenly composers discovered new values in old music, especially baroque music. Suddenly the much-used and abused triads acquired a new charm. And even such shopworn devices as the consecutive runs of diminished-seventh chords (they were known in operatic parlance as *accorde di stupefazione* — the chords of stupefaction — for they were habitually employed in highly dramatic operatic episodes) acquired a new dignity.

With the restoration to fashion of baroque music came the revival of the classical art of counterpoint. The last great contrapuntist of the 20th century was Max Reger. (He was quite a humorist, quipping that his name was a musical palindrome, for it read the same backwards.) Reger's revered teacher Hugo Riemann told him in a moment of effusive confidence: "Max, if you want, you can be a second Bach!" Reger did not become a Bach, but he continues to be venerated in Germany. Only Paul Hindemith, among modern composers, admired Reger unequivocally. And perhaps Hindemith was the last great neoclassicist among 20th-century composers, even though he did not shrink from using harsh dissonances. When Richard Strauss heard Hindemith's earlier chamber music at one of those modern music festivals that sprouted all over Europe after the end of the First World War, he asked him, almost compassionately: "Why do you do this? After all, you have talent."

The emancipation of dissonance in vertical harmony was inexorably followed by the emancipation of tonality in melodic progressions. Why be a slave to the tonic-dominant complex? Why be confined to the corridors of major or minor scales? Eureka! Let us throw off the chains of the major tetrachord and its minor relative under which we languished for a thousand years since Guido from the little Italian town of Arezzo began teaching his famous singing method. And so in the early decades of the present century a declaration of liberty, fraternity and equality of all chromatic notes was made; it took its practical form in a system that its originator, Arnold Schoenberg, described as a method of composition with 12 tones related only to one another.

Schoenberg was not alone in formulating this principle of composition. He had several precursors, competitors and claimants of priority. Schoenberg's method, which became known as dodecaphony (from the Greek *dodeca*, 12, and *phone*, sound), was presaged early in the century by, among others, the Italian theorist Domenico Alaleona, who published an article in 1911 in which he used the term *dodecafonia*. The Russian composer Nicolas Obouhov, a mystic who called himself "Nicolas l'illumine," and who marked rehearsal numbers in his score *Le livre de vie* with his own blood, demonstrated his system of 12 different notes without duplication as early as 1916. Then there was the Austrian composer Josef Matthias Hauer, who declared himself "the spiritual begetter and despite numerous bad imitators, still forever, the only one who knows how to use the music of 12 tones."

When the astronomer Christian Huygens discovered the rings of Saturn with his primitive telescope, he was careful to put this discovery in the form of a Latin anagram so that he could prove his priority in case someone else observed the rings. Gottfried Wilhelm von Leibniz and Isaac Newton contested the invention of differential calculus. Schoenberg took the precaution of handing a note to one of his students at a seminar in Berlin, specifically mentioning the inception of the method of composition with 12 tones. Schoenberg denied his role as a musical revolutionary. "What I did was neither revolution nor anarchy," he wrote in a letter addressed to me, in English, dated June 3, 1937. "I possessed, from my very first start, a thoroughly developed sense of form and a strong aversion [to]. . . exaggeration. There is no falling into order, because there was never disorder. There is no falling at all, but on the contrary, there is an ascending to higher and better order."

Schoenberg's sensibility in asserting his priority in the discovery of his method led to an extraordinary exchange of letters with Thomas Mann. It all started with the publication of Mann's novel *Doktor Faustus*, centering on a mythical German composer of 12-tone music named Adrian Leverkuhn. After he read the book, Schoenberg exploded in wrath, writing a letter to the editor of the *Saturday Review of Literature*:

> In his novel *Doktor Faustus*, Thomas Mann has taken advantage of my literary property. He has produced a fictitious composer as the hero of his book; and he made him the creator of what one erroneously calls my system of 12 tones, which I call method of composing with 12 tones. He did this without my permission and even without my knowledge. In other words, he borrowed it in the absence of the proprietor. . . . Leverkuhn is depicted from beginning to end as a lunatic. I am 74 and I am not insane, and I have never acquired the disease from which this insanity stems. I consider this an insult.

Schoenberg was persuaded to make peace with Mann on the promise that the next edition of Mann's novel would carry a note giving him credit for his method. Schoenberg wrote:

> I was satisfied by this promise because I wanted to be noble to a man who was awarded the Nobel Prize. But Mr. Mann was not as generous as I, who had given him good chance to free himself from the ugly aspect of a pirate. He gave an explanation in a few lines which he hid at the end of the book on a page where no one ever would see it. Besides, he added a new crime to his first. In the attempt to belittle me, he calls me a (!) contemporary composer and theoretician. In two or three decades, one will know which of the two was the other's contemporary.

Thomas Mann answered Schoenberg's letter in a philosophical mode, reiterating his belief in Schoenberg's greatness but adding:

> It is a sad spectacle to see a man of great worth whose all-too-understandable hypersensitivity grows out of a life suspended between glorification and neglect, almost willfully yield to delusion of persecution and of being robbed, and involve himself in rancorous bickering.

Like many great men, Schoenberg was subject to superstitious fears. He had triskaidekaphobia, the fear of number 13. In order to exorcise it, he cut out the second letter in the name Aaron in the title of his work *Moses und Aron* when he noticed that it otherwise would number 13 letters. When a friend remarked on Schoenberg's 76th birthday that the digits of his age added up to 13, Schoenberg seemed genuinely upset. He died on July 13, 1951, reportedly 13 minutes before midnight, at the age of 76.

What establishes Schoenberg as the true creator of the dodecaphonic method is his adoption of the time-honored contrapuntal devices of inversion, retrograde and retrograde inversion. Just using 12 different notes in a melody is no great task, but to invert a subject that would be fertile when turned melodically upside down or played backward or played backward upside down requires great power of imagination. There are 479,001,600 possible combinations of arranging 12 different tones (or tone rows, as they are usually described), and it requires the highest degree of perspicacity to select one that would lend itself to fruitful transformations. When I sent a copy of my *Thesaurus of Scales and Melodic Patterns* to Schoenberg, he paid me a left-handed compliment. "You have in all probability organized every possible succession of tones," he wrote. "This is an admirable feat of mental gymnastics. But as a composer, I must believe in inspiration rather [than] in mechanics." Schoenberg's emphasis on inspiration is revealing, since he was constantly accused of being a cerebral composer.

What distinguishes Schoenberg's method from similar dodecaphonic theories is its comprehensive extension into the field of counterpoint and harmony, so that the entire musical structure becomes a multiple function of the original series. The basic tone row and its three transformations — inversion, retrograde and retrograde inversion — become the ingredients of the contrapuntal and harmonic structure of a dodecaphonic piece of music. Thus, a 12-tone series can be represented contrapuntally, or harmonically, by six units of 2 notes each, four units of 3 notes each, three units of 4 notes each, two units of 6 notes each or a single unit of 12 notes. (Luckily for Schoenberg and his disciples, 12 is divisible by 2, 3, 4 and 6.)

In his practice Schoenberg excludes the major triad and its inversions, as well as minor triads in their fundamental positions, allowing occasional inversions, especially the second inversion of a minor triad in passing. Why this exclusion? Schoenberg could say, and actually did say, that major triads have been overworked and ought to be given a rest. Of course, thematic octaves are inadmissible in a truly dodecaphonic composition. I was horror-struck when I discovered, while rehearsing Schoenberg's symphonic piece entitled *Accompaniment to a Motion Picture Scene* (needless to say, it was never used in an actual movie), that two trumpets in the score were both playing C at an octave's distance. I approached Schoenberg to ask him what was wrong. "Oh," he said, "das ist falsch!" But what was the intended interval that was not "falsch"? I asked. "That I cannot remember," Schoenberg replied. I summoned Roger Sessions, a profound theorist as well as a remarkable composer, to help me solve the puzzle, and after an hour or so at my piano, we traced back the basic tone row and determined that the shocking interval of a perfect octave should have been a diminished octave, C over C-sharp. Problem solved, dodecaphonic syllogism resolved.

Schoenberg is described in most music courses and books as the founder of the second Viennese school, a successor to the old romantic school of Viennese composers. He and his star pupils Alban Berg and Anton von Webern, great composers in their own right, have been irreverently referred to as God the Father, God the Son and the Holy Ghost. Since the son of God was human, Alban Berg allowed himself to taste forbidden fruits, such as triads. And since the Holy Ghost is the least tangible of the Trinity, Anton von Webern evolved the most profoundly abstruse system of dodecaphonic application. Strangely enough, it was Webern who eventually exercised the most profound influence on composers around the world. Let the theologians figure out how a ghost, however holy, could have become so powerful.

It was not long after Schoenberg's death that his method of composing with 12 tones became a dominant tool of modern composers. His greatest posthumous victory was the conversion to dodecaphony of its principal opponent, Igor Stravinsky himself! Stravinsky even expressed his willingness to forgive Schoenberg his mocking choral canon in which Stravinsky was ridiculed as Mr. Modernsky, who put on a wig so as to look just like Papa Bach. It was a very fine contrapuntal piece, Stravinsky opined and said he was proud of having inspired its composition.

Only the Russians were adamant in their refusal to accept Schoenberg and his handiwork. Nikita Khrushchev made a pun: "You call it dodecaphony, but we call it plain cacophony" (the two words rhyme in Russian). And suddenly the dam broke. Dmitri Shostakovich himself began using occasional dodecaphonic passages in his later symphonies; and after him many other Soviet composers began to use dodecaphonic melodies.

An inevitable reaction set up against Schoenberg's dodecaphony; it suddenly became old-fashioned. Pierre Boulez, the standard-bearer of all that is modern under the sun, published an essay brutally entitled "Schoenberg Is Dead."

With dissonances safely emancipated and the chromatic tones of the scale democratically rendered equal, the modern techniques seemed to reach an impasse. What next? Why, split the semitones into quarter tones and even smaller fractions. This was the task of an enterprising Czech composer and teacher, Alois Haba, who was the first to publish a textbook on fractional tones. The Mexican composer Julian Carrillo was another pioneer; he published a magazine entitled *Sonido 13*, symbolically indicating divisions beyond the available 12 chromatic notes, and he constructed instruments that were supposed to produce such fractional tones. Still another composer of quarter-tone music was Ivan Wyschnergradsky, a Russian living in Paris, who constructed pianos tuned a quarter tone apart. A surprising adherent to the technique of composition in quarter tones was a grandson of Rimsky-Korsakov, Georgi, who published a book on the subject. The American Harry Partch built instruments that were supposed to produce 43 equal intervals to an octave. However, all these fractional intervals were approximations of the true tuning; only with the advent of electronic instruments did an exact division of an octave into fractional intervals become possible. Ernst Krenek, a composer of extraordinary power of invention who belonged to the Schoenberg school of composition, contributed pieces in such true divisions of an octave using electronic instruments.

There are in mathematics some formulas that connect seemingly unrelated symbols in a rather elegant equation; such is the Euler formula, which brings together the imaginary number, the ratio of the circumference of a circle to its diameter and the base of natural logarithms. There are similar surprises in music theory. For instance, the diminishing arithmetic progression with a semitone as the difference between two adjacent members, beginning with 9 and ending with 3, forms a bitonal chord — e.g. (from bass up), C-sharp, A-sharp, F-sharp, C-sharp, G, C, E, G.

Dodecaphony opposes triadic forms, but it is possible to split a chromatic scale into four mutually exclusive triads — e.g., C major, F-sharp major, D minor and G-sharp minor. Furthermore, it is possible to construct a chord including four triads connected by thirds, modeled after familiar seventh or ninth chords — e.g., F-sharp major triad, E major triad, D minor triad and C minor triad. (This is, incidentally, the only possible chord of this nature, verified by a computer, which after hours of electronic labor confirmed that there is no other combination satisfying these requirements.)

Natura non facit saltum, says the ancient adage enunciated long before Darwin. Nature does not make a leap in the arts either. The tolerance of dissonances came gradually; polytonality and atonality crept into music little by little. But there are exceptions both in the theory of evolution and in the arts, manifested by a sudden emergence of a new phenomenon unrelated to existing species. In music such a phenomenon was Charles Ives.

Nothing in his early life presaged Ives' eventual rise as a great American composer. He played the organ in village churches near his home in Connecticut; he entered Yale and graduated in musical composition in the class of Horatio Parker. But music was not a career for an American boy early in the century. Accordingly Ives went into the insurance business and made a success of it. During his leisure time he composed. Then suddenly he suffered a massive heart attack, which was complicated by a chronic case of diabetes. His wife, providentially named Harmony, took care of him, but he had to stop composing. He decided to publish, at his own expense, 104 of his songs as well as his *Concord Sonata*, in four movements, each named after a writer in Concord, Massachusetts: Emerson, Hawthorne, the Alcotts and Thoreau. Both the volume of songs and the *Concord Sonata* were obtainable gratis from the composer; Ives did not intend to make money from his music, even if he had to go to considerable lengths to avoid doing so. Because of his illness, he became practically a recluse, dividing his time between his summer home in Connecticut and a brownstone he owned in New York. Some sympathetic friends, to whom he played his pieces on his rickety upright piano, asked him why he had to compose music that is so hard on the ear. "I hear it this way," he invariably replied. When an overzealous copyist tried to change a particularly dissonant note in his manuscript, Ives wrote in the margin: "Please do not correct! The wrong notes are right!"

Virtually all of Ives' works are instilled with American themes; he quotes American church hymn tunes, popular ballads and military marches, but he invests them with highly dissonant harmonies and often changes them melodically. As a boy he arranged the American national anthem in strikingly discordant harmonies. Long before *polytonality, asymmetrical rhythms, atonality* and *polyrhythms* became accepted terms, Ives employed such devices in his compositions. It may be said that his harmonies followed the increasingly complex social movements of American life; that may be the reason why the music of Ives, written years ago, sounds contemporary to late 20th-century ears.

American music in the 19th century was but a faint reflection of German music. Edward MacDowell, regarded as the first American composer of stature, received his musical training in Germany; his harmonies follow the Germanic mold. It was only after the First World War that the German influence on American music began to wane, and this was due to a large extent to the fact that German conductors, performers and teachers, who had dominated the American musical horizon, suddenly found themselves enemy aliens, and several of them were forcibly dismissed from their posts; among them was the great conductor of the Boston Symphony Orchestra, Karl Muck, who was arrested and interned as a spy for the kaiser.

But even when such ridiculous episodes were relegated to the shameful past, German music had irretrievably lost its influence in America. Young composers and performers flocked to Paris for their instruction and enlightenment. Nadia Boulanger became the wet nurse of a generation of American composers; among her students were Aaron Copland, Walter Piston, Roy Harris, Virgil Thomson, Elliott Carter, Elie Siegmeister and many others. Of these, Aaron Copland became the most famous. His career was extraordinary. Fresh from Paris, he played a piano concerto of his own composition with the Boston Symphony, conducted by Serge Koussevitzky. It was dubbed a jazz concerto, because it had a lot of syncopation, and it shocked the prim, grim Boston audiences, who expressed their dismay openly. But Copland was not to be frightened away by such a show of horror and continued to compose in a modern American manner. He emphasized distinctly American subjects in such works as *Appalachian Spring, Billy the Kid, Lincoln Portrait* and *Rodeo*. His *Fanfare for the Common Man* for brass and percussion became famous.

A different type of American is reflected in the works of Roy Harris. He believed it was providential that he was born on Lincoln's birthday in Lincoln County, Oklahoma. He gave ostentatiously American titles to his symphonies and other works: *Folksong Symphony, Gettysburg Address, Abraham Lincoln Symphony, American Creed*. He was also preoccupied with creating a genuine type of American modality based on old church modes but arranged rhythmically and melodically in an American manner.

Walter Piston resolutely declined to write stereotypically American music. He felt that any music written by an American was *ipso facto* American and remarked somewhat sarcastically that one does not have to chase buffalo on the prairie to qualify as an American; reading books in the Boston Athaeneum was as American a pastime as any activity in the wild west. He wrote a number of remarkable symphonies, concertos and chamber music, but his most popular piece remains a ballet score entitled *The Incredible Flutist*. During a recording of this work, a dog barked, and Piston was persuaded to include the bark in the score.

Samuel Barber never studied with Nadia Boulanger, but he achieved fame by following his natural flair for lyric melody. He studied voice as well as composition and even gave a vocal recital as a young man. His music possesses a quality of natural birth; whatever he wrote — symphony, concerto, piano sonata or symphonic sketch — seems flawless in its technical brilliance. His most famous piece was an adagio from his early String Quartet; arranged for string orchestra, it was played by Arturo Toscanini and immediately became popular. Barber was not averse to exploring jazz; some of his pieces are cunningly peppered with jazzy syncopation.

The most versatile and the most celebrated American composer is, beyond any cavil or doubt, Leonard Bernstein. His success has no precedent in the annals of American music. He is known to the world as a charismatic conductor and is beloved by the masses for his musicals, such as *West Side Story*, which contains some of the most fetching American tunes after Gershwin. But Bernstein has also composed symphonic works, among them the remarkable score for *The Age of Anxiety*. It must be added that Bernstein is a successful lecturer and a television personality who knows how to communicate musically and verbally with the young. No American musician has ever collected such a grand garland of popular achievement.

Experimentation was the soul of American music in the new modern century. George Antheil, an American who spent much of his youth in Paris, where he became associated with James Joyce and other leaders of new art, set for himself the task of reflecting the age of the machine in music. The most celebrated product of this endeavor was his *Ballet mecanique*, scored for a variety of percussion instruments, 16 pianos and airplane propellers *ad libitum*. A *succes de scandale* was a natural consequence of this assault on the tender ears of peaceful concert goers. The *Ballet mecanique* was a futuristic event; indeed its attempt to glorify the mechanical world was close to the "art of noises" of the Italian futurist composers, who shocked the world with their exhibitions before the murderous noise of the First World War. But all the futurists could work with were drums and old-fashioned phonograph horns and megaphones; there was simply no technique available to deafen the audience with sound. Still the Italian futurists aroused their public sufficiently to start a number of fist-fights; in a communique they claimed victory over the audience.

The true apostle of modern music was Henry Cowell, who challenged the listening world with things like tone clusters, which he invented as a teen-ager in San Francisco. Tone clusters are produced by playing on the piano keyboard with fists, elbows and whole lengths of forearm, either on white or black keys. His pioneer composition with tone clusters was entitled *Amiable Conversation*. Amazingly enough, it was published in Germany by the most dignified publishing house of Breitkopf & Hartel. Cowell also enhanced the sound production of the piano by playing glissando directly on the strings under the lid of an open grand piano. He also plucked on the strings, or else he placed things like paper clips, darning eggs and coins on the strings to alter the tone color. I risked my own reputation (such as it was) when I engaged Cowell in 1928 to be soloist in his own work, replete with tone clusters and such, with my Chamber Orchestra of Boston. This event produced Cowell's favorite headline in the Boston *Post*: "USES EGG TO SHOW OFF PIANO." But tone clusters eventually became a legitimate means of tone production, and the term was included in most music encyclopedias.

Cowell had to pay out of his own pocket for the publication of his book *New Musical Resources*, in which he offered all kinds of novel suggestions, such as splitting the binary or ternary meters into sections, generating new rhythmic divisions. This book has now become a standard work for modern musicians.

Cowell's most faithful and most inventive follower was John Cage. Starting off with Cowell's metapianistic techniques, he inaugurated a prepared piano, which altered the piano sonorities far beyond Cowell's modest efforts. With Karlheinz Stockhausen, Gyorgy Ligeti, Mauricio Kagel and others, John Cage became the begetter of aleatory techniques. The word itself comes from the Latin *alea*, meaning dice. For his aleatory compositions John Cage used both dice and an old Chinese book of games that gave a table of all possible combinations of numbers.

At about the same time, the idea of total serialism was developed by Milton Babbitt and his followers and associates. To the "classical" serialization of 12 different notes was added the serial distribution of 12 different intervals. A new commandment was added to the dodecaphonic manual: Thou shalt not use an interval twice in succession. This meant good-bye to consecutive melodic fourths, so beloved by early practitioners of atonality. The palm of invention of intervallic serialism should be tendered to Fritz Heinrich Klein, an Austrian composer who used the nom de plume Heautontimorumenos, a Greek word that means self-tormentor. His musical self-flagellation paid off. He constructed a chord containing all different intervals and all different notes, a tonal matrix that he appropriately entitled *Mutterakkord*. (I went him one better by constructing a *Grossmutterakkord*, which not only contained all 12 different notes and all 11 different intervals but was also integrally invertible. This gimmick was not infertile; it was used as a foundation of an interplanetary opera, *Aniara*, by the Swedish composer Karl-Birger Blomdahl.)

Marching on toward total serialism, Milton Babbitt serialized tone colors and dynamics, note values and rest values. This simply meant that no self-respecting serialist should use the same tone color, or instrument, twice in succession or the same degree of dynamics, whether forte, piano or their gradations. The serialization of note values required that no two notes of equal value should be used until all other rhythmic subdivisions have been exhausted. The same rule of exclusion applied to the duration of each individual rest.

Outcries, sighs or even death rattles have been stock and trade for operatic composers for centuries. Schoenberg initiated a new form of vocalization, the *Sprechstimme* — half-spoken, half-sung sounds — and he applied it magisterially in his *Pierrot lunaire*. Obouhov added cries, groans, moans, shouts and other human and inhuman sounds to his vocabulary of vocal expression. Hans Werner Henze made use of clicks, screams, bellowing and snorting in some of his scores.

One of the most successful composers of enhanced vocal music is George Crumb, who makes effective use of explosive shrieks, hissing and whispering in fractional intervals. He also orders the pianist to shout at certain points of a piano piece. Wonders never cease.

Paul Wittgenstein declared in one of his cryptic utterances: "Whereof one cannot speak thereof one must be silent." John Cage followed Wittgenstein's dictum literally in composing his celebrated composition entitled *4 Minutes 33 Seconds*. It is scored for one piano or several pianos, or any other group of instruments, and is in three movements. The printed edition, retailing at 50 cents, contains two blank pages. The piece was first unplayed (though not necessarily unheard, since there were incidental noises) by Cage's faithful assistant David Tudor in Woodstock, New York on August 29, 1952.

Closely related to aleatory composition is the graphic notation of music, in which geometric figures suggest a variety of possible sounds to be freely interpreted by the performer. One of the earliest proponents of graphic notation was the American composer Earle Brown, who generated the concept of "open-end" composition; as early as 1952 he outlined a theory of musical space relative to conceptual mobility and transformation of events in arbitrary, unstable time.

By and large, modern music remains identifiable by written musical notes and markings indicating meter, rhythm and dynamics. In old music the number of beats in a bar was indicated by the time signature, and it was usually set in binary or ternary bars, with some simple combinations thereof. There were march meters, polka meters, waltz meters, jig meters and occasional syncopated meters in which the stress did not coincide with the strong beat of the bar. When Tchaikovsky dared to write a scherzo in his *Symphonie pathetique* in 5/4, he was taken to task by the famous Viennese critic Eduard Hanslick for making the piece unplayable. All he had to do, Hanslick urged, was to add a beat and convert the movement into a rolling barcarolle. But Tchaikovsky was dead by the time Hanslick happened to hear his symphony.

Rimsky-Korsakov went Tchaikovsky one better by writing a chorus in his opera *Sadko* in 11/4 time. To master this meter, the choristers sang it to the words, "Rimsky-Korsakov is altogether mad," which has 11 syllables in both the Russian original and the present English translation. In the finale of *Le Sacre du printemps*, Stravinsky really made conductors sweat it out, for its metrical plan constitutes a succession of such time signatures as 5/16, 2/8, 3/16 and even 1/16.

Meters in prime numbers, such as quintuple time signatures, are not the product of modern invention. They are found in natural folk rhythms of many lands. Two bars of 3/8 and a bar of 2/8, aggregating to a sum of three and five beats to a bar, are common in southeastern Europe. The great Hungarian composer Bela Bartok spent many years collecting folk songs in his native Transylvania and adjacent regions, a task in which he was aided by another great Hungarian Zoltan Kodaly. Bartok, and to a lesser extent Kodaly, made use of these natural melodies and rhythms in their own works. But being a product of the 20th century, Bartok also made use of consistent noneuphonious counterpoint, freely employing major sevenths and minor ninths in his works. Kodaly, who was an educator by nature, refrained from such extreme modernities, but he also made a significant contribution to modern meters and

rhythms. In folk music and in modern works based on folk melodies, different rhythms combined freely, giving the rise to polymeters and polyrhythms.

The great explorer of complex rhythms and meters combined with a totally liberated spirit of dissonance, Edgar Varese dispensed with the term *composition* in his works. He called his music "organized sound." It is completely removed from the world of sounds observable in nature. Even in a score that bears the seemingly descriptive title *Ameriques*, Varese tends to represent the conceptual Americas as the birthplace of new science, new technology and new sound. His other works bear such scientific titles as *Integrals* and *Hyperprism* (a projection of a prism into higher dimensions). His unique score entitled *Ionisation* is arranged for pitchless percussion instruments and two sirens. The title refers to the disintegration of atomic nuclei.

Schoenberg, Varese and, before them, Scriabin, regarded folk songs as raw material of no value to musical science. For Scriabin music was a union with eternity; for Schoenberg it was a logical continuation of previous historic achievements. It is significant that even in works in which he renounced tonality, Schoenberg adhered to classical forms, including an old-fashioned reprise; Alban Berg and Anton von Webern followed this formality of design. Varese, on the other hand, pursued the ideal of total abstraction, arranging his themes by successive agglutination.

Folklore and abstraction are not necessarily irreconcilable. If folklore represents an irreversible past and abstraction a conjectural vista of an idealized future, there is a way of reconciling these sources. A modern poet, painter or composer in search of a future simplicity and clarity can dip into the remote past for unadorned primitives. It is not for nothing that Stravinsky's ultramodern score *Le Sacre du printemps* was subtitled *Scenes of Pagan Russia*. This reference allowed him to use crude chunks of primordial material, stumps of tetrachords without elaboration and without subjection to rules of harmony or counterpoint.

Popular songs of the remote past may serve handily in lieu of folk songs. Carl Orff delved into a collection of medieval student songs in the German monastery of Benedictbeuren and concocted an effective scenic oratorio *Carmina Burana* (i.e., songs of Benedictbeuren), which enjoyed tremendous success despite the fact that the words, in Latin and early romance languages, cannot be understood without an interlinear translation. Other composers followed this example by arranging old sacred and secular music in a form that became known as "realizations." There is more than one way to cook a goose.

When the great Brazilian composer Heitor Villa-Lobos was asked, "What is folklore?" he answered, "I am folklore!" Indeed, Villa-Lobos rarely, if ever, used actual folk tunes in his works but rather approximated the Brazilian rhythms and melodic patterns in his own inventive fashion. Carlos Chavez, the towering figure in Mexican music, made use of a few Mexican tunes in some of his Mexican-flavored scores, but most of his music was self-made.

George Gershwin, like his predecessor Stephen Foster, did not have to borrow tunes from American life; he created the music of modern America out of his own

American imagination. And with all that, his music is authentically modern. His dissonances are mostly of the euphonious kind; he made ample use of the blue notes, a lowered seventh and a lowered third. The lowered seventh can be explained in terms of the overtones series as an approximation of the seventh overtone occurring below the octave. Gershwin's rhythmic sense was very precise. His song "I Got Rhythm," which is all too frequently mongrelized by the big bands as a mere syncopation, is an example of Gershwin's inventiveness. Cast in the framework of common time, it represents the following succession of rhythmic values: an eighth-note rest, followed by four dotted eighth notes and again an eighth-note rest, adding up to 16/16 — i.e., 4/4. In his song "Fascinating Rhythm," Gershwin performs an acrobatic stunt by intercalating a three-beat thematic passage within a bar of 4/4 time. And in his "Rhapsody in Blue," Gershwin made, as one critic remarked, an honest woman out of jazz.

Jazz and its healthy predecessor, ragtime, formed the art or urban folklore, alive with its syncopated rhythms, added sixths and sevenths, and its general air of aggressive vitality. Soon jazz spread all over the world, penetrating even Russia, which resisted its incursion for years. Ernst Krenek wrote an opera entitled *Jonny spielt auf*, which portrayed a black American jazz player who conquers Europe, seducing European maidens and riding roughshod over the world. In the finale he sits atop a huge globe, symbolizing his conquest. The idea of a black man doing such things made it necessary for the Metropolitan Opera House to delegate the part of the conquering jazz hero to a blackface musician.

Then came rock 'n' roll. Lamentably, it lost the virility, the fertility and the felicity of jazz and became a monstrously aggrandized and enhanced beat. It made up in loudness what it lost in syncopated vitality. Rock music impaired the hearing of the performers themselves; as protection against the assault of its deafening decibels, the frequenters of rock concerts are sometimes provided with cotton earplugs. But the most pitiful loss of all was the abandonment of the syncopated jazzy beat and a gradual reduction of the music to a uniform blast in 4/4 time. This is not to say that all rock musicians are brutal savages. Most of them yearn for musical education and even try to read the hefty volumes of Joseph Schillinger's *System of Musical Composition*, although they can hardly fathom Schillinger's algebraic formulas, which are unnecessarily strewn across the pages of this learned treatise. Schillinger, it must be recalled, was the musical guru of the jazz age; even Gershwin went to him for help. Schillinger's great idea was to reduce melodies to diagrams and charts; thus, he drew on graph paper the musical counterpart of the 1929 stock market crash.

With the renunciation of folklore as raw material of sophisticated composition, a surrogate had to be found. It was provided in the form of technological music, which originated in Paris under the name *musique concrete*; it was the creation of a French radio engineer, and it postulated that any noise, intentional or unintentional, produced in the studio could be used as *materia musica*. This material could then be transmogrified by electronics and arranged as a "composition." After all, the word *composition* means simply putting together, and it does not necessarily connote rational organization. Accordingly, it was possible for the American composer Richard Maxfield to collect assorted sounds recorded during a modern dance recital and arrange them in a work entitled *Cough Music*. (Poor Maxfield! He committed self-defenestration from a Los Angeles hotel room.)

Another way of providing raw material is the method of *objets trouves*. This allows a composer to pick up musical quotations from established works and insert them into his own production. Luciano Berio did that in his *Sinfonia*, putting in snatches from Gustav Mahler, Claude Debussy and others. In one of his piano pieces, George Crumb helped himself to the middle section of Chopin's *Fantaisie-impromptu*, commonly known among the *hoi polloi* by the tune of the popular song "I'm Always Chasing Rainbows." Of course, composers of all times have made surreptitious use of other people's tunes in their own works, and musicologists are still trying to discover who stole what from whom among great composers. (Handel was quite adept at that variety of petty larceny).

The originator of the method of *objets trouves*, along with much other nonsense, was that great clown of modern French music, Erik Satie. He was sadly aware of his lack of theoretical knowledge of music, which he tried to remedy by going to school to learn counterpoint at the age of 40, but he compensated for it by proclaiming that art must provide entertainment. He amused himself by deliberately hoodwinking the public through such shenanigans as inserting a learned footnote declaring that a certain passage was a funeral march by Franz Schubert when it was nothing of the sort. In one such moment of playful distraction, he created the concept of "furniture music." Music should be treated like furniture, Satie declared, demonstrating this conceit by placing several groups of musicians in different rooms of an art gallery, instructing them to play anything they wanted without paying attention to each other. Satie was not modest in proclaiming his own greatness. He instructed that the curtain at one of his stage productions should bear the legend: "Anyone who does not believe that Erik Satie is the greatest composer living is asked to leave the hall without delay."

Satie surrounded himself with talented young composers who shared his belief that music ought to be fun. These composers, five young men and one young woman, became known as Les Six. Three of them became famous: Darius Milhaud, Arthur Honegger and Francis Poulenc. Less famous was Georges Auric; even less famous was Germaine Tailleferre; and quite obscure was Louis Durey. The French Six tried to simplify music, but their styles were quite different. Milhaud composed works of huge dimensions awash with polytonal complexities; Honegger glorified the American locomotive in his symphonic poem *Pacific 231*; Poulenc wrote charming pieces, free from modernistic gargoyles, quite tonal in harmony and symmetric in form.

Years passed; another war was fought; and a new wave of modern composers appeared on the musical horizon. New resources had to be found in unexplored lands. The

American composer Steve Reich went to Ghana to study African drumming; he demonstrated that music can produce a deep impression by sheer repetition. Reich became known as a minimalist. Another American composer, Philip, Glass, espoused a homophony of an even starker type. His surrealist score entitled *Einstein on the Beach* became a huge success in Europe as well as in America.

Curiouser and curiouser. La Monte Young, of the same generation as Reich and Glass, made irrationality the cornerstone of his method of composition. Sometimes he dispensed with musical notes altogether and limited himself to verbal instructions, such as "Push the piano to the wall; push it through the wall; keep pushing." He sought to achieve immortality simply by claiming it. He supplied this bit of information for one of his compositions: "This piece of music may play without stopping for thousands of years." One seems to perceive the eerie ghost of Satie in the ectoplasm of such proclamations.

The begetter of new simplicity, as it was termed in Paris in the 1920s, was the brilliant American Virgil Thomson, grand master of sophisticated bedazzlement and befuddlement. In Paris he became associated with the French modern composers of the time; he could indeed be called the seventh member of the French Six. Like his Paris contemporaries, he preached hedonism — that is, an art for art's pleasure. He became an intimate of Gertrude Stein, but in his compositions he reversed Gertrude's famous equation of identity "Rose is a rose is a rose is a rose," making it "Rose is not a rose is not a rose is not a rose." Thus, in his famous opera *Four Saints in Three Acts*, there are at least a dozen saints among the *dramatis personae*, and there are four acts in the opera, not three. As to the harmonic content of the score, Thomson seems to be saying, "Major triad is a major triad is a major triad is a major triad." The prolixity of naked triads in Virgil Thomson's music is indeed astounding, and it also serves to deflect invidious criticism. If a Schoenbergian were to use a triad by inadvertence, he would be hurled into the Gehenna of disgrace, but then Thomson was never a Schoenbergian; when he used dodecaphonic constructions at all, they were apt to appear in a series of four mutually exclusive triads. ("Nicolas, did you hear your little triads in my piece?" he asked me after the performance of one of his symphonic works; indeed, he borrowed his mutually exclusive triads from my *Thesaurus of Scales and Melodic Patterns*.)

The animating spirit of modern composers is frugality. The staging is often reduced to a few symbolic trees, benches and occasional ladders. Gian-Carlo Menotti in America and Benjamin Britten in England reduced the orchestras in their operas to a minimal number, usually 13, and they practically eliminated the chorus. If comment was required in dramatic situations, it was usually entrusted to a single voice, much in the manner of Greek drama or, for that matter, the Prologue in Ruggero Leoncavallo's *Pagliacci*. Michael Tippett of England is also apt to reduce his orchestral and choral equipment to a minimum. The ultimate of this musical anorexia is reached in *The Four-Note Opera*, by the American composer Tom Johnson. This is not a spoof a la Virgil Thomson; Johnson actually uses only four notes in his opera. All that is left of old-

fashioned grand opera is the Gran' Ol' Opry of Nashville, Tennessee.

If hedonists and minimalists represent the infrared of the musical spectrum, then computerized music can be placed in the ultraviolet portion of it. The sudden availability of an infinite variety of serial sequences in computer technology naturally excited many composers, who ceased to trust their own inspiration. The trouble with computer music is that it has to be programmed by humans, so that many allegedly computerized compositions reflect the limited imagination of the technicians who programmed the music. To be sure, though, technicians and composers can program a computer to compose a certain number of dissonances, followed by a certain number of consonances, and they can even specify what kind of dissonant or consonant chords are to be used.

Another development of specialized serialism is music in space. In this category of composition, each instrument is assigned its place on the podium or in a room. Its justification is vectorial sound, so that the listeners hear each instrument from its assigned direction. My nephew, the Soviet composer Sergei Slonimsky, wrote a sort of ambulatory string quartet in which the instrumentalists are placed in the audience and advance toward the stage one after another, playing their assigned parts until they are all assembled together. Well, Haydn composed ambulatory music some 200 years before my nephew in his *Farewell Symphony*, in which musicians extinguished their candles (this was the 18th century, remember) and left the stage, one by one, until only the silent conductor was left with his purposeless baton to bid farewell to the audience.

Then there is serialism by appointment, whereby each player is assigned a certain interval and is not allowed to deviate from it throughout the duration of the music. A cello, say, would be confined to perfect fourths, a viola to tritones, a violin to semitones, etc. Vectorial sound projection will help to sort out the serial intervals. But even this assignment of specific intervals to selected instruments is not new. A string quartet ascribed to Benjamin Franklin (he never wrote it, but that is beside the point) was scored for open strings only, so that any amateur group can perform it with perfect ease; besides, the instruments are each tuned differently from one another in fifths or fourths, so that surprising dissonances result. Another example of instrumental serialism by special assignment was the peasant orchestras maintained by rich landowners in Russia in the first half of the 19th century. The musicians were recruited from among the serfs; each was assigned a single note to play, so that no one had to learn to read music. Such serfs were known by the notes they played; when two of them escaped, their owner advertised: "Escaped E-flat and F-sharp from the owner's orchestra. Reward."

Intervallic specialization in modern compositions signaled new and original possibilities in contrapuntal writing just in time to save fugal counterpoint from extinction. The great master of this sort of spatial and intervallic techniques is Elliott Carter. His concertos and other works are not mere *jeux d'esprit* but works of great musical interest. Stravinsky, who rarely found merit in American music, declared one of Carter's concertos to be the first American masterpiece.

The ultimate in spatial music is environmental music, in which objects surrounding the composer's workroom are declared by creative fiat to be parts in the score. This concept has enabled one composer from San Francisco to write a work scored for skyscrapers, airplanes, helicopters and automobiles. The Italian futurists of the time before the First World War would have hailed this method of composition with loud cries of delight.

Can a musical style be legislated? Certainly the Catholic Church gave strict prescriptions for proper ecclesiastical part writing; the norms of Gregorian chant were strictly defined by the church. But even the most pious composers were free to write different types of secular music. In modern times an attempt was made by Soviet authorities to establish an obligatory type of composition defined by Russian theorists as socialist realism, a method of composition based on the concrete representation of Soviet reality. But what Soviet reality? In the early years of the Russian Revolution, composers tried to imitate actual sounds of the streets, factories and weapons. They put factory whistles and steel sheets in their scores but still failed to achieve the desired reflection of the life of the masses. A militant group called Proletarian Organization of Musicians made an earnest attempt to define music according to dialectical materialism. March time was good; waltz time was suspect as bourgeois in essence. Major keys were good for the masses; minor keys tended to weaken spiritual energy. Still, doubts emerged. Why should the proletarian masses like the music of Tchaikovsky? Simple: In his symphonies and operas, Tchaikovsky celebrated the funeral of his class, and the proletarians could not help enjoying such a burial of class enemies.

Serge Rachmaninoff was out as a poet of decadence and a sworn enemy of the Soviet Union; he left Russia, never to return, on the day of the October Revolution and settled in the United States, the archfoe of the Bolsheviks. Beethoven was all right; he was a revolutionary at heart, even though he did write the opening movement of his *Heroic* symphony in 3/4 time. Mikhail Glinka, the father of Russian music, was all right, too, even though he did compose an opera entitled *A Life for the Tsar*. That little predicament was easily corrected, however, by changing the title to *Ivan Susanin*, a patriotic peasant who misled the Polish commando raiders intent upon killing, not the Tsar, of course, but the leader of the Russian people named Minin. Other operas were similarly revised. Tosca was now a member of the Paris Commune who killed General Galliffet, who suppressed the commune in 1871 (never mind the historical fact that Galliffet died peacefully in bed in 1909; this is mere pedantic bourgeois detail). Finally, the Soviet authorities became sick and tired of this proletarian nonsense and disbanded the Proletarian Organization of Musicians. One Soviet composer exclaimed: "Now I can write music in 3/4 time!"

Russian music split in two: Many Russian composers joined the emigration, most of them to Paris and America. Rachmaninoff's departure was followed by the emigration of Alexander Glazunov, Alexander Gretchaninoff, Nicolas

and Alexander Tcherepnin (father and son), and Sergei Prokofiev. However, Prokofiev had second thoughts and soon returned to Russia, where he was welcomed as a prodigal son, with honors and praise. After a musical honeymoon he was attacked by extreme radicals for his alleged addiction to Western ways of making music. After the infamous decree of 1948, Prokofiev found himself in a camp of "formalists," a code word applied to those who strayed from the proper path of Russian traditionalism. Prokofiev tried to ingratiate himself with Joseph Stalin by writing an overture for the Soviet ruler's sixtieth birthday, but somehow it lacked true Stalinist spirit and was never performed. Then he wrote an opera to a libretto depicting the heroic deed of a Soviet pilot who lost both legs in combat but, after having artificial legs made, reenlisted in the Soviet air force and scored several victories. But the opera never went beyond a preliminary performance; it was declared formalist in its style and idiom and unworthy of its heroic subject. Prokofiev died on the same day as Stalin, March 5, 1953. When he was safely dead, Stalin was disgraced as a tyrannical madman, while Prokofiev was posthumously glorified. The tenth anniversary of Prokofiev's and Stalin's death was celebrated with ample tribute to Prokofiev in the Soviet press, while Stalin was all but ignored.

A close contemporary of both Stravinsky and Prokofiev was Nikolai Miaskovsky, who remained in Russia. He wrote 27 symphonies, all of which were published, recorded and performed in Russia, but he remained virtually unknown outside his native land.

While Stravinsky left Russia before the revolution and Prokofiev spent half his life abroad, a true Soviet composer was Dmitri Shostakovich, who was never tempted to leave his country and labored valiantly to effect a decent compromise between his original rebellious nature and the requirements of the official Soviet line. He was damned for his opera *Lady Macbeth of the District of Mtinsk*, which was denounced by an anonymous writer in *Pravda* as being both cacophonous and obscene (there were suggestive trombone glissandi in an orchestral interlude). Shostakovich then wrote a ballet on the subject of a collective farm; it was dismissed as an unworthy attempt to depict Soviet workers. Shostakovich was rehabilitated with his symphonies; his Seventh Symphony in particular, dedicated to the heroes of the Leningrad siege, became a display piece of Soviet patriotism. But his Thirteenth Symphony was criticized for his having used a poem mourning the Jews massacred at Babi Yar. The critics pointed out the poem's inequity, in that it only commemorated Jews, whereas there were also Ukrainians and Russians among the victims. Shostakovich agreed to fix the text; it did not help. Still, Shostakovich was given honors and distinctions, including the Order of Hero of Socialist Labor. A man of frail physique, he traveled little, but in 1973 he did make a trip to America to accept an honorary degree of doctor of fine arts from Northwestern University; a more compelling reason for this visit was to consult an American cancer specialist. But his illness was beyond remedy, and he died in 1975. A postage stamp was issued in his memory bearing a quotation from his Seventh Symphony and his typically bespectacled visage.

It would be most instructive to trace influences of modern techniques on composers whose style was fully formed in the 19th century. Gustav Mahler wrote music that departed widely from his immediate forerunners, but still he never went beyond harmonies that were traditionally justified — not until his unfinished Tenth Symphony, which employed dissonances that appeared quite unheralded by his previous music. Ralph Vaughan Williams accepted the previously illegal parallel triadic progressions; Frederick Delius, who always affected lyrical moods with traditional modalities, made use of whole-tone groups that deviated from tonality; even Jean Sibelius made a perilous leap into the unknown in his Fourth Symphony, using whole-tone passages and their related augmented triads. Ernest Bloch accepted and brilliantly used an implied bitonality of triads at a tritone's distance; in his last string quartet he even experimented with 12-tone melodies, although he never developed them in a Schoenbergian way. And of course, Richard Strauss never hesitated to project the sharpest dissonances when he needed them for purposes of illustration.

The 20th century has been the most turbulent period in all musical history. The variety of musical compositions produced in every country in the world has been more ample than in any previous century. What kind of music will emerge in the future as a result of all these conflicting tendencies? Being a man of the present, I cannot predict.

In my first published book, *Music Since 1900*, I attempted to draw a panorama of modern music. I took into consideration the intrinsic importance of each musical event in my chronology, as well as its impact on the contemporary audience. Whenever suitable, I quoted critical reviews in contemporary newspapers. Inevitably I selected adverse criticism to point out the irony of nonrecognition of works that subsequently proved to be masterpieces. The same penchant toward rejection of music that was startlingly new on the contemporary scene was revealed in the numerous reviews I collected for my *Lexicon of Musical Invective*. *La mer* of Debussy was dubbed *Le mal de mer* by a critic who intended to be witty, and *Le Sacre du printemps* was described as *Le Massacre du printemps*. In an index of these invectives, I tried to prove my thesis of "non-acceptance of the unfamiliar" in music as in other arts.

Someday I hope to bring up to date the events tabulated in *Music Since 1900*. In the meantime Richard Burbank has assembled a compendium of events in music and related arts that is immensely larger and more comprehensive in scope. And his quotations from the contemporary press, both in praise of the events and otherwise, provide a panorama of extraordinary effect of an art in flux, an evolution of new forms, an emergence of new ideas. It is invaluable for scholars and fascinating for music lovers. As an early worker in the field of creative chronology of music, I salute the author and the publisher for the completion and publication of this truly remarkable accomplishment.

Nicolas Slonimsky
Author of *Music Since 1900*

Los Angeles, 1983

1900 Opera

Jan. 1 *Chris and the Wonderful Lamp*, by John Philip Sousa, receives its world premiere in New York City. This operetta, based on *Arabian Nights*, has a book by Glen Mac-Donough. Sousa, now 45, has played in the Marine Band and has conducted vaudeville in Washington, D.C. He also performed with Jacques Offenbach during Offenbach's American tour in 1877 and performed at the Chicago World's Fair (1893).

Jan. 14 Giacomo Puccini's *Tosca* premieres at the Teatro Costanzi in Rome. The libretto is by Giuseppe Giacosa and Luigi Illica and is based on the play *La Tosca* by Victorien Sardou (1887). Leopoldo Mugone conducts. The verismo style of *Tosca* marks Puccini's departure from the lyric sentimentality of his previous operas. The opera is subsequently performed in London, and J.F. Runciman, critic for the *Saturday Review* (New York) says of that performance that the composer "... represents evil art — Italian music, to wit — and his success would have meant the preponderating influence in England of that evil art." Later the opera premieres in New York, and the New York *Sun* calls it "... a melodrama, in the truest sense. The music is almost entirely subordinated to the drama." Puccini is now 41 years old and studied at the Istituto Musicale of Lucca and the Milan Conservatory where he was a pupil of

GIACOMO PUCCINI

Amilcare Ponchielli. He is now a solidly established opera composer, having triumphed with *Manon Lescaut*, premiered in 1893, and *La Boheme*, premiered in 1896.

Jan. 18 *Thyl Uylenspiegel* is performed for the first time in Brussels. This three-act opera, by Flemish composer Jan Blockx, is set during the Dutch revolt against the Spaniards between 1568 and 1573. It includes Flemish folk dances.

Jan. 22 Alexander von Zemlinsky's opera *Es war einmal* is produced at the Vienna Opera. Gustav Mahler conducts. Zemlinsky has studied at the Vienna Conservatory. This year the 28-year-old musician becomes conductor of the Karlstheater in Vienna.

Feb. 2 *Louise*, an opera in four acts by Gustave Charpentier written to his own libretto, premieres at the Opera-Comique in Paris. Charpentier's first opera, *Louise* is the story of a love affair between a seamstress, Louise, and a bohemian poet, Julien, in Paris toward the end of the 19th century. It also raises the question of a woman's right to make her own decisions. A story about the lives of ordinary people, *Louise* marks the beginning of naturalism in French opera. The performance is conducted by Andre Messager. Commenting on a New York performance in 1908, Krehbiel of the New York *Tribune* says, "... the music may also be set down as immoral...." Charpentier studied with Jules Massenet at the Paris Conservatoire and won the Grand Prix de Rome in 1887. In addition to his

HARICLEA DARCLEE, THE FIRST TOSCA

musical activities, he is extremely concerned with the plight of the poor.

Feb. 22   *La Cenerentola* — an opera by Ermanno Wolf-Ferrari — receives its world premiere at the Teatro la Fenice in Venice. The libretto, by Pezze-Pascolato, is based on the fairy tale by Charles Perrault. Wolf-Ferrari composer studied with Josef Rheinberger in Munich. He moved to Venice last year.

Aug. 27   Gabriel Faure's first opera, *Promethee* premieres in the Roman arena at Beziers. The libretto, by Paul Duval, is based on a previous treatment by Ferdinand Herold. In this opera Faure uses a mixture of song and spoken dialogue. This grandiose work, a loose adaptation of the classical myth of Prometheus, calls for 700 performers. A violent storm breaks during the first performance, and it is postponed, but tomorrow it is performed before 10,000 enthusiastic spectators. Due to the difficulties of staging *Promethee*, a scaled-down version is created in 1917 by Jean-Jules Roger-Ducasse for performance in indoor theaters. The 55-year-old Faure studied composition with Camille Saint-Saens. He has held various positions as an organist and became a professor of composition at the Paris Conservatoire four years ago.

Sep. 28   Mikhail Ippolitov-Ivanov's opera *Asya* is performed in Moscow, marking the opera's world premiere. The second opera by this composer, it is based on a love story by Turgenev. Ippolitov-Ivanov is a product of the Saint Petersburg Conservatory where he was a protege of Nikolai Rimsky-Korsakov. Now 40 years old, he has taught at the Music School in Tiflis and joined the faculty of the Moscow Conservatory seven years ago.

Nov. 3   Nikolai Rimsky-Korsakov's opera *The Tale of Tsar Saltan* premieres at the Solodovnikov Theater in Moscow.

The libretto by Vladimir Bielsky is based on a poem by Pushkin — a tale about Tsar Saltan, his wife Militrissa, their hero-son Guidon, Militrissa's wicked sisters and cousin, and a beautiful Swan Princess. The opera was written to celebrate the centenary of Pushkin's birth and is remembered today chiefly for the third-act interlude known as the "Flight of the Bumblebee." Rimsky-Korsakov graduated from the Saint Petersburg Naval School in 1862 and promptly went on a clipper voyage before returning to Russia two and a half years later. His interest in music manifested itself in his childhood. Among the musicians he met and found influential were Mily Balakirev, Cesar Cui and Alexander Borodin. After being appointed to the faculty of the Saint Petersburg Conservatory in 1871, he left the Navy to devote himself to music. His only remaining contact with the Navy was as an inspector of military orchestras. At this point in time, he is conducting as well as composing and attracting considerable attention, principally as a conductor of his own works.

Nov. 10   *Zaza* by Ruggero Leoncavallo premieres at the Teatro Lirico in Milan, with Rosina Storchio in the title role and Leoncavallo conducting. The libretto, written by the composer, is based on a play by Charles Simon and Pierre Berton about Zaza, a successful cafe singer, and her love for Milio Dufresne, a happily married man with a family. Next to *Pagliacci*, *Zaza* is Leoncavallo's most successful opera and is often performed in Italy. Leoncavallo, who studied at the Naples Conservatory, has toured as a pianist. Until 1892, when *Pagliacci* premiered and brought him outstanding success, he earned his living as a cabaret pianist. In 1897, his opera *La Boheme* received its world premiere but was overshadowed by Giacomo Puccini's opera of the same title which premiered a year earlier.

1900 Dance

Jan. 17   *Les Ruses d'amour* — a ballet by choreographer Marius Petipa — is produced for the first time today at the Hermitage Theater in Saint Petersburg. The lead dancers are Italian ballerina Pierina Legnani, Marie Petipa, Lubov Petipa and Nadejda Petipa. The one-act ballet, also known as *The Trial of Damis*, is about a duchess's daughter who poses as a chambermaid to make sure her beloved marquis loves her. Petipa bases his ballet on a 1760 Jean-Georges Noverre production entitled *La Toilette de Venus*. Music to this ballet is by Alexander Glazunov. Petipa, one of the seminal choreographers in ballet history, is currently in the evening of his career. He choreographed many works in Saint Petersburg including Tchaikovsky's *Sleeping Beauty*.

Feb. 10   *Les Millions d'Arlequin* — a two-act ballet with choreography by Marius Petipa and music by Riccardo Drigo — premieres at the Hermitage Theater, Saint Petersburg. Lead dancers in this work, based on traditional commedia dell'arte, are Mathilda Kschessinska and Olga Preobrajenska.

Feb. 20   *Les Saisons* a ballet by Marius Petipa, premieres today at the Hermitage Theater in Saint Petersburg. Music is by Alexander Glazunov; the principal dancer is Mathilda Kschessinska. Several ballets with this title and theme (the four seasons) are choreographed throughout the century.

1900   Instrumental and Vocal Music

Feb. 3   George Whitefield Chadwick's overture *Adonais* is premiered by the Boston Symphony Orchestra. This composer, a leading American musician, becomes a member of the Boston Academy of Arts and Letters. Chadwick studied at the Leipzig Conservatory with Carl Reinecke and Salomon Jadassohn. He also studied in Munich with Josef Rheinberger. Now 45 years old, he has been on the faculty of the New England Conservatory of Music for the past 20 years.

March 14   *Hiawatha's Wedding Feast* — the first part of Samuel Coleridge-Taylor's trilogy for soli, chorus and orchestra — receives its first American performance in Boston. The Cecilia Society performs under the baton of B.J. Lang. Coleridge-Taylor, now 25 years old, is a British composer of African extraction. The complete trilogy premieres on March 22 in London.

March 22   *Hiawatha's Departure* — a large scale work for soli, chorus and orchestra by Samuel Coleridge-Taylor, receives its first performance at Royal Albert Hall, London. The Royal Choral Society performs the work and the composer conducts. This piece is the third of a trilogy, *The Song of Hiawatha*, which includes *Hiawatha's Wedding Feast*, *The Death of Minnehaha*, and *Hiawatha's Departure*. Today's performance of the entire trilogy marks the first time the work is performed complete. This event substantially enhances the prestige of this composer. The trilogy receives its first American performance on November 16, 1904.

July 2   *Finlandia*, by Jean Sibelius, receives its world premiere in Helsinki, Finland. Robert Kajanus conducts the Helsinki Philharmonic. Inspired by a Russian attempt to suppress freedom of speech in Finland, the work is a revised version of the fourth movement, "Suomi," of his suite *Finland Awakes* (composed 1899). The piece is tremendously successful and comes to be internationally identified with struggles for freedom. Sibelius began as a law student but found it so boring that he dropped out before completing his first semester. His formal musical conservatory training, which began at that time, was preceded by his childhood and adolescent studies of piano and violin. He has also studied in Berlin and in Vienna (with Karl Goldmark). He is now 34.

Oct. 3   Edward Elgar's *The Dream of Gerontius*, Op. 38, receives its world premiere at the Birmingham Festival in England. Hans Richter conducts the oratorio, scored for solo voices, chorus and orchestra. The text is a poem by Cardinal Newman in which Gerontius prays in Latin and English and explores the meaning of Purgatory; the music consists of lyric and dramatic episodes cast in a Wagnerian blend. The work is a failure, largely because the Birmingham public had been anticipating a Handelian oratorio replete with arias, choruses and the like. It is not until next year, when the work is performed in Germany, that it makes a strong impression. Richard Strauss subsequently describes it as a "masterpiece." Elgar, 43, is on the verge of becoming known as the most prominent English composer of his day. He initially studied law while playing organ in church. He later studied violin and then returned to Worcester, where he conducted the band at the County Lunatic Asylum. In 1889 he married a daughter of Sir Henry Roberts, attempted to gain recognition in London, but failed. He settled in Malvern in 1891, where he now lives. To date, he has gained considerable, but not international, recognition for the following works: *Froissart*, an overture, premiered in 1890; the cantata *The Black Knight*, premiered in 1893; the cantata *Scenes from the Saga of King Olaf*, premiered in 1896; and the *Enigma Variations*, premiered in 1899.

Nov. 24   The Symphony No. 1 in E Minor, Op. 26 by Alexander Scriabin is performed at the Russian Symphony Concerts in Saint Petersburg, with Anatoly Liadov conducting. The sixth movement (a choral movement) is not performed today; it is finally performed on March 29 of next year at a concert in Moscow conducted by Vassily Safonov. Scriabin is now 28 years old and has studied with Sergei Taneyev. He also studied piano with Vassily Safonov at the Moscow Conservatory. His composition studies at the conservatory with Anton Arensky, however, led to disappointment when he failed his examinations and forfeited his diploma. His career began when he met publisher Mitrofan Belaiev who gave him a contract. His Concerto for Piano and Orchestra, Op. 20, premiered three years ago, was his first major composition. That year he married pianist Vera Isakovich. Despite his failure to obtain his diploma from the Moscow Conservatory, he was invited to join the faculty in 1898. He now teaches piano there.

Dec. 9   "Nuages" and "Fetes", the first two sections of Claude Debussy's symphonic suite *Nocturnes*, receive their world premiere at the Concerts Lamoureux in Paris. Camille Chevillard conducts. The third of the *Nocturnes* (later to be titled *Trois Nocturnes*) is "Sirenes," which receives its first performance on October 27 of next year.

Dec. 15   The second and third movements of Serge Rachmaninoff's Concerto No. 2 in C Minor for Piano and Orchestra, Op. 18, receive their world premiere in Moscow. Rachmaninoff performs at a concert organized by the Moscow Prison Philanthropic Committee. These movements were composed before the first movement; a complete premiere of the work, one of the composer's most famous, takes place next November 9.

1900 Births, Deaths and Debuts

Jan. 7   American baritone and opera teacher John Brownlee is born in Geelong, Australia.

March 2   Composer Kurt Weill is born in Dessau, Germany.

March 19   Charles-Louis Hanon, 81, dies in Boulogne-sur-Mer, France. A composer and teacher, Hanon's famous piano method books have become standard literature. His best known publication is *Le Pianiste-virtuose*.

March 21   Conductor Paul Kletzki is born in Lodz, Poland.

April 2   German musicologist Heinrich Besseler is born in Horde, Dortmund.

April 10   Scottish-American soprano Mary Garden makes her operatic debut in *Louise* at the Opera-Comique in Paris. This event takes place two months after the premiere of this work. Garden is called in today at the last minute to replace Marthe Rioton in the middle of the performance.

April 14   Bass Salvatore Baccaloni is born in Rome, Italy.

April 17   Composer Willy Burkhard is born in Leubringen bei Biel, Switzerland.

April 23   Composer Henry Barraud is born in Bordeaux, France.

April 26   Violinist Joseph Fuchs is born in New York.

May 5   Conductor Hans Schmidt-Isserstedt is born in Berlin, Germany.

May 13   German conductor Hermann Levi, 60, dies in Munich. He was conductor of the Munich court theater and was noted for performing the works of Richard Wagner and Johannes Brahms. On July 26, 1882 he led the first production of Richard Wagner's *Parsifal* at Bayreuth. He also conducted at Wagner's funeral. Correspondence between Levi and Brahms is subsequently published in *Brahms Briefwechsel* (Volume 7, Berlin, 1912).

May 17   Composer Nicolai Berezowsky is born in Saint Petersburg, Russia.

May 28   Sir George Grove, 79, who established the famous *Dictionary of Music and Musicians*, dies in London. Associated much of his life with the Crystal Palace concerts in London, he was also a biblical scholar. The first edition of his music dictionary was published in 1879.

June 15   Composer Otto Luening is born in Milwaukee, Wisconsin.

June 17   Composer Hermann Reutter is born in Stuttgart, Germany.

June 22   Mezzo-soprano Jennie Tourel is born in Saint Petersburg, Russia.

June 26   Tenor Richard Crooksis born in Trenton, New Jersey.

July 8   Composer George Antheil is born in Trenton, New Jersey.

July 9   Swiss composer Robert Oboussier is born in Antwerp, Belgium.

Aug. 23   Composer Ernst Krenek is born in Vienna, Austria.

Sep. 3   Conductor Eduard van Beinum is born in Arnhem, Holland.

Oct. 19   Soprano Erna Berger is born in Dresden, Germany.

Nov. 7   Conductor Efrem Kurtz is born in Saint Petersburg.

Nov. 12   Russian pianist Ossip Gabrilowitsch makes his American debut at Carnegie Hall, New York.

Nov. 14   Composer Aaron Copland is born in Brooklyn, New York.

Nov. 14   American contralto Louise Homer makes her American debut with the Metropolitan Opera, while that company is on tour in San Francisco. She sings Amneris in *Aida*.

SIR ARTHUR SULLIVAN

Nov. 22   Sir Arthur Sullivan, 58, dies in London. After studies at the Royal Academy of Music and the Leipzig Conservatory, Sullivan first attracted attention in 1864 with a performance of his cantata *Kenilworth* at the Birmingham Festival. Soon thereafter, he met and established a friendship with Sir George Grove, with whom he traveled to Vienna and discovered the lost manuscript of Franz Schubert's *Rosamunde*. Sullivan began to collaborate with humorist W.S. Gilbert in 1875. Together the team of Gilbert and Sullivan went on to attract international attention for their comic operas. In 1876 Richard D'Oyly Carte formed a special company just for Gilbert and Sullivan, which produced *H.M.S. Pinafore* in 1878 and all their other popular operettas. Sullivan, also known as a conductor and educator, received many honorary degrees and awards (Queen Victoria knighted him in 1883). Among his best-known works are *The Pirates of Penzance, Iolanthe, The Mikado, The Yeomen of the Guard* and *Patience*. He also composed cantatas, including *The Golden Legend*; songs, the most popular being "The Lost Chord"; oratorios, such as *The Light of the World*; and a grand opera, *Ivanhoe*.

Nov. 25   Composer, violinist and conductor Tibor Serly is born in Losonc, Hungary.

Nov. 27   Conductor Leon Barzin is born in Brussels, Belgium.

Dec. 19   English soprano Audrey Mildmay is born in Hurstmonceaux.

Dec. 22   English composer Alan Bush is born in Dulwich, England.

Dec. 25   Mezzo-soprano Gladys Swarthout is born in Deepwater, Missouri.

Dec. 27   Conductor Willem van Otterloo is born in Winterswijk, Holland.

1900 Related Events

Jan. 23   The Pittsburgh Symphony Orchestra makes its Carnegie Hall debut as Victor Herbert conducts. This orchestra was founded in 1894 when Frederick Archer became its first music director. A reviewer states after attending tonight's event: "At present there are four cities which can pride themselves in a permanent orchestra — Boston, Cincinnati, Chicago and Pittsburgh."

May   The famous dog trademark "His Master's Voice" is registered this year in the United States by Joseph Berliner. The same trademark was registered in England by the Gramophone Company after it had purchased the original painting of the dog "Nipper" from the artist Francis Barraud last year. (Nipper also dies this year and is buried at Kingston-on-Thames.) Other developments in the recording industry are the publication of a 5,000-entry catalog by the Gramophone Company (based in London); the introduction of paper labels for recordings, which replace the old method of hand-scratching information onto the wax centers of records; the introduction of a wax mastering process for discs by Eldridge R. Johnson; the establishment of the Consolidated Talking Machine Company; the founding of the Berliner Phonograph archives by Karl Stumpf; the publication of the first issue of *Phonographische Zeitschrift* (a new trade journal about the industry); and the introduction of a molded celluloid cylinder by Thomas B. Lambert. These events mark the beginning of increased sales of music and monologue records for home entertainment and spark the founding of many new recording companies, both in America and in Europe.

May 15   Ignace Paderewski establishes a new prize: The Paderewski Fund Prize for American composers of orchestral compositions. The fund is based in New York, and the award is to be made on an annual basis.

May 22   The Dallas Symphony Orchestra gives its first concert. Held in Turner Hall, Dallas, Texas, it is conducted by Hans Kriessig. The program includes music by Rossini, Wagner, Haydn and Mascagni, and also a piece entitled *Allons Dance* by the conductor.

June 18   The New York *Times* reports that farmers in upstate New York have discovered an effective way of killing unwanted insects: Have a brass band march around the orchards playing music at a loud volume. The report goes on to say that the farmers suspect the musical vibrations of this sonic insecticide may be a potent weapon in killing other forms of life, but that they cannot predict when the effect may become reversed and "set in motion a desire on the part of the animal capable of resisting them to kill the performer."

Oct. 15   Symphony Hall, Boston becomes the new home of the Boston Symphony Orchestra. The building's acoustics are praised, and it is subsequently ranked as one of the best concert halls in the world, along with the Concertgebouw in Amsterdam, Musik-Verein-Saal in Vienna and Carnegie Hall in New York.

Nov. 16   The first concert of the Philadelphia Orchestra takes place in that city. Fritz Scheel conducts a program of music featuring Beethoven's Fifth Symphony and Tchaikovsky's First Piano Concerto. Pianist Ossip Gabrilowitsch, 22, performs as soloist.

Nov. 22   The University of Cambridge, England awards the honorary degree of Doctor of Music to Edward Elgar.

1901 Opera

Jan. 17   *Le Maschere* by Pietro Mascagni premieres simultaneously in six different Italian cities; the conductor in Milan is Arturo Toscanini and in Rome, Mascagni. The libretto, by Luigi Illica, is a comedy of errors concerning Florindo and Rosaura — young lovers — and their attempts to outwit their elders in order to marry. Mascagni is now 37 years old. His father wanted him to becomes a baker but eventually gave in to his son's musical desires. Mascagni studied with Amilcare Ponchielli at the Milan Conservatory before dropping out because he disliked discipline. His opera *Cavelleria Rusticana* was premiered in Rome in 1890 — that event catapulted him to national attention because it introduced the "verismo" style.

March 31   *Rusalka*, by Antonin Dvorak premieres at the National Opera House in Prague. The libretto, by Jaroslav Kvapil, is based on a popular fairy tale about the love of a water sprite, Rusalka, for a mortal prince. It is the best-known of Dvorak's nine operas and is performed frequently in Czechoslovakia. Dvorak's father wanted him to become a butcher but Antonin persisted with music and entered the Prague Organ School at age 16. After 1873 when his first important work — *Hymnus* for mixed chorus and orchestra — premiered, his career steadily moved forward and involved conducting as well as composing. He is now 59 years old.

May 29   Ignace Jan Paderewski's *Manru* premieres at the Dresden Opera. The libretto by Alfred Nossig is based on a novel by Kraszewski about the gypsy Manru and the young woman, Ulana, who marries him against her mother's wishes. Paderewski, 40 years old, began to explore music at age 3. He made his first public appearance as a pianist at 12 and was helped by wealthy patrons until he arrived at the Conservatory of Warsaw, where he studied the trombone. He argued with the faculty about rehearsals and was expelled, but later readmitted and appointed to the faculty. After further studies he gave a successful concert in 1887 in Vienna. Since then he has toured extensively as a pianist and has been extremely well received. He began composing at age 7. His goal has always been to be a famous composer.

May 30   *Much Ado About Nothing* — a new four-act opera by composer Charles Villiers Stanford — premieres today at Covent Garden, London. Based on the play by William Shakespeare, the opera is performed once more at Covent Garden and is dropped from the repertoire. Stanford studied piano with Ernst Pauer in London. He then studied organ at Queens College, Cambridge and later, composition with Carl Reinecke in Berlin. He received honorary doctorates from Oxford and Cambridge in the 1880s. This year he becomes principal conductor of the Leeds Festival.

Sep. 26   George W. Chadwick's opera *Judith* premieres in a concert version at the Worcester, Massachusetts Music Festival. An American composer born in 1854, Chadwick's music is conservative in style. He studied composition with Carl Reinecke and Salomon Jadassohn at the Leipzig Conservatory. He also studied organ and composition with Josef Rheinberger in Munich before returning to Boston and joining the faculty of the New England Conservatory of Music.

Oct. 23   Camille Saint-Saens' *Les Barbares* is produced at the Paris Opera. The opera consists of a prologue and three acts, with text by V. Sardou and P.B. Gheusi. The story of the work, which takes place in 105 B.C., deals with Teutonic and Roman warriors who fight over a priestess. Saint-Saens is a product of the Paris Conservatoire; he studied there with Jacques Halevy. Since his graduation, he has become known as an organist and pianist as well as a composer. His only disappointment has been his failure, twice, to win the Grand Prix de Rome.

Nov. 9   Hans Pfitzner's opera *Die Rose vom Liebesgarten* premieres in Elberfeld, Germany. Conducted by the composer, the two-act opera is about a magical rose that creates love. Pfitzner studied at the Hoch's Conservatory in Frankfurt. He has conducted at the Municipal Theater in Mainz and has taught at the Conservatory of Coblenz and at the Stern's Conservatory in Berlin. He is now 32 years old.

Nov. 20   *Griselidis* by Jules Massenet, premieres at the Opera-Comique in Paris; the conductor is Andre Messager. The libretto, by Armand Silvestre and Eugene

PIETRO MASCAGNI

Morand, is based on a medieval legend of the virtuous Gri-selda, which appeared in several versions, from the *Lais of Marie de France* to Chaucer's *Canterbury Tales*. The cast is headed by Lucienne Breval and Lucien Fugere. Massenet entered the Paris Conservatoire at the age of 9 and won a Grand Prix de Rome at the age of 20. He has been teaching at that conservatory since 1878; he is now 59 years old.

Nov. 21   Richard Strauss' opera *Feuersnot* premieres at the Konigliches Opernhaus in Dresden conducted by Ernst von Schuch. The opera tells the story of sorcerer Kunrad and his love for Diemut (a burgomaster's daughter) and how he magically extinguishes all fires in the town, sing-ing that this lack of fire (*Feuersnot*) will continue until Die-mut yields to him. For this early work — his third opera — Strauss uses a libretto by Ernst von Wolzogen. The musi-cal style shows a variety of influences, among them Gus-tav Mahler, Richard Wagner and Anton Bruckner. The opera is not praised by critics. Strauss' education was begun at the instigation of his father, the horn player Franz Strauss. He studied violin, harp and composition. At age 16, he enjoyed the rare privilege of having one of his compositions, *Festmarsch* for Orchestra, Op. 1, published.

Nov. 24   Cesar Cui's one-act opera *A Feast in Time of Plague* is performed for the first time in Moscow. The opera, about the plague of London (1665), is set to Pushkin's dra-matic text. Pushkin's play had been based on *The City of Plague*, a tragedy by John Wilson. This work was originally written as a dramatic cantata. Cui studied engineering at the Saint Petersburg Engineering Academy for six years and is an expert typographer and specialist in military for-tification. He taught fortification to Czar Nicholas II. While in his early 20s, he met Mily Balakirev who coached him in composition. He has also worked as a music critic for the *Vyedomosti* (Saint Petersburg) but discontinues that activity this year. He is now 65 years old.

1901   Dance

Jan. 1   *Soldiers of the Queen* is produced at the Alhambra Theater, London. This ballet spectacle displays costumed dancers who represent the Queen's parade, complete with drums and fife. It features 250 dancers. The ballet is a tre-mendous success because of the patriotic fervor it evokes (the Boer War is now taking place).

March 18   *Les Papillons* — a ballet divertissement in two scenes — is produced at the Empire Theater, London. Mu-sic is by Leopold Wenzel, book and costumes by C. Wil-helm, scenery by Joseph Harker and choreography by Katti Lanner. This is one of many spectacle ballets per-formed since the late 1800s that mark the Empire Theater as a ballet center in London along with the Alhambra The-ater — theaters that specialize in historical and patriotic pageants. Today's performance stars Adeline Genee (who dances the part of Vanessa Imperialis, Queen of Butterfly Land) and whose performances in *The Press* (1898) and *Monte Cristo* (1897) brought her to national attention. The London *Times* says Genee "... gives a number of very charming dances. . . . " It also says of Will Bishop (who dances the part of the Grasshopper) that he "... conducts the revels with the greatest spirit and drollery. . . ." Dancer Adeline Genee is now 23 years old and made her debut in Oslo, Norway, when she was 10 years old. In 1896, she danced the role of Swanilda in *Coppelia* at the Munich Court Opera — a role that became her most famous to date. She is now the most popular dancer of London's Em-pire Theater.

Dec. 15   The ballet *Sylvia*, to music by Leo Delibes, is staged for the Maryinsky Theater in Saint Petersburg. The choreography for this version is by Lev Ivanov, who died before the completion of the ballet. Pavel Gerdt also con-tributes to the choreography. Originally premiered on June 14, 1876 at the Paris Opera, this version is staged as a benefit for the ballerina Olga Preobrajenska.

1901   Instrumental and Vocal Music

Feb. 3   Gabriel Faure's orchestral suite *Pelleas et Melisande* premieres at the Concerts Lamoureux in Paris. The music is adapted from incidental music to the drama by Maurice Maeterlinck.

Feb. 7   Claude Debussy's *Chansons de Bilitis* receives its first performance in Paris. Based on poems by Pierre Louys, this piece is scored for two flutes, two harps and celesta but is different from another work of the same name by Debussy, which is a group of songs. Today's per-formance includes narrator and mime; Debussy later in-corporates the music into his *Six epigraphes antiques* for piano duo.

Feb. 17   *Das klagende Lied*, by Gustav Mahler, receives its world premiere by the Vienna Philharmonic in that city, Mahler conducting. Mahler wrote his own text to this piece, which was completed in 1880 and is based on a fairy tale by Ludwig Bechstein about murder.

March 29   Alexander Scriabin's Symphony No. 1 in E Minor, Op. 26, is performed in its complete version in Moscow. Today's performance is conducted by Vassily Safonov and includes "*Hymn to Art* — the last choral movement. The work had been performed without this movement last November 24, in a performance by the Russian Symphony Concerts, conducted by Anatoly Liadov in Saint Petersburg.

May 3   Marcel Dupre's oratorio *La Vision de Jacob* premieres in France with Dupre playing the organ part himself. This is also the composer's 15th birthday.

June 20   Edward Elgar's *Cockaigne Overture* receives its world premiere as Elgar conducts the London Philharmonic.

June 23   Ernest Bloch's symphonic *Vivre Aimer* premieres at the Second Festival of Swiss Music in Geneva. He has studied solfeggio with Emile Jaques-Dalcroze and violin with Eugene Ysaye. He moves to Germany this year to study at the Hoch Conservatory in Frankfurt.

Oct. 19   Edward Elgar's first two *Pomp and Circumstance* marches premiere in Liverpool.

Oct. 27   Claude Debussy's *Trois Nocturnes* is given in its first complete performance as Camille Chevillard conducts the Lamoureux Orchestra in Paris. This performance includes "*Sirenes* — the third nocturne — which was not premiered with the other two last December. *Trois Nocturnes* is the composer's most impressive work at this point in his career. The pieces are dedicated to his wife, Rosalie Texier.

Nov. 9   Serge Rachmaninoff performs the solo part in his Concerto No. 2 in C Minor for Piano and Orchestra with Alexander Siloti conducting the Moscow Philharmonic. This event marks the first complete performance of this work. The concerto had been composed while Rachmaninoff was suffering from severe depression, and he dedicated it to his doctor, Dr. Dahl, for helping him recover and gain self-confidence. The work subsequently becomes a world favorite. It is probably Rachmaninoff's most popular and frequently performed composition.

Nov. 25   Gustav Mahler's Symphony No. 4 in G Major receives its world premiere in Munich, the composer conducting. This symphony features a soprano soloist in the last movement. Critics do not like the music: Theodor Kroyer says in *Die Musik* that the piece is ". . . a morbid, tasteless supermusic." A reviewer in the *Musical Courier* (New York) compares it to a "circus scene" and says ". . . it was a shock and an unpleasant one."

Dec. 20   Henry Hadley's *Symphony No. 2* (*The Four Seasons*) is performed by Emil Paur and the New York Philharmonic. The work wins this year's Paderewski Prize. Hadley has studied with George Whitefield Chadwick at the New England Conservatory (Boston). He is currently teaching at Saint Paul's School, Garden City, N. Y.

1901   Births, Deaths and Debuts

GIUSEPPE VERDI

Jan. 11   Russian composer Vassili Kalinnikov, 34, dies of tuberculosis at Yalta, the Crimea. He earned his living primarily as a bassoon player. Kalinnikov composed two symphonies, two symphonic poems, a cantata and other works. His Symphony in G Minor, premiered in 1897, remains his best-known work.

Jan. 22   Composer Hans Erich Apostel is born in Karlsruhe, Austria.

Jan. 27   Italian composer Giuseppe Verdi, 87, dies in Milan, Italy. Verdi studied organ with a local church organist and began composing at age 16. He went to Milan, where he was rejected by the Milan Conservatory for being almost incompetent at the keyboard; it was determined that he had talent but not enough technical skill as a composer to justify admission. Verdi then studied privately with Vincenzo Lavigna, began to become interested in opera and began conducting in 1834.

His first opera, *Oberto, conte di San Bonifacio*, premiered at La Scala in 1839. His first real success was with *Nabucco*, premiered at La Scala in 1842. This led to a secure position as a composer of Italian opera. He continued composing and producing operas with mixed results; most did not enhance his career until the appearance of *Rigoletto* in 1851. Following *Rigoletto* came *Il Trovatore* and *La Traviata*. These three operas established him internationally as a leading opera composer. *Un ballo in maschera* reflected his newfound interest in Italian independence. *Aida*, premiered in 1871, was composed for the opening of the Suez Canal. In 1887 Verdi's opera *Otello* premiered at La Scala — Verdi was then 73. His last opera, *Falstaff*, was composed when he was 80. In all, Verdi composed 26 operas.

Verdi was the most magnificent figure in Italian opera since Claudio Monteverdi. He combined unrestrained, passionate music with powerful drama and simple melody. Verdi's death symbolizes the end of a musical era. The 19th century closes. No composer of Italian opera after Verdi succeeds in achieving and maintaining the almost sacred status Verdi enjoyed. Shortly after Verdi's death, the preeminence of Italian opera soon surrenders to French impressionism and Viennese atonal-expressionism.

Jan. 26 Music scholar and composer Ervin Major is born in Budapest, Hungary.

Feb. 2 Violinist Jascha Heifetz is born in the Polish-Lithuanian town of Vilna.

March 8 Flemish composer Peter Benoit, 66, dies in Antwerp. A product of the Brussels Conservatory, his first opera, *A Mountain Village*, was produced in 1856. He later won a Prix de Rome with his cantata *Le meurte d'Abel*. In 1867 he founded the Flemish Music School in Antwerp (this institution became the Royal Flemish Conservatory in 1898) and became its director. As a composer he advocated a national Flemish school of composition. Through his music, essays and articles, he came to be known as the originator of this goal in Belgium. His music is also heavily influenced by French and German works. His masterpiece is the oratorio *Lucifer* (premiered in 1866). He also composed other oratorios, operas, cantatas, a few instrumental works and many songs.

March 15 Composer Colin McPhee is born in Montreal, Canada.

March 16 Czech contralto Marta Krasova is born in Protovin.

March 19 Edwin Francis Hyde, 81, dies in New York City. He was president of the Philharmonic Society of New York from 1888 to 1901.

March 22 Musicologist William Oliver Strunk is born in Ithaca, New York.

March 31 Sir John Stainer, 60, dies in Verona, Italy. At age 7 he sang as a chorister in London at Saint Paul's Cathedral, eventually rising to become that cathedral's organist. At age 47, suffering from poor vision, he resigned from Saint Paul's and was immediately knighted. He then taught at Oxford University. His music includes oratorios and cantatas on religious themes, canticles, anthems, songs, and books on harmony and other musical subjects.

April 4 German musicologist Adam Adrio is born in Essen.

May 7 Composer Marcel Poot is born in Vilvorde, Belgium.

May 17 Composer Werner Egk is born in Auchsesheim, Germany.

May 17 Tenor Max Lorenz is born in Dusseldorf, Germany.

May 18 Composer Henri Sauguet is born in Bordeaux, France.

May 23 Composer Edmund Rubbra is born in Northampton, England.

June 24 Composer Harry Partch is born in Oakland, California.

July 3 Composer Ruth Crawford Seeger is born in East Liverpool, Ohio.

July 14 Composer Gerald Finzi is born in London, England.

July 16 Conductor Fritz Mahler, a nephew of Gustav Mahler, is born in Vienna.

Aug. 16 Composer-conductor Olav Kielland is born in Trondheim, Norway.

Aug. 17 Composer Henri Tomasi is born in Marseilles, France.

Aug. 21 Violinist John Corigliano, Sr. is born in New York City.

Oct. 15 Geraldine Farrar makes her operatic debut in Berlin as Marguerite in Gounod's *Faust*. Karl Muck conducts the Berlin Royal Opera. The critics send Farrar to fame. One writes, ". . . no degree of trickery on the stage could have shaken her confidence or repose."

Nov. 1 Music critic and writer Hans Heinz Stuckenschmidt is born in Strasbourg, Germany.

Nov. 25 Composer Josef Gabriel Rheinberger, 62, dies in Munich. This internationally famous composer of organ music earned his living (in his early years) at the Munich Gesangverein working as an accompanist. He also conducted and taught piano and composition. Among his organ works are 20 organ sonatas and 2 organ concertos. Other compositions include operas, as well as orchestral, piano and chamber works.

Dec. 11 Lev Ivanov, one of the great choreographers of the Saint Petersburg Russian Imperial Ballet, dies in Saint Petersburg at the age of 67. Appointed second ballet master under Marius Petipa in 1885, Ivanov was responsible for some of the most important ballets in the Russian classical repertoire. His most important works were *The Nutcracker* and *Swan Lake* (acts 2 and 4), which he staged with Petipa.

Dec. 22   Russian-American conductor Andre Kostelanetz is born in Saint Petersburg, Russia.

Dec. 26   Composer and writer Georgi Rimsky-Korsakov is born in Saint Petersburg. He is the grandson of Nikolai Rimsky-Korsakov.

1901 Related Events

JEAN DE RESZKE

March 29   Jean de Reszke's final performance of the season with the Metropolitan Opera turns into his farewell performance with that company as he sings the title role in Richard Wagner's *Lohengrin*. Though not announced as his final Met appearance, he does not return except for a brief appearance this April. W.J. Henderson says of the tenor in The New York *Times*, "He was an ideal Knight of the Grail." Henry Krehbiel notes in the New York *Tribune*, "There were flowers for everybody and joy and peace and goodwill."

April 29   World-famous tenor Jean de Reszke returns to the stage to sing the second act of Richard Wagner's *Tristan und Isolde* at the Metropolitan Opera in New York. Anticipating his retirement after his final performance with the Met last month, the audience jams the opera house; 16 women faint; applause for this singer and his brother Edouard continues for a half hour. W.J. Henderson of the New York *Times* describes the ovation as "frantic."

May 17   The Benedictine monks of Solesmes are publicly lauded by Pope Leo XIII for their scholarly work on Gregorian chant. He sets up their work as a model for further scholarly research on the subject and says, in part (in a letter entitled *Nos quidem* addressed to Dom Paul Delatte, abbot of Solesmes), "All undertakings which aim towards explaining and propagating the science of the plainchant, this companion and auxiliary science, deserve praise not only because of the cleverness and for the energy expended, but also, and this is much more important, because from them we hope for an increase in divine worship."

June 1   The music publisher Universal Edition is officially founded today in Vienna. This publishing house consistently advances the cause of new music by publishing many important new works as the 20th century unfolds.

June 30   Maurice Ravel scores third place (deuxieme second) in the annual Prix de Rome competition. The assigned cantata subject, *Myrrha*, is judged by the panel of the Academie des Beaux-Arts, including Camille Saint-Saens and Jules Massenet. Charles-Marie Widor and Gabriel Faure serve as additional judges.

July 1   The French government enacts its "Law of Associations." This anti-clerical legislation prohibits the formation of new monastic orders and congregations without direct government approval. Old orders are allowed to continue, provided they submit annual lists of their membership to the government. The legislation is subsequently amended to prohibit all congregations from pursuing educational activities. As a direct result of today's action, the Benedictine monks of Solesmes go into exile: they are invited by Dom Mocquereau (a Roman Catholic monk and specialist on sacred music) to move to the Isle of Wight where they are entrusted with the preparation of the new Vatican edition of the chant books. Other male religious orders go into exile; female orders remain in France but become nursing congregations. This legislation ultimately leads to the final break between Church and State in France, which occurs four years from now. The monks of Solesmes return to France on April 1, 1922.

Sep. 20   The German music periodical *Die Musik*, an illustrated journal, is published for the first time in Berlin. Issued on a bimonthly basis, the magazine's purpose is to become a first-rate music periodical and rank with similar magazines about the other arts.

Oct.   The Columbia Phonograph Company (founded as a subsidiary sales organization of the North American Phonograph Company in 1889) issues the first recordings under its Climax label. In other developments in the recording industry this year: Eldridge Johnson establishes the Victor Talking Machine Company and is permitted to use the dog trademark "His Master's Voice." The National Gramophone Company issues the first celebrity red-label discs featuring artists from the Russian Imperial Opera, the first 10-inch discs ever manufactured. The International Zonophone Company is established.

Dec.   The Wa-Wan Press opens for business this month. Founded by Arthur Farwell, the music publishing house specializes in works of American composers who incorporate folk tunes of America (especially Indian) in their work. In addition to focusing on musical source material of American Indians, the company also seeks works reflecting cowboy songs. Rubin Goldmark and Henry Gilbert have works published by this house. Music is published on a quarterly basis until 1907, when it appears monthly.

Dec. 11   Guglielmo Marconi transmits the first transatlantic radio signal from Poldhu, Cornwall, England, to Saint John's, Newfoundland.

1902 Opera

JULES MASSENET

Feb. 18   Jules Massenet's *Le Jongleur de Notre Dame* premieres at the Theatre de Casino in Monte Carlo. The libretto by Maurice Lena is based on a medieval miracle play in which the Virgin blesses a lowly juggler, Jean, for paying homage to her in the only way he knows — with his juggling tricks — much to the dismay of the monks at Cluny. The opera is notable in that originally all the roles were written for men, although Mary Garden later persuaded Massenet to adapt the role of Jean for soprano voice.

April 9   English composer Ethel Smyth's one-act opera *Der Wald*, composed to her own libretto (in German), premieres in Berlin. Karl Muck conducts the work at the Royal Opera. The composer had learned German during her studies in Leipzig. A critic for *The Musical Courier* (New

York) terms the work ". . . a fiasco the like of which I have never witnessed." Smyth studied at the Leipzig Conservatory. Her first big success came in 1893 with the premiere of her *Mass* for vocal soloists, chorus and orchestra.

April 12   *Los amores de la Ines* by Manuel de Falla and Amadeo Vives, to a libretto by Emilio Dugi, premieres at the Teatro Comico in Madrid. This is the only one of the five zarzuelas written by de Falla and Vives to be performed.

April 30   Claude Debussy's only opera, *Pelleas et Melisande* premieres at the Opera-Comique in Paris. The libretto is

MARY GARDEN IN *LE JONGLEUR DE NOTRE DAME*

based on Maurice Maeterlinck's play about the love of Pelleas, a prince, for his brother's wife, Melisande. The revolutionary impressionistic style of the opera gives rise to great controversy; another controversy results from Maeterlinck's desire to have Georgette Leblanc — his mistress — sing the role of Melisande. Opera manager Albert Carre decides to hire Mary Garden, and Maeterlinck allegedly challenges Carre to a duel. All of this attracts the public, and performances are quickly sold out (Mary Garden sings the lead role). The opera subsequently enjoys 14 performances during the next two months and reappears next season, again selling out. Today's performance is conducted by Andre Messager.

Critics, however, pan the music. Andre Corneau, of *Le Matin* (Paris), says the opera ". . . never escapes the world of reverie." Eugene d'Harcourt says in *Le Figaro* (Paris) that the work is ". . . worthy of inclusion as a curiosity in all music libraries." A London review published in *Era* says, "The effect is quite bewildering, almost amusing in its absurdity." Arthur Pougin of *Le Menestrel* (Paris) says Debussy's ". . . music is vague, floating, without color and without shape, without movement and without life." The *Revue des Deux Mondes* (Paris) publishes a review by Camille Bellaigue in which he says of Debussy's orchestration: "When it pretends to caress, it scratches and hurts."

Oct. 14   Nikolai Rimsky-Korsakov's *Servilia* premieres at the Imperial Opera in Saint Petersburg. The five-act opera is about a maiden in Nero's Rome who dies of a broken heart.

Nov. 26   *Adriana Lecouvreur* by Francesco Cilea premieres at the Teatro Lirico in Milan. The libretto by Arturo Colautti is based on a play by Eugene Scribe and Ernest Legouve, in which Adriana, an actress at the Comedie Francaise, and the Princess de Bouillon are rivals for the love of Maurizio, count of Saxony. The premiere, conducted by Cleofonte Campanini, features Enrico Caruso as Maurizio and Giuseppe De Luca as Michonnet. This work is Cilea's most famous composition. He studied at the Naples Conservatory and is currently teaching harmony at the Istituto Musicale in Florence.

Nov. 28   Carl Nielsen's first opera, *Saul og David*, is produced in Copenhagen. The four-act opera is about the biblical characters. Nielsen studied violin and trumpet and, at the age of 14, was playing trumpet with the Odense military band. He then studied at the Royal Conservatory in Copenhagen. He is currently a violinist with the Royal Chapel Orchestra in Copenhagen.

Dec. 16   Mikhail Ippolitov-Ivanov's *Potemkin Holiday* is produced in Saint Petersburg. The four-act opera is about Fieldmarshal Potemkin's triumphs in 1791. Ivanov is also a professional music critic.

Dec. 25   Nikolai Rimsky-Korsakov's *Kashchei the Immortal* premieres in Moscow. Mikhail Ippolitov-Ivanov conducts the opera, about a Russian princess and a possessive wizard. It is in one act with three tableaux.

1902 Dance

Feb. 2   Alexander Gorsky's revised version of *Don Quixote* opens in Moscow. Based on a staging of the ballet by Marius Petipa that was performed in 1871, this is the first performance of a ballet on this theme in the 20th century. Music is by Alois Minkus.

April 21   *In Japan* is produced by the Alhambra Theater, London. Carlo Coppi choreographs music by Louis Ganne. The dance includes a "Ballet of Blossoms" with special effects. It is a half-hour long. The London *Times* says it ". . .

is free from Wardour Street Orientalism." It is revived at La Scala, Milan next year.

June 16   Carlo Coppi's last piece of choreography for London's Alhambra Ballet — *Britannia's Realm* — premieres today. This event takes place on the occasion of King Edward VII's coronation. Landon Ronald writes the music to this spectacle featuring a Canadian skating scene and an Indian jewel divertissement. Charles Wilson "invents" this ballet in prologue and four scenes. The final scene has the full cast of colorful dancers forming the Union Jack.

1902 Instrumental and Vocal Music

Jan. 25   Franz Schmidt's Symphony No. 1 in E Major premieres in Vienna. Schmidt, an Austrian composer, has studied composition with Anton Bruckner, music theory with Robert Fuchs, and piano with Theodor Leschetizky. He has also studied organ and cello at the Vienna Conserv-

atory. He is presently a cellist with the Vienna Philharmonic Orchestra.

Jan. 25   Alexander Scriabin's Symphony No. 2 in C Minor premieres as Anatoly Liadov conducts the music at the Russian Symphony Concerts in Saint Petersburg. A critic of the *Russian Musical Gazette* (Saint Petersburg) states that the composer "... deliberately flaunts dissonances at the public...."

March 1   Sergei Vassilenko's cantata *The Legend of the Great City of Kitezh and the Calm Lake Svetoyar* receives its first performance in Moscow. This is Vassilenko's diploma work for the Moscow Conservatory.

March 8   Symphony No. 2 in D Minor by Jean Sibelius premieres in Helsinki, the composer conducting. The four-movement symphony is an example of this composer's preference for massive orchestral sonorities and spectacular closing movements. Thirty-eight years from now, American composer and music critic, Virgil Thomson writes in the New York *Herald-Tribune* that the symphony is "... vulgar, self-indulgent, and provincial beyond all description."

March 10   Ralph Vaughan Williams' *Bucolic Suite* premieres in Bournemouth, England. The four-movement orchestral suite is based on English folksong materials. Vaughan Williams, now 29 years old, has studied with Sir Charles Villiers Stanford and Sir Charles Hubert Hastings Parry at the Royal College of Music in London. He also studied with Max Bruch in Berlin.

March 18   Arnold Schoenberg's *Verklarte Nacht* receives its world premiere in Vienna, as the Rose String Quartet and two players from the Vienna Philharmonic perform. The work is scored for string sextet (two violins, two violas and two cellos). Schoenberg completed the piece in 1899 at age 25; it was inspired by Richard Dehmel's poem about a woman who bears the child of one other than her lover.

April 5   Maurice Ravel's *Jeux d'eau* is premiered by pianist Ricardo Vines, who performs the work at the Societe Nationale de Musique in Paris. This piano piece is one of Ravel's first employing massive keyboard sonorities dispersed over the full registral spread of the instrument. Ravel's principal composition teacher was Gabriel Faure at the Paris Conservatoire. He composed his *Pavane pour une Infante defunte* in 1899 and made his first appearance as a conductor that same year. He is now 26 years old.

April 18   *The Celestial Country*—a cantata by Charles Ives—receives its first performance at Central Presbyterian Church, New York. Composed between 1888-1899, it is scored for large chorus with string quartet, trumpet, euphonium, tympani and organ and has seven sections. The work, early and conservative for this composer, is well received. Ives is now living at his "poverty flat" in New York City, beginning his double life as an insurance salesman during the day and composer during the evenings. He is now 27 and has met his future insurance partner, Julian Myrick. He is also working as an organist at Central Presbyterian Church, at Broadway and 57th Street, New York City.

June 9   Gustav Mahler's Symphony No. 3 in D Minor, subtitled *Ein Sommermorgentraum*, receives its world premiere in Krefeld. Mahler, who also conducts this performance, composed the work between 1893 and 1896.

Aug. 17   Camille Saint-Saens' incidental music *Parysatis* premieres at the Grand Roman Arena in Beziers, France.

Dec. 1   Symphony No. 2 (*The Four Temperaments*), by Carl Nielsen, receives its first performance in Copenhagen, the composer conducting.

1902   Births, Deaths and Debuts

Jan. 6   Composer Mark Brunswick is born in New York.

Jan. 9   Operatic impresario Rudolf Bing is born in Vienna, Austria.

Jan. 11   Organist and composer Maurice Durufle is born in Louviers, France.

Feb. 17   Contralto Marian Anderson is born in Philadelphia, Pennsylvania.

March 29   Composer William Turner Walton is born in Oldham, Lancashire, England.

March 29   Conductor Mario Rossi is born in Rome, Italy.

April 8   Conductor Josef Krips is born in Vienna, Austria.

May 11   Soprano Bidu Sayao is born in Rio de Janeiro, Brazil.

June 15   Conductor Max Rudolf is born in Frankfurt, Germany.

June 26   Tenor Hugues-Adhemar Cuenod is born in Corseaux-sur-Vevey, Switzerland.

Aug. 6   Contralto Margarete Klose is born in Berlin, Germany.

Aug. 9   Violinist Zino Francescatti is born in Marseilles, France,

Aug. 9   The pianist Solomon (originally named Solomon Cutner) is born in London, England.

Aug. 23   Teresa Stolz, 68, dies in Milan, Italy. This soprano, a favorite of Giuseppe Verdi, was renowned for her performances of Aida and Leonora (*La Forza del destino*). Although her career began in Russia, the bulk of her singing took place in Italy. She gave her farewell performance in 1879, singing in the Manzoni *Requiem* by Verdi.

Aug. 25   Composer Stefan Wolpe is born in Berlin, Germany.

Sep. 7   Franz Wullner, 70, dies in Braunfels-on-the-Lahn, Germany. The conductor of the first performances of Richard Wagner's *Das Rheingold* and *Die Walkure* in Munich, he became director of the Cologne Conservatory in 1884.

Nov. 1   Conductor Eugen Jochum is born in Babenhausen, Germany.

Nov. 22   Austrian cellist Emanuel Feuermann is born in Kolomea, Galicia.

Nov. 22   Composer Joaquin Rodrigo is born in Sagunto, Spain.

Dec. 4   Feodor Ignatievich Stravinsky, 59, dies in Saint Petersburg. This noted Russian bass was the finest prior to the appearance of Feodor Chaliapin. His most famous role was as Mephistopheles in Charles Gounod's *Faust*. He sang a total of 64 roles and made 1,235 appearances. His son, Igor, is now 20.

Dec. 19   Soprano Dusolina Giannini is born in Philadelphia, Pennsylvania.

1902   Related Events

Walter Damrosch (son of conductor Leopold Damrosch) replaces Emil Paur as music director of the New York Philharmonic Society. Andrew Carnegie a close friend, helped get him his appointment. Damrosch had previously encouraged Carnegie to build Carnegie Hall, which has been the home of this orchestra since its opening in 1891. His appointment lasts one season.

March 10   Gustav Mahler and Alma Maria Schindler are married. Mahler is 41; Schindler, 23.

April 11   Enrico Caruso makes his first recordings in Milan. He records 10 selections for the Gramophone and Typewriter Company and is paid the exorbitant sum of £100. The records are released next month in England to coincide with the tenor's British debut. They create a sensation, and the company soon realizes a profit of £15,000. Other developments in the recording industry this year include: An arrangement is made between Victor and Columbia to pool lateral-cut disc patents (becoming effective in 1903); Thomas Edison perfects a copying process for master cylinders — it is used to manufacture two-minute recordings, which are sold in England for 2 shillings each; Edison and Columbia produce their first molded-wax cylinders — these have a playing speed of 160 RPM, making obsolete the earlier standard of 120 RPM; the first Nellie Melba recordings are issued; the public begins to lose interest in the cylinder phonograph.

April 11   Cambridge University bestows the honorary degree of Doctor of Music upon American composer Horatio Parker. Parker was professor of music at Yale University.

May 17   Pianist and conductor Alfred Cortot, after studying the music of Richard Wagner at Bayreuth in 1898, conducts the French premiere of *Gotterdammerung* at the Theatre du Chateau d'Eau.

1903   Opera

Jan. 7   *L'Etranger*, by Vincent d'Indy, premieres at the Theatre de la Monnaie in Brussels. D'Indy himself wrote the libretto, a bizarre, symbolic story of a man — the stranger — who perpetually sails the seas in pursuit of an ideal.

Jan. 17   Cesar Cui's *Mam'zelle Fifi* premieres in Moscow.

Feb. 16   *Tapu*, an opera by New Zealand composer Alfred Hill, premieres in Wellington, New Zealand. This work, considered the first authentic New Zealand opera, has a libretto about Maori Indians by the composer and J.C. Williamson. Hill conducts. A review in *The New Zealand Times Wellington* says the opera is of "unique interest" and "is full of melody." Born in 1870 in Australia, Alfred Hill came to New Zealand at the age of 2. He subsequently returns to Australia.

March 3   The first staged version of Sergei Vassilenko's *The Legend of the Great City of Kitezh and the Calm Lake Svetoyar* is produced in Moscow.

Oct. 27   Alexander Gretchaninoff's *Dobrinya Nikititch* premieres at the Bolshoi Theater, Moscow, with Feodor Chaliapin singing the lead role.

Nov. 15   *Tiefland* by Eugene d'Albert, premieres at the Neues Deutsches Theater in Prague. The libretto, by Ru-

ERMANNO WOLF-FERRARI

dolf Lothar, is based on a Catalan play. Sebastiano, a tyrannical landowner, decides to marry off his mistress, Marta, to the simple shepherd Pedro, thus keeping her available to himself without preventing his marriage to a rich heiress. It is the most successful of d'Albert's operas.

Nov. 27   *Le Donne curiose*, by Ermanno Wolf-Ferrari, premieres at the Residenztheater in Munich in a German version. The libretto, by H. Teibler, is based on an 18th-century Italian comedy, in which a group of Venetian gentlemen rent a house where they can enjoy each other's company without the presence of their wives, who suspect infidelity and spy on them.

Nov. 30   Ernest Chausson's three-act opera, *Le Roi Arthur*, receives its first performance at the Theatre de la Monnaie, Brussels. The libretto, based on the medieval legend of King Arthur, is by the composer. This opera is performed posthumously — Chausson died in a bicycle accident in 1899 (at the age of 44). It is his only opera.

Dec. 7   O'Brien Butler's opera *Muirgheis* is produced in Dublin. It is the first opera composed to a Gaelic libretto. Butler has studied at the Royal College of Music in London where his teachers included Sir Charles Villiers Stanford. He composed this opera while in India.

Dec. 19   Umberto Giordano's opera *Siberia* receives its premiere at the Teatro alla Scala in Milan. The libretto, by Luigi Illica, deals with Stephana, a courtesan who abandons her wealth to follow Vassili, her love, to Siberia, where he is imprisoned for wounding Prince Alexis (Stephana's former lover). Rosina Storchio, Giovanni Zenatello and Giuseppe De Luca star.

Dec. 20   Nikolai Lissenko's five-act opera *Taras Bulba* receives its initial performance in Kiev. It is based on the epic novel by Gogol and has a Ukrainian libretto. The opera, which was composed 12 years ago, has a plot centering on a 17th-century Cossack who falls in love with a Polish woman.

1903   Dance

Jan. 12   *The Devil's Forge* is produced by the Alhambra Ballet, London. Choreography is by Lucia Cormani, the theater's new prima ballerina, and music by George Byng. The ballet tells the story of a young man who meets a mountain fairy and finds out how to win her love. It is the first work to be produced under the leadership of Cormani, who functions as choreographer, dancer and, on occasion, manager.

May 7   *Carmen* — a new ballet by the Alhambra Ballet — premieres in London. Lucia Cormani choreographs music by Georges Bizet arranged by George Byng. Dancer Rosario Guerro plays Carmen.

1903   Instrumental and Vocal Music

Jan. 3   Alexander Glazunov's Symphony No. 7 in F Major and the orchestral suite *From the Middle Ages* are premiered. The composer conducts the works at the annual Russian Symphony Concerts in Saint Petersburg.

Jan. 16   Reinhold Gliere's Symphony No. 1 in E-flat Major premieres in Moscow.

Feb. 11   Anton Bruckner's unfinished Symphony No. 9 in D Minor premieres posthumously in Vienna. Conducted by Ferdinand Loewe, today's performance substitutes the composer's *Te Deum* for the unfinished last movement of this symphony.

March 8 The two *Rumanian Rhapsodies* by Georges Enesco are performed for the first time in Bucharest, the composer conducting. These pieces subsequently become very popular. Enesco has a colorful background: He studied violin with a Rumanian gypsy violinist by the name of Nicolas Chioru before entering the Vienna Conservatory. He later studied at the Paris Conservatoire with Gabriel Faure and Jules Massenet. He also plays cello, piano and organ and has won several prizes at the Paris Conservatoire for performing on these instruments.

March 21 Ermanno Wolf-Ferrari's oratorio *La Vita Nuova* premieres in Munich.

May 5 Samuel Coleridge-Taylor's trilogy *The Song of Hiawatha* receives its first American performance as Charles E. Knauss conducts the Orpheus Oratorio Society in Easton, Pennsylvania.

Sep. 9 *The Atonement* — a cantata by Samuel Coleridge-Taylor — receives its first performance at the Hereford Festival in Hereford, England. The composer conducts, and the performance is tremendously successful.

Oct. 8 Carl Nielsen's overture *Helios* premieres in Copenhagen, the composer conducting.

Oct. 14 *The Apostles*, by Edward Elgar, receives its world premiere at the Birmingham Festival in England. The oratorio deals with the birth of Christ and the beginnings of the church; it also includes an ancient Hebrew melody with Elgar's personal harmonies. A review in the *Pall Mall Gazette* (London) calls it "a masterpiece"; *The Globe* (London) terms the orchestration "dazzling." The *Saint James Gazette* (London) says, ". . . it is a deeply intellectual work, a work of which Dr. Elgar and England may be proud. . . ." *The Observer* (London) says, "It speaks volumes for the intellectual discernment and genius of the Worcester composer that the most thrilling moment in his work is that in which he has given musical expression to the establishment of the Church of Christ."

1903 Births, Deaths and Debuts

Jan. 6 Conductor Maurice Abravanel is born in Salonika, Greece.

Jan. 10 Conductor Jean Morel is born in Abbeville, France.

Jan. 19 Composer Boris Blacher is born in Newchwang, China.

HUGO WOLF

Jan. 19 Pianist Erwin Nyiregyhazi is born in Budapest, Hungary.

Feb. 6 Pianist Claudio Arrau is born in Chillan, Chile.

Feb. 22 Hugo Wolf, 42, dies in an insane asylum in Vienna. Born in 1860, he received encouragement from Richard Wagner at about age 15. He was thrown out of the Vienna Conservatory for charging the faculty with incompetence. He had been advised by Johannes Brahms not to compose until he was a master of counterpoint. Wolf became bitter and vented his anger in his music criticism, especially against Brahms. Having had a difficult time trying to get his music performed, Wolf's first real success came in 1889, when many of his songs were finally published. He is also said to have had a bad encounter with Gustav Mahler, who was contemplating the production of Wolf's opera *Der Corregidor*. The opera was not produced. Wolf then began to assert that he was the new director of the Vienna Opera. His delusions led him to an asylum, a suicide attempt and a tragic end at a young age. His songs remain important and are frequently performed.

March 28 Pianist Rudolf Serkin is born in Eger, Bohemia of Russian parents.

April 10 Opera director Herbert Graf is born in Vienna, Austria.

April 17 Composer Nicolas Nabokov is born near Lubcha, Russia. He is the cousin of the renowned writer Vladimir Nabokov.

April 17 Cellist Gregor Piatigorsky is born in Ekaterinoslav, Russia.

May 12   Composer Lennox Berkeley is born in Boar's Hill, England.

May 15   American soprano Sibyl Sanderson, 37, dies in Paris. Born in San Francisco, she was later taken by her mother to Paris, where she studied with Jules Massenet and Mathilde Marchesi. She was a favorite of Massenet, who wrote *Thais* and *Esclarmonde* for her, and of Saint-Saens, who wrote his opera *Phryne* for her. She came to the Metropolitan in 1895 but did not become popular with the American public.

May 20   Composer Jerzy Fitelberg is born in Warsaw, Poland. His father is the conductor Gregor Fitelberg.

May 28   Composer Walter Goehr is born in Berlin, Germany.

June 4   Conductor Evgheny Mravinsky is born in Saint Petersburg, Russia.

June 6   Russian-Armenian composer Aram Khachaturian is born in Tiflis.

July 3   Opera administrator David Webster is born in Dundee, Scotland.

July 4   Composer and organist Flor Peeters is born in Thielen, Belgium.

July 28   French mezzo-soprano Rosine Stoltz, 97, dies in Paris. This woman led an extraordinary private life: She had affairs with the manager of the Paris Opera (Leon Pillet) and the emperor of Brazil (Don Pedro), eventually becoming Baroness von Ketschendorf (after having been given a castle by Ernest Ketschendorf). She was also married to Duke Carlo Lesignano and had at least one other marriage. Her operatic debut was in Brussels (1836) as Rachel in *La Juive*.

Aug. 17   Composer and pianist Abram Chasins is born in New York City.

Aug. 23   Violist William Primrose is born in Glasgow, Scotland.

Sep. 6   Hungarian composer and pianist Pal Kadosa is born in Leva (which subsequently becomes Levice), Czechoslovakia.

Sep. 11   Musician and philosopher Theodor Adorno is born in Frankfurt, Germany as Theodor Wiesengrund.

Oct. 10   Composer Vladimir Dukelsky is born at the train station of Parfianovka, Russia. He later adopts the name Vernon Duke.

Oct. 19   Composer Vittorio Giannini is born in Philadelphia, Pennsylvania.

Nov. 6   Soviet dancer, ballet master and teacher Asaf Messerer is born in Vilna.

Nov. 20   Musicologist Jacob Maurice Coopersmith is born in New York City.

Nov. 23   Enrico Caruso makes his debut with the Metropolitan Opera, New York, singing the role of the Duke of Mantua in *Rigoletto*. Reviews are mostly good: Krehbiel says in the New York *Tribune*, "He was musically the finest Duke New York has heard for a generation." W.J. Henderson says in the New York *Sun* that the singer "has a pure tenor voice of fine quality... without the typical Italian bleat."

Nov. 25   Soprano Olive Fremstad debuts at the Metropolitan Opera as Sieglinde in *Die Walkure*. Krehbiel writes in the New York *Tribune* that the soprano "... took rank with most of her predecessors in the part...."

Dec. 12   Musicologist Francisco Curt Lange is born in Eilenburg, Germany.

Dec. 12   Christian Johansson, 85, dies in Saint Petersburg. One of the great teachers of the Imperial Ballet School, he was responsible for training such dancers as Pavel Gerdt and Mathilde Kschessinska.

1903 Related Events

The New York Philharmonic Society dispenses with having a regular music director due to declining ticket sales. Walter Damrosch leaves, and the next three seasons are handled by guest conductors, including Richard Strauss, Felix Weingartner, Vassily Safonov and Willem Mengelberg.

Jan. 1   The French government awards the Cross of Chevalier de la Legion d'Honneur to Claude Debussy.

Jan. 28   *Ernani* — an opera by Giuseppe Verdi — receives its first New York performance at the Metropolitan Opera.

The cast includes Edouard de Reszke, Marcella Sembrich and Antonio Scotti.

April 30   Victor cuts its first Red Seal recordings. Soprano Ada Crossley records music at the Carnegie Hall studio, New York City. Other developments in the recording industry this year include: The first celebrity discs by Victor and Columbia are recorded and issued in America; the International Talking Machine Company (Odeon/Parlophone) is established by Carl Lindstrom in Berlin; the Victor Talking Machine Company and the Gramophone Company take control of Zonophone; Victor develops a tapered tone arm; the Gramophone Company issues the first 12-inch discs ever, with the introduction of its Monarch label; the Italian branch of "His Master's Voice" issues a 40 single-side-disc recording of Giuseppe Verdi's *Ernani*, marking the first complete opera recording; Barnet, Samuel and Sons, London, manufactures the Decca portable gramophone; Thomas A. Edison issues the first 80 RPM recordings, which are vertical-cut discs; and Odeon releases its first symphonic recordings (two Beethoven symphonies).

June 27   Raoul Laparra is awarded the first Grand Prix de Rome by the Academie des Beaux-Arts in Paris. Maurice Ravel was a contestant.

July   *The Act of Touch in All Its Diversity* by pianist Tobias Matthay, is published in London by Longmans, Green and Co. Subtitled *An Analysis and Synthesis of Pianoforte Tone-Production*, this book is an explication of his theories of piano playing in all its aspects.

Nov. 5   Emil Oberhoffer conducts the first concert of the newly established Minneapolis Symphony Orchestra.

Nov. 10   Arthur Nikisch and the Berlin Philharmonic record Ludwig van Beethoven's Symphony No. 5 for the Gramophone Company. This is the first recording of a complete symphony.

Nov. 22   Pope Pius X issues his moto propio, *Tra le sollicitudini* a papal document in which he puts forth rules for performance and interpretation of Gregorian chant. It states in part, "since modern music has become chiefly a secular art, greater care must be taken, when admitting it that nothing profane, vulgar, or theatrical be allowed, nothing that is reminiscent of theatrical pieces, nothing based as to its form on the style of secular compositions. These are the aria, the cavatina, the cabaletta, and the like. In the church it is forbidden to use the piano, and also all the instruments which are too noisy or nimble, such as drums, kettledrums, bells, cymbals, triangles, and the like. Bands are strictly forbidden to play in church."

Dec. 24   The Metropolitan Opera in New York City gives the first performance outside Bayreuth of Richard Wagner's *Parsifal*, despite copyright objections raised by Cosima and Siegfried Wagner. The cast includes Milka Ternina, Ludwig Burgstaller, Anton Van Rooy and Robert Blass and is conducted by Alfred Hertz. Richard Aldrich says of the performance in The New York *Times*, "It was without doubt the most perfect production ever made on the American lyric stage."

Dec. 29   The Seattle Symphony Orchestra gives its first concert. Conducted by Harry West, the program includes music by Jules Massenet, Max Bruch, Schubert and Rossini. The concert is performed at Christensen's Hall, Seattle.

1904   Opera

Jan. 21   The Deutsches National Theater in Brno premieres Leos Janacek's *Jeji pastorkyna* (later known as *Jenufa*). The libretto, by the composer, deals with a pregnant young woman whose fiance deserts her to marry a wealthy woman. She is accused of killing her child but is eventually cleared and marries her stepbrother. The opera marks the development of Janacek's original style. Criticized when submitted to the Czech National Theater, it receives a triumphant premiere.

Feb. 17   *Madama Butterfly*, by Giacomo Puccini, premieres at the Teatro alla Scala in Milan. The libretto, in two acts, is by Giuseppe Giacosa. The performance is conducted by Cleofonte Campanini and features Rosina Storchio, Giovanni Zenatello and Giuseppe De Luca. The opera is about a geisha girl who marries a U.S. Navy lieutenant and, years later, kills herself when he returns with his legally wedded American wife. The opera is a failure; the audience boos to the point of screaming. Critic Gian Battista Nappi says in *Perseveranza* "The personality of Puccini sins on the side of uniformity." A critic in *La Lombarda* says, "Butterfly is coated with Japanese lacquer amalgamated with American rubber. . . ." Giovanni Pozza says in *Corriere della Sera* that the public condemned Puccini when he appeared on the stage but that he believes the opera will revive itself.

Feb. 18   Camille Saint-Saens' *Helene* premieres in Monte Carlo. The opera is written for Australian soprano Nellie Melba, who creates the title role.

March 25   Antonin Dvorak's last opera, *Armida*, is produced in its original Czech version in Prague. The four-act opera is about a crusader who falls in love.

March 30   The first opera of Frederick Delius — *Koanga* — premieres at the Stadttheater in Elberfeld, Germany. Originally written in English, it is translated into German for the premiere. It tells the tragic love story of two slaves, forbidden to marry by their master.

May 28   A revised three-act version of Giacomo Puccini's *Madama Butterfly* is performed in Brescia, with Cleofonte Campanini conducting. Unlike its world premiere nearly four months ago, it is received with enormous praise: The composer takes 10 curtain calls. Puccini later writes to his publisher (Guilio Ricordi), "Viva *Butterfly* forever!"

Oct. 16   *Pan Voyevoda*, a four-act opera by Nikolai Rimsky-Korsakov, receives its first performance in Saint Petersburg. The opera is about a feudal lord who stumbles on a beautiful woman while hunting. The music includes Polish dances.

Nov. 4   Franco Alfano's four-act opera *Risurrezione* receives its first performance in Turin. The work is to a libretto by Cesare Hanau based on the Tolstoi novel of the same name. One of Alfano's early operas, it is regarded as his best. Today's performance receives favorable reviews.

Dec. 13   Ruggero Leoncavallo's opera *Der Roland von Berlin* premieres in Berlin. German Emperor Wilhelm II commissioned this work, which is based on a theme of German history. The opera is a failure.

1904 Dance

Feb. 4   Jules Massenet's ballet *La Cigale* is performed for the first time at the Opera-Comique in Paris. Based on a fable by La Fontaine, it is about a grasshopper and an ant who become people.

Dec. 26   Isadora Duncan makes her Russian debut in Saint Petersburg. Duncan dances to music by Frederick Chopin, including some of his nocturnes, mazurkas, preludes and one polonaise. Her costume is minimal, displaying bare legs and feet.

The performance attracts hundreds, including Serge Diaghilev and Michel Fokine. Diaghilev later says, "Duncan's influence on him (Fokine) was the initial basis of his entire creation.... Isadora gave the classical ballet of Imperial Russia a shock from which it could never recover."

Critics rave, and Duncan immediately becomes famous in Russia. N. Georgievich (real name Nicolai Georgievich Shebuyev) will write tomorrow in *Peterburgskaya Gazeta*, "Yesterday all fashionable Petersburg assembled in the Hall of the Nobles prepared to see La Duncan dance some kind of virginal cancan."But he says of the dancer, "Her body is as though bewitched by the music.... Duncan's bare legs and bare feet are like those of a rustic vagabond: they are innocent: it is not nudity that arouses sinful thoughts, but rather a kind of incorporeal nudity.... Duncan has no ballet technique... but there is so much sculpture in her, so much color and simplicity, that she fully deserves the capacity audience...."

1904 Instrumental and Vocal Music

Jan. 9   *Estampes*, by Claude Debussy, receives its initial performance at the Societe Nationale de Musique in Paris. Pianist Ricardo Vines performs. This three-movement piano suite is impressionistic. Its movements are entitled "Pagodes", "Soiree dans grenade" and "Jardins sous la pluie."

Jan. 13   Bela Bartok's *Kossuth* receives its first performance in Budapest. The music scandalizes the performing musicians, many of them German, because it parodies the German national anthem. Bartok, 22, has studied with Hans Koessler at the Royal Academy of Music in Budapest.

Feb. 8   Jean Sibelius conducts the premiere of his Violin Concerto in D Minor, Op. 47 in Helsinki, Finland. Victor Novacek is soloist. This work is later revised for a 1906 performance. A reviewer from the New York *Tribune* later says of the piece that the soloist has little chance to make his instrument "... speak in tones of beauty... " and compares the accompaniment to "... a mutter or a growl."

Feb. 28   Symphony No. 2 in B-flat Major, Op. 57, by Vincent d'Indy, is performed for the first time by the Lamoureux Orchestra in Paris. The symphony consists of three movements and appears some 17 years after his First Symphony, of 1886. The music blends chromatic harmo-

nies and whole-tone melodies. It is performed in America in January 1905 in Boston; critics are not especially fond of it. W.J. Henderson of the New York *Sun* says the music gives "... galvanic shocks to the nerves...." Louis Elson of the *Boston Daily Advertiser* says the music "... certainly could not soothe a heartache...."

Feb. 29   Bela Bartok's *Scherzo* for Piano and Orchestra, Op. 2, premieres in Budapest. This work was composed two years ago.

March 5   Maurice Ravel's String Quartet receives its first performance in Paris, given by the Societe Nationale de Musique. The only string quartet by this composer, it is in four movements and uses parallel chord progressions. A New York *Tribune* review later compares the music to an "algebra problem" and says it lacks "emotional nuance."

March 16   The Halle Orchestra of Manchester gives the first performance of *In the South*, by Edward Elgar, conducted by the composer. The performance takes place at Covent Garden, London. This orchestra was founded in 1848 by Charles Halle, who was knighted in 1888 and died in 1895 at the age of 76.

March 18   Anatoly Liadov's symphonic poem *Baba-Yaga* premieres in Saint Petersburg. This piece is a fairy tale for orchestra about a flying witch (Baba-Yaga) whose house is made of bones. Liadov, who studied with Nikolai Rimsky-Korsakov, had been suspended from the Saint Petersburg Conservatory for cutting classes and failing to finish assignments. In 1877 he completed *The Bride of Messina*, which was so successful that it resulted in his being hired by the same conservatory to teach theory and harmony.

March 21   *Symphonia domestica*, by Richard Strauss, receives its premiere at Carnegie Hall, New York City. Conducted by the composer, this event also marks the composer's first visit to the United States. Strauss conducts the Wetzler Symphony Orchestra and also includes on the program his *Also sprach Zarathustra* and *Don Juan*. Critic Henry T. Finck of the New York *Sun* says of the new piece that it "... is either a deplorable aberration of taste or else a clever method of courting publicity."

April 25   Jean Sibelius' *Valse Triste* premieres in Helsinki, Finland, the composer conducting. Today's performance is of the chamber orchestra version.

May 10   Hugo Alfven's *Midsommarvaka* premieres in Stockholm. This work is a rhapsody for orchestra.

May 17   Maurice Ravel's *Sheherazade* and Albert Roussel's *Resurrection* are premiered on the same program at a concert of the Societe Nationale de Musique in Paris. *Sheherazade* was first performed as an overture on May 27, 1899, the composer conducting. Today's version is a song cycle for orchestra and voice composed from some of the materials of the earlier overture. The piece sets three texts of Tristan Klingsor: "Asie," "La flute enchantee" and "L'indifferent."

May 17   Vincent d'Indy's *Choral varie*, a composition featuring the saxophone as solo instrument, premieres in Paris.

Sep. 7   Sir Hubert Parry's choral work *The Love that Casteth Out Fear* premieres at the Gloucester Music Festival. This work, about the passion of Christ, has a text by the composer and is scored for contralto, bass, chorus and orchestra.

Oct. 18   Gustav Mahler conducts the world premiere in Cologne of his Symphony No. 5 in C-sharp Minor, a work that subsequently becomes a showpiece for conductors and orchestras around the world. A 1906 review in the *Musical Courier* (New York) says that the listener "... has to cling by one's teeth, so to speak, to a shred of theme here and there...."

Nov. 10   Ferruccio Busoni's Piano Concerto receives its world premiere in Berlin. The composer is soloist in this performance conducted by Karl Muck. The concerto, in five movements, concludes with "Hymn to Allah," featuring a male chorus finale. A review in *Die Tagliche Rundschau* describes the music as "a flood of cacophony."

Nov. 13   *Caprice andalou*, by Camille Saint-Saens, receives its initial performance in Paris. This work is scored for violin and orchestra.

Nov. 29   Ernst von Dohnanyi's *4 Rhapsodies* for Piano, Op. 11, are premiered in Vienna, the composer performing.

FACSIMILE OF HUGO ALFVEN'S *SVENSK RHAPSODY* FROM *MIDSOMMARVAKA*

1904 Births, Deaths and Debuts

Jan. 2   Music publisher Peter Jurgenson, 67, dies in Moscow. He published many works by Tchaikovsky.

Jan. 10   Russian music publisher Mitrofan Belaiev, 67, dies in Saint Petersburg. Son of a wealthy lumber dealer, he patronized Russian composers by financing the publication and performance of their works. Composers who received his help include Nikolai Rimsky-Korsakov, Alexander Glazunov, Anatoly Liadov, Alexander Scriabin, Sergei Taneyev and Nicolas Tcherepnin. His famous "Belaiev Editions" helped promote nationalism in Russian music.

Jan. 13   Composer Richard Addinsell is born in London, England.

Jan. 15   Soviet dancer, choreographer and ballet master Leonid Jacobson is born in Moscow.

Jan. 22   George Balanchine, one of the seminal figures in the history of ballet, is born Georgi Melitonovich Balanchivadze in Saint Petersburg, Russia. He is the son of Meliton Balanchivadze, a Georgian composer.

Feb. 3   Italian composer Luigi Dallapiccola is born in Pisino, Italy.

Feb. 8   Soprano Malwine Schnorr von Carolsfeld, 71, dies in Karlsruhe, Germany. She was most famous for having created the role of Isolde in Wagner's *Tristan und Isolde* in Munich in 1865. At that same performance her husband, Ludwig, created the part of Tristan. He died a month later of rheumatic fever.

March 8   Composer Nikos Skalkottas is born in Euboca, Greece.

April 15   Frances Alda makes her operatic debut at the Opera-Comique in Paris, performing in *Manon*, by Jules Massenet.

May 1   Composer Antonin Dvorak, 62, dies in Prague. Dvorak left home at age 16 to study organ at the Prague Organ School. He also played the violin and viola, to earn money. On March 9, 1873 his work for mixed chorus and orchestra, *Hymnus*, premiered and attracted much attention. The following year, he received the Austrian State Prize for his Symphony in E-flat.

Dvorak quickly became known as a composer who imbued his music with Czech nationalism. He was elevated to the status of an international symbol of Czech nationalism largely through the efforts of Franz Liszt, Johannes Brahms and Hans von Bulow. His status motivated the Prague Conservatory to engage him as a teacher.

In 1892 he went to New York to direct the National Conservatory. While there he wrote his most famous work, Symphony in E Minor *(From the New World)*, Op. 95.

ANTONIN DVORAK

That work was premiered by the New York Philharmonic in 1893. It inspired some American composers to begin contemplating American 'nationalism in their music.

Dvorak's article "Music in America" (*Harper's New Monthly Magazine*, February 1895) asserted that American composers were backward-looking musicians satisfied with imitating European models and lacking in creative drive and originality. He believed that melodic materials from Indian and Negro folk song should constitute the basis of an American national style. The article created within musical circles in America a hostility toward Dvorak that would persist for 20 years.

Dvorak returned to the Prague Conservatory in 1895 and became artistic director in 1901. He became a member of the Austrian House of Lords — the first musician to be so honored. His music is rooted in the harmonic language of Brahms and Wagner; his inventive use of Czech folk song and ability to create powerful, emotion-filled moments enabled him to stand out as a Czech master. To a large degree, Dvorak's musical legacy is continued by Leos Janacek, now 49. Dvorak's works consist of nine operas (including *Rusalka*), seven symphonies, many symphonic poems, overtures and concertos, choral works (including his cantata *The American Flag*) and other pieces.

May 2   Czech soprano Emmy Destinn makes her Covent Garden debut as Donna Anna in Mozart's *Don Giovanni*.

May 25   Choral conductor Kurt Thomas is born in Tonning, Germany.

June 3   Tenor Jan Peerce is born in New York City.

June 13   Conductor Oliviero De Fabritiis is born in Rome, Italy.

July 9   Conductor Robert Whitney is born in Newcastle-on-Tyne, England.

July 15   Soviet dancer, choreographer and ballet master Vladimir Bourmeister is born in Moscow.

July 16   Composer Goffredo Petrassi is born in Zagarolo, Italy.

July 18   Musicologist and music librarian Harold Spivacke is born in New York City.

July 24   Dancer, choreographer and teacher Anton Dolin is born in Slinfold, England. His name at birth is Sydney Francis Patrick Chippendall Healey-Kay.

Aug. 6   Critic Eduard Hanslick, 78, who wrote the critique on musical aesthetics *The Beautiful in Music* and who rejected Richard Wagner's theory of music drama as the ultimate in art, dies in Vienna. Wagner's character of Beckmesser in *Die Meistersinger* was a caricature of Hanslick. This critic taught at Vienna University (1861–95) and was also principal critic for the *Neue Freie Presse.*

Sep. 2   Tenor Set Svanholm is born in Vasteras, Sweden.

Sep. 17   British dancer-choreographer Frederick Ashton is born in Guayaquil, Ecuador.

Oct. 1   Pianist Vladimir Horowitz is born in Berdichev, Russia.

Oct. 26   Conductor Boris Khaikin is born in Minsk, Russia.

Nov. 20   Dancer and teacher Alexandra Danilova is born in Peterhof, Russia.

Dec. 30   Soviet pianist and composer Dmitri Kabalevsky is born in Saint Petersburg, Russia.

Dec. 31   Violinist Nathan Milstein is born in Odessa, Russia.

1904 Related Events

The Heckelphone is introduced this year by Wilhelm Heckel and his sons. This double-reed woodwind instrument was conceived by Heckel after he had spoken to Richard Wagner in 1879. Wagner had expressed his annoyance that baritone double-reed instruments were not powerful enough to cut through heavy orchestral textures in performance. The three-section instrument features a larger diameter than the oboe with a large air column and bassoon-type reed.

Jan. 28   The Russian Symphony Orchestra gives its first concert today. Formed by conductor Modest Altschuler to promote Russian music, the concert takes place at Cooper Union in New York City. The orchestra is American with a Russian name, not a Russian orchestra touring America.

Feb. 1   Enrico Caruso records the aria "Vesti la giubba" from Ruggero Leoncavallo's *Pagliacci* for the Victor Company. This event marks his first recording in America.

March 2   Emma Calve sings Carmen at the New York Metropolitan Opera. This is her farewell performance with this opera company.

May 16   The Diamond Jubilee of violinist Joseph Joachim's first appearance in England is celebrated at Queen's Hall, London. British Prime Minister Balfour presides over the event and honors Joachim with a portrait painted by J.S. Sargent.

June 9   The newly formed London Symphony Orchestra gives its inaugural concert under the leadership of Hans Richter.

June 15   The first transmission of wireless telegraphy featuring music and dialogue takes place in Salzburg with Otto Nussbaumer making the transmission.

July 5   Edward Elgar is knighted in Great Britain by King Edward VII.

PROGRAM FOR THE FIRST CONCERT OF THE RESIDENTIE-ORKEST (THE HAGUE)

Aug. Columbia issues its first double-faced trial recordings (the first double-faced discs to be issued on a nontrial basis are produced by Odeon, also this year). Other developments in the recording industry this year are: 20-inch, long-playing, vertical-cut discs are issued by the Neophone Company, London; the Gramophone Company records an 18-side session at the Sistine Chapel, Vatican City; The Societa Italiana di Fonotipia (which subsequently becomes Odeon's Italian division) is founded to cut celebrity vocal recordings.

Nov. 16 Samuel Coleridge-Taylor, on his first trip to America, conducts the first American performance of his *The Song of Hiawatha* (complete trilogy). This event marks the opening of the Coleridge-Taylor Festival, which features two concerts in Washington, D.C., and a third in Baltimore. Today's opening concert takes place in Convention Hall, Washington, and employs musicians from the U.S. Marine Band. The audience of 4,000 people is approximately two-thirds negro. The Washington correspondent of the *Georgia Baptist* [Atlanta] writes: "It was the first time that a man of African blood held a baton over the heads of the members of this great Marine Band."

Nov. 20 The Hague Philharmonic Orchestra gives its inaugural concert. Conducted by Henri Viotta, the program consists of music by Mendelssohn, Tchaikovsky, Wagner and Beethoven and takes place in the Gebouw voor Kinsten en Wetenschappen, the Hague. This orchestra subsequently becomes internationally known.

Dec. 10 Serge Rachmaninoff, Sergei Taneyev and Alexander Scriabin are among the winners of the first annual Glinka Prize for best compositions by Russian composers. Rachmaninoff wins for his Second Piano Concerto, and Scriabin for his Third and Fourth Piano Sonatas. Both collect 500 rubles, but Taneyev walks off the big winner, with 1000 rubles for his Symphony, Op. 12.

1905 Opera

Feb. 14 Jules Massenet's *Cherubin* premieres in Monte Carlo. The three-act opera is about a young man who cannot stop making love.

March 12 Ottorino Respighi's first opera, *Re Enzo*, receives its initial performance in Bologna. The three-act opera is about the imprisoned poet Enzo, emperor of Sardinia. Born in 1879, Respighi studied with Nikolai Rimsky-Korsakov. His work exhibits imaginative effects of instrumental colors.

March 16 Pietro Mascagni's lyric drama *Amica* premieres at the Theatre du Casino, Monte Carlo. The libretto tells the story of Amica, who runs off with her lover, Rinaldo. Her uncle eventually persuades Rinaldo to abandon her, and in her attempts to reach him, Amica dies.

April 14 Engelbert Humperdinck's three-act comic opera *Die Heirat wider Willen* receives its initial performance at the Royal Opera in Berlin. The libretto is by the composer's wife, based on *Les demoiselles de Saint-Cyr*, by Alexandre Dumas. The opera is about two young men opposed to marriage who change their minds after they are forced to marry.

May 25 Emile Jaques-Dalcroze's opera *Onkel Dazumal* is produced in Cologne. His third opera, the work is performed under the title *Le Bonhomme Jadis* in Paris next year.

Dec. 1 The first opera by an American composer ever to be staged in Europe is produced today in Bremen. It is the three-act opera *Zenobia*, by Louis Adolphe Coerne, a native of Newark, New Jersey. The opera is about a Syrian queen who rejects the romantic advances of a Roman Emperor (Aurelian) who had killed her Greek lover. Coerne, 34, had previously studied with Josef Rheinberger.

Dec. 9 Richard Strauss' one-act musical drama *Salome* receives its initial performance at the Konigliches Opernhaus, Dresden. It is based on an Oscar Wilde play. The combination of Wilde's lurid play and Strauss's sensuous and erotic music shocks many, and the premiere, originally scheduled for Vienna, is moved to Dresden in order to circumvent the censors. It is an international triumph. Marie Wittich, Karl Burrian and Carl Perron head the cast. Ernst von Schuch conducts. Criticism is mixed. Paul Pfitzner says in *Musikalisches Wochenblatt* (Berlin) that '. . . further

ENGELBERT HUMPERDINCK

progress in the same direction must end in the destruction of all musical law and order. . . . " Arno Kleffel of *Allgemeine Musik-Zeitung* (Berlin) says the opera ". . . fascinates one not so much with the importance of its themes as through the masterful manner in which he uses his thematic material and the glittering brilliancy of its orchestral dress."

Dec. 26   Charles-Marie Widor's four-act opera *Les Pecheurs de Saint-Jean* receives its first performance at the Opera-Comique in Paris. The opera is about a young mariner who wins his love by saving her father from drowning.

Dec. 28   *Die lustige Witwe* by Franz Lehar, receives its first performance in Vienna. This operetta, Lehar's most successful work, is about the romance of a handsome prince and a wealthy, merry widow.

1905   Dance

Feb. 27   *My Lady Nicotine* is produced at the Alhambra Theater, London. Choreography is by Lucia Cormani, music by George Byng.

Dec. 11   *Parisiana* is produced at the Alhambra Theater, London. Alfredo Curti choreographs music by Glover. The ballet, whose scenery and dancing span recent Parisian history, includes a minuet, polka and maxixe.

1905   Instrumental and Vocal Music

Jan. 8   Florent Schmitt's symphonic poem *Le Palais hante*, based on a story by Edgar Allen Poe, premieres at the Concerts Lamoureux in Paris.

Jan. 26   Arnold Schoenberg's brilliantly orchestrated symphonic poem, based on the play by Maurice Maeterlinck, *Pelleas und Melisande* premieres in Vienna, the composer conducting. The piece, which uses leitmotivs, gravitates toward the key of D minor. Ludwig Karpath of the *Signal fur die Musikalische Welt* (Berlin) calls it ". . . a protracted discord lasting fifty minutes."

Feb. 5   Camille Saint-Saens' Concerto No. 2 in D Minor for Cello and Orchestra premieres in Paris.

Feb. 25   Concerto for Double Bass and Orchestra by Serge Koussevitzky premieres in Moscow, with the composer as soloist.

March 4   Concerto in A Minor for Violin and Orchestra, Op. 82, by Alexander Glazunov, receives its world premiere in Saint Petersburg, the composer conducting. It is dedicated to violinist Leopold Auer, who also performs as soloist.

March 8   Edward Elgar's Introduction and Allegro for string quartet and string orchestra and *Pomp and Circumstance No. 3* are premiered as the composer conducts the London Symphony Orchestra.

May 29   Alexander Scriabin's Symphony No. 3 in C Major *The Divine Poem*), Op. 43, is performed for the first time by Arthur Nikisch in Paris. This work reflects the composer's attraction to philosophy and mysticism. The tone poem-like symphony has three movements, entitled "Struggles," "Delights," and "Divine Play." Scriabin's

common-law wife, Tatiana Schloezer, describes the music as representing "the evolution of the human spirit which, torn from an entire past of beliefs and mysteries which it surmounts and overturns, passes through pantheism and attains to a joyous and intoxicated affirmation of its liberty and its unity with the universe (the divine "Ego")."

FRAGMENT OF THE MANUSCRIPT OF DEBUSSY'S *LA MER*

Sep. 29　George Whitefield Chadwick's symphonic poem *Cleopatra* premieres at the Worcester Music Festival in Massachusetts.

Oct. 8　Max Reger's *Sinfonietta in A Major*, Op. 90, is premiered by Felix Mottl in Essen. This German composer studied with Hugo Riemann and made his first big impression with his European tours as a pianist in 1901. He subsequently becomes a professor of counterpoint and receives honorary degrees. Critic Carl Krebs says today's new piece suffers from "...astounding aridity and poverty of invention." One year later critic Rudolf Louis says in the *Munchener Neuste Nachrichten* (Munich) that Reger "...is taking us for fools." Reger replies: "I am sitting in the smallest room of my house. I have your review before me. In a moment it will be behind me."

Oct. 15　Claude Debussy's *La Mer* receives its world premiere in Paris as Camille Chevillard conducts the Lamoureux Orchestra. This three-part, impressionistic work reflects the composer's love for the ocean. It was composed over the last two years. The movements are entitled "De l'aube a midi sur la mer," "Jeux de vagues" and "Dialogue du vent et de la mer." J. Jemain says in *Le Menestrel* [Paris] of the piece, "The composer, by a preconceived notion, avoids all that might resemble a melody...." Louis Schneider says in *Gil Blas* (Paris), "... one encounters here and there some phrases lost in orchestral foam."

Oct. 19　A revised final version of Jean Sibelius' Violin Concerto in D Minor, Op. 47, premieres in Berlin with Varl Halir as soloist.

Oct. 21　*Turandot Suite*, by Ferruccio Busoni, receives its first performance in Berlin. This work is an orchestral suite in eight movements arranged from earlier incidental music he composed.

1905　Births, Deaths and Debuts

Jan. 2　Composer Michael Kemp Tippett is born in London, England.

Jan. 4　Conductor Theodore Thomas, 69, dies in Chicago. He was originally a violinist who came from Germany to the United States at age 10 with his family. He played with various orchestras and in 1862 organized his own orchestra, which gave popular summer concerts in New York. He was conductor of the New York Philharmonic Society from 1877 to 1878 and then founded the Cincinnati College of Music. In 1891 he moved to Chicago, where he founded what is now known as the Chicago Symphony Orchestra. He introduced to America many works by Tchaikovsky, Antonin Dvorak, Anton Bruckner, Camille Saint-Saens and Richard Strauss.

Jan. 16　Composer Ernesto Halffter is born in Madrid, Spain.

Feb. 10　German conductor Felix Weingartner conducts for the first time in America with the New York Philharmonic Orchestra.

Feb. 25　Dancer, choreographer, ballet master and director and teacher Harald Lander is born Alfred Bernhardt Stevnsborg in Copenhagen, Denmark.

March 2　Composer Marc Blitzstein is born in Philadelphia, Pennsylvania.

March 18　Pianist John Kirkpatrick is born in New York City.

March 22　Dancer, choreographer and ballet director Ruth Page is born in Indianapolis, Indiana.

April 2　Choreographer and dancer Serge Lifar is born in Kiev, Ukraine.

April 2　Conductor Kurt Herbert Adler is born in Vienna, Austria.

April 3　Pianist Lili Kraus is born in Budapest, Hungary.

May 2　Composer Alan Rawsthorne is born in Haslingden, England.

May 4　Composer Matyas Seiber is born in Budapest, Hungary.

May 9　Austrian pianist Ernst Pauer, 78, dies in Jugenheim, Germany. A piano pupil of Wolfgang Amadeus Mozart Jr. (Mozart's son), he devoted his life to the performance of music for piano and harpsichord. He taught at the Royal Academy of Music (London) and made internationally known arrangements of Beethoven and Schumann symphonies for piano eight hands, piano four hands and piano solo.

May 24　Pianist Sascha Gorodnitzki is born in Kiev, Ukraine.

May 31　German horn virtuoso Franz Strauss, 83, dies in Munich. This musician — father of Richard Strauss — performed at the Hofoper in Munich. He hated Richard Wagner's work, although Wagner did not hate his; Wagner employed Strauss as principal hornist in the world premiere performances of *Tristan und Isolde*, *Die Meistersinger* and *Parsifal*. Strauss also composed, and his Horn Concerto in C Minor is a standard piece for students of the instrument.

June 4　Cuban-American pianist Jose Echaniz is born in Havana, Cuba.

June 6   Music scholar Arthur Mendel is born in Boston, Massachusetts.

June 13   Czech music critic, editor and composer Frantisek Bartos is born in Brnenec.

June 18   Soviet dancer, choreographer, ballet director and teacher Leonid Lavrovsky is born in Saint Petersburg, Russia.

July 14   Pianist Nadia Reisenberg is born in Vilnius, Russia.

Aug. 8   Composer Andre Jolivet is born in Paris, France.

Aug. 23   Composer Constant Lambert is born in London, England.

Aug. 31   Italian tenor Francesco Tamagno, 54, dies in Varese, Italy. Best known as the creator of Otello in the Verdi opera, he was, as a child, a baker's apprentice. After studies at the Turin Conservatory, his appearance in *Un Ballo in maschera* in Palermo attracted a great deal of attention, and his career took off. His powerful voice and stage presence made his interpretation of Otello the yardstick by which future performances were measured.

Oct. 23   Conductor Alexander Melik-Pashayev is born in Tiflis, Georgia.

Nov. 12   English musicologist Arthur Hedley is born in Shiremoor, England.

1905   Related Events

Among the developments in the recording industry this year are the following: Victor issues the first 8- and 14-inch discs; the decision to make 78 RPM a standard speed is made by recording executives; the first disc players with a "coin-in-slot" fixture appear.

The Cortot-Thibaud-Casals Trio is established this year by pianist, Alfred Cortot, violinist, Jacques Thibaud and cellist, Pablo Casals.

Feb. 2   The Moscow paper *Nashi Dni* publishes an open letter signed by 29 prominent Moscow musicians, including Serge Rachmaninoff, Feodor Chaliapin, Sergei Taneyev, Alexander Gretchaninoff and Reinhold Gliere, which says, "We are not free artists but, like all Russian citizens, victims of today's abnormal social conditions. In our opinion, there is only one solution: Russia must at last embark on a road of basic reforms. . . . "

March 19   Nikolai Rimsky-Korsakov is dismissed from the faculty of the Saint Petersburg Conservatory. He had asked that his name be attached to the open musicians' letter published February 2, supported students who went on strike demanding reforms and called for the resignation of the conservatory's director, August Bernhard, and internal autonomy for the conservatory. Alexander Glazunov and Anatoly Liadov later resign as well. There is great public indignation, and Bernhard's resignation is later accepted as a gesture of appeasement.

March 27   A performance of Nikolai Rimsky-Korsakov's *Kashchei the Immortal* becomes the scene of a heated public demonstration as a result of recent events at the Saint Petersburg Conservatory. The police interrupt the event by lowering the curtain and dispersing the audience. Rimsky-Korsakov is put under police surveillance, and the governor-general subsequently forbids performances of the composer's music.

April 15   The Conservatory of Geneva gives the first public demonstration of Emile Jaques-Dalcroze' *eurythmics*. This method of teaching rhythm through bodily movement subsequently receives international attention. Serge Diaghilev later has his leading dancers study this method.

April 30   Louis Adolphe Coerne is awarded a Ph.D. for his dissertation *The Evolution of Modern Orchestration*. His is the first doctoral dissertation in music to lead to the degree. The work spans the history of instrument-making and orchestration in the 18th and 19th centuries. Its purpose is to make available a comprehensive "history of the orchestra and orchestration" in English. It is published by The Macmillan Company in 1908.

ALEXANDER GLAZUNOV

June 26   Gabriel Faure succeeds Theodore Dubois as director of the Paris Conservatoire.

Sep.   The autocratic directorship of Vassily Safonov at the Moscow Conservatory is intensely resented by liberal faculty and students. Teacher and composer Sergei Taneyev resigns after leading the opposition and attacking Safonov in the press. Safonov leaves his post to become music director of the New York Philharmonic Orchestra and is succeeded by composer Mikhail Ippolitov-Ivanov.

Sep. 8   Double-bass virtuoso Serge Koussevitzky marries Natalie Ushkov, the daughter of a wealthy tea merchant.

Oct. 4   Enrico Caruso, now in Vienna, denies claims of music critics in Budapest that he "had to have morphine injected" in order to cope with the fact that his recent performances there were not sold out. (Caruso admits that ticket prices were too costly for audiences to afford.) He sang Rhadames in *Aida* at a fee of $2,400 per performance. Of the morphine charge, Caruso states: "Of course, not a word of it is true. I was as well as ever, and sang my best."

Oct. 29   The first concert of the New Symphony Orchestra of London occurs at the Coronet Theater, London.

Dec. 5   Alexander Glazunov is elected director of the Saint Petersburg Conservatory after the conservatories are granted limited autonomy. His first action is to ask Nikolai Rimsky-Korsakov to rejoin the faculty. Perturbed by the reactionary atmosphere of the conservatory and refusing to abandon his liberal positions, Rimsky-Korsakov nevertheless agrees to rejoin.

1906   Opera

Jan. 24   Serge Rachmaninoff's two one-act operas *The Miserly Knight* and *Francesca da Rimini* are premiered in Moscow, the composer conducting.

Jan. 31   American composer Frederick Converse's one-act opera *The Pipe of Desire* premieres in Boston. The opera is about an elderly, pipe-playing man who is adored by nymphs and other creatures of the forest.

Feb. 24   The opera *L'Ancetre*, by Camille Saint-Saens, is produced in Monte Carlo. The three-act work is set to a text by L. Auge de Lassus and deals with family vendettas.

March 1   English composer Nicholas Comyn Gatty's one-act opera *Greysteel* premieres in Sheffield, England during the University Opera Week. The opera is based on an Icelandic saga in which a magic sword is used to free an enslaved people and unite two lovers.

March 10   *Don Procopio*, an opera buffa written by Georges Bizet, is premiered posthumously at the Theatre du Casino, Monte Carlo. The two-act opera, written during Bizet's student days, had not been discovered until 30 years later.

March 19   The premiere of *I quattro rusteghi* (or *Die Vier Grobiane*), by Ermanno Wolf-Ferrari, takes place at the Hoftheater in Munich. The libretto, by Giuseppe Pizzolato, is based on a popular play of the same name by Carlo Goldoni. The German version is by H. Teibler. The story is a comedy concerning plotting and scheming on behalf of young lovers in 18th-century Venice.

March 27   John Philip Sousa's comic opera *The Free Lance* receives its initial performance in Springfield, Massachusetts. This work is one of 11 comic operas by Sousa and the first to be premiered since *Chris and the Wonderful Lamp* (1900). A brief review in *Musical America* (New York) says it ". . . possesses the spirit, swing, and dash characteristic of the bandmaster."

April 8   Vincenzo Tommasini's *Medea* premieres at the Teatro Verdi in Trieste. The libretto, written by the composer, is based on the Greek myth of Medea.

Oct. 15   Giacomo Puccini's *Madama Butterfly* receives its first American performance. The Henry W. Savage Opera Company performs the opera in Washington, D.C.

Oct. 27   Enrique Granados'zarzuela *Gaziel* is produced in Barcelona. This Spanish composer had earned his living by

SERGE RACHMANINOFF

EMMY DESTINN AS SALOME

playing "cocktail" piano in restaurants. His opera *Maria del Carmen* (1898) made him famous.

Oct. 31   Jules Massenet's *Ariane* has its premiere at the Paris Opera. The libretto, by Catulle Mendes, is based on the Greek myth of Ariadne. The opera is one of Massenet's minor works.

Nov. 11   *Strandrecht*, by Ethel Mary Smyth, premieres in Leipzig at the Konigliches Opernhaus. The libretto — based on a Cornish drama, *Les Naufrageurs*, by Henry Brewster — is about Cornish villagers who support themselves by robbing and killing sailors who have been shipwrecked on their coast, and about two villagers, Thirza and Mark, who try to prevent this. The opera is first performed in a German version and later translated into English.

Nov. 11   *Maskarade*, a three-act opera by Carl Nielsen, receives its first performance in Copenhagen, the composer conducting. The opera is about a prearranged marriage to which the man in question objects. He then falls in love with a masked woman who turns out to be the woman chosen for him by his parents. Nielsen composed the work over the last two years.

Dec. 5   Richard Strauss' *Salome* receives its first Berlin performance today; it stars Emmy Destinn and is so successful that, over the next 27 years, it is performed 285 times in Berlin alone.

Dec. 8   *Moloch*, an opera by Max von Schillings, receives its first performance in Dresden. It is about a priest, seeking to teach those oppressed by the Romans, who becomes frustrated and commits suicide. Schillings' musical style resembles that of Richard Wagner.

Dec. 27   *Matteo Falcone*, a dramatic scene by Cesar Cui, is performed for the first time in Moscow. The operatic work is based on a novella by Prosper Merimee about Corsicans.

1906 Dance

Jan. 6   *Cinderella* — another new production of the Empire Theater — premieres today in London. It stars Adeline Genee and is presented as a fairy ballet in five scenes. Choreography is by Fred Farren, costumes by C. Wilhelm and music by Sidney Jones. Genee is a smash hit, and the scenery captivates viewers. The London *Times* says that although it is set in the period of Louis XV, '. . . the ballet in its more boisterous moments becomes frankly 20th century."

Jan. 14   *The Debutante* is produced at London's Empire Theater. Scenery, costumes and book are by C. Wilhelm, music by Cuthbert Clarke and G.J.M. Glaser. The lead dancer is Fred Farren. The story is about a ballet dancer and how he wins his favorite ballerina. The London *Times* calls it ". . . full of contrast, not overlaid with incident, gracious, bright, and interesting."

Jan. 28   *Radha* — a modern dance work by Ruth Saint Denis — is performed for the first time today at a private performance at the New York Theater in that city. Music is by Leo Delibes (a subsequent version features music by Jess Meeker). The dance is set in a temple in which Radha awakens as priests enter. She dances "The Dance of the Touch," "The Dance of Taste" and "The Delirium of the Senses." The work is tremendously successful and brings Ruth Saint Denis to national attention. She subsequently considers the work to be her masterpiece.

March 26   Choreographer Ruth Saint Denis has two premieres: *The Cobras* and *The Incense*. Performed at the Hudson Theater in New York City, the music to *The Cobras* is by Leo Delibes and the music to *The Incense* is by Harvey Worthington Loomis.

RUTH ST. DENIS IN HER BALLET, *RADHA*

May 14   The London public sees its first complete performance of *Coppelia* as Adeline Genee recreates her famous role at the Empire Theater.

Aug. 6   *Fete Galante* premieres at the Empire Theater, London. This ballet is an expanded version of the first scene of *Cinderella*, produced at the same theater on January 6 of this year.

1906   Instrumental and Vocal Music

Jan. 15   Excerpts from Arthur Nevin's opera *Poia* are premiered in concert form by the Pittsburgh Symphony Orchestra. The work is produced in its entirety by the Berlin State Opera in 1910. Attracted to American Indian music and themes, this American composer spends time living on Indian reservations.

Jan. 21   Georges Enesco's Symphony No. 1 in E-flat Major premieres in Paris. The work has three movements.

Jan. 27   Ernest Bloch's symphonic work *Hiver-Printemps* premieres in Geneva, the composer conducting.

Feb. 6   Karol Szymanowski's *Concert Overture* is premiered by Gregor Fitelberg in Warsaw. Szymanowski becomes the most important composer in Poland in the 1920s. His use of Polish themes and his mazurkas help to establish him on the international scene. Of today's premiere, critic Aleksander Polinski (in Warsaw) writes: "I did not doubt even for a moment that I was faced with a composer whose talent is of no common order. Everything he writes bears the stamp of genius."

Feb. 18   Vincent d'Indy's symphonic work *Jour d'ete à la montagne* premieres at a Colonne concert in Paris.

March 7   Ernst von Dohnanyi's Concerto for Cello and Orchestra premieres with Hugo Becker as soloist and the composer conducting the Budapest Philharmonic.

March 11   Alexander Glazunov's *Russian Fantasy*, featuring the balalaika and composed for Vasily Andreyev and his Great-Russian Orchestra, premieres in Saint Petersburg.

May 24   *Sea Drift*, by Frederick Delius, is performed for the first time at the music festival in Essen, Germany. Scored for baritone solo, chorus and orchestra, the piece is a choral rhapsody. The text is by Walt Whitman.

May 27   Gustav Mahler's Symphony No. 6 in A Minor premieres in Essen, Germany, the composer conducting. The Andante of this symphony employs cowbells, evoking sounds of Mahler's youth, and interweaves these sounds with Mahlerian melodies. It becomes the composer's most neglected symphony. One critic — Julius Korngold, *Neue Freie Presse* (Vienna) — picks up the musical tension of the work and says it ". . . surpasses its predecessors in the solidity of structure but also in its realism and nerve-wracking intensity. It operates like an alarm."

Aug. 23   *Norfolk Rhapsody No. 1* in E Minor receives its first performance at a Promenade Concert in London. The work, by Ralph Vaughan Williams, is based on Norfolk folk tunes. Twenty years from now, after a performance by Serge Koussevitzky and the Boston Symphony Orchestra, a New York *Herald Tribune* review of that concert reports, "This seemed an appealing work, with skillful use of the tuneful material. . . . "

Dec. 22   Alexander Glazunov's Symphony No. 8 in E-flat Major premieres in Saint Petersburg, the composer conducting. This four-movement symphony is his last.

Dec. 27   Florent Schmitt's *Psalm XLVII* premieres at a Paris concert of music by the winners of the Prix de Rome.

Dec. 29   Jean Sibelius' symphonic work *Pohjola's Daughter* premieres in Saint Petersburg, the composer conducting.

1906   Births, Deaths and Debuts

Jan. 8   Pianist Arthur Rubinstein plays Camille Saint-Saens' Piano Concerto at his New York debut.

Jan. 17   Felix Weingartner makes his Boston debut conducting the New York Symphony Orchestra in a program that includes *Symphonie fantastique* by Hector Berlioz. A review in the Boston *Transcript* says, "By keenness, weight, and pliancy of mind, he grasps the design and proportions, the development and thought. . . of music."

Jan. 21   Pianist and composer Gunnar Johansen is born in Copenhagen, Denmark.

Jan. 21   Soviet dancer, choreographer and ballet director Igor Moiseyev is born in Kiev, Russia.

Jan. 27   Russian pianist Josef Lhevinne makes his American debut with the Russian Symphony Orchestra, conducted by Vassily Safonov in New York. He performs music by Mozart, Chopin and Alexander Scriabin. In the *Evening Post* (New York), Henry T. Finck compares him to Anton Rubinstein and states, "He has the great Anton's technique, his dash and his bravura, his brilliancy, and a good deal of his leonine power."

Feb. 1   Pianist and composer Pierre Capdevielle is born in Paris, France.

Feb. 8   Pianist Artur Balsam is born in Warsaw, Poland.

Feb. 25   Russian composer Anton Arensky, 44, dies of tuberculosis in Terijoki, Finland. A pupil of Nikolai Rimsky-Korsakov at the Saint Petersburg Conservatory, he later taught harmony at the Moscow Conservatory. At the turn of the century, he conducted the Imperial Choir at the Saint Petersburg Conservatory. His music, romantic in style, includes three operas and two symphonies, but he is best known for his pieces in smaller forms — string quartets, piano suites and songs. His book, *Manual of Harmony*, was translated into German.

March 29   Organist E. Power Biggs is born in Westcliff-on-Sea, England.

April 8   Tenor Raoul Jobin is born in Quebec, Canada.

April 9   Conductor Antal Dorati is born in Budapest, Hungary.

April 25   American composer John Knowles Paine, 67, dies in Cambridge, Massachusetts. Paine studied in Berlin, performed there and in America as an organist, and settled in Boston. He joined the faculty of Harvard University in 1862. In 1875 he became the first American composer to hold a professorship in music at Harvard. His pupils included John Alden Carpenter and Frederick S. Converse. As a composer, he wrote several sacred works for chorus and orchestra, a number of cantatas, two symphonies, symphonic poems, one opera (*Azara*, premiered in 1907), chamber music and songs. His work is not in any sense revolutionary but is in a conservative, somewhat academic style. His influence was largely as a music educator.

May 5   Soprano Maria Caniglia is born in Naples, Italy.

May 17   Soprano Zinka Milanov is born in Zagreb, Yugoslavia.

July 1   Manuel Patricio Garcia, 101, dies in London. He invented the laryngoscope — a medical instrument that enabled doctors to view the human vocal cords and determine, among other things, what was wrong with a singer's voice. Konigsberg University awarded Garcia an honorary doctorate for this invention. Garcia was the son of a famous singer of the same name and brother of two of the most famous 19th century singers, Maria Malibran and Pauline Viardot-Garcia. He himself taught singing in London and Paris. His most famous pupil was Jenny Lind.

July 9   Composer Elisabeth Lutyens is born in London, England.

July 12   Music critic Cecil Smith is born in Chicago, Illinois.

July 19   Composer Klaus Egge is born in Gransherad, Norway.

July 24   Cellist Pierre Fournier is born in Paris, France.

July 25   American composer Arthur Kreutz is born in La Crosse, Wisconsin.

Sep. 1   Tenor Aksel Schiotz is born in Roskilde, Denmark.

Sep. 25   Composer Dmitri Shostakovich is born in Saint Petersburg, Russia.

Oct. 5   Music critic Alfred Frankenstein is born in Chicago, Illinois.

Oct. 10   Composer Paul Creston is born Joseph Guttoveggio in New York City.

Oct. 23   Russian critic Vladimir Stasov, 82, who coined the phrase "the mighty five of Russian music," dies in Saint Petersburg. He wrote many books — both biographical and analytical — about nationalism in Russian music. The most important are *Art in the 19th Century* and *Russian Music During the Last 25 Years* (both published in 1905).

Nov. 26   Geraldine Farrar makes her Metropolitan Opera debut as Juliette in Charles Gounod's *Romeo et Juliette*. Samuel Bovy conducts a cast that also includes Charles Rousseliere and Pol Plancon. Krehbiel says in the New York *Tribune*, "Had she been one half less consciously demonstrative. . . one half less sweeping in her movements and gestures. . . she would have been twice as admirable." *Musical America* (New York) says, "In appearance and demeanor she was an ideal Juliette," but "her voice is essentially unsuited for coloratura passages."

Dec. 2   Electronic and recording engineer Peter Carl Goldmark is born in Budapest, Hungary.

Dec. 5   Lina Cavalieri makes her debut at the Metropolitan Opera singing the title role in Umberto Giordano's opera *Fedora*. Enrico Caruso sings the role of Loris Ipanov in this performance, which marks the opera's first appearance in America.

Dec. 7   Soprano Elisabeth Hongen is born in Gevelsberg, Germany.

Dec. 20   Alexander Scriabin makes his American debut as a pianist in New York City. He plays his own piano concerto as Modest Altschuler conducts the Russian Symphony. Scriabin is traveling with a woman to whom he is not married. This results in a scandal that forces the composer to cancel the rest of his American tour. The woman — Tatiana Schloezer — is Scriabin's common-law wife; their relationship results in three children.

Dec. 23   Composer Ross Lee Finney is born in Wells, Minnesota.

1906   Related Events

Vassily Safonov becomes the new music director of the New York Philharmonic Society, after a three-year period during which guest conductors led this orchestra. He lasts three seasons.

Feb. 19   Jean de Reszke, teaching voice in Paris, comments that ". . . the atmosphere of the girls' Christian associations does not promote the growth of the artistic temperament." He makes this remark in criticizing American patrons who make contributions to such organizations as a means of financing the musical education of young American females.

April 2   Mayor Schmitz of San Francisco gives a lavish dinner party for the purpose of raising money to build a new opera house. Violinist Jan Kubelik is the guest of honor. The evening is a tremendous success, and the guests pledge $10,000 each to launch the project. Construction of the new opera house is temporarily preempted by the most devastating earthquake in San Francisco's history, which occurs on April 18.

April 17   Enrico Caruso sings the role of Don Jose in a Metropolitan Opera Company production of *Carmen* in San Francisco. The opera house is packed due to his appearance. A earthquake destroys the city tomorrow, when the opera house is empty.

April 18   A catastrophic earthquake hits San Francisco. Leading opera stars of the New York Metropolitan Opera are in the Palace Hotel, which suddenly begins to rock and sway; large chunks of plaster and wall hangings become missiles and hit several Metropolitan stars as they try to run for cover. Enrico Caruso, Louise Homer, Marcella Sembrich, Olive Fremstad and Emma Eames are among the traumatized celebrities. Most are quickly gathered together by the management and moved to another hotel not in the path of raging fires (but which, soon, does catch fire). The Palace Hotel catches fire late this afternoon, consuming many personal effects of these singers that had been left behind during their hasty departure. They are later shuttled off to Oakland and put on a train heading east. News of the earthquake sends the New York opera crowd into a frenzy; the first substantive report from San Francisco, which comes to Steinway & Sons at 3 p.m. today, says that the Palace Hotel is in flames and that the situation is "precarious." The New York opera public assumes the principals are still inside the hotel.

Losses to music are heavy: The Grand Opera House, where Caruso performed last night, is destroyed by fire, which starts at noon today. Costumes and scenery for twelve operas go up in smoke, resulting in a loss of $125,000 for the Conreid Opera Company. The Metropolitan Opera had scheduled a matinee performance of *The Marriage of Figaro* and an evening performance of *Lohengrin* for today; it was hoped that the Met would earn about $160,000 on this tour to help cover losses from the recent tours of Pittsburgh, St. Louis and Kansas City.

Caruso's fee for each of his two performances was $1,200, and despite the fact that he survived the earthquake, he is reportedly irritated that he must sleep in Golden Gate Park tonight and tomorrow night. He later recounts the adventure in *Musical America* (New York), describing how, in his nightclothes, he had pulled his revolver on three Chinese to prevent them from stealing his trunks. Marcella Sembrich notes that a piano was thrown across her room by the force of the quake. Olive Fremstad, staying at the Saint Dunstan Hotel, departs the city via Chinatown and later comments "There were thousands of Chinamen on the roofs and running about in the streets, their little pigtails streaming out in the wind." Louise Homer dons a pair of her husband's trousers, and the two flee the dancing furniture.

May 29   Oxford University awards an honorary Doctor of Music degree to Edvard Grieg.

June 20   Anton von Webern's doctoral dissertation is approved by his doctoral advisors at the Musicological Institute of the University of Vienna. The dissertation is an edition of the second volume of Heinrich Isaac's *Choralis Constantinus* — a three-volume collection of polyphonic settings of church Offices. The dissertation is published three years from now in the 16th annual publication *Denkmaler der Tonkunst in Osterreich*. Webern, along with Alban Berg, has been studying musical composition for almost two years with Arnold Schoenberg (now 32) at the Schwarzwald School in Vienna while pursuing his university studies.

July   The flexible, laminated disc is issued by Columbia this month — Guglielmo Marconi helped the firm develop it. Other developments in the recording industry this year include: The first console gramophone is released (known as the Victrola, it is a horn-enclosed phonograph, approximately four feet high, manufactured by Victor; Victor publishes its first issue of its house organ, entitled *Voice of the Victor*; Zonophone issues a complete recording of *Aida* (26 discs).

Nov. 16   In what becomes known as the "monkey-house scandal," Enrico Caruso is arrested by a New York City police officer on a charge of making improper advances to a passer-by, Mrs. Hannah Stanhope. The arrest, taking place in the monkey house of the Central Park Zoo (New York City), sparks a scandal that threatens to reduce sales at the Metropolitan Opera box office. Caruso claims that his faulty English had prevented him from explaining why the charges were untrue. He is not required to appear in court, but is convicted and fined. The manager of the Metropolitan Opera, Heinrich Conried, now has this scandal to cope with in addition to competition from Oscar Hammerstein's Manhattan Opera House. All parties eagerly await the public's response to Caruso's next appearance, scheduled for November 28th.

Nov. 28   Enrico Caruso sings Rodolfo in *La Boheme*, by Giacomo Puccini. This is his first appearance after having been arrested, convicted and fined for making improper advances to a woman in the Central Park Zoo on November 16th. His appearance tonight is immediately greeted with applause and, although his performance begins with some nervousness, he virtually brings down the house. The "monkey-house scandal" is quickly forgotten and Caruso's stature remains unaffected.

Dec. 1   The celebrated soprano Adelina Patti gives her farewell concert at the Albert Hall in London. Including in her program "Home Sweet Home" and "Comin' Through the Rye," she moves the audience to applause and praise that lasts over half an hour. Patti cries and says after the concert, "My voice is no longer for sale, but I shall always be ready to sing for charity."

Dec. 3   Impresario Oscar Hammerstein opens the Manhattan Opera House to compete with the Metropolitan Opera in New York City. The first presentation is Bellini's *I Puritani*. Hammerstein hires tenor Alessandro Bonci, who advertises himself as a better singer than Enrico Caruso. A review in *Musical America* (New York) calls Bonci's voice "one of considerable lyrical beauty" but goes on to say, "It is, however, a small voice and at times impresses one as being of a pallid quality." The opera house and its planned productions cost over $2 million. People affiliated with this new company hope that perhaps a new group of wealthy patrons, who may have been rejected by the Metropolitan Opera social circles, will help finance productions in this recently opened opera house.

1907 Opera

Jan. 22   Richard Strauss' new opera *Salome* receives its first American performance at the Metropolitan Opera House. Audiences are shocked by the production, which includes dancing and costumes considered too erotic. The cast includes Olive Fremstad, Marion Weed, Karl Burrian, Anton Van Rooy and Andreas Dippel. The conductor is Alfred Hertz. H.E. Krehbiel writes in the New York *Tribune* that there ". . . is not a whiff of fresh and healthy air blowing through *Salome* except that which exhales from the cistern. . . ." W.J. Henderson of the New York *Sun* says the composer ". . . has a mania for writing ugly music." This production causes one of the greatest scandals in the company's history: It is subsequently banned from the repertory (five days from today).

Feb. 7   Jules Massenet's *Therese* is produced in Monte Carlo. The two-act opera is about lovers during the French Revolution.

Feb. 20   *The Legend of the Invisible City of Kitezh* by Nikolai Rimsky-Korsakov premieres at the Maryinsky Theater in

Saint Petersburg. The libretto, by Vladimir Bielsky, based on religious legends, is the story of a prince and a simple forest maiden who become engaged, and of what happens to them after a Tartar raid on their city. It is considered one of Rimsky-Korsakov's greatest works and one of the best Russian operas.

Feb. 21   Frederick Delius' opera *Romeo und Julia auf dem Dorfe* has its premiere at the Komische Oper in Berlin. The composer's own libretto is based on a story by Gottfried Keller. It is the tale of the children of feuding parents who fall in love and choose to die together rather than be separated. It is considered Delius' best operatic work.

April 23   Excerpts from Arthur Nevin's *Poia* are premiered at the White House. President Theodore Roosevelt listens as the composer performs at the piano in the ab-

sence of an orchestra. The opera is premiered in full in 1910, when it becomes the first American opera performed in Berlin. The story centers on a Blackfoot Indian, his love for a squaw, and her death.

May 10   *Ariane et Barbe-Bleue*, by Paul Dukas, premieres at the Paris Opera-Comique. The libretto is based on the play by Maurice Maeterlinck about Ariane, the sixth wife of Bluebeard, who finds his other wives locked in a vault and frees them. It is the only opera Dukas wrote and is considered one of his best works. Gabriel Faure comments in *Le Figaro* (Paris), "How I rejoice in seeing our music enriched by such a gem!"

Nov. 9   Umberto Giordano's *Marcella* is produced at La Scala in Milan. The opera, in three episodes, is about the love affair between an artist and his model.

1907 Dance

Feb. 23   The ballet *Chopiniana* premieres at the Imperial Opera House in Saint Petersburg. Anna Pavlova and Mikhail Obukhov dance the leads. The choreography, which has a strong character element, is by Michel Fokine. It is reworked as a "white ballet" in 1909, when it is called *Les Sylphides*.

April 28   Michel Fokine presents a ballet for students at the Saint Petersburg Imperial Ballet Theater entitled *The Animated Goblins*. The piece features music by Nicolas Tcherepnin. Tcherepnin subsequently introduces Fokine to Alexandre Benois, and the three collaborate to produce (on November 25 of this year) *Le Pavillon d'armide* — a tremendously successful work that is an expanded and embellished version of today's student piece.

Nov. 25   *Le Pavillon d'armide* receives its world premiere at the Maryinsky Theater in Saint Petersburg. The choreography is by Michel Fokine and the music by Nicolas Tche-

repnin. This is the first work by Alexandre Benois, who writes the book and designs the scenery and costumes. Lead dancers are Anna Pavlova, Pavel Gerdt, and Vaslav Nijinsky. Based on the story *Omphale*, By Gautier, the ballet is about a glorious tapestry whose goblins come to life. It is Fokine's first major ballet.

Dec. 22   Michel Fokine's *The Dying Swan* premieres at the Hall of the Noblemen in Saint Petersburg. Anna Pavlova dances to music by Camille Saint-Saens. Perhaps the most famous solo dance of the century, it lasts approximately three minutes. Fokine created the choreography in a few minutes at the request of Pavlova. Fokine comments on this work 24 years later in *Dance Magazine*, saying that this piece became "the symbol of the new Russian ballet." French critic Andre Levinson later describes the soloist's role as "the aerial creature struggling against earthly bonds."

1907 Instrumental and Vocal Music

Jan. 12   Maurice Ravel's song cycle *Histoires naturelles* premieres at a concert of the Societe Nationale de Musique in Paris.

Feb. 3   *Asrael* (Symphony No. 2 in C Minor), by Josef Suk, is performed for the first time today in Prague. The symphony, in five somber movements, is dedicated to the composer's deceased wife Otilie and to Antonin Dvorak (Suk's father-in-law). Dvorak had criticized Suk for attempting to write a five-movement symphony — today's premiere is the realization of that effort.

Feb. 3   Maurice Ravel's orchestral version of *Une Barque sur l'ocean* is premiered by Gabriel Pierne in Paris. This work is one movement from his piano suite *Miroirs*.

Feb. 5   Arnold Schoenberg's String Quartet No. 1 in D Minor, Op. 7, premieres in Vienna.

Feb. 8   Arnold Schoenberg's *Kammersymphonie*, Op. 9, premieres in Vienna. This is one of the last works he composes with a key signature. The melodies and harmonies feature fourths and fifths, and the parts, for 15 instruments, display soloistic writing for each instrument.

Feb. 22   Maurice Ravel's *Introduction and Allegro* premieres at the Cercle Musical in Paris. The chamber work is scored for harp, string quartet, flute and clarinet.

March 1   Claude Debussy's *La Mer* receives its American premiere as it is performed by Karl Muck and the Boston Symphony Orchestra in Boston. Elson of the Boston *Daily Advertiser* says, "It was not so long, but it was terrible while it lasted."

March 21   Claude Debussy's *La Mer* receives its New York premiere, with Karl Muck and the Boston Symphony Orchestra performing the work. The New York *Times* calls it "persistently ugly"; the New York *Post*, "the dreariest kind of rubbish"; the New York *Sun*, "that painted mud-puddle." Krehbiel writes in the New York *Tribune* that "Debussy's ocean was a frog pond."

April 20   Vincent d'Indy's *Souvenirs* premieres in Paris. This symphonic work is dedicated to the memory of his wife.

April 27   Igor Stravinsky's Symphony No. 1 in E-flat Major is premiered by the Imperial Chapel Orchestra in Saint Petersburg at a private concert. The work consists of four movements and is dedicated to Nikolai Rimsky-Korsakov. Stravinsky, now 23, recently left law studies to devote himself to composition. This event marks his first important premiere; the same work is performed publicly on February 5, 1908.

Aug. 24   Edward Elgar's *Pomp and Circumstance No. 4* premieres in London.

Sep. 25   Jean Sibelius conducts the world premiere of his Symphony No. 3 in C Major, Op. 52, today in Helsinki, Finland. This symphony has three movements.

Sep. 27   *Norfolk Rhapsody No. 2* and *Norfolk Rhapsody No. 3*, by Ralph Vaughan Williams, are premiered at the Cardiff Festival. The composer conducts. Vaughan Williams subsequently discards both scores, and the works are not published.

Oct. 8   Havergal Brian's overture *For Valor* premieres in London, with Henry Wood conducting. This composer, virtually unknown, bases the piece on "Drum Taps," by Walt Whitman.

Nov. 7   Anton von Webern's Quintet — scored for two violins, viola, violoncello and piano — receives its first performance at the Gremium Hall of the Wiener Kaufmannschaft in Vienna. This premiere is part of a concert of new music by students of Arnold Schoenberg and attendance is by invitation only. The Quintet is one of Webern's early works (composed before he began using opus numbers). Gustav Grube writes of it in *Neue Zeitschrift fur Musik* (Leipzig), "The principal theme. . . while not badly invented, lost itself very soon in wild confusion." This event marks the first time Webern's music is reviewed by a critic.

Nov. 9   *La tragedie de Salome* — a ballet by French composer Florent Schmitt — is premiered at a concert in Paris. Today's performance is a chamber orchestra version, without dancers. It contains five symphonic movements.

Nov. 22   American composer Charles Martin Loeffler's *A Pagan Poem* is premiered by Karl Muck and the Boston Symphony Orchestra. Scored for orchestra and piano obbligato, it was inspired by Virgil's *8th Eclogue*. Louis C. Elson writes in the Boston *Advertiser* that Loeffler "is not purely so cerebral as the bitter Vincent d'Indy and he is fully as romantic as the fawning Debussy."

Dec. 14   *The Wand of Youth* — an orchestral suite by Edward Elgar — receives its first performance in London. The music is in seven movements and is subtitled *Music to a Child's Play*. It was composed when Elgar was 12 years old.

Dec. 27   Symphony No. 3 in B Minor, by Henry Hadley, receives its first performance by the Berlin Philharmonic, the composer conducting. The symphony has four movements.

1907   Births, Deaths and Debuts

Jan. 4   Greek musicologist Thrasybulos Georgiades is born in Athens.

Jan. 7   Harpist Nicanor Zabaleta is born in San Sebastian, Spain.

Jan. 17   Dutch composer Henk Badings is born in Bandung, Indonesia.

Feb. 1   Swiss-Hungarian composer Sandor Veress is born in Kolozsvar, Hungary.

Feb. 12   Conductor-composer Ennio Gerelli is born in Cremona, Italy.

Feb. 15   Composer Jean Langlais is born in La Fontenelle, France.

March 19   Edward Elgar conducts a New York performance of his oratorio *The Apostles* with the Oratorio Society of New York City. This event marks Elgar's first conducting appearance in America. A review in the New York *World* says the work is not as good as his *The Dream of Gerontius* and that Elgar ". . . conducted in a somewhat academic manner. . . . He seems to figure more as a composer than as a leader." The New York *Telegram* says, "As a conductor Sir Edward qualifies, yet does not shine. . . he enters at once upon his interpretation, of which an abstract spirituality is the dominant feature."

April 4   Lucile Grahn, one of the major ballerinas of the Romantic Era, dies in Munich at the age of 87. A protegee of August Bournonville, she created the title role in the version of *La Sylphide* which he choreographed. Grahn left Denmark in 1839 to pursue an international career. She was one of the four ballerinas to take part in Jules Perrot's famous *Pas de Quatre* in London in 1845.

April 18   Composer Miklos Rosza is born in Budapest, Hungary.

May 5   Composer Yoritsune Matsudaira is born in Tokyo, Japan.

May 18   Pianist Clifford Curzon is born in London, England.

July 15   Gustav Schirmer, 43, dies in Boston. Founder of the Boston Music Company in that city, he was also a partner in the Schirmer (New York) company that his father had created.

Aug. 15   Hungarian violinist Joseph Joachim, 76, dies of asthma in Berlin. A world-renowned artist known for his precise intonation in performance, he was once accompanied at the piano by Felix Mendelssohn. He became especially famous in England, where he was praised for his technique, which combined virtuosity with a scholarly approach — attempting to communicate the intentions of the composer to the audience. He owned three Stradivarius violins, made several recordings in Berlin (1903) and was the first violinist to record unaccompanied violin music of Bach.

JOSEPH JOACHIM

EDVARD GRIEG

Aug. 20   Conductor Anatole Fistoulari is born in Kiev, Russia. His father is opera conductor Gregory Fistoulari.

Sep. 4   Norwegian composer Edvard Hagerup Grieg, 64, dies near Bergen, Norway. Grieg was partly of Scottish heritage — his grandfather, Alexander Grieg, emigrated from Scotland to Norway around 1765. He first studied with his mother, an amateur pianist. The Norwegian violinist Ole Bull suggested that Grieg be sent to the Leipzig Conservatory; he was and studied with Ernest Ferdinand Wenzel (piano), Moritz Hauptmann and Carl Reinecke (theory).

At this time he became interested in the music of Felix Mendelssohn and Robert Schumann. He went to Copenhagen in 1863 and studied with Niels Gade. While there, he also organized (with Norwegian composer Rikard Nordraak) the Euterpe Society, to promote Scandinavian music. Grieg married Nina Hagerup, a cousin, in 1867. A year later he performed as a soloist in his Concerto in A Minor for Piano and Orchestra. That event established him as a major young composer (he was then 25). He later composed incidental music to Henrik Ibsen's *Peer Gynt* and arranged it into two orchestral suites. They are among his most famous works. He received an annual grant of 1,600 crowns from the Norwegian government, allowing him to focus almost exclusively on composition. His music began to enjoy frequent performances in Germany and England. However, he shunned celebrity life in favor of peace and quiet and spent his final years at Troldhaugen.

His importance as a composer rests largely on his intense Norwegian nationalism. His music is imbued with a Norwegian sound without invoking the common practice of citing folk song materials. In addition to many orchestral works, he wrote a great deal of chamber music. His songs (25 sets) and piano works (including 10 sets composed between 1867 and 1901) are examples of his miniatures.

Oct. 5   Irish tenor John McCormack makes his English operatic debut as Turiddu in *Cavalleria Rusticana* at Covent Garden, London.

Oct. 12   Composer Wolfgang Fortner is born in Leipzig, Germany.

Oct. 27   Composer and organist Helmut Walcha is born in Leipzig, Germany.

Nov. 15   English pianist Myra Hess makes her debut in London playing Beethoven's Fourth Piano Concerto. Thomas Beecham conducts. The pianist is 17 years old.

Nov. 20   Feodor Chaliapin makes his American debut at the Metropolitan Opera House in *Mefistofele*. Henry Kreh-

biel writes in the New York *Tribune* that Chaliapin "Calls to mind, more than anything else, the vulgarity of conduct which his countryman Gorki presents with such disgusting frankness in his pictures of Russian low life. . . . "

Nov. 22   Alessandro Bonci makes his Metropolitan Opera debut as the Duke in *Rigoletto.*

Nov. 25   Mary Garden makes her American debut singing the American premiere of Jules Massenet's *Thais* at the Manhattan Opera House. The performance is conducted by Cleofonte Campanini. *Musical America* (New York) calls her ". . . a personality of compelling interest. . . " and an artist possessing ". . . dramatic resources rarely met with on the opera stage."

1907   Related Events

Jan. 27   Following protests by the board of directors that the opera was indecent, the executive committee of the Metropolitan Opera Company of New York removes Richard Strauss' *Salome* from the repertory and begins issuing refunds to holders of tickets for the remaining three performances.

Jan. 28   An investigation into the degree of obscenity in Richard Strauss' *Salome* is opened by the New England Watch and Ward Society in an effort to halt the Boston production.

March 5   The first wireless broadcast of a piece of music takes place as a performance of Rossini's *William Tell* overture is transmitted from New York Telharmonic Hall to the Brooklyn Navy Yard by an American, Lee de Forest.

May 16   The first of a series of five concerts is presented by Serge Diaghilev in Paris. Sponsored by the Societe des Grandes Auditions Musicales de France, this concert series

features Russian music, including works of Nikolai Rimsky-Korsakov, Alexander Glazunov, Serge Rachmaninoff, Mikhail Glinka, Alexander Borodin, Mily Balakirev, Modest Mussorgsky, Cesar Cui, Tchaikovsky, Alexander Scriabin and others. The first three conduct their own music. Arthur Nikisch also conducts. Feodor Chaliapin sings operatic excerpts, creating a sensation.

June 12   Cambridge University awards the honorary degree of Doctor of Music to Alexander Glazunov.

June 18   Oxford University awards the honorary degree of Doctor of Music to Alexander Glazunov.

June 26   Oxford University awards the honorary degree of Doctor of Music to Camille Saint-Saens.

Oct. 15   Gustav Mahler conducts his last performance as Music Director of the Vienna Opera. He subsequently departs to become music director of the New York Philharmonic.

1908   Opera

Feb. 19   Claude Debussy's *Pelleas et Melisande* receives its first American performance at the Manhattan Opera House in New York. Today's performance is in French, and the cast includes Mary Garden, Jean Perier, Jeanne Gerville-Reache and Hector Dufranne — the four original stars of the Opera-Comique production. *Musical America* (New York) calls the premiere ". . . one of the most noteworthy in the annals of opera in America." W.J. Henderson of the New York *Sun* describes it as ". . . a strange conception, solitary in spirit, tinged with the neutral colors and flaccid forms of the pre-Raphaelite school. . . . " Finck

of the *Evening Post* (New York) says, "Debussy eliminates the melodic element, and this marks a step backward."

March 30   *Les Jumeaux de Bergame,* by Emile Jaques-Dalcroze, receives its first performance in Brussels. The two-act opera is his last stage work.

May 19   Serge Diaghilev introduces the Parisian public to Russian opera. The new impresario brings a company of Russian singers to the Paris Opera to sing Modest Mussorgsky's *Boris Godunov.* The cast includes Feodor Chaliapin, Dimitri Smernov, Ivan Altchevsky, Natalia Yuzhina and

Vladimir Kastorsky. The settings are by Alexandre Benois, Alexander Golovine and Juon. The chorus is made up of singers from the Bolshoi Opera and the conductor is F.M. Blumenfeld. For this production, Diaghilev asked Nikolai Rimsky-Korsakov, who had already reorchestrated the opera, to add additional music to the coronation scene. Benois later recalls the sensation the opera had made on the public. After Chaliapin's singing of Boris's clock scene, "the audience went wild."

Oct. 8   Edvard Grieg's *Olav Trygvason*, his only opera, is produced posthumously in Christiania, Norway. It is about the first Christian king of Norway.

Nov. 27   *Le Jongleur de Notre-Dame*, a three-act opera by Jules Massenet, receives its first American performance at the Metropolitan Opera. Mary Garden sings the role of Jean (which was originally a tenor role). The conductor is Cleofonte Campanini.

Nov. 28   Riccardo Zandonai's *Il grillo del focolare*, to a libretto adapted from Dickens' *The Cricket on the Hearth*, premieres in Turin. This former pupil of Pietro Mascagni writes music imbued with passion. The opera is the composer's first.

1908   Dance

Feb. 9   Ruth Saint Denis' *The Yogi*, with music by Metrowitz, premieres in Vienna.

March 21   *Une nuit d'Egypte* is produced at the Maryinsky Theater in Saint Petersburg to music by Anton Arensky. The choreographer is Michel Fokine, and the lead dancers are Anna Pavlova and Pavel Gerdt, with Vaslav Nijinsky dancing a minor role. The set used in the ballet is taken from the Maryinsky production of *Aida*. Also performed today, is a revised version of *Chopiniana*. Michel Fokine revives the romantic spirit of last year's version by developing new choreography to some additional music by Frederick Chopin. Lead dancers are Olga Preobrajenska, Anna Pavlova, Tamara Karsavina and Vaslav Nijinsky.

Sep. 7   *The Dryad*, a pastoral fantasy in two scenes, is produced for the first time today at the Empire Theater in London. Alexandre Genee choreographs Dora Bright's music. The dancers are Adeline Genee and Gordon Cleather. It is about a wood nymph locked in an oak tree who gets out one night every 10 years. On one of her nights out she is seen by a shepherd who, of course, falls in love with her. The ballet is based on *Libussa*, by Musaus.

1908   Instrumental and Vocal Music

Jan. 2   "El albaicin," "El polo" and "Lavapies" — the three pieces comprising the third book of Isaac Albeniz' piano suite *Iberia* — are performed for the first time in Paris, at the salon of arts patron Armande de Polignac. Pianist Blanche Selva performs. Five years from now, Claude Debussy reviews "El albaicin" in *Bulletin francais de la Societe Independante de Musique* (Paris) and says, "It is like the muffled sounds of a guitar complaining in the night."

Jan. 18   Frederick Delius' *Brigg Fair* is premiered by Granville Bantock in Liverpool, England.

Jan. 23   Reinhold Gliere's four-movement Symphony No. 2 is premiered by Serge Koussevitzky in Berlin as Koussevitzky debuts as a conductor for the first time outside of Russia.

Feb. 7   George Whitefield Chadwick's *Symphonic Sketches* is premiered by Karl Muck and the Boston Symphony Orchestra. Performed today in its complete version, the work had been performed in a partial version (two of the sketches) in 1904.

Feb. 8   Symphony No. 2 in E Minor by Serge Rachmaninoff receives its world premiere as the composer conducts the Moscow Philharmonic. The symphony has four movements and was finished by the composer while he was in Dresden last month.

Feb. 29   *Le Faune et la Bergere*, by Igor Stravinsky, receives its initial performance by the Russian Symphony Society in Saint Petersburg. The work is scored for mezzo soprano and orchestra and consists of three songs to poems by Aleksander Pushkin.

March 15   Maurice Ravel's *Rhapsodie espagnole* is premiered by Edouard Colonne at a Paris concert. The symphonic suite has four movements.

March 22   Albert Roussel's Symphony No. 1 premieres in Brussels. This composer left the navy to embrace music and was a student as late as age 38. The work is subtitled "Le poeme de la foret."

May 4   Sergei Vassilenko's *The Garden of Death* premieres in Moscow. The piece is a symphonic poem.

June 4   The second part of *A Mass of Life*, by Frederick Delius, receives its first performance in Munich. The complete oratorio — scored for soloists, chorus and large orchestra — receives its world premiere on June 7, 1909.

June 17   Igor Stravinsky's short tone poem *Fireworks* premieres in Saint Petersburg.

Sep. 19   Gustav Mahler's Symphony No. 7 premieres in Prague, the composer conducting. The work is in five movements — "Langsam," "Nachtmusik," "Schatten-haft," "Nachtmusik" and "Rondo-Finale."

Oct. 13   Max Reger's Violin Concerto in A Major, Op. 101, is performed for the first time, with Henri Marteau as soloist and Arthur Nikisch conducting the Gewandhaus Orchestra of Leipzig. A review published in the *Leipziger Zeitung* claims that Reger's "... powerful presentation of polyphonic forms..." and the "... expansive mobility of his melismatic writing..." make him "... the blessed inheritor of Bach's treasure."

Oct. 24   Edward MacDowell's symphonic poem *Lamia* is presented for the first time by the Boston Symphony Orchestra, in a posthumous performance.

Nov. 4   *Passacaglia* for orchestra, Op. 1, by Anton von Webern, receives its first performance in the main hall of the Musikverein, Vienna. The composer conducts the Tonkunstlervein Orchestra. The piece is scored for woodwinds, four horns, three trombones, bass tuba, timpani, percussion, harp and strings, and features a passacaglia subject in D minor and in duple meter, which undergoes 23 variations. Lasting approximately eight minutes, it is one of the longest single-movement compositions by this composer and is also one of the last pieces he writes that is firmly anchored in tonality. The concert attracts the composer's pupils and provokes opinionated reviews. Although the critic of the *Wiener Illustriertes* (Vienna) says Webern cannot justify calling the work a passacaglia, Elsa Bienenfeld of the *Neues Wiener Journal* (Vienna) writes a favorable review, saying that despite the music's chord progressions and unusual harmonies, it succeeds in evoking moods.

Dec. 3   Havergal Brian's tone poem *Hero and Leander* is premiered by Thomas Beecham in London. The parts and score mysteriously vanish just after the performance.

Dec. 3   Symphony No. 1 in A-flat Major, Op. 55 by Edward Elgar, receives its initial performance in Manchester, England. Hans Richter conducts the Halle Orchestra of Manchester. The work is in four movements and is the first of two symphonies composed by Elgar. Richter and Elgar had had a falling-out after Richter conducted a disastrous rendition of Elgar's *The Dream of Gerontius* at the turn of the century. His performance today restores Elgar's respect.

Dec. 10   Alexander Scriabin's Symphony No. 4, Op. 54, *Le Poeme de l'Extase*, receives its world premiere by Modest Altschuler and the Russian Symphony Orchestra of New York City. W.J. Henderson of the New York *Sun* describes the music as containing "... formless melodies..." with "... acrid harmonies...."

Dec. 11   *In a Summer Garden*, by Frederick Delius, receives its first performance as the composer conducts the London Philharmonic. A review in the London *Times* asks, "... what is the object of employing so many players to say so very little?"

Dec. 18   Claude Debussy's *The Children's Corner* is premiered by pianist Harold Bauer at the Cercle Musical in Paris. This piano suite is in six movements.

Dec. 21   Arnold Schoenberg's String Quartet No. 2 in F-sharp Minor Op. 10, is presented for the first time in Vienna, the Rose String Quartet performing with Marie Gutheil-Schroder, soprano soloist. Based on a text by Stefan George, this work is the last the composer writes with a key signature. Karpath says in *Signale* (Berlin), "If I nevertheless abandoned my customary reserve, I only proved by it that I suffered physical pain, and as one cruelly abused, despite all good intentions to endure even the worst, I still had to cry out."

1908   Births, Deaths and Debuts

Jan. 1   Gustav Mahler conducts *Tristan und Isolde* at the Metropolitan Opera in New York. This event marks his first conducting appearance in America. Henry Krehbiel says in the New York *Tribune* of Mahler's conducting: "It was a strikingly vital reading which he gave to Wagner's score.... Mr. Mahler did honor to himself, Wagner's music and the New York public."

Jan. 6   Russian bass Feodor Chaliapin makes his debut at the Metropolitan Opera singing Mefistofele in Arrigo Boito's opera. Krehbiel writes in the New York *Tribune*, "... he calls to mind, more than anything else, the vul-garity of conduct which his countryman Gorki presents in his pictures of Russian low life...."

Jan. 12   Conductor Leopold Ludwig is born in Witkowitz, Austria.

Jan. 12   Dancer, choreographer and teacher Jose Limon is born in Culiacan, Mexico.

Jan. 15   The New York debut of Luisa Tetrazzini takes place as she performs in Verdi's *La Traviata* at the Manhattan Opera House.

EDWARD MACDOWELL

Jan. 23   American composer Edward MacDowell, 47, dies in New York City after a sustained period of mental collapse. He began as a pianist after studies with Teresa Carreno. Further studies took him to France (Paris Conservatoire) and Germany (Frankfurt Conservatory). In 1882 he met Franz Liszt, who helped him gain a performance of his *Modern Suite* for piano at the Allgemeiner Musikverein that same year. MacDowell soon married, and the couple settled in Boston, where his music was performed regularly by the Boston Symphony Orchestra. He was appointed a member of the music faculty at the new department of music of Columbia University in 1896. Toward the end of his life, he went insane. At his death $50,000 was raised to establish the MacDowell Memorial Association, part of which — the MacDowell Colony (Peterborough, N.H.) — is a retreat for composers and other artists.

His music is characteristically romantic and emotionally exciting. Famous pieces include the symphonic poems *Lamia* and *Hamlet and Ophelia*, the choral works *Love and Time* and *The Rose and the Gardener,* and the six songs comprising *From an Old Garden.* He composed an enormous amount of piano music.

Jan. 23   Conductor Serge Koussevitzky conducts the Berlin Philharmonic for the first time, thus launching his international career. The program (all Russian music) includes the world premiere of Reinhold Gliere's Second Symphony.

Feb. 2   Italian composer Renzo Rossellini is born in Rome.

Feb. 22   Music critic and writer Irving Kolodin is born in New York City.

April 4   British dancer, choreographer and teacher Antony Tudor is born in London.

April 5   Conductor Herbert von Karajan is born in Salzburg, Austria.

April 11   Conductor Karel Ancerl is born in Tucapy, Czechoslovakia.

May 15   Composer Lars-Erik Larsson is born in Akarp, Sweden.

May 30   Pianist Beveridge Webster is born in Pittsburgh, Pennsylvania.

June 7   Pianist Boris Goldovsky is born in Moscow, Russia.

June 21   Russian composer Nikolai Rimsky-Korsakov, 64, dies in Liubensk, in the vicinity of Saint Petersburg. In 1862 he was a naval officer; by 1871 he was a professor of composition at the Saint Petersburg Conservatory, where he remained for life (except for a brief period in 1905 when his support for student causes got him temporarily fired). He is considered to have been one of the masters of Russian music: His style was a blend of Oriental melodic materials and Russian folk music. He rose to the pinnacle of international fame with his dazzling orchestrations. He was also considered to be a great teacher — Igor Stravinsky was one of his students, as were Alexander Glazunov, Anatoly Liadov, Anton Arensky, Mikhail Ippolitov-Ivanov and Nikolai Miaskovsky. Famous works include the operas *The Maid of Pskov* (1895) and *Kaschei the Immortal* (1902), three symphonies, the *Russian Easter Overture* and *The Flight of the Bumble Bee.* He was extremely prolific and also wrote books, such as the *Foundations of Orchestration* (two volumes, 1913).

June 24   Organist and composer Hugo Distler is born in Nuremberg, Germany.

Aug. 3   Choreographer and dancer Birgit Cullberg is born in Nykoping, Sweden.

Sep. 20   Spanish violinist Pablo Sarasate, 64, dies in Biarritz. He studied at the Paris Conservatoire, soon obtained a Stadivarius violin and he toured Europe, North and South America, South Africa and the Orient, being widely acclaimed on each tour. Camille Saint-Saens composed *Rondo capriccioso* for him. His playing was known for its technical brilliance and exquisite tone. He arranged a number of works, including operatic airs for violin, and also composed works for violin and orchestra. His best-known work is *Zigeunerweisen* for violin and orchestra.

Sep. 26   Harpsichordist Sylvia Marlowe is born in New York City.

Sep. 30   Violinist David Oistrakh is born in Odessa, Russia.

Oct. 1   Russian pianist Benno Moiseiwitsch makes his debut in Reading, England.

Oct. 7   Conductor Nikolai Rabinovich is born in Saint Petersburg, Russia.

Oct. 21   Violinist Alexander Schneider is born in Vilna, Russia.

SCENE FROM THE METROPOLITAN OPERA PRODUCTION OF *AIDA*

Oct. 26   Baritone Igor Gorin is born in Grodek, Ukraine.

Oct. 31   Spanish soprano Lucrezia Bori makes her operatic debut as Micaela in *Carmen* at the Teatro Costanzi in Rome.

Nov. 4   Conductor August Vianesi, 70, dies in New York City. He conducted the opening night performance (*Faust*) at New York's Metropolitan Opera House on October 22, 1883.

Nov. 8   Conductor Alberto Erede is born in Genoa, Italy.

Nov. 16   Italian conductor Arturo Toscanini and Czech soprano Emmy Destinn make their Metropolitan Opera debuts in New York, Toscanini conducting and Destinn singing Aida. Also in the cast are Enrico Caruso, Louise Homer and Antonio Scotti. This event marks the first appearance of Toscanini in America and also the first opera presented by the new manager of the Metropolitan Opera, Giulio Gatti-Casazza. Henry Krehbiel says in the New York *Tribune*, "Of the new conductor it must be said that he is a boon to Italian opera as great and as welcome as anything that has come out of Italy since Verdi laid down his pen." Richard Aldrich says of Destinn in the New York *Times* that she is a "... singer of keen musical feeling and intelligence."

Nov. 20   Italian baritone Pasquale Amato makes his Metropolitan Opera debut in *La Traviata* with Marcella Sembrich and Caruso.

Nov. 22   French flutist and conductor Paul Taffanel, 63, dies in Paris. He coauthored (with Phillippe Gaubert) *Methode complete de flute.*

Nov. 26   American bass Herbert Witherspoon makes his Metropolitan Opera debut as Titurel in Richard Wagner's *Parsifal.*

Nov. 28   Soprano Rose Bampton is born in Cleveland, Ohio.

Dec. 7   Soprana Frances Alda debuts at the Metropolitan Opera singing Gilda in *Rigoletto* opposite Enrico Caruso. Henry Krehbiel writes in the New York *Tribune* that "... her tones were marred by a vibrato, and they were often sharpened to a keen edge that cut shrilly upon the ear."

Dec. 10   Mischa Elman makes his American debut as he performs as soloist in the Tchaikovsky Violin Concerto with the Russian Symphony Society in New York City.

Dec. 10   Olivier Messiaen is born in Avignon, France, to poetess Cecile Sauvage, whose poem "L'Ame en bourgeon" is dedicated to the newborn's "burgeoning soul."

Dec. 11   Composer Elliott Carter is born in New York City.

Dec. 13   Pianist Victor Babin is born in Moscow, Russia.

Dec. 31   Sergei Prokofiev, 17, premieres seven of his own piano compositions at a concert of the Society for Con- temporary Music in Saint Petersburg. This event marks the musician's first public appearance.

1908   Related Events

Amberol cylinders (four minutes each, with a 200-line-per-inch cut) are produced by Thomas Edison. These microgroove wax cylinders increase the short playing time of previous discs. Edison also produces an adapter for his Gem, Standard, and Home phonograph models to enable listeners to play both the two- and four-minute cylinders. In another recording industry development, Columbia and Victor release double-faced discs for public purchase (Victor does not do this, however, for its Red Seal discs, which are still single-faced).

Jan. 20   Claude Debussy and Mme Emma Bardac are married. Debussy divorced Rosalie Texier because he found her boring.

June 15   Erik Satie, now 42, successfully completes a course in counterpoint at the Schola Cantorum in Paris. His professors were Albert Roussel and Vincent d'Indy. Satie's music has already become well-known for its simplicity and almost popular appeal — two of his *Gymnopedies* are orchestrated by Claude Debussy.

July 1   The University of Vienna awards an honorary degree of Doctor of Music to Max Reger.

1909   Opera

Jan. 25   *Elektra* by Richard Strauss, premieres in Dresden at the Konigliches Opernhaus. The one-act opera, based on the Greek drama, is the first collaboration of Strauss and Hugo von Hofmannsthal. Krehbiel says in a dispatch to the New York *Times*, "It is fortunate for hearers the piece is no longer for it would else be too nerve wracking." In the cast are Anny Krull (Elektra), Ernestine Schumann-Heink (Klytamnestra), and Margarethe Siems (Chrysothemis). The conductor is Ernst von Schuch.

Feb. 19   *The Bartered Bride* — an opera by Bedrich Smetana first performed on May 30, 1866 — receives its first Metropolitan Opera performance today in New York City. Gustav Mahler conducts a cast including Emmy Destinn, Robert Blass, Marie Mattfeld and Adolph Muhlmann. W.J. Henderson writes in the New York *Sun* that the opera displays an "incessant flow of charming melody... It ought to have a prosperous career."

April 4   Henry Hadley's *Safie* is premiered in Mainz with the composer conducting. The score features lush romantic harmonies. The German libretto is about a princess from Persia who is poisoned. The opera does not receive another performance.

April 26   Camille Saint-Saens' *Samson et Dalila* is performed at Covent Garden, marking the first performance on an English stage of an opera depicting a biblical character after a ban on such depictions had been removed by the Lord Chamberlain.

May 5   Jules Massenet's *Bacchus*, to a libretto based on Catulle Mendes, is produced at the Paris Opera. The four-act opera takes place in India and on Olympus.

Oct. 7   Nikolai Rimsky-Korsakov's *Le Coq d'or* is premiered posthumously at the Solodovnikov Theater in Mos-

BEDRICH SMETANA

cow. The libretto, by Vladimir Bielsky, is based on a story by Alexander Pushkin. It is a satirical fairy tale which enraged the Russian authorities, who managed to keep it from the stage until the offensive sections were revised.

Nov. 11   Josef Holbrooke's *Pierrot and Pierrette* premieres at Her Majesty's Theatre in London. The libretto, by Walter Grogan, concerns the lovers Pierrot and Pierrette; the Stranger, who represents evil, tries to separate them by showing Pierrot the pleasures of the world, but love wins out. This opera establishes itself as the composer's best-known work.

Dec. 4   A three-act opera entitled *La Sina d'Vargoun*, by Francesco Balilla Pratella, receives its initial performance in Bologna. The composer writes his own libretto. The opera, about lovers and murder, contains Italian folk melodies and is couched in a verismo style. It wins the Baruzzi prize of 10,000 lire (Baruzzi was a revered citizen in Bologna). Pratella is in the process of embarking on his "futurist" movement and, next year, comments that Italy is "in the position of absolute inferiority in the futurist evolution of music among nations."

Dec. 4   *Il Segreto di Susanna* by Ermanno Wolf-Ferrari, to a libretto by Enrico Golisciani, has its premiere at the Hoftheater in Munich. It is a comedy about a young woman, Susanna, whose husband suspects her of having a lover because of her secretive behavior; in reality, she just wants to smoke her cigarettes.

1909 Dance

May 19   Serge Diaghilev stuns the world with the official opening performance of his new company, the Ballets Russes, at the Theatre du Chatelet in Paris. Huge sums of money have been spent recarpeting and redecorating the entire theater. The program consists of three ballets — *Le Pavillon d'Armide*, *Polevetsian Dances* (from *Prince Igor*) and *Le Festin*.

Le Pavillon d'Armide is based on the Maryinsky Theater production of November 25, 1907. Alexandre Benois creates new scenery, and Michel Fokine makes some choreographic changes. The lead dancers are Vera Karalli, Mikhail Mordkin, Alexis Bulgakov, Tamara Karsavina, Alexandra Baldina and Vaslav Nijinsky. Nicolas Tcherepnin conducts. Vaslav Nijinsky's appearance in the pas de trois causes tumultuous applause.

Although this ballet had been promoted as the main attraction of tonight's event, its success is eclipsed by the second ballet on the program — *Polovtsian Dances* from *Prince Igor*, by Alexander Borodin. The bass Zaporojetz plays Khan Kontchak in the entire Polovtsian act from *Prince Igor*. The sets and costumes for this ballet, designed by Nicholas Roerich, create as much of a sensation as the dancing itself. The lead dancers are Sophia Fedorova, Helen Smirnova and Adolph Bolm. The choreography, by Michel Fokine, breaks with the tradition of Marius Petipa and restores the male dancer to prominence on the ballet stages. (The ballet is revived many times by choreographers throughout the course of the century.) It displays savage dancing in the Tartar style that brings down the house as the entire cast, in a final fit of energy and movement, ends the ballet by rushing to the footlights.

Le Festin closes tonight's program and features Michel Fokine's original choreography in the finale. The rest of the ballet is a divertissement composed of dances from the repertory of the Maryinsky Theater, with music by various composers. The scenery from the first act of the Maryinsky production of the *Russlan and Ludmilla*, is repainted for tonight's production. It is the least successful ballet of the evening. A public *repetition generale* of this program had been given last night before scores of Parisian celebrities (including Auguste Rodin and Maurice Ravel) assembled by impresario Gabriel Astruc, who also provided substantial financial backing for the event. Jean Cocteau designed an illustrated brochure advertising the spectacle.

Critics go wild and wake up a city that had completely forgotten about ballet. Marcel Prevost says, "After a long eclipse dance will reign again over Paris." Henri Gauthier-Villars of *Commedia* (Paris) calls Vaslav Nijinsky "the wonder of wonders." Robert Brussel writes in *Le Figaro* (Paris) of Tamara Karsavina that her ". . . subtle technique and marvellous sense of music are combined with expressive grace and poetic feeling." Camille Mauclair says, "Nijinsky can alone give us the idea of what a Vestris must have been."

June 2   Michel Fokine's *Cleopatre* receives its world premiere today at the Theatre du Chatelet in Paris. The ballet is a revision of *Une nuit d'Egypte*. Music is by Anton Arensky, Sergei Taneyev, Nikolai Rimsky-Korsakov, Mikhail Glinka and Alexander Glazunov, costumes and scenery by Leon Bakst. The lead dancers are Anna Pavlova, Ida Rubinstein, Michel Fokine, Tamara Karsavina and Vaslav Nijinsky. The work, about a love affair between Cleopatra and her slave, Amour, is a big success; Bakst's imposing sets and Rubinstein's dancing enchant the audience. Also on the program is Fokine's *Les Sylphides*. With costumes and scenery by Benois, the ballet is danced by Pavlova, Karsavina and Nijinsky. The program is completed by a performance of the first act of Glinka's *Russlan and Ludmilla*.

1909 Instrumental and Vocal Music

Jan. 14   Samuel Coleridge-Taylor's cantata *Bon-Bon Suite* is performed for the first time in its full orchestral version at the Brighton Music Festival in England. The work, in six movements, is scored for baritone, chorus and orchestra. It had been performed on December 9 of last year in an arrangement for voices and two pianos.

Feb. 3   Sergei Vassilenko's symphonic poem *Hircus Nocturnus* premieres in Moscow.

Feb. 6   Igor Stravinsky's *Scherzo fantastique* is premiered by Alexander Siloti in Saint Petersburg. The work is scored for full orchestra, including three harps and celesta.

Feb. 12   Ignace Paderewski's Symphony in B Minor is premiered by Max Fiedler and the Boston Symphony Orchestra; Paderewski is also soloist in Camille Saint-Saens' Fourth Piano Concerto. Paderewski uses Polish melodic themes in this three-movement symphony reflecting Polish nationalism.

Feb. 21   Anatoly Liadov's orchestral piece *Enchanted Lake* is premiered by Nicolas Tcherepnin in Saint Petersburg.

Feb. 22   Ralph Vaughan Williams's *In the Fen Country* is premiered by Thomas Beecham in London. This symphonic work was composed five years ago.

March 9   Max Reger's *Prologue to a Tragedy*, Op. 108, is performed for the first time in Cologne. Critic Walter Niemann of Leipzig notes next month that, to him, the music

IGNACE PADEREWSKI

"... lacks, as does all of Reger's music, the warm rays of a more genuine, greater and simpler art."

March 26   Karol Szymanowski's Symphony No. 1 in F Minor is premiered by Gregor Fitelberg conducting the Warsaw Philharmonic Orchestra.

April 9   Claude Debussy's *Trois chansons de Charles d'Orleans* premieres at the Concerts Colonne in Paris, the composer conducting. The music is scored for chorus a cappella.

April 23   Mily Balakirev's Symphony No. 2 in D Minor is premiered by Sergei Liapunov in Saint Petersburg. The work is in four movements — Allegro ma non troppo, Scherzo alla Corsacca, Romanza and Finale (Tempo di Polacca) — and was composed when Balakirev was 70. He founded the "Balakirev circle" in 1862 to advance Russian national music.

May 1   Serge Rachmaninoff's symphonic poem *The Isle of the Dead* premieres in Moscow, the composer conducting.

June 7   *A Mass of Life*, by Frederick Delius, receives its first performance (in its complete version) in London. Conducted by Thomas Beecham, the work is scored for soloists, chorus and large orchestra and is based on Nietzsche's *Also sprach Zarathustra*. A review in the Glasgow *Herald* says, "The ear in listening to the choral climaxes in *A Mass of Life* is bewildered that any man should consider this ugly featureless noise as music."

July 13   Edward Elgar's *Elegy for Orchestra* premieres in London.

Aug. 7   *Drei Klavierstucke*, Op. 11 (Three Piano Pieces), are completed today by Arnold Schoenberg. These little pieces — forming a suite — mark the composer's departure from traditional tonality and signal what is to come from Schoenberg's pen. Schoenberg later says in a program note, "I am following an inner compulsion. . . ." Eight years from now, a review of this piece in the New York *Post* says, "Schoenberg's compositions show a characteristic disregard of other people's happiness."

Sep. 7   *Dance Rhapsody No. 1*, by Frederick Delius, premieres at the Hereford Music Festival, the composer conducting. A London *Times* review says the music "... only served to impress the mind with the second-hand character of the tunes."

Nov. 15   Ralph Vaughan Williams' *On Wenlock Edge* premieres in London. This suite in six sections is scored for tenor, piano and string quartet.

Nov. 22   Bela Bartok's Second Suite for small orchestra premieres in Budapest.

Nov. 26   *The Wasps*, by Ralph Vaughan Williams, premieres at the University of Cambridge, England. This incidental music is scored for tenor, baritone, male quartet and orchestra.

Nov. 28   Serge Rachmaninoff performs the solo part in the world premiere of his Concerto No. 3 in D Minor for Piano and Orchestra, Op. 30. Walter Damrosch conducts the New York Symphony Orchestra. This concerto comes eight years after his second one. A review in the New York *Times* calls it ". . . rambling in texture and unstereotyped in its makeup."

Dec. 12   Anatoly Liadov's *Kikimora* is premiered by Alexander Siloti in Saint Petersburg. It is a scherzo for orchestra.

1909   Births, Deaths and Debuts

American dancer and choreographer Erick Hawkins is born in Trinidad, Colorado.

American dancer and choreographer Agnes de Mille is born in New York City.

Jan. 11   Danish composer Gunnar Berg is born in Saint Gall, Switzerland.

Jan. 15   French composer Louis-Etienne-Ernest Reyer, 85, dies in Le Lavandou, France. This composer worked as a music librarian and as a critic. His real name was Rey but he added the suffix er because he revered Richard Wagner. His music was characteristically French and reflected his attraction to exotic subjects. He composed six operas (the most famous of which is *Sigurd*, premiered in 1884), several choral works, church music and other works.

Jan. 15   Composer Elie Siegmeister is born in New York City.

Jan. 19   Baritone Hans Hotter is born in Offenbach, Germany.

Feb. 5   Polish composer and pianist Grazyna Bacewicz is born in Lodz.

Feb. 17   Soprano Marjorie Lawrence is born in the vicinity of Melbourne, Australia.

March 3   Bruno Walter conducts the Royal Philharmonic Society in London, marking his first performance in England.

April 9   Dancer, choreographer, ballet director and actor Robert Helpmann is born in Mount Gambier, Australia.

April 27   Opera manager Heinrich Conried, 60, dies in Meran, Tyrol. After a start as an actor in Vienna, he came to the United States in 1878 and managed the Germania Theater in New York. From 1903 to 1908 he was manager of the Metropolitan Opera. During his administration many great singers joined the company. He was responsible for the first performance outside Bayreuth of Richard Wagner's *Parsifal* and the American premiere of *Salome*, both of which caused scandals. Due to falling receipts at the box office, Conried and the Metropolitan parted ways in 1908, and he retired to Europe.

May 6   Fanny Cerito, one of the famous Italian ballerinas of the Romantic period, dies in Paris. Among her most famous roles were Ondine and La Vivandiere. She was one of the four ballerinas to participate in Jules Perrot's famous *Pas de Quatre* in London in 1845.

May 9   American dancer and choreographer Lew Christensen is born in Brigham City, Utah.

May 18   Spanish composer Isaac Albeniz, 48, dies in Campos-les-Bains (Pyrenees). This composer travelled widely in his youth after having left home at age 13. He went to Puerto Rico, Cuba, America, Brussels, Leipzig and Budapest — places where he studied and worked — and eventually settled in Paris. He composed several operas and an operatic trilogy, *King Arthur* (incomplete); works for piano and orchestra, his famous piano piece *Iberia*, and many other different compositions. His music, impressionistic and incorporating Spanish melodic and rhythmic materials, bears the influence of Claude Debussy and Felipe Pedrell. Along with Pedrell, his mark on the international music scene was primarily as a champion of nationalism in Spanish music.

May 20   Bass-baritone Erich Kunz is born in Vienna, Austria.

June 1   Giuseppe Martucci, 53, dies in Naples. This pianist, conductor and educator promulgated the cause of German music and was the first to produce Richard Wagner's *Tristan und Isolde* in Italy. His compositions include symphonies, concertos, and chamber and piano music.

June 16   Conductor and violinist Willi Boskovsky is born in Vienna, Austria.

June 24   Violist and conductor Milton Katims is born in New York City.

July 13   Composer Paul Constantinescu is born in Ploesti, Rumania.

July 25   Conductor Gianandrea Gavazzeni is born in Bergamo, Italy.

Aug. 6   Composer and pianist Karl Ulrich Schnabel is born in Berlin, Germany. He is the son of pianist Artur Schnabel.

Aug. 22   Pianist Vitya Vronsky is born in Evpatoria, Russia.

Oct. 6   Dudley Buck, 70, dies in Orange, New Jersey. A composer of much sacred music, a pianist and an organist, he received his training in Leipzig. Buck was respected by his students for bringing German attitudes about music to his teaching.

Nov. 4   Serge Rachmaninoff gives a piano recital at Smith College, Northampton, Massachusetts. This event marks his first appearance in the United States.

Nov. 8   Composer, author, music theorist and educator Norman Lloyd is born in Pottsville, Pennsylvania.

Nov. 10   John McCormack makes his American debut as Alfredo in *La Traviata* at the Manhattan Opera House, New York City. Luisa Tetrazzini also stars. The New York *Sun* says McCormack has "a lyric tenor voice of much natural beauty." The New York *Herald Tribune* says his voice possesses "rare sweetness."

Nov. 16   Alma Gluck makes her Metropolitan Opera debut as Sophie in a performance of *Werther*, by Jules Massenet. Her performance is praised by critics.

Nov. 17   Austrian tenor Leo Slezak makes his New York debut at the Metropolitan Opera as Othello. Also in the cast are Antonio Scotti and Frances Alda. The conductor is Arturo Toscanini. Krehbiel, in the New York *Tribune*, comments on the tenor's massive physical size and says, ". . . it is doubtful if anyone expected the colossus that appeared." He also states that Slezak is a "splendid actor" and has a "voice of fine power."

Dec. 5   English music theorist and teacher Ebenezer Prout, 74, dies in London. He is best known for his edition of *Messiah* and his books about music, which include *Instrumentation* (1876), *Harmony: Its Theory and Practice* (1889), *Counterpoint: Strict and Free* (1890) and *Double Counterpoint and Canon* (1891).

Dec. 10   Baritone Otakar Kraus is born in Prague, Czechoslovakia.

Dec. 15   Francisco Tarrega, 57, Spanish guitarist and composer, who advanced the instrument to the status of "classical," dies in Barcelona.

1909 Related Events

Gustav Mahler becomes music director of The New York Philharmonic Society, succeeding Vassily Safonov. This event also marks the expansion of the orchestra's concert season from 18 to 54 concerts. Mahler remains at the post for two years.

This year's developments in the recording industry include the following: The Gramophone Company (England) begins using the famous dog label, replacing its Recording Angel trademark; Odeon releases the first full orchestral recording — Tchaikovsky's *Nutcracker Suite*, performed by Hermann Finck conducting the London Palace Orchestra — a double-faced disc.

Jan. 1   Ives & Myrick, an insurance company, comes into existence today. It is run by American composer Charles Ives and his business associate Julian Myrick.

Feb. 6   Polish-born soprano Marcella Sembrich sings her farewell to the stage at the Metropolitan Opera. In one of the scenes from *La Traviata*, the minor roles are taken by Geraldine Farrar, Antonio Scotti, Pasquale Amato, Adamo Didur and Enrico Caruso.

Feb. 12   F.T. Marinetti publishes his "First Futurist Manifesto" in *Le Figaro* (Paris), advocating futurist drama, literature, art and music.

Feb. 15   Soprano Emma Eames gives her farewell performance at the Metropolitan Opera singing Tosca. Her departure is due to disagreements with the new management of Giulio Gatti-Casazza.

PROGRAM FOR A CONCERT OF THE PHILHARMONIC SOCIETY OF NEW YORK CONDUCTED BY GUSTAV MAHLER

COURT SQUARE THEATRE
FEBRUARY 24, AT 8:15 P. M.

FIRST TIME
IN
SPRINGFIELD

The
Philharmonic Society
of New York

FOUNDED 1842

Gustav Mahler, Conductor

CORINNE RIDER-KELSEY
SOPRANO

AND THE ENTIRE
PHILHARMONIC ORCHESTRA
ONE HUNDRED PERFORMERS

Administrative Manager   Business Manager
RICHARD ARNOLD   FELIX F. LEIFELS

March 16   Natalie and Serge Koussevitzky establish the music publishing house Editions Russes de Musique, based in Moscow with offices in Germany and France. The first composer to receive a contract is Alexander Scriabin.

April 9   The first wireless broadcast of the human voice takes place as Enrico Caruso sings through two microphones at the Metropolitan Opera House in New York to the home of radio pioneer Lee de Forest.

May 22   Richard H. Stein's brochure detailing his system of composing in quarter tones is completed. This German music theorist is the first to have a quarter-tone composition published. He also built a quarter-tone clarinet.

July 1   The United States copyright law takes effect today. This law protects composers and/or publishers against infringement for a period of 28 years and is renewable for the same period of time. It also secures exclusive rights to print, publish, copy, vend, arrange, record and perform for profit.

July 24   Walter Damrosch conducts the New York Symphony Orchestra in a program of music at Chautauqua, New York. The concert is so successful that local people decide to form an annual Chautauquan music festival. It is not until some years later that the *Chautauqua Festival* is fully underway as an annual event.

Sep. 14   Sergei Prokofiev, a piano and composition student at the Saint Petersburg Conservatory, is graduated.

Oct. 6   Pianist Ossip Gabrilowitsch and Clara Clemens are married. Clara Clemens is the daughter of Mark Twain.

Nov. 8   A performance of Amilcare Ponchielli's *La Gioconda* marks the official opening of the Boston Opera House. The million-dollar building is packed with high-society and opera lovers from New York, Baltimore, Washington, D.C. and Philadelphia. Single-seat tickets go for a low of $40 to a high of $200. The cast includes Lillian Nordica, Louise Homer and Florencio Constantino. The director and organizer of the opera company is Henry Russell. *Musical America* (New York) says, "No auditorium of this city has seen a more brilliant audience than that assembled for this *premiere* performance."

1910 Opera

Jan. 15   Ruggero Leoncavallo's *Maia*, to a libretto by French publisher Paul Choudens, receives its first performance in Rome. Pietro Mascagni conducts this opera, which is a three-act love story involving suicide.

Jan. 19   Ruggero Leoncavallo's *Malbruk*, adapted from a story of Boccaccio, is produced in Rome. This three-act comic opera is about a king, a damsel and a harem. This is the second Leoncavallo opera to be produced in this city within a week.

Jan. 22   Ernst von Dohnanyi's *Der Schleier der Pierrette*, based on a fairy tale by Arthur Schnitzler, is premiered by Ernst von Schuch at the Dresden Opera. Now 33 years old, this Hungarian composer and pianist has studied with Karl Forstner and Eugene d'Albert. He becomes well-known through international tours as a pianist.

Feb. 19   Jules Massenet's *Don Quichotte* premieres in Monte Carlo. Feodor Chaliapin sings the title role in this opera based on scenes from Cervantes.

March 17   Umberto Giordano's *Mese mariano* premieres in Palermo, Sicily. The opera, whose title means "Mary's month," is about orphans in an asylum. The brief work is not a success, and Giordano fades until *Madame Sans-Gene* is produced in 1915.

March 18   Frederick Converse becomes the first American composer to have an opera produced by the Metropolitan Opera Company in New York, as *The Pipe of Desire* opens today. Giulio Gatti-Casazza oversees the production.

April 23   Arthur Finley Nevin's *Poia*, an opera about an Indian, premieres in a German version at the Royal Opera of Berlin. Nevin had spent time on Indian reservations studying American Indian music. This event marks the first opera by an American composer to be staged in Berlin.

FEODOR CHALIAPIN AS DON QUICHOTTE

GABRIEL PIERNE

May 30 Gabriel Pierne's lyric comedy *On ne badine pas avec l'amour*, after a story by Alfred Musset, premieres at the Opera-Comique in Paris, the composer conducting. A stu- dent of Cesar Franck and Jules Massenet, Pierne was an organist and conductor. He succeeded Edouard Colonne as conductor of the Concerts Colonne.

Oct. 4 Erich Wolfgang Korngold's *Der Schneemann* receives its first performance at the Vienna Opera. Alexander von Zemlinsky conducts. The work is a classical commedia dell'arte pantomime composed by Korngold who is 12 (Zemlinsky did the orchestration). Korngold is the son of music critic Dr. Julius Korngold of the *Neue Freie Presse* (Vienna), who succeeded Eduard Hanslick. It is with this performance that Dr. Korngold decided it was time to bring his son to the attention of the Vienna music public.

Nov. 20 Ottorino Respighi's three-act opera *Semirama* premieres in Bologna. In recent years Respighi has been earning his living as a string player.

Nov. 30 Ernest Bloch's only opera — *Macbeth* — has its premiere at the Opera-Comique in Paris. Edmond Fleg's libretto is based on Shakespeare, keeping close to the original text but condensing it to the most essential scenes. The opera is not a a great success but eventually comes to be regarded as an important work by this composer. Arthur Pougin says in *Le Menestrel* (Paris), "It is not merely capricious, but incoherent throughout, by virtue of incessant modifications of meter. As to harmonic progressions, they are no less extraordinary, and they may well be termed as savage. The music of Ernest Bloch seems to be a parody of Richard Strauss. It is simply noise for the sake of noise,

ENRICO CARUSO, EMMY DESTINN AND PASQUALE AMATO IN *LA FANCIULLA DEL WEST*

and the abuse of trumpets would break the sturdiest ear drums."

Dec. 2 Alexander von Zemlinsky's *Kleider machen Leute* premieres in Vienna. The three-act opera satirizes equality.

Dec. 8 Richard Strauss' *Salome* receives its first London performance at Covent Garden. Thomas Beecham conducts a cast including Aino Ackte and Clarence Whitehall. The opera house is surrounded by hundreds of people, many of whom are not able to get in. Previously censors had prevented the opera from being performed, but changes are made to satisfy them. This production deletes any mention of the name *John the Baptist* and instead substitutes *the prophet*. The head of John the Baptist on a silver tray is not shown. Ackte sings "to death let me follow the prophet" instead of "I want to kiss thy lips, Jochanaan." The principals receive 16 curtain calls. A London dispatch to *Musical America* (New York) calls Ackte's Salome "a painfully vivid realization of the varying moods of hate, cajolery and revenge...." The reviewer also praises Whitehall and Beecham.

Dec. 10 Giacomo Puccini's *La fanciulla del west* has its premiere at the Metropolitan Opera House in New York City.

The libretto, by Carlo Zangarini and Guelfo Civinini, is based on David Belasco's play. The cast features Emmy Destinn, Enrico Caruso and Pasquale Amato; Arturo Toscanini conducts. The opera is tremendously successful; there are 47 curtain calls. Despite its opening night popularity with the audience, *The Musical Courier* (New York) says, "The play caters to a depraved taste, and the music is without any appeal beyond that of emphasizing the meretricious elements in the libretto."

Dec. 28 *Die Konigskinder*, an opera by Engelbert Humperdinck, premieres at the Metropolitan Opera House in New York, Alfred Hertz conducting. The libretto, by Elsa Bernstein, is a fairy tale about a prince who falls in love with a goose girl, who in turn, is the prisoner of a wicked witch. Like *Hansel and Gretel*, it is a children's opera and for a while enjoys success all over the world (translated into seven languages). Geraldine Farrar is the goose girl and appears for curtain calls holding a live goose. Others in the cast include Hermann Jadlowker, Otto Goritz and Louise Homer. Henry Krehbiel of the New York *Tribune* reviews the opera, stating, "Though the composer hews to a theoretical line he does it freely, naturally, easily and always with the principles of musical beauty as well as that of dramatic truthfulness and propriety in view."

1910 Dance

Feb. 28 Choreographer Arthur Saint-Leon's *Coppelia* — starring Anna Pavlova and Mikhail Mordkin — is performed at the Metropolitan Opera House in New York City, marking the first American performance of the Russian Imperial Ballet version of this work.

March 5 Michel Fokine's *Carnaval* receives its first performance at a charity ball in Saint Petersburg. The one-act ballet uses dancers from the Imperial Ballet, who, not permitted to dance outside of the Maryinsky Theater during the season, appear masked. Using the piano piece by Robert Schumann, this commedia dell'arte ballet features Tamara Karsavina as Columbine, Vaslav Nijinsky as Florestan, and the actor and director Meyerhold as Pierrot.

May 20 Serge Diaghilev presents Michel Fokine's *Carnaval* on stage in its first theatrical performance at the Teater des Westens, Berlin. With an orchestration of the Robert Schumann piece by Alexander Glazunov, Nikolai Rimsky-Korsakov, Anatoly Liadov and Nicolas Tcherepnin, and decor by Leon Bakst, Diaghilev's cast includes Lydia Lopokova as Columbine, Leonide Leontiev as Harlequin and Adolph Bolm as Pierrot.

June 4 Serge Diaghilev's Ballets Russes premieres Michel Fokine's *Scheherazade* at the Paris Opera. The one-act ballet, to music by Nikolai Rimsky-Korsakov (using three of the four movements of his symphonic suite of the same name), deals with the infidelity of the wife and con-

cubines of Shah Sharyar. The libretto is by Alexandre Benois. The decor and costumes, by Leon Bakst, are among the finest and most lavish of the Diaghilev era. Ida Rubinstein (Zobeide), Vaslav Nijinsky (Favorite Slave) and Enrico Cecchetti (Chief Eunuch) have the main roles. The work causes an uproar because of its voluptuousness. Also receiving its first Paris performance on today's program is *Carnaval*.

June 18 *Giselle* is performed in a version by Serge Diaghilev's Ballets Russes in Paris. Choreography is by Michel Fokine, designs by Leon Bakst. Tamara Karsavina and Vaslav Nijinsky star.

June 25 Michel Fokine's *The Firebird* receives its world premiere at the Grand Opera in Paris performed by Serge Diaghilev's Ballets Russes. The music by Igor Stravinsky is his first score for ballet. Costumes and scenery are by Alexander Golovine. Fokine and Tamara Karsavina lead the cast. This is the first of Serge Diaghilev's ballets with a score specially commissioned by him. (Stravinsky is now 28 years old and dedicated this music to Nikolai Rimsky-Korsakov's son Andrei.) Both the music and the dancing make a powerful impression on the Parisians. Also premiered today is *Les Orientales*, a divertissement containing a group of dances. The music is a combination of works by Alexander Glazunov, Christian Sinding, Anton Arensky,

Edvard Grieg and Alexander Borodin. Nijinsky and Tamara Karsavina lead the cast.

Dec. 12 Ruth Saint Denis' *Egypta*, music by Meyrowitz, receives its first performance in New York City. This

dance, originally inspired by an advertisement for Egyptian cigarettes, was to have been her first composition, but was not produced until now because of its expense.

1910 Instrumental and Vocal Music

Feb. 3 Samuel Coleridge-Taylor's cantata *Endymion's Dream* receives its initial performance in Brighton, England. The work is scored for women's voices, chorus and orchestra; the text is by John Keats.

Feb. 8 Anton von Webern's *Five Movements for String Quartet*, Op. 5, are premiered in Vienna. The third movement of his work is 35 seconds long. Webern subsequently transcribes the piece for string orchestra.

Feb. 20 Claude Debussy's *Iberia* receives its first performance at a Colonne Concert in Paris. A movement from the orchestral suite *Images*, today's performance is the premiere of this movement.

Feb. 21 Ernst von Dohnanyi's Suite for Orchestra in F-sharp Minor Op. 19, premieres in Budapest with the composer conducting.

Feb. 23 Max Reger's *Psalm 100* premieres at Chemnitz in its first complete performance with the composer conducting.

March 2 Claude Debussy's *Rondes de Printemps*, the third movement of *Images*, premieres in Paris at a concert organized by French music publisher Marie-August Durand.

March 26 Alexander Glazunov's *Finnish Fantasy* premieres in Saint Petersburg.

April 6 Gustav Holst's *A Somerset Rhapsody* and *Songs of the West* receive their premiere at Queen's Hall in London. Now 34 years old, Holst had conducted and performed as an organist since age 19 and studied at the Royal College of Music with Charles Villiers Stanford. He successfully earned a living as a trombonist in his youth.

April 20 Christine Verger, age 6, and Germaine Durant, age 10, play the premiere of Maurice Ravel's *Ma Mere l'Oye* (for piano four hands) in Paris. This event is also the first concert of the Societe Musicale Independante in Paris, a group that seceded from the Societe Nationale de Musique.

April 23 Alfredo Casella's Symphony No. 2 in C Minor, Suite in C Major and *Italia* are premiered as the composer conducts these works and others in Paris. This Italian modernist is a concert pianist, conductor and teacher who won first prize in piano at the Paris Conservatoire in 1899.

May 25 Claude Debussy's first book of piano Douze preludes is premiered in excerpts. The composer performs

the music at a concert of the Societe Musicale Independante in Paris.

June 12 *Bamboula Rhapsodic Dance* — an orchestral rhapsody by Samuel Coleridge-Taylor — receives its first performance in the choral shed in Litchfield, Connecticut. The piece had been composed from Indian folk song materials compiled by the composer. Musicologist Carl Stoeckel had invited the composer to conduct his *Hiawatha* trilogy here to celebrate the 20th anniversary of the Litchfield Choral Union. Coleridge-Taylor immediately began composing a new orchestral rhapsody to bring along, and first rehearsals were held at Carnegie Hall, New York City, where the musicians referred to Coleridge-Taylor as "the African Mahler." Today's concert is a thundering success, and Coleridge-Taylor is praised by composers George W. Chadwick and Horatio Parker.

Sep. 6 *Fantasia on a Theme by Thomas Tallis*, by Ralph Vaughan Williams, receives its first performance at Gloucester Cathedral as part of the Gloucester Music Festival. Vaughan Williams conducts. The piece is scored for double stringed orchestra and is based on a theme Tallis wrote in 1567.

Sep. 12 Gustav Mahler's Symphony No. 8 in E-flat, the *Symphony of a Thousand*, receives its world premiere at the Exposition Concert Hall in Munich, Mahler conducting. This performance employs 1,003 performers, including 8 soloists. The symphony is one of two giant choral symphonies written by this composer (the other being his Second Symphony, the *Resurrection*). A review in the *Neue Freie Presse* (Vienna) says, "Flames seemed to dart from Mahler as he conducted; a thousand wills obeyed his will."

Oct. 12 Ralph Vaughan Williams' Symphony No. 1 (*A Sea Symphony*) premieres at the Leeds Festival with the composer conducting. The music — scored for soprano, baritone, chorus and orchestra — is set to texts of Walt Whitman.

Nov. 10 Edward Elgar's Concerto for Violin and Orchestra is premiered by Fritz Kreisler and the London Philharmonic. The composer conducts this performance in London.

Nov. 17 Piano Trio in D Major, Op. 1, by Erich Wolfgang Korngold, receives its initial performance in New York. The Margulies Trio performs. Korngold is now 13. W.J. Henderson writes in the New York *Sun*, "If we had a little boy of 12 who preferred writing this sort of music to hearing a good folk tune or going out and playing in the park, we should consult a specialist."

Nov. 25   Serge Rachmaninoff's *Liturgy of Saint John Chrysostom* premieres in Moscow. The work is scored for *a cappella* chorus.

Dec. 5   *Dreams* — a symphonic poem — and Piano Sonata in F Minor, both by Sergei Prokofiev, are performed for the first time as Prokofiev conducts and plays the piano at the Saint Petersburg Conservatory, where he is still a student.

Dec. 15   *Bourgogne* — a symphonic poem by Edgar Varese — receives its first performance; Josef Stransky conducts the piece in Berlin. This is the first major work by Varese, who has studied with Vincent d'Indy, Albert Roussel and Charles-Marie Widor. Bruno Schrader says in *Zeit am Montag* (Berlin) that the music is ". . . infernal noise, cat music." Also premiered today (in Leipzig) is Max Reger's Concerto for Piano and Orchestra in F Minor, Op. 114. Frieda Kwast-Hodapp is the soloist, and Arthur Nikisch conducts the Gewandhaus Orchestra. A review published in the Leipzig *Tageblatt* calls the music ". . . another abortion of Reger's Muse degenerated through constant inbreeding."

1910   Births, Deaths and Debuts

Jan. 8   The great Soviet prima ballerina assoluta Galina Ulanova is born in Saint Petersburg, Russia.

Jan. 10   Conductor and composer Jean Martinon is born in Lyons, France.

Feb. 20   Soviet dancer, choreographer and ballet director Konstantin Sergeyev is born in Saint Petersburg, Russia.

March 9   Composer Samuel Barber is born in West Chester, Pennsylvania.

March 12   Soviet dancer, choreographer and ballet master Vakhtang Chabukiani is born in Tiflis.

March 24   Conductor and musicologist Jacques Chailley is born in Paris, France.

March 28   Edouard Colonne, 71, dies in Paris. The conductor was founder of the Colonne Concerts, which furthered the work of French composers, Claude Debussy among them. He studied at the Paris Conservatoire, became the principal violinist of the Paris Opera and, during his conducting career, toured Britain, Russia and the United States.

April 13   Julius Ferdinand Bluthner, 86, dies in Leipzig. The piano firm of the same name was noted for its instruments of resonance, resulting from Bluthner's patent of the aliquot stringing system.

May 18   Pauline Viardot-Garcia, 88, dies in Paris. This French mezzo-soprano was the daughter of the Spanish impresario and singer Manuel del Popolo Vicente Garcia and wife of the French impresario Louis Viardot. She was the creator of the role of Fides in Meyerbeer's *Le Prophete* and was also a famous interpreter of *Fidelio*. She studied the piano with Franz Liszt.

May 29   Mily Balakirev, 73, dies in Saint Petersburg. Composer and member of the "Mighty Five," he taught Nikolai Rimsky-Korsakov, was Modest Mussorgsky's mentor and composed two symphonies, piano music, overtures and other works. After his early years of musical activity and his championing of the Russian nationalistic school, he suddenly took a hiatus from composing at age 35 and spent several years working as a clerk and as a music inspector in women's schools, eventually resuming his musical life. Balakirev often worked slowly, taking as long as 32 years to complete his Symphony in C. Although few of his compositions are played today, his influence on 19th-century Russian music was enormous.

June 14   Conductor Rudolf Kempe is born in Niederpoyritz, Germany.

June 22   Tenor Peter Pears is born in Farnham, England.

June 29   Singer Anna Sutter is murdered by Aloys Obrist, custodian of the Liszt Museum in Weimar. The man had allegedly gone insane from jealousy.

July 14   Marius Petipa dies in Gurzuf, the Crimea at the age of 92. One of the greatest choreographers in the history of ballet, Petipa developed what has come to be known as the Russian classical ballet. During his nearly 50 years as a choreographer, he created many of the ballets that have become part of the standard ballet repertoire including *Don Quixote*, *La Bayadere*, *Raymonda*, *Paquita*, *Swan Lake* and *The Sleeping Beauty*. Petipa's choreography is characterized by great musicality, geometric precision and elegance. His choreography subordinated mime to pure dance.
    Petipa was born in Marseilles in 1819 and danced at the Paris Opera with Fanny Elssler in 1841. In 1847 he signed a contract first as dancer and then instructor and choreogra-

pher with the Saint Petersburg Imperial Ballet, where he remained until his death. In 1862 he was appointed choreographer-in-chief. Under his direction Russian ballet reached its height. He brought the Italian and French styles to Russia and helped develop the classical Russian technique. During his tenure, the Theater produced some of Russia's greatest dancers, including Pavlova, Nijinsky and Fokine.

In 1903 he retired from the theatre as a result of the failure of one of his ballets, *The Magic Mirror*. At the time of his retirement, Petipa's ballets were considered old fashioned and he, himself, was out of favor. However, with the export of his ballets to the west beginning with Diaghilev, Petipa regained his popularity, and his choreography was established as the foundation for many classical ballet companies and an inspiration for many choreographers.

Aug. 2   Dancer Margot Lander is born in Copenhagen, Denmark.

Aug. 4   Composer William Schuman is born in New York City.

Aug. 14   Acoustician and inventor Pierre Schaeffer is born in Nancy, France.

Aug. 31   Pierre Aubry, 36, French musicologist and paleographer dies in a fencing accident in Dieppe. He published many writings on medieval music.

Sep. 1   Dancer, teacher, and ballet director Peggy van Praagh is born in London, England.

Sep. 5   Franz Xaver Haberl, 70, dies in Regensburg, Germany. This theorist and music editor took holy orders at the age of 22 and worked as a church musician. At age 35, he founded what would become an internationally famous school of sacred music in Regensburg. His knowledge of the history of Roman Catholic sacred music enabled him

to edit leading periodicals, including *Musica sacra*, *Musica divina* and *Kirchenmusikalisches Jahrbuch*. In 1879 he founded the Palestrina Society and edited a complete edition of Palestrina's works, published by Breitkopf & Hartel. He prepared a new edition of *Editio Medicea* (a collection of plainchant melodies), which was published between 1871 and 1881. This edition was found to be corrupt. Papal sanction was immediately revoked and given, instead, to the Benedictine monks of Solesmes, who were asked to prepare the new *Editio Vaticana*. As a result of this scandal, Haberl's editions have been suppressed, and all of his writings on plainchant are no longer considered valid in the eyes of the Church. These writings include Haberl's *Magister Choralis*, published in 12 editions between 1865 and 1899 and translated into English, French, Spanish, Polish and Hungarian.

Oct. 25   Dancer, choreographer David Lichine is born David Liechtenstein in Rostov-on-Don, Russia.

Nov. 29   Irish tenor John McCormack makes his Metropolitan Opera debut as Alfredo in *La Traviata* singing opposite Nellie Melba. Krehbiel praises McCormack in the New York *Tribune*, saying, "His delicate phrasing and the feeling and tenderness... were as evident as ever... his performance brought forth much praise...."

Dec. 1   Dancer Alicia Markova is born Lillian Alicia Marks in London, England.

Dec. 7   Conductor Richard Franko Goldman is born in New York City. His father is conductor Edwin Franko Goldman.

Dec. 15   Mezzo-soprano Giulietta Simionato is born in Forli, Italy.

Dec. 29   Italian tenor Giovanni Martinelli makes his operatic debut at the Teatro Dal Verme, Milan in Verdi's *Ernani*.

1910   Related Events

Jan. 13   The first radio broadcast takes place from the stage of the Metropolitan Opera in New York. Emmy Destinn and Riccardo Martin sing parts of *Cavalleria Rusticana*, and Enrico Caruso and Pasquale Amato sing music from *Pagliacci*. About 50 radio amateurs near New York City hear the broadcast, as do sailors aboard the SS *Avon* at sea.

April 17   Gustav Mahler conducts the orchestra of Concerts Colonne in a performance of his Second Symphony. This event marks his first appearance in Paris.

Sep. 7   The Dresden Opera Company notifies Richard Strauss that it refuses to produce *Der Rosenkavalier* because of his stipulation that *Salome* and *Elektra* also be produced four times annually for 10 years.

Oct. 3   Emile Jaques-Dalcroze leaves Geneva with his disciples for Hellerau, Germany to establish his Institute of Eurythmics.

Oct. 12   Max Reger is awarded the honorary degree of doctor of medicine by the University of Berlin. The faculty of medicine asserts that his music has the ability to relieve stress.

Nov. 12   Gabriel Faure conducts a program of his orchestral works in Saint Petersburg. This event marks the composer's first visit to Russia.

1911 Opera

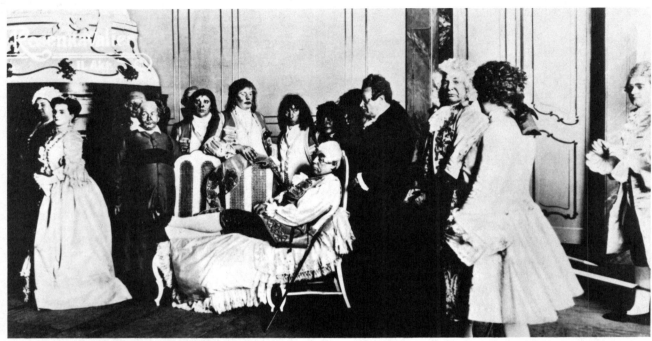

A SCENE FROM THE FIRST PRODUCTION OF *DER ROSENKAVALIER*

Jan. 26   *Der Rosenkavalier*, by Richard Strauss, to a text by Hugo von Hofmannsthal, receives its world premiere at the Konigliches Opernhaus in Dresden. The action is set in Vienna during the reign of Maria Theresa. The opera, coming after *Salome* and *Elektra*, causes some controversy among the critics because of the differences in style, but it is received enthusiastically by the public and becomes probably the most popular of any 20th-century German opera. The cast includes Carl Perron (Ochs), Margarethe Siems (Marschallin), Minnie Nast (Sophie) and Eva von der Osten (Octavian). Ernst von Schuch conducts.

Feb. 27   Cesar Cui's *The Captain's Daughter*, based on a tale by Pushkin, premieres in Saint Petersburg.

March 3   Frederick Converse's *The Sacrifice*, to his own libretto, premieres in Boston. The three-act opera is about an American military officer who falls in love with a Mexican woman.

March 14   *Dejanire*, by Camille Saint-Saens, premieres in Monte Carlo at the Theatre du Casino. Saint-Saens writes the libretto himself, having been asked by the prince of Monaco for a new work. He adapts it from the play by Louis Gallet based on the Greek myth of Hercules.

April 26   Raoul Laparra's *La Jota*, to his own libretto, premieres at the Opera-Comique in Paris. This opera is the composer's sequel to his *La Habenera*.

May 19   Maurice Ravel's one-act opera *L'Heure espagnole* premieres at the Opera-Comique in Paris. The libretto, based on the play by Maurice Etienne Legrand, is a complicated comedy about a watchmaker in 18th-century Spain; his wife, Concepcion; and her various lovers. The opera is not well received but subsequently becomes an established favorite.

May 22   *Le Martyre de Saint-Sebastien*, by Claude Debussy, receives its world premiere at the Theatre du Chatelet in Paris. The text, in French, is by Gabriele d'Annunzio and is written as a medieval mystery play with both pagan and Christian elements. The premiere creates a scandal, in part because it defies the archbishop's request of May 8 asking people not to attend the premiere because the leading role is played by Ida Rubinstein who is a Jew. The work is an important one in Debussy's artistic development, although it never becomes popular. As expected, reviewers talk more about Ida Rubinstein than about the music.

Critic Henri Bidow says in *Journal des Debats* (Paris) that Rubinstein ". . . is beneath the level of being merely repellent. She even failed to present a plastic composition of her role." Jean Cocteau, however, comes to her rescue, saying in *Comoedia* (Paris) that she ". . . makes one think of a miraculously animated stained-glass window whose image is full of immobile memory, mute, translucid, and sacred."

June 2   *Isabeau*, by Pietro Mascagni, premieres at the Teatro Coliseo in Buenos Aires, conducted by the composer. The libretto, by Luigi Illica, is the story of a proud princess, Isabeau; the knights who compete for her hand; and the young falconer with whom she falls in love. The opera is well received in Argentina but is not successful elsewhere.

Oct. 14   *Conchita*, by Riccardo Zandonai, premieres in Milan at the Teatro dal Verme. The libretto, by Maurizio Vaucaire and Carlo Zangarini, is based on a play by Pierre Louys about a poor cigar maker, Conchita, who rejects a rich suitor because she doesn't believe in his sincerity.

Dec. 23   *I Gioielli della Madonna*, by Ermanno Wolf-Ferrari, premieres in a German version in Berlin at the Kurfurstenoper. The text, by Enrico Golisciani and Carlo Zangarini, is the story of a blacksmith, Gennaro, who commits sacrilege by stealing the jewels from the statue of the Madonna for Maliella, the girl he loves.

CESAR CUI

1911 Dance

April 19   Tamara Karsavina and Vaslav Nijinsky dance the premiere of Michel Fokine's one-act ballet *Le Spectre de la Rose* in Monte Carlo. The libretto is by Jean-Louis Vandoyev. The romantic pas de deux, to Carl Maria von Weber's piano piece *Invitation to the Dance* (orchestrated by Hector Berlioz), tells of a young girl who comes back from a ball with a rose, falls asleep and dreams of the spirit of the rose. The ballet, designed by Leon Bakst, was created to show off Nijinsky's technique and Karsavina's romantic style.

April 26   *Narcisse* is premiered by Serge Diaghilev's Ballets Russes in Monte Carlo. Michel Fokine choreographs music by Nicolas Tcherepnin, who conducts the premiere. Amid sets by Leon Bakst, Narcissus (Vaslav Nijinsky) rejects the love of Echo (Tamara Karsavina), falls in love with his own reflection and is turned into a flower. The ballet is not a success.

June 6   The submarine act of *Sadko* is performed for the first time by Serge Diaghilev's Ballets Russes in Paris. Michel Fokine choreographs music by Nikolai Rimsky-Korsakov.

June 13   *Petrouchka* — a ballet by Igor Stravinsky — receives its world premiere by Serge Diaghilev's Ballets Russes in Paris. The choreography is by Michel Fokine, costumes and scenery by Alexandre Benois. The ballet, about a puppet imbued with human love, is considered to be one of Fokine's and Stravinsky's masterpieces. Lead dancers are Vaslav Nijinsky, Tamara Karsavina, Alexandre Orlov and Enrico Cecchetti. Pierre Monteux conducts. *Comoedia* (Paris) publishes a glowing review that says, "Instrumental timbres flow in a stream in a most novel fashion. These sonorities engender among the audience a sense of inexpressible exhilaration. Not a single measure remains indifferent. And what boldness in the handling of the instruments! What eloquence! What life! What youthfulness!"

June 21   Serge Diaghilev's Ballets Russes opens its first London season at Covent Garden. Performing *Le Pavillon d'Armide*, *Carnaval* and *Prince Igor*, dancers Vaslav Nijinsky, Tamara Karsavina, Adolph Bolm and others of the company star in leading roles. A review in the London *Times* the next day says, "It has been obvious for some years that Russians are the ideal dancers of the world. . . . "

Nov. 30   *Swan Lake* is performed for the first time by Serge Diaghilev's Ballets Russes at Covent Garden, London. Music is by Tchaikovsky. Vaslav Nijinsky and Mathilda Kschessinska star. The choreography by Marius Petipa is used with additional dances by Michel Fokine.

Dec. 19   Peter Ilyich Tchaikovsky's *Swan Lake* receives its first American performance in New York City. This production is staged by Mikhail Mordkin with scenery by James Fox.

1911   Instrumental and Vocal Music

Feb. 26   *Aux Etoiles*, by Henri Duparc, receives its first performance at a Lamoureux Concert in Paris. This work is the composer's second and final orchestral piece.

March 3   Alexander Gretchaninoff's cantata *19 February 1861* premieres in Saint Petersburg. The work is named after the date of the emancipation manifesto of the tsar. Gretchaninoff's music, influenced by the late Russian romantic composers, also contains elements of impressionism.

March 11   Enrique Granados' piano suite *Goyescas* is premiered by the composer in Barcelona. Considered his masterpiece, these pieces are based on paintings by the Spanish artist Goya.

March 15   Alexander Scriabin's Symphony No. 5, Op. 60 (Prometheus-The Poem of Fire) premieres as the composer plays the piano part and Serge Koussevitzky conducts in Moscow. The score contains a part for a color keyboard, which is supposed to create lighting changes along with the music. As it is not possible to build this instrument, the performance is given without lighting. A review published in the *Musical Courier* says, "The work is condemned for the present." Four years from now critic Frederick Corder will comment on the piece in the *Musical Quarterly*, his article entitled "On the Cult of Wrong Notes," saying the piece "is the product of a once fine composer suffering from mental derangement."

March 22   French organist and composer Charles-Marie Widor's *Symphonie antique* premieres in Paris.

April 2   Maurice Ravel's suite from *Daphnis et Chloe* is premiered by Gabriel Pierne at a Colonne Concert in Paris. This performance is not the premiere of the full work — only of the first suite ("Nocturne," "Interlude" and "Danse guerriere"). The complete ballet (one act and three tableaux) will receive its world premiere next June.

April 3   Jean Sibelius conducts in Helsinki the world premiere of his Symphony No. 4 in A Minor, Op. 63. The four movements of this work are built on the augmented fourth, or tritone, generating tonal uncertainty throughout much of the symphony. The piece is eventually considered the most modernistic and original of this composer's symphonies because of the way Sibelius develops his musical gestures using this interval as a seed.

April 7   Karol Szymanowski's Symphony No. 2 in B-flat Major premieres in Warsaw.

April 24   Alban Berg's String Quartet, Op. 3, receives its world premiere at the Ehrbar Hall in Vienna. The concert is held under the auspices of the Society for Art and Culture. The Rose Quartet, scheduled to perform the work, cancelled five days ago and a pick-up ensemble had to be assembled. A Vienna critic claims that Berg "mishandled" the idiom. The two-movement work is the last Berg composes while a full-time pupil of Arnold Schoenberg. Music philosopher Theodor Adorno subsequently describes Berg's compositional process in this piece as "liquidating the sonata." Today's event takes place shortly before Berg's marriage to Helene Nahowski and a month before Gustav Mahler's death.

April 24   Anton von Webern's Four Pieces for Violin and Piano, Op. 7, premieres in Vienna.

May 24   Granville Bantock's symphonic poem *Dante and Beatrice* premieres in Glasgow, the composer conducting.

May 24   Edward Elgar's Symphony No. 2 in E-flat Major, Op. 63 premieres at the London Music Festival with the composer conducting. In four movements like his earlier symphony, this work establishes itself as a favorite and helps deflect the criticism that Elgar was a poor man's Brahms. The four-movement symphony is dedicated to "the memory of His Late Majesty King Edward VII."

June 6   Henry Hadley's Symphony No. 4 premieres at the Norfolk, Connecticut Music Festival, the composer conducting. The work is subtitled "North, East, South, West."

June 13   Nikolai Miaskovsky's symphonic poem *Silence* premieres in Moscow. This prolific composer was influenced first by Tchaikovsky and Chopin and later by impressionism.

June 22   Edward Elgar's *Coronation March* premieres today at the coronation of King George V and Queen Mary.

Aug. 1   Sergei Prokofiev's *Autumn* premieres in Moscow. This work is a symphonic tableau.

Nov. 20   *Das Lied von der Erde*, by Gustav Mahler, is premiered posthumously in Munich. Bruno Walter conducts this work scored for tenor, contralto and orchestra. The text is a German translation of 18th-century Chinese poems. The six sections are entitled "Drinking Song of Earthly Anguish," "Solitary Soul in Autumn," "Of Youth," "Of Beauty," "The Drunkard in Springtime" and "The Farewell." Mahler regarded this work as a symphony, and the composition is often thought of by musicologists as Mahler's masterpiece.

Dec. 14   Erich Wolfgang Korngold's *Schauspiel-Ouverture*, Op. 4, is premiered by Arthur Nikisch in Leipzig. The composer, 14 years old, is already writing accomplished works in the Strauss idiom.

Dec. 23   Engelbert Humperdinck's music to *The Miracle*, a mystery play with a scenario by Max Reinhardt and a libretto based on medieval poems, premieres in London in its full-play version, as Protestants protest with signs saying "No Popery."

1911   Births, Deaths and Debuts

Feb. 2   Tenor Jussi Bjorling is born in Stora Tuna, Sweden.

March 8   Composer Alan Hovhaness is born in Somerville, Massachusetts of Scottish-Armenian descent.

March 11   American conductor-cellist Howard Mitchell is born in Lyons, Nebraska.

March 17   Swiss composer Raffaele d'Alessandro is born in Gallen.

March 17   Pianist Robert Goldsand is born in Vienna, Austria.

March 29   Alexandre Guilmant, 74, dies in Meudon. This French organist cofounded the Schola Cantorum along with Charles Bordes and Vincent d'Indy.

March 31   Soprano Elisabeth Grummer is born in Diedenhofen, Alsace.

April 1   Opera director Gunther Rennert is born in Essen, Germany.

April 5   American recording executive and composer Goddard Lieberson is born in Hanley, England.

April 17   Russian musicologist and critic Izrail Nestyev is born in Kerch, Russia.

April 21   Baritone Leonard Warren is born in New York City.

May 18   Austrian composer Gustav Mahler, 50, dies in Vienna. A product of the Vienna Conservatory, where he studied piano, harmony and composition, Mahler was not a student of any world-renowned composer. He began conducting at age 20 and at 25 was appointed conductor of the Prague Opera, succeeding Anton Seidl. There he focused on Wagnerian opera. Three years later he became music director of the Royal Opera, Budapest, where he completely reorganized the opera house. This in turn led to important operatic conducting posts in Hamburg and then at the Vienna Court Opera — a position he held for a decade. His tenure in Vienna brought that company international acclaim.

In 1908 he made his debut as principal conductor of the Metropolitan Opera, New York, and a year later was appointed principal conductor of the New York Philharmonic Society.

As a composer Mahler was the last giant of the Viennese postromantic school. His music, employing Austrian folk materials and rooted in the Germanic tradition of Wagner, was often scored for massive ensembles. His work, in mood, often gravitated toward the morbidity of death and also reflected, to some degree at least, the conflict of his religious pursuits.

Born a Jew, he converted to Roman Catholicism and often contemplated Pantheism. His intense romanticism and grandness of musical gesture exerted an influence on younger Austrian composers who would later become revolutionary: Arnold Schoenberg and Alban Berg, in particular.

Although Mahler composed a great deal of vocal music (he began three operas but destroyed the scores), his contribution was principally as a symphonist — nine complete; one unfinished (No. 10); and *Das Lied von der Erde*, which, though technically not a symphony, was considered one by the composer.

May 29   Librettist Sir William Schwenck Gilbert, 74, dies of a heart attack after rescuing a young woman from drowning at Harrow Weald, Middlesex, England. In 1891 he met Arthur Sullivan, and they began their collaboration on the comic operas including *H.M.S. Pinafore*, *The Pirates of Penzance* and *Iolanthe*, that have remained popular through the years.

June 10   Harpsichordist and musicologist Ralph Kirkpatrick is born in Leominster, Massachusetts.

June 29   Composer-conductor Bernard Hermann is born in New York City.

June 30   English pianist Solomon makes his debut playing the Tchaikovsky Piano Concerto No. 1 in London. He is 8 years old.

July 2   Austrian conductor Felix Mottl, 54, dies in Munich. After studies at the Vienna Conservatory, he was engaged as an assistant at the first Bayreuth Festival. He later conducted there as well as in London and was often associated with performances of Wagner's operas. In 1905 he conducted the first complete performance of *Les Troyens* (by Hector Berlioz) in Germany. He also composed three operas, none of which was very successful.

July 7   Composer and librettist Gian Carlo Menotti is born in Cadegliano, Italy.

FELIX MOTTL

Aug. 12   American music writer Edward Downes is born in Boston, Massachusetts.

Oct. 27   Alexander Glazunov's Violin Concerto is the featured music as violinist Efrem Zimbalist makes his American debut with the Boston Symphony Orchestra. The performance also marks the American premiere of this concerto.

Nov. 3   Composer Vladimir Ussachevsky is born in Hailar, Manchuria.

Nov. 13   German contralto Margarete Matzenauer makes her Metropolitan Opera debut as Amneris in *Aida*, conducted by Arturo Toscanini. The cast also includes Enrico Caruso, Emmy Destinn, Adamo Didur and Pasquale Amato. Krehbiel writes in the New York *Tribune* that Matzenauer sang "... with a large and luscious voice, with ample evidences of a fine knowledge of the art of singing, and acted it so as to make it something more than an operatic marionette."

Dec. 3   Italian composer Nino Rota is born in Milan.

Dec. 28   Italian coloratura soprano Luisa Tetrazzini debuts at the Metropolitan Opera as Lucia. The New York *Tribune* publishes its review by Henry Krehbiel, asserting that much can be said "... in praise of her command of artistic device, in dispraise of the inequalities of her voice; in praise of the fine texture of her upper tones, in regret because of the infantile character of her lower...."

1911   Related Events

Jan. 26   The *Petersburgskaya Gazeta* announces Vaslav Nijinsky's dismissal from the Imperial Ballet at the Maryinsky Theater because he danced *Giselle* in a costume considered indecent. Serge Diaghilev subsequently establishes his own ballet company, of which Nijinsky becomes the star.

March 19   Gustav Mahler performs his final New York concert as music director of the New York Philharmonic. The concert takes place at the Brooklyn Academy of Music, and the program includes music of Dvorak, Bruch, Mendelssohn and Wagner.

March 20   Russia's first copyright law takes effect. The legislation extends protection to composers and authors in any nation under obligation by international copyright.

May 8   In reaction to the upcoming scheduled premiere of Claude Debussy's *Le Martyre de Saint-Sebastien*, the archbishop of Paris asks Roman Catholics not to attend because the part of the saint is to be performed by Jewish star Ida Rubinstein.

May 17   Josef Stransky becomes music director of the New York Philharmonic, succeeding Gustav Mahler. Stransky continues in this capacity for 12 years.

July 1   Arnold Schoenberg's first book, *Harmonielehre*, is completed in Vienna. The book explores traditional harmony within the context of recent musical developments. It is subsequently translated into English and published as *Theory of Harmony* (New York, 1947). This month reviewer G.B. Weston writes of the book in the *Harvard Musical Review* (Cambridge), "It is not so often that any author so obligingly furnishes the reductio ad absurdum of his own work as does the naive writer of this rambling grammar of cacophony."

Dec. 8   The San Francisco Symphony Orchestra gives its first concert. The conductor is Henry Hadley, also a composer, who came to this position after having been a conductor of the Seattle Symphony. The program consists of music by Wagner, Tchaikovsky, Haydn and Liszt. The San Francisco *Chronicle* praises the performance. Hadley remains as music director until 1915.

1912 Opera

Feb. 17   Jules Massenet's five-act opera *Roma* receives its initial performance in Monte Carlo. The opera is set in 216 B.C.

March 14   Horatio Parker's *Mona* premieres at the Metropolitan Opera House in New York City. The three-act opera, which had been awarded the Metropolitan Opera Prize of $10,000, is about a British woman in love with a Roman soldier. Louise Homer and Herbert Witherspoon lead a cast conducted by Alfred Hertz. Parker later tells the press that he associated different keys with different characters as a compositional device. W.J. Henderson writes of the opera, "Mr. Parker's musical design [was] fundamentally untheatrical." The opera is not a great success and has only four performances.

April 13   Ferruccio Busoni's three-act opera *Die Brautwahl* receives its first performance in Hamburg. It is about a bride and her problems.

June 24   Ruggero Leoncavallo's operetta *La reginetta delle rose* is performed for the first time simultaneously in Rome and Naples. A love story set during the Portuguese Revolution of 1910, the opera is unsuccessful.

Aug. 10   *The Atonement of Pan*, by Henry Hadley, receives its initial performance in San Francisco. The work is a musical drama in three scenes and is performed under the auspices of San Francisco's Bohemian Club.

Aug. 17   Armenian composer Armen Tigranian's opera *Anush* receives its first performance in Alexandropol. This

RUGGERO LEONCAVALLO

musician founded a choral society in 1902 to advance the cause of Armenian music.

Sep. 16   Ruggero Leoncavallo's two-act opera *Zingari*, based on a poem by Pushkin, receives its first performance in London. It is about life in a gypsy camp.

Oct. 15   Walter Damrosch's *The Love of Peace* premieres in Philadelphia. This opera is one of five composed by this musician, who is principally known as a conductor. Son of conductor-violinist Leopold Damrosch, he has conducted the New York Oratorio Society, the New York Symphony Society, the New York Philharmonic Society and at the Metropolitan Opera. In 1894 he founded the Damrosch Opera Company, which for five seasons toured the United States presenting German operas.

Oct. 25   The first version of *Ariadne auf Naxos*, by Richard Strauss receives its premiere performance in Stuttgart with the composer conducting. Hugo von Hofmannsthal writes the libretto. This version consists of incidental music to Moliere's play, *Le Bourgeois Gentilhomme*, and a one-act opera which is played as a postlude to the play. Today's performance proves impractical because both a theatrical and an operatic company are required on stage for the same production. (A revised version of the opera will be produced at the Vienna Hofoper on October 4, 1916.) The cast for today's performance includes Maria Jeritza, Margarethe Siems and Hermann Jadlowker.

RICHARD STRAUSS

Oct. 25   Alexander Gretchaninoff's *Soeur Beatrice*, to Maurice Maeterlinck's play, premieres in Moscow. The three-act opera is suppressed after three performances because it attacks religion.

Nov. 13   Riccardo Zandonai's *Melenis* premieres in Milan. In three acts, it is about a Greek woman who commits suicide because her lover falls in love with another woman.

Dec. 21   Vincent d'Indy's *Le Chant de la cloche*, to Schiller's text, premieres in Brussels at the Theatre de la Monnaie.

1912   Dance

March 11   *Bakawali*, choreographed by Ruth Saint Denis, receives its world premiere in New York City. Her *O-Mika* also premieres on the same program.

April 22   Paul Dukas' symphonic poem *La Peri* and Maurice Ravel's *Adelaide, ou le langage des fleurs* premiere in Paris at a dance concert by Russian ballerina Natacha Trouhanova. Each composer conducts his own music.

May 14   Serge Diaghilev's Ballets Russes premieres *Le Dieu bleu*, by Michel Fokine. The work is to music by Venezuelan-born composer Reynaldo Hahn, with sets and costumes by Leon Bakst and a libretto by Jean Cocteau. It tells the story of two lovers saved from death by the intervention of Hindu gods. Tamara Karsavina (the Young Girl), Lydia Nelidova (the Goddess), Vaslav Nijinsky (the Blue God) and Max Frohman (the Young Priest) star. It is one of Fokine's minor works.

May 20   *Thamar*, a one-act ballet choreographed by Michel Fokine, receives its first performance by Serge Diaghilev's Ballets Russes at the Theatre du Chatelet in Paris. It is about a queen who murders her lovers and throws their bodies out of the castle. Tamara Karsavina and Adolph Bolm star. Music is by Mily Balakirev.

May 29   Vaslav Nijinsky's first ballet — *L'Apres-midi d'un faune* — with music by Claude Debussy and settings by Leon Bakst, premieres with Serge Diaghilev's Ballets Russes in Paris. The choreography, inspired by ancient Greek friezes, consists mainly of angular movements and poses. It is a complete departure from classical dance, which stresses rounded, flowing movement. That, combined with an erotic gesture by Nijinsky at the end of the dance, causes a scandal. Nijinsky, who dances the lead, speculates that his choreography is a failure, and Diaghilev orders the immediate repetition of the 12-minute ballet. Despite generally favorable reviews, the editor Calmette of *Le Figaro* (Paris) says of Nijinsky and his choreography, "We are shown a lecherous faun, whose movements are filthy and bestial in their eroticism, and whose gestures are as crude as they are indecent. That is all."

VASLAV NIJINSKY, RIGHT, IN HIS BALLET *L'APRES-MIDI D'UN FAUNE.*

June 8   *Daphnis and Chloe*, with choreography by Michel Fokine, receives its premiere at the Theatre du Chatelet, during the Diaghilev Ballets Russes' Paris season. Maurice Ravel composed the commissioned score (he took two years to write it and scored it for orchestra and chorus); Leon Bakst designed the costumes; and Pierre Monteux conducts. The scenario, based on a tale by the Roman author Longus, tells the story of a young shepherd, Daphnis, who is in love with Chloe. She is captured by pirates, but is reunited with Daphnis after the intervention of Pan.

Tamara Karsavina (Chloe) and Vaslav Nijinsky (Daphnis) dance the title roles. Adolph Bolm plays Dorkon. The conflict between Fokine and Diaghilev over Daphnis and Nijinsky's "Greek" ballet (Nijinsky's style of choreography as evidenced in *L'Apres-midi d'un faune*) forces Fokine to leave the company a few days from now. Jean Marnold writes in *Mercure de France*, "The score abounds in tableaux of the most exquisite plastic beauty."

Nov. 30   Reinhold Gliere's ballet *Chrysis*, based on a tale by Pierre Louys, premieres in Moscow.

1912 Instrumental and Vocal Music

Jan. 21   Maurice Ravel's *Ma mere l'oye* premieres in its orchestral version in Paris.

Jan. 26   Frederick Converse's symphonic poem *Ormazd* is premiered by Max Zach and the St. Louis Symphony Orchestra.

Feb. 28   Carl Nielsen's Symphony No. 3, subtitled *Sinfonia Espansiva*, and his Violin Concerto premiere in Copenhagen. The composer conducts, and the violinist is the composer's son-in-law, Emil Telmanyi.

March 11   Edward Elgar's *The Crown of India* receives its first performance at the London Coliseum in that city. Elgar describes it as an "imperial masque." The work was composed to celebrate King George V's visit to India.

March 23   Symphony No. 3 in B Minor, Op. 42, (*Ilya Murometz*) by Reinhold Gliere, receives its first performance in Moscow. Emil Cooper conducts the Russian Musical Society. It is in four movements and depicts the life of an 11th-century Russian warrior. The symphony is awarded the Glinka prize.

May 1   Gustav Holst's suite *Beni Mora* premieres in London.

May 18   Albert Roussel's symphonic *Evocations* premieres in Paris.

June 4   George Chadwick's symphonic fantasy *Aphrodite* premieres at the Norfolk, Connecticut Music Festival.

June 20   Eugene Goossens, 19 years old, conducts the premiere of his first orchestral piece at the Royal College of Music in London. The piece, entitled *Variations on a Chinese Theme*, is influenced by French impressionism.

June 26   Gustav Mahler's Symphony No. 9 in D is premiered posthumously by Bruno Walter, conducting the Vienna Philharmonic in Vienna. The four-movement work — the composer's last complete symphony — was composed during the last few years of Mahler's life and has been characterized as a musical bridge between the 19th and 20th centuries. Its outer slow movements enclose two scherzo-type movements.

July 23   Ralph Vaughan Williams' symphonic suite version of *The Wasps* premieres in London, the composer conducting.

July 24   Nikolai Miaskovsky's Symphony No. 2 in C-sharp Minor premieres in Moscow.

Aug. 7   Piano Concerto No. 1 in D-flat Major, by Sergei Prokofiev, receives its initial performance in Moscow, with Prokofiev as soloist. This concerto is in one movement. The composer, now a student at the Saint Petersburg Conservatory, performs this piece again at his graduation, in 1914. Critic Leonid Sabaneyev writes in *Voice of Moscow* of today's performance that the music "scarcely merits an honorable title."

SELF-PORTRAIT OF ARNOLD SCHOENBERG

Sep. 3   *Five Pieces for Orchestra*, Op. 16, by Arnold Schoenberg, receives its world premiere in London. Sir Henry Wood conducts the piece at a Promenade Concert. This work is Schoenberg's first orchestral composition written in an atonal style. The third piece, with its dynamic markings never exceeding a "mezzo piano," displays static harmonies with shimmering instrumental colors, producing what Schoenberg describes as "the quivering reflection of the sun upon calm water." A program note to the performance says, "This music seeks to express all that swells in us subconsciously like a dream." The titles to each of the five pieces are added later by the publisher, C.F. Peters. The music provokes scathing reviews. The London *Globe* reports it "resembled the wailings of a tortured soul, and suggested nothing so much as the disordered fancies of delirium or the fearsome, imaginary terrors of a highly nervous infant."

Sep. 5   English theorist and composer John Foulds' symphonic suite *Music Pictures*, containing quarter-tones in the second movement, premieres at the Promenade Concerts in London.

Sep. 24   Frank Bridge's orchestral suite *The Sea* is premiered by Sir Henry Wood in London.

Oct. 4   Max Reger's orchestral work *Konzert in alten Stil*, Op. 123, is premiered by Willem Mengelberg in Frankfurt.

Oct. 11   Max Reger's *Romantische Suite*, Op. 125, premieres in Dresden. Scored for orchestra, this piece has three movements.

Oct. 16   *Pierrot Lunaire* — a revolutionary composition consisting of 21 musical melodramas — receives its world premiere today in Berlin. Albertine Zehme performs as soloist. The composer, Arnold Schoenberg, required 40 rehearsals prior to this premiere performance. The music, set to poetry by Albert Giraud (translated into German by Otto Erich Hartleben), describes the reflection of moonlight. The work is scored for piano, flute, piccolo, clarinet, bass clarinet, violin, viola, cello and spoken voice. The voice part — *sprechstimme* — substitutes a speech-song of sliding pitches for fixed-pitch melody. This piece is one of two Schoenberg introduces this year that spark controversial reaction (the other being the *Five Pieces for Orchestra*, Op. 16). A review in the *Signale fur die musikalische Welt* (Berlin) says, "One must first learn the new alphabet to approach this new frightful Schoenberg." Arthur M. Abell writes in *The Musical Courier* (New York) that Albertine Zehme performed while the players ". . . discoursed the most ear-splitting combinations of tones that ever desecrated the walls of a Berlin music hall."

Oct. 25   Richard Strauss' incidental music to Moliere's *Le Bourgeois Gentilhomme* premieres in Stuttgart, the composer conducting. This suite was arranged from music written for the first version of *Ariadne auf Naxos*.

Nov. 15   Frederick Delius' *Lebenstanz* receives its first performance in Berlin. This tone poem is a revised version of his work entitled *The Dance Goes On*, composed in 1900.

Dec. 5   Sir Charles Hubert Parry's Symphony-Fantasy in B Minor premieres in London, the composer conducting.

Dec. 8   Anatoly Liadov's symphonic poem *From the Apocalypse* is premiered by Alexander Siloti in Saint Petersburg.

1912 Births, Deaths and Debuts

Jan. 5   Pianist Wilhelm Backhaus performs Beethoven's *Emperor* Concerto with the New York Symphony Orchestra, marking his American debut.

Feb. 4   Conductor Erich Leinsdorf is born in Vienna, Austria.

Feb. 7   Italian soprano Claudia Muzio makes her operatic debut in *Manon Lescaut* in Arezzo.

Feb. 11   Pianist Rudolf Firkusny is born in Napajedla, Czechoslovakia.

March 13   Dancer and teacher Igor Youskevitch is born in Piriatin, Russia.

March 25   Soprano Magda Olivero is born in Saluzzo, Italy.

April 22   English contralto Kathleen Ferrier is born in Higher Walton, Lancashire, England.

May 3   Organist Virgil Fox is born in Princeton, Illinois.

May 15   Composer and music writer Arthur Berger is born in New York City.

May 16   Conductor Felix Prohaska is born in Vienna, Austria.

May 23   Composer Jean Francaix is born in Le Mans, France.

May 26   Flemish composer Jan Blockx, 62, dies in Antwerp, Belgium. A pupil of Peter Benoit, he promulgated national Flemish music and composed operas and cantatas to Flemish texts.

May 30   Countertenor Alfred Deller is born in Margate, England.

June 9   Composer Ingolf Dahl is born in Hamburg, Germany.

June 22   American dancer, choreographer and ballet director Katherine Dunham is born in Chicago, Illinois.

July 27   Composer and conductor Igor Markevitch is born in Kiev, Ukraine.

Aug. 13   French composer Jules Massenet, 70, dies in Paris. He entered the Paris Conversatoire at age 9 and won the Grand Prix de Rome at age 21. At 36 he became professor of composition at the Paris Conservatoire and that same year was elected to the Academie des Beaux-Arts. His pupils included Gustave Charpentier, Gabriel Pierne and Alfred Bruneau. Massenet's influence was both as a teacher and as a composer who had a substantial impact on French opera: His melodies rivaled those of Camille Saint-Saens — his only real competitor. Shortly after the turn of the century, Massenet's influence began to fade due to the appearance of new trends in French opera, particularly Claude Debussy's *Pelleas et Melisande*. Massenet composed approximately 200 songs, 25 operas (including *Manon, Werther* and *Thais*), 3 ballets and numerous oratorios, choral works, orchestral works and incidental pieces. He also orchestrated and finished the opera *Kassya*, by Leo Delibes.

Aug. 21   Soviet dancer and ballet mistress Natalia Dudinskaya is born in Kharkov, Russia.

Aug. 31   Tenor Ramon Vinay is born in Chillan, Chile.

Sep. 1   British composer Samuel Coleridge-Taylor, 37, dies in Croydon, England. The composer was of African extraction; his father was a native of Sierra Leone. Coleridge-Taylor studied violin at the Royal Academy of Music (where he later taught) and studied composition with Charles Villiers Stanford. He organized a successful orchestra at Croydon, where he decided to settle. Edward Elgar helped him by recommending his music for performances at the Gloucester Festival. Three tours to America also helped establish him as a young composer of merit. His works include the opera *Thelma*, two operettas, the famous trilogy *The Song of Hiawatha* and a host of other works for chorus, orchestra, voice and various ensembles. The style of his music resembles, to some degree, that of Edward Elgar, yet his attraction to Indian themes added a non-English element to his music's sound.

Sep. 5   Composer John Cage is born in Los Angeles, California.

Sep. 21   Pianist Gyorgy Sandor is born in Budapest, Hungary.

Oct. 11   Leopold Stokowski, 30, makes his debut as the new music director of the Philadelphia Orchestra. A review in the *Public Ledger* (Philadelphia) says Stokowski "dispensed with the score by virtue of infallible memory, and held his men and his audience from first note to last firmly in his grasp."

Oct. 13   Composer Hugo Weisgall is born in Ivancice, Czechoslovakia.

Oct. 21   Conductor Georg Solti is born in Budapest, Hungary.

Oct. 27   Composer Conlon Nancarrow is born in Texarkana, Arkansas.

Oct. 28   Russian violinist Jascha Heifetz creates a debut sensation playing the Tchaikovsky Concerto in Berlin under Arthur Nikisch. He is 11 years old.

Nov. 6   Ukrainian composer Nikolai Lissenko, 70, dies in Kiev. As a youth, he was strongly influenced by Ukrainian folk song. His formal training in Russia was in the natural sciences, and in his mid-twenties he worked as a justice of the peace. He then went to Leipzig Conservatory, where he studied piano with Carl Reinecke. His orchestration studies were with Nikolai Rimsky-Korsakov, in Saint Petersburg. In addition to many songs, operas (including *Taras Bulba, Natalie from Poltava* and *Sappho*), cantatas, orchestral works and piano pieces, he wrote his famous pamphlet, "The Characteristics of the Ukrainian Dumki" (1874). In this pamphlet he asserts that the Ukrainian modes were derived from ancient Greek music and that symmetrical rhythms and antiphonal features distinguish Ukrainian songs from Russian songs. Lissenko's influence was largely that of a Ukrainian nationalist composer whose work helped identify Ukrainian musical themes and materials.

Nov. 11   Lucrezia Bori makes her American debut as Manon in *Manon Lescaut*. Henry Krehbiel writes in the New York *Tribune* that she has "fine vocal skill, displayed at crucial moments."

Nov. 25   Dancer, choreographer, teacher and ballet director Alwin Nikolais is born in Southington, Connecticut.

Dec. 27   A performance of *Les Huguenots*, by Giacomo Meyerbeer, at the Metropolitan Opera House of New York features Frieda Hempel, making her American debut. Henry Krehbiel, of the New York *Tribune*, says, "her voice in its high register is of power and better quality."

Dec. 29   Composer Peggy Glanville-Hicks is born in Melbourne, Australia.

1912 Related Events

Several developments take place in the recording industry this year: Thomas A. Edison introduces his new Blue Amberol cylinders, which are unbreakable; Columbia (USA) stops distributing cylinder recordings; and the first edition of the *Victor Book of the Opera* is published.

The Wa-Wan Press, suffering from lack of subscriptions and financial difficulties, is acquired by G. Schirmer of New York.

March 12   Henry Cowell, 15 years old, demonstrates his tone clusters at the San Francisco Music Club. These sonorities involve playing the piano with fists and forearms.

April 15   The *SS Titanic* sinks in the North Atlantic. Among those who perish are British musicians W. Hartley, J. Hume, P.C. Taylor, J.W. Woodward, R. Bricoux, F. Clarke, G. Krins and W.T. Brailey.

June 14   Arthur Nikisch conducts the London Symphony Orchestra in a pianola performance of Edvard Grieg's Piano Concerto. The pianola is played by Easthope Martin. This event marks the first solo performance of the pianola.

July 18   Francesco Pratella's manifesto "Destruction of Quadrature" is issued in Milan. It proposes a "new musical order of disorder."

July 23   English composer Ethel Smyth is arrested in London on a charge of attempted arson. She was involved in a suffragist demonstration 10 days ago and allegedly attempted to set fire to the house of the secretary of state for the colonies, Lewis V. Harcourt.

Dec. 21   Arnold Schoenberg's *Pelleas und Melisande* is conducted by the composer in Saint Petersburg. This event marks the first Russian performance of this work as well as the composer's first and only Russian tour. He is well received.

1913 Opera

Jan. 9   The first staged performance of *Une Education manquee*, by Alexis Emmanuel Chabrier, takes place in Paris. The libretto, by Eugene Leterrier and Albert Vanloo, is about a young couple engaged to be married who do not know what they are supposed to do on their wedding night. This opera was written while Chabrier was still working in the civil service before turning to music as a full-time occupation. Originally written in 1879, it was performed at that time privately with piano accompaniment.

Jan. 20   *Tante Simona*, a one-act comic opera by Ernst von Dohnanyi, receives its first performance in Dresden. It is about an Italian spinster who tries to protect the virginity of her niece.

Feb. 20   *Ugale fortuna*, an opera buffa by Vincenzo Tommasini, receives its first performance in Rome. The opera won the Verdi contest this year and is produced as the first-prize composition.

Feb. 27   The Metropolitan Opera in New York premieres Walter Damrosch's *Cyrano de Bergerac* to a libretto based on a play by Edmond Rostand. Conducted by Alfred Hertz, the cast includes Pasquale Amato and Frances Alda. The opera is about the long-nosed soldier who writes love letters to the woman he adores. Henry Krehbiel of the New York *Tribune* says of this work: "It offers nothing which points even remotely to a solution of the problem of English or American opera. . . . "

Feb. 28   Erik Satie's one-act operetta *Coco-Cheri* receives its first performance in Monte Carlo.

March 4   Gabriel Faure's opera *Penelope* premieres at the Theatre du Casino at Monte Carlo. The libretto, by Rene Fauchois, is based on the story of Ulysses' return to Penelope after his long journey home from the Trojan War. It is considered by Faure's admirers to be one of his most important works, but his detractors finds it dull and without dramatic interest. The cast includes Lucienne Breval and Charles Rousseliere. Leon Jehin conducts.

March 28   *Le Chateau de la Grande Breteche*, a new opera by Albert Dupuis, receives its first performance in Nice. The work is based on a novella by Balzac. Dupuis is Belgium's most prolific 20th-century composer of opera.

April 1   *La vida breve*, by Manuel de Falla, receives its premiere at the Theatre de l'Opera in Nice. The libretto, by Carlos Fernandez Shaw, is a story of a young girl, Salud, who discovers that her lover, Paco, is engaged to a rich girl. It is de Falla's first opera and is well received by both the public and the critics. The opera had won an award given by the Academia de Bellas Artes (Madrid, 1905).

THE INTERIOR OF THE TEATRO ALLA SCALA IN MILAN, ITALY

April 10   Italo Montemezzi's opera *L'Amore dei tre re* (libretto by Sem Benelli) premieres at the Teatro alla Scala, in Milan. Fiora, an Italian princess, is in love with Avito but is forced to marry the son of Archibaldo, the blind conqueror of Italy. The suspicious father-in-law eventually strangles her for her infidelity. This work is considered one of the best products of 20th-century Italian opera. Tullio Serafin conducts.

April 14   *Mimi Pinson*, by Ruggero Leoncavallo, premieres in Palermo, Italy. This work, originally entitled *La Boheme*, is a new version of the composer's 1897 opera of that title. The composer changed the title in order to avoid its association with Puccini's more successful *La Boheme*.

April 25   A new opera by Jules Massenet, entitled *Panurge*, premieres posthumously in Paris. The opera, in four acts, is based on a satire by Rabelais.

June 4   *Julien*, by Gustave Charpentier, premieres in Paris at the Opera-Comique. The composer writes his own libretto, which is intended as a sequel to his earlier opera *Louise*, but which falls far short of the success established by his earlier work. *Julien* becomes a rarely performed opera.

June 24   Serge Diaghilev opens his London season with a presentation of Modest Mussorgsky's *Boris Godunov*, starring Feodor Chaliapin. The London *Times* writes the following day, "It is difficult to say how far Mussorgsky, how far the extraordinarily powerful acting of M. Chaliapin and the other principals, the fine singing, and natural action of the crowds, or the beauty of the scenery were responsible for the effect."

Oct. 8   *The Fair at Sorochinsk*, by Modest Mussorgsky, receives its world premiere in Moscow. Based on Gogol's tale, it was unfinished at the time of Mussorgsky's death, and this three-act version is assembled by various musicians. Another version, put together by Cesar Cui, will be performed in Saint Petersburg in 1917. The opera will also be produced in a version by Vissarion Shebalin in 1931.

Nov. 22   Belgian composer Flor Alpaert's opera *Shylock*, to a Flemish libretto after Shakespeare, premieres in Antwerp. Alpaert's music is influenced by Flemish folk songs.

Dec. 4   *L'Amatore medico*, an opera buffa by Ermanno Wolf-Ferrari, premieres in a German version entitled *Der Liebhaber als Arzt*. The comedy, based on a work of Moliere, tells the story of the lovesick Lucinda. She is cured by her lover (disguised as a doctor), who prescribes marriage.

Dec. 9   The Metropolitan Opera in New York gives the first American performance of Richard Strauss' *Der Rosenkavalier*. Featuring lead singers Frieda Hempel, Otto Goritz, Margarete Ober and Hermann Weill, the production is conducted by Alfred Hertz. Richard Aldrich of the New York *Times* assesses the work: "This music is not his most distinguished in invention, his most fortunate in ideas."

Dec. 15   Pietro Mascagni's four-act opera *Parisina* receives its first performance in Milan at the Teatro alla Scala. The text is by the Italian poet Gabriele d'Annunzio. It is the tragic story of Ugo, a young nobleman, the illegitimate son of Niccolo d'Este, who falls in love with his father's young wife, and she with him.

1913 Dance

May 10   *Papillon,* a one-act ballet choreographed by Michel Fokine, receives its first performance at the Maryinsky Theater in Saint Petersburg. Music is by Robert Schumann. The sets are by Mstislav Doboujinsky and the costumes by Leon Bakst. It is about a man walking in a park who encounters young women whom he thinks are butterflies. Tamara Karsavina and Fokine star. Fokine restages the work for Serge Diaghilev on April 16th of next year.

May 15   *Jeux* is performed for the first time at the Theatre des Champs-Elysees, in Paris. Danced by Serge Diaghilev's Ballets Russes, the music is by Claude Debussy, with choreography by Vaslav Nijinsky and costumes and scenery by Leon Bakst. The one-act "poeme dansee" is a dance of love involving a game resembling tennis and featuring one male and two females. The dancers are Nijinsky, Tamara Karsavina and Ludmilla Schollar. Pierre Monteux conducts.

May 29   Serge Diaghilev's Ballets Russes premieres *Le Sacre du printemps* at the Theatre des Champs-Elysees in Paris, with music by Igor Stravinsky, choreography by Vaslav Nijinsky, and costumes and decor by Nicholas Roerich. The conductor is Pierre Monteux. The choreography, which evokes prehistoric Russia, continues Nijinsky's departure from classicism. The dancers, in bare feet, stomp around the stage in movements designed to show the brutality and eroticism of barbarian fertility rites. The audience provides a negative reaction, so loud that the dancers are unable to hear the music. Reports of fistfighting and verbal smears emerge from the theater, as Stravinsky's music coupled with Nijinsky's choreography, invoke one of the most infamous reactions of the century.

Critical reaction to Stravinsky's music is fierce. Pierre Lalo writes in *Le Temps* (Paris), "Never has the cult of the wrong note been applied with such industry, zeal and ferocity." H. Quittard of *Le Figaro* (Paris) asks, "Does Stravinsky really believe that a melody would become more intense if it is doubled for fifty bars by a second above it, a second below it, or both?"

June 12   Serge Diaghilev presents *La Tragedie de Salome* at the Theatre des Champs-Elysees in Paris. Choreographed by Boris Romanov to music of Florent Schmitt, the decor is by Serge Soudeikine. Tamara Karsavina dances the role of Salome.

July 12   *The Impromptu,* choreographed by Ruth Saint Denis, premieres in Chicago.

1913 Instrumental and Vocal Music

Jan. 3   Havergal Brian's overture *Doctor Merryheart* premieres at the Annual Conference of the Incorporated Society of Musicians, Birmingham, England.

Feb. 4   A revised version of Ralph Vaughan Williams' Symphony No. 1 (*Sea Symphony*) is performed in London.

Feb. 23   Franz Schreker conducts the premiere of Arnold Schoenberg's *Gurre-Lieder* in Vienna. Set to texts by Danish poet Jen Peter Jacobsen, the oratorio depicts the life of Denmark's King Waldemar and his love for Tove. One of Schoenberg's massive works, it includes a part for chain (in the percussion section) and is scored for five solo voices, speaking voice, three male choirs, mixed chorus of eight parts and huge orchestra.

Feb. 26   Bela Bartok's symphonic *Deux images* premieres in Budapest.

March 30   Joaquin Turina's symphonic poem *La procesion del rocio* receives its world premiere in Madrid.

March 31   *Six Pieces for Orchestra,* Op. 6, by Anton Webern, receives its world premiere under the auspices of The Academic Society for Literature and Music at the large hall of the Musikverein in Vienna. These pieces, composed in 1909, are a bridge from Webern's *Passacaglia,* Op. 1, to his *Three Little Pieces,* Op. 11, for piano and cello: They display intense sonorities with virtually no repetition or motivic development. Scored for an orchestra of four flutes, two piccolos, one alto flute, two oboes, two English horns, three clarinets, one E-flat clarinet, two bass clarinets, two bassoons, one contrabassoon, six horns, six trumpets, six trombones, six tubas, two harps, celesta, timpani, percussion and strings, it is the largest ensemble Webern ever uses. These six pieces last approximately 10 minutes. The fourth — a funeral march — features massive brass statements over a percussion ostinato.

This music, in addition to the other works on the program (*Four Orchestral Songs on Poems of Maeterlinck,* by Alexander von Zemlinsky; *First Chamber Symphony,* by Arnold Schoenberg; two of *Five Orchestral Songs on Picture-Postcard Texts of Peter Altenberg,* by Alban Berg; and *Kindertotenlieder,* by the late Gustav Mahler), provokes one of the greatest scandals of the century. Critics immediately go on the offensive. In a dispatch from Vienna, the Boston *Evening Transcript* says of the *Six Pieces for Orchestra,* "[Webern] chose to write them with an instrumentation which can only be described in terms of the barnyard." Auguste Spanuth writes in *Signale* (Berlin), "Fifteen brave musicians presented to us Schoenberg's Chamber Symphony. 'Chamber-of-Horrors Symphony' would be a more fitting title."

A group of composers and musicians, mostly unknown and conservative, attend this concert intent on causing a disturbance. Hissing, laughter and applause vie for prominence during and immediately after the new Webern pieces are performed. Fistfighting breaks out in the second balcony at the conclusion of the Schoenberg piece. During the performance of the Berg work, Schoenberg stops the orchestra and threatens to have the Vienna police evict unruly listeners. This sparks a melee. Webern shouts from his seat that the human baggage must be removed from the concert hall. The police arrive and are ineffective in securing order. The musicians, almost in shock, exit. Mahler's *Kindertotenlieder* is not performed, and the evening ends in chaos. Two of the disorderly listeners are required to appear in court (where a physician who also attended the concert tells the judge that music of this kind is "harmful to the nervous system"), and each is fined 100 kronen. Anton Webern collects his wife and children and flees to a spa at Portorose, near Trieste, to recuperate.

April 18   Jean-Jules Roger-Ducasse's symphonic poem *Au jardin de Marguerite*, composed between 1901 and 1905, receives its first performance in Paris. This work was inspired by the story of Faust's visit to the garden of Marguerite.

May 15   Gian Francesco Malipiero's symphonic *Impressioni dal vero* (first set only) premieres in Milan. This work imitates the sound of birds.

June 5   American composer Henry F. Gilbert conducts the New York Philharmonic in the world premiere of his *Negro Rhapsody* in Norfolk, Connecticut. This student of Edward MacDowell uses Negro melodies and rhythms in his work.

June 7   Josef Matthias Hauer's Symphony No. 1 premieres in Sankt Polten, Austria. Subtitled *Nomos*, the work is by the man who subsequently claims he was the first to use the 12-tone method of composition. Although Hauer calls the work a symphony, it is scored for two pianos, four hands.

June 19   Claude Debussy's second book of Preludes *pour piano* is partially premiered at a concert in Paris, with the composer at the keyboard. The concert is prefaced by an explanatory lecture given by Emile Vuillermoz, a French music critic. The preludes premiered today are entitled "Canope," "La Terrasse des audiences du clair de lune" and "Hommage a Pickwick, Esq."

Sep. 5   Sergei Prokofiev, 22, performs the solo part in the world premiere of his Piano Concerto No. 2 in G Minor for piano and orchestra. The concert takes place in Saint Petersburg. Prokofiev revises this work in 1924. A review appearing in the Saint Petersburg *Gazetta* says the music is "... cacophony which has nothing to do with cultural music. His cadenzas are unsufferable. The Concerto is filled to overflow with musical mud, produced, one may imagine, by accidental spilling of ink on music paper."

Oct. 2   Edward Elgar conducts the premiere of his *Falstaff* at the Leeds Festival. Described by the composer as a "symphonic study in C minor with two interludes in A minor," the music is an orchestral portrait of the Shakespearean character.

Oct. 2   *On Hearing the First Cuckoo in Spring* and *Summer Night on the River* receive their initial performances in Leipzig. Composed by Frederick Delius, these pieces are both symphonic.

Oct. 12   Max Reger conducts his *4 Tondichtungen nach Arnold Bocklin* at its world premiere in Essen.

Dec. 3   Franz Schmidt's Symphony No. 2 receives its initial performance in Vienna. This three-movement symphony features a middle movement consisting of a theme with 10 variations.

Dec. 13   Serge Rachmaninoff conducts the premiere of his symphonic poem *The Bells* in Saint Petersburg. It is set to a Russian translation of Edgar Allan Poe's poem and features vocal soloists and chorus.

1913   Births, Deaths and Debuts

Jan. 24   Composer Norman Dello Joio is born in New York City.

Jan. 25   Composer Witold Lutoslawski is born in Warsaw, Poland.

Feb. 17   Composer, conductor and musicologist Rene Leibowitz is born in Warsaw, Poland.

March 2   Austrian tenor Richard Tauber makes his operatic debut at Chemnitz, singing Tamino in *The Magic Flute*.

March 27   Composer Godfrey Turner is born in Manchester, England.

April 2   Danish singer Lauritz Melchior makes his operatic debut as a baritone at the Royal Opera in Copenhagen as Silvio in *Pagliacci*.

April 13   Hungarian-American composer, cellist and conductor George Barati is born in Gyor, Hungary.

May 1   Conductor Walter Susskind is born in Prague, Czechoslovakia.

May 21   Pianist Gina Bachauer is born in Athens, Greece.

June 10   Composer Tikhon Khrennikov is born in Elets, Russia.

June 11   Mezzo-soprano Rise Stevens is born in New York City.

July 10   Soprano Ljuba Welitsch (real name Velitchk-ova) is born in Borisovo, Bulgaria.

July 22   Soprano Licia Albanese is born in Bari, Italy.

Aug. 7   David Popper, 70, dies in Baden. Born in Prague, he became a virtuoso cellist, composer of music for that instrument and a professor at the conservatory of Budapest. Among his most notable pieces are *Serenade orientale*, *Gavotte*, *Tarentelle*, *Elfentanz*, *Im Walde* and *Ungarische Rhapsodie*.

Aug. 14   Tenor Feruccio Tagliavini is born in Reggio, Italy.

Aug. 28   Tenor Richard Tucker (real name Reuben Ticker) is born in Brooklyn, New York.

Sep. 21   Musicologist Vincent Duckles is born in Boston, Massachusetts.

Oct. 5   Danish dancer, choreographer and ballet master Niels Bjorn Larsen is born in Copenhagen.

Oct. 15   Composer Henry Brant is born in Montreal, Canada.

Oct. 24   Baritone Tito Gobbi is born in Bassano del Grappa, Italy.

Nov. 17   Mathilde Marchesi, 92, dies in London. A noted voice teacher, she taught Nellie Melba, Emma Calve and other famous vocalists. She wrote instructional and autobiographical books and taught at the Vienna Conservatory and privately in Paris. Her own teacher was Manuel Garcia. She was married to Italian baritone Salvatore Marchesi de Castrone.

Nov. 20   Italian tenor Giovanni Martinelli makes his Metropolitan Opera debut as Cavaradossi in *Tosca*. Richard

MATHILDE MARCHESI AND NELLIE MELBA

Aldrich writes in the New York *Times*: "Martinelli here showed considerable power. His voice is of very good quality in the higher range, which he uses naturally and easily."

Nov. 22   Composer Benjamin Britten is born in Lowestoft, England.

Nov. 28   Rosa Raisa makes her American debut performing in *Aida* with the Chicago Opera.

Dec. 10   Composer Morton Gould is born in New York City.

1913   Related Events

A new annual opera festival begins this year at the Arena in Verona. Open-air performances begin with *Aida*. The festival was organized largely through the efforts of tenor Giovanni Zenatello. Performances are interrupted during the war years.

The San Francisco Symphony Orchestra purchases the library of the Pittsburgh Symphony Orchestra (that orchestra went out of business in 1910). This event substan-tially enhances Henry Hadley's ability, as music director, to be more flexible in programming.

Jan. 11   Camille Saint-Saens is awarded the Grand Croix of the Legion d'Honneur.

March 11   Italian futurist musician Luigi Russolo issues a manifesto entitled "The Art of Noises," which says in part, "We must break out of this narrow circle of pure musical sounds, and conquer the infinite variety of noise sounds."

June 2   Luigi Russolo premieres his ensemble of noise-makers in Modena. Built in collaboration with Ugo Piatti, these instruments can out-sound an audience.

June 21   The Houston Symphony Orchestra gives its first concert. Conducted by Paul Blitz, the program features music of Mozart, Bizet and Tchaikovsky.

July 6   Lili Boulanger receives the Premier Grand Prix de Rome. Each contestant composed a setting of "Faust and Helen" based on the tale by Goethe. Nadia Boulanger accompanies the performance of her sister's work. The vote, 31 to 5, makes Boulanger the first woman ever to receive this award.

Sep. 10   Romola de Pulszky marries Vaslav Nijinsky at City Hall in Buenos Aires after a voyage from Cherbourg during which the lady wooed the dancer-choreographer.

Sep. 18   The Gesellschaft der Musikfreunde of Donaueschingen is organized to perform modern music.

Oct. 19   The aerophor, invented by flutist Bernard Samuels, is used in a concert for the first time during the premiere of Richard Strauss' *Festival Prelude*. The invention sustains breathing and playing of wind instruments by allowing the player to pump additional air into his mouth from a foot pump attached to a tube, which, in turn, is attached to the instrument's mouthpiece. The invention does not become standard orchestral equipment. This event also marks the inaugural concert of the Konzert-Haus in Vienna.

Dec. 3   Serge Diaghilev, angered by Vaslav Nijinsky's marriage, dismisses the dancer from his company on the pretext that Nijinsky deliberately missed a performance in Buenos Aires.

Dec. 10   Claude Debussy conducts Serge Koussevitzky's orchestra in a program of his own music in Moscow. This marks the composer's first conducting appearance in Russia. He later states in his article "Lettre de Russie," published in the monthly bulletin of Societe Internationale de Musique in 1914, that the peasant audiences liked his music so much that they were reluctant to applaud."

1914 Opera

Jan. 2   *L'Amore dei tre rei*, an opera by Italo Montemezzi, receives its first American performance at the Metropolitan Opera in New York City. Arturo Toscanini conducts. The cast includes Lucrezia Bori, Edoardo Ferrari-Fontana, Pasquale Amato and Adamo Didur. Henry E. Krehbiel writes in the New York *Tribune* that the opera "would have delighted the soul of Verdi" and calls Montemezzi a genius.

Jan. 24   Gian Francesco Malipiero's *Canossa* premieres in Rome. The opera is about an emperor and a pope. Malipiero allegedly destroys the manuscript immediately because he is dissatisfied with the music.

Feb. 19   *Francesca da Rimini*, by Riccardo Zandonai, receives its premiere in Turin at the Teatro Regio. The text is by Tito Ricordi, based on the tragedy by Gabriele d'Annunzio. The libretto, based on part of Dante's *Divine Comedy*, is the story of Francesca, for whom a marriage has been arranged with Giancotto, who is lame; she is led to believe that she is going to marry Paolo, with whom she falls in love.

Feb. 23   Jules Massenet's final opera, *Cleopatre*, premieres in Monte Carlo. In three acts, it is about Cleopatra and her last lover.

April 1   Franz Schmidt's opera *Notre Dame*, with a libretto based on Victor Hugo's novel, premieres in Vienna. It is in two acts.

May 10   Engelbert Humperdinck's *Die Marketenderin* premieres in Cologne.

May 15   The premiere performance of *Marouf, Savetier du Caire*, by Henri Rabaud, takes place in Paris at the Opera-

EDOARDO FERRARI-FONTANA AND LUCREZIA BORI IN A SCENE FROM *L'AMORE DEI TRE RE*

Comique. Lucien Nepoty's libretto is based on a story from *The Arabian Nights* about a poor cobbler who leaves home to get away from his bad-tempered wife and ends up marrying a princess and finding a magic ring.

May 17 Felix Weingartner's one-act opera *Kain und Abel*, with his own libretto, premieres in Darmstadt.

May 26 *Le Rossignol*, an opera-ballet by Igor Stravinsky, is given its first performance at the Paris Opera by Serge Diaghilev's Ballets Russes. The libretto, written by the composer and Stephan Mitusov, is based on a fairy tale by Hans Christian Andersen about a nightingale who sings for the Emperor of China. Pierre Monteux conducts. The work is considered a masterpiece of both brilliance and discipline and enjoys frequent revivals; it is performed as a ballet in 1920. Critics pounce, however. Moreno says in *Le Menestrel* (Paris), "There reigns insufferable cacophony, an accumulation of bizarre chords which succeed one another without rhythm or justification; it seems like a wager that one can make the gullible public and the snobs swallow anything at all in our concert halls."

Aug. 26 *The Immortal Hour*, by Rutland Boughton, premieres in Glastonbury, England. The libretto, written by Fiona Macleod (the pseudonym of William Sharp), deals with an ill-fated marriage between a fairy princess and a mortal king.

Oct. 10 Joaquin Turina's opera *Margot* premieres in Madrid. After studies at the Madrid Conservatory and with Vincent d'Indy in Paris, this composer writes characteristically Spanish music.

1914 Dance

April 16 *Les Papillons* — a one-act ballet choreographed by Michel Fokine — is performed by Serge Diaghilev's Ballets Russes in Monte Carlo. This is a retitled and re-staged version of Fokine's *Papillon*, premiered last May 10th.

May 14 Richard Strauss' *La legende de Joseph* is premiered by Serge Diaghilev's Ballets Russes in Paris, the composer conducting. The choreography is by Michel Fokine. Leonide Massine plays Joseph in his debut with Diaghilev's company.

May 21 Serge Diaghilev's Ballets Russes premieres Michel Fokine's staging of *Le coq d'or* (an opera, but performed today as a ballet) at the Paris Opera. Music is by Nikolai Rimsky-Korsakov, decor by Nathalie Gontcharova. The production has two casts, one singing and one dancing. The evening-length work, based on a narrative poem by Pushkin, tells the story of a Russian tsar who is given a golden cockerel that will crow when his kingdom is in danger. Despite the bird's warnings, the tsar loses his kingdom and his bird. The principal dancers are Tamara Karsavina (Queen of Shemakhan), Alexis Bulgakov (King Dodon) and Enrico Cecchetti. This ballet performance brings the work to world attention: Its original premiere as an opera (October 7, 1909 at the Bolshoi Theater in Moscow) was not very successful.

June 2 *Midas*, choreographed by Michel Fokine, receives its first performance by Serge Diaghilev's Ballets Russes in Paris. Tamara Karsavina and Adolph Bolm star. The music is by Maximilian Steinberg, the decor by Mstislav Doboujinsky. This is the last ballet Fokine choreographs for this company.

Dec. 3 Isadora Duncan's *Ave Maria*, with music by Franz Schubert, receives its world premiere at Carnegie Hall, New York City.

1914 Instrumental and Vocal Music

Feb. 17 Ernst von Dohnanyi's *Variations on a Nursery Song* premieres in Berlin with the composer performing the part for solo piano. The work parodies a number of musical styles. In *Essays in Musical Analysis*, Sir Donald Tovey will comment 25 years from now, "Dohnanyi's Variations must rank high among the modern classics in one of the severest of art forms."

March 11 Sergei Liapunov's symphonic poem *Hashish* premieres in Saint Petersburg.

March 27 Symphony No. 2 (*A London Symphony*), by Ralph Vaughan Williams, receives its world premiere in London, Geoffrey Toye conducting. Scored for large orchestra with heavy percussion, the four-movement symphony was inspired by the London life of this composer. Vaughan Williams revises the symphony four times.

March 29 Alfredo Casella's *Notte di Maggio* is premiered by the orchestra of Concerts Colonne in Paris, the composer conducting. The work is scored for voice and orchestra.

April 5 Igor Stravinsky's *Le Sacre du printemps* is performed as a concert work for the first time by Pierre Monteux in Paris.

April 21 Luigi Russolo's *Networks of Noises* premieres in Milan. The music features thunderers, exploders, whistlers, gurglers, snorers. Audience reaction is extremely negative.

June 2 Nikolai Miaskovsky's Symphony No. 1 in C Minor premieres in Pavlovsk, in the vicinity of Saint Petersburg. First performances of his symphonies do not necessarily occur in the order in which they were composed. His Second Symphony premiered back in 1912.

June 4 Jean Sibelius' *Oceanides* premieres at a concert featuring other music of this composer at the Litchfield County Choral Union in Norwalk, Connecticut, the composer conducting. This event marks the composer's first visit to America.

July 10 Herbert Howells' Piano Concerto in C Minor premieres with Arthur Benjamin, soloist, in London. This piece was written while Howells was a student at the Royal College of Music in London where he studied with Charles Villiers Stanford and Sir Charles Hubert Parry. He writes choral as well as instrumental music.

Oct. 13 Eugene Goossens' symphonic work *Perseus* premieres at a Promenade Concert in London.

Dec. 2 Igor Stravinsky's *Three Poems from the Japanese* premieres in Petrograd. These songs are scored for soprano, two flutes, two clarinets, piano and string quartet.

Dec. 7 Edward Elgar's *Carillon* premieres at a Promenade Concert in London. The patriotic work is scored for voice and orchestra.

Dec. 18 Arnold Schoenberg's *Five Pieces for Orchestra*, Op. 16, receives its first American performance as Karl Muck conducts the Boston Symphony Orchestra in Boston. Originally premiered on September 3, 1912 in London, today's performance provokes a similarly nasty reaction from the critics. Louis Elson writes in the Boston *Daily Advertiser*, "It has been said that it is difficult to score a noise well... Schoenberg has certainly succeeded in doing this." The Boston *Globe* says of Schoenberg, "his emotions are fit subjects for a vacuum cleaner." Olin Downes writes in the Boston *Post*, "it appears as the music of raw and tortured nerves."

1914 Births, Deaths and Debuts

Jan. 17 Arnold Schoenberg makes his London debut as a conductor, conducting his *Five Pieces for Orchestra*, Op. 16. The world premiere of this work also took place in London on September 3, 1912. Of today's performance, the *Daily Telegraph* (London) says the music "suggested feeding time at the zoo; also a farmyard in great activity while pigs are being ringed and geese strangled." The concert is also reported in *Musical America* (New York), whose headlines state the work is "Reminiscent of a Nightmare."

Feb. 10 Harmonica player Larry Adler is born in Baltimore, Maryland.

Feb. 26 Polish composer-conductor Witold Rowicki is born in Taganrog, Russia.

March 6 Conductor Kiril Kondrashin is born in Moscow, Russia.

May 9 Conductor Carlo Maria Giulini is born in Barletta, Italy.

May 10 American soprano Lillian Nordica, 56, dies in Batavia, Java, during a world concert tour. Born Lillian Norton, she made her operatic debut in 1879 in Milan and became one of the great Wagnerian sopranos of her time.

May 10 Austrian conductor Ernst von Schuch, 67, dies in Dresden, where he had spent most of his career. As conductor of the Dresden Court Opera for 40 years, he led the world premieres of several Strauss operas — *Salome, Elektra* and *Rosenkavalier* — and introduced many Italian works to Germany. He was considered one of the finest operatic conductors of his time.

May 18 Bass Boris Christoff is born in Plovdiv, Bulgaria.

June 26 Tenor Wolfgang Windgassen is born in Annemasse, Haute Savoie, France.

June 29 Conductor Rafael Kubelik is born in Bychory, Czechoslovakia. He is the son of violinist Jan Kubelik.

Aug. 2 French composer Gabriel Dupont, 36, dies in Paris. A pupil of Charles-Marie Widor, he went on to compose piano and orchestral music, and put great effort into his opera *Antar*, which is in rehearsal and is indefinitely postponed due to his death and the outbreak of World War I.

Aug. 9 Conductor Ferenc Fricsay is born in Budapest, Hungary.

Aug. 12 French bass Pol Plancon, 63, dies in Paris. Known for his elegant singing and strong stage personality, he debuted in 1877. He became famous as Mephistofeles in Gounod's *Faust*, a part that served as his debut role in London (1891) and New York (1893). He elected to stay in America at the Metropolitan Opera until he retired in 1906.

Aug. 28   Russian composer Anatoly Liadov, 59, dies in Novgorod. Son of an opera conductor and grandson of the Saint Petersburg Philharmonic Society's conductor, he studied at the Saint Petersburg Conservatory and was a composition pupil of Nikolai Rimsky-Korsakov. He was a truant and was expelled, but was later allowed to take his final examinations, graduated and was appointed to the faculty as a teacher of harmony and theory. He held this position throughout his life. His pupils included Sergei Prokofiev, Nikolai Miaskovsky and Boris Asafiev. As a composer, he was attracted to Russian folklore. This is reflected especially in his arrangements of Russian songs. He was not a prolific composer and is best known for his works in smaller forms; these include the piano cycle *Birulki* and the orchestral tableaux *Baba Yaga, Enchanted Lake* and *Kikimora.*

Sep. 3   Composer Alberic Magnard, 48, is shot and killed in his home on the Marne, France, as he combats the invading German troops. Trained at Ramsgate and at the Paris Conservatoire under Theodore Dubois and Jules Massenet, he later studied with Vincent d'Indy. His work includes chamber music, symphonies and an opera, *Yolande.*

Sep. 5   American composer Gail Kubik is born in South Coffeyville, Oklahoma.

Sep. 19   Serbian composer Stevan Mokranjac, 58, dies in Skopje, Yugoslavia. He was a prolific composer of church music.

Sep. 24   Composer Andrzej Panufnik is born in Warsaw, Poland.

Oct. 27   Austrian composer Richard Heuberger, 64, dies in Vienna. He is noted especially for his operetta *Das Opern-*

ball. Heuberger taught at the Vienna Conservatory (1902), conducted the Mannergesangverein (1902–9) and also wrote criticism for the *Wiener Tageblatt,* the *Neue Freie Presse* and other tabloids.

Oct. 30   Composer and conductor Marius Flothius is born in Amsterdam, Holland.

Nov. 15   Pianist Jorge Bolet is born in Havana, Cuba.

Nov. 20   Elisabeth Schumann makes her Metropolitan Opera debut as Sophie in *Der Rosenkavalier.* W.J. Henderson, in the New York *Sun,* says she has "A light lyric soprano voice of beautiful natural quality."

Dec. 14   Italian pianist and composer Giovanni Sgambati, 73, dies in Rome. A pupil of Franz Liszt, he conducted the first Rome performance of Beethoven's Third Symphony in 1866. Between his concertizing as a pianist and conductor, he quickly established himself as the one Italian conductor of his generation to bring a wide variety of symphonic music before the Italian public. His piano class at the Accademia de Santa Cecilia, Rome led to the recognition of the Liceo Musicale as Italy's foremost music school. Two symphonies, a piano concerto, a string quartet, nocturnes, two piano quintets (his two most famous works) and other pieces comprise his output.

Dec. 14   Pianist and harpsichordist Rosalyn Tureck is born in Chicago, Illinois.

Dec. 16   Croatian composer Giovanni von Zaytz (born Ivan Zajc), 83, dies in Zagreb. He was a conductor of the Zagreb Opera and composed over 1,200 works. His opera *Nikola Subric Zrinski,* premiered November 4, 1876, was the first Croatian national opera. He also directed the Zagreb Conservatory until 1908.

1914   Related Events

Feb. 13   ASCAP — the American Society of Composers, Authors, and Publishers — is established at the Hotel Claridge, New York City. The purpose of this organization is to protect the performing rights of its members and distribute royalties to them. Victor Herbert is named director.

March 7   Cecil Forsyth completes the Preface to his book *Orchestration,* published this year by Macmillan and Company (London). The book is one of the first on orchestration published this century that attempts to describe the origin, technological developments and sonic characteristics of modern orchestral instruments.

March 29   Writer Felix Borowski's article "The New Futurism" is published in the Chicago *Record Herald.* He says, "Mr. Schoenberg, apostle of queer harmony, is not the true futurist." He goes on to say that Balilla Pratella probably stands a greater chance of becoming the true futurist.

April 23   Soprano Olive Fremstad sings her farewell performance at the Metropolitan Opera as Elsa in *Lohengrin.* Krehbiel of the New York *Tribune* writes, "The asbestos curtain was lowered four times in an effort to halt the cheers. . . but not until Mme. Fremstad had appeared and bowed more than forty times would her admirers depart from the house. . . . It was a superb tribute to the woman who has been one of the chief glories of the Metropolitan."

May 24   Sergei Prokofiev performs his Piano Concerto No. 1 in D-flat Major at a commencement ceremony at the Saint Petersburg Conservatory and wins a grand piano as the Rubinstein Prize.

June 1   The Fifth Congress of the International Musical Society meets in Paris. This event marks the final congress of the society prior to its termination due to World War I.

June 14   Richard Strauss is awarded the order of Chevalier of the Legion d'Honneur by the French government.

June 17   Jean Sibelius is awarded the honorary degree of doctor of music by Yale University.

July 10   Pope Pius X confers a new title on the Superior School of Religious Music in Rome. As of today it is the Pontifical Institute of Sacred Music and has, by papal approval, the power to grant masters and doctoral degrees in composition, organ and Gregorian chant.

July 15   Violinist Efrem Zimbalist and Alma Gluck are married in London.

Aug. 1   Germany declares war on Russia marking the beginning of World War I.

Aug. 15   Edward Elgar's *Sospiri* and Tchaikovsky's *Capriccio italien* are substituted for Richard Strauss' *Don Juan* at the first concert of the season of the Promenade Concerts in London. Due to the outbreak of the war, the substitution follows British policy not to perform music by German composers.

Sep. 19   Camille Saint-Saens publishes an article in *L'Echo de Paris* urging that Richard Wagner's operas not be performed in France and condemning German art and music.

Sep. 30   The International Musical Society is officially disbanded due to World War I. German music publisher Breitkopf & Hartel makes the announcement. This society was founded (in 1899) to create an international federation of musicians and music lovers who would work to further musicological research. It held periodic congresses and issued various publications, including *Zeitschrift der Internationalen Musikgesellschaft* (*ZIM* — a monthly periodical) and *Sammelbande der Internationalen Musikgesellschaft* (*SIM* — a quarterly).

1915 Opera

Jan. 25   *Madame Sans-Gene*, by Umberto Giordano, has its first performance at the Metropolitan Opera in New York. It is conducted by Arturo Toscanini. The libretto — written by Renato Simoni, based on the play of the same name by Victorien Sardou and Emile Moreau — is set in France during and after the revolution. The opera is very well received but does not become a favorite. Geraldine Farrar, Giovanni Martinelli and Pasquale Amato star. Henry Krehbiel writes in the New York *Herald-Tribune*, "there are many pages of ''Sans-Gene'' which we would gladly exchange for any one of the melodies of 'Le coq'."

March 20   *Fedra*, by Ildebrando Pizzetti, premieres at the Teatro alla Scala in Milan. The text, by Gabriele d'Annunzio, is based on the Greek myth of Phaedra. The opera is well received by both the critics and the public.

July 1   Horatio Parker's *Fairyland* premieres in Los Angeles. The opera is about a nun who takes a lover — a lover who is a fairy. The work was awarded the $10,000 prize of the National Federation of Women's Clubs. Like Parker's first opera, *Mona*, it is not very successful.

Sep. 26   *Mona Lisa*, a two-act opera by Max von Schillings, receives its first performance in Stuttgart, the composer conducting. The opera is about a couple on their honeymoon who hear the story of Mona Lisa and become the contemporary counterparts of Mona Lisa and Gi-

ocondo. The text is by Beatrice Dovsky. The cast includes Hedy Iracema-Brugelmann and John Forsell.

GERALDINE FARRAR, GIOVANNI MARTINELLI AND PASQUALE AMATO IN A SCENE FROM *MADAME SANS GENE*

1915 Dance

Jan. 19   Isadora Duncan's *Dionysion* premieres at the Metropolitan Opera House in New York City.

Feb. 22   *The Garden of Kama* — a modern dance work choreographed by Ruth Saint Denis and Ted Shawn — receives its first performance in San Francisco. This year, these choreographers open their school — Denishawn — in Los Angeles.

April 15   Manuel de Falla's *El amor brujo* premieres at the Teatro Lara in Madrid. Scored for mezzo-soprano and orchestra, the ballet is choreographed and danced by Pastora Imperio. The one-act work, which features Spanish dance rhythms, also includes the "Ritual Fire Dance." The libretto is by G. Martinez.

Dec. 20   Leonide Massine's ballet *La soleil de nuit* receives its first performance by Serge Diaghilev's Ballets Russes at the Grand Theater in Geneva. The one-act work uses music from *Snegourotchka*, an opera by Nikolai Rimsky-Korsakov. This is Massine's first ballet.

1915 Instrumental and Vocal Music

Jan. 24   Ottorino Respighi's *Sinfonia drammatica*, a three-movement orchestral work, premieres in Rome.

Feb. 5   Max Reger's *Variationen und Fuge uber ein Thema von Mozart*, Op. 132, and *Eine vaterlandische Ouverture* receive their first performances in Berlin with Reger conducting. The latter piece is dedicated to the German army, which, at the moment, is engaged in World War I. The overture incorporates patriotic German songs, including "Deutschland, Deutschland, uber alles."

Feb. 27   Nikolai Miaskovsky's Symphony No. 3 in A Minor premieres in Moscow. This romantic symphony, composed last year, is in two movements.

March 10   Serge Rachmaninoff's *Vesper Mass* receives its first performance in Moscow. It is scored for *a capella* chorus.

March 15   *Paraphrases of the National Anthems of the Allied Nations*, by Alexander Glazunov, receives its first performance at the Petrograd Conservatory, the composer conducting. This concert had been organized for patriotic reasons (World War I is in progress). The composition incorporates passages from the national anthems of Japan, Belgium, England, France, Montenegro, Serbia and Russia.

March 19   John Alden Carpenter's orchestral suite *Adventures in a Perambulator* is premiered by the Chicago Symphony Orchestra. The music is impressionistic in style. A former pupil of Edward Elgar, Carpenter earns his living in the shipping industry.

March 20   Alexander Scriabin's *Prometheus (The Poem of Fire)* receives its first American performance by Modest Altschuler and the Russian Symphony Orchestra at Carnegie Hall, New York City. This performance attempts to use the composer's lighting changes, which are projected onto a screen. The light apparatus (a keyboard, which — when played — produces lights as well as sound) was devised by the Electrical Testing Laboratories at the request of the conductor and does not work properly. Altschuler also insists that this performance is the real world premiere of *Prometheus* because it is the first to use colored lights. The work is played twice, some critics noting that the color combinations are different with each rendition. H.T. Finck writes in the *Evening Post* (New York), "The whole thing seemed childish, and it certainly was a bore long before it was over." *Musical America* (New York) says *Prometheus* is "unquestionably one of those hot-house products which the spiritually stagnant and mephitic atmosphere of Europe before the war engendered in large numbers."

March 28   Symphony No. 2 in A Major, by Georges Enesco, now 33, premieres in Bucharest, the composer conducting. The symphony is both romantic and neobaroque.

April 14   Sergei Taneyev's cantata *At the Reading of the Psalms* receives its first performance by Serge Koussevitzky in Moscow. The music, based on the modes of Russian Orthodox liturgy, is Taneyev's last piece.

June 19   Camille Saint-Saens' *Hail, California!* premieres at the Panama-Pacific International Exposition as a specially commissioned work. The composer conducts.

July 6   Edward Elgar's symphonic poem *Polonia* premieres in London. The work was composed for the benefit of the Polish Relief Fund.

Oct. 28   *Eine Alpensinfonie*, by Richard Strauss, is premiered in Berlin by the Berlin Philharmonic Orchestra, the composer conducting. This work is scored for large orchestra and additional percussion — wind and thunder machines. Leopold Schmidt writes of it in the *Berliner Tageblatt* (Berlin), ". . . it is at present the first and the only towering musical monument from the great era in which we live."

Nov. 10   Claude Debussy's *Douze Etudes* for piano are performed for the first time by Marguerite Long at a concert of the Societe Nationale de Musique in Paris. The *etudes* range in difficulty from simple five-finger exercises to rapid, repeated rhythmic arpeggiations and chromatic passages.

Dec. 8   Symphony No. 5 in E-flat Major, by Jean Sibelius, is performed for the first time in Helsinki, the composer conducting. This three-movement symphony reflects the composer's nationalistic sentiments. It will be performed in a revised version on December 14, 1916.

1915   Births, Deaths and Debuts

Jan. 2   Austro-Hungarian composer Karl Goldmark, 84, dies in Vienna. This composer studied violin in his youth and received formal training at the Vienna Conservatory. When he was 35, his overture *Sakuntala* premiered, bringing him his first fame. Ten years later his opera *Die Konigin von Saba* brought him to international attention. He composed a total of eight operas, seven overtures and various other works. He was also the uncle of American composer Rubin Goldmark.

Feb. 9   American dancer, choreographer and teacher Anna Sokolow is born in Hartford, Connecticut.

Feb. 11   Percy Grainger makes his debut in New York City, giving his first piano recital in America. The concert takes place at Aeolian Hall. His program includes music by Ferruccio Busoni, Johann Sebastian Bach, Edvard Grieg, Maurice Ravel and others. A review by Herbert F. Peyser in *Musical America* [New York] says, "Grainger's performances are surcharged with electricity, with veritable musical ozone."

Feb. 16   Alsatian composer Emil Waldteufel, 77, dies in Paris. Known principally as a composer of waltz music and a pianist, he studied at the Strasbourg and Paris Conservatories. Waldteufel spent virtually his entire life in Paris, where Parisians loved his waltzes. He made occasional tours to London, Berlin and Vienna and, at age 28, was selected by Empress Eugenie (director of court balls) to be one of her chamber musicians. His dances number at least 268 (most for large orchestra), and his music successfully (but briefly) competed with that of Johann Strauss.

Feb. 19   French musicologist and music writer Jules Ecorcheville, 42, dies in combat at the battle of Perthesles-Hurlus in Champagne. A pupil of Cesar Franck, his writings include studies of Lully and Rameau as well as a 10,000-item catalog of ancient materials in the Bibliotheque Nationale.

March 4   Spanish-American composer Carlos Surinach is born in Barcelona, Spain.

March 10   Conductor Charles Groves is born in London, England.

March 20   Pianist Sviatoslav Richter is born in Zhitomir, Russia.

April 27   Russian composer Alexander Scriabin, 43, dies in Moscow from blood poisoning, resulting from a lip abscess. He studied composition with Sergei Taneyev and piano with Vassily Safonov at the Moscow Conservatory. His career got underway when Mitrofan Belaiev financed a European tour for him. Scriabin's debut as a composer-pianist was in Paris (1895). His first important composition (Concerto for Piano and Orchestra, Op. 20) premiered in Odessa (1897).

Scriabin later met Serge Koussevitzky, who became one of his strongest supporters, both in terms of financing the publication of his works and conducting performances of his music. Koussevitzky and Scriabin later severed their professional relationship over financial quarrels and ego conflict.

Scriabin was fascinated by color and developed specific correspondences between color and pitch. He attempted on several occasions to perform with a color organ and colored lights to communicate his vision, but these experiments were largely failures.

Scriabin's impact on 20th-century music was due, in part, to his approach to harmony: intense chromaticism coupled with chords built on fourths. His "mystic chord" became a harmonic trademark of his *Promethee*.

May 6   Composer and theorist George Perle is born in Bayonne, New Jersey.

May 7   Irish composer O'Brien Butler goes down with the SS *Lusitania*. His exact date of birth is unknown, though the year is presumed to have been 1870. His studies included work at the Royal Academy of Music (London). His opera *Muirgheis* (produced in 1903) was the first Irish opera with a Gaelic libretto.

June 6   Composer Vincent Persichetti is born in Philadelphia, Pennsylvania.

June 19   Russian composer and teacher Sergei Taneyev, 58, dies in Dyudkovo, near Moscow. A pupil of Peter Ilyich Tchaikovsky (of whom he became a close friend) at the Moscow Conservatory, he made his debut in that city in 1875 as a pianist. After several tours he joined the faculty of the Moscow Conservatory, teaching harmony, orchestration and piano. He soon devoted himself to composition and to writing treatises on music. His book *Convertible Counterpoint in the Strict Style* (originally published in

Russian in 1909; in English in 1962) is one of several such systematic presentations of his compositional techniques. As a composer, his style blended Russian elements with a German approach to counterpoint. Although his work quickly became revered in Russia, its recognition elsewhere was minimal. His *Oresteia* trilogy, based on Aeschylus and premiered in 1895, is probably his best-known work.

June 25   Hungarian-American pianist Rafael Joseffy, 62, dies in New York City. He studied at the Leipzig Conservatory with E.F. Wenzel and later with Karl Tausig in Berlin and Franz Liszt in Weimar. His debut came in Berlin (at age 18), and nine years later he made his American debut performing under Leopold Damrosch in New York City. His career in America eventually became solidified, and he taught, wrote and composed as well as performed. He also edited a renowned 15-volume edition of Chopin's compositions.

July 9   Composer David Diamond is born in Rochester, New York.

July 27   Tenor Mario Del Monaco is born in Florence, Italy.

Aug. 25   Violist Walter Trampler is born in Munich, Germany.

Aug. 26   Composer Humphrey Searle is born in Oxford, England.

Sep. 23   Flutist Julius Baker is born in Cleveland, Ohio.

Oct. 14   Hungarian pianist Erwin Nyiregyhazi makes his debut with the Berlin Philharmonic playing Beethoven's Third Piano Concerto. He is 12 years old.

Nov. 11   Brazilian pianist Guiomar Novaes makes her New York debut.

Nov. 13   Heitor Villa-Lobos makes his debut as a composer in Rio de Janeiro. The concert features his Piano Trio No. 1 and the Sonata No. 2 for violin and piano. Other works on the program include songs. Now 28, Villa-Lobos has dropped out of the National Music Institute (Rio de Janeiro) because of his temper and his disagreements with his professors.

Nov. 14   Austrian pianist and teacher Theodor Leschetizky, 85, dies in Dresden, Germany. A pupil of Carl Czerny, he began teaching when he was 15 years old. He later taught at the Saint Petersburg Conservatory and in Vienna. His students included Ignace Paderewski, Ossip Gabrilowitsch and Artur Schnabel. Known for his arched-hand technique of piano playing, he emphasized free wrist movement for playing octaves and chords.

Nov. 18   Austrian conductor Artur Bodanzky makes his Metropolitan Opera debut conducting *Die Gotterdammerung*. Richard Aldrich says in the New York *Times* that Bodanzky's conducting is full of "the red blood of dramatic power... "and pulses"... with the ebb and flow of passion."

Nov. 25   Italian baritone Giuseppe De Luca makes his Metropolitan Opera debut as Figaro in *The Barber of Seville*. Richard Aldrich writes in the New York *Times* that De Luca has "... intelligence and comic power...."

Nov. 26   Pianist Earl Wild is born in Pittsburgh, Pennsylvania.

Nov. 29   Music critic Harold Schonberg is born in New York City.

Dec. 9   Soprano Elisabeth Schwarzkopf is born in Jarotschin, near Poznan, Germany.

1915 Related Events

The recording industry witnesses the birth of a new recording company — Garrard Engineering — which is founded as a subsidiary of Garrard & Company Crown Jewellers. Events this year also include the beginnings of the recording industry in Argentina.

The Interpretation of the Music of the XVIIth and XVIIIth Centuries, by Arnold Dolmetsch, is published this year by Novello & Company in London. The book, edited by Ernest Newman, is devoted to unraveling notation problems in order to postulate correct performance practice for music of the 17th and 18th centuries. Its chapters cover expression, tempo, alterations of rhythm, ornamentation, figured basses, fingering position and musical instruments of those centuries.

The Longy School of Music is founded this year in Cambridge, Massachusetts.

Jan. 1   G. Schirmer publishes the first issue of *The Musical Quarterly*, edited by Oscar George Sonneck of the Library of Congress.

Feb. 8   Richard Wagner's *The Ride of the Valkyries* is featured as a Ku Klux Klan call in D.W. Griffith's film *The Birth of a Nation*, which opens a national run today in America.

Feb. 8   Music of Manuel de Falla, Enrique Granados and Joaquin Turina is featured at the first concert of the Sociedad Nacional de Musica in Madrid. This society is formed to promote Spanish music.

April 15   Alexander Scriabin performs his last recital in public, playing his *Five Preludes*, Op. 74, at the Petrograd Conservatory. The preludes are polytonal and atonal. This set of preludes is also his last composition — within the next few days Scriabin develops an abscess on his lip, which leads to blood poisoning and death.

May 7   Upon hearing the news of the torpedoing of the *Lusitania*, Charles Ives commits the tragedy to music, titling his Second Orchestral Set "From Hanover Square North at the End of a Tragic Day the Voice of the People Again Arose."

May 14   Karl Muck conducts the Boston Symphony Orchestra in the first of a series of 13 concerts in San Francisco. These concerts feature music of all countries and are performed at the Panama-Pacific International Exposition.

May 29   The Lewisohn Stadium of the College of the City of New York opens. A gift of Adolph Lewisohn, its summer concerts are scheduled to begin in 1917.

June 9   A charge of treason is placed against Riccardo Zandonai by the Austrian governor of the province of Trieste for having composed a hymn that advocates the regaining of lost provinces by Italy. The composer was born in Tyrol.

July 14   The ashes of French composer Claude-Joseph Rouget de Lisle are transferred from Choisy-le-Roi, France to the Invalides in Paris, marking the final recognition of "La Marseillaise" as being an original tune by this composer. He was born in 1760 and wrote the words and music to "La Marseillaise" on April 25, 1792. He was imprisoned by Robespierre because he supported the French monarchy. He then lived in virtual poverty until he finally received a pension from Louis-Philippe. It was only through the efforts of his nephew, Amedee Rouget de Lisle, that "La Marseillaise" was finally attributed to its composer.

Oct. 12   Emile Jaques-Dalcroze's Institute for Eurythmics moves from Hellerau, Germany, to Geneva, Switzerland, due to the war.

Oct. 12   Alfred Hertz — a conductor from the Metropolitan Opera of New York — becomes music director of the San Francisco Symphony Orchestra. He holds this post for 15 years, during which he hires the first woman player in a major American symphony orchestra.

Dec. 1   American inventor Lee de Forest states that he has created lovely sounding musical tones produced by vacuum tubes. He describes this in an article, "Audion Bulbs as Producers of Pure Musical Tones," published in *The Electrical Experimenter*.

1916   Opera

Jan. 14   Charles Villiers Stanford's *The Critic, or an Open Rehearsal* is premiered by Eugene Goossens in London. This two-act comic opera is about two characters who debate the meaning of art. Based on a play by Richard Brinsley Sheridan, the text is by Lewis Cairns James. The cast includes Frank Mullings, Percy Hemming and Frederick Ranalow.

Jan. 28   *Goyescas* by Enrique Granados, premieres at the Metropolitan Opera House in New York. The characters and setting for the opera were inspired by the works of Goya, the Spanish painter, and the music was adapted from a set of piano pieces Granados had written on the themes of several of Goya's paintings. The cast of today's production includes Anna Fitziu (who makes her Metropolitan debut), Giovanni Martinelli and Giuseppe De Luca. Herbert F. Peyser writes in *Musical America* (New York), "The little work possesses some decided merits and appealing beauties, but it also has a number of egregious flaws. . ." *Goyescas* is also Granados' last opera. It is premiered in New York rather than Paris, as had been originally planned, because of the war. Granados is invited to New York for the premiere, and on his way back to Europe his boat is torpedoed by the Germans, and he and his wife perish.

Jan. 28   Ethel Mary Smyth's *The Boatswain's Mate* receives its premiere at the Shaftesbury Theatre in London. The composer writes her own libretto, basing it on W.W. Jacobs' *Captains All*, about a pompous boatswain, Harry Benn, who persuades Travers, a former soldier, to help him in a scheme to persuade a Mrs. Waters to marry him. The scheme backfires.

Feb. 23   Felix Weingartner's opera *Dame Kobold* receives its initial performance in Darmstadt. The composer wrote the libretto to this three-act opera.

March 5   Eugene d'Albert's one-act opera with prologue *Die toten Augen* premieres in Dresden. It is about a blind woman cured by Jesus who later stares at the sun until she again becomes blind. The work was completed three years ago.

March 24   *Master-Builder*, by Greek composer Manolis Kalomiris, is premiered in Athens. This two-act opera, the first by Kalomiris, is about a young architect who rejects love for art. Born in Turkey in 1883, Kalomiris settled in

Greece in 1910 and sparks nationalism in Greek music through the use of Greek folk tunes.

March 28   *Violanta* and *Der Ring des Polykrates* — two one-act operas by Erich Wolfgang Korngold — receive their first performances in Munich. *Violanta* is about chastity, passion, revenge and murder. *Der Ring des Polykrates* is about an emotional conflict between a drummer, a maidservant and a kapellmeister. Korngold is now 18.

Oct. 4   The second version of *Ariadne auf Naxos*, by Richard Strauss, receives its first performance in Vienna at the Hofoper. In this version an operatic prelude is added to eliminate the requirement of having both an operatic and a theatrical company perform simultaneously. The earlier version of the opera, performed on October 25, 1912, was conceived as a postlude for Moliere's *Le Bourgeois Gentilhomme*. The cast of today's performance includes Maria

Jeritza, Selma Kurz and Lotte Lehmann. Franz Schalk conducts.

Nov. 21   Mikhail Ippolitov-Ivanov's four-act opera *Ole from Nordland* receives its first performance in Moscow. It is about a Norwegian fisherman in love.

Dec. 5   The first performance of *Savitri*, by Gustav Holst, takes place in London at Wellington Hall. The libretto is based on a tale from the Indian epic poem *Mahabharata*, about a woman who defeats Death's attempt to take her husband away from her. The opera is very well received in England.

Dec. 6   *Elga*, an opera in seven scenes by Erwin Lendvai, is performed for the first time in Mannheim. It is based on the play by Gerhardt Hauptmann. Lendvai is currently teacher of dramatic composition at the Hoch's Conservatory in Frankfurt.

1916   Dance

Jan. 17   Michel Fokine's *The Firebird* receives its first American performance as Serge Diaghilev's Ballets Russes performs the work in New York City. Leonide Massine and Xenia Maclezova are the lead dancers. Also performed during the next week on this tour engagement are Vaslav Nijinsky's *L'Apres-midi d'un Faune*, Fokine's *Carnaval*, and Igor Stravinsky's *Petrouchka*. The last ballet features Massine, Lydia Lopokova, and Adolph Bolm.

Jan. 20   *Les Sylphides* receives its American premiere. It is performed by Serge Diaghilev's Ballets Russes in New York City and supersedes the performance by Gertrude Hoffman of 1911 that had not been authorized.

July 29   *Life and Afterlife in Egypt, Greece and India* is performed for the first time in Los Angeles. The modern dance work is choreographed by Ruth Saint Denis and Ted Shawn.

Oct. 23   Vaslav Nijinsky's *Til Eulenspiegel*, with costumes and scenery by Robert Edmond Jones, is performed for the first time by Serge Diaghilev's Ballets Russes in New York to music by Richard Strauss. Nijinsky had been in Budapest and was promptly interned by the Hungarian government when World War I broke out. Although Diaghilev has severed relations with Nijinsky because the latter decided to get married, he nevertheless helped Nijinsky get out of Hungary so he could fulfill the requirement of the Metropolitan Opera that Nijinsky dance with the company during its engagement.

SERGE DIAGHILEV (RIGHT OF CENTER) WITH SOME OF HIS COMPANY ON TOUR IN THE UNITED STATES. LEONIDE MASSINE IS THIRD FROM THE LEFT.

1916 *Instrumental and Vocal Music*

Jan. 17   Ferruccio Busoni's *Indianische Fantasie* premieres in Zurich, with the composer as soloist. Composed in 1913, it is scored for piano and orchestra. Now living in Zurich, Busoni is attracting many students who are fascinated with his new ideas about musical esthetics.

Jan. 17   *Hebridean Symphony*, by Granville Bantock, receives its first performance in Glasgow. The piece, in four movements, includes pentatonic melodies and Wagnerian harmonies.

Jan. 29   The world premiere of *Scythian Suite*, by Sergei Prokofiev, takes place as the composer conducts the work in Petrograd. Originally intended as a ballet, it is subtitled "Ala and Lolli" and contains music depicting an evil dance, sun worshipping, a sunrise and a nocturne. It is Prokofiev's first important orchestral composition. A reviewer for the *Petrograd Listok* says, "It produces some kind of aggressive, crude sound which expresses nothing but infinite braggadocio." Also on today's program is the first performance of Nicolas Tcherepnin's *The Masque of the Red Death*. The composer conducts this piece, which he describes as a "choreographic poem"; it is based on the tale by Edgar Allan Poe.

Feb. 1   Carl Nielsen's Symphony No 4 (*The Inextinguishable*) receives its first performance in Copenhagen with the composer conducting. Nielsen, now 50, is conducting the Music Society (Musikforeningen) in Copenhagen.

March 10   John Alden Carpenter's *Concertino* for piano and orchestra is premiered by Percy Grainger and the Chicago Symphony Orchestra.

March 13   Frank Bridge's tone poem *Summer* receives its premiere in London, the composer conducting.

April 9   Manuel de Falla's *Noches en los jardines de Espana* is premiered by Enrique Fernandez Arbos, with Jose Cubiles as piano soloist. The Orquesta Filarmonica of Madrid performs. This piece, a suite for piano and orchestra, is in three movements.

Oct. 29   Charles Stanford Skilton's *Two Indian Dances* premieres in Minneapolis. The work is in two parts, and today's performance constitutes Part 1. Skilton studied with Dudley Buck and is now teaching organ at the University of Kansas in Lawrence.

Dec. 10   Sergei Prokofiev's song "The Ugly Duckling" is performed for the first time in Saint Petersburg. Scored for voice and piano, the piece is based on the fable by Hans Christian Andersen. Maxim Gorky is in the audience and later says "Prokofiev meant himself in the music!"

1916 *Births, Deaths and Debuts*

Jan. 12   Spanish-born mezzo-soprano Conchita Supervia sings Carmen with the Chicago Opera Association in that city. Supervia has been learning the role since age 14 (she is now 21), and this performance is her debut with this opera company. Her initial debut took place last year at La Scala.

Jan. 15   Russian playwright and librettist Modest Tchaikovsky, 65, dies in Moscow. Brother of the famous composer, he was his brother's biographer and also librettist of *The Queen of Spades*.

Jan. 16   British dance notator Rudolf Benesh is born in London.

Jan. 22   Composer Henri Dutilleux is born in Angers, France.

March 24   Spanish composer Enrique Granados, 48, and his wife die in the English Channel as their ship, the SS *Sussex*, is torpedoed by a German submarine. The composer and his spouse were on their way home from the premiere of *Goyescas* at the Metropolitan Opera in New York (January 28th). Granados was a pupil of Felipe Pedrell at the Madrid Conservatory. By the age of 33 he had established himself as a teacher, opera composer and conductor. His masterpiece — *Goyescas* — is a series of piano pieces based on paintings by Goya (this work was later transformed into the opera mentioned). His work was postromantic, with a heavy emphasis on Spanish dance rhythms. He was a fairly prolific composer, producing operas, symphonic works, chamber and choral music.

April 11   Composer Alberto Ginastera is born in Buenos Aires, Argentina.

April 22   Violinist Yehudi Menuhin is born in New York City.

April 30   Conductor Robert Shaw is born in Red Bluff, California.

May 10   Composer, theorist and music writer Milton Babbitt is born in Philadelphia, Pennsylvania.

May 11   German composer Max Reger, 43, dies of heart paralysis in Leipzig. As a youngster he heard *Die Meistersinger* and *Parsifal* at Bayreuth and decided to pursue a career in music. He studied with Hugo Riemann at the Sonderhausen Conservatory and the Wiesbaden Conservatory. He began to be noticed in his late twenties, when he toured as a pianist. He subsequently taught composition at many academies and universities. His output was exceptionally prolific, yet his music never captivated the world of his day, despite his musical style, which was largely postromantic.

May 28   Albert Lavignac, 70, dies in Paris. This French musician was noted especially for his book *Encyclopedie de la musique et Dictionnaire du Conservatoire* (1913). He was also largely responsible for musical dictation becoming a required subject in European conservatories with the publication of his six-volume work *Cours complet theorique de dictee musicale* (1882).

July 17   Soprano Eleanor Steber is born in Wheeling, West Virginia.

July 23   Composer Ben Weber is born in St. Louis, Missouri.

July 27   German pianist Karl Klindworth, 85, dies in Stolpe, near Potsdam. As a youth, he studied with Franz Liszt and, in his mid-twenties, made a notable reputation for himself in London as a piano teacher. At this time, he befriended Richard Wagner (who was also in London) and undertook the herculean task of arranging (in vocal scores) Wagner's *Ring* cycle. At the age of 38, he joined the faculty of the Moscow Conservatory. He eventually returned to Germany in his early fifties and conducted the Berlin Philharmonic. His Klavierschule (founded in 1884) later merged with the Scharwenka Conservatory (Berlin). Klindworth's transcriptions of Wagner's operas and his other arrangements and editions become highly valued musical contributions.

Sep. 28   Soviet ballerina and teacher Olga Lepeshinskaya is born in Kiev.

Oct. 17   Pianist Mischa Levitzki makes his American debut at Aeolian Hall, New York City.

Oct. 19   Pianist Emil Gilels is born in Odessa, Russia.

Nov. 18   Amelita Galli-Curci makes her American debut as Gilda in Giuseppe Verdi's *Rigoletto* with the Chicago Opera.

Nov. 23   Conductor Eduard Napravnik, 77, dies in Saint Petersburg. This celebrated musician was the first conductor of the Russian Imperial Opera — a post he held for 47 years. While there he conducted the premieres of *Boris Godunov*, *The Queen of Spades* and many other important Russian operas. During that period he conducted over 3,000 performances. Also a composer, he wrote four operas, four symphonies, chamber and choral music.

Dec. 4   Italian soprano Claudia Muzio makes her Metropolitan Opera debut as Tosca. Also in the cast are Enrico Caruso and Antonio Scotti. Richard Aldrich of the New York *Times* says the coloring of her voice "... suit[s] the dramatic intention of the moment...."

Dec. 5   German conductor Hans Richter, 73, dies in Bayreuth, Germany. This musician was a favorite of Richard Wagner — he played French horn in Wagner's ensembles and worked for him as a music copyist. He was also involved in the first Bayreuth Festival of 1876 and was chosen to conduct the first *Ring* performances at that festival. Later he led the Halle Symphony Orchestra in England and conducted Wagner's operas at Covent Garden. His last performance was of *Die Meistersinger* at the Vienna Opera in 1912, after which he retired to Bayreuth.

1916   Related Events

The Mannes College of Music is established this year in New York City.

Jan. 1   Thomas Beecham is knighted for his service to music.

Feb. 11   The first concert of the Baltimore Symphony Orchestra takes place as Gustav Strube conducts a program of Beethoven, Mozart, Saint-Saens, Delibes and Wagner at the Lyric Theater in Baltimore, Maryland. The orchestra has 53 musicians.

June 7   Maurice Ravel voices opposition to the campaign against the performance of German and Austrian music and insists that the work of foreign colleagues exerts a healthy influence on French music. The protest is lodged in a letter to the Ligue Nationale pour la Defense de la Musique Francaise.

July 15   A German hymn praising hatred for Great Britain is published in Leipzig. It is entitled *Gott strafe England*.

Oct. 9   Pierre Monteux refuses to conduct Richard Strauss' *Till Eulenspiegel* in a New York Ballets Russes production. He is replaced by German conductor Anselm Goetz and returns to conduct the remainder of the program, which features Russian music.

Nov. 19   Arturo Toscanini conducts a performance of "Siegfried's Funeral March" from *Gotterdammerung* in Rome. An Italian soldier allegedly cries, "In memory of our battalions!" and the event comes to provoke the prohibition of the performance of German music in Italy until the war is over.

Dec. 12   A scheduled performance of Sergei Prokofiev's *Scythian Suite* is canceled due to a substantial number of orchestral players' having been drafted into the Russian army. Serge Koussevitzky was to have conducted. Russian music critic Leonid Sabaneyev, intent on attacking Prokofiev, publishes a scathing review of the piece without intending to attend the concert and without knowing that the concert was canceled. The review ignites one of the biggest scandals in the history of 20th-century music criticism. Sabaneyev writes, in *News of the Season*, that the music "is magnificently barbaric, the world's best barbaric music. But if I am asked whether this music gives me pleasure or artistic satisfaction, if it produces a profound impression, I must categorically say no. The composer conducted himself with barbaric abandon." Sabaneyev, now on the board of the Moscow Institute of Musical Science, seriously damages his own career as a result of writing and publishing this review. Prokofiev publicly responds next month on January 30.

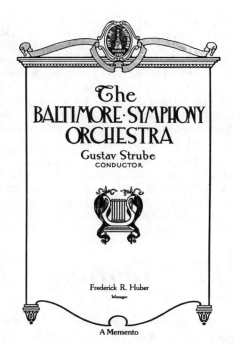

PROGRAM FOR THE FIRST CONCERT OF THE BALTIMORE SYMPHONY ORCHESTRA.

1917 Opera

Jan. 30   *Eine florentinische Tragodie*, an opera in one act by Alexander von Zemlinsky, receives its first performance in Stuttgart. Zemlinsky is currently conductor of the German Opera in Prague.

March 8   *The Canterbury Pilgrims*-a four-act opera by Reginald De Koven premieres at the Metropolitan Opera in New York. Based on the tales by Chaucer, the libretto is by Percy MacKaye. Artur Bodanzky conducts a cast including Margarete Ober, Edith Mason, Johannes Sembach and Basil Rysdael. This production is the result of efforts by Giulio Gatti-Casazza, the general manager, who is determined to produce new American operas from time to time. The last was four seasons ago. Gatti-Casazza says after this performance, "The public received it well." The opera is performed six times. At the sixth performance, the management announces that the United States has entered World War I. Ober immediately faints, and other German singers in the production quickly become indisposed. The remaining scheduled performances of this opera are canceled.

March 27   The premiere of *La Rondine*, by Giacomo Puccini, with a libretto by Giuseppe Adami, takes place in

Monte Carlo at the Theatre du Casino. The work is conceived as a light operetta in the Viennese style. The subject is a courtesan, Magda de Chivry, who leaves her opulent life in Paris for the love of Ruggiero Lastouc but then renounces him because she feels she is unworthy. Although the opera is very enthusiastically received, it does not receive many performances after today.

April 30   Pietro Mascagni's *Lodoletta* premieres at the Teatro Costanzi in Rome. The libretto, by Giovacchino Forzano, is based on the novel *Two Little Wooden Shoes*, by Louise de la Ramee, under the pen name Ouida. The opera is about a Dutch girl who dies for the love of a French painter.

May 11   The premiere of Ferruccio Busoni's *Turandot* takes place in Zurich at the Stadttheater. The composer writes his own version of Carlo Gozzi's play about a proud princess who rejects all suitors who cannot answer her three riddles. Busoni originally wrote incidental music for Gozzi's play and later expanded it into this opera. Also performed for the first time today is his *Arlecchino* (or *Die Fenster*). Busoni again writes his own libretto, using classic commedia dell'arte figures of Harlequin and Columbine. It is a humorous, ironic treatment of Italian melodrama.

June 12   The premiere of Hans Pfitzner's *Palestrina* takes place at the Residenztheater in Munich, with Bruno Walter conducting. Pfitzner's libretto, which he writes himself, is based on Palestrina's saving the art of counterpoint from condemnation by the church with his composition of the *Missa Papae Marcelli*. The opera is well received in Germany, although it falls out of favor in years to come. It is probably Pfitzner's most famous work. The composer, now 48, has recently been conductor of the Strasbourg Opera and director of the Strasbourg Conservatory.

Oct. 26   Modest Mussorgsky's *The Marriage* is performed posthumously in Petrograd. The opera, written in 1864, is based on a comedy by Gogol. Mussorgsky never finished the work (today's performance is of Act 1 only). The opera is subsequently completed and orchestrated by Alexander Tcherepnin and is performed in that version in 1937. Also premiered is Mussorgsky's unfinished *The Fair of Sorochinsk*, with sections completed by Cesar Cui for this performance. Another version of this opera is made by Nicolas Tcherepnin and produced in Monte Carlo in 1923.

Dec. 11   Hans Pfitzner's opera *Das Christ-Elflein* is performed in its revised version in Dresden. The two-act work is about divinity and magic, in which a Christmas tree is brought to a sick child. It was first premiered on December 11, 1906.

Dec. 26   Henry Hadley's three-act grand opera *Azora, Daughter of Montezuma* receives its first performance in Chicago, the composer conducting. Hadley is now between conducting jobs: He left the San Francisco Symphony Orchestra in 1915 and will join the New York Philharmonic (as associate conductor) in 1920.

1917   Dance

April 12   *The Good-Humored Ladies* premieres by the Ballets Russes de Serge Diaghilev at the Teatro Costanzi in Rome. Choreography and libretto are by Leonide Massine, music by Domenico Scarlatti arranged by Vincenzo Tommasini. It is a one-act ballet about two lovers outmaneuvering parental objection. Massine, Lydia Lopokova, Lubov Tchernicheva, Enrico Cecchetti, Stanislas Idzikowski and Leon Woizikovsky star. This is one of the first ballets in which Massine is both choreographer and lead dancer. He now embarks on a double career doing both.

May 11   Serge Diaghilev's Ballets Russes gives the first performance of Leonide Massine's *Contes Russes* at the Theatre du Chatelet, Paris. The music is by Anatoly Liadov and decor by Mikhail Larionov. The ballet, based on various Russian folktales, is one of Diaghilev's favorites. Lydia Sokolova (Kikimora), Stanislas Idzikowski (Cat), Lubov Tchernicheva (Swan Princess), Leonide Massine (Bova Korelevich) and Nicolas Kremnev (Baba-Yaga) star.

May 12   Bela Bartok's *The Wooden Prince* receives its first performance in Budapest. The libretto is by Bela Balasz, choreography by Otto Zobisch and decor by Count Banffy. This one-act ballet is about a prince who wins his beloved by carving a wooden model of himself and giving it to her. Lead dancers are Anna Palley, Emilia Nirschy, Ede Brada and Boriska Hormat.

May 18   *Parade*, choreographed by Leonide Massine, receives its initial performance by Serge Diaghilev's Ballets Russes at the Theatre du Chatelet, Paris. The ballet is one of the most renowned collaborations of the Diaghilev period. Erik Satie writes the music, which includes such sound effects as sirens and a typewriter, Jean Cocteau writes the scenario and libretto. The scenery and costumes are by Pablo Picasso. The ballet deals with a street circus in Paris, where hustling managers display their troup's talents to persuade passers-by to come inside. The work is a landmark, introducing cubism in the theater. Describing the work in the program, Guillaume Apollinaire uses the word *surrealism* for the first time. The opening night cast includes Leonide Massine, Lydia Lopokova, Nicholas Zverev, Maria Chabelska and Leon Woizikovsky. A lighting failure sparks an audience riot, and a subsequent review calls Satie, Cocteau and Picasso derogatory names. Satie responds to another review, by Jean Poueigh, with a nasty postcard, is taken to court by the critic and sentenced to eight days in jail. He never serves the sentence.

SCENE FROM *PARADE*

1917 Instrumental and Vocal Music

Jan. 17   Leo Sowerby's concert overture *Comes Autumn Time*, *The Irish Washerwoman*, an orchestral scherzo and a piano concerto are premiered by pianist Eric De Lamarter in Chicago. The composer conducts. The concerto includes an obbligato soprano part.

Jan. 20   Symphony No. 3 (*Song of the Night*), by Karol Szymanowski, receives its initial performance in Petrograd. Alexander Siloti conducts this three-movement work scored for tenor solo, chorus and orchestra. The text consists of poetry by Persian poet Jalal al-Din Rumi (1207–73).

March 11   Ottorino Respighi's tone poem *Fountains of Rome* receives its world premiere at the Augusteo in Rome. The work was inspired by four Roman fountains and, along with *The Pines of Rome*, remains more popular than any of his operas or ballets. Respighi is now teaching at the Academy of Santa Cecilia in Rome.

March 11   Gian Francesco Malipiero's second part of *Impressioni dal vero* premieres in Rome. This part consists of "Colloquio di Campane", "I Cipressie e il Vento" and "Baldoria campestre."

March 23   *Trois poemes juifs*, by Ernest Bloch, receives its first performance, with Bloch conducting the Boston Symphony Orchestra. This work is the first identified with the composer's Jewish heritage. A review in the New York *Evening Post* says, "The rambling cacophonies. . . produced no effect except boredom. . . . Are there not enough horrors assailing the world at present without adding those of unnecessary harmonies?"

April 3   Arthur Honegger's *Aglavaine et Selisette* receives its first performance at the Paris Conservatoire, the composer conducting. This overture, based on Maurice Maeterlinck's drama, is the composer's first symphonic work. Honegger is now 25 years old.

April 9   Igor Stravinsky's orchestral arrangement of *The Volga Boatman's Song* is featured at a benefit for the Italian Red Cross given by Serge Diaghilev in Rome. Ernest Ansermet conducts.

May 3   Ernest Bloch's *Schelomo* receives its first performance, conducted by Artur Bodanzky in New York City at a concert of the New York Society of the Friends of Music. The composer describes this piece as a "Hebrew rhapsody" for cello and orchestra. It was inspired by a sculpture of Catherine Barjansky. Also on the all-Bloch program are the first two movements of his *Israel Symphony*, *Three Jewish Poems* and *Three Psalms*. A review in the New York *Evening Post* says, "Mr. Bloch's ideal of the Jewish music of the future is apparently the grotesque, hideous, cackling dispute of the Seven Jews in Richard Strauss' *Salome*."

May 5   Claude Debussy's Violin Sonata premieres in Paris with Gaston Poulet as soloist and the composer playing the piano part. This event marks the composer's last public appearance in Paris. Debussy is dying of cancer.

July 2   Pietro Mascagni's *Rapsodia satanica* premieres in Rome. This orchestral work was composed as film music.

Nov. 11   Alexander Glazunov's Piano Concerto No. 2 in B Major premieres at the Petrograd Conservatory, the composer conducting. Glazunov has been working on this piece, a single-movement concerto, since 1894.

Nov. 14   Leos Janacek's *Fiddler's Child* premieres in Prague. This orchestral piece is called a ballad and was composed in 1912.

Nov. 24   Edward Elgar's *The Spirit of England* receives its first performance in its complete version in London at the Royal Albert Hall. Text for this orchestral trilogy is by the poet Lawrence Binyon and is from his collection called "The Winnowing Fan." The score features a soprano or tenor soloist.

Dec. 11   Francis Poulenc's *Rapsodie negre*, for small orchestra, premieres in Paris, the composer singing the vocal part in the movement entitled "Honolulu." Poulenc is now 18 years old.

1917 Births, Deaths and Debuts

Jan. 5   Composer and theorist Reginald Smith-Brindle is born in Bamber Bridge, England.

Jan. 5   Richard Wagner's grandson — Wieland Wagner — is born in Bayreuth. He eventually becomes director of the Bayreuth Festival.

Jan. 7   Composer Ulysses Kay is born in Tucson, Arizona.

Jan. 12   Conductor Walter Hendl is born in West New York, New Jersey.

Jan. 13   German tenor Albert Niemann, 86, dies in Berlin. After starting his career as an actor, he took singing lessons in Paris and joined the Royal Court Opera in Berlin. He was chosen by Richard Wagner to sing the first performances of *Tannhauser* in Paris and Siegmund in *Die Walkure* at Bayreuth. At the Metropolitan Opera, Niemann sang the first American performance of *Tristan und Isolde* and *Gotterdammerung* in 1888.

Feb. 10   French composer and harmony teacher Emile-Louis-Fortune Pessard, 73, dies in Paris. In 1866 he won the Grand Prix de Rome for his opera *Dalila*. Regarded as a first-rate songwriter, he taught at the Paris Conservatoire.

Feb. 12   Conductor Thomas Scherman is born in New York City.

Feb. 28   Conductor and harpsichordist George Malcolm is born in London, England.

March 2   Composer John Gardner is born in Manchester, England.

April 1   Pianist and composer Dinu Lipatti is born in Bucharest, Rumania.

April 1   Black American composer Scott Joplin, 49, dies in New York. After studies in Texarkana, he ran away to St. Louis at age 17 and played piano in the local bordellos. He later studied further at George Smith College and in 1895 wrote his most famous composition, the "Maple Leaf Rag." He continued to write numerous rags as well as two operas. The opera *Treemonisha* was perhaps his most ambitious composition. As a result of syphilis, he dies insane in a state hospital.

April 22   French dancer and teacher Yvette Chauvire is born in Paris.

May 4   Composer and theorist Edward T. Cone is born in Greensboro, North Carolina.

May 14   Composer Lou Harrison is born in Portland, Oregon.

May 23   Soviet dancer and teacher Tatiana Riabouchinska is born in Moscow.

May 25   Polish bass Edouard de Reszke, 63, dies in Garnek, Poland. Along with his brother Jean, he was one of the most popular singers of the late 19th and early 20th centuries. He made his operatic debut in Paris in 1876 singing the King in *Aida* in the Paris premiere of the work directed by Giuseppe Verdi himself. He later sang in America with great success, appearing there often with his brother until 1903. He retired to an estate in Poland, where World War I brought him dire poverty and failing health.

June 4   Baritone Robert Merrill is born in Brooklyn, New York.

June 12   Pianist, composer, soprano and conductor Teresa Carreno, 63, dies in New York. Having made her debut as a pianist at age 8, she studied singing and made some operatic appearances. She conducted opera for her husband's troupe and finally went back to the piano. Carreno also wrote a number of compositions, some of which

TERESA CARRENO

were published. She was married four times to various musicians. Known as "the Valkyrie of the piano," Carreno was famous for her fiery playing. She was revered in Venezuela, the country of her birth.

July 16   Polish-German composer Philipp Scharwenka, 70, dies in Bad Nauheim. In addition to his instructional piano music, he also composed a symphony and other orchestral music. Among his most famous orchestral pieces are *Dramatische Fantasie, Arkadische Suite* and *Fruhlingswogen*.

Aug. 11   Pavel Gerdt, one of the greatest dancers in the history of the Saint Petersburg Russian Imperial Ballet, dies in Vommaca, Finland at the age of 72. Noted for his elegance and ability as a mime, he was the leading dancer in a number of Petipa's most famous ballets, including *Swan Lake* and *The Sleeping Beauty*.

Aug. 16   Composer Roque Cordero is born in Panama.

Sep. 13   Composer Robert Ward is born in Cleveland, Ohio.

Sep. 17   Composer Isang Yun is born in Tong Young, Korea.

Sep. 20   Opera impresario and manager Goeran Gentele is born in Stockholm, Sweden.

Sep. 28   Dancer and ballet director Michael Somes is born in Horsley, England.

Oct. 27   Violinist Jascha Heifetz, now 16, makes his New York debut after escaping from Russia via Siberia and the Orient. The concert takes place at Carnegie Hall.

Oct. 31   Conductor Peter van Anrooy makes his debut as the new music director of the Hague Philharmonic Orchestra, conducting a program of music by Smetana, Tchaikovsky and Mahler at the Gebouw voor Kunsten en Wetenschappn, The Hague.

Dec. 7   Austrian composer Alois Louis Minkus, 91, dies in Vienna. A violinist by profession, he traveled to Russia, where he performed with Prince Yusupov's serf orchestra in Saint Petersburg and later became the Bolshoi Theater's concertmaster. He composed ballet music, and his *Don Quixote* was a signal success, which remained in the Russian repertory. *La Bayadere* was subsequently produced by

Marius Petipa in Saint Petersburg and was also successful. After the production of *La Fiametta*, Minkus became court composer of ballet music for Saint Petersburg's imperial theaters. It was only in his final years that he returned to Vienna. His music, though rooted in 19th-century Austrian romanticism, was suited to the tasks of Russian choreographers because of its superficial rhythms and accessible melodies.

Dec. 21   Dancer and teacher Andre Eglevsky is born in Moscow, Russia.

1917   Related Events

The Manhattan School of Music is founded this year in New York City.

The San Francisco Conservatory of Music is founded this year in San Francisco.

Jan. 22   Supreme Court Justice Oliver Wendell Holmes rules in the case of *Victor Herbert* v. *The Shanley Company* that the performance of a copyrighted musical composition in a hotel or restaurant for entertainment purposes without an admission charge constitutes an infringement of copyright. Herbert's march *From Maine to Georgia*, performed in the dining room of the Vanderbilt Hotel, New York City without remuneration for the composer, had sparked the controversy.

Jan. 30   Sergei Prokofiev responds to Leonid Sabaneyev's scathing review of his *Scythian Suite*, which was published without Sabaneyev's realizing that the concert had been canceled. Prokofiev's statement, published in *Musikalny Sovremennik* (Petrograd), says in part: "the critic could not possibly acquaint himself with the music because the only manuscript score of the work is in my possession." Prokofiev is 25 years old.

March 17   Lionel de la Laurencie becomes the first president of La Societe Francaise de Musicologie, founded today in Paris.

March 31   Geraldine Farrar defends herself against rumor that she is pro-German. Shortly after the outbreak of World War I, there had been circulated in London and the United States copies of a letter, supposedly written by Farrar, that purportedly contained the following comments: "I am a Germanophile through and through. I am much too loyal to Germany to amuse the American people, or to oblige them." She goes on to say (today) that suspicion may have lingered because her operatic debut took place in Berlin (1906) and because of her subsequent association with Karl Muck and the Berlin Royal Opera.

May 8   Serge Koussevitzky becomes music director of the former Imperial Court Orchestra in Petrograd. He was offered the position by Alexander Kerensky's provisional government of Russia.

Sep. 10   Leopold Stokowski and the Philadelphia Orchestra begin recording for Victor, in Camden, New Jersey. The first recording is Hungarian Dance No. 1, by Johannes Brahms. Violinist Jascha Heifetz also makes his first recording for Victor this year.

Sep. 18   The ukelele is patented as a musical instrument. The patent holder is the Honolulu Ad Club. A four-stringed, guitar-like instrument, it was originally imported to Hawaii in the early 1880's from Madeira.

Sep. 25   Paul Hindemith's Three Pieces for Cello and Piano, Op. 8, is published by Breitkopf & Hartel, Leipzig. This date marks the first composition by Hindemith to be published.

Oct. 25   Walter Damrosch urges that the music of Bach, Beethoven and Brahms not be censored in the United States due to the war.

Nov. 7   Singing the role of Philip II in Giuseppe Verdi's *Don Carlo* at the Winter Palace, Feodor Chaliapin calms the audience as the cruiser *Aurora*, anchored in the river Neva, fires a salvo signaling the beginning of the Russian Revolution.

Nov. 8   Anatol Lunacharsky becomes commissar of public education in Russia, enabling him to exert a strong influence on musical and cultural events in the Soviet Union.

Nov. 9   The Philadelphia Orchestra management conforms to the Pittsburgh Orchestra Association's request not to perform German music on its upcoming November 19 concert and will instead substitute American music.

Nov. 17   Reinhold Faust, a German, sends a bomb down the aisle at a war benefit performance of the Chicago Opera Company. It does not explode.

Nov. 22   The new Soviet government officially takes over the theaters, in what it says is an effort to meet the needs of the working population.

Dec. 1   Anatol Lunacharsky publishes in *Pravda* an appeal asking painters, musicians and artists to fulfill their civic obligations by reporting to the office of the commissar of public education in the Winter Palace in order to "... work towards the rapprochement of the broad popular masses with art in all its aspects...."

Dec. 8   German conductor Ernst Kunwald, director of the Cincinnati Symphony Orchestra, is apprehended as an enemy alien, freed on bail, allowed to conduct two concerts and then asked to resign.

Dec. 10   The Vatican decrees that the tango and maxixe should not be danced in public or at home by Roman Catholics.

1918 Opera

Jan. 5   *A Daughter of the Forest*, a one-act opera by Arthur Finley Nevin, is performed for the first time in Chicago. It is a story involving love, pregnancy and suicide during the Civil War. Nevin, now 46, is teaching at the University of Kansas.

March 6   Adolph Bolm's staging of an opera-pantomime version of *Le Coq d'or* is performed at the Metropolitan Opera House in New York City. Pierre Monteux conducts this first American performance of the work. The cast includes Maria Barrientos and Adamo Didur.

March 10   Eugene d'Albert's three-act opera *Der Stier von Olivera* premieres in Leipzig.

March 23   American composer Charles Wakefield Cadman's *Shanewis* receives its first performance at the Metropolitan Opera in New York City. This two-act opera is about an Indian girl whose non-Indian lover is killed by a tribesman. Sophie Breslau, Marie Sundelius and Paul Althouse star. This performance also includes the premiere of the ballet-pantomime *The Dance in Place Congo*, by Henry F. Gilbert. Roberto Moranzoni conducts both.

April 25   Franz Schreker's three-act opera *Die Gezeichneten* receives its first performance in Frankfurt. Schreker writes the libretto to this work about a female cripple yearning for a lovely, healed body.

May 24   The premiere of Bela Bartok's *Duke Bluebeard's Castle* takes place in Budapest at the Kiralyi Operhaz. The text, by Bela Balasz, is based loosely on the legend of Bluebeard. It was composed in 1911 but was banned by the Hungarian Commission of Fine Arts. It is rediscovered in 1918 by its Italian conductor, Igisto Tango; after another period of oblivion it is eventually recognized as one the greatest of Hungarian operas.

Aug. 18   Franz Schubert's *Fernando* premieres in Magdeburg. This event marks the first performance of this opera since its completion 103 years ago.

Oct. 18   *Bianca*, a one-act opera by Henry Hadley, receives its first performance in New York City. Based on Carlo Goldoni's play *La Locandiera*, the opera is a love story.

Nov. 1   Italo Montemezzi's opera *La nave* premieres at La Scala, Milan, with a libretto by Gabriele d'Annunzio. The opera — one of six by this composer — is about a Venetian woman who seeks revenge on a merchant for torturing her parents. She winds up tied to the front of her enemy's ship and dies.

Dec. 14   Giacomo Puccini's *Il Trittico*: *Il Tabarro*, *Suor Angelica* and *Gianni Schicchi* premieres at the Metropolitan Opera in New York. Giuseppe Adami's libretto for *Il Tabarro* is based on Didier Gold's *La Houppelande*, about a woman who betrays her husband with one of his employees. The libretto for *Suor Angelica*, written by Giovacchino Forzano, is about a noblewoman who gave birth to an illegitimate son and was forced to retire to a convent. The text for *Gianni Schicchi*, also by Forzano, is based on an episode from Dante's *Inferno*. *Il Trittico* is intended to be performed as a single work but is broken up after its premiere and the three operas performed separately. Roberto Moranzoni conducts all three. The lead singers are Luigi Montesanto, Giulio Crimi (*Il Tabarro*); Geraldine Farrar, Flora Perini (*Suor Angelica*); Giuseppe De Luca, Florence Easton (*Gianni Schicchi*). Henry Krehbiel writes in the New York *Tribune* of *Gianni Schicchi* that the opera is "a modern effort in the line of the old Italian opera buffa, though in a different musical speech."

1918 Dance

Sep. 28   Igor Stravinsky's *L'histoire du soldat* receives its first performance in Lausanne, Switzerland. Choreographed by Ludmilla Piteov, this work is about attempts by the devil to manipulate an ordinary soldier into giving up his cherished violin and his soul. The devil wins. The music is subsequently performed many times as an instrumental suite. Scored for narrator and seven instruments, it reflects Stravinsky's recent change toward economy of instrumentation, which he attributes partly to wartime economics. Ten years from now, Lawrence Gilman will review a performance of this work and write, in the New York *Herald-Tribune*, "It is probably the nearest that any composer of consequence has ever come to achieving complete infantilism. . . . "

1918 Instrumental and Vocal Music

Jan. 27   Gian Francesco Malipiero's *Pause del silenzio* (first part only) premieres in Rome. This subsequently becomes the composer's best-known orchestral work.

Feb. 11   Carl Nielsen's pastoral piece *Pan and Syrinx* premieres in Copenhagen. The composer is currently head of the Music Society of Copenhagen.

March 23   American composer John Powell's *Rapsodie negre* is performed for the first time by the Russian Symphony Orchestra in New York, the composer playing the solo piano part. The work is based on the novel *Heart of Darkness*, by Joseph Conrad.

April 21   Sergei Prokofiev's *Classical Symphony* in D Major receives its first performance in Petrograd, the composer conducting. This four-movement work becomes one of the composer's most popular compositions.

April 23   Dutch composer Willem Pijper's Symphony No.1 (*Pan*) which has four movements, is premiered by Willem Mengelberg and the Concertgebouw Orchestra in Amsterdam. Pijper is now 23.

Sep. 29   Gustav Holst's *The Planets* premieres in a private performance in London. The work will receive its first public performance on November 15, 1920.

Dec. 15   Dutch composer Daniel Ruyeman's *Hieroglyphs* premieres in Amsterdan. The work — scored for two guitars, two mandolins, piano, harp, celesta and three flutes — also has a part for cup-bells. Controversy arises about the source of the bells — some claim they are from J. Taylor & Company, London; others say they were bought in a thrift store. The bells are destroyed in an air attack on Rotterdam in 1940 and subsequently the part is played on the vibraphone.

1918 Births, Deaths and Debuts

Olga Alexandrovna Spessivtseva becomes prima ballerina of the Maryinsky Theater this year. Born in 1895, she has studied at the Saint Petersburg Imperial Ballet Academy.

Jan. 21   Conductor and cellist Antonio Janigro is born in Milan, Italy.

Jan. 24   Austrian composer Gottfried von Einem is born in Bern, Switzerland.

Jan. 28   Amelita Galli-Curci's New York debut takes place as she performs in Giacomo Meyerbeer's *Dinorah*.

March 13   Lili Boulanger, 24, dies in Paris. A pupil of Paul Vidal at the Paris Conservatoire, she composed a cantata entitled *Faust et Helene*, which won her the Grand Prix de Rome in 1913 (making her the first woman to receive this award). She was the sister of Nadia Boulanger.

March 20   Composer Bernd Alois Zimmermann is born in Bleisheim, Germany.

March 25   French composer Claude Debussy, 55, dies in Paris. He began studying at the Paris Conservatoire at the age of 10. He was patronized by Mme. Nadezhda von Meck (who also patronized Tchaikovsky) and taken to Italy, Switzerland and Russia. At age 22 he won the Grand Prix de Rome for his cantata *L'Enfant prodigue*. In his late twenties, he became enamored of Mallarme's poetry and the French impressionist movement. This development soon led to his maturation as a composer.

Early impressionistic works include *Ariettes oubliees* (1888) and *Suite bergamasque* (which includes his famous "Clair de lune"). In 1894 another famous piece — *Prelude a l'Apres-midi d'un faune* — was premiered, and his only opera, *Pelleas et Melisande*, was begun.

At the beginning of the 20th century, Debussy's major work was *Trois Nocturnes*. Subsequent works (*La Mer, Images* and the ballet *Jeux*) helped establish him as one of the most important French composers of his time. He virtually introduced and developed impressionism in French music, although he disliked the term. Musical elements invoked to achieve this style include pentatonic and whole-tone scales (common to Oriental music); shimmering orchestrations; chord progressions emphasizing fourths and fifths moving in consecutive and parallel motion; and unresolved dissonance.

March 26   Russian composer Cesar Cui, 83, dies in Petrograd. Cui was trained as a military man, studying warfare and topography. As a musician, he was largely self-taught. It was not until age 21, when he met Mily Balakirev, that he had any formal training in composition. He then simultaneously pursued composition, music criti-

CLAUDE DEBUSSY

fluenced by German and French music. His opera *Mefistofele* (produced in 1868 at La Scala) revealed these influences and also became his most important work. (It was revised due to audience reaction and then performed widely.) In 1862 Boito began composing *Nerone*, an opera he would work on for more than 50 years and never finish. He was also a poet, novelist and librettist; his masterpieces are considered to be his librettos for Giuseppe Verdi's operas *Falstaff* and *Othello*. His many awards include that of Inspector-General of Italian Conservatories (1892).

July 5   Composer George Rochberg is born in Paterson, New Jersey.

July 6   Pianist Eugene List is born in Philadelphia, Pennsylvania.

July 6   Soprano Dorothy Kirsten is born in Montclair, New Jersey.

July 24   Violinist Ruggiero Ricci is born in San Francisco, California.

July 27   Cellist Leonard Rose is born in Washington, D.C.

July 27   New York music critic and writer Gustav Kobbe, 61, is killed in his sailboat by the maneuvers of a Navy seaplane off the shore of southern Long Island, New York. His writings include the *Complete Opera Book* (New York, 1919), which was tremendously successful and was later republished in an expanded version entitled *Kobbe's Complete Opera Book* (compiled by the Earl of Harewood, and published in 1954).

Aug. 25   Pianist, composer and conductor Leonard Bernstein is born in Lawrence, Massachusetts.

Sep. 18   English composer and organist Ernest Bristow Farrar, 33, is killed in the Battle of Somme, France. He studied with Charles Villiers Stanford at the Royal College of Music; was organist at the English Church in Dresden; and composed cantatas, orchestral works, chamber music, songs and organ preludes. He received the Carnegie Award for his orchestral suite *English Pastoral Impression*.

Sep. 19   English singer and composer Liza Lehmann, 56, dies in London. Her work includes the song cycle *In a Persian Garden*, text from *Rubaiyat* of Omar Khayyam. She was the first woman composer from England to become a success in America as well as in her native country. With the exception of a few piano pieces, all of her music is for voice.

Sep. 19   Mezzo-soprano Blanche Thebom is born in Monessen, Pennsylvania.

Oct. 7   English composer Sir Hubert Parry, 70, dies in Knight's Croft, Rustington, England. A director of the Royal College of Music, he became a professor of music at Oxford in 1900. His work includes much choral and orchestral music. Among his most famous compositions are *Blest Pair of Sirens* and his rendition of Blake's *Jerusalem*. He was knighted in 1898. He also wrote several books and

cism and military endeavors through the turn of the century. At age 45 he tutored Tsar Nicholas II in the science of military fortification. At the same time he was composing his orchestral work *Marche solennelle*. His well-publicized attacks on German music enabled him to become one of the Russian "Mighty Five" (the others were Nikolai Rimsky-Korsakov, Modest Mussorgsky, Alexander Borodin and Mily Balakirev) who championed the Russian nationalistic school. He viciously attacked Richard Wagner, Richard Strauss and Max Reger. His music, though not as forceful as that of the remaining. "Mighty Five," helped establish a Russian national school. His best-known works include the piano piece *Orientale* (from *Kaleidoscope*, Op. 50). He also composed 14 operas, orchestral works, chamber music and songs.

April 3   Conductor-pianist Sixten Ehrling is born in Malmo, Sweden.

April 25   Soprano Astrid Varnay is born in Stockholm, Sweden.

May 3   Tenor Leopold Simoneau is born in Quebec City, Canada.

May 17   Soprano Birgit Nilsson is born near Karup, Sweden.

June 10   Italian composer Arrigo Boito, 76, dies in Milan. A product of the Milan Conservatory, he first made an impression in his late teens with the cantatas *Il 4 Giugno* and *Le Sorelle d'Italia*. He went to Paris on a government grant and then to other countries. During his travels, he became in-many articles (especially for *Grove's Dictionary of Music and Musicians*).

Oct. 9   After retraining his voice, Lauritz Melchior makes his debut as a tenor at the Royal Opera, Copenhagen, in *Tannhauser*.

Oct. 11   American dancer, choreographer and ballet director Jerome Robbins is born in New York.

Nov. 14   Contralto Jean Madeira is born in Centralia, Illinois.

Nov. 15   American soprano Rosa Ponselle makes her Metropolitan Opera debut in the first Metropolitan pro-duction of *La forza del destino*. Also in the cast are Enrico Caruso, Giuseppe De Luca and Jose Mardones. James G. Huneker, of the New York *Times*, calls her voice "vocal gold" and says it "may prove a gold mine."

Nov. 20   Sergei Prokofiev makes his American debut playing a program of his own music, including his Sonata No. 2 for Piano, at Aeolian Hall in New York City. In reviewing the concert, Richard Aldrich writes in the New York *Times* that Prokofiev is ". . . a psychologist of the uglier emotions. . . ."

1918   *Related Events*

The Starr Piano Company — manufacturer of Gennett Records — wins a lawsuit against Victor. It sued to break Victor's monopoly of the lateral-cut disc process, which was jointly held by Victor and Columbia.

Jan. 5   Serge Rachmaninoff departs from the Soviet Union, marking his farewell to his native country.

Jan. 10   The chorus of the Maryinsky Theater in Petrograd goes on strike to protest government directives. The government subsequently threatens dismissal, and the strike soon ends.

Jan. 15   Arthur Honegger suddenly becomes known in France as he participates today in a concert of new music in Paris. Entitled Nouveaux Jeunes, the program features new works by young French composers.

Jan. 21   The New York Philharmonic management bans the performance of music by German composers.

Feb. 14   Igor Stravinsky, Leon Bakst, operatic soprano Felia Litvinne, Ida Rubinstein and other prominent artists living in France publish a joint statement of principle, which is released today: "At this grave and sad hour in the history of Russia, our martyred country, we, Russian citizens of the liberal professions, having the great good fortune to enjoy the fraternal hospitality of beloved France, believe it our duty to declare solemnly that we repudiate the sinister band of Bolsheviki who are momentarily in

LEWISOHN STADIUM

power at Petrograd and that we will never recognize the government of the vile traitor Lenin and his associates."

March 14   A Boston Symphony Orchestra concert in New York City is conducted by Karl Muck despite patriotic protests to have him removed.

March 24   The Paris Opera resumes performances in spite of German cannon fire.

March 25   Music director Karl Muck of the Boston Symphony Orchestra is arrested at his home as an enemy alien. Henry Higginson, the orchestra's founder, resigns and sets up a board of directors to govern the orchestra. This event marks the end of the continuous line of German conductors leading this orchestra that began with George Henschel in 1881. Reaction to the arrest is swift: The Boston *Herald* says the American authorities ". . . consider it an established fact that his Boston residence was part of the Kaiser's policy of some years ago of 'planting' musicians, college professors and other men of great accomplishments and culture in various countries as part of his gorgeous scheme of eventual world-wide conquest."

June 10   The Rotterdam Philharmonic Orchestra gives its first concert. Conducted by Willem Feltzer, the program consists of music by Beethoven, Cherubini and others. The orchestra becomes one of 16 professional orchestras in Holland.

June 23   The Adolph Lewisohn Stadium opens with a new annual series of summer concerts by the New York Philharmonic.

July 12   Vladimir Lenin and Anatol Lunacharsky declare the conservatories of Moscow and Petrograd state institutions of higher learning. Nationalization of private music schools, publishing houses, printing establishments, instrument factories, libraries, archives and concert institutions subsequently follows; works of deceased composers also become state property.

July 29   Responding to the government decree of July 12, Alexander Glazunov bids farewell to the Russian Musical Society, saying he desires "to express thanks to the Directorate of the Russian Musical Society for the more than fifty years of trusteeship of the Petrograd Conservatory."

Sep. 16   Mrs. Elizabeth Sprague Coolidge opens her Berkshire Music Center on her estate near Pittsfield, Massachusetts. These concerts are to feature classical and modern American and European music. The concerts are subsequently held in Washington, D.C. The Tanglewood summer sessions will begin on July 8, 1940, under the direction of Serge Koussevitzky.

Sep. 23   In response to a protest by Alexander Glazunov that conservatory admission standards have been lowered in order to admit more students from working-class and peasant backgrounds, Anatol Lunacharsky (Soviet commissar of public education) concedes and issues a special dispensation to allow conservatories to continue their policy of requiring entrance examinations. Lunacharsky's original interference was empowered by changes in government resulting from the Russian Revolution last year (Vladimir Lenin ordered all admissions examinations to institutions of higher learning abolished in order to eliminate "privileges of the moneyed classes"). Lunacharsky's stated purpose was to "democratize" the conservatories and "provide a broader service to fulfill the musical needs of the working populations."

Nov. 1   Arnold Schoenberg's plan to give musicians and interested people a "real and exact knowledge of modern music" is realized today as the Society for Private Musical Performances is established in Vienna, with Schoenberg as president. The society forbids applause and does not permit music critics to attend.

Nov. 11   The Allies sign an armistice with Germany. This event brings an end to World War I.

Nov. 14   The musical affairs of Germany are presided over by a Provisional Central Musical Council in Berlin, formed today, three days after the Armistice.

Nov. 30   Ernest Ansermet conducts the inaugural concert of the Societe de l'Orchestre de la Suisse Romande in Geneva.

Dec. 11   The Cleveland Symphony Orchestra gives its first concert at Gray's Armory in Cleveland, Ohio. Nikolai Sokoloff conducts a program of music by Franz Liszt, Georges Bizet, Tchaikovsky, Anatoly Liadov and Victor Herbert. A reviewer for the *Plain Dealer* (Cleveland) says of Sokoloff, "He hitches his chariot to a star." The orchestra subsequently becomes known as the Cleveland Orchestra.

1919   Opera

Jan. 14   French composer Henri Fevrier's three-act opera *Gismonda* receives its first performance by the Chicago Opera Company, with Mary Garden in the title role. The opera is about a duchess who is in conflict with a goddess for ordering the destruction of a statue. Fevrier was a student of Gabriele Faure, Andre Messager and Jules Massenet.

March 12   Two one-act operas by American composers are produced by the Metropolitan Opera. They are *The Legend*, by Joseph Carl Breil (a love story including murder), and *The Temple Dancer*, by John Adam Hugo (about a Hindu priestess who commits theft and is struck by lightning). Both are examples of American operas by relatively unimportant American composers, who, apart from today's event, achieve little in terms of important performances of their works. Breil's most famous pieces are the film scores to D.W. Griffith's *The Birth of a Nation* and *Intolerance*. The operas were programmed by Giulio Gatti-Casazza, who is determined to stage new operas by American composers from time to time. Rosa Ponselle stars in *The Legend*; Florence Easton and Morgan Kingston star in *The Temple Dancer*.

March 18   Engelbert Humperdinck's opera *Gaudeamus* premieres in Darmstadt.

April 7   *Monsieur Beaucaire*, a three-act opera by Andre Messager, is performed for the first time in an English version (translated by Newton Booth Tarkington) in Birmingham, England with the composer conducting. The opera is about a relative of Louis XV who masquerades as a barber while in England and encounters a noblewoman. This musician is now living in Paris after having spent last year touring America as a conductor.

May 20   *Soeur Beatrice* — a three-act opera by Dimitri Mitropoulos, now 23 years old — receives its first performance at the Odeon in Athens. The opera is based on the play by Maurice Maeterlinck.

July 29   *La Via della finestra*, a three-act opera by Riccardo Zandonai, receives its first performance in Pesaro. This is Zandonai's fifth opera.

Oct. 10   *Die Frau ohne Schatten*, by Richard Strauss with a text by Hugo von Hofmannsthal, receives its world premiere at the Vienna Staatsoper. It is a kind of symbolic fairy tale about a spirit who is married to a mortal emperor. The spirit has no shadow, and in order to be permitted to remain with her husband she must find one, or he will be turned to stone. The opera is unanimously acclaimed. The cast includes Lotte Lehmann, Maria Jeritza, Lucie Weidt, Karl Oestvig and Richard Mayr. Franz Schalk conducts.

Oct. 21   *Fennimore und Gerda* — a two-act opera by Frederick Delius, to the composer's German libretto — is performed for the first time in Frankfurt. The opera, based on a novel by Danish writer Jens Peter Jacobsen, is a love story about a poet and a painter who both desire a woman called Fennimore. The poet eventually falls in love with Gerda, his childhood sweetheart. The opera — the last by Delius — is not a great success.

1919 Dance

June 5   Serge Diaghilev's Ballets Russes gives the first performance, at the Alhambra Theater in London, of Leonide Massine's *La Boutique fantasque*. The ballet deals with two dolls in a toy shop who are in love with each other. The toys revolt to prevent them from being sold to different families. Enrico Cecchetti (Shopkeeper), Lydia Lopokova and Leonide Massine (Can-Can Dancers), Lydia Sokolova and Leon Woizikovsky (Tarantella Dancers), Stanislas Idzikowski (Snob), Nicholas Zverev (Cossack Chief), Vera Nemchinova, Lubov Tchernicheva and Serge Grigoriev star. The music, by Gioacchino Rossini, is arranged by Ottorino Respighi.

July 22   Serge Diaghilev's Ballets Russes premieres *The Three-Cornered Hat*, a farcical ballet about an adulterous governor. Choreography is by Leonide Massine, music by Manuel de Falla, decor by Pablo Picasso. The performance takes place at the Alhambra Theater, London. Lead dancers are Massine, Tamara Karsavina, Leon Woizikovsky and Stanislas Idzikowski. This version of the ballet is the final one — an earlier production entitled *El corregidor y la molinera* took place in Madrid in 1917.

Nov. 3   Ted Shawn's modern dance piece *Juinar of the Sea* receives its first performance in Los Angeles. Music is by Louis Horst.

Dec. 10   *La boite a joujoux* — a ballet in four scenes with choreography and decor by Andre Helle — receives its first performance at the Theater du Vaudeville in Paris. This ballet, with music by Claude Debussy, is about a love affair between three dolls in a box of toys. Andre Caplet arranges the music for orchestra from Claude Debussy's piano score and also conducts. Today's premiere is not overly successful. Jean Borlin will later choreograph the ballet for the Ballets Suedois in 1921 — a performance that is well received.

Dec. 23   John Alden Carpenter's ballet-pantomime *The Birthday of the Infanta* premieres in Chicago. The dance, based on the short story by Oscar Wilde, is the first of three ballets the composer writes. Carpenter is now 42.

1919 Instrumental and Vocal Music

Jan. 11   *Eventyr*, a symphonic poem by Frederick Delius, receives its first performance in London. Sir Henry Wood conducts the music at a Promenade Concert. This impressionistic work is based on Norwegian fairy tales.

Jan. 30   American composer Rubin Goldmark's *Requiem* receives its first performance by the New York Philharmonic in that city. This work is based on Lincoln's Gettysburg Address. Goldmark studied composition in New York with Antonin Dvorak.

Feb. 2   Anton Webern's two-piano, six-hand arrangement of his *Passacaglia* for orchestra, Op. 1, premieres in a private performance at the Society for Private Musical Performances in Vienna. The performers are Eduard Steuermann, Ernst Bachrich and Paul A. Pisk.

Feb. 15   Carl Nielsen's symphonic suite *Aladdin* is performed for the first time in Copenhagen, the composer conducting. The suite has five movements.

Feb. 18   *Through the Looking Glass* — a suite for chamber orchestra — is performed for the first time in New York City. This work, by Deems Taylor, is subsequently revised for full orchestra. Taylor is a product of New York University and worked as a war correspondent during the First World War. His career as a music critic (as well as a composer) is now taking shape.

March 14   Gabriel Faure's *Ballade* for piano and orchestra premieres in Paris, with Alfred Cortot as soloist and the composer conducting.

April 30   *Anti-Symphonie*, subtitled "*Musical Circular Guillotine*", by Jefim (Jef) Golyscheff, receives its first performance at a Dada exhibition in Berlin. The movements of the work are entitled "Provocational Injections"; "Chaotic Oral Cavity", or Submarine Aircraft"; and "Clapping in Hyper F-sharp Major". Golyscheff was born in Kherson, Russia and studied violin in Odessa before Russian anti-Jewish activity forced him to move to Berlin. He is a composer, theorist and painter who, in 1914, composed a string

trio containing what he called "Zwolftondauer-Komplexen" — passages in the music in which the 12 tones of the chromatic scale have different durations. Like Austrian composer Josef Matthias Hauer, who in 1912 composed a piano piece entitled *Nomos (Law)* which used six-note tropes, Golyscheff's work is part of the beginnings of 12-tone music, or dodecaphony. Arnold Schoenberg (now 44) who recently organized the Society for Private Musical Performances in Vienna, is now in the process of eclipsing both Golyscheff (now 21) and Hauer (now 35) in terms of developing this revolutionary musical system.

May 11   Claude Debussy's *Rhapsody for Saxophone*, orchestrated by Jean-Jules Roger-Ducasse, is premiered posthumously by the Societe Nationale de Musique in Paris. The piece had been requested by Mrs. Elisa Hall of Boston in 1903.

May 14   Gabriel Faure's *Fantasie*, Op. 111, receives its first performance by the Societe Nationale de Musique in Paris, with Alfred Cortot as soloist. Scored for piano and orchestra, the one-movement work is in G major.

May 24   *Keuchmaneuver (Cough Music)* by Jef Golyscheff, premieres at a Dada soiree in Berlin.

May 25   Georges Enesco's Symphony No. 3 in C Major premieres in Bucharest, the composer conducting. The symphony — scored for organ, piano, wordless chorus and orchestra — depicts the first fifth of the century: peace, war and peace.

GEORGES BARRERE WITH PIANIST INEZ CARROLL

June 6   Anton Webern's Five Songs from *Der siebente Ring* by Stefan George, Op. 3, premiere in Vienna.

July 20   Colombia's foremost composer, Guillermo Uribe-Holguin, now 39, conducts the premiere of his impressionistic Symphony No. 1 in Bogota.

Oct. 27   Edward Elgar's Concerto for Violoncello and Orchestra in E Minor, Op. 85, premieres in London, with Felix Salmond as soloist. This work is the last Elgar composes of real importance — his wife dies next year and he becomes despondent.

Nov. 16   *Poem for Flute and Orchestra*, by Charles Tomlinson Griffes, receives its first performance, with Georges Barrerre as soloist, in New York City. This work is impressionistic in style. Griffes, now 35, has studied composition with Engelbert Humperdinck in Berlin. He has been earning his living — barely — as a teacher.

Nov. 28   *The Pleasure Dome of Kubla Khan*, a symphony poem by Charles Tomlinson Griffes, receives its first performance by the Boston Symphony Orchestra. Pierre Monteux conducts. The piece is based on a poem by Samuel Taylor Coleridge.

Dec. 6   Igor Stravinsky's *Le Chant du rossignol* is premiered by Ernest Ansermet and the L'Orchestre de la Suisse Romande in Geneva. Today's performance is of a three-part suite from the opera *Le Rossignol*, which premiered on May 26, 1914.

Dec. 14   Symphony No. 3 (*Sinfonia brevis de Bello Gallico*) by Vincent d'Indy, is premiered by the Societe Nationale de

VINCENT D'INDY

Musique in Paris. The four-movement symphony, concluding with a fanfare, was composed during World War I.

Dec. 19   *The White Peacock*, by Charles Tomlinson Griffes, receives its first concert performance, with Leopold Stokowski conducting the Philadelphia Orchestra. This music exists in a piano version and was also performed as a ballet in New York in June of this year. The work features impressionistic harmonies.

1919   Births, Deaths and Debuts

Jan. 24   Composer Leon Kirchner is born in Brooklyn, New York.

Feb. 2   Composer Xavier Leroux, 55, dies in Paris. A pupil of Jules Massenet and teacher of Alfredo Casella, he won the first Prix de Rome in 1885. He composed 14 operas, including two that were performed in America (*La Reine Fiamette* and *Le Chemineau*), both staged at the Metropolitan Opera in New York City.

April 9   Conductor and musicologist Noah Greenberg is born in New York City.

April 16   American dancer and choreographer Merce Cunningham is born in Centralia, Washington.

April 18   American dancer, choreographer and ballet master John Taras is born in New York City.

April 23   Composer Bulent Arel is born in Istanbul, Turkey.

April 24   French composer Camille Erlanger, 55, dies in Paris. A pupil of Leo Delibes at the Paris Conservatoire, he won a Grand Prix de Rome at age 25. His opera *Le Juif polonaise* premiered in 1900 with great success. He composed several other operas, but none became as popular as *Le Juif polonaise*. He also composed several symphonic poems and a French requiem. A minor composer, he had no impact on the international music scene.

April 25   Augustus D. Juilliard, 83, dies in New York City. This millionaire established in his estate the fund for what is to become The Juilliard School.

May 10   Conductor Peter Maag is born in Saint Gallen, Switzerland.

May 18   Margot Fonteyn is born as Peggy Hookham in Reigate, England.

May 30   Baritone George London is born in Montreal, Canada.

July 6   Tenor Ernest Haefliger is born in Davos, Switzerland.

July 10   German musicologist Hugo (Carl Wilhelm Julius) Riemann, 69, dies in Leipzig. As a youngster, he studied music theory, piano, law, philosophy and history before entering the Leipzig Conservatory. He later conducted and taught and lectured at various conservatories. In 1914 he became director of the Forschungsinstitut fur Musikwissenschaft. Riemann's impact on 20th-century music was as a theorist as well as a musicologist. His extensive studies and writings cover the scientific aspects of music and laid the foundations for contemporary music theory. His *Musik-Lexikon* was first published in 1882 and quickly became a standard reference work.

July 31   Conductor Norman Del Mar is born in London, England.

Aug. 1   Impresario Oscar Hammerstein, 73, dies in New York. Born in Germany, he came to America and first worked in a cigar factory. After building several theaters and producing plays and operas, he opened the Manhattan Opera House, presenting famous singers such as Nellie Melba, Lillian Nordica and Mary Garden. During its four seasons, his company gave the American premieres of five operas by Jules Massenet, Charpentier's *Louise* and Debussy's *Pelleas et Melisande*. In 1910 he was bought out by the Metropolitan Opera with the proviso that he not produce operas in New York for 10 years. Hammerstein was the uncle of playwright and librettist Oscar Hammerstein.

Aug. 9   Italian composer Ruggero Leoncavallo, 62, dies in Montecatini, Italy. He studied at the Naples Conservatory, made his debut as a pianist at age 16 and traveled widely before settling in Paris. He became involved in a massive operatic project shortly after discovering the music of Richard Wagner — the trilogy *Crepusculum*, about the Italian renaissance — which, after six years, he took to the publisher Ricordi in Italy. Ricordi expressed an interest but was carefully noncommittal. Leoncavallo then composed *Pagliacci* and submitted it to the publisher Sonzogno. The opera was premiered in 1892 and, along with Mascagni's *Cavalleria Rusticana*, signaled the arrival of Italian "verismo." Leoncavallo's success peaked here; some 15 other operas followed *Pagliacci*, but none was nearly as successful.

Sep. 27   Italian coloratura soprano Adelina Patti, 76, dies in Brecknock, Wales. Born in Madrid to Italian parents, she began singing in public at the age of 7. One of the most famous singers of the 19th century, she made her operatic debut in New York in 1859 and her London debut in 1861. Her success was great enough to rival that of Giulia Grisi, and she soon conquered the European operatic capitals as well. Not known for her acting ability or her musical intelligence, she won over her audiences by the sheer beauty and purity of her voice. She retired in 1907.

Oct. 9   Soprano Irmgard Seefried is born in Kongetried, Bavaria.

Nov. 15   Boston Symphony Orchestra founder Henry Lee Higginson, 84, dies in Boston. A banker by profession, he was a strong supporter of German music and saw to it that German conductors always directed the Boston Symphony Orchestra. Higginson resigned from the management of the orchestra when Karl Muck was arrested as an enemy alien last year.

Nov. 29   Pianist Benno Moiseiwitsch makes his American debut at Carnegie Hall in New York City.

Dec. 18   American composer and teacher Horatio Parker, 56, dies in Cedarhurst, New York. A pupil of George Whitefield Chadwick and Josef Rheinberger, his first success came with the premiere of his oratorio *Hora Novissima* (1893). One year later, he joined the faculty of Yale University and was affiliated with that institution until today. Parker championed the music of Charles Ives while adhering to his conservative musical style influenced by German models. His music, largely choral, also includes orchestral and chamber pieces.

Dec. 19   Italian-American conductor Cleofonte Campanini, 59, dies in Chicago. A product of the Parma and Milan Conservatories, he made his debut in 1883, conducting *Carmen* in Parma. His American debut (*Otello*) was with the Metropolitan Opera in 1888. He then toured until Oscar Hammerstein engaged him to conduct at the Manhattan Opera House. After splitting with Hammerstein, he joined the Chicago Opera Company. He established himself as a first-rate conductor of opera and introduced Claude Debussy's *Pelleas et Melisande* to America.

Dec. 29   Composer and music writer Roman Vlad is born in Cernauti, Rumania.

Dec. 30   Conductor David Willcocks is born in Newquay, England.

1919 Related Events

The major development of the year in the recording industry is the formation of the Radio Corporation of America (RCA). Other developments include experimentation in electrical recording, carried out by Henry C. Harrison and Joseph P. Maxfield of Bell Laboratories.

The Busch Quartet is organized this year by violinist Adolf Busch.

Hugo Riemann's *Musik-Lexikon*, one of the standard reference works on music, is published in its ninth edition this year. This is the first edition that Alfred Einstein edits.

Jan. 17   The first musician to become a head of state in this century is inaugurated today, as Ignace Paderewski officially becomes premier of Poland.

Jan. 26   Ludwig van Beethoven's *Egmont Overture* is performed in Rome, marking the end of an Italian ban on German music due to the war.

March 3   The Saint Thomas Choir School is established in New York. English organist and composer T. Tertius Noble had asked the church (Saint Thomas Episcopal Church in New York City) to help him organize an English cathedral choir for the parish. The church responds by establishing a boarding school for boy singers. The school subsequently becomes known as one of the finest of its kind in the world.

April 11   Edgard Varese conducts the first concert of the newly formed New Symphony Orchestra in New York City.

Aug. 22   The famous Academy of Santa Cecilia, Rome, is renamed Regio Conservatorio Musicale di Santa Cecilia.

Oct. 24   The Los Angeles Philharmonic gives its first concert, performing in Trinity Auditorium, Los Angeles. The program is conducted by Walter Henry Rothwell, who remains music director of this orchestra until 1927, when he is succeeded by Georg Schneevoight. The orchestra is founded with the help and generosity of William Andrews Clark, Jr., a bibliophile and amateur musician who donates $3 million to the orchestra over the next 15 years.

Oct. 28   After intense protests by the American Legion, the Star Opera Company of New York City cancels its season. The company had scheduled a season of operas in German.

Nov. 8   The performance of Richard Wagner's music is resumed in Paris.

Nov. 27   Ignace Paderewski resigns his position as Polish premier to resume his musical career. During his 10 months in office, he participated in the Versailles treaty conference. Georges Clemenceau allegedly said to Paderewski at that conference, "You, a famous pianist, and now Prime Minister — what a comedown!"

Dec. 2   The Latvian National Opera House opens in Riga.

Dec. 2   Due to winter weather conditions and shortages of fuel, the former Imperial Opera House in Petrograd stops performances.

Dec. 29   Vaudeville and light music theaters are closed by order of the Council of People's Commissars of the Russian Soviet Socialist Republic on the grounds that their performances are educationally unhealthy for the masses.

1920 Opera

Jan. 2   Reginald De Koven's opera *Rip Van Winkle* is premiered by the Chicago Opera Company. This three-act opera is based on the tale by Washington Irving.

Jan. 31   The Metropolitan Opera premieres Henry Hadley's two-act opera *Cleopatra's Night*. The libretto, based on a story by Theophile Gautier, tells of an Egyptian who wins Cleopatra for one night in return for his death in the morning. It is Hadley's most popular opera. The conductor is Gennaro Papi; lead singers are Frances Alda and Orville Harrold. Critic W.J. Henderson calls the libretto "stilted and unnatural."

March 7   *Andrea Chenier* by Umberto Giordano, is performed by the Metropolitan Opera in New York. The performance takes place some 24 years after the work's original premiere at La Scala. Today's performance — the first of this opera by this company — is not the American premiere of the work; that took place on November 13, 1896 at the New York Academy of Music. Today's cast includes Giuseppe Danise, Kathleen Howard, Claudia Muzio and Ellen Dalossy; the conductor is Roberto Moranzoni.

April 23   Leos Janacek's *Excursions of Mr. Broucek* premieres in Prague. This opera is really two distinct operas — *Mr. Broucek's Flight to the Moon* and *Mr. Broucek's Trip to the 15th*

Century. Both satirical, they are about a European's time-travel imaginings.

May 22   Spanish composer Jesus Guridi's *Amaya* premieres in Bilbao. This event marks the first production of an opera set to a Basque libretto. In three acts, it is about religious conflict among Christians and pagans.

May 29   Alfred Kalnins' *Banjuta* — an opera in four acts — premieres at the new Latvian National Opera House in Riga. This production is the first national Latvian opera composed to a libretto about Livonian life in medieval times. The story is one of passion, involving murder and rape.

June 9   Vincent d'Indy's *La Legende de Saint-Christophe* premieres at the Paris Opera. The composer bases his libretto on the 13th-century *Legenda Aurea* by Jacopo da Varazzi.

July 7   Dutch composer Carolus Hacquart's 1680 opera

Love's Triumph premieres in a new version arranged by P.A. von Westhreen in Arnhem. This libretto was written in Dutch to celebrate the Peace of Nymwegen (1679). The original libretto is by D. Buijsero. It is an example of a piece that had to wait 240 years to be performed.

Dec. 4   *Die tote Stadt* — a three-act opera by Erich Wolfgang Korngold — receives its world premiere simultaneously in Hamburg and Cologne. The libretto is by Paul Schott. The opera, based on *Bruges-la-Morte*, a novel by G.R.C. Rodenbach, is about love, murder, a widower and a ballerina. The productions mark the composer's greatest success. The Hamburg cast includes Maria Olczewska and Richard Schubert; the conductor is Egon Pollack. The Cologne production is conducted by Otto Klemperer.

Dec. 13   Ruggero Leoncavallo's *Edipo re* premieres posthumously in Chicago. The last stage work by this composer, the one act opera is based on a tale by Sophocles.

1920 Dance

Feb. 2   *Le Chant du rossignol* receives its world premiere by Serge Diaghilev's Ballets Russes at the Paris Opera. Igor Stravinsky's music is choreographed by Leonide Massine. Henri Matisse creates the decor for this one-act ballet

IGOR STRAVINSKY AND LEONIDE MASSINE

based on the fairy tale by Hans Christian Andersen. It is about an emperor of China who receives a mechanical nightingale, banishes the real bird until he becomes ill and then discovers he needs the original. The music is composed from materials from Stravinsky's 1914 opera *Le Rossignol*. Tamara Karsavina, Lydia Sokolova and Stanislas Idzikowski star. Diaghilev, in 1925, commissions George Balanchine to rechoreograph the work.

HUGO ALFVEN

Feb. 21   *Le Boeuf sur le toit* — a new ballet with music by Darius Milhaud — is performed for the first time by the Fratellini brothers and the Comedie des Champs-Elysees, Paris. The production and libretto are by Jean Cocteau, decor by Guy-Pierre Fauconnet and Raoul Dufy. The work is a pantomimic divertissement featuring Brazilian rhythms and melodies juxtaposed with scenery of an American tavern during Prohibition. Its characters include a dwarf, a transvestite and a policeman.

May 15   Serge Diaghilev's Ballets Russes premieres Leonide Massine's one-act ballet *Pulcinella*. The ballet is based on one of the characters in commedia dell'arte. In the first performance Massine dances the title role with Tamara Karsavina as Pimpinella. Vera Mentchinova, Lubov Tchernicheva, Enrico Cecchetti, Stanislas Idzikowski, Sigmund Novak and Nicholas Zverev are also in the cast. Pablo Picasso designs the decor. The music is by Igor Stravinsky.

Oct. 25   *La Nuit de Saint Jean* — a one-act ballet by Swedish choreographer Jean Borlin — receives its first performance by a new ballet company, Les Ballets Suedois, at the Theatre des Champs-Elysees in Paris. The music, by Swedish composer Hugo Alfven, was originally an orchestral rhapsody entitled *Midsommarvaka*, which incorporates elements of Swedish folk song. Today's premiere is tremendously successful; the ballet is performed 134 times this season alone. Also premiered today is Borlin's *Iberia*, with music by Isaac Albeniz orchestrated by Desire Inghelbrecht. The dancers include Borlin and Carina Ari. Borlin, a student of Michel Fokine, founded the company with the help of Swedish patron Rolf de Mare. Les Ballets Suedois lasts four years.

1920   Instrumental and Vocal Music

Jan. 3   *Le Chant de Nigamon* — a symphonic poem by Arthur Honegger — is performed for the first time in Paris. The music, which uses pentatonic scales, describes Indians at war.

Jan. 26   Sergei Prokofiev's *Overture on Hebrew Themes* is premiered in New York City by Jewish-American students who studied at the Saint Petersburg Conservatory. This work is scored for a chamber ensemble of clarinet, two violins, viola, cello and piano.

Jan. 30   Frederick S. Converse's Symphony No. 1 is premiered by the Boston Symphony Orchestra. The work is romantic in character.

Feb. 14   Erik Satie's *Socrate* is premiered in a voice and piano version by the Societe Nationale de Musique in Paris. The work is scored for four sopranos and chamber orchestra. It receives its first performance with a full complement of musicians this June. Later this month, French critic Jean Marnold says in *Le Mercure de France* "Impotence would not be too harsh a word to characterize the nullity of the whole thing."

Feb. 28   Maurice Ravel's *Le Tombeau de Couperin* is premiered by the Pasdeloup Orchestra in Paris. This orchestral suite was arranged from four earlier piano pieces ("Prelude", "Forlane", "Rigaudon" and "Menuet").

March 5   Leo Sowerby's Piano Concerto is premiered in its revised version by the Chicago Symphony Orchestra.

March 8   Erik Satie's *Musique d'ameublement* is premiered at the Galeries Barbezanges in Paris. Described as "furniture music," the musical aesthetic is that music be considered a practical part of the environment; musicians are placed in different areas of the room, enabling the sauntering listener to perceive individual tunes of the players.

April 11   Ottorino Respighi's symphonic poem *Ballata delle gnomidi* is premiered by Bernardino Molinari at the Augusteo in Rome.

April 27   *Ragtime* — a work for 11 instruments (including cimbalom) by Igor Stravinsky — receives its first performance, in London, as Arthur Bliss conducts. The piece was inspired by American dance music and reflects Stravinsky's current preoccupation with economy of instrumentation (largely due to budgetary constraints). It was composed two years ago.

May 14   Symphony No.2 (*A London Symphony*), by Ralph Vaughan Williams, is performed in its revised version in London. Its first performance was on March 27, 1914.

June 7   Erik Satie's *Socrate* is performed in its full orchestral version for the first time.

July 18   Nikolai Miaskovsky's Symphony No. 5 in D Major premieres in Moscow. The four-movement work contrasts with his earlier symphonies by emphasizing a major key.

Sep. 11   Joaquin Turina's symphonic *Sinfonia sevillana* is premiered by Fernandez Arbos under its original title *Sevilla* in San Sebastian, Spain.

Oct. 29   Arnold Bax' symphonic poem *The Garden of Fand* is premiered by the Chicago Symphony Orchestra. The work is based on an Irish legend about a girl who has magical powers, lives on a magical island and amuses herself with the crew of a ship that she captures.

Nov. 5   Ernest Bloch's Suite for Viola and Orchestra premieres in New York City. The piece, an orchestral version of his earlier work Suite for Viola and Piano (which won the Coolidge Prize last year), has four movements.

Nov. 15   Gustav Holst's *The Planets* is performed in its first complete public performance, with Albert Coates conducting in London. (In September 1918 the work was premiered at a private performance.) The music consists of seven movements — "Mars, the Bringer of War"; "Venus, the Bringer of Peace"; "Mercury, the Winged Messenger"; "Jupiter, the Bringer of Jollity"; "Saturn, the Bringer of Old Age"; "Uranus, the Magician"; and "Neptune, the Mystic" (Pluto has not yet been discovered). The composition is subsequently performed frequently and becomes a favorite of the music public.

Nov. 23   John Alden Carpenter's symphonic poem *A Pilgrim Vision* is performed for the first time by the Philadelphia Orchestra. The performance commemorates the tercentenary Mayflower Celebration.

Dec. 12   *La valse* — a new work by Maurice Ravel — receives its first performance as Camille Chevillard conducts the Lamoureux Orchestra in Paris. Based on the Viennese waltz, the music evokes the grand events of an imperial court with dancing couples luxuriating in its music. It becomes one of Ravel's most frequently performed works.

1920   Births, Deaths and Debuts

Jan. 5   Pianist Arturo Benedetti Michelangeli is born in Brescia, Italy.

Jan. 16   American composer Reginald De Koven, 60, dies in Chicago. He was best known as a successful composer of operettas — one of these is *Robin Hood* (produced in 1890 in London). "O Promise Me," a song he later added to *Robin Hood*, became a standard favorite. Two of his operas — *Rip Van Winkle* and *The Canterbury Pilgrims* — were performed by major American opera companies. He also composed approximately 400 songs. As a conductor, he organized the Philharmonic Orchestra in Washington, D.C. He was also a music critic, who wrote for the New York *World*, the Chicago *Evening Post* and *Harper's Weekly*.

Jan. 17   American dancer Nora Kaye is born Nora Koreff in New York City.

Jan. 22   Baritone William Warfield is born in Helena, Arkansas.

Jan. 30   American dancer and teacher Rosella Hightower is born in Ardmore, Oklahoma.

Feb. 13   Soprano Eileen Farrell is born in Willimantic, Connecticut.

Feb. 14   Louis Charles Elson, 71, dies in Boston. Author, music editor and critic, he was a particularly outspoken critic and exerted a substantial influence on American musical life for many years. He was also on the faculty of the New England Conservatory. His wife, Bertha L. Elson, subsequently bequeaths funds to provide for lectures on music and musical literature to take place at the Library of Congress, Washington, D.C. in memory of her husband. These lectures begin in 1946.

March 24   British dance notator Joan Benesh is born as Joan Rothwell in Liverpool.

April 8   American composer Charles Tomlinson Griffes, 35, dies in New York City. After studying in Berlin, he returned to the United States to teach in Tarrytown, New York. He was an impressionist, whose music includes orchestral, string and piano music as well as many songs. His most important works are the ballets *The Kairn of Koridwen* and *Sho-Jo* and the orchestral works *The White Peacock* and *The Pleasure Dome of Kubla Khan*.

April 21   Italian composer Bruno Maderna is born in Venice.

April 27   Conductor Guido Cantelli is born in Novara, Italy.

June 14   Czech pianist Rudolf Firkusny makes his concert debut in Prague, performing a Mozart piano concerto with the Prague Philharmonic Orchestra.

July 21   Violinist Isaac Stern is born in Kremenetz, Russia.

Aug. 4   Russian composer Vladimir Rebikov, 54, dies in Yalta, the Crimea. His music includes pieces composed with tone clusters and whole-tone scales. Along with a great deal of piano music, he composed what he termed "rhythmo-declamations" and "musical psychological sketches". The waltz from his opera *The Christmas Tree* lives as a favorite of the music public. Although his early works were romantic, with influence of Tchaikovsky apparent, he later wrote music reflecting the influence of impressionism.

Aug. 11   American pianist William Masselos is born in Niagara Falls, New York.

Aug. 20   Coloratura soprano Etelka Gerster, 65, dies near Bologna, Italy. She made her debut in 1876 as Gilda in *Rigoletto* (Venice). She was especially known as a singer with Colonel Henry Mapleson's Opera Company. She also taught at the New York Institute of Musical Art.

Sep. 29   American dancer and choreographer John Butler is born in Memphis, Tennessee.

Oct. 2   German composer Max Bruch, 82, dies in Berlin. His notable works include *Kol Nidre*, a romance for violin and orchestra, and the Violin Concerto in G Minor, a frequently performed favorite of violinists. He wrote his first symphony when he was 14 and established himself as a world-touring conductor as well as a composer and violinist. The Berlin Musikhochschule appointed him to its faculty in 1891. He subsequently received honorary awards from the University of Cambridge and the French Academy.

Oct. 31   American dancer and teacher Leon Danielian is born in New York City.

Nov. 26   Italian tenor Beniamino Gigli makes his debut at the Metropolitan Opera singing Faust in Boito's *Mefis-*

tofele. Richard Aldrich writes in the New York *Times* that he has "... many of the inclinations and manners of his kind, such as a persistent disposition to sing to the audience, to the neglect of Margherita or whomever else the dramatic situation requires him to address...."

Dec. 6   Czech composer and conductor Karel Kovarovic, 57, dies in Prague. Also a conductor of the National Opera in Prague, his work includes many operas. He studied with Zdenko Fibich and was particularly noted for his renditions of music by Bedrich Smetana and Antonin Dvorak.

1920   Related Events

Les Ballets Suedois is founded this year in Paris by Swedish art patron Rolf de Mare, who is director of this new ballet company. Jean Borlin is choreographer and lead dancer. The company pursues works of a novel, avant-garde style. Its premiere performance takes place this October 25.

The Cleveland Institute of Music is founded this year in Cleveland, Ohio.

Jan. 1   The first issue of the quarterly *Music and Letters* is published in London. Arthur Henry Fox-Strangeways is editor. The periodical features articles on musical aesthetics and history and examines aspects of both contemporary and noncontemporary music.

Jan. 16   In an article in the theatrical daily *Comoedia* (Paris), French music critic Henri Collet groups together six young French composers who reject the musical esthetic of Claude Debussy and espouse a simpler, more popular sounding music: Darius Milhaud, Louis Durey, Georges Auric, Arthur Honegger, Francis Poulenc and Germaine Tailleferre. He decides to call this group of composers "Les Six." The designation remains.

Feb. 1   The new German modern music periodical *Melos* begins publication in Berlin. Hermann Scherchen is editor, and the publisher is Melos-Verlag. The magazine is devoted to espousing new musical trends.

May 20   Camille Saint-Saens participates as a pianist and conductor at a festival of his music in Athens, beginning today. He is now 84 years old.

June 8   American composer Charles E. Ives circulates his proposal for a 20th amendment to the United States Constitution at the Republican National Convention in Chicago. His proposal had been turned down for publication by eight leading tabloids in New York City. The amendment would require American citizens over the age of 21 to vote on all important issues, with the results to be submitted to Congress. William Howard Taft (now at Yale University) replies to Ives in a letter stating that he opposes the idea because the proposed amendment would introduce "the principle of the referendum," which, ac-

cording to Taft, does not secure the "real opinion of the people." Ives' proposal fails to find support.

June 27   The Cincinnati Opera gives its very first production: *Martha*, by Friedrich von Flotow. The conductor and stage director is Ralph Lyford, and the cast includes Melvena Passmore, Elaine de Sellem, Salvatore Sciarretti, Robert Maitland and Paolo Quintana. The performance takes place at the Cincinnati Zoo.

July 20   The S.S Victoria becomes the first ship to host a wireless musical broadcast from sea as it steams to Canada from England.

Aug. 5   Russian electrical engineer Leon Theremin, 23, demonstrates his new invention — the Theremin — before the Physico-Technical Institute in Petrograd. It was originally called the etherophone and later the Thereminovox. Musical tones are produced by electronic impulses interacting with ultrasonic circuits, oscillating radio tubes and hand movements of the player. The instrument, never used extensively, is one of many inventions in this area.

Aug. 22   The first Salzburg Festival begins today as the medieval morality play *Everyman* is performed in a production by Max Reinhardt. The play was recreated by Hugo von Hofmannsthal. The festival subsequently becomes what is perhaps the most famous annual music event in the world: Artists of the highest caliber are engaged to display their talent, and audiences compete months in advance for tickets to each event of the festival. The Berlin Philharmonic becomes the principal orchestra associated with the festival, although other famous orchestras, such as the New York Philharmonic, also participate. Today's performance of *Everyman* takes place in front of the Salzburg Cathedral; over the next 60 years, various concert halls are constructed in Salzburg to accommodate the festival's audiences and performers.

Sep. 16   Enrico Caruso makes his last recordings. Other developments in the recording industry this year include the appearance of two new labels in Czechoslovakia: Ultraphon and Esta; an export department specializing in international series recordings is established by Victor.

Oct. 1   The Paris Conservatoire appoints Henri Rabaud as its new director.

Nov. 10   The City of Birmingham Symphony Orchestra (England) gives its first concert tonight. Edward Elgar conducts the orchestra in a program of his own music. Critics offer mixed reactions. The Birmingham *Mail* says, "Its playing was a credit to the city." The Birmingham *Gazette* says of Elgar's conducting, "... his beat is erratic." The Manchester *Guardian* says Elgar "... is conducting with a more decided power than ever."

Dec. 11   Enrico Caruso suffers a throat hemorrhage while performing in *L'elisir d'amore*, by Gaetano Donizetti, at the Brooklyn Academy of Music in New York. His disease is diagnosed as intercostal neuralgia. He sings for the final time on December 24 and, after surgery and decline, dies in August of next year.

Dec. 24   While in great pain, Enrico Caruso sings his last performance at the Metropolitan Opera House in New York, as Eleazar in *La Juive*, by Jacques Halevy. It is his 607th performance at this theater.

Dec. 28   Arturo Toscanini begins an American tour conducting the La Scala orchestra in New York City. Although his American debut was in 1908 (conducting at the Metropolitan Opera), and his symphonic-conducting debut (in America) was in 1913, today marks the first time he brings a foreign orchestra to America.

Dec. 31   Kaunas, Lithuania becomes the home of the newly organized Lithuanian National Opera.

Dec. 31   The Association of Operatic Dancing is established by Adeline Genee, Tamara Karsavina, Phyllis Bedells, E. Espinosa and Philip John Sampney Richardson. The association advances the cause of classical dance in Great Britain and refines approaches to teaching.

1921 Opera

March 21   Reynaldo Hahn's one-act opera *La colombe de Bouddha* is performed for the first time in Cannes. It is about a buddha and his sacred bird.

April 15   *Der Vetter aus Dingsda*, a light opera by German composer Eduard Kunneke, receives its first performance in Berlin. Like his singspiel which premiered last year (*Das Dorf ohne Glocke*), it is tremendously successful.

May 2   *Il piccolo Marat*, by Pietro Mascagni, premieres in Rome at the Teatro Costanzi. It is the story of Mariella, the niece of the president of the revolutionary committee, and her efforts to help a young aristocrat free his mother from prison. The libretto, written by Giovacchino Forzano and Giovanni Targioni-Lozzetti, is based partly on Victor Martin's book *Sous la Terreur*. The composer conducts the performance.

May 15   *Die Prinzessin Girnara*, an opera by Egon Wellesz, based on a play by Jakob Wassermann, premieres in Hannover. The two-act opera is about human and ghostlike characters that interact through dissonant music. Critic Richard Ohlekopf writes in *Signale fur die musikalische Welt* (Berlin), "The opera is blatant nonsense of unspeakable hideousness."

May 16   Eugene d'Albert's *Sirocco* premieres in Darmstadt. This three-act opera tells the story of a woman from Paris and her relations with North African soldiers.

May 21   *Prince Ferelon*, by Nicholas Comyn Gatty, has its first performance in London at the Old Vic. It is a fairy story, written by the composer, about a princess who rejects all suitors because she believes they do not love her. The opera wins the Carnegie Award in 1922.

June 4   Paul Hindemith's *Morder, Hoffnung der Frauen* and *Das Nusch-Nuschi* are performed for the first time in Stuttgart. These are two one-act operas. The first is about a man and woman who decide that murder is the only way women can ever achieve fulfillment. The second includes marionettes, a giant rat and an alligator who becomes a powerful ruler.

June 11   Arthur Honegger's opera *Le Roi David* premieres at the Theatre Jorat in Mezieres, Switzerland. The libretto, by Rene Morax, is based on biblical texts. It is not often performed as an opera, although it has been adapted for performance as an oratorio.

Nov. 19   *Die tote Stadt*, by Erich Wolfgang Korngold, receives its first American performance at the Metropolitan Opera House. The cast includes Maria Jeritza and is conducted by Artur Bodanzky. Richard Aldrich writes in the New York *Times* that Korngold "plunges, as into his own native element, into the unplumbed seas of modern dissonance."

Nov. 23   Leos Janacek's *Katya Kabanova* receives its premiere at Brno. The libretto, written by the composer, is based on V. Cervinka's translation of Alexander Ostrovsky's *The Storm*. It is the story of a young married woman, Katya, who is driven by her unhappiness to fall in love with another man.

Dec. 10   *La Leggenda di Sakuntala*, by Franco Alfano, has its premiere at the Teatro Communale in Bologna. The composer adapts his libretto from the play *Sakuntala*, by the fifth-century Indian poet Kalidasa. The composer's first successful work, it is performed throughout Europe and in South America. It is rewritten after World War II, when the only complete score was destroyed, and is subsequently performed in 1952 as *Sakuntala*. Tullio Serafin conducts the premiere.

Dec. 30 Sergei Prokofiev's *The Love for Three Oranges* premieres at the Chicago Opera House. Prokofiev writes his own libretto based on a comedy by Carlo Gozzi. It is a fairy tale about a prince who is suffering from melancholy and can only be cured if he can be made to laugh. The opera has a mixed reception, both in Chicago and later in the Soviet Union. Since then, however, it has come to be appreciated and enjoys frequent revivals. Nina Koshetz stars, and the composer conducts. Richard Aldrich says in the New York *Times* "... it seldom produces any effect but that of disagreeable noise...." Edward Moore says in the Chicago *Tribune* that the composer "... might well have loaded up a shotgun with several thousand notes of varying lengths and discharged them against the side of a blank wall."

1921 Dance

Jan. 31 Ted Shawn's *The Abduction of Sita* is performed for the first time by the Denishawn, dance company in San Diego. This modern dance work features Siamese music arranged by Louis Horst.

May 17 *Le chout* — a new ballet with music and libretto by Sergei Prokofiev — receives its first performance by Serge Diaghilev's Ballets Russes at the Theatre Gaite-Lyrique in Paris. The ballet, in six scenes with five symphonic interludes, is based on a medieval Russian fairy tale about eight buffoons. The score features asymmetrical rhythms. Choreography is by Tadeo Slavinsky and Mikhail Larionov. Lead dancers are Katharina Devilier and Slavinsky. The production is not a success, and the ballet is not revived until 1957, when Gertrud Steinweg's version is produced at the Berlin Comic Opera.

June 6 *L' homme et son desir* — a surrealist ballet with music composed by Darius Milhaud — premieres in Paris. It is based on a poem by Paul Claudel about a man and his fantasies of nudes. The score includes a hammer striking a wooden plank and castanets. Claudel comments that the poem was inspired by his experience of being in the jungles of Brazil with friends and of feeling "submerged." Choreography is by Jean Borlin, with decor by Andree Parr. The Ballets Suedois performs the work at the Theatre des Champs-Elysees. The lead dancers are Borlin and Carina Ari.

June 19 *Les Maries de la Tour Eiffel* — featuring music of Georges Auric, Arthur Honegger, Darius Milhaud, Francis Poulenc and Germaine Tailleferre — is premiered at the Theatre des Champs-Elysees by the Ballets Suedois in Paris. Jean Borlin choreographs this one-act ballet with a libretto by Jean Cocteau (who also conceived the spectacle). Costumes are by J. Hugo, sets by Irene Lagut. The ballet is about a photographer perched on the Eiffel Tower who tries to photograph a wedding party and has trouble because he is a hunchback. The piece is an artistic statement by "Les Six," although Louis Durey does not participate.

Nov. 2 Tchaikovsky's *The Sleeping Beauty* receives its first performance in Western Europe, by Serge Diaghilev's Ballets Russes at the Alhambra Theater in London. First offered in 1890 by the Russian Imperial Ballet, the original Marius Petipa choreography is recreated by Nicholas Sergeyev, with additional choreography by Bronislava Nijinska, The costumes and scenery are by Leon Bakst. The production is a critical and popular failure, and although the ballet is performed at the Alhambra 115 times, Diaghilev leaves London £7,000 in debt. Dancing the famous fairy tale are Olga Spessivtzeva, making her debut with the company; Pierre Vladimiroff; Lydia Lopokova ; and Stanislas Idzikowski.

SCENE FROM *LES MARIES DE LA TOUR EIFFEL*

1921 Instrumental and Vocal Music

Jan. 10 Norwegian composer Christian Sinding's Symphony No. 3 premieres in Berlin. The Berlin Philharmonic is conducted by Arthur Nikisch.

March 17 Pantcho Vladigerov's Piano Concerto No. 1 is premiered by the Berlin Philharmonic with the 22-year-old Bulgarian composer playing the solo part.

June 10 Igor Stravinsky's *Symphonies of Wind Instruments* receives its first performance in London. Serge Koussevitzky conducts. The piece, which is dedicated to the memory of Claude Debussy, is built on static rhythms; its sonorities move in distinct blocks of sound. Stravinsky composed this work almost simultaneously with his ballet *Pulcinella*.

July 31 String Quartet No. 4 , by Alois Haba, and Ernst Krenek's *Serenade* for clarinet and string quartet are premiered at the first concert of the first festival for the promotion of contemporary music in Donaueschingen, Germany. The Haba work employs quarter tones, as is characteristic of this composer. This festival quickly establishes itself as one of the world's major annual festivals.

Aug. 1 Paul Hindemith's String Quartet No. 3 premieres at the Donaueschingen Festival.

Oct. 9 *Taras Bulba*, a symphonic work by Leos Janacek, is performed for the first time in Brno. This rhapsody, scored for large symphony orchestra, is based on the tale by Gogol. The work contains characteristically Slavic rhythms.

Oct. 29 Albert Roussel's symphonic poem *Pour une fete de printemps* is premiered by Gabriel Pierne at a Colonne Concert in Paris. This piece is composed from musical materials the composer had been reserving for a movement of his Second Symphony.

Oct. 30 *Horace Victorieux*, by Arthur Honegger, receives its first performance in Lausanne, Switzerland with Ernest Ansermet conducting. This symphonic work depicts an ancient tale of a warrior who kills his sister.

Nov. 17 Henry Hadley's symphonic poem *The Ocean* is premiered by the New York Philharmonic with the composer conducting.

Dec. 1 Vincent d'Indy's *Poeme des rivages* is performed for the first time by the New York Symphony with the composer conducting. This symphonic suite has four movements — with geographical titles — and is based on d'Indy's travels with his wife.

Dec. 8 Marcel Dupre's live improvisatory *Symphonie-Passion* premieres in Philadelphia. Musicians in the audience supply the themes. This event is part of the organist's first American tour.

ALOIS HABA

Dec. 16   Sergei Prokofiev's Piano Concerto No. 3 in C Major in three movements is premiered by the Chicago Symphony Orchestra, with the composer as soloist. The most popular of his piano concertos, it was composed between 1911 and this year. This work marks his renewed interest in composing a virtuoso concerto.

1921   Births, Deaths and Debuts

Jan. 15   English tenor Gervase Elwes, 54, dies after being hit by a train in Boston, Massachusetts. Elwes decided to devote his life to music after serving as a diplomat and toured Germany and the United States as a singer. He was especially known as a singer of oratorio, having performed in approximately 150 performances of Edward Elgar's *The Dream of Gerontius*.

Feb. 3   Austrian conductor Max Zach, 56, dies in Saint Louis, Missouri. He studied at the Vienna Conservatory and became a violist with the Boston Symphony Orchestra after emigrating to America. He was also the violist of the Adamowski Quartet and conducted the Boston Pops. His principal impact was as a conductor of the St. Louis Symphony Orchestra, a post he received in 1907. While there, he advanced the cause of new music by American composers, including Ernest Bloch, John Alden Carpenter, Charles Tomlinson Griffes, and others.

Feb. 9   James Gibbons Huneker, 61, dies in Brooklyn, New York. Musical aesthetician, critic and author, he was noted for his opposition to the modern music of his day, most especially that of Richard Strauss and Claude Debussy. His criticism was published in the New York *Times*, the New York *World* and the Philadelphia *Press*.

March 12   Composer Ralph Shapey is born in Philadelphia, Pennsylvania.

March 21   Violinist Arthur Grumiaux is born in Villers-Perwin, Belgium.

March 24   French composer Deodat de Sevarac, 48, dies in Caret, the Pyrenees. Having studied with Vincent d'Indy, he wrote piano music, songs, chamber music and symphonic poems. His works include the opera *Le Coeur du moulin* (1909) and the symphonic poem *Nymphes au Crepuscule*. His music is marked by impressionism, but in a light, almost popular vein.

May 17   French-horn player Dennis Brain is born in London. He is the son of another famous French-horn player, Aubrey Brain.

June 25   Dancer, choreographer and ballet director Celia Franca is born in London, England.

July 30   Pianist Grant Johannesen is born in Salt Lake City, Utah.

Aug. 2   The great Italian tenor Enrico Caruso, 48, dies in Naples, Italy. Born the 18th child (the first to survive) of a working-class family in Naples, he made his debut in 1884

ENRICO CARUSO IN *PAGLIACCI*

in Naples. Chosen to create the tenor role in Umberto Giordano's *Fedora* in 1898, he was a huge success and was then hired to sing in Russia, South America and, in 1900, at La Scala. In 1902 he created the role of Maurizio in *Adriana Lecouvreur* and also that year made his Covent Garden debut in *Rigoletto*. His greatest successes were in the United States, where he first sang in 1903. He left an enormous catalog of phonograph records, which helped to popularize that medium. One of the highest-paid singers in the world, he received as much as $16,000 for a single performance and made over $100,000 a year from his recordings alone. He possessed ringing high notes combined with a baritonal quality in his lower register. His recordings remain models of bel canto singing.

Aug. 8   Arthur Pougin, 87, dies in Paris. A critic who often assailed Claude Debussy's music, he opposed the work of any composer he perceived as departing from his conception of traditional music. He began the *Revue de la Musique* (1876), which went out of business in six months. Most of his memorable reviews were published in *Le Menestrel*, *Le Soir*, *La Tribune*, *L'Evenement* and *Journal Officiel*.

Sep. 3   Musicologist and harpsichordist Thurston Dart is born in London, England.

Sep. 27   German composer Engelbert Humperdinck, 67, dies in Neustrelitz, Germany. He first studied architecture but was brought into music by Ferdinand Hiller of the Cologne Conservatory. At age 27 he won the Meyerbeer Prize (7,600 marks). Soon after, he traveled to Italy to meet Richard Wagner and subsequently helped Wagner with the preparation of the score of *Parsifal*. His opera *Hansel and Gretel*, produced in 1893, was a tremendous success and quickly became internationally known. In 1897 Humperdinck became preoccupied with the relation between speech, song and music and developed an approach to rhythmic and pitch inflections that he called "sprechnoten"; his opera *Konigskinder* is the result of this pursuit. He also wrote criticism for the *Frankfurter Zeitung* and worked for the Schott music publishing house.

Oct. 2   American baritone David Bispham, 63, dies in Philadelphia, Pennsylvania. After studies in Italy and England, he made his operatic debut in London in 1891 and later became famous for his interpretation of Wagnerian roles. He was strongly in favor of opera in English, and after his death the Opera Society of America established the Bispham Memorial Award for the writing of an opera in English by an American composer. He was also the first American baritone to sing with the Metropolitan Opera.

Oct. 24   Soprano Sena Jurinac is born in Travnik, Yugoslavia.

Nov. 14   Amelita Galli-Curci makes her Metropolitan Opera debut as Violetta in *La Traviata*. W.J. Henderson writes in the New York *Sun*, "The natural beauty of her voice was all that it used to be, and it is one of the most beautiful voices this public has heard."

Nov. 19   Pianist Geza Anda is born in Budapest, Hungary.

Nov. 19   Moravian soprano Maria Jeritza makes her Metropolitan Opera debut in the American premiere of Erich Wolfgang Korngold's *Die tote Stadt*. Richard Aldrich writes in the New York *Times* that Korngold's opera "is the

product of no mean talent" but that Jeritza's voice, though powerful, "degenerated unpleasantly into stridency. . . ."

Nov. 22   Swedish soprano Kristina Nilsson, 79, dies in Stockholm. She debuted in Paris in 1864 and later sang in Europe and America. She opened the Metropolitan Opera House on October 22, 1883 singing Marguerite in Charles Gounod's *Faust*.

Dec. 16   French composer Camille Saint-Saens, 86, dies in Algiers. He began to compose at age 6 and made his debut as a pianist at age 11. He studied with Jacques Halevy and won prizes for organ performance. At age 29, while an emerging composer, he failed a second time to win the Grand Prix de Rome; he subsequently worked as an organist and teacher. It was not until 1877 (at age 42) that he decided to devote himself entirely to composition and conducting. He helped establish the Societe Nationale de Musique (to encourage French composers) but resigned when Vincent d'Indy tried to bring in foreign composers. During his lifetime he was extremely well known as a virtuoso performer and composer. His music is characterized by lush harmonies and orchestrations. He revered German music until Germany invaded France in World War I. Saint-Saens was extremely prolific, with his work also known for its classical character. He disliked the work of Claude Debussy and opposed modernism in music. Symphony No. 3 (with organ), *Carnival of the Animals* and the opera *Samson et Dalila* are among his most famous compositions.

Dec. 21   Cuban dancer and ballet director Alicia Alonso is born Alicia Ernestina de la Caridad dei Cobre Martinez Hoyo in Havana.

Dec. 25   Swiss composer Hans Huber, 69, dies in Locarno. His composition teachers at the Leipzig Conservatory included Carl Reinecke. Huber's music is noted for its use of Swiss folk themes and for its Lisztian virtuosity. His output — including 8 symphonies, 5 operas, and 48 preludes and fugues for piano four hands — is prolific. After his death, his work is very highly regarded in Switzerland, though it is not performed much in other parts of the world.

1921 Related Events

The Composers' Society of Rumania is founded this year to protect composers' rights and further the cause of a national school of Rumanian music. The composer behind the organization is Georges Enesco. The society subsequently becomes the Union of Rumanian Composers and expands its functions to include control over conditions of performance and the establishment of social requirements for composers.

The Eastman School of Music is founded this year as part of the University of Rochester in New York.

Jan. 28   Music publisher G. Ricordi & Company is awarded $25,000 in a fine imposed on music publisher J.H. Remick & Company by the federal court of New York City. The popular song "Avalon," published by J.H. Remick & Company, was judged to be a plagiarized version of the aria "E lucevan le stelle," from Giacomo Puccini's *Tosca*, published and copyrighted by G. Ricordi & Company.

April 22   The Concerts Koussevitzky are inaugurated in Paris by Serge Koussevitzky. He is the founder of this new orchestra, which he dedicates to promoting new works by contemporary composers, including Arthur Honegger, Maurice Ravel, Sergei Prokofiev, Albert Roussel, Igor Stravinsky and Germaine Tailleferre.

May 3   The International Composers' Guild is organized in New York City by Edgar Varese to further the interests of contemporary composers.

June 14   The inaugural concert of the British Music Society is given in London. The program includes *The Planets*, by Gustav Holst; *The Eternal Rhythm*, by Eugene Goossens; and *The Lark Ascending*, by Ralph Vaughan Williams.

June 16   The first Zurich International June Festival begins today, as Arthur Nikisch conducts the Tonhalle-Orchester in a performance of Beethoven's Ninth Symphony. Events at this festival also include conducting appearances by Gabriel Pierne, Sir Henry J. Wood and Bruno Walter. The festival subsequently becomes an annual event, attracting musicians and music lovers from around the world.

June 24   Fontainebleau becomes the home of the American Conservatory of Music which is established today in France.

July 20   Music of George Chadwick, Henry F. Gilbert, Frederick S. Converse, Arthur Foote, Edward Burlingame Hill, Leo Sowerby and others is featured at Plymouth, Massachusetts to recall the landing of the Pilgrims 300 years ago.

Sep. 25   Moscow becomes the home of the State Institute of Musical Science. Its purpose is to advance and systematize the study of musicology in the Soviet Union. It is established through the efforts of Anatol Lunacharsky (People's Commissar of Public Education) and composer Boris Asafiev.

Oct. 4   Leo Sowerby becomes the first composer to receive a fellowship from the American Academy in Rome, founded today.

Nov. 11   Rudolph Ganz leads his first concert as permanent conductor of the St. Louis Symphony Orchestra. His program consists of music by Bizet, Tchaikovsky and Wagner. Ganz made his initial debut as a pianist with the Berlin Philharmonic Orchestra in 1899. He comes to St. Louis as an internationally recognized musician and was second choice after Fritz Kreisler, whom the orchestra's management failed to attract. Ganz remains six years, during which he introduces his audiences to music of Igor Stravinsky, Arnold Schoenberg and other living composers; audience attendance eventually declines, and he is asked to resign.

Dec. 9   Feodor Chaliapin returns to the Metropolitan Opera for the first time since 1908, singing the title role in *Boris Godunov*. Krehbiel writes of the performance in the New York *Times*, ". . . the effect upon the Russians in the audience was akin to frenzy. . . . [the performance] was heartbreaking in its pathos, terrible in its vehemence and agony."

Dec. 26   Arturo Toscanini conducts a performance of Giuseppe Verdi's *Falstaff* at La Scala, Milan. This event marks the reopening of La Scala which was closed in 1917 due to World War I and for reorganizational purposes. It is now a self-governing body, with Toscanini as artistic director. His orchestra numbers 100 players; his chorus, 120 voices. Italian baritone Mariano Stabile, who has been singing since 1909, has a huge success as Falstaff. Stabile's debut took place in Palermo in 1909.

1922 Opera

Feb. 14   The premiere of *Giulietta e Romeo*, by Riccardo Zandonai, takes place at the Teatro Costanzi in Rome. The libretto, by Arturo Rossato, is based on Shakespeare. The composer conducts a cast that includes Gilda Dalla Rizza and Miguel Fleta.

March 26   *Sancta Susanna*, a one-act opera by Paul Hindemith, receives its first performance in Frankfurt. A young nun, struggling to find her faith, decides to remove the garment from Christ's body on the crucifix. The opera is scored for speaking parts and a female chorus as well as soloists and orchestra.

April 1   The posthumous premiere of *Adamis*, by Jules Massenet, occurs at the Theatre du Casino in Monte Carlo. The libretto, by Jules Claretie, is based on a 15th-century romance by Garcia Ordonez de Montalero. It is one of Massenet's minor works.

April 13   Ottorino Respighi's opera *La bella addormentata nel bosco* premieres in Rome at the Teatro Odescalchi. Gian Bistolfi's libretto is based on the fairy tale of *The Sleeping Beauty*, by Charles Perrault. Featuring the puppeteer work of Vittorio Podrecca, the opera is enthusiastically received and is performed all over the world.

May 13   Karol Szymanowski's one-act opera *Hagith* premieres in Warsaw. It is a biblical story involving David and Abishag, his concubine. The 39-year-old composer

INTERIOR OF THE PARIS OPERA HOUSE

wrote this opera while he was living in Vienna (1912–14). Today's event marks the premiere of his first opera.

May 28   Alexander von Zemlinsky's *Der Zwerg* premieres in Cologne. This one-act opera is based on the story entitled "The Birthday of the Infanta," by Oscar Wilde.

June 3   *Mavra* — an opera by Igor Stravinsky — is performed for the first time at the Paris Opera by Serge Diaghilev's Ballets Russes. The text is by Boris Kochno, and the work is based on Pushkin's poem "The Little House at Kolomna," about a Russian village girl, Parasha, and her lover, the hussar Vassily. Principal singers include Russian soprano Oda Slobodskaya. The conductor is Gregor Fitelberg.

July 11   Ralph Vaughan Williams' *The Shepherds of the Delectable Mountains* — based on *Pilgrim's Progress*, by John Bunyan — premieres in London.

Aug. 26   Rutland Boughton's opera *Alkestis* premieres in Glastonbury, England. He composed this opera and established the theater at which today's performance takes place in an unsuccessful effort to create a British opera event comparable to Bayreuth.

Dec. 16   Ildebrando Pizzetti's *Debora e Jaele* receives its first performance at La Scala in Milan. The libretto, by the composer, is based on the story of Jaele from the Book of Judges. Arturo Toscanini conducts.

1922   Dance

Jan. 20   *Skating Rink*, a ballet choreographed by Jean Borlin to music by Arthur Honegger, is performed for the first time by the Ballets Suedois in Paris. The libretto of this one-act ballet is by Riciotto Canudo; decor, by Fernand Leger. Yoland Figoni, Kay Smith and the choreographer dance the lead roles in this production at the Theatre des Champs-Elysees. The ballet features dancers caricaturing people at a skating rink.

May 12   *Scaramouche* — a ballet in three scenes with music by Jean Sibelius — receives its initial performance in Copenhagen. The libretto is by Paul Knudsen; choreography, by Emilie Walbom. The Royal Danish Ballet performs. A demonic fiddler seduces an upper-class woman who desires to kill him but, because of his haunting music, dances herself to death. This work, composed in 1913, is the only ballet score Sibelius writes.

May 18   Serge Diaghilev and his Ballets Russes present the world premiere of *Renard* at the Paris Opera. The new one-act burlesque (technically an opera but premiered as a ballet, with powerful choreography by Bronislava Nijinska) is by Igor Stravinsky. The work is based on a Russian folk tale about a fox, a cock and a goat who engage in things naughty and nice. Stravinsky also writes the text to this piece, which is performed with singers (placed in the orchestra), acrobats and dancers. Mikhail Larionov creates the decor, and Ernest Ansermet conducts. Lead dancers are Nijinska and Stanislas Idzikowski. Also premiered at today's event is *Aurora's Wedding*, a divertissement from the last act of *The Sleeping Beauty*. Vera Trefilova and Yuri Vladimirov star.

1922   Instrumental and Vocal Music

Jan. 9   Bela Bartok's orchestral suite *Four Orchestral Pieces* receives its first performance. The Philharmonic Society of Budapest is conducted by Ernst von Dohnanyi. The work has four movements: "Preludio," "Scherzo," "Intermezzo" and "Marcia funebre."

Jan. 24   William Walton's *Facade* premieres in a private performance in London. Set to poetry by Edith Sitwell, the work is scored for reciting voice, flute, clarinet, trumpet, saxophone, cello and percussion. It is subsequently performed in a ballet version choreographed by Frederick Ashton.

Jan. 24   Symphony No. 5, by Carl Nielsen, receives its first performance in Copenhagen with the composer conducting. The new two-movement work incorporates a snare drum part that the composer states is "to be played in its own rhythm as though intended at all costs to disrupt the music."

Jan. 26   Ralph Vaughan Williams' Symphony No. 3 (*Pastoral Symphony*) is premiered by Adrian Boult in London. This four-movement symphony features a soprano solo in its final movement.

Feb. 5   Ottorino Respighi's *Concerto gregoriano* premieres in Rome. The work is scored for violin and orchestra.

Feb. 26   *Carnival of the Animals*, by Camille Saint-Saens, is premiered posthumously by Gabriel Pierne at a Colonne Concert in Paris. The piece is scored for celesta, xylophone, harmonium, clarinet, flute, strings and two pianos. It contains 14 tableaux depicting various animals. Saint-Saens considered the piece, composed in 1886, to be a mild amusement, not a serious work. For this reason, he prohibited its performance during his lifetime.

March 4   Albert Roussel's Symphony No. 2 in B Major receives its first performance in Paris. Its three movements represent three stages of life: youth, middle age and old age.

March 16   *English Suite No. 3*, by Havergal Brian, premieres in Bournemouth, England. The work employs English folk melodies.

March 23   Frederick Delius' *Requiem* for chorus and orchestra premieres in London. This work is dedicated to artists who perished in the First World War. The text, in German, includes Latin extractions from the Book of Ecclesiastes.

April 7   Leo Sowerby's Symphony No. 1 is premiered by Frederick Stock, who conducts the Chicago Symphony Orchestra.

April 21   Frederick Converse's Symphony No. 2 is premiered by the Boston Symphony Orchestra with Pierre Monteux conducting. This symphony omits percussion (except kettledrums) because, in the composer's words, "I am tired of the cheap, conventional effects obtained by their use." The work is in E Major and spans a variety of moods from suffering to joy. Henry Levine writes in *Musical America* (New York), "The music strains and stresses with a complaining fervor, almost operatic in its grandiloquent heights."

July 30   Ernst Krenek's *Symphonic Music for Nine Solo Instruments* premieres at the Second Chamber Music Festival for the Promotion of Contemporary Music in Donaueschingen.

July 31   Paul Hindemith's *Kammermusik No. 1* premieres at the Donaueschingen Festival.

Sep. 7   Arthur Bliss conducts the premiere of his *Colour Symphony* at the Three Choirs' Festival in Gloucester, England.

Oct. 19   Maurice Ravel's orchestration of Modest Mussorgsky's *Pictures at an Exhibition* receives its first performance as Serge Koussevitzky conducts the work in Paris. The piece, originally written by Mussorgsky for piano, was inspired by a series of paintings by Victor Hartmann. Koussevitzky paid Ravel a commission of 10,000 francs for his work. This orchestration brings the music to world attention, and the work immediately enters the repertory of major orchestras.

Nov. 2   Dutch composer Willem Pijper's Symphony No. 2 is performed for the first time by Willem Mengelberg and the Concertgebouw Orchestra in Amsterdam. The symphony's two movements are entitled "Allegro maestose" and "Lento molto rubato."

Dec. 2   Symphony No. 1 in E-flat Major, by Arnold Bax, premieres in London. This piece, which includes a heckelphone and a sarrusophone, contains three movements. (The sarrusophone is a member of the oboe family that is made of brass, not wood.)

Dec. 7   Arnold Schoenberg's arrangement of Bach's *Two Chorale Preludes* is performed for the first time by Josef Stransky and the New York Philharmonic. The chorale preludes are "Schmucke dich, O liebe Seele" and "Komm, Gott, Schopfer, Geist." Schoenberg scored the music for large orchestra, including glockenspiel, celesta and a triangle.

Dec. 15   Heitor Villa-Lobos' *Fantasia dos movimentos mixtos* premieres in Rio de Janeiro. The three-movement work is scored for violin and orchestra.

1922 Births, Deaths and Debuts

Jan. 7   Flutist Jean-Pierre Rampal is born in Marseille, France.

Jan. 19   Italian baritone Titta Ruffo makes his Metropolitan Opera debut in *The Barber of Seville*. Henderson writes in the New York *Sun*: "it can be recorded that Mr. Ruffo's Figaro was pleasing in its glee, its vivacity, its genuine humor, and its touches of a hitherto unrevealed skill."

Jan. 23   Hungarian conductor Arthur Nikisch, 66, dies in Leipzig. The first "star" conductor, Nikisch started as a child prodigy on the violin and then turned to conducting. Among the many posts he held in his lifetime were conductor of the Leipzig Theater, the Boston Symphony, the Budapest Opera, the Gewandhaus Concerts and the Berlin Philharmonic. Nikisch was the first conductor to achieve the kind of acclaim usually reserved for virtuosos, with his performances being known for their romanticism and profundity.

Feb. 1   Soprano Renata Tebaldi is born in Langhirano, Parma, Italy.

Feb. 16   Baritone Geraint Evans is born in Pontypridd, Wales.

April 14   Hindu instrumentalist Ali Akbar Khan is born in Shibpore, Bengal.

April 21   Alessandro Moreschi, 63, dies in Rome. This event marks the death of the last castrato. He sang soprano at the Sistine Chapel and in 1902 made recordings of 19th-century sacred music on the G. & T. record label. The sound of his voice earned him the nickname "the angel of Rome."

May 16   Australian soprano Florence Austral makes her operatic debut as Brunnhilde at Covent Garden.

May 29   Composer and theorist Iannis Xenakis is born in Braila, Rumania.

Aug. 15   Composer-conductor Lukas Foss is born in Berlin, Germany as Lukas Fuchs.

Aug. 19   Spanish composer and musicologist Felipe Pedrell, 81, dies in Barcelona. This musician was known as much for his writings about music as for his musical compositions. His first opera, *El ultimo Abencerraje*, premiered in Barcelona when Pedrell was 33; 14 years later he began his *Ilustracion musical hispano-americana*, a publication he edited

for many years. His operatic trilogy *Los Pirineos* (1889–91) employs Spanish folk song elements. He was encouraged by the clergy to bring about the reform of Spanish sacred music and edited the journal *Musica religiosa* at the end of the 19th century. His work — both as a composer and as a writer — was praised by his contemporaries; his pupils included Isaac Albeniz, Enrique Granados, Manuel de Falla and Roberto Gerhard.

Sep. 11   American composer Louis Adolphe Coerne, 52, dies in Boston. He studied violin with Franz Kneisel and composition with J.K. Paine (Harvard University) and Josef Rheinberger (Munich). He was the first American musician to receive a Ph.D. in music from an American university and the first American composer to have an opera staged in Europe (*Zenobia*, Bremen, 1905). Other works include his symphonic poem *Hiawatha* and the hymn "Beloved America," for male chorus and orchestra. He was also on the faculties of Harvard University, Smith College and the University of Wisconsin.

Sep. 20   Pianist William Kapell is born in New York City.

Sep. 22   English baritone Charles Santley, 87, dies in Hove, England. He studied in Milan and then with Manuel Garcia in London and made his debut in 1857 singing in Haydn's *Creation*. After making his stage debut at Covent Garden in 1850, he joined the Carl Rosa Company and toured the world for several years. He was knighted in 1907. Santley published several books on singing and two volumes of autobiography.

Sep. 24   Baritone Cornell MacNeil is born in Minneapolis, Minnesota.

Nov. 22   German soprano Elisabeth Rethberg makes her Metropolitan Opera debut as Aida. Richard Aldrich, of the New York *Times*, writes that her singing displays ". . . high, clear, liquid tones of a singular brightness floating above Verdi's orchestration with unforced ease."

1922   Related Events

This year Fritz Busch becomes the principal conductor of the Dresden Opera, and Wilhelm Furtwangler succeeds Arthur Nikisch as conductor of the Berlin Philharmonic.

Hugo Riemann's *Musik-Lexikon*, one of the standard reference works on music, is published in its 10th edition this year. This is the second edition that Alfred Einstein edits.

Nauko o hudebnich formach, (*Treatise on Musical Forms*) by Czech composer Karel Jirak, is published this year in Prague. The book explores various musical forms and approaches to composing in them. It is subsequently published in five editions, all in Czechoslovakian. Jirak is now a professor of composition at the Prague Conservatory.

Jan. 10   The clavilux — an instrument correlating sound and color by projecting onto a screen colors that are coordinated and articulated by a keyboard — is demonstrated in New York City by Thomas Wilfred, its inventor.

Jan. 17   In an open letter to the German music magazine *Melos*, Ferruccio Busoni attacks the extremes in new music and says in part: "When a physician recommends wine to a patient, he does not intend to make him drunk. Anarchy is not liberty."

Feb. 13   Beethoven's music is featured at the opening concert in Moscow of the Pervyi Symphonichesky Ensemble (Persymfans), founded to demonstrate that a music director is unnecessary in a proletarian state orchestra. One of many experiments in this century that seeks to eliminate the conductor, it fails. The NBC Symphony tries a similar venture after the death of Arturo Toscanini.

April 1   After spending 21 years of exile on the Isle of Wight the Benedictine monks of Solesmes return to their monastery in France. While on the Isle of Wight, they diligently prepared the new Vatican Edition of the chant books. The edition, a combined result of Benedictine and Solesmes scholarship, included *Kyriale* (1905), *Cantus Missae* (1907), *Graduale Vaticanum* (1907), *Officium Defunctorum* (1909), *Cantorinus* (1911), and *Antiphonale Diurnum Romanum* (1912).

April 11   Willem Mengelberg conducts the New York Philharmonic in a recording of Beethoven's *Coriolan Overture* for the Victor Company. This event marks the first recording made by this orchestra.

April 22   Geraldine Farrar gives her final Metropolitan Opera performance, singing the title role in Ruggero Leoncavallo's *Zaza*. People on the street offer to pay as much as $200 for a pair of last-minute tickets, and the entrance to the opera house is decorated with banners reading "Farrar, Hurrah!!! Hurrah, Farrar!"

July 11   German conductor Alfred Hertz conducts the inaugural concert of the new Hollywood Bowl.

Aug. 7   The International Festival of Contemporary Music is inaugurated today in Salzburg. The first concert includes performances of Darius Milhaud's Sonata (for flute, oboe, clarinet and piano); *Rout*, by Arthur Bliss — a work for soprano and 10 instruments (featuring a soprano part with a meaningless text exploiting the sounds of word syllables); and Bela Bartok's Sonata No. 1 for violin and piano.

Aug. 19   The Drottningholm Court Theater (Sweden) reopens after a period of dormancy lasting more than 100 years. This baroque theater was built in 1754, destroyed by fire in 1762 and reopened in 1766. Approximately 35 stage settings from the 18th century that survived the fire were discovered in 1921 (along with baroque machinery by the Italian, Donato Stopani) by the scholar Agne Beijer, who immediately realized that the "pile of junk" had great historical value (the theater had been abandoned since the assassination of King Gustav III). Swedish authorities permit Beijer to head the restoration team; the only change is the replacement of wax candles with low-watt electric bulbs to approximate candlelight and reduce the risk of fire. This event marks the 150th anniversary of King Gustav III's palace revolution.

Oct. 23   Isadora Duncan is prohibited by Mayor James Curley from performing in Boston after she danced in a transparent costume and spoke favorably of the Soviet government.

THE DROTTNINGHOLM COURT THEATER

Nov. 11   The BBC begins wireless broadcasting of music.

Nov. 12   Columbia (U.S.) sells its British division to Louis Sterling; this year Columbia also issues laminated-stock discs. Other recording industry developments include the development, by Noel Pemberton-Billing (in England), of the constant linear-speed disc, which appeared on the British market in October. The success of this disc motivates recording entrepreneurs in France and Belgium to apply for similar patents in their countries. Billing's success leads him to introduce his "World" label — a recording requiring his special record controller attachment for gramophones. The catalog of the Vienna Phonogram Archiv also appears this year.

1923   Opera

March 23   *El retablo de Maese Pedro*, by Manuel de Falla, premieres at the Teatro S. Fernando in Seville. De Falla's libretto is based on parts of Cervantes' *Don Quixote*. This premiere is in concert form and features vocalists and marionettes.

April 26   *Belfagor*, by Ottorino Respighi, is performed for the first time at La Scala in Milan. The text, by Claudio Guastella, is based on a comedy by Ercole Luigi Morselli, which, in turn, is based on a tale by Machiavelli about the devil attempting to marry.

May 14   Gustav Holst's *The Perfect Fool* receives its first performance at Covent Garden in London. The composer writes his own libretto — a folk tale about a fool who captures the heart of a princess. The opera is praised but subsequently fades away.

June 1   *Padmavati* premieres at the Paris Opera. Composed by Albert Roussel to a libretto by Louis Lalay, it is based on a historical event in 13th-century India. The work is an opera-ballet.

June 25   Manuel de Falla's *El retablo de Maese Pedro* is performed privately at the salon of the Princesse de Polignac, in Paris. This opera, for singers and marionettes, features traditional Castillian music. It was performed in concert form last March; the first public stage performance comes this November.

Oct. 27   The first performance of *Holofernes*, by Emil Nikolaus von Reznicek, takes place at the Hoftheater in Berlin. The composer writes his own libretto, based on the play *Judith*, by Friedrich Hebbel, which, in turn, is based on the *Book of Judith*.

Dec. 16   Siegfried Wagner's opera *Der Schmied von Marienburg* premieres in Rostock.

Dec. 22   *Diana* — a one-act opera about infidelity by 29-year-old Hungarian composer Eugen Zador — is performed for the first time in Budapest.

1923   Dance

Jan. 31   *La Bayadere*, choreographed by Alexander Gorsky and Vasilii Tikhomirov, is performed for the first time by the Bolshoi Ballet in Moscow. The music is by Alois Minkus and the decor by Konstantin Korovin. This event marks the first Soviet version of this work, which was originally choreographed in 1877 by Marius Petipa.

March 7   Feodor Lopokov's ballet *Dance Symphony, The Greatness of Creation* is premiered at the Maryinsky Theatre in Leningrad. Among the dancers are Georgi Balanchivadze (George Balanchine), Alexandra Danilova and Leonid Lavrovsky. The ballet is danced to Beethoven's Fourth Symphony. Its sections are entitled "Birth of Light," "Triumph of Life Over Death," "Awakening of Nature in the Sun of Spring," and "The Cosmogonic Spiral." The work is one of the first attempts at a truly symphonic ballet. The choreography progresses from classical ballet steps to free movement and arises from the orchestral texture of the piece. Balanchine, at this point just out of school, is greatly influenced by the work. *Dance Symphony* is condemned as obscene and contrary to Bolshevik ideals. It does not receive another performance.

June 5   *Old King Cole*, by Ralph Vaughan Williams, premieres in Cambridge, England. The ballet, scored for orchestra and chorus, is the first of three by this English composer.

June 13   Bronislava Nijinska's *Les Noces* receives its premiere performance by Serge Diaghilev's Ballets Russes at the Theatre Gaite-Lyrique in Paris. The score is by Igor Stravinsky; decor and costumes by Nathalie Gontcharova. A stern, austere stylization of a wedding in ancient Russia, *Les Noces* contains some of Nijinska's most revolutionary choreography. In it she breaks with the soft rounded style, and while still retaining the use of point, uses bold, basic motions and silences to create a picture of solemnity and humor of an important rite. The principal dancers are Felia

Dubrovska (the Bride) and Leon Woizikovsky (the Bridegroom). The ballet is scored for chorus, vocal soloists, 4 pianos and 17 percussion instruments.

Sep. 10   Anna Pavlova's production of Alexander Tcherepnin's *The Ajanta Frescoes* premieres in London, with Pavlova playing the part of the princess.

Oct. 25   *La creation du monde*, by Darius Milhaud, receives its first performance by the Ballets Suedois at the Theatre des Champs-Elysees in Paris. This one-act ballet has a libretto by Blaise Cendrars and choreography by Jean Borlin. Decor is by Fernand Leger. The dance is a rendition of how an African Negro might conceive creation. The music contains jazz elements — the first major work to incorporate jazz within the context of serious symphonic music. The ballet comes to be ranked among Milhaud's finest music — perhaps his masterpiece. Ebon Strandin and Jean Borlin star. Six years from now, Max Chop says of this ballet in *Signale* (Berlin), "A more brutal self-accusation of sinning against the spirit of true art is difficult to find."

Dec. 16   Henry Cowell accompanies a concert of dances to his own music, choreographed by Yvonne Daunt, at the Salon d'Automne in Paris.

1923   Instrumental and Vocal Music

Jan. 6   Kurt Atterberg's Symphony No. 5 (*Sinfonia funebre*) premieres in Stockholm.

Jan. 18   Rubin Goldmark's *Negro Rhapsody* is performed for the first time by Josef Stransky and the New York Philharmonic. He is the nephew of the Austro-Hungarian composer Karl Goldmark.

Feb. 19   Symphony No. 6 in D Minor, Op. 104, by Jean Sibelius, receives its first performance in Helsinki, with Sibelius conducting. The work has four movements.

March 4   *Hyperprism* — a new work by Edgard Varese — is premiered by the International Composers' Guild in New York City. Scored for 18 percussion instruments and 9 winds, this "organized sound" composition is a spatial and static exploration of extremes of register and does not employ melodic themes. Olin Downes writes of this music in the New York *Times*, "[*Hyperprism*] reminded us of election night, a menagerie or two and a catastrophe in a boiler factory."

March 4   Ottorino Respighi's *La Primavera* premieres in Rome. This work is a cantata for soloists, chorus and orchestra.

March 10   Deems Taylor's *Through the Looking Glass* is premiered in a revised version for full orchestra by Walter Damrosch and the New York Symphony Society Orchestra.

March 18   Anton Bruckner's Symphony in F Minor premieres in Klosterneuberg, Germany. This event marks the premiere of a work composed some 60 years earlier. Like his Symphony in D Minor, this is one of two early symphonies Bruckner discarded.

May 3   Arthur Honegger's *Chant de joie* is performed for the first time by Serge Koussevitzky in Paris. This piece is a symphonic movement in three sections.

May 30   Howard Hanson's Symphony No. 1 in E Minor (*Nordic Symphony*) premieres in Rome with the composer conducting. Hanson, now 26, is residing in that city after having won the American Rome Prize.

June 12   William Walton's *Facade*, to poems by Edith Sitwell, with Sitwell herself performing as speaker, receives its first public performance in London.

June 17   Paul Hindemith's *Das Marienleben* receives its first performance at the third Donaueschingen Festival. The cycle consists of 15 songs and is scored for violin and piano. The text describes the life of the Blessed Virgin. Hindemith, now 27, subsequently revises the work.

June 24   Ernst Toch's chamber symphony *Die Chinesische Flote* receives its first performance in Frankfurt. This is a work for 14 instruments and soprano soloist.

July 4   Ralph Vaughan Williams' *English Folk Song Suite*, commissioned by the Royal Military School of Music, premieres in London.

Aug. 6   Ferruccio Busoni's piano work *Fantasia contrappuntistica* premieres at today's concert of the first International Society for Contemporary Music festival. This piece, in 12 sections, is modeled on Bach's *Art of the Fugue*. The music is tonal and cast in a neoclassical style.

Oct. 18   *Octet*, by Igor Stravinsky, is performed for the first time in Paris. The composer conducts. The three-movement work is scored for flute, clarinet, two bassoons, two trumpets and two trombones. This piece, composed six years ago, is one of Stravinsky's first neoclassical works and is considered to be one of his most important instrumental compositions. Sergei Prokofiev's Violin Concerto No. 1 in D Major also premieres at the same concert, with Marcel Darrieux as soloist and Serge Koussevitzky conducting.

Nov. 11   *Quintete*, by Ernest Bloch, receives its initial performance in New York at the inaugural concert of the League of Composers. The work, scored for piano and string quartet, has three movements and employs quarter tones.

Nov. 19   Ernst von Dohnanyi's *Festival Overture*, Zoltan Kodaly's *Psalmus Hungaricus*, and Bela Bartok's *Five Dances* are premiered in Budapest at a 50th-anniversary celebration of the union of the Yugoslavian twin cities Buda and Pest.

Dec. 1   Florent Schmitt's ballet *Le Petit Elfe Ferme-l'oeil* premieres in a concert version at a Colonne Concert in Paris.

Dec. 18   Frederick S. Converse's symphonic piece *Scarecrow Sketches* premieres in Boston. This work was composed using materials from one of his earlier pieces, *Puritan Passions*.

1923   Births, Deaths and Debuts

Pierina Legnani, Italian ballerina assoluta, dies in Milan this year. Legnani became prima ballerina of La Scala in 1892. She appeared in Saint Petersburg the following year where her technical brilliance, particularly her ability to execute 32 fouettes, challenged the Russians to emulate her technical feats. She created the role of Odette in the Petipa-Ivanov version of *Swan Lake* in 1895. Legnani was appointed prima ballerina assoluta the same year.

Jan. 20   American tenor George Hamlin, 55, dies in New York City. He was one of the earliest singers to present the songs of Richard Strauss in the United States.

Feb. 2   French dancer, choreographer and actor Jean Babilee is born in Paris.

Feb. 10   Bass Cesare Siepi is born in Milan, Italy.

Feb. 12   Russian bass Alexander Kipnis makes his American debut with the German Opera Company in New York singing Pogner in *Die Meistersinger*.

May 17   American composer Peter Mennin is born in Erie, Pennsylvania as Peter Mennini.

May 23   Pianist Alicia de Larrocha is born in Barcelona, Spain.

July 13   Danish composer Asger Hamerik, 80, dies in Frederiksberg. His work includes seven symphonies, four operas and two choral trilogies. He had also been knighted by the king of Denmark. Born Asger Hammerich, he stud-

GIUSEPPE VERDI AND VICTOR MAUREL

ied orchestration with Hector Berlioz in 1864. He lived for 26 years in Baltimore, where he was director of the Peabody Conservatory.

Sep. 15   Austrian composer and organist Anton Heiller is born in Vienna.

Oct. 22   French baritone Victor Maurel, 75, dies in New York. Starting his career in Paris in 1868, Maurel was best known for creating the roles of Iago in Verdi's *Otello* and the title role in Verdi's *Falstaff*. He emigrated in 1909 to America, where he taught voice. In 1919 he designed the scenery for a production of Charles Gounod's opera *Mireille* for the Metropolitan Opera.

Nov. 1   Soprano Victoria de Los Angeles is born in Barcelona, Spain.

Dec. 3   Soprano Maria Callas (nee Kalogeropoulos) is born in New York City.

Dec. 8   Dom Joseph Pothier, 78, dies in Conques, Belgium. He joined the Order of the Benedictines at the Abbey of Solesmes at age 24 and relocated to Belgium (the other monks went to the Isle of Wight) when the Law of Associations, enacted in France in 1901, forced many religious orders into exile. Pope Pius X, in 1904, appointed him to oversee publication of the *Editio Vaticana* — the Vatican edition of the chant books. Dom Andre Mocquereau was one of Pothier's proteges.

1923   *Related Events*

Due to a failing market, Columbia (U.S.) goes into receivership; recent public interest in recordings has become secondary in preference to radio listening. Other events in the recording industry this year include: the publication of the first issue of *The Gramophone* (England), a periodical about recordings; the first recording made by members of the British royal family (Queen Mary and King George V).

The Belgrade Philharmonic is founded this year. Composer Stevan Hristic is the first music director of this Yugoslavian orchestra.

Jan. 4   A radio program originating at New York station WEAF is transmitted by Boston station WNAC. This event marks the first radio network broadcast.

Jan. 8   The first wireless broadcast of a full opera takes place as the BBC broadcasts Mozart's *The Magic Flute* from a London concert hall.

April 11   The League of Composers is created in New York City to advance new music of moderate trends. A

faction of the International Composers' Guild of New York, it also emphasizes heavy contact with the public.

May 5   Nikolai Rimsky-Korsakov's grandson Georgi Rimsky-Korsakov becomes director of the new Society of Quarter-Tone Music, founded today in Petrograd. Its purpose is to advance quarter-tone music, both through performances and the publication of articles. The Soviet Commissar of Public Education, Anatol Lunacharsky, calls it "one of the most important phenomena in the formal development of our music."

June 14   Erik Satie announces the formation of the Ecole d'Arcueil in Paris. Dedicated to this composer's aesthetic ideals, the group includes Henri Cliquet-Pleyel, Roger Desormiere, Maxim Jacob and Henri Sauguet.

Nov. 1   Hugo Gernsback's staccatophone is demonstrated in New York City via radio broadcast. The musical instrument is an electronic piano that replaces strings with vacuum tubes. Gernsback is also a well-known science fiction writer.

1924   *Opera*

Feb. 14   Belgian composer Leon Jongen's four-act opera *Thomas l'Angelet*, premieres in Brussels. It is an adventure story taking place during the Franco-Spanish War. A French soldier who desires a Spanish lady captures and kills her male relatives when she refuses to show him affection. He is eventually hanged.

March 19   French organist Charles Tournemire's opera *Les Dieux sont morts* receives its first performance at the Paris

Opera. This two-act opera, composed 12 years ago, is about pagan gods dying at the time of the birth of Jesus.

May 2   The posthumous premiere of *Nerone*, by Arrigo Boito, takes place at the Teatro alla Scala in Milan. The composer bases his libretto on the story of the Roman emperor Nero. It is revised by Arturo Toscanini, who conducts this performance.

June 6   Arnold Schoenberg's monodrama *Erwartung* premieres in Prague at the Neues Deutsches Theater. Schoenberg commissioned the young poet Marie Pappenheim to write the text for the opera. There is only one character — a woman who goes through the woods at night to meet her lover, whom she finds murdered by the side of the road.

June 9 Ernst Krenek's comic opera *Der Sprung uber den Schatten* receives its initial performance in Frankfurt. The composer writes this detective story. Krenek later says the work satirizes corruption, occultism and snobbism. This is Krenek's first opera, and it incorporates jazz elements within an atonal context.

July 14 The first professional performance of Ralph Vaughan Williams' *Hugh the Drover, or Love in the Stocks* is given in London at His Majesty's Theatre. The traditional love story, by Harold Child, is set in England at the beginning of the 19th century. The opera is not successful. An earlier dress rehearsal performance took place 10 days ago.

Sep. 19 Giacomo Puccini's *Tosca* is performed in Leningrad in a Russian version by Moscow stage director Nikolai Vinogradov. It is called *Struggle for the Commune*. Fourteen performances are given.

Oct. 14 Arnold Schoenberg's one-act opera *Die gluckliche Hand* receives its first performance in Vienna. The opera, about a man who desires but is rejected by a woman, has a libretto by the composer. The work waited 11 years to be performed. It is the second of four operas written by Schoenberg. The cast includes Alfred Jerger and is conducted by Fritz Stiedry. Austrian dancer Hedy Pfundmayr also

performs. Six years from now, W.J. Henderson writes of this opera, "The wailing complaints of the man and the caterwauling of the chorus have neither musical nor dramatic value."

Nov. 4 *Intermezzo*, an opera by Richard Strauss, is performed for the first time at the Dresden Staatsoper. The libretto, by the composer, is based on an incident from his own marriage. (Strauss had received an anonymous love letter from a female admirer — a letter that had been delivered to him by mistake). The two-act opera stars Lotte Lehmann (who sings the role of the composer's wife, Pauline) and Joseph Correck (who sings the role of Strauss). The conductor is Fritz Busch.

Nov. 6 Leos Janacek's *The Cunning Little Vixen* receives its world premiere in Brno. The composer adapts the libretto from a story by R. Tesnohlidek about a forester who captures a fox and tries to domesticate her. It is considered one of the great Czech operas of the century and one of Janacek's most lyrical works.

Dec. 3 Mikhail Glinka's *A Life for the Tsar* premieres in Odessa in a revised Soviet version entitled *For the Hammer and the Sickle*.

Dec. 20 *La cene delle beffe* a four-act opera by Umberto Giordano, receives its first performance at La Scala, Milan. Arturo Toscanini conducts. This love story is Giordano's last success.

1924 Dance

Jan. 6 Serge Diaghilev's Ballets Russes premieres Bronislava Nijinska's *Les Biches*, with a commissioned score by Francis Poulenc and decor by Marie Laurencin. The ballet, which has no plot, revolves around a series of meetings between individuals at a house party. It is a masterful satire of the mores of the 1920s. Alexandra Danilova, Ninette de Valois, Felia Dubrovska, Natalie Komarova, Vera Nemchinova, Alice Nikitina, Bronislava Nijinska, Lubov Tchernicheva, Leon Woizikovsky, Anatole Vilzak and Nicholas Zverev star.

Jan. 19 *Les Facheux*, a one-act ballet with music by Georges Auric, receives its first performance in Monte Carlo. Lubov Pavlova Tchernicheva, Anatole Josifovich Vilzak and Anton Dolin star in this production by Serge Diaghilev's Ballets Russes. Bronislava Nijinska emphasizes mime in her choreography. The decor is by Georges Braque, libretto (based on the comedy by Moliere) by Boris Kochno. The ballet is about a lover who desires to be with his beloved and is distracted by irritating people who delay his visit. The work is not successful, but Diaghilev likes the ballet and three years from now commissions Leonide Massine to create a new version.

Feb. 26 *Les Elfes*, a one-act ballet choreographed by Michel Fokine to music by Felix Mendelssohn, is performed for the first time at the Metropolitan Opera House in New York by the Fokine Ballet. Mendelssohn's overture from *A Midsummer Night's Dream* and the Andante and Allegro movements of his "Violin Concerto in D Major form the sonic backdrop to the plotless choreography.

May 9 Heinrich Kroller's two-act ballet *Schlagobers* receives its initial performance at the State Opera in Vienna. This work, set to music by Richard Strauss with decor by Ada Nigrin, is about a child who eats too much whipped cream. It is one of two ballets by Strauss. Lead dancers are Gusti Pichler, Hedy Pfundmayr, Tilly Losch, Toni Birkmeyer (of the famous Viennese family of dancers) and Willy Franzl.

June 15 *Mercure* — a new ballet choreographed by Leonide Massine — receives its world premiere at the Theatre de la Cigale, Paris. This production is part of the short ballet season, Les Soirees de Paris, organized by Count Etienne de Beaumont. Music is by Erik Satie, decor by Pablo Picasso. Massine also writes the libretto to this ballet, consisting of a tableau in three scenes depicting various aspects of Mercury's mystical personality (magic, theft,

SCENE FROM *RELACHE*

fertility and communication with the gods). The ballet has an unexpected result: Picasso's cubist decor grips the audience, overpowers Massine's choreography and substantially enhances Picasso's stature. Serge Diaghilev decides to produce this work for his Ballets Russes three years from now.

June 20   Bronislava Nijinska's *Le Train bleu* receives its world premiere by Serge Diaghilev's Ballets Russes. The performance takes place at the Theatre des Champs-Elysees in Paris. Music is by Darius Milhaud, libretto by Jean Cocteau and curtain (with two giant females escaping from excited males) by Pablo Picasso. This one-act ballet is about the train that shuttles the wealthy between Paris and the Riviera. Lead dancers are Nijinska, Anton Dolin and Leon Woizikovsky.

Oct. 29   Soviet composer Vladimir Deshevov's ballet *The Red Whirlwind* receives its first performance in Leningrad. Feodor Lopokov choreographs and supplies the libretto. Decor is by L. Tshupiatov. Pavel Gerdt and Victor Semenov star. The production — featuring dance, acrobatics, song and speech — is subtitled *Bolsheviki* and is based on

the Russian Revolution. It receives only two performances.

Nov. 19   Alfredo Casella's *La giara*, based on a tale by Luigi Pirandello, receives its initial performance by the Ballets Suedois in Paris. Pirandello writes the libretto. This one-act ballet, about a hunchback in a jar, is also known as *La jarre*, or *The Jar*. Choreography is by Jean Borlin, decor by Giorgio di Chirico. Inger Fris, Eric Viber and the choreographer star in this production at the Theatre des Champs-Elysees.

Dec. 4   *Relache* — an "instantaneous" ballet in two acts, featuring a cinematic entr'acte by Rene Clair — receives its world premiere by the Ballets Suedois at the Theatre des Champs-Elysees in Paris. Choreography is by Jean Borlin, music by Erik Satie, libretto and decor by F. Picabia. The ballet is an expression of the "carpe diem," or live-for-the-day, philosophy cast in Dadaist fantasy. Lead dancers are Borlin and Edith Bonsdorff. The curtain is decorated with the following inscription: "Erik Satie is the greatest musician in the world; whoever disagrees with this notion will please leave the hall."

1924 Instrumental and Vocal Music

Jan. 6   Jacques Ibert's symphonic piece *Escales* premieres at the Concerts Lamoreux in Paris.

Jan. 13   *Octandre*, by Edgard Varese, is performed for the first time in New York City. Scored for flute, piccolo, clari-

net, piccolo clarinet, oboe, bassoon, horn, trumpet, trombone and double bass, the music moves in blocks and displays repeated pitch and rhythmic patterns, with the musical material of the third section derived from that of the first two sections. W.J. Henderson writes of it in the

New York *Herald*: "An Octandre is a flower having eight stamens. Mr. Varese's *Octandre* was no flower; it was a peach."

Jan. 26   Alexander Tcherepnin's Piano Concerto No. 2 is premiered by the Societe Nationale de Musique in Paris, with the composer as soloist and Nadia Boulanger conducting.

Feb. 2   Franz Schmidt's *Concertante Variationen uber ein Thema von Beethoven* premieres in Vienna, with Paul Wittgenstein as soloist. The music is composed for the left hand for this one-handed pianist.

Feb. 12   American composer George Gershwin performs as soloist in the world premiere of his *Rhapsody in Blue*. Paul Whiteman conducts in Aeolian Hall, New York City. Based on jazz themes, this music establishes itself as a favorite not only among American audiences but internationally as well. Lawrence Gilman writes of it in the New York *Tribune*; "Its gorgeous vitality of rhythm and of instrumental color is impaired by melodic and harmonic anemia of the most pernicious kind. . . ." Deems Taylor writes in the New York *World*, "It was crude, but it hinted at something new. . . ."

March 24   Symphony No. 7 in C Major, Op. 105, by Jean Sibelius, receives its world premiere in Stockholm with the composer conducting. This single-movement symphony has four sections. This is Sibelius' last symphony.

April 26   Maurice Ravel's *Tzigane* is premiered in London by Hungarian violinist Jelly d'Aranyi, with the composer at the keyboard. This work becomes a popular showpiece for violinists. A critic writes in the London *Times*, "Either the work is a parody of all the Liszt-Brahms-Joachim school of Hungarian violin music, or it is an attempt to infuse into his [Ravel's] work a little of that warm blood it needs."

May 2   Soviet composer Andrei Pashchenko's *Symphonic Mystery* premieres in Leningrad. It is the first time a symphonic work features a solo electronic instrument — in this case, the Thereminovox.

May 4   Nikolai Miaskovsky's Symphony No. 6 in E-flat minor premieres in Moscow. This is one of the composer's most important symphonies — it reflects his impressions of the Russian Revolution, which he later describes as a "submissive attitude." The work has four movements.

May 8   The revised version of Sergei Prokofiev's Piano Concerto No. 2 in G Minor is performed in Paris with Serge Koussevitzky conducting. The first version was performed on September 5, 1913. Also premiered at today's concert is Arthur Honegger's *Pacific 231*. The music is about a locomotive; a film version using the same music is later created. In a subsequent interview in the Geneva magazine *Dissonances*, the composer says: "I have always loved locomotives passionately. For me they are living beings whom I love as others love women or horses."

May 22   Igor Stravinsky performs as soloist in his *Concerto for Piano and Winds*. The world premiere of this three-movement work is conducted by Serge Koussevitzky in Paris.

May 27   *From the Northland* — an orchestral suite by Leo Sowerby — premieres at the American Academy in Rome. This piece was inspired by the composer's impressions of Canadian geography. Howard Hanson conducts.

May 29   *Seven, They Are Seven* — a cantata by Sergei Prokofiev — is performed for the first time by Serge Koussevitzky in Paris. The piece is scored for tenor solo, chorus and orchestra and was composed six years ago. Set to poetry by Constantin Balmont, it is one of the most modernistic compositions of Prokofiev's early period, combining intense dissonance with highly animated rhythms. Special effects in this eight-section piece include a chorus whispering a glissando.

May 29   Alexander Gretchaninoff's Symphony No. 3 in E Major, Op. 100 premieres in Kiev, the composer conducting. The work was composed between 1920 and 1923.

July 19   Anton Webern's *Six Bagatelles for String Quartet*, Op. 9, is premiered by the Amar Quartet in Donaueschingen, at the new music festival. These pieces, composed between 1911 and 1913, last approximately two minutes and employ all 12 tones of the chromatic scale without repeating any until each has been sounded. Reviews are largely favorable. A critic of the *Dresdner Neuste Nachrichten* (Dresden) writes that the pieces go "beyond all usual concepts."

July 20   *Serenade*, Op. 24, by Arnold Schoenberg, receives its first performance at the fourth Donaueschingen Festival. This work, in seven sections, is the first by this composer that fully uses his 12-tone method. It is scored for guitar, mandolin, bass clarinet, clarinet, cello, violin and baritone. Also premiered today is Anton Webern's *Six Songs on Poems of Georg Trakl*, Op. 14. The composer conducts and Clara Kwartin is soloist.

Oct. 9   Anton Webern's *Five Sacred Songs*, Op. 15, premieres in Vienna, with the composer conducting, Felicie Huni-Mihacsek as soloist and members of the Vienna Opera as instrumentalists. These songs are settings of poems of a religious nature and are scored, in varying combinations, for soprano, flute, clarinet, bass clarinet, trumpet, harp, violin and viola. The last song, entitled "Arise in the Name of the Lord," employs a double canon. Webern enters the piece, composed between 1917 and 1922, in this year's Berkshire Chamber Music Competition. The score is misplaced by the administrators of the contest and eventually returned to him without having been considered (the winning work is Wallingford Riegger's *La belle* *dame sans merci*, which received its first performance in Pittsfield, Massachusetts, on September 19; that work is scored for four solo voices and chamber orchestra.

Oct. 9   Marcel Dupre's improvisatory *Symphonie-Passion* is performed in its notated version at Westminster Abbey, London.

Oct. 12   Gustav Mahler's Symphony No. 10 (two movements — Adagio, and Purgatorio — both dating from 1910) receives its first performance by Franz Schalk in Vienna. Unfinished at Mahler's death, this version was completed by Ernst Krenek. The manuscript of these two movements is subsequently published in facsimile this year by Alma Mahler; Deryck Cooke prepares a performing edition of Mahler's draft for the whole work which is first heard in 1960.

Oct. 12   Anton Bruckner's Symphony in D Minor premieres in Klosterneuberg, Germany. This event marks the work's first public performance since its composition in 1864 and revision in 1869. Like his Symphony in F Minor premiered on March 18 of last year, this is one of two early symphonies Bruckner discarded.

Oct. 16   Ernst Krenek's cantata *Zwingburg*, based on a story by Franz Werfel, premieres in Berlin. The piece is about a rebellion. Krenek is now 24.

Oct. 20   Bela Bartok's Violin Sonata No. 2 premieres at a concert of the Society of Rumanian Composers. This is the first concert given by this new society.

Nov. 15   Claude Debussy's *Khamma* premieres posthumously in Paris. This work had originally been composed for piano, but today's version has been orchestrated by Charles Koechlin.

Nov. 17   Ernst von Dohnanyi's symphonic suite *Ruralia Hungarica* premieres in Budapest, the composer conducting. The seven-movement work is performed today in its orchestral version. The composer based this work on earlier piano pieces.

Dec. 2   Anton Webern's *Three Little Pieces for Violoncello and Piano*, Op. 11, premieres in Mainz.

Dec. 7   *Men and Mountains*, by American composer Carl Ruggles, receives its first performance in New York City. This symphonic suite contains three movements: "Men," "Lilacs" and "Marching Mountains."

Dec. 14   Ottorino Respighi's *Pines of Rome* is performed for the first time in Rome with Bernardino Molinari conducting. This Italian impressionistic music is made up of four tone paintings ("I pini di Villa Borghese," "Pini presso una catacomba," "I pini del Giancolo" and "I pini di Via Appia"). Along with *The Fountains of Rome*, this piece becomes one of Respighi's best-known compositions.

1924   Births, Deaths and Debuts

Jan. 13   Dancer, choreographer and ballet director Roland Petit is born in Villemomble, France.

Jan. 14   Hungarian pianist and composer Count Geza Zichy, 74, dies in Budapest. He studied with Franz Liszt. Zichy lost his right arm at age 14, and thereafter became a well-known left-handed pianist. He was president of the National Conservatory in Budapest for 43 years. Most of his music is either operatic or for piano.

Feb. 23   German bass-baritone Friedrich Schorr, who made his Metropolitan Opera debut a few days earlier, sings his first Hans Sachs in *Die Meistersinger* at this theater. Lawrence Gilman writes in the New York *Tribune*, "Some of his mezza-voce and pianissimo singing yesterday was of astonishing delicacy, purity, and finesse...."

March 6   Conductor and opera director Sarah Caldwell is born in Maryville, Missouri.

March 29   English composer Sir Charles Villiers Stanford, 71, dies in London. His works include seven operas, seven symphonies, piano concertos and chamber music. Also an organist and conductor, he led many of the Leeds Festivals and toured internationally. He taught composition at the Royal College of Music. His romantic style incorporates English and Irish folk elements.

April 7   Spanish guitarist Andres Segovia gives his first recital in Paris.

May 26   Composer Victor Herbert, 65, dies in New York. As a youngster, he studied cello and later performed in various European orchestras. He studied composition with Max Seifritz at the Stuttgart Conservatory. After marrying singer Therese Forster in 1886, he became a cellist in the Metropolitan Opera Orchestra and his wife was invited to sing with that company. Once they came to New York, he began conducting light music and forming ensembles. He conducted the Boston Festival Orchestra, the 22nd Regiment Band and the Pittsburgh Symphony Orchestra. He then began composing operettas, the activity for which he is most remembered. These include *Prince Ananias*, *Babes in Toyland*, *It Happened in Nordland*, *Miss Dolly Dollars*, *Naughty Marietta* and *Mlle. Modiste*. His music is marked by simple, diatonic melody, symmetric rhythms and simple harmonies.

July 13   Tenor Carlo Bergonzi is born in Parma, Italy.

July 24   French dancer, choreographer, and ballet director Janine Charrat is born in Grenoble.

July 27   Ferruccio Busoni, 58, dies in Berlin. This half-Italian, half-German pianist and composer made his debut as a pianist at age 8 in Trieste. He conducted his *Stabat Mater* at age 12 in Graz, Austria. He then performed in Leipzig, Helsingfors and Moscow. He taught at the New England Conservatory of Music and performed with the Boston Symphony Orchestra. Eventually he settled in Berlin. As a pianist, he was internationally known. In France he was the third musician of Italian extraction to be made Chevalier de la Legion d'Honneur (Rossini and Verdi were the other two). Busoni advanced the cause of new music (though not overtly radical new music) both in his writings and in his performances. He composed several operas, two symphonic suites, a piano concerto with male chorus, other concertos, string quartets, piano music and various smaller works.

Oct. 10   Serge Koussevitzky, 50, debuts as the new music director of the Boston Symphony Orchestra. H.T. Parker writes in the Boston *Evening Transcript*, "Koussevitzky Superbus, as the old Romans might have written; but Koussevitzky passioning for his music — not for himself."

Nov. 3   Italian conductor Tullio Serafin makes his Metropolitan Opera debut conducting *Aida*. This performance also marks his American debut. Serafin's La Scala debut took place in 1909.

Nov. 4   Gabriel-Urbain Faure, 79, dies in Paris. A pupil of Camille Saint-Saens and teacher of Georges Enesco, Nadia Boulanger, Maurice Ravel and Florent Schmitt, he was a professor at the Paris Conservatoire and also an organist. He became director of the Paris Conservatoire in 1905 and held that position until 1920. He also wrote occasional criticism for *Le Figaro* and became a Commandeur de la Legion d'Honneur in 1910. His music was impressionistic before that movement took root; it involved the use of modes and coloristic instrumental writing. Faure's best-known works include his *Requiem* and his songs.

Nov. 8   Russian pianist and composer Sergei Liapunov, 64, dies in Paris. He studied with Sergei Taneyev and taught at the Saint Petersburg Conservatory before relocating to Paris after the Russian Revolution. The Imperial Geographic Society commissioned him to collect folk songs which were published in 1897. He composed many orchestral pieces as well as piano pieces that reflect Russian nationalism. His First Piano Concerto (performed in 1890) quickly entered and remained in the repertory.

Nov. 14   Violinist Leonid Kogan is born in Dniepropetrovsk, USSR.

Nov. 29   Italian composer Giacomo Puccini, 65 (full name Giacomo Antonio Domenico Secondo Maria Puccini), dies of throat cancer in Brussels. He was trained at the Milan Conservatory (the same conservatory that rejected Giuseppe Verdi) and studied with Antonio Bazzini and Amilcare Ponchielli. Puccini's first tremendous success was his four-act opera *Manon Lescaut* (produced in Turin, 1893); *La Boheme* (produced in Turin, 1896) catapulted him to international fame. *Tosca* was his next opera, to be followed by *Madama Butterfly* which was poorly received initially. With its revision came Puccini's ascension to the top of the world of Italian opera. Other operas include *La Fanciulla del West*, *La Rondine*, *Il Tabarro*, *Suor Angelica*, *Gianni Schicchi* and *Turandot* (unfinished, completed by Franco Alfano).

Dec. 8   Franz Xaver Scharwenka, 74, dies in Paris. Born in Poland, the pianist, composer and teacher was a co-founder with his brother Philipp of the Scharwenka Conservatory in Berlin. As a pianist, he was considered a German romantic, in the tradition of Robert Schumann. As a teacher, he was a follower of Carl Czerny.

Dec. 28   Russian painter and designer Leon Bakst, 58, dies in Paris. This artist was known in music and dance circles principally for his association with Serge Diaghilev's Ballets Russes. He created the decor for many of Diaghilev's most spectacular productions, including *Carnaval*, *Spectre de la Rose*, *L'Après-midi d'un faune*, and *Daphnis and Chloe*.

1924   *Related Events*

Sir Edward Elgar is appointed Master of the King's Musick this year.

The Curtis Institute of Music is founded this year in Philadelphia.

The St. Louis Institute of Music is founded this year in St. Louis, Missouri.

Jan. 17   Emil Leichner establishes the Czech Nonet. This chamber ensemble quickly becomes internationally known and commissions nonets from famous composers, including Alois Haba, Witold Lutoslawski and Bohuslav Martinu.

Feb. 25   The League of Composers' *Review* issues its first quarterly in New York City. It is subsequently called *Modern Music*.

March 18   German piano maker August Foerster's quarter-tone piano is patented. This event marks the first time a patent is granted for a quarter-tone piano.

May   Bell Laboratory engineers Henry C. Harrison and Joseph P. Maxfield (who have been experimenting with electrical recordings since 1919) are granted a patent for their work on recordings. Other developments in the recording industry this year include: Columbia (U.S.) renames itself Columbia Phonograph Company; His Master's Voice recording label issues the smallest gramophone disc pressed to date — a one and three-quarter inch diameter disc featuring "God Save the King"; the first "record club" appears, as the National Gramophone Society (England) introduces a prepaid subscription plan; and the "exponential folded horn" is introduced by Bell Telephone

(the device subsequently becomes part of the Orthophonic Victrola, manufactured by the Victor Company).

July 22   Richard Wagner's *Die Meistersinger von Nurnberg* is performed at the Bayreuth Festival. This event marks the reopening of this theater which has been closed for 10 years.

1925 Opera

Feb. 19   Ermanno Wolf-Ferrari's *Gli Amanti sposi* receives its initial performance in Venice. This three-act opera is based on Carlo Goldoni's *Il ventaglio*.

March 7   The first performance of Riccardo Zandonai's four-act opera *I cavalieri di Ekebu* takes place in Milan at La Scala. The text, written by Arturo Rossato, is based on the novel by Selma Lagerlof entitled *Gosta Berling*. The highly successful opera is written in honor of Lagerlof's 70th birthday. Arturo Toscanini conducts.

March 21   Maurice Ravel's *L'Enfant et les sortileges* is given its world premiere in Monte Carlo; Victor De Sabata conducts. This famous two-act opera is based on a fairy tale by Colette, which tells of the imagined joys and adventures of a little boy. Human voices are used, in part, to imitate the sound of crickets. The work is subsequently performed as a ballet as well as an opera.

April 3   Gustav Holst's one-act opera *At the Boar's Head* receives its world premiere in Manchester, England. The libretto, by the composer, is based on Shakespeare's *Henry IV*. Malcolm Sargent conducts the British National Opera Company, whose cast, for this production, includes Constance Willis, T. Davies and Norman Allin.

April 22   La Scala premieres Adriano Lualdi's *Il diavolo nel campanile*. The libretto, by the composer, is based on a story by Edgar Allan Poe.

April 24   Arseny Gladkovsky and Eugene Prussak's *For Red Petrograd* premieres in Leningrad. It is the first opera composed on a Soviet revolutionary subject. The score uses the whole-tone scale.

April 30   Charles Villiers Stanford's four-act opera *The Travelling Companion* receives its initial performance by an amateur ensemble in Liverpool. This opera, set to a libretto by Henry Newbolt, is based on a fairy tale by Hans Christian Andersen.

May 19   Charles Koechlin's one-act opera *Jacob chez Laban* receives its world premiere in Paris, years after it was finished. The work is based on the biblical tale.

May 21   Ferruccio Busoni's *Doktor Faust* premieres posthumously at the Dresden Staatsoper. The composer's libretto is based on Marlowe's *Doctor Faustus* and on the character of Faust in an old puppet play. Philipp Jarnach completes this unfinished work. The opera is considered

one of the composer's best compositions. Fritz Busch conducts a cast that includes Meta Seinemeyer.

July 1   Albert Roussel's *La Naissance de la lyre* premieres at the Paris Opera. The one-act opera is based on a recently discovered play by Sophocles.

Nov. 5   The complete version of Gian Francesco Malipiero's opera *L'Orfeide* is performed for the first time in Dusseldorf. The work, written to the composer's own libretto, is a symbolic trilogy about the conflict between the theater and reality. The second part, *Sette Canzoni*, had been performed in Paris in 1920.

Nov. 11   Leos Janacek's tragic *Sarka* premieres in Brno. This three-act opera, completed in 1887, is about the love between Sarka and a warrior. Frantisek Neumann conducts.

LEOS JANACEK

Dec. 14   Alban Berg's opera *Wozzeck* receives its world premiere at the State Opera in Berlin. The cast includes Fritz Sȯot and Leo Schutzendorf. Erich Kleiber conducts. Based on a play by Georg Buchner, it is about a soldier who loses his mind from jealousy and murders his love. The opera is praised and vilified both for its dramatic nature and for its musical style. Universal Edition later publishes the angry reviews in a pamphlet entitled "Wozzeck and the Music Critics." One of two operas by this composer, it contains a passacaglia with 29 variations. It is considered to be one of the most important operas of the cen-

tury. Paul Zschorlisch says of the opera in *Deutsche Zeitung*, "The perpetrator of this work builds securely upon the stupidity and charity of his fellow-men, and for the rest relies on God Almighty and the Universal Edition. I regard Alban Berg as a musical swindler and a musician dangerous to the community." Despite many negative reviews, the production brings him international fame.

Dec. 24   Raoul Laparra's *Le Joueur de viole* receives its first performance at the Opera-Comique in Paris. The four-act work has a libretto by the composer.

1925 Dance

March 3   *Joseph the Beautiful* receives its initial performance by the Experimental Theater in Moscow. The ballet features choreography and book by Kasian Goleizovsky, with music by Sergei Vassilenko. The designs are by B. Erdman. The ballet, in two acts and five scenes, is based on the biblical story. Its erotic choreography sparks controversy.

April 28   Leonide Massine's one-act ballet *Zephyr et Flore* is premiered by Serge Diaghilev's Ballets Russes in Monte Carlo. The music is by Vladimir Dukelsky and the libretto by Boris Kochno. Sets and costumes are by Georges Braque. The ballet attempts to reconstruct Didelot's ballet of the same name, premiered in 1796. The dancers include Alice Nikitina, Anton Dolin and Serge Lifar, in his first important solo role.

June 17   Serge Diaghilev's Ballets Russes presents Leonide Massine's *Les Matelots* in Paris. The music is by Georges Auric, the book by Boris Kochno, and the costumes and decor by Pedro Pruna. The ballet tells of a young girl, engaged to a sailor, whose fidelity is tested by

the sailor and his friends. Vera Nemchinova, Lydia Sokolova, Leon Woizikovsky, Tadeo Slavinsky and Serge Lifar star. Also premiered today is a revised version of Igor Stravinsky's *Le chant du rossignol*, based on a fairy tale by Hans Christian Andersen. The choreography, by George Balanchine, is his first for Diaghilev. The ballet is set to a symphonic poem based on Stravinsky's opera. It tells the story of a Chinese emperor who — when given a bejewelled, mechanical nightingale — banishes the real nightingale. He is forced to call her back when the mechanical nightingale will not sing to charm death from his door. Alicia Markova, 15, dances the Nightingale.

Dec. 11   George Balanchine's *Barabau* is premiered by Serge Diaghilev's company at the Coliseum Theater in London. The music to this one-act ballet is by Vittorio Rieti and the sets and costumes by Maurice Utrillo. The lead dancers in this burlesque are Serge Lifar, Tatiana Channie and Leon Woizikovsky. Despite its success, the ballet is soon withdrawn because of the difficulties of using a singing chorus in addition to the dancers.

1925 Instrumental and Vocal Music

Jan. 11   *Symphony for Organ and Orchestra*, by Aaron Copland, receives its world premiere in New York City. Performed by Nadia Boulanger at the organ and conducted by Walter Damrosch, the work is dedicated to Boulanger. The concerto, in three movements, is diatonic and includes asymmetric rhythms. Of today's performance, Lawrence Gilman writes in the New York *Herald-Tribune*, "Let us get used to the fact that it is as normal for the youth of 1925 to write in two keys simultaneously as it was for the youth of 1825 to confine himself frugally to one."

Jan. 31   Jacques Ibert's three-piece suite, *Les Bouquetieres*, *Creoles* and *Les Bavardes*, receives its first performance in Paris.

Feb. 8   Nikolai Miaskovsky's Symphony No. 4 in E Minor and Symphony No. 7 in B Minor receive their first performances in Moscow. Miaskovsky subsequently becomes known as the Soviet Union's most prolific symphonist.

Feb. 13   Leopold Stokowski and the Philadelphia Orchestra premiere Leo Ornstein's Piano Concerto No. 2, assembled from an earlier piano sonata. The composer is the soloist. Ornstein, now 32, is currently thought of as a prophet of new music. He quickly fades.

Feb. 15   Mexican composer Julian Carrillo's *Preludio a Cristobal Colon* has its initial performance in Mexico City. This work features quarter tones, eighth tones and sixteenth tones. The piece is an overture to an opera the composer intends to write.

March 1   *Integrales*, by Edgard Varese, receives its first performance in New York City. The work's title reflects the composer's preoccupation with the creative use of concepts from physics and mathematics. He describes the work as "organized sound." The piece is scored for a large ensemble, including 11 wind instruments and 17 percussion instruments (featuring Chinese blocks, sleigh bells and chains). It is the largest ensemble piece Varese composes. W.J. Henderson, in the New York *Sun*, compares one moment of the piece to "an injured dog's cry of pain or a cat's yell of midnight rage. . . ." Ernest Newman writes in the New York *Evening Post*: "It sounded a good deal like a combination of early morning in the Mott Haven freight yards, feeding time at the zoo and a Sixth Avenue trolley rounding a curve, with an intoxicated woodpecker thrown in for good measure."

May 23   Serge Koussevitzky conducts the premiere of Arthur Honegger's *Concertino for Piano and Orchestra* in Paris. Andree Vaurabourg, the composer's fiancee, is the soloist in the three-movement work.

May 30   Serge Koussevitzky premieres the Piano Concerto, by Germaine Tailleferre, the female member of "Les Six." The performance takes place in Paris, with the composer as soloist.

June 1   Ernest Bloch conducts the world premiere of his *Concerto Grosso* in Cleveland. The work is neobaroque in style and is scored for string orchestra and piano obbligato.

June 6   Serge Koussevitzky conducts the world premiere of Sergei Prokofiev's Symphony No. 2 in D Minor in Paris. This symphony is unusual because it is composed of only two movements. Critics pan the work. Prokofiev, in his *Autobiography*, later says of this experience: "This was perhaps the only time it occurred to me that I might be destined to be a second-rate composer."

June 11   Arthur Honegger's incidental music to *Judith* premieres in Mezieres, Switzerland, with the composer conducting. The music is based on a play by Rene Morax, which, in turn, is based on the biblical tale.

July 25   Paul Hindemith's *Concerto* for orchestra — with oboe, bassoon and violin soli — premieres in Duisberg.

Oct. 7   Gustav Holst's *Choral Symphony* receives its first performance at the Leeds Festival. Scored for soprano, chorus and orchestra, the text consists of poems by John Keats.

Oct. 16   Austrian pianist Paul Wittgenstein premieres a newly commissioned arrangement of *Symphonia domestica*, by Richard Strauss. His right arm lost in combat, Wittgenstein performs a version for piano left hand and orchestra entitled *Parergon zur Symphonia Domestica*.

Oct. 19   Ralph Vaughan Williams' *Flos Campi* receives its world premiere in London. The work is scored for viola, small chorus and small orchestra.

Oct. 28   Charles Loeffler's *Canticle of the Sun*, Frederick Stock's *Rhapsodic Fantasy* and Frederick Jacobi's *Two Assyrian Prayers* are premiered as the Elizabeth Sprague Coolidge Foundation sponsors a new Festival of Chamber Music at the Library of Congress, Washington, D.C.

Nov. 6   *Concerto Accademico in D Minor*, by Ralph Vaughan Williams receives its first performance in London, with Hungarian violinist Jelly d'Aranyi as soloist. The three-movement work is scored for violin and string orchestra.

Nov. 20   Serge Koussevitzky and the Boston Symphony Orchestra give the first performance of Aaron Copland's *Music for the Theater* in Boston. The work, in five movements, is scored for small orchestra and piano. Copland dedicated the score to Koussevitzky. This is the first Copland piece to be premiered by this world-famous conductor. The resultant exposure substantially enhances Copland's career.

Dec. 3   George Gershwin is soloist at the world premiere of his Concerto in F for piano and orchestra, as Walter Damrosch conducts the New York Symphony. This three-movement work evokes the chromaticism of American blues music.

Dec. 6   Gabriel Pierne premieres Jacques Ibert's *Feerique*, a symphonic scherzo, at a Colonne Concert in Paris.

Dec. 11   Carl Nielsen's Symphony No. 6 receives its first performance in Copenhagen with the composer conducting. Subtitled "Sinfonia Semplice," the symphony had been completed just six days prior to its world premiere.

Dec. 23   Reinhold Gliere conducts the premiere of his *The Cossacks of Zaporozh* in Odessa. This symphonic work was inspired by a painting by Repin.

Dec. 31   The New York Philharmonic premieres Ottorino Respighi's *Concerto in modo misolidio*. Respighi performs the solo piano part.

1925   Births, Deaths and Debuts

Jan. 2   The young American baritone Lawrence Tibbett creates a sensation at the Metropolitan Opera as a last-minute substitution as Ford in a revival of *Falstaff*. He upstages Antonio Scotti, Beniamino Gigli, Lucrezia Bori and Frances Alda. The conductor is Tullio Serafin. W.J. Henderson writes in the New York *Sun* that "Mr. Tibbett's performance won him an unprecedented ovation. . . . it was Mr. Tibbett who stepped alone before the curtain to receive thunderous applause from an enthusiastic audience who had called insistently for all of fifteen minutes in a darkened house for the young man from California."

Jan. 8   Igor Stravinsky conducts the New York Philharmonic in a concert of his music at Carnegie Hall in New York City. This event marks his first American appearance as a conductor. The program includes *Fireworks, Scherzo fantastique* (first American performance), the suite from *Pulcinella, Le chant du rossignol* and the suite from *The Firebird*. Lawrence Gilman reviews the concert and remarks, "It would be excessive to say that he threw much new light upon the question of the interpretation of his works."

Jan. 24   American dancer Maria Tallchief is born in Fairfax, Oklahoma.

Feb. 7   Rumanian-born French composer Marius Constant is born in Bucharest, Rumania.

Feb. 20   Italian composer Enrico Bossi, 63, dies at sea aboard the SS *De Grasse*. He studied at the Liceo Rossini in Bologna and with Amilcare Ponchielli in Milan. Other studies included violin and organ. He was known principally as a teacher and taught at the Royal Conservatory San Pietro in Naples, the Liceo Benedetto Marcello in Venice, the Liceo Musicale in Bologna and the Saint Cecilia Academy Music School in Rome. He also toured internationally as an organist and a pianist. He was largely a composer of operas and oratorios. These include the operas *Paquita* and *L'angelo della notte*; the mystery play *Giovanna d'Arco*; and *Il paradiso perduto*, scored for chorus and orchestra.

March 4   Silesian pianist and composer Moritz Moszkowski, 70, dies in Paris. His first public appearance was in Berlin in 1873; he later settled in Paris. His *Spanish Dances* and his opera *Boabdil der Maurenkonig* are his best-known works.

March 26   Composer-conductor Pierre Boulez is born in Montbrison, France.

April 3   Polish tenor Jean de Reszke, 75, dies in Nice, France. One of the best-loved singers of the 19th century, he made his debut as a baritone in 1874 in Venice. He started singing tenor roles in 1879. His creation of the role of John the Baptist in Massenet's *Herodiade* in 1884 caused a sensation. After a visit to Bayreuth in 1888, he studied the Wagnerian repertoire and gained worldwide renown as a Wagnerian tenor. After his retirement, he taught singing in Paris. A true "Golden Age" singer, he was known for beauty of voice, elegance of phrasing, clarity of enunciation and a powerful stage presence.

April 22   French composer Andre Caplet, 46, dies in Paris. A friend of Claude Debussy, he began his studies at the Paris Conservatoire and was awarded the Prix de Rome in 1901. As a conductor, he led operatic performances in America and England. His music is impressionistic and employs whole-tone scales.

May 28   Baritone Dietrich Fischer-Dieskau is born in Berlin, Germany.

July 1   French composer Erik Satie, 59, dies in Paris. After studies at the Paris Conservatoire, he played in various Parisian cabarets and then began writing short piano pieces with peculiar names (*Trois morceaux en forme de poire*).

His ridiculing of both the modern movement and classical stuffiness gained him many admirers among early 20th-century French composers. He wrote several ballets for Serge Diaghilev's Ballets Russes, including *Parade*, which introduced jazz elements for the first time in a ballet. He was a sponsor of the group of French composers known as "Les Six," although not a member of that group.

Satie's work reflects a sensitivity to various stimuli. These include associations of color, rhythm, predictability and graphic design. His personality and originality surface in his music, which has a hypnotic and attractive quality. The appeal and accessibility of his music angered other composers not enjoying popularity, and on occasion, they accused Satie of being an uneducated composer who concealed his ignorance with frivolity.

His most famous compositions include the piano suite *Gymnopedies*; the ballets *Relache* and *Mercure*; and *Socrate*, a musical drama for four sopranos and chamber orchestra. He also wrote manifestos featuring prose and poetry that assailed modernism in music. One literary piece is *Memoirs d'un amnesique*, a satirical autobiography.

July 4   American mezzo-soprano Cathy Berberian is born in Attleboro, Massachusetts.

July 11   Tenor Nicolai Gedda is born in Stockholm, Sweden.

Aug. 15   Pianist Aldo Ciccolini is born in Naples, Italy.

Aug. 23   Avant-garde composer Wlodzimierz Kotonski is born in Warsaw, Poland.

Sep. 11   Composer Harry Somers is born in Toronto, Canada.

Oct. 24   Composer Luciano Berio is born in Oneglia, Italy.

Nov. 2   Mezzo-soprano Irina Arkhipova is born in Moscow, Russia.

Nov. 20   Soviet dancer Maya Plisetskaya is born in Moscow.

Nov. 26   Pianist Eugene Istomin is born in New York City.

1925 Related Events

March 25   Pianist Alfred Cortot makes the first classical electrical recording, as he records an impromptu by Frederick Chopin and music by Franz Schubert at the Victor Company's Camden, New Jersey studio. This is an important year for the recording industry. Other developments include: Victor officially adopts the electrical recording process, and the English division of Columbia obtains electrical recording rights by buying up its American counterpart (Columbia, U.S.); the Brunswick Company introduces an all-electric record player, known as the Panotrope, as well as an experimental 78 RPM long-playing record lasting 40 minutes; Victor introduces a new recording process to accommodate its new Orthophonic Victrola, officially released this year; the first complete recording of all nine Beethoven symphonies is made by the Parlaphone Company. As a result of the advent of electrical recording technology, the playing speed of 78.26 RPM, compatible with 60-cycle AC line frequency, emerges as an industry standard. The labels Ultraphon and Electrola are established in Germany.

April 1   Composers Alexander Davidenko, Boris Schechter and Victor Byely organize the Soviet Society for Promotion of Proletarian Music, Production Collective (Procoll), in Moscow.

April 13   The Dubrovnik Philharmonic Orchestra gives its first concert today, as Polish conductor Tadeusz Sygietynski conducts a program of music by Mendelssohn, Mozart, Weber and others. This orchestra has been assembled by students and professional musicians of Dubrovnik who wish their city to have a symphony orchestra. After World War II this semi-professional symphony is replaced by the professional Dubrovnik Symphony Orchestra.

May 1   The Gervex Pavilion at the Paris Exhibition features a demonstration of the scie musicale. It is a musical saw, whose range is three octaves and can accommodate tunes in both tempered and nontempered scales.

Aug. 27   After winning a voice contest against 300 contenders, Marian Anderson is the soloist at a concert of the New York Philharmonic at Lewisohn Stadium.

Oct. 28   The new Coolidge Auditorium of the Music Division of the Library of Congress, Washington, D.C. is inaugurated.

1926 Opera

Feb. 13   *Judith* receives its first performance in Monte Carlo at the Theatre du Casino. The opera, composed by Arthur Honegger to a libretto by Rene Morax, is based on the story of Judith in the Apocrypha. The work was originally a play with incidental music but was later expanded. This revised version is well received.

March 24   *Tre commedie goldoniane* — an opera trilogy by Gian Francesco Malipiero — premieres in its entirety at the Hessisches Landestheater in Darmstadt. The composer creates a text that is based freely on Goldoni's plays *La Bottega del Caffe*, *Sior Toxero Brontolon* and *Le Baruffe Chiozzotti*. All are set in 18th-century Venice and portray aspects of Venetian life.

March 27   Kurt Weill's one-act opera *Der Protagonist* receives its initial performance in Dresden. Georg Kaiser writes the libretto to this opera about jealousy and murder. The opera casts a drama within an opera (the opera singers are the audience for the drama). One of Weill's earliest stage works, it is modernistic.

April 25   Giacomo Puccini's three-act opera *Turandot* receives its first performance at La Scala in Milan. The libretto, by Giuseppe Adami and Renato Simoni, is based on the play by Carlo Gozzi. Puccini dies before the score is finished, and Franco Alfano completes it. At today's premiere, however, Arturo Toscanini puts down his baton at the end of Puccini's music and announces to the audience that this is where the opera ends. The cast includes Rosa Raisa, Maria Zamboni and Miguel Fleta.

May 7   The first performance of Darius Milhaud's *Les maltheurs d'Orphee* takes place in Brussels' Theatre de la Monnaie. The libretto, by Armand Lunel, is a modern-day version of the legend of Orpheus, in which Orpheus is an animal healer and Eurydice is a gypsy.

June 19   *Krol Roger* a three-act opera by Karol Szymanowski premieres in Warsaw. The libretto, by the composer and his cousin, Jaroslaw Iwaskiewicz, is based on an anonymous 12th-century German poem recounting the deeds of King Roger II of Sicily.

Oct. 16   Zoltan Kodaly's *Hary Janos* is performed for the first time at the Budapest Opera. The libretto, by Bela Paulini and Zsolt Harsanyi, is based on a poem by Janos Garay about a Hungarian folk character, the prodigious liar Hary Janos. The opera achieves lasting success in Hungary.

Nov. 9   Paul Hindemith's three-act opera *Cardillac* premieres at the Stadttheater in Zurich. Ferdinand Lion's libretto is based on an E.T.A. Hoffmann story about a series of murders in 17th-century France. The cast includes Claire Born, Grete Merram-Nikisch, Max Hirzel and Robert Burg. Fritz Busch conducts. The opera is subsequently revised by the composer.

Nov. 11   Alban Berg's *Wozzeck* receives its first Prague performance, in a Czech version. It is conducted by Otakar Ostrcil at the National Theater. The audience demands between 30 and 40 curtain calls. The third Prague performance (on November 16), however, results in a melee.

Nov. 14   Eugene d'Albert's three-act opera *Der Golem* is performed for the first time in Frankfurt. The opera is about a rabbi of Prague who indulges in black magic.

Nov. 27   Ernst Krenek's opera *Orpheus and Eurydike* premieres in Kassel.

Dec. 8   Charles Wakefield Cadman's *A Witch of Salem* is premiered by the Chicago Civic Opera Company.

Dec. 18   *The Makropulos Affair*, a three-act opera by Leos Janacek, receives its world premiere in Brno. It is based on a play by Karel Capek about a woman who, 300 years ago, was given the secret of eternal life. She attests to events that took place long ago, and others desire to possess her secret. Finding eternity boring, she dies at the end of the opera when her secret formula is destroyed. This is Janacek's penultimate opera. Frantisek Neumann conducts.

1926 Dance

Feb. 19   John Alden Carpenter's *Skyscrapers* is premiered by the Metropolitan Opera Company in New York City. This work is performed as a ballet and traces contemporary American civilization through dance and music. It is scored for large orchestra with saxophones and a banjo.

May 4   English composer Constant Lambert's first ballet *Romeo and Juliet* is premiered by Serge Diaghilev's Ballets Russes in Monte Carlo.

July 3   *Jack-in-the-Box*, a ballet in three scenes, receives its initial performance at the Theatre Sarah Bernhardt in

SCENE FROM *SKYSCRAPERS*

Paris. George Balanchine choreographs music by Erik Satie. Decor is by Andre Derain. The ballet is a divertissement about a playful jumping-jack and three ballerinas. Alexandra Danilova, Lubov Tchernicheva, Felia Doubrovska and Stanislas Idzikowski star.

Nov. 28 *The Miraculous Mandarin,* a one-act ballet with music by Bela Bartok, receives its world premiere in Cologne. Dancers include Ernst Zeiller and Wilma Aug. Menyhert Lengyel writes the libretto; Hans Strohbach directs. Konrad Adenauer — lord mayor of Cologne — bans

the work because it is about a prostitute who is forced by her pimps to rob her customers. The score is eventually the inspiration for several choreographers.

Dec. 3 George Balanchine's *The Triumph of Neptune* at the Lyceum Theatre in London. Serge Diaghilev's Ballets Russes performs. Music is by Lord Berners and decor by Prince A. Shervashidze. The commedia dell'arte piece parodies mythological characters in opera. Alexandra Danilova, Lubov Tchernicheva, Evgenia Sokolova, Serge Lifar and Balanchine star.

1926 Instrumental and Vocal Music

Jan. 30 *Aeroplane,* by Emerson Whithorne, receives its first performance in Birmingham, England. Adrian Boult conducts this symphonic movement based on an earlier piano piece of the same title.

Feb. 6 Kurt Weill's orchestral work *Quodlibet, eine Unterhaltungsmusik* premieres in Coburg, Germany. It was composed in 1924.

Feb. 12 Leos Janacek's *Concertino* for piano, two violins, viola, clarinet, bassoon and horn receives its first performance in Brno. Although it is tonal, key signatures are absent. It is in four movements and includes Moravian melodic source material.

March 13 American composer Emerson Whithorne's *Saturday's Child* based on poetry by Negro poet Countee Cullen, is premiered by the League of Composers in New York City. The piece is scored for mezzo-soprano, tenor and chamber orchestra.

April 9 Leopold Stokowski and the Philadelphia Orchestra premiere *Ameriques* — a symphonic poem by Edgard Varese. This work is scored for large orchestra. Reaction to this composer's music has been consistently negative. Stokowski is one of the few top conductors in America who programs new works by Varese. Samuel Chotzinoff says in the New York *World,* "*Ameriques* seemed to depict the progress of a terrible fire in one of our larger zoos."

May 7 *Sancta Civitas* is performed for the first time in Oxford. This oratorio, by Ralph Vaughan Williams, is scored for tenor, baritone, mixed chorus and distant chorus.

May 12 Nikolai Malko and the Leningrad Philharmonic premiere Dmitri Shostakovich's Symphony No. 1 in F Minor. The four-movement symphony was composed as a graduation piece at the Leningrad Conservatory. Shostakovich is now 19 years old. Alexander Glazunov, one of the faculty judges, comments that Shostakovich is "a bright, outstanding creative talent."

May 23 Nikolai Miaskovsky's Symphony No. 8 in A Major premieres in Moscow. This four-movement symphony is based, in part, on Russian folk songs.

June 3 Russian expatriate Nicolas Obouhov's *Preface au Livre de Vie* premieres at a Koussevitzky Concert in Paris, with the composer and Nicolas Slonimsky as piano soloists. Scored for orchestra, two pianos and four soloists, the work employs hisses and shrieks.

June 19 George Antheil's *Ballet mecanique* and Symphony in F are performed for the first time by Vladimir Golschmann in Paris. *Ballet mecanique* was composed as film music for an abstract film by F. Leger. Consequently, this performance is not choreographed or danced. It is scored for eight pianos, player piano and various percussion instruments and becomes Antheil's best-known piece.

June 22 *Five Pieces for Orchestra* , Op. 10, by Anton Webern, receives its world premiere. Webern conducts the Tonhalle-Orchester of Zurich at the fourth festival of the International Society for Contemporary Music in Zurich. The pieces are scored for flute, piccolo, oboe, clarinet, bass clarinet, E flat clarinet, horn, trumpet, trombone, harmonium, celesta, harp, mandolin, guitar, percussion and strings (one each, solo). The five pieces last a total of 6 minutes, with the fourth piece ("Fliessend, ausserst zart") lasting approximately 18 seconds. These pieces had been composed between 1911 and 1913 and had to wait 13 years for their premiere. The performance creates a sensation, and Webern suddenly becomes internationally famous. Reviews are largely favorable, especially those published in the *Berliner Tageblatt* (Berlin) and the *Christian Science Monitor* (United States), which appears next month. The reviewer for the latter writes, "Only a true musical poet would give us these fugitive glimpses of a new and fascinating world of sound."

June 22 William Walton's overture *Portsmouth Point* premieres at the concert of the fourth festival of the International Society for Contemporary Music.

June 29 *Sinfonietta,* by Leos Janacek, receives its first performance in Prague. This five-movement orchestral work, with its famous fanfare opening, becomes the composer's most popular instrumental composition. Janacek is now 72.

July 17   Danish composer Knudage Riisager's Symphony No. 1 premieres in Copenhagen. It is in three movements.

July 30   Emerson Whithorne's orchestral suite *New York Days and Nights* premieres at the Sesquicentennial International Exposition in Philadelphia. Originally written for piano, the work is characteristic of Whithorne's modernist style.

Oct. 8   Ernst Toch's Piano Concerto No. 1 premieres in Dusseldorf, with Walter Gieseking as soloist.

Oct. 21   Concerto for Flute and Orchestra, by Carl Nielsen, receives its initial performance in Paris. Nielsen later decides to rewrite the conclusion of this two-movement concerto.

Oct. 28   Dutch composer Willem Pijper's Symphony No. 3 receives its first performance in Amsterdam. The four-movement symphony is conducted by Pierre Monteux. This work becomes Pijper's most frequently performed piece.

Nov. 5   The Concerto for Harpsichord, Flute, Oboe, Clarinet, Violin and Cello, by Manuel de Falla, receives its world premiere in Barcelona, the composer conducting. Composition of this work had been suggested by harpsichordist Wanda Landowska, who is today's soloist. The concerto evokes, to some degree, the keyboard clarity of Domenico Scarlatti's music. The work quickly establishes itself as one of the composer's best.

Nov. 13   The Symphony in F Minor, by Vissarion Shebalin, and *Revolutionary Episode*, by Lev Knipper — both Soviet composers — are premiered in Leningrad.

Nov. 19   Serge Koussevitzky and the Boston Symphony Orchestra give the first American performance of Anton Webern's *Five Pieces for Orchestra*, Op. 10. Also receiving its first American performance is William Walton's overture *Portsmouth Point*. Lawrence Gilman says in the New York *Herald Tribune*, "Webern's *Five Pieces for Orchestra* were as clearly significant and symptomatic as a toothache." Warren Storey Smith says in the Boston *Post* of the Webern work, "Inevitably these faint rustlings, these tiny squeaks and titterings called to mind the activities of insects. . . ."

JEAN SIBELIUS

Nov. 27   Louis Gruenberg's *The Creation*, set to a text by James Weldon Johnson, is premiered by the League of Composers in New York City. The music is scored for baritone and eight instruments.

Dec. 9   Darius Milhaud's *Le Carnaval d'Aix*, based on his ballet *Salade*, is premiered by Willem Mengelberg and the New York Philharmonic, with the composer at the piano.

Dec. 15   *Choros No. 10*, by Heitor Villa-Lobos, receives its first performance in Rio de Janeiro. The piece is scored for orchestra and mixed chorus. This is one of Villa-Lobos' "Choros" compositions, evoking the Brazilian dance form of the same name and characterized by indigenous Brazilian rhythms and balladlike melodies.

Dec. 26   *Tapiola*, a symphonic poem by Jean Sibelius, receives its first performance by Walter Damrosch and the New York Symphony Society Orchestra.

1926   Births, Deaths and Debuts

Jan. 6   French composer and educator Emile Paladilhe, 81, dies in Paris. Winner of the Prix de Rome at age 16, he later became a professor at the Paris Conservatoire and composed many operas, two masses, a symphony and many songs.

Jan. 8   Greek composer Jani Christou is born in Heliopolis, Egypt.

Jan. 20   Avant-garde pianist and composer David Tudor is born in Philadelphia, Pennsylvania.

Feb. 3   American dancer, choreographer and ballet director Glen Tetley is born in Cleveland, Ohio.

Feb. 5   Andre Gedalge, 69, dies in Paris. After beginning his musical studies at the late age of 28, he won a Prix de Rome. He composed symphonies, operas and other works, many of which do not receive frequent performances.

Author of the *Traite de fugue*, a standard work on counterpoint and fugue, his pupils included Maurice Ravel, Georges Enesco, Darius Milhaud and Arthur Honegger.

Feb. 17   Danish tenor Lauritz Melchior makes his debut at the Metropolitan Opera as Tannhauser. Olin Downes writes of the performance in the New York *Times*, "The tone was forced and rough in quality and the melodic line suffered."

Feb. 22   Pianist Walter Gieseking makes his American debut at Aeolian Hall in New York City.

March 26   Rumanian violinist Franz Kneisel, 61, dies in New York City. He debuted in 1882 in Vienna. In 1885 he became concertmaster of the Boston Symphony Orchestra. The following year he founded the Kneisel Quartet, which flourished until 1917. His efforts advanced the cause of chamber music in America. Both Princeton and Yale universities awarded him an honorary doctorate.

March 29   American dancer and teacher Diana Adams is born in Stanton, Virginia.

June 6   Conductor Klaus Tennstedt is born in Merseburg, Germany.

July 1   Composer Hans Werner Henze is born in Gutersloh, Westphalia.

Aug. 15   Pianist Julius Katchen is born in Long Branch, New Jersey.

Sep. 3   American conductor Ralph Lyford, 45, dies in Cincinnati, Ohio. He was the first conductor of the Cincinnati Opera, which he helped establish and form. He was also an associate conductor of the Cincinnati Symphony Orchestra under Fritz Reiner and composer of the opera *Castle Agrazant*, which won the American Opera Society's Bispham Silver Medal.

Sep. 10   Danish dancer and teacher Fredbjorn Bjornsson is born in Copenhagen.

Sep. 12   Operatic baritone Henri Albers, 59, dies in Paris. This vocalist was especially noted for having been the first Wotan to sing Wagner's *Ring* cycle in French when it came to France. He also sang at the Metropolitan Opera in 1898.

Oct. 25   Soprano Galina Vishnevskaya is born in Leningrad, Russia.

Nov. 1   Italian bass Ezio Pinza makes his Metropolitan Opera debut as Pontifex Maximus in Gaspare Spontini's *La Vestale*. The cast also includes Rosa Ponselle, Giacomo Lauri-Volpi, Giuseppe De Luca and Margarete Matzenauer. The conductor is Tullio Serafin. Lawrence Gilman writes of Pinza in the New York *Herald-Tribune*, "This new singer is an imposing figure, he has an excellent voice, and he sings with brains and discretion."

Nov. 7   Soprano Joan Sutherland is born in Sydney, Australia.

Nov. 14   Soprano Leonie Rysanek is born in Vienna.

Dec. 26   Composer Earle Brown is born in Lunenburg, Massachusetts.

1926   Related Events

Hungarian dancer, choreographer, ballet master and dance theoretician Rudolf von Laban's *Choreographie* is published this year in Jena. This book is devoted to the creation of a scientific approach to dance notation. In it Laban develops symbols set down in three vertical lines that run parallel to the musical staves. The symbols represent the left, central and right parts of the dancer's body. He later calls his system kinetographie; it also becomes known as Labanotation. This is the first comprehensive approach to dance notation in this century.

Dance Lovers Magazine begins publication this year. It is a monthly featuring articles on various aspects of theatrical dance. It ceases publication in 1932 due to the Depression and is resurrected as *Dance Magazine* in 1941.

The dramatic impact of radio broadcasting on recording sales peaks this year, as record sales are at their lowest point since the recording industry's development during the first quarter of the century. In spite of this, the industry does not die. Wilhelm Furtwangler makes his first recordings with the Berlin Philharmonic, of Beethoven's Fifth Symphony and Weber's *Freischutz Overture*. Eldridge Johnson sells the Victor Talking Machine Company to Seligman banking interests and retires. Thomas A. Edison introduces his long-playing-diamond discs, which feature 450 grooves per inch and 20 minutes per side at 80 RPM. Many recording companies buy other recording companies to expand their business: The Lindstrom companies (Germany) are bought by Columbia (England); the General Phonograph Company and its Okeh subsidiary are bought by the Columbia Phonograph Company (U.S.); and Brunswick buys Vocalion.

Ninette de Valois establishes her Academy of Choreographic Art in London this year. This academy eventually leads to the establishment of the Royal Ballet. This year she also begins collaboration with Lilian Baylis on dance productions at the Old Vic. This theatre is rebuilt over the next five years.

Jan. 1   The Leningrad Association for Contemporary Music is officially created under the leadership of Boris Asafiev. Asafiev subsequently withdraws to head a factional constituency, entitled Circle for New Music, dedicated to more radical musical trends.

April 7   The Stockholm Concert Hall at Haymarket, Stockholm is inaugurated today, as Franz Berwald's overture *The Queen of Golconda* is performed there by the Stockholm Philharmonic Orchestra. The architect chosen for the job was Ivar Tengbom, who wanted to "raise a Greek temple near the Arctic Circle." The project took 47 years to complete due to financial problems.

May 2   Richard Hageman conducts a free concert given by the Pittsburgh Symphony Orchestra at the Syria Mosque in that city, marking the rebirth of this orchestra, which, because of financial problems, disbanded in 1910.

June 8   Soprano Nellie Melba gives her farewell performance at a gala in her honor at Covent Garden, London. She sings scenes from Puccini's *La Boheme* and Verdi's *Otello*. She subsequently returns to her native Australia where she becomes the President of the Melbourne Conservatory.

July 25   Jorg Mager's electronic instrument the spharophon is displayed at the Donaueschingen Festival. One of three electronic instruments built by this electronic music

specialist (the other two being the elektrophon and the partiturophon), it produces microtonal intervals.

Aug. 6   Henry Hadley becomes the first musician to be featured as a conductor in a full-sound motion picture. He conducts the New York Philharmonic in a film entitled *Don Juan*, by the Vitaphone Company, released today.

Nov. 15   Walter Damrosch conducts the New York Symphony Orchestra, Albert Stoessel the New York Oratorio Society and Edwin Franko Goldman the Goldman Band in the first chain broadcast by the National Broadcasting Company in New York City.

Nov. 16   Alban Berg's *Wozzeck*, receiving its third Prague performance, sparks a riotous reaction. At the onset of Act III, a group of individuals, determined to restrict the National Theater to performances of works by native Czech composers, begins to create a loud disturbance. The music is stopped, and the police are summoned. Remaining scheduled performances are canceled. Alma and Franz Werfel witness the riot. The press quickly refers to Berg as "Aaron Berg, the Jew from Berlin" (Berg is not Jewish). Letters of support for Berg from leading Czech musicians, including Leos Janacek, fail to help get the opera rescheduled.

1927 Opera

Jan. 28   *Angelique*, a one-act opera by Jacques Ibert, premieres in Paris at the Theatre Beriza. It is a comedy about the owner of a china shop, Boniface, who wants desperately to get rid of his bad-tempered wife, Angelique, but even the devil won't take her. The work is a big success. Vladimir Golschmann conducts.

Feb. 10   *Jonny spielt auf*, an opera by Ernst Krenek, receives its world premiere at the Leipzig Opera House. The opera, in two acts and 11 scenes with a libretto by the composer, is about a jazz-band leader who steals a violin and inspires the world to dance the Charleston. It is also about a love affair between a moody musician, Max, and a singer, Anita. The opera includes jazz elements to depict certain settings but is not a "jazz opera." Fritz Ohrmann writes of the work in *Signale* (Berlin), "The art that Schubert glorified as holy, that should be a Queen, is debased to a prostitute."

Feb. 17   Deems Taylor's new opera *The King's Henchman* receives its world premiere in New York City, performed by the Metropolitan Opera. The text, by Edna Saint Vincent Millay, is a variation on the story of *Tristan and Isolde*, set in medieval England. It is the first American opera produced by this house in almost 10 years. Tullio Serafin conducts a cast that includes Lawrence Tibbett, Edward Johnson and Florence Easton. Reviews are largely favorable. W.J. Henderson says it is "the best American opera this public has heard." Pitts Sanborn writes in the *Telegram* that

the opera "is based firmly on Wagner." The opera runs for three seasons.

March 2   Kurt Weill's *Royal Palace* premieres in Berlin. This one-act opera is about a woman who possesses men from her past, present and future.

March 5   Franco Alfano's comic opera *Madonna Imperia* based on a tale by Balzac, premieres in Turin.

April 16   Darius Milhaud's *Agamemnon* receives its first performance in Paris. This work is the first part of a trilogy entitled *Orestea*, and in this part Clytemnestra seeks revenge on Agamemnon for sacrificing Iphegenia to his ambitions.

April 21   Ermanno Wolf-Ferrari's *Veste di cielo* premieres in a German version in Munich, under the title *Das Himmelskleid*.

April 27   *Svanda dudak*, by Jaromir Weinberger, premieres in Prague at the Czech National Theater. The libretto, by Milos Kares and Max Brod, is based on a folk tale by Tyl. The opera subsequently enjoys great success in Czechoslovakia. Otakar Ostrcil conducts the two-act opera.

May 21   Ernst Krenek's *Der Sprung uber den Schatten* is performed in Leningrad. This event marks the first time a modern European opera is produced in the Soviet Union. Critic Igor Glebov writes of the opera in *Krasnaya Gazeta* that the composer "is a master of the stage and a musician

JAROMIR WEINBERGER

Die Prinzessin auf der Erbse are premiered at a festival of new music in Baden-Baden. This is the short version of Weill's opera; it is subsequently lengthened and performed in Leipzig in 1930.

Oct. 7   *Das Wunder der Heliane*, a three-act opera by Erich Wolfgang Korngold, premieres in Hamburg. It is about a woman combating the devil.

Nov. 18   Ottorino Respighi's *La campana sommersa*, receives its world premiere at the Stadttheater in Hamburg. The libretto to this four-act opera is by Claudio Guastella and is based on Gerhart Hauptmann's play *Die versunheve Geocke*, about a blacksmith who falls in love with a fairy and leaves his family to follow her into the mountains. The opera is enthusiastically received.

Nov. 27   *Les Eumenides*, a three-act opera by Darius Milhaud, receives its first performance in Antwerp. This is the third part of his operatic trilogy based on Aeschylus's *Orestea*. The other two parts are *Agamemnon* and *Les Choephores*.

Dec. 16   *Le pauvre matelot*, a three-act opera by Darius Milhaud, receives its first performance at the Opera-Comique in Paris. Jean Cocteau writes the libretto, which is based on a newspaper story about a sailor whose wife does not recognize him when he pretends to be a wealthy friend. While in bed, he is murdered by his wife, who decides to steal his jewels to finance her husband's trip home. She does not realize that she is killing her husband.

Dec. 28   Arthur Honegger's *Antigone* premieres in Brussels at the Theatre de la Monnaie. The libretto, by Jean Cocteau, is based on the tragedy by Sophocles. The opera does not receive many performances after today's premiere.

Dec. 29   Ermanno Wolf-Ferrari's three-act opera, *Sly* premieres at La Scala in Milan. This opera is based on the prologue to Shakespeare's *The Taming of the Shrew*.

who has succeeded in returning the opera to healthy Mozartean traditions." Anatol Lunacharsky (Soviet commissar of education), however, comments in *Krasnaya Gazeta* (Leningrad): "Krenek's opera is rather confused in its plot, and it is in this respect a perfect counterpart of contemporary European culture, which is incapable of creating anything of the least value."

June 10   Vincent d'Indy's three-act opera *Le Reve de Cyniras* premieres in Paris.

July 17   Kurt Weill's *Mahagonny*, Paul Hindemith's *Hin und Zuruck*, Darius Milhaud's *L'Enlevement* and Ernst Toch's

1927 Dance

April 27   Feodor Lopokov's *The Ice Maiden*, with music by Edvard Greig arranged by Boris Asafiev, premieres in Leningrad at the Kirov Ballet. Alexander Golovine creates the designs. The ballet, in three acts and five scenes, is about a fairy who attracts young men to their death. Lopokov's acrobatic choreography sparks controversy. Lead dancers are Olga Mungalova and Pytor Gusey.

April 30   George Balanchine's *Le chatte* receives its world premiere by Serge Diaghilev's Ballets Russes in Monte Carlo. Henri Sauguet writes the music and Naum Gabo and Antoine Pevsner create the decor. The story is based on an Aesop fable in which a youth falls in love with a cat, who, upon his request, is changed into a girl by the gods. During their lovemaking, the girl leaves the youth to pursue a mouse. She is then changed back into a cat, and the

youth dies. Olga Spessivtzeva and Serge Lifar dance the lead roles. This is also Sauguet's first ballet and his first big success. He composes six other ballets.

June 7   *Le Pas d'acier* receives its initial performance by Serge Diaghilev's Ballets Russes at the Theatre Sarah Bernhardt in Paris. Leonide Massine choreographs music by Sergei Prokofiev. The ballet, in two scenes, has no specific plot but depicts Soviet life and concludes with machines dancing in a factory. Lead dancers are Massine, Serge Lifar, Alexandra Danilova and Leon Woizikovsky. Although the ballet was intended to compliment life in the Soviet Union, Soviet critics are not especially flattered. Yuri Keldysh writes two years from now in the *Proletarian Musician* (Moscow), "The musical characterizations. . . are so monotonously similar, so completely submerged in buffoonery and persiflage that it is difficult to distinguish among them." In the spring of 1929, Prokofiev is interviewed in Moscow and asked whether the workers depicted in his ballet are "capitalist slaves" or "Soviet masters." Prokofiev replies, "This is a political and not a musical question, and I will not answer it."

June 14   The Bolshoi Theater gives the initial performance of *The Red Poppy* in Moscow. It deals with a Chinese dancer exploited by a vicious capitalist. She eventually gives her life to save the revolutionary leader and thus helps in the liberation of China. It is the first "revolutionary" ballet in the Soviet Union. Yekaterina Geltzer (Tao Hoa) and Alexis Bulgakov (Captain) lead the cast. The choreography is by Vasili Tikhomirov and Lev Laschilin to music by Reinhold Gliere. The ballet is in three acts and eight scenes. Revivals feature a different title — *The Red Flower* — to avoid an association with opium.

1927   Instrumental and Vocal Music

Jan. 8   *Lyric Suite*, by Alban Berg, receives its world premiere by the Kolisch Quartet in Vienna. This six-movement composition, scored for string quartet, is the first work Berg composes in the 12-tone method. The composer later arranges three of its movements for chamber orchestra. American composer George Perle and musicologist Douglass M. Green subsequently discover a vocal part to the work. This is publicly presented in 1979.

Jan. 21   Albert Roussel's orchestral *Suite in F* is premiered by Serge Koussevitzky and the Boston Symphony Orchestra. Roussel's first neoclassical work, it is in three movements.

Jan. 22   *Scarlattiana*, by Alfredo Casella. receives its first performance by Otto Klemperer and the New York Philharmonic. Casella plays the piano part. The music, based on themes from sonatas by Domenico Scarlatti, is scored for piano and chamber orchestra.

Jan. 28   Piano Concerto, by Aaron Copland, receives its world premiere by Serge Koussevitzky and the Boston Symphony Orchestra, with the composer as soloist. This two-movement concerto includes jazz elements while adhering to a sonata form. Reaction is immediate and largely unfavorable. Philip Hale writes in the Boston *Herald*, "Copland's Piano Concerto shows a shocking lack of taste, of proportion."

Jan. 29   The second movement of Charles Ives' Symphony No. 4 is premiered by Eugene Goossens in New York City. The work was completed in 1916. This movement includes various American tunes sounding in conflict with each other. They include "Marching Through Georgia" and "Columbia, Gem of the Ocean." Alfred J. Frankenstein calls it "a wild, senseless frenzy of noise." Due to the complexity of the score, the full symphony is not premiered until April 26, 1965.

This performance is one of the few of Ives' works that occurs during the first half of the century. Despite his importance, Ives is still relatively unknown and obscure. Other works he has composed so far include a Trio for violin, clarinet and piano; *Prelude from Pre-first Sonata*; *Thanksgiving and/or Forefather's Day*; *3-Page Sonata*; *The Pond*; *Pre-Second String Quartet*; *Calcium Light Night*; *Central Park in the Dark*; *The Unanswered Question*; *Space and Duration*; *All the Way Around and Back*; *The Innate*; Violin Sonata No. 1; *Some Southpaw Pitching*; *The Anti-Abolitionist Riots*; and Piano Sonata No. 1. None of these works have been premiered to date — many of them and some of his subsequent compositions are not premiered until after his death in 1951. *The Unanswered Question* and *Central Park in the Dark* later become very famous works.

Feb. 25   Ottorino Respighi's *Vetrate di chiesa* receives its first performance by Serge Koussevitzky and the Boston Symphony Orchestra. The piece consists of orchestral impressions.

March 5   Danish composer Knudage Riisager's Symphony No. 2 premieres in Copenhagen. This symphony is in one movement.

March 18   Serge Rachmaninoff's Piano Concerto No. 4 in G Minor receives its first performance by Leopold Stokowski and the Philadelphia Orchestra. Rachmaninoff is the soloist.

March 18   Polish composer Alexandre Tansman's Symphony No. 1 in A Minor is premiered by Serge Koussevitzky and the Boston Symphony Orchestra. The symphony has four movements.

March 20   Alban Berg's *Kammerkonzert* receives its initial performance in Berlin. Hermann Scherchen conducts this work scored for piano, violin and 13 wind instruments. Dedicated to Arnold Schoenberg, it is in three movements. The melodic themes of the piece are derived from correspondences between pitches and letters of the names Schoenberg, Berg and Webern.

March 20   William Grant Still's *From the Black Belt* receives its first performance in New York City, by the Barrere Little Symphony. The piece has seven sections and is based on Negro themes and spirituals.

April 1   Bela Bartok's *The Miraculous Mandarin* is performed in its orchestral suite version by Fritz Reiner and the Cincinnati Symphony Orchestra.

April 2   The Concerto for Piano, Flute, Violoncello and String Orchestra, by Vincent d'Indy, receives its first performance in Paris.

April 8   *Arcana*, a symphonic poem by Edgard Varese, receives its first performance by Leopold Stokowski and the Philadelphia Orchestra. This work is scored for large orchestra and includes parts for 40 percussion instruments. Edward Cushing writes of the piece in the Brooklyn *Daily Eagle*, "The score is long and infinitely wearying in its revelations of the unspeakably hideous." Oscar Thompson, in *Musical America*, says, "There was no mercy in its disharmony, no pity in its successions of screaming, clashing, clangorous discords. . . ."

April 10   Anton Webern's *Entflieht auf leichten Kähnen*, Op. 2, receives its world premiere in Furstenfeld, Austria. Scored for *a capella* mixed chorus, it is a setting of a poem cycle by Stefan George. The piece was composed in 1908 and had to wait 19 years for its premiere because of its intense chromaticism and intonation problems. It is also the last piece Webern composes under Arnold Schoenberg's supervision.

April 15   Frederick S. Converse's *Flivver 10,000,000, a Joyous Epic: Fantasy for Orchestra* is premiered by Serge Koussevitzky and the Boston Symphony Orchestra.

April 17   The Concerto for Harp and Wind Instruments, by Carlos Salzedo, receives its initial performance by Artur Rodzinski at Aeolian Hall in New York City. Salzedo plays the harp part, featuring novel effects. This harpist and composer later writes a book on harp technique that becomes a standard reference work on this instrument.

April 22   Roger Sessions' Symphony No. 1 in E Minor is performed for the first time by Serge Koussevitzky and the Boston Symphony Orchestra. The symphony is neoclassical in style and has three movements. Sessions is now 30 years old.

May 30   The first performance of Igor Stravinsky's opera-oratorio *Oedipus Rex* takes place in concert form in Paris at the Theatre Sarah Bernhardt with the composer conducting. The libretto, based on the tragedy by Sophocles, is a French text by Jean Cocteau that has been translated into Latin by Jean Danielon. *Oedipus Rex* receives its first stage performance in 1928. A year from now, Samuel Chotzinoff writes of the piece in the New York *Telegram*, "At the finish one is only conscious of a presumptuous drive with nothing of any consequence to back it up."

May 30   Maurice Ravel's Sonata for Violin and Piano premieres in Paris. Georges Enesco plays the violin part, and the composer is at the piano.

July 1   Bela Bartok's Piano Concerto No. 1 is premiered by Wilhelm Furtwangler, with the composer as soloist, at the International Society for Contemporary Music festival in Frankfurt.

Sep. 3   Knudage Riisager's *T-DOXC* is performed for the first time in Copenhagen. The work is subtitled *Poeme mecanique*. It is scored for orchestra and reflects the composer's interest in things futuristic.

Sep. 19   Arnold Schoenberg's String Quartet No. 3, Op. 30, receives its first performance by the Kolisch String Quartet in Vienna. The quartet has four movements. Next month, a review in the New York *Times* comments on the piece: "Behind this music stands a man who can give expression to the utmost depths of feeling."

Oct. 24   *Choros No. 8*, by Heitor Villa-Lobos, is performed for the first time in Paris. This piece is scored for two pianos and full orchestra.

Oct. 29   Alexander Tcherepnin's Symphony No. 1 is performed for the first time in Paris. It is in four movements. This Tcherepnin (son of Nicolas) made his first American tour last year.

Nov. 6   Dmitri Shostakovich's Symphony No. 2 (*To October*) receives its world premiere in Leningrad at a festival celebrating the 10th anniversary of the Russian Revolution. It is in one movement. Next February a review of the piece appears in the *Christian Science Monitor*. It says the symphony "might be described as the negation of harmonic development."

Nov. 18   Bohuslav Martinu's *La Bagarre* is premiered in Boston by Serge Koussevitzky and the Boston Symphony Orchestra. This impressionistic symphonic rondo depicts the landing of Charles Lindbergh at Le Bourget airport in Paris.

Dec. 5   *Glagolitic Mass*, by Leos Janacek, receives its world premiere in Brno. Scored for soloists, chorus, organ and orchestra, it is in eight sections (five choral) and includes an organ solo. The text is in old Slavonic, and the mass is virtually the most important piece of sacred music Janacek composes. It is also his last piece. This massive work enters the standard repertory and becomes a showpiece for orchestras and vocalists around the world.

1927 Births, Deaths and Debuts

Jan. 1   French choreographer and ballet director Maurice Bejart is born Maurice Berger in Marseilles, France.

Jan. 2   Soviet dancer, choreographer and ballet director Yuri Grigorovich is born in Leningrad.

Feb. 10   Soprano Leontyne Price is born in Laurel, Mississippi.

Feb. 23   Soprano Regine Crespin is born in Marseilles, France.

Feb. 26   American bass-baritone Donald Gramm is born in Milwaukee, Wisconsin.

March 10   German conductor Fritz Busch makes his American debut with the New York Symphony Society.

March 20   South African composer John Joubert is born in Cape Town, South Africa.

March 27   Cellist and conductor Mstislav Rostropovich is born in Azerbaijan, Baku, USSR.

May 31   Italian baritone Giuseppe Campanari, 68, dies in Milan. Having begun as a cellist at La Scala, he eventually sang at the Metropolitan Opera for many years. He made his debut in 1893 in New York as Tonio in *Pagliacci*.

June 20   Dancer and ballet director Sonia Arova is born in Sofia, Bulgaria.

July 16   Conductor Serge Baudo is born in Marseilles, France.

July 27   Pianist Jean Casadesus is born in Paris, France.

Aug. 15   Dancer, choreographer and ballet director John Cranko is born in Rustenburg, South Africa.

Aug. 20   Pianist Fannie Bloomfield Zeisler, 63, dies in Chicago. She made her debut in 1875 in Chicago and enhanced her reputation by concertizing in Europe.

Sep. 14   Isadora Duncan dies as a result of an accident near Nice at the age of 49. She is strangled when her scarf is caught in the rear wheel of her car. One of the important influences on the development of modern dance and ballet, Duncan broke away from conventional ballet to develop a style of her own. She made an unsuccessful debut in Chicago in 1899 and then danced in Europe where she

was well received. She founded her school of dance in Berlin in 1904. The following year Duncan appeared in Russia, where she had a strong influence on Michel Fokine.

Duncan's dance, which she called "free dance" was based on a vaguely articulated theory that movement should express an inner impulse or emotion. Duncan broke with convention by using the music of major composers for her work. She was the first Western dancer to appear barefoot on the stage. Her standard costume was a version of a Greek tunic.

Duncan's pieces, which involved mime more than conventional dance techniques, were little more than repeated improvisations. Because her art was extremely personal, little of her choreography survived. However, her influence — in terms of freeing dancers from conventional movements and stressing the emotional content of the work — was profound.

Sep. 25   Conductor Colin Davis is born in Weybridge, Surrey, England.

Sep. 26   American dancer and choreographer Carolyn Brown is born in Fitchburg, Massachusetts.

Oct. 6   Pianist Paul Badura-Skoda is born in Vienna, Austria.

Oct. 27   Composer Dominick Argento is born in York, Pennsylvania.

Nov. 25   Violinist Yehudi Menuhin, 11, makes his New York debut playing a Beethoven concerto with the New York Symphony, conducted by Fritz Busch. He has already been playing in public for four years.

Dec. 25   Soprano Bethany Beardslee is born in Lansing, Michigan.

1927   Related Events

Conductor Georg Schneevoight becomes music director of the Los Angeles Philharmonic Orchestra this year. He succeeds Walter Henry Rothwell and lasts two seasons.

The Chamber Orchestra of Boston is established this year by Nicolas Slonimsky. The ensemble specializes in presenting new works by contemporary composers.

Feb.   The two factions of the divided Leningrad Association for Contemporary Music reunite to pursue a common cause dedicated to the performance of new music. Non-Soviet composers now featured include Alban Berg, Ernst Krenek and Paul Hindemith.

May   Deutsche Grammophon establishes its Japanese branch — Nippon Polydor. The recording industry is now slowly expanding and recovering from a period of serious decline. New and important recordings this year include the first complete electrical recording of an opera — *Pa-*

gliacci, sung in English by the British National Opera and conducted by Eugene Goossens. Columbia (England) makes its first complete electrical recordings of all nine Beethoven symphonies. Victor releases its first automatic orthophonic record changer. The beginnings of the magnetic recording process take place in Germany, with experimentation involving coated plastic tape. An American patent makes first mention of the term *dummy head* (binaural stereo); the patent is granted to Bartlett Jones of Chicago. Columbia (U.S.) buys United Independent Broadcasters (CBS).

Aug. 24   Feodor Chaliapin is barred from being called a People's Artist by the Soviet government because he had allegedly made anti-Soviet remarks.

Sep. 30   Guido Adler becomes honorary chairman of the new International Musicological Society in Basel. This event marks the resumption of this organization, which had suspended its activities since the outbreak of World War I.

Oct. 15   The first issue of *New Music* is published. A new quarterly devoted to modern American music, the journal is edited by Henry Cowell. It publishes new music scores rather than articles, and this issue features Carl Ruggles' *Men and Mountains.*

1928 Opera

Jan. 31   Alexander Tcherepnin's three-act opera *Ol-Ol,* based on a drama by Leonid Andreyev, premieres in Weimar. It is about students in Russia before the revolution. A dispatch to the New York *Times* says of this composer's first opera, "It is unlikely that the composition will have a long life."

Feb. 16   Modest Mussorgsky's *Boris Godunov* is performed in Leningrad. This event marks the first performance of the opera in Leningrad in its original form. Previous performances had included alterations by Nikolai Rimsky-Korsakov.

Feb. 18   Kurt Weill's *Der Zar lasst sich Photographieren* receives its world premiere at the Neues Theater in Leipzig. Set to a libretto by Georg Kaiser, it is a satire about an anarchist plot to assassinate the tsar.

March 29   Eugen Zador's *The Isle of Death* premieres in Budapest. The opera is in two acts.

March 31   Gian Francesco Malipiero's opera *Filomela e l'Infatuato* premieres in Prague.

April 20   Darius Milhaud's *L'abandon d'Ariane* is performed for the first time in Wiesbaden. The libretto, by Henri Hoppenot, is a satirical treatment of the myth of Ariadne. Also premiered on the same program is Milhaud's *La deliverance de Thesee.*

May 6   Ernst Krenek's *Der Diktator; Das geheime Konigreich;* and *Schwergewicht, oder die Ehre der Nation* are premiered at a modern-music festival in Wiesbaden. These are three short operas.

May 16   The first performance of *Fra Gherardo,* by Ildebrando Pizzetti, takes place at La Scala in Milan. The libretto, by the composer, is based on an episode from the 13th-century *Chronica da Fra Salimbene da Parma.* This opera subsequently becomes Pizzetti's most famous composition. Arturo Toscanini conducts a cast that includes Ebe Stignani, Antonin Trantoul and Salvatore Baccaloni.

June 6   Richard Strauss' *Die agyptische Helena* receives its world premiere at the Dresden Staatsoper. The text, by Hugo von Hofmannsthal, is an imaginary sequel to the myth of Helen of Troy. The cast, which includes Elisabeth Rethberg, is conducted by Fritz Busch.

Aug. 1   Slovak composer Viliam Figus-Bystry's *Detvan* premieres in Bratislava. This event marks the first time a stage work is set to the Slovak language.

Aug. 3   Kurt Weill's *Die Dreigroschenoper* premieres at the Theater am Schiffbauerdamm in Berlin. The text, by Bertolt Brecht, is a free adaptation of John Gay's *The Beggar's Opera.* It is a political singspiel, with sung and spoken parts. The cast includes Weill's wife, Lotte Lenya. The work is given a mixed reception, with wild enthusiasm on one side and abusive criticism on the other. It features the tune "Mack the Knife" and becomes one of the composer's most popular pieces. This opera, in a prologue and eight scenes, is Weill's first great success.

Sep. 2   A revised version of Egon Wellesz' *Die Prinzessin Girnara* premieres in Mannheim.

Sep. 5   Brazilian composer Francisco Mignone's *L'innocente* receives its first performance in Rio de Janeiro. This is Mignone's second opera.

Dec. 1   Eugen d'Albert's three-act opera *Die schwarze Orchidee* receives its initial performance in Leipzig. It is about a thief who inherits a fortune.

KURT WEILL

1928 Dance

April 27   Igor Stravinsky's *Apollon Musagete* premieres at the Library of Congress in Washington, D.C. The work was commissioned by the Elizabeth Sprague Coolidge Foundation. Adolph Bolm choreographs this two-scene ballet, with decor by Nicholas Remisoff. It is about Apollo and the various stages of his education, culminating in his ascent to Mount Parnassus. Lead dancers are Ruth Page, Berenice Holms and Elise Reiman.

June 6   Leonide Massine's two-act ballet *Ode or Meditation at Night on the Majesty of God as Revealed by the Aurora Borealis*, set to a poetic text by Mikhail Lomonov, receives its first performance by Serge Diaghilev's Ballets Russes at the Theatre Sarah Bernhardt in Paris. Music is by Nicolas Nabokov (now 25 years old) with a libretto by Boris Kochno and decor by Pavel Tchelitchev and Pierre Charbonnier. The ballet, about the harmony and beauty of nature, stars Ira Beliamina and Serge Lifar.

June 12   Serge Diaghilev's Ballets Russes presents the first European performance of Igor Stravinsky's *Apollon Musagete* at the Theatre Sarah Bernhardt in Paris. The choreography is by George Balanchine; decor, by Andre Bauchant. The ballet focuses on the growth of the god Apollo, supported by three muses. This cast includes Serge Lifar (Apollo), Alice Nikitina (Terpsichore), Lubov Tchernicheva (Polyhymnia) and Felia Doubrovska (Calliope). The ballet is one of the most significant of the 20th century.

July 16   George Balanchine's one-act ballet *The Gods Go A-Begging*, to music by Handel arranged by Thomas Beecham, is performed for the first time by Serge Diaghilev's Ballets Russes in London. Scenery is by Leon Bakst and costumes are by Juan Gris. The ballet, about a shepherd and a serving woman who reveal themselves as gods, is danced by Alexandra Danilova and Leon Woizikovsky.

Oct. 28   Choreographer Doris Humphrey's *Water Study*, costumes by Pauline Lawrence, is premiered by the Humphrey-Weidman Concert Group in New York City. This modern dance composition explores motion. Humphrey, now 33, studied at the Francis W. Parker School in Chicago and joined the Denishawn Company in 1917. This year, she and Charles Weidman formed their performing group. Weidman, now 27, has studied at Denishawn and with Eleanor Frampton.

Nov. 4   *El fuego nuevo*, a ballet by Mexican composer Carlos Chavez, premieres in Mexico City, the composer conducting.

Nov. 22   The Ida Rubinstein Company stars in the first production of Bronislava Nijinska's *The Beloved*, to music by Franz Schubert and Franz Liszt. The ballet, produced at the Paris Opera, focuses on a poet and his muse reminiscing about his youth. Rubinstein and Anatole Vilzak dance the lead roles. Also premiered at today's performance is Maurice Ravel's *Bolero*, which had been commissioned by Ida Rubinstein. The choreography is by Bronislava Nijinska and the decor (set in a Spanish tavern) by Alexandre Benois. The ballet becomes a big favorite and is subsequently performed both as a concert work and as a ballet. Its driving, repetitive rhythms captivate audiences on a basic level. Anatole Vilzak and Rubinstein are the lead dancers.

Nov. 27   *Le baiser de la fee* — based on *The Ice Maiden*, by Hans Christian Andersen — receives its initial performance by the Ida Rubinstein Company at the Paris Opera. The ballet, in one act and four scenes, has music by Igor Stravinsky, who also conducts. The choreography is by Bronislava Nijinska; decor, by Alexandre Benois. Lead dancers are Ida Rubinstein, Ludmilla Schollar and Anatole Vilzak.

1928 Instrumental and Vocal Music

Jan. 16   Anton Webern's String Trio, Op. 20, is premiered by Rudolf Kolisch, Eugen Lehner and Benar Heifetz at the small hall of the Musikverein in Vienna. This piece contains two movements — a sonata rondo with variations and a movement in sonata form — and is based on a 12-tone row, which undergoes mosaiclike transformations. The music provokes negative reviews, which, over the course of the next six months, continue to be published. The *Hamburger Fremdenblatt* (Hamburg) says Webern played a "bad joke with patient listeners."

Feb. 12   Gustav Holst's symphonic poem *Egdon Heath* is premiered by Walter Damrosch and the New York Symphony Orchestra.

Feb. 16   Anton Webern's *Four Songs for Voice and Orchestra*, Op. 13, is premiered by Hermann Scherchen in Winterthur, with Clara Wirz-Wyss as soloist.

March 2   Leos Janacek's *Capriccio* is performed for the first time by pianist Otakar Hollmann in Prague. Composed two years ago, the work is scored for piano left hand, flute, two trumpets, three trombones and tuba.

Hollmann's right hand was incapacitated during World War I.

March 23   Walter Piston's *Symphony Piece* and Filip Lazar's *Music for an Orchestra* are premiered by the Boston Symphony Orchestra.

March 25   Pantcho Vladigerov's symphonic work *Vardar* is performed for the first time in Prague. This rhapsody is constructed from an earlier work for piano and violin. Vladigerov, a Bulgarian composer, is now 29.

April 5   *Dances africanas*, by Heitor Villa-Lobos, receives its first performance in Paris. It is an orchestral suite in three sections.

April 7   Nikolai Miaskovsky's Symphony No. 10 in F Minor premieres in Moscow. This one-movement symphony depicts conflict in the life of Peter the Great.

April 29   Nikolai Miaskovsky's Symphony No. 9 in E Minor is performed for the first time in Moscow, just 22 days after the premiere of his Tenth Symphony. It is in four movements.

June 16   *Impressioni brasiliane*, a symphonic suite by Ottorino Respighi, receives its initial performance in Sao Paulo, the composer conducting. Respighi is now touring Brazil.

Sep. 14   William Walton's first orchestral suite from *Facade* receives its first performance at the International Society for Contemporary Music festival in Siena.

Sep. 14   Carl Nielsen's *Clarinet Concerto* premieres in Copenhagen. It is in one movement.

Oct. 15   Swedish composer Kurt Atterberg's Symphony in C Major is performed for the first time in Cologne. On

KURT ATTERBERG

August 17 the piece was awarded the Schubert Memorial Prize. Ernest Newman reviews today's performance in the London *Times* saying, "Atterberg may have looked down the list of judges, and slyly made up his mind that he would put in a bit of something that would appeal to each of them in turn. . . ."

Oct. 19   Arthur Honegger's *Rugby* is premiered in Paris by the Orchestre Symphonique de Paris. The piece is a symphonic movement.

Dec. 2   Arnold Schoenberg's *Variations for Orchestra*, Op. 31, receives its world premiere as Wilhelm Furtwangler conducts the Berlin Philharmonic. This is Schoenberg's first orchestral work composed in his 12-tone method and employs the standard operations on 12-tone rows associated with this method: inversion, retrograde and retrograde-inversion. Scored for large orchestra plus flexaton and mandolin, it consists of an introduction, theme, nine variations and a finale. At one point a trombone sounds the BACH theme (B, A, C, B-flat), which is later stated frequently by other instruments of the orchestra.

The performance provokes a reaction that has become almost customary at concerts of new works by this composer. Paul Schwers asks in *Allgemeine Musikzeitung* (Berlin): "How long can the untenable situation be tolerated whereby a person like Arnold Schoenberg, lost to the world of music, continues to lead a master class in composition in a state-supported academic institution where he may cause incalculable harm to innocently trustful youth? Let Schoenberg be given a decent financial settlement, or a state pension, but let us, for God's sake, remove him, and very soon, from his teaching post."

Dec. 2   Franz Schmidt's Symphony No. 3 in A Major premieres in Vienna. This event marks the performance of the work awarded the Schubert Centennial Prize for the Austrian Section by the Columbia Phonograph Company in New York City.

Dec. 13   George Gershwin's *An American in Paris* receives its world premiere by Walter Damrosch and the Philharmonic Symphony Society of New York. This orchestral work depicts the sounds and life of Parisian streets as heard by an American tourist. It becomes one of Gershwin's most popular compositions. Herbert F. Peyser says in the New York *Telegram* that the work "is a nauseous claptrap, so dull, patchy, thin, vulgar, long-winded and inane, that the average movie audience would be bored by it."

Dec. 14   Bohuslav Martinu's *La symphonie* is premiered by Serge Koussevitzky and the Boston Symphony Orchestra.

Dec. 20   The New York Philharmonic premieres Ernest Bloch's symphonic piece *America*. This work had been awarded the Musical America prize for reflecting the ideals of American life. It is performed tomorrow simultaneously in Boston, Philadelphia, Chicago and San Francisco.

1928   Births, Deaths and Debuts

Jan. 12   Russian pianist Vladimir Horowitz makes his American debut playing Tchaikovsky's First Piano Concerto under Thomas Beecham.

Jan. 14   Dancer-choreographer Gerald Arpino is born in West Brighton, Staten Island, New York.

Jan. 17   French composer Jean Barraque is born in Paris.

Feb. 7   American soprano Grace Moore makes her Metropolitan Opera debut as Mimi in *La Boheme*. Francis Perkins writes in the New York *Herald-Tribune*, "The Metropolitan's roof still remains in place, but the audience, which included a Tennessee delegation headed by both United States Senators, did not economize its applause."

March 16   Mezzo-soprano Christa Ludwig is born in Berlin, Germany.

March 24   Pianist Byron Janis is born in McKeesport, Pennsylvania.

May 11   German composer-conductor Emil Bohnke, 40, dies in Pomerania. He was a conductor of the Berlin Symphony Orchestra.

May 19   American composer Henry F. Gilbert, 59, dies in Cambridge, Massachusetts. A pupil of Edward MacDowell, he first earned his living by working in factories, the real estate business and other enterprises. It was not until the age of 33 that he decided, despite economic hardship, to devote himself completely to musical composition. His music, incorporating Negro melodic and rhythmic elements, helped move American musical styles away from European models. Some of his works were published by the short-lived Wa-Wan Press. He composed one opera, many orchestral works, piano pieces and songs.

June 13   Swiss composer and scholar Wolfgang Graeser, 21, commits suicide in Nikolassee. This musician orchestrated Bach's *Kunst der Fuge* and systematically studied relationships between the various arts.

July 23   Pianist Leon Fleischer is born in San Francisco, California.

July 16   Dancer and teacher Patricia Wilde is born in Ottawa, Canada.

Aug. 12   Czech composer Leos Janacek, 74, dies in Ostrava. A choirmaster of a monastery at age 16, he later studied in Leipzig, Vienna and Prague before settling in Brno. At age 27 he began conducting the Czech Philharmonic (Brno) and subsequently joined the faculty of the Brno Conservatory. His first big success as a composer came at the age of 40, when his opera *Jenufa* premiered in Brno. This event quickly established him as an important Czech nationalist composer. Like many important Eastern European composers, he was strongly influenced by the folk songs of his native land. It was only in the last year of his life that he became acquainted with French impressionism and reflected this new influence in his music.

His impact on the international music scene was principally as a Czech nationalist composer, creating works that are imbued with the musical and cultural elements common to Moravian life. His output includes nine operas, many choral works (six cantatas, his monumental *Glagolitic Mass*), chamber pieces, orchestral works and piano pieces.

Aug. 22   German composer Karlheinz Stockhausen is born in Modrath, near Cologne.

Sep. 6   Conductor Evgeny Svetlanov is born in Moscow, Soviet Union.

Oct. 3   Dancer and ballet master Erik Bruhn is born in Copenhagen, Denmark.

Nov. 7   The great Italian baritone Mattia Battistini, 71, dies in Collebaccaro, Italy. After first studying medicine in Rome, he decided to become a singer. He debuted in Rome in 1878 and eventually became known worldwide as an outstanding exponent of bel canto. His career lasted for 50 years, up to the time of his death.

Nov. 13   Italian ballet master and teacher Enrico Cecchetti, 78, dies in Milan, Italy. He made his debut as a dancer in 1879 at La Scala and then appeared as a guest artist throughout Europe. In 1887 he appeared in Saint Petersburg, where he stayed to teach and work as a ballet master at the Imperial Theatre. Cecchetti was one of the most important teachers in ballet history. He helped introduce Italian technique to Russia and developed a style, emphasizing strength and placement, that provided the technical basis for some of the most brilliant dancers of the late 19th and early 20th centuries. His pupils included Anna Pavlova, Tamara Karsavina, Michel Fokine, Vaslav Nijinsky, Leonide Massine, Anton Dolin and Serge Lifar. In 1910 Serge Diaghilev hired him to be ballet master of the Diaghilev Ballets Russes. Eight years later he opened his own school in London. Checchetti's technique is still the basis of the curriculum at the school of the Royal Ballet.

Nov. 15   American violinist Ruggiero Ricci makes his concert debut in San Francisco, accompanied by his teacher, Louis Persinger. He is 10 years old.

Dec. 17   Austrian conductor Herbert von Karajan makes his conducting debut in Vienna conducting the orchestra of the Vienna Music Academy.

1928   Related Events

The rapid expansion of the recording industry through the buying and selling of recording companies that began two years ago continues as the Radio Corporation of America (RCA) buys the Victor Talking Machine Company, thereby beginning RCA Victor. Columbia (England) buys Pathe Freres, and Columbia (U.S.) sells CBS, which it bought only last year. This year's technological developments in the industry include the development of a vertical-lateral pickup by W.B. Jones and Western Electric's introduction of its 618A dynamic microphone.

Mexican composer Carlos Chavez is appointed director of the Conservatorio Nacional de Musica and organizes the Orquesta Sinfonica de Mexico this year.

English composer Eric Fenby moves to Grez-sur-Loing, France, this year to work with Frederick Delius who is now suffering from syphilis and going blind. Fenby subsequently takes note-by-note dictation from Delius in an effort to help him complete his final works. Fenby is now 22, Delius, 66.

March 11   The Nazi song "Lied der Sturmkolonnen" is sung to the melody of the "Internationale" in Bernau and features new words praising Adolf Hitler.

March 21   A performance of Ernst Krenek's *Jonny spielt auf* is interrupted by protesters of new music, who release a stink bomb in the Budapest Opera Theater.

March 29   Carlos Salzedo demonstrates his new harp at a National Harp Festival in Philadelphia. The instrument enables the harpist to produce new sounds evoking percussive and delicate sonorities. He names these novel effects the eolian flux, eolian chords, gushing chords, etc.

March 30   The Philharmonic Society of New York (Willem Mengelberg, music director) and the New York Symphony Society (Leopold Damrosch, music director) merge to become the Philharmonic-Symphony Society of New York, Inc. This merger substantially strengthens the orchestra both musically and financially (Damrosch's orchestra had been the major competition). Arturo Toscanini is principal conductor; Walter Damrosch, guest conductor.

April 20   The ondes musicales is demonstrated in Paris. Invented by Maurice Martenot, the instrument subsequently becomes known as the ondes Martenot. This electronic instrument operates with electric valve oscillators to produce an eerie sound that is used in science fiction films as well as in performances of new music.

April 25   The first performance of more than one electronic instrument takes place as six dynamophones are assembled as an orchestra. Rene Bertrand supervises the event which takes place in Paris.

May 5   The Teatro Colon in Buenos Aires opens its new concert hall.

June 15   Alexander Glazunov, an appointee to the Schubert Centennial, leaves Leningrad, marking his final departure from the Soviet Union.

Oct. 10   *L' eau du Nil*, the first French film to include a synchronized sound track, premieres in Paris.

Oct. 20   As of today, celibacy is no longer required of contestants in the Prix de Rome competition.

Nov. 1   The National Opera House, Tashkent, Uzbek Soviet Republic, Central Asia, opens today.

Dec. 11   The Library of Congress in Washington D.C. becomes the home of the Society of Friends of Music, founded today in that city.

Dec. 31   Arthur Honegger's *Rugby* is performed as a special event at an intermission of the International Rugby Match of the French and British competition.

1929   Opera

Jan. 19   Ernst Krenek's *Jonny spielt auf* premieres in an English version at the Metropolitan Opera in New York. Artur Bodanzky conducts a cast that stars Michael Bohnen, Walter Kirchhoff and Florence Easton. W.J. Henderson writes in the New York *Sun*, "The applause signified a deep satisfaction derived from the disclosure of what Dr. Burney might have called the present state of music in Germany."

Feb. 1   English composer Josef Holbrooke's *Bronwen, Daughter of Llyr* premieres in Huddersfield. This opera is part of the composer's trilogy *The Cauldron of Annwyn*.

Feb. 9   Felice Lattuada's *Le preziose ridicole* premieres at La Scala in Milan. Arturo Rossato's libretto is based on Moliere's *Les précieuses ridicules*. The cast includes Mafalda Favero, Ebe Stignani, Jan Kiepura and Salvatore Baccaloni. The conductor is Gabriele Santini.

Feb. 9   Ernst von Dohnanyi's three-act opera *Der Tenor* receives its first performance in Budapest. It is about a German tenor who is successful in attracting women, but not the music public, with his voice.

March 21   The premiere of *Sir John in Love*, by Ralph Vaughan Williams, takes place at the Royal College of Music in London. The composer chose the text from many plays, including William Shakespeare's *The Merry Wives of Windsor*. The four-act opera is conducted by Malcolm Sargent. A London dispatch to the New York *Times* says of the opera, "None of the music seems to express the characters."

April 29   Sergei Prokofiev's *Igrak* receives its premiere performance at the Theatre de la Monnaie in Brussels. The composer adapts the text from Dostoyevsky's story "The Gambler." The opera had originally been composed in 1915 and 1916. This performance is of a revision that was made in 1927.

May 15   Jacques Ibert's two-act opera *Andromede ou le plus heureux des trois* premieres at the Paris Opera. It is about a Parisian female who overpowers her captor.

May 23   *Son of the Sun*, a four-act opera by Sergei Vassilenko, receives its first performance in Moscow, the composer conducting. The opera, set during the Boxer Rebellion in China, is about a Chinese scientist who opposes foreign diplomats and missionaries.

June 8   *Neues vom Tage*, a 3-act opera by Paul Hindemith, receives its first performance at the Kroll Theater in Berlin. The libretto, by Marcellus Schiffer, is a satirical account of everyday life. Otto Klemperer conducts a cast that includes Sabine Kalter, Fritz Krenn and Dezso Ernster. This is the last of Hindemith's operas to be premiered in Germany until Hitler is defeated.

June 25   Eugene Goossens' *Judith* with a libretto based on the novel by Arnold Bennett, premieres at Covent Garden in London, the composer conducting. The opera is in one act.

1929 Dance

Jan. 12   The Ida Rubinstein Company premieres Bronislava Nijinska's version of Maurice Ravel's *La Valse* in Monte Carlo. Decor is by Alexandre Benois. Ida Rubinstein and Anatole Vilzak star.

March 4   Ten French composers premiere their collectively composed music as an opera-ballet. Entitled *Jeanne's Fan*, the work is dedicated to Mme. Jeanne Dubost by the composers Florent Schmitt, Albert Roussel, Maurice Ravel, Jacques Ibert, Alexis Roland-Manuel, Darius Milhaud, Marcel Delannoy, Francis Poulenc, Georges Auric and Pierre Octave Ferroud. The Paris Opera performs the piece.

March 31   Doris Humphrey's *Air on a Ground Bass, Gigue, Speed* and *Life of a Bee* are performed for the first time in New York City. *Compassion*, by Charles Weidman, is also premiered on the same program.

May 7   Serge Diaghilev's Ballets Russes premieres George Balanchine's *Le Bal* to music by Vittorio Rieti. The libretto is by Boris Kochno. The decor is by Giorgio di Chirico. Alexandra Danilova, Alice Nikitina, Lydia Sokolova, Anton Dolin and Serge Lifar star.

May 21   George Balanchine's *The Prodigal Son* receives its world premiere by Serge Diaghilev's Ballets Russes at the Theatre Sarah Bernhardt in Paris. The music is by Sergei Prokofiev, with costumes and scenery by Georges Rouault. Based on the biblical story, it is one of the most important ballets of the twentieth century. The lead dancers are Serge Lifar and Felia Doubrovska. It is the last ballet produced by Diaghilev. Also premiered at the same theater is Serge Lifar's version of Igor Stravinsky's *Le Renard*, with roles played by acrobats. At the Paris Opera, Georges Auric's ballet *Les Enchantements d'Alcine* receives its initial performance by Ida Rubinstein.

June 19   *Aubade* receives its first performance at the home of the Vicomtesse de Noailles in Paris. Choreographed by Bronislava Nijinska to music by Francis Poulenc (scored for piano and 18 instruments), the "concerto choreographique" is about the myth of Diana and Actaeon. Poulenc also writes the libretto; decor is by J.M. Franck.

Aug. 6   The Denishawn company premieres Ted Shawn's *Pacific 231*, choreographed to the rhythmic score by Arthur Honegger.

1929 Instrumental and Vocal Music

Jan. 18   In Moscow Procoll (Production Collective of the Soviet Union) premieres its first work composed collectively by nine composers, entitled *The Path of October*. The work's composers are Victor Biely, Henrik Bruck, Alexander Davidenko, Marian Koval, Zara Levina, Sergei Riausov, Vladimir Tarnopolsky, Nicolai Tchemberdzhi and Boris Schekhter.

Jan. 21   Alban Berg's *Lyric Suite* is performed in its version for chamber orchestra in Berlin. This version is the composer's arrangement of three movements of the suite.

Jan. 27   Hermann Scherchen premieres Anton Webern's revised version of his *Six Pieces for Large Orchestra*, Op. 6, in Berlin.

Feb. 21   Ottorino Respighi's symphonic *Feste romane* is premiered by Arturo Toscanini and the New York Philharmonic. This is the third in a series of tone poems also comprising *The Pines of Rome* and *The Fountains of Rome*.

Feb. 28   Ildebrando Pizzetti's *Concerto dell'estate* is performed for the first time by Arturo Toscanini and the New York Philharmonic. The piece is a symphonic triptych.

March 11   Colin McPhee's Concerto for Piano and Wind Octet premieres in Boston.

March 29   Leo Sowerby's Symphony No. 2 in B Minor premieres in Chicago.

May 3   Francis Poulenc's three-movement *Concerto Champetre* receives its initial performance in Paris. Pierre Monteux conducts the Orchestre Symphonique de Paris. Wanda Landowska is harpsichord soloist. Today's performance features a harpsichord designed by Landowska who also commissioned this piece. In this concerto Poulenc attempts to evoke, in a contemporary vein, the virtuosic style of 17th-century French keyboard music.

May 30   Heitor Villa-Lobos' symphonic poem *Amazonas* premieres in Paris.

July 28   *Lindberghflug* — a radio cantata composed by Paul Hindemith and Kurt Weill, with a text by Bertolt Brecht — premieres in Baden-Baden. The cantata depicts the transatlantic flight of Charles Lindbergh.

Oct. 3   Viola Concerto, by William Walton, premieres in London, with Paul Hindemith as soloist. The three-movement concerto is neoclassical in style.

Oct. 12   The Delius Festival begins today in London. Sir Thomas Beecham and the London Symphony Orchestra perform and premiere various works by Frederick Delius, who has been brought from France to hear the performances. *A Late Lark*, for tenor and orchestra, premieres on to-

day's program. Other first performances on succeeding concerts of the festival include *Air and Dance*, for string orchestra; *Cynara*, for baritone and orchestra, and a revised Piano Concerto. The festival enhances the composer's stature in England.

Nov. 12   Josef Matthias Hauer's one-movement Violin Concerto receives its first performance in Berlin. The dodecaphonic work is subtitled *Zwolftonmusik for Orchestra with a Solo Instrument*. It uses one 12-tone row to generate 112 others, which appear at various places throughout the concerto.

Dec. 6   Igor Stravinsky's *Capriccio* scored for piano and orchestra, receives its initial performance by Ernest Ansermet and the Orchestre Symphonique de Paris, with the composer as soloist.

Dec. 12   Constant Lambert's symphonic cantata *Rio Grande* premieres in Manchester, England. The work, scored for solo piano, chorus and orchestra, incorporates jazz elements. The piece was inspired by a poem by Sacheverell Sitwell. It is extremely successful. Lambert is now 24.

Dec. 13   Arnold Bax's Symphony No. 2 is premiered by Serge Koussevitzky and the Boston Symphony Orchestra. This symphony has three movements.

Dec. 15   Darius Milhaud's Viola Concerto is premiered by Pierre Monteux and the Concertgebouw Orchestra, with Paul Hindemith as soloist.

Dec. 18   Symphony, Op. 21, by Anton Webern, receives its world premiere at Town Hall, New York City. Alexander Smallens conducts an ensemble organized under the auspices of the League of Composers, which pays Webern an honorarium of $350 for the work. The two-movement symphony marks a breakthrough for Webern, who is moving toward distillation and compression of the 12-tone method. Webern views his goal as music governed by the laws of nature and reflected, in this composition, through canonic imitation, mirror inversion and variation. The symphony's first movement is divided into two parts — statement and development; the second movement consists of a theme, seven variations and a coda. Olin Downes reviews the concert in the New York *Times* and says that Webern ". . . has achieved the perfect fruition of futility and written precisely nothing."

Dec. 22   Sergei Prokofiev's four-movement, symphonic *Divertissement* premieres in Paris, the composer conducting. The first and third movements are taken from his ballet *Trapeze*, composed four years ago.

1929   Births, Deaths and Debuts

Feb. 24   French composer-conductor Andre Messager, 75, dies in Paris. A pupil of Camille Saint-Saens, he worked as a church organist and choirmaster before conducting at the Opera-Comique at age 45. He later conducted at the Paris Opera. In 1924 he conducted one season of Serge Diaghilev's Ballets Russes. His importance as a composer was overshadowed by his conducting achievements. Although he wrote at least 13 operas, 6 operettas and 9 ballets, these eclectic and characteristically French works did not have an international impact.

March 4   Conductor Bernard Haitink is born in Amsterdam, Holland.

April 6   Conductor, pianist and composer Andre Previn is born in Berlin, Germany.

May 16   German soprano Lilli Lehmann, 80, dies in Berlin. The famous singer, who made her debut in 1865, was chosen by Wagner to sing in the first Ring cycle at Bayreuth in 1876. She then became a lifetime member of the Berlin Opera and appeared to great acclaim all over Europe and America. Her repertoire was vast, consisting of 170 roles in works from Mozart to Puccini as well as some 600 songs. She was at home in many styles, displaying consummate musicianship and a beautiful voice. Among her pupils were Geraldine Farrar and Olive Fremstad.

May 25   American soprano Beverly Sills is born in Brooklyn, New York.

July 11   Baritone Hermann Prey is born in Berlin, Germany.

Aug. 19   Serge Diaghilev, 57, dies in Venice. One of the great impresarios of ballet history, he became a catalyst of all the most important trends in music, dance and art during the first three decades of the 20th century. Under his direction, ballet in Europe regained its integrity and seriousness. With choreographer Michel Fokine, he helped develop modern ballet, a unity of choreography, dance and design.

Born in the Novgorod district of Russia, Diaghilev studied law and associated himself with a circle of young writers, musicians and painters promoting reform in the arts. He co-founded the art journal *Mir Iskusstva (The World of Art)* in 1899. From 1899 to 1901 he was an artistic advisor to the Maryinsky Theatre. In 1908 he began his career as an international impressario, bringing a production of *Boris Godunov*, featuring Feodor Chaliapin, to Paris. The following year he formed the Diaghilev Ballets Russes which presented a season in Paris in May. The season was a triumph for Diaghilev and the company and proved a turning point in the history of ballet. It reintroduced ballet to most of Western Europe and ushered in a period of tremendous artistic creativity in many of the arts.

Diaghilev nurtured and introduced some of the greatest talents of the 20th century. Among his choreographers were Michel Fokine, Vaslav Nijinsky, Leonide Massine, Bronislava Nijinska and George Balanchine. Designers used in his productions included Alexandre Benois, Leon Bakst, Nicholas Roerich, Pablo Picasso and Henri Matisse. Diaghilev commissioned many of Igor Stravinsky's important ballets including *Le Sacre du printemps* and *Petroushka*. He also commissioned scores from Sergei Prokofiev, Darius Milhaud, Francis Poulenc, Georges Auric, Maurice Ravel and Manuel de Falla. The Ballets Russes developed such talents as Vaslav Nijinsky, Tamara Karsavina, Alicia Markova and Anton Dolin. Diaghilev was a seminal figure not only for ballet but also for music and art.

Aug. 28   Conductor Istvan Kertesz is born in Budapest, Hungary.

Sep. 13   Bass Nicolai Ghiaurov is born in Velimgrad, Bulgaria.

Sep. 19   British dancer, choreographer and ballet director Peter Darrell is born in Richmond, Surrey.

Oct. 2   Ballerina Tanaquil LeClerq is born in Paris, France.

Oct. 24   Composer George Crumb is born in Charleston, West Virginia.

Oct. 28   Russian violinist Nathan Milstein makes his American debut with the Philadelphia Orchestra. He is soloist in Alexander Glazunov's Concerto in A Minor, Op. 82. Milstein has studied with Leopold Auer and Eugene Ysaye.

Nov. 4   Yehudi Menuhin, 13, makes his London debut performing the Brahms Violin Concerto with the London Symphony Orchestra at Queen's Hall, London.

Nov. 21   Alexander Glazunov conducts the Detroit Symphony Orchestra in a performance of his Sixth Symphony. This event marks his first American appearance.

Dec. 11   Dancer, choreographer and ballet director Kenneth MacMillan is born in Dunfermline, Scotland.

Dec. 29   Russian cellist Gregor Piatigorsky makes his New York debut with the New York Philharmonic.

1929   Related Events

Arturo Toscanini becomes music director of the New York Philharmonic this year. It is under his leadership that this orchestra becomes internationally known. He presides over the orchestra's first European tour and the beginning of its nationwide radio broadcasts.

Hugo Riemann's *Musik-Lexikon,* one of the standard reference works on music, is published in its 11th edition this year. This is the third edition that Alfred Einstein edits.

Artur Rodzinski becomes music director of the Los Angeles Philharmonic Orchestra this year. He succeeds Georg Schneevoight and holds this post until 1933.

Serge Lifar is appointed ballet master of the Paris Opera Ballet this year. During his 15 years in this post, he thoroughly reorganizes this ballet company.

Jan. 1   The first issue of the Association of Proletarian Musicians' (RAPM's) new journal *The Proletarian Musician* is published in Moscow. Its purpose is to prevent young Soviet composers from becoming "decadent," to encourage them to inherit past musical trends and to create a new proletarian type of music.

Jan. 17   Alexander Alexandrov becomes music director of the Red Army Ensemble, founded today in Moscow to encourage military musical events.

Feb.   The Decca Gramophone Company, Ltd. is born in England. Musical instrument makers Barnet, Samuel and Sons create this new recording company and select its name — Decca — by combining letters from the names of portable gramophones developed since 1913. Other events in the recording industry this year include the first complete recording of Beethoven's String Quartets (Capet and Lener String Quartets — Columbia, England); the establishment in France of the Polydor label, which is a subsidiary of Deutsche Grammophon (Germany); the development in Germany of a steel tape magnetic record/playback machine called the blattnerphon; and the cessation of Thomas A. Edison's active work in the recording industry.

March 1   Frederick Delius becomes the first composer to be made a Companion of Honour by royal decree. Instituted in 1917, this British order now has 40 members.

May 7   At a performance of Kurt Weill's *Die Dreigroschenoper* at the Berlin State Opera, Hitler's brownshirts express their anti-Semitism by throwing stink bombs into the theater.

May 10   The first meeting of the Acoustical Society of America takes place at the Bell Telephone Laboratories in New York City. The purpose of this new organization is to increase and spread the knowledge of acoustics and to promote its practical applications.

May 13   The Inglis Collection is bequeathed to the National Library of Scotland in Edinburgh. It contains approximately 740 items of Scottish and English printed music and manuscripts from the 18th and 19th centuries. The collection had formerly belonged to Alexander W. Inglis of Glencourse, commissioner of supply and an officer in the Royal Scots Militia.

May 20   The Cowan Collection is bequeathed to the National Library of Scotland. This collection of over 1,100 items was bequeathed by William Cowan, author of *The Bibliography of the Book of Common Order and Psalm Book of the Church of Scotland, 1556–1644* (1913) and (with James Love) of *The Music of the Church Hymnary* (1901). The collection consists mainly of liturgies, psalm and hymn books, and books on church ceremony, ranging from the 16th to the 20th centuries.

June 1   Hermann Scherchen writes the Preface to his *Handbook of Conducting,* published this year in a German edition entitled *Lehrbuch des Dirigierens.* The book is divided into three sections: "On Conducting," "The Science of the Orchestra" and "Conductor and Music." It distills Scherchen's experience as a conductor and offers both technical and aesthetic information aimed at one goal: realizing exactly what the composer's intentions were in terms of performance. The book is published in an English edition in 1933.

Aug. 4   The final performance of Serge Diaghilev's Ballets Russes takes place in Vichy. Due to the death of Diaghilev 15 days from today, the company disbands.

Oct. 6   The Sonneck Memorial Fund is established at the Library of Congress in Washington, D.C. Harold Bauer, president of the Beethoven Association of New York, gives the library a check for $10,000 to advance musicology by awarding annual prizes for scholarly research in the field. The fund is named after Oscar G. Sonneck, first chief of the library's Music Division.

Nov. 4   The new Chicago Civic Opera House opens with a production of Giuseppe Verdi's *Aida.* Giorgio Polacco conducts a cast that includes Rosa Raisa. The building cost $20 million and rises 45 stories above street level (the upper floors contain studios and offices for both opera and commercial businesses). The opera house seats 3,471 and features a movable stage and a steel curtain displaying a medley of operatic characters painted by Jules Guerin of New York City.

Dec. 28   Soprano Frances Alda sings her farewell performance at the Metropolitan Opera in *Manon Lescaut.*

1930 Opera

Jan. 12   Dmitri Shostakovich's *The Nose* premieres at the Maly Theater in Leningrad. The libretto, by J. Preis, is based on the story by Nikolai Gogol. The opera was written when the composer was 20 years old.

Jan. 19   Ernst Krenek's *Leben des Orest* premieres in Leipzig. This five-act opera is about the Greek myth of Orestes.

Feb. 1   Arnold Schoenberg's *Von Heute auf Morgen* premieres in Frankfurt. The text is written by Schoenberg's wife, Gertrud Kolish, who uses the pseudonym Max Blonda. It is a story about the everyday relations between husband and wife. William Steinberg conducts.

March 9   Kurt Weill's *Aufstieg und Fall der Stadt Mahagonny* is performed in its expanded version at the Neues Theater in Leipzig. The first version had been premiered on July 17, 1927 in Baden-Baden. The libretto, by Bertolt Brecht is a satire about a city built by thugs and con artists. The opera causes an uproar in Leipzig and is banned by the Nazis, who later attempt to destroy all copies of the score; the original is saved and rediscovered after the war.

March 15   Polish composer Witold Maliszewski's opera-ballet *Boruta* premieres in Warsaw. The composer receives the Polish State Music Award of 1931 for this work.

April 12   Leos Janacek's opera *From the House of the Dead* premieres posthumously in Brno. The composer wrote his own libretto, which is based on a book by Feodor Dostoyevsky. The opera shows scenes of life in a Russian prison camp. It is considered one of Janacek's finest achievements.

April 17   Charles Stanford Skilton's one-act opera *The Sun Bride* receives its initial performance over radio in New York. The work incorporates American Indian melodic materials.

April 29   Ildebrando Pizzetti's two-act opera *Lo Straniero* receives its first performance in Rome. The opera is the third part of an operatic trilogy and is composed in the style of Greek tragedy, using a chorus to punctuate the drama.

May 5   Darius Milhaud's *Christophe Colomb* receives its world premiere at the Staatsoper in Berlin. Paul Claudel's German libretto is a fictionalized account of the life of Christopher Columbus after he discovered America. The opera contains 26 scenes.

May 15   Vladimir Deshevov's opera *Ice and Steel* premieres in Leningrad. The four-act work is about a 1921 revolt against the Soviet government by a splinter group of the Soviet Navy. The opera includes a 12-tone row and tone clusters played on the piano.

May 24   *X-mal Rembrandt* receives its initial performance in Gera, Germany. This opera-burlesque by Eugen Zador depicts a painter copying a Rembrandt self-portrait in a German museum in order to steal the original after replacing it with his copy. He later discovers that the original is also a fake, and that this particular variety of theft has occurred many times; the original thief chants at the end of the opera: "One time Rembrandt, two times Rembrandt, X times Rembrandt" — the title of the opera is derived from that character's line.

May 25   George Antheil's three-act opera *Transatlantique* premieres in Frankfurt, Germany. The opera includes jazz elements and satirizes an American presidential election. It is also known as *The People's Choice*.

June 8   Ernst Toch's *The Fan* receives its first performance in Konigsberg, at the Allgemeiner Deutscher Musikverein festival. This three-act opera is about a Chinese widow who struggles with thoughts of being chaste after her husband's death.

June 21   Paul Hindemith's *Wir bauen eine Stadt* premieres in Berlin. This neobaroque children's opera is about the construction of a city.

June 30   *Der Jasager*, by Kurt Weill, receives its premiere performance in Berlin. Bertolt Brecht's libretto to this two-act opera is based on a 15th-century Japanese drama. Weill considers it a children's opera. Like Weill's other works, it is condemned by the Nazis.

Dec. 10   Karol Rathaus' first opera, *Fremde Erde* premieres in Berlin. The four-act work is about Russian immigrants travelling to America who hope to make millions. The opera includes ragtime and blues rhythms.

Dec. 10   American composer Hamilton Forrest's *Camille*, with a libretto by the composer, receives its first performance by the Chicago Civic Opera Company, in a French version with Mary Garden in the lead role.

Dec. 12   Arthur Honegger's *Les Aventures du Roi Pausole* receives its initial performance in Paris. Based on a novel by Pierre Louys, it is the composer's first operetta and deals with life in a nudist colony.

Dec. 13   *The Measures Taken*, by 32-year-old Hanns Eisler, with text by Bertolt Brecht, receives its first performance in Berlin. The operatic play — scored for three speakers, tenor chorus and orchestra — was composed as a propaganda device for the German Communist Party. A review applauding the work's purpose is published in *Die rote Fahne* (Berlin); it says, "Here is at least an ideologically mature and artistically perfect choral work for workers."

1930 Dance

Feb. 25   The Ballet Club gives its first public performance at the Lyric Theatre, Hammersmith, England. The Rambert dancers premiere Frederick Ashton's *Capriole Suite*, to music by Peter Warlock. The plotless work is a suite of old dances. Andree Howard, Diana Gould, Harold Turner, Frederick Ashton and William Chappell appear in the opening night cast.

Marie Rambert began organizing this dance company in 1926 (when it was called the Marie Rambert Dancers). It is England's oldest ballet company. After a series of productions featuring excerpts from the classics, complete versions of traditional ballets later enter the repertoire.

Marie Rambert was born in Warsaw in 1888. Her dance studies were influenced by Isadora Duncan and Emile Jaques-Dalcroze. At age 25 she was hired by Serge Diaghilev to coach Vaslav Nijinsky on the rhythmic intricacies of Igor Stravinsky's *Le Sacre du printemps*. She subsequently went to London, married dramatist Ashley Dukes at age 30 and then focused her energies on forming her own company. The company is renamed Ballet Rambert in 1935.

April 11   *Le Sacre du printemps* is revised by Leonide Massine and performed in Philadelphia in a version featuring Martha Graham as lead dancer. This version is presented under the auspices of the League of Composers.

April 11   Doris Humphrey's *Die gluckliche Hand* — with music by Arnold Schoenberg and Robert Edmond Jones, — premieres at the Philadelphia Opera House.

June 22   Ted Shawn, and Margarete Wallman premiere their new modern dance work *Orpheus Dionysos* at the third German Dance Congress in Munich.

June 24   Choreographer Mary Wigman's *Das Totenmal* is performed for the first time in Munich at the third German Dance Congress. Now 43, Wigman has studied with Emile Jaques-Dalcroze and Rudolf von Laban. Since the end of World War I, she has established a reputation for herself as Germany's most famous expressionist dancer. Her dance school, founded in 1920 in Dresden, has expanded internationally to include more than 2,000 pupils.

Aug. 12   *Angkor-Vat*, choreographed by Ruth Saint Denis, receives its first performance at Lewisohn Stadium in New York.

Oct. 26   Choreographer Vasily Vainonen's *The Golden Age*, with music by Dmitri Shostakovich, is premiered by the Kirov Ballet in Leningrad. It also features choreography by Leonid Yacobson and V. Chesnakov. The libretto, which resulted from a competition for new ballet stories based on Soviet themes, deals with class conflict and the ideological differences between communism and fascism.

Nov. 12   The Humphrey-Weidman company presents Doris Humphrey's *The Shakers*, set to music by Pauline

MARY WIGMAN

Lawrence (who also designs the costumes). The modern dance work is a depiction of Shaker religious rites. The one-act ballet is performed at Hunter College in New York.

1930   Instrumental and Vocal Music

Jan. 21   Dmitri Shostakovich's Symphony No. 3 (*May First*) is premiered by Alexander Gauk and the Leningrad Philharmonic. The work, in one movement, is subsequently considered ideologically weak by Soviet authorities and is no longer performed.

Feb. 15   Florent Schmitt's *Cancunik* receives its first performance in Paris. Translated from the French, the title (phonetically spelled) means "one-way street." The piece is a humorous symphonic sketch.

Feb. 16   Nicolas Nabokov's *Symphonie lyrique* in three movements receives its initial performance by the Orchestre Symphonique de Paris, in that city. Pierre Monteux conducts.

Feb. 20   Randall Thompson's Symphony No. 1 receives its first performance by the Rochester Philharmonic, Howard Hanson conducting. The work was completed last year.

March 13   *Fantasia on Sussex* by Ralph Vaughan Williams is premiered by John Barbirolli and the Royal Philharmonic Orchestra, with Pablo Casals as soloist. This piece is scored for violoncello and orchestra.

March 28   American composer Walter Piston conducts the world premiere of his Suite for Orchestra with Boston Symphony Orchestra. Piston is now a professor of music at Harvard University.

March 28   *Konzertmusik* for viola and chamber orchestra, by Paul Hindemith, is performed for the first time in Hamburg.

April 3   *Summer Evening*, a symphonic tone poem by Zoltan Kodaly, receives its first performance in New York City, as Arturo Toscanini conducts the New York Philharmonic.

April 3   Gustav Holst's *Double Concerto* for two violins and orchestra is premiered by Adila Fachiri and Jelly d'Aranyi in London, at Queen's Hall.

April 14   Alban Berg's *Drei Orchesterstucke*, Op. 6, premieres in its complete and final version in Oldenburg. The first two sections were performed in 1923.

June 4   Alban Berg's *Der Wein*, set to poems by Baudelaire and translated by Stefan George, receives its initial performance in Konigsberg. This dodecaphonic work is scored for voice and orchestra.

June 17   *Fuge aus der Geographie*, by Ernst Toch, receives its world premiere at the first concert of the Festival der neuen Musik in Berlin. The festival's purpose is to explore utilitarian music. This fugue, scored for *a capella* chorus, is based on names of geographical locales and uses the chorus to articulate them in an asyllabic counterpoint Toch calls "Gesprochene Musik."

July 6   Dutch composer Henk Badings' Symphony No. 1 premieres in Amsterdam, as Willem Mengelberg conducts the Concertgebouw Orchestra. Badings, 23, is studying composition with Willem Pijper. He subsequently destroys the score of this symphony. It is the first of 14 symphonies he writes.

Sep. 20   Edward Elgar's fifth and final march of the orchestral series *Pomp and Circumstance* premieres in London.

Sep. 24   Henry Hadley's symphonic suite *Streets of Peking* receives its initial performance in Tokyo with the composer conducting. This work includes pentatonic harmonies.

Oct. 22   *Morning Heroes* premieres in Norwich, England at the Norwich Festival. This work, by Arthur Bliss, is a symphonic piece in six sections scored for orator, chorus and orchestra. It is dedicated to soldiers killed in combat. The composer's brother suffered that fate.

Oct. 24   Albert Roussel's Symphony No. 3 in G Minor receives its initial performance by Serge Koussevitzky and the Boston Symphony Orchestra.

Oct. 25   Ernst von Dohnanyi's *Missa in Dedicatione Ecclesiae*, scored for soloists, chorus and orchestra, is premiered as a special event of consecration of the Cathedral of Szeged.

Nov. 6   Arnold Schoenberg's *Music for a Film*, Op. 34, is premiered by Otto Klemperer and the Berlin State Opera Orchestra in Berlin. Conceived as background music for a cinematic scene, it has three sections. Walter Herschberg writes in *Signale fur die musikalische Welt* (Berlin), "This is absolute Unmusic."

Nov. 7   Ottorino Respighi's orchestral work *Metamorphosen, Modi XII* is premiered by Serge Koussevitzky and the Boston Symphony Orchestra as a commissioned work celebrating the 50th anniversary of the orchestra's founding. The work is a theme and variations.

Nov. 7   Igor Stravinsky's orchestral arrangements of his *Four Etudes, Three Pieces for String Quartet, Study for Pianola, Cantique* and *Madrid* are premiered in Berlin.

Nov. 14   Serge Koussevitzky and the Boston Symphony Orchestra give the first performance of Sergei Prokofiev's Symphony No. 4 in C Major. The work incorporates part of Prokofiev's ballet *L'enfant prodigue*.

Nov. 28   Zoltan Kodaly's symphonic *Dances of Marosszek* receives its first performance in Dresden. These symphonic dances are based on folk songs that Ernst von Dohnanyi collected in Transylvania.

Nov. 28   Howard Hanson's Symphony No. 2 (*Romantic*) is performed for the first time by Serge Koussevitzky and the Boston Symphony Orchestra. The composer employs strong melodic configurations and angular rhythms. It is one of Hanson's most successful compositions.

Nov. 30   Jacques Ibert's symphonic suite *Divertissement* receives its first performance in Paris. The music is extracted from his score *Le Chapeau de paille d'Italie* — instrumental music for a farce.

Dec. 1   English composer Kaikhosru Sorabji performs his massive piano work entitled *Opus Clavicembalisticum*. The event takes place in Glasgow under the auspices of the Active Society for the Propagation of Contemporary Music. The piece contains a theme with 44 variations and a passacaglia with 81 variations. It is dedicated to "the everlasting glory of those few men blessed and sanctified in the curses and execrations of those many whose praise is eternal damnation." Born in Chingford, England in 1892, this composer's real name is Leon Dudley.

Dec. 5   Darius Milhaud's two-movement Concerto for Percussion and Chamber Orchestra is performed for the first time in Paris.

Dec. 13   Igor Stravinsky's *Symphony of Psalms* premieres in Brussels. Dedicated to the Boston Symphony and to "the glory of God," the piece is scored for chorus and orchestra (without violins or violas) and uses the Latin text of the psalms. This piece reflects Stravinsky's recently renewed interest in the Russian Orthodox faith of his youth and is, to some degree, in dramatic contrast to his ballets, which display powerful dance rhythms. This "symphony", which is austere in its vocal solemnity, features the lower registers of the orchestra. It comes at the midpoint of Stravinsky's career — he is now 48.

Dec. 19   Igor Stravinsky's *Symphony of Psalms* is performed by the Boston Symphony Orchestra, for whose 50th anniversary celebration it was composed. Serge Koussevitzky conducts this first American performance of the piece. It was originally scheduled for December 12 — a performance that was canceled due to Koussevitzky's indisposition.

Dec. 22   *Hymn to Bolivar* premieres in Caracas. Franco Alfano conducts this performance of his latest work, which he composed to celebrate the centennial of Simon Bolivar's death. It is scored for chorus and orchestra.

Dec. 28   Henry Cowell's Piano Concerto is performed in its complete version by the Havana Philharmonic, with the composer as soloist. The work includes keyboard techniques of playing with fists and forearms to generate tone clusters. A partial performance took place earlier this year.

1930 Births, Deaths and Debuts

Jan. 18   Dom Andre Mocquereau, 80, dies in Solesmes, France. This scholar joined the Order of the Benedictines at the Abbey of Solesmes at age 26 and, under the aegis of Dom Joseph Pothier, studied the intricacies and musicological problems of Gregorian chant. He also directed the abbey's choir. After passage of the *Law of Associations* legislation in France, he became prior of Quarr Abbey, Isle of Wight, where the monks stayed while in exile. Mocquereau's writings on chant are extensive: He founded and edited the 17-volume *Paleographie musicale* and authored his famous scholarly work *Le nombre musical gregorien ou rythmique gregorienne* (1908–27).

Jan. 28   Czech soprano Emmy Destinn, 52, dies in Budejovice, Czechoslovakia. This distinguished singer, known for her vocal and dramatic abilities, made her debut in Berlin in 1898 as Santuzza. She was later chosen by Cosima Wagner to sing Senta in the first Bayreuth production of *The Flying Dutchman* and by Richard Strauss for the Berlin premiere of *Salome*. She was successful in England, where she sang the first English performance of *Madama Butterfly*, and in the United States, where she created the title role in Puccini's *Girl of the Golden West*. After her retirement in 1921, she wrote a play, a novel and some

poetry. According to the pianist Arthur Rubinstein, who seems to have been on intimate terms with her, she had a tattoo of a snake running up one of her legs.

Feb. 26   Pianist Lazar Berman is born in Leningrad, USSR.

March 6   Conductor Lorin Maazel is born in Neuilly, France of American parents.

March 9   Conductor Thomas Schippers is born in Kalamazoo, Michigan.

April 1   Cosima Wagner, 92, wife of Richard Wagner, dies at Bayreuth. The daughter of Franz Liszt, she was first married to conductor Hans von Bulow, during which time she had two children by Wagner. She and von Bulow were eventually divorced, and a few weeks later she married Wagner. After his death, she ran the Bayreuth Festival and controlled all rights to Wagner performances throughout the world. An intelligent and autocratic personality, she effectively promulgated the Wagner operas well into the 20th century.

April 3   Canadian soprano Dame Emma Albani, 82, dies in London. Born in Montreal, she made her debut in 1870 in Messina (as Amina in *La Sonnambula*) and repeated this role at Covent Garden. After performances in Russia, she again sang Amina in New York, marking her American operatic debut (1874). Her Metropolitan Opera debut came in 1891. This led to many performances at that house. She was known for her powerful, emotional singing and accurate vocal technique. At age 78 she was made a dame of the British Empire.

April 9   French soprano Rose Caron, 72, dies in Paris. She made her debut as Alice in *Robert le Diable* (1884). Many years later, at Giuseppe Verdi's request, she sang Desdemona in *Othello*'s Paris premiere. She also created Brunhilde in Louis-Etienne-Ernest Reyer's *Sigurd*. She joined the faculty of the Paris Conservatoire in 1902.

May 8   Soprano Heather Harper is born in Belfast, Ireland.

May 8   Joseph Adamowski, 67, dies in Cambridge, Massachusetts. A cellist on the faculty of the New England Conservatory and a member of the Adamowski Trio, he was married to the only female pupil of Ignace Paderewski, Antoinette Szumowska.

May 14   E. Power Biggs gives his first New York recital at the Wanamaker Auditorium, performing organ works by Liszt, Marcel Dupre and Bach. Rave reviews include one in the New York *World* that says Biggs is "... one of the foremost organists of the day."

July 3   Conductor Carlos Kleiber is born in Berlin. He is the son of conductor Erich Kleiber.

July 15   Leopold Auer, 85, dies in Loschwitz, in the vicinity of Dresden. A famous violinist and teacher, his pupils included Mischa Elman, Jascha Heifetz and Efrem Zimbalist. The Tchaikovsky Violin Concerto had been dedicated to him, but the dedication was later revoked due to Auer's criticism of the piece.

July 25   Contralto Maureen Forrester is born in Montreal, Canada.

July 29   American dancer, choreographer and ballet director Paul Taylor is born in Allegheny County, Pennsylvania.

Aug. 4   Siegfried Wagner, 61, dies in Bayreuth. Son of Richard and Cosima Wagner, his grandfather was Franz Liszt. He took over the management of Bayreuth 24 years after his father's death and conducted many performances. Also a composer, his principal works are operas, *Der Barenhauter* among them.

Nov. 17   American composer David Amram is born in Philadelphia, Pennsylvania.

Nov. 27   American tenor Richard Crooks makes his American debut as Cavaradossi in *Tosca* with the Philadelphia Grand Opera Company.

Dec. 17   English composer Philip Heseltine, 36, commits suicide in his London apartment by turning on the stove and inhaling gas. He worked under the pseudonym of Peter Warlock. Heseltine's music was strongly influenced by Frederick Delius and Bernard van Dieren. He also wrote many articles and books, including *Carlo Gesualdo, Prince of Venosa, Musician and Murderer* with Cecil Gray; (London, 1926).

Dec. 24   American dancer, choreographer, teacher and ballet director Robert Joffrey is born Abdulla Jaffa Anver Bey Khan in Seattle, Washington.

Dec. 24   Czech violist, composer and conductor Oscar Nedbal, 55, commits suicide in Zagreb. A performer with the Bohemian String Quartet, he also studied composition with Antonin Dvorak and conducted the Tonkunstler Orchestra in Vienna. His work includes many ballets, operettas and instrumental pieces.

1930   Related Events

Bell Laboratories features the dummy head (binaural stereo) at an exhibition in Chicago. Other events in the recording industry this year include: The Phonycord Company introduces its flexible disc in England (Columbia [U.S.] preceded this development by several years with its Marconi Velvetone disc); Okeh and Columbia (U.S.) merge; the Brunswick Company is bought by Warner Brothers.

English conductor Basil Cameron becomes music director of the San Francisco Symphony Orchestra this year, succeeding Alfred Hertz. This arrangement lasts one season. Next year he shares the podium with Issay Dobrowen.

Friedrich Trautwein exhibits his Trautonium this year in Berlin. This electronic musical instrument is comprised of an oscillator which produces a tone. Pitch indications of the chromatic scale are indicated on a part of the instrument the player touches. Trautwein, an inventor, views the trautonium as a melodic instrument. Richard Strauss and Paul Hindemith subsequently compose music for it (in combination with other instruments).

Adrian Boult is appointed music director of the BBC (British Broadcasting Corporation) and conductor of the BBC Symphony Orchestra this year.

Feb. 27   During a concert with the Berlin Philharmonic, Greek conductor Dimitri Mitropoulos substitutes for pianist Egon Petri playing Sergei Prokofiev's Piano Concerto No. 3 while conducting from the keyboard.

March 29   The Music Supervisors National Conference in Chicago officially opposes using "The Star-Spangled Banner" as the American national anthem. Congress is currently considering a bill that would make the tune the national anthem. The society opposes it on the grounds that the text reflects "a single war-time event which cannot fully represent the spirit of a nation committed to peace and good will". It also maintains that the tune "is not suitable for frequent singing in school rooms and assemblages of many kinds where a national anthem is needed."

May 7   Arthur Fiedler becomes music director of the Boston Pops. Founded in 1885, this orchestra has had 17 previous music directors, including Alfredo Casella, Max Zach and Franz Kneisel. Fiedler joined the Boston Symphony Orchestra in 1915 as a violinist under Karl Muck and founded the Boston Sinfonietta in 1924. Fiedler also founded the Esplanade Concerts last year — these events are summer concerts by the Boston Pops at the Hatch Memorial Shell on the east bank of the Charles River.

June 24   The Orquesta Sinfonica Venezuela gives its inaugural concert at the Teatro Nacional in Caracas. Conducted by Vicente Martucci and Vicente Emilio Sojo, the program consists of music by Weber, Mozart, Bach and Beethoven.

Aug. 22   Music Mountain (Falls Village, Connecticut) holds its first concert today. Violinist Jacques Gordon organized this festival, which is the first music festival in America. The Gordon Quartet performs music for string quartet.

Oct. 19   The Camargo Society gives its inaugural performance in London with works by Adeline Genee, Ninette de Valois and Frederick Ashton. The organization was formed in an effort to create a national ballet for Great Britain.

Oct. 20   Kurt Weill is judged victorious in a lawsuit he filed against the Nero Film Company. The company tried to change the score of Weill's *Threepenny Opera* for its screen version.

Oct. 28   The National Orchestral Association gives its first concert. Conducted by Leon Barzin in Carnegie Hall, the orchestra performs works of Beethoven and Wagner. Barzin comes from a musical family — his father played violin with the Metropolitan Opera orchestra and his mother was a ballerina. He has played first viola with the New York Philharmonic.

Nov. 2   The Indianapolis Symphony Orchestra gives its first concert. The event conducted by Ferdinand Schaefer, takes place in the Caleb Mills Hall at Shortridge High School in Indianapolis. This orchestra is one of four American symphony orchestras founded during the Great Depression; the others are the Rochester Civic Philharmonic Orchestra, the National Symphony Orchestra and the Kansas City Philharmonic Orchestra.

1931 Opera

Feb. 7   Deems Taylor's three-act opera *Peter Ibbetson*, based on a novel by George du Maurier, receives its first performance at the Metropolitan Opera. The opera is about a young architect threatened with execution for killing his uncle. Tullio Serafin conducts a cast that includes Lucrezia Bori, Edward Johnson and Lawrence Tibbett. Olin Downes writes of the opera, "Taylor assembled a very affecting drama with slow music, and some fast music too." The opera receives a total of 16 performances in 4 seasons, making Deems Taylor the most performed American composer at this famous opera house.

March 5   Ermanno Wolf-Ferrari's *La vedova scaltra* premieres at the Opera in Rome. The libretto, by Mario Ghisalberti, is an adaptation of a play by Carlo Goldoni about a beautiful widow who tests the constancy of her four suitors.

April 18   Eugen Zador's *Dornroschens Erwachen*, a fairy opera in two acts, premieres in Saarbrucken, Germany. Its plot is a variation of *The Sleeping Beauty*.

May 15   Gian Francesco Malipiero's *Torneo notturno* receives its first performance in Munich at the National Theater. The libretto, written by the composer, consists of seven encounters between the two main characters, Mr. Despair and Mr. Heedless. The message of the work is that external events do not affect the passions that torment the human soul. It is considered one of Malipiero's best works.

May 17   A new 10-scene opera by Czech composer Alois Haba entitled *Die Mutter* receives its premiere today in Munich in a German version. (The opera receives its first Czech performance in Prague on May 27, 1947.) The libretto, by Haba, deals with a family's domestic problems. This opera is the first stage work to systematically employ quarter tones.

June 20   *Die Bakchantinnen*, by Egon Wellesz, is performed for the first time in Vienna.

June 23   Arthur Honegger's *Amphion* receives its first performance at the Paris Opera. The text is by Paul Valery. It is moderately well received but is seldom performed. The character of Amphion is mimed by Ida Rubinstein.

Nov. 12   *Das Herz*, a three-act opera by Hans Pfitzner, receives its initial performance in Munich. The supernatural opera is about a doctor in 17th-century Germany who decides to become involved in heart transplants.

1931 Dance

Feb. 2   *Primitive Mysteries*, a ballet in three sections choreographed by Martha Graham, receives its initial performance by Martha Graham and Group at the Craig Theater in New York City. Graham also designs the costumes. The music is by Louis Horst. The three sections — entitled "Hymn to the Virgin," "Crucifixus" and "Hosannah" — reflect a religious simplicity. This event marks the premiere of Graham's first major ensemble piece. Graham, now 36, has studied at Denishawn and has performed with that dance company. She has also taught at the Eastman School of Music in Rochester, New York and founded her own school of contemporary dance in 1927. She formed her own company two years ago.

Feb. 4   Henry Cowell's *Steel and Stone* (later renamed *Dance of Work*), choreographed by Charles Weidman, premieres at the Craig Theater in New York City.

Feb. 6   The Ballet Club stages Frederick Ashton's *La Peri* to Paul Dukas' tone poem of the same name. The ballet deals with a man searching for the flower of immortality. Frederick Ashton and Alicia Markova star.

MARTHA GRAHAM IN THE 1920S, WHEN SHE WAS A MEMBER OF THE DENISHAWN COMPANY.

April 5   *Comedians*, a ballet by Reinhold Gliere, receives its initial performance in Moscow. It is based on the play *La fuente ovejuna*, by Lope de Vega, in which a feudal lord requires young brides to let him undo their virginity. The work, featuring Spanish dance rhythms, is subsequently renamed *A Daughter of Castile* and produced on May 28, 1955 in Moscow.

April 8   Choreographer Feodor Lopokov's *Bolt* — with music by Dmitri Shostakovich, book by V. Smirnov and designs by G. Gorshykov and Tatiana Bruni — is premiered by the Kirov Ballet in Leningrad. It concerns saboteurs trying to stop Soviet progress by putting a bolt in a factory machine.

April 26   The Camargo Society premieres Frederick Ashton's *Facade*. John Armstrong creates the decor for this one-act ballet. The music, by William Walton, was originally written as an accompaniment to poems by Edith Sitwell, which also form the basis for the ballet. This slight work establishes Ashton as a creative force. It has been termed the beginning of British ballet. Lydia Lopokova, Pearl Argyle, Alicia Markova and Frederick Ashton dance the lead parts.

May 5   The company soon to be known as the Vic-Wells gives its first full evening of ballet at the Old Vic in London. The group descended from the Academy of Choreographic Art organized in 1926 by Ninette de Valois, had occasionally performed and was also used by Lilian Baylis, director of the Old Vic, to dance in plays presented there. The program includes *Les petits riens, Danse sacree et profane, Hommage aux Belles Viennoises, The Jackdaw and The Pigeons, Faust, Scene de ballet, Bach Suite of Dances* and *The Faun* (all choreographed by de Valois) as well as a Spanish solo by Anton Dolin. The dancers include de Valois, Dolin, Beatrice Appleyard, Ursula Moreton, Sheila McCarthy, Joy Newton, Leslie French and Stanley Judson. Constant Lambert conducts.

May 22   *Bacchus and Ariane*, a two-act ballet choreographed by Serge Lifar, receives its first performance at the Paris Opera. Music is by Albert Roussel, libretto by Abel Hernant and decor by Giorgio di Chirico. Based on the Greek legend, the work closes with a bacchanal. Lifar, Olga Spessivtzeva and Serge Peretti star.

July 5   London's Camargo Society premieres Ninette de Valois' *Job* in London. The music is by Ralph Vaughan Williams, with costumes and scenery by Gwendolen Raverat, the principal dancer is Anton Dolin. The ballet, based on the biblical tale, is a masque in eight scenes.

Aug. 7   Choreographer Jose Limon's *B Minor Suite* receives its first performance by *The Little Group* in Westport, Connecticut. Born in Mexico in 1908, this Mexican-American choreographer, dancer and teacher begins to choreograph this year. He has studied with Doris Humphrey and Charles Weidman.

1931   Instrumental and Vocal Music

Jan. 4   *Piano Variations*, by Aaron Copland, receives its first performance in New York City, at a concert held under the auspices of the League of Composers. The composer performs as soloist. The music reflects Copland's current attraction to a rigorous, abstract style. It is also performed twice next year at the first Yaddo Festival. Critic Paul Rosenfeld writes in *The New Republic* after those performances that the work is a "gorgeous piece, stark and structural and solid as an Empire State Building."

Jan. 10   *Three Places in New England*, by Charles Ives, receives its world premiere by Nicolas Slonimsky and the Boston Chamber Orchestra at Town Hall in New York City. This work, depicting three American locales and personalities ("Colonel Shaw and his Colored Regiment," "Putnam's Camp" and "The Housatonic at Stockbridge"), was composed between 1906 and 1914. Musically, the work includes expansion of triadic structures, asymmetric rhythms, polymetric passages and folk song quotations. Ives rescored the original instrumentation (which was for large orchestra) for a smaller ensemble in order to make today's premiere possible. He subsequently renames the piece *Orchestral Set No. 1*.

Feb. 9   Ernst Toch's orchestral piece *Kleine Theater-Suite* is premiered by Wilhelm Furtwangler and the Berlin Philharmonic.

Feb. 13   *Le chemin de la croix*, by French organist-composer Marcel Dupre, receives its world premiere today as Dupre improvises the music in Brussels. The piece is subsequently notated and performed in a definitive version next year in Paris.

Feb. 13   Arthur Honegger's Symphony No. 1 (*Symphonie*) is premiered by Serge Koussevitzky and the Boston Symphony Orchestra. The work celebrates the orchestra's 50th anniversary.

Feb. 19   French composer Olivier Messiaen's *Les Offrandes oubliees* receives its first performance at the Theatre des Champs-Elysees in Paris. The work is a symphonic meditation on Jesus Christ. Walter Strarem conducts. This event marks the premiere of the first major work by this composer, now 22, who is organist at Trinity Church in Paris. At age 11, Messiaen entered the Paris Conservatoire, where he studied with Marcel Dupre and Paul Dukas, and won prizes in composition, organ and improvisation.

March 19   George Dyson's oratorio *The Canterbury Pilgrims* receives its first performance in Winchester, England. The work, scored for chorus, soloists and orchestra, is based on poetry by Geoffrey Chaucer. It is Dyson's most famous work. Dyson studied at, and was later a director of, the Royal College of Music in London.

April 3   Paul Hindemith's *Konzertmusik* is premiered by Serge Koussevitzky and the Boston Symphony Orchestra. The work is scored for brass instruments and string orchestra.

April 13   Anton Webern's Quartet, Op. 22, receives its first performance at the small hall of the Musikverein in Vienna. The performers are Rudolf Kolisch (violin), Johann Low (clarinet), Leopold Wlach (tenor saxophone) and Eduard Steuermann (piano). Dedicated to architect Adolf Loos to celebrate his 60th birthday, this two-movement work was composed last year. The first movement sets the two hands of the pianist off against the three single-line parts of the other players, creating a duo against a trio. The second movement, a rondo with variations, creates an improvisatorylike sound by dispersing motivic imitations among the various parts without the confinement of strict canonic imitation. Reaction is not favorable: Dr. Friedrich Bayer, of the *Neues Wiener Extrablatt* (Vienna), writes that the music demonstrates "amazing similarity to certain vital human utterances of an indecent nature."

June 2   *Gris du monde*, a stage oratorio by Arthur Honegger, receives its first performance in Paris. The piece depicts a recluse trying to escape the real world.

June 6   Henry Cowell's *Synchrony* receives its world premiere performance. Nicolas Slonimsky conducts it at a two-day Paris presentation of new music (mostly American) sponsored by the Pan-American Association of Composers. Reviews are not favorable: Paul Zschorlisch writes in *Deutsche Zeitung* (Berlin), "The musical inmates of a madhouse seem to have held a rendezvous on this occasion."

June 11   *Energia*, a new work by Carlos Chavez, receives its first performance at the second concert of new music in Paris. Nicolas Slonimsky conducts this piece as well as a rendition of Cuban composer Alejandro Caturla's *Bembe*. Philip Hale writes in the Boston *Daily Advertiser* that Slonimsky, ". . . indefatigable in furthering the cause of the extreme radical composers, has brought out in Paris orchestral compositions by Americans who are looked on by our conservatives as wild-eyed anarchists."

Sep. 17   Frederick Delius' orchestral piece *A Song of Summer* premieres in London. The work is dedicated to Eric

Fenby, the composer's amanuensis, who patiently took dictation from the blind and incapacitated composer.

Oct. 10   *Belshazzar's Feast*, an oratorio by William Walton, receives its first performance at the Leeds Festival. Malcolm Sargent conducts. Scored for baritone, chorus and orchestra, the work's text is culled by Osbert Sitwell from biblical sources and deals with Isaiah and prophecy. The oratorio incorporates rhythms and harmonies characteristic of Walton's other works. The piece is tremendously successful and is immediately compared to Edward Elgar's *The Dream of Gerontius*.

Oct. 16   The Boston Symphony Orchestra performs Gustav Mahler's Symphony No. 9 in D in Boston. Conducted by Serge Koussevitzky, the event marks the first American performance of this work.

Oct. 23   Igor Stravinsky's *Concerto in D for Violin and Orchestra* receives its first performance in Berlin. Samuel Dushkin is the violin soloist, and Stravinsky conducts. Herbert F. Peyser writes next month in the New York *Times* that the piece ". . . stands in the vanguard of Stravinsky's most regrettable aberrations."

Oct. 29   William Grant Still's *Afro-American* Symphony is premiered by Howard Hanson and the Rochester Philharmonic. In four movements, it depicts the musical world of American blacks.

Nov. 13   Serge Koussevitzky and the Boston Symphony Orchestra premiere Ottorino Respighi's symphonic piece *Five Picture Studies*.

Nov. 21   *Das Unaufhörliche*, an oratorio by Paul Hindemith, premieres in Berlin. The work, based on a mystic poem by Gottfried Benn, is neomedieval in style.

Nov. 22   Ferde Grofe's *Grand Canyon Suite* receives its first performance by Paul Whiteman in Chicago. This piece becomes a favorite of American audiences because of its orchestral depiction of American moods and places. The five movements are entitled "Sunrise," "Painted Desert," "On the Trail," "Sunset" and "Cloudburst."

Dec. 11   Dmitri Kabalevsky's Piano Concerto No. 1 in A Minor premieres in Moscow, with the composer as soloist.

1931   Births, Deaths and Debuts

Jan. 3   French coloratura soprano Lily Pons makes her Metropolitan Opera debut as Lucia. Olin Downes writes in the New York *Times* that she ". . . is not, and will not be a Patti or a Tetrazzini."

ANNA PAVLOVA AND LAURENT NOVIKOFF IN A SCENE FROM *AUTUMN LEAVES*

Jan. 5   Pianist Alfred Brendel is born in Wiesenberg, Moravia.

Jan. 5   Dancer-choreographer Alvin Ailey is born in Rogers, Texas.

Jan. 23   Anna Pavlova dies in The Hague of pneumonia at the age of 50. The greatest dancer of the early twentieth century, she was prima ballerina of the Maryinsky Theatre from 1906 to 1913. Among her most important roles were *Giselle, Paquita, Raymonda* and *The Sleeping Beauty*. Beginning in 1907 she toured outside Russia, appearing with the Diaghilev Ballets Russes during its initial Paris season in 1909 and performing at New York's Metropolitan Opera House in 1910. During the years from 1914 until her death, Pavlova travelled all over the world bringing ballet to millions of people in small towns as well as large cities.

Pavlova's dancing was characterized by its lightness, absence of visible effort and concern for the style and atmosphere of the work. A brilliant performer, but not a particularly strong technician, she subordinated her vituosity to the role as a whole.

Conservative in terms of choreography and music, Pavlova took little part in the reforms of the Fokine and Diaghilev era. Few of her signature pieces survive except Fokine's *Dying Swan*. Her artistic legacy lies in her ability to find and cultivate audiences for the ballet. For many, Pavlova was the first contact with ballet. For others she was an example to follow, an inspiration to a ballet career. Her appearances enabled millions to experience the highest standards of ballet performance.

NELLIE MELBA

Feb. 23   Australian soprano Nellie Melba, 69, dies in Sydney, Australia. One of the biggest stars of her generation, she studied with Mathilde Marchesi in Paris and later made a series of sensational debuts in Brussels, London, Paris, Milan and New York. She lived like a true prima donna, traveling in her own luxurious railway car and associating with high society. She was popular enough to have had peach melba and melba toast named after her. She retired in 1926 and became the director of the Melbourne Conservatory. Melba possessed a pure, true, extremely flexible voice.

April 4   American composer George Whitefield Chadwick, 76, dies in Boston. He studied composition and organ with Josef Rheinberger and made his debut conducting his overture *Rip van Winkle* in Leipzig (1879). He was a prominent musician in Boston throughout the later period of his life, receiving many prestigious awards, including the Gold Medal of the American Academy of Arts and Letters (1928). He was also director of the New England Conservatory of Music. His music is romantic, with Wagnerian harmonies. Chadwick composed a large number of pieces, among them four operas, three symphonies and much chamber and choral music. He is credited with having been one of the first American composers to encourage and cultivate a national American musical style.

April 27   American concert manager Loudon Charlton, 51, commits suicide in Stamford, Connecticut. He managed the American tours of such artists as Nellie Melba, Pablo Casals, Dame Clara Butt and Arturo Toscanini.

May 12   Belgian violinist Eugene Ysaye, 72, dies in Brussels. The internationally known virtuoso studied with Henryk Wieniawski and Henri Vieuxtemps. He gave many chamber music recitals with pianist Raoul Pugno and with his own quartet, formed in 1886. With this group he premiered Claude Debussy's String Quartet in 1893. Turning to conducting, he led the Cincinnati Orchestra from 1918 to 1922. Ysaye was a player of the romantic school, excelling in the elusive art of rubato.

May 28   American composer and pedagogue Peter Westergaard is born in Champaigne, Illinois.

Aug. 2   Baritone John Shirley-Quirk is born in Liverpool, England.

Sep. 10   British dancer, choreographer and ballet director Norman Morrice is born in Agua Dulce, Mexico.

Oct. 3   Danish composer Carl Nielsen, 66, dies in Copenhagen. He studied at the Royal Conservatory in Copenhagen and performed (in his youth) as a trumpeter, violinist and conductor. His early music reflects the influences of Franz Liszt, Johannes Brahms and Edvard Grieg, but his later music includes entirely different harmonies, with dissonance and chromaticism. He did not receive great acclaim in his lifetime. His music becomes internationally known in 1965 when a centennial festival celebrates his work. He composed six symphonies, two operas and scores of other pieces — concertos, choral works, etc. He is subsequently ranked as one of the most important Danish composers.

Oct. 20   Emanuel Moor, 68, dies in Mont-Pelerin, in the vicinity of Vevey, Switzerland. A Hungarian pianist and composer, he also invented a two-keyboard piano called the duplex pianoforte.

CARL NIELSEN

Oct. 30   Eugene Ormandy, who had been conductor of the Capital Theater Orchestra, conducts the Philadelphia Orchestra for the first time.

Nov. 21   Australian composer Malcolm Williamson is born in Sydney.

Nov. 30   French composer and writer Marc Delmas, 46, dies in Paris. In addition to composing operettas, he wrote biographies of Georges Bizet and Gustave Charpentier. He also won several important awards, including the Grand Prix de Rome (1919).

Nov. 30   John J. Hattstaedt, 79, dies in Chicago. He was founder and president of the American Conservatory of Music in Chicago.

Dec. 2   Vincent d'Indy, 79, dies in Paris. Born Paul-Marie-Theodore-Vincent, he studied composition with Cesar Franck and did musical analysis with Henri Duparc. He met Richard Wagner, Franz Liszt and Johannes Brahms in 1873 and soon began an annual pilgrimage to Bayreuth to hear all music by Wagner. He helped establish the Schola Cantorum in 1896 and became known as a conductor of his own works, though not as a first-rate conductor of works by other composers. He toured Russia and the United States twice. His music for large instrumental forms generated more recognition for him than all of his other music, which constitutes a considerable amount of work. He was also a writer on music and authored the multivolume treatise *Cours de composition musicale* (1903–9). His influence as a composer was as a Frenchman who composed music rooted in the Germanic tradition combined with elements of Gregorian chant. His work also reflects the strong influence of Cesar Franck.

Dec. 15   Igor Markevitch, 19, conducts a suite from his ballet *Rebus* in Paris. This conducting debut leads to the nickname "Igor II" (Stravinsky being "Igor I"). The ballet was commissioned by Serge Diaghilev, who does not live to see it staged.

1931   Related Events

Vladimir Golschmann becomes music director of the St. Louis Symphony Orchestra, after a 4-year period during which the ensemble had been conducted by seven guest conductors, including Eugene Goossens, Bernardino Molinari and George Szell. During his 27-year tenure, many famous soloists (including Ossip Gabrilowitsch, Vladimir Horowitz, Serge Rachmaninoff, Jascha Heifetz, Yehudi Menuhin and Sergei Prokofiev) appear in concert.

Basil Cameron and Issay Dobrowen become co-music directors of the San Francisco Symphony Orchestra this year. Dobrowen had been a conductor of the Moscow Opera and is also a composer. He becomes sole music director next year.

The Huelgas Codex — a Spanish collection of polyphonic and monodic medieval music — is published by Higini Angles this year in Barcelona. The collection includes 55 motets and a three-voice *Credo* reflecting the style of the early *ars nova*. It is also the only collection of polyphonic music to have been preserved in its place of origin.

Jan. 6   The Sadler's Wells Theatre reopens in London with a performance of *Twelfth Night*, by William Shakespeare. The theater, which closed in 1906, was used by Lilian Baylis for occasional dance productions in recent years. Opera and dance events alternate with Shakespearean productions for three years, after which the Sadler's Wells features only music and dance. The new theater seats 1,548.

Feb. 5   Severance Hall, the new home of the Cleveland Symphony Orchestra, opens today in that city, with the orchestra playing the premiere performance of *Evocation*, by Charles Martin Loeffler.

March 3   The U.S. Senate passes a bill officially naming "The Star Spangled Banner" the American national anthem.

May 14   Arturo Toscanini refuses to conduct "Giovinezza," a fascist song, in Bologna and is subsequently physically attacked by a fascist youth.

July 21   The quarter-tone piano designed by Hans Barth is patented.

Sep. 17   RCA Victor demonstrates its first 33.3 RPM standard groove long-playing record and soon releases several titles for commercial marketing. Performed by the Victor Concert Orchestra, they include "To a Wild Rose," by American composer Edward MacDowell. Other developments in the recording industry this year include the following: Electrical and Musical Industries (EMI) is created as a result of the merger of the Gramophone Company (HMV) and Columbia Gramophone Company; the Gramophone Company (HMV) also releases its first music society recordings of songs by Hugo Wolf; the first stereo disc patents are issued to Alan Dower Blumlein of EMI (England); the Capehart turnover record changer is marketed in America; the Kantorei (Berlin) label is founded; Allgemeine Electricitaets Gesellschaft (AEG) and I.G. Farben (Germany) continue experiments with magnetic tape and playback; record sales are at their lowest since 1926, due to the Great Depression.

Nov. 2   The National Symphony Orchestra gives its first official concert as a new American orchestra. Conducted by Hans Kindler, the program includes music by Weber, Beethoven, Mussorgsky and Tchaikovsky. The concert takes place at Constitution Hall in Washington, D.C. Attempts had been made since 1902 to organize a symphony orchestra that would have the nation's capital as its home. This concert marks the realization of that goal. Hans Kindler remains music director until 1949.

1932 Opera

Jan. 4   *Maximilien*, a three-act opera by Darius Milhaud, receives its initial performance at the Paris Opera. Based on the play *Juarez und Maximilian*, by Franz Werfel, the opera is about Napoleon III and the Archduke of Austria, whom Napoleon positions as emperor of Mexico, knowing he will be executed by Juarez' forces. Reaction is not favorable. P.B. Gheusi writes in *Le Figaro* (Paris), "We clutched our chair. But we were hurled out of it by such a hurricane of wrong notes that we found ourselves half dead, on the stairway, without knowing how we could fall down quite so far." Emile Vuillermoz says of Milhaud, "his talent offered no originality."

March 10   Kurt Weill's three-act opera *Die Burgschaft* premieres in Berlin. The opera is about gold bullion used to finance a war. It is scored for voices, electrically amplified pianos and jazz band.

March 16   *Maria Egiziaca*, an opera by Ottorino Respighi, is performed in a concert version at Carnegie Hall in New York City. The work concerns the repentance of Maria, who had paid for a trip to the Holy Land with sex. The work receives its first staged performance in Venice on August 10 of this year.

March 17   Alfredo Casella's *La donna serpente* receives its first performance at the Opera in Rome. The libretto, by Cesare Lodivici, is based on a fairy tale by Gozzi in which Miranda, a fairy princess, wants to become a mortal and marry Altidor, King of Teflis.

March 23   Pietro Mascagni's two-act opera *Pinotta* premieres in San Remo. This opera had been composed in 1880, and its score had only recently been found.

April 24   *Szekely fono*, by Zoltan Kodaly, premieres at the Hungarian Opera Theater in Budapest. The libretto, by Bence Szbolisi, consists of scenes from village life.

Sep. 6   The first performance of Alfredo Casella's chamber opera *La favola d'Orfeo* takes place in Venice at the Teatro Goldoni. Also premiered is *Pantea*, a work by Gian Francesco Malipiero scored for baritone, chorus, orchestra and solo ballerina.

Oct. 29   Franz Schreker's *Der Schmied von Gent* is performed for the first time in Berlin. The three-act opera is loosely based on the Faust legend. Schreker wrote his own libretto.

Dec. 15   Gian Francesco Malipiero's trilogy *Il mistero di Venezia* receives its first complete performance in Coburg. Its three parts are entitled "Le Aquile de aquileia," "Il finto Arlecchino" (first performed in Mainz on March 8, 1928) and "I Corvi di San Marco." Today's production is in German.

1932 Dance

Jan. 5   Henry Cowell's *Dance of Sports*, choreographed by Charles Weidman, premieres at the New School in New York.

April 12   George Balanchine's *La concurrence* — with music by Georges Auric and costumes, scenery and libretto by Andre Derain — is premiered by the Ballets Russes de Monte Carlo in Monte Carlo. This ballet, about two tailors who fight for new customers, is in one act. The cast includes Irina Baronova, Tamara Toumanova and Leon Woizikovsky.

April 21   The Ballets Russes de Monte Carlo gives the first performance of George Balanchine's one-act *Cotillion*, set to music by Emmanuel Chabrier, in Monte Carlo. This plotless ballet, which takes place in a ballroom, is one of Balanchine's finest early works. Valentina Blinova, Lubov Rostova, Tamara Toumanova, David Lichine and Leon Woizikovsky lead the cast.

July 3   *The Green Table* receives its world premiere at the Theatre des Champs-Elysees in Paris. This antiwar work is considered to be the choreographic masterpiece of Kurt Jooss. The music is by Fritz Cohen and the costumes by Hein Heckroth. In eight scenes, it depicts diplomats engaged in useless discussions, leading to war and catastrophe. The ballet is so successful that it becomes the hallmark of the Ballets Jooss. It wins a major award for choreography administered by Rolf de Mare and Les Archives Internationales de la Danse in Paris. Jooss, Ernst Uthoff and Lisa Czoble star.

Oct. 9   The Ballet Club premieres Frederick Ashton's *Foyer de danse* at the Mercury Theater in London. The work, set to music by Lord Berners, deals with occurrences at a ballet rehearsal. It was inspired by the paintings of Edgar Degas. Alicia Markova and Ashton star.

Nov. 7   Vasily Vainonen's *Flames of Paris* premieres at the Kirov Theater in Leningrad. The ballet, in four acts and five scenes, has music by Boris Asafiev. It takes place during the French Revolution and contains a virtuoso pas de deux, which enters the repertoire of a large number of companies. Vakhtang Chabukiani (Jerome), Olga Jordan (Jeanne), Nina Anisimova (Therese) and Galina Ulanova (Mireille de Poitiers) star.

Nov. 21   The Ballets Jooss gives the premiere performance of Kurt Jooss' *Big City*, to music by Alexander Tans-

man. It tells the story of a young girl in love with a workman who is dazzled by a libertine into adventure in the dance halls, where she finds disillusionment. Mascha Lidolt, Sigurd Leeder and Ernst Uthoff star. The premiere takes place at the Folkwang Dance Stage in Cologne, Germany.

Dec. 16   Sergei Prokofiev's ballet *Sur le Borysthene*, choreographed by Serge Lifar, receives its initial performance at the Paris Opera. The ballet is about a soldier's love for a girl. Lifar offered Prokofiev 100,000 francs for composition and exclusive performing rights to the ballet. Today's premiere is a miserable failure, and Lifar pays Prokofiev only 70,000 francs. Prokofiev sues, and the courts resolve the case on January 5, 1937.

1932   Instrumental and Vocal Music

Jan. 5   Maurice Ravel's Concerto in D Major for Piano Left Hand and Orchestra receives its world premiere in Vienna. Paul Wittgenstein (who also commissioned the work) is soloist. The one-movement concerto includes a jazz episode derived from themes in the introduction, as well as a middle section evoking improvisation. Wittgenstein and Ravel find themselves engaged in contretemps over this work: The pianist demands that changes be made; Ravel refuses. Pianist Jacques Fevrier is later coached by the composer to execute another performance of the concerto next year. Ravel's other piano concerto — Concerto in G Major for Piano and Orchestra — premieres less than two weeks from today, on January 14.

Jan. 14   Concerto in G Major for Piano and Orchestra, by Maurice Ravel, receives its first performance in Paris, with Marguerite Long as soloist and the composer conducting. This three-movement concerto was composed over a two-year period and gave Ravel a good deal of trouble; he was concerned with making this piece the perfect expression of his compositional craft, evoking the spirit of Mozart and Camille Saint-Saens. French critic Henri Prunieres says of the second movement that it "consists of one of those long cantilenas which Ravel knows so well how to write." The concerto does not become popular.

Jan. 29   Serge Koussevitzky and the Boston Symphony Orchestra premiere George Gershwin's *Rhapsody No. 2 for Piano and Orchestra*. Gershwin performs as soloist. The piece, commissioned for the 50th anniversary of this orchestra, is based on a theme Gershwin composed for a motion picture. The work is not successful.

Feb. 18   Ernest Bloch's symphonic piece *Helvetia, the Land of Mountains, and Its People* is premiered by Frederick Stock and the Chicago Symphony Orchestra. It is based on Helvetian folk songs. The work won a $5,000 prize administered by the Victor Talking Machine Company.

Feb. 19   Aaron Copland's *Symphonic Ode* receives its first performance by Serge Koussevitzky and the Boston Symphony Orchestra. Another of many works commissioned by this orchestra for its 50th-anniversary celebration, it is composed from materials from Copland's Nocturne for Violin and Piano. Copland is now helping to establish the Yaddo Festival, which has its first concert on April 30 of this year.

Feb. 25   *Sun-Treader*, a symphonic poem by American composer Carl Ruggles, receives its first performance by Nicolas Slonimsky and the Orchestre Symphonique de Paris. This work is based on a line of poetry by Robert Browning and has atonal, pandiatonic and tonal moments. Although the work is eventually considered to be the composer's most important, it is not performed in America until January 24, 1966. Paul Schwers says in *Allgemeine Musikzeitung* (Berlin): "*Sun-Treader* by Carl Ruggles should have been surely renamed "Latrine-Treader." I, for one, had only the impression of bowel constrictions in an atonal Tristanesque ecstasy. Theodore Strongin, however, says of the music in the New York *Times*, "Craggy, rangy, it is all contained power."

March 16   Basil Cameron and the San Francisco Orchestra premiere Sir Arnold Bax's Symphony No. 4. The three-movement symphony is in E-flat.

March 24   Randall Thompson's Symphony No. 2 is premiered by Howard Hanson and the Rochester Philharmonic, in Rochester, New York. The symphony is the composer's first significant work and establishes him as a major American composer. Thompson is now 32. The symphony becomes extremely popular and, over the next 10 years, receives more than 500 performances in America and Europe.

April 15   Paul Hindemith's *Philharmonisches Konzert* is premiered by Wilhelm Furtwangler and the Berlin Philharmonic. This neoclassical work was commissioned to celebrate the 50th anniversary of this orchestra.

June 1   Nikolai Miaskovsky's Symphony No. 12 in G Minor premieres in Moscow. This three-movement work, subtitled *Collective Farm Symphony*, depicts agricultural life in the Soviet Union.

Aug. 16   Albert Coates premieres George Gershwin's *Cuban Overture* at Lewisohn Stadium in New York City. This work features Cuban percussion instruments playing rumba rhythms.

Sep. 12   *Bachianas Brasileiras No. 1*, by Heitor Villa-Lobos, receives its initial performance by Burle Max and the Philharmonic Orchestra of Rio de Janeiro. This three-movement work, scored for eight cellos, is the first of a series of nine such pieces by Villa-Lobos that blend Brazilian folk elements with the contrapuntal style of Johann Sebastian Bach.

Oct. 9   Karol Szymanowski's *Symphonie Concertante* for piano and orchestra receives its first performance today in Poznan, Poland. Gregor Fitelberg conducts, and the composer is piano soloist. The piece is well received, and Szymanowski travels to Brussels, London and Paris to perform it.

Oct. 21   John Alden Carpenter's *Patterns* for piano and orchestra is premiered by Serge Koussevitzky and the Boston Symphony Orchestra, with the composer as soloist.

Oct. 31   Sergei Prokofiev's Piano Concerto No. 5 in G Major receives its initial performance by Wilhelm Furtwangler and the Berlin Philharmonic. The composer performs as soloist. In this concerto Prokofiev employs percussive writing for the piano. The work is unusual in that it has five, not three, movements.

Nov. 9   Dmitri Kabalevsky's Symphony No. 1 in C-sharp Minor premieres in Moscow.

FLORENT SCHMITT (PAINTING BY PAUL BRET)

Nov. 25   Florent Schmitt's *Symphonie Concertante* is premiered by Serge Koussevitzky and the Boston Symphony Orchestra, with the composer as soloist. This event marks the composer's only tour of America.

Dec. 16   Laszlo Lajtha's String Quartet No. 3, Arthur Honegger's *Sonatine* for violin and cello, and Albert Roussel's String Quartet receive their premiere performances at the first concert of Triton, a new Parisian music society designed to further the cause of new chamber music.

1932   Births, Deaths and Debuts

Jan. 28   Conductor Franz Xavier Arens, 75, dies in Los Angeles. In 1900 he founded the New York People's Symphony Concerts. Tickets for these concerts were priced between 5 cents and 50 cents.

Feb. 7   Conchita Supervia makes her New York debut at Town Hall in a program of Italian and Spanish songs. The audience is pleased enough to tolerate the long intermissions necessary for Supervia's costume changes. Francis D. Perkins says in the New York *Herald-Tribune* that her voice is "... of good size and rather dusky in color." Olin Downes says in the New York *Times* that she belongs "... on the operatic and not on the concert stage."

Feb. 22   German Wagnerian soprano Johanna Gadski, 59, is killed in an automobile accident in Berlin. She started her career in Berlin at age 17 in 1889 and later had successes at the Metropolitan Opera and Covent Garden. She continued to sing until 1931.

March 3   German pianist and composer Eugene d'Albert, 67, dies in Riga, Latvia. A music theory pupil of Sir Arthur Sullivan and piano pupil of Franz Liszt, he appeared as piano soloist at London's Crystal Palace in a performance of Schumann's Piano Concerto (1881). That same year he performed as soloist in his own piano concerto which was praised by critics. The Hochschule fur Musik in Berlin appointed him director in 1907. Although born in Glasgow, Scotland, he was sympathetic to German music and culture. He openly sided with Germany during World War I, and his insulting remarks about English music led to rejection of his work by the English music public. Among his most successful works are the operas *Tiefland* and *Die toten Augen*. Not considered overly original, his style blended melodic and contrapuntal elements of Italian and German music of the period. One of his wives was vocalist Hermine Finck; another was pianist Teresa Carreno. There were four others.

March 6   John Philip Sousa, 77, dies in Reading, Pennsylvania. As a youth, he studied wind instruments and was playing in the Marine Band by the time he was 13. He then conducted vaudeville and performed as a violinist during Jacques Offenbach's American tour. He began conducting at the 1893 Chicago World's Fair, the 1900 Paris Exposition, and then made many international tours. He composed a great deal of march music. "The March King" and "The Stars and Stripes Forever" rival the march music of any other composer of this century. He also wrote 11 comic operas (*El Capitan* being the most successful), waltzes, songs, other marches, an autobiography and five novels.

March 9   Soprano Berta Ehnn, 86, dies near Vienna. A singer with the Vienna Imperial Opera, she sang Elisabeth in *Tannhauser* under Wagner's baton in 1868.

March 14   American industrialist George Eastman, 77, commits suicide in Rochester, New York after learning that he has cancer. With an endowment of $3,500,000, he established the Eastman School of Music at the University of Rochester, which quickly became one of the nation's leading institutions of music education.

April 22   Composer Michael Colgrass is born in Chicago, Illinois.

May 12   Andreas Dippel, 65, dies in Los Angeles. He made his debut in Bremen in 1887 as the Steersman in a production of *The Flying Dutchman*. He was a tenor with the Metropolitan Opera and, in 1910, he became manager of the Chicago Opera.

July 11   Dancer, choreographer and ballet director Hans van Manen is born in Nieuwer Amstel, The Netherlands.

July 20   Korean-American avant-garde composer Nam June Paik is born in Seoul.

July 23   French soprano Maria Delna, 57, dies in Paris. Her debut came in 1892, when she played Dido in Berlioz' *Les Troyens* at the Opera-Comique in Paris. She sang at the Metropolitan Opera House in New York in 1910 as Orfeo (Gluck) and soon began complaining that only Italian singers were granted decent opportunities at that opera house; she then returned to France and resumed singing at the Opera-Comique.

July 27   Dancer David Blair is born in Halifax, Canada.

Aug. 2   Composer Marvin David Levy is born in Passaic, New Jersey.

Sep. 1   Austrian-Polish soprano Irene Abendroth, 60, dies in Vienna. The first soprano to sing the role of Tosca in German (1902), she was a famous star of the Vienna and Dresden operas.

Sep. 2   American composer John S. Fearis, 65, dies in Lake Geneva, Wisconsin. A composer of church music, he also composed *Beautiful Isle of Somewhere*, which was played at President McKinley's funeral.

Sep. 24   Dancer Svetlana Beriosova is born in Kaunas, Lithuania.

Sep. 25   Pianist Glenn Gould is born in Toronto, Canada.

Oct. 20   Dancer and teacher Claude Bessy is born in Paris, France.

Oct. 31   Russian-born pianist Anton Luis Dahl, 57, dies in Los Angeles. A pupil of Edvard Grieg, he went on to play before all the crowned heads of Europe.

Nov. 1   Alsatian-born Charles Munch makes his professional conducting debut with the Straram Orchestra in Paris.

Nov. 28   Dutch bass-baritone Anton Van Rooy, 62, dies in Munich. In 1897 he made an auspicious operatic debut at the Bayreuth Festival singing Wotan in the *Ring*. The following year he came to the Metropolitan, remaining there until 1908 and singing in London and Bayreuth during the summer seasons. He then joined the Frankfurt opera as lead baritone. Although famous for his Wagnerian performances, he also sang in some French operas and in oratorio.

Nov. 29   Italian conductor Agide Jacchia, 56, dies in Siena, Italy. Known principally as a conductor of opera, he was a personal friend of Pietro Mascagni. He was associated with the Montreal Opera and the Boston National Opera, and also conducted the Boston Pops between 1918 and 1926.

Dec. 16   Soviet composer Rodion Shchedrin is born in Moscow.

Dec. 19   American bass Clarence Whitehill, 51, dies in New York. After studies in Paris, he was the first American singer to appear at the Opera-Comique. He decided on further study and went to Bayreuth, where he learned the Wagnerian repertoire from Cosima Wagner. He was a member of the Cologne Opera (1903–8), the Chicago Opera (1911–15) and sang at the Metropolitan in 1909 and again from 1914 to 1932. He also sang in the Metropolitan premieres of *Louise* and *Pelleas et Melisande*.

1932   Related Events

Rene Blum forms the Ballets de Theatre de Monte Carlo this year. This ballet company is an outgrowth of Serge Diaghilev's Ballets Russes, which disbanded after Diaghilev's death in 1929, and it is a competitor to the first resurrection of Diaghilev's company — L'Opera Russe a Paris. The latter, founded by Prince Zeretelli, gave one London summer season last year. Upon recently learning of Blum's new company in Monte Carlo, Colonel de Basil, an associate of Zeretelli, rushed there and persuaded Blum to make him co-director of the company; its name quickly becomes the Rene Blum and Colonel de Basil Ballets Russes de Monte Carlo and — with choreographers George Balanchine and Leonide Massine and dancers Alexandra Danilova, Irina Baronova, Tamara Toumanova and Tatiana Riabouchinska — establishes itself as the best Russian-oriented ballet company outside of the Soviet Union. Next year the company drops the s from its title and becomes known as the Rene Blum and Colonel de Basil Ballet Russe de Monte Carlo. Over the next three years, the company tours America (by arrangement with impresario Sol Hurok). It is tremendously successful, largely because of its revivals of ballets from the Diaghilev era and because of Massine's impressive choreography. Rene Blum leaves the company in 1936, when the company becomes known as Colonel de Basil's Ballet Russe. He then forms the Rene Blum Ballets Russes de Monte Carlo. That event ignites a "ballet war" that continues for 30 years.

Issay Dobrowen becomes sole music director of the San Francisco Symphony Orchestra this year. Last year he shared the post with Basil Cameron. Dobrowen holds this post for two seasons.

Events in the recording industry this year include the following: Leopold Stokowski and the Philadelphia Orchestra (with choir and soloists) record Arnold Schoenberg's *Gurre-Lieder* for RCA Victor — the recording is issued in both 78 RPM and long-playing formats; the Gramophone Company HMV issues its first recordings of its new Beethoven Sonata Society — they feature Artur Schnabel; the Telefunken label comes into existence as a result of the merger of Ultraphon and Musica Sacra; BSR (British Sound Reproducers) is established — its first item produced is a transformer; Garrard Company (England) introduces its first drop-type record changer; Union Carbide Company (USA) develops a vinyl compound for the manufacture of recordings.

The American Library of Musicology in New York publishes *A Theory of Evolving Tonality*, by musicologist Joseph Yasser. In this book Yasser explores the origins of the heptatonic and pentatonic scales and delineates his theory justifying a scale of 19 tones.

Choreographer Harald Lander is appointed ballet master of the Royal Danish Ballet School. He revives the work of August Bournonville and choreographs approximately 30 ballets. The ballet school flourishes under his leadership; he holds this post for 19 years.

Spanish dancer La Argentinita and Federico Garcia-Lorca establish the Ballet de Madrid this year.

Jan. 10   The National Socialist Symphony Orchestra presents its inaugural concert. Performing in Munich, this orchestra was organized by Nazi officials.

March 11   Contralto Ernestine Schumann-Heink makes her last appearance at the Metropolitan Opera, singing Erda in Wagner's *Siegfried*. She is 70 years old. Olin Downes writes in the New York *Times*, "no other artist in the cast. . . so held and captured the imagination of the audience."

April 17   Wilhelm Furtwangler receives a gold medal from President von Hindenburg to celebrate the 50th anniversary of the Berlin Philharmonic.

April 23   The Central Committee of the Soviet Communist Party terminates all conflicts among creative and proletarian organizations in the arts by dissolving all such proletarian groups. The resolution, entitled "On the Reconstruction of Literary and Artistic Organizations," marks the end of proletarian-dominated influence on Soviet music.

April 30   The first Yaddo Festival of Contemporary Music opens near Saratoga Springs, New York. It includes performances of music by Aaron Copland, Walter Piston, Virgil Thomson, Charles Ives, Robert Russell Bennett, Roger Sessions, Roy Harris, Carlos Chavez, Wallingford Riegger, Louis Gruenberg, Nicolai Berezowsky, Marc Blitzstein, Silvestre Revueltas, Henry Brant, and others.

Aug. 28   To placate irate patrons of Philadelphia Orchestra concerts, the orchestra's management states that performances of new music will be curtailed in the future.

Oct. 7   Sir Thomas Beecham conducts the first concert of the London Philharmonic. Beecham establishes this orchestra this year.

Oct. 23   German soprano Gertrud Bindernagel, 38, is shot by her husband, banker Wilhelm Hintze, for infidelity. The event occurs after a performance of *Siegfried* featuring Bindernagel as Brunnhilde. She subsequently dies.

Oct. 30   Walter Wilson Cobbett is awarded a silver medal by the Elizabeth Sprague Coolidge Foundation at the Library of Congress in Washington, D.C. for his contribution to the promotion of chamber music. In 1925 Miss Coolidge had won the Cobbett Medal for services to chamber music.

1933 Opera

Jan. 7   Louis Gruenberg's *The Emperor Jones*, a two-act opera (with prologue and interlude), receives its initial performance at the Metropolitan Opera. Based on a play by Eugene O'Neill, it is about a negro pullman porter who is charged with murder, escapes to the Caribbean and eventually commits suicide. Tullio Serafin conducts a cast that stars Lawrence Tibbett, Marek Windheim and Pearl Besuner. The role of the Witch Doctor is danced by Hemsley Winfield — the first negro to perform in a production at this opera house. The opera was originally scheduled for premiere in Berlin; Erich Kleiber, the scheduled conductor, canceled the premiere because he felt the Nazi government might object to an opera whose main character was a negro. Of today's performance, Pitts Sanborn writes in the *World-Telegram* (New York) that the opera is "a remembered convention."

Feb. 22   Riccardo Zandonai's *La farsa amorosa* premieres in Rome. In three acts, five scenes and three comic interludes, the opera is about a Spanish official who tries to seduce a woman.

March 17   Alexander Tcherepnin's three-act opera *Die Hochzeit der Sobeide*, based on a play by Hugo von Hof-

mannsthal, premieres in Vienna. The opera is about a married woman who falls in love with a young man and commits suicide.

May 20   *Merry Mount*, a new four-act opera by Howard Hanson, receives its world premiere at the University of Michigan in Ann Arbor. Today's performance is in concert form. The opera receives its Metropolitan Opera premiere — conducted by Tullio Serafin — next February 10.

July 1   *Arabella* premieres at the Dresden Staatsoper. The music is by Richard Strauss and the libretto by Hugo von Hofmannsthal — their last collaboration. It is a comedy of errors about a retired officer in 19th-century Vienna who hopes to find rich husbands for his daughters. The cast includes Viorica Ursuleac, Alfred Jerger and Margit Borkor. The conductor is Clemens Krauss.

July 23   Ottorino Respighi's *Maria Egiziaca* receives its first performance in Buenos Aires. This one-act opera has a text by C. Guastalla. The cast includes Gilda Dalla Rizza and is conducted by Gino Marinuzzi. The work was first performed in a concert version at Carnegie Hall in New

SCENE FROM *MERRY MOUNT*

York City on March 16, 1932. Respighi conducted that performance.

Oct. 14   Alexander von Zemlinsky's *Der Kreidekreis*, with a libretto by the composer, premieres in Zurich. This three-act opera is about murder in Manchuria. Zemlinsky returns to Vienna this year, after having been conductor (for five years) of the Berlin State Opera.

Nov. 5   E.T.A. Hoffmann's *Aurora* premieres in Bamberg. The score to this 1811 opera had been found in 1907.

Nov. 4   Paul von Klenau's three-act opera *Michael Kohlhaas* premieres in Stuttgart. The composer wrote his own libretto to this opera about oppression in medieval Germany. The work includes a theme based on a 12-tone row and vocal passages in Sprechstimme.

1933 Dance

March 21   *Coppelia* is performed by the Vic-Wells Ballet in London, marking its first performance in London by that company. Lydia Lopokova performs as a special guest.

April 13   The Ballet Russe de Monte Carlo gives the first performance of Leonide Massine's *Les Presages* in Monte Carlo. Set to Tchaikovsky's Fifth Symphony, it is Massine's first symphonic ballet. Nina Verchinina, Irina Baronova, Tatiana Riabouchinska and David Lichine head the cast.

April 15   The restaged version of Leonide Massine's *Le Beau Danube* is given by the Ballet Russe de Monte Carlo. The ballet, set to music by Johann Strauss, takes place in a Viennese garden. There a woman wins back a Hussar after he flirts with a street dancer. Alexandra Danilova (Street Dancer), Leonide Massine (Hussar), Tatiana Riabouchinska (Daughter), Irina Baronova (First Hand) and David Lichine (King of the Dandies) star. Danilova becomes renowned for her role as the Street Dancer.

June 7   Les Ballets 1933 premieres George Balanchine's *Seven Deadly Sins* in Paris at the Theatre des Champs-Elysees. Tilly Losch and Lotte Lenya lead the cast. The scenario, by Bertolt Brecht, tells the story of a young American girl who encounters each of the seven deadly sins during her journey through America back to the small town in which she was born. The music is by Kurt Weill. This is the last collaboration between Weill and Brecht.

Sep. 19   Bohuslav Martinu's song cycle *Spalicek*, for women's chorus and orchestra, featuring dancing and miming, premieres in Prague.

Oct. 24   Leonide Massine's *Choreartium* receives its initial performance by the Ballet Russe de Monte Carlo in London. The plotless work is to Brahms' Symphony No. 4 in E Minor. It is Massine's second symphonic ballet. Alexandra Danilova, Tatiana Riabouchinska, Nina Verchinina, Vera Zorina, Roman Jasinski, David Lichine, Paul Petroff and Yurek Shabelevski star.

Dec. 5   Frederick Ashton premieres his *Le rendezvous* with the Sadler's Wells Ballet. The music, by Francois Auber, sets the mood for the ballet, which is a suite of dances for young couples set in a park. Alicia Markova, Stanislas Idzikowski, Ninette de Valois and Robert Helpmann star.

1933 Instrumental and Vocal Music

Jan. 16   Symphony No. 11 in E Minor, by Nikolai Miaskovsky, premieres in Moscow. This symphony has three movements.

Jan. 31   *Sinfonietta*, for chamber orchestra, by Benjamin Britten, receives its first performance in London. The work exploits motivic use of the interval of the major seventh.

Feb. 1   Piano Concerto in C Major, by Ralph Vaughan Williams, is performed for the first time by Adrian Boult and the BBC Symphony Orchestra. Harriet Cohen is soloist. This concerto is unusual in that it has four movements.

Feb. 5   Alexander Tcherepnin's Piano Concerto No. 3 premieres in Paris, with the composer as soloist. This three-movement concerto employs a motive derived from an Egyptian folk song.

Feb. 12   Olivier Messiaen's symphonic poem *Le Tombeau resplendissant* premieres in Paris.

March 3   Abram Chasins' Piano Concerto No. 2 is premiered by Leopold Stokowski and the Philadelphia Orchestra at the Philadelphia Academy of Music. The composer is soloist.

March 6   *Ionisation* receives its world premiere in New York City. Composed by Edgard Varese, the work is conducted by Nicolas Slonimsky (to whom it is eventually dedicated). Carlos Salzedo, Henry Cowell, Paul Creston and William Schuman also participate as instrumentalists in this performance sponsored by the Pan-American Association of Composers. Scored for 41 percussion instruments, it is the first Western composition (apart from folk music) to be scored only for percussion instruments. It depicts, in sonic terms, the ionization of molecules as electrons are dispersed through the process of atomic change. The instruments include anvils, gongs, tamtams, sirens, Chinese blocks and lion's roar. The work is quickly considered one of the century's masterpieces. The writer Henry Miller describes its sound as "a sock on the jaw." Paul Rosenfeld says, "*Ionisation* sets living forces in action whose effects will never cease to be felt."

March 27   Arthur Honegger's *Mouvement symphonique No. 3* receives its initial performance by Wilhelm Furtwangler and the Berlin Philharmonic.

April 5   Sergei Vassilenko's *Arctic Symphony* receives its premiere in Moscow. His fourth symphony, it depicts Soviet scientists exploring the Arctic.

April 10   George Gershwin's *Cuban Overture* receives its first Cuban performance by Nicolas Slonimsky in Havana.

Aug. 30   Samuel Barber's *Overture to the School for Scandal*, based on the play by Richard Brinsley Sheridan, receives its first performance by the Philadelphia Orchestra. This overture evokes a baroque style. It is the first piece he composes that marks him as a noteworthy young composer. (Barber is now 23.) He is a product of the Curtis Institute of Music where he studied with Rosario Scalero (composition), Emilio de Gorgoza (voice) and Isabelle Vengerova (piano).

Oct. 3   Frederick Delius' *Idyll*, based on a text by Walt Whitman, is premiered by Henry Wood at a London Promenade Concert. The piece is scored for soprano, baritone and orchestra.

Oct. 5   Henk Badings' Symphony No. 2 is performed for the first time in Amsterdam.

Oct. 6   Karol Szymanowski's Violin Concerto No. 2 is premiered by Gregor Fitelberg and the Warsaw Philharmonic, with Paul Kochanski as soloist. The concerto, in one movement, is dedicated to Kochanski.

Oct. 14   Alexander Glazunov's *Concerto-Ballata* for cello and orchestra premieres in Paris, with Maurice Eisenberg as soloist and the composer conducting.

Oct. 15   Dmitri Shostakovich's *Piano Concerto No. 1* for piano, strings and solo trumpet premieres in Leningrad, with the composer as soloist. The concerto is in four movements.

Nov. 30   John Alden Carpenter's symphonic poem *Sea-Drift*, after Walt Whitman, is premiered by Frederick Stock and the Chicago Symphony Orchestra. The composer is awarded an honorary doctorate from the University of Wisconsin this year.

Nov. 30   German composer Richard Trunk's choral work *Feier der neuen Front*, with text by Baldur von Schirach, premieres in Berlin. The movements are entitled "Hitler," "Des Fuhrers Wachter," "O Land" and "Horst Wessel." The work praises Adolf Hitler. Critic Arthur Egidi writes of the piece in *Musik im Zeitbewusstsein* that it is". . . a worthy tribute to the Fuhrer and serves as the mirror of his spirit and his deeds."

Dec. 15   Carlos Chavez' *Sinfonia de Antigona* receives its initial performance in Mexico City, the composer conducting. This composer is now principal conductor of the Orquesta Sinfonica de Mexico, which he organized five years ago.

1933   Births, Deaths and Debuts

Jan. 6   Russian pianist Vladimir de Pachmann, 84, dies in Rome. Best known for his peculiar behavior, he would, while playing a concert, yell "bravo" at himself when he played a piece well and make faces when he thought he played badly. He would sometimes hunt under the piano for the wrong notes he'd played. He also took considerable liberties with the music. He married so often that no one is quite sure how many wives he actually had.

Jan. 16   German soprano Frida Leider makes her Metropolitan Opera debut as Isolde. Lawrence Gilman, in the New York *Herald-Tribune*, writes that *Tristan und Isolde*, ". . . due to [her] participation — was one of the most eloquent performances of the incomparable music-drama that New York has witnessed since the fabulous days before the war."

Jan. 27   Soviet dancer Nicolai Fadeyechev is born in Moscow.

Feb. 12   French composer Henri Duparc, 85, dies in Paris. Born Marie Eugene Henri Fouques, he composed many songs and was a founder of the National Music School. His work is considered noteworthy because his vocal melodies are beautifully crafted over modal harmo-

HENRI DUPARC

nies. Duparc suffered from nervous exhaustion and had to flee to Switzerland to relax. Cesar Franck — his teacher — considered Duparc to be his best student. Among Duparc's famous songs are "Invitation au voyage," "Extase," "Chanson triste" and "La Vie anterieure."

March 1   British bass Robert Radford, 58, dies in London. He was principal basso at Covent Garden Opera House for over 25 years and also sang with the Beecham Opera Company.

April 21   Composer Easley Blackwood is born in Indianapolis, Indiana.

April 27   Thomas Stanley Chappell, 72, dies in London. He was chairman of Chappell & Company, a music publishing firm that was founded in 1810 by Samuel Chappell and others. Thomas Stanley Chappell became chairman of the board at the turn of the century, when the company became incorporated.

May 10   Coloratura soprano Selma Kurz, 58, dies in Vienna. She debuted in Hamburg in 1895 and later was hired by Gustav Mahler to sing at the Vienna Court Opera. She also sang in London at Covent Garden, and in America.

May 22   German-born conductor Emil Oberhoffer, 65, dies in San Diego. He was the first conductor of the Minneapolis Symphony Orchestra.

May 22   Soviet dancer Irina Kolpakova is born in Leningrad, USSR.

May 23   American violinist Estelle Gray-Lhevinne, 41, dies in Boston. After making her debut at the age of 7 with the San Francisco Symphony Orchestra, she became the youngest graduate of the College of the Pacific (age 11). She was the first American instrumentalist to perform at La Scala.

June 26   Conductor Claudio Abbado is born in Milan.

July 18   Composer R. Murray Schafer is born in Sarnia, Ontario, Canada.

July 24   German composer Max von Schillings, 65, dies in Berlin. He studied art, literature, law and philosophy at the University of Munich and decided to devote his life to music after meeting Richard Strauss. Known principally as a conductor, he was associated with the operatic life of Stuttgart, Bayreuth and the Berlin State Opera. His own music was derivative of Richard Wagner's; as a composer he had little impact on the music of his day. He wrote five operas, of which Mona Lisa was the most successful. Other works include symphonic fantasies, a violin concerto and various smaller pieces.

July 29   Norwegian composer Gerhard Schjelderup, 73, dies in Benedikbeuren, Bavaria. A pupil of Jules Massenet, he later settled in Bavaria, where he lived until today. His music was influenced by Edvard Grieg and Richard Wagner, about whom he wrote books. Like Max von Schillings (who died five days ago), he composed five operas and some symphonic and chamber music but had little impact on the international music scene.

Aug. 4   Dancer, choreographer and ballet director Rudi van Dantzig is born in Amsterdam, The Netherlands.

Aug. 21   Mezzo-soprano Janet Baker is born in Hatfield, Yorkshire, England.

Sep. 5   French bass Marcel Journet, 66, dies in Vittel, France. The celebrated singer, who made his debut in France in 1891, was a star at all the world's major opera houses. He sang in the world premieres of La Navarraise, Samson et Dalila, Nerone and Thais. His repertoire included about 100 roles in French, Italian and German.

Nov. 13   Milton Aborn, 68, dies in New York City. He was active in campaigning for performances of grand opera in English and was a comanager of the Century Opera Company in New York.

Nov. 20   American singer, voice teacher and music writer Perley Dunn Aldrich, 70, dies in Philadelphia. He was the first chairman of the Voice Division of the Curtis Institute of Music.

Nov. 23   Polish composer Krzysztof Penderecki is born in Debica, Poland.

1933   Related Events

Ted Shawn establishes his All-Male Dancers Group after splitting up the Denishawn company which he founded with Ruth Saint Denis in 1915. He also acquires Jacob's Pillow, a Massachusetts farm, which he turns into a dance studio. His all-male company is highly effective in stemming prejudice in America directed at male dancers.

Dance Observer is founded this year by American musican Louis Horst. Its purpose is to promote modern dance.

Otto Klemperer becomes music director of the Los Angeles Philharmonic Orchestra this year. He succeeds Artur Rodzinski and continues in this post for six years. Klemperer, a refugee from the Nazis, comes to America directly from Switzerland.

Sergei Prokofiev decides to return to the Soviet Union this year and subsequently settles in Moscow. He tells the French critic, Serge Moreux, "The air of foreign lands does not inspire me because I am Russian, and there is nothing more harmful to me than to live in exile."

FM radio is conceived and developed, to be introduced some five years from now. Other developments in the recording industry this year include the following: BASF (Badische Analin und Soda Fabrik) (Germany) pursues development of magnetic tape; Alan Dower Blumlein's stereo disc patents of two years ago result in the first stereo discs produced by EMI (Electrical & Musical Industries, England); BSR (British Sound Reproducers) expands and produces PA amplifiers, which it markets as "Birmingham Sound Reproducers."

American inventor Laurens Hammond develops the Hammond organ. This electronic keyboard instrument uses wheel revolution in a magnetic field to produce tones. Loudspeakers amplify the tones. The instrument (technically not an organ) becomes enormously popular and is the first commercial hit in the field of electronic musical instruments.

Jan. 20   Italian baritone Antonio Scotti gives his farewell performance at the Metropolitan Opera after singing there for 35 years. He sings in an obscure opera by Franco Leoni called *L'Oracolo*. Olin Downes, reviewing the performance in the New York *Times*, says Scotti is an artist whose like we shall never see again. The Metropolitan should "destroy the scenery" forever now that Scotti will no longer be around to sing the "second-rate work."

Feb. 23   *Sovietskaya Musica* publishes its first issue today. This journal exists to encourage "socialist realism" and discourage the study of Western European techniques.

March 8   The New York *Times* reports that German conductor Fritz Busch has been removed by the Nazis from his conducting post at the Dresden Opera because he is thought to be anti-Nazi.

March 11   Berlin Municipal Opera director Carl Ebert and conductor Fritz Stiedry are fired by the Nazis and forced to leave the opera company.

March 16   The Nazi government cancels a Leipzig concert that was to be conducted by Bruno Walter due to what it considers might be negative audience reaction sparked by the sight of a Jew conducting.

March 21   Kurt Weill and his wife, Lotte Lenya, flee to Paris to escape Nazi persecution.

April 1   In a cable to Adolf Hitler, the musicians Arturo Toscanini, Walter and Frank Damrosch, Serge Koussevitzky, Artur Bodanzky, Alfred Hertz, Fritz Reiner, Ossip Gabrilowitsch, Harold Bauer, Charles Martin Loeffler and Rubin Goldmark appeal to him to end persecution of Jews.

April 4   The Berlin Radio's Nazi chief responds to the musicians' protest of April 1 by banning all compositions and recordings of the protesters.

April 10   Dr. Joseph Goebbels reaffirms the exclusion of Jewish artists and continues to reject Wilhelm Furtwangler's appeal against his action. Max Reinhardt, Otto Klemperer and Bruno Walter are subsequently denied the same artistic freedoms as non-Jewish artists.

May   The Delius Society is formed this month in London for the purpose of promoting, studying, performing and recording the music of Frederick Delius. Sir Thomas Beecham is artistic director.

May 30   Arnold Schoenberg and Franz Schreker are fired from their teaching posts at the Prussian Academy of Arts in Berlin by the Nazis.

June 5   To protest the Nazi persecution of Jewish musicians, Arturo Toscanini cancels his scheduled conducting engagement at Bayreuth.

July 24   Arnold Schoenberg reconverts from Roman Catholicism to Judaism, the religion of his birth. The event takes place in a Paris synagogue. Marc Chagall is a witness.

July 30   Tribschen, on Lake Lucerne, Switzerland becomes the home of the new Wagner Museum, which opens today. Richard and Cosima Wagner lived at Tribschen from 1866 to 1874.

Sep. 22   Adolf Hitler signs a decree establishing the Reichsmusikkammer, which empowers the Ministry of Propaganda to have six Reich Culture Chambers, one of which is for music.

Oct. 23   German composer Horst Gerlach's "Hermann Goring March" is published in Nazi Germany.

Oct. 31   Arnold Schoenberg arrives in America, fleeing the Nazis. This event marks his farewell to Germany.

Nov. 15   Dr. Joseph Goebbels organizes the Reichsmusikkammer in Berlin for the purpose of controlling racial and aesthetic aspects of German music. He names Richard Strauss president, Paul Graener vice-president, Wilhelm Furtwangler general music director, Fritz Stein and Gustav Havemann members, and Heinz Ihlert secretary.

1934   Opera

Jan. 13   Gian Francesco Malipiero's three-act opera *La favola del figlio cambiato* receives its first performance in Brunswick, Germany. Composed to a libretto by Luigi Pirandello, it is performed today in a German version entitled *Die Legende vom vertauschten Sohn*. It is performed this March in Rome, where Benito Mussolini attends the performance and the audience boos the music. Mussolini later bans further performances in Italy on the grounds that Pirandello's libretto expresses "moral incongruity."

Jan. 22   The first performance of Dmitri Shostakovich's four-act opera *Lady Macbeth of the District of Mtsensk* takes place in Leningrad at the Maly Theater. The libretto, written by the composer with A. Preis, is based on a story by Nicolai Liskov. The opera receives a mixed reception, and repeat performances go on for nearly a year. In 1936 the opera is banned by the government but is again performed after Joseph Stalin's death. It is presented in Moscow under the title *Katerina Ismailova* two days from today. In an article published in the program notes to today's performance, A. Ostretzov writes, "Shostakovich reveals himself in his opera as a powerful satirist." W.J. Henderson also reviews the piece in the New York *Sun* and says, "The whole scene is little better than a glorification of the sort of stuff that filthy pencils write on lavatory walls."

Jan. 23   Ottorino Respighi's *La Fiamma* premieres in Rome. Claudio Guastella's libretto is based on a play by Hans Wiers Jenssen called *The Witch*. The opera is enthusiastically received.

Feb. 8   Virgil Thomson's *Four Saints in Three Acts*, based on a story by Gertrude Stein, premieres in Hartford, Connecticut. Described by the composer as "an opera to be sung," the work is set in Spain and features Saint Theresa and Saint Ignatius (of Antioch). The black cast is dressed in cellophane costumes. The performance is by the Society of Friends and Enemies of Modern Music. Lawrence Gilman says the opera has a "suave and charming score." It is highly successful and moves to Broadway later this month.

Feb. 10   Howard Hanson's opera *Merry Mount* receives its Metropolitan Opera premiere in New York City. The work received its world premiere (in concert form) on May 20, 1933 at the University of Michigan in Ann Arbor. Conducted by Tullio Serafin, the cast includes Arnold Gabor, James Wolfe, Irra Petina and Giordano Paltrinieri. The opera is based on the tale "The Maypole of Merrymount," by Nathaniel Hawthorne. Pitts Sanborn says of today's performance in the New York *Telegram*, "True, there is oftener the suggestion of Mussorgsky than of Massachusetts, but who would be so ungracious as to object to that?"

Feb. 28   George Antheil's three-act opera *Helen Retires*, based on a novel by John Erskine, premieres at the Juilliard School in New York.

March 24   *Il Dibuc*, a three-act opera by Lodovico Rocca, premieres in Milan at the Teatro alla Scala. Renato Simoni's libretto is based on a Yiddish story by Shalom An-ski.

Sep. 18   Leos Janacek's *Osud* premieres in a concert version over Brno Radio. The opera had been written in 1903–4.

Oct. 20   Vittorio Giannini's *Lucedia* premieres in a German version in Munich. This three-act opera is about a girl who loses her virginity and dies.

1934   Dance

Jan. 30   Choreographer Nicholas Sergeyev's *The Nutcracker* is performed for the first time in London. The music is by Tchaikovsky. Hedley Briggs creates the costumes for this production performed by the Sadler's Wells Ballet. The choreography is based on Lev Ivanov's 1892 work. Alicia Markova and Harold Turner lead the cast.

March 21   *Fadetta*, a ballet choreographed by Leonid Lavrovsky to music by Leo Delibes, Jules Massenet and others is premiered by dancers of the Leningrad Choreographic School at the Leningrad State Academic Theater of Opera and Ballet. The ballet is based on *Little Fadette*, by George Sand, with designs by N. Nikiforov.

April 3   The Vic-Wells Ballet premieres Ninette de Valois' *The Haunted Ballroom*. Music is by Geoffrey Toye, and costumes and scenery by Motley. The lead roles are danced by Robert Helpmann, Alicia Markova and William Chappell. The ballet, in one act and two scenes, is a death dance.

April 6   Leonide Massine's *Union Pacific* — with music by Nicolas Nabokov, costumes by Irene Sharaff and scenery by Albert Johnson, — is performed for the first time by the Ballet Russe de Monte Carlo in Philadelphia. This work is Massine's first to be choreographed on an American theme. Tamara Toumanova, Andre Eglevsky, David Lichine and Massine are the lead dancers, portraying workers who lay track for first transcontinental railroad in America.

April 30   The first performance of Igor Stravinsky's *Persephone* takes place at the Paris Opera. Andre Gide's libretto is based on a work of Homer. Persephone is more of a secular oratorio than an opera, incorporating mime, spoken dialogue, dance and song. It was composed at the request of Ida Rubinstein. The choreographer is Kurt Jooss. A. Mangeot says in *Le Monde Musical* (Paris) of the work, "During the last scene, in which Persephone descends into Hell for the second time, someone was heard to whisper: 'Let's hope she stays there.' "

May 11   Ida Rubinstein performs a dance recital in Paris featuring Florent Schmitt's dance tragedy *Oriane*, which also serves as material for a later ballet entitled *Oriane et le prince*. Also premiered today is Arthur Honegger's *Semiramis*, based on a poem by Paul Valery. Ida Rubinstein dances the lead role. The work also features the ondes Martenot.

May 15   Ninette de Valois' *Bar aux Folies-Bergere* is given its premiere by Marie Rambert's Ballet Club at the Mercury Theater in London. The work, to Emmanuel Chabrier's *Dix pieces pittoresques*, involves characters from Toulouse-Lautrec. It is the only work de Valois choreographs for Rambert. Alicia Markova (Le goulue), Pearl Argyle, Diana Gould, Frederick Ashton and Oliver Reynolds lead the cast.

June 9   The students of the School of American Ballet present the first performance (private premiere) of George Balanchine's *Serenade* in White Plains, New York. The abstract work is set to Tchaikovsky's *Serenade for String Orchestra* in C Major. It is Balanchine's first work in the United States and receives its first public performance on December 6 of this year.

Sep. 28   *The Fountain of Bakhchisaray*, a four-act ballet choreographed by Rostislav Zakharov to music by Boris Asafiev, receives its first performance in Leningrad. The love story is based on the Pushkin poem of the same name. Galina Ulanova, Tatiana Vetschlova and Mikhail Dudko star.

Oct. 28   Antony Tudor presents *The Planets* with the Ballet Club. Set to Gustav Holst's score of the same name, it is considered Tudor's first major work. Pearl Argyle, William Chappell, Maude Lloyd, Hugh Laing, Diana Gould, Kyra Nijinsky and Tudor star.

Nov. 20   The Sadler's Wells Ballet performs *Swan Lake* in London. This production includes the Petipa-Ivanov choreography reproduced by Nicholas Sergeyev, with costumes and scenery by Hugh Stevenson. The event marks the first complete performance of the ballet in England. Alicia Markova and Robert Helpmann lead the cast.

Dec. 6   The American Ballet, formed by Lincoln Kirstein and Edward M.M. Warburg, gives its first performances during a three-day engagement in Hartford, Connecticut. The program consists of the first public performance of George Balanchine's *Serenade* and the premiere of *Alma Mater*, also by Balanchine. Also on the program is *Mozartiana*, another work choreographed by Balanchine, to music by Tchaikovsky.

1934   Instrumental and Vocal Music

Jan. 10   Franz Schmidt's Symphony No. 4 in C Major, known also as his *Requiem Symphony*, is premiered by Oswald Kabasta in Vienna. The music is dedicated to this conductor.

Jan. 12   Ernest Bloch's *Sacred Service* premieres in Turin, Italy with the composer conducting. Scored for baritone, chorus and orchestra, this is a setting of Jewish liturgical text. The work, in five movements, is the largest of his Hebraic pieces. Bloch took two years to compose it.

Jan. 14   George Gershwin's *Variations on ''I Got Rhythm''* for piano and orchestra is premiered by the Leo Reisman Orchestra in Boston. Gershwin conducts and plays the solo piano part.

Jan. 15   Sir Thomas Beecham and the London Philharmonic premiere Arnold Bax's Symphony No. 5. This three-movement symphony is dedicated to Jean Sibelius.

Jan. 21   Vissarion Shebalin's *Lenin* — a symphonic work with narrator and chorus and with text by Vladimir Mayakovsky — receives its first complete performance in Leningrad (part of the work was premiered in Moscow last year). Dmitri Kabalevsky's Symphony No. 3 premieres in Moscow. Both works commemorate the 10th anniversary of Vladimir Lenin's death.

Jan. 26   Symphony No. 1 by Roy Harris, receives its initial performance by Serge Koussevitzky and the Boston Symphony Orchestra. The work, subtitled *1933*, is in three movements and depicts the energy and will of human life. Harris, now 35, has studied in Paris with Nadia Boulanger. This is the first of many symphonies he composes.

Feb. 25   Georges Enesco's Symphony in D Minor premieres in Bucharest with the composer conducting. This work had been composed when Enesco was 14.

March 6   Walter Piston's neobaroque Concerto for Orchestra premieres in Cambridge, Massachusetts. The composer conducts the Boston Symphony Orchestra.

March 11   Sergei Prokofiev's symphonic suite *Sur le Borysthene*, arranged from his ballet of that title, is performed for the first time in Paris with the composer conducting.

March 12   Paul Hindemith's symphonic piece *Mathis der Maler* is performed for the first time by Wilhelm Furtwangler and the Berlin Philharmonic. This work is a three-movement piece from his as yet unperformed opera of the same name.

March 20   The Uzbek Symphony Orchestra premieres Mikhail Ippolitov-Ivanov's *Uzbekistan* in Tashkent. This symphonic poem is based on Russian themes.

April 2   Gian Francesco Malipiero is the only composer to have a world premiere at this year's 12th International Society for Contemporary Music Festival, held in Florence, Italy. His Symphony No. 1 is the featured work. Subtitled "In Four Movements Like Four Seasons," it features special percussion effects.

April 14   Sergei Prokofiev's *Symphonic Song* premieres in Moscow.

April 15   *Ecuatorial*, a symphonic poem by Edgard Varese, receives its first performance by Nicolas Slonimsky in New York. The work is scored for bass voice, brass ensemble, percussion and Thereminovox and is set to Mayan texts.

May 25   *Cantata Profana*, by Bela Bartok, receives its first performance in London. Composed four years ago, it is scored for chorus and orchestra.

Aug. 20   Ernst Toch's Symphony for Piano and Orchestra receives its first performance in London, with the composer as soloist. Toch has now left Nazi Germany for the United States — this premiere comes as he makes his way west.

Sep. 27   *Fantasia on Greensleeves*, by Ralph Vaughan Williams, receives its world premiere in London. The composer conducts the BBC Symphony Orchestra. The work, adapted from his opera *Sir John in Love*, is scored for strings and harp.

Oct. 11   Symphony No. 2 by Kurt Weill, is premiered in Amsterdam by Bruno Walter and the Concertgebouw Orchestra.

Oct. 16   Nikolai Miaskovsky's Symphony No. 13 in B-flat Minor is premiered by Hermann Scherchen and the Musikkollegium in Winterthur, Switzerland. This three-movement symphony was composed last year.

Nov. 7   Serge Rachmaninoff's *Rhapsody on a Theme by Paganini* in A Minor is premiered by Leopold Stokowski and the Philadelphia Orchestra, with the composer at the piano. Two years from now Pitts Sanborn says in the New York *World-Telegram*, "Rachmaninoff's *Rhapsody on a Theme by Paganini* sometimes sounds like a plague of insects in the Amazon valley, sometimes like a miniature of the Day of Judgment. . . and for a change goes lachrymose."

Nov. 12   Ralph Vaughan Williams' *Suite for Viola and Chamber Orchestra* is performed for the first time by violist Lionel Tertist in London. The piece is a stylization of English dances.

Nov. 22   Sir Donald Francis Tovey's Cello Concerto receives its initial performance by Pablo Casals and the Reid Symphony Orchestra in Edinburgh with the composer conducting. This musician, known principally as a musical scholar, founded this orchestra in 1917.

Nov. 23   Marguerite Long premieres Darius Milhaud's Piano Concerto No. 1 in Paris.

Nov. 23   Aaron Copland's *Short Symphony* is premiered in Mexico. Carlos Chavez conducts.

Nov. 25   Saxophonist Sigurd Rascher premieres Alexander Glazunov's last composition — Concerto for Saxophone in E-flat Major, Op. 109 — in Nykoping, Sweden.

Nov. 30   Alban Berg's *Symphonic Suite*, using music from his incomplete opera *Lulu*, receives its initial performance by Erich Kleiber in Berlin.

Dec. 1   Maurice Ravel's *Don Quichotte a Dulcinee* premieres in Paris. It consists of three songs with orchestral accompaniment.

ALBAN BERG

Dec. 3   Sir Hamilton Harty and the BBC Symphony Orchestra premiere William Walton's Symphony No. 1.

Dec. 15   Jean Francaix' *Concertino* for Piano and Orchestra, a work in four movements, premieres in Paris, with the composer as soloist. Francaix is now 22 years old.

Dec. 20   Ernst Toch's *Big Ben* receives its first performance by Richard Burgin and the Boston Symphony Orchestra in Cambridge, Massachusetts. The neoromantic music is a symphonic fantasy based on the changing bells of Westminster Abbey.

Dec. 25   Albert Coates premieres Dmitri Kabalevsky's three-movement Symphony No. 2 in Moscow. Now 29, Kabalevsky is an instructor in composition at the Moscow Conservatory.

1934   Births, Deaths and Debuts

Jan. 11   German soprano Lotte Lehmann makes her Metropolitan Opera debut as Sieglinde in Wagner's *Die Walkure*. Hubbard Hutchinson writes in the New York *Times* that she "had an electrifying quality that swept [the critical] faculty away for once and made even the guarded listener a breathless participant in the emotions of the anguished Sieglinde."

Jan. 16   Soprano Marilyn Horne is born in Bradford, Pennsylvania.

Jan. 18   Czech violinist and teacher Otakar Sevcik, 81, dies in Pisek. Having begun his studies at the Prague Conservatory, he later became a faculty member of the Kieff, Prague and Vienna conservatories and was a teacher of Jan Kubelik. His method of instruction centered on perfecting chromatic chord progressions — he expounded these ideas in his instructional writings, published in German, Bohemian, French, Russian and English.

Jan. 24   Czech conductor Rafael Kubelik makes his debut with the Czech Philharmonic in Prague.

Feb. 3   American mezzo-soprano Eleanora de Cisneros, 53, dies in New York City. She was the first American singer without European training to appear at the Metropolitan Opera.

Feb. 23   English composer Sir Edward Elgar, 76, dies in Worcester, England. Trained by his father, he studied organ and violin and in his early twenties conducted the band at the Worcester County Lunatic Asylum. His first success came at age 32 with his overture *Froissart*, premiered in 1890. Six years later, his fame increased substantially with his cantata *Scenes from the Saga of King Olaf*. In 1900 his masterpiece, *The Dream of Gerontius*, premiered.

Elgar's music was distinctly romantic, marked by melodic grace and harmonies rooted in the 19th century. He excelled at secular drama, often using this medium for his oratorios, such as *The Apostles*. His two symphonies achieved great notice in England. His works include four oratorios and six cantatas as well as choral, orchestral and chamber works. His awards were many and included honorary music doctorates from Cambridge, Oxford and Yale universities. He was also made Master of the King's Musick in 1924.

Feb. 24   Soprano Renata Scotto is born in Savona, Italy.

March 4   Argentine composer Mario Davidovsky is born in Buenos Aires.

March 16   Arnold Schoenberg's early works comprise today's program of the Boston Symphony Orchestra with the composer conducting. This event marks the composer's first appearance in America as a conductor.

March 21   Austrian composer Franz Schreker, 55, dies in Berlin. He began his studies at the Vienna Conservatory and later became conductor of the Vienna Philharmonic Chorus. At age 42 he became director of the Hochschule fur Musik (Berlin), where he taught Ernst Krenek, Karol Rathaus and Alois Haba. He was later ousted by the Nazis from a similar position at the Prussian Academy of Arts. He wrote nine operas, one ballet and many orchestral and chamber works. His music is markedly neoromantic, with expressionist tendencies. The operas, in particular, are rooted in the harmonic fields of Wagner while portraying subjects of psychological controversy that are associated with German expressionism. With the rise of the second Viennese school (Arnold Schoenberg, Alban Berg and Anton Webern), his work quickly disappears.

April 12   American inventor Dr. Thaddeus Cahill, 67, dies in New York City. He invented the dynamophone (also known as the telharmonium) — an electrical instrument capable of producing combinations of tones at various dynamic levels by electromagnetic induction. The instrument weighed more than 200 tons and took up enormous space. It was also used to broadcast concerts over telephone lines, but because of interference with telephone communications, that application was abandoned. The dynamophone was a forerunner of the Hammond organ (1929), the RCA synthesizer (Columbia-Princeton Electronic Music Center, 1960) and the Moog synthesizer (1969).

May 2   German musicologist Dr. Max Friedlander, 81, dies in Berlin. A noted writer on music, he was a specialist on the work of Franz Schubert. He taught at Harvard in 1911 but was mainly associated with Berlin University. His seven-volume edition of Schubert's songs features more than 100 songs by that composer that had been discovered by Friedlander.

May 25   English composer Gustav Holst, 59, dies in London. His formal training as a composer began at age 19, when he entered the Royal College of Music in London and studied with Sir Charles Villiers Stanford. His skillful playing enabled him to earn money as a trombonist. At age 33 he was appointed music director of Morley College in London and at age 45 joined the faculty of the Royal College of Music. Four years later he embarked on an American tour, lecturing and performing at Harvard University and the University of Michigan.

Holst's music reflects a blend of several distinct influences: literature, philosophy, English folklore and oriental themes. Works reflecting oriental themes include his chamber opera *Savitri*. Two other works — *Saint Paul's Suite* and *The Planets* — are his most popular. *The Planets*, in particular, reflects Holst's preoccupation with mysticism; its movements depict the planets as mystical symbols.

Holst was one of the most important English composers during the first third of the century. Holst composed at least nine stage works, including two choral ballets (*The Morning of the Year* and *The Golden Goose*) and one operetta (*Lansdown Castle*, premiered in 1893) as well as many orchestral pieces, chamber music and piano music.

June 10   English composer Frederick Delius, 72 — blind and incapacitated from syphilis — dies in Grez-sur-Loing, France. In his youth he studied violin, piano and organ. After some time growing oranges in Florida, he went in 1886 to the Leipzig Conservatory, where he studied composition with Carl Reinecke, Hans Sitt and Salomon Jadassohn. He later met Edvard Grieg, who strongly influenced his work.

His illness began to affect his work at age 60; it was at this time that his amanuensis, Eric Fenby, began to take musical dictation from Delius to help him complete his late works. Seven years later, Sir Thomas Beecham held a Delius Festival in London, an event that substantially enhanced the composer's stature. Delius then returned to France, where his health slowly deteriorated.

He blended romanticism with impressionism, and his orchestral works often emphasize the colors of individual instruments. Despite his important blending of these styles, he did not have a major impact on the international music scene. Like the work of Gustav Holst, Delius' music was eclipsed in England by the work of Ralph Vaughan Williams.

Delius composed seven operas, many orchestral and vocal works, and various chamber and programmatic pieces, for which he is most noted (*On Hearing the First Cuckoo in Spring, North Country Sketches*, etc.). *A Mass of Life* is Delius' only piece conceived on a large scale.

June 15   French composer Alfred Bruneau, 77, dies in Paris. Born Louis Charles Bonaventure Alfred, he was known as the best cellist at the Paris Conservatoire. Jules Massenet was his composition teacher. His cantata *Sainte-Genevieve* won him a Prix de Rome when he was 24. He conducted at the Opera-Comique from 1903 and was later appointed to the faculty of the Paris Conservatoire. In the early days of his career, he also wrote music criticism for *Gil Blas, Le Figaro* and *Le Matin*. His career was enhanced by his foreign appearances as a conductor of his own works. He was made a member of the Academie des Beaux Arts at age 68. As a composer, his impact was on French opera. Drama, both in music and in acting, was his principal concern. This was shown in his coupling of dissonance with moments of dramatic intensity. He composed 12 operas, 2 ballets, overtures and various other works.

June 29   Ballet dancer Henning Kronstam is born in Copenhagen.

July 12   American pianist Van Cliburn (born Harvey Lavan Jr.) is born in Shreveport, Louisiana.

July 28   Dancer Jacques d'Amboise is born in Dedham, Massachusetts.

Aug. 7   Alton Gilbert Holt, 61, dies in Pittsfield, Massachusetts. He was president of the American Conservatory of Music.

Sep. 8   English composer Peter Maxwell Davies is born in Manchester, England.

Sep. 10   German conductor Sir George Henschel, 84, dies in Aviemore, Scotland. Having begun his career as a singer, he went on to become the Boston Symphony Orchestra's first conductor in 1881. He was knighted in 1914. Also a composer, he wrote approximately 200 songs.

Oct. 3   American composer, writer, critic and editor Benjamin Boretz is born in New York City.

Oct. 13   American-born, German-trained musicologist Theodore Baker, 83, dies in Dresden. This musician compiled the first edition of *Baker's Biographical Dictionary of Musicians*, first published in 1900 by G. Schirmer.

Oct. 21   Italian music historian and critic Gaetano Casari, 64, dies in Milan. He wrote studies of the 16th-century madrigal and was an editor of a collection of old Italian music entitled *Istituzioni e monumenti dell'antica musica italiana*, issued by Ricordi.

Nov. 1   English composer William Mathias is born in Whitland, Dyfed, Wales.

Nov. 30   American music critic Philip Hale, 80, dies in Boston. Before studying organ with Dudley Buck, he practiced law. He studied composition with Josef Rheinberger in Munich. His criticism is noted for its hatred of modern music and of Brahms (the common concertgoer's remark in Boston, "Exit in Case of Brahms," is attributed to Hale). He wrote criticism for many tabloids, including the Boston *Home Journal*, The Boston *Post* and the Boston *Herald*. He also edited songs, though none by Brahms.

Dec. 11   British-American composer Godfrey Winham is born in London.

Dec. 19   French pianist Francis Plante, 95, dies in Saint Avit, France. One of the more eccentric musical figures, he first studied at the Paris Conservatoire, where he won first prize after seven months. He then studied privately for the next 10 years and emerged as a polished musician. About

1900 he decided that he would never again be seen in public and retired. He did give several more concerts in 1915, but — true to his promise — he was hidden from the audience behind a screen.

1934   Related Events

The term high fidelity (hi-fi) becomes a household word this year as recording companies use it in extensive advertising and marketing. Other events in the recording industry include: The Decca Record Company (New York City) is established by Jack Kapp and releases discs at a price of 35 cents each; BASF (Badische Analin und Soda Fabrik) produces 50,000 meters of magnetic recording tape for AEG (Allgemeine Electricitaets Gesellschaft); RCA markets its "outboard" attachments for record players; the Filmon belt-type long-playing record is introduced in Japan.

Fundamentals of the Classic Dance, by Agrippina Vaganova, is published this year in Leningrad. The book's importance lies in its exposition of Vaganova's teaching methods which become the basis for the formulation of the Soviet style. It is published in an English edition in 1937.

Jan. 2   The School of American Ballet opens today in New York City. It was founded by George Balanchine and Lincoln Kirstein with financial help from Edward Warburg.

Jan. 17   Scientist Albert Einstein performs the second violin part in a Mozart quartet and Bach's Concerto for Two Violins at a private concert in New York given by Adolph Lewisohn. This event is a benefit for Jewish and non-Jewish scientists in Nazi Germany. It marks Einstein's American debut on the violin.

April 22   The Nazi government decrees that all choral organizations in Germany must now belong to the Sangerbund, for the purpose of employing music as a means of promoting Nazi doctrine.

May   The first Glyndebourne Festival begins this month and features performances of *The Marriage of Figaro* and *Cosi fan tutte*, both by Mozart. The manor house and estate are located on the Sussex Downs, near Lewes and is owned by the Christie family. The festival is founded by John Christie and his wife, soprano Audrey Mildmay. Fritz Busch conducts, Carl Ebert is producer, and Rudolf Bing, manager. The festival quickly establishes itself as one of the finest opera festivals in the world.

June 3   Carleton Sprague Smith becomes chairman of the American Musicological Society, founded today in New York City. The society is dedicated to "the advance-

ment of research in the various fields of music as a branch of learning." It holds regular meetings and an annual convention at which papers on musicological subjects are read. The society also publishes *Papers of the A.M.S.* (PAMS), *Bulletin of the A.M.S.* (BAMS) — both yearly publications — and, beginning in 1948, *Journal of the A.M.S.* (JAMS), published three times a year.

June 8   Arthur Henry Fox-Strangeways, an English writer and promoter of new music, writes a letter indirectly addressed to American composer Harry Partch and delivered through an intermediary. The letter is on the subject of just intonation. Partch had submitted, through the intermediary, an article to Fox-Strangeways that he hoped would be published in *Music and Letters* [London], which Fox-Strangeways edits.

Just intonation is a system of tuning in which every interval is derived from the pure or natural fifth or third. This method of tuning contrasts with equal temperament (the way a modern piano is tuned, for example) in which the octave is divided into 12 semitones and in which the octave is the only acoustically correct or pure interval. Fox-Strangeways rejects the article saying that modulation — the method of changing keys in the equal temperament system — is impossible in the system of just intonation and that displacing equal temperament would "scrap the music of two centuries." Partch contends that composers tend to think in terms of equal temperament because "it is all they have got to think in."

This event is one of a series during Partch's lifetime that prompts him to pursue his own musical beliefs. At the age of 28, Partch burned all of his early music in a pot-bellied stove and proceeded to build a number of musical instruments to accommodate his scale, divided into 43 tones. Over the next 30 years — except when Partch responds to poverty by becoming a hobo — he continues to build, compose for, and perform on these instruments.

June 10   Igor Stravinsky formally becomes a citizen of France.

June 11   Richard Strauss accepts an autographed photograph of Adolf Hitler and one of Joseph Goebbels as a 70th-birthday gesture from the Reich.

Oct. 1   New York City becomes the home of the Mutual Broadcasting System, inaugurated today.

Oct. 30 Oliver Strunk presents the Elizabeth Sprague Coolidge Medal to Alfredo Casella at the Library of Congress in Washington, D.C. for his contributions to musical art.

Oct. 31 As of today, the use of non-German pseudonyms by musicians becomes a punishable offense in Nazi Germany.

Nov. 1 German composers Rudolf Wagner-Regeny and Julius Weismann are commissioned to compose a new version of incidental music to Shakespeare's *A Midsummer Night's Dream*. Dr. Walter Strang, leader of the National-Socialist Kulturgemeinde, notes in today's issue of *Die Musik* that the Mendelssohn version does not advance Aryan racial purity.

Dec. 4 Wilhelm Furtwangler resigns from the German Reichsmusikkammer (he had become deputy president), the Berlin State Opera (he was director) and the Berlin Philharmonic (he was music director) because the Nazi government recently excluded Paul Hindemith from German musical life. In addition, as conductor, he had been unsuccessful in creating good working conditions for German musicians under the Nazi government.

Dec. 6 Paul Hindemith's opera *Neues vom Tage* is denounced by Joseph Goebbels, who says, in part, "Opportunity creates not only thieves but also atonal musicians. . . . "

1935 Opera

Jan. 16 *Nerone*, an opera by Pietro Mascagni, receives its first performance at La Scala. The libretto, by Giovanni Targioni-Tozzetti, is based on a comedy by Pietro Cassa. The composer conducts. The cast includes Lina Bruna Rasa, Margherita Carosio and Aureliano Pertile.

March 27 Darius Milhaud's *Les Choephores* (part two of his trilogy *Orestia*) receives its first staged performance at the Theatre de la Monnaie in Brussels. In this installment Orestes takes revenge on his mother and Aegisthus and is then tormented by the Furies.

May 5 Ildebrando Pizzetti's *Orseolo* premieres in Florence at the Teatro Communale. Pizzetti writes his own libretto, set in 17th-century Venice.

May 20 German composer Werner Egk's three-act opera *Die Zaubergeige* premieres in Frankfurt. Based on a Bavarian folk tale, the opera is about a farmer who is given a magical violin and becomes a virtuoso.

June 24 Richard Strauss' *Die schweigsame Frau* receives its first performance at the Dresden Staatsoper. Stefan Zweig writes the libretto which is based on the comedy *Epicoene*, by Ben Jonson. The opera is well received by the public but is soon banned by Adolf Hitler because Zweig is a Jew. Nazi harassment of Zweig causes Strauss to protest. Karl Bohm conducts a cast that includes Maria Cebotari, Erna Sack and Friedrich Plaschke.

Sep. 30 George Gershwin's three-act opera *Porgy and Bess* opens in Boston. The story is based on a novel by Du Bose Heyward, who, with the composer's brother Ira, turned it into an opera libretto. Alexander Smallens conducts. Lawrence Gilman says of it in the New York *Herald-Tribune*, "Perhaps it is needlessly Draconian to begrudge Mr. Gershwin the song hits which he has scattered through his score and which will doubtless enhance his fame and popularity."

Oct. 22 Russian composer Ivan Dzerzhinsky's four-act opera *Quiet Flows the Don* premieres in Leningrad. The opera, about the Russian Revolution, is based on a novel by Mikhail Sholokhov.

Oct. 26 Rumanian composer Paul Constantinescu's *O noapte furtunoasa* premieres in Bucharest. It is a comic opera about a young man who enters the wrong bedroom.

SKETCH BY DUBOSE HEYWARD FOR CATFISH ROW SET FOR *PORGY AND BESS*

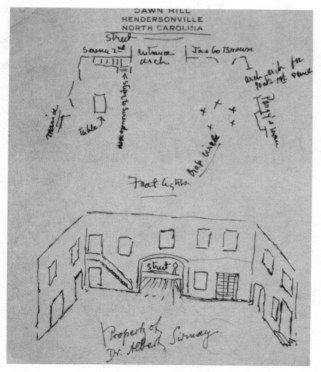

1935   Dance

Feb. 23   *Iphigenia in Aulis*, choreographed by Doris Humphrey and Charles Weidman, is performed for the first time in Philadelphia.

March 1   The American Ballet premieres George Balanchine's one-act abstract ballet *Reminiscence*, with music by Benjamin Godard. The work evokes echoes of the ballets Balanchine grew up with in Saint Petersburg. Holly Howard, Elise Reiman and William Dollar star.

March 20   Michel Fokine's *The Firebird* is performed in New York City. This version includes costumes and scenery by Nathalie Gontcharova and is performed by the Ballet Russe de Monte Carlo. Alexandra Danilova dances the role of the Firebird. Also receiving its first American performance is Leonide Massine's *La Boutique fantasque*.

April 4   Choreographer Feodor Lopokov's *The Bright Stream* — with music by Dmitri Shostakovich and designs by Mikhail Bobyshov — premieres at the Maly Theater in Leningrad. It is about life on a collective farm. *Pravda* subsequently publishes an article entitled "Choreographic Misrepresentation," which states that the ballet has "nothing to do with authentic folk dances on the Kuban River or any other place." Lopokov is fired as ballet chief of the Maly Theater. A New York *Times* review of the ballet, commenting that Joseph Stalin watched from his box, says, "The performance was received lukewarmly, so this revolutionary dance poem, despite some sprightly music, will probably end in the archives of the theatre."

April 28   Martha Graham presents her solo *Frontier*, a dance about a pioneer woman. It is one of her greatest early works and marks the beginning of her association with Isamu Noguchi, who designed the scenery. The music is by Louis Horst.

May 11   Karol Szymanowski's *Harnaise* premieres in Prague. This full-length ballet, by J. Nikolska, is about robbers in the Tatra district of Poland.

May 20   The Vic-Wells Ballet gives the first performance of Ninette de Valois' *The Rake's Progress*, to music by Gavin Gordon. The ballet is inspired by a series of paintings by William Hogarth. Walter Gore and Alicia Markova lead the cast, which includes Ailne Phillips, Ursula Moreton, Joy Newton and Harold Turner.

July 9   Serge Lifar's *Icare* receives its world premiere by the Paris Opera Ballet. The music, for percussion, is arranged by J.E. Szyfer; the costumes and scenery are by Eugene Berman. The work, which contrasts the art of choreography with that of musical composition, is about Icarus trying to fly with wings his father, Daedalus, made.

July 18   The Ballet Russe de Monte Carlo at Covent Garden premieres *The Hundred Kisses* in London. The work is based on a tale by Hans Christian Andersen. The choreography is by Bronislava Nijinska to music by Frederic d'Erlanger, with costumes and scenery by Jean Hugo. Irina Baronova and David Lichine star.

Nov. 26   Frederick Ashton's version of *Le Baiser de la fee* is given its first performance by the Sadler's Wells Ballet. The story, to music by Igor Stravinsky, concerns a fairy who claims a man on his wedding day. Margot Fonteyn plays the Bride in her first created ballerina role. Pearl Argyle and Harold Turner complete the cast.

Dec. 31   *Lost Illusions* is performed for the first time by the Kirov Ballet in Leningrad. Choreography is by Rostislav Zakharov; the music, by Boris Asafiev; the book and designs, by Vladimir Dmitriev. The work, based on the novel by Balzac, is about a composer who sacrifices love to get his work performed.

1935   Instrumental and Vocal Music

Jan. 13   Eugene Ormandy and the Minneapolis Symphony Orchestra premiere Roy Harris' overture *When Johnny Comes Marching Home*. The piece is a set of variations on the famous Civil War song — which is also an unusual martial tune in that it is in a minor key.

Jan. 26   Ernst Toch's Piano Concerto No. 2, in four movements, is premiered in Frankfurt by pianist Heida Hermanns and conductor William Steinberg. Toch has left

Germany. This performance takes place under the auspices of the Kulturbund deutscher Juden, a Jewish cultural group permitted to exist (at least temporarily) by the Nazi government.

Jan. 30   *Concertino for Flute, Harp, Celesta and Strings*, by Otto Luening, receives its first performance in Philadelphia. Luening is now 34 and has studied with Ferruccio Busoni and Phillipp Jarnach. He has also helped establish the Grand

Opera Company in Chicago and has, at this young age, already been on the faculties of the Eastman School of Music and the University of Arizona. He is currently teaching at Bennington College.

Feb. 24   Nikolai Miaskovsky's Symphony No. 14 in C Major is performed for the first time in Moscow. In five movements, it was composed two years ago.

Feb. 26   Georges Bizet's Symphony No. 1 in C Major receives its world premiere by Felix Weingartner in Basel, Switzerland. The score to this presumably discarded early work had been located in the Paris Conservatoire. The piece was composed 80 years ago.

March 23   The New York Philharmonic premieres Samuel Barber's *Music for a Scene from Shelley*. The neoromantic work is scored for full orchestra.

April 8   Bela Bartok's String Quartet No. 5 premieres during the Coolidge Festival at the Library of Congress in Washington, D.C. Commissioned by Elizabeth Sprague Coolidge, the five-movement piece was composed in one month.

April 10   Symphony No. 4 in F Minor, by Ralph Vaughan Williams, receives its initial performance by Adrian Boult and the BBC Symphony Orchestra in London. Containing four movements, the work features unusually complicated rhythms and jagged melodies. Vaughan Williams reportedly told the orchestra at rehearsal, "I don't even know if I like it." Eric Blom writes in the Birmingham *Post* that it is "harshly and grimly uncompromising in its clashing dissonant polyphony." The symphony, nevertheless, is a big success.

May 2   Symphony No. 3, by Henk Badings, premieres in Amsterdam.

May 18   Otto Klemperer and the Los Angeles Philharmonic premiere Arnold Schoenberg's Suite for String Orchestra. Schoenberg composed this work specifically for high school musicians, commenting in a foreword to the piece that the student should "acquire gradually a feeling for something more than the primitive symmetric construction, the unvaried and undeveloped melody, which give pleasure to mediocrities of all lands and peoples." He also writes on the title page of the manuscript, "The spots in this score are Klemperer's drops of perspiration." The piece has five movements and a key signature — the first time Schoenberg has used one since 1908.

May 25   Heitor Villa-Lobos' symphonic poem *Uirapuru* premieres in Buenos Aires.

June 2   Symphony No. 5 by Henry Hadley, premieres in Norfolk, Connecticut, the composer conducting. The three-movement symphony celebrates the tercentenary of the state of Connecticut.

Sep. 4   Anton Webern's Concerto, Op. 24, receives its world premiere in Prague. Heinrich Jalowetz conducts this work scored for flute, oboe, clarinet, horn, trumpet, trombone, piano, violin and viola. Composed last year, it is dedicated to Arnold Schoenberg in celebration of his 60th birthday. The music reflects Webern's strictest adherence to the 12-tone method and derives miniature gestures from one basic idea — the 12-tone row.

Oct. 10   Tikhon Khrennikov's Symphony No. 1 in B-flat Minor receives its initial performance in Moscow. This three-movement symphony is the composer's graduation piece for the Moscow Conservatory. He is now 22.

Oct. 19   Albert Roussel's Symphony No. 4 in A Major premieres in Paris. This four-movement symphony is performed by the Pasdeloup Orchestra with Albert Wolf conducting. It marks Roussel's movement away from impressionism and toward neoclassicism. The piece is successful: Shouts of "Encore" result in the third movement being performed twice.

Oct. 19   Arthur Honegger's *Radio-Panoramique* premieres in Paris. This piece is a symphonic sketch characterizing a listener switching radio stations.

Oct. 28   Nikolai Miaskovsky's Symphony No. 15 in D Minor is premiered by the Moscow Radio Orchestra. The work was composed last year.

Nov. 6   William Walton's Symphony No. 1 is performed in its complete version by Hamilton Harty and the BBC Symphony Orchestra. Today's performance includes the Finale. The other three movements were first performed on December 3 of last year. Walton is now 33.

Nov. 14   Paul Hindemith's viola concerto *Die Schwanendreher* is premiered by Willem Mengelberg and the Concertgebouw Orchestra in Amsterdam, with the composer as soloist.

Nov. 21   Igor Stravinsky's neobaroque Concerto for Two Pianos is performed for the first time unaccompanied in Paris. The composer and his son Sviatoslav Soulima-Stravinsky are soloists.

Nov. 21   In Brussels, Leon Jongen's symphonic piece *Malaise* receives its initial performance. It depicts the composer's impressions of his travels to Malaya.

Nov. 21   Knudage Riisager's Symphony No. 3 premieres in Copenhagen. The symphony has three movements.

Dec. 1   Sergei Prokofiev's Violin Concerto No. 2 in G Minor is premiered in Madrid.

1935   Births, Deaths and Debuts

Jan. 2   Austrian cellist Emanuel Feuermann makes his American debut with the New York Philharmonic.

Jan. 11   Soprano Marcella Sembrich, 76, dies in New York City. After first studying the piano and violin, she turned to singing on the advice of Franz Liszt. She debuted in Athens in 1877 in Vincenzo Bellini's *I Puritani*. Other European and American debuts soon followed, and she eventually became a member of the Metropolitan Opera Company in 1898. In 1909 she was given an extraordinary farewell there, and after her retirement, she taught at the Curtis Institute and the Juilliard School. She excelled at lyric coloratura roles in the Italian and French repertoires.

Jan. 14   Polish-Austrian music theorist Heinrich Schenker, 66, dies in Vienna. A student of Anton Bruckner, he was also a composer and editor of piano works. Schenker developed an approach to the understanding and analysis of tonal music through levels of rhythmic and harmonic motion that he called "surface," "middleground" and "background." His system was accompanied by graphic symbols and a unique vocabulary delineating these levels, leading to the notion that one triad is the essence of a musical composition. His principal treatise is entitled *Neue Musikalische Theorien und Fantasien* — its three volumes deal with harmony, counterpoint and

KIRSTEN FLAGSTAD AND LAURITZ MELCHIOR

free composition. His work has a greater impact on music education in the United States than in Europe.

Jan. 28   Russian composer and teacher Mikhail Ippolitov-Ivanov, 75, dies in Moscow. He studied with Nikolai Rimsky-Korsakov and years later (at the recommendation of Tchaikovsky) became director of the Moscow Conservatory. His interest in Caucasian folk music is reflected in his pieces, especially *Caucasian Sketches*. His pupils included Reinhold Gliere and Sergei Vassilenko. He composed six operas, many orchestral works, chamber music and a good number of choral pieces.

Feb. 2   Norwegian soprano Kirsten Flagstad, 40, makes a sensational debut at the Metropolitan Opera singing Sieglinde in Wagner's *Die Walkure*. Lawrence Gilman writes in the New York *Herald-Tribune*, "The singing that we heard yesterday is that of a musician with taste and brains and sensibility, with poetic and dramatic insight."

Feb. 27   Soprano Mirella Freni is born in Modena, Italy.

April 5   Polish composer and conductor Emil Mlynarski, 65, dies in Warsaw. A conductor of the Philadelphia Opera Company, he was also the first director of the Warsaw Philharmonic. In addition, he was a director of the Warsaw Conservatory and taught, too, at the Curtis Institute of Music in Philadelphia. He was also well-known as a conductor in Scotland, where he conducted the Scottish Orchestra.

May 10   Former singer Herbert Witherspoon, 61, who had been chosen to succeed Giulio Gatti-Casazza as general manager of the Metropolitan Opera, dies in his office at the opera house following six weeks of preparation for his first season. Before this post, he had been a successful bass, president of the Cincinnati Conservatory and artistic director of the Chicago Civic Opera.

May 17   French composer Paul Dukas, 69, dies in Paris. As a student at the Paris Conservatoire, he was noted for winning prizes and, at age 62, was appointed to that faculty. He was an unusual figure in that, although not prolific, he composed at least two works that have been acclaimed as extremely important. They are *The Sorcerer's Apprentice*, an orchestral scherzo noted for its orchestral brilliance, and *Ariane et Barbe-Bleue*, noted for being an excellent French impressionist opera (It is the only opera he composed.)

He made his career principally as an educator and music critic and had little impact on musical life outside of France. His other works include the ballet *La Peri*, three overtures, chamber music (including *Villanelle* for horn and piano — a favorite of horn students) and piano pieces.

May 19   American composer Charles Martin Loeffler, 74, dies in Medfield, Massachusetts. As a youth, he lived in Russia, Hungary, Switzerland and Germany. He studied violin with Eduard Rappoldi, Joseph Joachim and Lambert-Joseph Massart. In Paris he was a composition pupil of Ernest Guiraud and played violin with the Pasdeloup Orchestra. He later played violin in Russian Baron Paul von Derwie's private orchestra. Loeffler returned to America at age 20 and performed under Leopold Damrosch in New York. A year later he became second concertmaster of the Boston Symphony Orchestra. At age 42 he devoted himself to composing and teaching.

His work as a composer reflects the unusual influences of the many nations he lived in during his youth — this "international" background was extremely rare for an American composer of his generation. All of these influences are overshadowed by that of France: His music is impressionistic and reflects French tendencies in orchestration. Despite this extraordinary background, his music was not performed widely outside of Boston, nor did he have a formidable impact on the music of his age in an international context. His works comprise many orchestral pieces (including his most famous — *A Pagan Poem*) and a host of choral and chamber works.

May 29   Czech composer and violinist Josef Suk, 61, dies in Benesovo, near Prague. Having begun as a violinist, he studied composition with Antonin Dvorak and was married to Dvorak's daughter Otile. He was second violinist of the Bohemian String Quartet and later taught at the Prague Conservatory. As a composer, his works are post-romantic and heavily influenced by the style of his father-in-law. His works include overtures and two symphonies, two string quartets, piano pieces and other music.

JOSEF SUK

Aug. 15   French soprano Lucienne Breval, 64, dies in Paris. Known as one of the chief operatic singers of France, she created leading soprano roles in the first performances of Wagner operas at the Paris Opera.

Aug. 27   Conductor Adolfe Bracale, 62, dies in Bogota. Director of the National Opera of Colombia, he is especially noted for having brought about a production of *Aida* at the foot of the pyramids.

Sep. 1   Conductor Seiji Ozawa is born in Hoten, China of Japanese parents.

Oct. 1   Italian conductor Italo Azzoni, 82, dies in Parma. He was a teacher of Arturo Toscanini, a director of the Metropolitan Opera and a faculty member of the Arrigo Boito Conservatory.

Oct. 12   Tenor Luciano Pavarotti is born in Modena, Italy.

Oct. 14   Avant-garde composer La Monte Young is born in Bern, Idaho.

Oct. 30   Mme. Norma K. Lutge, 85, dies in Los Angeles. She was the first female impresario in America and made 128 trips to Europe arranging American concert tours for such artists as Ossip Gabrilowitsch and Jan Kubelik. She contended that women could bring peace to the world and founded the International Women's League to bring women of different nations together.

Nov. 5   Composer Nicholas Maw is born in Grantham, Lincolnshire, England.

Dec. 10   Soprano Licia Albanese makes her operatic debut singing *Madama Butterfly* in Parma.

Dec. 24   Austrian composer Alban Berg, 50, dies in Vienna from an infection at the base of his spine resulting from an insect bite. His education was undertaken largely with Arnold Schoenberg, of whom he became a steadfast disciple and friend. Berg helped organize the Society for Private Performances in Vienna (which prohibited music critics from attending).

His early pieces reflected the influence of Richard Wagner and Gustav Mahler — this influence was formative and would become apparent in his later 12-tone works through grandness of musical gesture. His opera *Wozzeck* — premiered 10 years ago — is his major work and becomes widely performed in America and Europe after World War II. His other opera, *Lulu,* is unfinished and is later completed by Friedrich Cerha. His Violin Concerto, which is premiered posthumously next April, is his last complete work and uses 12-tone principles in a free, unrestricted manner.

The youngest of the second Viennese school (the other two being Arnold Schoenberg and Anton Webern), Berg is the only one of the three whose music, in its maturity, embraced romantic sentiment within the context of dodecaphonic composition. His becomes the most popular of these three composers' work. He was, perhaps, a 20th-century romantic, in that he successfully combined the emotional intensity of 19th century music with the intellectual pursuits of the 20th-century theorist. His other pieces include songs, piano works, chamber and orchestral items, and various arrangements.

1935   Related Events

Due to the effects of the Great Depression, the San Francisco Symphony Orchestra almost goes bankrupt. To save the orchestra and reduce mounting deficits, Mrs. Lenore Wood Armsby — instrumental in saving the symphony — convinces the management of the orchestra to hire Pierre Monteux as music director. It is under Monteux's leadership that the orchestra begins to attract larger audiences from the areas outside San Francisco, largely because of new bridges spanning San Francisco Bay. Monteux remains music director until 1952.

Frederick Ashton becomes chief choreographer of the Vic-Wells Ballet this year.

The State Academic Theatre of Opera and Ballet (formerly the Maryinsky Theatre) changes its name to the Kirov Theatre of Opera and Ballet this year.

The first Mozart opera recordings are begun this year at the Glyndebourne Festival in England. Other developments in the recording industry include the following: Magnetic tape processing is perfected by BASF (Badische Analin und Soda Fabrik); AEG (Allgemeine Electricitaets Gesellschaft) participates in the Berlin Broadcasting exhibition and demonstrates its magnetophon; the first recordings of early music are launched as musicologist Curt Sachs begins his *Anthology Sonore* history.

Chroniques de ma vie, by Igor Stravinsky, is published this year in Paris. The composer's autobiographical work is in two volumes and is published in an English version next year in London.

Jan.   German theorist on national socialism Alfred Rosenberg's article "Esthetics or National Struggle?" is published this month in *Die Musik* (Berlin). Rosenberg comments on Wilhelm Furtwangler's resignation as conductor of the Berlin Philharmonic, due — to some degree — to Furtwangler's protest over the Nazi exclusion of Paul Hindemith from German musical life. He states, in part: "So when a man like Hindemith, after a few German beginnings, lives and works for fourteen years among Jews and feels himself at ease in such company, consorts almost exclusively with Jews, and is loved by them; when he, following the ideology of the Weimar Republic, commits the foulest perversions of German music, we have a right to reject him and his environment. The accomplishments of such a person under the Weimar Republic, and the laurels bestowed upon him by that now overthrown regime are of no value to our movement. It is a great pity that so great an artist as Dr. Wilhelm Furtwangler entered this controversy, and chose to identify himself with Hindemith's cause. Herr Furtwangler clings to his 19th-century ideas and has manifestly lost all sense of national struggle of our times."

April 25   Wilhelm Furtwangler resumes his position as Berlin Philharmonic music director after Nazi officials resolve their conflict with him. Furtwangler had protested Paul Hindemith's exclusion from German musical life. The reconciliation is temporary.

July 13   After a reported refusal to part with Jewish librettist Stefan Zweig and discontent with Nazi attitudes toward musical culture, the position of president of the Reichsmusikkammer becomes open as Richard Strauss resigns. Strauss claims old age as a reason for stepping down.

Aug. 1   The U.S. Emergency Relief Bureau opens a new branch, called the Federal Music Project today in Washington, D.C. Its purpose is to provide jobs for unemployed American musicians.

Aug. 30   Jews and all non-"Aryans" are prohibited from performing in German orchestras as of today by the Nazi Reichsmusikkammer.

Oct. 30   Music of Roy Harris comprises the first program of the Composers' Forum-Laboratory, connected with the Federal Music Project. The purpose of these concerts is to perform new American music and test audience reaction to it.

Dec. 16   Gertrude Clarke Whittall donates five Stradivari instruments to the Music Division of the Library of Congress and establishes the Whittall Foundation to finance concerts at which these instruments may be played.

Dec. 22   French composers Claire Delbos, Andre Jolivet, Paul le Flem, Jules Lefebvre, Edouard Sciortino, Georges Migot, Daniel Lesur and Olivier Messiaen offer a concert of their music. Known as La Spirale, the group's purpose is to advance modern music.

1936 Opera

Jan. 22   Franco Alfano's *Cyrano de Bergerac* premieres at the Teatro Reale in Rome. The libretto, written by Henri Cain, is based on the play by Edmond Rostand. The opera is well received but does not survive.

Feb. 8   *Giulio Cesare*, by Gian Francesco Malipiero, receives its first performance at the Teatro alla Felice in Genoa. Malipiero writes his own libretto, based on the play by Shakespeare.

Feb. 12   Ermanno Wolf-Ferrari's *Il Campiello* premieres at La Scala. Mario Ghisalberti's libretto is based on a comedy by Carlo Goldoni about a Neapolitan pursuing his amorous adventures in Venice. It is generally considered one of the composer's most successful works.

Feb. 28   Czech composer Josef Bohuslav Foerster's three-act opera *Bloud* premieres in Prague. The title means "The Simpleton." Foerster writes his own libretto, based on a tale by Tolstoy about a youth who helps a blind girl.

March 10   Georges Enesco's *Oedipe* is performed for the first time at the Paris Opera. It is a four-act opera based on the Greek play.

April 20   Bulgarian composer Pantcho Vladigerov's *Tsar Kaloyan* premieres in Sofia.

April 25   *Il notturno romantico*, by Riccardo Pick-Mangiagalli, premieres at the Opera in Rome. Arturo Rossato's libretto tells the story of a young man who has fallen in love with the niece of a former mistress.

May 12   The first performance of *The Poisoned Kiss*, or *The Empress and the Necromancer*, by Ralph Vaughan Williams, takes place in Cambridge, England. The libretto, written by Evelyn Sharp, is based on Richard Gornetis' story "The Poisoned Maid," from his collection *Twilight of the Gods*. The opera is not well received.

Oct. 15   Swiss composer Heinrich Sutermeister's *Die schwarze Spinne* receives its initial performance over radio in Bern. It is a one-act opera about a woman who gives birth to spiders.

Oct. 29   Alexander Borodin's opera *Bogatyri* — which includes music of Giacomo Meyerbeer, Giacchino Rossini, Jacques Offenbach, Giuseppe Verdi and Alexander Serov

GEORGES ENESCO

— premieres in Moscow. It was originally premiered in 1867; today's version features a new text by poet Demian Biedhy. Borodin had borrowed music from the above-named composers to create an operatic pasticcio.

Nov. 14   Albert Roussel's *Le testament de la tante Caroline* receives its world premiere in a Czech version in Olomoue, Czechoslovakia. This three-act comic opera is about three nieces who try to become pregnant in order to inherit their aunt's fortune.

Nov. 19   Kurt Weill's *Johnny Johnson* premieres in New York. His first work written for the American stage, it is about an American pacifist who tries to prevent war by using laughing gas.

Nov. 20   English conductor and composer Albert Coates' opera *Pickwick*, based on Charles Dickens, is performed for the first time in London.

1936 Dance

Jan. 26   Antony Tudor's *Lilac Garden* receives its world premiere by the Ballet Rambert. The music is by Ernest Chausson and the costumes and scenery by Hugh Stevenson. A Victorian story of love and anguish in a garden, the ballet is an enormously popular and important work, considered one of Tudor's greatest achievements. The lead dancers are Maude Lloyd, Hugh Laing, Peggy van Praagh and the choreographer.

Feb. 11   The Vic-Wells Ballet premieres Frederick Ashton's *Apparitions* at the Sadler's Wells Theater in London. The ballet, which deals with a poet's visions, is to music by Franz Liszt. Cecil Beaton provides the decor. The cast includes Margot Fonteyn, Robert Helpmann, Harold Turner and Maurice Brooke.

June 25   Rene Blum's Ballet Russe offers the premiere of Michel Fokine's *Don Juan*, based on Moliere's play. The music is from a ballet by Christoph Willibald Gluck. Anatole Vilzak, Jeannette Lauret and Andre Eglevsky have leading roles.

July 24   Leonide Massine's *Symphonie fantastique*, with music by Hector Berlioz and costumes and scenery by Christian Berard, is premiered by the Ballet Russe de Monte Carlo in London. Tamara Toumanova and the choreographer lead the company.

Nov. 10   The Vic-Wells Ballet premieres Frederick Ashton's *Nocturne* at the Sadler's Wells Theater in London. It is set to Frederick Delius' *Paris*. The ballet, in one act, is an atmospheric work, in which a poor girl watches wealthy individuals coming to a ball. A wealthy young man is attracted to her but leaves her when a rich woman lures him

TAMARA TOUMANOVA AND LEONIDE MASSINE IN *SYMPHONIE FANTASTIQUE*

back. Margot Fonteyn, June Brae, Robert Helpmann and Frederick Ashton lead the cast.

1936   Instrumental and Vocal Music

Jan. 19   Vittorio Giannini's symphonic work *In Memoriam: Theodore Roosevelt* premieres at the American Museum of Natural History in New York. The piece celebrates the dedication of the Theodore Roosevelt Memorial at this museum. The composer is now 32.

Jan. 22   Paul Hindemith's *Funeral Music* is performed for the first time in London, with the composer as viola soloist. He composed the piece in tribute to England's King George V, who died two days ago.

Jan. 23   Symphony No. 2 (*Sinfonia India*) by Carlos Chavez, receives its initial performance by the Columbia Broadcasting Symphony Orchestra in New York. The composer conducts. The one-movement work features Mexican percussion instruments, including Yacqui drums.

Feb. 28   Symphony No. 2, by Roy Harris, receives its first performance, as Richard Burgin conducts the Boston Symphony Orchestra. The symphony is in three movements.

Feb. 28   Another work by Roy Harris — Prelude and Fugue for String Orchestra — is premiered by Werner Janssen and the Philadelphia Orchestra.

April 11   Hans Lange and the New York Philharmonic premiere Otto Luening's *Two Symphonic Interludes* at Carnegie Hall.

April 19   The Violin Concerto, by Alban Berg, premieres posthumously at this year's International Society for Contemporary Music festival in Barcelona. American violinist Louis Krasner (who also commissioned the piece) is soloist. This two-movement work — Berg's last — is dedicated "to the memory of an angel" (Manon Gropius, daughter of architect Walter Gropius and Alma Mahler, who died of polio at age 18); each of the movements deals with Manon's life and death. The concerto incorporates both a 12-tone row and a chorale tune from a Bach cantata ("Es ist genug," from the cantata *O Ewigkeit, du Donnerwort*). Berg composed the piece at an unusually fast pace — approximately 3 1/2 months. Anton Webern had been scheduled to conduct the premiere but was replaced by Hermann Scherchen because Webern took too much time rehearsing the first few measures. Webern insisted that the Spanish musicians deliberately misinterpreted his instructions and tried to have the performance canceled. It is only the tears of Helene Berg that finally convince him to let another conductor save the premiere. Scherchen reluctantly accepts but insists that Krasner play the solo part from memory, which he does. Webern was also scheduled to conduct fragments from Ernst Krenek's opera *Karl V*; Ernest Ansermet assumes the podium instead.

May 2   The Moscow Philharmonic premieres Sergei Prokofiev's *Peter and the Wolf*, Op. 67. Scored for orchestra and narrator, this work is based on the famous fairy tale. Each character is portrayed in terms of a musical instrument, allowing the story to unfold in words and music. It becomes one of the composer's most popular pieces.

May 12   Dmitri Kabalevsky's Piano Concerto No. 2 in G Minor is premiered in Moscow.

Sep. 11   *Te Deum of Budavar* by Zoltan Kodaly, receives its first performance in Budapest. A hymn for soloists, chorus and orchestra, the text features the ancient Christian hymn *Te Deum laudamus* and celebrates Buda's defending the city from the Turks.

Sep. 25   Ralph Vaughan Williams' *Five Tudor Portraits*, to John Skelton's texts, premieres at the 34th Norwich Triennial Festival with the composer conducting. The work is a choral suite scored for soloists, chorus and orchestra.

Oct. 4   Antonin Dvorak's symphonic work *The Bells of Zlonitz* is premiered posthumously in Prague by the Czechoslovak State Radio Orchestra. The youthful work had been found in archives in Prague.

Oct. 8   Canadian composer Healey Willan's Symphony No. 1 in D Minor premieres in Toronto. Willan has been vice principal of the Royal Conservatory in Toronto since 1920.

Oct. 21   William Schuman's Symphony No. 1 receives its initial performance by the Gotham Symphony Orchestra in New York. This is the first of 10 symphonies by this prolific American composer, now 26. He has been an instructor at Sarah Lawrence College; this summer, he studies with Roy Harris.

Oct. 24   Nikolai Miaskovsky's Symphony No. 16 in F Major premieres in Moscow. It is dedicated to the Soviet air force.

Oct. 29   Sergei Prokofiev's *Russian Overture* premieres in Moscow. It is based on Russian melodies.

Nov. 6   Leopold Stokowski and the Philadelphia Orchestra premiere Serge Rachmaninoff's Symphony No. 3 in A Minor. This three-movement symphony is the last Rachmaninoff writes. Lawrence Gilman reviews the piece and says of it, "Somber, lyrical, defiant, it is a work wholly representative of the Slavic genius. . . ."

Nov. 24   Sergei Prokofiev's first orchestral suite, composed from his ballet *Romeo and Juliet*, premieres in Moscow.

Nov. 30   Leo Sowerby's Piano Concerto No. 2 premieres in Boston, as Serge Koussevitzky conducts the Boston Symphony Orchestra.

Dec. 10   *Pinocchio*, an overture by Ernst Toch, is premiered by Otto Klemperer and the Los Angeles Philharmonic. This is the first orchestral piece Toch composes after moving to California.

Dec. 13   Samuel Barber's *Symphony in One Movement* is premiered by Bernardino Molinari and the Augusteo Orchestra in Rome. Barber is now living in that city as a result of having been awarded an American Prix de Rome. He describes the work as "a synthetic treatment of the four-movement classical symphony." A New York *Times* review says, "The work, which in fact recalls the modern German school, especially the works of Paul Hindemith, may well be termed representative of our epoch for its nervous, tormented style."

1936 Births, Deaths and Debuts

Jan. 10   Dr. Carl Bunge, 80, dies in Chicago. A violinist and conductor, he is said to have studied with Franz Liszt, Richard Wagner, Tchaikovsky and Jules Massenet. He also conducted the Metropolitan Orchestra in Chicago and directed a music conservatory named after him.

Jan. 23   English contralto Dame Clara Butt, 62, dies in Worthsloke, Oxford, England. After studies in England and France, she made her debut in 1892 and continued to sing in opera and oratorio. Among the pieces written for her is Edward Elgar's *Sea Pictures*. She was over six feet tall and was a favorite of the royal family.

Feb. 5   German composer George Fuerst, 66, dies in Munich. Composer of the "Badenweiler March," he was one of Adolf Hitler's favorite composers.

Feb. 8   Mary E. Nolan, 80, dies in Brantford, Ontario. In addition to being a concert pianist, she was also the first person to transmit song over Alexander Graham Bell's new telephone line from Brantford to Hamilton.

Feb. 15   Charles David Isaacson, 44, dies in New York City. An opera impresario and radio director, he organized over a thousand free concerts for the New York music public.

Feb. 26   Italian baritone Antonio Scotti, 70, dies in Naples, Italy. After his operatic debut in Malta in 1889, he became an international star. He came to America in 1899 and was a member of the Metropolitan Opera for 35 years. He was the Rigoletto in Enrico Caruso's debut, sang Scarpia to 15 different Toscas and participated in many American operatic premieres. He excelled in the 19th-century Italian repertoire. For a while after World War I, he toured around the United States with his own company.

March 4   Composer and pianist Aribert Reimann is born in Berlin, Germany.

March 6   Composer Rubin Goldmark, 64, dies in New York. A pupil of Antonin Dvorak, he eventually became head of the composition department at the Juilliard School. His uncle was composer Karl Goldmark; his most famous pupil, Aaron Copland. Goldmark's pieces are largely for orchestra or piano.

March 21   Russian composer Alexander Glazunov, 70, dies in Neuilly-sur-Seine, France. He came from a wealthy family and, when he was 15, met Nikolai Rimsky-Korsakov, with whom he studied harmony, counterpoint and orchestration. He composed his first symphony at age 16 and was immediately proclaimed a genius by leading Russian composers, including Cesar Cui. Glazunov then went to Weimar, where he met Franz Liszt. He toured London and Paris before returning to Saint Petersburg, where he joined the faculty of the Saint Petersburg Conservatory. At age 64, Glazunov toured America, conducting the Detroit Symphony and the Boston Symphony Orchestra.

Glazunov's impact was principally as a teacher: He was considered an expert on counterpoint. His work, distinctly romantic, reflects the influences of Richard Wagner and Franz Liszt. He was a Russian national composer whose popularity rose at the end of the last century and lasted briefly into the present century. The ballet *Raymonda* is his most famous composition; other works include an extraordinary amount of orchestral music (including eight symphonies), vocal works, chamber music and piano pieces.

March 29   English composer Richard Rodney Bennett is born in Broadstairs, Kent, England.

March 30   Spanish mezzo-soprano Conchita Supervia, 40, dies in London. When she was 14 years old, she made her debut in Buenos Aires, and a year later she sang at La Scala in the Italian premiere of *L'heure espagnole*. She also sang in Paris, Chicago and at Covent Garden. Her vivacious personality and unique voice, with its pronounced vibrato, which was capable of executing difficult coloratura, made her very successful in the operas of Rossini. Her portrayal of Carmen was also memorable.

April 18   Italian composer Ottorino Respighi, 56, dies in Rome. He studied violin at the Liceo Musicale in Bologna and composition with Giuseppe Martucci. At age 21 he went to Russia, where he studied with Nikolai Rimsky-Korsakov and performed as a violist in the orchestra of the Imperial Opera in Saint Petersburg. At age 34 he joined the faculty of Santa Cecilia in Rome and remained there for 12

years, after which he concentrated on conducting and composing. Honors followed, including election to the Italian Royal Academy. He also toured America as a performer. Respighi's music is noted for brilliance of orchestration and for its lush harmonies — his early studies with Rimsky-Korsakov enabled him to become an Italian authority on orchestration throughout the first third of the century. His music, not of great intellectual power, attracted audiences with its simplicity and ability to depict Italian life and themes. His symphonic poems won him great acclaim. He also wrote many operas, several ballets, choral works, chamber music, songs, concertos and a host of various kinds of orchestral pieces.

April 24   Dutch-born composer, conductor and writer Bernard van Dieren, 51, dies in London. Known as an anti-Wagnerian and an opera hater, he wrote many essays, including the volume *Down Among the Dead Men* (1935). This book urges composers to return to polyphony and advances the notion that the modern composer could only find true freedom in the musical tradition of the Roman Catholic Church. He also worked for the recognition of the music of Frederick Delius.

April 29   Conductor Zubin Mehta is born in Bombay, India.

May 24   Italian soprano Claudia Muzio 47, dies in Rome. A singer of great expressive power, Muzio studied in Turin and made her Italian debut in 1912. She subsequently sang in Europe, England, South America and the United States — at the Metropolitan and the War Memorial Opera House in San Francisco, which she opened singing Tosca in 1932.

June 30   Danish dancer, choreographer and ballet director Flemming Flindt is born in Copenhagen.

July 4   Italian-born opera singer Edoardo Ferrari-Fontana, 58, dies in Toronto. He was considered the leading Wagnerian singer in Italy prior to World War II and was a Knight of the Italian Crown.

July 27   Soviet dancer Marius-Rudolph Liepa is born in Riga, Latvia.

Aug. 17   French composer Pierre-Octave Ferroud, 36, dies in the vicinity of Debrecen, Hungary in an automobile accident. A student of Florent Schmitt, he was also a music critic and is known for his skillful contrapuntal writing. His work, somewhat popular in style, includes several ballets.

Aug. 20   Dancer Carla Fracci is born in Milan, Italy.

Sep. 14   Russian pianist and conductor Ossip Gabrilowitsch, 58, dies in Detroit, Michigan. After studies with Anton Rubinstein and Theodor Leschetizky, he began a successful concert career in Europe and the United States. In 1909 he married Clara Clemens, a contralto and daughter of Mark Twain, and they often appeared in concert together. As a conductor, he was appointed director of the Detroit Symphony in 1928 and later also shared with

Leopold Stokowski responsibilities for conducting the Philadelphia Orchestra.

Nov. 5   British conductor John Barbirolli makes his debut with the New York Philharmonic and is so favorably received that he is picked to succeed Arturo Toscanini as musical director of that orchestra. He holds the post until 1943.

Nov. 14   Louis Geissler, 75, dies in Northport, Long Island. He was a music publisher and director of the Victor Talking Machine Company.

Nov. 16   Contralto Ernestine Schumann-Heink, 75, dies in Hollywood, California. The enormously popular singer started her career in 1878 and in the next two decades debuted in London, Bayreuth and the United States. She sang some 150 roles, including the premiere of Klytemnes-

tra in Strauss' *Elektra*. Doing that role was apparently a rather unnerving experience, since the composer is said to have yelled at the orchestra during a rehearsal, "Louder, I can still hear Mme. Schumann-Heink." She continued singing into her seventies, her vocal powers and temperament undiminished.

Dec. 4   American conductor William M. Daly, 49, dies in New York. He was a conductor of the Chicago Opera and a guest conductor of the New York Philharmonic and the Philadelphia Symphony Orchestra.

Dec. 21   Swedish contralto Kerstin Thorborg makes her Metropolitan Opera debut as Fricka in *Die Walkure*. Lawrence Gilman, in the *Tribune*, writes that she is a "woman of regal and distinguished beauty" who is an intelligent actress and who knows "the significance of what she is called upon to say and do."

1936   Related Events

John Barbirolli is appointed music director of The New York Philharmonic, succeeding Arturo Toscanini.

The Association of Operatic Dancing is granted a Royal Charter this year and becomes known as the Royal Academy of Dancing. Its first president is Adeline Genee.

Jan. 14   Arnold Schoenberg replies to Alban Berg's widow, Helene Berg, concerning her inquiry about the completion of the third act of *Lulu*. She had written Schoenberg suggesting he do the job and had Universal Edition send him the sketches and libretto. The candidates for the job are Arnold Schoenberg (now in California), Anton Webern, Alexander von Zemlinsky, Erwin Stein (a Universal Edition employee who prepared the piano-vocal score) and, later, Igor Stravinsky and Luigi Dallapiccola. Schoenberg originally expressed an interest but replies today that the work would involve more effort than he could give; Webern and Zemlinsky also soon refuse for other reasons. Universal Edition, the publisher, does not pursue further negotiations, despite the later interest of Stravinsky and Dallapiccola.

The intrigue fades until 16 years from now, when Helene Berg changes her mind and, in 1953, asserts that she is able to communicate with her dead husband's soul and that he does not want the opera finished. This attitude persists until Helene herself becomes part of the spiritual world, on August 30, 1976.

Jan. 28   Dmitri Shostakovich's *Lady Macbeth of the District of Mtsensk* is officially denounced as being too Western-sounding in an article in *Pravda* entitled "Confusion Instead of Music." The article says in part: "*Lady Macbeth* is highly successful with the bourgeois audiences abroad. It may be that this success is owing to the fact that Shostakovich's opera is utterly devoid of all political meaning,

and that it titillates the perverted tastes of the bourgeoisie with its fidgeting, screaming, neurasthenic music."

March 1   *Die Musik* publishes an article denouncing Jews as cultureless people and features caricatures of Felix Mendelssohn, Giacomo Meyerbeer, Jacques Offenbach, Gustav Mahler, Kurt Weill and Otto Klemperer. This journal is now under Nazi control.

March 14   Wilhelm Furtwangler cancels his contract to be music director of the New York Philharmonic for the 1936-37 season due to intense protest by the American public over his continued conducting in Nazi Germany.

March 29   Spanish soprano Lucrezia Bori is given a gala farewell at the Metropolitan Opera. Bori sings scenes from *La Traviata* and *Manon*, while other operatic scenes are sung by Elisabeth Rethberg, Ezio Pinza, Kirsten Flagstad, Lauritz Melchior, Rosa Ponselle and Giovanni Martinelli. The well-loved singer receives a 20-minute ovation.

April 3   The Nazi Reichsmusikkammer organizes its International Music Festival in Baden-Baden as a counter to the annual International Society for Contemporary Music festival. This Nazi festival features music of "Aryan" composers only.

April 9   AGMA (American Guild of Musical Artists) becomes the first organization to represent musical performers as a bargaining unit.

May 13   The final concert is held today at the Teatro Augusteo in Rome. The building is subsequently demolished to search for the tomb of Emperor Augustus.

July 17   The Ballet Caravan opens its first season in Bennington, Vermont. The organization, founded by Lincoln Kirstein, is designed as a showcase for American choreographers, designers and dancers.

Aug. 12   Ignace Paderewski makes his first film appearance performing Beethoven's *Moonlight* Sonata in a film studio in London.

Aug. 16   The Berlin Olympiad opens and celebrates Nazi life with music by approved "Aryan" composers: Richard Strauss, Lino Liviabella, Kurt Thomas, Werner Egk and Paul Hoeffer.

Aug. 29   The National Bureau of Standards broadcasts the 440-cycle *A* as a reference tone for tuning.

Sep. 14   The *Nototyp Rundslater* is patented in Berlin. This music typewriter is the first of its kind.

Nov. 5   The Buffalo Philharmonic Orchestra Society gives its first concert. Lajos Shuk conducts a program of music by Bach, Tchaikovsky, Debussy, Pierre Lalo and Jaromir Weinberger. Violinist Mischa Elman also performs. The concert takes place in Elmwood Hall in Buffalo, New York. Shuk is this orchestra's first music director and stays one season.

Nov. 14   Alexander Borodin's *Bogatyri* is denounced by the Council of People's Commissars of the Union of Soviet Socialist Republics for ideological reasons. All performances of the work are canceled. An article in *Pravda* explaining the decision says, in part, that the opera "tarnishes the image of Russian epic heroes. . . who personify in the popular imagination the inherent traits of the people of Russia."

Nov. 19   Sir Thomas Beecham and the London Philharmonic Orchestra perform Mozart's Thirty-ninth Symphony in Ludwigshafen, Germany. The concert is recorded on magnetic tape by BASF (Badische Analin und Soda Fabrik), marking the first magnetic tape recording of concert music by a major conductor and orchestra. Other developments in the recording industry this year include the establishment of the British Sound Recording Association (BSRA) at Shortlands, Kent (England); and the publication by the Gramophone Shop (New York City) of R.D.Darrell's *Gramophone Shop Encyclopedia of Recorded Music*, which is the first complete discography of electrical classical music recordings.

Nov. 27   Joseph Goebbels decrees that critics must now be at least 30 years old and must avoid extremes of praise and denunciation.

Dec. 8   Gottfried Sonntag's *Nibelungen-Marsch* is limited by the Nazi Ministry of Propaganda to being performed at selected important meetings of the Nazi Party. Adolf Hitler approved the decision last year. The march is derived from tunes in Richard Wagner's *Ring* cycle.

Dec. 26   Arturo Toscanini conducts the first concert of the Palestine Symphony Orchestra in Tel Aviv and refuses all remuneration. The orchestra is composed largely of refugees from Nazi Germany.

Dec. 29   The Mutual Broadcasting System is expanded today and becomes a coast-to-coast network. Inaugurated on October 1, 1934, it is the third radio network in America.

1937 Opera

Feb. 24   Ottorino Respighi's *Lucrezia*, completed by his widow Elsa Olivieri, premieres posthumously in Rome. It is a one-act opera about a woman who commits suicide.

March 5   Douglas Moore's operetta *The Headless Horseman* premieres in Bronxville, New York. The one-act work is based on *A Legend of Sleepy Hollow*, by Wasington Irving.

March 11   *L'Aiglon* receives its first performance in Monte Carlo. This is a five-act opera with three acts composed by Arthur Honegger and two acts composed by Jacques Ibert. It is based on a play by Edmond Rostand about Napoleons's son.

March 18   *Veselohrz na moste*, a one-act opera by Bohuslav Martinu, receives its first performance on the radio in Prague. It is a one-act opera satirizing war.

April 1   Gian-Carlo Menotti's one-act opera *Amelia al ballo* premieres at the Academy of Music in Philadelphia. Fritz Reiner conducts. Menotti's Italian libretto is translated into English by George Mead. The comedy is this composer's first successful opera. He is now 25.

April 21   Aaron Copland's *The Second Hurricane* is premiered by Lehman Engel at the Henry Street Music School in New York. The composer calls this piece a "school opera," to be performed by boys and girls.

May 6   Alfredo Casella's *Il deserto tentato* receives its initial performance in Florence at the May Festival. The composer says in a personal letter to Nicolas Slonimsky that the opera is his finest composition. It deals with Benito Mussolini's invasion of Ethiopia and is in one act.

May 12   The premiere of Walter Damrosch's opera *The Man Without a Country* takes place in New York City at the Metropolitan Opera. The libretto, by Arthur Guiterman, is based on a story by Edward Everett Hale. The composer conducts a cast headed by Helen Traubel, who is making her Metropolitan debut. Critic Lawrence Gilman says the opera has "an infectious gusto."

June 2   *Lulu*, an opera by Alban Berg, receives its world premiere posthumously at the Stadttheater in Zurich. The composer also wrote the libretto, which is based on two dramas by Frank Wedekind about a woman who destroys her lovers and is herself eventually killed by Jack the Ripper. Robert Denzler conducts a cast that includes Nuri Hadzic (Lulu). Stage direction is by Karl Schmidt-Bloss, designs by Roman Clemens. Berg did not complete the third act before his death. This premiere substitutes two fragments of the *Lulu Symphony* and a verbal onstage synopsis of the end of the opera; the final murder scene is sung with a backdrop suggestive of an attic. Berg began composing this opera nine years ago; he kept postponing its completion due to other commissions and projects, poor health and, perhaps, a lack of enthusiasm. The basic 12-tone row of the opera (Lulu's theme) is the musical source material from which the entire opera unfolds. The music includes a sonata, arioso, aria, rondo and interlude placed at various points throughout the opera. The opera is criticized for its lurid tone and violent subject matter. However, critic K.H. David writes in the *Schweizerische Musikzeitung* (Zurich) that the opera "is in no way politically dangerous; it is an exceptional work on purely artistic grounds, to be hailed or condemned as such." Due to the constraints placed on performance of the opera by the composer's widow, Helene Berg, the opera is not performed in its entirety until February 24, 1979.

June 16   Marc Blitzstein's two-act opera *The Cradle Will Rock*, with a libretto by the composer, premieres in New York. This event had been banned by the WPA branch of the Federal Theater because the opera's story, advancing union organization, was considered left-wing. This performance occurs without costumes and scenery and with performers singing their parts from places in the audience. The composer is at the piano.

June 24   *Don Juan de Manora*, a four-act opera by Eugene Goossens, is performed for the first time in London. It is about the loves of a man living in the 17th century.

Sep. 9   *Maria d'Alessandria*, by Federico Ghedini, premieres at the Teatro della Novita in Bergamo. Cesare Meneo's libretto is set in the fourth century. It is the story of a notorious prostitute who is moved to seek redemption by the sacrifice of a young man who loves her. It is Ghedini's earliest work for the stage.

Sep. 14   Modest Mussorgsky's unfinished comic opera *The Marriage*, this version finished by Alexander Tcherepnin, premieres in Essen, Germany.

Oct. 17   Louis Gruenberg's radio opera *Green Mansions* is premiered by CBS in New York. The work is described by the composer as "non-visual."

Oct. 23   Ivan Dzerzhinsky's *Soil Upturned* premieres in Moscow at the Bolshoi Theater. This opera is a sequel to *Quiet Flows the Don*. The composer's second opera, it is in four acts.

Nov. 30   The premiere of Ralph Vaughan Williams' one-act opera *Riders to the Sea* takes place in London at the Royal College of Music. The libretto, written by John Millington Synge, is about an old woman who has lost her husband and five sons to the sea. Malcolm Sargent conducts a cast that includes Olive Hall.

1937 Dance

Feb. 11   *The Sleeping Beauty* receives its American premiere. It is performed by the Philadelphia Ballet and features choreography by Catherine Littlefield.

Feb. 16   The Vic-Wells Ballet presents the first performance of Frederick Ashton's one-act ballet *Les Patineurs* to music by Giacomo Meyerbeer. The ballet is based on movements associated with ice skating. Harold Turner, Margot Fonteyn, Mary Honer, Elizabeth Miller, Pamela May and June Brae star. The performance takes place at the Sadler's Wells Theater in London.

Feb. 19   The Ballet Rambert gives the premiere of Antony Tudor's *Dark Elegies*. The work, to Gustav Mahler's *Kindertotenlieder*, is a powerful psychological study of grief. It becomes one of Tudor's greatest works. The Mahler piece includes a voice part for contralto soloist. Today's performance, however, features a baritone. Peggy van Praagh, Agnes De Mille, Maude Lloyd, Antony Tudor and Hugh Laing are in the opening cast. The one-act ballet is staged at the Duchess Theater in London.

Feb. 23   Choreographer Andree Howard's *Death and the Maiden*, set to music by Franz Schubert with costumes by the choreographer, is premiered by the Ballet Rambert in London. It is a one-act ballet about a young girl facing death.

April 23   The Littlefield Ballet Company premieres Catherine Littlefield's *Barn Dance* in Philadelphia. The work, which uses traditional music, becomes the signature piece of the Littlefield Company. Dorothie Littlefield and Thomas Cannon have the principal roles.

April 27   Frederick Ashton's *A Wedding Bouquet* is performed for the first time by the Vic-Wells Ballet in London. The scenery, costumes and music are by Lord Berners, and the words are by Gertrude Stein. The ballet is a comedy about a French wedding. Margot Fonteyn, Mary Honer, Robert Helpmann and June Brae star.

April 27-28   The American Ballet presents a Stravinsky festival of three ballets choreographed by George Balanchine: *Apollon Musagete*, *La Baiser de la fee* and *Jeu de cartes*. The composer conducts these works at the Metropolitan Opera House, New York. *Apollon Musagete*, with costumes and scenery by Stewart Chaney, is a restaging of Balanchine's 1928 ballet. *Le Baiser de la fee* is Balanchine's version of the

Stravinsky score originally choreographed by Bronislava Nijinska in 1928. *Jeu de cartes*, which is having its world premiere at this festival, has costumes and scenery by Irene Sharaff. The ballet is about a poker game with the dancers as playing cards. William Dollar heads the cast.

June 15   *Checkmate* is premiered during the Sadler's Wells Ballet's Paris tour. Ninette de Valois choreographs this one-act ballet (with prologue) to music by Arthur Bliss. Decor is by E. McKnight Kauffer. It is a dance in which chess pieces enact scenes of love and death. Robert Helpmann, June Brae, Pamela May and Harold Turner star.

Oct. 23   Michel Fokine's *Le coq d'or* is premiered by the Ballet Russe de Monte Carlo. The music is by Nikolai Rimsky-Korsakov; libretto by V. Byelsky, based on a poem by Pushkin; and costumes and scenery by Nathalie Gontcharova. Lead dancers are Irina Baronova and Tatiana Riabouchinska.

Nov. 20   The Ballets Polonais premieres Bronislava Nijinska's *Chopin Concerto*. The ballet, to the Concerto for Piano and Orchestra in E minor, is a plotless work in three movements. Olga Slawska, Nina Yuszkiewicz and Zbigniew Kilinski star. The piece is danced at the Theatre de Mogador in Paris.

1937 Instrumental and Vocal Music

Jan. 21   Ernest Bloch's *Voice in the Wilderness* (a symphonic poem for orchestra and cello obbligato) is premiered by Otto Klemperer and the Los Angeles Philharmonic, with Alexander Borisoff as soloist.

Jan. 21   The Cleveland Orchestra premieres Samuel Barber's Symphony No. 1. Artur Rodzinski conducts.

Jan. 21   Paul Sacher and the Chamber Orchestra of Basel give the first performance of Bela Bartok's *Music for Strings, Percussion and Celesta*. Composed last year, it includes a harp and piano.

Jan. 25   Russian-French composer Ivan Wyschnegradsky's quarter-tone pieces *Symphonic Fragments*, *Thus Spake Zarathustra*, *Etudes en forme de scherzo* and *Preludes* are premiered in Paris. The composer conducts.

Feb. 20   Sergei Prokofiev's symphonic piece *Lieutenant Kije*, using music previously composed for a film, receives its initial performance in Paris with the composer conducting.

March 19   Symphony No. 2 by Emerson Whithorne, is premiered by Eugene Goossens and the Cincinnati Symphony Orchestra.

March 24   David Diamond's Violin Concerto receives its first performance by violinist-composer Nicolai Berezowsky in New York. The composer conducts. Diamond, now 21, has studied with Bernard Rogers, Roger Sessions and Nadia Boulanger.

April 15   Sergei Prokofiev's second orchestral suite, taken from his ballet *Romeo and Juliet*, premieres in Moscow.

April 30   Symphony No. 1 by British composer Edmund Rubbra, premieres in London. This is a three-movement symphony. Rubbra, now 35, has studied with Cyril Scott, Gustav Holst, John Ireland, Eugene Goossens and Ralph Vaughan Williams.

May 9   William Walton's march *Crown Imperial* premieres over BBC Radio. The work was composed for the coronation of George VI.

May 12   *Festival Te Deum*, by Ralph Vaughan Williams, premieres at the coronation of King George VI along with the second performance of William Walton's *Crown Imperial*. Both works were composed especially for the coronation ceremonies.

May 23   William Grant Still's *Lenox Avenue* premieres over CBS Radio in New York. This symphonic piece depicts life in Harlem.

May 26   Vittorio Giannini's *Requiem* receives its first performance in Vienna, with Dusolina Giannini, his sister, as soprano soloist.

June 8   Carl Orff's *Carmina Burana* premieres in Frankfurt. This oratorio is set to Latin texts, some of which are quite ribald. It is scored for soloists, choruses, orchestra and expanded percussion. This is the first part of his "Trionfi" trilogy (the other two parts are *Catulli Carmina* and *Trionfo di Afrodite).*

June 20   Walter Piston's *Concerto for Piano and Chamber Orchestra* premieres over CBS Radio in New York with the composer conducting.

July 1   *Scaramouche*, Op. 165b, by Darius Milhaud, premieres in Paris. This suite for two solo pianos has three movements, the last of which features a samba. The piece was composed for pianists Ida Jankelvitch and Marcelle Meyer. Milhaud expected the work to be a failure because he thought it lacked popular appeal. It is highly successful, and he subsequently adapts it for saxophone (or clarinet) and orchestra.

July 5   Concerto for Piano and Orchestra, by Aram Khachaturian, receives its first performance in Leningrad, with the composer as soloist. The three-movement work is so successful that it establishes Khachaturian as an important

Armenian composer. Cast in a folklike mood, it becomes one of Khachaturian's most frequently performed works.

July 25   *Music for Radio*, by Aaron Copland, is premiered by the CBS Orchestra. A contest is subsequently held for a title to be given to the work. The winner is *Saga of the Prairie*.

Aug. 17   John Ireland's *A London Overture* receives its initial performance by Sir Henry Wood at a Promenade Concert in London.

Aug. 27   Aaron Copland's symphonic work *El salon Mexico* receives its world premiere by Carlos Chavez and the Orquesta Sinfonica de Mexico. Copland composed this piece after visiting Mexico five years ago. He describes the work as "a kind of modified potpourri in which Mexican themes and their extensions are sometimes inextricably mixed for use of conciseness and coherence."

Sep. 12   *Suite Provencal*, by Darius Milhaud, premieres in Venice, the composer conducting. It is an orchestral suite of eight dances based on 18th-century folk songs of Provence.

Sep. 19   The CBS Orchestra in New York premieres Howard Hanson's Symphony No. 3 (first three movements only). The composer conducts. The composer says the music "pays tribute to the epic qualities of the pio-

neers." A complete performance, including the Finale, takes place on March 26 of next year.

Oct. 1   Nikolai Miaskovsky's Symphony No. 18 in C Major premieres in Moscow. This three-movement symphony celebrates the 20th anniversary of the Russian Revolution and includes melodies indigenous to Russia.

Oct. 6   William Walton's *In Honour of the City of London* receives its initial performance at the Leeds Festival. The piece, scored for chorus and orchestra, has a text by William Dunbar.

Oct. 26   Peter Stadlen premieres Anton Webern's *Variations for Piano*, Op. 27, in Vienna.

Nov. 21   The Leningrad Philharmonic premieres Dmitri Shostakovich's Symphony No. 5. This event marks the composer's first performance since the official Soviet denunciation of his *Lady Macbeth of the District of Mtsensk*. The symphony reflects his adherence to and acceptance of "socialist realism." Fifteen years from now, the work is performed in America, and Warren Storey Smith writes in the Boston *Post*, "There are agreeable passages and also a deal of frivolity, of vulgarity and bombast."

Nov. 27   Alberto Ginastera's symphonic suite, from his ballet *Panambi*, premieres in Buenos Aires.

1937   Births, Deaths and Debuts

Jan. 4   Soprano Grace Bumbry is born in St. Louis, Missouri.

Jan. 10   American dancer Edward Villella is born on Long Island, New York.

Jan. 10   American organist and writer Clarence Eddy, 86, dies in Chicago. He performed at many world exhibitions, beginning with Vienna in 1873, and is credited with having played for more audiences than any other American organist of his day.

Jan. 18   Conductor David Wulstan is born in Birmingham, England.

Jan. 22   British music patron and writer Walter Wilson Cobbett, 89, dies in London. A contributor to Grove's *Dictionary of Music and Musicians*, he edited and published the *Cyclopedic Survey of Chamber Music*.

Feb. 13   Brazilian soprano Bidu Sayao makes her debut at the Metropolitan Opera in Jules Massenet's *Manon*. Olin Downes writes in the New York *Times*, "She made the woman real."

March 12   French organist, composer and teacher Charles-Marie Widor, 93, dies in Paris. Widor began organ improvisation when he was a child and received his first job as a church organist at age 14. At 23 he was appointed

organist at Saint-Sulpice in Paris and maintained that position for 60 years. He later taught counterpoint, fugue, composition and organ at the Paris Conservatoire. He also wrote music criticism and conducted. His impact was largely as a first-rate organist of his day. His compositions reflect a style distinctly French and highly idiomatic to the organ. Although he wrote several operas, a ballet, symphonic works and choral, chamber and piano music, he is best known for his organ symphonies. Albert Schweitzer was one of Widor's pupils. They collaborated on editing the first five volumes of the eight-volume edition of Johann Sebastian Bach's organ works.

March 16   Composer David Del Tredici is born in Cloverdale, California.

March 28   Polish composer Karol Szymanowski, 54, dies in Lausanne, Switzerland. He began to compose and play piano early in his childhood and had his first piano piece, Nine Preludes for Piano, Op. 1, published at age 24. He was heavily influenced by the music of Richard Strauss when he lived in Berlin in 1906 and 1908. A later influence was Alexander Scriabin. French impressionism began to attract him just before the Russian Revolution. During the revolution, he lost most of his property (his family owned land in Timovshovka). At age 44 he was appointed director of the Warsaw Conservatory.

Szymanowski established himself as the most important Polish composer of the first third of this century. Works such as the violin triptych *Mythes, Stabat Mater* and his ballet *Harnaise* attracted international attention; he was a composer favored by the International Society for Contemporary Music. His pieces reflect a profound sense of Polish nationalism within the context of harmonic innovation. Despite the formative influences of non-Polish music, he was able to retain his own identity and give Polish music a new image. He revered Chopin and often composed mazurkas (20 of them), though not in a style derivative of Chopin. Three operas, one ballet, three symphonies, two violin concertos, choral pieces, approximately 100 songs, chamber and piano music, and other pieces comprise his work.

April 8   American composer Arthur Foote, 84, dies in Boston. He was a university-trained composer and received the first A.M. degree ever given in America (Harvard University, 1875). His principal teacher was J.K. Paine. A year later, he went to Bayreuth for the Wagner Festival. He returned to America and settled in Boston, organizing concerts, performing as a pianist with the Kneisel Quartet and teaching. His honors were many: After being a founding member of the American Guild of Organists, he became its president; he was also a fellow of the American Academy of Arts and Sciences and a member of the National Institute of Arts and Letters. His career as a composer was greatly enhanced by the Boston Symphony Orchestra, which premiered many of his works.

His music is distinctly romantic, with fluid melodies and harmonies rooted in the 19th century. Despite the revolutionary musical events and movements taking place in Europe (particularly Vienna), he remained unaffected by the mark of formidable giants, such as Arnold Schoenberg. He composed a variety of orchestral works, choral pieces, chamber music and approximately 100 songs. Foote also wrote manuals on harmony, piano instruction, fugue and other musical subjects.

May 15   English organist, composer and writer on music John Ernest Borland, 71, dies in London. He assisted in composition of music for the coronations of Edward VII, George V and George VI. He also wrote *The Instruments of the Orchestra* and was an editor of *Musical News*.

May 15   Russian mezzo-soprano Jennie Tourel makes her Metropolitan Opera debut as Mignon.

May 18   Arnold Gantvoort, 79, dies in Los Angeles. He was chairman of a 1914 National Education Association committee to revise national songs, including the "Star Spangled Banner." He also published many books.

May 21   American Indian Lusschanya Mobley makes her debut singing the title role in *Aida* in Trieste, Italy. Of Chickasaw descent, she is believed to be the first American Indian to sing opera in Europe. She sings this performance after having won a scholarship offered by Benito Mussolini to study at the University of Rome. She had received permission from the American Consulate to participate in the competition.

June 5   American music critic William James Henderson, 81, commits suicide in New York City. This critic wrote principally for the New York *Times* and the New York *Sun*; he also wrote several books about music and some poetry. A graduate of Princeton University, he studied piano and voice. He hated contemporary music and used his writing skills to attack Claude Debussy and Richard Strauss. The reason for his suicide is not known.

July 6   Pianist Vladimir Ashkenazy is born in Gorki, Russia.

July 7   Soprano Elena Obraztsova is born in Leningrad, Russia.

July 11   American composer George Gershwin, 38, dies in Hollywood of a brain tumor. Gershwin began his piano performances at age 16 and, throughout his life, studied with many composers. These included Rubin Goldmark, Henry Cowell, Wallingford Riegger and Josph Schillinger. At age 19 his song "Swanee" was published — it sold over a million copies, as well as 2 1/4 million phonograph records. His career as a 20th-century classical composer was advanced with the premiere of *Rhapsody in Blue* (1924), although he was criticized for having the piece orchestrated by Ferde Grofe. Gershwin quickly began doing his own orchestrations. His music combines lyrical melodies, inventive rhythms, jazz and folk elements in an original fashion. He was not passionate about intellectual expression in music, though he did attempt to systematize his compositional technique by studying with Schillinger.

His impact in America was enormous: He was a figure who straddled the fence between popular music and serious concert music. His opera *Porgy and Bess*, perhaps his masterpiece, flourishes despite the mixed reaction it received at its premiere. Unlike Aaron Copland, who is two years younger, Gershwin did not (largely because of his premature death) have the opportunity to extend himself fully to the international world of contemporary music. Besides those mentioned, Gershwin's works include many musical comedies, film music, piano transcriptions and songs.

July 17   French composer Gabriel Pierne, 73, dies in Ploujean, Brittany, France. He was a product of the Paris Conservatoire, where his teachers included Cesar Franck and Jules Massenet. At age 19 he won the Grand Prix de Rome for his cantata *Edith*. He later became organist at Ste.-Clothilde, succeeding Cesar Franck. He also conducted. His composing output was substantial, yet he never made a mark on the world as an extremely important 20th-century composer. His most famous works are *La Croisade des enfants* (oratorio) and *Marche de petits soldats de plomb* (for piano). He composed 5 operas, 10 ballets (including pantomimes), much chamber music and piano music, as well as many oratorios and songs.

Aug. 23   French composer Albert Roussel, 68, dies in Royan, France. As a youngster, he had no formal conservatory training in music (apart from private organ study). He concentrated on mathematics and joined the French navy at age 18. While serving on the frigate *Iphigenie*, he vi-

ALBERT ROUSSEL

sited Indochina and was influenced by Oriental culture. It was not until age 25, after several naval assignments and voyages, that he decided to devote himself exclusively to musical composition. He went to Paris and studied with Vincent d'Indy. At age 37, he was engaged to teach counterpoint at the Schola Cantorum where his pupils included Erik Satie and Edgard Varese. He then went to India and was again influenced by foreign culture. After World War I he settled in Normandy.

Though he was not a formidable French composer, his work did evolve from French impressionism to neoclassicism. These stylistic changes, coupled with his attraction to Oriental subjects and ability to depict humor through music, made him a successful composer of stage works. He

composed numerous operas and ballet-pantomimes, four symphonies, other orchestral works, choral works, chamber music and songs.

Sep. 6   American composer Henry Hadley, 65, dies in New York. A pupil of George W. Chadwick at the New England Conservatory, he later traveled to Vienna and toured Germany as a conductor of his own pieces. He returned to America and was a conductor of the Seattle Symphony, the San Francisco Symphony Orchestra and the New York Philharmonic.

As a composer, he ascended to an unchallenged position in the United States for a composer of his generation. His music, though not by any means revolutionary, was performed internationally because Hadley often toured as a conductor and would schedule his own works. His works are often programmatic and sometimes include dense harmonies and impressionistic textures. His impact, both as a composer and as a conductor, was to substantially help American music gain a respected position in a European-dominated music world. He composed eight operatic works, five symphonies, overtures, tone poems, anthems, songs and piano pieces.

Oct. 6   Dancer Merle Park is born in Salisbury, Rhodesia.

Oct. 11   Violinist Isaac Stern makes his New York debut.

Cct. 21   American pianist Julius Katchen makes his d but with the Philadelphia Orchestra.

Nov. 9   Franco Autori conducts his first concert with the Buffalo Philharmonic Orchestra Society at Elmwood Music Hall in Buffalo, New York. The program consists of music by Beethoven and Brahms. Albert Spalding performs as violin soloist. Autori remains music director of this ensemble until 1945, when William Steinberg takes over.

Dec. 17   Yugoslavian soprano Zinka Milanov makes her Metropolitan Opera debut as Leonora in *Il Trovatore*.

1937   Related Events

The Philharmonic Radio of New York (marketing the home use of ultra-high quality sound reproducing equipment) is founded this year by Avery R. Fisher. The offset head pickup is developed this year by Benjamin Bauer.

Jan. 5   Sergei Prokofiev wins his lawsuit brought against Serge Lifar for failing to pay him the remaining 30,000 francs for his ballet *Sur le Borysthene*. The work premiered in Paris on December 16, 1932, and lack of public enthusiasm forced the production to close. Lifar had originally agreed to pay Prokofiev 100,000 francs for the music and for exclusive performance rights. When the work was panned, Lifar paid Prokofiev only 70,000 francs; Prokofiev sued for

the remaining 30,000. Lifar's defense was based on his assertion that the ballet failed because the music was weak. The judge disagrees and states, in part, "any person acquiring a musical work puts faith in the composer's talent, since there is no dependable criterion for the evaluation of the quality of a work of art, which is received according to individual tastes, history teaching us that the public is often mistaken."

Jan. 14   Anton Webern writes a letter to Nicolas Slonimsky thanking him for publishing the fourth piece ("Fleissend, ausserst zart") of his Five Pieces for Orchestra, Op. 10, on the children's page of the *Christian*

Science Monitor. He says, in part, "Yes, it is true that if the so-called adults, the grown-ups, had as few prejudices as children, then everything would be quite different."

Jan. 26   As of today, music of Brazilian composers is to be featured on music programs in that country. The ruling is handed down by the Brazilian Parliament.

Feb. 2   The New York *Times* reports that the Academy of Santa Cecilia has two new members — George Gershwin and Heitor Villa-Lobos.

April 23   The official German news agency announces that Jewish conductor Leo Blech is now retired from his post as music director of the Berlin Opera because of old age. A former pupil of Engelbert Humperdinck, Blech is 66 years old.

May 24   Nazi Germany's 1933 International Society for Promoting Cooperation Among Composers features a music festival in Dresden that includes music of Henk Badings, Carl Nielsen, Paul Graener, Jon Leifs and Bela Bartok. Pantcho Vladigerov, who is part Jewish, is given special permission to have his music performed at these concerts.

June 5   The BBC televises the third act of Charles Gounod's *Faust* to a local London studio. This event marks the first time part of an opera is televised.

June 12   A concert of modern Dutch music — which includes music of composers Henk Badings, Johan Wagenaar, Guillaume Landre and Bertus Van Lier — is given in Amsterdam. The group is entitled the Manifestatie Van Nederlandsche Toonkunst (Maneto). Today's concert is the group's first.

June 12   After 68 years of annual music festivals, the members of the German Tonkunstler Verein terminate the organization as a result of Nazi policies. Originated by Franz Liszt, the group held festivals in Darmstadt and Frankfurt.

July 6   Adolf Hitler signs a decree requiring Gottfried Sonntag's *Nibelungen-Marsch* to be performed at all Nazi Party meetings. The music has roots in Wagner's *Ring* cycle.

July 27   Igor Stravinsky receives 1 French franc in official resolution of the 300,000-franc suit he brought against Warner Brothers for having used *The Firebird* to suggest sexual seduction in its film of the same title.

Aug. 12   The first Tanglewood concert takes place as Serge Koussevitzky conducts the Boston Symphony Orchestra in an outdoor program of music by Richard Wagner. As the first piece on the program, *The Ride of the Valkyries*, is played, a fierce storm breaks. Rain pours on the musicians and audience, damaging many of the instruments and forcing a change in the second half of the program. Patrons, musicians and management subsequently voice the need to construct a permanent concert shed for these concerts. This is begun this December and completed next June. The inaugural concert at the new shed takes place on August 4 of next year at the first *Berkshire Festival.*

Nov. 2   The Louisville Orchestra (Louisville, Kentucky) gives its first concert today, Robert Whitney conducting.

Nov. 4   Nicolas Slonimsky's *Music Since 1900* is published in its first edition by W.W. Norton Company in New York. This book becomes a classic chronology of 20th-century music and documents thousands of musical facts in an often humorous style.

Nov. 28   Pianist Josef Hofmann gives his golden jubilee recital at the Metropolitan Opera House. He had played there as a child 50 years earlier.

Dec. 19   The American Composers' Alliance is established today in New York City. Its chairman is Aaron Copland. Its purpose is to protect the performing rights of composers who do not belong to ASCAP (American Society of Composers Authors and Publishers) and to promote the musical and financial interests of serious American composers.

Dec. 23   Giovanni Battista Pergolesi's *La Serva padrona* is televised in London. This marks the first time an opera is televised in its entirety.

Dec. 25   Italian conductor Arturo Toscanini conducts his first concert with the NBC Symphony Orchestra, a radio orchestra that had been organized as a vehicle for him.

1938   Opera

Jan. 1   Licinio Refice's *Margherita da Cortona* receives its first performance at La Scala. The libretto is by Emidio Mucci.

March 16   Bohuslav Martinu's *Julietta* premieres in Prague. This three-act opera is about a young man who dreams about a beautiful woman.

May 28   Paul Hindemith's opera *Mathis der Maler* receives its world premiere in Zurich, Switzerland. Robert Denzler conducts. Based on paintings by Mathis Grunewald, the opera depicts a peasant revolt in Germany. It is considered, perhaps, to be Hindemith's masterpiece. The opera is subsequently performed in Boston and critic Cyrus Durgin writes "*Mathis* is a heavy, German-style opera in the unique musical manner of the composer."

June 2   Vittorio Giannini's two-act opera *The Scarlet Letter*, based on the tale by Nathaniel Hawthorne, receives its first performance at the State Opera of Hamburg in a German version entitled *Das Brandmal*. Giannini is now 34 years old.

June 15   Ernst Krenek's *Karl V*, composed five years ago, receives its first performance in Prague. It is Krenek's first piece composed according to the 12-tone method. The story is about a Roman emperor who speaks to God.

July 24   *Friedenstag*, a one-act opera by Richard Strauss, receives its first performance at the Nationaltheater in Munich. The libretto, by Josef Gregor, is set in the besieged city of Bada at the end of the 30 Years' War. The opera is one of Strauss' least successful, due, in part, to a poor libretto. Clemens Krauss conducts.

Sep. 26   Kurt Weill's *Knickerbocker Holiday*, a musical that includes his tune "September Song," premieres in Hartford, Connecticut. Book and lyrics are by Maxwell Anderson, based on *Father Knickerbocker's History of New York*.

Oct. 15   *Daphne*, by Richard Strauss, is performed for the first time at the Dresden Staatsoper. Josef Gregor's libretto is based on the Greek myth of Apollo and Daphne. Karl Bohm conducts this one-act opera. The cast includes Marguerite Teschemacher and Torsten Ralf.

Nov. 24   Werner Egk's *Peer Gynt*, with a libretto based on Henrik Ibsen, premieres at the Berlin State Opera with the composer conducting. The three-act opera is denounced by the Nazis until Adolf Hitler attends a performance and decides he likes it.

Nov. 24   Vittorio Giannini's one-act opera *Beauty and the Beast* receives its first concert radio broadcast over CBS. Its first stage performance takes place in 1946.

1938 Dance

Jan. 6   *Filling Station* — a one-act ballet choreographed by Lew Christensen to music of Virgil Thomson, with costumes and scenery by Paul Cadmus and book by Lincoln Kirstein — is performed for the first time by the Ballet Caravan in Hartford, Connecticut. This work is a comedy involving cops and gangsters. The choreographer is the principal dancer.

Jan. 7   The Paris Opera premieres Serge Lifar's *Oriane et le Prince d'Amour*. Florent Schmitt composes the music to this choral ballet. It is about a woman who enjoys seducing men until she accidentally seduces Death and perishes. Schmitt is now 67 years old. The title was originally *Oriane la sans-egale*; Lifar suggested it be changed.

April 5   The Ballet Russe de Monte Carlo premieres Leonide Massine's *Gaite Parisienne*, to music by Jacques Offenbach, in Monte Carlo. The ballet, using some of the characters from Offenbach's *La Vie Parisienne*, deals with flirtations at a Paris nightclub. Nina Tarakanova, Eugenia Delarova, Lubov Roudenko, Leonide Massine, Frederic Franklin and Igor Youskevitch star.

April 14   *The Prisoner of the Caucasus* premieres at the Maly Theater in Leningrad. It is choreographed by Leonid Lavrovsky and I. Zilbershtein, with music by Boris Asafiev, book by Nikolai Volkov, and designs by Valentina Khodasevich. This is one of several ballets inspired by Pushkin's poem of the same title.

May 5   The Ballet Russe de Monte Carlo gives the initial performance in Monte Carlo of Leonide Massine's *Seventh Symphony*, set to Beethoven's Symphony No. 7. Decor is by Christian Berand. The abstract work in four movements deals with the creation and destruction of the Earth. Alicia Markova, Jeannette Lauret, Nini Theilande, Frederic Franklin and Igor Youskevitch have the lead roles.

May 30   Choreographer Jan Veen premieres his modern dance work *The Incredible Flutist* at a Boston Pops concert. The music is choreographed to the work of the same title by Walter Piston.

June 15   Antony Tudor's *The Judgment of Paris* premieres in London at the Westminster Theater. The music is by Kurt Weill and the costumes by Hugh Laing. Agnes de Mille, Charlotte Bidmead, Therese Langfield, Hugh Laing and Antony Tudor comprise the cast in this satirical treatment of Juno, Minerva and Venus.

June 19   The Educational Ballets in London gives the world premiere of Michel Fokine's one-act version of *Cinderella*. The ballet, with music by Frederic d'Erlanger and decor by Nathalie Gontcharova, stars Tatiana Riabouchinska and Paul Petroff.

June 19   *Frankie and Johnny*, a ballet choreographed by Ruth Page and Bentley Stone to music by Jerome Moross, is performed for the first time by the Page-Stone Ballet in Chicago. The scenery and costumes are by Paul Dupont. The libretto is based on the words of the popular song. The work is produced for a dance project of the WPA and is subsequently performed in New York City by the Ballet Russe de Monte Carlo in 1945.

June 28   *The Heart of the Hills* is performed for the first time by the Kirov Ballet in Leningrad. The work, in three acts and five scenes, is choreographed by Vakhtang Chabukiani to music by Andrei Balanchivadze (George Balanchine's brother). The story is one of Georgian history dealing with revolution against taxation. The designs are by Simon Virsaladze.

July 21   Leonide Massine presents his *Nobilissima visione*, a one-act ballet based on the life of Saint Francis of Assisi and set to music by Paul Hindemith. Massine, Jeannette Lauret, Lubov Rostova, Nini Theilade, Frederic Franklin and Simon Semenoff lead the Ballet Russe de Monte Carlo in the opening performance in Monte Carlo.

Aug. 6   *American Document* (choreographed by Martha Graham to music by Ray Green), Charles Weidman's *Opus* and Hanya Holm's *Dance Sonata* and *Metropolitan Day* receive their first performances at Bennington College in Bennington, Vermont. Holm was born in Worms, Germany in 1898. In 1921 she joined Mary Wigman's school and became a teacher and dancer, performing in premieres of Wigman's works. Holm inaugurated the New York branch of Wigman's school in 1931 and established her own dance studio two years ago.

Oct. 10   The Mordkin Russian Ballet premieres Alexander Tcherepnin's ballet *Trepak* in Richmond, Virginia.

Oct. 16   While on tour in Chicago, the Ballet Caravan premieres Eugene Loring's *Billy the Kid* , to music by Aaron Copland. The one-act ballet deals with the heroic myth of Billy the Kid. Loring, Marie Jeanne, Lew Christensen and

Todd Bolender dance the first performance. The music reflects Copland's ability to compose a full-length work incorporating American folk melodies without mere quotation and repetition.

Oct. 20   Leonide Massine's *Bogatyri*, with music by Alexander Borodin and costumes and scenery by Nathalie Gontcharova, is premiered by the Ballet Russe de Monte Carlo at the Metropolitan Opera House in New York. The ballet, about knights in a royal court, stars Alexandra Danilova.

Nov. 26   Antony Tudor premieres his ballet *Soiree musicale* during a Cecchetti Society matinee in London. The divertissement, to music by Benjamin Britten, stars Gerd Larsen, Hugh Laing, Maude Lloyd, Tudor, Peggy van Praagh, Monica Boam and Guy Massey.

Dec. 5   The London Ballet premieres Antony Tudor's *Gala Performance* at Toynbee Hall in London. The comic work, to Sergei Prokofiev's *Classical Symphony*, is a spoof on the characteristics of three schools of ballet — the Russian, Italian and French. Peggy van Praagh, Maude Lloyd, and Gerd Larsen star.

1938   Instrumental and Vocal Music

Jan. 5   Sergei Prokofiev's choral-orchestral work *Songs of Our Day* premieres in Moscow. This set of nine pieces includes a tribute to Joseph Stalin.

Jan. 16   Bela Bartok's Sonata for Two Pianos and Percussion receives its first performance in Basel, Switzerland with the composer and his wife as soloists. This three-movement work treats the piano as a percussion instrument and includes xylophone solos.

Feb. 11   The San Francisco Symphony Orchestra premieres Ernest Bloch's orchestral suite entitled *Evocation*. The work, which was composed between 1930 and 1937, has three sections, the last of which is about life in San Francisco.

Feb. 19   Egon Wellesz' symphonic poem *Prosperos Beschwörung*, based on Shakespeare's *The Tempest*, is premiered by Bruno Walter in Vienna. Anton Bruckner's Fourth Symphony is performed on the same program. This event marks the final concert Bruno Walter conducts with the Vienna Philharmonic prior to the Nazi takeover of Austria.

March 17   Ernst Krenek's Piano Concerto No. 2 receives its initial performance by Bruno Walter and the Concertgebouw Orchestra in Amsterdam, with the composer as soloist. This four-movement concerto is dodecaphonic.

March 26   Symphony No. 3, by Howard Hanson, receives its first performance in its complete version over ra-

dio by the NBC Symphony Orchestra in New York, the composer conducting. A partial performance of the work took place on September 19 of last year.

March 30   William Walton's second orchestral suite from *Facade* premieres in New York City.

April 2   The New York Philharmonic premieres Quincy Porter's Symphony No. 1. The composer conducts. Porter, now 41, succeeds Frederick Converse as dean of the New England Conservatory this year.

April 8   Walter Piston's Symphony No. 1 is premiered by the Boston Symphony Orchestra, the composer conducting. The three-movement symphony was composed last year. Today's performance does not attract great attention.

April 22   Serge Koussevitzky and the Boston Symphony Orchestra premiere Leo Sowerby's Concerto for Organ and Orchestra. E. Power Biggs is soloist.

April 27   Marcel Dupre's Concerto for Organ and Orchestra premieres in Groningen, Holland, with the composer as soloist.

May 8   Igor Stravinsky's Concerto in E-flat Major (*Dumbarton Oaks*) receives its world premiere in Washington, D.C. Nadia Boulanger conducts. The neoclassical piece is dedicated to Robert Woods Bliss (a wealthy patron) and is

ARTHUR HONEGGER

named for that man's estate. The three-movement work contains much fugal writing. Next month, the piece is performed in Paris, and critic Boris Schloezer says in his *Dernieres Nouvelles* that the music "sounds strangely dull. It abounds in scholastic cliches and banalities."

May 12   Arthur Honegger's *Jeanne d'Arc au Bucher* receives its world premiere in Basel, Switzerland. Paul Sacher conducts the Chamber Orchestra of Basel. The dramatic oratorio, completed three years ago, is set to a text by Paul Claudel and includes spoken dialogue within its prologue and seven scenes. It is about Joan of Arc and, in this piece, she performs her role on the stake. It becomes one of Honegger's most successful works. Ida Rubinstein performs the speaking role of Saint Joan. The "mimodrama" is most often performed as an oratorio.

May 25   William Schuman's Symphony No. 2 is premiered in New York by the Greenwich Orchestra.

June 15   Franz Schmidt's oratorio *Das Buch mit sieben Siegeln*, his last composition, premieres in Vienna. The text is from the New Testament.

June 17   Anton Webern's *Das Augenlicht*, Op. 26, receives its world premiere by Hermann Scherchen and the BBC Symphony Orchestra and chorus. The work, which includes canonic writing, is scored for mixed chorus and orchestra. Its text is by Hildegard Jone. The performance takes place as part of this year's International Society for Contemporary Music festival. The work is the first of three of the composer's last important vocal works (the other two are his cantatas).

July 31   Morton Gould's *Second American Symphonette* is premiered by the New York Philharmonic at Lewisohn Stadium, the composer conducting. The piece includes jazz elements. Gould is now 24 years old.

Aug. 18   Benjamin Britten's Piano Concerto is premiered by Sir Henry Wood in London, with the composer as soloist. The four-movement concerto is later revised by the composer. Britten is now 24.

Sep. 3   *Conquest of the Air*, a symphonic suite in six movements by Arthur Bliss, receives its first performance in London. Bliss conducts.

Sep. 22   Anton Webern's String Quartet, Op. 28, is performed for the first time by the Kolisch Quartet in Pittsfield, Massachusetts. Commissioned by and dedicated to Elizabeth Sprague Coolidge, it is the last of Webern's chamber works. Today's performance is part of the Tenth Berkshire Festival of Chamber Music. As is characteristic of this composer, the work is canonic within a dodecaphonic context.

Oct. 5   Ralph Vaughan Williams' *Serenade to Music*, based on Shakespeare's *The Merchant of Venice*, is premiered by Sir Henry Wood at a Promenade Concert in London. Scored for 16 solo voices and orchestra, it is praised as one of the composer's most sensuous works.

Nov. 5   Samuel Barber's *Adagio for Strings* and *First Essay for Orchestra* are premiered by Arturo Toscanini and the NBC Symphony Orchestra in New York. The *Adagio* is an arrangement for string orchestra of a movement from the composer's string quartet. It becomes one of the composer's most famous works and a favorite of the music public.

Nov. 26   Sergei Prokofiev's Concerto for Cello and Orchestra in E Minor is premiered by Mstislav Rostropovich in Moscow. The three-movement piece was composed between 1934 and 1938.

Nov. 29   Aram Khachaturian's symphonic work *A Poem About Stalin* premieres in Moscow at the Second Festival of Soviet Music. It praises Joseph Stalin.

Dec. 2   The Minneapolis Symphony Orchestra presents the first performance of Darius Milhaud's Piano Concerto No. 1. Dimitri Mitropoulos is both conductor and soloist.

Dec. 15   Ernest Bloch's Violin Concerto is premiered by Dimitri Mitropoulos and the Cleveland Orchestra, with Joseph Szigeti as soloist. The work employs Hebrew modes and is in three movements.

Dec. 16   *An Outdoor Overture* by Aaron Copland, premieres in New York at the High School of Music and Art. Composed specifically for young people to perform, it was written while Copland was working on *Billy the Kid*.

Dec. 16   Edmund Rubbra's Symphony No. 2 premieres in London. The symphony is in D major.

1938   Births, Deaths and Debuts

Jan. 4   Tenor Jussi Bjorling makes his formal New York recital debut at Town Hall, singing music of Mozart, Verdi, Puccini, Schubert and Hugo Alfven. *Musical America* (New York) says of the event: "It was immediately evident that once more, Scandinavia had sent us a singer of technical perfection."

Jan. 13   Rudolf Firkusny, 25, makes his American debut at Town Hall in New York City, performing works of Liszt (Sonata in B Minor), etudes and mazurkas of Chopin, and other pieces by Josef Suk, Debussy, Prokofiev, Bohuslav Martinu, Bedrich Smetana and Bach-Busoni. A review in *Musical America* (New York) says, "Interpretively, the pianist was more at home in compositions of smaller framework than among the more massive proportions of the Liszt sonata."

Jan. 21   Austrian conductor Erich Leinsdorf makes his American debut conducting *Die Walkure* at the Metropolitan Opera. Lawrence Gilman writes in the New York *Herald-Tribune* that "he [Leinsdorf] soon made it evident that he was entirely at home in the great work before him. . . . He knew what he wanted from his orchestra, and how to get it. . . . It was impossible to doubt that his ability was extraordinary. . . ."

Feb. 16   Composer John Corigliano Jr. is born in New York City.

March 17   Soviet dancer and choreographer Rudolf Nureyev is born on a train between Lake Baikal and Irkutsk, USSR.

RUDOLF FIRKUSNY

JUSSI BJORLING

March 18   English composer Cyril Rootham, 62, dies in Cambridge, England. His work includes chamber, orchestral and choral music as well as his opera, *The Two Sisters*. He was also an organist at Saint John's College, Cambridge.

April 12   Russian bass Feodor Chaliapin, 65, dies in Paris. Apprenticed to a cobbler at age 10, he was singing in the chorus of a traveling opera troupe in the company of Maxim Gorky by the time he was 14. By 1896 he was an established singer in Russia. He created a sensation in Paris when brought there by Serge Diaghilev in 1908 to sing *Boris Godunov* but failed to make a favorable first impression in America. By the 1920s, however, he was universally recognized as being one of the world's greatest singing actors. He wrote two autobiographical books: *Pages from My Life* and *Man and Mask*.

May 17   Dancer Paolo Bortoluzzi is born in Genoa, Italy.

May 25   Dom Paolo Feretti, 71, dies in Bologna. He was president of the Pontifical Institute of Sacred Music in Rome and taught at the Pius X School of Liturgical Music in New York City.

May 26   Soprano Teresa Stratas is born in Toronto, Canada.

May 30   Spanish tenor Miguel Fleta, 44, dies in La Coruna. Thought by some to be another Caruso, he sang with the Metropolitan Opera for two seasons before becoming involved in a lawsuit for breach of contract.

June 2   Hans von Wolzogen, 90, dies in Bayreuth. This individual is known for having made popular the term *leitmotiv* in relation to Wagner's music.

June 9   Composer Charles Wuorinen is born in New York City.

Aug. 14   Musicologist Abraham Zevi Idelsohn, 56, dies in Johannesburg, South Africa. He studied at the Leipzig Conservatory and sang as a baritone in addition to pursuing musicology. In 1910, he established the Institute for Jewish Music in Jerusalem. He later lectured in America at the Hebrew Union College in Cincinnati. He was known as an authority on Jewish music and wrote many books, including *History of Jewish Music* (1924), and the 10-volume *Thesaurus of Hebrew-Oriental Melodies* (1914-32).

Sep. 6   Danish dancer Niels Kehlet is born in Copenhagen.

Oct. 2   Giulio Setti, 69, dies in Turin. He was associated with Giulio Gatti-Casazza and Arturo Toscanini and was chorus master of the Metropolitan Opera for 27 years.

Nov. 11   Frits Schuurman makes his debut as new music director of the Hague Philharmonic Orchestra, conducting music by Dvorak, Rachmaninoff, and others, at the Stadsgehoorzaal, Leyden.

Nov. 21   Pianist Leopold Godowsky, 67, dies in New York. One of the pianistic giants of his time, he started as a child prodigy in Russia and played his first concert in America at age 14 in 1884. He taught in the United States and Europe and eventually settled in America at the beginning of World War I. He was known for his prodigious technique and wrote many extremely difficult piano pieces. His arrangements of the Chopin etudes, make them even more difficult than the originals.

Nov. 24   Swedish tenor Jussi Bjorling makes his Metropolitan Opera debut as Rodolfo in *La Boheme*. Olin Downes writes in the New York *Times* of him: "The sum of it was a tenor of ample tone and quality for the role, with a B-flat which rings and carries, and which has by no means reached the summit of its development."

Dec. 3   Uruguayan-American conductor and composer Jose Serebrier is born in Montevideo.

Dec. 12   Albert Carre, 86, dies in Paris. He was director of the Opera-Comique for 23 years and presided over premiere productions of operas by Claude Debussy, Paul Dukas, Camille Saint-Saens, Vincent d'Indy and others. He was the nephew of Michael Carre, the librettist of Charles Gounod's *Faust*.

1938 *Related Events*

Gweneth Lloyd and Betty Farrally establish the Winnipeg Ballet this year in Canada. It is one of the earliest first-rank Canadian ballet companies. It subsequently becomes known as the Royal Winnipeg Ballet.

Jan. 13   The ondes musicales is patented by Maurice Martenot. Designed to electronically produce intervals of the Hindu Scale (1/12 tones), it has a microtonal keyboard.

Jan. 30   Leonide Massine leaves Colonel de Basil's Ballet Russe. Massine and Colonel de Basil had been feuding over artistic matters ever since 1934, when Rene Blum left the company (it was originally established in 1932 as the Rene Blum and Colonel de Basil Ballets Russes de Monte Carlo). Massine immediately relocates to Monte Carlo and joins another ballet company recently organized by Rene Blum for the Monte Carlo Opera. Massine approaches Blum about collaborating, and another partnership is arranged. Blum's new partner is a corporation — World Art Inc., later known as Universal Art Inc. — whose two principal representatives are businessman Julius Fleischmann and the New York financier Sergei I. Denham. Massine becomes artistic director.

This creates intense competition for Colonel de Basil and ignites an all-out war next month, when many of Colonel de Basil's best dancers defect to join the Blum-Massine company, which becomes known as the Ballet Russe de Monte Carlo. The new name creates immense confusion because of its similarity to the name of the ballet company formed by Blum and Colonel de Basil in 1932.

Feb.   Ballet stars Alexandra Danilova, Tamara Toumanova and others leave Colonel de Basil's Ballet Russe (now completing an American tour) and join Leonide Massine and Rene Blum in Monte Carlo, where last month they entered into partnership with World Art Inc. to create a new ballet company, the Ballet Russe de Monte Carlo. Impresario Sol Hurok subsequently announces that he is engaging the Massine-Blum group for an American tour instead of Colonel de Basil's fading company (Massine is the artistic director of the new Monte Carlo-based group; dancers Alicia Markova, Serge Lifar, Igor Youskevitch and others also join its ranks).

March   Colonel de Basil, Rene Blum and Leonide Massine announce that their two companies (Colonel de Basil's Ballet Russe and the Ballet Russe de Monte Carlo, recently formed by Blum, Massine and World Art Inc.) will merge and that Colonel de Basil will be on the board of governors. The company will be known as the Ballet Russe de Monte Carlo. World Art Inc. changes its name to Universal Art Inc. and, this June 17, restrains Colonel de Basil from exercising any substantive power over Massine and Blum.

March 9   The National Library of Scotland acquires the Balfour Handel Collection. This collection of 650 volumes of George Frederick Handel's scores and librettos contains many early editions, including some unique items.

March 24   Nazi composer Paul Winter's hymn *Grossdeutschland zum 10 April* premieres over Vienna Radio. This music is designed to encourage the Austrian people to vote in favor of Adolf Hitler's annexation of Austria on April 10th.

April 18   Gertrude Clarke Whittall donates funds for the construction of the Whittall Pavilion at the Library of Congress to house the Stradivari instruments she donated in 1935. The Budapest Quartet becomes the first to regularly use the precious instruments and is succeeded in 1962 by the Juilliard Quartet. Whittall also donates funds that enable the Music Division of the Library of Congress to acquire valuable manuscripts of music by Beethoven, Mozart, Schubert, Haydn and Brahms.

May 1   As of today, Jewish music students are prohibited by the Reichsmusikkammer from being taught by "Aryan" teachers.

May 6   Italian opera composer Gino Marinuzzi conducts a concert in Rome on the occasion of Adolf Hitler's visit. The massive event consists of 10,000 performers, including 45 military bands.

May 22   The first-prize winner of the Concours Ysaye is pianist Emil Gilels, 21, who competes with 95 other pianists. Belgian composer Jean Absil's piano concerto had been given to the 12 finalists a week before public performance, which was to be accompanied by an orchestra.

May 22   Music scores of Ernst Krenek, Ernst Toch, Ernest Bloch, Igor Stravinsky, Paul Hindemith, Alban Berg, Josef Matthias Hauer, Arnold Schoenberg, Hanns Eisler and others, as well as articles and monographs by these musicians, are featured as being degenerate at a Nazi music exhibition in Dusseldorf. Also today, a celebration of Nazi music begins in the same city, featuring Otto Besch's *Ostmark-Overture*, composed as a tribute to the annexation of Austria.

June 17   Universal Art Inc. initiates legal proceedings to restrain Colonel de Basil from "producing, performing, or authorizing the production of certain ballets" for the Ballet Russe de Monte Carlo, the ballet company founded this year in Monte Carlo by Rene Blum and Leonide Massine. Although Colonel de Basil is on the board of governors of this new company and has officially merged his Colonel de Basil's Ballet Russe with the new company, he declares war on Universal Art Inc. by having his entourage (those dancers of the new company loyal to him) open a London season three days from today at the Covent Garden Royal Opera House. Members loyal to Blum and Massine (the more famous of the company's dancers) also open a London season next month at the Drury Lane Theater. Due to what might legally constitute a conflict of interest, Colonel de Basil renames his dancers the Royal Covent Garden Ballet Russe. In effect, he leaves Blum and Massine and creates a new ballet company for the purpose of overwhelming them with fierce competition. It is directed by Victor Dandre, German Sevastianov and Serge Grigoriev. Colonel de Basil states he has officially retired, enabling him to control the company from behind the scenes. This latest offensive in the continuing ballet war between these personalities results in the Ballet Russe de Monte Carlo (the Massine-Blum contingent) appearing in America this October.

Aug. 4   The inaugural concert in the music shed at Tanglewood (The Berkshire Festival) takes place as Serge Koussevitzky conducts the Boston Symphony Orchestra and the Cecilia Society in music by Bach and Beethoven. The shed, based on original designs by Eliel Saarinen, seats 5,090 people.

Sep. 23   A phonograph recording of *Finlandia*, by Jean Sibelius, is one of several works placed in a time capsule buried today at the New York World's Fair site. It is to be opened in A.D. 6938.

Oct.   The Ballet Russe de Monte Carlo, headed by Leonide Massine and Rene Blum, opens its American tour this month. Its cast includes Alexandra Danilova, Alicia Markova, Tamara Toumanova, Igor Youskevitch, Andre Eglevsky and Serge Lifar. The tour is the result of Colonel de Basil's having organized his Royal Covent Garden Ballet Russe in London last June. That company, in an effort to make a consistently new impression on the public and to confound Massine's efforts, changes its name from the Royal Covent Garden Ballet Russe to Educational Ballets Ltd. and later to Original Ballet Russe.

The name changes result in tremendous confusion. Colonel de Basil's efforts consistently fail, however, due to Massine's extraordinary choreography and his ability to hold the best dancers, particularly Danilova and Markova, Youskevitch and Eglevsky (Toumanova and a few others defect to Colonel de Basil). The ballet war between the two companies continues to be fought by each waging spectacular tours. Two years from now, Sol Hurok has both companies perform in New York back-to-back, creating the largest ballet season in New York City history. It is not until January 1948 that Colonel de Basil's Original Ballet Russe disbands.

Dec.   CBS acquires Columbia (U.S.) and, under the administration of Edward Wallerstein, becomes a formidable competitor in the American recording industry. Columbia also begins two-speed mastering, which later leads to the introduction of its LP disc. Other events in the recording industry this year include the implementation of FM broadcasting; the replacement of wax discs by flowed lacquer discs for master recordings; the use of cellulose acetate-based magnetic tape for music recording; and the development of inexpensive rim-drive motors for record players.

Dec. 24   George Balanchine marries Vera Zorina. The marriage lasts until January 17, 1946. Zorina is a ballerina and actress who has performed with the Ballet Russe de Monte Carlo (1934-36) and in films produced in Hollywood. She is now 21 years old.

1939   Opera

Jan. 26   *Re Hassan*, by Georgio Federico Ghedini, receives its first performance at the Teatro la Fenice in Venice. The libretto, by Tullio Rinelli, is set in 15th-century Spain and concerns a conflict between the Islamic leader Hassan and his son Hussein.

Feb. 1   Ermanno Wolf-Ferrari's *La donna boba* premieres at La Scala. This three-act comic opera is based on a comedy by Lope de Vega about love in Spain.

Feb. 5   The premiere of Carl Orff's three-act opera *Der Mond* takes place in Munich at the Nationaltheater. The libretto, written by the composer, is based on a fairy tale by the brothers Grimm about four boys who capture the moon. It is performed in a revised version in 1950, also in Munich. Clemens Krauss conducts a cast that includes Julius Patzak.

Feb. 17   Mikhail Glinka's *A Life for the Tsar* is performed in Moscow and entitled *Ivan Susanin*. This event marks the work's first public performance after the revolution in its original version. It is in four acts and was originally premiered in 1836.

March 16   Henri Sauguet's first opera, *La Chartreuse de Parme*, receives its initial performance at the Paris Opera. The four-act opera is based on the novel by Stendhal. Sauguet writes the opera in a simple, accessible style.

April 22   NBC premieres *The Old Maid and the Thief* over radio in New York. Composed by Gian-Carlo Menotti, the 14-section opera is about a man in a woman's bedroom. It was composed for the stage and is staged two years from now.

May 18   Douglas Moore's one-act opera *The Devil and Daniel Webster*, with a libretto by Stephen Vincent Benet, receives its initial performance in New York. The opera resembles, to some degree, the famous Faust legend, in that its central character signs a contract with the Devil.

Oct. 7   Erich Wolfgang Korngold's *Die Kathrin* premieres in Stockholm. The work had been scheduled for performance in 1939 in Vienna but was canceled by the Nazis because the composer is Jewish. The three-act opera is about military life in France. Korngold is now living in Hollywood.

Oct. 7   *Medee*, an opera by Darius Milhaud, receives its first performance in Antwerp. The opera is based on the Greek tale of Medea.

Oct. 8   *Columbus*, a one-act opera by Eugen Zador, premieres in an English version over NBC radio in New York. The opera is about Christopher Columbus. Zador is now living in America, after fleeing the Nazis.

Oct. 10   *During the Storm* by Tikhon Khrennikov, receives its initial performance in Moscow. In four acts, it is about agricultural events in the Soviet Union. In it Vladimir Lenin is portrayed as the hero of a Soviet opera for the first time.

1939   Dance

Feb. 2   The Sadler's Wells Ballet's version of *The Sleeping Beauty* premieres in London. This version includes costumes by Nadia Benois. Margot Fonteyn and Robert Helpmann head the cast. The choreography, based on the original by Marius Petipa, is by Nicholas Sergeyev.

March 22   Choreographer Vakhtang Chabukiani's *Laurencia* — with music by Alexander Krein, book by Yevgeny Mandelberg and designs by Simon Virsaladze — is premiered by the Kirov Ballet in Leningrad. Natalia Dudinskaya and Chabukiani dance the lead roles in this work, which tells the story of a revolutionary Spanish village girl.

May 4   The Ballet Russe de Monte Carlo gives the initial performance, in Monte Carlo, of La Argentinita's and Leonide Massine's *Capriccio espagnol* to Nikolai Rimsky-Korsakov's score of the same name. The ballet is a series of five divertissements. La Argentinita, Leonide Massine, Alexandra Danilova and Michel Panaieff star. The ballet is in one act.

May 11   The Ballet Russe de Monte Carlo gives the first performance of Leonide Massine's *Rouge et noir* in Monte Carlo. The abstract symphonic ballet in four movements is set to Dmitri Shostakovich's Symphony No. 1. Alicia Markova, Igor Youskevitch, Nathalie Krassovska, Frederic Franklin, Michel Manaieff and Marc Platoff star.

May 15   *Lady into Fox* is premiered by the Ballet Rambert in London. The choreography is by Andree Howard and the music by Arthur Honegger, with costumes and scenery by Nadia Benois. The ballet, in one act and three scenes, is about a woman tempted by infidelity.

May 19   The Committee of Friends and Enemies of Modern Music gives the premiere performance of *8 Column Line*. This modern dance work is choreographed by Alwin Nikolais to music by Ernst Krenek. Krenek's first major dance work composed in America, the piece is about meeting deadlines in a newspaper office. The performance takes place in Hartford, Connecticut. Nikolais, now 26, began as a piano accompanist for silent films and as a puppeteer. He then studied dance with Hanya Holm, Martha Graham and Doris Humphrey.

May 24   *Pocahontas*, by Elliott Carter, receives its first performance in New York City. The ballet is based on the Indian of that name, who lived between 1595 and 1617. Carter, now 30, is music director of the Ballet Caravan.

June 30   Michel Fokine's *Paganini* is premiered by Colonel de Basil's Ballet Russe at Covent Garden in London. The ballet is set to Serge Rachmaninoff's *Rhapsody on a Theme of Paganini*. It is based on the legends surrounding Paganini, who was reported to have sold his soul to the Devil in return for his talent. Dmitri Rostoff (Paganini), Irina Baronova (Divine Genius), Tatiana Riabouchinska (Florentine Beauty), Tamara Grigorieva (Guile) and Paul Petroff (Florentine Youth) are in the opening cast. The ballet is in one act and three scenes.

Oct. 26   The Ballet Russe de Monte Carlo premieres, at the Metropolitan Opera House in New York, Frederick Ashton's *Devil's Holiday*, with music by Vincenzo Tommasini, based on themes by Paganini. The plot revolves around the Devil's attempts to fix a love affair. Simon Semenoff (Old Lord), Alexandra Danilova (His Daughter), Frederic Franklin (Young Lover), George Zoritch (Fiance) and Marc Platoff (the Devil) star. The ballet is in three scenes and two entr'actes.

Oct. 31   The Ballet Russe de Monte Carlo premieres *Igrouchka* in New York City. The choreography and libretto are by Michel Fokine, with costumes and scenery by Nathalie Gontcharova. Originally produced in 1921, the music is by Nikolai Rimsky-Korsakov. Alexandra Danilova dances the lead role in this folk tale ballet.

Nov. 9   Leonide Massine's *Bacchanale* — to music by Richard Wagner, (*Tannhauser*), with libretto, costumes and scenery by Salvador Dali — is premiered by the Ballet Russe de Monte Carlo in New York. Dealing with the madness of King Ludwig of Bavaria, the ballet is surrealist.

Dec. 1   *The Prodigal Son* is performed by the Original Ballet Russe in a version choreographed by David Lichine in Sydney, Australia.

Dec. 27   Martha Graham presents *Every Soul Is a Circus*, with music by Paul Nordoff. The work focuses on the characteristics that have distinguished women throughout time. It is Graham's first lighthearted ballet. The ballet also introduces Merce Cunningham to the company. Graham (the Woman), Erick Hawkins (the Ringmaster) and Merce Cunningham (the Acrobat) star. The one-act work is performed at the Saint James Theater in New York.

1939 Instrumental and Vocal Music

Jan. 9   Bela Bartok's *Contrasts* for violin, clarinet and piano premieres in New York, with the composer at the keyboard; Joseph Szigeti, violinist; and Benny Goodman, clarinetist. The piece, based on Hungarian melodies and rhythms, is in three movements.

Jan. 20   *Concord Sonata* (Second Pianoforte Sonata, Concord, Massachusetts, 1840–60), by Charles Ives, receives its world premiere in New York. John Kirkpatrick performs. Written between 1909 and 1915, this piece consists of four movements, entitled "Emerson," "Hawthorne," "The Alcotts" and "Thoreau." The technical complexity of this work prevented it from being premiered until now. Ives says the work "is called a sonata for want of a more exact name." The music includes tempi that may be varied by the performer, a slab of wood to be depressed on the keyboard so a tone cluster will sound, a musical quotation from Beethoven's Fifth Symphony and, in the last movement, a flute part. The piece reflects the impact that transcendentalist philosophy had on Ives. He published the

score in 1919 at his own expense and offered it to anyone who wanted it. He also published separately *Essays Before a Sonata* (the music is dedicated "to those who can't stand the essays"; the essays, "to those who can't stand the music"; and both, "to those who can't stand either").

The premiere of this composition substantially enhances Ives' position as an American composer: He has been largely obscure until today and had virtually stopped composing after having suffered from a massive heart attack and diabetes. In reviewing today's premiere, Lawrence Gilman writes in the New York *Herald-Tribune*, "This Sonata is exceptionally great music — it is, indeed, the greatest music composed by an American, and the most deeply and essentially American in impulse and implication."

Feb. 15   Nikolai Miaskovsky's Symphony No. 19 in E-flat Major premieres in Moscow at the Comintern Radio Station. This four-movement symphony is scored for military band.

Feb. 20   Paul Creston's symphonic *Two Choric Dances* are premiered by Arthur Shepherd conducting the Cleveland Federal Orchestra. Creston is a largely self-taught composer. He has studied piano with Giuseppe Aldo Randegger and organ with Pietro Alessandro Yon. He was awarded a Guggenheim fellowship last year.

Feb. 24   Symphony No. 3, by Roy Harris, receives its world premiere in Boston, as Serge Koussevitzky conducts the Boston Symphony Orchestra. This work, in one movement and five sections, incorporates materials from an earlier violin concerto that had been composed for and then rejected by Jascha Heifetz for not being idiomatic to the instrument. Koussevitzky states in an interview that he considers it a great American work. The symphony immediately enters the repertoire and becomes the most popular symphony by Harris.

Feb. 26   Aaron Copland's Sextet for piano, clarinet and string quartet premieres in New York City. This piece was arranged from his *Short Symphony*.

March 25   *Bachianas Brasileiras No. 5* for voice and eight cellos, by Heitor Villa-Lobos, receives its world premiere in Rio de Janeiro, the composer conducting. This work, in two parts ("Aria" and "Danza"), is the most popular of his "Bachianas Brasileiras" suites.

April 19   Igor Stravinsky's *Zvezdoliki* is premiered by the Belgian State Radio Orchestra in Brussels. This cantata (also known as *Le Roi des etoiles*) was composed between 1911 and 1912. It is scored for male chorus and orchestra. The text is by Russian poet Constantin Balmont.

April 23   Bela Bartok's Violin Concerto receives its first performance by Willem Mengelberg and the Concertgebouw Orchestra in Amsterdam, with Zoltan Szekely as soloist. The concerto has three movements.

May 17   Sergei Prokofiev's cantata *Alexander Nevsky* premieres in Moscow, the composer conducting. Based on music written for the Sergei Eisenstein film of the same name, this piece for mezzo-soprano, chorus and orchestra becomes one of the composer's most popular works. It is in seven sections.

May 24   *Munchen Walzer*, an orchestral waltz suite by Richard Strauss, premieres in Munich. The work had been composed as music for a film about that city.

June 9   Arnold Bax's Symphony No. 7 in A-flat Major receives its first performance by Adrian Boult and the New York Philharmonic at the New York World's Fair inauguration of British Week. Eugene Goossens' Concerto for Oboe and Orchestra receives its first American performance at the same place and by the same orchestra.

June 10   Arthur Bliss's Piano Concerto and Ralph Vaughan Williams' *Five Variants on Dives and Lazarus* are premiered by Adrian Boult and the New York Philharmonic during the second British Week concert at the New York World's Fair.

June 17   Witold Lutoslawski's *Variations Symphoniques* premieres in Krakow. This composer is now 26.

Oct. 6   *American Festival Overture*, by William Schuman, receives its initial performance by Serge Koussevitzky and the Boston Symphony Orchestra. This piece depicts, in music, American life and street scenes.

Oct. 28   Mario Castelnuovo-Tedesco's Concerto in D for guitar and orchestra is premiered by Andres Segovia in Montevideo, Uruguay.

Nov. 3   Howard Hanson's Symphony No. 3 receives its first concert performance by the Boston Symphony Orchestra, the composer conducting.

Nov. 5   Symphony No. 6, by Dmitri Shostakovich, receives its world premiere in Leningrad. The three movements of this symphony conclude in D minor and D major. Originally conceived as a tribute to Vladimir Lenin, it was to have been scored for large chorus, orchestra and soloists. The final version, however, has no program and is purely instrumental.

Nov. 18   Manuel de Falla's symphonic suite *Homenajes* premieres at the Teatro Colon in Buenos Aires, the composer conducting. This event marks the composer's first conducting appearance since his arrival from Spain. The four sections of this work pay tribute to Claude Debussy, Enrique Fernandez Arbos, Paul Dukas and Felipe Pedrell. The work was originally composed for guitar in 1920.

Nov. 23   *Peacock Variations*, an orchestral work by Zoltan Kodaly, receives its world premiere by Willem Mengelberg and the Concertgebouw Orchestra in Amsterdam. The piece contains 16 brief sections, all based on the Hungarian folk song "Fly, Peacock, Fly." It was commissioned to celebrate this orchestra's 50th anniversary. Kodaly is now living in Budapest compiling folk songs. He decided to stay there despite the dangers resulting from World War II.

Dec. 7   William Walton's Violin Concerto is premiered by Artur Rodzinski and the Cleveland Orchestra, with Jascha Heifetz as soloist. The concerto is in three movements.

Dec. 9   *Imaginary Landscape No. 1*, by John Cage, is performed for the first time in Seattle, Washington. The piece is scored for suspended cymbal, muted piano and two phonograph turntables. This is the first of a group of works by the same title Cage composes that explore "surrealistic" combinations of sounds. It may be performed either as a recording or as a broadcast. Cage is now 27 and has been a dance accompanist at the Cornish School in Seattle for the past two years. He has been influenced by Arnold Schoenberg, Henry Cowell and others.

Dec. 21   Sergei Prokofiev's cantata *Zdravitza* premieres in Moscow. The work had been composed for Joseph Stalin's 60th birthday. The text of this piece is in Russian, Ukrainian, Byelorussian, Kurd, and several other languages.

1939   Births, Deaths and Debuts

Jan. 9   Austrian composer Julius Bittner, 64, dies in Vienna. A lawyer by profession, he later composed operas, as well as chamber and vocal music, and also edited a music journal. His early music studies were with Bruno Walter.

Jan. 13   American baritone Leonard Warren makes his operatic debut at the Metropolitan Opera singing the small part of Paolo in Giuseppe Verdi's *Simon Boccanegra*.

Feb. 1   Soviet dancer Yekaterina Maximova is born in Moscow.

Feb. 8   Arthur F. Hill, 79, dies in London. He wrote books on violins, including Stradivari instruments, and donated a priceless collection of such instruments to the Ashmolean Museum at Oxford.

Feb. 11   Austrian composer Franz Schmidt, 64, dies in Perchtoldsdorf, near Vienna. He was a pupil of Anton Bruckner at the Vienna Conservatory and played cello with the Vienna Philharmonic Orchestra. He earned his living principally as an instructor, teaching at the Vienna Academy of Music and at the Hochschule fur Musik. As a composer, he was strictly a product of the last century; his music is immersed in the romanticism associated with 19th-century Vienna and is largely derivative of Bruckner. He composed four symphonies, several operas, oratorios, concertos, string quartets and other works. His musical style established him as a favorite in Austria; yet, due to his myopic perception of a changing musical world, he failed to make any mark whatsoever on the international music scene.

Feb. 19   Soviet tenor Vladimir Atlantov is born in Leningrad.

Feb. 27   Ballerina Antoinette Sibley is born in Bromley, England.

March 2   Cuban composer Amadeo Roldan, 38, dies in Havana. He studied violin with Fernandez Bordes at the Madrid Conservatory and won the Sarasate Violin Prize. He later worked as a conductor and was associated with the Orquesta Filharmonica (Havana). His music is imbued with rhythms characteristic of African and Cuban culture. His ballet *La rebambaramba* employs many different Cuban percussion instruments.

April 18   Ballet dancer and director Marcia Haydee is born in Niteroi, Brazil.

April 22   Italian violinist and conductor Leandro Campanari, 81, dies in San Francisco. After making his debut with the Boston Symphony Orchestra, he joined the faculty of the New England Conservatory and the Cincinnati Conservatory. He also conducted at the Manhattan Opera House and conducted the Philadelphia Orchestra but was not well received.

May 21   Oboe player Heinz Holliger is born in Langenthal, Switzerland.

June 2   Spanish conductor and violinist Enrique Fernandez Arbos, 75, dies in San Sebastian. Known also as an orchestrator, his opera *El centro de la tierra* was premiered in 1895. He conducted many orchestras, including the Madrid Symphony Orchestra and the Glasgow Symphony Orchestra. His orchestral arrangement of *Iberia*, by Isaac Albeniz, has achieved great popularity.

June 2   Austrian composer Josef Reiter, 77, dies in Vienna. He composed *Festgesang an den Fuhrer des deutschen Volkes* — a work published by Nazi-controlled Universal Edition and dedicated to Adolf Hitler. He was also known as a choral conductor and, between 1908 and 1911, was director of the Mozarteum in Salzburg. He composed four operas and many other vocal works.

July 20   British conductor Sir Dan Godfrey, 71, dies in Bournemouth. He conducted the Bournemouth Municipal Orchestra for 41 years. His efforts were directed toward helping British composers gain recognition. He was knighted in 1922.

Aug. 14   Lorin Maazel, age 9, makes his conducting debut at the New York World's Fair. He conducts the National Music Camp Orchestra of Interlochen, Michigan, at the fair's Court of Peace. Louis Biancolli writes in the *World-Telegram* (New York), "You had to rub your eyes to believe it — this chubby little figure in a white linen suit pace-making for an orchestra of seventy, and giving every cue on the dot."

Aug. 18   Mme. Antoinette Szumowska Adamowska, 70, dies in Rumson, New Jersey. She was the only female pupil of Ignace Paderewski and a piano soloist with many American symphony orchestras. She was also on the faculty of the New England Conservatory and a member of the Adamowski Trio.

Nov. 20   Belgian composer Desire Paque, 72, dies in Bessencourt, France. A product of the Liege Conservatory, he lived in many cities during his youth. Most of his music is unpublished. His work includes eight symphonies, chamber music and atonal music for children considered to be the first of its kind, deploying a method of athematicism he termed "adjonction constante."

Nov. 23   Austrian conductor Artur Bodanzky, 61, dies in New York. Studies at the Vienna Conservatory and an early assistantship to Gustav Mahler led to other conducting positions. He eventually joined the Metropolitan Opera in 1915 where he was in charge of German repertory. He stayed there until his death. He made arrangements of several operas, among them, *Fidelio*, which he conducted at the Metropolitan. His conducting was noted for its Mahlerian focus on contrast and climax.

Dec. 6   French tenor Charles Dalmores, 68, dies in Hollywood. In his youth he was a French-horn player. He began singing in his twenties and made his debut at Rouen in 1899. He later went on to sing at Covent Garden, at the Manhattan Opera House and with the Chicago Opera Company. He was known principally for his roles in German and French operas.

Dec. 8   American pianist, conductor and composer Ernst Schelling, 63, dies in New York. He debuted at age 4 1/2 at the Academy of Music in Philadelphia. After a series of piano teachers, he studied with Ignace Paderewski. This led to tours and, in 1905, the beginnings of his career as a conductor-composer. He was associated as a conductor with the Baltimore Symphony Orchestra. His most successful composition is *A Victory Ball*, an orchestral fantasy.

Dec. 8   Flutist James Galway is born in Belfast, Ireland.

Dec. 19   Conductor, composer and pianist Eric Fogg, 37, dies in London. A pupil of Granville Bantock, he was a conductor with the BBC and conducted at the Promenade Concerts.

1939   Related Events

Otto Klemperer takes a leave of absence as music director of the Los Angeles Philharmonic Orchestra this year. No music director immediately succeeds him: Guest conductors are invited to perform until Alfred Wallenstein is hired as music director in 1943.

The Chapelle Musicale Reine Elisabeth is founded this year in the province of Barbant, Belgium. Established for postconservatory study by the Belgian queen, it accepts only 14 pupils. It is located on the outskirts of the Forest of Soignes.

Leopold Stokowski establishes the All American Youth Orchestra this year.

American dancer Anna Sokolow begins working in Mexico City this year as a choreographer and a teacher. She also appears there with Martha Graham's dance company and subsequently establishes her own school of modern dance in Mexico.

Jan. 2   Black contralto Marian Anderson is barred from singing at Constitution Hall in Washington, D.C. In protest, a group of citizens led by Eleanor Roosevelt organizes a concert for her at the Lincoln Memorial. It takes place on April 9. Roosevelt also resigns from the Daughters of the American Revolution, the organization that is the proprietor of the hall.

Jan. 5   An electronic instrument called the "Voder" is exhibited in Philadelphia at the Franklin Institute. This instrument produces the sound of the human voice by synthesizing it electronically. It is also known as the "vocoder."

Feb. 2   Laurens Hammond demonstrates his novachord in Washington, D.C. This electronic instrument produces timbres of musical instruments. This is one instrument of three associated with this man. The other two are the solovox and the Hammond organ.

Feb. 26   Ignace Paderewski performs Beethoven's *Moonlight Sonata* and other music during his first broadcast concert at New York's Radio City.

March 6   The Whittall Pavilion at the Music Division of the Library of Congress is informally opened to the public as Adolf Busch and Rudolf Serkin perform a recital of violin and piano music.

April 9   Marian Anderson performs an open-air recital in Lincoln Memorial Park, Washington, D.C. Attendance is listed at 75,000.

July 15   A Dusseldorf dispatch to the *Christian Science Monitor* says in discussing Werner Egk's opera *Peer Gynt* that Adolf Hitler ". . . asked to have the composer introduced, and is said to have made the statement that he was happy to have met such talent." The dispatch goes on to say that Egk subsequently received a commission of 10,000 marks to compose a new opera.

MARIAN ANDERSON

July 24   The estate of the Johann Strauss family is confiscated by the Nazis in Vienna and his step-daughter prevented from collecting the inheritance. She is adjudicated by the Nazis to be non-"Aryan."

Aug. 8   An attempt to kill the usage of musical nomenclature in the French language occurs in Rome as the Fascist Department of Education issues such an order.

Sep. 1   Nazi Germany invades Poland, marking the outbreak of World War II. Over the next six years, the world of contemporary music is thrown into turmoil. Many composers and musicians flee various parts of Europe and settle in England and America. Music, particularly concert programs, becomes subject to censorship and government control.

Sep. 4   Pope Pius XII refuses to grant the Hammond Organ Company permission to pursue sales and installment of their organs in Roman Catholic churches on the grounds that the electronic organ invented by Laurens Hammond does not produce the sound of a true pipe organ. Ten years from now, the church reverses itself and allows poorer parishes to purchase electronic organs for temporary use until they can afford a pipe organ.

Oct. 8   Manuel de Falla lands in Argentina after having sailed from Spain. This event marks his final departure from Spain, now controlled by the Falangists.

Oct. 14   BMI (Broadcast Music Inc.) is founded in New York City. This organization exists to further broadcasting of new music and is fresh competition for ASCAP (American Society of Composers, Authors and Publishers).

1940 Opera

Feb. 15   *La pulce d'oro*, by Giorgio Federico Ghedini, is premiered at the Teatro Carlo Felice in Genoa. Tullio Pinelli's libretto is about a young man who says that he keeps a golden flea whose bite will turn anything except food into gold.

May 18   Luigi Dallapiccola's one-act opera *Volo di notte*, with a libretto based on a tale by Antoine de Saint-Exupery, premieres in Florence. The opera is about an airplane flight over the Andes.

June 23   Sergei Prokofiev's *Simeon Kotko* premieres in Moscow at the Opernyi Teatr Stanislavsky. The libretto is

based on a story by V. Katayev, who, together with the composer, adapted it for the stage. The five-act opera is about civil war in the Ukraine between 1918 and 1920.

July 26   Heitor Villa-Lobos' *Magdelena* premieres in Los Angeles. This opera is about love south of the border. Its unusual sound effects include an old pianola and an automobile.

Oct. 22   *Guntram* is performed in a revised version in Weimar. The opera, premiered in 1894, was Richard Strauss' first. It is about a German knight.

1940 Dance

Jan. 11   The Ballet Theater gives its inaugural performance at the Center Theater in New York. Premiered at this performance is *The Great American Goof*, with music by Henry Brant, choreography by Eugene Loring, libretto by William Saroyan, and costumes and scenery by Boris Aronson. The ballet is a failure, one possible reason being that the dancers are called upon to speak as well as dance. The work is essentially a morality play on American life, and its dancer-speakers reflect the gamut of personality stereotypes.

Jan. 11   Leonid Lavrovsky's production of *Romeo and Juliet* receives its initial performance at the Kirov Theater in Leningrad. The score, commissioned for this production, is by Sergei Prokofiev. The work closely follows Shakespeare's play, with an emphasis on social conflict between the two families. Galina Ulanova, Konstantin Sergeyev, Andrei Lopokov and Sergei Koren star.

Jan. 13   Adolph Bolm's *Peter and the Wolf*, with book and music by Sergei Prokofiev and costumes and scenery by Lucinda Ballard, is premiered by the Ballet Theater in New York City. A favorite of children, the work stars William Dollar, Eugene Loring, Viola Essen, Nina Stroganova, Karen Conrad and Edward Caton.

Jan. 23   Frederick Ashton's *Dante Sonata* receives its initial performance by the Sadler's Wells Ballet in London. The work, using Franz Liszt's music, deals with the struggle between good and evil. As such, it has significance for war-torn Londoners. Margot Fonteyn, Pamela May, Robert Helpmann and Michael Somes star.

Feb. 28   *Graduation Ball* is performed for the first time by the Original Ballet Russe in Sydney, Australia. Choreographed by David Lichine to music by Johann Strauss, the

GALINA ULANOVA IN *ROMEO AND JULIET*

April 10   George Balanchine's *Le Baiser de la fée* is performed by the Ballet Russe de Monte Carlo in New York. This marks the work's first performance by this company.

July 4   The Sadler's Wells Ballet premieres Ninette de Valois' *The Prospect Before Us*. The music is by William Boyce, arrangement by Constant Lambert, and costumes and scenery by Roger Furse.

Aug. 11   Martha Graham's *Letter to the World* receives its world premiere at Bennington College in Vermont. The music is by H. Johnson, sets by Arch Lauterer and costumes by E. Gylfond. The one-act ballet is a choreographic exploration of the life of American poet Emily Dickinson. Graham, Jane Dudley, Erick Hawkins, and Merce Cunningham star.

Oct. 17   Tchaikovsky's *The Nutcracker* is performed for the first time in America. Danced by the Ballet Russe de Monte Carlo, the scenery and costumes are by Alexandre Benois. The principal dancers are Alicia Markova and Andre Eglevsky.

Nov. 16   Michel Fokine's *Cinderella* receives its first American performance by the Original Ballet Russe in New York. Music is by Sergei Prokofiev.

Dec. 6   *The Firebird* is performed in New York by the Original Ballet Russe. This performance utilizes the Nathalie Goncharova costumes and scenery that the Ballet Russe de Monte Carlo used in its 1935 New York performances. Irina Baronova dances the title role.

ballet is a comical look at a graduation ball. It features costumes by Alexandre Benois.

1940 Instrumental and Vocal Music

Jan. 8   Roger Sessions' neoclassical Violin Concerto premieres in Chicago.

Jan. 30   *Les Illuminations*, by Benjamin Britten, to poetic texts by Arthur Rimbaud, receives its initial performance in London. Scored for high voice and string orchestra, it is a suite of 10 pieces.

Feb. 4   Kurt Weill's cantata *The Ballad of Magna Carta*, with a text by Maxwell Anderson, premieres over radio in New York City. This work is about the signing of the Magna Carta by King John of England. The program on which it is broadcast is called "Pursuit of Happiness Radio Program." It advances commercial works with the themes of peace and opposition to tyranny.

Feb. 9   The Double Concerto for Timpani, Piano and two string orchestras by Bohuslav Martinu, is premiered by Paul Sacher and the Chamber Orchestra of Basel. This neobaroque work was composed two years ago.

Feb. 10   Anton Webern's *Five Songs on Poems of Stefan George*, Op. 4, scored for violin and piano, premieres in Basel. The

performers are Marguerite Gradmann-Luscher (violin) and Erich Schmid (piano). Composed between 1908 and 1909, these songs reflect an earlier stage in Webern's development: The music is based on central chords, which — though not tonal — give the harmony a sense of anchor.

March 1   Arthur Honegger's *La danse des morts*, with text by Paul Claudel, is premiered by Paul Sacher and the Chamber Orchestra of Basel. This work is an oratorio which includes melodies of French songs and also the *Dies Irae*. It is based on macabre drawings by Hans Holbein.

March 14   Paul Hindemith's Concerto for Violin and Orchestra, receives its first performance in Amsterdam, as Willem Mengelberg conducts the Concertgebouw Orchestra. Hindemith is soloist. The violin part features fluid melodic lines. This is the last piece Hindemith composes before coming to America. It is a tonal work in three movements.

March 18   Walter Piston's Violin Concerto is premiered by violinist Ruth Posselt in New York City. This neoclassical work is in three movements.

April 7   Heitor Villa-Lobos' *New York Skyline* is performed via radio broadcast from Rio de Janeiro to the Brazilian Pavilion at the New York World's Fair. This event marks the formal opening of this pavilion.

April 10   The first movement of Luigi Dallapiccola's *Canti di Prigionia*, entitled "Prayer of Mary Stuart," premieres in Brussels. This vocal cycle is performed in its entirety on December 11, 1941.

April 11   John Barbirolli and the New York Philharmonic premiere Bernard Herrmann's cantata *Moby Dick*. Herrmann, now 29, is chief conductor of the CBS Symphony Orchestra.

April 12   Eugene Goossens' Symphony No. 1 receives its initial performance by the Cincinnati Symphony Orchestra with the composer conducting.

April 16   *Aotearoa*, by Douglas Lilburn, receives its initial performance in London. This work is an overture based on Maori tribal musical themes. Lilburn, now 24, has studied composition with Ralph Vaughan Williams at the Royal College of Music in London.

April 17   Charles Munch premieres Alexander Tcherepnin's *Suite Georgienne* in Paris. This four-movement work is an orchestral depiction of a Caucasus landscape.

April 17   *Christophe Colomb* a radio play by Arthur Honegger, premieres on Radio Lausanne. Ernest Ansermet conducts. It is about the travels of Christopher Columbus.

April 25   Roy Harris' Symphony No. 4 (*Folk Song Symphony*), four choral movements only, is premiered by Howard Hanson at the American Spring Festival in Rochester, New York. The entire symphony is performed for the first time this December 26.

May 16   *Xochipilli Macuilxochitl*, by Carlos Chavez, scored for percussion orchestra, premieres at the Museum of Modern Art in New York City. The title of this work is the name of the Aztec god of music.

June 11   Paul Sacher and the Chamber Orchestra of Basel premiere Bela Bartok's *Divertimento for String Orchestra*. This three-movement work includes secundal harmonies (harmonies built on major seconds).

June 25   William Grant Still's *And They Lynched Him on a Tree*, Roy Harris' *1940* and Earl Robinson's *Ballad for Americans* are premiered by Artur Rodzinski and the New York Philharmonic at Lewisohn Stadium. The text to the Harris work is the Preamble to the U.S. Constitution.

July 5   William Schuman's cantata, *This Is Our Time*, receives its first performance by Artur Rodzinski, the People's Philharmonic Choral Society and the New York Philharmonic at Lewisohn Stadium.

Aug. 4   Darius Milhaud's orchestral work *Le cortege funebre* premieres over CBS Radio with the composer conducting. This event marks the composer's first appearance since his recent arrival in the United States. The music is an elegy about the surrender of France.

Oct. 10   Frederick Stock's *Festival Fanfare* premieres at the Chicago Symphony Orchestra's Jubilee Season opening concert. The composer (who is also the orchestra's director) conducts. This piece includes a part for an unusual percussion instrument called the Turkish Crescent (also known as the Schellenbaum, the Chinese Pavilion and the Jingling Johnny.) It is a "bell tree," with small and large bells suspended from a tentlike top attached to a pole.

Oct. 17   The Symphony No. 1, by Darius Milhaud, is premiered by the Chicago Symphony Orchestra, the composer conducting. The four-movement work is based on musical materials from Aix-en-Provence.

Oct. 24   Knudage Riisager's Symphony No. 4 receives its first performance in Copenhagen. It is in three movements. This Danish composer is now 43.

Oct. 24   John Alden Carpenter's Symphony in C is premiered by the Chicago Symphony Orchestra. This work celebrates the golden anniversary of this orchestra and was specifically commissioned for the occasion. It is in one movement.

Oct. 27   *Festmusik*, by Richard Strauss, receives its world premiere in Tokyo. It was written to celebrate the Imperial Dynasty of Japan.

Nov. 7   The Symphony No. 6, by Frederick S. Converse, is premiered posthumously by Fabien Sevitzky and the Indianapolis Symphony Orchestra.

Nov. 7   Igor Stravinsky's Symphony in C receives its initial performance by the Chicago Symphony Orchestra, the composer conducting. Like the composer's *Symphony of Psalms*, this work is dedicated to the glory of God and the anniversary of an American orchestra. The neoclassical work is in four movements. The third movement is composed of a minuet and a passapied.

Nov. 9   Spanish composer Joaquin Rodrigo's *Concierto de Aranjuez* for guitar and orchestra premieres in Barcelona. This three-movement concerto immediately becomes a favorite of guitarists. Its melodic and harmonic content reflects the folk life of Spain. Rodrigo, now 39, lost his sight while a child. He has studied composition with Paul Dukas in Paris.

Nov. 9   Aaron Copland's symphonic suite from *Billy the Kid* is premiered by William Steinberg and the NBC Symphony in New York.

Nov. 16   Nikolai Miaskovsky's Symphony No. 21 in F-sharp Minor and Aram Khachaturian's Violin Concerto are premiered at a festival of Soviet music in Moscow.

Nov. 23   Quintet for Piano and Strings, by Dmitri Shostakovich, receives its initial performance at the Moscow Festival, with the composer at the keyboard. The five-movement piece is subsequently awarded the Stalin prize (100,000 rubles).

Nov. 28   Nikolai Miaskovsky's Symphony No. 20 in E Major receives its initial performance in Moscow. This work, which is premiered 12 days after the premiere of his Twenty-first Symphony, has three movements. Miaskovsky composes an average of two symphonies per year.

Dec. 6   Leopold Stokowski and the Philadelphia Orchestra premiere Arnold Schoenberg's Violin Concerto. Louis Krasner is the soloist. This dodecaphonic work has three movements and was completed four years ago. Schoenberg later comments: "I believe that in my Violin Concerto I have created the necessity for a new kind of violinist. I am delighted to add another unplayable work to the repertoire." Edwin H. Schloss of the Philadelphia *Record* says of the concerto, "The effect on the vast majority of hearers is that of a lecture on the fourth dimension delivered in Chinese."

Dec. 15   Arnold Schoenberg's *Chamber Symphony*, No. 2, Op. 38, receives its initial performance by Fritz Stiedry and the New Friends of Music in New York. This two-movement work was begun in 1906, when Schoenberg was composing tonal music. He reconciles the two styles by using key signatures, but with elements of his 12-tone technique. The work is virtually a hybrid musical composition.

Dec. 15   Edmund Rubbra's Symphony No. 3 is premiered in Manchester, England.

Dec. 26   *Symphony No. 4 (Folk Song Symphony)*, by Roy Harris, for chorus and orchestra, is premiered in its complete version by the Cleveland Orchestra. This symphony was composed to enable high school choruses to perform with first-rate orchestras. The chorus sings in five of the seven movements. A partial performance took place eight months ago.

1940   Births, Deaths and Debuts

Jan. 5   Russian bass Alexander Kipnis makes his Metropolitan Opera debut as Gurnemanz in Wagner's *Parsifal*. Olin Downes, writing in the New York *Times*, describes Kipnis' performance as "one of the most authoritative and sympathetic representations of the character that the Metropolitan stage has seen in recent years."

Jan. 27   Russian-American pianist Alexander Kelberine, 36, commits suicide (by a sleeping pill overdose) after performing a recital at Town Hall in New York City. A pupil at the Kiev Conservatory and the University of Vienna, he also studied with Ferruccio Busoni in Berlin, Rubin Goldmark in New York and Ernst Toch. He suffered from severe depression and was distressed over romantic and financial problems. He programmed only works in minor keys for his last recital, concluding with *Totentanz*, by Franz Liszt.

Feb. 2   Soprano Martina Arroyo is born in New York City.

Feb. 9   Licia Albanese debuts at the Metropolitan Opera singing the role of *Madama Butterfly*.

Feb. 28   Arnold Dolmetsch, 82, dies in Haslemere, Surrey, England. Trained in both piano and violin, he became interested in antique instruments and eventually learned to play, restore and build them. He formed the Dolmetsch Trio to give performances of old music on original instruments. In 1925 he founded a festival of chamber music at Haslemere where old music was played on reconstructed instruments.

March 3   German conductor Karl Muck, 80, dies in Stuttgart, Germany. In his successful career he held such posts as conductor of the Berlin Opera (1892), the Vienna Philharmonic (1903–06) and the Boston Symphony Orchestra (from 1906). During World War I Muck was arrested in Boston as an enemy alien and detained until the end of the war. He was known as a disciplinarian and for his fine musicianship and taste.

April 18   Soviet dancer Vladimir Vasiliev is born in Moscow.

April 28   Italian coloratura soprano Luisa Tetrazzini, 58, dies in Milan. Her early training was at the Florence Conservatory. She made her debut in 1890, but her real successes came in 1905 while touring with an opera company in South America. She first sang in America in 1905 and at Covent Garden in 1907. In 1925 she sang in the first radio broadcast in England. After her retirement she taught singing in Milan.

May 23   Andrei Rimsky-Korsakov, 61, dies in Leningrad. Son of Nikolai Rimsky-Korsakov, he specialized in the history of Russian music. His famous magazine *The Musical Contemporary (Musikalny Sovremennik)* began publication in 1915 and stopped two years later, when the Russian Revolution occurred. Other writings include the catalog "Musical Treasures of the Catalogue Department of the Leningrad Public Library" and extensive biographical writings on the life and work of his father.

July 10   British musicologist Sir Donald Tovey, 64, dies in Edinburgh. He was a conductor, pianist, essayist and composer, his music including chamber and symphonic works and an opera entitled The Bride of Dionysus. He established The Chelsea Concerts in 1906 (London) and the Reid Symphony Orchestra in 1917 (Edinburgh). His books include the six-volume *Essays in Musical Analysis*, which he wrote between 1935 and 1939.

Aug. 4   American composer Charles Naginski, 31, commits suicide (by drowning) in the vicinity of Lenox, Massachusetts. He had been rejected from Paul Hindemith's class at Berkshire as a result of having failed a counterpoint test. He was a pupil of Rubin Goldmark at the Juilliard Graduate School in New York. His works include two symphonies, a ballet, *Minotaur* and various other pieces.

Aug. 8   Italian lyric tenor Alessandro Bonci, 70, dies in Milan. He made his debut in *Falstaff* in 1896 and went on to sing in many major opera houses around the world, including the Metropolitan Opera and La Scala. His New York debut at the Manhattan Opera House (1906) created competition for Enrico Caruso.

Aug. 10   Soviet dancer Yuri Soloviev is born in Moscow, Russia.

Sep. 2   Opera manager Giulio Gatti-Casazza, 72, dies in Ferrara, Italy. The director of La Scala from 1898 to 1908, he then became general manager of the Metropolitan Opera (from 1908 to 1935), where he was responsible for the most successful period in the house's history (both artistically and at the box office). He brought many great artists to the theater, including Arturo Toscanini, Rosa Ponselle, Leo Slezak, Lucrezia Bori and others. He opened the way for American operas and world premieres of European works, and during his tenure more than 100 unusual operas were performed. He was married to soprano Frances Alda. He spent his retirement in Italy.

Oct. 5   Mexican composer Silvestre Revueltas, 40, dies in Mexico City. Violinist, conductor and composer, he was noted for many short orchestral works. Revueltas studied violin and conducting and only began to compose at the age of 30. His music reflects Mexican cultural themes and includes melodic themes and rhythms indigenous to Mexico. He wrote several ballets and dance pieces, among them *El renacuajo paseador*.

Oct. 21   Ballerina Natalia Makarova is born in Leningrad, USSR.

Nov. 12   Cuban composer Alejandro Caturla, 34, acting as a judge in Remedios, is assassinated by a criminal about to receive a prison sentence. Caturla studied with Nadia Boulanger in Paris and was cofounder and conductor of the Orquesta de Conciertos de Caibarien in Cuba. His music blends Afro-Cuban rhythms with harmonic dissonance.

JAN KUBELIK

Dec. 5   Czech violinist Jan Kubelik, 60, dies in Prague. After studies in Prague and Vienna, he began an extraordinarily successful concert career in 1900. His popularity as a violinist rivaled that of Ignace Paderewski as a pianist. He wrote six violin concertos and other pieces as well. He was the father of conductor Rafael Kubelik. After marrying a Hungarian, he become a naturalized citizen of Hungary.

Dec. 21   Italian bass Salvatore Baccaloni makes his debut at the Metropolitan Opera as Don Pasquale in Gaetano Donizetti's opera buffa of the same name. Olin Downes writes in the New York *Times* that he "sings with admirable ease and variety of effect, and the voice is a very fine one."

1940   Related Events

The Dance Notation Bureau is established this year in New York City. Its principal founders are Rudolf von Laban and Kurt Jooss. Its purpose is to be a clearinghouse for research and analysis of movement and dance notation and to pursue copyright protection for choreographers' works. It also has a library and features training programs and instruction, particularly in Labanotation and kinetographie — the system of dance notation introduced and developed by Laban in 1926.

The Dance Archives Museum of Modern Art is established this year in New York City. It contains Lincoln Kirstein's private collection of dance memorabilia, which is subsequently divided into two collections and given to Harvard College (Theater Collection) and the New York Public Library (Dance Collection).

Jan. 5   Major Edwin H. Armstrong's frequency modulation techniques become the basis for the first successful shortwave radio station linking, which occurs today between Worcester, Massachusetts and New York City. The achievement eliminates background noise.

Feb. 1   *The Music Review* publishes its first issue today in Cambridge, England. Its editor is Geoffrey Sharp.

March 10   Ruggero Leoncavallo's *Pagliacci* becomes the first opera to be televised in America, as the Metropolitan Opera performs the work before cameras.

April 9   Carnegie Hall becomes the location of the first demonstration of stereophonic sound reproduction from sound film, achieved by Bell Telephone Laboratories.

May 14   German bombs destroy the Rotterdam City Centre, which includes the concert hall that is the home of the Rotterdam Philharmonic Orchestra. The music library and many musical instruments are also destroyed. This orchestra does not get a new home until 1966.

May 31   Arturo Toscanini sails to South America aboard the *S.S. Brasil* along with the NBC Symphony Orchestra. Beginning in Rio de Janeiro, this tour takes the maestro back to the city where, at 19 years of age, he conducted his first opera.

June 11   Richard Strauss gives his completed score of *Festmusik* to the Japanese ambassador in Berlin as a gesture of Axis unity. The work receives its premiere performance this October 27.

July 8   The Berkshire Festival opens in Tanglewood, Massachusetts, with Serge Koussevitzky as director.

Nov. 6   Ignace Paderewski arrives in New York City aboard the *S.S. Excambion*, which sailed from Lisbon. This event marks the end of this musician's hazardous journey through France and Spain to escape the Nazis.

Nov. 13   Walt Disney's *Fantasia* is released today by RKO in New York City. This feature-length film has a sound track recorded with multitrack stereo optical process. The music, including segments of famous musical compositions (such as Igor Stravinsky's *Le Sacre du printemps*), is performed by Leopold Stokowski and the Philadelphia Orchestra. (Mickey Mouse also stars.) Other events in the recording industry this year include the halving of record prices by Columbia and Victor and the levying of a 33.3 percent purchase tax on gramophone records.

Nov. 21   Richard Wagner's *Die Walkure* is performed at the Moscow Opera House. This event marks the first performance of one of Wagner's operas in the Soviet Union since December of 1925 and reflects the signing of the Soviet-Third Reich nonaggression treaty.

1941 Opera

Jan. 5   Marc Blitzstein's *No For An Answer*, with a libretto by the composer, premieres in New York. The composer is at the keyboard and conducts the vocalists. The opera is about Greek waiters who try to organize a union. Brooks Atkinson says in the New York *Times* that the work "... is a labor drama leaning so far to the left that it is practically horizontal."

Jan. 23   Kurt Weill's musical *Lady in the Dark*, receives its first performance in New York. In the cast are Gertrude Lawrence and Danny Kaye. It is about a magazine editor who undergoes psychoanalysis. She finds the experience ridiculous.

Feb. 11   The Philadelphia Opera Company gives the first stage performance of Gian-Carlo Menotti's *The Old Maid and the Thief*. The opera was premiered in concert form on April 22, 1939.

May 5   Benjamin Britten's *Paul Bunyan*, with a text by W.H. Auden, premieres at Columbia University in New York City. This "choral operetta" is about a lumberjack who likes to sing ballads. It is Britten's first operatic work.

May 13   *Tarquin*, a two-act opera by Ernst Krenek, receives its initial performance in a shortened English version at Vassar College, Poughkeepsie, New York. The Experimental Theater performs with the composer at the keyboard. The work, described by the composer as "a new opera for the modern stage," also contains a prologue and an epilogue. Krenek is now teaching at Vassar College. While there, he also composes his *Lamentatio Jeremiae Prophetae*, a setting of the lamentations of Jeremiah in which he applies the serial operation called rotation to hexachords derived from tones of the Gregorian modes.

1941 Dance

Jan. 22   The Original Ballet Russe premieres George Balanchine's *Balustrade* in New York. It is a work in four movements to parts of Igor Stravinsky's Concerto for Violin and Orchestra. The work takes its name from the balustrade that is the main decor. Tamara Toumanova, Roman Jasinski and Paul Petroff lead the cast. The work is a failure; Stravinsky later expresses disappointment because he considered the piece an excellent visualization.

Feb. 11   *Three Virgins and a Devil* receives its world premiere by the Ballet Theater in New York City. The choreography is by Agnes de Mille to music by Ottorino Respighi, with a scenario by Ramon Reed, costumes by Motley and scenery by Arne Lundborg. Agnes de Mille, Lucia Chase, Annabelle Lyon, Eugene Loring and Jerome Robbins dance this comic work about temptation.

May 29   The American Ballet Caravan premieres George Balanchine's *Concerto Barocco* to Bach's Concerto in D Minor for Two Violins. The plotless ballet is in Balanchine's purest, most abstract vein, offering the choreographer's interpretation of the music. Marie Jeanne, Mary Jane Shea and William Dollar are the principal dancers. This evening marks the first new production of this company, which is a merger of the American Ballet and the Ballet Caravan. The

performance takes place at an opera rehearsal at Hunter College in New York. Also premiered today is George Balanchine's *Ballet Imperial*. The abstract work in three movements is to Tchaikovsky's Piano Concerto No. 2 in G Major. The work is Balanchine's homage to the Imperial Russian Ballet tradition from which he came. The dancers are Marie Jeanne, Gisella Caccialanza and William Dollar.

Oct. 8   Leonide Massine's *Labyrinth* — to music by Franz Schubert, with costumes, scenery and book by Salvador Dali — is performed for the first time by the Ballet Russe de Monte Carlo at the Metropolitan Opera House in New York. It is an abstract rendition of the conflict between classicism and romanticism. Andre Eglevsky and Tamara Toumanova star.

Oct. 27   Michel Fokine's *Bluebeard* — with music by Jacques Offenbach and costumes and scenery by Marcel Vertes — is premiered by the Ballet Theater in Mexico City. Principal dancers include Jerome Robbins, Alicia Markova, Antony Tudor, Lucia Chase, Nora Kaye, Anton Dolin and Dimitri Romanoff. In two prologues, four acts and three interludes, it is based on Offenbach's opera *Barbe-bleu*, premiered in 1866; it involves a count who kills his wife.

1941 Instrumental and Vocal Music

Jan. 3   Serge Rachmaninoff's *Symphonic Dances*, based on materials from his ballet *The Scythians*, is premiered by Eugene Ormandy and the Philadelphia Orchestra. These dances depict various times of day.

Jan. 15   *Quartet for the End of Time*, by Olivier Messiaen, receives its world premiere at Stalag VIII-A, Gorlitz. Scored for violin, violoncello, clarinet and piano, the piece is in eight movements. The work was conceived and composed during Messiaen's captivity by the Germans. The performers are Jean Le Boulaire (violin), Henri Akoko (clarinet), Etienne Pasquier (cello) and the composer (piano). Inspired by an excerpt from the Revelation of Saint John, it reflects Messiaen's deep mysticism and contemplation of the Catholic faith. It is intended, in part, to draw the listener into a state of suspended time. It becomes one of the most famous chamber works composed this century. Critic Howard Taubman later reviews the work in the New York *Times* and writes, "This Quartet has memorable things — long-breathed passages full of mystery and poetry as well as pages of vibrant yet controlled fervor."

Jan. 28   Aaron Copland's *Quiet City* is premiered by the Saidenberg Little Symphony in New York. This instru-

mental suite is scored for trumpet, English horn and string orchestra.

Feb. 6   Frederick Stock and the Chicago Symphony Orchestra give the first performance of Zoltan Kodaly's Concerto for Orchestra. The work had been commissioned as a 50th anniversary celebration. The concerto includes pentatonic modes and Magyar dance rhythms.

Feb. 7   Paul Hindemith's Concerto for Violoncello and Orchestra receives its initial performance by Serge Koussevitzky and the Boston Symphony Orchestra. This event marks the premiere of the composer's first work written in the United States. Gregor Piatigorsky is soloist.

Feb. 7   Samuel Barber's Violin Concerto receives its initial performance by Eugene Ormandy and the Philadelphia Orchestra, with Albert Spalding as soloist. The three-movement concerto includes, in the last movement, a tarantella with kettledrums playing unaccompanied at one point. Barber is now 30. Twenty years from now, Paul Henry Lang reviews a performance of the piece, saying, in the New York *Herald-Tribune*, that it ". . . is a friendly work of aristocratic elegance, beautifully shaped, always euphonious. . . . ''

Feb. 9   Morton Gould's *Spirituals for String Choir and Orchestra* premieres in New York, the composer conducting. It has five movements.

Feb. 22   Paul Creston's Symphony No. 1, Roy Harris' *Ballad of a Railroad Man*, Henry Brant's Violin Concerto and Morton Gould's *Latin-American Symphonette* are premiered by Fritz Mahler and the National Youth Administration Symphony Orchestra in Brooklyn, New York. This concert is designed to advance American music. Fritz Mahler is the nephew of Gustav Mahler.

March 6   Leo Sowerby's Symphony No. 3 is premiered by Frederick Stock and the Chicago Symphony Orchestra. Sowerby is now 45 and teaching at the American Conservatory in Chicago.

March 23   *Fantaisie portugaise*, an orchestral fantasy by Ernesto Halffter, is performed for the first time in Paris. This Spanish composer is the brother of Rodolfo Halffter, another Spanish composer. Both brothers studied with Manuel de Falla.

March 27   Alfredo Casella's neoclassical Symphony No. 3 is premiered by Frederick Stock and the Chicago Symphony Orchestra.

March 29   John Barbirolli and the New York Philharmonic premiere Benjamin Britten's *Sinfonia da Requiem*. The three sections of this piece outline the Latin titles of the Requiem Mass, but the piece is not intended to be liturgical. It was inspired by the death of Britten's father.

April 3   William Walton's overture *Scapino* is premiered by Frederick Stock and the Chicago Symphony Orchestra.

May 10   American composer Robert Ward's Symphony No. 1 is premiered by the Juilliard Graduate School Orchestra in New York City, the composer conducting. This work is neobaroque. The composer, now 23, has completed his studies at the Eastman School of Music, where he studied with Howard Hanson and Bernard Rogers.

May 11   *Tales of the Countryside*, by Henry Cowell, receives its initial performance by Leopold Stokowski and the All-American Youth Orchestra in Atlantic City, New Jersey, with the composer at the keyboard. This event marks the inaugural concert of this orchestra. Cowell's piece is a suite for piano and orchestra and includes tone clusters characteristic of his music.

June 5   Paul Ben-Haim's Symphony No. 1 premieres in Tel Aviv, the composer conducting. This composer was born in Munich in 1897. The symphony depicts the agony of Nazi victims (Ben-Haim fled Nazi Germany in 1933).

June 10   The Concerto for Organ, Tympani and Strings, by Francis Poulenc, receives its world premiere in Paris. Charles Munch conducts, with Maurice Durufle as organ soloist. The piece, based on a four-note motto, alludes in one movement to Johann Sebastian Bach's G Minor Organ Fantasia. It becomes a favorite showpiece for organists.

July 18   Alberto Ginastera's *Concierto argentino* for piano and orchestra premieres in Montevideo.

Oct. 4   Manuel Ponce's *Concierto del sur* for guitar and orchestra premieres in Montevideo, the composer conducting. Andres Segovia is soloist, and the work is dedicated to him. Ponce has taught at the National Conservatory in Mexico and later went to France to study with Paul Dukas. He is now touring South America.

Oct. 17   William Schuman's Symphony No. 3 is premiered by Serge Koussevitzky and the Boston Symphony Orchestra. This two-movement symphony contains a passacaglia, fugue, chorale and toccata. The work is well received and wins the New York Critics Circle Award next year. It marks Schuman's first major success as a symphonist and is subsequently performed nationally and internationally.

Oct. 17   Jaromir Weinberger's *The Lincoln Symphony* is premiered by Eugene Goossens and the Cincinnati Symphony Orchestra.

Oct. 19   *Baal Shem* for violin and orchestra, by Ernest Bloch, receives its first performance in New York by Joseph Szigeti and the WPA Orchestra.

Oct. 21   Aaron Copland's Piano Sonata premieres in Buenos Aires, with the composer as soloist. This three-movement piece was commissioned by the American playwright Clifford Odets.

Oct. 30   Randall Thompson's String Quartet No. 1 in D Minor is premiered by the Coolidge Quartet in Washington, D.C.

Nov. 14   Serge Koussevitzky and the Boston Symphony Orchestra premiere *Concerto Grosso* for chamber orchestra, by Bohuslav Martinu. This three-movement piece had been scheduled for premiere three times (in Vienna, Prague and Paris) but was removed from the program each time by Nazi authorities.

Nov. 17   Virgil Thomson's Symphony No. 2 is premiered by Sir Thomas Beecham and the Seattle Symphony Orchestra. It is in three movements. This composer is now also writing music criticism for the New York *Herald-Tribune*.

Nov. 21   Symphony in E-flat, by Paul Hindemith, is premiered by Dimitri Mitropoulos and the Minneapolis Symphony Orchestra.

Nov. 28   Benjamin Britten's *Scottish Ballad* is premiered by Eugene Goossens and the Cincinnati Symphony Orchestra, with Ethel Bartlett and Rae Robertson as piano soloists. Derived from old Scottish tunes, the work is scored for two pianos and orchestra.

Dec. 11   Luigi Dallapiccola's *Canti di Prigionia* premieres in its complete version in Rome. Part of the work was premiered last year. This vocal cycle is scored for chorus, two pianos, two harps and percussion. It is about the anguish of Mary Stuart, Boethius and Savonarola. Dallapiccola adopted Arnold Schoenberg's 12-tone method last year.

Dec. 21   David Diamond's Symphony No. 1 is premiered by Dimitri Mitropoulos and the New York Philharmonic. The work, in three movements, attracts attention to this American composer, now 26.

1941   Births, Deaths and Debuts

Jan. 1   Italian tenor Mario Del Monaco makes his operatic debut in Milan singing Pinkerton in *Madama Butterfly*.

Jan. 10   English composer Frank Bridge, 61, dies in Eastbourne. Having studied at the Royal College of Music, he was also a violist and conductor, and conducted the Marie Brema opera in London as well as Promenade Concerts. His music — most often scored for easily available combinations of instruments and written in a practical manner — never achieved popularity during his lifetime. He is best remembered for being the teacher of Benjamin Britten. His songs (about 100) are often performed.

Jan. 21   Tenor Placido Domingo is born in Madrid, Spain.

Feb. 14   German conductor Bruno Walter leads his first operatic performance in America — *Fidelio* at the Metropolitan, with Kirsten Flagstad in the title role. Pitts Sanborn writes in the New York *World-Telegram*, "This performance brought the audience to such a pitch of enthusiasm that one trembled for the safety of the august house."

Feb. 15   Austrian musicologist Guido Adler, 85, dies in Vienna. He was a pupil of Anton Bruckner and Felix Otto Dessoff at the Vienna Conservatory and a founder of the Wagner Society. His important works include the publications *Der Stil in der Musik* and *Handbuch der Musikgeschichte*. He was an editor of the 83-volume *Denkmaler der Tonkunst in Osterreich*.

Feb. 19   Irish conductor and composer Sir Hamilton Harty, 61, dies in Brighton, England. Starting his career as an organist, he took up conducting and in 1920 became conductor of the Halle Orchestra, a position he held for 13 years. He was knighted in 1925. His best-known composition is *Irish Symphony*.

March 11   English organist, teacher and composer Sir Henry Walford Davies, 71, dies near Bristol, England. This musician was the 20th Master of the King's Music. He was also an organist and professor of counterpoint at the Royal College of Music. His oratorio *Everyman* is perhaps his best-known composition.

April 20   Baritone George London makes his professional debut in Albert Coates' opera *Gainsborough's Duchess* in Los Angeles.

June 1   Conductor Edo de Waart is born in Amsterdam.

IGNACE PADEREWSKI SHOWN SIGNING AUTOGRAPHS

June 29   Polish pianist Ignace Jan Paderewski, 80, dies in New York. After much musical study, he decided to become a pianist and took lessons from Theodor Leschetizky. Following his debut as a soloist in Vienna in 1889, he quickly made a reputation in Europe and America. An ardent Polish nationalist, he donated huge sums of money during his lifetime to help his country. He entered politics twice — first becoming prime minister of Poland in 1919–20 and then president of the Polish parliament in exile in 1940. During his lifetime he earned more money than any other musician up to that time. He was buried, by order of President Franklin Delano Roosevelt, in Arlington National Cemetery. As a composer, he is remembered especially for the *6 Humoresques* for piano.

July 19   Soviet dancer Natalia Bessmertnova is born in Moscow.

July 28   Conductor Riccardo Muti is born in Naples.

Aug. 10   American black conductor Dean Dixon conducts the New York Philharmonic at Lewisohn Stadium in New York. This event marks the first professional appearance of this conductor and the first time a black has conducted this orchestra.

Sep. 9   Dancer Karin von Aroldingen is born in Berlin, Germany.

Oct. 28   American pianist William Kapell makes his New York debut in Town Hall.

Nov. 29   American tenor Jan Peerce makes his Metropolitan Opera debut as Alfredo in *La Traviata*.

Dec. 3   Norwegian composer Christian Sinding, 85, dies in Oslo. After preliminary studies in Oslo, he went to the Leipzig Conservatory, where he studied orchestration

CHRISTIAN SINDING

with Carl Reinecke. Norwegian government subsidies enabled him to study further in Germany. His music is marked by a strong German influence, especially that of Robert Schumann and Franz Liszt. He became a leader of Scandinavian romanticism. Highly prolific, he composed two operas, many orchestral works, and chamber and piano music.

Dec. 6   Soprano Astrid Varnay makes her operatic debut singing Sieglinde in *Die Walkure*. She is a substitute for Lotte Lehmann, who had been scheduled to sing the performance. Noel Strauss writes in the New York *Times* that she is "remarkable considering the fact that this was her first appearance on any operatic stage."

1941   Related Events

The music directorship of the New York Philharmonic goes to guest conductors for the next two seasons. These conductors, replacing John Barbirolli, include Serge Koussevitzky, Bruno Walter, Fritz Reiner and Arturo Toscanini.

The Jacob's Pillow Dance Festival is established this year near Lee, Massachusetts. Ted Shawn is director. The annual summer festival quickly becomes one of the most famous in America.

Carl Fischer, Inc. publishes *The Schillinger System of Musical Composition*. This massive 2-volume publication contains a total of 12 books explaining Joseph Schillinger's approach to musical composition. It synthesizes music theory and recent theories of physics, psychology and mathematics

and makes an attempt at the scientific classification of musical resources. Henry Cowell, writing in his foreword to the treatise, describes Schillinger's work as possessing "a universality of esthetic concepts. . . ." In addition to expounding theories of rhythm, melody, harmony, counterpoint, pitch-scales, composition and orchestration, it also contains sections exploring musical techniques, such as "Variations of Music by means of Geometrical Projection." This work is considered Schillinger's masterpiece. It is subsequently criticized for being too mathematical. Despite this, many composers (including George Gershwin) found the approach extremely useful.

April 11   Arnold Schoenberg becomes a naturalized U.S. citizen.

May 10   Nazi bombs obliterate Queen's Hall in London this evening.

June 12   Myra Hess is made Dame Commander of the British Empire.

July   The Kirsova Ballet gives its first professional season. It is the first professional company founded in Australia.

Oct.   The Ballet Caravan disbands. It subsequently merges with the American Ballet.

Dec. 7   The Japanese attack Pearl Harbor this morning. The news is made public in Japan today while conductor Joseph Rosenstock is rehearsing an orchestra in Tokyo. Last night, the American ambassador to Japan, Joseph Clark Grew, was scheduled to attend a concert with his wife that was to be conducted by Rosenstock. The tickets had been sold by mistake to another party. Rosenstock telephoned the embassy several times to work out other arrangements for the ambassador's attendance. The Japanese had tapped the telephones and assumed the conversations about concert tickets were a code for wartime information. Rosenstock is arrested during today's rehearsal by Japanese authorities on grounds of espionage. He is sent to Karuizawa, a small town in northern Japan, where he copes with extremely cold winters for the duration of the war. While there, he composes *Variations on an Original Theme*. He is rescued in 1945.

Dec. 9   Tchaikovsky's *1812 Overture* is performed in Leningrad in an arrangement by Vissarion Shebalin. This event marks the first time this work has been performed in Russia since the revolution.

Dec. 15   Upon recapturing the town of Klin, the Red Army discovers the Tchaikovsky Musem to have been desecrated by the Nazis. Eugene Petrov subsequently reports in *Izvestia*: "They tore off the wall panels and used them for fuel.... Fortunately, Tchaikovsky's manuscripts, his library, his favorite piano, his writing desk, all had been previously evacuated."

1942 Opera

Jan. 21   Ivan Dzerzhinsky's *Blood of the People* receives its first performance by the Leningrad Opera Company in Leningrad. The one-act opera is about a Soviet heroine who dies at the hands of the Nazis.

Feb. 10   Deems Taylor's three-act opera *Ramuntcho* is premiered in Philadelphia. The composer's fourth opera, it is about a smuggler and a nun.

Feb. 20   Gian-Carlo Menotti's *The Island God*, with a libretto by the composer, receives its initial performance by the Metropolitan Opera in New York. The opera, in one act, is about a couple trapped on an island in the midst of World War II. The cast includes Leonard Warren, Raoul Jobin, Astrid Varnay and Norman Cordon. It is a more ambitious work than any of Menotti's previous operas. Virgil Thomson writes in the New York *Herald-Tribune* that it "sounds like an opera, reads like a short story, actually is a secular cantata."

Feb. 21   Sergei Vassilenko's *Suvorov* premieres in Sverdlovsk. This four-act opera is about Russians who fought Napoleon.

March 29   Randall Thompson's *Solomon and Balkis*, with a libretto based on a story by Rudyard Kipling, receives its initial performance over radio in New York. Based on Kipling's "The Butterfly That Stamped," it is about a butterfly and the 999 quarreling wives of Solomon.

Oct. 24   Gian Francesco Malipiero's *I Capricci di Callot* receives its first performance in Rome at the Opera. The composer writes his own libretto, set in Rome during carnival. The work is well received by the critics.

RICHARD STRAUSS

Oct. 28   The first performance of Richard Strauss' *Capriccio* takes place in Munich at the Nationaltheater. The libretto is written by conductor Clemens Krauss, with help from the composer. It concerns the comparative importance of the music and words in opera. *Capriccio* is Strauss' last opera. The cast includes Viorica Ursuleac and Hans Hotter. Krauss conducts.

Nov. 3 *The Opera Cloak*, by Walter Damrosch, premieres in New York with the composer conducting. The one-act work is about a seamstress, starving for love, who is swept off her feet by a fireman. The libretto is by the composer's daughter. Damrosch is now 80 years old.

Nov. 28 Dmitri Kabalevsky's *At Moscow* premieres in Moscow. It is about the Soviet counterattack against Nazi forces trying to invade Moscow. The four-act opera coincides with the 25th anniversary of the Russian Revolution. Kabalevsky is now a full professor of composition at the Moscow Conservatory.

1942 Dance

Jan. 14 The Sadler's Wells Ballet premieres Robert Helpmann's *Comus*, based on a masque by John Milton, to music by Henry Purcell. Robert Helpmann, Margot Fonteyn, John Hart, David Paltenghi, Margaret Dale and Moyra Fraser head the cast. It is Helpmann's first ballet.

April 8 The Ballet Theater gives the first performance of Antony Tudor's *Pillar of Fire*. It is performed to Arnold Schoenberg's *Verklarte Nacht*. The ballet follows the poem by Richard Dehmel upon which Schoenberg's composition was based. Hagar, afraid she will become a spinster and fearful that she is losing the love of her Friend, gives herself to a dissolute man. Later she finds love with the Friend. Nora Kaye, Lucia Chase, Annabelle Lyon, Antony Tudor and Hugh Laing star. It is one of Tudor's greatest works. The costumes and sets are by Jo Mielziner.

April 24 Choreographer Lew Christensen's one-act ballet *Jinx* is premiered by the Dance Players in New York City. Choreographed to music by Benjamin Britten, with scenery by James Stewart Morcom and costumes by Felipe Fiocca, the ballet is about a clown and superstition.

May 19 The Sadler's Wells Ballet premieres Robert Helpmann's one-act version of *Hamlet*. The music is by Tchaikovsky, with costumes and decor by Leslie Hurry.

Aug. 1 Bennington College hosts the premiere performances of *Seeds of Brightness* and *Credo in Us*, choreographed by Merce Cunningham and Jean Erdman. The latter work features music by John Cage.

Sep. 8 While on tour in Mexico City, the Ballet Theater premieres Leonide Massine's *Aleko*, to music by Tchaikovsky, with decor by Marc Chagall. The work, about a poet who joins a gypsy camp, becomes a vehicle for its stars, George Skibine, Alicia Markova, Hugh Laing, and Antony Tudor.

Oct. 12 *The Snow Maiden*, by Bronislava Nijinska, is premiered by the Ballet Russe de Monte Carlo. The work, based on a story by Alexander Ostrovsky, is set to music by Glazunov. Alexandra Danilova, Nathalie Krassovska and Igor Youskevitch star.

Oct. 16 The Ballet Russe de Monte Carlo gives the world premiere of Agnes De Mille's *Rodeo: The Courting at Burnt Ranch* to music by Aaron Copland. The scenario deals with courting at a ranch in the old West. The work, which is an immediate hit, introduces square dance forms to ballet. De Mille, Casimir Kokitch, Frederic Franklin and Milada Mladova star. Dance critic Walter Terry calls it a "danced dream."

Nov. 29 David Lichine's *Helen of Troy* receives its world premiere by the Ballet Theater in Mexico City. It is choreographed to music by Jacques Offenbach, with costumes and scenery by Marcel Vertes. The work is a broad comedy very loosely based on Greek legends. Lead dancers are Irina Baronova, Andre Eglevsky, Jerome Robbins and Simon Semenov. The ballet had been started by Michel Fokine, who was taken ill, and finished by Lichine.

Dec. 9 *Gayane* receives its world premiere by the Kirov Ballet. It is choreographed by Nina Anisimova to music by Aram Khachaturian. The costumes are by Tatiana Bruni and the decor by Natan Altman. The performance takes place in Perm where the ballet company has been evacuated during the war. In four acts and six scenes, the ballet is about a cotton picker married to a drunkard. This ballet includes the famous "Sabre Dance."

1942 Instrumental and Vocal Music

Jan. 1 The Piano Concerto, by Carlos Chavez, is premiered by Dimitri Mitropoulos and the New York Philharmonic, with Eugene List as soloist. This concerto incorporates rhythmic elements of Indian music. It was composed two years ago.

Jan. 7   Aaron Copland's symphonic suite *Statements for Orchestra* premieres in New York City, as Dimitri Mitropoulos conducts the New York Philharmonic. Each of the six episodes has a distinct character and a title designed to "help the public in understanding what the composer had in mind when writing these pieces." The music was composed between 1933 and 1935.

Jan. 12   Nikolai Miaskovsky's Symphony No. 22 in B Minor premieres in Tbilisi, Georgia, Soviet Union. Based on Caucasian folk songs, this three-movement symphony is subtitled *Symphonie-Ballade*.

Jan. 16   *Diversions on a Theme*, by Benjamin Britten, is premiered by Eugene Ormandy and the Philadelphia Orchestra, with Paul Wittgenstein as soloist. This work consists of 11 variations on one theme and is scored for orchestra and piano left-hand.

Jan. 22   William Schuman's Symphony No. 4 receives its initial performance by Artur Rodzinski and the Cleveland Orchestra. This work, in three movements, includes jazz rhythms.

Jan. 23   Bohuslav Martinu's *Concerto da camera* in F minor for violin, string orchestra, piano and timpani is premiered by Paul Sacher and the Chamber Orchestra of Basel, with Gertrude Flugel as soloist.

Feb. 8   Igor Stravinsky's *Danses concertantes* is premiered by the Janssen Symphony Orchestra in Los Angeles, the composer conducting. This neoclassical piece has five movements.

March 1   *Imaginary Landscape No. 3*, by John Cage, premieres in Chicago, the composer conducting. The third in a series of pieces with the same title, it includes sounds produced by audio frequency modulators, variable-speed turntables, Balinese gongs, tin cans and other sound-producing objects. Cage is now 29.

March 1   The Symphony No. 7 (*Leningrad*), by Dmitri Shostakovich, receives its world premiere in Kubischev. It was composed between July and December of last year, shortly after the Nazis invaded the Soviet Union and attacked Leningrad. Shostakovich says of his latest symphony, "it is a continuation of the emotions and moods of the Fifth Symphony."

March 26   Frank Martin's oratorio *Le vin herbe* premieres in Zurich. The piece is in three parts, with prologue and epilogue. This Swiss composer, now 51, bases his text for this work on the Tristan legend. Martin is appointed president of the Association of Swiss Musicians this year.

April 16   Samuel Barber's *Second Essay for Orchestra* receives its first performance by Bruno Walter and the New York Philharmonic. Like his first piece based on a literary form (the essay), this work introduces a musical thought and develops it to a conclusion. Of the two such works by this composer, today's premiere offers an orchestral chorale finale.

April 21   The Sonata for Clarinet and Piano, by Leonard Bernstein, receives its first performance in Boston, marking the emergence of this musician as a composer. For the past two summers, Bernstein has studied at the Berkshire Music Center at Tanglewood with Serge Koussevitzky. Prior to that he studied conducting with Fritz Reiner, orchestration with Randall Thompson, counterpoint and fugue with Walter Piston and orchestration with Edward B. Hill. He is now 23.

April 22   Francisco Mignone's symphonic suite *Festa das igrejas* is premiered by the NBC Symphony Orchestra in New York City, the composer conducting. The piece, in four movements, depicts impressions of Brazilian cathedrals. This Brazilian composer is now touring America.

May 12   Alberto Ginastera's *Sinfonia portena* premieres in Buenos Aires. The title means "Symphony of the Port of Buenos Aires."

May 14   *Lincoln Portrait*, by Aaron Copland, receives its world premiere by Andre Kostelanetz and the Cincinnati Symphony Orchestra. The work, commissioned by this conductor, is scored for narrator and orchestra. The text is culled from Abraham Lincoln's letters and speeches and concludes with the last lines of the Gettysburg Address. Copland later confirms that the title of this piece is *Lincoln Portrait*, not *A Lincoln Portrait*.

May 23   Arthur Honegger's Symphony No. 2 is premiered by Paul Sacher and the Chamber Orchestra of Basel. Written last year while the Nazis occupied Paris, the three-movement symphony tries to capture the French mood during that period.

June 6   *Bachianas brasileiras No. 4* for orchestra, by Heitor Villa-Lobos, premieres in New York, the composer conducting. This piece was begun in the 1930s as a piano work and was orchestrated by the composer last year.

June 14   *A Ceremony of Carols*, by Benjamin Britten, receives its initial performance in Aldeburgh. It is scored for teen-age boys' chorus and harp, with texts from medieval sources. It becomes one of Britten's most popular pieces.

June 26   Rodolfo Halffter's Violin Concerto is premiered by Carlos Chavez and the Orquesta Sinfonica de Mexico, with Samuel Dushkin as soloist. This concerto is in four movements. The composer, formerly active in defending the Loyalist government in Spain, settled in Mexico after its defeat. Two years ago he founded "La Paloma Azul," the first Mexican company devoted to contemporary ballet.

July 14   William Schuman's symphonic suite *Newsreel* premieres in New York City. The composer describes this work as a symphonic suite "in five shots."

July 15   *Choros* Nos. 6, 9 and 11 are performed for the first time in Rio de Janeiro. The composer, Heitor Villa-Lobos, conducts. The first two pieces are scored for orchestra; the third, for piano and orchestra. They are the least popular of the 14 "Choros" pieces he writes.

July 20   Nikolai Miaskovsky's Symphony No. 23 in A Minor premieres in Moscow. Like his last symphony, first performed in January, this one is in three movements and is derived from Caucasian folk melodies.

July 24   Alan Bush's Symphony No. 1 is premiered by the London Philharmonic, the composer conducting. Bush has studied piano with Artur Schnabel and composition with John Ireland. He joined the Communist Party in 1935 and, a year later, organized and became president of the Worker's Music Association in London. He is now 41.

Aug. 14   Edmund Rubbra's Symphony No. 4 premieres in London. This is a three-movement work.

Oct. 14   Concerto for Two Pianos, Percussion and Orchestra, by Bela Bartok, is premiered by Sir Adrian Boult and the Royal Philharmonic Orchestra, with Louis Kentner and Llona Kabos as soloists. This work is an orchestral arrangement of Bartok's Sonata for Two Pianos and Percussion.

Oct. 15   *Leningrad*, by Dmitri Shostakovich, receives its first performance in Moscow. It is a suite for chorus and orchestra that pays tribute to the citizens of Leningrad for opposing the Nazis.

Oct. 15   The Symphony No. 1, by Bohuslav Martinu, receives its initial performance by Serge Koussevitzky and the Boston Symphony Orchestra. The four-movement neoclassical work dispenses with key signatures but nevertheless gravitates toward the tonal centers of B and B-flat. It is the first of six symphonies Martinu composes. He arrived in New York last year after fleeing the Nazis.

Oct. 22   John Alden Carpenter's Symphony No. 2 is premiered by Bruno Walter and the New York Philharmonic. The three-movement work was based on a piano quintet Carpenter composed in 1934. It is the last symphony he composes.

Oct. 28   Andre Jolivet's cantata *La tentation derniere* premieres in Paris. It is based on the life of Joan of Arc.

Nov. 13   Darius Milhaud's Concerto for Two Pianos and Orchestra is premiered by Fritz Reiner and the Pittsburgh Symphony Orchestra, with Victor Babin and Vitya Vronsky as piano soloists.

Nov. 14   *Marco Takes a Walk*, by Deems Taylor, is premiered in New York by the New York Philharmonic. It depicts, through symphonic variations, a walk down a street.

Nov. 27   Paul Creston's *A Fanfare for Paratroopers* is premiered by Eugene Goossens and the Cincinnati Symphony Orchestra. The work is a tribute to American fighting men.

Dec. 11   *Fanfare de la liberte*, by Darius Milhaud, is premiered by Eugene Goossens and the Cincinnati Symphony Orchestra. Through music, it praises the French spirit for survival.

Dec. 17   Aaron Copland's *Danzon cubano* is premiered in a two-piano version by Leonard Bernstein and the composer in New York. Based on a Cuban dance form that attracted Copland when he visited Mexico, it was conceived as a birthday tribute to the League of Composers. Copland later creates an orchestral version of the piece.

1942 Births, Deaths and Debuts

Jan. 5   Pianist Maurizio Pollini is born in Milan, Italy.

Jan. 6   French soprano Emma Calve, 83, dies in Millau, France. Calve had made her debut in 1882. She created the title role in *Sapho* and Anita in *La Navarraise*, both by Jules Massenet. But she was best known for her portrayal of Carmen. She left an autobiography, *My Life*, and later another book of memoirs, *Sous tous les ciels j'ai chante*.

Feb. 24   American dancer, choreographer and ballet director John Neumeier is born in Milwaukee, Wisconsin.

March 15   Austrian composer Alexander von Zemlinsky, 70, dies in Larchmont, New York. Encouraged in his youth by Johannes Brahms, he was a product of the Vienna Conservatory. At age 35 he became conductor of the Vienna Volksoper and, two years later, of the Vienna Opera. He went on to conduct the Mannheim Opera, the German Opera in Prague and the Berlin State Opera. He taught Arnold Schoenberg and was often associated with concerts of new music by Schoenberg, Alban Berg and Anton Webern. Despite the fact that his music is romantic, he was able to be progressive within that context. His operas, according to Schoenberg, "satisfied the demands of the theater with better musical substance than any composer after Richard Wagner." His most successful work is the opera *Es war einmal*, premiered in 1900. He composed five other operas, three symphonies, chamber music, piano music, four string quartets and songs.

April 27   German pianist Emil von Sauer, 79, dies in Vienna. A student of Franz Liszt, he concertized from the 1880s until 1936. He was a teacher at the Meisterschule fur Klavierspiel in Vienna, wrote many pieces and also edited the piano works of Johannes Brahms.

May 7   German conductor Felix Weingartner, 78, dies in Winterthur, Switzerland. Through the recommendation of

EMMA CALVE

Franz Liszt, Weingartner became Hans von Bulow's assistant with the Meiningen Orchestra. In 1891 he became conductor of the Berlin Opera, and in 1908 he succeeded Gustav Mahler as conductor of the Vienna Philharmonic. He guest-conducted around Europe and the United States and eventually settled in Switzerland, where he founded a school of conducting. He was also a composer and librettist and wrote several books.

May 25   Austrian cellist Emanuel Feuermann, 39, dies in New York. After studies in Vienna and Leipzig, at age 16 he became a teacher at the Cologne Conservatory. He concertized in Europe and the United States and was a professor at the Berlin Hochschule fur Musik. He gave chamber music concerts with Artur Schnabel and Bronislaw Huberman.

June 5   American composer Charles Dodge is born in Ames, Iowa.

June 12   English composer Walter Leigh, 42, is killed in action in the vicinity of Tobruk, Libya. A pupil of Paul Hindemith, his work includes songs, piano music, and orchestral and choral works. His comic opera *Jolly Roger* is among his best-known compositions.

July 1   American dancer and choreographer Twyla Tharp is born in Portland, Indiana.

July 5   American dancer, choreographer and ballet director Eliot Feld is born in Brooklyn, New York.

Aug. 11   German composer and music theorist Richard Heinrich Stein, 60, dies at Santa Brigida, Canary Islands. This musician constructed a quarter-tone clarinet and published a quarter-tone work in 1906, making him the first composer to do so. Other works include approximately 100 piano pieces and 50 songs.

Aug. 12   Italian baritone Pasquale Amato, 65, dies in Queens, New York City. He made his singing debut in 1900 in Naples and later sang leading roles at the Metropolitan Opera until 1921. A highlight of his career was his creation of the role of Jack Rance in the world premiere of Giacomo Puccini's *Girl of the Golden West*.

Aug. 18   Czech composer Erwin Schulhoff, 48, dies in a concentration camp in Wulzburg, Bavaria. Schulhoff's teachers included Max Reger. This musician is especially noted for his cantata that sets the German text of the Communist Manifesto (1848) to music. Schulhoff also worked on quarter-tone music with Alois Haba. He wrote several ballets, an opera, many orchestral works (including seven symphonies) and much chamber music.

Aug. 22   Michel Fokine dies of pneumonia in New York City at the age of 62. Fokine is honored as a great choreographer and ballet reformer who brought ballet into the twentieth century. He graduated from the Imperial School of Ballet in Saint Petersburg and made his debut at the Imperial Theatre in 1898. One of the great dancers of his generation, he was known for his expressive dancing and solid technique.

In 1905 Fokine began choreographing for student performances and individual concerts. One of his earliest efforts was *The Dying Swan*, choreographed for Anna Pavlova in 1905. Two years later he staged his first ballet for the Imperial Theatre, *Le Pavillon d'Armide*. In 1909 Diaghilev invited him to stage several ballets for the Diaghilev Ballets Russes. His association with that company marks the beginning of Fokine's serious career as a choreographer and the opening of a new era in ballet. During his years with the company, Fokine produced some of the most important ballets of the twentieth century, including Le Spectre de la Rose, Petrouchka, Firebird, Scheherazade and Carnaval. These works were a dramatic departure from those of academic choreographers such as Petipa.

Fokine believed that a ballet should be a unity of choreography, music and design. The movement for each piece should be appropriate to the time and place of the action rather than conform to theoretical academic principles. He opposed the use of mime to tell a story and utilized movement and dramatic gesture involving the whole body to move the plot. Fokine liberated the corps de ballet from the static geometric patterns of previous choreographers and used the crowd as an integral dramatic element in his work.

Fokine's influence on ballet is profound, affecting the way in which most modern choreographers think of dance.

Aug. 24   Dancer Egon Madsen is born in Ringe, Denmark.

Nov. 1   German composer Hugo Distler, 36, commits suicide in Berlin. He was a product of the Leipzig Conservatory whose musical style was influenced by 16th-century polyphony. Most of his music (and there is not that much) is for the church. He composed three cantatas and an unfinished oratorio. It is only after his death that his works become known.

Nov. 15   Conductor-pianist Daniel Barenboim is born in Buenos Aires.

Dec. 25   Croatian composer Vojislav Vuckovic, 32, dies in Belgrade after having been shot by the Nazis during an attempt to escape from his place of hiding. This musician is known for his books dealing with Marxism and music. He studied with Josef Suk and composed two symphonies. In his early works he was moving into expressionism. His attraction to Marxism, however, convinced him to drop that musical style in favor of realism.

1942   Related Events

Dance News begins publication this year. This new periodical — which appears monthly (except July and August) — features articles on all aspects of theatrical dance. Its founder is Anatole Chujoy, a Latvian-American writer and critic.

Jan.   *Dance Index* begins publication this month. This infrequently published magazine is founded under the auspices of Ballet Caravan Inc. and is edited by Baird Hastings, Lincoln Kirstein and Paul Magriel. It features pieces on all aspects of theatrical dance approached from a scholarly perspective and becomes a highly important contribution to dance scholarship.

Jan. 13   Conductor Bruno Walter announces that he has been forbidden to conduct the nonunionized Boston Symphony Orchestra by James Petrillo, president of the American Federation of Musicians. Walter had joined the union last May when he signed a contract with the Boston Symphony.

March 7   The music department of the Bibliotheque Nationale is established in Paris. It is comprised of three sections — the Bibliotheque Nationale, the library of the Paris Conservatoire and the library of the Paris Opera. Music librarian Guillaume de Van is subsequently named curator of the department. Among the special collections this library acquires are manuscripts, correspondence and other materials relating to Arthur Honegger, Georges

Migot, Camille Saint-Saens, Serge Diaghilev, Serge Lifar, Jules Massenet and many others.

March 28   The organ in the Marienkirche in Lubeck is destroyed by Allied bombs. This event marks the unfortunate end of a magnificent musical instrument that had been played by Johann Sebastian Bach and Dietrich Buxtehude.

July 8   The president of the American Federation of Musicians, James Petrillo, announces that the 140,000 members of his union will be forbidden to make commercial recordings after July 31. This campaign is to force radio stations, bars and restaurants to employ union musicians.

Sep. 20   E. Power Biggs begins his Sunday morning series of organ recitals, playing at the Busch Reisinger Museum in Cambridge, Massachusetts. Broadcast nationally over radio by CBS and internationally by shortwave, these recitals result in a 16-year role for Biggs as a programmer of music for radio.

Nov. 25   The Boston Symphony, the only nonunionized major orchestra in the United States, agrees to join the American Federation of Musicians after the union agrees to let the orchestra hire musicians anywhere.

1943   Opera

Feb. 20   Carl Orff's *Die Kluge*, with a text by the composer and based on a tale by the Grimm brothers, premieres in Frankfurt. This opera, in six scenes, is about a king who puts riddles to a clever woman. In the end she gets what she wants — the king.

June 30   Gian Francesco Malipiero's *La vita e sogno* is premiered in a German version in Breslau. Based on a tale by Pedro Calderon, this opera is in three acts.

July 5   Ermanno Wolf-Ferrari's *Gli dei a Tebe* receives its initial performance in a German version entitled *Der Kukuck von Theban* in Hannover, Germany. This three-act opera is about Hera and Zeus. It is Wolf-Ferrari's last opera.

Sep. 8   Ivan Dzerzhinsky's *Nadezhda Svetlova*, with a libretto by the composer, is performed for the first time by the personnel of the Leningrad Opera in Orenburg. The three-act opera is about a surgeon and his daughter trapped in Leningrad by the Nazis.

Oct. 7   Kurt Weill's musical *One Touch of Venus*, starring Mary Martin premieres in New York. It is about a barber who places a ring on the finger of a statue of Venus. She comes to life and settles down with him.

Oct. 10   *Barbe-bleue*, a comic opera by Jacques Ibert, premieres over radio in Lausanne. It is about a man with six wives who ultimately winds up with a seventh. It is Ibert's last opera. The composer is now director of the Academy of Rome.

1943 Dance

March 11   *El salon Mexico*, to music by Aaron Copland, is performed for the first time as a one-act ballet, choreographed by Doris Humphrey. Florence Lessing and Jose Limon star in this production by the Jose Limon Dance Company at the Studio Theater in New York. The original premiere of the music was on August 27, 1937.

April 6   The Sadler's Wells Ballet gives the initial performance of Frederick Ashton's *The Quest*, to commissioned music by William Walton. The work tells the story of Saint George's triumph over the forces of evil. Margot Fonteyn, Robert Helpmann and Leslie Edwards lead the cast. The ballet is in five scenes.

April 6   Antony Tudor's version of *Romeo and Juliet* is performed by the Ballet Theater in New York. The one-act ballet, unfinished at its premiere, is set to music by Frederick Delius. The work is performed in full on April 10. Alicia Markova, Hugh Laing, Nicholas Orlov and Antony Tudor star.

June 19   *Suite en blanc* receives its first performance in Zurich. The Paris Opera Ballet performs this work choreographed by Serge Lifar to music by Edouard Lalo. This one-act ballet is a showpiece for technical brilliance. Solange Schwarz, Yvette Chauvire, Lycette Darsonval and Lifar head the cast.

July 18   Martha Graham premieres her *Deaths and Entrances*, with music by Hunter Johnson, at Bennington College. The work is a psychological analysis of the Bronte sisters. Graham, Jane Dudley and Sophie Maslow star.

Oct. 20   The Ballet Theater gives the first performance of Antony Tudor's *Dim Lustre* in New York. Set to Richard Strauss' *Burleske* for piano and orchestra, the one-act work deals with two people who meet at a ball. They are constantly carried back into the past by various small incidents. Nora Kaye and Hugh Laing star.

Dec. 26   *Salem Shore* — a new modern dance work choreographed by Martha Graham — receives its first performance in New York City. The music is by Paul Nordoff. It is a solo dance reflecting the longing of women for their husbands in battle.

1943 Instrumental and Vocal Music

Jan. 10   Tikhon Khrennikov's Symphony No. 2 in C Major — a four-movement work reflecting Soviet will to defeat the Nazis — premieres in Moscow. The finale is later revised.

Jan. 13   William Schuman's Concerto for Piano and Small Orchestra premieres in New York. The concerto was composed last year.

Jan. 15   Virgil Thomson's *Fanfare for Orchestra* is premiered by the Cincinnati Symphony Orchestra.

Jan. 21   Sergei Prokofiev's symphonic suite *1941* receives its initial performance in Sverdlovsk. The three-movement work reflects the anguish of the Soviet people after the Nazi invasion.

Jan. 22   Morton Gould's *Fanfare for Freedom* is performed for the first time by the Cincinnati Symphony Orchestra.

Jan. 31   *Divertimento for Chamber Orchestra* premieres in Vienna. Composed by Richard Strauss, it is based on themes of piano pieces composed by Francois Couperin.

Feb. 2   Alexander Tansman's Symphony No. 5 in D Minor is premiered by the National Symphony Orchestra in Baltimore, Maryland. This four-movement symphony is the first work written by this composer since he left Europe to flee the Nazis. Olin Downes writes in the New York *Times*, "The cyclic method is present in the structure."

Feb. 13   William Schuman's *Prayer in Time of War* premieres in Pittsburgh. The work is scored for orchestra.

Feb. 14   Swedish composer Kurt Atterberg's Symphony No. 7 premieres in Frankfurt. It is subtitled *Sinfonia romantica* and was composed last year. Atterberg is now secretary of the Royal Academy of Music.

Feb. 26   Roy Harris' Symphony No. 5 receives its first performance by Serge Koussevitzky and the Boston Symphony Orchestra. The three-movement symphony was inspired by Soviet resistance to Nazi aggression. Harris dedicates it to "the heroic and freedom-loving people of our great ally, the Union of Soviet Socialist Republics." The performance is transmitted by shortwave to the Soviet Union, and the work is subsequently transmitted 11 times by shortwave to the American armed forces.

March 3   Anton Webern's *Variations for Orchestra*, Op. 30, receives its world premiere by Hermann Scherchen and the Stadtorchester in Winterthur. Consisting of six variations on a theme, the work reflects Webern's intense concentration on the horizontal and vertical aspects of dodecaphonic composition. It was composed between April and November of 1940.

March 5   Morton Gould's Symphony No. 1 is premiered by the Pittsburgh Symphony Orchestra, the composer conducting.

March 12   Aaron Copland's *Fanfare for the Common Man* receives its world premiere by the Cincinnati Symphony Orchestra. This work becomes one of the most famous of the century and is included as part of his Third Symphony.

March 26   William Schuman's *A Free Song*, with a text by Walt Whitman, is premiered by Serge Koussevitzky and the Boston Symphony Orchestra. This piece is a secular cantata scored for mixed chorus and orchestra.

May 2   Walter Damrosch's *Dunkirk* is premiered by the NBC Symphony Orchestra in New York, the composer conducting. This ballad-poem is scored for baritone solo, chorus, piano and chamber orchestra. It is dedicated to the British heroes of the evacuation of Dunkirk.

May 10   *Visions de l'amen*, by Olivier Messiaen, premieres at the Concerts de la Pleiade in Paris. Yvonne Loriod and the composer are soloists. Scored for two pianos, it is a seven-movement work based on the composer's contemplations of Jesus Christ, saints, stars, Saturn, judgment and consummation. It is an example of Messiaen's attraction to keyboard music for both the piano and the organ.

May 12   Reinhold Gliere's Concerto for Soprano and Orchestra premieres in Moscow. The piece has no text, only vocalization, making it a "vocal concerto." It is in two movements.

May 27   Norwegian composer Harald Saeverud's Symphony No. 6 (*Sinfonia dolorosa*) premieres in Bergen, the composer conducting.

May 28   Aaron Copland's orchestral suite from his ballet *Rodeo* is premiered by Arthur Fiedler and the Boston Pops Orchestra. This four-movement piece was composed from materials from Copland's full-length ballet *Rodeo: The Courting at Burnt Ranch*, which premiered on October 16, 1942.

June 24   The Symphony No. 5 in D Major, by Ralph Vaughan Williams, receives its world premiere at a London Promenade Concert, the composer conducting. The four-movement work marks a return to the composer's conservative style, which was abandoned in his Fourth Symphony. The music reflects moods of serenity and the composer's attraction to modal harmony.

July 8   Lennox Berkeley's Symphony No. 1 is premiered in London with the composer conducting. It is in four movements. The composer, now 40, is on the staff of the music department of the BBC.

Aug. 11   Richard Strauss' Concerto No. 2 for French Horn and Orchestra premieres in Salzburg. Composed some 60 years after his only other horn concerto, this, like the first, is in E-flat major. It is one of the composer's last concertos.

Aug. 25   *I Hate Music (Five Kid Songs)*, by Leonard Bernstein, premieres at the Berkshire Music Center at Tanglewood, with Jennie Tourel as soloist. Considered an early and minor work, its premiere comes less than three months before Bernstein makes his surprise conducting debut in New York City. Today is Bernstein's 25th birthday.

Aug. 25   Morton Gould's *Interplay* for piano and orchestra premieres in New York with the composer conducting and Jose Iturbi at the keyboard.

Sep. 26   Robert Russell Bennett's *The Four Freedoms* is premiered by the NBC Symphony Orchestra in New York. This symphonic suite was inspired by Franklin Delano Roosevelt's speech of the same name.

Sep. 28   *Freedom Morning* for tenor, chorus and orchestra, by Marc Blitzstein, is premiered by the London Symphony Orchestra in London, with black vocalist Roland Hayes as soloist. A black chorus of 200 participants also performs. The work is based on Negro spirituals.

Oct. 8   Igor Stravinsky's *Ode* receives its first performance by Serge Koussevitzky and the Boston Symphony Orchestra. In three parts, it is dedicated to the memory of Natalie Koussevitzky, the deceased wife of the conductor.

Oct. 15   Benjamin Britten's *Serenade for Tenor, Horn and Strings* premieres in London. This composition becomes one of the composer's best-loved pieces. Its text includes material from Ben Jonson, William Blake, John Keats and Alfred, Lord Tennyson. Walter Goehr conducts; Peter Pears is tenor soloist; Dennis Brain, horn soloist.

Oct. 22   Nicolai Berezowsky's Symphony No. 4 is premiered by the Boston Symphony Orchestra with the composer conducting. It is the composer's last symphony.

Oct. 28   *Memorial to Lidice*, by Bohuslav Martinu, is premiered by Artur Rodzinski and the New York Philharmonic; his Symphony No. 2 is premiered by Erich Leinsdorf and the Cleveland Orchestra. These first performances coincide with the 25th anniversary of Czechoslovakia's birth.

Oct. 29   Samuel Barber's *Commando March* receives its initial performance by Serge Koussevitzky and the Boston

A SCENE FROM *CATULLI CARMINA*

Symphony Orchestra. The march is broadcast by short-wave radio to various parts of the world.

Nov. 4   The Symphony No. 8, by Dmitri Shostakovich, receives its world premiere in Leningrad with Evgheny Mravinsky conducting. The piece reflects the Soviet struggle against the Nazis. The composer also describes the music as an effort "to look into the future, into the postwar epoch."

Nov. 6   Carl Orff's *Catulli Carmina* premieres in Leipzig, Germany. This scenic cantata is based on Catullus. The work subsequently becomes part of Orff's trilogy entitled *Trionfi* (*Carmina Burana, Catulli Carmina* and *Trionfo di Afrodite*). It is scored for voices, four pianos and percussion.

Nov. 12   William Schuman's Symphony No. 5 (*Symphony for Strings*) receives its initial performance by Serge Koussevitzky and the Boston Symphony Orchestra.

Dec. 3   Howard Hanson's Symphony No. 4 receives its first performance by the Boston Symphony Orchestra, the composer conducting. Inspired by the death of the composer's father, it is based on the requiem mass.

Dec. 5   Anton Webern's *Three Songs from Viae inviae*, Op. 23, premieres in Basel, with Marguerite Gradmann-Luscher as soloist.

Dec. 6   *Opus Americanum* premieres in San Francisco. Pierre Monteux conducts the San Francisco Symphony Orchestra. Composed by Darius Milhaud, it is an orchestral tribute to the United States.

Dec. 8   Nikolai Miaskovsky's Symphony No. 24 in F Minor in three movements receives its first performance in Moscow.

Dec. 16   Bernard Hermann's symphonic piece *For the Fallen* is premiered by the New York Philharmonic, the composer conducting. The composer describes the piece as a "berceuse [lullaby] for those who lie asleep on the many alien battlefields."

Dec. 30   Aram Khachaturian's Symphony No. 2 (*Symphony of Bells*) premieres in Moscow, as Boris Khaikin conducts the Moscow Conservatory Orchestra. The symphony, in four movements, includes church bells. The composer states that the third movement depicts "the superhuman sufferings caused to the Soviet people by the Nazi monsters."

1943   Births, Deaths and Debuts

Feb. 16   Dancer Anthony Dowell is born in London, England.

March 16   Harpsichordist Rudolf Dolmetsch, 36, is reported missing at sea. A member of the musical antiquarian family, he is lost in combat as a gunner in the Royal Artillery.

March 23   Russian-born composer and theorist Joseph Schillinger, 47, dies in New York. He was a product of the Saint Petersburg Conservatory and later taught and conducted at the State Academy of Music in Kharkov. He left the Soviet Union in 1928 and came to America, where he settled in New York and taught at the New School for Social Research. He never established himself as an impor-

tant composer but wrote books and treatises on musical composition and analyses that attracted much attention (George Gershwin decided to study with him). These include *The Mathematical Basis of the Arts* and his masterpiece, *The Schillinger System of Musical Composition*.

March 28   Russian composer Serge Rachmaninoff, 69, dies in Beverly Hills, California. A product of the Saint Petersburg Conservatory, he also studied composition under Sergei Taneyev and Anton Arensky at the Moscow Conservatory. Tchaikovsky encouraged him to pursue a musical career, and at age 19 Rachmaninoff composed his Prelude in C-sharp Minor — a piece that quickly became internationally famous.

After he graduated, his First Symphony was premiered in 1897. It failed, and Rachmaninoff subsequently destroyed the score (it was reconstructed in 1945 from the orchestra parts, which survived). He then began touring successfully as a pianist. In 1901 he premiered his Second Piano Concerto, conducted by his cousin, Alexander Siloti. The concerto became the single work of its genre since 1900 to achieve a truly international appreciation. Rachmaninoff quickly became a legend and was compared to Franz Liszt.

Rachmaninoff was in demand as a conductor and twice turned down the position of music director of the Boston Symphony Orchestra. Other conducting positions he did accept were with the Bolshoi Theater (opera) and the Philharmonic Society Orchestra in Moscow.

He left the Soviet Union shortly after the revolution and never returned, settling first in Lucerne, Switzerland and later in Los Angeles. (He consistently opposed the Soviet regime. Despite this criticism, his music enjoyed great popularity in the Soviet Union and was not suppressed. His position of opposition to the Soviet government was somewhat toned down when Nazi Germany invaded the Soviet Union in 1941.)

As a composer, his music is clearly rooted in the 19th-century Russian romantic tradition. Like Gustav Mahler, he was the last great romantic composer of his nation who excelled both as a composer and as a conductor and whose romanticism was steeped in morbidity and melancholy. His soaring melodies and wide-spaced harmonies (minor keys prevail) were never allowed to give way to any modern trend or revolutionary approach to composition, such as those that, by the time of his death today, have become established, and even entrenched, in Western music. Rachmaninoff's works include three operas, three symphonies, four piano concertos and many other piano, choral, chamber and orchestral works.

April 4   French composer Raoul Laparra, 66, dies near Paris as a result of an Allied air raid. He had studied with Gabriel Faure and Jules Massenet. The composer was also a music critic for *Le Matin* (Paris). Laparra's music was mostly inspired by Spanish subjects. Best remembered for having won the Grand Prix de Rome in 1903, he composed six operas, some incidental music, piano music and other works.

April 25   Dancer Jean-Pierre Bonnefous is born in Bourg-en-Bresse, France.

April 28   Dancer Ivan Nagy is born in Debrecen, Hungary.

May 2   German soprano Irmgard Seefried makes her debut at the Vienna Opera as Eva in *Die Meistersinger*.

May 12   American composer-conductor Albert Stoessel, 48, dies in New York as he conducts a performance of Walter Damrosch's *Dunkirk*. At one time head of the music department at New York University, he composed chamber, choral and orchestral works.

June 23   Conductor and pianist James Levine is born in Cincinnati, Ohio.

July 13   German ethnomusicologist Kurt Huber, 49, is decapitated by the Gestapo in Munich. He had been found guilty of participating in an anti-Hitler student protest. He was a specialist on Bavarian folk songs and taught at Munich University.

Aug. 6   American dancer Carolyn Adams is born in New York City.

Oct. 29   American composer and music theorist Percy Goetschius, 90, dies in Manchester, New Hampshire. A product of the Stuttgart Conservatory, he eventually joined the faculties of Syracuse University, the New England Conservatory of Music and the New York Institute of Musical Art. A reactionary, he advocated resolution of all harmonic dissonance and wrote many books expounding such concepts. These include *The Homophonic Forms of Musical Composition*.

Nov. 14   Substituting for an indisposed Bruno Walter (he has the flu), Leonard Bernstein — 25 years old — conducts the New York Philharmonic Symphony Orchestra at Carnegie Hall and creates an overwhelming sensation. The event is broadcast nationally over radio. Bernstein conducts from memory and without a baton. The program includes music by Robert Schumann, Richard Strauss and the world premiere of *Theme, Variations and Finale* by Miklos Rozsa. Bernstein later says he was up till 4:30 a.m. the day of the concert studying, drinking coffee and dozing and that he was informed at 10 a.m. by the orchestra's management that he was to conduct.

Critics praise him, and the story makes the front page of the New York *Times*. In that article, Olin Downes says Bernstein is one of a new generation ". . . indubitably to be reckoned with."

Nov. 16   Canadian dancer David Adams is born in Winnipeg.

Nov. 20   Dancer and choreographer Meredith Monk is born in Lima, Ohio.

1943 Related Events

Artur Rodzinski becomes music director of the New York Philharmonic after a two-season period in which guest conductors led that orchestra. He holds this post until 1947. Alfred Wallenstein becomes music director of the Los Angeles Philharmonic Orchestra this year, ending a three-season period during which the orchestra had been conducted by guest conductors. He holds this post until 1956. Wallenstein's appointment is the result of long deliberation by the management of the orchestra.

Jan. 6   After having been prohibited from using Washington's Constitution Hall in 1939, black contralto Marian Anderson gives a concert there at the invitation of the Daughters of the American Revolution. She had demanded that the segregation policy be suspended. The integrated audience includes first lady Eleanor Roosevelt as well as members of the cabinet and the Supreme Court.

Feb. 1   Serge Rachmaninoff becomes a naturalized citizen of the United States. He lives another two months.

May 3   William Schuman is awarded the Pulitzer Prize for music for *Secular Cantata No. 2, A Free Song*.

June 21   Due to British composer Michael Tippett's failure to meet the requirements of his military registration as a conscientious objector, he is sent to the Wormwood Scrubs, Surrey prison for three months.

Aug. 16   The auditorium of the Teatro alla Scala in Milan is damaged by an Allied bomb.

Oct. 18   An Allied air raid obliterates the National Theater in Munich. This event marks the destruction of the home of the Staatsoper, constructed in 1818.

Nov. 4   Florence Foster Jenkins gives a recital at the Ritz-Carlton Hotel ballroom in New York City. She had planned to appear in one number as an "angel of inspiration," but did not. Robert Coleman writes in the *Daily Mirror* (New York), "We suspect that due to the war emergency she was unable to obtain the airplane wire required to support her angelic wings."

Nov. 15   The San Carlo Opera House in Naples resumes performances after the German retreat.

Nov. 21   American pianist Eugene Istomin plays Brahms' Second Concerto with the New York Philharmonic, winning the Leventritt Award.

Dec. 4   The offices of German music publisher Breitkopf and Hartel are destroyed by Allied bombs today in Leipzig. Many precious relics and engraved manuscripts are destroyed.

1944 Opera

July 4   Henri Sauguet's one-act opera *La Gageure imprevue* is premiered at the Opera-Comique in Paris. Sauguet is now 43.

1944 Dance

Feb. 25   Agnes De Mille's one-act ballet *Tally-Ho!* is premiered by the Ballet Theater in Los Angeles. The music is by Christoph Willibald Gluck and arranged by Paul Nordoff; the costumes and scenery are by Motley. It is about a young woman who tries to make her husband prefer her to his books. The cast includes the choreographer Hugh Laing, Anton Dolin, Lucia Chase and Muriel Bentley.

April 5   Merce Cunningham's *Spontaneous Earth* and *Triple Paced*, both to music by John Cage, are premiered in New York City.

April 18   *Fancy Free*, a one-act ballet choreographed by Jerome Robbins, is premiered by the Ballet Theater at the Metropolitan Opera House in New York. The ballet, set to music by Leonard Bernstein, deals with three sailors on shore leave. It is Robbins' first work. Harold Lang, John Kriza and Robbins are the sailors in the first cast.

Sep. 10   The Ballet Russe de Monte Carlo gives the world premiere of George Balanchine's *Danses concertantes* in New York. The plotless ballet in six movements is set to Igor Stravinsky's music of the same name. Alexandra Danilova and Leon Danielian have the lead roles.

Sep. 23   George Balanchine's *Le Bourgeois Gentilhomme* is given its initial performance by the Ballet Russe de Monte Carlo in New York. The ballet, based on a Moliere comedy, is to music by Richard Strauss. Nicholas Magallanes, Michel Katcharov, and Nathalie Krassovska star.

Oct. 26   The Sadler's Wells Ballet premieres the *Miracle in the Gorbals*. The choreography is by Robert Helpmann and the music by Arthur Bliss. The ballet depicts the inevitability of the death of Christ. The dancers include Helpmann, Moira Shearer, Alexis Rassine and David Paltenghi.

Oct. 30   Martha Graham presents *Appalachian Spring* during a concert at the Library of Congress in Washington, D.C. The work, which tells the story of a pioneer couple building a home in the West, is to a score by Aaron Copland. Sets are by Isamu Noguchi. The cast includes Graham, May O'Donnell, Merce Cunningham and Erick Hawkins. Commissioned by Elizabeth Sprague Coolidge, the ballet is one of the most significant of the 20th century. The title was chosen by Graham, who was inspired by a poem of Hart Crane containing those words. Critic John

Martin writes in the New York *Times*, "It is completely simple, homely, dedicated, and a lovelier work you would have to go far to find." The music wins the New York Critics Circle Award in 1945; it also wins a Pulitzer Prize for music.

Nov. 29   The Ballet Rambert gives the initial performance of Walter Gore's *Simple Symphony* in Bristol, England. The ballet, in one act, is set to Benjamin Britten's symphony of the same name. The abstract work has a nautical flavor. Sally Gilmour and Walter Gore star.

1944   Instrumental and Vocal Music

Jan. 5   William Grant Still's *In Memoriam: The Colored Soldiers Who Died for Democracy* is premiered by Artur Rodzinski and the New York Philharmonic. This orchestral work was commissioned by the League of Composers of New York and is dedicated to Negro soldiers who have perished in World War II. Still is known as "the dean of Afro-American composers."

Jan. 13   Igor Stravinsky's *Four Hungarian Moods* and the orchestral piece *Circus Polka* receive their first performance by the Boston Symphony Orchestra in Cambridge, Massachusetts, the composer conducting. The *Circus Polka* was commissioned by the Ringling Brothers Barnum and Bailey Circus to accompany an elephant ballet. Stravinsky begins the concert with his arrangement of *"The Star-Spangled Banner"* (he undertook the arrangement as his tribute to American patriotism). A performance of the arrangement scheduled for January 15 is canceled due to complaints that its harmonies are "queer."

Jan. 20   *Symphonic Metamorphoses on Themes by Carl Maria von Weber*, by Paul Hindemith, receives its initial performance by Artur Rodzinski and the New York Philharmonic. The piece is in four movements.

Jan. 28   *Jeremiah Symphony* (Symphony No. 1), by Leonard Bernstein, receives its world premiere in Pittsburgh. The composer conducts the Pittsburgh Symphony, and Jennie Tourel (singing in Hebrew) is soloist. The work — planned as a lamentation for soprano and orchestra — features a text from the Book of Lamentations. Reviews are favorable, and the symphony wins the New York Music Critics Circle Award for the 1943–44 season.

Feb. 6   Arnold Schoenberg's Piano Concerto, Op. 42, is premiered by Leopold Stokowski and the NBC Symphony Orchestra in New York, with Eduard Steuermann as piano soloist. Composed in 1942, this one-movement work has four sections. Although the concerto is dodecaphonic, triadic structures and tonal references are included.

Feb. 13   Symphony No. 4, by George Antheil, is premiered by Leopold Stokowski and the NBC Symphony Orchestra. Antheil is now 43.

Feb. 15   *Ludus Tonalis*, by Paul Hindemith, receives its world premiere by pianist Willard MacGregor at the University of Chicago. Subtitled *Studies on Counterpoint, Tonal Organization and Piano Playing*, this piece consists of 12 three-voiced fugues, each in a different key; "interludiums" are found between each fugue. A praeludium and postludium open and close the entire piece. In all, the work has 25 sections and a duration of about 45 minutes. It is compared to the art of Johann Sebastian Bach. A critic for the New York *Herald-Tribune* writes, "The 'Ludus' is entirely tonal, being written in the type of twelve-tone scale Hindemith now champions, which is based on acoustic laws."

Feb. 17   William Schuman's *William Billings Overture* is premiered by Artur Rodzinski and the New York Philharmonic. The symphonic piece is based on themes by the American composer William Billings.

Feb. 21   Sergei Prokofiev's cantata *Ballad of a Boy Who Remained Unknown* premieres in Moscow. It is scored for soprano, tenor, chorus and orchestra.

March 3   Samuel Barber's Symphony No. 2 receives its initial performance by Serge Koussevitzky and the Boston Symphony Orchestra. The three-movement symphony, composed on commission from the U.S. Air Corps, is a tribute to the Air Force and includes a part for electrical tone generator simulating a signal code. The Office of War Information subsequently broadcasts it internationally by shortwave radio. Barber later revises the symphony.

March 5   Walter Piston's Symphony No. 2 is premiered by Hans Kindler and the National Symphony Orchestra in Washington. It is in three movements.

March 13   *Bachianas Brasileiras No. 7*, by Heitor Villa-Lobos, receives its first performance in Rio de Janeiro, the composer conducting. Scored for orchestra, it concludes with a four-voiced fugue.

March 19   Michael Tippett's oratorio *A Child of Our Time*, with a libretto by the composer, receives its initial performance by Walter Goehr and a chorus at Morley College in London. Based on an incident between a Nazi diplomat and a Jewish youth, the oratorio reflects the composer's hatred of injustice. He also includes melodic references to Negro spirituals and writes the text himself. A critic for the *Times Educational Supplement* writes, "It is a silhouette of all persecuted humanity."

March 14   Symphony No. 6 (*Gettysburg Address Symphony*), by Roy Harris, is premiered by Serge Koussevitzky and the Boston Symphony Orchestra. Dedicated "to the Armed Forces of Our Nation," it was inspired by the life and work of Abraham Lincoln.

April 22   *U.S. Highball, a Musical Account of a Transcontinental Hobo Trip*, for chorus and instruments, receives its world premiere today at Carnegie Recital Hall, New York City. Composed by Harry Partch, it is scored for subjective voice (tenor-baritone), several objective voices (mostly baritones), kithara II, surrogate kithara, harmonic canon II, chromelodeon I, diamond marimba, boo, spoils of war, cloud-chamber bowls and bass marimba. The work is approximately 25 minutes long. Partch describes this piece as a "hobo allegro form," in which the subjective voice is the protagonist and the objective voices are the other hobos on the trip. The text includes graffiti from boxcars. Partch later says in his book *Genesis of a Music* (1949) that he considers the piece to be his most creative work.

Partch is largely self-taught and has spent years building his own instruments to accommodate his 43-tone scale and system of "just intonation." Also premiered on today's program are *Barstow — Eight Hitchhiker Inscriptions from a Highway Railing at Barstow, California* (composed in 1941 and later revised several times), *San Francisco — A Setting of the Cries of Two Newsboys on a Foggy Night in the Twenties* (composed in 1943) and *The Letter — A Depression Message from a Hobo Friend* (also composed in 1943). These four works comprise a set called *The Wayward*. In 1955 Partch composes another work entitled *Ulysses at the Edge*; that piece becomes the fifth component of *The Wayward*. *Yankee Doodle Fantasy* (composed this year) is another (unrelated) piece by Partch that receives its first performance at today's concert.

April 27   Elliott Carter's Symphony No. 1 receives its initial performance as Howard Hanson conducts in Rochester, New York. Inspired by "the characteristic beauties of Cape Cod," it has three movements. Carter is now 35.

May 12   Alberto Ginastera's symphonic overture *Obertura para el Faust criollo* premieres in Santiago, Chile.

May 15   Lukas Foss' orchestral suite *The Prairie* is performed in its complete version by Robert Shaw and the Collegiate Chorale in New York.

June 9   Tikhon Khrennikov's Symphony No. 2 in C Major is performed in a new version with a revised finale in Moscow.

June 18   *Sonatina No. 1* for 16 wind instruments by Richard Strauss is premiered in Dresden. It was composed last year.

Sep. 3   Paul Hindemith's *Theme and Variations According to the Four Temperaments* receives its initial performance by Richard Burgin and players from the Boston Symphony Orchestra. Lukas Foss plays the piano part. Consisting of three themes and four variations, the piece was originally conceived as a ballet, and its variations characterize people of "melancholic," "sanguine," "phlegmatic," and "choleric" moods.

Sep. 30   Ralph Vaughan Williams' Concerto in A Minor for Oboe and String Orchestra is premiered by Malcolm Sargent and the Liverpool Philharmonic Orchestra, with Leon Goossens as soloist.

Oct. 8   Samuel Barber's *Capricorn Concerto* is premiered in New York. It is scored for flute, oboe, trumpet and strings.

Oct. 13   Serge Koussevitzky and the Boston Symphony Orchestra premiere David Diamond's Symphony No. 2. The four-movement symphony includes atonal melodies.

Oct. 17   Aaron Copland's chamber version of *Letter from Home* is premiered by Paul Whiteman and the Philco Radio Orchestra.

Oct. 20   Arnold Schoenberg's *Theme and Variations for Orchestra*, Op. 43b, receives its first performance by Serge Koussevitzky and the Boston Symphony Orchestra. Notated with a key signature of G major, it marks a return to tonality (the second time Schoenberg has returned to tonality over the last 10 years). The work consists of a theme and seven variations.

Oct. 21   Walter Piston's *Fugue on a Victory Tune* is premiered by Artur Rodzinski and the New York Philharmonic.

Oct. 22   *Chant de liberation*, by Arthur Honegger, premieres in Paris. This choral work is scored for baritone, chorus and orchestra.

Oct. 24   Samuel Barber's *A Stopwatch and an Ordnance Map* is premiered in Columbus, Ohio. Composed as a wartime piece, it is a choral work scored for men's chorus and kettledrums.

Nov. 11   Elie Siegmeister's *Ozark Set* for orchestra is premiered by Dimitri Mitropoulos conducting the Minneapolis Symphony Orchestra.

Nov. 23   Arnold Schoenberg's *Ode to Napoleon Bonaparte*, Op. 41, receives its first performance by Artur Rodzinski and the New York Philharmonic. It is scored for string orchestra, piano and speaker, with a text by Byron. A review in *Musical America* (New York) says: "There are dark hints of sequential developments, and there are plain evidences of harmony! Is this work a confession, an armistice, or a revolution?"

Nov. 24   Dimitri Mitropoulos and the Minneapolis Symphony Orchestra premiere David Diamond's *Rounds for String Orchestra*. The piece consists of three uninterrupted movements.

Dec. 1   Bela Bartok's Concerto for Orchestra receives its world premiere by Serge Koussevitzky and the Boston Symphony Orchestra. The five-movement concerto is the first Bartok begins and completes in America. It was commissioned by the Koussevitzky Music Foundation. Bartok is now suffering from leukemia and severe depression. The concerto becomes one of his most popular pieces.

Dec. 10   George Antheil's *Nocturne*, based on his symphonic piece *Decatur at Algiers*, is premiered by Vladimir Golschmann and the St. Louis Symphony Orchestra.

Dec. 16   Vittorio Rieti's *Sinfonia tripartita* is premiered by Vladimir Golschmann and the St. Louis Symphony Orchestra. This work is the fourth of six symphonies he composes.

1944 — Births, Deaths and Debuts

Feb. 6   Victor Dandre, 74, dies in London. He was husband and manager of Anna Pavlova. After her death, he took over the Ballet Russe de Colonel de Basil, which then became the Royal Covent Garden Russian Ballet.

Feb. 8   Italian soprano Lina Cavalieri, 69, dies during an air raid in Florence, Italy. A great beauty, she became the toast of Paris after appearances at the Folies-Bergere. Her first husband, Russian Prince Bariatinsky, persuaded her to turn to opera. In 1906 she was engaged by the Metropolitan, where her beauty made more of an impression than her singing. She married American millionaire Winthrop Chandler and left him after a week, causing a huge scandal that resulted in her dismissal from the Metropolitan. She was also later married to French tenor Lucien Muratore.

CECILE CHAMINADE

Feb. 20   American pianist Byron Janis makes his debut with the Pittsburgh Symphony Orchestra playing Serge Rachmaninoff's Second Piano Concerto.

April 13   French composer Cecile Chaminade, 86, dies in Monte Carlo. She was known as a "salon" musician, and as a concert pianist (her American debut was in 1908); her career was made mostly in France, though her works gained recognition in England and America as well. *Etude symphonique*, *Valse-caprice* and *Les sylvans* were among her best-known works.

May 6   French-American music writer, bibliographer, editor and librarian Carl Engel, 60, dies in New York. He was chief of the Music Division of the Library of Congress, president of Schirmer Inc. and an editor of the *Musical Quarterly* to which he also contributed. He was also president of the American Musicological Society and a composer of impressionistic songs and chamber music.

May 8   English composer Ethel Mary Smyth, 86, dies in Woking, Surrey. She studied at the Leipzig Conservatory. Her first big success was with her Mass for solo voices, chorus and orchestra which premiered in London in 1893. She then became a composer of stage works. Several operatic successes culminated with *The Wreckers*, which premiered in Leipzig in 1906. She also wrote many orchestral works. Her music is characterized by German romanticism and English nationalist tendencies. With her music and her militant feminism, she made her way to international attention. Her battle song, "The March of the Women" advanced the cause of the suffrage movement. She was made a Dame of the British Empire in 1922. She also wrote autobiographical and humorous essays.

June 15   Italian composer Riccardo Zandonai, 61, dies in Pesaro, Italy. His principal teacher was Pietro Mascagni. Zandonai's first success came with his opera *Il grillo del focolare*, produced in 1908. The following year his opera *Conchita* was premiered. That event established him as a prominent member of the Italian operatic world. He became involved in politics during the First World War and campaigned for the return of former Italian provinces. He composed a total of 11 operas, including *Francesca da Rimini*; 4 symphonic poems; a requiem mass; concertos; and chamber music. As a composer, he was a flamboyant Italian romantic, who contributed to the modern verismo tradition.

July 14   Dancer, choreographer Mikhail Mordkin dies in Millbrook, New York at the age of 63. One of Anna Pavlova's partners, he was important in the development of ballet in the United States. Mordkin graduated from the Moscow Imperial School of Ballet in 1899 and joined the Bolshoi Theater. During 1909 he danced with Diaghilev's Ballets Russes but left the following year to tour with Anna Pavlova and then to form his own group of Russian ballet stars. He served as director of the Bolshoi Ballet from 1917 to 1923. That year he came to the United States where he spent the remainder of his life touring with his own companies, choreographing and teaching. In 1937 he established the Mordkin Ballet, which became the nucleus of Ballet Theater in 1939.

Aug. 19   English conductor Sir Henry Wood, 75, dies in Hitchin, Herts, England. Most famous for founding the Promenade Concerts in London in 1895, he also founded the Nottingham Orchestra in 1899 and was conductor of the Wolverhampton Festival Choral Society and the Norwich Festival. In 1923 he became professor at the Royal Academy of Music. He also composed under the name of Paul Klenovsky.

Aug. 23   Russian composer Nikolai Roslavetz. 63, dies in Moscow. His principal teacher was Sergei Vassilenko at the Moscow Conservatory. In 1913 his Violin Sonata was published (this piece was atonal — the first by a Russian composer). His work and intellectual nature helped him become a leader of the modern movement in Russia. Unfortunately, the results of the Soviet Revolution pushed his work out of prominence: He was severely criticized by the press once "socialist realism" was firmly entrenched. He then attempted to compose mindless operettas and ballets to satisfy the Soviet musical establishment; these efforts failed. His work, however, began to be performed in West Germany and later in America. Had he not been persecuted by the Soviet establishment, he might have become that nation's equivalent of Arnold Schoenberg. His work includes three string quartets, three piano trios, four violin sonatas, a symphony, symphonic poems (including *End of the World*), a violin concerto and other works.

Oct. 5   American dancer Richard Cragun is born in Sacramento, California.

Oct. 16   Polish-Jewish composer Hans Krasa, 44, dies in Auschwitz concentration camp. A pupil of Alexander von Zemlinsky, he was successful as a young conductor (Kroll Opera, Berlin). He was living and working in Prague, was interned two years ago by the Nazis and was executed today. His music, somewhat atonal, aims for a high level of entertainment.

Oct. 20   American composer William Albright is born in Gary, Indiana.

Nov. 4   American pianist Leon Fleischer, age 16, appears with the New York Philharmonic playing Concerto for Piano and Orchestra in D Minor by Johannes Brahms. Pierre Monteux conducts. Monteux subsequently calls Fleischer "the pianistic find of the century." Fleischer's official debut was with Monteux and the San Francisco Symphony Orchestra last year, but this performance creates a greater sensation.

Nov. 13   German composer Paul Graener, 72, dies in Salzburg. He achieved his success as an opera composer and was a director of the Mozarteum in Salzburg. He also taught at the Royal Academy of Music in London. Later, in 1920, he succeeded Max Reger at the Leipzig Conservatory. His music is romantic, in the German 19th-century tradition, and includes folk elements.

Nov. 14   Hungarian-born violinist Carl Flesch, 71, dies in Lucerne, Switzerland. He made his debut in 1895, was a court musician for the Queen of Rumania, a faculty member of the Curtis Institute of Music and a member of the Curtis Quartet. He wrote *The Art of the Violin* (a standard instructional book about that instrument) and edited much violin music.

Nov. 26   Coloratura soprano Florence Foster Jenkins, approximately 70, dies in New York City. This singer founded the Verdi Club in 1917 and gave many recitals in New York, often at the Ritz-Carlton Hotel ballroom. She was noted for her costumes, exhibiting extraordinary camp, and for her terrible voice. She financed her concerts with her wealth. Irving Johnson subsequently appraises her career in *The American Weekly* by writing, "Madame Jenkins was a soloist in the best tradition of the hoot owl and bullfrog, and the cash register jingled a merry roundelay whenever she exposed her robust shape to the soggy slings and arrows of outraged music-loving audiences."

Dec. 3   Russian pianist Josef Lhevinne, 69, dies in New York. He studied at the Moscow Conservatory and started a highly successful career in Europe and America. In 1899 he married and later concertized and taught with his wife, Rosina. After the First World War, he settled in America and taught at the Juilliard School. He was known for his beautiful singing tone, his virtuoso technique and his elegant phrasing.

Dec. 21   Conductor Michael Tilson Thomas is born in Hollywood, California. He is the grandson of Boris Thomashefsky, the founder of the Yiddish Theater in New York.

Dec. 30   French writer and musicologist Romain Rolland, 78, dies in Vezelay, France. His studies on Lully, Scarlatti, Luigi Rossi and Beethoven won him much praise and recognition as a musicologist. He organized the first International Congress of Music History (Paris, 1900) and the music division of the Ecole des Hautes Etudes Sociales. His writings include the novel *Jean-Christophe* and the analytical monograph *Beethoven: Le Chant de la resurrection* (devoted to Beethoven's last sonatas and the *Missa solemnis*).

1944   Related Events

The Dance Collection of the New York Public Library is established this year as part of the library's Music Division. It is devoted to collecting and cataloging materials on all aspects of dance, including literature and iconography. It subsequently becomes the leading dance library in the world.

Events in the recording industry this year include the release by Decca (England) of its full frequency range recording ("ffrr"), which features more accurate fidelity to true musical sounds. This process was created largely as a result of the work of Arthur Haddy and his associates at Decca and was based, in part, on techniques of submarine detection employed by the British military.

Jan. 15   Boston Police Commissioner Thomas F. Sullivan, Police Captain Thomas F. Harvey and six members of a "radical squad" appear at today's Boston Symphony Orchestra concert in Cambridge, Massachusetts, where a performance of Igor Stravinsky's arrangement of "The Star-Spangled Banner" has been programmed. Several listeners had complained to police authorities about the arrangement's harmonies. The police, prepared to file a complaint against Stravinsky (under Massachusetts law Chapter 264, Section 9, prohibiting rearrangement of the national anthem; fine — $100), back down when today's performance of the arrangement is canceled.

Feb. 21   The New York City Opera gives its first performance. Laszlo Halasz conducts Dusolina Gianinni, Ma-rio Berini and George Czaplicki in a performance of Giacomo Puccini's *Tosca* at the City Center. The cost of the production is $5,739.00. Oscar Thompson says in the New York *Sun* that Czaplicki is the greatest Scarpia since Antonio Scotti. *Time* magazine, in comparing the new company to the Metropolitan Opera, says the Gianinni and Czaplicki performances were "a notch higher than the Met's recent job."

May 1   Howard Hanson is awarded the Pulitzer Prize for music for his Symphony No. 4, Op. 34.

June 11   Richard Strauss celebrates his 80th birthday by conducting a performance of his opera *Salome* in Vienna. At this performance, soprano Ljuba Welitsch sings the role for the first time.

June 30   Karl Bohm conducts a performance of Richard Wagner's *Gotterdammerung* at the Vienna State Opera House. This is the last opera performance there. The house is hit by incendiary bombs in an air raid in March of next year.

July 28   Sir Henry Wood, founder of the Promenade Concerts in London, conducts the last of these concerts prior to his death a month from now.

Aug. 16   The final rehearsal of the three-act opera *Die Liebe der Danae*, by Richard Strauss, takes place in Salzburg. Strauss completed the opera two years ago. The Nazis close all German and Austrian theaters today and the

SCENE FROM THE NEW YORK CITY OPERA'S PRODUCTION OF *TOSCA*

scheduled world premiere is cancelled. The opera does not receive its first performance until August 14, 1952.

Aug. 24   Pierre Schaeffer, pioneer of "musique concrete," presides over a radio broadcast in Paris celebrating the liberation. He reads from Victor Hugo, plays *"La Marseillaise"* and asks priests to toll their church bells. French citizens join in by singing along with various tunes coming over the radio, opening their windows and creating a massive outpouring and mingling of musical sounds.

Sep. 1   It is reported from Helsinki that many manuscripts of Finnish composer Jean Sibelius were destroyed in an Allied bombing raid on Leipzig, Germany.

Oct. 26   Florence Foster Jenkins gives her final concert at Carnegie Hall, New York City, singing music by Gluck, Mozart, Rachmaninoff and others. She also includes a song by her accompanist, Cosme McCoon, entitled "Bishop's Love Has Eyes". Robert Bagar reviews the concert in the *World-Telegram* (New York) and writes, "Of all the singers appearing before the public today only Mme. Jenkins has perfected the art of giving added zest to a written phrase by improvising it in quarter-tones, either above or below the original notes."

Oct. 30   The Ballet International, founded by the Marquis George de Cuevas, gives its premiere season in New York. The season is a financial disaster, and the company disbands.

1945 Opera

June 7   The Sadler's Wells Theater in London reopens with the premiere of Benjamin Britten's *Peter Grimes*. Montagu Slater's libretto is based on the poem "The Borough," by George Crabbe. This opera catapults Britten to world attention. The work, about a fisherman accused of mistreating and murdering his apprentice, stars Peter Pears, Joan Cross and Owen Brannigan. The conductor is Reginald Goodall.

June 21   Estonian composer Eugene Kapp's *Tuleelegid* premieres in Tallin. The opera, in five scenes, is about Estonian patriots fighting in 1343.

1945 Dance

March 2   Choreographer Roland Petit's first ballet, *Les Forains* with music by Henri Sauguet and book by Boris Kochno, is premiered by the Ballets des Champs-Elysees in Paris. The scenery and costumes are by Christian Berard. The one-act ballet, about a group of traveling performers, is danced by Janine Charrat and Ethery Pagava.

April 10   Antony Tudor's *Undertow* receives its world premiere by the Ballet Theater in New York City. The music is by William Schuman, with costumes and scenery by Raymond Breinin. The story deals with the psychological development of a murderer. Alicia Alonso, Hugh Laing, Nana Gollner, Diana Adams, Lucia Chase and others lead the cast.

June 1   *Interplay* is performed for the first time as part of Billy Rose's *Concert Varieties* in New York City. Choreographed by Jerome Robbins to music by Morton Gould, the work is in three movements and a finale, entitled "Free Play," "Horseplay," "Byplay," and "Team Play." The star dancers are Robbins, John Kriza and Janet Reed.

Oct. 4   Choreographer Michael Kidd's one-act ballet *On Stage!* is performed for the first time by the Ballet Theater in Boston. The music is by Norman Dello Joio, the scenery by Oliver Smith and the costumes by Alvin Colt.

Nov. 21   *Cinderella*, choreographed by Rostislav Zakharov to music by Sergei Prokofiev, receives its first performance in Moscow. The sets are by Pyotr Williams. The two leads are danced by Olga Lepeshinskaya and Mikhail Gabovich.

1945 Instrumental and Vocal Music

Jan. 13   Sergei Prokofiev's Symphony No. 5, Op. 100, receives its world premiere in Moscow, the composer conducting. Prokofiev composed this four-movement symphony in one month during the summer of 1944. It reflects the composer's perception of the effects of war on the Soviet people.

Feb. 3   Igor Stravinsky's *Scenes de ballet*, originally composed for a Billy Rose revue entitled *The Seven Lively Arts*, is premiered by the New York Philharmonic, the composer conducting. This is the first performance of the complete score. An abbreviated version was used in the revue.

Feb. 4   Symphony in G, by Lukas Foss, receives its initial performance by the Pittsburgh Symphony Orchestra, the composer conducting.

Feb. 9   Kurt Atterberg's Symphony No. 8 premieres in Helsinki. It is this Swedish composer's penultimate symphony.

Feb. 15   Paul Creston's Symphony No. 2 in two movements is premiered by Artur Rodzinski and the New York Philharmonic. The composer states that it was "conceived as an apotheosis of the two foundations of all music: song and dance."

Feb. 21   Heitor Villa-Lobos' *Choros No. 12* receives its first performance by the Boston Symphony Orchestra, the composer conducting.

Feb. 22   Virgil Thomson's *Symphony on a Hymn Tune* receives its initial performance by the New York Philharmonic, the composer conducting. The four-movement work is based on Southern Baptist hymns.

Feb. 26   Leon Theremin's Concerto for the Thereminovox and Orchestra (orchestral part by Anis Fuleihan) is premiered by Leopold Stokowski and the New York Symphony Orchestra, with Clara Rockmore as Thereminovox soloist.

March 25   *Figure humaine*, a cantata by Francis Poulenc with a text by Paul Eluard, premieres over the BBC Radio in London. It is scored for double chorus *a cappella* and expresses the hope of the French people for liberation from Nazi occupation.

April 6   Gunther Schuller's Concerto for Horn and Orchestra is premiered by the Cincinnati Symphony Orchestra, with the composer as soloist. Schuller, now 19, is the first horn player of this orchestra.

April 21   Olivier Messiaen's *Trois petites liturgies de la Presence Divine*, with texts by the composer, premieres in Paris, as Roger Desormiere conducts at a Concert de la Pleiade. It is scored for celesta, vibraphone, maracas, gong, tam-tam, piano, ondes Martenot, string orchestra and female chorus.

May 8   Ralph Vaughan Williams' *Thanksgiving for Victory* is premiered over the BBC Radio to celebrate victory in Europe.

June 13   Benjamin Britten's symphonic suite from *Peter Grimes* premieres in Cheltenham, the composer conducting. The work is based on several orchestral interludes from the opera.

July 31   Ralph Vaughan Williams' symphonic suite, *The Story of a Flemish Farm*, premieres in London with the composer conducting.

Oct. 4   Aaron Copland's *Appalachian Spring* is performed in its symphonic suite version by the New York Philharmonic. Tomorrow it receives performances by both the Cleveland Orchestra and the Boston Symphony Orchestra.

Oct. 12   Bohuslav Martinu's Symphony No. 3 is premiered by Serge Koussevitzky and the Boston Symphony Orchestra.

Oct. 23   Vincent Persichetti's Concertino for Piano and Orchestra receives its first performance. Howard Hanson conducts in Rochester, New York, with the composer as soloist. Persichetti, now 29, studied piano with Olga Samaroff, composition with Paul Nordoff and Roy Harris, and conducting with Fritz Reiner.

Oct. 26   Ernest Bloch's *Suite symphonique* is premiered by Pierre Monteux and the Philadelphia Orchestra. It is in three movements.

Oct. 30   Reinhold Gliere's overture *Victory* premieres in Moscow. This overture celebrates the Soviet victory over the Nazis.

Nov. 2   Piano Concerto in F Major, by Gian-Carlo Menotti, receives its first performance by Richard Burgin and the Boston Symphony Orchestra, with Rudolf Firkusny as soloist.

Nov. 3   The Symphony No. 9, by Dmitri Shostakovich, receives its world premiere in Leningrad, as Evgheny Mravinsky conducts the Leningrad Philharmonic Orchestra. The work, which the composer describes as "a merry little piece," is in five movements. Also the shortest of his symphonies, it expresses joy over the Soviet victory against Nazi fascism. Soviet officials quickly call it "ideologically weak." Russian critic Izrail Nestyev attacks it as "bitter, ironic and not expressive of modern ideas."

Nov. 10   Sergei Prokofiev's *Ode to the End of War* premieres in Moscow. This work, celebrating Soviet triumph, is scored for large orchestra, including 4 pianos, 8 harps and 16 double basses (other strings are excluded).

Nov. 10   Ivan Wyschnegradsky's quarter-tone symphonic poem *Cosmos* and two other works entitled *Linnite* and *Five Variations* are premiered in Paris, the composer conducting. *Cosmos* is scored for four pianos; *Linnite* is a pantomime for three female voices and four pianos.

Nov. 16   Darius Milhaud's Suite for Violin and Orchestra is premiered by Eugene Ormandy and the Philadelphia Orchestra, with Zino Francescatti as soloist.

Nov. 18   The collaborative composition entitled *Genesis*, each of its seven scenes featuring an episode of the creation — composed by Arnold Schoenberg, Nathaniel Shilkret, Alexander Tansman, Darius Milhaud, Mario Castelnuovo-Tedesco, Ernst Toch and Igor Stravinsky — is premiered by Werner Janssen and Janssen Symphony in Los Angeles.

Nov. 24   Elie Siegmeister's *Western Suite* receives its first performance by Arturo Toscanini and the NBC Symphony Orchestra. The work features quotations from American folk songs. Siegmeister has studied composition with Wallingford Riegger and Nadia Boulanger.

Nov. 30   Bohuslav Martinu's Symphony No. 4 receives its initial performance by Eugene Ormandy and the Philadelphia Orchestra.

Dec. 6   Darius Milhaud's *La bal martiniquais* is premiered by the New York Philharmonic with the composer conducting. This piece, in two distinct sections, is based on rhythms indigenous to the island of Martinique.

Dec. 19   *Thunderbolt P-47* premieres in Washington, D.C. Composed by Bohuslav Martinu, this work is an orchestral scherzo.

1945   Births, Deaths and Debuts

Jan. 25   American tenor Richard Tucker makes his Metropolitan Opera debut as Enzo in *La Gioconda*.

Jan. 26   Cellist Jacqueline Du Pre is born in Oxford, England.

March 6   Czech composer Rudolf Karel, 64, dies in Terezin concentration camp, in the vicinity of Prague. The last pupil of Antonin Dvorak, he lived in Russia before returning to Prague in 1920 and teaching at the Prague Conservatory. Active in the Czech resistance, he was captured by the Nazis in 1943 and dies today, shortly before liberation. His music, which is programmatic and romantic, includes several operas and two symphonies. His last work, *Three Hairs of the Wise Old Man*, was composed while he was in the concentration camp.

April 8   Austrian conductor Leopold Reichwein, 64, commits suicide in Vienna. This musician had subscribed to Nazi policies and was facing charges of collaboration at the time of his suicide. He conducted the Vienna Opera and was president of the Gesellschaft der Musikfreunde in Vienna.

April 12   German conductor and music writer Peter Raabe, 72, dies in Weimar. This musician took over the position of president of the Reichsmusikkammer from Richard Strauss. He conducted the Netherlands Opera in Amsterdam and the Kaim Orchestra in Munich. He wrote several scholarly books on Franz Liszt and was a custodian of the Liszt Museum in Weimar. He dies just before the fall of Nazi Germany.

June 1   Austrian composer Frederick Block, 45, dies in New York City. In addition to his eight operas and three symphonies, he is known for having reconstructed three movements of Gustav Mahler's Tenth Symphony. This reconstruction was subsequently published by the Bruckner-Mahler Society of America.

June 26   Russian composer, conductor and teacher Nicolas Tcherepnin, 72, dies in Issy-les-Moulineaux, near Paris. He studied with Nikolai Rimsky-Korsakov at the Saint Petersburg Conservatory and later joined that faculty. Exposure came when he toured as a conductor with Serge Diaghilev's Ballets Russes. After the Russian Revolution he went to Tiflis (where he directed that city's conservatory) and later settled in Paris. His works — including two operas; three ballets; and orchestral, chamber, piano and vocal compositions — reflect Russian nationalism tempered by French impressionism: Melodies soar; harmonies are lush; orchestrations emphasize coloristic qualities of various instruments. Sergei Prokofiev was one of his students.

July 24   Italian soprano Rosina Storchio, 69, dies in Milan. She is best known for having created the title role in *Madama Butterfly* at La Scala in 1904.

Aug. 2   Italian composer Pietro Mascagni, 81, dies in Rome. He studied with Amilcare Ponchielli at the Milan Conservatory, dropped out and became a band conductor. His opera *Cavalleria rusticana* won first prize in a competition organized by Edoardo Sonzogno; it was premiered in 1890 and was tremendously successful. Several other operas followed, but none was as well received as the first. Mascagni continued to compose and conduct. He became a Knight of the Crown of Italy and was appointed director of the Rossini Conservatory in Pesaro. With the advent of Benito Mussolini, Mascagni embraced Italian fascism, only to be rejected by Arturo Toscanini and other prominent musicians. As a composer, he accomplished one spectacular thing: the introduction and climb to prominence of the style of opera known as "verismo." This style aims for realism, with dramatic action condensed to captivate audiences. His other operas include *L'Amico Fritz* and *Guglielmo Radcliff*. He wrote a total of 17 operas and various other works.

Aug. 2 Austrian composer Emil Nikolaus von Reznicek, 85, dies in Berlin. He composed many operas and was also a conductor. He taught at the Scharwenka Conservatory in Berlin and conducted the Warsaw Opera and the Komische Oper in Berlin; he later taught at the Hochschule fur Musik. His most successful work is the opera *Donna Diana* (1894).

Aug. 16 American dancer Suzanne Farrell is born in Cincinnati, Ohio.

Aug. 17 Italian composer Giuseppe Marinuzzi, 63, dies in Milan. He studied at the Palermo Conservatory and became internationally known as a conductor after touring Spain and South America. He later became director of the Liceo Musicale in Bologna, was artistic director of the Chicago Opera Association and was chief conductor of the Rome Opera and of La Scala. Never especially popular as a composer, he wrote three operas and several orchestral pieces. False reports about his death state that he was assassinated by Italian anti-Fascists for supporting Benito Mussolini. It is later discovered that he died of hepatic anemia in a Milan hospital.

Aug. 23 Leo Borchard, a conductor of the Berlin Philharmonic, is shot to death by an American soldier. His car had been ordered to stop and did not.

Aug. 31 Violinist Itzhak Perlman is born in Tel Aviv, Israel.

Sep. 15 Austrian composer Anton Webern, 61, is accidentally shot to death by an American military policeman in Mittersill, Austria. Born Anton von Webern, he dropped the "von" in 1918. He was a product of the University of Vienna, where he studied musicology with Guido Adler. (He was one of the first revolutionary composers of the century to be university, not conservatory, trained.) He studied composition privately with Arnold Schoenberg, quickly becoming a disciple of Schoenberg. Along with Alban Berg he became part of the Second Viennese School. (Webern is the second of the three to die; Schoenberg, the oldest and perhaps the most important, is now 70 and living in California.)

Webern began conducting theater orchestras in Vienna, Prague and in Germany before settling in Modling, near Vienna, after World War I. He helped organize the Society for Private Musical Performances and also organized concerts of the Workers' Chorus and Orchestra in Vienna. He later conducted the BBC Orchestra. During World War II he remained in Austria and eventually left Vienna, moving to Mittersill.

A man of political naivete, he has been criticized for being pro-Nazi (the Library of Congress in Washington, D.C. has letters from Webern to his friend, pianist Eduard Steuermann, in which Webern suggests that Steuermann return to Austria on the grounds that things are not so bad under the Nazis); on the other hand, he has been docu-

mented to have helped Jewish friends escape the Nazis (he consistently tried to help his Jewish friend Josef Polnauer obtain an exit visa to go to America). Webern is shot tonight as he steps outside his house, unaware that American occupation forces have established a curfew (the detailed circumstances of this event are later documented by musicologist Hans Moldenhauer).

Webern's music is often mistakenly described as *pointillistic* (a term borrowed from painting), instead of being correctly described as "light-textured." His melodies, not confined to any one voice or instrument, are dispersed over a vastly wider registral range than is the diatonic and chromatic music of the 19th century. Webern also introduced the 12-tone pitch extension known as "derivation" — an operation that generates new 12-tone sets from segments of sets, usually trichords, tetrachords and hexachords. His work exerts a profound influence on the younger generation of European composers — in particular, Pierre Boulez (now 19 and a recent graduate of the Paris Conservatoire, where he studied with Olivier Messiaen) and Karlheinz Stockhausen (now 16).

Webern was not prolific (the duration of all of his works, back-to-back, is approximately three hours); yet his compositions embrace a shift from traditional harmony to the beginnings of the era of sound now being developed by Edgard Varese. Webern's music focuses on "the single musical event" and employs silence as a structural, essential component of content and form. His pieces are scored for various groupings of voices and instruments, chorus *a cappella*, orchestra and piano (his two cantatas are premiered posthumously, as are some of his very early works later discovered). It is only after his death today and the end of World War II that his music emerges as a major force of the century.

Sep. 16 Irish tenor John McCormack, 61, dies in Glena, Booterstown, Ireland of bronchial pneumonia. After winning a gold medal at the National Irish Festival in 1904 without any previous training, McCormack went to Italy to study. He debuted there in 1905 and was soon at Covent Garden, where he became a great favorite. In 1907 he appeared in America, also scoring a huge success. After World War I he left the operatic stage and devoted himself to recitals. He made many radio appearances and one movie, *Song of My Heart*. His voice was of the purest quality, and his exquisite phrasing brought him success in the operas of Mozart and Puccini. In 1928 he was lauded by Pope Pius XI and became a papal chamberlain.

Sep. 26 Hungarian composer Bela Bartok, 64, dies in New York. A pupil at the Royal Academy of Music in Budapest, Bartok composed his early works in the style of Johannes Brahms. His attraction to Hungarian, Transylvanian, Rumanian and Slavonic folk music surfaced in his youth and became a lifelong preoccupation. With Zoltan Kodaly, he traveled these areas to collect folk songs and with him published a taxonomy of folk songs in 1906. He then joined the faculty of the Royal Academy of Music and, after World War I, became a director, along with Kodaly and Ernst von Dohnanyi, of the same institution. He performed widely as a pianist but mostly programmed

BELA BARTOK

structures. Though not a revolutionary (like Anton Webern, who died 11 days ago), he was a titan in that he was the most important nationalistic composer of the century. He was able to create an original idiom from a wide variety of influences — the pianistic, technical brilliance of Franz Liszt, the French impressionism of Claude Debussy, the melodic and rhythmic characteristics of Eastern European folk music.

His output is vast and includes many works for orchestra, chamber pieces, folk song collections, six string quartets and other works. He composed one opera, *The Castle of Duke Bluebeard*. His famous six-volume collection of 153 progressive piano pieces — *Mikrokosmos* — was composed between 1926 and 1937.

Oct. 16   Conductor Carl Alwin, 54, dies in Mexico City. An assistant to Karl Muck at the Hamburg Opera, he also conducted the Vienna State Opera and was the first conductor of the Mexican Opera Nacional.

Nov. 16   Dancer Martine van Hamel is born in Brussels, Belgium.

Dec. 8   Russian pianist and conductor Alexander Siloti, 82, dies in New York. This musician was a pupil of Liszt and first cousin of Serge Rachmaninoff. He taught at the Juilliard School of Music.

Dec. 14   English pianist and teacher Tobias Matthay, 86, dies in High Marley, England. After early studies at the Royal Academy of Music and with other teachers, (including Ebenezer Prout and Arthur Sullivan), he was appointed teacher of piano at that academy in 1876. In 1880 he started his concert career, which lasted only 15 years. After that he confined himself to teaching and founded the Matthay system, which became well known in Europe and America. Among his many compositions are some 100 piano pieces; he also wrote several books on the principles of piano playing.

Dec. 15   American baritone Robert Merrill makes his Metropolitan Opera debut as Germont in *La Traviata*.

his own works. He came to America in 1940, experienced extreme financial hardship and suffered severe depression. It is only after his death that recognition and honors attest to his importance.

Influenced by French impressionism, his music is tonal and exploits extreme registers of instruments, especially that of the piano. His rhythms are asymmetric and evoke a Slavic character; his melodies, sometimes bordering on being atonal (emphasizing all 12 notes of the chromatic scale), are underpinned with tone clusters and polytonal

1945   Related Events

The Smetana Quartet is established this year. Its violist — Vaclav Neumann — subsequently becomes music director of the Czech Philharmonic in 1948.

The Czech Philharmonic Orchestra is nationalized this year to create what its management and the Czech government call "the best possible conditions for further artistic development." This orchestra also incorporates the Prague Philharmonic Choir, the Kuhn Children's Choir and the Smetana Quartet.

Jan. 24   Ernst Krenek is naturalized as an American citizen.

Feb. 3   The Cracow Philharmonic Orchestra gives its first concert. This orchestra assumes the role of restoring symphonic life to Poland. Warsaw is in a state of ruin as a result of World War II. The orchestra subsequently performs in Warsaw and other Polish cities and becomes a regular participant in the "Warsaw Autumn" International Festival of Contemporary Music.

March   The Ballets des Champs-Elysees gives its inaugural season in Paris this month, with Roland Petit as choreographer, director and lead dancer. It disbands in 1951, three years after Petit leaves the company.

March 12   The Vienna State Opera House is hit by incendiary and explosive bombs during an air raid on Vienna. The interior of the house (the auditorium and stage facilities) is completely destroyed. The exterior, however (especially the front) is largely undamaged. This theater was built between 1861 and 1869 by architects August Siccard von Siccardsburg and Eduard van der Null.

May 7   The Pulitzer Prize for music is given to Aaron Copland for his ballet *Appalachian Spring*.

May 8   Subsequent to Germany's surrender yesterday, V.E. Day occurs today. World War II is over in the European theater. This catastrophic war had a devastating effect on music as well as on humanity: Many composers and musicians were displaced, executed, died in combat or suffered severe hardship. Music buildings, including opera houses and concert halls, were bombed and in some cases demolished. Music publishing houses, some containing precious engraved plates of famous musical manuscripts, were also damaged in bombing raids.

May 12   Music of David Diamond, Howard Hanson, Henry Brant and Walter Piston is featured at Columbia University in New York today at the First Annual Festival of Contemporary American Music.

May 25   In the course of an allied air raid on Tokyo, most of Japanese composer Koscak Yamada's musical manuscripts are destroyed.

June 9   Norwegian soprano Kirsten Flagstad — bitter because of the arrest of her husband, who is accused of Nazi collaboration — says she never wants to sing in Norway again and hopes to settle in the United States.

July 3   Music of Roy Harris, Wallingford Riegger, Samuel Barber, Elie Siegmeister and George Gershwin is performed by the State Symphony Orchestra of Moscow as a token of global friendship between the U.S. and the Soviet Union.

July 14   As of today, Nazi songs and martial music are prohibited by Allied occupation authorities in Germany.

Aug. 14   After the United States dropped two atomic bombs on Japan, that nation surrenders, marking the end of World War II. Losses to music from the atomic bomb attacks were minimal, since both Hiroshima and Nagasaki were chosen because they were industrial centers.

Sep. 3   Warsaw becomes the home of the Union of Polish Composers, founded today.

Oct. 14   The first postwar concert at the Great Concert Hall (Grosser Musikvereinsaal) in Vienna takes place as Josef Krips conducts. Krips had been assigned the task of restoring musical life to Vienna after the war ended (he reopened the Volksoper last May).

Nov. 9   William Steinberg conducts his first concert as the new music director of the Buffalo Philharmonic Orchestra Society. Steinberg remains music director of the orchestra until 1952, when Josef Krips succeeds him.

Dec. 14   Ernst von Dohnanyi is officially cleared by the Hungarian Ministry of Justice of charges of Nazi affiliation. This Hungarian composer had been accused of belonging to the Hungarian Arrow-Cross Party, a pro-Nazi organization.

Dec. 28   Igor Stravinsky becomes a naturalized citizen of the United States.

1946 Opera

Feb. 14   Vittorio Giannini's *Beauty and the Beast* is performed in its full stage version in Hartford, Connecticut.

April 20   Healey Willan's *Deirdre* is premiered in concert form over radio by the CBC in Toronto.

May 8   *The Medium*, a two-act opera by Gian-Carlo Menotti, is performed for the first time in New York at the Barrymore Theater. Menotti writes his own libretto, about a woman pretending to be a medium who becomes a victim of her own tricks. Despite mixed reviews, the opera is a huge success with the public. It receives over 1,000 performances during the next few years and is later made into a film.

June 12   The first staged performance of Sergei Prokofiev's opera *War and Peace* takes place in Moscow. The li-

bretto, adapted from the Tolstoi novel of the same title, is by the composer and Mira Mendelssohn. This performance includes only the first 8 scenes of the total 13; a second version is performed on April 1, 1955 in Leningrad — this second version is the complete opera. Soviet critic A. Khokhlovkin says it "is a work of tremendous significance."

July 12   *The Rape of Lucretia*, composed by Benjamin Britten, premieres at the Glyndebourne Festival. The libretto is by Ronald Duncan, based on *Le viol de Lucrece*, by Andre Obey. The work is enthusiastically received and is performed 80 times within three months of its premiere. The cast includes Joan Cross and Peter Pears.

Nov. 3   The first performance of Sergei Prokofiev's opera *Betrothal in a Convent* takes place in Leningrad at the Kirov

Theater. The libretto is by Mira Mendelssohn, based on Richard Sheridan's *The Duenna*. The work is regarded as one of Prokofiev's finest.

Dec. 20   Boris Blacher's *Die Flut*, based on a tale by Guy de Maupassant, premieres over radio in Berlin. The one-act chamber opera involves murder and lust.

1946 Dance

Jan. 23   Martha Graham premieres *Dark Meadow*, to a score by Carlos Chavez in New York. The work, in four sections, is a celebration of the phases of life. Graham, May O'Donnell and Erick Hawkins star. A critic for the New York *Times* writes, "[*Dark Meadow*] leaves one exhausted rather than entertained."

Feb. 20   The Sadler's Wells Ballet performs *The Sleeping Beauty* in a version similar to its production of February 1939, but with additional choreography by Frederick Ashton and Ninette de Valois. Costumes and scenery are by Oliver Messel. This performance, danced by Margot Fonteyn and Robert Helpmann, celebrates the reopening of the Royal Opera House, Covent Garden after World War II.

Feb. 27   George Balanchine's *Night Shadow* is premiered by the Ballet Russe de Monte Carlo in New York. It is set to music from Vincenzo Bellini's operas, arranged by Vittorio Rieti. The one-act ballet deals with a Poet at an evening party who meets a mysterious Sleepwalker, the wife of the Baron. The Baron, enraged, kills the Poet and the Sleepwalker. Alexandra Danilova, Nicholas Magallanes, Maria Tallchief and Michel Katcharov star. In 1961 Balanchine renames the work *La somnambula*.

April 24   Frederick Ashton's *Symphonic Variations*, with music by Cesar Franck and costumes and scenery by Sophie Fedorovitch, is performed for the first time. The Sadler's Wells Ballet dances the work with Margot Fonteyn and Michael Somes leading the cast. Matching rhythm to mood, this classical one-act ballet has come to be considered one of the choreographer's masterpieces.

May 5   The Nouveau Ballet de Monte Carlo premieres Serge Lifar's *Chota Roustaveli* in Monte Carlo. The ballet, in four acts, is to music by Arthur Honegger, Alexander Tcherepnin and Tibor Harsanyi. Based on the Georgian poem "A Hero in a Leopard's Skin," it tells the story of a poet and Queen Thamar. It is one of the earliest modern evening-length ballets to be created outside the USSR. Lifar, Yvette Chauvire, Sirene Adjemova and Alexandre Kalioujny star.

May 10   Martha Graham's *Serpent's Heart* — to music by Samuel Barber, with sets by Isamu Noguchi and costumes designed by Edythe Gilfond and Graham — premieres at the McMillin Theater, Columbia University in New York. The theme of the dance is Medea's revenge. Graham subsequently changes the title to *Cave of the Heart*. Graham, Erick Hawkins, Yuriko and May O'Donnell star.

MARGOT FONTEYN AND ROBERT HELPMANN IN *SLEEPING BEAUTY*

June 25   *The Young Man and Death*, choreographed by Roland Petit to music by Bach, is premiered by the Ballets des Champs-Elysees in Paris. The book is by Jean Cocteau, with costumes and scenery by Georges Wakhevitch. About the suicide of a young artist, the work was rehearsed to jazz rhythms; the music of Bach was heard by the dancers for the first time at the dress rehearsal.

Oct. 1   Choreographer John Taras' *Camille* — with music by Franz Schubert, arrangement by Vittorio Rieti, and costumes and scenery by Cecil Beaton — is premiered by the Original Ballet Russe in New York. The principal dancers are Alicia Markova and Anton Dolin.

Oct. 24   Jerome Robbins' *Facsimile* — with music by Leonard Bernstein, costumes by Irene Sharaff and scenery by Oliver Smith — is premiered by the Ballet Theater in New York City. The composer conducts. The work, in one scene, depicts a sexual triangle and is danced by Robbins, Nora Kaye and John Kriza.

Nov. 12   The Sadler's Wells Ballet gives the first performance, at Covent Garden of Frederick Ashton's *Les sirenes*, set to a commissioned score by Lord Berners. The work is an Edwardian romp on a French beach. Margot Fonteyn, Robert Helpmann, Frederick Ashton, Beryl Grey and Michael Somes star. In the work Helpmann sings an aria. It marks the first time a lead dancer sings in an opera house.

Nov. 20   The Ballet Society gives the world premiere, in New York, of George Balanchine's *The Four Temperaments*. The abstract work, to music by Paul Hindemith, is in four sections: "Sanguine," "Melancholic," "Phlegmatic" and "Choleric." Gisella Caccialanza, Georgia Hiden, Rita Karlin, Tanaquil LeClerq, Mary Ellen Moylan, Elise Reiman, Beatrice Tompkins, Todd Bolender, Lew Christensen, Fred

ALEXANDRA DANILOVA AND NICHOLAS MAGALLANES IN *NIGHT SHADOW*

Danieli, William Dollar, Jose Martinez and Francisco Moncion are in the first night cast. It is one Balanchine's greatest works.

Nov. 26   The Ballet Society in New York, premieres George Balanchine's *The Spellbound Child*, set to the opera *L'enfant et les sortileges* by Maurice Ravel. The opera-ballet is about a child for whom everyday objects come to life through magic. Gisella Caccialanza, Georgia Hiden, Elise Reiman, Beatrice Tompkins, Paul d'Amboise, William Dollar and John Scancarella are in the opening night cast.

1946   Instrumental and Vocal Music

Jan. 24   The New York Philharmonic premieres Igor Stravinsky's Symphony in Three Movements. The composer conducts. Stravinsky states, "Each episode in the Symphony is linked in my imagination with a specific cinematographic impression of the war."

Jan. 25   Richard Strauss' *Metamorphosen* for string orchestra receives its first performance in Zurich, as Paul Sacher conducts the Collegium Musicum. Composed between March and April of last year, it reflects the end of the Third Reich and the occupation of Germany by Allied forces. Strauss is now living in Zurich.

Feb. 8   Bela Bartok's Third Concerto for Piano and Orchestra is premiered posthumously by Eugene Ormandy and the Philadelphia Orchestra, with Gyorgy Sandor as soloist. The piece was composed while Bartok was dying. Tibor Serly completed the final 17 measures.

Feb. 17   Aaron Copland's *Danzon cubano* is performed in its symphonic version by Reginald Stewart and the Baltimore Symphony Orchestra.

Feb. 26   Richard Strauss' Concerto for Oboe and Chamber Orchestra premieres in Zurich.

March 6   Dutch composer Guillaume Landre's Symphony No. 2 premieres in The Hague. This is the second of four symphonies by this composer, who is currently teaching economics in Amsterdam.

March 7   American composer Halsey Stevens' Symphony No. 1 receives its initial performance in San Francisco, the composer conducting. This composer, now 37, has studied with Ernest Bloch and is currently on the faculty of the University of Southern California in Los Angeles.

March 8   Sergei Prokofiev's third symphonic suite from his ballet *Romeo and Juliet* premieres in Moscow.

March 22   *Scherzo a la Russe*, by Igor Stravinsky, is performed in its orchestral version for the first time by the San Francisco Symphony Orchestra. Stravinsky conducts. Originally composed for band two years ago, this piece is based on popular Russian tunes.

March 23   Marc Blitzstein's *Airborne Symphony* receives its first performance by Leonard Bernstein and the New York City Symphony Orchestra. Scored for narrator, singers and orchestra, it depicts the history of aviation. The work is the result of a commission Blitzstein received while with the U.S. Eighth Air Force in England. He states: "I call *The Airborne* a symphony (even though none of its three movements is strictly in the same form) in the same way that Liszt named the *Faust Symphony* and Stravinsky the *Symphony of Psalms.*"

March 25   *Sonatina No. 2* by Richard Strauss, premieres in Winterthur, Switzerland. It is scored for 16 wind instruments.

March 25   Igor Stravinsky's *Ebony Concerto* receives its initial performance by Woody Herman's band at Carnegie Hall. Scored for clarinet and band, the concerto includes jazz elements and has three movements.

April 5   Samuel Barber's Cello Concerto receives its first performance by Serge Koussevitzky and the Boston Symphony Orchestra, with Raya Garbousova as soloist. The concerto uses the interval of the tritone as a focal point. Twelve years from now, critic Howard Taubman reviews the work in the New York *Times* and says, "There are flashes of engaging writing in the first movement, but here, as in the flimsy final section, the ideas are not always compelling."

April 5   The Symphony No. 3, by Charles Ives, receives its world premiere in New York, as Lou Harrison conducts the Little Symphony of New York. The three movements are entitled "Old Folks Gatherin'," "Children's Day" and "Communion." The music contains unorthodox chord progressions and many cross-rhythms. It was composed 42 years ago. Its premiere today finally establishes Ives, beyond any doubt, as a major American composer. The work is subsequently awarded the Pulitzer Prize for music and receives a special citation from the New York Critics Circle.

May 5   Douglas Moore's Symphony No. 2 in A Major premieres in Paris, as Robert Lawrence conducts the Paris Broadcasting Orchestra. Moore is now head of the music department at Columbia University.

May 14   Paul Hindemith's *When Lilacs Last in the Dooryard Bloom'd*, with a text by Walt Whitman, receives its initial performance by Robert Shaw and the Collegiate Chorale in New York. Shaw commissioned this work, subtitled *A Requiem for Those We Love*. It is scored for soprano, contralto, baritone, chorus and orchestra and has four sections. Howard Taubman writes in the New York *Times*: "When the composer brings together the full potential of chorus and orchestra, he sometimes achieves an unforgettable effect."

May 17   Frank Martin's *Petite symphonie concertante* is premiered by Paul Sacher and the Chamber Orchestra of Basel, in Zurich. This neoclassical work is scored for harp, harpsichord, piano and two string orchestras.

May 26   Darius Milhaud's Piano Concerto No. 3 premieres at the Spring Festival in Prague.

May 31   *Sinfonia elegiaca* by Alberto Ginastera, receives its first performance in Buenos Aires. This is a one-movement piece.

July 12   *First Cantata*, Op. 29, by Anton Webern, is premiered posthumously by Karl Rankl and the BBC Symphony Orchestra and Chorus in London, with Emelie Hooke as soprano soloist. Composed between 1938 and 1939, this is one of two cantatas Webern composed. The text, by Hildegard Jone, was inspired by characters from Greek mythology (Apollo, Charis); it deals with the meaning of grace. The performance takes place as part of the 20th International Society for Contemporary Music festival. Consisting of three movements, the cantata reflects the final stages of Webern's craftsmanship and application of the 12-tone system. Webern commented some six years ago to Hildegard Jone: "Musically there is not a single center of gravity in this piece. The harmonic construction (as it results from the individual voices) is such that everything remains in a floating state."

Before his death Webern campaigned vigorously for a performance of this cantata; it was turned down for various reasons by Paul Sacher and others. Humphrey Searle subsequently reviews the music in *The Monthly Musical Record* and writes: "Throughout the whole work, one is fascinated by the remarkable sonorities achieved. Like most of Webern's later music, the work is built up like a mosaic from small fragments contributed by the different instruments; yet this is done not in any impressionist or pointillist manner, but architecturally, and the crystal-clear structure holds together as logically as any Bach fugue."

Aug. 17   Charles Munch premieres Arthur Honegger's *Symphonie liturgique* (Third Symphony) in Zurich. The symphony is dedicated to Munch, who later says the work "poses the problem of humanity vis-a-vis God."

Oct. 18   Serge Koussevitzky and the Boston Symphony Orchestra premiere Aaron Copland's Symphony No. 3. Copland began this piece two years ago. It incorporates, in toto, his earlier *Fanfare for the Common Man*, which appears in the last movement. Koussevitzky describes it as "the greatest American symphony — it goes from the heart to the heart." It was commissioned by the Koussevitzky Music Foundation and is dedicated to the memory of Mme. Natalie Koussevitzky.

Oct. 22   Belgian composer Marcel Poot's *Sinfonietta* is premiered by Desire Defauw and the Chicago Symphony Orchestra. Now 45, Poot is on the staff of the Brussels Conservatory.

Oct. 30   Cello Concerto in E Major by Aram Khachaturian, premieres in Moscow.

Nov. 22   Piano Concerto No. 3 by Ernst Krenek, receives its first performance by Dimitri Mitropoulos and the Minneapolis Symphony Orchestra. It is a five-movement concerto.

Nov. 28   Artur Rodzinski and the New York Philharmonic premiere Darius Milhaud's Concerto No. 2 for Violoncello and Orchestra. Edmund Kurtz, who commissioned the piece, is soloist. The concerto has three movements.

Dec. 11   Arthur Honegger's *Serenade a Angelique* premieres in Paris. This piece is a symphonic scherzo.

Dec. 14   Vissarion Shebalin's cantata *Moscow* premieres in that city, celebrating the 800th anniversary of its founding. The patriotic cantata has five movements and calls for churches to ring their bells.

Dec. 19   Norman Dello Joio's *Ricercari* for piano and orchestra is premiered by George Szell and the New York Philharmonic. The composer performs as soloist. The three-movement work is based on the 16th- and 17th-century musical form of the same name. Dello Joio has recently been teaching at Sarah Lawrence College.

Dec. 20   Darius Milhaud's Symphony No. 2 is premiered by the Boston Symphony Orchestra, the composer conducting. The five-movement work was composed on commission from the Koussevitzky Music Foundation.

Dec. 29   Elie Siegmeister's *Prairie Legend* (second part only) is premiered by Leopold Stokowski and the New York Philharmonic.

1946   Births, Deaths and Debuts

Jan. 21   Pianist Gina Bachauer makes her London debut with the New London Orchestra, conducted by Alec Sherman, who later becomes her husband.

Feb. 6   Austrian conductor Oswald Kabasta, 49, commits suicide in Munich. This musician had voluntarily become a member of the Austrian Nazi Party and killed himself because the Nazis lost the war. He was a conductor and director of the Gesellschaft der Musikfreunde in Vienna, as well as a conductor of the Vienna Radio Orchestra and the Munich Philharmonic. He also performed at two Bruckner Festivals in Linz.

June 1   Austrian tenor Leo Slezak, 72, dies in Egern-on-the-Tegernsee, Bavaria. He debuted in 1896 as Lohengrin at the Brno Opera. Later appearances were with the Berlin Opera and the Vienna Opera. Before singing in England and America, he went to Paris to study with Jean de Reszke. He performed with the Metropolitan Opera in 1910 and later sang in Russia. In addition to having a fine voice, he was noted for his acting ability: He acted in several motion pictures (his son Walter became a well-known actor). Slezak published several volumes of memoirs.

June 20   Pianist Andre Watts is born in a U.S. Army camp in Nuremberg, Germany. He is the son of a Hungarian mother and an American black soldier.

July 8   American dancer Cynthia Gregory is born in Los Angeles, California.

Aug. 19   Violinist Ben Stad, 61, dies in Gloucester, Massachusetts. He founded the American Society of the Ancient Instruments, which, like the similar society founded by Arnold Dolmetsch, was concerned with reviving, preserving and recording old music written for unusual musical instruments. Examples of such instruments are the viola da gamba, viola d'amore and the pardessus de viole.

Sep. 3   Polish pianist Moriz Rosenthal, 83, dies in New York. A pupil of Karol Mikuli, who himself was a student of Frederic Chopin, he later took additional lessons from Franz Liszt. He was known as a great virtuoso. He toured the United States many times, eventually settling there in 1938. His pupils included Charles Rosen.

Oct. 9   American opera singer Enrica C. Dillon, 65, dies in Harrison, Maine. Known for having brought opera to the American public by singing in small theaters throughout the country, she sang some 1,800 performances, was decorated in Buckingham Palace by King George V, directed many opera societies and yet never became a great opera star.

Oct. 16   English composer Sir Granville Bantock, 78, dies in London. He was a product of the Royal Conservatory of Music in London, whose early work included the Egyptian ballet suite *Ramses II*. He later became founder and editor of *New Quarterly Musical Review* (1893) and toured as a conductor. Most of his conducting involved performances of works by young British composers. After succeeding Sir Edward Elgar as composition professor at the University of Birmingham, he visited India and Australia. He was knighted in 1930. Like Gustav Holst, he was attracted to things Oriental — many of his works reflect programmatic ideas and titles based on Oriental mythology and literature. His music is characteristically British in terms of its harmonies and melodies and includes three operas, three ballets, five tone poems, overtures, choral works with and without orchestra, chamber music and other pieces. Soon after his death the Bantock Society is founded to produce recordings of his works. Jean Sibelius is the society's first president.

Oct. 27   Dancer and choreographer Peter Martins is born in Copenhagen, Denmark.

Nov. 14   Spanish composer Manuel de Falla, 69, dies in Alta Gracia, Argentina. A pupil of Felipe Pedrell, he first attracted attention in 1905 when he won the Academia de Bellas Artes Prize for composition and the Ortiz y Cuso Prize for piano. He then went to Paris and was helped by Claude Debussy, Paul Dukas and Maurice Ravel — which exposed him to French impressionism. He returned to Spain and settled in Granada until the end of the Spanish civil war, when he relocated to Argentina. Although Falla's early works were rooted in Spanish folk song elements, his later works clearly display the influence of French impressionism. His pieces for keyboard (*4 pieces espagnoles: Aragonesa, Cubana, Montanesa, Andaluza*) bear a likeness to the work of Domenico Scarlatti, who also lived in Spain and was influenced by Spanish folk music. Falla's most famous works include the ballet *El amor brujo* and the opera *La vide breve*. His output also includes *El retablo de Maese Pedro* (an opera for singers and marionettes); the ballet *El sombrero de tres picos*; various orchestral, guitar, piano, and chamber works and songs.

Nov. 15   Zoltan Kodaly's *Dances of Galanta* are performed by the Pittsburgh Symphony Orchestra with the composer conducting. This event marks this musician's American debut as a conductor. The music was composed in 1933 and is based on childhood memories of Hungary. Since the death of Bela Bartok last year, Kodaly has become Hungary's most prominent composer.

Dec. 27   Charles Munch conducts the Boston Symphony Orchestra in his first appearance with that orchestra.

Dec. 30   American composer Charles Wakefield Cadman, 65, dies in Los Angeles. This composer often employed music featuring Indian themes and is known for his tune "At Dawning." He studied composition with Emil Paur. Cadman's grandfather was Samuel Wakefield — the inventor of "buckwheat notation." Cadman's most successful work was the opera *Shanewis*. He composed four other operatic works, many orchestral pieces, and a host of piano and choral works, including approximately 180 songs.

1946 *Related Events*

The Czech Philharmonic celebrates its 50th anniversary this year by organizing the Prague Spring International Music Festival.

Benjamin Britten, John Piper and Eric Crozier establish the English Opera Group this year to encourage the creation of new contemporary operas and librettos. The organization later plays a role in the establishment of the Aldeburgh Festival.

Birgit Cullberg becomes director of the Swedish Dance Theatre this year.

The Sadler's Wells Ballet moves to Covent Garden this year.

The first issue of *Ballet Today* is published this month. The editor of this new British dance magazine is P.W. Manchester. The publication lasts until 1970.

March 24   John Cage is interviewed in the newspaper *PM*. He states that the elimination of harmony is his principal contribution to musical composition.

April   The Welsh National Opera is established this month in Cardiff, Wales.

April 25   The first of the Louis Charles Elson Memorial Fund Lectures takes place at the Library of Congress in Washington, D.C., as Otto Kinkeldey delivers a talk entitled "Early Ensembles: The Forerunners of the Orchestra."

May 6   Leo Sowerby is awarded the Pulitzer Prize for music for his *Canticle of the Sun*.

May 11   Music of Gioacchino Rossini, Giuseppe Verdi, Arrigo Boito and Giacomo Puccini is conducted by Arturo Toscanini at La Scala in Milan. This event marks the unofficial and preliminary reopening of this opera house since its auditorium was destroyed by Allied bombs.

July 15   Lincoln Kirstein and George Balanchine form the Ballet Society to encourage the production of new works.

Aug. 1   The Salzburg Festival reopens in Salzburg, Austria. This is the first performance there since the Nazi annexation of Austria.

Oct. 1   Soviet composers Dmitri Shostakovich and Sergei Prokofiev decline an invitation from conductor Serge Koussevitzky to be guest conductors of the Boston Symphony Orchestra.

Oct. 8   John Philip Sousa's "Stars and Stripes Forever" is released on an RCA recording. This event marks this company's billionth recording.

Oct. 22   Wolfgang Amadeus Mozart's *Little Masonic Cantata* becomes the musical material for a new Austrian national anthem. With text by Paul Preradovic, it is entitled "Land der Berge, Land am Strome" and is adopted today by the Austrian government.

Oct. 26   The New Zealand Symphony Orchestra is formed today. Andersen Tyrer is appointed conductor, and the ensemble gives its first concert next March.

Nov. 29   The British-produced film *Instruments of the Orchestra* is released today in London. The music for the film is by Benjamin Britten and is subsequently called *The Young Person's Guide to the Orchestra*, variations on a theme by Henry Purcell. The music is later performed as a concert piece.

Dec. 17   Wilhelm Furtwangler is officially cleared of charges of Nazi collaboration in Berlin. Furtwangler issues a statement to the world press, saying: "What made me remain in Germany was my anxious desire to preserve the integrity of German music. When Thomas Mann asks,

'How can Beethoven be played in Himmler's Germany?' I answer, 'When was the music of Beethoven more needed than in Himmler's Germany?' I could not therefore leave Germany in her hour of greatest need, and I have no regrets for having stayed at my post."

Dec. 26   Giuseppe Verdi's *Nabucco* is conducted by Tullio Serafin at La Scala. This event marks the official reopening of this world-renowned opera house, which had been closed due to the war.

1947 Opera

Jan. 2   *L'oro*, by Ildebrando Pizzetti, premieres in Milan at the Teatro alla Scala. As is customary with Pizzetti, he writes his own libretto: This one is the story of a rich landlord who discovers gold in his backyard.

Jan. 4   Andre Jolivet's *Dolores* premieres over radio in Paris. This one-act opera buffa is about an ugly woman who works hard to attract men.

Jan. 9   *Street Scene* by Kurt Weill, premieres in New York. This folk opera, with a book by Elmer Rice, tells the story of a man who kills his wife and her lover. It is set in a New York tenement.

Feb. 18   The first performance of Gian Carlo Menotti's *The Telephone* (subtitled *L'amour a trois*) occurs at the Heckscher Theater in New York City. The libretto, by the composer, is the love story of Ben and Lucy and a telephone that interrupts the marriage proposal. It is performed with a revised version of *The Medium* and is lauded by critics.

April 18   Roger Sessions' one-act opera *The Trial of Lucullus* receives its initial performance at the University of California in Berkeley. Composed to a radio play by Bertolt Brecht, it is about a Roman general on trial for crimes against humanity and is an anti-Hitler allegory. Critic Alfred J. Frankenstein writes in the San Francisco *Chronicle*, "The remarkable feature of the opera from a purely aesthetic point of view is the unparalleled suppleness of its declamation."

April 19   *Rachel*, based on a tale by Guy de Maupassant, premieres in its stage version in Moscow. This one-act opera, by Reinhold Gliere, takes place in 1871 and is about the assassination of a Prussian lieutenant.

May 7   Virgil Thomson's *The Mother of Us All*, with a text by Gertrude Stein, receives its world premiere at Columbia University in New York. The three-act opera is about Susan B. Anthony and women's suffrage. The cast includes Marilyn Horne. Olin Downes says Thomson's music is "built upon the simple harmonic lines, with the admirable

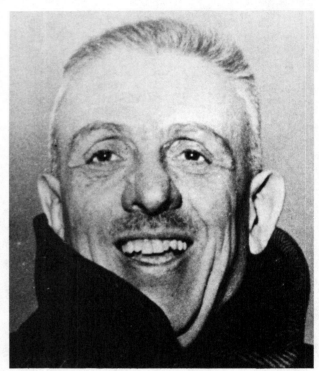

FRANCIS POULENC

prosody of which he is a master, and a knowledge of singing use of the language."

June 3   The first performance of Francis Poulenc's *Les Mamelles de Tiresias* is given at the Opera-Comique in Paris. The text, a surrealistic drama by Guillaume Apollinaire written in 1903, is a satire on role reversal. Albert Wolff conducts a cast that includes Denise Duval.

June 15   Carl Orff's *Die Bernauerin* premieres in Stuttgart. This work — a folk opera in two parts and seven scenes — is about a Bavarian duchess, living in 1435, who is killed by her father. It is dedicated to the memory of German ethnomusicologist Kurt Huber, who was executed by the Nazis in 1943.

June 20   *Albert Herring*, a comic opera in three acts by Benjamin Britten, premieres at Glyndebourne. The libretto, by Eric Crozier, is adapted from a short story by Guy de Maupassant, "Le rosier de Madame Husson." The work is a great success with critics and public alike. Britten conducts a cast that includes Joan Cross and Peter Pears.

Aug. 6   *Dantons Tod*, by Gottfried von Einem, receives its initial performance at the Salzburg Festival. The libretto, by the composer and Boris Blacher, is adapted from the play by Georg Buchner. Danton opposes Robespierre during the French Revolution. The cast includes Maria Cebotari, Paul Schoeffler and Julius Patzak. The conductor is Ferenc Fricsay.

Sep. 28   Vano Muradelli's four act opera *Great Friendship* premieres in Stalino, USSR. After subsequent performances in other Soviet cities this year, the opera is denounced as having historically misrepresented the ethnicity of the Caucasian people. At a later meeting of the General Assembly of Composers, Muradelli agrees that he has failed and even states in his speech to the committee, "How could it have happened that I failed to introduce a single folk song in the score of my opera?"

1947 *Dance*

Jan. 13   The Ballet Society premieres George Balanchine's *Divertimento*, a themeless work in five parts to music by Alexei Haieff. Mary Ellen Moylan and Francisco Moncion lead the cast. Also performed is Balanchine's version of Igor Stravinsky's *Le renard*. Lew Christensen, Fred Danieli, John Taras and Todd Bolender lead the cast.

Feb. 27   Martha Graham and her company premiere *Cave of the Heart*, to music by Samuel Barber. The Greek myth of Medea's vengeance on Jason provides the basis for a study of the self-destructiveness of hate. Graham, Erick Hawkins, Yuriko and May O'Donnell star. This is a revised version of *Serpent's Heart*, performed last year.

Feb. 28   Martha Graham presents *Errand into the Maze*, to music by Gian-Carlo Menotti, in New York. This duet, based on the legend of the Minotaur, is a psychological exploration of fear. Graham and Mark Ryder are the first cast. Isamu Noguchi creates the sets; Edythe Gilfond the costumes.

May 3   Martha Graham presents *Night Journey*. Based on the Oedipus myth, it is set to a score by William Schuman. Graham, Erick Hawkins, and Mark Ryder star. The performance takes place in Cambridge, Massachusetts at a Harvard Symposium on Music Criticism.

May 13   Merce Cunningham's *The Seasons*, to music by John Cage and with designs by Isamu Noguchi, receives its first performance by the Ballet Society in New York City. Leon Barzin conducts. The dancers are Tanaquil LeClerq, Beatrice Tompkins and Cunningham. This piece was the first for large orchestra by John Cage; it lasts 18 minutes. Critic Alfred J. Frankenstein writes, "Its score is an extraordinary structure of rippling, prickling, pointed and drawn-out sounds, complex, crashing resonances, and firmly structural melodies."

June 2   *The Sailor's Return* is given its initial performance by the Ballet Rambert in London. The work — by Andree Howard, to commissioned music by Arthur Oldham — deals with a sailor who brings home his African bride. She is initially accepted by the population, but gradually prejudice reveals itself. Sally Gilmour, Walter Gore, Frank Staff and John Gilpin star.

July 11   *Fables for Our Time*, a four-part ballet choreographed by Charles Weidman, receives its initial performance by the Charles Weidman Dance Theater Company at Jacob's Pillow Dance Festival. The ballet is based on tales by James Thurber and becomes one of Weidman's most popular pieces. Weidman and Betty Osgood star.

July 28   The Paris Opera presents George Balanchine's *Palais de cristal*, an abstract work in four movements, to music by Georges Bizet. Tamara Toumanova, Lycette Darsonval, Micheline Bardin, Madeleine Lafon, Jacqueline Moreau, Denise Bourgeois, Alexandre Kalioujny, Michel Renault, Max Bozzoni and Roger Ritz are in the opening night cast. The work is restaged next year for the Ballet Society as *Symphony in C*.

Aug. 19   Jose Limon's modern dance work *Song of Songs*, with music by Lukas Foss, receives its first performance in Boston.

Sep. 27   George Balanchine's *Theme and Variations* — to music by Tchaikovsky and with costumes and scenery by Woodman Thompson — is performed for the first time by the Ballet Theater in Richmond, Virginia. It is an abstract work featuring Alicia Alonso and Igor Youskevitch.

Nov. 12   George Balanchine's *Symphonie concertante*, with music by Mozart and costumes and scenery by James Stewart Morcom, is premiered by the Ballet Society in New York City. The plotless ballet stars Maria Tallchief,

Tanaquil LeClerq and Todd Bolender. It is in three movements.

Dec. 14   Merce Cunningham's *The Open Road* and his *Dromenon* are premiered in New York City. The first is to music by Lou Harrison; the second, to music by John Cage.

Dec. 15   Serge Lifar's *Les mirages* is premiered by the Paris Opera Ballet in Paris. The music is by Henri Sauguet, with costumes and scenery by A.M. Cassandre. Yvette Chau-

vire leads the ballet, which is about a young man's dreams and disillusionment.

Dec. 21   The Jose Limon Dance Company gives the premiere performance of Doris Humphrey's *Day on Earth*, to Aaron Copland's Piano Sonata. The work traces the cycle of life. Limon, Letitia Ide, Miriam Pandor and Melisa Nicholaides star. The work was performed at the Beaver County Day School in Brookline, Massachusetts this past May; today's performance is considered its premiere.

1947   Instrumental and Vocal Music

Jan. 9   Pierre Monteux and the San Francisco Symphony Orchestra premiere Roger Sessions' Symphony No. 2. Composed between 1944 and 1946, this symphony is dedicated to the memory of Franklin Delano Roosevelt. It later wins the New York Music Critics Circle Award.

Jan. 18   Elie Siegmeister's *Prairie Legend* is premiered in its complete version by Leopold Stokowski and the New York Philharmonic. The piece received a partial performance last year.

Jan. 21   Igor Stravinsky's Concerto in D for String Orchestra (Basler Concerto), Bohuslav Martinu's *Toccata e due canzoni* and Arthur Honegger's Symphony No. 4 are premiered by Paul Sacher and the Chamber Orchestra of Basel. This event marks the 20th anniversary celebration of this orchestra.

Feb. 1   *Symphonia serena*, by Paul Hindemith, is premiered by Antal Dorati and the Dallas Symphony Orchestra. The four-movement piece, which includes a march theme Beethoven composed between 1809 and 1810, was commissioned by Dorati.

Feb. 9   George Antheil's Concerto in D for Violin and Orchestra premieres in Dallas.

Feb. 16   Morton Gould's Symphony No. 3 receives its initial performance by the Dallas Symphony Orchestra. The composer conducts. In four movements, it includes jazz elements.

Feb. 19   Heitor Villa-Lobos' *Bachianas Brasileiras No. 3* for piano and orchestra is premiered by the Columbia Broadcasting System Orchestra in New York.

Feb. 27   The Concerto for Piano and Orchestra, by Paul Hindemith, receives its initial performance by George Szell and the Cleveland Orchestra, with Jesus Maria Sanroma as soloist. This neoclassical piece was completed in 1945 and consists of three movements. The last movement is a medley on the 14th century dance theme "Tre fontane." Also performed at this concert is Aaron Copland's *Letter from Home* in its full symphonic version.

Feb. 27   Walter Hendl and the New York Philharmonic premiere Peter Mennin's Symphony No. 3. This three-movement symphony brings this American composer to national attention. Virgil Thomson calls it "an accomplished work." Mennin is now 23.

March 6   Nikolai Miaskovsky's Symphony No. 25 in D-flat Major premieres in Moscow. This symphony, in three movements, is uncharacteristic of the composer in that it is relaxed and idyllic. It expresses Miaskovsky's relief that the war is over. His biographer, Tamara Livanova, later describes it as being "beautiful and transparent, but not sufficiently democratic and bright."

March 7   Lukas Foss's cantata, *The Song of Songs*, is premiered by Serge Koussevitzky and the Boston Symphony Orchestra, with soprano Ellabelle Davis as soloist. The four-movement piece is based on biblical themes.

March 16   Piano Sonata No. 2, by Roger Sessions, premieres at the Museum of Modern Art in New York. Andor Foldes is soloist.

April 11   Ernst Krenek's *The Santa Fe Time Table* receives its first performance at the University of Chicago with the composer conducting. It is an *a cappella* choral work, with a text culled from timetables of that railroad.

May 1   Harvard University features a three-day Symposium on Music Criticism for the purpose of aiding the lay listener's understanding of new music. Walter Piston's String Quartet No. 3, Arnold Schoenberg's String Trio, Op. 45, and Bohuslav Martinu's String Quartet No. 6 are all premiered at a concert held today in connection with the symposium. Each work was commissioned for the symposium.

May 2   Paul Hindemith's *Aparebit repentina Dies*, Gian Francesco Malipiero's *La terra* and Aaron Copland's *In the Beginning* are premiered at the second concert held during the Harvard Symposium on Music Criticism.

May 27   The Symphony No. 5, by Bohuslav Martinu, receives its world premiere. Rafael Kubelik conducts in Prague. It is a three-movement symphony. After having stayed in New York during the war, Martinu visited Prague last year and is now spending most of his time in Switzerland.

May 28   Darius Milhaud's Suite for Harmonica and Orchestra receives its premiere in Philadelphia. The piece was written for harmonica player Larry Adler, who performs it with the Philadelphia Orchestra. It was performed as a concerto for violin and orchestra in 1945.

Aug. 6   *Bachianas Brasileiras No. 8*, by Heitor Villa-Lobos, premieres in Rome with the composer conducting. Scored for orchestra, it is in four movements.

Oct. 11   Sergei Prokofiev's Symphony No. 6 in E-flat Minor receives its world premiere in Leningrad. The three-movement work is in contrast to his last symphony in that, according to Nikolai Miaskovsky, it is "harsh and metallic; the sonorities of the low brass instruments are snarling, and those of the high woodwinds shrill." Four months from now, the Soviet Communist Party decides to crack down on composers: This symphony becomes a target.

Oct. 20   David Diamond's *Romeo and Juliet*, Norman Dello Joio's Concerto for Harp and Orchestra, and Douglas Moore's *Farm Journal* are premiered by Thomas K. Scherman and the Little Orchestra Society in New York. The event marks the first concert of this organization.

Oct. 21   Vincent Persichetti's Symphony No. 1 receives its initial performance by Howard Hanson in Rochester, New York. The one-movement symphony is neoclassical.

Oct. 24   Richard Burgin and the Boston Symphony Orchestra premiere Henry Cowell's *Short Symphony*.

Oct. 30   Elie Siegmeister's Symphony No. 1 is premiered by Leopold Stokowski and the New York Philharmonic at Carnegie Hall. The composer describes the four-movement work as follows; "I might simply say that it deals with the spirit, the struggle, the hope of man."

Oct. 30   Darius Milhaud's Symphony No. 3 (*Hymnus ambrosianus*) premieres in Paris. The four-movement work celebrates the liberation of France from the Nazis and was commissioned by the French government.

Oct. 31   *Toccata for Percussion Instruments*, by Carlos Chavez, premieres in Mexico City. Scored for 11 types of percussion instruments, it includes Yaqui drums, rattles and gongs and is in three movements. Chavez is now director of the Instituto Nacional de Bellas Artes in Mexico.

Nov. 9   Andrzej Panufnik's *Berceuse* premieres over radio in Cracow, the composer conducting. The music is scored for two harps and 29 stringed instruments and features quarter-tone harmonies. Panufnik, now 33, has studied at the Warsaw Conservatory and has also studied conducting with Felix Weingartner in Vienna. He remained in Warsaw during the Nazi occupation and is now conductor of the Warsaw Orchestra.

Nov. 9   Alexander Tcherepnin's cantata *Les Douze*, with a text by Alexander Blok, premieres in Paris. This work is scored for narrator, strings, harp, piano and percussion and depicts the Red army as apostles of Jesus Christ.

Nov. 21   Eugene Ormandy and the Philadelphia Orchestra premiere Vincent Persichetti's Symphony No. 3. Composed over a four-year period, this four-movement work brings the composer to national attention. He is now 32.

Nov. 27   Ernst Krenek's Symphony No. 4 receives its initial performance by Dimitri Mitropoulos and the New York Philharmonic. The three-movement work is dodecaphonic. The composer states he uses that technique to generate a "very high amount of logical coherence and intelligible significance." Reviews are not favorable. John Briggs says in the New York *Post*, "Krenek's Fourth Symphony is so removed from the listener's normal experience that one has a feeling of suddenly being transported to Mars not knowing whether to be amused or infuriated." Virgil Thomson says in the New York *Herald-Tribune* that the music "... is a pseudo-masterpiece, with about as much savor to it as a pasteboard turkey."

1947   Births, Deaths and Debuts

Jan. 26   American soprano Grace Moore, 48, is killed in an airplane crash on her way from Copenhagen to Stockholm. Starting her career in musical comedy, she debuted

successfully at the Metropolitan Opera in 1928. She also made guest appearances in Europe and made several motion pictures.

Jan. 28   French composer Reynaldo Hahn, 72, dies in Paris. Born in Caracas, Venezuala, Hahn moved with his family to Paris when he was 5. His fine young voice attracted immediate attention, and he made a recording in 1910. He later studied composition with Jules Massenet at the Paris Conservatoire. He pursued conducting and began conducting operas and writing criticism for *Le Figaro* (Paris). During the Nazi occupation of Paris, he remained there, despite his father's Jewish ancestry. He became a director of the Paris Opera in 1945 and also that year was elected a member of the Institut de France. He was a close personal friend of Marcel Proust. His music is known for its romantic flavor and facile melodies. He composed seven operas, several operettas, ballets, orchestral works and other pieces. He is best remembered for his songs (for example, "Les chansons grises," composed while he was still a conservatory student) and for his criticism.

Feb. 4   Italian composer Luigi Russolo, 61, dies in Cerro, Italy. This composer was known for his futurist tendencies and machinations. He joined the futurist movement in 1909 and in 1916 published his book *L'arte dei rumori*, in which he formulated his principles of the "art of noises." His concerts generated such a negative response that he was once physically attacked by members of a Paris audience. His machine, the "Russolophone," was constructed in 1929. The appeal of this noisemaker began to wane after a few concerts and ironically, with the emergence of airplanes and automobiles, his movement lost its novelty and faded.

His contribution — along with that of other futurists, such as Filippo Marinetti — was in terms of helping give birth to the era of sound, a trend that would quickly lead to the introduction and development of electronic music. Their credo was: "To present the musical soul of the masses, of the great factories, of the railways, of the transatlantic liners, of the battleships, of the automobiles and airplanes. To add to the great cultural themes of the musical poem the domain of the machine and the victorious kingdom of Electricity." As soon as 20th-century technology surpassed his revolutionary capabilities, Russolo became a painter and enjoyed successful exhibitions in Paris and New York. His paintings, reflecting trends of the modern French School, are known for their colors.

Feb. 26   Alexis Kudisch, 65, dies in Brooklyn, New York. A composer and violinist, he studied composition with Nikolai Rimsky-Korsakov and founded the New York Polyphonic Symphony Orchestra and the American String Quartet.

March 5   Italian composer Alfredo Casella, 63, dies in Rome. He studied at the Paris Conservatoire with Gabriel Faure and soon toured Europe and Russia as a pianist and conductor. He later taught at Santa Cecilia in Rome and founded what would become the Italian section of the International Society for Contemporary Music. For a time he conducted the Boston Pops, but his efforts to introduce new works aroused hostility from the Boston public. He later won several awards, including the Coolidge Prize

(1934). Casella was prolific both as a writer and as a composer. His music, neoclassical in style, exhibits modernist influences (expecially in his early works). He composed three operas, four ballets, three symphonies, many other orchestral works and chamber works. He also made a four-hand piano arrangement of Gustav Mahler's Seventh Symphony.

March 18   Dutch composer Willem Pijper, 52, dies in Leidschendam, Netherlands. He studied at the Toonkunst School of Music in Utrecht and later wrote music criticism for several Dutch newspapers and periodicals. He taught at the Amsterdam and Rotterdam conservatories. Most of his works were destroyed by the German bombings of Rotterdam in 1940. His music is essentially romantic, with the added influence of French impressionism. He had a favorite scale, which he called the "Pijper scale"; Nikolai Rimsky-Korsakov used the same scale in Russia and called it the "Rimsky-Korsakov scale" (it consists of alternating whole tones and semitones). Pijper's "germ-cell" theory postulates that a chord or motive opening a composition generates the entire musical composition — a notion similar to that system developed by the Austrian theorist Heinrich Schenker. Pijper was prolific: His work includes two operas, three symphonies and much incidental music as well as chamber, piano and choral music. His work is remembered in Holland, though not much elsewhere.

March 21   Czech dancer and choreographer Jiri Kylian is born in Prague.

April 19   American pianist Murray Perahia is born in the Bronx, New York City.

May 6   American contralto Louise Homer, 75, dies in Winter Park, Florida. After studying singing in America and Europe, she debuted in Vichy in 1898 in *La favorita*. After engagements at Covent Garden and in Brussels, she made her American debut in 1900. She sang with the Metropolitan Opera until 1919 and again from 1927 to 1930, and also appeared in other American and European houses. She participated in many notable productions, including a revival of Gluck's *Orfeo ed Euridice*, conducted by Arturo Toscanini. She was noted for the beauty of her voice and for maintaining the highest artistic standards.

June 12   American dancer and choreographer John Clifford is born in Hollywood, California.

June 15   Polish violinist Bronislaw Huberman, 64, dies in Corsier-sur-Vevey, Switzerland. After studies in Warsaw and then with Joseph Joachim in Berlin, he began playing at age 11 in the European capitals. In 1895 he was chosen by Adelina Patti to play at her farewell concert in Vienna and, the following year, was complimented by Brahms after playing his Violin Concerto. In 1936 he founded the Palestine Symphony Orchestra with Jewish musicians who had fled the Nazis.

July 24   Pianist Peter Serkin is born in New York, the son of pianist Rudolf Serkin.

Aug. 3   Soprano Maria Callas makes her Italian operatic debut as La Gioconda in Verona.

Sep. 20   Bulgarian soprano Ljuba Welitsch makes her London debut on tour with the Vienna State Opera, singing Donna Anna in a performance of *Don Giovanni*.

1947   Related Events

The Royal Philharmonic is organized this year by Sir Thomas Beecham.

Events in the recording industry this year include the following: Magnetic recordings (both wire and tape) begin appearing on the American market; General Electric's variable reluctance pickup cartridge is introduced; RCA Victor's red vinyl pressing series is introduced; the Audio Engineering Society (AES) is founded in the United States.

The Komische Oper is established in Berlin this year. Walter Felsenstein is head of the company. The opera company subsequently becomes one of the most respected in Europe.

The Edinburgh Festival is established this year in Scotland. This annual summer music festival is financed by Audrey Christie and the Glyndebourne Society Ltd., and Rudolf Bing, who is its first director.

Schoenberg et son ecole, by Rene Leibowitz, is published this year in Paris. This is the first book on Schoenberg; it becomes a classic. It is published in an English edition two years from now.

The Ballet Annual begins publication this year. Arnold Haskell is editor. The publication ceases in 1963.

Feb. 3   Polish conductor Artur Rodzinski resigns as music director of the New York Philharmonic in the middle of the fourth year of his leadership because of differences with the management. Bruno Walter succeeds him, but as "music advisor." This arrangement lasts two years.

Feb. 6   The Pittsburgh Symphony Orchestra, under the baton of its music director Fritz Reiner, gives a concert at the Palacio de Bellas Artes in Mexico City. This event marks the first time a major American orchestra performs in Mexico. The event coincides with the fiesta celebrating the signing of the Mexican constitution.

Feb. 7   Three days after resigning his post of music director of the New York Philharmonic, Artur Rodzinski signs a contract to head the Chicago Symphony.

March 6   The New Zealand Symphony Orchestra gives its inaugural concert today in Wellington Town Hall, Wellington, New Zealand. Conducted by Andersen Tyrer, the program includes music by Antonin Dvorak, Johannes Brahms, Georges Enesco, Richard Wagner and others.

May 5   The Pulitzer Prize for music is awarded to Charles Ives for his Third Symphony. Ives is 72 years old.

May 9   Black singer Paul Robeson sings a church-sponsored concert in a school auditorium in Albany, New York. He had been barred from singing in Illinois after a congressional group named him cosponsor of the "communist" American Youth for Democracy.

May 10   Tullio Serafin announces his resignation as artistic director of La Scala. He cites conflicts between the management and his artistic leadership.

May 20   Donemus is established today in Amsterdam. This new organization is a clearinghouse for contemporary Dutch music. It publishes and records new music; develops an extensive library of new works by Dutch composers; and publishes various periodicals, including *Key Notes*, which publicize new music and report explorations in contemporary music theory by Dutch composers and musicians.

Nov. 20   Pope Pius XII issues a papal encyclical entitled *Mediator Dei*. This document clarifies directions for active participation of the congregation in music for worship. In the section entitled "The Other Arts in the Liturgical Cult," he states, "Modern art should be given free scope in the due and reverent service of the church" so long as "the needs of the Christian community are taken into consideration rather than the particular taste or talent of the individual artist."

Nov. 28   The Vienna Philharmonic gives its first concert under this name. It had originally been founded in 1842 and called the Philharmonische Akademie (with Otto Nicolai as its music director). Since then its music directors have included Hans Richter, Gustav Mahler, Ernst Schuch, Felix Mottl, Karl Muck, Arthur Nikisch, Felix Weingartner, Wilhelm Furtwangler and others.

1948 Opera

March 15 The Budapest Opera premieres Zoltan Kodaly's *Czinka Panna*. The opera is about a young gypsy woman who motivates Hungarian soldiers to victory over the Austrians in the battle of 1703.

May 5 Otto Luening conducts the premiere performance of his opera *Evangeline* at the first concert of the Fourth Annual Festival of Contemporary Music in New York. Based on the poem by Longfellow, the work features church music and Indian howls. Virgil Thomson subsequently says, "Otto Luening is an original composer, and his textures are both highly personal and expressive."

May 24 Benjamin Britten's new version of John Gay's *The Beggar's Opera* premieres in Cambridge, England, the composer conducting.

July 15 Kurt Weill's folk opera *Down in the Valley* premieres at Indiana University in Bloomington. The libretto is by Arnold Sundgaard. The opera, in one act, is about love and murder and incorporates Kentucky mountain folk songs.

Oct. 14 Swiss composer Heinrich Sutermeister's two-act opera *Raskolnikoff* receives its world premiere in Stockholm. It is based on Dostoevski's *Crime and Punishment*. Sutermeister has studied philology at the Sorbonne and musical composition with Carl Orff.

Oct. 28 Czech composer Rudolf Karel's *Three Hairs of the Old Wise Man* premieres posthumously in Prague. The composer died after writing this work in a concentration camp.

Dec. 3 Sergei Prokofiev's *A Story of a Real Man* is premiered for a selected audience in Leningrad. The work is scorned by Soviet officials for being dissonant. It does not receive its first public performance until October 8, 1960. Of today's performance, Tikhon Khrennikov writes in *Pravda* that the composer ". . . is still interested solely in the external effects of dramatic action and in naturalistic details."

Dec. 18 In Berlin, Werner Egk conducts the premiere of his *Circe*, an opera based on the Homeric tale.

1948 Dance

Jan. 15 Harald Lander's *Etudes* is premiered by the Royal Danish Ballet. The plotless ballet, to music by Knudage Riisager based on Carl Czerny piano etudes, shows the development of ballet technique through a ballet class. Hans Brenaa, Margot Lander and Svend Erik Jensen lead the cast.

Feb. 6 John Taras' *Designs with Strings* premieres in Edinburgh, Scotland, danced by the Metropolitan Ballet to music of Tchaikovsky. The plotless ballet is danced by Erik Bruhn, Svetlana Beriosova, Sonia Arova, Celia Franca, Delysia Blake and David Adams.

Feb. 11 Margot Fonteyn and Michael Somes head the opening night cast of Frederick Ashton's *Scenes de ballet*. The work is set to Igor Stravinsky's *Scenes de ballet*, originally composed for Billy Rose's revue *Seven Lively Arts* produced in 1944. This is the first ballet using the complete score.

March 22 George Balanchine's *Symphony in C* receives its American premiere as it is performed by the Ballet Society in New York City. Originally entitled *Le palais de cristal*, it was first performed last year by the Paris Opera Ballet. The dancers include Maria Tallchief, Tanaquil LeClerq and Nicholas Magallanes. The ballet is in four movements.

April 14 Antony Tudor premieres *Shadow of the Wind* with the Ballet Theater at the Metropolitan Opera House in New York. The one-act ballet, in six episodes, is based on poems by Chinese poet Li Po. The work is set to Gustav Mahler's *Das Lied von der Erde*. Alicia Alonso, Nana Gollner, Muriel Bentley, Igor Youskevitch and Hugh Laing star. The work, which is the first balletic treatment of Mahler's score, is unsuccessful.

April 22 Agnes De Mille's *Fall River Legend* is performed for the first time by the American Ballet Theater in New York City. It features music by Morton Gould, scenery by Oliver Smith and costumes by Miles White. The lead dancers are Alicia Alonso, John Kriza, Muriel Bentley, Peter Gladke and Diana Adams. Nora Kaye subsequently dances the star role, but she is too ill to dance the first performance. The ballet is about Lizzie Borden.

April 28 The Ballet Society in New York presents George Balanchine's *Orpheus*, to music by Igor Stravinsky. It is based on the Greek legend. Nicholas Magallanes, Maria Tallchief, Francisco Moncion and Herbert Bliss star.

May 22 The Ballets de Paris premieres Roland Petit's *Les Demoiselles de la Nuit* to music by Jean Francaix in Paris. The story, by Jean Anouilh, is about a young man who falls in love with a cat who assumes human characteristics. She tries to be faithful but is enticed to freedom by the cries of tomcats. He tries to catch her but falls to his death. She then jumps to her death. Margot Fonteyn, Petit and Gordon Hamilton star. This performance is the first of Ballets de Paris. Roland Petit decided to break with Les Ballets des Champs-Elysees and has established this dance company.

Aug. 13   The Martha Graham Company premieres her *Diversion of Angels* (under the title *Wilderness Stair*), with music by Norman Dello Joio, in New London, Connecticut. The plotless work deals with first love. May O'Donnell, Pearl Lang, Helen McGehee, Erick Hawkins and Robert Cohan lead the cast.

Aug. 13   *Dramatic Etude*, choreographed by Alwin Nikolais, and *Xochipili*, choreographed by Hanya Holm, are performed for the first time in Colorado Springs. Both works are danced to percussion music.

Aug. 20   Merce Cunningham's *A Diversion*, with music by John Cage, premieres at Black Mountain College.

Aug. 27   Ted Shawn's *Minuet for Drums* receives its first performance at Jacob's Pillow in Lee, Massachusetts.

Nov. 16   Andree Howard's *Selina* premieres with the Sadler's Wells Ballet in London. The ballet, in one act and set to music from various Rossini operas, is a satire of the ro-

mantic tradition. Elaine Fifield, Hans Zullig, Stanley Holden and Pirmin Trecu star.

Nov. 25   Frederick Ashton premieres his *Don Juan* with the Sadler's Wells Ballet in London. The one-act work is to Richard Strauss' tone poem of the same name. Its theme deals with Don Juan's love affair with death. Margot Fonteyn, Moira Shearer and Robert Helpmann star.

Dec. 13   Choreographer Jean Babilee's *L' amour et son amour*, with music by Cesar Franck and costumes and scenery by Jean Cocteau, is premiered by Les Ballets des Champs-Elysees in Paris. It tells the story of Cupid and Psyche. Nathalie Phillippart stars. The ballet is in two scenes.

Dec. 23   The Sadler's Wells Ballet gives the world premiere of Frederick Ashton's evening-length *Cinderella*, to music by Sergei Prokofiev. In this brilliant production, the ugly stepsisters are played *en travesti* in the tradition of English pantomime. This is the first evening-length ballet choreographed by a British choreographer. Moira Shearer replaces the indisposed Margot Fonteyn. Michael Somes, Pamela May, Robert Helpmann and Frederick Ashton also star.

1948   Instrumental and Vocal Music

Jan. 9   Serge Koussevitzky and the Boston Symphony Orchestra premiere Walter Piston's Symphony No. 3 in E. The symphony is highly successful: It receives the Hornblit Award and the Pulitzer Prize.

Jan. 23   Heitor Villa-Lobos' symphonic poem *Mandu-Carara* is given its first performance in New York. The music is based on a Brazilian tale about two children who are haunted by an evil spirit. It is scored for mixed choir, children's chorus, two pianos and percussion.

Jan. 23   The Symphony No. 4, by David Diamond, is premiered by Leonard Bernstein and the Boston Symphony Orchestra. It is in three movements.

Jan. 25   Hans Kindler and the National Symphony Orchestra premiere Robert Ward's Symphony No. 2 in Washington, D.C. This three-movement work expounds music "in older forms treated in a new way."

Jan. 30   American composer Henry Brant's Symphony No. 1 receives its world premiere by Thor Johnson and the Cincinnati Symphony Orchestra.

Feb. 8   Henri Sauguet's *Symphonie expiatoire* receives its world premiere in Paris. According to the composer, the music is an expression of the anguish the French experienced during the Nazi occupation.

Feb. 22   The Berlin Philharmonic gives the first performance of Wilhelm Furtwangler's Symphony No. 2 with the

composer conducting. The work is based on the 19th-century model of the German romantic symphony.

Feb. 24   The Kansas City Philharmonic presents Virgil Thomson's symphonic poem *The Seine at Night*. The composer states that the music he composed in Paris is ". . . in one way or another about Kansas City."

Feb. 27   Serge Koussevitzky and the Boston Symphony Orchestra give the first performance of Gian Francesco Malipiero's Symphony No. 4, subtitled *In Memoriam*. Each movement of the work ends in a minor key. The piece had been commissioned by the Koussevitzky Foundation.

March 23   Swedish composer Hilding Rosenberg's opera-oratorio *Joseph and His Brethren*, based on the novel by Thomas Mann, premieres in Stockholm. Rosenberg conducts. The complete work is eight hours long; this performance features only the last part.

April 1   Witold Lutoslawski's Symphony No. 1 premieres in Katowice, Poland. Composed between 1941 and 1947, it is the first of two symphonies he writes. He is now 35.

April 2   German composer Karl Amadeus Hartmann's Symphony No. 4 for strings, in three movements, premieres in Munich.

April 4   The Palestine Symphony Orchestra gives the first performance of Karol Rathaus' *Vision dramatique* in Tel

Aviv. This work is a symphonic movement. Rathaus is now teaching at Queens College of the City University of New York.

April 4   Richard Strauss' *Duet Concertino* is presented for the first time over Radio-Swizzera Italiana. The work is scored for clarinet, bassoon, string orchestra and harp.

April 9   Serge Koussevitzky and the Boston Symphony Orchestra give the first performance of Samuel Barber's *Knoxville: Summer of 1915*. Eleanor Steber is soloist. It is scored for soprano and orchestra, with text from James Agee's *A Death in the Family*. This work becomes one of the composer's best-loved compositions.

April 21   Sir Adrian Boult and the Royal Philharmonic premiere Ralph Vaughan Williams' Symphony No. 6 in E Minor. The performance takes place in London. The symphony is considered one of the composer's greatest works. He completed it at age 75.

April 23   Andre Jolivet's Concerto for Ondes Martenot and Orchestra is presented for the first time in Vienna. This three-movement work features an extensive percussion section.

May 16   Dean Dixon and the CBS Symphony Orchestra present Wallingford Riegger's Symphony No. 3 and Quincy Porter's Concerto for Viola and Orchestra in New York City. Riegger's piece wins the Naumburg Award and the New York Music Critics Circle Award.

May 20   Darius Milhaud conducts his Symphony No. 4 at its premiere in Paris. The work, subtitled *1848*, was commissioned by the French government to commemorate the revolt against King Louis Philippe.

June 5   Benjamin Britten's cantata *Saint Nicolas* with text by Eric Crozier, premieres at the Aldeburgh Music Festival. This work, in nine movements, is scored for tenor solo, mixed chorus, two pianos, strings, percussion and organ.

June 30   John Barbirolli conducts the world premiere of Australian composer Arthur Benjamin's Symphony No. 1 at the Festival of Contemporary British Music in Cheltenham. Benjamin studied composition with Charles Villiers Stanford at the Royal College of Music in London and has recently completed his tenure as conductor of the Vancouver Symphony Orchestra (Canada).

July 1   Alan Rawsthorne's Violin Concerto, in two movements, premieres at the Cheltenham Festival. This English composer began studying music when he was 21. He is a product of the Royal Manchester College of Music and studied piano with Egon Petri in Berlin.

Aug. 25   Hans Werner Henze's Symphony No. 1 receives its initial performance at Bad Prymont. Henze, who fought on the Russian front with the German army, is now 21. He studied with Wolfgang Fortner.

Oct. 5   Pierre Schaeffer's first *Concert de bruit* receives its world premiere over radio in Paris. The work involves the simultaneous playing of five randomly selected phonograph records, as well as other sonic additives, such as coughing and a tampered-with piano.

Oct. 10   Leonard Bernstein's *La bonne cuisine* is premiered by soprano Marion Bell at Town Hall in New York City.

Oct. 22   Andre Jolivet's *Suite delphique* premieres in Vienna. It is scored for wind instruments, harp, Ondes Martenot and percussion.

Oct. 24   Conductor Roger Desormiere and the BBC Symphony Orchestra premiere Francis Poulenc's *Sinfonietta* in London. The four-movement piece is scored for orchestra.

Oct. 27   Ernest Ansermet gives the first performance of Igor Stravinsky's *Mass* in Milan. The work is scored for tenors and basses and a children's chorus of trebles and altos. A double wind quintet is also included. It is Stravinsky's first major liturgical work. Next year the piece is performed in New York. Of that performance, Noel Strauss writes in the New York *Times*, "It is largely bereft of either spirituality or human feeling." Arthur Berger, however, writes in the New York *Herald-Tribune* that it is of "uncommon purity and remarkably unforced religious sentiment."

Oct. 29   Dmitri Kabalevsky's Violin Concerto premieres simultaneously in Leningrad and Moscow. This is the first of three concertos the composer writes for Soviet youth.

Nov. 4   Kurt Frederick and the Albuquerque Civic Symphony Orchestra give the world premiere of Arnold Schoenberg's *Survivor of Warsaw*. The text, in English, is by the composer. It is scored for narrator, men's chorus and orchestra and depicts life in the Warsaw ghetto. Olin Downes, about a year and a half from now, reviews a performance of the piece in the New York *Times* and says, "It is poor and empty music, even though it be couched in the most learned Schoenbergian formulas of craftsmanship."

Nov. 23   Norman Del Mar and the Chelsea Symphony Orchestra give the first performance of Ernst von Dohnanyi's Symphony No. 2 in E Major.

Nov. 26   Eugene Ormandy and the Philadelphia Orchestra premiere Virgil Thomson's Suite for Orchestra, drawn from materials from his film score *Louisiana Story*.

Dec. 7   Virgil Thomson's *Wheat Field at Noon* is premiered by the Louisville Orchestra with the composer conducting. The music features variations on a theme made up of the 12 notes of the chromatic scale.

Dec. 12   Hans Werner Henze's Violin Concerto receives its first performance in Baden-Baden.

Dec. 28   Nikolai Miaskovsky's Symphony No. 26, premieres in Moscow. The work, in C major, is deliberately conservative to satisfy the recommendations of the February 1948 Soviet Communist Party resolutions on musical style. It is in three movements and is Miaskovsky's penultimate symphony.

Dec. 31   Rudolf Firkusny and the Boston Symphony Orchestra premiere Howard Hanson's Piano Concerto. On the same program, Lukas Foss conducts the premiere of his own symphonic piece *Recordare*, which is dedicated to the memory of Mahatma Gandhi.

Dec. 31   Eugene Ormandy and the Philadelphia Orchestra premiere George Antheil's Symphony No. 5. This three-movement symphony is subtitled *Joyous*.

1948   Births, Deaths and Debuts

Jan. 8   Austrian tenor Richard Tauber, 55, dies in London. After an enormously successful debut in Chemnitz, he was engaged by the Dresden Opera and, two years later, by the Berlin Royal Opera. The height of his popularity came with his many performances in Viennese operetta. To escape the Nazis, in 1938 he settled in London, where he wrote and starred in an operetta called *Old Chelsea*. He sang Italian, French and German operas; was particularly admired for his Mozart singing; and was also capable as a recitalist.

Jan. 21   Italian composer Ermanno Wolf-Ferrari, 72, dies in Venice. A pupil of Josef Rheinberger in Munich, he lived at various times during his career in Venice and Neu-Biberg (near Munich). His initial success came with the premiere of his oratorio *La sulamite* (Venice, 1899). His opera, *Cenerentola*, premiered in 1900. His first big success came in 1903, when the opera *Le donne curiose* was staged in Munich. Between 1906 and 1911 several of his operas brought Wolf-Ferrari to the attention of the public. *Il segreto di Susanna* — a one-act verismo opera buffa — quickly came to be considered a small masterpiece. *I Gioielli della Madonna* (premiered in Berlin in 1911) soon became an international favorite. Although he composed 13 operas and

several cantatas, as well as orchestral, chamber and other works, his impact was negligible compared to that of Richard Strauss, whose operatic efforts also peaked in 1911 with *Der Rosenkavalier*. Wolf-Ferrari's subjects were mostly of a light, comedic nature and did not, as with Strauss, include much powerful psychological drama. He made absolutely no contribution to contemporary music theory.

Jan. 27   Dancer Mikhail Baryshnikov is born in Riga, USSR.

Feb. 14   Italian-born composer Aldo Franchetti, 65, dies in Hollywood. His opera *Namiko-San* is considered to be among his best-known works.

March 26   Violinist Kyung-Wha Chung is born in Seoul, Korea.

March 30   American tenor John H. Bieling, 79, dies in Hempstead, New York. He was a pioneer in early recordings and made early cylindrical recordings in the laboratory of Thomas A. Edison in 1894.

April 24   Latvian composer Joseph Wihtol, 84, dies in Lubeck. Teacher of Sergei Prokofiev and Nikolai Miaskovsky, he also founded a Latvian Conservatory in Riga. He was a pupil of Nikolai Rimsky-Korsakov at the Saint Petersburg Conservatory and later wrote music criticism in Germany, where he settled after 1944. His music is clearly in the Russian romantic tradition and includes Latvian folk elements. He composed orchestral, choral and piano works, as well as arrangements of approximately 200 Latvian folk songs.

April 24   Mexican composer Manuel Ponce, 65, dies in Mexico City. A pupil of Enrico Bossi in Bologna and, much later, of Paul Dukas in Paris, he taught piano at the National Conservatory in Mexico. His works — including many orchestral pieces, chamber and piano works, songs and folk song arrangements — reveal a Mexican musical mind tempered by French impressionism. He was Mexico's first 20th-century composer to enter the realm of a new musical language: economy of form and an emphasis — to some degree, at least — on animated musical rhythms. His song "Estrellita," highly popular, never made him any money because he was negligent about filing a copyright registration form.

May 2   English writer on music Arthur Henry Fox-Strangeways, 88, dies in Dinton, near Salisbury, England. A critic for the *London Times* and the *Observer*, he also

RICHARD TAUBER

founded the quarterly *Music and Letters* in 1920. He was an expert on Indian music and wrote many books on the subject.

June 27 American composer George Templeton Strong, 92, dies in Geneva. Born of a father who hated the music of Franz Liszt and Richard Wagner, he studied in Leipzig with Salomon Jadassohn and began to revere the work of Liszt. He was acquainted with Edward MacDowell while in Wiesbaden (1886 to 1889). He returned to America to teach at the New England Conservatory of Music. After becoming enraged at the lack of recognition given American composers in the United States, he moved to Switzerland and became a watercolor painter. He wrote three symphonies, two symphonic poems and other works.

July 16 Violinist Pinchas Zuckerman is born in Tel Aviv, Israel.

Sep. 15 American violinist Nicholas Gordon, 49, dies in Great Barrington, Massachusetts. He founded the annual Music Mountain festival some years after arriving in America from Odessa, Russia. He studied with Franz Kneisel at the Institute of Musical Art in New York City and was a soloist with the Russian Symphony Orchestra. Gordon also performed as second violinist with the Berkshire String Quartet, which had been founded by Elizabeth Sprague Coolidge. He later became concertmaster of the Chicago Symphony Orchestra. Music Mountain came into existence in 1930 with the financial help of Sears, Roebuck & Company.

Oct. 24 Austrian operetta composer Franz Lehar, 78, dies in Bad Ischl. He studied at the Prague Conservatory and later studied composition with Zdenko Fibich. He was also encouraged by Antonin Dvorak. His operetta *Kukusche* premiered in 1896. Great success came in 1905 with the premiere of *Die lustige Witwe*. Two years later that same operetta was being performed simultaneously in five languages in Buenos Aires. His music is noted for its simple, diatonic melody and lively rhythm. Combined with nostalgic subjects and humor, Lehar's work was thoroughly embraced by the Viennese music public during the early part of the century. In addition to many operettas, he also wrote a few orchestral works, marches and dances.

Nov. 12 Italian composer Umberto Giordano, 81, dies in Milan. He studied at the Naples Conservatory and had his first opera, *Mala Vita*, staged in Rome in 1892. He revised that work, and soon after, composed *Regina Diaz*, bringing him some success. *Andrea Chenier* was premiered in 1896 — this opera brought him to international attention. *Fedora* also brought success, but did not remain as popular as *Andrea Chenier*. He then entered a period of decline, recapturing the music public in 1915, with *Madame Sans-Gene*. Of his final operas, *La cena delle beffe* was the only one attracting notice. He was, in his last years, elected a member of the Accademia Luigi Cherubini. Giordano was one of the last heralded composers of Italian opera whose works entered the repertoire of major opera houses. His theatrical skill and lyric expression made him one of the finest modern Italian opera composers. Like Ruggero Leoncavallo and Pietro Mascagni he did not however, have anywhere near the international impact that Giacomo Puccini enjoyed.

Dec. 1 Dancer Eva Evdokimova is born in Geneva, Switzerland.

Dec. 7 British composer Godfrey Turner, 35, commits suicide in New York City. A pupil of Nadia Boulanger and E.J. Dent, he had been an editor at Boosey and Hawkes, a faculty member of the San Francisco Conservatory and an employee of the American Music Center in New York.

1948 Related Events

The Ballet Society becomes the *New York City Ballet* this year. Lincoln Kirstein, George Balanchine and Jerome Robbins are in charge. This event is the culmination of a progression of different names for the evolving ballet company. It began as the School of American Ballet (1934), then became the American Ballet (1935), then the Ballet Caravan (1936) and the Ballet Society (1946).

The Ballet Alicia Alonso is established this year in Havana by Alicia Alonso. She and Fernando Alonso direct, and Alberto Alonso is principal choreographer. The company changes its name in 1955 to Ballet de Cuba. In 1959 it becomes Ballet Nacional de Cuba.

The Robert Shaw Chorale is established this year.

Violist and conductor, Vaclav Neumann, becomes music director of the Czech Philharmonic Orchestra this year. He was formerly a member of the Smetana Quartet.

Philosophy of Modern Music, by Theodor W. Adorno, is published this year in Tubingen. The book was written while Adorno was living in Los Angeles to escape the Nazis. It analyzes in depth the music of Arnold Schoenberg and Igor Stravinsky and explores their work in terms of sociological and political phenomena. Adorno asserts that these two giants are in dialectical opposition to one another. Schoenberg is depicted as progressive, Stravinsky as reactionary. Thomas Mann later writes of this book "Its spirit was remarkably forward-looking, subtle, and deep."

Jan. Colonel de Basil's ballet company — Original Ballet Russe — disbands in France after a period of tours that included Mexico, South America, the United States and Europe. The disbanding comes largely as a result of Colonel de Basil's personality problems and his inability to attract first-rate impresarios who would work with him. Colonel de Basil's great competitor — Leonide Massine — is still prominent with his Ballet Russe de Monte Carlo; that company celebrates its 10th anniversary this year and is officially directed by Sergei I. Denham, the financier who helped bring it into existence. Its 10th anniversary marks its peak of fame in America, however. The company begins to fade and finally ceases to perform in 1962 (although it does maintain a ballet school in New York City after 1962).

Jan. 13   The management of the Chicago Symphony announces the dismissal of its new conductor, Artur Rodzinski, for policy disagreements. He had not yet finished his first season in this post.

Jan. 27   The Bach Aria Group makes its New York debut at Carnegie Recital Hall.

Feb. 11   Three Soviet composers — Dmitri Shostakovich, Sergei Prokofiev and Aram Khachaturian — are rebuked by the Communist Central Committee for writing unharmonious, "anti-democratic" music. They are accused of forsaking Russian traditional melody and writing a "cacophonic and chaotic heaping of sounds," which "strongly smells of the spirit of current modernistic bourgeois music of Europe and America." All composers of Russian music are ordered to eschew modernism.

Feb. 21   It is reported that Soviet composers Dmitri Shostakovich, Aram Khachaturian and Sergei Prokofiev have thanked the Communist Party for criticizing their music and have promised to correct their mistakes.

March 20   Eugene Ormandy conducts the Philadelphia Orchestra in a concert transmitted over television by CBS to New York City. Arturo Toscanini's televised concert by NBC to Philadelphia, Schenectady, Buffalo and Washington begins one hour later. These events mark the first television broadcasts of a symphony orchestra performance.

March 26   Hanns Eisler leaves America after being charged with Communist associations and perjury by the House of Representatives' Committee on Un-American Activities. In a subsequent article before leaving, the composer says that Adolf Hitler had placed a price on his head during the days of the Third Reich.

April 3   Walter Piston is awarded the Pulitzer Prize for music for his Symphony No. 3.

April 11   In a letter to *Izvestia*, Soviet composers Dmitri Shostakovich, Sergei Prokofiev, Aram Khachaturian and Nikolai Miaskovsky accuse the 20th Century Fox film studio of unauthorized use of their music in the film *The Iron Curtain*.

April 15   French radio engineer Pierre Schaeffer's concept of "musique concrète" — which he defines as a mixture of natural, random and recorded sounds combined in some aesthetic way — is concretized today. Schaeffer gives this date as the movement's advent in his *Introduction a la musique concrete.*

May 29   In an attempt to make music accessible to the world public, composers and musicologists prepare a proclamation of aims at the Second International Congress of Composers and Musicologists, beginning today in Prague and continuing for 10 days. The four principal aims are (1) avoidance of subjectivism; (2) cultivation of national flavor in music; (3) pursuance of well-known forms; and (4) increased activity by composers and critics in music education.

June 8   Richard Strauss is cleared of charges of Nazi collaboration in Munich, despite his having accepted the presidency of the Reichsmusikkammer under Dr. Joseph Goebbels and having accepted autographed photographs of both Adolf Hitler and Goebbels on Strauss's 70th birthday.

June 15   The first Holland Festival begins today. It includes symphony, opera, ballet and chamber music, and participating ensembles include the Concertgebouw Orchestra, the Rotterdam Philharmonic Orchestra, The Hague Philharmonic Orchestra and the Nederlandsche Opera. This festival celebrates music for one month.

June 21   Columbia (U.S.) announces its vinyl microgroove long-playing disc (developed by Dr. Peter Goldmark and associates, this is the first record capable of playing up to 45 minutes) along with inexpensive "outboard" players (which had been manufactured first by Philco) and a large catalog of available recordings of this type. Other events in the recording industry this year include Magnecord's introduction of its PT6 tape recorder; the appearance and proliferation of competitive new recording firms in America (Capitol, MGM and Mercury); and the establishment of the Charles Cros Recording Award in France.

July 29   Igor Stravinsky sues Leeds Music Company of New York City for $250,000. This company published a tune entitled "Summer Moon," which Stravinsky claims is from *The Firebird* and insults his reputation as a serious composer. The case is dismissed in March of next year.

Sep. 30   In one of the most selfish gestures in the history of music in Western civilization, the Stradivarius violin belonging to deceased Italian-American violinist Louise Terzi is placed in her casket and buried with her, as per her orders. She is buried in Los Angeles.

Oct.   The Ballet Alicia Alonso gives its first season in Havana.

Oct. 11   The New York City Ballet (formerly the Ballet Society) gives its first performance under that name at the City Center in New York. The program includes *Concerto Barocco*, *Orpheus* and *Symphony in C*. The company appears as an affiliate of the resident opera company but performs as an independent part of the City Center starting in January.

Oct. 14   Charles Munch conducts a concert of the Orchestre National de France in Bridgeport, Connecticut. It marks the first concert of this orchestra's tour and the first time since 1919 that a French orchestra tours the United States.

Nov. 29   A British film, *Scott of the Antarctic*, receives its premiere in London. The score is by Ralph Vaughan Williams, who subsequently uses material from it in his Symphony No. 7. subtitled *Sinfonia antartica*.

Dec. 19   In an article entitled "One Always Returns," published today in the New York *Times*, Arnold Schoenberg comments on his recent return to tonality as found in his *Theme and Variations for Orchestra*, Op. 43b, indicating that such a return was perhaps influenced by nostalgia. He states, in part: "A longing to return to the older style was always vigorous in me, and from time to time I had to yield to that urge. This is how and why I sometimes write tonal music. To me stylistic differences of this nature are not of special importance. I do not know which of my compositions are better; I like them all, because I liked them when I wrote them."

Dec. 29   At the conclusion of its Moscow convention, the Union of Soviet Composers issues another formal resolution praising "socialist realism" and denouncing intellectualism in music. It says in part: "Defeated ideologically, formalism still lingers in Soviet music."

1949 Opera

Feb. 9   Douglas Moore's *White Wings* premieres in Hartford, Connecticut. This chamber opera is about a young woman in love with a sanitation worker.

March 2   Heinrich Sutermeister's one-act opera *Die schwarze Spinne* receives its first performance in Saint Gall, Switzerland. It is about a woman who is transformed into a spider by the Devil.

March 31   *The Troubled Island*, by William Grant Still, receives its world premiere by the New York City Opera at the City Center, New York. The three-act opera, with libretto by Langston Hughes, is about Haitian independence. Robert Weede, Marie Powers, Oscar Natzka and Francis Bible perform. Although the opera is not successful, it is the first opera by an American composer to be premiered by this relatively new opera company.

May 7   Hans Werner Henze's *Das Wundertheater*, with a libretto based on Miguel de Cervantes, premieres in Heidelberg.

May 12   *Il Cordovano*, by Goffredo Petrassi, premieres in Milan at the Teatro alla Scala. The one-act opera buffa is based on a play by Miguel de Cervantes entitled *The Jealous Old Man*.

June 14   The first performance of Benjamin Britten's *Let's Make an Opera* is held at Aldeburgh. It is a two-part entertainment for young people written to a libretto by Eric Crozier. The first part of the work is actually the rehearsal for the second part, entitled *The Little Sweep*. Adults, children and the audience participate in the second part. The second part is the opera itself, about an 8-year-old apprentice chimney sweep.

June 21   Reynaldo Hahn's *Le oui des jeunes filles*, partially orchestrated by Henri Busser, premieres posthumously at the Opera-Comique in Paris. It is three-act lyric comedy.

Aug. 9   *Antigonae*, by Carl Orff, receives its first performance in Salzburg. The opera is based on Friedrich Holderlin's translation of the tragedy by Sophocles. The instrumentation to this musical play is unusual: It includes six pianos, four harps, African drums, Javanese gongs, xylophones and an anvil.

Sep. 7   Giorgio Federico Ghedini's *Billy Budd* premieres in Venice at the Teatro La Fenice. The libretto is based on the novel by Herman Melville. The work is originally conceived as a stage oratorio but is later performed as an opera in one act.

Sep. 29   The first performance of *The Olympians*, by Arthur Bliss, takes place at Covent Garden in London. The libretto, by J.B. Priestley, is a story about the gods of Olympus who have fallen from power and are forced to make their living as strolling minstrels. Once a year they return to their former glory for a single night.

Oct. 11   Marc Blizstein's opera *Regina*, based on *The Little Foxes* by Lillian Hellman, premieres in Boston. It is about the members of a southern family who wallow in hatred for each other. Ten years from now, Virgil Thomson comments in the *Saturday Review*: "Here is a work that fills an operatic stage and fulfills the listener."

Oct. 30   *Lost in the Stars*, an operetta by Kurt Weill, receives its initial performance in New York.

Dec. 4   Luigi Dallapiccola's *Il prigioniero*, based on tales by Villiers de l'Isle-Adam and Charles de Coster, is premiered over Turin radio. Composed between 1944 and 1948, the one-act opera with prologue is about a prisoner of Philip II in 16th-century Flanders during the Inquisition. The opera receives its first stage production on May 20 of next year.

1949 Dance

Jan. 20   Jerome Robbins' *The Guests*, to music by Marc Blitzstein, is premiered by the New York City Ballet in New York City. This is Robbins' first ballet for this company. Although the ballet is plotless, its theme is prejudice and discrimination. The dancers are Maria Tallchief, Francisco Moncion and Nicholas Magallanes.

Feb. 21   Choreographer Roland Petit's *Carmen* — to music by Georges Bizet, with costumes and scenery by Antoni Clave — is premiered by Roland Petit's Ballets de Paris in London. Renee Jeanmaire, Roland Petit and Serge Perrault star.

Feb. 24   William Dollar's one-act ballet *Le combat*, to music by Rafaello de Banfield, is premiered by Roland Petit's Ballets de Paris in London. The pas de deux, suggested by the story of Tancredi and Clorinda from Torquato Tasso's *Jerusalem Delivered*, is danced by Janine Charrat and Vladimir Skouratoff.

March 14   The Kirov Theater Ballet premieres Rostislav Zakharov's *The Bronze Horseman* in Leningrad. The full-length ballet, with music by Reinhold Gliere, is based on a poem by Aleksander Pushkin. Konstantin Sergeyev and Natalia Dudinskaya lead the cast.

March 31   Choreographer Jose Limon's *La Malinche* — to music by Norman Lloyd, with costumes by Pauline Lawrence — is premiered by the Jose Limon Dance Company in New York City. The dancers — Limon, Pauline Koner and Lucas Hoving — enact a modern dance story of Aztecs being conquered by Spaniards.

July 18   The Sadler's Wells Ballet gives the first performance of John Cranko's *Sea Change*. The ballet, to music by Jean Sibelius, is Cranko's view of life in a fishing village. It is the choreographer's first major work. Sheila O'Reilly, Michael Hogan, Jane Shore and Hans Zullig lead the cast.

Aug. 17   *The Moor's Pavane* is premiered by the Jose Limon Dance Company at Connecticut College. The choreography is by Limon, the costumes by Pauline Lawrence and the music by Henry Purcell, arranged by Simon Sadoff. Danced by Limon, Betty Jones and Lucas Hoving, it is based on Shakespeare's *Othello*.

Oct. 9   The Sadler's Wells Ballet opens its first North American tour at the Metropolitan Opera House, New York with Nicholas Sergeyev's production of *Sleeping Beauty*. Margot Fonteyn and Robert Helpmann star. Fonteyn is a revelation to the American public. Walter Terry of the New York *Herald Tribune* calls her "a star, a ballerina among ballerinas."

Nov. 9   Choreographer Jean Babilee's *Til Eulenspiegel* — to music by Richard Strauss, with costumes and scenery by Tom Keogh — is premiered by the Ballets des Champs-Elysees in Paris. Babilee dances the role of Til, whose flouting of authority ends in his hanging.

Nov. 27   George Balanchine premieres his version of Igor Stravinsky's *Firebird* with the New York City Ballet. Maria Tallchief and Francisco Moncion lead the cast. This is a shortened version arranged by the composer.

Dec. 1   The New York City Ballet premieres George Balanchine's *Bourree Fantasque*, to music by Emmanuel Chabrier. The plotless ballet, in three movements, contains satirical pieces on dance as well as a romantic pas de deux. Tanaquil LeClerq, Jerome Robbins, Maria Tallchief, Nicholas Magallanes, Janet Reed and Herbert Bliss star.

Dec. 20   John Cranko's *Beauty and the Beast* receives its first performance by the Sadler's Wells Theater Ballet in London. The ballet is set to portions of Maurice Ravel's *Mother Goose Suite*. It is one of the few ballets to use only two people to tell the story. Patricia Millar and David Poole star in the premiere.

1949 Instrumental and Vocal Music

Jan. 5   Henry Cowell's Symphony No. 5 premieres in Washington, D.C.

Jan. 6   Pierre Monteux and the San Francisco Symphony premiere Morton Gould's symphonic suite from his ballet *Fall River Legend*.

Jan. 7   Serge Koussevitzky and the Boston Symphony Orchestra give the world premiere of Leo Sowerby's Symphony No. 4. It is in three movements.

Jan. 26   Edmund Rubbra's Symphony No. 5 in B-flat Minor premieres in London. It is a four-movement symphony. This English composer is now on the faculty of Oxford University.

Feb. 10   George Antheil's Symphony No. 6 receives its initial performance by Pierre Monteux and the San Francisco Symphony Orchestra. The three-movement work was inspired, in part, by Eugene Delacroix's painting *Liberty Leading the People*.

Feb. 11   Gian Francesco Malipiero's Symphony No. 6 is premiered by Paul Sacher in Basel. It is scored for strings only and is in four movements.

Feb. 12   Darius Milhaud's Concerto for Marimba, Vibraphone and Orchestra is premiered by the St. Louis Symphony Orchestra.

Feb. 27   William Schuman's Symphony No. 6 receives its first performance by Antal Dorati and the Dallas Symphony Orchestra. Its one movement is subdivided into six sections.

March 6   Alan Hovhaness' *Sosi* for Violin, Piano, Percussion and Strings premieres in New York City.

March 15   Dmitri Kabalevsky's Concerto for Cello and Orchestra in G Minor Op. 49, premieres in Moscow. Sviatoslav Knusheitzky is soloist. It is one of a trilogy of concertos dedicated to Soviet youth (the other two are Concerto for Violin and Orchestra, Op. 48, and Piano Concerto No. 3, Op. 50).

March 24   *Tragic Overture*, by Andrzej Panufnik, premieres in New York City. It is dedicated to the memory of those who died in the 1943 Warsaw uprising.

April 5   Roy Harris' symphonic scherzo *Kentucky Spring* is premiered by the Louisville Orchestra, the composer conducting.

April 8   Leonard Bernstein's Symphony No. 2 (*The Age of Anxiety*) is premiered by Serge Koussevitzky and the Boston Symphony Orchestra. Bernstein performs as piano soloist. Scored for piano and orchestra, the piece features jazz rhythms. It was inspired by W.H. Auden's poem "The Age of Anxiety." The symphony subsequently receives the Hornblit Prize.

April 29   Frank Martin's oratorio *Golgotha* premieres in Geneva. Neobaroque in style, it is based on texts by Saint Augustine.

May 6   George Perle's *Two Songs in German*, to a text by Rainer Maria Rilke, premieres at Temple Emanu-El in New York City. Perle, now 33, has studied with Ernst Krenek and is a graduate of the American Conservatory of Music in Chicago.

May 7   Ned Rorem's *Overture in C* is premiered at Carnegie Hall, New York City.

May 13   Andrzej Panufnik's *Sinfonia rustica* receives its initial performance in Warsaw with the composer conducting.

May 15   Randall Thompson's Symphony No. 3 in A Minor receives its first performance by Thor Johnson and the CBS Orchestra at McMillan Theater, Columbia University in New York City. Composed between 1944 and 1948, it is in four movements. Irving Kolodin writes in the New York *Sun* that it "flows freely and powerfully from the source — in the composer's imagination — to the point where it joins the open seas of musical creation."

May 15   *Concerto for 4 Winds, Harp and Orchestra*, by Paul Hindemith, receives its initial performance in New York.

May 18   Darius Milhaud's *Sabbath Morning Service* premieres at the Temple Emanu-El in San Francisco, the composer conducting.

June 27   Symphony No. 2 by Alan Bush, is premiered at Nottingham, England. It is based on the legend of Robin Hood.

July 14   Benjamin Britten's *Spring Symphony* premieres at the Holland Festival in Amsterdam. This work, set to texts by various English poets, is scored for soprano, alto, tenor, mixed chorus and orchestra.

Aug. 10   Darius Milhaud's String Octet is premiered by the Budapest and Paganini Quartets at Mills College in Oakland, California.

Sep. 3   Ernest Bloch's *Concerto symphonique* premieres at the Edinburgh Music Festival, the composer conducting. The piece, in three movements, is scored for piano and orchestra.

Oct. 29   *Ollantay*, by Alberto Ginastera, premieres in Buenos Aires. It is a symphonic triptych.

Nov. 3   Gian Francesco Malipiero's Symphony No. 7 premieres in Milan. It has four movements.

Nov. 6   *Song of Friendship*, by Alan Bush, is premiered by the Choirs and Orchestra of the Workers' Music Association in London, the composer conducting. This choral work is scored for bass, chorus and band and is dedicated to socialist ideas. Bush is now a member of the British Labor Party.

Nov. 15   Dmitri Shostakovich's oratorio *Song of the Forests* receives its first performance in Leningrad. The oratorio is scored for tenor, bass, boys' chorus, mixed chorus and full orchestra. It is the composer's first large composition for chorus and depicts reforestation of Soviet desert land. It is also the first piece Shostakovich composed after having been rebuked by Soviet authorities for composing "abstract" music. The oratorio is awarded the Stalin Prize.

Nov. 20   Bohuslav Martinu's Concerto No. 3 for Piano and Orchestra is premiered by Walter Hendl and the Dallas Symphony Orchestra, with Rudolf Firkusny as soloist.

Nov. 24   Carl Ruggles' *Organum* is premiered by Leopold Stokowski and the New York Philharmonic at Carnegie Hall in New York City. This orchestral piece is the composer's last work. He gives up musical composition and devotes himself to painting.

Dec. 1   Hans Werner Henze's Symphony No. 2 premieres in Stuttgart. It is a three-movement work.

OLIVIER MESSIAEN

Dec. 2   *Turangalila-symphonie* — a massive symphony for piano, Ondes Martenot and orchestra — receives its world premiere in Boston, as Leonard Bernstein conducts the Boston Symphony Orchestra. The composer is Olivier Messiaen. The title of the piece means love song in Hindi. The work has 10 movements and was completed last year. Its rhythms are based on the rhythmic modes Messiaen describes in his two-volume publication *Technique de mon langage musical.*

Dec. 2   Bela Bartok's Viola Concerto receives its first performance in Minneapolis. Antal Dorati conducts, with William Primrose as soloist. This unfinished work was orchestrated and assembled by Tibor Serly. Next year Olin Downes reviews the work in the New York *Times* and says, "The concerto proved pronouncedly agreeable and much less problematical at first hearing than, for example, the violin concerto."

Dec. 7   Henk Badings' Symphony No. 5 is premiered by the Concertgebouw Orchestra in Amsterdam.

Dec. 22   Alexander Tansman's *Ricercari* is premiered by Vladimir Golschmann and the St. Louis Symphony Orchestra. This orchestral work is in four movements.

1949   Births, Deaths and Debuts

Jan. 14   Spanish composer Joaquin Turina, 66, dies in Madrid. He studied at the Madrid Conservatory and later with Vincent d'Indy in Paris. While in Paris he met Isaac Albeniz and Manuel de Falla and became dedicated to nationalism in Spanish music. His music reflects, within that context, the coloristic orchestrations of French impressionism and romantic tendencies. He joined the faculty of the Madrid Conservatory in 1931. His work comprises two operas, many orchestral pieces (including the symphonic poems *La procession del rocio* and *Sinfonia sevilliana*) and chamber music (including *Escena andaluza* for viola, string quartet and piano), as well as piano and guitar music.

Jan. 15   By invitation of Arturo Toscanini, Guido Cantelli makes his American debut conducting the NBC Symphony Orchestra in New York.

Jan. 27   Russian composer and writer Boris Asafiev, 64, dies in Moscow. A pupil of Anatoly Liadov at the Saint Petersburg Conservatory, he also studied history and philology at the University of Saint Petersburg. He adopted the pseudonym "Igor Glebov" for his music criticism and published a considerable amount of work under that name. Asafiev was also an editor of *Novaya Musica*, a music journal, and became dean of the music department of Petrograd's Institute of History of Arts in 1920. He published books on many composers, including Frederic Chopin, Franz Liszt, Nikolai Rimsky-Korsakov, Alexander Scriabin and Modest Mussorgsky. As a composer, he was a Russian nationalist. His ballets, including *The Fountain of*

Bakhtchisaray and *The Prisoner of the Caucasus*, reflect this goal. He wrote 25 other ballets and 9 operas, as well as orchestral and chamber music. His impact was largely in terms of his contribution as a historian of Russian music — his books won acclaim and respect. These include an early monograph on Igor Stravinsky (in which he praises Stravinsky; he later retracted that view), a catalog of Russian vocal music entitled *The Russian Poets in Music* and *Glinka* (which won the Stalin Prize — the only book about music to have received that award).

Feb. 4   Bulgarian soprano Ljuba Welitsch making her American debut and Fritz Reiner making his Metropolitan Opera conducting debut create a sensation with a performance of *Salome.* Olin Downes writes in the New York *Times* that Welitsch has ". . . eloquence and fire which distinguished the interpretation. . . . "

Feb. 11   Italian tenor Giovanni Zenatello, 72, dies in New York. Having started as a baritone, he restudied as a tenor and made his debut in *Pagliacci* in 1901. In 1904 he created the role of Pinkerton in *Madama Butterfly.* In 1905 he debuted at Covent Garden and in 1907 at the Manhattan Opera House in New York. He later retired in New York and taught singing.

April 2   Willem van Otterloo makes his debut as the new music director of The Hague Philharmonic Orchestra, conducting a program of music by Mozart and Beethoven. The concert takes place at the Gebouw voor Kunsten en Wetenschappen in The Hague.

May 14   American music publisher Charles Healy Ditson, 84, dies in New York City. His will bequeaths $100,000 for music education to each of the following institutions: Yale University, Harvard University, Princeton University, Columbia University, the New England Conservatory of Music, the Chicago Musical College, the College of Music in Cincinnati and the Ann Arbor School of Music of the University of Michigan.

May 22   German composer Hans Pfitzner, 80, dies in Salzburg. He studied piano in Frankfurt with James Kwast and later married that pianist's daughter. He began conducting in Mainz and taught at the Stern's Conservatory in Berlin. This led to conducting jobs at the Theater des Westens, the Kaim Concerts in Munich and the Strasbourg Opera. His last teaching post (before he concentrated mostly on composition) was at the Akademie der Tonkunst in Munich. Shortly before his death, he was accused of Nazi collaboration but was cleared.

As a composer, he was successful at an early age: In 1893 his first concert took place in Berlin to rave reviews. Two years later his opera *Der arme Heinrich* was praised by Engelbert Humperdinck. Between 1895 and 1911 his rise to operatic success rivaled that of Richard Strauss (who dies later this year). Pfitzner's fame peaked in 1917 with his opera *Palestrina*. He was thought to be a musical cohort of Strauss in that his harmonies and power of musical gesture reflected a deep immersion in German postromanticism. However, after *Palestrina*, none of his works (which included one further opera, *Das Herz*) came close to the stature and frequent appearances in the repertory that the music of Strauss maintained. Pfitzner composed many orchestral pieces, concertos, chamber works, choral works and 106 songs for voice and piano. He also published editions and arrangements and wrote pamphlets assailing new ideas in music theory.

June 8   Pianist Emanuel Ax is born in Lvov, USSR.

July 8   Bohemian-Italian composer and pianist Riccardo Pick-Mangiagalli, 66, dies in Milan. After studying at the Conservatory Giuseppe Verdi, he eventually became its director. He composed four operas, several dance pieces, many orchestral works, chamber music and songs. Pick-Mangiagalli is noted principally for being the first composer to have an opera premiered over radio — *L'ospite inatteso* (1931).

July 18   Czech composer Vitezslav Novak, 78, dies in Skutec, Slovakia. A pupil of Antonin Dvorak, he also studied philosophy and jurisprudence. He was discovered and helped by Johannes Brahms, who introduced him to the publisher Simrock. Although influenced by German postromanticism, his work is immersed in Czech nationalism. He composed several operas, two ballets, orchestral works and chamber music. He was made National Artist of the Republic of Czechoslovakia in 1946.

Sep. 8   German composer Richard Strauss, 85, dies in Garmisch-Partenkirchen. Son of the horn player Franz Strauss, he studied violin and composition in his childhood and composed his first work (*Polka in C*) when he was 6. After finishing school (Gymnasium), he studied

VITEZSLAV NOVAK

philosophy in Munich. His first major work — Symphony in D Minor — was performed when he was 17. That event, plus the premiere of his Violin Concerto two years later, established him as an important young composer. When he was 20, his Symphony in F Minor was performed in New York. He later became assistant to conductor Hans von Bulow.

Through the efforts of musician and poet Alexander Ritter, Strauss became deeply aware of the philosophical, literary and musical depth of the work of Richard Wagner and Franz Liszt. He combined conducting (at the Court Opera in Munich and later at the Weimar Court Orchestra) and composing, attracting attention as a multifaceted musician. His mentor, Hans von Bulow, called him "Richard the Second" (after Wagner, who was "Richard the First") and helped Strauss all he could. (Strauss succeeded von Bulow as conductor of the Berlin Philharmonic in 1894.)

Between 1886 and 1890 he composed his first tone poems — *Macbeth*, *Don Juan* and *Death and Transfiguration*. Then came *Till Eulenspiegel's Merry Pranks*, *Also sprach Zarathustra*, *Don Quixote* and *Ein Heldenleben*. His first opera, *Guntram*, premiered in 1894 (its lead part was sung by Pauline de Ahna, who became Strauss' wife). Other orchestral works followed, including *Symphonia domestica* and *Eine Alpensinfonie*. His opera *Salome*, combining psychologicial drama with lush orchestrations and depicting extreme eroticism, was received with shock in New York in 1907. *Elektra* also reflected his ability to combine dramatic conflict (in this case, matricide) with powerful music. His next opera, *Der Rosenkavalier*, with its extraordinary gracefulness, marked a departure from this style. With *Elektra* Strauss began his collaboration with librettist Hugo von Hofmannsthal (Stefan Zweig and Josef Gregor became Strauss' librettists after Hofmannsthal's death in 1929). *Capriccio* was the composer's final opera; it was premiered in 1942. Strauss flourished in many conducting positions and survived the Third Reich, becoming president of the Reichsmusikkammer and later leaving the post.

Despite the waning of 19th-century romanticism in the last decades of that century, Strauss' postromantic work reflects a powerful attempt to connect the old romanticism with 20th-century musical trends. Like Gustav Mahler and Hugo Wolf, he was a leader of postromanticism in Germany. He developed the concept of "program in music" to its extreme and was, to some degree, a forerunner of the trend toward using novel sounds in musical compositions, having included sound effects imitating wind and animal noises (these are mostly found in his orchestral works). His orchestral sonorities are massive and include solo parts for trombones, tubas and double basses, bringing the large orchestra of Hector Berlioz to new heights. His genius enabled him to combine the coloristic orchestral effects of French music with the poignant emotional force of Italian music; this resulted in a music energized by violent rhythms, and an extraordinary sense of timing. His harmonies seemed at first unorthodox but later became familiar and were no longer shocking. He was sometimes accused of being sensational but this never bothered him. He composed a total of 15 operas, 2 ballets, many orchestral works, choral works, chamber music, piano pieces and other works (including editions and arrangements).

Sep. 11   French composer Henri Rabaud, 74, dies in Paris. A pupil of Jules Massenet and winner of the Prix de Rome, he was also a well-known conductor, conducting the Opera-Comique and the Paris Opera. He later succeeded Karl Muck as conductor of the Boston Symphony Orchestra. His final job was as director of the Paris Conservatoire. His most successful work was the opera *Marouf, Savetier du Caire*. He composed many other operas; orchestral, choral, chamber and piano works; and songs.

Sept. 19   Greek composer Nikos Skalkottas, 45, dies in Athens of a strangulated hernia. A pupil of Arnold Schoenberg and Kurt Weill, he quickly adopted Schoenberg's 12-tone method of composition. Most of his music was composed after 1933, when he returned to Athens and after Schoenberg left Vienna to flee the Nazis. Skalkottas eventually departed from 12-tone composition and based his music on Greek modalities and Balkan folk sources. He was quite prolific and composed many orchestral and chamber works. His Piano Concerto No. 3, with 10 winds and percussion (1939), requires a different soloist for each movement because the work is so long.

Oct. 28   French violinist Ginette Neveu, 30, dies in an air crash in the vicinity of the Azores. A relative of Charles-Marie Widor, she performed with the Colonne Orchestra in Paris at age 7. She graduated from the Paris Conservatoire and won several prizes. After an appearance with the Boston Symphony Orchestra two years ago, her career was firmly established.

1949   Related Events

Dimitri Mitropoulos and Leopold Stokowski are appointed principal conductors of the New York Philharmonic. This one-season arrangement supersedes the "musical advisor" leadership of Bruno Walter.

Conductor Howard Mitchell becomes music director of the National Symphony Orchestra in Washington, D.C., succeeding Hans Kindler. Mitchell holds this post until 1969.

Genesis of a Music, by Harry Partch, is published by the University of Wisconsin Press in Madison. This book expounds, in great depth, the Partch approach to musical composition and his belief that "just intonation" comprises the truth of temperament. American composer and pioneer of electronic music Otto Luening comments in the Introduction: "If, in the future, these [Partch's] ideas are used in conjunction with electronic and other scientific developments in sound, one may expect a strange and beautiful music to result."

Jan.   RCA releases its first 45 RPM 7-inch (17.8-cm) disc in America to undermine sales of Columbia's long-playing discs. The resultant "battle of the speeds" has a devastating effect on sales for both companies, and they subsequently agree to use 45 RPM for popular music, LPs for classical. Other events in the recording industry this year include Magnecord's introduction of its staggered-head, two-track stereo tape recorder; the first appearance of Deutsche Grammophon's *Archiv Production* (an anthology of pre-19th-century classical music); the introduction by Ampex of its Model 300 studio tape recorder (which establishes itself as a standard piece of equipment for almost a decade); the founding of Westminster Records — one of many new labels resulting from recent advances in tape/ LP technology; and the publication of the first Schwann Long Playing Record Catalog. The first Audio Fair (held in New York City) also takes place this year.

Jan. 19   Wilhelm Furtwangler withdraws as a guest conductor of the Chicago Symphony Orchestra because of a threatened boycott by famous soloists and conductors who accuse him of Nazi collaboration.

Jan. 25   Pianist Walter Gieseking, who arrived in the United States on January 22, leaves the country rather than face a deportation hearing. Although he was cleared by a denazification court, veterans' groups accused Gieseking of having been an active Nazi.

Feb. 14   Paul Hindemith conducts the Berlin Philharmonic in a concert of his own works in Berlin. This event marks his first return to Germany since the rise of Adolf Hitler and the beginning of World War II. Joseph Goebbels had accused Hindemith of being a cultural Bolshevik (Hindemith was married to a woman whose father was a Jew). Since 1934, when Hindemith left Germany, he has been involved in establishing the music curriculum at Ankara Conservatory, Turkey, after having been invited there by the Turkish government. He also performed in Switzerland and America. He is currently a professor of musical composition at Yale University.

March 9   The Superior Court of Los Angeles dismisses Igor Stravinsky's lawsuit against the Leeds Music Company on the grounds that the composer was aware of the commercial nature at the time he voluntarily embarked on the venture with Leeds. Stravinsky sued the firm on July 29 of last year for using his name on a watered-down tune (which Leeds called "Summer Moon") from his work *The Firebird*. Stravinsky's score was not copyrighted.

May 2   Virgil Thomson is awarded the Pulitzer Prize for music for *Louisiana Story*.

May 17   The First Congress of Dodecaphonic Music, which lasts four days, begins in Milan. It includes performances of music by Wallingford Riegger, Josef Matthias Hauer, Ernst Krenek, Arnold Schoenberg, Luigi Dallapiccola and Hans Erich Apostel. Schoenberg sends the following telegram: "Proudly I greet my companions who aim to present musical ideas with new tools of musical logic — good luck!"

June 30   The enormous music encyclopedia *Die Musik in Geschichte und Gegenwart* is begun in Kassel by the Barenreiter Verlag. Its editor is Friedrich Blume.

Aug. 1   The War Memorial Opera House in San Francisco reverses its ban on Norwegian soprano Kirsten Flagstad in order to keep the season from being canceled. The Norwegian government was reported to have cleared her of suspicion of having participated in her husband's wartime pro-Nazi activities.

Dec. 20   Margaret Truman, daughter of President Harry Truman, sings at Carnegie Hall in New York in a half-hour, commercially sponsored broadcast. She performs a Puccini aria and two Christmas carols. The critical reception is mixed.

1950   Opera

Feb. 7   Hal Overton's *The Enchanted Pear Tree* premieres over radio in New York City. This is a one-act opera composed specifically for radio broadcast.

Feb. 24   Tikhon Khrennikov's *Frol Skobeyev* premieres in Moscow. This four-act comic opera concerns serfs in 17th-century Russia.

March 1   Gian-Carlo Menotti's *The Consul* premieres in Philadelphia at the Shubert Theater. Menotti himself writes the libretto, which is about a patriot living in a police state. The three-act opera is a great success and is subsequently translated into many foreign languages. Olin Downes says it was "written from the heart, with a blazing sincerity and a passion of human understanding."

May 4   *L'allegra brigata*, by Gian Francesco Malipiero, receives its first performance at La Scala. The composer's libretto concerns a group of young people telling stories in a puppet theater in a park while the stories are acted out by the puppets above them.

May 9   Norman Dello Joio's *The Triumph of Saint Joan* premieres at Sarah Lawrence College in Bronxville, New York. This chamber opera is later used as material for a symphonic work and a ballet, both with the same title.

May 12   *Bolivar*, an opera by Darius Milhaud, is performed for the first time in Paris. The text is based on the play by Jules Supervielle about the life of Simon Bolivar. The work is the third in a trilogy of operas about the lives of famous men in the history of Latin America.

May 18   *The Jumping Frog of Calaveras County*, by Lukas Foss, receives its first performance at the University of Indiana in Bloomington. The text is by Jean Karsavina, based on the story by Mark Twain. It is Foss's first opera, and the music is well received.

May 20   The first staged performance of Luigi Dallapiccola's *Il prigioniero* takes place in Florence at the Teatro Communale. The composer bases his libretto on two plays — *La legende d'Ulenspiegel et de Lamme Gvedzac*, by Charles de Coster, and *La torture par l'esperance*, by Villiers de l'Isle-Adam. The subject is a prisoner under the Inquisition. It had been premiered over radio on December 4, 1949. Italian critics reacted negatively to the opera, but it is acclaimed abroad. Hermann Scherchen conducts. Next year the work is performed in New York. Howard Taubman writes of that performance in the New York *Times*, "It is a work that, in its music and its bare, symbolic action, projects the horror of a fear-ridden world."

July 16   Ernst Krenek's opera *Tarquin* premieres in its full stage version in Cologne.

July 20   Estonian composer Eugen Kapp's *Freedom's Singer* receives its first performance in Tallinn. This event marks the premiere of the first Estonian opera based on a Soviet subject. It is about the Nazi invasion of 1941.

Oct. 24   Goffredo Petrassi's *La morte dell'aria* has its premiere performance at the Teatro Eliseo in Rome. T. Scialojas' libretto is based on a true incident that occurred in Paris at the turn of the century, in which an inventor flung himself off a high tower to test a parachute garment he had invented.

Nov. 7   Dmitri Kabalevsky's opera *The Family of Taras* premieres in Leningrad. It incorporates materials from his earlier operas *In the Fire* and *At Moscow*. In four acts, it is about Soviets fighting the Nazis.

1950 Dance

Jan. 4   Martha Graham's *Judith* — with music by William Schuman, sets by Charles Hyman and William Sherman, and costumes designed by the choreographer — premieres at the Columbia Auditorium in Louisville, Kentucky.

Jan. 15   Merce Cunningham's *Before Dawn* and his *Pool of Darkness* premiere at the Hunter College Playhouse in New York City. The music to *Pool of Darkness* is by Ben Weber.

Jan. 24   Herbert Ross's *Caprichos* receives its premiere at the Choreographer's Workshop in New York City. The work, based on four comments by Goya on his paintings, is to Bela Bartok's *Contrasts* for piano, clarinet and violin. Ilona Murai, Emy Saint Just, Gina Synder, Alice Temkin, Dorothy Hill, Frank Glass, Leslie Harris, Herbert Ross, Joseph Stember, Larry Stevens and George Wood are in the opening night cast. This ballet is in four episodes and an epilogue.

Feb. 2   Choreographer Ninette de Valois' version of *Don Quixote*, with music by Roberto Gerhard, is premiered by the Sadler's Wells Ballet in London. Costumes and scenery are by Edward Burra. Robert Helpmann (Don Quixote),

Margot Fonteyn (Dulcinea) and Alexander Grant (Sancho Panza) star.

Feb. 25   John Taras' *Designs with Strings* receives its American premiere by the Ballet Theater in New York City. This event features costumes by Irene Sharaff. The dancers are Erik Bruhn, Michael Lland, Diana Adams, Norma Vance, Lillian Lanese and Dorothy Scott.

Feb. 26   Choreographer Jerome Robbins' *The Age of Anxiety* — with music by Leonard Bernstein, costumes by Irene Sharaff and scenery by Oliver Smith — is premiered by the New York City Ballet. The principal dancers are Jerome Robbins, Todd Bolender, Tanaquil LeClerq and Francisco Moncion. Four strangers meet, looking in vain for companionship. The ballet is in six scenes and is based on Leonard Bernstein's Second Symphony.

March 1   Choreographer Birgit Cullberg's *Miss Julie* — with music by Ture Rangstrom and costumes and scenery by Sven Erixon — is premiered by the Swedish Ballet. Based on a play by August Strindberg, the work, in one act and four scenes, blends modern and classical movements in a story of seduction and suicide. It becomes part of the standard repertory.

SCENE FROM *AGE OF ANXIETY*

March 2   Frederick Ashton's one-act ballet *Illuminations* is performed for the first time by the New York City Ballet in New York. It is choreographed to music by Benjamin Britten composed on poems of Rimbaud, with costumes and scenery by Cecil Beaton. This work is noted for its blend of pantomime, classical steps and free movement. It is also the first ballet that the company commissions from a foreign choreographer. The lead dancers are Nicholas Magallanes, Tanaquil LeClerq, Melissa Hayden and Robert Barnett.

March 18   *Opening Suite* — a modern dance work choreographed by Alwin Nikolais — receives its first performance at the Henry Street Playhouse in New York City.

June 14   Serge Lifar's *Phedre* — with music by Georges Auric and libretto and decor by Jean Cocteau — is premiered by the Paris Opera Ballet. The lead dancers are Tamara Toumanova and Lifar. The ballet is done largely in mime.

June 28   The Kirov Ballet presents Leonid Yacobson's three-act ballet *Shurale* in Leningrad. The ballet, based on Tartar folklore, is set to music by Farid Yarullin. Natalia Dudinskaya and Konstantin Sergeyev star.

Aug. 11   *The Exiles*, a ballet choreographed by Jose Limon to music of Arnold Schoenberg, receives its initial performance by the Jose Limon Dance Company at Connecticut College. The costumes are by Pauline Lawrence, and the decor is by Anita Weschler. The ballet is about Adam and Eve.

Oct. 31   Choreographer Birgit Cullberg's *Medea*, to music by Bela Bartok orchestrated by Herbert Sandberg, is performed for the first time in Gaevle, Sweden. Dancing the legend of the vengeful mother are Anne-Marie Lagerborg, Maurice Bejart and Inga Noring. In one act and five scenes, it is choreographed to selected parts of Bartok's *Mikrokosmos*.

1950 Instrumental and Vocal Music

Jan. 6   Charles Munch and the Boston Symphony Orchestra give the first performance of Francis Poulenc's Piano Concerto. The composer is soloist. The last movement of the concerto includes an interpolation of the French song known as "A la claire fontaine."

Feb. 1   David Diamond's *Timon of Athens* is premiered by the Louisville Orchestra. This work is a symphonic portrait based on Shakespeare.

Feb. 10   William Schuman's Violin Concerto is premiered by Charles Munch and the Boston Symphony Orchestra, with Isaac Stern as soloist. It is in two movements.

March 1   Paul Hindemith's *Sinfonietta* in E receives its initial performance by the Louisville Orchestra with the composer conducting. Based on the 18th-century concept of an "entertainment piece," it has four movements.

March 3   Darius Milhaud's Piano Concerto No. 4 is premiered by Charles Munch and the Boston Symphony Orchestra, with Zadel Skolovsky as soloist.

March 4   Virgil Thomson's Cello Concerto is premiered by Eugene Ormandy and the Philadelphia Orchestra in Philadelphia. Paul Olefsky is the soloist. The finale includes two familiar melodies ("Yes, Jesus Loves Me" and a Beethoven piano sonata theme). Olin Downes writes of the piece: "The themes fit in well with the other scraps of folksy tunes that prattle along, side by side, or in combination, in this amusing finale."

March 10   *Song of Anguish*, by Lukas Foss, is premiered by the Boston Symphony Orchestra, the composer conducting. This work is a biblical cantata scored for baritone and orchestra. The text is from the Book of Isaiah.

March 16   Ernst Krenek's Symphony No. 5 is premiered by the Albuquerque Symphony Orchestra. This atonal work has five movements.

March 18   Pierre Schaeffer and Pierre Henry collaborate in a program of music concrete at the Ecole Normale de Musique in Paris. The works are entitled *Symphonie pour un homme seul*, *Concerto des ambiguites* and *Bidule en ut*. This music combines chance combinations of various recorded noises, melodies and fragments of human speech played foward, in reverse, and at various speeds.

May 18   The Symphony No. 2 in C Minor, by Healey Willan premieres in Toronto.

May 20   American composer William Bergsma's Symphony No. 1 premieres over radio in New York City.

May 22   Richard Strauss' *Vier letzte Lieder* for soprano and orchestra is premiered posthumously by Wilhelm Furtwangler, with Kirsten Flagstad as soloist. The performance takes place in London.

June 8   The Concerto for French Horn and Orchestra, by Paul Hindemith, premieres in Baden-Baden.

June 23   *Second Cantata*, Op. 31, by Anton Webern, receives its world premiere (posthumously) by Herbert Hafner and the NIR Chamber Orchestra and Chorus in Brussels. Ilona Steingruber and Otto Wiener perform as soprano and bass soloists. The performance takes place as part of this year's International Society for Contemporary Music festival. Larger than Webern's *First Cantata*, it has six movements, the last of which is a double canon (tenor and soprano, alto and bass) featuring low dynamic levels and shifting accents. The text, based on the story of Christ, is from six different poem cycles by Hildegard Jone, and the music was composed between 1941 and 1943. The work is considered Webern's crowning achievement.

Sep. 5   Australian composer Arthur Benjamin's Piano Concerto is premiered by Eugene Goossens and the Sydney Symphony Orchestra.

Oct. 27   Paul Creston's Symphony No. 3 (*Three Mysteries*) receives its world premiere at a Worcester Festival Concert, as Eugene Ormandy conducts the Philadelphia Orchestra. In three movements, it is based on Gregorian chant fragments, including the Easter sequence "Victimae Paschali Landes." Robert Sabin says of the work in *Musical America* (New York) that it has ". . . glib Hollywoodisms of orchestration. . . ."

Oct. 29   Aaron Copland's Quartet for Piano and Strings premieres at the Coolidge Festival at the Library of Congress in Washington, D.C. This is the composer's first 12-tone work. The three-movement piece was commissioned by the Elizabeth Sprague Coolidge Foundation.

Oct. 31   *Job* receives its first performance in Rome. Composed by Luigi Dallapiccola, the work is a dramatic oratorio for solo voices, chorus and orchestra. The piece, which the composer describes as a "sacred representation," was inspired by Jacob Epstein's sculpture *Behold the Man*. The work is dodecaphonic.

Nov. 3   David Diamond's Symphony No. 3 is premiered by Charles Munch and the Boston Symphony Orchestra. The music has five sections.

Nov. 6   Aaron Copland's Concerto for Clarinet and String Orchestra receives its first performance by Fritz

Reiner and the NBC Symphony Orchestra in New York City. Benny Goodman (who commissioned the work) is soloist. The concerto includes Brazilian melodic material.

Nov. 18   *Concerto grosso*, by Ralph Vaughan Williams, is premiered by Adrian Boult in London. This five-movement work was composed for amateur musicians.

Nov. 21   Knudage Riisager's Symphony No. 5 premieres in Copenhagen. This is the last symphony this prolific Danish composer writes.

Dec. 2   Ernest Bloch's *Scherzo fantastique* for piano and orchestra is premiered by the Chicago Symphony Orchestra.

Dec. 5   Symphony No. 27 in C Minor, by Nikolai Miaskovsky, is premiered posthumously in Moscow. The symphony, which was finished last year, is this composer's last (to date he has been the Soviet Union's most prolific symphonist). The piece is greeted as a masterpiece, largely because Miaskovsky, in attempting to conform to Joseph Stalin's concept of an acceptable musical style, composed the work in a traditional language.

Dec. 8   Bohuslav Martinu's *Sinfonia concertante* for violin, cello, oboe, bassoon and orchestra premieres in Basel.

Dec. 11   Paul Hindemith's Clarinet Concerto is premiered by Eugene Ormandy and the Philadelphia Orchestra, with Benny Goodman as soloist.

Dec. 19   Sergei Prokofiev's cantata *On Guard for Peace* premieres in Moscow. This is an oratorio for mezzo-soprano, narrators, mixed chorus, boys' chorus and orchestra and has 10 sections.

BOHUSLAV MARTINU

Dec. 20   Symphony No. 1, by Ernst Toch, receives its initial performance in Vienna. The work has four move-ments. Toch, now 63, has recently returned to Vienna after living in California.

1950   Births, Deaths and Debuts

March 15   American baritone Cornell MacNeil makes his professional debut in Gian-Carlo Menotti's opera *The Consul* in New York.

March 19   American black baritone William Warfield gives his first New York song recital.

April 3   German composer Kurt Weill, 50, dies in New York City. A pupil of Engelbert Humperdinck (for one semester at the Berlin Hochschule fur Musik), he went to Dessau and worked as an opera coach. He later studied with Ferruccio Busoni in Berlin. At an early age he was attracted to innovations in theater and started writing brief modernistic operas that were based on satirical themes. He often collaborated with Bertolt Brecht, and together they created *The Threepenny Opera*, Weill's first signal success. This work was performed (in translated versions) in Poland, Holland, Denmark, Hungary, Russia, France and England (it was also performed in America with a new libretto by Marc Blitzstein).

Weill and Lotte Lenya, his wife, fled Germany when the Nazis came to power and went to Paris, London, and finally, New York. His popularity was swift and lasting in America, largely due to his ability to create musical plays that reflected and satirized American life and because his music often included jazz elements as well as other approaches to musical composition. Unlike many composers in New York associated with "musical plays," he refused to let other musicians tinker with his orchestrations. His 1948 production *Down in the Valley* was highly successful and was performed widely in the United States. In addition to operas and much vocal music, he also composed a ballet, *Die sieben Todsunden*, a string quartet, symphonies and piano pieces.

Weill's work changed from an early interest in serious concert pieces to cabaret-type music and, finally, to musical comedy. Despite a musical evolution from what some might consider serious to unserious, his work in each stage included elements of atonality, polytonality and unconventional rhythm. Weill succeeded at being an innovator of the American musical and composed original music for that genre without forfeiting originality and without becoming mediocre.

April 8   Vaslav Nijinsky dies in London at the age of 60. Nijinsky, who came to epitomize great male dancing, was closely associated with the Diaghilev Ballets Russes, for which he was leading dancer and, for a brief period, its choreographer. While with the Diaghilev company, he was the vehicle for much of Fokine's greatest choreography, including *Spectre de la Rose*, *La Pavillon d'Armide*, and *Petrouchka*. In 1912 he choreographed his first ballet, *L'Apres-midi d'un faune*. This short work was a departure from traditional choreographic style, emphasizing angular, jerky movements rather than smooth, rounded, elongated lines. It also introduced an explicit sexual element into choreography for the first time.

Nijinsky choreographed only two other pieces for Diaghilev, *Le Sacre du printemps*, which created a scandal during its first performance, and *Jeux*. Both, continuing Nijinsky's innovations, received only a few performances. In 1913 Nijinsky was dismissed from the company following his marriage. The dismissal effectively marked the end of his career, although he continued to perform occasionally until 1919, when he was forced to retire because of mental illness.

Nijinsky was the greatest male dancer of his generation. Appearing in Europe during a period when male dancing in general was at a low ebb, his extraordinary technique and acting ability was a revelation. He was known for his virtuosity, particularly his elevation and ballon, and his ability to assume the personality of the character that he danced. Tragically, his career ended before he reached artistic maturity. Consequently, although his legend continues, his actual impact on ballet is modest.

April 19   British composer Lord Berners, 66, dies in London. Born into wealth, Gerald Hugh Tyrwhitt-Wilson, attended Eton. His music teachers were Ralph Vaughan Williams (composition) and Igor Stravinsky and Alfredo Casella (orchestration). His music reflected an attraction to the titles of works by Erik Satie (his *3 Funeral Marches* for piano are entitled "For a Statesman," "For a Canary," and "For a Rich Aunt"). He also wrote novels and a two-volume autobiography, and painted in oils. His music includes one opera, many ballets (including *The Triumph of Neptune*, produced by Serge Diaghilev's Ballets Russes), and other pieces.

July 1   Emile Jaques-Dalcroze, 84, dies in Geneva. He studied with Anton Bruckner in Vienna and later studied orchestration with Leo Delibes in Paris. His interest in rhythm manifested itself at an early age, and with his first teaching position at the Geneva Conservatory, he began developing his "eurythmics" method. This involved translating rhythm into movements of the entire human body (these movements were called "gymnastique rhythmique") and was developed in collaboration with French psychologist Edouard Claparide. His method did not win the approval of other faculty members. That led to his resignation and the establishment of his own school of rhythm, first founded in Hellerau, near Dresden. Branches of the school opened in France, Russia, Germany, England and America. World War I disrupted his school, and he

EMILE JAQUES-DALCROZE

reopened in Geneva and later in Paris. His Hellerau school reopened in Vienna after the war. His work had an important effect on dance: Among his hundreds of pupils were those who would use his methods in some fashion as they molded modern dance; these include Mary Wigman, Hanya Holm, Yvonne Goergi and Marie Rambert. Jaques-Dalcroze was also a composer and wrote many operas and songs incorporating Swiss folk song materials. Surprisingly, he wrote virtually no ballet or dance music.

Aug. 8   Russian composer Nikolai Miaskovsky, 69, dies in Moscow. In his childhood he lived in Orenburg and Kazan. His father, an officer in the department of military fortification, sent him to military school. Miaskovsky developed an interest in music at the time of his graduation and found himself attracted to the music of Frederick Chopin and Tchaikovsky. He studied with Reinhold Gliere before entering the Saint Petersburg Conservatory where he studied with Anatoly Liadov and Nikolai Rimsky-Korsakov. During the First World War he served in the Russian army. After the revolution he joined the composition faculty of the Moscow Conservatory, where he remained until his death. During that period, he embarked on a symphonic journey that would result in the composition of 27 symphonies, making him the most prolific symphonist since Haydn. Miaskovsky composed music in a traditional, almost 19th-century style. He avoided modernisms and adhered to tonality with occasional forays into Russian folk elements. Despite his many symphonies, he was eclipsed by Sergei Prokofiev and Dmitri Shostakovich. He also composed 13 string quartets, sonatas, piano works, song cycles, etc. Between 1953 and 1956 his collected works are published in a 12-volume edition.

Aug. 26   Italian baritone Giuseppe De Luca, 73, dies in New York City. After studies at the Santa Cecilia Academy in Rome, he made his debut in 1897. He created baritone roles in *Adriana Lecouvreur*, *Madama Butterfly* and *Gianni Schicchi*, among others. He made his last appearance at age 71 when he sang a golden jubilee concert in 1947. He was known for his elegant musicianship and bel canto singing.

Oct. 23   Soprano Eileen Farrell gives her first formal New York recital in Carnegie Hall, singing music of Beethoven, Giuseppe Verdi, Samuel Barber and Olivier Messiaen (*Chants de terre et de ciel*). Anthony Bruno says in *Musical America* (New York) that Farrell possesses a ". . . big, sensuous voice." He goes on to note that her performance of contemporary music overcomes ". . . stylistic obstacles. . . with consummate success. . . " and describes the Messiaen piece as ". . . monotonous meanderings in mysticism. . . . "

Oct. 24   Spanish soprano Victoria de los Angeles makes her American debut at Carnegie Hall with a program of songs and arias. She receives a thunderous ovation. Cecil Smith says of her in *Musical America* (New York) that her musical and facial expression is ". . . as seraphic as that of a madonna."

Oct. 29   Greek pianist Gina Bachauer's American debut takes place at Town Hall in New York City, as she performs a brief program of music by Bach-Busoni, Brahms, Maurice Ravel, Haydn, Liszt and Chopin. Anthony Bruno says in *Musical America* (New York) that Bachauer is ". . . among the foremost pianists of the day."

Nov. 2   Italian pianist Aldo Ciccolini makes his American debut with the New York Philharmonic playing the Tchaikovsky Piano Concerto No. 1.

Nov. 17   Roberta Peters, 20, makes her Metropolitan Opera debut as Zerlina in Mozart's *Don Giovanni*. She suddenly replaces Nadine Connor, who became indisposed with food poisoning at 3 o'clock this afternoon. Reviewer Quaintance Eaton says in *Musical America* (New York), "... her fresh youth, pretty voice, and stage wisdom provided the chief interest of the evening."

Nov. 20   Italian composer Francesco Cilea, 84, dies in Varazze. Among his most famous music is his opera *Adriana Lecouvreur*. He had been made a member of the Order of the Italian Crown and was also director of the Palermo Conservatory. He composed in the Italian verismo style.

Nov. 26   French baritone Gerard Souzay gives his first New York recital at Town Hall, singing Spanish, French, German and Italian songs. Robert Sabin of *Musical America* (New York) notes that Souzay, who studied with Pierre Bernac, has Bernac's "... infallible taste and interpretive insight...." Sabin goes on to say that Souzay is a finer vocalist.

Dec. 2   Pianist and composer Dinu Lipatti, 33, dies in Chene-Bourg, Switzerland. Lipatti, who came from a musical family, studied at the Bucharest Conservatory and then with Alfred Cortot. During World War II he taught piano at the Geneva Conservatory and after the war concertized in Europe and Great Britain. He also composed numerous pieces, mostly for the piano. His playing was marked by the most refined elegance and musical sensitivity.

Dec. 22   German-American conductor Walter Damrosch, 87, dies in Rome. He studied with his father Leopold and with Hans von Bulow. His career came to prominence when he began conducting the New York Oratorio Society and the New York Symphony Society.

This led to conducting performances of German operas at the Metropolitan Opera House of New York. He formed his own opera company in 1894. He specialized in performances of Wagner operas and brought famous artists to America for the first time including Katharina Klafsky, Johanna Gadski and Milka Ternina. He introduced *Parsifal* to America in concert form for the first time (March 3, 1886). He also conducted the New York Philharmonic Society and established schools for bandmasters at the request of General John Pershing. He received honorary doctorate degrees from Princeton University, Columbia University, Brown University, Dartmouth College, and New York University. As a composer, he wrote five operas (some of which were staged at the Metropolitan Opera), incidental music, choral music and songs.

Dec. 23   Italian composer Vincenzo Tommasini, 71, dies in Rome. His most famous teacher was Max Bruch. Tommasini became an opera composer in the Italian romantic tradition. He composed a total of 10 operas and various other orchestral and chamber works, of which his best-known piece is *Le donne di buon umore*, based on music by Domenico Scarlatti; Serge Diaghilev staged this work as a ballet in 1917. During Tommasini's lifetime, his music was popular and enjoyed frequent performances.

Dec. 31   French composer Charles Koechlin, 83, dies in Canadal, Var, France. A pupil of Jules Massenet, he later became a writer on music. He was a prolific composer and an expert orchestrator. Although interested in modern music, he adhered to a style reflecting French impressionism: His works are tonal and do not involve complicated rhythms. He composed many orchestral and chamber works and ballets (including *La foret paienne*) and also wrote many educational treatises (including a four-volume treatise on orchestration).

1950 Related Events

Dimitri Mitropoulos becomes principal conductor of the New York Philharmonic. He becomes music director of this orchestra next year.

Ernst Krenek deposits his recently completed autobiography in the Library of Congress, Washington, D.C. Although he subsequently publishes excerpts with the title *Self-Analysis*, he instructs the library not to open the autobiographical materials until 15 years after his death.

Jan.   *Dance & Dancers* begins publication in London this month. This British monthly dance magazine features articles on various aspects of theatrical dance and is edited by dance writer Peter Williams.

Jan. 10   The Argentine government, led by President Juan Peron, decrees that all musical entertainment in Argentina must consist of music that is at least 50 percent the work of native composers.

Feb. 2   Wagnerian tenor Lauritz Melchior quits the Metropolitan Opera after 24 years over contract differences with the incoming general manager, Rudolf Bing.

Feb. 8   Hanns Eisler's setting of Johannes R. Becher's hymn "Auferstanden aus Ruinen und der Zukunft zugewandt" becomes the official national anthem of the German Democratic Republic.

March 8   Soviet composer Dmitri Shostakovich is awarded the Stalin Prize for his *Song of the Forests* and his music for the film *Fall of Berlin*.

May 1   Gian-Carlo Menotti is awarded the Pulitzer Prize for music for *The Consul*.

June   Decca (England) issues its first long-playing records this month. RCA Victor, this year, begins to manufacture its first long-playing records. Other recording industry developments this year include the introduction of nickel facing for metal stamper matrices and the appearance of new labels in Europe: Teldec, Philips, Argo and Nixa. Sales of 78 RPM records decline, and they begin to become collectors' items.

June 1   Rudolf Bing becomes general manager of the Metropolitan Opera in New York, succeeding Edward Johnson. Bing began in opera management at age 18 and later worked at the Glyndebourne Opera (1936–39; 1946–49) and Edinburgh Festival (1947). Today marks the beginning of his 22 seasons as general manager of the Met. He subsequently brings in directors and designers from Broadway and puts into practice his belief that opera is theater. Prices at the Met for this upcoming season are $7.50 for the best seats in the house.

June 26   The first Moravian Music Festival takes place in Bethlehem, Pennsylvania. This festival celebrates the history and practice of Moravian and church music. Thor Johnson — conductor of the Cincinnati Symphony Orchestra — leads the participants.

July 18   Austrian conductor Josef Krips is deported from the United States due to charges of left-wing political associations. He returns to Vienna today after having been in America two days.

Sep. 8   Dutch astronomer Christian Huygens' (1629–95) system of intonation dividing the octave into 31 unequal degrees is realized today as an organ built to accommodate this system is demonstrated in Rotterdam.

Oct. 24   London's Festival Ballet begins its inaugural season. Alicia Markova, Anton Dolin, John Gilpin and Nathalie Krassovska are the principal dancers. Leonide Massine, David Lichine and Tatiana Riabouchinska are guest artists.

Nov. 20   Violinist Joseph Szigeti is cleared of unspecified charges after having been held in detention for five days at Ellis Island. The U.S. Immigration authorities invoked the McCarran Act and apprehended Szigeti as he disembarked from the ocean liner *Ile de France* upon his return from a European concert tour. The clause of the McCarran Act that was invoked requires investigation of aliens for membership in fascist or communist organizations. Szigeti's status (since 1941) is that of permanent resident of the United States. He is not yet an American citizen — although he has applied twice for citizenship. He states that concert tours took him out of Los Angeles both times he was called in for examination.

1951 Opera

Jan. 16   Soviet composer Herman Zhukovsky's three-act opera *From All Our Hearts* premieres at the Bolshoi Theater in Moscow. It relates the story of life on a collective farm. At first the work is well received and is awarded a prize of 25,000 rubles. Suddenly, however, on April 19, *Pravda* tears the opera apart.

March 9   Germaine Tailleferre's *Il etait un petit navire* premieres at the Opera-Comique in Paris. This satirical opera in three acts features the French folk tune of the same title.

March 17   *Das Verhor des Lukullus*, by Paul Dessau, written to a libretto by Bertolt Brecht, premieres in Berlin at the Staatsoper. This opera offends the East German military government and is subsequently withdrawn from the repertoire. It was originally broadcast over radio in 1939. A reviewer writes in *Neues Deutschland* (East Berlin), "As for the music, it follows Igor Stravinsky, a composer resident in the U.S.A., who is a fanatical destroyer of all European musical traditions."

March 28   The Opera Workshop of Columbia University gives the world premiere of Douglas Moore's *Giants in the Earth*, based on the book by the same title.

April 26   *The Pilgrim's Progress* — a morality play in four acts, by Ralph Vaughan Williams — premieres at Covent Garden in London. The composer writes the libretto, basing it on John Bunyan's allegory. The opera includes "The Shepherds of the Delectable Mountains." Originally premiered in 1922, this is a revised version.

May 2   The Opera Workshop of the University of Southern California premieres Ernst Krenek's *Dark Waters*. This one-act opera, with libretto by the composer, tells the tale of a runaway heiress who gets shot.

May 4   Ildebrando Pizzetti's *Ifigenia* receives its first stage performance in Florence. Conducted by the composer, the opera is about Agamemnon's daughter sacrificed to satisfy Artemis. In one act, it was premiered over radio last year.

May 28   *Veselohra na moste*, an opera by Bohuslav Martinu, is performed in its English version, entitled *Comedy on the Bridge*, at Hunter College in New York City.

June 27   Spanish composer Roberto Gerhard's opera *The Duenna*, based on a play by Richard Brinsley Sheridan, is premiered as part of this year's International Society for Contemporary Music festival in Wiesbaden. Gerhard has studied with Enrique Grandos and Felipe Pedrell. A Catalonian by birth, he is now a British subject. He also studied with Arnold Schoenberg and composes using his own modified approach to dodecaphonic principles.

July 1   Jean Francaix' comic opera, *L'Apostrophe*, based on a story by Balzac, receives its first stage performance at the Holland Music Festival in Amsterdam.

Sep. 11   The first performance of Igor Stravinsky's *The Rake's Progress* is given in Venice at the Teatro La Fenice. The libretto, by W.H. Auden and Chester Kallman, was inspired by a series of engravings by the 18th-century artist Hogarth. The composer conducts a cast that includes Robert Rounseville, Elisabeth Schwarzkopf, Otakar Kraus and Jennie Tourel. In three acts and an epilogue, it is Stravinsky's first opera in 29 years and his first full-length opera. Critic Ronald Eyer subsequently writes in *Musical America* (New York) that the composer's "harmony, though by no means atonal, is mostly free and astringent; the rhythm is also free and in constant mutation among all the varieties of duple and triple meters." The opera is successful; it is Stravinsky's last neoclassical work.

Oct. 12   Georges Bizet's four-act opera *Ivan le Terrible* premieres in Bordeaux. Presumed lost, the score was recently discovered among the property of a distant relative of Bizet that had been given to the Paris Conservatoire.

Nov. 6   *Acres of the Sky*, an opera-ballad by Arthur Kreutz, receives its first performance in Fayetteville, Arkansas. It is about family life in that state.

Dec. 1   Benjamin Britten's four-act opera *Billy Budd* receives its world premiere at Covent Garden in London. The libretto, by E.M. Forster and Eric Crozier, is based on the novel by Herman Melville. The composer conducts an all-male cast, which includes Peter Pears, Theodor Uppman, Frederick Dalberg and Geraint Evans. English critic Richard Capell says the opera's "incidental felicities are innumerable and many things are in the best vein."

Dec. 5   Egon Wellesz' atonal opera, *Incognita*, receives its world premiere in Oxford. It is based on a tale by Congreve.

Dec. 24   Gian-Carlo Menotti's *Amahl and the Night Visitors* premieres on national television. The one-act opera, the first composed specifically for that medium, had been commissioned by the National Broadcasting Corporation. The story, about a crippled boy who is cured after offering his crutch as a gift to the Christ child, is repeated on 13 consecutive Christmas eves. Olin Downes writes in the New York *Times*, "television, operatically speaking, has come of age."

SCENE FROM *THE RAKE'S PROGRESS*

1951 Dance

Feb. 18   George Balanchine's *Pas de Trois* — with music by Alois Minkus and costumes by Karinska — is premiered by the New York City Ballet. This performance stars Maria Tallchief, Nora Kaye and Andre Eglevsky.

Feb. 20   *La Valse* receives its world premiere in New York. Danced by the New York City Ballet, the choreography is by George Balanchine to music by Maurice Ravel. Costumes are by Karinska. The one-act ballet with its sinister overtones, closes with the appearance of Death, danced by Francisco Moncion. Other lead dancers include Tanaquil LeClerq and Nicholas Magallanes.

March 13   John Cranko's *Pineapple Poll* is premiered by the Sadler's Wells Ballet in London. The music is by Arthur Sullivan from several Gilbert and Sullivan operettas, arranged by Charles Mackerras. The ballet tells the story of a sea captain who is so irresistible to women that all the ladies of the town join his crew, only to find out that he has been married that morning. Elaine Fifield (Poll), David Blair (Captain Belaey) and David Poole (Jasper) star. Cranko is the first choreographer to use Sullivan's music after the copyright expired. The ballet is in one act and three scenes.

April 5   Frederick Ashton's version of *Daphnis and Chloe* is premiered by the Sadler's Wells Ballet in London. Margot Fonteyn (Chloe), Michael Somes (Daphnis), John Field (Dorkon) and Alexander Grant (Pirate Chief) star. Chloe becomes one of Fonteyn's greatest roles.

June 12   The New York City Ballet premieres Ruthanne Boris' *Cakewalk* in New York. The work — with music by Louis Gottschalk, arranged by Hershey Kay — is a spoof of a minstrel show. Frank Hobi (Mr. Interlocutor), Tanaquil LeClerq and Beatrice Tompkins (End Men), Janet Reed (Wallflower Waltz), Patricia Wilde (Wild Pony and Leader in Freebee), Yvonne Mounsey (Venus), Janet Reed (Hortense, Queen of the Swamp Lilies) and Herbert Bliss (Harolde, the Young Poet) star.

June 14   Nora Kaye stars in the premiere of Jerome Robbins' *The Cage*, to Igor Stravinsky's Concerto in D for Strings. The plot, involving female insects who lure a male to his death, is an allegory of woman destroying man. Nicholas Magallanes (Second Intruder), Yvonne Mounsey (Queen) and Michael Maule (First Intruder) also have lead roles. The ballet is in one act.

Oct. 17   Ruth Page's *Revenge* receives its initial performance by the Ballet des Champs-Elysees in Paris. The music is by Giuseppe Verdi, with costumes and scenery by Antoni Clave. The ballet, whose plot is similar to *Il Trovatore*, stars Sonia Arova, Jacqueline Moreau, Vladimir Skouratoff and Gerard Ohn.

Nov. 14   George Balanchine's *Tyl Ulenspiegel* receives its first performance by the New York City Ballet in New York. This production features costumes and scenery by Esteban Frances and music by Richard Strauss. Jerome Robbins dances Tyl in this lavish production.

Nov. 20   George Balanchine's one-act version of *Swan Lake* is premiered by the New York City Ballet in New York. Dancing to music from the second and fourth acts of Tchaikovsky's famous ballet are Maria Tallchief and Andre Eglevsky.

Dec. 4   *The Pied Piper* — choreographed by Jerome Robbins to music by Aaron Copland — is performed for the first time by the New York City Ballet in New York. Diana Adams, Jillana, Roy Tobias, Janet Reed, Nicholas Magallanes, Todd Bolender, Robbins, Herbert Bliss, Tanaquil LeClerq and Melissa Hayden dance to clarinettist Edmund Wall's mesmerizations.

Dec. 5   Martha Graham's *The Triumph of Saint Joan* — with music by Norman Dello Joio and costumes designed by the choreographer — premieres at the Columbia Auditorium in Louisville, Kentucky. The work, which was commissioned by the Louisville Arts Council, is a solo danced by the choreographer.

Dec. 12   Leonide Massine's *Donald of the Burthens* — set to music by Ian Whyte, with costumes and scenery by Robert Colquhoun and Robert MacBryde — receives its world premiere by the Sadler's Wells Ballet in London. The story resembles the Faust legend in a Scottish setting and uses Scottish dances. The dancers include Beryl Grey, Alexander Grant and Leslie Eduards. The ballet is in one act and two scenes.

1951 Instrumental and Vocal Music

Jan. 22   The Florida State Symphony Orchestra premieres Ernst von Dohnanyi's Piano Concerto No. 2 in B minor in Tallahassee. The composer is soloist.

Feb. 22   Leonard Bernstein and the New York Philharmonic perform Charles Ives' Symphony No. 2 which took five years to compose. The world premiere takes place some 50 years after the work was finished. It climaxes with a rousing version of *Columbia, The Gem of the Ocean* built into the score. Ives listens to the performance from a radio in his kitchen.

Feb. 23   Jacques Ibert's *Symphonie concertante* for oboe and string orchestra premieres in Basel.

Feb. 28   The Louisville Orchestra gives the world premiere of Arthur Honegger's *Suite Archaique*.

March 9   Arthur Honegger's Symphony No. 5 is premiered by Charles Munch and the Boston Symphony Orchestra. The work, commissioned by the symphony, is in three movements, all of which end on *d*.

March 21   Gian Francesco Malipiero's Symphony No. 8 (*Di un tempo*) premieres in Rome. This symphony's movements are played without a break.

March 30   The Minneapolis Symphony, conducted by Antal Dorati, presents the world premiere of Walter Piston's Symphony No. 4. This work, in a neo-classical style, celebrates the centennial of the University of Minnesota.

March 31   Richard Strauss' *Munchen Walzer* is performed posthumously in its 1945 revised version in Vienna. An additional section in G minor was added after a 1945 Allied air attack on Munich. The music was originally composed for a film about Munich.

April 4   Zoltan Kodaly's *Kallo Double* premieres in Budapest. Based on a Hungarian tune, the composition features humming sounds of the human voice and is scored for chorus and small orchestra. The Hungarian People's Ensemble performs.

April 20   The Radio Orchestra of Warsaw gives the first performance of Witold Lutoslawski's *Petite Suite* for orchestra. The work is thought to be one of the composer's best pieces.

April 21   German composer Karl Amadeus Hartmann's Symphony No. 5 (*Symphonie concertante*) premieres in Stuttgart. A three-movement work, it is scored for cellos, double basses and winds.

May 2   *Imaginary Landscape No. 4*, by John Cage, receives its world premiere in New York City, the composer conducting. The work is scored for 12 radios operated by 24 performers. One performer manipulates the dynamics of each radio while the other adjusts the dial. The resultant sound, or "music", depends entirely on what the radio stations "tuned in" happen to be broadcasting. The work is thus indeterminate and is composed of a chance combination of music, speech, static and so forth.

Another work by Cage composed this year — *Music of Changes* — and two other works — Karlheinz Stockhausen's *Kreuzspiel* and Pierre Boulez' *Structures I* — signal the beginnings of aleatoric, or chance music. Serialism in America, however, continues to flourish: Milton

Babbitt, in particular, is in the process of developing his "time-point system," an approach to rhythm in serial music that generates rhythmic patterns and structures through a correlation with intervals between pitch classes. In 1947 Babbitt's *Three Compositions for Piano* and in 1948 his *Composition for Four Instruments* were the first integrally serialized works — the first to have all dimensions of their musical structure (pitch, rhythm, dynamics, instrumentation, register, etc.) serialized. Those pieces preceded both Olivier Messiaen's *Mode de valeurs et d'intensites* and Pierre Boulez' *Structures I*, which are advertised by European serialists as being the first integrally serialized compositions. Morton Feldman's *Projections I* and *Projections II* are also composed this year — these pieces explore varying degrees of indeterminacy.

May 2   Howard Hanson conducts the first performance of Ulysses Kay's three movement Symphony in E in Rochester, New York.

May 6   Ralph Vaughan Williams' cantata *The Sons of Light* is premiered by the London Symphony Orchestra and 1,000 British children in London.

May 25   Andrzej Panufnik's *Symphony of Peace* for chorus and orchestra premieres in Warsaw. This text declares that peace is the responsibility of the people.

June 2   Swiss composer Othmar Schoeck's *Festlicher Hymnus* for orchestra receives its first performance in Grossmunster, Switzerland. The work celebrates the 600th anniversary of Zurich's joining a Swiss confederation of towns.

June 12   Arthur Honegger's *Monopartita* premieres in Zurich. Like the Othmar Schoeck premiere of 10 days ago, this work celebrates the Swiss confederation. It is in eight contiguous movements.

June 13   Francis Poulenc's *Stabat Mater*, scored for soprano, mixed choir and orchestra, receives its world premiere in Strasbourg.

June 16   Rafael Kubelik and the Concertgebouw Orchestra in Amsterdam premiere Guillaume Landre's Symphony No. 3.

June 17   Alan Rawsthorne's neo-classical Piano Concerto No. 2 is premiered by Malcolm Sargent and the London Symphony Orchestra. Clifford Curzon is soloist.

June 19   Andre Jolivet's Piano Concerto (*Equatoriales*) receives its world premiere in Strasbourg with the composer as soloist. The work evokes geographical areas that inspired the composer.

July 2   Arnold Schoenberg's "Dance Around the Golden Calf," from his opera *Moses und Aron*, is performed for the first time in Darmstadt. The opera premieres over radio on March 12, 1954 (two completed acts — Schoenberg dies before finishing it).

July 6   Malcolm Arnold conducts the world premiere of his three-movement Symphony No. 1 at the Cheltenham Festival.

Aug. 5   Anton Webern's *Five Canons on Latin Texts*, Op. 16, is premiered posthumously in New York with Jacques Monod as conductor and Bethany Beardslee as soloist. Scored for soprano, clarinet and bass clarinet, the work was composed between 1923 and 1924. The texts are from the Holy Week liturgy of the Christian church.

Aug. 26   Czech composer Karel Jirak's Symphony No. 5 receives its premiere at the Edinburgh International Festival. The work expresses the composer's relief at the termination of World War II. Jirak is now living in Chicago.

Oct. 6   This year's Donaueschingen Festival of Contemporary Music begins today. It features five first performances: Ernst Krenek's *Double Concerto*, Rolf Liebermann's Piano Sonata, Pierre Boulez' *Polyphonie X*, Hermann Reutter's *Der Himmlische Vagant* and Marcel Mihalovici's *Etude*.

Oct. 7   Lukas Foss' Piano Concerto No. 2 premieres in Venice, the composer at the keyboard. The work is described as a virtuoso piece and is in three movements.

Oct. 7   Hans Werner Henze's Symphony No. 3 is given its world premiere at the final Donaueschingen Festival concert. Works of Tibor Harsanyi and Arthur Honegger are also performed.

Oct. 11   Knudage Riisager's Violin Concerto in two movements is premiered in Copenhagen.

Oct. 14   Pablo Casals conducts the premiere of his *La Sardana* in Zurich. The orchestra consists of 123 cellists.

Oct. 19   Gian-Carlo Menotti's symphonic poem *Apocalypse* premieres in Pittsburgh.

Nov. 1   Stefan Wolpe's first suite from his ballet *The Man from Midian* is premiered by Dimitri Mitropoulos and the New York Philharmonic at Carnegie Hall in New York City. After fleeing the Nazis in Germany, Wolpe studied with Anton Webern in Vienna before going to Palestine to teach at the Jerusalem Conservatory. He later came to America and is now teaching at the Philadelphia Academy of Music.

Nov. 7   The Louisville Orchestra premieres Heitor Villa-Lobos' symphonic poem *Erosion*.

Nov. 29   Hans Werner Henze's radio cantata *Eine Landarzt* premieres over Hamburg Radio. Based on a story by Franz Kafka, the work is dodecaphonic.

Nov. 30   Leopold Stokowski and the Pittsburgh Symphony Orchestra give the world premiere of Mexican composer Julian Carrillo's *Horizontes*. It features a zither tuned in 16th-tones, a cello tuned in quarter-tones and a violin.

1951   Births, Deaths and Debuts

March 12   Pianist Harold Bauer, 77, dies in Miami, Florida. After making his debut as a violinist, he studied piano with Ignace Paderewski and debuted as a pianist in 1893. In 1918 he founded the Beethoven Association in New York and later edited the piano works of Franz Schubert and Johannes Brahms.

March 17   Spanish soprano Victoria de los Angeles makes her Metropolitan Opera debut as Marguerite in Gounod's *Faust*. Virgil Thomson writes in the New York *Herald-Tribune* of de los Angeles that "she made everybody else on the stage seem, both musically and dramatically, a little amateurish."

March 21   Dutch conductor Willem Mengelberg, 79, dies in exile in Chur, Switzerland. After studies at the Conservatory of Utrecht and the Cologne Conservatory, he was appointed head of the Concertgebouw Orchestra in 1895 at the age of 24. Mengelberg frequently appeared as a guest conductor in Europe and America until World War II. Because of his Nazi sympathies, he was prevented from conducting in Holland after the war. He was a romanticist, whose performances of Beethoven, Mahler and Tchaikovsky were famous for their emotional power. Mengelberg was also conductor of the choral group Toon-

kunst. He received an honorary doctorate from Columbia University. Richard Strauss dedicated *Ein Heldenleben* to him.

April 21   Russian-Jewish composer Alexander Krein, 67, dies in Moscow. A cello student at the Moscow Conservatory, his work includes much use of ancient synagogue melodies. He was extensively involved in the Jewish Drama Theater in Moscow after the revolution. In addition to using Hebrew melodic materials, he was influenced by Claude Debussy and Alexander Scriabin. He composed many operas, Jewish plays (including *Sabbati Zewi*), symphonies, chamber music and songs.

April 21   Soprano Olive Fremstad, 79, dies in Irvington-on-Hudson, New York. Born in Sweden, she was brought to the United States by her adoptive parents. After studies in the United States and with Lilli Lehmann in Berlin, she made her debut as a contralto in *Il Trovatore* in Cologne in 1895. After restudying as a soprano, she sang at the Metropolitan and elsewhere with growing acclaim until her retirement in 1920. Her performances, especially of Wagner's music, established the highest standards, to the detriment of many later singers of these roles.

April 26   American composer John Alden Carpenter, 75, dies in Chicago. A product of Harvard University (he studied with John Knowles Paine), he later took lessons from Sir Edward Elgar. He continued composing while earning his living in his father's shipping supply business. It was only after his retirement in 1936 that he was able to devote himself fully to composition. His music reflects a combination of several distinct influences — French impressionism, modernism and American jazz. Although his work had little influence on younger composers or the international music scene, he composed one piece that was considered a musical stereotype of American life — *Skyscrapers* (1926). Other works include ballets; orchestral, choral and chamber music; piano pieces; and songs.

May 29   Czech composer Josef Bohuslav Foerster, 91, dies in Novy Vestec. After studying organ, he began conducting and taught at the Hamburg Conservatory. His wife, singer Berta Lauterer, was hired by Gustav Mahler at the Vienna Court Opera. Foerster's career was both as a teacher and as a composer. His music was heavily influenced by Czech nationalism and includes melodic materials characteristic of that nation. He composed six operas, four masses, five symphonies, four string quartets, chamber music, incidental music and other works.

May 30   Greek composer Dimitri Levidis, 65, dies in Athens. A pupil at the Athens Conservatory, he was the first to compose for electronic instruments in symphonic music. One such work is *Poeme symphonique pour solo d'Ondes musicales et orchestre*. He also composed chamber music, song cycles and piano works.

June 4   Conductor Serge Koussevitzky, 76, dies in Boston, where he had been music director of the Boston Symphony for 25 years. Starting in Russia as a bass player with the Bolshoi Theater Orchestra, he eventually turned to conducting. In 1909 he put together his own orchestra in Moscow and featured new works by his contemporaries (he did a great deal to help Alexander Scriabin). After the Russian Revolution he moved to Paris, where he again organized his own ensemble, playing many new works by French and Russian composers. In 1924 he was named conductor of the Boston Symphony. During his tenure there he commissioned many new works from composers such as Aaron Copland, Roy Harris, Walter Piston, Samuel Barber, William Schuman, Igor Stravinsky, Paul Hindemith, Sergei Prokofiev, George Gershwin, Maurice Ravel and many others. He was a conductor in the romantic tradition. Leonard Bernstein was his protege.

July 13   Austrian composer Arnold Schoenberg, 76, dies in Los Angeles. This revolutionary composer studied counterpoint for a few months with Alexander von Zemlinsky — his only training apart from some violin and cello lessons at the Realschule in Vienna. He first worked as a bank clerk and as an arranger of popular songs and operettas. His String Quartet in D Minor (composed in 1897, no opus number) was well received, largely because of its familiar romantic sound. Soon, however, his intellectual bent began to manifest itself, and his early songs began to provoke hostile responses.

ARNOLD SCHOENBERG

Schoenberg began conducting amateur groups near Vienna around 1900. In 1901 he relocated to Berlin and began an enterprise known as "Uberbrettl," which — with other artists as well as himself running it — was a kind of artistic cabaret. While there, he conducted light music and wrote a cabaret song with trumpet obbligato. Soon thereafter he met Richard Strauss, who helped him locate a teaching position at the Sterns Conservatory. A year later (1903) he moved back to Vienna and met Gustav Mahler. Mahler was then at the apogee of his career and helped Schoenberg meet important performers. Schoenberg then began painting, and his visual works revealed strong expressionist tendencies.

Anton Webern, Alban Berg, Ernst Krenek and Egon Wellesz soon found themselves gravitating toward Schoenberg and studied with him. Schoenberg joined the faculty of the Vienna Academy in 1910. The following year he went back to Berlin to teach privately and lecture at the Sterns Conservatory; his disciples followed him there. He also conducted in important European cities — Amsterdam, London, Saint Petersburg — before joining the military during World War I. After the war he returned to teaching and organized — with Anton Webern, Alexander von Zemlinsky and Alban Berg — the Society for Private Musical Performances, a group that prohibited applause and the presence of critics. Schoenberg was given a master class at the Prussian Academy of Arts in Berlin in 1925; in 1933 he was fired by the German Ministry of Education, controlled by the Nazis. He went to Paris and immediately converted back to Judaism (born a Jew, he had converted to Roman Catholicism earlier in his life). Cellist

Joseph Malkin invited him to teach at the newly established Malkin Conservatory in Boston; he accepted and stayed there one season. He then settled in Hollywood and taught at the University of Southern California and later at the University of California at Los Angeles. He became an American citizen and changed his name from Schonberg to Schoenberg.

Schoenberg was perhaps the most important composer of the first half of the century. Rooted in Viennese postromanticism, he blossomed into an artist whose work would have a dramatic effect on the music of Western civilization. He combined an intense visionary approach to music with an intellectual preference for abstraction. The result was a system of composition that in its complexity rivaled any in the history of Western music.

Schoenberg underwent four periods of development and transformation: postromanticism, atonal-expressionism, introduction and development of the strict 12-tone method and his American period. His postromantic period was anchored in the music of Richard Wagner, Richard Strauss and Gustav Mahler. Schoenberg first composed music that was tonal, with key signatures, that employed massive orchestras and exploited a full range of orchestral sonorities. During this period he produced works such as *Verklarte Nacht*, Op. 4 (composed in 1899); *Pelleas et Melisande*, Op. 5 (composed in 1902); and *Gurre-Lieder* (composed between 1900 and 1911). Also during this period he began to pursue an interest in chamber music — these pieces embody components such as vocal lines with wide intervals — which became characteristic of his later work. Examples of such chamber pieces are *Eight Songs*, Op. 6 (composed in 1905); the String Quartet No. 1 in D Minor, Op. 7 (composed in 1904); and the String Quartet No. 2 in F-sharp Minor (composed in 1907). This latter work includes a vocal part that, in the final movement, contains the famous line by Stefan George: "I feel the air of another planet."

Schoenberg's second period — atonal-expressionist — is characterized by an increased absence of tonality and an almost equal presence of consonance and dissonance within the pitch environment. This period witnessed a preoccupation with chamber works that enabled Schoenberg to unmask his deepening pursuit of musical abstraction. *Three Piano Pieces*, Op. 11 (composed in 1909); *Das Buch der hangenden Garten*, Op. 15 (composed in 1908), which also introduces the requirement that vocalists have absolute pitch to negotiate jagged vocal lines; *Erwartung*, Op. 17 (composed in 1909); *Five Pieces for Orchestra*, Op. 16 (composed in 1909 and revised in 1949); *Pierrot lunaire*, Op. 21 (composed in 1912), which introduces "Sprechstimme," a kind of voice production involving elements of both song and speech (and which Anton Webern described as "the prose of music"); and Four Songs for Voice and Orchestra, Op. 22 (composed in 1914-15), are works that, while not all chamber pieces, characterize his second period.

His third period constitutes the one in which he made his most noteworthy contribution — the 12-tone method. During this period he systematized the technique of musical composition that would have a devastating effect on postromanticism and completely shatter the notion that only a traditional approach to harmony and counterpoint can lead to the limits of great music. His 12-tone system ushered in a new musical universe, whose outer edges connected atonal music with the chromatic music that would emerge from the pens of composers in the second half of the 20th century — music that, like its late 19th- and early 20th-century predecessors and its middle and late 20th-century offspring — is based on the 12 tones of the chromatic scale. Schoenberg's system involved four basic operations: the set, or row (the use of all 12 tones of the chromatic scale arranged in any order selected by the composer), stated in its original form; the set's inversion form; the set's retrograde form; and the set's retrograde inversion form. The set, or row, in any of its forms, may begin on any degree or tone of the chromatic scale. His method enabled the composer to order the 12 pitch classes of the chromatic scale and then create, through melody and counterpoint, a music that would embrace "perpetual variation" — variation in which these 12 pitch classes would be in constant flux, not repeated before each of the others had been stated, and not confined to what Schoenberg and his disciples viewed as the unbearable constraints of the hierarchical pitch relationships found in the diatonic scale and tonal music. The 12-tone system captivated many post-World War II composers in both Europe and America, including Pierre Boulez, Karlheinz Stockhausen, Milton Babbitt and Charles Wuorinen. Works Schoenberg composed during this period include the Quintet for Flute, Oboe, Clarinet, Bassoon and Horn, Op. 26 (composed in 1924); and *Variations for Orchestra*, Op. 31 (composed in 1927–28).

Schoenberg's last period dates from 1933, when he relocated to America. During this time he continued to pursue his 12-tone method and yet, somewhat surprisingly, began once again to incorporate tonal elements in his music. This period brought forth works that were rigidly 12-tone, such as the String Quartet No. 4, Op. 37 (composed in 1936), and the String Trio, Op. 45 (composed in 1946); as well as works that permitted key signatures, such as *Kol Nidre* for speaker, chorus and orchestra, Op. 39 (composed in 1938), and *Theme and Variations* for orchestra, Op. 43b (composed in 1943). In *Ode to Napoleon*, Op. 41 (composed in 1942), and *A Survivor from Warsaw*, Op. 46 (composed in 1947), he used the 12-tone method but in a simplified manner, allowing references to tonality to occur. Pierre Boulez later describes Schoenberg's last period as "terribly academic."

Schoenberg's work also embraced the beginnings of combinatoriality — the art of combining set forms such that the resultant pitch content meets certain criteria desired by the composer. Schoenberg composed prolifically for the stage as well as for orchestra, chorus, chamber ensemble, voice and keyboard (despite his impact on music, he composed no works for electronic instruments); he also wrote prolifically — essays, books and articles. One of his maxims: "Genius learns only from itself, talent chiefly from others."

Schoenberg had a paranoid fear of the number 13 (triskaidekaphobia) and believed that he would be fine if he survived July 13 because the digits of his age — 7 and 6 — add up to 13; he dies at 13 minutes to midnight.

July 27   Ballet director Colonel W. de Basil dies in Paris at the age of 63. Rumored to have been a Cossack general, he became assistant to Prince Zeretelli, director of the Russian Opera, in 1925. In 1932 he became co-director of the Ballets Russes de Monte Carlo with Rene Blum. In 1939 he obtained control of the Original Ballet Russe, which he directed until its demise in 1948.

Aug. 15   Austrian pianist Artur Schnabel, 79, dies in Morschach, Switzerland. After studying with Theodor Leschetizky in Vienna, he became a child prodigy, concertizing in Europe. In addition to his solo career, he played much chamber music. He taught at the Hochschule fur Musik in Berlin from 1925 to 1933 and then, fleeing the Nazis, settled in Switzerland, where he gave summer master classes. During the war Schnabel lived in America but afterward returned to Europe. He was famous for his interpretations of Schubert, Mozart, Brahms and, especially, Beethoven. He also composed in the atonal idiom and edited the piano sonatas of Beethoven.

Aug. 21   English conductor and essayist Constant Lambert, 45, dies in London. Also a composer and critic, he was a pupil of Ralph Vaughan Williams at the Royal College of Music. One of his best-known books is *Music Ho!: A Study of Music in Decline* (London, 1934). In 1926 Serge Diaghilev commissioned him to compose a ballet (*Romeo and Juliet*); Lambert then devoted most of his time to composing and conducting ballets. His music is noted for its inclusion of jazz elements.

Sep. 14   German conductor Fritz Busch, 61, dies in London. A product of the Cologne Conservatory, he conducted in Russia, Aachen and with the Stuttgart and Dresden Opera companies before leaving Germany in 1933 to become a Swiss citizen. He then conducted in various European countries, in South America and at the Metropolitan Opera in New York. He was the brother of violinist Adolf Busch and cellist Hermann Busch.

Nov. 5   Agrippina Vaganova, one of the most important teachers in the history of ballet, dies in Leningrad at the age of 72. A dancer at the Imperial Ballet in Saint Petersburg from 1897 to 1915, she began teaching after the Revolution. In 1934 she became director of Leningrad school. During her tenure, she developed the teaching system that has become the basis for ballet education in the Soviet Union and in many areas of Eastern Europe. Expanding on the systems developed by Enrico Cecchetti and Olga Preobrajenska, her technique focuses on the harmonious, fluid movement of the body. Her students were noted for their strong, supple backs which enabled them to soar in the air. Her technique contributed to the development of the virtuosity that is the hallmark of Soviet ballet. Among her pupils were Galina Ulanova, Natalia Dudinskaya and Irina Kolpakova.

Nov. 13   Russian composer Nikolai Medtner, 71, dies in London. A pupil of Vassily Safonov and Sergei Taneyev at the Moscow Conservatory, he quickly achieved success in Europe as a pianist. After teaching at the Moscow Conservatory, Medtner lived in Berlin and Paris before settling in London. He avoided nationalism in his music and attempted to create a personal style blending classicism and romanticism; this style is reflected in his *34 Fairy Tales* for piano, composed between 1905 and 1929. His early works remain his best. Although he wrote much for piano (including three piano concertos), he also composed 104 songs, other vocal works and chamber music. He wrote essays, too.

Nov. 13   German-American music scholar Hugo Leichtentritt, 77, dies in Cambridge, Massachusetts. Noted for having written books about motets, he also composed operas and other music and wrote music criticism. Among his most famous writings are *Music, History and Ideas* (Cambridge, Massachusetts, 1938), *Handel* (Berlin, 1924) and *Geschichte der Motette* (Leipzig, 1908).

Nov. 23   French music critic and composer Henri Collet, 66, dies in Paris. This critic came up with the designation "Les Six" for that group of composers: Louis Durey, Germaine Tailleferre, Francis Poulenc, Georges Auric, Darius Milhaud and Arthur Honegger. Erik Satie was a sponsor of this group but not a member. Collet's criticism was often vituperous, especially when aimed at great composers. His music was light and not very successful. He composed in a style reminiscent of Spanish folk music.

Dec. 6   French bass Leon Rothier, 76, dies in New York. After making his operatic debut in 1899 at the Opera-Comique, he was chosen a few months later to appear in

SELIM PALMGREN

the world premiere of *Louise*. In 1910 he came to the Metropolitan Opera, where he sang in a large variety of operas until 1939. After his retirement he remained in New York as a teacher and coach and appeared in the play *A Bell for Adano*. He was heavily decorated by the French government.

Dec. 13   Finnish composer Selim Palmgren, 73, dies in Helsinki. His most famous teacher was Ferruccio Busoni. He conducted in Helsinki and Turku and, in 1921, toured America as a pianist. He taught composition and piano at the Eastman School of Music, Rochester, New York, between 1923 and 1926. He then returned to Finland where he remained until his death. His music is characterized by Finnish melodic fragments and impressionist elements, including whole-tone scales. He composed much piano music (five piano concertos, two sonatas, 24 preludes, 24 etudes), two operas, and other works. Although highly esteemed in Finland, his work has little impact on the international stage.

1951   Related Events

Dimitri Mitropoulos becomes music director of the New York Philharmonic. He holds this position until 1957, when Leonard Bernstein succeeds him.

CeBeDem — Belgian Center for Music Documentation — is founded this year in Brussels. This nonprofit organization consists of Belgian, French and Dutch composers and musicians who work to promote performance of new music. The center also develops a music and a recording library and publishes works of its members.

Les Ballets des Champs-Elysees disbands this year. Roland Petit — its choreographer, director and lead dancer — left the company to form the Ballets de Paris, making it impossible for the company to continue, although after his departure it did carry on briefly under the direction of Jean Robin.

Niels Bjorn Larsen is appointed artistic director of the Royal Danish Ballet this year.

The National Ballet of Canada is established this year in Toronto. Celia Franca is director. The new company is created as an eastern Canadian equivalent of western Canada's Royal Winnipeg Ballet.

Royal Festival Hall opens this year in London.

Jan. 7   Soviet musicologist and critic Izrail Nestyev's article called "Dollar Cacophony" is published in *Izvestia*. It is largely an attack on the music of Igor Stravinsky. Nestyev calls Stravinsky "the shameless prophet of bourgeois modernism." Soviet attacks on Stravinsky increase as Stravinsky embraces the 12-tone method of composition.

Feb. 3   The Canadian League of Composers is created today in Toronto.

Feb. 16   Soprano Lotte Lehmann announces her retirement during a recital in New York's Town Hall. Her career spanned 40 years.

April 19   *Pravda* denounces Herman Zhukovsky's opera *From All Our Hearts* by asserting that "the score, weak from a professional standpoint, compounds the ideological falsity of the libretto in its portrayal of the Soviet people as devoid of all individuality." Zhukovsky's 25,000-ruble prize is subsequently revoked, and the humiliating episode is published in both *Pravda* and *Isvestia*.

April 24   The chairmen of the Soviet All-Union Arts Committee and the director of the Bolshoi are dismissed because they produced Herman Zhukovsky's *From All Our Hearts* — which *Pravda* denounced as "falsely portraying" collective farm life. Zhukovsky's career is now displaced and remains so until May 28, 1958, when a resolution of the Soviet Communist Party's Central Committee modifies its position of this past April 19.

May 7   Douglas Moore is awarded the Pulitzer Prize for Music for *Giants in the Earth*.

THE FOUNDERS OF THE MARLBORO MUSIC FESTIVAL: (LEFT TO RIGHT) MARCEL MOYSE, LOUIS MOYSE, RUDOLF SERKIN, BLANCHE MOYSE, ADOLF BUSCH, HERMAN BUSCH (WITH CELLIST NATHAN CHAIKIN SECOND FROM LEFT).

June 2   The British Institute of Recorded Sound is established today. Other developments in the recording industry this year include the following: EMI (Electrical & Musical Industries) demonstrates its "stereosonic" open-reel tapes; HMV (The Gramophone Company, England) demonstrates its first stereo tapes; Columbia's 45-RPM records are added to its catalog; the wet silvering process for plating is introduced by many firms; the first issue of *High Fidelity* magazine is published in America.

July 8   The first concert of the Marlboro Music School and Festival takes place at Marlboro, Vermont. The Busch-Serkin Trio performs music of Beethoven and Schubert. The members of the trio are Rudolf Serkin, Adolf Busch and Hermann Busch. This festival subsequently becomes internationally known and attracts scores of young and adult professional musicians from around the world. There are no predetermined programs, no teachers, no lessons — only music making.

Oct. 1   Herbert Eimert introduces the term *electronic music* today in a radio lecture in Germany entitled "Die Klangwelt der elektronischen Musik." This German music theorist is now 54 and has studied musicology and philosophy at the University of Cologne.

Oct. 7   The Colosseum in Rome becomes an active theater after 19 centuries of disuse. The first performance features parts of Verdi's operas sung by the Rome Opera House chorus.

Oct. 25   Conductor Manuel Rosenthal of the Seattle Symphony Orchestra is fired for living with a woman — French singer Claudine Pillard Verneuil.

1952 Opera

Feb. 11   American composer Hugo Weisgall's *The Tenor* premieres in Baltimore, the composer conducting. This one-act opera is based on Frank Wedekind's novella *Der Kammersanger*. It is about a tenor who, while rushing to the opera house to sing Tristan, stumbles on the corpse of one of his mistresses. The music combines ballad singing with atonality. Weisgall, now 39, is appointed chairman of the faculty at the College of Jewish Music in New York this year.

Feb. 17   *Boulevard Solitude* enjoys its premiere performance. Composed by Hans Werner Henze, the work is performed at the Landestheater in Hannover. The libretto, by Greta Weil, is based on A.J. Prevost's *L'histoire du Chevalier des Grieux et de Manon Lescaut*. The music receives critical approval, despite its dodecaphonic sound.

March 17   Argentine composer Juan Jose Castro's *Proserpina e lo straniero* premieres in Milan at the Teatro alla Scala, conducted by the composer. The libretto, by Omar del Carlo, tells the story of a young prostitute in Buenos Aires. The work wins a prize offered by La Scala in honor of the 50th anniversary of the death of Giuseppe Verdi. In the cast are Giulietta Simionato, Cloe Elmo and Rosanna Cartieri. It is the composer's most successful work.

March 25   *Leonore 40/45*, by Rolf Liebermann, premieres in Basel at the Stadttheater. Heinrich Strobel's libretto is the story of a romance between a French girl and a German soldier during and after World War II. The two-act opera quotes music from Beethoven's *Fidelio*.

June 12   Leonard Bernstein's *Trouble in Tahiti* premieres at Brandeis University in Waltham, Massachusetts. This event marks the opening of the Festival of Creative Arts at this university. The opera is about marital troubles in American suburbia. Howard Taubman, in the New York *Times*, writes that Bernstein "seeks to reach more deeply into the hearts of his principal characters and in a long aria for the wife his music becomes searching and affecting."

June 14   Kurt Weill's *Die Dreigroschenoper* receives its first English-language performance. It is entitled *The Threepenny Opera* and has a libretto in English by Marc Blitzstein. The cast includes Weill's widow, Lotte Lenya. The work is performed at the Brandeis University Festival.

June 20   *Cardillac*, by Paul Hindemith, is performed in a revised version in Zurich. The original version was premiered in Dresden in 1926.

LOTTE LENYA

Aug. 9   Hugo Weisgall's *The Stronger*, based on a play by Strindberg, premieres in Westport, Connecticut, the composer conducting. The one-act opera is about two women who struggle for psychological dominance. The music is atonal and includes jazz elements.

Aug. 13   *The Farmer and the Fairy*, an opera by Alexander Tcherepnin, receives its initial performance in Aspen, Colorado. It is about a promiscuous female.

Aug. 14   *Die Liebe der Danae*, by Richard Strauss, is performed for the first time at the Salzburg Festival. The libretto, by Josef Gregor, is a variation on the myth of Danae. The opera never finds a place in the repertoire. Although the composer had seen the work staged at a dress rehearsal in 1944, he had never seen a public production of it during his lifetime. It was scheduled for performance in August of 1944; however, the Nazis closed down theaters in Austria and Germany, and the performance was canceled.

Nov. 5   Ildebrando Pizzetti's *Cagliostro*, with a libretto by the composer, premieres over Italian radio. The four-act opera is about a charlatan who attempts to gain influence with Marie Antoinette. The opera is performed in a stage version on January 24, 1953.

1952 Dance

Feb. 14   Jerome Robbins' *Ballade* — to music by Claude Debussy, with orchestrations by Ernest Ansermet and costumes and scenery by Boris Aronson — receives its initial performance by the New York City Ballet in New York. Nora Kaye and Tanaquil LeClerq star.

Feb. 19   The New York City Ballet presents George Balanchine's *Caracole* (later known as *Divertimento No. 15* to Mozart's *Divertimento* in B-flat major. The plotless ballet, in five movements, is one of the choreographer's most brilliant works. Maria Tallchief, Melissa Hayden, Patricia Wilde, Diana Adams, Tanaquil LeClerq, Andre Eglevsky, Nicholas Magallanes and Jerome Robbins are in the cast.

Feb. 26   Antony Tudor's *La gloire* is premiered by the New York City Ballet in New York. In the cast are Nora Kaye, Hugh Laing, Jacques d'Amboise and Francisco Moncion. The dramatic ballet combines the personal life of a great tragedienne with some of the characters she plays on stage. It is set to music from Beethoven overtures. This is the last ballet created by Tudor for this company. The work is in one act and three scenes.

Feb. 28   Frederick Ashton's *Picnic at Tintagel* — to music by Arnold Bax, with costumes and scenery by Cecil Beaton — receives its first performance by the New York City Ballet in New York. This ballet is a modern retelling of the Tristan story, and the lovers are danced by Diana Adams and Jacques d'Amboise. It is in one act and three scenes.

March 14   *Oedipus* — a dance-drama by Harry Partch — receives its world premiere at Mills College in Oakland, California. Marjorie Swaezey conducts, with the part of Oedipus danced and played by Allan Louw. The music is scored for voices, clarinet, bass clarinet and many of Partch's specially built instruments (gourd tree and cone gongs are added to a later — 1967 — version of the piece to replace the cloud chamber bowls, which, when played, have a tendency to shatter). The work is approximately 75 minutes long and is based on the Greek tragedy.

April 22   The Martha Graham Dance Company premieres her one-act ballet *Canticle for Innocent Comedians* to music by Thomas Ribbink in New York. The plotless work is in praise of the cycle of life. Pearl Lang, Yuriko, Helen McGehee, Mary Hinkson, Bertram Ross, Stuart Hodes and Robert Cohan lead the cast.

May 21   Alicia Alonso's version of *La fille mal gardee*, based on the choreography of Bronislava Nijinska, is performed for the first time by the Ballet Alicia Alonso in Havana.

June 14   Merce Cunningham premieres a new work at Brandeis University. It is *Collage*, with music by Pierre Henry and Pierre Schaeffer. The dance concert takes place as part of the Brandeis University Festival. Maurice Bejart subsequently choreographs the complete Schaeffer music; that premiere takes place in 1955, under the title *Symphonie pour un homme seul*.

Sep. 3   Frederick Ashton's version of *Sylvia* to music by Leo Delibes, is premiered by the Sadler's Wells Ballet in London. Costumes and scenery are by Robert and Christopher Ironside. Margot Fonteyn and Michael Somes lead the cast.

Oct. 1   *The Harvest According* is premiered by the Ballet Theater in New York City. The work is choreographed by Agnes De Mille, with music by Virgil Thomson and costumes and scenery by Lemuel Ayres. Gemze de Lappe, Ruth Ann Koesun, Jenny Workman and Kelly Brown head the cast. The ballet fuses modern dance, classical ballet and folk dance to tell a story of war, women and soldiers.

Nov. 11   Choreographer Walter Gore's *Street Games* — to music by Jacques Ibert, with costumes and decor by Ronald Wilson — is premiered by the New Ballet Company in London.

Nov. 11   The New York City Ballet premieres George Balanchine's *Scotch Symphony*, in New York, to Felix Mendelssohn's Symphony in A Minor. The plotless work hints at the romantic era. Maria Tallchief, Patricia Wilde, Andre

Eglevsky, Michael Maule and Frank Hobi lead the cast. The ballet is in three movements.

Nov. 25   George Balanchine's *Metamorphoses* is performed for the first time by the New York City Ballet. The music is by Paul Hindemith and costumes are by Karinska. The ballet, showing the transformation of larvae into butterflies and dragonflies, is danced by Tanaquil LeClerq, Todd Bolender and Nicholas Magallanes.

Dec. 23   John Taras' *Piege de lumiere* — to music by Jean-Michel Damase, with costumes by Andre Levasseur and decor by Felix Labisse — is premiered by the Marquis de Cuevas Ballet in Paris. The ballet is about escaped convicts trying to capture butterflies and is one of Taras's best works. The dancers include Rosella Hightower, Serge Golovine and Vladimir Skouratoff.

1952   Instrumental and Vocal Music

Jan. 7   *Symphonie-Concertante*, by Gail Kubik, receives its world premiere in New York City.

Jan. 11   Ernst Toch's Symphony No. 2 premieres in Vienna. The four-movement work is dedicated to Albert Schweitzer.

Jan. 24   Paul Hindemith's *Die Harmonie der Welt*, Frank Martin's Violin Concerto and Goffredo Petrassi's Concerto No. 2 for Orchestra are premiered by Paul Sacher and the Chamber Orchestra of Basel. This event marks the 25th anniversary of this ensemble.

Jan. 26   Ernst von Dohnanyi's Violin Concerto No. 2 premieres in San Antonio, Texas. Dohnanyi completed this work two years ago while in Tallahassee, Florida. It is a four-movement concerto scored for orchestra (no violins) and violin soloist.

Jan. 26   Reinhold Gliere's Concerto for Horn and Orchestra premieres in Moscow, the composer conducting.

Jan. 30   Symphony No. 4, by Paul Creston, is premiered by Howard Mitchell and the National Symphony Orchestra in Washington, D.C.

Feb. 8   Arnold Schoenberg's String Quartet in D Major is performed posthumously at the Library of Congress in Washington, D.C. This event marks the reintroduction of a work thought for many years to have been lost. Schoenberg brought the score with him to America, and it was recently purchased by the Music Division of the Library of Congress. The piece was first performed in Vienna during the 1897–98 season.

Feb. 10   Pianist David Tudor premieres new works by American composers at the Cherry Lane Theater in New York City. They are *Three Pieces for Piano*, by Earle Brown; *Intermissions* III, IV and V, by Morton Feldman; *Fugue for Piano*, by Lou Harrison; and *For Piano I*, by Christian Wolff. Brown has studied mathematics and engineering at Northeastern University and is concerned with aspects of musical space. He has been influenced by abstract expressionist painting, modern sculpture, surrealism and neo-Dadaism. He builds a model of musical space this year, which he describes as "relative to conceptual mobility and transformation of events in arbitrary, unstable time."

Feldman has studied with Wallingford Riegger and Stefan Wolpe and was also influenced by abstract expressionist painting. His music explores relationships between predetermined musical events and indeterminacy, and his approach to notation indicates only approximations of musical "actions." Harrison has studied with Henry Cowell and Arnold Schoenberg and has been a diligent champion of the music of Charles Ives. Wolff has studied at Harvard University and with John Cage. He confines his piano piece premiered today to nine different notes.

Feb. 18   Sergei Prokofiev's Symphony-Concerto in E Minor for Violoncello and Orchestra, Op. 125, receives its world premiere by cellist Mstislav Rostropovich in Moscow. This work incorporates materials from Prokofiev's earlier Concerto for Cello and Orchestra. Composed over the past two years, it is in three movements. Prokofiev considers the piece as much a symphony as a concerto.

Feb. 22   Sergei Prokofiev's overture *The Meeting of the Volga with the Don River* premieres over Moscow radio.

Feb. 29   Carlos Chavez' Violin Concerto receives its initial performance in Mexico City, with Viviane Bertolami as soloist. The concerto has eight contiguous sections. It is later revised and performed in its new version in 1965.

March 4   Luigi Dallapiccola's *Tartiniana* for violin and orchestra premieres in Bern, Switzerland. The piece is based on themes composed by Giuseppe Tartini, who founded an Italian school of virtuoso violin playing.

March 16   Anton Webern's *Three Songs on Poems of Hildegard Jone*, Op. 25, is premiered posthumously by Jacques Monod in New York, with Bethany Beardslee as soloist. Also premiered posthumously on the same program is Webern's *Three Traditional Rhymes*, Op. 17, complete version (these songs were composed between 1924-25 and the second was performed last year). Beardslee has studied at Michigan State University and at the Julliard School. She specializes in contemporary music.

March 20   Alexander Tcherepnin's Symphony No. 2 receives its first performance by Rafael Kubelik and the Chicago Symphony Orchestra. Composed between 1945 and 1951, it is in four movements and is dedicated to the memory of Tcherepnin's father, Nicolas.

April 13   Morton Gould's Symphony No. 4 premieres at the U.S. Military Academy at West Point, the composer conducting. Composed for West Point's sesquicentennial, it is a two-movement work.

April 30   Swedish composer Hugo Alfven's Symphony No. 5 in A Minor premieres in Stockholm.

May 2   *Water Music*, by John Cage, receives its first performance at the New School for Social Research in New York City. Pianist David Tudor performs. The work requires the pianist to use a deck of cards, whistles, a radio and a Chinese book of oracles. Cage later sends a letter to Nicolas Slonimsky inviting him to attend another performance of the work. He writes, "Unlike Handel's, it actually splashes." Also premiered on today's concert is Morton Feldman's *Extension 3*.

May 3   Ralph Vaughan Williams' *Romance in D-flat* for harmonica, string orchestra and piano is premiered by the Little Symphony Orchestra in New York City, with Larry Adler as soloist.

May 8   Milton Babbitt's *Du* (setting of seven brief poems by August Stramm) premieres at Barnard College in New York City. Babbitt is now 37.

May 13   Darius Milhaud's *Cantata from Proverbs* receives its initial performance by Isadore Freed and the United Temple Chorus of Lawrence, Long Island. This three-movement choral work is scored for women's chorus, oboe, cello and harp.

May 30   Henry Cowell's *Fantasy*, Darius Milhaud's *West Point Suite* and Roy Harris' *Symphony in One Movement* are premiered by the U.S. Military Academy Band at West Point, New York. This event is a celebration of the sesquicentennial of West Point.

Aug. 29   John Cage's *4'33"* is premiered by pianist David Tudor in Woodstock, New York. This event marks the premiere of a silent musical composition scored for any instrument or combination of instruments — the performer(s) merely attending their instruments for the specified time and then leaving, awaiting applause. An unidentified reviewer allegedly writes in an unidentified New York newspaper, "The difficulty to judge John Cage's *4'33"* is that it is impossible to tell what music has *not* been played."

Oct. 11   Symphony No. 7 in C-sharp Minor, by Sergei Prokofiev, receives its world premiere in Moscow. This four-movement work is his last symphony. *Pravda* praises the music and says Prokofiev composed "delicate music able to satisfy the aesthetic demands and artistic tastes of the Soviet people." A year from now the piece is performed in America. Olin Downes then says, "The symphony must remain an enigma to the warmest admirers of Prokofiev."

Oct. 28   Leopold Stokowski conducts a concert at the Museum of Modern Art in New York City. Receiving their world premieres are new electronic works: Vladimir Ussachevsky's *Sonic Contours* and Otto Luening's *Low Speed*, *Invention* and *Fantasy in Space*. Also on the program is Ben Weber's *Symphony on Poems of William Blake*, Op. 33, with baritone Warren Galjow as soloist. This event marks one of the first concerts of electronic music in America to establish this new medium as a noteworthy phenomenon.

Stokowski introduces the event with the following remarks: "I am often asked: What is tape music, and how is it made? Tape music is music that is composed directly with sound instead of first being written on paper and later made into sound. Just as the painter paints his picture directly with colors, so the musician composes his music directly with tone. In classical orchestral music many instruments play different groups of notes which sound together. In tape music several or even many tapes are superimposed; the tapes sound together the groups of tones that are recorded on them. So, essentially, it is a new way of doing what has been done for centuries by old methods."

Critics rave. Jay Harrison writes in the New York *Herald-Tribune*, "It has been a long time in coming, but music and the machine are now wed." *Time* magazine reports, "The twentieth-century instrument is the record machine — phonograph or tape recorder." Italian composer Luciano Berio (now unknown) is in today's audience; the event prompts him to form an electronic music studio in Italy — the Studio di Fonologia Musicale is established within two years. The program is later broadcast over WNYC in New York and WGBH in Boston. The composers are also interviewed on Dave Garroway's *Today* program on NBC television.

Nov. 11   Igor Stravinsky's *Cantata* premieres in Los Angeles, the composer conducting. Scored for soprano, tenor, female chorus and instrumental guitarist, it is in nine sections and uses poetry of four anonymous 15th and 16th-century English poets as texts. Mildred Norton writes in the *Daily News* (Los Angeles), "Stravinsky's Cantata. . . is a mercilessly dull, wholly unleavened essay in boredom. . . ."

Nov. 13   Ben Weber's film score *Image in the Snow* premieres at Cinema 16 in New York City.

Nov. 20   Symphony No. 7, by Roy Harris, receives its first performance by Rafael Kubelik and the Chicago Symphony Orchestra. The single-movement work has a passacaglia with five variations. Harris states: "In this work I have hoped to communicate the spirit of affirmation as a declaration of faith in Mankind." He later revises the symphony — the new version is performed on September 15, 1955 in Copenhagen.

Nov. 25   Henry Cowell's Symphony No. 7 for chamber orchestra premieres in Baltimore, as Reginald Stewart conducts the Baltimore Symphony Orchestra. The four-movement work is one of Cowell's most successful.

Dec. 12   Swedish composer Karl-Birger Blomdahl's Symphony No. 2 premieres in Stockholm.

1952 Births, Deaths and Debuts

Jan. 11   Italian tenor Aureliano Pertile, 67, dies in Milan. His greatest successes began in 1921, when he was engaged by Arturo Toscanini for La Scala. There he won applause for his performances in *Il Trovatore*, *Mefistofele*, *Manon Lescaut* and *Nerone*, among other operas. He sang his farewell as Otello in 1940 and later became a singing teacher at the Milan Conservatory.

Jan. 20   American composer and music educator Arthur Farwell, 79, dies in New York City. He was a pupil of Engelbert Humperdinck. Farwell's music includes elements from his study of American Indian music. He is noted for encouraging American composers to develop a style that would be characteristically American. He taught at Cornell University and at the University of California at Berkeley. He also wrote for *Universal America*. In 1936 he established a press in East Lansing, Michigan so he could print his own music.

Feb. 13   German lexicographer and music scholar Alfred Einstein, 71, dies in El Cerrito, California. This musician was an editor of Hugo Riemann's *Musiklexikon* and revised Ludwig von Kochel's catalog of Mozart's compositions. He was a cousin of the scientist Albert Einstein. He also wrote music criticism for the *Berliner Tageblatt* between 1927 and 1933; he later taught at Smith College in America.

Feb. 17   German conductor Bruno Walter, 86, dies in Beverly Hills, California. An early post as assistant to Gustav Mahler at the Hamburg Stadttheater played an important role in his life. He was subsequently a fervent supporter of Mahler's music and conducted premieres of several of his works. Other important positions included conductor of the Berlin Opera in 1900, music director of the Munich Opera from 1914 to 1922, conductor of the Leipzig Gewandhaus Orchestra from 1929 until the Nazi regime relieved him of that post, and music director of the Vienna Opera from 1936 until the Nazi annexation of Austria. From 1922 he was a regular conductor at the Salzburg Festival, where his Mozart performances set the highest standards. He also conducted frequently in England and America. During World War II he settled in the United States and often conducted the New York Philharmonic and at the Metropolitan Opera. His interpretations of Mozart, Beethoven and Mahler were renowned.

April 23   German soprano Elisabeth Schumann, 67, dies in New York. The silvery-voiced singer started her career in Hamburg in 1911 and later, at the recommendation of Richard Strauss, joined the Vienna State Opera. After the Nazi annexation of Austria she settled in America, eventually becoming the head of the voice department of the Curtis Institute in Philadelphia. She excelled in operas of Mozart and Strauss and was one of the great lieder singers of her generation.

May 15   Italian composer Italo Montemezzi, 76, dies in Visagio, near Verona, Italy. A product of the Milan Conservatory, he composed a work for chorus and orchestra entitled *Cantico dei Cantici* as his graduation piece. It was conducted by Arturo Toscanini. He quickly began composing operas. His operas are not in the least cerebral and do not pursue sentimentality to an excessive degree. *L'Amore dei tre re* is his best-known work and is also considered his masterpiece. Although its tale is medieval, it is a verismo opera. He wrote five other operas and two symphonic poems.

June 9   Violinist Adolf Busch, 60, dies in Gilford, Vermont. After studying in Cologne and Bonn, he became concertmaster of the Vienna Konzertverein. He later taught at the Musikhochschule in Berlin. In 1919 he helped create the Busch Quartet and the Busch-Serkin Trio.

June 10   Hans Beck dies in Copenhagen at the age of 91. One of the greatest dancers and ballet masters in the history of the Royal Danish Theatre, Beck was known primarily for his preservation of August Bournonville's ballets. It is due to his work that ballets such as *Napoli* are presented with the original choreography and in the original style. Beck was appointed ballet master in 1894 and served until 1915. Following his retirement he continued to supervise rehearsals until his death.

June 13   American soprano Emma Eames, 87, dies in New York. A pupil of Mathilde Marchesi, she was selected by Charles Gounod to sing Juliet in Paris in 1889, which was her operatic debut. Engagements in London and New York quickly followed. She was known for the beauty and clarity of her voice, if not for her histrionic ability or her warmth. A critic reviewing her performance of *Aida* once said, "There was skating on the Nile last night."

June 17   Argentine composer Alberto Williams, 89, dies in Buenos Aires. A pupil at the Paris Conservatoire, he studied organ with Cesar Franck. He founded his own conservatory in Argentina in 1893 and soon established 100 branches. He also organized a music publishing house called La Quena. He composed music that blended French impressionist elements, such as whole-tone scales and parallel chord progressions, with rhythmic elements common to Argentine dance music. He was Argentina's most prolific composer, having written nine symphonies, several dance suites, three violin sonatas and a great deal of piano music. He was also a poet.

June 18   Heinrich Schlusnus, 63, dies in Frankfurt. He was a baritone with the Berlin Opera and the Nuremberg Opera and sang at other leading opera houses in Europe. He also performed with the Chicago Opera.

Sep. 18   Soprano Frances Alda, 68, dies in Venice. Born in New Zealand in 1883, she studied with Mathilde Marchesi and made her debut as Manon at the Opera-Comique in 1904. She later married Giulio Gatti-Casazza, the manager of the Metropolitan Opera, from whom she was divorced in 1928. She left an autobiography entitled *Men, Women and Tenors.*

Dec. 14   Norwegian composer Fartein Valen, 65, dies in Haugesund, Norway. Valen was a pupil of Max Bruch. His early music reflected the influence of Brahms. He was later influenced by Arnold Schoenberg and developed an approach that he called "atonal polyphony." His work at-

tracted non-Norwegian performers, and a Valen Society was founded both in England and in Norway. His work includes five symphonies as well as choral and chamber music.

Dec. 25   Italian conductor Bernardino Molinari, 72, dies in Rome. He conducted many world-famous orchestras in South America and in Europe (including the Augusto Orchestra in Rome). His American debut was with the New York Philharmonic in 1928. He is especially known for conducting premiere performances of works by Ottorino Respighi and Gian Francesco Malipiero.

1952   Related Events

Iceland's first symphony orchestra is organized this year in Reykjavik by Norwegian conductor-composer Olav Keilland. Keilland has conducted the Oslo Philharmonic Orchestra (1931–45) and also this year becomes music director of the Bergen Philharmonic.

American conductor and musicologist Noah Greenberg establishes the New York Pro Musica Antiqua in New York this year. This ensemble specializes in medieval and renaissance music and employs authentic instruments in its productions. It also revives medieval liturgical music drama.

Merce Cunningham forms his own modern dance group this year.

Jan. 26   Black contralto Marian Anderson sings before the first integrated audience in Miami, Florida. Refunds are given to 250 whites who bought tickets before they learned there would be no segregation.

May 5   Gail Kubik is awarded the Pulitzer Prize for music for *Symphonie-Concertante.*

May 6   Charles Munch conducts the Boston Symphony Orchestra in Paris in a program of 20th-century music including works by Arthur Honegger, Samuel Barber, Maurice Ravel, Claude Debussy and Walter Piston. This event marks the first foreign tour of this orchestra.

May 8   A performance of Igor Stravinsky's *Le Sacre du printemps* takes place in Paris, conducted by Pierre Monteux. This event occurs thirty-nine years after the original premiere that sparked one of the greatest scandals of the century. Commenting on today's applause and bravos, Monteux says, "There was just as much noise the last time, but of a different tonality!" Monteux had conducted the world premiere on May 29, 1913.

May 9   Vladimir Ussachevsky publicly demonstrates some examples of his electronic music at the McMillan Theatre, Columbia University, New York City. The event also includes conventional instruments. Until last year, Ussachevsky was preoccupied with the composition of

"traditional" music. He arrived in America in 1930 and studied at Pomona College; he later earned his Ph.D. at the Eastman School of Music, Rochester, New York, with Howard Hanson and Bernard Rogers. Columbia University purchased an Ampex tape recorder (7 1/2 and 15 ips.) which Ussachevsky began experimenting with and found "that the tape recorder could be treated as an instrument of sound transformation," superimposing sounds to generate new, complex, and fascinating sonorities. Henry Cowell subsequently comments next year in the *Musical Quarterly*, "Ussachevsky is now in the process of incorporating some of these sounds into a composition. The pitfalls are many; we wish him well." Today's development is a sensation and quickly attracts the American Composer's Alliance and Broadcast Music, Inc., now sponsoring and organizing a concert to be directed by Leopold Stokowski this October.

May 19   Zwolftonspiel-Manifest, a manifesto by Josef Matthias Hauer, is publicized by the composer in Vienna. In it, Hauer claims to be the first to introduce the 12-tone method of musical composition. He writes, in part, "Zwolftonspiel performs the functions of galaxies and constitutes the formative dynamic centers of organic processes." Hauer then contests Arnold Schoenberg about who was first in introducing this method. In fact, Hauer's approach involves constructing 12-tone subjects, or themes, from 6-note tropes, or hexachords, and permits unrestricted permutation of each trope. Schoenberg's method, with its four basic operations applied to ordered 12-tone sets, solidifies the basis of what has become a new musical language.

May 28   Conductor and music director of the New York City Opera, Laszlo Halasz, is awarded $15,324.80 in a suit he brought against the management of the opera company. He was discharged on grounds that his conduct was "a threat to the prosperity and advancement of the City Center." He was accused of cost overruns, use of foul language and autocratic leadership. The American Guild of Musical Artists (AGMA) was also involved in the complaints. Although the jury awards Halasz the money, and press support for him is high, his tenure is over (he was officially dismissed and accepts the financial settlement stipulated by the jury). Halasz is succeeded by Joseph Rosenstock.

Oct.   HMV (The Gramophone Company, England) releases its first 45-RPM records this month. Other events in the recording industry this year include the appearance of EMI's (Electrical & Musical Industries) first 33 1/3-RPM long-playing discs; the publication of Volume I of Clough & Cumming's *World Encyclopedia of Recorded Music* — a complete classical music discography of different kinds of discs developed since the early part of the century; and the appearance of Cinerama, a new multitrack sound process for movies.

Dec. 11   *Carmen* becomes the first opera in history to be televised simultaneously in 27 cities and 31 movie houses across America. The opera is broadcast on a closed circuit by the Metropolitan Opera.

1953   Opera

Jan. 9   George Antheil's *Volpone* premieres at the University of Southern California at Los Angeles. The three-act opera is about an old man who engages in psychological manipulation of his heirs. It is based on the play of the same name by Ben Jonson.

Jan. 31   Vittorio Giannini's opera *The Taming of the Shrew*, premieres in Cincinnati, Ohio.

Feb. 7   *The Marriage*, by Bohuslav Martinu, with an English libretto based on a tale by Nikolai Gogol, premieres over television in New York City. This one-act opera was composed and designed specifically for television.

Feb. 21   Nicolai Berezowsky's opera *Babar the Elephant* receives its initial performance at Hunter College in New York City. Performed by the Little Orchestra Society and conducted by Thomas Scherman, it is based on the Babar stories of Jean de Brunhoff. The work is a children's opera, with a libretto by Dorothy Heyward and additional lyrics by Judith Randal. It is Berezowsky's most successful work.

March 11   Hanns Eisler's *Johannes Faustus* is performed for the first time in East Berlin. It is an opera that is based on the Faust legend but takes place on the island of Atlantis. Communist critics attack it, charging that its characters resemble American capitalists.

May 4   *The Mighty Casey*, by William Schuman, receives its world premiere in Hartford, Connecticut. The "baseball opera" is about a game in 1887 during which a pitcher's skill causes Casey to strike out. This was the same baseball game that inspired Ernest L. Thayer to write his famous poem "Casey at the Bat."

SCENE FROM *GLORIANA*

May 4   Frederick Delius' *Irmelin*, with a libretto by the composer, is premiered posthumously by Sir Thomas Beecham in Oxford. The three-act opera is about a young woman awaiting Mr. Right. It was composed 60 years ago.

May 25   Marc Blitzstein's one-act opera *The Harpies* receives its initial performance at the Manhattan School of Music in New York. He writes his own libretto. The opera, about a Greek man harassed by harpies, was composed in 1931, when it was commissioned by the League of Composers.

June 8   The first performance of Benjamin Britten's *Gloriana* takes place at Covent Garden in London. William Plomer writes the libretto, basing it on Lytton Strachey's *Elizabeth and Essex*. The three-act opera is commissioned by the Arts Council of Great Britain for the occasion of the coronation of Queen Elizabeth II. The gala opening marks the first time since 1736 that a British composer's opera is honored by the attendance of the reigning monarch.

June 23   Yuri Shaporin's grand opera *Decembrists* premieres at the Bolshoi Theater in Moscow. It is about five men who rebelled against Tsar Nicholas I in 1825. The work was performed in an earlier version in 1925, under the title *Paulina Goebel*. Shaporin has been working on today's version since 1947. The libretto underwent constant change and emendation — Aleksei Tolstoi even had his hands in it. Nevertheless, the libretto is considered weak,

and the music is regarded as more oratoriolike than operatic.

June 28   Boris Blacher's *Abstrakte Oper No. 1* receives its first performance at a festival of new music in Frankfurt. This unusual opera has a libretto by composer Werner Egk and is scored for three vocalists, two speakers, chorus and orchestra. The libretto is written of nonsense syllables, and the "abstraction" in the opera's title refers to scenes being communicated via emotions. The scenes are titled "Fear," "Love No. 1," "Pain," "Paris" and "Love No. 2."

Aug. 17   *Der Prozess*, by Gottfried von Einem, premieres at the Salzburg Festival. The libretto is by Boris Blacher and Heinz von Cramer and is based on the novel *The Trial*, by Franz Kafka. Although successful at this festival, the opera does not enter the repertoire.

Oct. 20   Carl Orff's *Astutuli* premieres in Munich. This opera is, according to Orff, "a Bavarian comedy." He writes his own text and scores the work for voices and 24 percussion instruments, including glasses and a beer stein. It is about a charlatan who manipulates local people to keep himself in women and liquor.

Dec. 4   Hans Werner Henze's *Das Ende einer Welt* is performed for the first time in Hamburg. This opera, composed for radio, is about doomsday and includes jazz elements.

1953   Dance

Jan. 6   George Balanchine's *Valse-fantaisie* — to music by Mikhail Glinka, and with costumes by Karinska — is performed for the first time by the New York City Ballet in New York. Tanaquil LeClerq, Melissa Hayden, Diana Adams and Nicholas Magallanes comprise the cast in this work.

Jan. 19   Erick Hawkins' modern dance work *Opening of the Eye* premieres in New York City. Music is by Lucia Dlugoszewski.

Jan. 26   Alwin Nikolais premieres new works at the Henry Street Playhouse in New York City. They are *Aqueonscape*, *Noumenon Mobilius*, and *Masks, Props and Mobiles*.

Feb. 1   *Somnambulism*, a one-act ballet choreographed by Kenneth MacMillan, receives its world premiere by the Sadler's Wells Choreographic Group in London. Music is by Stan Kenton. Three dancers express their anxieties and discover they are dreaming. It is MacMillan's first ballet. Maryon Lane, David Poole and MacMillan star.

March 3   John Cranko's ballet *The Shadow* is premiered by the Sadler's Wells Ballet at Covent Garden in London. The one-act ballet, set to Ernst von Dohnanyi's Suite for Orchestra in F Minor, deals with a young man unable to accept love until he faces the fears that beset him. Philip

Chatfield, Svetlana Beriosova, Rosemary Lindsay, and Bryan Ashbridge star.

March 10   Choreographer Lew Christensen's *Con amore* — to music by Rossini, with a libretto by James Graham-Lujan and costumes and scenery by James Bodrero — is premiered by the San Francisco Ballet in San Francisco. This spoof of love is danced by Nancy Johnson, Leon Danielian and Sally Bailey.

March 24   *Suite by Chance*, choreographed by Merce Cunningham, is performed for the first time in Urbana, Illinois. The music is by Hugo Wolf.

April 15   Doris Humphrey's *Ritmo jondo*, to music by Carlos Surinach, premieres in New York City.

May 14   The New York City Ballet premieres Jerome Robbins' *Afternoon of a Faun* to music by Claude Debussy. In this version of the ballet, the faun and nymph are two dancers who meet by chance in a studio. They ignore the romantic possibilities of the situation and focus on the image of themselves in the mirror. Tanaquil LeClerq and Francisco Moncion star.

May 23   Choreographer and dancer Alwin Nikolais premieres new modern dance compositions in New York

City. Presented at the Henry Street Playhouse, the works are entitled *Kaleidoscope* and *Forest of Three*.

June 2   The New York City Ballet premieres Jerome Robbins' *Fanfare* to celebrate the coronation of Queen Elizabeth II. The ballet uses Benjamin Britten's *Young Person's Guide to the Orchestra*, with the dancers representing the various instruments. Yvonne Mounsey, Irene Larsson, Jillana, Jacques d'Amboise, Todd Bolender, Herbert Bliss and Frank Hobi lead the cast.

June 2   Frederick Ashton's *Homage to the Queen* is performed for the first time by the Sadler's Wells Ballet in London. With music by Malcolm Arnold and costumes and scenery by Oliver Messel, the work celebrates the coronation of Queen Elizabeth II. The elements Air, Earth, Water and Fire salute the queen. Margot Fonteyn and Michael Somes are among the lead dancers.

Aug. 20   The Jose Limon Dance Company offers the first performance of Doris Humphrey's *Ruins and Visions* in New London, Connecticut. It is performed to Benjamin Britten's String Quartet. The abstract work is based on a series of poems by Stephen Spender. Jose Limon, Pauline Koner, Lucas Hoving and Lavina Nielsen lead the cast.

Aug. 21   *Hommage a Chopin* is performed by Les Ballets de l'Etoile at the Theatre de l'Etoile in Paris. The production is a group of three ballets choreographed by Maurice Bejart. This is the inaugural performance of this new ballet company established in Paris by Maurice Bejart and Jean Laurent. The company changes its name to Ballet-Theatre de Paris in the summer of 1957. The company dancing today is a distinct company from Ballet des Etoiles de Paris, which is established by Milorad Miskovitch and Irene Lidova in 1956 as Ballets 1956 de Paris.

Nov. 19   *Plectra and Percussion Dances*, by Harry Partch, receives its world premiere at International House in Berkeley, California. This dance piece consists of three sections: "Castor and Pollux," "Ring Around the Moon" and "Even Wild Horses." "Castor and Pollux" is a follow-up to Partch's earlier work *Oedipus* and is based on the satyr plays that followed Greek tragedy. Its dances depict the seduction of Leda by Zeus.

1953 Instrumental and Vocal Music

Jan. 1   *Suite hebraique* for viola and orchestra, by Ernest Bloch, receives its first performance in Chicago. Rafael Kubelik conducts the Chicago Symphony Orchestra.

Jan. 14   Symphony No. 7 (*Sinfonia Antartica*), by Ralph Vaughan Williams, receives its world premiere by Sir John Barbirolli and the Halle Orchestra in Manchester. The five-movement symphony was composed from Vaughan Williams' earlier film music to *Scott of the Antarctic*, which opened on December 30, 1948. The piece includes parts for chorus and wordless soprano.

Feb. 1   Dmitri Kabalevsky's Piano Concerto No. 3 in D Major premieres in Moscow, with the composer conducting and Vladimir Ashkenazy as soloist. This work is the last in a trilogy of concertos; the other two are for violin and orchestra and violoncello and orchestra.

Feb. 11   Carlos Chavez' Symphony No. 4 (*Sinfonia romantica*) is premiered by the Louisville Orchestra, the composer conducting. The three-movement symphony features melodies with tritones. Howard Taubman writes in the New York *Times*: "The piece is tonal, melodic, agreeably worked out and scored."

Feb. 13   Carl Orff's *Trionfo di Afrodite* — based on Catullus, Sappho and Euripides — premieres in Milan. The third part of a trilogy entitled *Trionfi* (which includes *Carmina Burana* and *Catulli Carmina*), the work is a depiction of the marriage ceremony. Howard Taubman writes in the New York *Times* (after the piece receives its American premiere three years from now): "It has to be conceded that Orff's techniques generate excitement and overwhelming waves of sound."

March 1   Henry Cowell's Symphony No. 8 premieres in Wilmington, Ohio. This four-movement work includes a mixed chorus that sings nonsense syllables.

March 11   *A Parable of Death*, by Lukas Foss, receives its initial performance in Louisville, Kentucky. Robert Whitney conducts, and Vera Zorina is the narrator. The work is a cantata for narrator, tenor, chorus and orchestra. Its text is based on several stories and poems by Rainer Maria Rilke.

March 13   Ernst Krenek's *Medea* for contralto and orchestra is premiered by the Philadelphia Orchestra. This is a dodecaphonic cantata.

April 11   Ernest Bloch's *Sinfonia breve* and *Concerto Grosso No. 2* for strings in G minor are premiered by Sir Malcolm Sargent and the BBC Symphony Orchestra.

April 11   Arthur Berger's *Ideas of Order* for orchestra, based on poetry of Wallace Stevens, is premiered by Dimitri Mitropoulos and the New York Philharmonic.

April 27   Robert Starer's Symphony No. 2 is premiered by Erich Leinsdorf in Tel Aviv, Israel.

May 26   *Kontra-Punkte*, by Karlheinz Stockhausen, receives its world premiere at the Electronic Studio of the West German Radio in Cologne. Scored for 10 instruments, the music generates counterpoint by a serially organized interplay between horizontal and vertical lines. It is Stockhausen's first serial composition. He later revises the work after Pierre Boulez remarks that it is too rigid. Stockhausen, now 24, has studied piano at the Musik-hochschule in Cologne and composition with Frank Martin, Olivier Messiaen and Darius Milhaud. He was also strongly influenced by the music of Anton Webern.

June 2   Alberto Ginastera's *Variaciones concertantes* is premiered by Igor Markevitch in Buenos Aires. This piece is a suite for chamber orchestra in 11 variations.

June 9   Scottish composer Iain Hamilton's Symphony No. 2 receives its first performance at the Cheltenham Festival in England.

July 26   Henri Sauguet's *Concerto d'Orphee* for violin and orchestra premieres at Aix-en-Provence, France. This work is in one movement.

Aug. 15   Arthur Benjamin's Concerto for Harmonica and Orchestra is premiered by Basil Cameron and the London Symphony Orchestra, with Larry Adler as soloist.

Oct. 1   Israeli composer Oedoen Partos' symphonic fantasy, *Ein-Gev* is premiered by Leonard Bernstein and the Israel Philharmonic Orchestra. This work receives the Unesco Prize and the Israeli State Prize.

Oct. 11   Olivier Messiaen's *Le reveil des oiseaux* for piano and orchestra premieres at the Donaueschingen Festival. This work is one of two by Messiaen that contain music derived entirely from bird song (the other is *Oiseaux exotiques*). The composer describes it as concerning "the awakening of birds at the beginning of a spring morning."

Oct. 16   Darius Milhaud's Symphony No. 5 premieres over Italian radio in Turin with the composer conducting. The work has four movements.

Oct. 19   *Praeludium*, by Igor Stravinsky, receives its initial performance. Robert Craft conducts in Los Angeles. This event is part of a program of the "Evenings on the Roof" series of concerts, founded in 1939 by Canadian-born music writer Peter Yates. *Praeludium* is scored for four saxophones, three trumpets, two trombones, strings, celesta, guitar and drums. Also performed on today's program is a new version, prepared by Stravinsky, of his *Tango*, originally composed in 1940.

Nov. 18   Peter Mennin's Symphony No. 6 is premiered by the Louisville Orchestra. This neobaroque piece is in three movements.

Dec. 1   Carlos Chavez' Symphony No. 5 receives its first performance by the Chamber Orchestra of Los Angeles, the composer conducting. This work is neoclassical.

Dec. 6   Henry Brant's *Rural Antiphonies* premieres in New York City. Brant is concerned with antiphonal music and concepts of universal space. This work is scored for five orchestras and five conductors, each with its own set of musical instructions relative to meter and tempo.

Dec. 12   Arthur Honegger's *Une cantate de Noel* is premiered by Paul Sacher and the Chamber Orchestra of Basel. Based on Christmas carols, the piece is scored for baritone solo, children's voices, mixed chorus, organ and orchestra.

Dec. 17   Symphony No. 10 by Dmitri Shostakovich, receives its world premiere in Leningrad. This is his first symphony in about 10 years. Shostakovich describes it as expressing the "thoughts and aspirations of our contemporaries" regarding peace. It is in four movements and features motivic material derived from the composer's "motto" theme — D, E-flat, C, B — formulated from letters of the composer's name. He has used this theme in several other works. The symphony is the first of the composer's new works to be premiered after the death of Joseph Stalin. It causes a stir in Soviet music circles, receiving both favorable and unfavorable criticism. Shostakovich survives the criticism and, next summer, is given the title "People's Artist of the USSR," signaling a liberalized attitude toward music by party officials in the early post-Stalin period.

1953   Births, Deaths and Debuts

Jan. 10   Austrian pianist Paul Badura-Skoda makes his New York recital debut. He later becomes artist-in-residence at the University of Wisconsin.

March 5   Russian composer Sergei Prokofiev, 61, dies in Moscow. His early training was with his mother, an amateur pianist. By the time he was 9, he had composed an opera, *The Giant*. He composed another opera, *Ondine*, and several other works and studied with Reinhold Gliere before entering the Saint Petersburg Conservatory at age 13. There he studied composition (with Nikolai Rimsky-Korsakov, Anatoly Liadov and others) and conducting with Nicolas Tcherepnin. He graduated in 1914, winning a grand piano (the Anton Rubinstein Prize) for his First Piano Concerto. His postgraduation piano works — *Visions fugitives* and *Sarcasms*, in particular — displayed a percussive use of the piano without forfeiting melodic grace.

Scythian Suite was his first notable orchestral work; by age 26 he had completed his *Classical Symphony* (this was premiered in 1918), after which Prokofiev left the Soviet Union via Siberia and Japan for America, where he performed in several cities, including New York and Chicago. He then proceeded to Paris and collaborated with Serge Diaghilev on the ballet *Chout* and on two other ballets. Serge Koussevitzky found himself attracted to Prokofiev's music and began publishing and commissioning his works.

Between 1921 and 1932 Prokofiev toured and lived in several places: Chicago, the Soviet Union and Paris, finally settling in the Soviet Union and occasionally making concert appearances in other countries. He married Spanish soprano Lina Llubera in 1923; after staying with her for about 17 years, he lived with Myra Mendelson, a writer (he did not divorce Llubera). During his Soviet years (1932–53) he was often the target of Soviet music critics bent on turning him away from any approach to composition that was remotely intellectual. Prokofiev resisted, for the most part, and remained true to his art, composing music that was decisively modern and yet flourished in spite of the varying temperamental attitudes of the Soviet music establishment. Virtually all of his works were performed and published and had a strong influence on younger Soviet composers. Several of his pieces — *Classical Symphony* (composed in 1916–17), Piano Concerto No. 2 (premiered in 1913), *Love for Three Oranges* (premiered in 1921) — entered the international repertoire immediately after their premieres.

As a composer, he remained untouched by the work of formidable contemporaries, such as Arnold Schoenberg. His music evolved in a distinct progression from tonality to polytonality to atonality but was never dodecaphonic. His rhythms — largely asymmetrical — evoked a powerful sense of movement that sometimes bordered on primitivism. His melodies traversed wide intervals and, combined with often scintillating orchestrations, sometimes empowered orchestral sonorities to become overwhelming. His idiomatic writing for instruments was always practical. Prokofiev considered his best piece, according to Dmitri Kabalevsky, to be his opera *War and Peace*. Parts of the opera were performed during his lifetime — the complete opera is premiered two years from now.

Prokofiev was extremely prolific and composed for virtually every combination of voices and instruments. These works include eight operas, seven ballets, seven symphonies, three piano concertos, two string quartets, nine piano sonatas and an extraordinary number of incidental, choral, orchestral, chamber and piano pieces and songs. He also composed a good deal of film music and, in collaboration with Soviet filmmaker Sergei Eisenstein, enabled the Soviet Union to move into the foreground of this new art form. Two such examples are *Alexander Nevsky* and *Ivan the Terrible*. Prokofiev's last years were under the oppressive torment of Joseph Stalin and Stalin's influence on musical life in the Soviet Union. Prokofiev's death today occurs, ironically, less than one hour before the death of Stalin.

July 5 Italian baritone Titta Ruffo, 76, dies in Florence, Italy. He made his debut in 1898 and then sang in the European houses. He first came to America in 1912 to sing with the Philadelphia-Chicago Opera Company and, in 1922, with the Metropolitan Opera in New York. After his retirement in 1929, he appeared in several movies. He made his last public appearance at the opening of Radio City Music Hall in New York in 1932. He had an enormously powerful voice and excelled in verismo roles.

Aug. 14 German bass-baritone Friedrich Schorr, 64, dies in Farmington, Connecticut. A specialist in Wagnerian roles, he started his career in 1911 and later became a member of the Berlin State Opera. He came to the Metropolitan Opera in 1924 and remained there until 1943. He sang four seasons at the Bayreuth festival. Schorr had a voice of exceptional beauty. This, combined with a fine musical sensibility and a noble quality, made him one of the finest Wagnerian baritones of the century.

Aug. 27 Russian-born composer Nicolai Berezowsky, 53, dies in New York City from an overdose of sedatives. He was a graduate of the Court Chapel of Saint Petersburg and, in his early years, performed as a violinist. He left the Soviet Union in 1920. He settled in New York, where he again worked as a violinist and studied composition with Rubin Goldmark at the Juilliard Graduate School. In addition to performing in the violin section of the New York Philharmonic and as a member of the Elizabeth Sprague Coolidge String Quartet, he conducted radio performances. His music is rooted in Russian nationalism. His opera *Babar the Elephant*, premiered this past February 21, is his best-known piece. Other works include four symphonies, several concertos, orchestral overtures, two string quartets, a cantata (*Gilgamesh*) and chamber music. Besides the opera mentioned, only his chamber music remains in the repertoire.

Sep. 1 French violinist Jacques Thibaud, 72, dies in an airplane crash on his way to French Indochina. Heard playing in a cafe by Edouard Colonne, he was hired to play in Colonne's orchestra. He made a solo debut in 1898 and was very successful thereafter in both Europe and America. Later he, Alfred Cortot and Pablo Casals formed a trio and set musical standards that are still being aspired to by players of chamber music.

Sep. 13 Hungarian conductor Georg Solti makes his American debut at the San Francisco Opera.

Oct. 3 English composer Sir Arnold Bax, 69, dies in Cork, Ireland. A product of the Royal Academy of Music, he quickly became enamored of Irish folk song and incorporated such materials in his music. He visited Russia in 1910 and composed a few works (including *In a Vodka Shop*) in a style reminiscent of Russian postromantic music. Although he was a fine conductor and pianist, his shy nature prevented him from appearing as a soloist. He was knighted in 1937 and became Master of the King's Musick in 1941, succeeding Sir Walford Davies. He was quite prolific and wrote neoromantic music enhanced by elements of French impressionism. He composed two ballets, seven symphonies, many symphonic poems and orchestral works (including *Tintagel* and *Coronation March*), concertos, vocal music, three string quartets and much chamber music. He also wrote an autobiography, *Farewell My Youth* (London, 1943).

Oct. 8 English contralto Kathleen Ferrier, 41, dies of cancer in London. Known for her taste and musicianship, she was at home in oratorio, opera and on the recital stage. She did not take singing lessons until age 25 but quickly became successful. She sang in the premiere of Benjamin Britten's *Rape of Lucrezia.*

Oct. 29   American pianist William Kapell, 31, is killed in an airplane crash near San Francisco on his way back from a concert tour in Australia. After encouragement from Artur Rubinstein and studies with Olga Samaroff at the Philadelphia Conservatory of Music, Kapell debuted in 1941. His early death ends a brilliant career.

Nov. 4   Elizabeth Sprague Coolidge, 90, dies in Cambridge, Massachusetts. Patroness of a great deal of new music, she was also a composer. She was responsible for the establishment of the Berkshire Music Festival. She created a medal, which is administered by the Music Division of the Library of Congress for services in the field of chamber music. In music circles she was known as "the fairy godmother of chamber music."

Dec. 4   American composer Daniel Gregory Mason, 80, dies in Greenwich, Connecticut. The grandson of organist, composer and conductor Lowell Mason, nephew of music educator William Mason and son of Henry Mason (a cofounder of the piano firm Mason & Hamlin), he was a product of Harvard University. He later studied with Percy Goetschius (theory), George Whitefield Chadwick (orchestration) and Vincent d'Indy. He joined the faculty of Columbia University in 1910 and remained there until 1942. His music is rooted in German postromanticism; he also combined melodic materials from New England and the South and strictly opposed a pluralistic esthetic for American music, speaking out against the inclusion of African and Jewish melodies and harmonies. Despite the accessiblity of his tunes, his work quickly fades into oblivion because of its lack of original character. He composed three symphonies, several orchestral works and a great

deal of chamber music. His best-known works are a clarinet sonata (composed in 1915) and *Chanticleer,* an orchestral overture (premiered in 1928). He also wrote many books and articles about music.

Dec. 9   Russian conductor Issay Dobrowen, 61, dies in Oslo, Norway. Born Issay Barabeichek, he studied at the Nizhy-Novgorod Conservatory and the Moscow Conservatory. He became conductor of the Moscow Opera and conducted the first German performance of Modest Mussorgsky's *Boris Godunov* at the Dresden State Opera in 1922. He then conducted in Berlin and Sofia before making his American debut in 1931. His American appearances were not well received, and he returned to Europe. He conducted the Budapest Opera between 1936 and 1939, and when World War II began, he conducted in Sweden. This led to his period of greatest success, in terms of conducting both opera and symphonic music: He conducted the Stockholm Opera and the Philharmonic of Goteborg. He was also an active composer and wrote romantic concertos, piano pieces and other works.

Dec. 11   English composer and conductor Albert Coates, 71, dies in Milnerton, South Africa. This musician studied at Liverpool University and studied cello, piano and conducting (with Arthur Nikisch) at the Leipzig Conservatory. He made his conducting debut with the Leipzig Opera and, in 1910, became a co-conductor of the Dresden Opera. After conducting the Imperial Opera of Saint Petersburg, he began specializing in Wagnerian operas and in the music of Alexander Scriabin. After some work in America, he conducted the Berlin State Opera and the Vienna Philharmonic before settling in South Africa, where he was conductor of the Johannesburg Symphony Orchestra. He also composed a great deal of music but wrote nothing that entered the repertoire.

1953   *Related Events*

Sir Arthur Bliss is named Master of the Queen's Musick this year. He succeeds Sir Arnold Bax.

The Dance Museum opens this year at the Royal Theater in Stockholm. It features a display of Asian dance materials, including instruments, masks and costumes collected by Rolf de Mare, founder of the Ballets Suedois.

Technological developments in the recording industry this year include the appearance of the Neumann M-49 condenser microphone for recording and the adoption (by the Recording Industry Association) of playback curve as an equalization standard for the record industry in America. The first issue of the Bielrfelder Katalog — a

German version of the American Schwann Catalog — is published in Germany this year.

Karlheinz Stockhausen succeeds Herbert Eimert as director of the Cologne Studio in West Germany.

Nicolas Slonimsky's book, *Lexicon of Musical Invective, Critical Assaults on Composers Since Beethoven's Time,* is published this year. The book contains nasty and humorous reviews about many famous composers, including many 20th century composers. Slonimsky asks in his opening section, "Why do music critics, who are in private life, most of them, the mildest of creatures, resort so often to the language of vituperation?" The book also contains an "Invecticon," in which reviews are indexed alphabetically according to derogatory terms mentioned in the review, such as "amoeba weeps," "massacre du printemps," and "whole-tone daisy chains."

Jan. 1 Choreographer George Balanchine marries dancer Tanaquil LeClerq.

Sep. 27 Wagnerian soprano Helen Traubel announces her refusal to sign a contract with the Metropolitan Opera

because its manager, Rudolf Bing, has criticized her for playing in nightclubs.

Nov. 19 Tenor David Poleri walks off the stage in a fit of temper during a performance of *Carmen* with the New York City Opera Company in Chicago, leaving Carmen to stab herself to death. He is later dismissed by the company.

1954 Opera

March 12 *Moses und Aron*, a 12-tone opera by Arnold Schoenberg, receives its posthumous world premiere over radio in Hamburg (the section entitled "Dance Around the Golden Calf" was performed separately on July 2, 1951 — 11 days before Schoenberg's death). The opera has two acts (Schoenberg intended a third but never finished it; he left instructions that if his death occurred before the third act was completed, that act should be played as spoken drama). The first two acts were completed in 1932, but because of the musical complexity of the score, the opera had to wait 22 years for its premiere. It is based on Exodus and is about the struggle between Moses, God and Aron (Schoenberg spells Aron with one *a* because, with two, the title would have 13 letters — he was superstitious about the number 13). The entire opera is based on one 12-tone row, or set, and features Sprechstimme. The interlude between the two acts contains a double fugue.

Today's performance is not very successful — in part, because the radio premiere precludes the visual impact of dramatic staging. Today's performance is conducted by Hans Rosbaud. Peter Gradenwitz subsequently writes in the New York *Times*, "The opera, when performed only as a monumental fragment, without the final act, puts Schoenberg's own credo into a somewhat faulty perspective."

April 1 *The Tender Land*, a three-act opera by Aaron Copland, receives its world premiere at the New York City Opera. Horace Everett's libretto is the story of the protected life of a midwestern farm girl. It was commissioned by Rodgers and Hammerstein for the 30th anniversary of the League of Composers.

April 4 American composer Peggy Glanville-Hicks' *The Transposed Heads*, based on the story by Thomas Mann, premieres in Louisville, Kentucky.

June 1 Darius Milhaud's *David* premieres in a concert version in Jerusalem. Armand Lunel wrote the libretto, which is based on the first and second books of Samuel and on the Book of Kings. The work, in five acts, was commissioned for the King David Festival by the Koussevitzky Foundation.

June 17 *A Dinner Engagement*, a one-act comedy by Lennox Berkeley, premieres at the Aldeburgh Festival, England. Paul Dehn's libretto is a comedy about an impoverished couple's attempt to marry off their daughter to a wealthy prince.

July 28 George Antheil's opera *The Brothers* premieres in Denver, Colorado.

Aug. 7 Jean Francaix' *Paris a nous deux* receives its initial performance in Fontainebleau at the American Conservatory. The farcical opera satirizes Parisian society.

Aug. 17 Rolf Liebermann's *Penelope* has its premiere performance in Salzburg at the Festspielhaus. The libretto, by Heinrich Strobel, is a modern version of the myth of Penelope and Ulysses. The conductor is George Szell.

Sep. 14 The first performance of Benjamin Britten's *The Turn of the Screw* takes place at the Teatro la Fenice in Venice. Myfanwy Piper's libretto is based on the story by Henry James. The opera is well received and enjoys frequent performances. Scored for 13 instruments, the opera is constructed from 12-tone variations. Three years from now, Ross Parmenter writes in the New York *Times*: "Whatever one might think of the work as an opera, one thing is clear: it is a remarkably sensitive piece of music."

Sep. 22 Lennox Berkeley's *Nelson* premieres in London. The three-act opera is about Admiral Nelson's affair with Lady Hamilton.

Dec. 3 *Troilus and Cressida*, a three-act opera by William Walton, premieres in London at Covent Garden. The libretto, which was adapted from Chaucer's *Troilus and Criseyde*, is by Christopher Hassall. Today's premiere is heralded with more publicity than any operatic premiere in London since Benjamin Britten's *Peter Grimes*. Ronald Eyer comments on Walton's music, writing in *Musical America* (New York) that Walton "is rarely British, frequently Italian, but most consistently German and middle European in his derivations."

BILLBOARD POSTER FOR *THE SAINT OF BLEECKER STREET*

Dec. 4   Ildebrando Pizzetti's *La figlia de Jorio* is performed for the first time in Naples at the Teatro San Carlo. Pizzetti adapted the libretto from a tragedy by Gabriele d'Annunzio. A story involving sorcery, murder and a burning at the stake, it is considered one of Pizzetti's better works.

Dec. 23   Bernard Herrmann's *A Christmas Carol* is broadcast over CBS TV in New York City. This work is a musical play composed specifically for television. The libretto is based on the tale by Charles Dickens.

Dec. 27   Gian-Carlo Menotti's *The Saint of Bleecker Street* receives its first performance in New York City at the Broadway Theater. Menotti writes his own text and directs the production about a religious woman in New York City's Italian immigrant community who receives the stigmata. Thomas Schippers conducts. The work is enthusiastically received and runs for 100 performances. It wins the 1954 Drama Critics Circle Award for finest musical play and a Pulitzer Prize for music. Olin Downes says the music "dexterously underscores every word of dialogue and every instant of action."

1954 Dance

Jan. 19   The premiere performance of George Balanchine's *Opus 34* is danced by the New York City Ballet in New York. The music, Arnold Schoenberg's *Musical Accompaniment to a Motion Picture Scene*, is played twice — once for each section of the dance. The dancers — suggesting surgeons, dancing corpses and nurses — include Diana Adams, Patricia Wilde, Nicholas Magallanes, Francisco Moncion, Tanaquil LeClerq and Herbert Bliss.

Jan. 29   Jose Limon's modern dance piece *Ode to the Dance*, to music by Samuel Barber, premieres in New York City.

Feb. 2   George Balanchine's *The Nutcracker* receives its premiere by the New York City Ballet in New York. The costumes are by Karinska and the lavish settings by Horace Armistead. This production is noted for using the full score, including a singing chorus, and 39 children as well as adults. The star dancers are Maria Tallchief, Nicholas Magallanes and Tanaquil LeClerq. Choreography for the battle between the Nutcracker and the Mouse King is by Jerome Robbins.

Feb. 12   The Bolshoi Ballet premieres Leonid Lavrovsky's evening-length ballet *The Stone Flower*. The work, set to music by Sergei Prokofiev, was inspired by folk tales of the Ural Mountains. Galina Ulanova, Maya Plisetskaya, Vladimir Preobrazhensky and Alexei Yermolaev have the principal roles. The work is deemed a failure and is soon taken out of the repertoire.

Feb. 18   Jerome Robbins' *Quartet*, to music by Sergei Prokofiev, is premiered in New York by the New York City Ballet. The plotless ballet contains elements of folk dancing. The dancers include Patricia Wilde, Jillana, Jacques d'Amboise and Todd Bolender.

Feb. 25   John Cranko's *The Lady and the Fool* is premiered by the Sadler's Wells Theater Ballet in Oxford. It is choreographed to music by Giuseppe Verdi, arranged by Charles Mackerras, with scenery and costumes by Richard Beer. The dancers are Patricia Miller, Kenneth MacMillan and Johaar Mosaval. A lady, taking two clowns to a ball, falls in love first with one, then with the other.

Aug. 19   Jose Limon's one-act ballet *The Traitor* — to music by Gunther Schuller, with decor by Paul Trautvetter and costumes by Pauline Lawrence — is performed for the first time by the Jose Limon Dance Company in New London, Connecticut. Jose Limon and Lucas Hoving lead the cast in this work based on the tale of Jesus' betrayal by Judas.

Sep. 14   George Balanchine's *Ivesiana*, choreographed to various compositions by Charles Ives, receives its world premiere by the New York City Ballet in New York. This work incorporates images suggested to Balanchine by the music and creates a choreographic ebb and flow with and against the music. The principal dancers include Janet

Reed, Francisco Moncion, Patricia Wilde, Jacques d'Amboise, Allegra Kent, Todd Bolender, Diana Adams, Herbert Bliss and Tanaquil LeClerq. The ballet is in six episodes.

Dec. 8   Merce Cunningham premieres his modern dance work *Minutiae* at the Brooklyn Academy of Music. The music is by John Cage, costumes by Remy Charlip and scenery by Robert Rauschenberg and Jasper Johns.

1954 Instrumental and Vocal Music

Jan. 9   Carlos Surinach's *Sinfonietta flamenca* premieres in Louisville, Kentucky. This work includes flamenco rhythms.

Jan. 17   Symphony No. 6, by Edmund Rubbra, premieres in London. The work is neoromantic.

Jan. 23   Heitor Villa-Lobos' overture *Alvorado na floresta tropical* premieres in Louisville, Kentucky. The work depicts birds in the jungles of Brazil.

Jan. 23   Igor Stravinsky's Septet receives its first performance at the Dumbarton Oaks estate in Washington, D.C. with the composer conducting. Scored for violin, viola, cello, clarinet, horn, bassoon and piano (or harpsichord), it is in three movements and is based on baroque dance forms.

Feb. 1   Havergal Brian's Symphony No. 8 is premiered by Sir Adrian Boult and the London Philharmonic Orchestra. This one-movement symphony is in the key of B-flat minor. It was inspired by Goethe's ballad "Die Braut von Corinth." Brian is now 78.

Feb. 8   Anton Webern's Three Songs, Op. 18, is premiered posthumously by Robert Craft in Los Angeles, with Grace-Lynne Martin as soloist.

Feb. 13   *O Frabulous Day! (The Jabberwock)*, by Harry Partch, is performed for the first time at a Young People's Concert of the Mill Valley Outdoor Art Club. It is scored for intoning voice, harmonic canon and bass marimba and — along with *The Mock Turtle Song* (not premiered today) — comprises Partch's two-part piece *Two Settings from Lewis Carroll*.

Feb. 13   Wallingford Riegger's Variations for Piano and Orchestra is performed for the first time by the Louisville Orchestra.

Feb. 20   Concerto for Orchestra, by Alan Hovhaness, receives its first performance in Louisville, Kentucky.

Feb. 21   Ernst van Dohnanyi's *American Rhapsody* receives its initial performance in Athens, Ohio with the composer conducting. This is Dohnanyi's first orchestral piece composed in America.

March 4   Ernst Krenek's Cello Concerto premieres in Los Angeles.

March 13   Cristobal Halffter's neobaroque Piano Concerto premieres in Madrid.

March 17   Quincy Porter's Concerto for Two Pianos and Orchestra is premiered by the Louisville Orchestra. The

work was commissioned by this orchestra and subsequently wins a Pulitzer Prize for music.

March 20   *Rhapsodic Variations* — a work mixing tape-recorded music with live symphony orchestra — receives its world premiere in Louisville, Kentucky. Otto Luening and Vladimir Ussachevsky co-composed the work; it is conducted by Robert Whitney. This event marks the first performance of tape-recorded music with a full symphony orchestra. Six and one-half years from now, the work is reviewed in *De Nieuwe Dag* (Amsterdam): "In our opinion it seems to be a morganatic marriage. . . ."

May 6   Hans Werner Henze's *Ode an den Westwind* for cello and orchestra premieres in Bielefeld. The piece was inspired by Percy Bysshe Shelley's poem "Ode to the West Wind."

May 29   Henry Cowell's Symphony No. 11 (*Seven Rituals of Music*) receives its first performance in Louisville, Kentucky. The symphony depicts what Cowell describes as the seven stages of life: grief, work, love, dance, magic, war and death.

May 30   *Odisseia de uma raca*, by Heitor Villa-Lobos, receives its world premiere at the opening concert of the 28th festival of the International Society for Contemporary Music in Haifa, Israel. The work is a symphonic poem that expresses the composer's respect for the state of Israel. Villa-Lobos states, "When the Universe was formed, God created a heroic race which lived and suffered, and became victorious in Israel."

June 3   Japanese composer Yoritsune Matsudaira's *Metamorphoses on Saibara* and Israeli composer Josef Tal's Viola Concerto receive their initial performance at this year's International Society for Contemporary Music festival in Haifa.

June 13   Ralph Vaughan Williams' Concerto for Tuba and Orchestra is premiered by Sir John Barbirolli and the London Symphony Orchestra, with Philip Catelinet as soloist. The three-movement work is one of the few tuba concertos ever composed.

Aug. 14   Alexander Tcherepnin's *The Lost Flute* premieres in Fish Creek, Wisconsin. Thor Johnson conducts, and his wife, Hsien Ming, is narrator. The work, featuring six Chinese poems, is scored for narrator and orchestra.

Aug. 25   Luigi Nono's oratorio *La victoire de Guernica*, with a text by Paul Eluard, premieres in Darmstadt. The music was inspired by the pre-World War II air raid on Guernica,

Spain, which also inspired Pablo Picasso's famous painting *Guernica*. Today's concert takes place as part of the International Festival for New Music.

Aug. 28   Vincent Persichetti's Symphony No. 5 (*Symphony of Strings*) receives its first performance by the Louisville Orchestra. The symphony has one movement.

Sep. 8   *Hodie*, by Ralph Vaughan Williams, premieres at the Worcester Cathedral, the composer conducting. This Christmas cantata is scored for soprano, tenor, baritone, mixed chorus, boys' voices and orchestra. The texts are from Milton, other English poets and the Bible. Today's performance takes place as part of the Three Choirs Festival.

Sep. 12   Leonard Bernstein's *Serenade* for violin, string orchestra, harp and percussion receives its initial performance by Isaac Stern in Venice, the composer conducting. The concert takes place as part of an international festival of contemporary music. It is in five movements and was inspired by Plato's *Symposium*. Bernstein comments in the program notes, "The music, like the dialogue, is a series of related statements in praise of love, and generally follows the Platonic form through the succession of speakers at the banquet."

Sep. 18   Virgil Thomson's Concerto for Flute, Strings, Harp, Celesta and Percussion premieres in Venice, where an international festival of contemporary music is taking place. The composer describes the three-movement piece as "a portrait conceived as a concerto for nightingale and strings."

Sep. 20   Igor Stravinsky's *In Memoriam Dylan Thomas* receives its initial performance in Los Angeles. Robert Craft conducts. Scored for tenor, string quartet and four trombones, its text is Dylan Thomas' famous poem "Do not go gentle into that good night." In this work, Stravinsky subjects a pentad (a group or segment of five notes) to various serial operations, including rotation (the operation in which the notes involved are rotated one or more positions).

Oct. 3   Luigi Dallapiccola's *Variazioni per orchestra* premieres in Louisville, Kentucky. The music is composed from a 12-tone row, or set, with the tritone occurring between the first and last elements.

Oct. 17   Rolf Liebermann's Concerto for Jazz Band and Symphony Orchestra premieres at the Donaueschingen Festival. This unusual work is dodecaphonic and has eight movements. The piano part deploys the 12-tone row, or set, vertically; the muted divisi strings deploy it horizontally. Also premiered at this festival today are two works by American composers. They are John Cage's *34' 46.776"* and Morton Feldman's *Intersection for Magnetic Tape*. The title of the Cage piece refers to its duration, derived by observing imperfections on a sheet of paper and from *I Ching*, the Chinese book of oracles. Feldman's title was inspired by the moment a green traffic light flashes at a street intersection. Also this year, Cage composes *Williams Mix* — his first fully electronic composition.

Oct. 19   Karlheinz Stockhausen's *Studie I* and *Studie II*, Herbert Eimert's *Glockenspiel, Etude uber Tongemische* and Henri Posseur's *Seismogramme* are among the musical works comprising a concert of electronic music called "Music of Our Time" broadcast by Cologne Radio in West Germany. This event marks the major official broadcast illuminating the new form commonly known as electronic music.

Oct. 20   Alberto Ginastera's symphonic pastorale *Pampeana No. 3* premieres in Louisville, Kentucky. The work is based on a 12-tone row, or set.

Nov. 17   *Fantasy for Piano and Orchestra*, by Roy Harris, receives its initial performance in Hartford, Connecticut.

Nov. 17   *Ahavah*, by David Diamond, receives its first performance in Washington, D.C. The piece is scored for narrator and orchestra.

Nov. 17   Edmund Rubbra's Symphony No. 6 premieres in London. This four-movement work is based on a four-note motive.

Nov. 26   Witold Lutoslawski's Concerto for Orchestra receives its first performance in Warsaw. The music, in three movements, is based on Polish folk themes. Lutoslawski is now 41.

Dec. 2   *Deserts*, by Edgard Varese, receives its world premiere in Paris, as Hermann Scherchen conducts at the Theatre des Champs-Elysees. Scored for wind instruments, percussion and electronic sounds, it is one of the first works scored for prerecorded magnetic tape and orchestral instruments (*Rhapsodic Variations*, by Otto Luening and Vladimir Ussachevsky, scored for magnetic tape and full orchestra, premiered this past March 20). Varese states that the title refers to "that remote inner space no telescope can reach, where man is alone, a world of mystery and essential loneliness." A reviewer in *High Fidelity* magazine subsequently writes, "these powerfully imagined instrumental sounds are brilliantly dovetailed with the taped interludes through skillful use of percussion." The performance creates a sensation; it results in Varese being invited to Germany and to Bennington College.

Dec. 3   Samuel Barber's oratorio *Prayers of Kierkegaard* receives its initial performance by Charles Munch and the Boston Symphony Orchestra. Leontyne Price is soloist. It is scored for soprano solo, chorus and orchestra. The texts are from the Danish philosopher's writings. Olin Downes writes in the New York *Times*, "Universality is the suggestion, a universality that does not dismiss but includes inevitably the consciousness of the infinite mercy, the infinite tenderness, the cosmic design."

Dec. 11   Carlos Chavez's Symphony No. 3 premieres in Caracas, the composer conducting. Commissioned by Claire Booth Luce, the work has four movements.

Dec. 17   Vincent Persichetti's Symphony No. 4 receives its initial performance by Eugene Ormandy and the Philadelphia Orchestra. It is a four-movement work. Persichetti recently became director of publications at Elkan-Vogel Company, a music publishing house in Philadelphia.

1954   Births, Deaths and Debuts

March 14   Polish composer Ludomir Rogowski, 72, dies in Dubrovnik, Yugoslavia. A pupil of Hugo Riemann in Leipzig, he later founded and conducted the Vilna Symphony Orchestra in Poland. He composed four operas, two ballets, six symphonies, two string quartets, choral and chamber music.

April 5   French composer Claude Delvincourt, 66, is killed in an auto crash in Bivio de Albinia, Orbetello, Italy. He was a pupil of Charles-Marie Widor, a winner of the Prix de Rome, and a director of the Paris Conservatoire. He is best known for his stage works, including the mystery play *Lucifer.* He also composed some orchestral and chamber music.

May 16   Austrian conductor Clemens Krauss, 61, dies in Mexico City. This eminent conductor held such posts as director of the Vienna State Opera and conductor of the Vienna Philharmonic, music director of the Munich Opera and of the Mozarteum in Salzburg. He was a friend of Richard Strauss and wrote the libretto for his opera *Capriccio.*

May 19   American composer Charles Ives, 79, dies in New York City. He was the son of a bandleader of the First Connecticut Heavy Artillery, which played throughout the Civil War. Ives studied piano and cornet with his father in his early teens. By age 13 he was playing organ at the Danbury Church. During this period he began to improvise music that mixed and mismatched keys — this approach would lead to a compositional style that was radical and exceptionally unorthodox. He composed *Variations on America* for organ at age 17. After attending Danbury High School, he went to Yale and studied organ with Dudley Buck and composition with Horatio Parker. It was his studies with Parker that instilled in Ives a traditional approach to musical composition — an approach he assimilated and later discarded. While at Yale, he composed his first two symphonies (the second was not premiered until three years ago). Ives graduated in 1898 and entered the insurance business, believing that although he desired a vocation in music, it was unfair to subject his family to the economic hardships of that vocation. He would later marry Harmony Twitchell and adopt a daughter. He co-founded the insurance firm of Ives & Myrick in 1907 and played organ at the Central Presbyterian Church in New York City. As a businessman, he was highly successful; he aggressively pursued both insurance and composition (composing in the evenings and on weekends) until he suffered a serious heart attack in 1918. He also began suffering from diabetes and, between the two health problems, was forced to minimize both pursuits. By 1930, when he retired from business, he had all but stopped composing.

In 1919 he published the *Concord Sonata,* copies of which he distributed free of charge to his friends and to anyone who wanted them; he did the same thing in 1922 with his collection *114 Songs.* Ives lived the life of a recluse, never attending concerts and never purchasing a record player. His personality was that of an intense introvert who valued privacy, home and family and who could care less about the musical establishment. For this reason (and also because of his health) his music had to wait until the 1940s and 1950s to come before the world.

Ives was the most important American composer of the first half of the century. His work explored polytonality, atonality and the beginnings of the 12-tone system. His *Tone-Roads,* composed between 1911 and 1915, includes the use of a 12-tone row, or set; Schoenberg's introduction of the 12-tone system would come some 10 years later. Unlike Schoenberg, Ives did not introduce a new grammar and syntax of harmony but related the 12 pitch classes of the chromatic scale to one another in a similar premise as an experiment. Ives also employed other devices that could be termed anticipatory of unfolding trends in 20th-century music: cross rhythms, different meters and rhythmic devices operating simultaneously (such as syncopation to displace accents); tone clusters to create percussive sounds; notation freely mixing sharps and flats, often without key signatures and chords spelled contextually rather than according to some pervasive tonal center or key signature; dynamics that spanned the spectrum of intensities and were notated with great care; the use of the piano in massive orchestras; antiphonal placement of ensembles and orchestras, sometimes demanding at least two conductors; and employment of quarter tones in some works.

His works include four symphonies and incomplete fragments of another, the *Universe Symphony.* Like Alexander Scriabin's *Mysterium,* which was conceived to be performed in the Himalaya mountains but was never begun because of Scriabin's death, Ives' *Universe Symphony* was conceived to employ 6 to 10 orchestras performing on different mountaintops, each in its own "independent time orbit." Other works include *Calcium Light Night* for chamber orchestra (composed in 1898–1907); *The Pond* (composed in 1906); *Space and Duration* for string quartet and a "very mechanical piano" (composed in 1907); four violin sonatas; two string quartets; *Psalm 67* (composed in 1898); *Psalm 90* (composed in 1898–1901, later revised); and *Three Quarter-tone Piano Pieces* (composed in 1903–24).

June 13   Russian composer Nicolas Obouhov, 62, dies in Paris. A pupil of Nicolas Tcherepnin at the Saint Petersburg Conservatory, he later studied with Maurice Ravel in Paris. Obouhov was somewhat bizarre: He would use his blood to mark places in his scores and often signed his name "Nicolas l'illumine." The finale of his 2,000-page score *Le livre de vie* represented a Russia in which both prerevolutionary and postrevolutionary groups in Russian and Soviet life would be reconciled. This work occupied him for his entire life; the massive score is subsequently cataloged in the Bibliotheque Nationale in Paris. He also employed shouting and screaming and developed his own special notation for his system called "absolute harmony," which features harmonies constructed of the 12 pitches of the chromatic scale without duplications. He invented an electronic instrument called the croix sonore," an ether-wave device using valve oscillators to combine two electric currents of varying frequency to produce sound; the instrument was in the form of a cross. He also wrote the monograph *Traite d'harmonie tonale, atonale et totale* (Paris, 1946).

June 27   Composer-conductor Francois Louis Casadesus, 83, dies in Suresnes, France. A pupil at the Paris Conservatoire, he later conducted the Opera-Comique and founded the American Conservatory at Fontainebleau. He frequently conducted music over radio and also wrote music criticism. His compositions include four operas, several symphonic works, chamber music and songs.

July 19   French composer Jean-Jules Aimable Roger-Ducasse, 81, dies in Bordeaux, France. He studied with Gabriel Faure at the Paris Conservatoire and later succeeded Paul Dukas as a music composition professor. His music is impressionistic, though not especially ingenious or original. He composed operatic, symphonic and choral music as well as songs. He also wrote many exercises for piano.

Oct. 27   Italian composer Franco Alfano, 78, dies in San Remo, Italy. He studied composition with Salomon Jadassohn in Leipzig and immediately began devoting himself to opera. The composition of two operas — *Miranda* and *La Fonte di Ensir* — preceded his visit in 1900 to Paris, where he became attracted to light theater music. His ballet *Napoli* was staged at the Folies-Bergeres the following year and enjoyed 160 performances. His opera *Risurrezione* followed and was a sensation. That was his summit. Thereafter, he composed and taught at the Liceo Musicale in Bologna and the Turin Conservatory and was director of the Rossini Conservatory in Pesaro. His best-known achievement was his completion of Giacomo Puccini's opera *Turandot*. Alfano composed a total of 10 operas, 3 symphonies, 3 string quartets and 2 ballets, as well as orchestral and chamber music.

Nov. 21   Polish-American composer Karol Rathaus, 59, dies in New York. A pupil of Franz Schreker in Berlin and in Vienna, he traveled to Paris and London before arriving in New York. There he joined the faculty of Queens College of the City University of New York, where he stayed until his death. His music is postromantic, tonal and characterized by distinct contrapuntal control. He composed one ballet, one opera, five string quartets, many orchestral works, four piano sonatas, choral works and chamber music.

Nov. 30   German conductor Wilhelm Furtwangler, 68, dies in Baden-Baden, Germany. After studies in Munich, he began as an opera conductor in Zurich, Strasbourg and Lubeck. In 1919 he was appointed music director of the Berlin State Opera, and in 1922 he succeeded Arthur Nikisch as conductor of the Berlin Philharmonic and the Leipzig Gewandhaus Orchestra. He made his American debut in 1925 and in 1936 was offered the leadership of the New York Philharmonic, but his association with the Nazis prevented his acceptance of that post. He continued to conduct in Germany during World War II, and although he was absolved of Nazi collaboration after the war, he was not allowed to conduct in the United States. His position of preeminence in Western Europe, however, remained untarnished. He was finally set to tour the United States with the Berlin Philharmonic in 1955, but unfortunately, he died. Also a composer, Furtwangler wrote two symphonies and a piano concerto. He excelled in the music of Richard Wagner and Beethoven, his readings being highly personal and romantic.

1954   Related Events

Spanish conductor Enrique Jorda becomes music director of the San Francisco Symphony Orchestra this year, succeeding Pierre Monteux. He holds this post until 1963.

Conductor Josef Krips becomes music director of the Buffalo Philharmonic Symphony Society. He holds the position for nine years.

Developments in the recording industry this year include the following: Audiosphere (America) releases its first stereo tapes for commercial sales; Deutsche Grammophon expands its Archive Series to include commercial releases in England; the Fidelipac endless-loop tape cartridge is developed by George Eash; the Royal National Institute for the Blind and Saint Dunstans (England) devises a new tape cassette system featuring 20 hours of recording availability on 0.5 inch, 18-track tape; the first stereo recording sessions of EMI (Electrical and Musical Industries) take place; and the first transistor radios appear.

Paul Hindemith receives the Sibelius Award this year for distinguished service to music. One of the most prestigious awards in music and science, it is a prize of $35,000.

Jan. 13   The first concert of Domaine Musicale takes place in Paris. The program consists of music by Igor Stravinsky, Karlheinz Stockhausen, Luigi Nono and Anton Webern. This new music series, organized by Pierre

Boulez and financed by his patron Jean-Louis Barrault and later, Suzanne Tezenas, is first called Les Concerts du Petit-Marigny (named after the theater where it is held). The series becomes one of the century's most famous. Boulez, Hermann Scherchen and Hans Rosbaud do most of the conducting. Boulez describes the series as "a means of communication between the composers of our time and the public that is interested in its time." He focuses on the music of Arnold Schoenberg, Alban Berg and Anton Webern and, over the next 10 years, performs approximatley 60% of their combined works (Webern's music, in particular, is still relatively unknown in France). Nadia Boulanger becomes involved in the enterprise and becomes fond of telling Boulez "You are occupying yourself with scientific music." Boulez is now 28 years old and already the most prominent musician of the French avant-garde.

March 13   The first color television broadcast of an opera takes place as Vittorio Giannini's *The Taming of the Shrew* is broadcast by NBC in New York City.

April 4   Arturo Toscanini conducts the NBC Symphony Orchestra at Carnegie Hall, New York, in a performance of Richard Wagner's *Tannhauser* Overture. He becomes confused to the extent that the performance is interrupted and a recording of Brahms' First Symphony is substituted for broadcast. This event marks Toscanini's last public appearance.

May 3   Quincy Porter is awarded the Pulitzer Prize for music for *Concerto for Two Pianos and Orchestra*.

June 12   Scandinavian music is featured on the first program of the First International Council of Composers in Reykjavik, Iceland.

Sep. 11   Loew's Inc. is sued for $9 million by grandchildren of composer Robert Schumann in New York City. Contending that Loew's movie *Song of Life* depicts Schumann as a lunatic, they hold that the resultant humiliation they have suffered justifies the financial compensation. The law suit is subsequently dismissed upon documentation that Schumann was, in fact, insane.

Oct. 27   The Symphony of the Air (formerly the NBC Symphony Orchestra), which had been disbanded by NBC following Arturo Toscanini's retirement, plays a concert without a conductor in Carnegie Hall in an effort to sustain itself. The musicians decided to appoint no permanent conductor during Toscanini's lifetime. The effort is unsuccessful largely because audiences pay to watch conductors as well as to listen to performances.

1955 Opera

Jan. 27   *The Midsummer Marriage* — an opera with music and words by Michael Tippett — premieres at Covent Garden in London. It is a symbolic fairy tale inspired by Mozart's *The Magic Flute*. Singers include Joan Sutherland; the conductor is John Pritchard. This is Tippett's first opera.

Feb. 24   Carlisle Floyd's *Susannah*, with a libretto written by the composer, premieres at Florida State University in Tallahassee. The opera is about a beautiful woman from Tennessee who struggles to overcome the jealousy of others. Floyd describes the opera's theme as "persecution and the concomitant psychological ramifications." The opera is subsequently performed in New York and becomes a tremendous success — it receives the New York Music Critics Circle Award and three years from now is performed in Belgium at the Brussels World's Fair Exposition. This is Floyd's first and greatest success. He is on the faculty of Florida State University.

April 1   Sergei Prokofiev's opera *War and Peace* is performed posthumously in its complete version in Leningrad. It had been performed in a partial version in 1944.

April 2   George Antheil's one-act opera *The Wish*, with a libretto by the composer, premieres in Louisville, Kentucky. It is about the death of two young lovers in New York City.

May 9   American composer Theodore Chanler's *The Pot of Fat* receives its first performance in Cambridge, Massachusetts. The chamber opera is about a cat and a mouse who survive on a pot of fat. The performance takes place at the Longy School of Music. Chanler, now 53, studied with Ernest Bloch at the Cleveland Institute of Music and with Nadia Boulanger in Paris.

May 10   The Punch Opera in New York City performs Ned Rorem's *A Childhood Miracle*. The one-act opera is based on "The Snow Image," by Nathaniel Hawthorne. It is scored for 6 instruments and 13 voices. It is Rorem's first opera. Also on today's program is the first performance of Bernard Roger's opera *The Nightingale*.

May 13   Norman Dello Joio's opera *The Ruby* premieres in Bloomington, Indiana.

May 20   Bohuslav Martinu's one-act opera *What Men Live By*, based on a tale by Tolstoy, is premiered at Hunter College, New York City. The work is about a cobbler who helps people and receives a vision of Jesus.

Aug. 17   The first performance of Werner Egk's opera *Irische Legende* is given in Salzburg.

Sep. 14   Sergei Prokofiev's *The Flaming Angel* has its first staged performance at the Teatro la Fenice in Venice. The libretto, by the composer, is based on the novel by Valery Bryusov about a young woman who, ever since she was a child, has been visited by an angel. Prokofiev spent three years in seclusion working on the opera, but it is not staged until 30 years after its completion. This work was partially premiered on June 14, 1928 by Serge Koussevitzky; a concert version of the full opera was performed on November 25, 1954 in Paris.

Oct. 17   The Hamburg State Opera premieres Ernst Krenek's *Pallas Athene weint* in Hamburg with a libretto written by the composer. This three-act opera with prologue is set during the Peloponnesian War in 404 B.C. Socrates and Pallas Athene mourn the loss of Athens. The music is dodecaphonic.

Nov. 6   Lukas Foss's *Griffelkin*, a fantasy opera in three acts, is premiered on NBC-TV in New York City. The opera, which is about a devil who enjoys one day on Earth, was commissioned by NBC for telecast. The libretto is by Alastair Reid, of Sarah Lawrence College. Robert Sabin writes in *Musical America* (New York) that the music has "rhythmic ingenuity and transparency of texture."

1955 Dance

Jan. 6   The Sadler's Wells Ballet produces Frederick Ashton's *Rinaldo and Armida* in London to a commissioned score by Malcolm Arnold. The one-act ballet is based on Torquato Tasso's *Gerusalemme Liberata*. Svetlana Beriosova, Michael Somes, Julia Farron and Ronald Hynd star.

Jan. 18   Kenneth MacMillan presents his version of *Danses concertantes*, choreographed to Igor Stravinsky's score, at the Sadler's Wells Ballet Theater in London. Maryon Lane, Donald Britton and David Poole have the lead roles.

Feb. 1   The National Ballet of Canada gives the initial performance of Antony Tudor's *Offenbach in the Underworld*. The ballet, to the score for *Gaiete parisienne*, takes place in a fashionable Paris cafe. Celia Franca, Angela Leigh, Lillian Jarvis, David Adams and Earl Kraul star.

Feb. 24   Anna Sokolow presents *Rooms*, to music by Kenyon Hopkins. The modern dance work deals with loneliness in the big city. Beatrice Seckler, Eve Beck, Donald McKayle, Jeff Duncan, Jack Moore, Sandra Pine, Judith Coy and Paul Sanasardo are in the opening night cast.

Feb. 27   George Balanchine's *Western Symphony* — to music by Hershey Kay and with scenery by John Boyt and costumes by Karinska — is officially premiered by the New York City Ballet in New York. Although there are folk elements in the music, the dance movements are mostly classical. Diana Adams, Herbert Bliss, Janet Reed, Nicholas Magallanes, Patricia Wilde, Andre Eglevsky, Tanaquil LeClerq and Jacques d'Amboise lead the cast. The work was informally premiered last September in rehearsal costumes.

March 1   The New York City Ballet gives the first performance of George Balanchine's *Pas de trois* in New York. The music is by Mikhail Glinka, and costumes are by Karinska. The work features Andre Eglevsky, Melissa Hayden and Patricia Wilde.

May 8   The Martha Graham Dance Company performs Martha Graham's *Seraphic Dialogue*, to music by Norman Dello Joio, in New York. One of Graham's major works, it deals with three aspects of Joan of Arc — the maid, the warrior and the martyr. Linda Margolies, Patricia Birsh, Mary Hinkson, Matt Turney and Bertram Ross star.

May 19   Frederick Ashton's version of *Romeo and Juliet* is premiered by the Royal Danish Ballet in Copenhagen. The work is set to Sergei Prokofiev's score. Mona Vangsaa, Henning Kronstam, Frank Schaufuss and Niels Bjorn Larsen star.

May 24   Merce Cunningham's *Springweather and People* choreographed to music by Earle Brown, premieres at Bard College. The costumes are by Robert Rauschenberg, Remy Charlip, Ray Johnson and Vera Williams.

July 26   *Symphonie pour un homme seul*, a one-act ballet choreographed by Maurice Bejart to music by Pierre Henry and Pierre Schaeffer, receives its first performance by Les Ballets de l'Etoile in Paris. The ballet is about a man in conflict with sex and technology. It stars Bejart and Michele Seigneuret. It is Bejart's first major success.

Aug. 3   The Dance Drama Company presents Todd Bolender's *The Still Point* during the Jacob's Pillow Festival. The work, about young love, is set to the first three movements of Claude Debussy's String Quartet. Emily Frankel and Mark Ryder star. The work is added to the repertoire of the New York City Ballet next year.

Nov. 9   The New York City Ballet gives the first performance of George Balanchine's *Pas de dix* in New York City, to music by Alexander Glazunov and with costumes by Esteban Frances. The lead dancers are Maria Tallchief and Andre Eglevsky.

Nov. 15   Todd Bolender's *Souvenirs*, set to music by Samuel Barber, is premiered by the New York City Ballet in New York. The light-hearted ballet is set in a resort hotel shortly before World War I. Irene Larsson and Carolyn George star.

1955 *Instrumental and Vocal Music*

Jan. 7 Bohuslav Martinu's Symphony No. 6 (*Fantaisies symphoniques*) is premiered by Charles Munch and the Boston Symphony Orchestra. The work has three movements and was completed two years ago. Martinu originally scored it for large orchestra and three pianos but abandoned the pianos because he was "frightened by the three big instruments on the stage." The symphony is one of many works performed to celebrate the 75th anniversary of the Boston Symphony Orchestra. It also receives the New York Music Critics Circle Award.

Jan. 14 Heitor Villa-Lobos conducts the Philadelphia Orchestra in the first performances of his Symphony No. 8 and Concerto for Harp and Orchestra. Harpist Nicanor Zabaleta is soloist.

Jan. 15 Alexander Tcherepnin's Symphony No. 3 in F-sharp is premiered by Fabien Sevitzky and the Indianapolis Symphony Orchestra. It has four movements.

Jan. 23 Georges Enesco's *Symphonie de chambre* in E Major receives its first performance in Paris. Scored for 12 instruments, it is Enesco's last piece — he dies this May. This composition was completed last year, before Enesco suffered a debilitating stroke.

Feb. 18 Howard Hanson's Symphony No. 5 (*Sinfonia sacra*), Op. 43, is premiered by Eugene Ormandy and the Philadelphia Orchestra in Philadelphia. The symphony is in one movement, subdivided into three sections performed contiguously. It was inspired by the story of Easter related in the gospel of Saint John. Olin Downes writes in the New York *Times* that Hanson "is not trying to go archaic. . . ."

Feb. 21 Igor Stravinsky's *Four Russian Songs* drawn from his 1919 songs of the same title and the remaining two from his 1917 *Three Tales for Children* — is performed for the first time in Los Angeles, Robert Craft conducting. The work is scored for sopranos, flute, harp and guitar.

March 18 Randall Thompson's orchestral fantasy *A Trip to Nahant* is premiered by Eugene Ormandy and the Philadelphia Orchestra in Philadelphia.

March 21 The first performance of Olivier Messiaen's *Livre d'orgue* is given in Paris at the Trinite, with the composer at the organ. The piece has seven movements.

May 11 Arthur Bliss' Violin Concerto premieres in London.

May 28 The Louisville Symphony Orchestra premieres Ned Rorem's *Design for Orchestra* in Louisville, Kentucky.

May 30 Luigi Nono's *Incontri for 24 instruments* premieres in Darmstadt.

June 18 *Le Marteau sans Maitre*, by Pierre Boulez, receives its world premiere at this year's International Society for Contemporary Music festival in Baden-Baden. This event catapults Boulez to world attention. Pitch, rhythm, timbre and register are serialized in this nine-movement composition, which derives its inspiration from a text by Rene Char written in 1934. The work is scored for alto flute, vibraphone, viola, contralto, guitar and percussion. Boulez sets the text in a "surrealistic, interior" fashion. He later comments on the criticism that his setting of the text is incomprehensible by saying: "If you wish to 'understand' the text, then read it or speak it: there can be no better solution. I am now proposing that knowledge of the poems has already been acquired."

Sep. 13 Franz Andre and the Orchestra of the Belgian Institute National de Radiodiffusion premiere Darius Milhaud's Symphony No. 7 in Venice. The work has three movements.

Sep. 15 A revised version of Roy Harris' Symphony No. 7 is presented by Eugene Ormandy and the Philadelphia Orchestra in Copenhagen. It was performed in its original version on November 20, 1952.

Sep. 24 The Louisville Orchestra in Louisville, Kentucky premieres Andre Jolivet's orchestral *Suite transoceane.*

Oct. 7 Darius Milhaud conducts the Boston Symphony Orchestra in the premiere of his Symphony No. 6. The performance of this four-movement work takes place almost a month after the premiere of his Symphony No. 7.

Oct. 29 The first performance of Dmitri Shostakovich's Concerto in A Minor for Violin and Orchestra is given in Leningrad. The violinist is David Oistrakh; Evgheny Mravinsky conducts. The concerto has four movements.

Nov. 4 William Schuman's orchestral work *Credendum* is premiered by Thor Johnson and the Cincinnati Symphony Orchestra. The three-movement piece was commissioned by the American government for UNESCO.

Nov. 25 Charles Munch and the Boston Symphony Orchestra premiere Walter Piston's Symphony No. 6. The four-movement work celebrates the 75th anniversary of this orchestra.

Nov. 26 The premiere of Boris Liatoshinsky's symphonic ballad *Grazina* is presented in both Kiev and Moscow.

Dec. 2 The Symphony No. 3, Op. 75, by Ernst Toch, is performed for the first time by the Pittsburgh Symphony Orchestra, William Steinberg conducting. Inspired by Goethe's *The Sorrows of Werther*, the three-movement piece includes sound effects produced by a tank of carbon dioxide with a valve and a wooden box containing croquet balls. His most famous symphony, it was commissioned by the American Jewish Tercentenary Committee of Chicago. Toch is subsequently awarded the Pulitzer Prize for music for this work.

Dec. 31   Japanese composer Michio Miyagi's concerto *Har no Umi*, featuring the koto, is premiered by Andre Kos-

telanetz and the New York Philharmonic, with Shinichi Yuize as soloist. The work is scored for koto soloist, flute and orchestra. Miyagi, who became blind at age 7, has composed hundreds of works for the koto.

1955   Births, Deaths and Debuts

Jan. 7   Marian Anderson becomes the first black to sing at the Metropolitan Opera House. She debuts as Ulrica in Giuseppe Verdi's *A Masked Ball*. A reviewer writes in the *Christian Science Monitor* that she "graced the stage with force of personality, dignity of stage presence, and vocal artistry."

March 26   Conductor Thomas Schippers leads his first concert with the New York Philharmonic. At age 25 he is one of the youngest conductors to lead that orchestra.

May 2   German baritone Dietrich Fischer-Dieskau makes his American debut giving a lieder recital at Town Hall, New York. He sings Franz Schubert's song-cycle *Die Winterreise*. Jay S. Harrison writes in the New York *Herald Tribune*, "Such musicianship as his knows no vocal gates. . . ."

May 4   Rumanian composer Georges Enesco, 73, dies in Paris. He studied with Nicolas Chioru, a Rumanian gypsy violinist, when he was 4 years old. He later studied at the Vienna Conservatory and at the Paris Conservatoire, with Gabriel Faure and Jules Massenet. After receiving several prizes for his violin, cello, organ and piano playing, he de-

voted himself to composition, conducting and teaching. The queen of Rumania appointed him court violinist. He gave master classes in violin and taught Yehudi Menuhin. After several successful tours of Europe and America (both as a conductor and as a violinist), he returned to Rumania, where he stayed during World War II. He then enjoyed another highly successful tour of America and settled in Paris. His native country honored him by naming a street in Bucharest after him and holding festivals in his name. His music, largely neoromantic, includes extensive use of Rumanian folk materials and occasionally quarter tones (his opera *Oedipe*, for example, produced in 1936). He composed five symphonies plus three early symphonies he did not number; many other orchestral works (including his famous *Rumanian Rhapsodies*); a great deal of chamber music and music for piano; as well as vocal music and song cycles.

May 18   Italian composer and writer Francesco Balilla Pratella, 75, dies in Ravenna, Italy. He studied with Pietro Mascagni at the Liceo Rossini in Pesaro and eventually became director of the Istituto Musicale in Lugo and the Liceo Musicale G. Verdi in Ravenna. At about age 30 he became enamored of Luigi Russolo's movement known as "futurism" and joined forces with that musician. He composed operas, incidental music, and orchestral and chamber music (these pieces include the orchestral works *Romagna*, *La guerra* and *5 poemi musicali*) but is most noted for his connection with futurism.

June 11   French composer Marcel Samuel-Rousseau, 72, dies in Paris. He studied with Charles Lenepveu and composed operas and ballets, most of which were premiered in Paris. He was elected to the Academie des Beaux-Arts in 1947.

June 18   Swiss composer Willy Burkhard, 55, dies in Zurich. He studied in Leipzig and Paris before returning to Switzerland and eventually became a teacher at the Bern Conservatory and the Zurich Conservatory. He was extremely prolific and is considered one of the most important Swiss composers. His music, which is neoclassical in style, comprises one opera (*Die Schwarze Spinne*), many oratorios and cantatas (including his masterpiece, the oratorio *Das Gesicht Jesajas*), other vocal works, orchestral pieces, chamber works and piano and organ music.

Oct. 7   German coloratura soprano Frieda Hempel, 70, dies in Berlin. She studied piano at the Leipzig Conserva-

DIETRICH FISCHER-DIESKAU

tory and singing with Frau Nicklass-Kempner in Berlin. She debuted in *Merry Wives of Windsor* in 1905. She then sang at the Court Opera in Schwerin, the Royal Opera in Berlin and the Metropolitan Opera, New York, where she made her debut with that company in 1912. During the Jenny Lind contenary celebration (1920) she impersonated Lind in 70 concerts.

Nov. 22   French composer Guy Ropartz, 91, dies in Lanlouppar-Plouha, France. Although he studied with Jules Massenet at the Paris Conservatoire, his principal influence was Cesar Franck, with whom he studied composition and organ. He was director of the Paris Conservatoire between 1894 and 1919 and then devoted himself to composing and conducting. His most important opera is *Le pays*, produced in 1913. He also wrote five symphonies, incidental music, six string quartets, other chamber music, piano music and songs.

Nov. 27   French composer Arthur Honegger, 63, dies in Paris. He studied at the Zurich Conservatory and at the Paris Conservatoire with Andre Gedalge and Charles Ma-

rie Widor. He later studied with Vincent d'Indy. He began to become noticed toward the end of the second decade of the century, when he belonged to the group "Nouveaux Jeunes" and later to "les Six." *Pacific 231* was extremely successful in 1924. Honegger then went on to compose a great deal of music, expecially cantatas, oratorios, incidental music, film music, orchestral works, (including five symphonies), choral and vocal works (including *Chant de liberation*, three string quartets and a host of other chamber pieces, piano music and songs. His work in its early stages reflected the then-current preoccupation with depicting, through music, the machine age and the advent of 20th-century technology (George Antheil was another composer identified with this trend). Honegger did not, however, make this preoccupation a lifelong habit. His later music, beginning with works composed about 1930, reveals an attraction to neoclassical models. His music was never dodecaphonic, although he did employ atonal melodies and polytonal harmonies. Honegger may have been acutely aware of Igor Stravinsky's presence in Paris and his impact on the world of music; this may, in turn, have attracted Honegger to neoclassicism.

1955 Related Events

The East German State Opera House reopens this year.

Les Ballets Chiriaeff is established this year by dancer and ballet director Ludmilla Chiriaeff.

Recording industry companies in America introduce price slashing this year as a means of creating competition in the record market. The Columbia Record Club begins merchandising its long-playing records by mass mail.

Die Reihe begins publication this year in Vienna. This new music journal is edited by Herbert Eimert and Karlheinz Stockhausen. Its first issue is devoted to electronic music.

Feb. 27   The Berlin Philharmonic Orchestra gives its first American concert in Washington, D.C. The conductor is Herbert von Karajan. He replaces Wilhelm Furtwangler, who died before the tour. The State Department rejects protests by Jewish War Veterans and the Musicians' Union that von Karajan is an ex-Nazi.

March 19   Austrian conductor Erich Kleiber quits his post with the Berlin State Opera in East Berlin and flees to Cologne. He says the Communist authorities were forcing him to subordinate art to propaganda. Kleiber had left the same opera in 1935 in protest against the Nazis and had refused to conduct at La Scala in 1936 in protest against anti-Semitism.

May 2   Gian Carlo Menotti is awarded the Pulitzer Prize for music for his opera *The Saint of Bleecker Street.*

June 17   The basic tuning pitch "A" is changed from 435 cycles to 440 cycles by 37 nations at the International Standards Organization in Stockholm.

June 26   American composer Cecil Effinger's invention, the musicwriter — a typewriter of musical notation — is displayed in Denver, Colorado.

Nov. 5   The Vienna State Opera House reopens after having been hit by bombs in 1945. *Fidelio*, by Beethoven, is performed. The rebuilt theater seats 2,209, and the total stage area is 20,000 square feet. The music is broadcast to an overflow crowd in the street outside the opera house.

Nov. 6   The Chicago Opera Ballet, organized by Ruth Page, gives its inaugural performance at the Chicago Lyric Opera. Alicia Markova is guest artist in a performance of *The Merry Widow.*

Dec. 26   A new small opera house adjacent to La Scala, called La Piccola Scala, opens in Milan. A performance of Domenico Cimarosa's *Il matrimonio segreto* is featured.

Dec. 26   George Gershwin's *Porgy and Bess* receives its first performance in Leningrad by an all-black American company, which also tours Europe, the Middle East and Latin America. This event marks the first time an American operatic company visits the Soviet Union. The performance takes place at the Leningrad Palace of Culture.

THE VIENNA STATE OPERA

1956   Opera

Feb. 25   *La guerra*, by Renzo Rossellini, premieres in Rome. The libretto, by the composer, is the story of a wartime romance. The cast includes Magda Olivero.

March 10   *L'ipocrita felice*, by Giorgio Ghedini, receives its first performance in Milan at La Piccola Scala. The libretto, by F. Antonicelli, is based on Max Beerbohm's *The Happy Hypocrite*. The cast includes Tito Gobbi and Graziella Sciutti.

April 8   Norman Dello Joio's opera *The Trial at Rouen* premieres over NBC-TV in New York City.

May 17   Robert Ward's *Pantaloon* is premiered in New York City by the Columbia University Opera Workshop. The three-act opera is about a clown in love.

June 17   *Der Sturm* by Frank Martin receives its first performance in Vienna at the Staatsoper. The libretto is based on Schlegel's translation of Shakespeare's *The Tempest*. It is in three acts. Rudolf Klein, writing in *Oesterreichische Musik-*

zeitschrift, describes Martin's technique as "unending melody combined with recitative."

June 27   Paul Constantinescu's *Pana Lesnea Rusalim* premieres in Bucharest. The three-act opera is about a Rumanian peasant girl who fights the Turks.

July 7   Douglas Moore's *The Ballad of Baby Doe* receives its world premiere at the Tabor Opera House in Central City, Colorado. The story — based on the rise and fall of silver magnate Horace Tabor and his love, Baby Doe — is sung in the opera house named after the lead character. The libretto is by John Latouche. Howard Taubman writes in the New York *Times*: "The score makes us attempt to pursue advanced techniques."

Sep. 23   Hans Werner Henze's *Konig Hirsch* premieres in Berlin at the Stadtische Oper. The libretto, by Heinz von Cramer, is based on the fairy tale *Il re cervo*, by Carlo Gozzi.

The musical style is eclectic, blending avant-garde elements with popular and traditional music.

Oct. 29   *Candide* receives its world premiere at the Colonial Theater in Boston. This comic operetta has music by Leonard Bernstein, book by Lillian Hellman, lyrics by Richard Wilbur, John Latouche, Dorothy Parker, Hellman and Bernstein. It is based on the satire by Voltaire and contains many songs that become famous, including "Glitter, and Be Gay." It is revised in 1973.

Nov. 18   *The Men of Blackmoor*, by Alan Bush, premieres in a German version entitled *Die Manner von Blackmoor* in Weimar. The three-act opera is about striking mine workers in England. The libretto is by the composer's wife, Nancy Bush.

Dec. 4   Robert Starer's one-act opera *The Intruder* premieres in New York City. This is Starer's first opera. He has studied in Vienna, Jerusalem and at the Juilliard School in New York and is now on the Juilliard faculty.

1956 Dance

Feb. 15   Frederick Ashton's *La Peri* — to music by Paul Dukas and with costumes and scenery by Andre Levasseur — is performed in a new version by the Sadler's Wells Ballet in London. Margot Fonteyn and Michael Somes dance this ballet about an oriental fairy, a magical flower and a poet called Iskender.

March 1   The New York City Ballet gives the premiere, in New York, of *Allegro Brillante*. This abstract work for a lead couple and an ensemble of eight is choreographed by George Balanchine to Tchaikovsky's Third Piano Concerto. Maria Tallchief and Nicholas Magallanes star.

March 6   The New York City Ballet stages Jerome Robbins' *The Concert* in New York. The comic ballet is a series of sketches showing people's fantasies while listening to a recital of Chopin's piano pieces. Hershey Kay contributes some of the orchestrations. Tanaquil LeClerq, Yvonne Bolender, Robert Barnett, Richard Thomas and John Mandia lead the cast.

April 20   Choreographer Jose Limon's *There Is a Time* — to music by Norman Dello Joio and with costumes by Pauline Lawrence — is premiered by the Jose Limon Dance Company in New York City. This modern dance composition is based on Ecclesiastes.

April 20   Doris Humphrey's *Theatre Piece #2* to music by Otto Luening, is performed for the first time in New York City.

May 5   The Sadler's Wells Ballet performs Frederick Ashton's *Birthday Offering* to celebrate its 25th birthday. The plotless ballet, to music by Alexander Glazunov, is designed as a showcase for the company's seven ballerinas — Margot Fonteyn, Beryl Grey, Violetta Elvin, Nadia Nerina, Rowena Jackson, Svetlana Beriosova and Elaine Fifield.

May 18   A modern dance concert of new works by the prolific Merce Cunningham is held at the University of Notre Dame in South Bend, Indiana. The compositions are entitled *Lavish Escapade, Suite for Five in Space and Time* and *Galaxy*.

June 7   Kenneth MacMillan's ballet *Solitaire* is premiered by the Sadler's Wells Ballet in London. The work, set to music by Malcolm Arnold, deals with a girl who tries to join in the play of others but always finds herself alone. Margaret Hill, Sara Neil and Donald Britton star.

July 11   Merce Cunningham's modern dance piece *Nocturnes* — to music by Erik Satie and with scenery by Robert Rauschenberg — premieres at Jacob's Pillow, Lee, Massachusetts.

July 12   Jose Limon's *The Emperor Jones* — to music by Heitor Villa-Lobos and with designs by Kim Swados — premieres at the Empire Street Music Festival in Ellenville, New York. This dance is based on the play of the same name by Eugene O'Neill. It is about an emperor in the Caribbean who is being pursued by local people. The piece is subsequently filmed.

Dec. 19   George Balanchine's *Divertimento No. 15*, (formerly titled *Caracole*), receives its world premiere by the New York City Ballet in New York. This version, created anew because Balanchine forgot the original choreography, features new costumes by Karinska. The lead dancers are Melissa Hayden, Diana Adams and Patricia Wilde.

Dec. 27   The Kirov Ballet gives the first performance, in Leningrad, of Leonid Yacobson's *Spartacus*, set to music by Aram Khachaturian. The evening-length work tells the story of a slave who incites his fellow slaves to revolt but is eventually killed. Yacobson's choreography is unsuccessful, but the score remains popular. Askold Makarov, Inna Zubkovskaya and Alla Shelest star.

1956 Instrumental and Vocal Music

Jan. 14   Roger Sessions' orchestral work *Idyll of Theocritus*, scored for soprano and orchestra, premieres in Louisville, Kentucky.

Feb. 2   Samuel Barber's full, large orchestral version of his ballet *The Serpent Heart* is premiered by Dimitri Mitropoulos and the New York Philharmonic.

Feb. 15   Ernest Bloch's Symphony in E-flat is performed for the first time in London. The four-movement work was completed last year.

Feb. 23   Leon Kirchner's Piano Concerto is premiered by Dimitri Mitropoulos and the New York Philharmonic, with the composer as soloist. The three-movement work is neoclassical in style. Kirchner is currently on the faculty of Mills College in Oakland, California.

Feb. 24   Symphony No. 5, by Walter Piston, receives its world premiere in New York City. The work was commissioned to celebrate the 50th anniversary of the Juilliard School.

March 2   The Boston Symphony Orchestra premieres Heitor Villa-Lobos' Symphony No. 11. The composer conducts. The four-movement work celebrates the 75th anniversary of this American orchestra.

March 10   French composer Jean Barraque's *Sequence* premieres in Paris. The work, considered his most important, is scored for soprano, piano, harp, violin, cello and percussion. The text is from works by Nietzsche. The music is atonal and offsets the intervals of the major seventh and the tritone. Barraque, now 28, studied with Jean Langlais and Olivier Messiaen. *Sequence* was composed between 1950 and 1955.

March 31   Carl Orff's *Comoedia de Christi resurrectione* premieres over radio in Munich. The Easter cantata is a surrealistic rendition of the resurrection of Christ. It is scored for soloists, mixed chorus and children's voices, three pianos, two harps, four double-basses and percussion.

April 4   Ernest Bloch's Symphony for Trombone and Orchestra receives its initial performance in Houston, Texas. The work has three movements.

April 4   Paul Creston's Symphony No. 5 premieres in Washington, D.C., as Howard Mitchell conducts the National Symphony Orchestra. The composer describes the three-movement work as expressing "spiritual conflicts."

April 16   Vincent Persichetti's Symphony No. 6 (*Symphony for Winds*) premieres in St. Louis, Missouri. The Washington University Band performs. Persichetti is now 40 years old.

April 21   Elliott Carter's *Variations for Orchestra* receives its world premiere in Louisville, Kentucky, as Robert Whit-

ney conducts the Louisville Orchestra. The piece is comprised of an introductory thematic statement and 10 variations. Carter describes the work as a "large, unified musical action of gesture." William Mootz writes in the Louisville *Courier-Journal*, ". . . the composer is a more accomplished craftsman and a man more passionately devoted to the art of composition than most of the music makers the Louisville Orchestra commissions these days."

May 2   Ralph Vaughan Williams' Symphony No. 8 in D Minor is premiered by conductor John Barbirolli in Manchester, England. The four-movement work is the composer's penultimate symphony. The first movement of the symphony is subsequently characterized as "seven variations in search of a theme."

May 5   Dominick Argento's ballet suite *The Resurrection of Don Juan* premieres in a concert version at the Festival of American Music in Rochester, New York.

May 27   Igor Stravinsky's arrangement of Johann Sebastian Bach's *Choral-Variationen uber das Weihnachtslied* premieres in Ojai, California.

May 30   Herbert Eimert's *5 Stucke*, Gottfried Michael Konig's *Klangfiguren II*, Karlheinz Stockhausen's *Der Gesang der Junglinge* and Ernst Krenek's *Spiritus Intelligentiae Sanctus* are among the works premiered at the Westdeutscher Rundfunk electronic music concert in Cologne. The Stockhausen piece is scored for boy soprano and electronic tape. Stockhausen requests it be performed through a five-channel stereophonic system.

June 4   Ralph Vaughan Williams' *A Vision of Aeroplanes* premieres in London. It is a motet scored for chorus and organ and has a text from the Book of Ezekiel.

June 25   Darius Milhaud's Piano Concerto No. 5 is premiered by Pierre Monteux and the Stadium Symphony Orchestra with Stell Anderson as soloist, at Lewisohn Stadium in New York City.

Aug. 5   Ned Rorem's Symphony No. 2 receives its first performance in La Jolla, California.

Sep. 5   Sergei Prokofiev's Concerto No. 4 for Piano and Orchestra in B-flat Major, Op. 53, for left hand only, receives its initial performance by Siegfried Rapp in Berlin. The four-movement work, originally commissioned by Paul Wittgenstein, was composed 25 years ago. Its premiere never took place during Prokofiev's lifetime because Wittgenstein viewed the music as too modern and refused to perform it. Prokofiev did not pursue performance of the work.

Sep. 11   Alexander Tcherepnin's Concerto for Harmonica and Orchestra premieres in Venice.

Sep. 13   Igor Stravinsky's *Canticum sacrum ad honorem Sancti Marci nominis*, with texts in Latin and culled from the Vulgate, receives its initial performance at San Marco in Venice. This event marks the premiere of the first dodecaphonic work by Stravinsky. It is scored for tenor, baritone, chorus and orchestra. The Cardinal of Venice gave him special permission to conduct the performance in the church of San Marco. The piece has five sections, of which the middle three are strictly dodecaphonic. *Time* magazine (New York) headlines its review "Murder in the Cathedral." Two years from now, Soviet musicologist and critic Izrail Nestyev reviews this work in *Sovetskaya Muzyka*. His article is entitled "Holy Cacophony" and he asks: "How ravaged, how emasculated must have been the soul of the composer capable of creating such dreadful music?"

Sep. 25   William Walton's *Johannesburg Festival Overture* premieres in that South African city. The music incorporates South African melodic materials and celebrates the 70th anniversary of Johannesburg.

Oct. 4   Rudolf Firkusny performs as soloist in the world premiere of Bohuslav Martinu's Piano Concerto No. 4, as Leopold Stokowski conducts the Symphony of the Air at the Metropolitan Museum of Art in New York City. The concerto is subtitled *Incantation*. Edward Downes says of the work in the New York *Times*: ". . . it is chic, but it gives you the feeling that somewhere you've seen that dress before. And you have." He goes on to remark that the applause for the Martinu piece was largely intended for Firkusny.

Oct. 17   Dmitri Kabalevsky's Symphony No. 4 premieres in Moscow. The work is in four movements.

Oct. 24   Luigi Nono's *Il canto sospeso* receives its first performance at the first concert of the Musik der Zeit in Cologne. Based on texts of letters by Nazi resisters sentenced to death, the work is dodecaphonic and is scored for three voices, chorus and orchestra.

1956 Births, Deaths and Debuts

Jan. 3   Russian composer Alexander Gretchaninoff, 91, dies in New York. After studies with Vassily Safonov and Anton Arensky at the Moscow Conservatory, and with Nikolai Rimsky-Korsakov at the Saint Petersburg Conservatory, he taught at the Moscow Institute. He then moved to Paris before touring and finally settling in America. He wrote an autobiography entitled *My Life*, which contains a complete list of his works. Gretchaninoff's early music reflects the influence of Tchaikovsky and Rimsky-Korsakov. At about age 45 he began adopting a style similar to French impressionism. This did not attract attention, and he then devoted himself to the sacred music for which he is most noted. He composed masses that introduce native Russian melodic materials and instrumen-

GUSTAVE CHARPENTIER

tal accompaniment into the Russian Orthodox liturgy. These pieces were rejected by that church for liturgical use because of their addition of instrumental accompaniment. Gretchaninoff then began incorporating musical elements common to other religions, which musicologist Joseph Yasser termed "heterodox." His *Missa oecumenica* is an example of these pieces. In addition to his sacred music, he also composed operas, 5 symphonies, other orchestral works, 84 choruses, 14 vocal quartets, 258 songs, 4 string quartets, piano works and a new Russian national anthem for Siberian exiles entitled "Hymn of Free Russia."

Jan. 27   Austrian conductor Erich Kleiber, 65, dies in Zurich, Switzerland. After studying in Prague, he became a conductor at the Prague National Theater in 1911. As music director of the Berlin State Opera, he conducted the world premiere of Alban Berg's *Wozzeck* in 1925. Escaping the Nazis, he went to South America in 1935 and returned to Europe after the war. He was also a composer and wrote a number of chamber works, several concertos, piano pieces and songs.

Feb. 18   French composer Gustave Charpentier, 95, dies in Paris. He studied composition with Jules Massenet at the Paris Conservatoire and quickly became preoccupied with the problems of the poor. Charpentier is an example of a composer who enjoyed longevity but whose work is marked by only two successes — he won the Grand Prix de Rome while in his twenties and composed one opera that would achieve world fame, *Louise*. He was not prolific.

March 11   Soviet composer Sergei Vassilenko, 83, dies in Moscow. After law studies at Moscow University and private composition studies with Alexander Gretchaninoff, he studied with Sergei Taneyev, Mikhail Ippolitov-Ivanov and Vassily Safonov at the Moscow Conservatory. He later taught orchestration at that conservatory and conducted in Moscow and Berlin. He helped musicians in Tashkent, Uzbekistan form a national school of musical composition. His music blends Russian folk song with eastern subjects and French impressionistic harmonies. He wrote six operas, six ballets, five symphonies, many other orchestral works, three string quartets and numerous songs, including the famous "*A Maiden Sang in a Church Choir*" (composed in 1908).

June 23   Russian composer Reinhold Gliere, 81, dies in Moscow. He was a pupil of Anton Arensky, Sergei Taneyev and Mikhail Ippolitov-Ivanov at the Moscow Conservatory and graduated with a gold medal. He lived and worked in Berlin for two years before teaching at the Kiev Conservatory and becoming its director. After 1920 he became director of the Moscow Conservatory. Being fond of folk melodies, he traveled widely throughout Russia and Europe to collect such tunes. His music is distinctly Russian, embodying 19th-century Russian harmonic language and avoiding all revolutionary innovations taking place in 20th-century music. He is best known for his symphonies and orchestral works but also wrote operas, ballets, incidental music, chamber music (including 5 string quartets) and approximately 200 songs and 200 piano pieces. His Symphony No. 3 (*Ilya Murometz*) and his

Soviet ballet *The Red Poppy* are among his most famous compositions. Gliere is one of three Russian composers associated with Moscovian musical life to die this year — the other two are Alexander Gretchaninoff and Sergei Vassilenko.

Oct. 12   Italian composer Don Lorenzo Perosi, 83, dies in Rome. This musician is noted especially for having composed music emulating that of Palestrina. He was also a priest and music director of the Sistine Chapel. He suffered a severe mental breakdown in 1915 but regained his health and continued to pursue a style of sacred music consonant with the teachings of the Roman Catholic Church. *La passione di Christo*, a trilogy, is considered his masterpiece.

Oct. 26   Pianist Walter Gieseking, 60, dies in London. Born in France to German parents, he studied in Hannover, served in World War I and then started his successful concert career. In 1949 he was forced to cancel an American appearance because of protests against his alleged Nazi collaboration during World War II, but he was later cleared by an Allied court and finally returned to the United States in 1953. A refined musician, he was known for his interpretations of Claude Debussy and Mozart, among others. He also wrote an autobiography, which is published in 1963.

Oct. 29   Maria Callas makes her Metropolitan Opera debut in the title role of *Norma*. Although she was offered a contract with the Metropolitan in 1945, she elected to return to Italy, where she began her extraordinary career. Paul Henry Lang writes in the New York *Herald-Tribune* that "Miss Callas is undoubtedly a great artist... with a commanding dramatic personality.... But it is not a beautiful voice and it has many limitations...."

Nov. 13   Italian tenor Carlo Bergonzi makes his Metropolitan Opera debut as Radames in *Aida*.

Nov. 24   Italian conductor Guido Cantelli, 36, dies in an airplane crash at Orly airport. He was flying to the United States for conducting engagements. Cantelli studied at the Milan Conservatory. The Nazis sent him to the Stettin concentration camp during World War II. In 1949 Arturo Toscanini invited him to conduct the NBC Symphony Orchestra in New York. That event was so successful Cantelli became known as "piccolo Toscanini." He was especially known for his musical memory.

Dec. 9   Pianist and composer Hans Barth, 59, dies in Jacksonville, Florida. After studies with Carl Reinecke at the Leipzig Conservatory, he went to America. In 1928 he built a quarter-tone piano with help from George L. Weitz. He then composed music for this instrument and performed it in New York. His work is largely devoted to quarter-tone composition and includes a piano concerto with string orchestra tuned in quarter-tones. He also wrote essays on music.

1956   Related Events

Herbert von Karajan becomes music director of the Vienna State Opera and the Salzburg Festival this year.

Eduard van Beinum becomes music director of the Los Angeles Philharmonic Orchestra this year. He succeeds Alfred Wallenstein and holds the post for three seasons, until his death. Van Beinum comes to this position from the Amsterdam Concertgebouw Orchestra, where he was principal conductor.

The Nippon Philharmonic Orchestra is established this year by Japanese conductor Akeo Watanabe. Watanabe is music director until 1968.

John Field is appointed director of the Sadler's Wells Theatre Ballet this year.

RCA Victor (Electrical Musical Industries) and EMI break partnership. EMI subsequently establishes the Angel label in America, and RCA Victor counters by releasing its first commercial stereo tapes.

The Caramoor Festival (New York State) begins this year. The estate was acquired in 1922 by Lucie Bigelow and Walter Tower Rosen. It subsequently becomes an internationally known festival.

Jan. 1   Queen Elizabeth II installs ballerina Margot Fonteyn as a Dame Commander of the Order of the British Empire. Vienna-born Rudolf Bing, general manager of the Metropolitan Opera, is made a Commander of the Order of the British Empire.

Jan. 31   H.F. Olson and H. Belar's RCA electronic music synthesizer is demonstrated for the first time by General David Sarnoff at a meeting of the Institute of Electrical Engineers in New York City.

Feb. 22   The Yale University Music Library acquires the Charles Ives papers. This collection includes musical manuscripts, printed works, correspondence, photographs, diaries, programs, reviews, etc., and is given to the library by the composer's wife, Harmony Ives.

March 9   Eugene Goossens is forced into resigning his positions as head of the New South Wales Conservatorium of Music and music director of the Sydney Symphony Orchestra after Australian officials find over a thousand imported pornographic photographs in his luggage in Sydney.

May 3   Violinist Isaac Stern gives a concert in Grand Conservatory Hall in Moscow. He is the first American artist to appear there in 10 years.

May 7   Ernst Toch is awarded the Pulitzer Prize for music for Symphony No. 3.

June 2   The first Festival International de Lausanne begins in that Swiss city today, as Ernest Ansermet conducts a performance of *Le roi David*, by Arthur Honegger. The music is performed by L'Orchestre de la Suisse Romand. This festival quickly establishes itself as a major summer international musical attraction and becomes an annual event.

Sep. 6   Charles Munch conducts the Boston Symphony Orchestra in a concert of music by Walter Piston, Beethoven, Maurice Ravel and Paul Dukas at the Leningrad Conservatory. This event marks the first time an American orchestra performs in the Soviet Union.

Oct. 10   Beginning today, music of Arnold Schoenberg, Alban Berg, Bela Bartok, Karol Szymanowski, Maurice Ravel, Arthur Honegger, Benjamin Britten, Georges Enesco, Dmitri Shostakovich, Aram Khachaturian, Sergei Prokofiev, Darius Milhaud, Georges Auric, Olivier Messiaen and others is featured at the International Festival of Contemporary Music — the first Warsaw Autumn Festival — in that city.

Oct. 31   By royal charter, the Sadler's Wells Ballet changes its name to The Royal Ballet.

1957   Opera

Jan. 26   Francis Poulenc's *The Dialogues of the Carmelites* receives its world premiere in Italian at the Teatro alla Scala in Milan. Emmet Lavery's libretto is based on the play by Georges Bernanos, which, in turn, was inspired by Gertrud von Le Fort's *Die Letzte am Schafatt*. These pieces were all based on the actual execution on July 17, 1794 of 16 Carmelite nuns in Paris. The cast includes Virginia Zeani, Leila Gencer and Fiorenza Cossotto. Nino Sanzogno conducts. The work, considered one of Poulenc's best, is his first full-length opera. Howard Taubman later writes in the New York *Times*: "When he is dealing with emotion, particularly with the spiritual feelings of the nuns, Poulenc is a rare artist."

March 17   Ernst Krenek's opera *The Bell-Tower* premieres at the University of Illinois in Urbana.

May 6   Dominick Argento's opera *The Boor* — based on a play by Anton Chekhov, with a libretto by John Olon-

Scrymgeour — premieres at the Festival of American Music in Rochester, New York. Critic Jay S. Harrison later says, "*The Boor*, in short, is a bore and not even the elegant settings and polished performance could drape its faults and relieve its monotony."

May 9   *Panfilo and Lauretta*, a three-act opera by Carlos Chavez, premieres at Columbia University in New York City. It is about aristocrats trying to avoid pestilence in the 14th century.

May 9   Werner Egk's *Der Revisor* premieres in Schwetzingen. The five-act comic opera is about corruption in tsarist Russia.

May 22   *Una domanda di matrimonio*, a one-act opera buffa by Luciano Chailly, premieres in Milan at La Piccola Scala. Claudio Fino's libretto is based on a play by Anton Chekhov, *The Proposal*. The work is the second of Chailly's compositions for the theater and is well received.

May 24   George Antheil's opera *Venus in Africa* receives its first performance at the University of Denver, Colorado. It is about a young American in Tunis who asks a statue of Venus for help in finding love.

May 25   *Die Bluthochzeit*, by Wolfgang Fortner, premieres in Cologne. This opera is a revised version of his earlier opera *Der Wald*, which premiered in 1953.

May 25   Vissarion Shebalin's *The Taming of the Shrew* premieres in Kuibishev, Soviet Union. It is a four-act comic opera.

June 6   The first staged performance of Arnold Schoenberg's *Moses und Aron* takes place at the Stadttheater in Zurich. The text is by the composer and is based on the Book of Exodus. The work was begun in 1926 as a cantata but evolved into an opera in three acts. Schoenberg left the opera unfinished at his death. It had been performed over the radio in 1954.

Aug. 2   American composer Marvin David Levy's *The Tower* is premiered by the Santa Fe Opera Company in Santa Fe, New Mexico. This is his second one-act opera. Levy has studied with Otto Luening.

Aug. 11   *Die Harmonie der Welt*, by Paul Hindemith, is given its world premiere at the Prinzregententheater at the Munich Festival. The composer conducts. Hindemith writes his own libretto, incorporating two historical figures — the astronomer/astrologer Johannes Kepler (1571–1630) and General Albrecht von Wallenstein (1538–1634). Critic Everett Helm describes the five-act opera in the New York *Times* as "a pageant of events and conditions."

Aug. 17   Rolf Liebermann's three-act opera buffa *Schule der Frauen*, based on a play by Moliere, receives its first stage performance in Salzburg. It is scored for six singers and chamber orchestra.

Oct. 26   Tikhon Khrennikov's *Mother*, based on a novel by Maxim Gorky, premieres at the Bolshoi Theater in Moscow. The four-act opera is about striking factory workers and includes melodic quotations from various revolutionary songs.

Nov. 22   American composer Jack Beeson's opera *The Sweet Bye and Bye* premieres in New York City. The three-act opera is about the disappearance of revivalist Aimee Semple MacPherson in 1926.

1957 Dance

Jan. 1   John Cranko's *The Prince of the Pagodas* — to music by Benjamin Britten, with scenery by John Piper and costumes by Desmond Heeley — is premiered by The Royal Ballet in London. The evening-length ballet is a fairy tale. It is danced by Svetlana Beriosova, Julia Farron and David Blair.

March 26   *The Bewitched*, a dance satire, receives its world premiere at the University of Illinois. Alwin Nikolais choreographs music by Harry Partch. The 80-minute score was composed between 1952 and 1955. According to the composer, the piece is about "the transmission of perception." Its central character is a witch (solo soprano) who bewitches the musicians.

April 27   The Kirov Ballet presents Yuri Grigorovich's version of Sergei Prokofiev's *The Stone Flower*. Irina Kolpakova, Alla Osipenko, Alexander Gribov and Anatoli Grindin star. The ballet is about a stonecutter who leaves home to pursue his ideal. This version becomes the standard. Soviet critics consider it one of the most important ballets of the Soviet era.

April 27   Maurice Bejart's ballet *Sonate a trois* is performed for the first time in Essen. Adapted from Jean-Paul Sartre's *No Exit*, it deals with three people who have to share a small room from which there is no escape. The work is set to Bela Bartok's Sonata for 2 Pianos and Percussion. Michele Seigneuret, Tania Bari and Bejart star.

May 13   Choreographer Herbert Ross' *The Maids* — to music by Darius Milhaud, with decor by William Atkins — is performed for the first time by the Ballet Theater in New York City. The dance is based on a play by Jean Genet. Paul Olsen and Loren Hightower head the cast.

Nov. 16   *Medusa*, a ballet in three scenes, premieres at the State Opera in Vienna. Choreography is by Erika Hanka, and music is by Gottfried von Einem. It is about the myth-

SCENE FROM *AGON*

ological figure who has the effect of turning people who gaze on her to stone. Christl Zimmerl stars.

Nov. 21   The New York City Ballet dances George Balanchine's *Square Dance*. The work, set to music by Arcangelo Corelli and Antonio Vivaldi, is a classical ballet performed in square dance formations. Many of the steps are called out by a caller. Patricia Wilde and Nicholas Magallanes star.

Nov. 22   *The Moon Reindeer*, by Birgit Cullberg, receives its first performance at the Royal Danish Ballet in Copenhagen. The ballet, with music by Knudage Riisager, is based on a Lapp legend in which a young girl under the spell of a sorcerer is turned into a reindeer that lures men to their deaths. However, one man fights the sorcerer, and the girl is permitted to resume her own form. Mona Vangsaa, Henning Kronstam and Fredbjorn Bjornsson star.

Nov. 24   Erick Hawkins' modern dance work *Here and Now with Watchers*, to music by Lucia Dlugoszewski, premieres in New York City.

Nov. 29   The Paliashvili Theater of Opera and Ballet in Tbilisi, Soviet Union presents the first performance of Vakhtang Chaboukiani's four-act ballet *Othello*. It is set to music by Alexei Machavariani. Chaboukiani dances the title role.

Dec. 1   The New York City Ballet gives the official premiere of George Balanchine's *Agon* (there had been a public preview on November 27). The score, commissioned by the ballet company, is by Igor Stravinsky. The abstract work — a series of intricate ensembles, pas de deux, pas de trois, pas de quatre and solos — is considered one of the major dance works of the 20th century. Diana Adams, Melissa Hayden, Barbara Walczak, Barbara Milberg, Todd Bolender, Roy Tobias, Jonathan Watts, Arthur Mitchell, Roberta Lubell, Francia Russell, Dido Sayers and Ruth Sobotka are in the opening night cast. Mildred Norton writes in the *Saturday Review* (New York) that *Agon* "possesses the crystalline texture and rhythmic elan that vivify Stravinsky's writing for the theater. . . ."

1957 Instrumental and Vocal Music

Jan. 11   Henk Badings' Symphony No. 8 premieres in Hannover, Germany.

Jan. 20   Morton Gould's symphonic piece *Declaration* is premiered by Howard Mitchell and the National Symphony Orchestra at Constitution Hall in Washington,

D.C. This concert is held to celebrate the second inauguration of President Dwight D. Eisenhower.

Jan. 25   William Walton's Cello Concerto receives its first performance by Charles Munch and the Boston Symphony Orchestra, with Gregor Piatigorsky as soloist.

Feb. 2   Dimitri Mitropoulos and the New York Philharmonic premiere Morton Gould's orchestral work *Jekyll and Hyde Variations*.

Feb. 26   Kurt Atterberg's *Sinfonia visionaria* (Ninth Symphony) premieres in Helsinki. This is the Swedish composer's last symphony.

March 3   Henry Brant's *All Souls Carnival* receives its initial performance at Carnegie Recital Hall in New York with the composer conducting.

March 8   David Diamond's Symphony No. 6 is premiered by Charles Munch and the Boston Symphony Orchestra. The two themes of the first movement form the basis of the entire three-movement symphony.

March 15   Symphony No. 2 in E Major, by Ernst von Dohnanyi, is performed in a revised version by Antal Dorati and the Minneapolis Symphony Orchestra. An earlier version was performed in 1948.

April 4   Heitor Villa-Lobos' Symphony No. 10 premieres in Paris. The music celebrates Sao Paulo's 400th anniversary and is scored for soloists, chorus and orchestra.

April 9   Howard Hanson's *Song of Democracy*, with a text by Walt Whitman, premieres in Washington, D.C., the composer conducting. It celebrates the centennial of the National Education Association of America.

April 12   Symphony No. 4, by Wallingford Riegger, premieres at the University of Illinois in Urbana. The three-movement symphony was commissioned by the Fromm Music Foundation for the Festival of Contemporary Arts at that university. The second movement contains material from Riegger's ballet *Chronicle*, which he composed for Martha Graham in 1936.

April 20   Dominick Argento's *Ode to the West Wind* (Concerto for Soprano and Orchestra), based on poetry by Percy Bysshe Shelley, premieres at the Festival of American Music in Rochester, New York.

May 10   Concerto No. 2 in E Major for Piano and Orchestra, by Dmitri Shostakovich, receives its world premiere in Moscow, with the composer's son MaximShostakovich as soloist. The three-movement work is scored for piano and small orchestra. Maxim Shostakovich is now 19 years old.

June 17   Igor Stravinsky's *Agon* is premiered in a concert version conducted by Robert Craft in Los Angeles. The choreographed production by George Balanchine takes place this December 1.

June 26   *Dos movimientos*, by Cristobal Halffter, premieres in Madrid. The piece is scored for kettledrum and string orchestra.

Oct. 1   Edmund Rubbra's Symphony No. 7 receives its initial performance by Andrzej Panufnik and the Birmingham Symphony Orchestra in Birmingham, England. The work has three movements. Rubbra is currently teaching at Oxford University.

Oct. 24   Jean Martinon's cantata *Le lis de Saron* premieres in Paris, the composer conducting.

Oct. 25   Aaron Copland's *Fantasy for Piano* receives its first performance by William Masselos in New York City. This event is a celebration of the Juilliard School's 50th anniversary.

Oct. 30   Symphony No. 11, in G Minor (1905), Op. 103, by Dmitri Shostakovich, receives its world premiere in Moscow. Composed to commemorate the 1905 Russian Revolution, the work's four movements are entitled "Palace Square," "January 9," "Eternal Memory," and "Alarm." Ross Parmenter later characterizes the work in the New York *Times* as "vividly pictorial."

Nov. 18   Leo Sowerby's cantata *The Throne of God* premieres in Washington, D.C. It is scored for mixed voices and orchestra and was commissioned to celebrate the 50th anniversary of the National Cathedral in that city.

Nov. 22   Ernst Toch's Symphony No. 4 is premiered by Antal Dorati and the Minneapolis Symphony Orchestra. The symphony has three movements.

Dec. 6   Symphony No. 3, by Roger Sessions, receives its initial performance by Charles Munch and the Boston Symphony Orchestra. The four-movement work uses a 12-tone row as a structural element.

1957   Births, Deaths and Debuts

Jan. 16   Italian conductor Arturo Toscanini, 89, dies in New York. Originally a cellist, he began his conducting career as a last-minute substitute in Rio de Janeiro in 1886. During his long life he held musical directorships with many musical organizations — La Scala (1898–1903, 1906–8, 1921–29), the Metropolitan Opera (1908–15), the New York Philharmonic (1928–36) and the NBC Symphony Orchestra (1937–54). In each post he demanded, and received, the highest standards from his musicians and singers — a perfection that was attained both by his inspiration and by his awesome temper. Toscanini conducted the world premieres of *Pagliacci*, *La Boheme*, *The Girl of the Golden West*, *Madame Sans-Gene* and Arrigo Boito's *Nerone*. A foe of the Nazis, he refused to conduct in Germany under their regime and settled in America during World War II. His interpretations — the opposite of the expansive German romantic school of conducting — were characterized by lean, textured, taut performances. He committed all music he conducted to memory because of severe myopia.

Jan. 20 Daniel Barenboim makes his American debut as a pianist at Carnegie Hall in New York. He plays Sergei Prokofiev's First Piano Concerto, conducted by Leopold Stokowski. Barenboim is 14 years old.

Feb. 16 Polish pianist Josef Hofmann, 81, dies in Los Angeles. A child prodigy, he first performed in public at age 6. At age 11 he toured the United States, but after criticism by the Society for the Prevention of Cruelty to Children and an offer by Alfred Corning Clark of $50,000 for the continuance of his education, Hofmann returned to Europe to study with Moritz Moszkowski and Anton Rubinstein. He returned to the stage when he was 18 and was eventually regarded as one of the greatest pianists of his time. He was head of the piano department at the Curtis Institute of Music in Philadelphia from 1926 to 1938.

March 8 Swiss composer Othmar Schoeck, 70, dies in Zurich. He studied at the Zurich Conservatory and with Max Reger in Leipzig. He earned his living largely as a conductor in Zurich and in Saint Gall. In addition to 5 song cycles, he wrote more than 120 songs. Other works include 6 operas, 2 string quartets and concertos. He is considered to have been Switzerland's best composer of songs.

May 2 Polish composer Tadeusz Kassern, 53, dies in New York. He studied at the Lwow Conservatory and in Poznan before moving to Paris. He later went to New York and became the Polish consulate's cultural attache. He then severed his relationship with Communist Poland and, last year, became an American citizen. His music reflects an attraction to Polish folk song but is couched in some of the harmonic and rhythmic trends of contemporary European music, including bitonality and neoclassicism. He wrote two operas and many other pieces, especially concertos.

May 6 Soviet composer Mikhail Gnessin, 74, dies in Moscow. A student of Anatoly Liadov and Nikolai Rimsky-Korsakov at the Saint Petersburg Conservatory, he traveled to Germany and Palestine and became preoccupied with socialism. His music is romantic in style, with some of his works reflecting an interest in Jewish folk song. He wrote an opera, *Abraham's Youth*; a string quartet entitled *Variations on a Jewish Theme*; and many other works scored for a variety of voices and instruments. He also authored a monograph on Rimsky-Korsakov.

May 9 Italian bass Ezio Pinza, 64, dies in Stamford, Connecticut. After a brief career as a professional bicycle racer, he studied singing and eventually made his debut in 1921 as King Mark in *Tristan and Isolde* in Rome. After several seasons at La Scala, he was engaged in 1926 by the Metropolitan, where he sang until 1947. He also made guest appearances in Europe. He was famous for roles in operas by Giuseppe Verdi and Charles Gounod, as Boris Godunov and especially as Don Giovanni and Figaro in the Mozart operas, which he sang in famous performances at Salzburg in the 1930s as well as at other opera houses. In 1949 he became a matinee idol because of his appearance

in the Broadway musical *South Pacific*. He was known for his beautiful voice, his imposing stage appearance and his good looks. He could not read a note of music.

May 30 Renata Scotto makes her London debut as she sings the role of Adina in Gaetano Donizetti's *L'elisir d'amore*. Desmond Shawe-Taylor of *Opera* (London) calls her". . . the discovery of the whole season." Scotto's initial debut took place at the Teatro Nuovo in Milan, when she sang Violetta in *La traviata* in 1954.

June 9 Swiss composer Robert Oboussier, 56, is stabbed to death by his roommate in Zurich. A pupil of Philipp Jarnach at the Conservatory of Zurich, he also conducted and wrote about music. He was an editor of the *Deutsche allgemeine Zeitung* between 1922 and 1928 and a music critic. He was also director of the *Central Archive of Swiss Music*. His music incorporates stylistic elements of Germanic and southern European culture. He wrote one opera, *Amphitryon* (premiered in 1951), as well as orchestral, choral and piano pieces.

July 6 French opera composer Henri Fevrier, 81, dies in Paris. His principal teachers at the Paris Conservatoire were Gabriel Faure and Jules Massenet. He composed five operas and many operettas. He also wrote a book about Andre Messager.

Sep. 1 French-horn player Dennis Brain, 36, dies in an automobile accident in Hatfield, Hertfordshire, England. He was the first horn player of the Royal Philharmonic and later the Philharmonic Orchestra. He gave the first performance of Benjamin Britten's *Serenade for Tenor, Horn*

JEAN SIBELIUS

and Strings, which was written for him. He was also known for his performances of the Mozart and Strauss horn concertos. Along with his father, Aubrey Brain, he was one of the few players of the French horn to gain international recognition.

Sep. 3   Renata Scotto, 23, replaces an indisposed Maria Callas as Amina in a performance of *La sonnambula* during the Edinburgh Festival. Scotto later says she learned the role in three days. Harold Rosenthal of *Opera* (London) states: "Never were Callas's gifts and faults so much in evidence as on this occasion in her absence!"

Sep. 20   Finnish composer Jean Sibelius, 91, dies in Jarvenpaa, Finland. After less than a year studying law, he entered the local conservatory to study music, his childhood love. After studies in Finland, Germany and Vienna, he started composing music inspired by Finnish legends. By 1893 he was appointed to the faculty of the Helsinki Conservatory. In 1897 was awarded an annual salary of 2,000 marks for 10 years by the Finnish government.

His nationalistic work *Finlandia* (premiered in 1900) so stirred the emotions that its performance was prohibited by the tsarist government during periods of civil strife. He composed his last piece in 1929 and inexplicably spent his final 30 years in retirement.

His music belongs to the postromantic tradition, and his seven symphonies remain the most impressive of his output. The early nationalistic works were inspired by the geography, sagas and sentiments of the Finnish people. These include *En Saga* (composed in 1892), *The Swan of Tuonela* (composed in 1893) and *Pohjola's Daughter* (composed in 1906). His music expressed the intensity of arctic light and dark and, like that of Edvard Grieg, the depth of Scandinavian emotion. He was the last important composer of the generation of Richard Strauss — the generation that connected the romantic age to the 20th century by forging the stylistic trends of postromanticism. These trends included massive orchestras, heavy orchestral textures and, perhaps most important, some immersion in nationalism expressed through music. Sibelius achieved enormous popularity in Scandinavia, England and America. His music is seldom performed in other parts of Europe, however. He is considered to have been the towering figure in Finnish music.

Nov. 29   Austrian composer Erich Wolfgang Korngold, 60, dies in Hollywood, California. After studies with Alexander von Zemlinsky, he was billed as a "wunderkind" — his piano trio, composed at age 12, was immediately published. A series of quick successes — including performances conducted by Arthur Nikisch and Felix Weingartner — established Korngold as a young composer by the time he was 20. Gustav Mahler proclaimed him a genius, and this endorsement, along with the 1928 premiere of his opera *Die tote Stadt*, catapulted Korngold to international attention.

Korngold first went to Hollywood in 1934 to work on a film version of *A Midsummer Night's Dream*. He traveled back and forth between Europe and Hollywood before finally deciding to remain in Hollywood, where he worked principally as a composer of film music. Despite his accessible film music, Korngold was somehow unable to maintain his success in the opera house and concert hall. This may have been due to the style of his work — Viennese romanticism — which he never changed. He composed six operas, many orchestral works, and chamber and piano pieces.

Nov. 30   Italian tenor Beniamino Gigli, 67, dies in Rome. One of the most popular tenors of the century, Gigli debuted in 1914 in Rovigo, Italy. He came to America in 1920, just a month before Enrico Caruso's last appearance, and was considered by many to be his successor. After refusing to take a cut in salary requested by the Metropolitan during the depression, he returned to Europe to sing, coming back to the United States in 1938. He was much criticized for his support of the fascists during World War II. He sang up to his death, his voice remaining intact. Although afflicted with a penchant for holding on to high notes and excessive sobbing, he was the possessor of a beautiful and expressive voice.

Dec. 21   English composer and violist Eric Coates, 71, dies in Chichester, England. After studies at the Royal Academy of Music, he joined the Hambourg String Quartet and later the Queen's Hall Orchestra. He also toured the United States and South America as a conductor. His music, mostly for orchestra, is of a light, semiclassical nature and quickly attained popularity for this reason. Examples of such pieces are *Sleepy Lagoon*, a serenade-waltz, and the march "Knightsbridge," from his *London Suite*.

1957   Related Events

Leonard Bernstein becomes music director of the New York Philharmonic, succeeding Dimitri Mitropoulos. Bernstein is the first American-born conductor to assume this position, which he holds for 11 years.

The International Summer Academy of Dance is established this summer in Krefeld, Germany. It subsequently moves to Cologne and becomes known as the best summer dance school in Europe.

Luciano Berio and Bruno Maderna establish the Studio di Fonologia Musicale this year in Milan. This is a new electronic music studio.

Ballet Theatre changes its name to American Ballet Theatre this year.

Les Ballets Chiriaeff changes its name this year to Les Grandes Ballets Canadiens.

Construction begins on the Sydney Opera House this year in Sydney, Australia. The project takes 16 years to complete.

The Audio Engineering Society convention takes place in New York City. Organized by Decca (England) and Westrex, the convention features demonstrations of stereo discs. To attenuate the "battle of the speeds," Westrex's 45/45 cutting system is adopted internationally. A new stereo disc manufactured by Westrex is marketed this year by Sidney Frey's Audio Fidelity firm in America.

American composers and computer specialists Lejaren Hiller and Leonard M. Isaacson create their *Illiac Suite* for string quartet this year. The title is an abbreviation of "Illinois accumulator." The computer-generated music involves programming the computer to compose music according to predetermined rules, selecting pitches at random, storing them in a memory (but rejecting them if they violate the rules) and "assembling" them into a composition. The computer printout is then transcribed into notation for conventional instruments. The results, while not satisfying to every music lover, achieve a high degree of notoriety for Hiller. He devotes much of his time and energy to computer music as well as to his earlier field, chemistry. Hiller's work was preceded — to some degree, at least — by that of John Pierce and M.E. Shannon, of Bell Laboratories, who experimented with computer-generated chance music six years ago.

May 6   Norman Dello Joio is awarded the Pulitzer Prize for music for *Meditations of Ecclesiastes*.

May 15   Franz Josef Haydn's Concerto in D Major for Violoncello and Orchestra is performed in its authentic version by Enrico Mainardi in Vienna. The original manuscript has recently been found, and the attribution of its composition to Anton Kraft is now discredited (Kraft was principal cellist in Haydn's Esterhazy Orchestra).

May 28   The Philharmonia Hungarica gives its first concert today as Zoltan Rozsnyai conducts a program of music by Haydn, Antonin Dvorak, Bela Bartok, and Zoltan Kodaly in the Large Concert Hall of the Konzerthaus in Vienna.

Les Ballets de l'Etoile, founded in 1953 by Maurice Bejart and Jean Laurent, changes its name this month to Ballet-Theatre de Paris.

Aug. 31   The first international Gaudeamus Music Week begins today. The festival, which takes place in Bilthoven, the Netherlands, becomes an annual event. This year's celebration features music (mostly chamber music) of European composers. Gaudeamus Music Weeks was initiated on a national basis in 1945. Until last year, there were no plans to expand the festival to an international basis.

Sep. 9   *Life* magazine reports that Carnegie Hall in New York City is to be torn down to make way for a new office building. This announcement results in an outburst of protest from music lovers throughout the world. Violinist Isaac Stern immediately organizes a campaign to save Carnegie Hall. His efforts are hampered by the powerful forces supporting construction of Lincoln Center for the Performing Arts, which do not want unnecessary competition (the Rockefeller family has invested heavily in the future of Philharmonic Hall — the new home of the New York Philharmonic). Stern's group wins, and he subsequently becomes president of Carnegie Hall. The crisis also results in the formation of the Carnegie Hall Corporation — a nonprofit organization to protect, manage and rent the concert hall; the corporation is officially established on July 1, 1960.

1958 Opera

Jan. 15   The world premiere of *Vanessa*, by Samuel Barber, takes place at the Metropolitan Opera House in New York City. Gian-Carlo Menotti writes the libretto, and Cecil Beaton designs the costumes and sets. The opera is heaped with praise. Some critics say that this opera, which later receives the Pulitzer Prize, should have been called "Erika," because she is the character the opera focuses on. The opening night cast includes Eleanor Steber, Rosalind Elias and Nicolai Gedda. Dimitri Mitropoulos conducts. Several noteworthy facts surround this opera. It is the composer's first, and it quickly becomes known as one of the finest examples of an opera written by an American composer. It is the first world premiere offered under the leadership of Rudolf Bing. It is also the first American opera to be staged at the Met in 11 years and the first American opera to be produced at the Salzburg Festival. The five-voice fugue — "To Leave, To Break, To Find, To Keep" — sung near the end of the opera, becomes known as one of the finest examples of Barber's musical craftsmanship and skill in writing for the human voice.

Feb. 6   Deems Taylor's chamber opera *The Dragon* is premiered in a piano-organ version with singers by the New York University Opera Workshop. The one-act work is about a princess pursued by a dragon and the prince who saves her.

March 1   *Assassinio nella cattedrale*, by Ildebrando Pizzetti, premieres in Milan at La Scala. The libretto is by the composer, based on T.S. Eliot's *Murder in the Cathedral* — the story of Thomas a Becket. The opera is well received.

March 19   Douglas Moore's *Gallantry* premieres in New York City. The one-act opera is about a surgeon who desires a nurse. The composer characterizes it as a "soap opera."

April 14   Ned Rorem's *The Robbers*, with a libretto by the composer, and Vittorio Rieti's *The Pet Shop* are premiered at Mannes College of Music in New York. In the first, three robbers fight among themselves for their stolen money. In the second, a woman tries to influence the judge of a dog show by marrying him.

May 4   Marvin David Levy's one-act opera *Escurial* premieres in New York City.

June 18   Benjamin Britten's *Noye's Fludde* premieres at Oxford, England. This "miracle play," in one act, is based on the biblical tale of Noah and the Ark. Charles Mackerras conducts a cast that includes Owen Brannigan and Gladys Parr.

June 20   *The Scarf*, a one-act opera by Lee Hoiby, libretto based on a tale by Anton Chekhov, receives its initial performance in Spoleto at the First Festival of Two Worlds. It is about a woman who kills her husband so she can have the mailman.

July 16   Carlisle Floyd's three-act opera *Wuthering Heights* is premiered by the Santa Fe Opera in New Mexico. The composer writes his own libretto to the opera, which is based on the novel by Emily Bronte. Floyd later decides to revise the work, and Howard Taubman writes of the revision in the New York *Times* that although the vocal writing is "gray and differentiated," the opera has "warmth and sincerity."

Aug. 20   Gian-Carlo Menotti's *Maria Golovin* is performed for the first time in Brussels at the American Pavilion of the World's Fair. Menotti's libretto is the story of a love affair between Donato, a young blind man, and Maria, the wife of a prisoner of war. Irving Kolodin subsequently writes of it in *Saturday Review* magazine: "Menotti's flow is cleverly diverted into some channels and areas he has not previously been able to navigate."

Oct. 3   Humphrey Searle's *The Diary of a Madman*, based on a tale by Nikolai Gogol, is premiered by Hermann Scherchen in Berlin. The one-act opera is about a government clerk in Russia who is demented.

Oct. 25   Leos Janacek's *Osud* is performed posthumously in its stage version in Brno. The opera is about a frustrated composer. Composed between 1903 and 1904, it was premiered over radio in 1934.

1958 Dance

Jan. 4   The Kirov Theater in Leningrad presents the first performance of Konstantin Sergeyev's *The Path of Thunder*. The three-act ballet, to music by Kara Karayev, tells the tragic story of the love between a white girl and a black boy.

Jan. 8   George Balanchine's *Gounod Symphony* — to music by Charles Gounod, with scenery by Horace Armistead and costumes by Karinska — is premiered by the New York City Ballet in New York. The lead dancers are Maria Tallchief and Jacques d'Amboise.

Jan. 17   *Stars and Stripes* — a ballet choreographed by George Balanchine to music by John Philip Sousa arranged and orchestrated by Hershey Kay, with scenery by David Hays and costumes by Karinska — is premiered by the New York City Ballet in New York. Allegra Kent, Robert Barnett, Diana Adams, Melissa Hayden and Jacques d'Amboise dance the lead roles in this colorful tribute to American symbols and sounds.

Feb. 1   A new version of Maurice Ravel's *La Valse*, with choreography by Frederick Ashton, is premiered by the La Scala Opera Ballet in Milan.

April 1   Martha Graham premieres her *Clytemnestra*, to music by Halim El-Dabh, in New York. The ballet, in two acts with prologue and epilogue, is based on the Aeschylus

trilogy. It is the first evening-length modern dance work. Martha Graham, Bertram Ross, Paul Taylor and Yuriko star.

April 3   The Martha Graham Dance Company presents *Embattled Garden*, to music by Carlos Surinach, in New York. It is a satirical view of the garden of Eden. Matt Turney, Yuriko, Bertram Ross and Glen Tetley star.

April 11   Jose Limon's *Missa Brevis* is performed for the first time at the Juilliard Dance Theater in New York City. The music is by Zoltan Kodaly, and lighting projections are by Ming Cho Lee. Limon dances the lead role in this modern dance work about the spirit of man.

May 21   Merce Cunningham's modern dance piece *Suite for Two*, to music by John Cage, premieres at the University of Pittsburgh.

July 26   John Cranko's version of Sergei Prokofiev's *Romeo and Juliet* is premiered by the La Scala Opera Ballet in Venice.

Aug. 14   Merce Cunningham's modern dance piece *Antic Meet*, to music by John Cage, receives its first performance at Connecticut College.

Aug. 17   *Summerspace*, a plotless work, receives its first performance by Merce Cunningham and Company at

Connecticut College in New London, Connecticut. The music is by Morton Feldman, the choreography by Merce Cunningham, the lighting by Nicolas Cernovich, and the costumes and decor by Robert Rauschenberg. The choreographer, Viola Farber, Carolyn Brown, Marilyn Wood, Cynthia Stone and Remy Charlip lead the cast.

Sep. 5 Merce Cunningham continues his premiere performances with his latest dance work — *Night Wandering*. This takes place in New London, Connecticut.

Oct. 27 Margot Fonteyn stars in the premiere of Frederick Ashton's *Ondine*, with the Royal Ballet at Covent Garden in London. The music is by Hans Werner Henze. The ballet tells the story of Ondine, a naiad, who tries unsuccessfully to lure Palemon away from his fiancee. On his wedding day he kisses Ondine, dies and is taken to live with Ondine in the sea. Ondine is considered Fonteyn's greatest creation. Michael Somes, Julia Farron and Alexander Grant star with Fonteyn in the opening night cast.

1958 *Instrumental and Vocal Music*

Jan. 23 Howard Hanson's *Mosaics* for orchestra is premiered by the Cleveland Orchestra, George Szell conducting. The composer interweaves various instrumental timbres to create a sense of color interplay. The work was commissioned to celebrate the 40th anniversary of this orchestra and was inspired by the mosaics at the Cathedral of Parma.

Jan. 24 Bohuslav Martinu's cantata *The Epic of Gilgamesh* and Ernst Krenek's *Kette, Kreis und Spiegel* are premiered by Paul Sacher and the Chamber Orchestra of Basel. The Krenek work is scored for orchestra.

Jan. 30 William Walton's *Partita for Orchestra* is premiered by the Cleveland Orchestra with George Szell conducting. The work has three parts and was commissioned to celebrate the 40th anniversary of the orchestra. Critic Howard Taubman says the music has "the tang of our century."

Feb. 5 Michael Tippett's Symphony No. 2 receives its world premiere by Sir Adrian Boult and the BBC Symphony Orchestra. The four-movement work took five years to compose and was completed last year. The musicians and conductor inadvertently lose their places during the first movement. Boult stops the orchestra, apologizes to the audience, and starts over. Tippett is now 53 years old.

Feb. 10 Henry Brant's *Mythical Beasts* — a work for mezzo-soprano and instruments — is performed for the first time by the New Century Players at Carnegie Hall in New York City.

March 5 *Orchestral Variations*, by Aaron Copland, receives its initial performance in Louisville, Kentucky, as Robert Whitney conducts the Louisville Orchestra. This work is an orchestrated version of Copland's *Piano Variations*, composed in 1930. Whitney asked Copland to orchestrate it. Critic Howard Taubman says the music has "dignity and becoming richness of effect."

March 16 *Doubles*, by Pierre Boulez, receives its world premiere in Paris. The symphonic variations involve different figures, or "doubles," that the composer says "pass each other's prisms." It alters the traditional seating arrangement of the orchestra, and musicians periodically shift their positions. This piece subsequently becomes the central movement of his three-section orchestral work *Figures, Doubles, Prismes*.

March 22 Havergal Brian's Symphony No. 9 receives its first performance by Norman Del Mar and the London Symphony Orchestra in London. The work has three movements and was composed in 1951. Brian, now 82 years old, has been living in virtual seclusion, composing symphony after symphony. So far, he has composed 12 of them.

March 28 George Rochberg's Symphony No. 1 premieres in Philadelphia. The work has three movements.

April 2 Symphony No. 9 in E Minor, by Ralph Vaughan Williams, receives its world premiere by Sir Adrian Boult and the London Philharmonic Orchestra in London. The four-movement work is the composer's last symphony. It is scored for large orchestra, including three saxophones and a fluegel-horn (a bugle-type instrument). A reviewer for *Musical America* (New York) writes that the music contains "those winding figures, of which Vaughan Williams is so fond, which do not have a striking profile...."

April 15 Ernest Bloch's Quintet No. 2 for Piano and Strings premieres at the University of California in Berkeley.

April 18 Quincy Porter's symphonic suite *New England Episodes* premieres in Washington, D.C. This event marks the opening of the first Inter-American Music Festival, sponsored by the Pan American Union.

April 20 Heitor Villa-Lobos' Symphony No. 12 and Camargo Guarnieri's *Choro* for clarinet and orchestra are premiered in Washington, D.C. at the Inter-American Music Festival.

April 22 Darius Milhaud's Symphony No. 8 (*Rhodanienne*) and Andrew Imbrie's Violin Concerto No. 1 are premiered by Enrique Jorda and the San Francisco Symphony Orchestra. The Milhaud symphony, in four movements, was inspired by the flow of the Rhone River.

April 29   Russian-American composer Lazare Saminsky's Symphony No. 5 (*Jerusalem*) premieres in New York City. Composed between 1929 and 1930, it has two sections and is scored for orchestra and chorus.

May 15   *Concert for Piano and Orchestra*, by John Cage, receives its first performance in New York. The piece combines electronic and aleatoric, or chance, elements. Cage states it can be performed "in whole or part, any duration, any number of performers, as a solo, chamber ensemble, symphony, concerto for piano and orchestra, etc." It utilizes unusual piano sonorities, such as the instrument's strings being plucked and strummed. The other performers are also expected to produce unusual sonorities — the tuba player is expected to play two tubas at once, and the violist is required to play the instrument tucked between his or her knees. Virgil Thomson says the music "is a far cry from the poverty of electronic sound. It is human, civilized, and sumptuous."

May 22   Randall Thompson's *Requiem* premieres as the concluding work of the University of California Music Festival in Berkeley. It is scored for double chorus *a cappella*.

May 30   Bela Bartok's Violin Concerto No. 1 premieres in Basel. The work was composed between 1905 and 1908 for violinist Geyer Steffy. Steffy held the manuscript in her possession without performing it. She died last year, and the score was then located. The concerto has two movements.

June 6   Rolf Liebermann's *Geigy Festival Concerto* premieres at the Musiksaal in Basel. Scored for orchestra and "Basel drum," the work was commissioned by J.R. Geigy and Company (the chemical firm) to celebrate its anniversary.

June 15   Florent Schmitt's Symphony No. 2, Op. 137, receives its first performance by Charles Munch and the Boston Symphony Orchestra in Strasbourg. This event marks the conclusion of this year's International Society for Contemporary Music festival. The three-movement piece is Schmitt's last symphonic work. He is now 87 years old.

Sep. 23   Igor Stravinsky's *Threni* receives its world premiere in Venice, the composer conducting. This is the composer's first integrally serial piece. The texts, from the lamentations of Jeremiah, are in Latin. It is scored for six soloists, chorus and orchestra. Stravinsky's *Canticum sacrum ad honorem Sancti Marci nominis*, premiered on September 13, 1956, is also dodecaphonic but not integrally serialized (all parameters of the music serialized, not just pitch). The work is performed in America next year. Critic Howard Taubman then says, "Stravinsky has a gift for saying much with few notes and voices."

Oct. 7   Henk Badings' electronic work *Genese* premieres in Brussels. This piece is scored for five oscillators and was recorded in Eindhoven. It is subsequently used as a ballet score with the title *Der Sechste Tag*.

Oct. 16   Benjamin Britten's *Nocturne* premieres in Leeds at the Centennial Music Festival. These songs for voice and small orchestra are to texts from various English poets.

Oct. 19   *Poesie pour pouvoir*, by Pierre Boulez, receives its world premiere at the Donaueschingen Festival. The composer and Hans Rosbaud conduct. The music is scored for two orchestras and nine loudspeakers, one of which is suspended from the ceiling and rotates. The loudspeakers emit the sounds of a taped text comprised of a French poem by Henri Michaux about a curse. The tape-manipulated text focuses on the sounds of the poem's syllables and is largely unintelligible in this presentation. Otto Tomek, a music director of the Cologne Radio, attends and later comments, "It was music that took you not only by the ears and mind but by the entire body."

Oct. 24   *Symphony of Chorales for Orchestra*, by Lukas Foss, based on chorales by Johann Sebastian Bach, is premiered by the Pittsburgh Symphony Orchestra with the composer conducting.

Nov. 3   Havergal Brian's Symphony No. 10 premieres in London. The single-movement work is romantic in style.

Dec. 2   Anton Webern's *Satz fur Klavier* is premiered posthumously by Else Stock-Hug in Vienna. The music was composed in 1906.

Dec. 5   Alexander Tcherepnin's Symphony No. 4 in E, Op. 91, is premiered by Charles Munch and the Boston Symphony Orchestra in Boston. The three-movement work was commissioned by this orchestra and wins the prestigious Glinka Prize. Critic Harold Rogers writes in the *Christian Science Monitor* that it is "artistically built."

1958   Births, Deaths and Debuts

Feb. 20   French pianist Isidor Philipp, 94, dies as a result of a fall in the Paris subway. He studied with Camille Saint-Saens, among others and, after a brief career as a pianist, turned to teaching at the Paris Conservatoire. He also made two-piano arrangements of famous works and published exercise books for piano students.

March 25   American composer Emerson Whithorne, 73, dies in Lyme, Connecticut. Born Emerson Whittern, he later changed his name to the original name of his paternal grandfather. After studies in Cleveland and appearances as a pianist in Chautauqua, he went to Vienna and studied piano with Theodor Leschetizky and composition with

Robert Fuchs. He also studied with Artur Schnabel. He later lived in London before settling in New York and becoming an active participant in the League of Composers. His music, often inspired by oriental melodies, is modernistic and embraces the "machine-music" style popular in the 1920s and 1930s. *The Aeroplane* is an example of a piece in this style. Whithorne was eclipsed, however, by George Antheil, who pursued and developed this style to a much higher degree of success. Whithorne's other works include various orchestral pieces, chamber and piano music, and songs.

May 19   Pianist Van Cliburn gives a debut concert at Carnegie Hall in New York. It is a triumphant return for Cliburn after winning first prize in the Tchaikovsky competition in Moscow. He plays the Tchaikovsky Concerto No. 1 and the Rachmaninoff Third Concerto. The NBC Symphony Orchestra is conducted by Kiril Kondrashin. The concert sells out so quickly that a second one is scheduled.

June 23   Finnish conductor and composer Armas Jarnefelt, 88, dies in Stockholm. He studied at the Helsinki Conservatory and later with Ferruccio Busoni and Jules Massenet. He then worked as an opera coach before becoming conductor of the Stockholm Opera, a post he held for 25 years. His music, little-known outside of Finland, is nationalistic in character.

July 31   English writer and lexicographer Percy Scholes, 80, dies in Vevey, Switzerland. He wrote *The Oxford Companion to Music*, was a recipient of many honorary degrees, wrote music criticism and founded the Anglo-American Music Education Conferences. His impact on the field of music was one of scholarly contribution and eloquent writing.

Aug. 5   English composer Josef Holbrooke, 79, dies in London. He was largely concerned with composing music that would entertain the masses. Although he enjoyed a following during his lifetime, his music fades away after today. He composed operas and ballets, orchestral and chamber music. His best-known work is probably his operatic trilogy *The Cauldron of Anwyn*, produced between 1912 and 1929.

Aug. 17   French composer Florent Schmitt, 87, dies in Neuilly, near Paris. After studies with various teachers, including Jules Massenet and Gabriel Faure, and after winning a few prizes, he went to Italy, Germany, Austria, Hungary and Turkey before settling in Paris. He was extraordinarily prolific and composed for virtually every combination of voices and instruments. His music is largely impressionistic in style but is fashioned of strong counterpoint and asymmetrical rhythms. He also included unusually heavy percussion parts in his orchestral textures. He wrote a great deal on music and was an important critic for *Le Temps* (Paris). His work includes several ballets, vocal music, vocal music with orchestra, chamber works, piano pieces and songs.

Aug. 24   German conductor and composer Leo Blech, 87, dies in Berlin. He studied composition with Engelbert Humperdinck and conducted opera in Berlin, Prague, Stockholm and Riga. His output as a composer includes operas and other compositions. His most successful work is *Das war ich*, an "opera-idyll." His music was Wagnerian in style.

Aug. 26   English composer Ralph Vaughan Williams, 85, dies in London. As a youngster he studied composition with Sir Charles Hubert Hastings Parry and Sir Charles Villiers Stanford. He then studied for a short time with Max Bruch in Berlin and Maurice Ravel in Paris. He became interested in English folk material, and much of his music reflects this interest.

His works embrace a variety of styles, from the Elizabethan modes of his *Fantasia on a Theme by Tallis* (premiered in 1910) to the more modern harmonies of his middle and late symphonies. Symphony No. 4 in F Minor (premiered in 1935) and Mass in G Minor (composed in 1923) are considered to be among his best works. His music includes use of parallel chord progressions and is often through-composed. He dedicated his Symphony No. 5 in D Major (premiered in 1943) to Jean Sibelius, to whom he was frequently compared. Both were intensely nationalistic in attitude, and both reflected this attitude in their music.

Unlike Sibelius, who died last September, Vaughan Williams frequently incorporated native folk melodies into his work. Vaughan Williams taught at the Royal College of Music in London, conducted the London Bach Choir and toured America three times. He was prolific and wrote a number of operas and three ballets in addition to his extensive list of symphonic and vocal works.

Oct. 16   Canadian soprano Teresa Stratas makes her debut with the Toronto Opera singing Mimi in *La Boheme*.

Nov. 27   Polish conductor Artur Rodzinski, 66, dies in Boston. He made his conducting debut in Lwow in 1921 and in 1926 became assistant to Leopold Stokowski with the Philadelphia Orchestra. Thereafter he was the music director of the Los Angeles Philharmonic, the Cleveland Orchestra, the New York Philharmonic and the Chicago Symphony. He was forced to leave the last two posts because of disagreements with the managements and afterward confined most of his work to Europe. Rodzinski was the first major conductor to introduce the performance of operas in concert form.

Dec. 29   Doris Humphrey, one of the most important personalities in the development of modern dance, dies in New York City at the age of 63. Humphrey danced with the Denishawn company from 1917 to 1928, during which time she was encouraged by Ruth Saint Denis to develop her choreographic skills. In 1928 she left Denishawn to found a company and school with Charles Weidman. Through experimentation, she developed a theory that the area of movement lay in the "arc between two deaths" — ranging from balance to imbalance, from fall to recovery.

This theory became the basis of her choreography. Humphrey was particularly adept in choreographing for mass groups. During her mature years, she developed a growing interest in the field of gesture and created a number of dramatic pieces while experimenting in this area. Among her greatest works are *The Shakers, Passacaglia* and her trilogy, *Theatre Piece, With My Red Fires* and *New Dance.*

Humphrey retired from performing in 1945 as a result of a hip injury and increasingly severe arthritis. She continued teaching and choreographing as director of the Jose Limon company until her death.

1958   Related Events

Ballets: U.S.A. is founded this year by Jerome Robbins. It is created to perform at the Brussels Worlds Fair and at the Festival of Two Worlds in Spoleto, Italy. Its first appearances create a sensation and the company continues after these two festival events are over.

George Skibine is appointed ballet-master of the Paris Opera Ballet this year.

The New York Philharmonic, under the leadership of Leonard Bernstein, begins its televised "Young People's Concerts." The program immediately becomes an American favorite and wins every major award for educational television.

Edouard van Remoortel becomes music director of the St. Louis Symphony Orchestra this year. This conductor remains in the post for four years. Van Remoortel succeeds Vladimir Golschmann and does not get on well with the orchestra.

Dance Perspectives begins publication this year. A quarterly devoted to different aspects of contemporary dance, it is edited by S.J. Cohen. It subsequently becomes one of the most famous dance publications of the century.

The Festival of Two Worlds is established this year in Spoleto, Italy by composer and librettist Gian Carlo

SPOLETO—HOME OF THE SPOLETO FESTIVAL

Menotti. The festival is devoted to performances of old and new music.

Pianist Van Cliburn becomes the first American and the first musician to have a recording of classical music (Tchaikovsky's Piano Concerto No. 1 in B-flat Minor) achieve sales of 1 million records. Other developments in the recording industry this year include: the release of stereo records by EMI (Electrical and Musical Industries) and Decca; RCA Victor's introduction of its 1/2 track, 3.75 ips speed cartridge and player; and the mass manufacturing of stereo disc playback hardware.

Max Mathews, J.R. Pierce and others at Bell Laboratories in New Jersey begin creating music by computer this year. Mathews is an electrical engineer and director of the Behavioral Research Department of Bell Laboratories. This development is an outgrowth of his research and the acoustical research of Dr. Harvey Fletcher. Computers are now used to produce musical sounds. The approach is subsequently refined by Godfrey Winham and Hubert S. Howe of Princeton University.

Jan. 2   Soprano Maria Callas causes a near riot at the Rome Opera when she walks out in the middle of a performance of *Norma*. Doctors say she is suffering from temporary hoarseness, but house superintendent Carol Lattini says Callas had celebrated the "start of the New Year until a late hour."

Jan. 13   Conductor Pietro Cimara collapses from a stroke on the podium while conducting a performance of *La Forze del destino* at the Metropolitan Opera House. The performance continues without interruption when second violinist Walter Hagen conducts the rest of the act from memory.

Feb.   Milton Babbitt's article "Who Cares if You Listen?" is published this month in *High Fidelity* (New York). Babbitt discusses the schism between the contemporary composer and the musical public, and argues that the "isolation" of composers is inevitable and ultimately advantageous. He states that developments in 20th century music are comparable to those that took place in theoretical physics in the middle of the 19th century and contends that the "fall from musical innocence" is irreversible and "disquieting" to the average concertgoer. He concludes, in part, "And so, I dare suggest that the composer would do himself and his music an immediate and eventual service by total, resolute, and voluntary withdrawal from his public world to one of private performance and electronic media, with its very real possibility of complete elimination of the public and social aspects of musical composition."

The article is one of the most controversial on music in this century and brings Babbitt into the foreground of renewed debate and discussion about contemporary music and contemporary composers. This year, Babbitt composes *Sounds and Words*, a work for voice and piano whose text consists of different syllables.

April 13   American pianist Van Cliburn wins the Tchaikovsky International Piano Contest in Moscow. He is the first American to receive this prestigious prize. He performed the Tchaikovsky First Piano Concerto and the Rachmaninoff Third Piano Concerto.

May 5   Samuel Barber is awarded the Pulitzer Prize for music for his opera *Vanessa*.

May 20   Van Cliburn is lauded in New York City with a ticker-tape parade for his having won the Tchaikovsky competition. This event marks the first time an American musician receives such a tribute.

May 28   A resolution is issued by the Central Committee of the Soviet Communist Party effectively nullifying its earlier resolution of February 10, 1948, which attacked various operas by Soviet composers as displaying the wrong musical tendencies. These operas included Herman Zhukovsky's *From All Our Hearts*. The earlier document also attacked Sergei Prokofiev, Dmitri Shostakovich, Aram Khachaturian and Nikolai Miaskovsky for being submissive to Western decadence. Today's resolution admits "blatant errors" in some of the committee's previous judgments and attempts to reconcile Soviet composers with their government. It also states that music by the composers mentioned may have been wrongly denounced "as the representations of a formalist anti-people trend." Prokofiev and Miaskovsky are dead and cannot respond. Shostakovich responds, in part, to today's development by saying in *Pravda*, "The resolution wipes out the unfair and sweeping appraisals of various Soviet composers."

June 2   Herman D. Kenin is elected to succeed James C. Petrillo as president of the American Federation of Musicians. This event takes place in Philadelphia at the 61st convention of the national organization.

June 6   Jerome Robbins' company, Ballets: USA gives its premiere performance at the Teatro Nuovo in Spoleto, dancing works by Todd Bolender and Robbins.

Sep. 3   Mechanical instruments, including tape recorders, are prohibited in services of holy worship by the Vatican. The instruction is issued by the Congregation of Rites and includes electronic organs and microphones to amplify sermons.

Oct. 4   H.F. Olson and H. Belar, inventors at the Acoustical and Electromechanical Research Laboratory of the Radio Corporation of America, patent their invention — the RCA electronic music synthesizer. This synthesizer produces and manipulates timbre, reverberation, dynamics, speed and rhythm.

Nov. 6   Soprano Maria Callas is dropped from her Metropolitan Opera contract by manager Rudolf Bing. She had refused to sing the lead role in *La Traviata* as well as the heavier role of Lady Macbeth in the same season.

1959 Opera

Feb. 6   *La voix humaine*, by Francis Poulenc, premieres in Paris at the Opera-Comique. The text is from the play by Jean Cocteau. The opera has only one character, a woman who is saying good-bye to her lover over the telephone. Poulenc creates the opera for soprano Denise Duval. A Paris critic characterizes the work as "Melisande on the telephone."

April 26   Hugo Weisgall's *Six Characters in Search of an Author*, based on the play by Luigi Pirandello, premieres at the New York City Opera in New York. The characters are members of an opera company. Weisgall has studied at the Peabody Conservatory and at the Curtis Institute of Music. He is currently teaching at the Juilliard School.

May 14   Lou Harrison's opera *Rapunzel* receives its first performance at the YMHA in New York City. It is his first opera.

May 17   Bohuslav Martinu's opera *Mirandoline*, based on a comedy by Carlo Goldoni, premieres in Prague.

May 31   *Aniara* — a new futuristic opera by Swedish composer Karl-Birger Blomdahl — receives its world premiere today in Stockholm. Based on a science fiction novel by Harry Martinson about space travel, it includes electronic sound. The opera depicts a bleak future of atomic war and the struggle for survival of the remaining population, which leaves the planet for greener pastures. The seed of the music is an all-interval set and a 12-tone row. The opera immediately catapults Blomdahl to international fame and is subsequently performed throughout Europe.

June 17   Samuel Barber's *A Hand of Bridge*, to a libretto by Gian-Carlo Menotti, is performed for the first time at the Teatro Caio Melisso in Spoleto. The action consists of the dialogue that takes place between bridge players. The work is scored for chamber orchestra and four solo voices.

June 19   Henk Badings' electronic opera *Salto mortale*, with a libretto by the composer, premieres on Dutch television. This is the first opera featuring a score recorded electronically. It is scored for five voices and electronic tape and is about a biochemistry professor who brings a suicide victim back to life. When the suicide victim, a poet, pursues the professor's laboratory assistant, the professor decides to kill him.

Oct. 23   Lee Hoiby's *Beatrice*, based on a play by Maurice Maeterlinck, premieres in Louisville, Kentucky. The three-act opera is about a nun who falls from grace by visiting bordellos.

Oct. 28   *Panfilo and Lauretta*, an opera by Carlos Chavez, is performed in a revised version in Spanish in Mexico City, the composer conducting. It was previously performed in 1957.

Oct. 30   The first performance of Luciano Chailly's *Procedura penale* is held at the Como Festival in Italy. The libretto, by Dino Buzzati, concerns the desperation of conventional, superficial lives. It is considered the most successful product of the collaboration between Chailly and Buzzati. Besides studies in Italy, Chailly studied with Paul Hindemith.

Nov. 27   Nicolas Nabokov's *Der Tod des Grigori Rasputin* premieres in Cologne. This three-act opera is based on materials from his earlier opera *The Holy Devil* and is about the murder of Rasputin.

Dec. 11   Carl Orff's *Oedipus der Tyrann*, based on Sophocles, premieres in Stuttgart. Orff characterizes this opera as a "funeral play."

Dec. 15   *Blue Flame*, by Alan Hovhaness, receives its initial performance in San Antonio, Texas. The opera has four scenes. Hovhaness, now 48 years old, studied composition with Frederick S. Converse and Bohuslav Martinu. His music combines musical elements of Oriental cultures, Armenian rhythms, thematic repetition and dynamic contrast.

Dec. 22   Vissarion Shebalin's *The Sun over the Steppe* receives its first stage performance in Moscow. The three-act opera, about Bolsheviks and civil war, was premiered in a concert version last June.

KARL-BIRGER BLOMDAHL

1959 Dance

March 22   Alwin Nikolais' modern dance piece *Finials* receives its first performance on the "Steve Allen Show," on WNBC-TV. Over the next year, many of this choreographer's works make their first appearances on this program.

April 16   The Bolshoi Ballet performs *Romeo and Juliet* in New York City. This event marks the work's American premiere and the first time the Russian company has performed in the United States. The lead dancers are Galina Ulanova and Yuri Zhdanov.

April 17   The Ballets de Paris de Roland Petit premieres Petit's evening-length ballet *Cyrano de Bergerac*, set to music by Marius Constant, in Paris. Petit, Renee Jeanmaire and George Reich star. The ballet has three acts.

May 9   The Juilliard Dance Theater hosts the first performance of Doris Humphrey's *Brandenberg Concerto*. It is her last work, completed after her death by Ruth Currier.

May 10   The Donald McKayle Dance Company gives the world premiere of his *Rainbow Round My Shoulder* in New York. The work is a dance translation of traditional southern prison songs. McKayle and Mary Hinkson lead the cast.

May 14   *Episodes* receives its world premiere by the New York City Ballet in New York. Choreographed by George Balanchine and Martha Graham to music of Anton Webern, the ballet marks the first time these choreographers

collaborate and the first choreography created by Graham for a ballet company other than her own. The story in the Graham section deals with Mary, Queen of Scots, reliving her life while on her way to the scaffold; the Balanchine choreography is abstract. Costumes are by Karinska, scenery by David Hays. Dancers include Graham, Jacques d'Amboise, Melissa Hayden and guest Paul Taylor.

July 3   Jerome Robbins' ballet *Moves* receives its first performance at the Festival of Two Worlds in Spoleto. The work explores liberty of movement within the context of silence.

Nov. 19   Choreographer John Butler's version of *Carmina Burana* — to music by Carl Orff, with costumes by Ruth Morley and decor by Paul Sylbert — receives its initial performance at the New York City Opera. Dancers include Carmen DeLavallade, Glen Tetley, Veronika Mlaker and Scott Douglas. Set to Orff's erotic and compelling music, the sensual work has established itself as a major modern dance piece.

Nov. 28   Talley Beatty premieres *Road of the Phoebe Snow* in New York, with music by Duke Ellington and Billy Strayhorn. The ballet, in a jazz style, deals with incidents that take place near a railroad track. Candace Caldwell, Georgia Collins, Tommy Johnson and Herman Howell lead the cast.

1959 Instrumental and Vocal Music

Jan. 30   Paul Hindemith's symphonic piece *Pittsburgh Symphony* is premiered by the Pittsburgh Symphony Orchestra with the composer conducting. The three-movement work celebrates the bicentennial of Pittsburgh and includes melodic materials from Pennsylvania Dutch songs.

Jan. 31   Bohuslav Martinu's *Fantasia concertante* for piano and orchestra premieres in Berlin, with Margrit Weber as soloist. The neobaroque piece has three movements.

Feb. 24   Symphony No. 2, by Lennox Berkeley, premieres in Birmingham, England. The four-movement work is neoclassical in style.

Feb. 26   George Rochberg's Symphony No. 2 is premiered by George Szell and the Cleveland Orchestra. This symphony uses a 12-tone row as its structural base.

March 1   Rolf Liebermann's *Capriccio* for soprano, violin and orchestra receives its initial performance in Paris. It uses themes from two of his earlier works — the operas *Leonore 40/45* and *Penelope*.

March 1   Gottfried von Einem's orchestral and choral suite *Das Stundenlied*, with a text by Bertolt Brecht, premieres in Hamburg. The work depicts the passion of Jesus Christ in the context of a socialist hero persecuted by nonsocialist religious forces.

March 3   Henry Cowell's Symphony No. 13 (*Madras Symphony*) receives its first performance by Thomas Scherman and the Little Orchestra Society, in Madras, India. The music includes Indian melodic and rhythmic elements Cowell observed in Indian music while on tour there in 1956. Scherman's orchestra is now touring India.

March 4   Klaus Egge's Symphony No. 3 premieres in Louisville, Kentucky. The work was inspired by a viewing of the aurora borealis which the composer witnessed while in an airplane. It has one movement. This Norwegian composer studied in Berlin and became president of the Society of Norwegian Composers in 1945. He combines modern harmonies, sometimes dissonant, with Scandinavian modes and scales.

March 10   Howard Hanson's *Summer Seascape* is premiered by the New Orleans Symphony Orchestra. This piece is a symphonic sketch.

March 15   Symphony No. 7 by Karl Amadeus Hartmann, premieres in Hamburg. The three-movement symphony is dodecaphonic.

March 24   *Gruppen*, by Karlheinz Stockhausen, receives its world premiere in Cologne. This work features three conductors conducting three chamber orchestras, each punctuating time in three different tempi. Meter, rhythm, intervalic structure, dynamics and instrumentation are serialized. This is the first piece Stockhausen composes that explores the "spatial dimension in music." The three orchestras surround the audience and perform independently of each other; though at times they meet with, echo and call to each other. Critic Peter Heyworth reviews a subsequent London performance of this work in the *Observer* (London). He writes "If Bernstein and the Beatles had appeared simultaneously, the applause could hardly have been louder or more sustained."

April 15   Olivier Messiaen's *Catalogue d'oiseaux* for piano receives its first performance by Yvonne Loriod at a concert of the Domaine Musicale. This work was inspired by bird calls.

April 16   Ned Rorem's Symphony No. 3 is premiered by Leonard Bernstein and the New York Philharmonic in New York.

May 3   Gunther Schuller's *Little Fantasy* receives its initial performance by the New York Chamber Symphony in New York City.

July 3   Robert Starer's Concerto for Viola, Strings and Percussion premieres in Geneva. The concerto has four movements.

July 5   Heitor Villa-Lobos' orchestral piece *Concerto grosso* premieres in Pittsburgh.

July 13   *Saint Michael*, a sonata for 17 wind instruments, by Peter Maxwell Davies, receives its initial performance by the London Symphony Orchestra. The work was composed two years ago. Davies, now 24 years old, is music director at the Cirencester Grammar School in England.

July 22   Benjamin Britten's *Missa brevis* premieres at the Westminster Cathedral in London. Britten sets the Roman Catholic Latin text, without the Credo. The piece is scored for 3-part boys' voices and organ.

Aug. 25   Igor Stravinsky's *Le Sacre du printemps* and Charles Ives' *The Unanswered Question* are performed by Leonard Bernstein and the New York Philharmonic in Moscow. This event marks the first performance of the former work since the Soviet Revolution and the first Soviet performance of the latter work.

Sep. 17   Krzysztof Penderecki's *Strophes* premieres at the contemporary music festival in Warsaw. The piece is scored for soprano, speaker and 10 instruments and uses biblical texts. It also employs serial and aleatoric techniques.

Oct. 3   Andre Jolivet's Symphony No. 2 receives its first performance in Berlin. The three-movement work is the second of his three numbered symphonies. For the past 16 years, Jolivet has been music director of the Comedie-Francaise.

Oct. 4   Dmitri Shostakovich's Concerto for Cello and Orchestra, Op. 107, is premiered by Mstislav Rostropovich in Leningrad. It has four movements and was composed specifically for Rostropovich.

Oct. 17   Igor Stravinsky's *Epitaphium fur das Grabmal des Prinzen Max Egon Furstenberg* premieres at the first concert of this year's Donaueschingen Festival. The dodecaphonic work is scored for flute, clarinet and harp. It was composed as a tribute to the patron of this annual music festival.

Oct. 21   Tikhon Khrennikov's Violin Concerto premieres in Moscow.

Oct. 23   Ned Rorem's symphonic poem *Eagles* is premiered by the Philadelphia Orchestra. Rorem is 36 years old today.

Oct. 23   *Three New England Sketches*, by Walter Piston, is premiered by Paul Paray and the Detroit Symphony Orchestra in Worcester, Massachusetts. It is an orchestral suite inspired by the composer's impressions of New England.

Oct. 24   Vincent Persichetti's Symphony No. 7, Op. 80 (*Liturgical*), receives its initial performance by the St. Louis Symphony Orchestra in St. Louis. Edouard van Remoortel conducts. The five-movement work is largely constructed from Persichetti's earlier work *Hymns and Responses for the Church Year*, Op. 68, composed in 1955.

Oct. 28   Roberto Gerhard's Symphony No. 2 premieres in London. The dodecaphonic symphony is the second of five he composes.

Nov. 5   Havergal Brian's Symphony No. 11 and Symphony No. 12 receive their first performances in London. The former was composed in 1954; the latter, in 1957.

Nov. 13   *Ommaggio a Cage*, by Nam June Paik, receives its world premiere in Dusseldorf. Paik, while at the keyboard, throws eggs at a mirror, rosary beads at the audience, and attacks the piano with large scissors. The score also requires a motorcycle to blast its engines. (Because of fear of audience asphyxiation the motorcycle part is deleted at a performance of the work next year in Cologne celebrating the 34th International Society for Contemporary Music festival.)

Nov. 27 Gunther Schuller's *Seven Studies on Themes of Paul Klee* receives its world premiere by Antal Dorati and the Minneapolis Symphony Orchestra in Minneapolis. The music, inspired by seven of Klee's paintings, is highly successful, despite its serial technique of composition. It is soon performed by other major American symphony orchestras and is also performed at next year's festival of the International Society for Contemporary Music.

Dec. 9 Henri Dutilleux's Symphony No. 2 is premiered by Charles Munch and the Boston Symphony Orchestra.

The three-movement piece is scored for 12 solo instruments and orchestra.

Dec. 11 Henry Cowell's *Mela and Fair* premieres in New Delhi. This event marks the opening of the American exhibit of the World Agricultural Fair in that city. The piece is an orchestral essay.

Dec. 24 Frank Martin's oratorio *Le mystere de la nativite*, based on a 15th-century play about the nativity, premieres in Geneva. Martin uses modal melodies and harmonies to depict heaven and atonal melodies and harmonies to depict hell.

1959 Births, Deaths and Debuts

Feb. 5 Curt Sachs, 77, dies in New York City. He was a German music critic and later a musicologist who specialized in the history and development of musical instruments. After Adolf Hitler came to power Sachs traveled to America and joined the faculties of New York University and Columbia University. He was a head of the American Musicological Society and wrote many musicological books, essays and articles. Among his best-known books are *Reallexikon der Musikinstrumente* (1913) and *The Rise of Music in the Ancient World* (1943).

Feb. 12 American composer George Antheil, 58, dies in New York. A pupil of Ernest Bloch, Antheil began experimenting with new approaches to musical composition in his youth. He toured Europe as a pianist and composer before living in Paris and befriending Ezra Pound, Jean Cocteau and James Joyce. The premiere of his *Ballet mecanique* startled Parisians in 1926. He then returned to New York, attracting publicity with the same object. He began an opera based on Joyce's *Ulysses*, which he called *Mr. Bloom and the Cyclops*, but never finished it. His opera *Transatlantique*, premiered in 1930, brought him once again to international attention. In 1936 Antheil went to Hollywood and began composing film music. He also wrote about music and, with actress Hedi Lamarr, amused himself by trying to invent a device that would improve torpedoes. The military did not express an interest, however. Antheil devoted himself to composing music of an accessible style, blending neoclassicism, romanticism and impressionism. He is best known as an *enfant terrible* whose work dramatically but only temporarily had an impact on the middle years of the century's first half. He composed operas, one ballet, symphonies, string quartets, songs, and chamber and piano pieces.

Feb. 17 Australian soprano Joan Sutherland scores a huge success singing Lucia at her Covent Garden debut in London.

Feb. 25 Pianist and teacher Gustav Becker, 97, dies in Epsom, Surrey, England. He made his debut at age 11 and studied in New York and Berlin. He was an assistant to

Rafael Joseffy at the National Conservatory in New York. After some concertizing, he became known principally as a teacher and also composed (his piano pieces number approximately 200). In addition, he wrote manuals on piano playing.

March 17 Swiss composer Raffaele d' Alessandro, 48, dies in Lausanne. He studied in Zurich and with Nadia Boulanger in Paris. He later studied organ with Marcel Dupre. He spent most of his life in Lausanne and performed as a pianist and organist in addition to composing. He wrote one ballet (*Isla persa*), two symphonies, many orchestral works, two string quartets, and a host of chamber and keyboard pieces.

April 11 English music writer and editor Eric Blom, 70, dies in London. This musician is especially noted for having edited an edition of *Grove's Dictionary of Music and Musicians*. He was also a music correspondent for the Manchester *Guardian*, a music critic for the Birmingham *Post* and *The Observer*, and an editor of *Music & Letters*.

April 13 Dutch conductor Eduard van Beinum, 58, dies in Amsterdam. In 1945 he replaced Willem Mengelberg as the conductor of the Concertgebouw Orchestra of Amsterdam. He was known for his cerebral and balanced interpretations and was at home with music from all periods of the orchestral repertoire.

July 7 English music critic Ernest Newman, 90, dies in Tadworth, Surrey. In addition to writing books on opera and on Richard Wagner, Newman was a critic for the London *Sunday Times* for 39 years. He was born William Roberts and constructed his nom de plume from the words *earnest new man*.

July 15 Composer Ernest Bloch, 78, dies in Portland, Oregon. He studied solfeggio with Emile Jaques-Dalcroze, violin with Eugene Ysaye and composition with Ludwig Thuille. His early pieces, including *Historiettes au crepuscule* (a group of songs composed in 1903), show the influence of French impressionism. He began conducting and, in 1916, toured America with dancer Maude Allen. He returned to

ERNEST BLOCH

Geneva a year later but was immediately offered a teaching position at the Mannes School of Music in New York, which he accepted. It was in the early 1920s when Bloch incorporated Jewish musical elements in his work. Examples of these pieces are *Trois poemes juifs* and *Schelomo* (both premiered in 1917). The latter work, a Hebrew rhapsody for cello and orchestra, would become a standard in the repertoire.

Young composers — including Roger Sessions, George Antheil and Leon Kirchner — found themselves attracted to his work and studied with him. In 1920 Bloch became director of the Cleveland Institute of Music and later the San Francisco Conservatory. In the 1930s he again lived in Switzerland but finally settled in Oregon.

Bloch's music is characterized by bitonal harmonies and mild dissonance. Like many composers aware of the revolutionary impact of the 12-tone system, Bloch experimented with this technique in his later works but never adopted it. He also experimented with quarter tones. He wrote one opera, *Macbeth* (premiered in 1910); a few piano and vocal pieces; and an extremely large number of orchestral and chamber works.

Aug. 16   Chilean composer Pedro Humberto Allende, 74, dies in Santiago, Chile. A product of the National Conservatory in Santiago, he quickly became interested in Chilean folk song and incorporated such elements in his music. In 1928, he was Chilean delegate to the Congress of Popular Arts, held in Prague under the auspices of the League of Nations. He later taught at the National Conservatory in Santiago. His music casts Chilean folk melodies in an impressionistic style. He composed many different types of pieces, the most famous of which is *12 tonadas de character popular chileno* (composed between 1918 and 1922), for piano.

Aug. 16   Harpsichordist Wanda Landowska, 81, dies in Lakeville, Connecticut. After studying the piano in her native Warsaw and in Berlin, she became interested in early music and had a harpsichord built for her by the firm of Pleyel. In 1925 she established a school for the study of early music near Paris and also gave concerts there. Although well-known for her performances of old music, particularly that of Bach, she commissioned new works from such composers as Manuel de Falla and Francis Poulenc. At the outbreak of World War II, she came to America and settled in Connecticut to teach and record. Up to her death she was considered the greatest 20th-century exponent of early keyboard music. She singlehandedly made the harpsichord popular in this century. She also wrote numerous articles on the interpretation of this music.

Aug. 28   Czech composer Bohuslav Martinu, 68, dies in Liestal, Switzerland. He studied violin at the Prague Conservatory and performed as a violinist with the Czech Philharmonic in that city but left in 1914 to avoid the draft. He returned after World War I and studied with Josef Suk. Failing to graduate, he went to Paris and studied composition with Albert Roussel. He was fortunate in having his work performed in Paris and remained there until 1940, when he fled the Nazis. He came to America via Portugal and taught at the Berkshire Music Center in Tanglewood and at Princeton University. He spent his final years in Switzerland. Martinu's music is characterized by Bohemian rhythms and melodies — to some degree, at least, it reflects a concern with Czech nationalism. These

JOSEF MATTHIAS HAUER

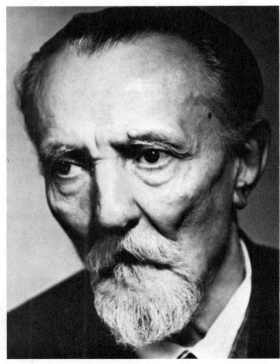

elements are couched in a neoclassicism that is heavily contrapuntal. He was exceptionally prolific and wrote works for almost every genre and medium. These include 16 operas, many ballets, 6 symphonies, concertos, song cycles, 7 string quartets and many keyboard works.

Sep. 22   Austrian composer Josef Matthias Hauer, 76, dies in Vienna. Largely self-taught in music, Hauer began experimenting with mathematical structures and then basing musical compositions on them. He developed a personal method involving six-note tropes and wrote a series of articles describing this method and claiming discovery of what would become known as dodecaphony. He went public with his manifesto, *Zwolftonspiel-Manifest*, presented in Vienna on May 19, 1952. Hauer's music, not what might be termed "accessible", attracted attention largely because of the clamor he created in contesting Arnold Schoenberg on the discovery of the 12-tone system. Schoenberg, however, succeeded in creating a new musical language — an enormously important contribution that

Hauer steadfastly failed to acknowledge. Hauer composed almost 1,000 works of all types. Each was subtitled "Zwolftonspiel." These pieces include oratorios, orchestral fantasies, concertos, chamber pieces and several sets of piano works entitled *Nomoi*.

Nov. 17   Brazilian composer Heitor Villa-Lobos, 72, dies in Rio de Janeiro. With a keen interest in Brazilian folk music and lacking much formal education, Villa-Lobos went on to compose a huge catalog of music flavored with Brazilian rhythms and melodies without actually having to quote folk tunes directly. Championed by pianist Artur Rubinstein, he was given a grant by the Brazilian government to live in Paris, where he stayed from 1923 to 1930, eventually returning to Brazil. There he became director of music education, introducing bold new methods of teaching music. In 1945 he established the Brazilian Academy of Music in Rio de Janeiro. Probably best known for his *Bachianas brasileiras*, he composed over 2,000 works in all forms.

1959   Related Events

Benjamin Harkarvy establishes the Netherlands Dance Theater this year. The company, largely formed of dancers from Het Netherlands Ballet, is based in The Hague.

Galina Ulanova becomes ballet mistress of the Bolshoi Ballet this year. She is also currently known as "prima ballerina assoluta of Soviet ballet."

The first volume of Hugo Riemann's *Musik-Lexikon*, one of the standard reference works on music, is published in its 12th edition this year. The complete edition is in three volumes and is edited by Wilibald Gurlitt. The other two volumes are published over the next eight years. Carl Dahlhaus edits a two-volume supplement, which is published in the early 1970s.

Jan. 8   Columbia University and Princeton University receive a $175,000 grant from the Rockefeller Foundation to establish an electronic music center. The grant covers a five-year period and is to finance space, electronic equipment, technical assistants and materials enabling composers to work at the center without paying fees. It also finances the purchase of 19 loudspeakers and a control console and recommends the procurement of the Mark II RCA Synthesizer (capable of producing, mixing and modifying sounds through complex electronic connections — this synthesizer becomes an integrated component of the center next year). Otto Luening and Vladimir Ussachevsky (who is also chairman of the project) of Columbia University and Milton Babbitt and Roger Sessions of Princeton University comprise the committee of direction. The directors immediately invite additional composers to pursue their work at this installation. These include Muchiko Toyama (Japan), Bulent Arel (Turkey),

Mario Davidovsky (Argentina), Halim El-Dabh (Egypt) and Charles Wuorinen (America — who, like Davidovsky, later wins a Pulitzer Prize for a work composed there). The center — officially called the Columbia-Princeton Electronic Music Center — gives its first concert on May 9, 1961.

March 2   The musicians of the St. Louis Symphony Orchestra vote not to perform under their new music director, Edouard van Remoortel, because of his intention to fire 42 of the 85 players. Van Remoortel lowers the figure to approximately 17, and the orchestra subsequently plays the next concert "under protest." The event becomes public, and the orchestra members make no secret of their contempt for their new music director. The conflict soon results in 2 resignations, 3 retirements, 2 players being put on probation, 2 being retained and the other 8 being reauditioned and given consideration for rehire.

April 28   American lyricist Stanley Adams is elected president of ASCAP (American Society of Composers, Authors and Publishers).

May 4   John La Montaine is awarded the Pulitzer Prize for music for *Concert for Piano and Orchestra*.

May 14   President Dwight D. Eisenhower breaks ground for the Lincoln Center for the Performing Arts in New York City, at the site of what is to become Philharmonic Hall (subsequently Avery Fisher Hall), the new home of the New York Philharmonic.

Sep.   Garrard Engineering issues its magazine-type tape cassettes this month. Featuring a playing speed of 3.75 IPS and 0.25-inch tape, the magazines foreshadow development of the audio cassette. In another development, Decca (England) releases a stereo recording of Richard Wagner's *Das Rheingold,* and its success inaugurates mass production and marketing of stereo records.

1960 Opera

Feb. 8   *La notte de un nevrastenico,* by Nino Rota, is performed for the first time at La Piccola Scala in Milan. Riccardo Bacchelli's libretto is about a man obsessed by a need for silence and the precautions he takes when he rents a room in a hotel. The opera had won the 1959 R.A.I. Premio Italia prize.

May 19   Sir Arthur Bliss' *Tobias and the Angel* receives its world premiere in London. The two-act opera deals with exorcism.

May 22   Hans Werner Henze's *Der Prinz von Homburg* receives its initial performance in Hamburg. The three-act opera moves from a tonal beginning to a 12-tone ending. Based on a melodrama by Heinrich von Kleist, it tells the story of a soldier neglecting duty for love.

June 11   The premiere of *A Midsummer Night's Dream,* by Benjamin Britten, takes place at Aldeburgh, England. The libretto is adapted from Shakespeare's play by Britten and Peter Pears. Britten conducts the three-act opera, featuring Pears as a lead vocalist.

June 15   Henk Badings' *Martin Korda, D.P.* premieres in Amsterdam. Featuring electronic music, the three-act opera is about a displaced person at the end of World War II.

This event marks the opening of Amsterdam's Holland Festival.

Sep. 21   Boris Blacher's opera *Rosamunde Floris,* about premarital sex and love affairs, premieres in Berlin.

Oct. 8   *A Story of a Real Man,* by Sergei Prokofiev, is revived posthumously at the Bolshoi Theater in Moscow. The opera was originally premiered for a selected audience on December 3, 1948 but was severely censured by Soviet critics. Today's event marks its first public performance. *Pravda* responds by calling it "a great event in the cultural life of the capital."

Oct. 21   Arthur Honegger's *Le Roi David* receives its first operatic stage performance at the Opera in Paris. Originally premiered in 1921, it had also been performed as an oratorio and a symphonic psalm prior to this staged version.

Dec. 11   Carl Orff's *Ludus de nato infante mirificus,* with a libretto by the composer, premieres in Stuttgart, the composer conducting. Orff's style has been termed neoarchaic by some. This nativity play features church Latin in its libretto.

1960 Dance

Jan. 28   The Royal Ballet presents Frederick Ashton's version of *La fille mal gardee,* set to music by Francois Joseph Herold, reorchestrated and with additional music by John Lanchberry. It tells the humorous story of how Lise and her lover, Colas, foil her mother's attempts to have her marry a wealthy farmer's son. The work is the first British ballet to use traditional British folk dances as a source. The opening night cast is headed by Nadia Nerina, David Blair, Stanley Holden and Alexander Grant.

Jan. 29   *Totem* — a modern dance work choreographed by Alwin Nikolais — is performed for the first time at the Henry Street Playhouse in New York City.

Jan. 31   The Alvin Ailey Dance Theater presents the world premiere of Alvin Ailey's *Revelations* in New York. The abstract work, which reflects traditional Negro spirituals, becomes one of this choreographer's most successful.

March 4   The Bolshoi Ballet performs *The Humpbacked Horse* in Moscow. Originally choreographed by Arthur Saint-Leon to Cesare Pugni's music, the work had been premiered as early as 1864 by the Russian Imperial Ballet in Saint Petersburg. It was the first classical ballet derived from a native Russian story. Today's version is choreographed by Alexander Radunsky to music by Rodion Shchedrin. The work is subsequently made into a film featuring Maya Plisetskaya.

March 29   George Balanchine's classical *Tchaikovsky Pas de Deux,* with music by Tchaikovsky, is premiered by the New York City Ballet. Violette Verdy and Conrad Ludlow are the first cast.

April 7   Leonid Lavrovsky premieres his version of *Paganini* at the Bolshoi Theater in Moscow. He uses Serge Rachmaninoff's *Rhapsody on a Theme by Paganini* to explore the theme of the ecstasy of creation. Yaroslav Sekh dances the title role.

April 12   Kenneth MacMillan's version of Igor Stravinsky's *Le baiser de la fee* is performed for the first time by The Royal Ballet in London. Svetlana Beriosova, Lynn Seymour and Donald MacLeary star.

April 20   *Lady from the Sea* is performed for the first time by the American Ballet Theater in New York City. It is choreographed by Birgit Cullberg, to music by Knudage Riisager, and with decor and costumes by Kerstin Hedeby. The dancers are Lupe Serrano, Glen Tetley and Royes Fernandez. The tale, based on the play by Ibsen, is about a woman torn between her love for her husband and family and her love for a sailor.

April 27   Martha Graham's *Acrobats of God* is performed for the first time in New York. It is a celebration of the dance, whose performers include Graham, Helen McGehee, Mary Hinkson, Bertram Ross and Paul Taylor.

April 29   Martha Graham's *Alcestis* — to music by Vivian Fine, with sets by Isamu Noguchi and costumes designed by the choreographer — premieres at the 54th Street Theater in New York City. Graham uses the Greek legend as a metaphor for the coming of spring. The dancers include Graham, Bertram Ross and Paul Taylor.

Oct. 11   Kenneth MacMillan's *The Invitation* receives its initial performance by The Royal Ballet in Oxford, Eng-

land. Choreographed to music by Matyas Sieber, with scenery by Nicholas Georgiadis, the ballet deals with human relationships. The lead dancers are Lynn Seymour, Christopher Gable, Desmond Doyle and Anne Heaton.

Nov. 16   The New York City Ballet premieres George Balanchine's *Donizetti Variations* in New York. The one-act plotless work uses music from *Don Sebastian*. Melissa Hayden and Jonathan Watts lead the cast. Also premiered today is Balanchine's *Monumentum pro Gesualdo*, a plotless work for one couple and a corps of 12. The score is Igor Stravinsky's recomposition of three madrigals by Gesualdo di Venosa. Diana Adams and Conrad Ludlow lead the cast.

Nov. 22   George Balanchine's *Liebeslieder Walzer* receives its first performance by the New York City Ballet in New York. Featuring music by Brahms, costumes by Karinska and decor by David Hays, the work also includes onstage musicians. Today's cast is made up of Diana Adams, Melissa Hayden, Jillana, Violette Verdy, Bill Carter, Conrad Ludlow, Nicholas Magallanes and Jonathan Watts.

Dec. 7   Choreographer John Taras' *Ebony Concerto* — to music by Igor Stravinsky, with decor by David Hays — is premiered by the New York City Ballet in that city.

1960 Instrumental and Vocal Music

Jan. 2   Roger Sessions' Symphony No. 4 receives its initial performance by Antal Dorati and the Minneapolis Symphony Orchestra. The three-movement work celebrates the centennial of the state of Minnesota.

Jan. 5   La Monte Young's *Poem for Tables, Chairs and Benches* premieres at the University of California in Berkeley. The piece involves moving furniture. Young, an extremely avant-garde composer, has studied at the University of California (Los Angeles and Berkeley) and at the New School for Social Research in New York. He is now 24 years old.

Jan. 10   Igor Stravinsky's *Movements for Piano and Orchestra* premieres in New York City. The composer conducts with pianist Margrit Weber as soloist. Stravinsky states that the piece, in part, explores harmonies that are more complicated than much of his previous work and that the music is serialized to some degree on all levels. He also says its most significant aspect is its "anti-tonality."

Jan. 15   Leonard Bernstein and the New York Philharmonic premiere Gunther Schuller's *Spectra*. The work, in seven parts, sonically reflects the colors of the rainbow. Schuller later comments that "composers think now in kaleidoscopically varied, intricate networks rather than in well-proportioned blocks of tone."

Jan. 31   Henry Brant's *Atlantis* is premiered by Claude Monteux, the Hudson Valley Philharmonic Orchestra and the Hudson Valley Chorale in Poughkeepsie, New York. It is a work for chorus and orchestra.

Feb. 1   Alan Hovhaness' symphonic poem *Arjuna* premieres in Madras, India, with the composer at the piano. It includes a part for the mridongam, an Indian instrument.

Feb. 25   David Tudor premieres John Cage's *Music for Amplified Toy Pianos* in Middletown, Connecticut. The music, of extremely high decibel levels, is transmitted from local loudspeakers in the audience connected to microphones on stage.

March 1   Robert Whitney and the Louisville Orchestra give the world premiere of Paul Hindemith's *Sinfonietta in E*. The piece has four movements.

March 18   Mstislav Rostropovich plays the world premiere of Sergei Prokofiev's *Concertino for Cello and Orchestra*, Op. 132, in Moscow. This work, unfinished at the time of Prokofiev's death, was completed by the cellist.

March 20   *Concerted Piece*, by Otto Luening and Vladimir Ussachevsky, receives its first performance by Leonard Bernstein and the New York Philharmonic. The work is scored for tape recorder and symphony orchestra, and today's event is a televised "Young People's Concert,"

DARIUS MILHAUD

bringing the new medium of electronic music before a young audience.

March 28   Leopold Stokowski and the Houston Symphony Orchestra give the first performance of Henry Cowell's Symphony No. 12.

March 29   Darius Milhaud's Symphony No. 9 is premiered by Mario di Bonaventura and the Ft. Lauderdale Symphony Orchestra. Commissioned by this orchestra, the work is in three movements.

April 23   Ferde Grofe conducts the San Francisco Symphony Orchestra in the premiere of his *San Francisco Suite*. The composition depicts an earthquake, which Grofe scores for percussion.

May 14   Virgil Thomson conducts the first performance of his *Missa pro Defunctis* in Potsdam, New York. Scored for chorus and orchestra, the work is imbued with triadic and tonal references.

May 27   Vittorio Giannini's Symphony No. 4 receives its first performance in New York City.

June 11   *Kontakte*, by Karlheinz Stockhausen, receives its world premiere at this year's International Society for Contemporary Music festival in Cologne. Scored for piano, percussion and electronic sounds, it explores what the composer says are not only "contacts between electronic and instrumental sound groups but also contacts between autonomous, very characteristic, moments." Four years from now, the work is performed in America. Critic Raymond Ericson then writes that the music "suggested an aural landscape of considerable fascination." In New York, in 1964, the piece is also used as background music to a play entitled *Originale*. The neodadaistic play features a chimpanzee on the cymbals. Also receiving its first perfor-

mance at today's concert is *Anagram*, by Mauricio Kagel. Scored for four voices, speaking chorus and instruments, it was inspired by surrealistic poems in different languages.

June 13   *Pli selon pli*, by Pierre Boulez, receives its world premiere at the 34th International Society for Contemporary Music festival in Cologne. The title means "fold according to fold," and the music was inspired by poetry of Stephane Mallarme. The one-hour work for orchestra and soprano consists of five movements and was begun in 1958. The three middle movements are titled "Improvisation sur Mallarme I, II and III," and the entire piece reflects Boulez' musical rendition of a line of poetry by Mallarme describing how the town of Bruges emerges from a mist — Boulez does not use that specific line in the music but takes his inspiration from it. *Pli selon pli* is promptly termed the most important score since the end of World War II. However, Igor Stravinsky, present at today's premiere, is reportedly disappointed, contending that *Le marteau sans maitre* — Boulez's last big piece — indicated a more powerful work would follow.

Quaderni for orchestra, by Luciano Berio, also receives its first performance at today's concert. This is a piece in which the composer constructs musical images inspired by a gyrating mobile.

June 17   *Fioriture*, an orchestral work by Karl-Birger Blomdahl, receives its initial performance at this year's International Society for Contemporary Music festival in Cologne.

June 19   The 34th International Society for Contemporary Music festival concludes in Cologne. Gyorgy Ligeti's *Apparitions* is performed at today's concert and creates a sensation. It is his first work for conventional instruments to be performed by live players (as opposed to electronic composition) in four years and is a static, interwoven network of density and color full of inner detail without resembling traditional melody, rhythm or harmony. Ligeti later tells a reporter that the piece is like a childhood dream he had in which a thick web prevented him from climbing into the safety of his bed.

In a postfestival concert held at the studio of Mary Bauermeister, unusual pieces are played, including Sylvano Bussotti's *Five Pieces for David Tudor*; the work features a gong immersed in water. This festival and associated concerts represent perhaps the culmination of what some in the world of contemporary music consider to be the outrageous musical experiments of the 1950s and the hopeful beginnings of a more sensible, appealing, though still somewhat cerebral, approach to musical composition in the 1960s, particularly in light of Ligeti's work.

June 23   Bohuslav Martinu's *Suite on the Frescoes of Piero della Francesca* premieres posthumously in Granada, Spain. Featured as the composition that opens Granada's Ninth Festival of Music and Dance, the three-movement work sonically displays a painter's moods.

July 1   Benjamin Britten's *Cantata academica* premieres in Basel. It is one of the few works by Britten that involves 12-tone materials. The Latin text is taken from the charter of the University of Basel.

July 9   Polish composer Wlodzimierz Kotonski's *Etude concrete pour un seul coup de cymbale* premieres in Darmstadt. This integrally serial work is generated from one stroke of a cymbal and lasts slightly more than 2 1/2 minutes. The original sonorities produced by the cymbal stroke are electronically transposed to the different pitches of the chromatic scale.

July 14   Reginald Smith-Brindle's symphonic piece *Cosmos*, inspired by "spiritual and cosmic thoughts," premieres in Cheltenham, England. The work's performance concludes Cheltenham's 16th Festival of British Contemporary Music.

July 14   Dominick Argento's *Songs About Spring* (*A Song Cycle for Soprano and Chamber Orchestra*), with a text by e.e. cummings, premieres at the Eastman School of Music in Rochester, New York.

Sep. 2   William Walton's Symphony No. 2 is premiered by John Pritchard and the Liverpool Philharmonic Orchestra in Edinburgh. A large-scale tonal composition, this three-movement symphony is featured at this year's Edinburgh Festival. Critic Peter Heyworth notes, "Walton has come to accept the basically romantic roots of his idiom with increasing frankness."

Sep. 3   Humphrey Searle's Symphony No. 3 premieres in Edinburgh. The work takes its inspiration from the death place of Agamemnon. Searle is currently honorary secretary of the Liszt Society.

Sep. 18   Krzysztof Penderecki's *Dimensions of Time and Silence* for chorus and instruments receives its world premiere at the Warsaw Autumn Festival. The composer states that the work creates a "space of sonic matter." The piece was conceived as a musical counterpart to paintings by Paul Klee.

Sep. 27   Igor Stravinsky's *Monumentum pro Gesualdo di Venosa ad CD Annum* premieres in Venice, the composer conducting. Based on three madrigals by Gesualdo, the instrumental work celebrates the 400th anniversary of his birth. It is performed as a ballet for the first time this November 16.

Sep. 30   Ernst Krenek conducts the world premiere of his *Quaestio Temporis* in Hamburg. Scored for chamber orchestra, the work is composed of an all-interval set whose intervals are symmetrically invertible. It also deploys a pattern of speed changes derived from the Fibonacci series — an arithmetic series of integers in which each constituent is the sum of the previous two.

Sep. 30   Eugene Ormandy and the Philadelphia Orchestra give the world premiere of Samuel Barber's *Toccata festiva* at the first concert of the orchestra's 61st season. The music celebrates a new cathedral organ, built at a cost of $175,000. The music was commissioned by Mrs. Mary Curtis Zimbalist.

Oct. 14   Walter Piston's Violin Concerto No. 2 is premiered by William Steinberg and the Pittsburgh Symphony Orchestra, with Joseph Fuchs as soloist.

Oct. 15   Wolfgang Fortner's *Five Bagatelles* for Wind Quintet, Bohuslav Martinu's String Quartet No. 4, Bo Nilsson's *Szene I* and Alois Haba's String Quartet No. 12 are among the works premiered at today's opening concert in Donaueschingen of the Musiktage fur die zeitgenossische Tonkunst.

Oct. 16   Krzysztof Penderecki's *Anaklasis* for strings and percussion is performed for the first time, with Hans Rosbaud conducting, at the Donaueschingen Festival. Involving quarter tones, harmonics, tremolos, glissandi and a host of other special effects, some novel, the piece elicits hisses and boos from the audience. Rosbaud deliberately gives it an encore. Also premiered today are Japanese composer Yoritsune Matsudaira's *Suite of Dances* and Olivier Messiaen's *Chronochromie*.

Oct. 20   *Time Cycle*, by Lukas Foss, receives its world premiere by Leonard Bernstein and the New York Philharmonic, with Adele Addison as soprano soloist and the composer at the piano. Involving the juxtaposition of improvisations and composed sections, the work uses texts by W.H. Auden, Franz Kafka, A.E. Housman and Nietzsche. It becomes the first work ever to be repeated on the premiere program by the New York Philharmonic, after the conductor proposes to the audience that the piece be played twice. Pianist Glenn Gould subsequently calls it "the most important work in the last ten years." *Time Cycle* is performed in Boston two years from now — the audience walks out. It wins the New York Music Critics Circle Award for 1961.

Oct. 21   William Schuman's Symphony No. 7 is premiered by Charles Munch and the Boston Symphony Orchestra.

Oct. 22   George Rochberg's symphonic work *Time-Span* is premiered by the St. Louis Symphony Orchestra. This serial piece is in one movement.

Oct. 28   *Carre*, by Karlheinz Stockhausen, receives its initial performance in Hamburg. It is scored for four orchestras, four choruses and four conductors placed along four walls of a mess hall. The audience is seated in rows of chairs placed at 90 degrees to each other. The composer states that the music is based on a correspondence between pitch and duration.

Nov. 2   Malcolm Arnold's Symphony No. 4 receives its initial performance by the BBC Symphony Orchestra in London, the composer conducting. The symphony has four movements and a scherzo with a 12-tone row which, according to the composer, is used to express unpleasant emotions."

Nov. 17   Paul Creston's Violin Concerto No. 2 is premiered by Michael Rabin and the Los Angeles Philharmonic.

Dec. 17   Pablo Casals' oratorio *El Pesebre* receives its first performance in Acapulco, Mexico, the composer conducting. Involving folk themes, it is a Christmas work.

Dec. 17   Henk Badings' Symphony No. 9 premieres in Amsterdam. The work is scored for string orchestra.

Dec. 19   Gustav Mahler's Symphony No. 10 (a version made by Deryck Cooke) is performed by Berthold Goldschmidt and the Philharmonic Orchestra of London.

Cooke is both praised and criticized for his version, with some saying that it is remarkably close to Mahler's orchestral handwriting and others asserting that it sounds nothing like the work of the great master. Alma Mahler praises Cooke and removes earlier restrictions she had placed on the symphony's performance.

1960   Births, Deaths and Debuts

Jan. 24   Swiss pianist Edwin Fischer, 73, dies in Zurich. Besides being a pianist, known for his interpretations of Bach, Mozart and Beethoven, he was also a conductor and a noted teacher. His pupils included Daniel Barenboim and Alfred Brendel.

Feb. 9   Hungarian pianist, composer and conductor Ernst von Dohnanyi, 82, dies in New York City. After studies at the Budapest Conservatory of Music, he studied with Eugene d'Albert. He made his debut as a pianist in Berlin in 1897 and then toured Europe and America. He joined the faculty of the Berlin Hochschule fur Musik and later became director of the Budapest Conservatory and conductor of the Budapest Philharmonic. He was also director of the Hungarian Academy. He taught in Argentina and finally joined the music faculty of Florida State University at Tallahassee. Dohnanyi was the last of the Hungarian composers to subscribe to the romantic tradition. His music was influenced by that of Johannes Brahms and employed traditional harmonies.

March 4   American baritone Leonard Warren, 48, dies onstage during a performance of *La forza del destino* at the Metropolitan Opera in New York. After studying at the

ERNST VON DOHNANYI

Greenwich House Music School in New York, he undertook further studies in Milan. He toured South America, Canada and the Soviet Union in addition to singing in America and Europe. He was best-known for his roles in the operas of Giuseppe Verdi.

March 30   German composer Joseph Haas, 81, dies in Munich. He studied with Max Reger and studied organ with Karl Straube before teaching at the Stuttgart Conservatory. He was a highly prolific composer and was greatly revered as a teacher. He also wrote articles on music and authored a biography of Reger. Especially noted for his liturgical music, he taught at the Institute of Church Music in Munich.

May 8   Swedish composer Hugo Alfven, 88, dies in Faluns, Sweden. He studied at the Stockholm Conservatory and was awarded many government stipends, which enabled him to study in various European countries. His music is nationalistic and traditional — its roots are in the work of Edvard Grieg and Jean Sibelius. Primarily a symphonist, he was also a violinist and director of music at the University of Uppsala.

May 14   Spanish soprano Lucrezia Bori, 72, dies in New York City. After singing successfully from 1908 to 1915, she was forced to stop singing for several years because of a growth in her throat. She returned to the stage in 1918 and sang until her gala farewell in 1936. She helped raise money to save the Metropolitan Opera during the Depression and, after her retirement, became a member of its board of directors.

July 9   American composer Edward Burlingame Hill, 87, dies in Francestown, New Hampshire. His teachers included John Knowles Paine, George W. Chadwick and Charles-Marie Widor. Hill was a member of the faculty at Harvard University; his work includes symphonies, piano and choral music, and other works. He also wrote a book entitled *Modern French Music*. His music was strongly influenced by French impressionism — this is especially apparent in his orchestral pieces, such as the symphonic poem *Lilacs*.

July 15   American baritone Lawrence Tibbett, 63, dies in New York. After a brief career as an actor, he studied voice and made his operatic debut at the Metropolitan in 1923, singing small roles for several years. As a last-minute replacement as Ford in Giuseppe Verdi's *Falstaff*, he created a sensation and from then until 1950 sang many leading baritone roles at that theater. He sang in the world premieres of *The Emperor Jones* and *Peter Ibbetson* as well as in Metropolitan premieres of many other operas. He was also a recitalist and appeared in several movies.

Aug. 7   French composer Andre Bloch, 87, dies in Paris. His teachers at the Paris Conservatoire included Jules Massenet. He won the Premier Grand Prix de Rome in 1893 and later conducted at Fontainebleau. He was also a scientist, who is said to have developed a listening device for use aboard submarines. His best-known work is *Suite palestinienne*.

Sep. 9   Swedish tenor Jussi Bjorling, 48, dies in Siaro, Sweden. After studying with his father, he traveled with the Bjorling quartet, which consisted of his two brothers, his father and himself. He made his operatic debut at the Royal Theater in Stockholm and then began his international career. He was known for his warm, lyrical singing and his fine musicianship.

Sep. 12   Italian tenor Dino Borgioli, 69, dies in Florence, Italy. He sang at La Scala, Covent Garden and with other companies. He also performed with Nellie Melba in Australia on her farewell tour. He spent his last years teaching voice in London.

Sep. 20   Russian dancer and actress Ida Rubinstein dies in Vence on the French Riviera. Her age is not disclosed. Originally trained in mime and recitation, she later studied privately with Michel Fokine. After dancing with Serge Diaghilev's Ballets Russes from 1909 to 1911, she formed her own company and commissioned works from many new composers, such as Claude Debussy, Maurice Ravel, Igor Stravinsky, Arthur Honegger and Jacques Ibert. She was especially noted for her commanding stage presence and her extraordinary beauty.

Sep. 24   Hungarian composer Matyas Seiber, 55, is killed in Johannesburg, South Africa in an automobile crash. Trained as a cellist, he studied composition with Zoltan Kodaly and subsequently became a faculty member of the Frankfurt am Main Conservatory. He conducted the Dorian Singers. Seiber's work includes symphonic, chamber and orchestral music. The style of his music went from Hungarian nationalism to the addition of jazz and oriental melodic and harmonic elements to the inclusion of 12-tone procedures in his late works.

Oct. 30   Australian composer and conductor Alfred Hill, 89, dies in the vicinity of Sydney, Australia. He studied at the Leipzig Conservatory and later taught at the Sydney Conservatory. His output includes 12 symphonies, operas, cantatas, ballets and 17 string quartets. His music reflects the influence of the Maori music of New Zealand. Hill became one of the most prominent Australian composers.

Nov. 2   Greek conductor Dimitri Mitropoulos, 64, dies in Milan while conducting a rehearsal of Gustav Mahler's Symphony No. 3 at La Scala. Also a composer, Mitropoulos studied in Greece, Belgium and Germany (where he studied piano with Ferruccio Busoni); in the 1930s he began to gain recognition for his conducting. He debuted in the United States in 1937 and was so successful that he was engaged as music director of the New York Philharmonic, where he often presented modern works, including a concert performance of Alban Berg's *Wozzeck*. He also guest-conducted in Europe and at the Metropolitan Opera. His conducting was from memory and without a score.

Dec. 6   Soprano Eileen Farrell makes her Metropolitan Opera debut in Gluck's *Alcestis*. Winthrop Sargeant writes in the *New Yorker* magazine that Farrell "is the most powerful dramatic-soprano voice to be heard at the Met since Kirsten Flagstad."

Dec. 7   Rumanian pianist Clara Haskil, 64, dies in Brussels. She studied at the Paris Conservatoire and later with Ferruccio Busoni and subsequently had an international career, which was intermittently interrupted by a muscular disease. She was a fine musician, particularly noted for her performances of Mozart and Beethoven.

1960   Related Events

The Ballet of the 20th Century (Ballet du XXe Siecle) is established this year by Maurice Bejart.

April   Milton Babbitt's article "Twelve-Tone Invariants as Compositional Determinants" is published this month in the *Musical Quarterly*. One of Babbitt's most important essays, it outlines the basic ideas of his "total serialism." He also composes *Composition* for voice and six instruments this year.

May 2   Elliott Carter is awarded the Pulitzer Prize for Music for his String Quartet No. 2.

May 25   American pianist Malcolm Frager, 25, wins the Queen Elisabeth International Music Competition in Brussels after giving the premiere of Marcel Poot's Piano Concerto. The work was composed especially for this event.

July 1   The Carnegie Hall Corporation is officially established to protect, manage and rent Carnegie Hall in New York City. This new nonprofit corporation is the result, in part, of the attempt to demolish the concert hall and the struggle to preserve it that ensued in the late fifties. This corporation is established by special state legislation, which permits the City of New York to purchase the concert hall from private ownership. The corporation is also permitted to sponsor special events. Isaac Stern, who led the fight to save the building, is immediately elected president of the corporation. This event helps lead to the eventual granting of landmark status to Carnegie Hall in 1964.

July 27   The governor of Florida proclaims today "Dohnanyi Day" to honor the 83rd birthday of the deceased composer. Ernst von Dohnanyi had taught at Florida State University.

Aug. 14   An American balloon, *Echo I*, transmits the first satellite broadcast of music by sending "America the Beautiful" from Holmdel, New Jersey to Goldstone, California.

Oct. 11   The English Chamber Orchestra gives its first concert today. Conducted by Raymond Leppard, the concert takes place at Festival Hall in London and includes music by Claudio Monteverdi. This orchestra was formerly known as the Goldsborough Orchestra — founded by conductor Arnold Goldsborough in 1950.

1961   Opera

Jan. 31   Cooper Union in New York City plays host to the premieres of Dick Higgins' *The Peaceable Kingdom*, a spoken opera with bells, and his *Amazing Grace* and David Jonson's electronic *Cough Music* and *Two Sounds*.

Feb. 17   Hugo Weisgall's *Purgatory*, with a libretto based on a play by William Butler Yeats, premieres in Washington, D.C. at the Library of Congress. The one-act opera is about murder and revenge.

March 2   Bohuslav Martinu's one-act *Ariadne* premieres posthumously in Gelsenkirchen, Germany. The opera is about Theseus, whose ego kills its own id, and Ariadne's role in the trauma. The opera was composed in 1958.

March 11   *Uno Sguardo del Ponte*, by Renzo Rossellini, premieres in Rome. The opera is based on a play by Arthur Miller.

March 23   *Il calzare d'argento*, by Ildebrando Pizzetti, premieres at La Scala. The two-act musical play is about an impoverished man accused of theft. Jesus Christ comes to life on a crucifix in the Lucca Cathedral to defend him.

April 13   Luigi Nono's *Intoleranza 1960* receives its world premiere at the Teatro La Fenice in Venice. The text incorporates works of Bertolt Brecht, Jean-Paul Sartre and other revolutionary poets. The principal figure in the opera is an emigrant miner who survives brutality and brainwashing to rediscover the strength of human feeling. The opera is revised several times after its premiere today and subsequently becomes known as *Intoleranza 1971*. It is an example of a major work by a composer who embraces the politics of the left; Nono's music, however, is not often performed in the Soviet Union because of its avant-garde style and lack of immediate popular appeal. Nono says in

SCENE FROM *THE CRUCIBLE*

his notes about this opera that 12-tone music is "only a distribution of notes contrasting with one another and demonstrating what happens when democracy is carried into the field of music."

May 20   Hans Werner Henze's *Elegy for Young Lovers* is performed in a German version entitled *Elegie fur junge Liebende* in Schwetzingen. The three-act opera, with a libretto by W.H. Auden and Chester Kallman, is about an old poet who sends a mistress and her lover into a snowstorm. They die. It is performed in English at Glyndebourne in July.

May 25   Mario Castelnuovo-Tedesco's *Il mercante di Venezia* premieres in Florence at the Maggio Musicale. The three-act opera is based on Shakespeare's *The Merchant of Venice*. It won first prize in an international competition sponsored by the manufacturer of the aperitif campari.

July 20   *Lavinia*, an opera-buffa by Henry Barraud, premieres in Aix-en-Provence.

Sep. 18   Norman Dello Joio's opera *Blood Moon* receives its first performance in San Francisco. It is about an actress during the Civil War who discovers she is part Negro.

Oct. 12   Douglas Moore's *The Wings of the Dove*, based on a novel by Henry James, premieres at the New York City Opera. Ethan Ayer wrote the text to this opera in six scenes. It is a love story involving wealth and death. Critic Miles Kastendieck writes in the *Journal American*, "This is music drama in the best modern style."

Oct. 26   *The Crucible* — by Robert Ward, based on a play by Arthur Miller — receives its initial performance in New York City. The libretto, by Bernard Stambler, deals with the Salem witch trials. Irving Kolodin says the opera leaves the observer with "some sense of exaltation." The opera, in three acts, was commissioned by the Ford Foundation and wins the Pulitzer Prize for music as well as a citation from the New York Music Critics Circle.

COMPOSERS PAUL HINDEMITH AND IGOR STRAVINSKY

Nov. 25   Vittorio Giannini's *The Harvest* is premiered by the Chicago Lyric Opera Company, the composer conducting. It is about love and conflict on an American farm at the turn of the century.

Dec. 17   Paul Hindemith's *The Long Christmas Dinner* receives its initial performance in Mannheim. The libretto, by the composer, is based on the play by Thornton Wilder. The action takes place at a Christmas dinner table, telescoping 90 Christmas dinners in the history of a family into one. This is Hindemith's last opera; he had planned a companion piece but dies before the idea could become music.

1961 Dance

Feb. 14   Frederick Ashton's version of *Two Pigeons* is premiered by The Royal Ballet in London. The music is by Andre Messager and the decor by Jacques Dupont. Louis Merante choreographed the original ballet, about a young couple and the gypsy that comes between them, in 1886. Lynn Seymour and Christopher Gable head today's cast.

March 22   The New York City Ballet premieres *Electronics*, a ballet in three movements by George Balanchine, in New York. The music, by Remi Gassamann, is the first electronic score for an American ballet. Diana

Adams, Jacques d'Amboise, Violette Verdy and Edward Villella lead the cast.

March 23   Yuri Gregorovich's *Legend of Love* — to music by Arif Melikov, with book by Nazim Khikmet and designs by Simon Virsaladze — is premiered by the Kirov Ballet in Leningrad. Irina Kolpakova, Inna Zubkovskaya and Alexander Gribov dance the story of Queen Mehmene-Banu, who sacrifices her beauty and happiness to save her sister.

April 14   Igor Belsky's *Seventh Symphony* is given its initial performance at the Kirov Theater in Leningrad. The abstract work, set to the first movement of Dmitri Shostakovich's Symphony No. 2 (*Leningrad*), is based on Leningrad's resistance to the Nazi invasion during World War II. Alla Sizova and Yuri Solovyov lead the cast.

April 16   Martha Graham presents *Visionary Recital* in New York, to music by Robert Starer. The work deals with three aspects of Samson. Bertram Ross, Paul Taylor, Dan Wagoner, Martha Graham, Matt Turney and Akiko Kanda star.

Oct. 4   Choreographer Birgit Cullberg's *Adam and Eve*, to Hilding Rosenberg's Concerto for String Orchestra, is premiered by the American Ballet Theater in New York City. The costumes and sets are by Per Falk.

Dec. 7   The New York City Ballet premieres George Balanchine's *Raymonda Variations*, to music from Alexander Glazunov's *Raymonda*. The abstract ballet is loosely based on Marius Petipa's *Raymonda*. Patricia Wilde, Jacques d'Amboise, Victoria Simon, Suki Schorer, Gloria Govrin, Carol Sumner and Patricia Neary lead the cast.

1961 Instrumental and Vocal Music

Jan. 5   American composer Easley Blackwood's Symphony No. 2 is premiered by George Szell and the Cleveland Orchestra. The three-movement symphony, romantic in style, was commissioned by the music publishing house G. Schirmer to celebrate its centennial.

Jan. 20   Francis Poulenc's *Gloria* receives its world premiere by Charles Munch and the Boston Symphony Orchestra. This work — scored for soprano solo, chorus and orchestra — becomes one of the composer's most often performed compositions. The music is dedicated to the memory of Serge and Natalie Koussevitzky. Poulenc states he attempted to "write a joyous hymn to the glory of God."

Feb. 8   Roberto Gerhard's *Collages* receives its initial performance by the BBC Symphony Orchestra in London. It is a serially organized work scored for orchestra and tape-recorded sounds and was inspired by abstract expressionist painting. A critic for *Musical Opinion* (London) writes, "If ever the BBC has wasted public money on the rehearsal and performance of absolute rubbish, it was on this occasion."

Feb. 10   Walter Piston's Symphony No. 7 is premiered by Eugene Ormandy and the Philadelphia Orchestra. The three-movement symphony wins the Pulitzer Prize for music, the second time Piston wins that award. Harold C. Schonberg writes in the New York *Times* that the piece is "smoothly constructed, well orchestrated, shapely in form and always well-bred."

Feb. 10   Ferde Grofe's *Niagara Falls Suite* is premiered by the Buffalo Philharmonic, the composer conducting. The four-movement piece celebrates the opening of the Niagara Power Project.

March 2   Aaron Copland's *Nonet for Strings* receives its initial performance in Georgetown at the Dumbarton Oaks Research Library, near Washington, D.C. Scored for three cellos, the work is neobaroque in style.

March 31   *L'horloge de flore*, by Jean Francaix, is premiered by Eugene Ormandy and the Philadelphia Orchestra, with John de Lancie as oboe soloist. The neoclassical suite is scored for solo oboe and small orchestra. Its seven movements are named after flowers.

April 4   Darius Milhaud's Symphony No. 10 is premiered by Piero Bellugi and the Portland Symphony Orchestra in Portland, Oregon. The work was commissioned by the Oregon State Centennial Commission. Milhaud correlates letters of the alphabet with musical pitches to create a theme that spells "Oregon."

April 20   George Szell and the Cleveland Orchestra premiere Walter Piston's *Symphonic Prelude*.

April 24   Witold Lutoslawski's symphonic suite *Jeux venitiens* is premiered by the Cracow Philharmonic Orchestra in Venice. The music has aleatoric moments and reflects the influence of John Cage (Lutoslawski recently heard Cage perform at Darmstadt). He tells an interviewer, "The experience provided a spark that ignited a powder keg in me."

April 27   Henry Cowell's Symphony No. 14 and Roy Harris' *Give Me the Splendid Silent Sun* are premiered by Howard Hanson and the Eastman School of Music Philharmonic. This event occurs during this year's Inter-American Music Festival in Washington, D.C.

April 30   Alberto Ginastera's *Cantata para America magica* receives its initial performance in Washington, D.C. at the Inter-American Music Festival. Ginastera writes his own text to this piece, scored for soprano and a percussion orchestra numbering 53 players.

May 31   Krzysztof Penderecki's *Threnody for the Victims of Hiroshima* receives its world premiere over Warsaw radio. Scored for 24 violins, 10 violas, 10 cellos and 8 double basses, the work is intended to evoke a sense of human catastrophe in the aftermath of the atomic bomb attack on Hiroshima in 1945. Its special effects include tapping, scraping and snapping of parts of musical instruments. This composition becomes the composer's most frequently played piece.

June 5 Heitor Villa-Lobos' Concerto for Harmonica and Orchestra is premiered posthumously by conductor Guillermo Espinosa, with John Sebastian as soloist, in Cartagena, Colombia.

June 9 Bohuslav Martinu's *The Greek Passion*, based on a novel by Nikos Kazantzakis, is premiered posthumously by Paul Sacher and the Zurich Opera. The piece, scored for voices and orchestra, is the last Martinu composed.

June 16 Arnold Schoenberg's *Die Jakobsleiter*, completed by Winfried Zillig, premieres at today's concert of this year's International Society for Contemporary Music festival, which began five days ago. Schoenberg's oratorio is based on the biblical tale of Jacob and his dream. He began the piece in 1915 and worked on it intermittently until his death.

June 24 Symphony No. 1 (*Gothic*), by Havergal Brian, receives its initial performance in Westminster, England. The performers are amateurs. The piece receives a fully professional performance in 1966. It is scored for vocal soloists, chorus, four mixed choirs, children's choir, four brass bands and large orchestra. The last of its four movements is a protracted *Te Deum*. The symphony was composed 42 years ago.

Aug. 3 *Atlas Eclipticalis*, by John Cage, receives its world premiere in Montreal, Canada, the composer conducting. The work is based on the positions of stars in an astronomical atlas, with Cage having applied chance operations to the pages of the atlas as a source for the music. It is scored for electronic instruments (loudspeakers, amplifiers and microphones) and orchestra and was commissioned by the Montreal Festivals Society.

Aug. 16 Zoltan Kodaly's *Szimfonia* premieres in Lucerne. Kodaly's first symphony, this piece has three movements. It is dedicated to the memory of Arturo Toscanini.

Sep. 6 Elliott Carter's *Double Concerto for Harpsichord and Piano with Two Chamber Orchestras* receives its world premiere in New York City. Charles Rosen and Ralph Kirkpatrick perform as soloists, and Gustave Meier conducts. The music was commissioned by the Fromm Music Foundation and performed for the eighth congress of the International Society for Musicology. The piece has seven sections, and

Carter states he "tried to present a musical analogue to the human experience of time both in brief moments and in the longer pattern of evolving events." Eric Salzman writes in the New York *Times* that it is "a breathtaking panorama of flashing textures and rhythms. . . ."

Oct. 1 Dmitri Shostakovich's Symphony No. 12 (*1917*) receives its world premiere in Leningrad. The four-movement work is a sequel to his last symphony and is dedicated to the memory of Vladimir Lenin.

Oct. 7 Henry Cowell's Symphony No. 15 (*Thesis*) receives its initial performance in Murray, Kentucky, as Robert Whitney conducts the Louisville Orchestra.

Oct. 18 The Louisville Orchestra premieres Lou Harrison's *Suite for Symphonic Strings*.

Oct. 21 *Structures, Book II*, for two pianos, by Pierre Boulez, is among the works performed and premiered at this year's Donaueschingen festival, beginning today. The work includes aleatoric elements, offering the pianists various choices at certain moments. Boulez asks in a program note, "Is a musical work conceivable only in one precise and organized direction?" The pianists are Yvonne Loriod and the composer.

Oct. 22 Gyorgy Ligeti's *Atmospheres* for orchestra, Luciano Berio's *Epifanie* for orchestra and Gunther Schuller's *Contrasts* are premiered at the closing concert of the Donaueschingen festival. The Ligeti work attracts much attention, with the composer later commenting that he conceived the music a decade ago but needed the technical means available in the West to transcribe his "musical hallucination" into musical notation. The piece is subsequently performed widely and is used, in part, by filmmaker Stanley Kubrick in the sound track to the space odyssey *2001*.

Oct. 26 David Diamond's Symphony No. 8 is premiered by Leonard Bernstein and the New York Philharmonic. The two-movement work is dedicated to Aaron Copland.

Dec. 19 John Corigliano Jr.'s *Fern Hill* for chorus and orchestra premieres in New York City. The text consists of words by Dylan Thomas. Corigliano has studied with Otto Luening at Columbia University, Vittorio Giannini at the Manhattan School of Music and privately with Paul Creston. His music is tonal and traditional.

1961   Births, Deaths and Debuts

Jan. 27 Black American soprano Leontyne Price makes her Metropolitan Opera debut in *Il trovatore*. Irving Kolodin writes in the *Saturday Review* magazine (New York) that her voice embodies "glistening sound and warm artistry."

Feb. 20 Australian-born composer and pianist Percy Grainger, 78, dies in White Plains, New York. After making a smashing American debut in New York in 1915, he

went on to teach and to establish a museum in Australia for his manuscripts and memorabilia. He was known to be eccentric and wanted his skeleton shown in his museum after his death. This never came to pass, but his eccentricity and flash abound in his music, which includes works for orchestra, chorus, chamber groups, electronic instruments and band. Next year, the National Library of

Scotland in Edinburgh receives a collection of Grainger's manuscripts. The gift is made possible by Grainger's widow in accordance with the composer's known wishes. The works are those inspired by Scotland or by Scottish melodies.

Feb. 22   Ballet impresario and director Marquis George de Cuevas dies in Cannes at the age of 75. He founded the Ballet Institute and Ballet International in 1943. Four years later he took over the Nouveau Ballet de Monte Carlo and changed its name to Grand Ballet de Monte Carlo. In 1950 it became Le Grand Ballet du Marquis de Cuevas and, in its final years, International Ballet of the Marquis de Cuevas. Under his direction, the company became a showcase for major international stars such as Alicia Markova, Leonide Massine and Erik Bruhn. It was also the first European ballet company with a strong American contingent, including George Skibine, William Dollar, Marjorie Tallchief and Rosella Hightower. The artistic output of the company was minimal. Cuevas, who dictated the company's policies, relied on the box-office appeal of big-name stars rather than on choreography to attract audiences.

March 3   Austrian pianist Paul Wittgenstein, 73, dies in Manhasset, New York. A student of Theodor Leschetizky, he made his debut in 1913. During World War I he lost his right arm and subsequently commissioned a number of left-hand concertos from such composers as Maurice Ravel, Richard Strauss, Erich Korngold and Benjamin Britten.

March 8   Sir Thomas Beecham, 81, dies in London. Born into wealth, he could pursue music without economic worries. His first major performance came in 1905, when he conducted the Queen's Hall Orchestra in London. By 1910 he had become an opera impresario and produced and conducted the first British performance of *Elektra* and other operas by Richard Strauss. In 1929 he founded the Delius Festival. Eventually he conducted in America and led such ensembles as the Seattle Symphony and the Metropolitan Opera. As a conductor, he was known for his charisma and excellent technique. He was often hailed as the conductor who bridged the gap between music of the past and present. He also wrote an autobiography entitled *A Mingled Chime* (1943).

April 2   American composer Wallingford Riegger, 75, dies in New York City. Percy Goetschius was his principal composition teacher. Riegger composed music under many different pseudonyms and spent much of his adult life in obscurity. The year 1948 brought him to public attention when he won the New York Music Critics Circle Award for his Symphony No. 3. He wrote music in a number of very different styles with equal skill and had a considerable influence on the development of atonal American music. He was also an ardent supporter of Charles Ives.

JOAN SUTHERLAND RECEIVES AN OVATION AFTER HER METROPOLITAN OPERA DEBUT.

April 14 Japanese conductor Seiji Ozawa, assistant conductor of the New York Philharmonic, makes his conducting debut with that orchestra at Carnegie Hall.

June 30 American inventor Lee de Forest, 87, dies in Hollywood. He was known as the "father of the radio" for adding a grid to the cathode and anode of a vacuum tube, thus making radio possible. In 1909 de Forest presided over the first broadcast of a human voice (Enrico Caruso, from the Metropolitan Opera House in New York). His work laid the foundation for advancements in sound motion pictures and television.

July 19 Danish prima ballerina Margot Lander dies in Copenhagen at the age of 50. Lander became a solo dancer (the equivalent of principal dancer) in 1931 and was named prima ballerina in 1942. She is the only Danish dancer ever to officially hold the title. Known for her brilliance and poetry, Lander's outstanding roles were in *Napoli, Swan Lake, Giselle* and *Coppelia*. She was one of the few Danish women of her generation to dance the Petipa ballets successfully.

July 27 American composer Theodore Chanler, 59, dies in Boston. His principal composition teacher was Ernest Bloch, and he also studied with Nadia Boulanger. His output includes songs, which are considered examples of lyrical American writing; other choral works; a ballet, and an opera. His music is polytonal, without dense harmony.

Nov. 26 Australian soprano Joan Sutherland receives an ovation after her Metropolitan Opera debut in *Lucia di Lammermoor.*

1961   Related Events

The Deutsche Oper reopens this year in Berlin. Formerly known as the Stadtische Oper, the theater was destroyed in an air raid in 1944 and reopened after World War II as Theater des Westens (in a different building). The rebuilt theater is on Bismarckstrasse. Gustav Sellner is Intendant.

Het Amsterdam Ballet and Het Nederlands Ballet merge to form Het Nationale Ballet. Sonia Gaskell is director.

John Cranko is appointed director of ballet at the Wurtemburg State Opera in Stuttgart this year.

FM broadcasting in stereo multiplex begins this year.

May 1 Walter Piston is awarded the Pulitzer Prize for music for his Symphony No. 7.

May 9-10 The Columbia-Princeton Electronic Music Center gives its first two initial concerts. Taking place at the McMillan Theater at Columbia University in New York City, the programs consist of the following works: *Electronic Study No. 1*, by Mario Davidovsky; *Leiyla and the Poet*, by Halim El-Dabh; *Creation-Prologue*, by Vladimir Ussachevsky; *Composition for Synthesizer*, by Milton Babbitt; *Stereo Electronic Music No. 1*, by Bulent Arel; *Gargoyles for Violin Solo and Synthesized Sound*, by Otto Luening, with Max Polikoff performing the violin part; and *Symphonia sacra*, by Charles Wuorinen. Today's event helps establish this electronic music center as one of the finest in the world.

June 12 The Institute of Sonology is established at the University of Utrecht, the Netherlands. The institute explores — through courses, concerts, writings and other presentations — the relationship between music, sound production, electro-acoustics and mathematics. It has studios for the composition of electronic and computer music and is designed as an internationally oriented center of musical thought and experimentation.

June 16 Rudolf Nureyev, 23, a star of the Kirov Ballet, flees the company as it is about to board a plane in Paris. He asks for political asylum in France.

July 23 American singer Grace Bumbry creates a sensation when she sings the role of Venus in *Tannhauser* at the

COMPUTER STUDIO AT THE INSTITUTE OF SONOLOGY, UNIVERSITY OF UTRECHT

Bayreuth Festival. She is the first black American singer to appear at this festival.

Dec.   Zubin Mehta, 24, is appointed director of the Los Angeles Philharmonic Orchestra this month.

1962   Opera

Feb. 15   Vittorio Giannini's *Rehearsal Call* premieres in New York City at the Juilliard School. The three-act opera buffa is about young aspiring singers working their way to the stage.

May 10   Wolfgang Fortner's comic opera *In seinem Garten liebt Don Perlimpin Belison*, based on a tale by Federico Garcia Lorca, receives its initial performance in Schwetzingen, Germany. The serial work is about a schizophrenic husband. It is Fortner's third opera based on Lorca (*Der Wald* and *Die Bluthochzeit* are the other two).

May 29   *King Priam*, by Michael Tippett, receives its world premiere at the Coventry Theatre in Coventry, England. The libretto is based on the story of King Priam of Troy. The opening night cast includes Marie Collier, Josephine Veasey and Richard Lewis. John Pritchard conducts.

June 27   Ernst Krenek's *Ausgerechnet und verspielt*, with a libretto by the composer, premieres over Vienna television.

It is about a mathematician who devises a formula to win money at gambling but loses.

Aug. 12   *Constantin Palaeologus*, by Manolis Kalomiris, premieres posthumously in Athens. The opera, the composer's last, is about the fall of Byzantium.

Oct. 11   Carlisle Floyd's *The Passion of Jonathan Wade* receives its initial performance by the New York City Opera in New York. It is about a northern colonel in South Carolina just after the Civil War. Ross Parmenter, in the New York *Times*, calls it "pretty and melodious."

Dec. 30   Dmitri Shostakovich's *Katerina Ismailova* premieres in Moscow. This opera is a toned-down version of the composer's *Lady Macbeth of the District of Mtsensk*, originally produced in 1934, which shocked the Soviets by portraying violence and adultery.

1962   Dance

Jan. 17   George Balanchine premieres his evening-length *A Midsummer Night's Dream* with the New York City Ballet in New York. The work is set to music by Mendelssohn. Edward Villella, Melissa Hayden and Arthur Mitchell star. The work is in two acts and six scenes.

March 4   Martha Graham premieres *Phaedra*, in New York, to music by Robert Starer. Graham, Paul Taylor, Bertram Ross, Ethel Winter and Helen McGehee star. The work is based on the Greek legend of Phaedra and her love for Hippolytus, her stepson.

March 6   Martha Graham's *Samson Agonistes*, a revised version of *Visionary Recital* — to music by Robert Starer, with sets by Rouben Ter-Arutunian and costumes designed by the choreographer — premieres at the Broadway Theater in New York City.

May 5   Arnold Schoenberg's *Pierrot Lunaire* is performed as a ballet for the first time. The choreography is by Glen Tetley, and he and his company dance the performance in New York. The decor for today's presentation is by Rouben Ter-Arutunian.

May 8   *Le Sacre du printemps* is performed by The Royal Ballet in London. This version is choreographed by Kenneth MacMillan and features scenery and costumes by

Sidney Nolan. Monica Mason dances the role of the Chosen Maiden.

June 10   Choreographer John Cranko's *Coppelia* is premiered by the Stuttgart Ballet in Stuttgart. This is another version of this famous work, first danced in 1870 in Paris.

June 14   Igor Stravinsky's *Noah and the Flood*, choreographed by George Balanchine, receives its world premiere over CBS television, the composer conducting. The biblical spectacle includes narration, mime, song and dance. It is based on the tale of Noah and the ark and uses some Latin texts, mixing diatonic writing with 12-tone procedures. Paul Henry Lang of the New York *Herald-Tribune* pans the music. Stravinsky responds by cable from Germany to that newspaper, "The only blight on my eightieth birthday is the realization that my age will probably keep me from celebrating the funeral of your senile music columnist." Lang quickly responds to Stravinsky's cable by writing, "Stravinsky is a man trapped in his own narrowness and intolerance, so blinded by the praise of sycophants who want to vindicate his joining the twelve-tone camp that he leaps to an instantaneous attack upon everyone who dares to express an independent opinion about his work."

July 15 John Cranko's version of *Daphnis and Chloe*, to music by Maurice Ravel, receives its world premiere by the Stuttgart Ballet. The decor for this version is by Nicholas Georgiadis.

Aug. 4 The Paul Taylor Company presents the world premiere of *Aureole*, a "white" abstract modern dance work to music by Handel. Taylor, Elizabeth Walton, Dan Waggoner, Sharon Kinney and Renee Kimball are in the cast. The one-act ballet is performed at the American Dance Festival held at Connecticut College.

Aug. 17 The Martha Graham Company performs *Secular Games* at Connecticut College. The abstract work, in three movements, deals with play. It is set to Robert Starer's *Concerto a tre*. Robert Powell, David Wood, Richard Kuch, Richard Gain, Clive Thompson, Dudley Williams, Petero Randazzo, Helen McGehee, Lois Schlossberg and Juliet Fisher are in the opening night cast.

Sep. 17 The Bolshoi Ballet premieres Asaf Messerer's *Ballet School* in New York City. The work, which describes a dancer's training, is the first Soviet ballet to be premiered outside the USSR. It is performed to music by Anatoly Liadov, Sergei Liapunov, Alexander Glazunov and Dmitri Shostakovich. Maya Plisetskaya, Yekaterina Maximova, Maya Samokhvalova, Margarita Smirnova, Nina Fedorova, Tatiana Papko, Nicolai Fadeyechev, Vladimir Vasiliev, Vladimir Nikonov and Mikhail Lavrovsky head the cast. The performance takes place during a visit of the Bolshoi Ballet to the United States.

Sep. 30 In a workshop performance, the Robert Joffrey Ballet premieres Alvin Ailey's *Feast of Ashes* in New York. The work is based on Federico Garcia Lorca's *House of Bernarda Alba*, with a score by Carlos Surinach. Francoise Martinet, Lisa Bradley and Paul Sutherland star. Also premiered tonight is Joffrey's *Gamelan*. This work, dealing with colors and images evoking Japanese culture, features music by American composer Lou Harrison and costumes by Willa Kim.

Dec. John Cranko unveils his second production of Sergei Prokofiev's ballet *Romeo and Juliet* at the Wurttemberg Staatstheater in Stuttgart this month.

Dec. 12 The Royal Ballet produces Frederick Ashton's version of the "melodrama" *Persephone*. The ballet, to Igor Stravinsky's music, is part of worldwide homage to the composer on his 80th birthday. Based on the legend of Persephone, it is rarely performed because of the need to find a ballerina who can speak Andre Gide's poem. Svetlana Beriosova, Keith Rosson, Alexander Grant, Gerd Larsen and Derek Rencher star.

Dec. 27 Paul Taylor's modern dance work *Piece Period*, to music by Isang Yun, premieres in New York City.

1962 Instrumental and Vocal Music

Jan. 17 Symphony No. 8 (*San Francisco Symphony*), by Roy Harris, receives its initial performance by Enrique Jorda and the San Francisco Symphony Orchestra. Based on the life of Saint Francis of Assisi (who is also the patron saint of San Francisco), it celebrates the San Francisco Symphony's 50th anniversary.

Jan. 19 The Violin Concerto, by Egon Wellesz, premieres in Vienna. The piece has four movements.

Jan. 20 Dmitri Shostakovich's Symphony No. 4 is finally presented for the general public in Moscow. Rehearsed in 1936, the symphony was not performed because of the reaction of Soviet musicians and officials.

Jan. 26 David Diamond's Symphony No. 7 is premiered by Eugene Ormandy and the Philadelphia Orchestra. The symphony has three movements.

Feb. 6 Dmitri Kabalevsky's Sonata for Cello in B-flat Major, Op. 72, is premiered by Mstislav Rostropovich at the Moscow Conservatory.

Feb. 16 Darius Milhaud's Symphony No. 12 (*Rural*) is premiered by Enrique Jorda and the San Francisco Symphony Orchestra in Davis, California.

Feb. 20 David Amram's String Quartet receives its first performance by the Beaux Arts Quartet at Town Hall in New York City.

Feb. 23 *A Sermon, a Narrative and a Prayer*, by Igor Stravinsky, receives its world premiere by Paul Sacher and the Chamber Orchestra of Basel in Basel. Scored for tenor, contralto, narrator, chorus and orchestra, the work has three sections. Stravinsky describes it as a "meditation of the New Testament virtue of hope." Peter Heyworth writes in the New York *Times* that the piece is "one of the most impressive examples of twentieth-century religious art."

Feb. 26 Havergal Brian's Symphony No. 18 is premiered by Brian Fairfax and the Polyphonia Symphony Orchestra in London. The work has three movements. Brian is now 86 years old.

March 1 *Invocation and Dance*, an orchestral work by William Mathias, receives its initial performance at the Cardiff Festival in Wales. Mathias has studied with Lennox Berkeley at the Royal Academy of Music.

March 9 Norman Dello Joio's *Fantasy and Variations* for piano and orchestra receives its initial performance by the Cincinnati Symphony Orchestra, Max Rudolf conducting.

Lorin Hollander is soloist. The piece was commissioned by the Baldwin Piano Company.

March 21   *Quintet for Winds*, by Michael Colgrass, receives its first performance by the Dorian Wind Quintet at the Kaufman Concert Hall in New York City. Colgrass has studied with Darius Milhaud, Lukas Foss, Wallingford Riegger and Ben Weber. He also studied at the University of Illinois and at the Berkshire Music Center in Tanglewood. He is a professional percussion player as well as a composer.

April 16   Krzysztof Penderecki's *Polymorphie* premieres in Hamburg. This work is scored for 48 string instruments.

May 15   Otto Luening's *Sonority Canon for Four Solo Flutes Accompanied by 33 Flutes on Tape* premieres at Columbia University in New York City.

May 19   Joseph Haydn's Concerto for Violoncello and Orchestra in C Major premieres in Prague after the recent discovery of a copy of the original manuscript at the National Museum of Prague.

May 21   *Momente* by Karlheinz Stockhausen premieres in Cologne. It is composed for soprano, four choruses, 13 players and percussion. The choral parts ask the singers to speak, whisper, laugh, scream, clap and stamp as well as sing. The piece is revised in 1965.

May 25   Anton Webern's symphonic poem *Im Sommerwind* premieres at the University of Washington in Seattle. This event marks the opening of the first International Anton Webern Festival. The manuscript of the Webern work had been discovered by scholar and musicologist Hans Moldenhauer.

May 25   Sir Arthur Bliss' cantata *The Beatitudes* premieres at the Coventry Cathedral Festival. This event celebrates the opening of the new cathedral built on the site of the original, which was obliterated by Nazi bombs in 1941.

May 26   Anton Webern's *Three Poems for Voice and Piano*, *Three Songs After Poems by Ferdinand Avenarius*, String Quartet (1905) and *Five Songs After Poems by Richard Dehmel* are premiered posthumously at the first International Anton Webern Festival in Seattle, Washington.

May 27   Anton Webern's *Eight Early Songs* and his *Langsamer Satz* for string quartet are premiered posthumously at the first International Anton Webern Festival in Seattle, Washington.

May 30   *War Requiem*, Op. 66, by Benjamin Britten, set to Latin texts and poems of Wilfred Owen, receives its world premiere at Coventry Cathedral, the composer conducting. This event marks the consecration of this reconstructed cathedral. Scored for soprano, tenor, baritone, mixed chorus, boy's choir, full orchestra and chamber orchestra, it is considered one of Britten's most important works.

June 26   Krzysztof Penderecki's cantata *Psalmy Dawida* premieres in Cracow. This cantata is based on texts from the psalms of David. It includes whispering and shouting.

July 5   American composer Leslie Bassett's orchestral suite *Five Movements* premieres in Rome. The composer describes the work as "pyramid sounds." Bassett studied with Ross Lee Finney, Arthur Honegger and Nadia Boulanger. He was awarded an American Prix de Rome last year.

Aug. 10   *Dance Overture*, by William Mathias, receives its first performance in London.

Aug. 22   Luigi Nono's *Three Songs of Life and Love* premieres at this year's Edinburgh Festival.

Sep. 20   Krzysztof Penderecki's *Canon* premieres at this year's music festival in Warsaw. It is scored for orchestra and magnetic tape.

Sep. 23   Aaron Copland's *Connotations for Orchestra* receives its world premiere by Leonard Bernstein and the New York Philharmonic. This event marks the inauguration of Lincoln Center for the Performing Arts in New York City. The piece is Copland's first 12-tone work for orchestra and the first orchestral work he has composed since 1946.

Sep. 24   Samuel Barber's Concerto for Piano and Orchestra, Op. 38, is premiered by Erich Leinsdorf and the Boston Symphony Orchestra, with John Browning as soloist. The three-movement concerto celebrates the opening of Philharmonic Hall at Lincoln Center in New York City. It was commissioned by G. Schirmer music publishers. Barber subsequently receives a Pulitzer Prize for it, his second in five years.

Sep. 25   Walter Piston's *Lincoln Center Festival Overture* is premiered at Philharmonic Hall at Lincoln Center in New York City, as Eugene Ormandy conducts the Philadelphia Orchestra.

Sep. 28   American composer William Bergsma's *Toccata for the Sixth Day* and William Schuman's *Song of Orpheus* receive their first performances by the Juilliard School Orchestra in Philharmonic Hall at Lincoln Center in New York City. Schuman is now president of Lincoln Center.

Oct. 4   William Schuman's Symphony No. 8 receives its initial performance by Leonard Bernstein and the New York Philharmonic at Lincoln Center in New York City. The three-movement symphony was commissioned by this orchestra. A reviewer for *Musical America* (New York) calls the composer "America's greatest symphonist."

Nov. 3   Aram Khachaturian's *Concerto-Rhapsody* for violin and orchestra premieres in Moscow, with Leonid Kogan as soloist. The composer later tells Nicolas Slonimsky, "A concerto is music with chandeliers burning bright; a rhapsody is music with chandeliers dimmed."

Nov. 8   Humphrey Searle's Symphony No. 4 premieres in Birmingham, England, the composer conducting. The four-movement work is based on a 12-tone row.

Dec. 4   Mario Castelnuovo-Tedesco's Concerto for Two Guitars and Orchestra premieres in Toronto.

Dec. 18   Symphony No. 13, Op. 113, by Dmitri Shostakovich, with texts by Evgeny Evtushenko, premieres in Moscow. Evtushenko's text, about the Nazi massacre of Jews at Babi Yar, is condemned by Soviet leader Nikita Khrushchev, and the poem is rewritten to follow the party line. The symphony is scored for bass soloist, male voices and orchestra. It has five movements.

1962   Births, Deaths and Debuts

Jan. 29   Austrian violinist Fritz Kreisler, 86, dies in New York. He studied in Vienna and Paris and won gold medals in both cities for his playing. His first visit to America was in 1888, and he eventually became one of most popular violinists of his time. He received many awards from many countries, was the owner of numerous original manuscripts, including that of the Brahms Violin Concerto (which he gave to the Library of Congress in 1949), and of several celebrated instruments, including a Guarneri violin. His repertoire was vast, and he also wrote numerous pieces for violin that became very popular.

Feb. 5   French composer Jacques Ibert, 71, dies in Paris. He studied with Gabriel Faure and others at the Paris Conservatoire and won the Prix de Rome in 1919. He held directorships of the Academy of Rome and the Paris Opera. His music includes operas and ballets, as well as orchestral, chamber and piano works. Ibert's music is a blend of French impressionism and neoclassicism. It exhibits craftsmanship and an ability to convey humor.

Feb. 17   German conductor Bruno Walter, 85, dies in Beverly Hills, California. He was an assistant conductor to Gustav Mahler at the Hamburg Stadttheater and later conducted premieres of important Mahler works. He performed at the Vienna Opera and all over Europe, eventually accepting the position of court conductor in Munich. He left Germany when Adolf Hitler came to power, went to France and later to America, where he worked with the Metropolitan Opera and the NBC Symphony. He also led the New York Philharmonic from 1947 through 1949. A composer of symphonies and other music, his real name was B.W. Schlesinger.

March 10   Rudolf Nureyev makes his U.S. debut with the Chicago Opera Ballet in a performance of the *Don Quixote* pas de deux with Sonia Arova.

April 3   Greek composer Manolis Kalomiris, 78, dies in Athens. He founded the Conservatory of Athens in 1926 and is noted for having sparked a school of nationalistic Greek composition. He was enormously prolific, with his own music incorporating folk song melodies and rhythms. His harmonies, however, reflect the influence of German and Russian culture.

June 12   English composer John Ireland, 82, dies in Wash, England. He studied composition with Charles Villiers Stanford at the Royal College of Music and later joined the faculty, teaching Benjamin Britten and others. He destroyed some of his early scores, and his later music is heavily influenced by English folk tunes, with modal and pentatonic harmonies and elements of French impressionism.

June 13   English composer and conductor Sir Eugene Goossens, 69, dies in London. He studied at Bruges Conservatoire and the Royal College of Music and conducted some of Sir Thomas Beecham's opera productions from 1915 to 1920. He came to America and conducted the Rochester Philharmonic and the Cincinnati Symphony Orchestra (1931–46). He was knighted in 1955. As a composer, his work was influenced by Claude Debussy and, later, by the neoclassical movement. His music was tonal but occasionally approached atonality.

June 15   Pianist Alfred Cortot, 84, dies in Lausanne, Switzerland. After making his debut as a pianist in 1896, he became a champion of the music of Richard Wagner and conducted performances of that composer's works in France. He formed a trio in 1905 with Pablo Casals and Jacques Thibaud, founded the Ecole Normale de Musique in 1919 and was famous also as a teacher. His piano playing was known for its romanticism and its beautiful tone.

July 4   John Christie, 80, dies in Glyndebourne, England. An opera impresario, he founded the Glyndebourne Festival and was responsible for some operas at the Edinburgh Festival.

Sep. 6   German composer Hanns Eisler, 64, dies in Berlin. He studied with Arnold Schoenberg at the Vienna Academy of Music and came to America in 1933 to lecture at the New School for Social Research. Later he was music assistant to Charlie Chaplin in Hollywood. He was deported ("voluntary deportation") from America in 1948 for having been involved in radical politics. His vocal music praising the Red Army achieved popularity in the Soviet Union. His symphonic works, on the other hand, are largely 12-tone and reflect the influence of Schoenberg. He also composed the music to *Auferstanden aus Ruinen* — the German Democratic Republic's national anthem, adopted in 1949. A three-volume *Hanns Eisler Archive* is published in 1968 in East Berlin. He was a prolific composer, whose work also includes approximately 40 film scores.

Nov. 19   French soprano Regine Crespin makes her Metropolitan Opera debut as the Marschallin in Richard Strauss' *Der Rosenkavalier*.

Dec. 7   Norwegian soprano Kirsten Flagstad, 67, dies in Oslo, Norway. After a relatively obscure career of 22 years, she made her Metropolitan Opera debut at age 40 and became an overnight sensation. Until her retirement, she was considered the finest Wagnerian soprano in the world as well as one of opera's brightest stars. She returned to her native Norway during the Second World War, and her husband was accused of collaboration with the Nazis. Because of this, she was not allowed to sing in the United States again until 1951. She continued making recordings until shortly before her death.

Dec. 29   Austrian conductor Hans Rosbaud, 67, dies in Lugano. After studies at the Hoch Conservatory in Frankfurt, he became director of the Mainz municipal music school and a conductor of radio performances broadcast in Munster and Frankfurt. After World War II he became director of the Munich Konzertverein and later, music director of the festival at Baden-Baden. He excelled as a conductor of new works of all styles.

1962   Related Events

Charles Wuorinen and Harvey Sollberger establish the Group for Contemporary Music in New York this year. Based at the McMillan Theater of Columbia University, the ensemble's purpose is to exercise direct control over the performance of their music and the conditions under which it is presented.

Georges Auric is appointed general administrator of both the Grand Opera and the Opera-Comique in France. This year he is also elected a member of the Academie des Beaux-Arts.

The Institute of Choreology is founded this year by British dance notators Rudolf and Joan Benesh. Its purpose is to advance the "Benesh System of Dance Notation" (also known as "choreology"), which involves writing dance movements onto a musical staff with special symbols (they copyrighted this system of dance notation in 1955 and have used it at the London Royal Academy of

Dancing and The Royal Ballet School). The institute offers diplomas and places graduates with prominent dance companies. Along with Labanotation (also known as kinetographie), developed by Rudolf von Laban, the Benesh method becomes an internationally known 20th-century system of dance notation.

Perspectives of New Music is founded this year by American music critic, editor and composer Benjamin Boretz. This periodical explores aspects of contemporary music and music theory and quickly establishes itself as one of the most sophisticated such journals in the world.

Introduction to the Sociology of Music, by Theodor W. Adorno, is published this year in Frankfurt am Main. The book is comprised of a series of lectures recently delivered at Frankfurt University. The essays, covering every aspect of music, define a sociology of music in terms of societal structures and social elements embodied in musical forms. Adorno then attempts to demonstrate the effects of such a sociology of music on people's lives and minds.

Serial Composition and Atonality (subtitled *An Introduction to the Music of Schoenberg, Berg, and Webern*), by George Perle, is published this year by the University of California Press. In it Perle explores the basics of serial composition and atonality and examines works by composers such as Alexander Scriabin, Bela Bartok and Igor Stravinsky as well as Arnold Schoenberg, Alban Berg and Anton Webern. He posits that serial techniques are not necessarily unique to 12-tone composition. The book is extremely well received and is praised by critics. It is subsequently published in three new editions and culminates in the book *Twelve-Tone Tonality*, published in 1977. Perle is now on the music faculty of Queens College of the City University of New York.

Feb. 21   Rudolf Nureyev and Dame Margot Fonteyn begin their legendary partnership with a performance of *Giselle* at Covent Garden.

May 7   Robert Ward is awarded the Pulitzer Prize for music for his opera *The Crucible*.

GEORGES AURIC

June 30   The Marquese de Cuevas disbands the Ballet International de la Marquese de Cuevas following the death of her husband, its patron.

July 23   "The Battle Hymn of the Republic", sung by the Mormon Tabernacle Choir, becomes the first tune to be telecast by the American satellite Telstar.

July 9   Milton Babbitt's article "Twelve-Tone Rhythmic Structures and the Electronic Medium" is published this month in *Perspectives of New Music*. In this article, one of Babbitt's most important contributions to the literature on contemporary music theory, he details his serial approach to rhythm, also known as "the time-point system." The fundamental principle of the system is the transference of pitch relations to time relations by a correspondence of time interval to pitch interval. Recent works by Babbitt include *Composition for Synthesizer* and *Vision and Prayer*, a song for soprano and synthesized magnetic tape. Both were composed last year.

Sep. 26   Igor Stravinsky conducts a program of his music in Moscow. This event marks the composer's first appearance in the Soviet Union in 48 years. Nikita Khrushchev invites the composer to meet with him. Stravinsky accepts and later reports that music was not the topic of conversation because "Mr. Khrushchev is not a musician."

ERIK BRUHN

Nov. 2   The Australian Ballet begins its initial season in Sydney with Erik Bruhn and Sonia Arova as guest artists. The company's director is Peggy van Praagh.

1963 Opera

March 3   Gian-Carlo Menotti's *Labyrinth*, with a libretto by the composer, premieres over NBC television. The one-act work is about a couple on their honeymoon encountering different characters who represent different facets of life. It is Menotti's first opera in six years. He describes it as an "operatic riddle." Irving Kolodin writes in the *Saturday Review* (New York), "Traditional opera is spoofed broadly and subtly."

March 16   Gian Francesco Malipiero's one-act opera *Il Capitan Spavento* premieres in Naples.

April 23   *Monsieur de Pourceaugnac*, by Frank Martin, receives its first performance at the Grand Theater in Geneva. The libretto is based on the comedy by Moliere.

May 13   William Grant Still's *Highway No. 1, U.S.A.* premieres in Miami, Florida. The one-act opera is about the highway on the East Coast of America.

May 31   Dominick Argento's *Christopher Sly*, with a libretto by John Manlove, receives its initial performance at the University of Minnesota in Minneapolis.

Oct. 21   Gian-Carlo Menotti's *Le dernier sauvage* receives its first performance at the Opera-Comique in Paris. The opera, originally commissioned by the Paris Opera, was deemed more suitable to be performed at this theater. The libretto, by the composer, was originally written in Italian and translated into French for the premiere. It is a satirical portrayal of the American upper class. Harold C. Schonberg writes in the New York *Times* that Menotti's opera is a "Broadway musical masquerading as an opera."

Nov. 27   *Die Verlobung in San Domingo*, a two-act opera by Werner Egk, is performed for the first time at the Bavarian National Opera Theater in Munich. The libretto is by the composer, who also conducts the performance. Based on a novella by Heinrich von Kleist, the opera is about a revolt during the 19th century in which the French authorities arrest and execute an innocent man. Featuring a half-hour of recorded Dominican music, the opera is premiered just four days after this theater was reopened — it was rebuilt after having been destroyed by bombs in 1943.

Dec. 2   Carlisle Floyd's opera *The Sojourner and Mollie Sinclair* premieres in Raleigh, North Carolina. The one-act work is about problems of Scottish settlers in the South. It was commissioned by the Carolina Charter Tercentenary Commission.

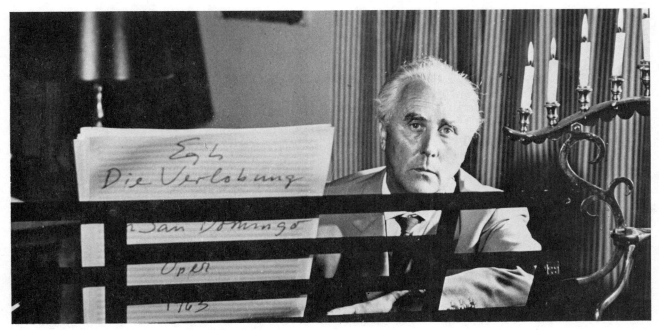

WERNER EGK

1963 Dance

March 12   *Marguerite and Armand* receives its first performance by the Royal Ballet. It is choreographed by Frederick Ashton to music of Franz Liszt arranged by Humphrey Searle, with decor and costumes by Cecil Beaton. Michael Somes, Margot Fonteyn and Rudolf Nureyev perform this ballet, which becomes a showcase for Fonteyn and Nureyev. The story is that of Camille. Armand is the first role created by Nureyev outside the Soviet Union. The one-act ballet is performed at Covent Garden in London.

March 13   Jose Limon's version of *The Demon*, to music by Paul Hindemith, premieres in New York City. The work, originally performed in 1923 as a dance-pantomime, is about a demon who enslaves a succession of women.

March 20   George Balanchine's *Bugaku* is premiered by the New York City Ballet. The work, with music by Toshiro Mayzumi, is reminiscent of the Japanese court dance. Allegra Kent and Edward Villella star. The one-act ballet is performed at the City Center in New York.

April 9   Igor Stravinsky's *Movements for Piano and Orchestra* is performed as a ballet for the first time, with choreography by George Balanchine. Lighting and decor are by David Hays and Peter Harvey. Today's work, in combination with Stravinsky's *Monumentum pro Gesualdo*, is subsequently performed as a single piece. This presentation is by the New York City Ballet in New York. Suzanne Farrell and Jacques d'Amboise star.

April 12   Choreographer Konstantin Sergeyev's *A Distant Planet* — set to music by B.S. Maizel, with a libretto by the choreographer and the composer — receives its world premiere by the Kirov Ballet in Leningrad. The designs are by Valery Dorrer.

July 13   *Las Hermanas* is performed for the first time by the Stuttgart Ballet in Stuttgart. It features choreography by Kenneth MacMillan, music by Frank Martin, and costumes and decor by Nicholas Georgiadis. The story is based on Federico Garcia Lorca's *The House of Bernarda Alba*.

July 17   Merce Cunningham's *Field Dances* — to music by John Cage, with designs by Robert Rauschenberg — is performed for the first time at the University of California in Los Angeles.

Sep. 6   Martha Graham premieres her *Circe*, to a commissioned score by Alan Hovhaness, at the Prince of Wales Theater, in London. The work is based on the Greek legend. Mary Hinkson, Bertram Ross, Clive Thompson, Robert Powell, Richard Gain, Gene McDonald and Peter Randazzo are in the opening night cast.

Sep. 28   The Royal Swedish Ballet gives the initial performance of Antony Tudor's *Echoing of Trumpets*, to Bohuslav Martinu's *Fantaisies symphoniques*. The source of the ballet is the Nazi destruction of Lidice, Czechoslovakia during World War II. Gerd Andersson, Svante Lindberg, Annette Wiedersheim-Paul, Kari Sylwan and Mario Mengarelli star. The one-act work is performed at the Royal Swedish Opera House in Stockholm.

Nov. 14   The Stuttgart Ballet premieres John Cranko's version of *Swan Lake* in Stuttgart. The costumes are by Jurgen Rose.

Nov. 27   Rudolf Nureyev's version of the white act from *La Bayadere* is performed by The Royal Ballet. The work

becomes the basis for the development of the company's corps de ballet which is subsequently judged the best in the world. Margot Fonteyn and Nureyev are the principal dancers.

Dec. 10   George Balanchine's *Meditation* — to music by Tchaikovsky, with costumes by Karinska — is performed for the first time by the New York City Ballet, at the City Center in New York. Suzanne Farrell and Jacques d'Amboise dance this pas de deux.

1963   Instrumental and Vocal Music

Jan. 18   Symphony No. 9 (*1963*), by Roy Harris, is premiered by Eugene Ormandy and the Philadelphia Orchestra. The symphony was commissioned by this orchestra and is dedicated to "the city of Philadelphia as the cradle of democracy."

Jan. 25   Jacques Ibert's *Mouvement symphonique (Bostoniana)* is premiered by Charles Munch and the Boston Symphony Orchestra. This is the first movement of a proposed larger work for this orchestra. The piece was not finished because of Ibert's death.

Feb. 6   A concert of new music by Canadian composers features R. Murray Schafer's orchestral work *Canzoni for Prisoners* and Harry Somers' *Five Concepts for Orchestra*. V. Feldbrill conducts the Montreal Symphony Orchestra in that city.

Feb. 8   Anton Webern's *Klavierstuck* (1925) for piano and his *Satz fur Streichtrio* (1925) are premiered posthumously in Vienna.

Feb. 9   Dmitri Kabalevsky's *Requiem* receives its world premiere in Moscow, Vladislav Sokolov conducting. The piece is scored for solo voices, chorus and orchestra and is dedicated to the Soviet soldiers who died in World War II. The requiem has three movements. Soviet critic A. Medvedev says it has "clarity and simplicity."

March 8   William Walton's *Variations on a Theme by Hindemith* is premiered by the London Philharmonic, the composer conducting. Walton's theme was derived from the second movement of Paul Hindemith's Cello Concerto and from his opera *Mathis der Maler*.

March 19   Harry Somers' *Stereophony for Orchestra* is premiered by the Toronto Symphony Orchestra in Toronto. Somers studied at the Royal Conservatory in Toronto and with Darius Milhaud in Paris. He is now 37 years old.

March 21   Henry Cowell's *Symphony No. 16 (Icelandic)* premieres in Reykjavik, Iceland. The piece has five movements.

March 27   Concerto for Cello, by Anatol Vieru, receives its first performance in Geneva. The one-movement work

was completed last year. It combines neobaroque and impressionistic elements within a dodecaphonic pitch environment.

March 28   Alan Hovhaness' Symphony No. 15 (*Silver Pilgrimage*) premieres in New York City.

April 2   Bohuslav Martinu's choral and orchestral piece *Prophecy of Isaiah* premieres posthumously in Jerusalem. The work, with a biblical text, is Martinu's last.

April 4   Samuel Barber's *Andromache's Farewell* Op. 39, based on Euripides, receives its initial performance by Thomas Schippers and the New York Philharmonic. Martina Arroyo is soprano soloist.

April 13   Alberto Ginastera's *Quintet for Piano and Strings* is premiered at this year's contemporary music festival in Venice.

April 16   American composer Morton Subotnick's *Serenade No. 2* premieres at this year's contemporary music festival in Venice.

April 23   Gian Francesco Malipiero's *Abracadabra* and Iannis Xenakis' *Strategie* are premiered at this year's contemporary music festival in Venice.

April 24   Hans Werner Henze's cantata *Novae de infinito laudes* receives its first performance at today's concert of this year's contemporary music festival in Venice. The work includes both tonal and nontonal elements.

April 25   Concerto for Organ and Orchestra, by Paul Hindemith, is premiered by the New York Philharmonic, the composer conducting. This orchestra commissioned the four-movement concerto. Hindemith is now visiting America for the last time — he dies this December.

May 16   Hans Werner Henze's Symphony No. 5 receives its initial performance by Leonard Bernstein and the New York Philharmonic. Henze deletes clarinets and bassoons from the orchestration. The piece is atonal and marks a departure from his previous dodecaphonic works.

May 18   Gian-Carlo Menotti's cantata *Death of the Bishop of Brindisi* premieres in Cincinnati. Max Rudolf conducts the work, which was commissioned by the Cincinnati Musical Festival Association. It is scored for soprano, bass, children's chorus, chorus and orchestra. Harriet Johnson of the New York *Post* writes, "The music is more compassionate than powerful."

July 6   Leslie Bassett's *Variations for Orchestra* receives its first performance in Rome, as Ferruccio Seaglia conducts the Radio Orchestra of Rome (RAI). The composer, now at the American Academy after winning a Prix de Rome, writes that the variations are built from musical "areas," not a theme. The work subsequently wins a Pulitzer Prize for music.

Aug. 28   Michael Tippett's Concerto for Orchestra receives its initial performance at the Edinburgh Festival of Music and Drama. The three-movement neobaroque piece was commissioned by the Edinburgh Festival Society.

Sep. 1   Benjamin Britten's *Cantata Misericordium* is premiered by Ernest Ansermet and L'Orchestre de la Suisse Romande in Geneva. Peter Pears and Dietrich Fischer-Dieskau are the soloists. The work — scored for tenor, baritone, mixed chorus and orchestra — condemns the inhumanity of war. The Latin text was adapted by Peter Wilkenson. Raymond Ericson writes in the New York *Times* after the work's New York premiere that it is "pervaded by a sweetness and gentleness that echo the ending of the War Requiem."

Oct. 3   Olivier Messiaen's *Sept Haikai* is performed for the first time by conductor Pierre Boulez at a concert of the Domaine Musicale in Paris. The piece is scored for piano, xylophone, marimba and instruments.

Oct. 3   Alberto Ginastera's Violin Concerto is premiered by Leonard Bernstein and the New York Philharmonic, with Ruggiero Ricci as soloist.

Oct. 6   Jacques Ibert's *Symphonie marine* premieres posthumously in Paris.

Oct. 9   Symphony No. 4, by Hans Werner Henze, premieres in Berlin, the composer conducting. The three-movement symphony incorporates materials from his opera *Konig Hirsch*. Peter G. Davis writes in *High Fidelity* magazine that, in terms of the composer's orchestral writing, the symphony is his "greatest achievement."

Oct. 11   Morton Feldman's *Vertical Thoughts, Straits of Magellan,* and *The Swallows of Salangan*; and Earle Brown's *December 1952, Pentathis, Available Forms I,* and *From Here* are premiered at a concert of avant-garde music in New York City.

Oct. 22   Otto Luening's *Synthesis for Orchestra and Electronic Sound* premieres in Erie, Pennsylvania.

Oct. 23   Alan Hovhaness' Symphony No. 17 (*Symphony for Metal Orchestra*) receives its initial performance in Cleveland, Ohio.

Nov. 11   Lukas Foss' *Echoi* premieres in New York City, with the composer playing the piano part. The four-movement suite is scored for piano, clarinet, cello, assorted percussion and garbage can.

Nov. 12   Paul Hindemith's *Mass* for a cappella mixed choir receives its world premiere by the Vienna Chamber Chorus, the composer conducting. This event marks both the composer's final public appearance and the performance of his last work.

Nov. 17   David Diamond's *The Sacred Ground* is premiered by the Buffalo Philharmonic Orchestra. The piece — scored for orchestra, chorus and male voice — is a setting of Abraham Lincoln's Gettysburg Address.

Dec. 3   Darius Milhaud's *Murder of a Great Chief of State. In Memory of John F. Kennedy* premieres in Oakland, California, as Bernard Samuel conducts the Oakland Symphony. Milhaud composed it in two days — the piece lasts 3 1/2 minutes.

Dec. 3   Aaron Copland's *Dance Panels in Seven Movements* premieres in Munich, the composer conducting. Although the work was conceived as a ballet, this performance is a concert version of the piece.

Dec. 10   Leonard Bernstein's Symphony No. 3 (*Kaddish*) receives its world premiere in Tel Aviv, the composer conducting the Israel Philharmonic Orchestra. Jennie Tourel is soprano soloist, Hannah Rovina is the speaker. The work is scored for orchestra, mixed chorus, boy's choir, speaker and soprano solo. This symphony, in memory of John F. Kennedy, was inspired by the "Kaddish" — the traditional Jewish prayer for the dead. Ross Parmenter subsequently writes in the New York *Times*: "The music is decidedly more palatable than the text. . . ."

Dec. 10   Howard Hanson's cantata *Song of Human Rights* premieres in Washington, D.C. The piece was commissioned by the United Nations Human Rights Organization.

Dec. 20   Darius Milhaud's *Pacem in terris,* Op. 404, is premiered by Charles Munch at the new Paris Radio Hall. The choral symphony, in seven sections, uses a text from an encyclical of Pope John XXIII.

Dec. 28   Paul Constantinescu's *Triple Concerto* for violin, piano, cello and orchestra premieres posthumously in Bucharest.

1963   Births, Deaths and Debuts

Jan. 4   Italian baritone Giuseppe Danise, 79, dies in New York City. After he made his debut in Naples in 1906, his first big success was in 1913. Beginning in 1915 he sang on an annual basis at the Teatro Colon. He sang with the Metropolitan Opera in New York for 12 years and also sang regularly at the Ravinia Festival. Danise was married to Brazilian soprano Bidu Sayao. His voice was praised for its warm tone. His dramatic ability and general musicality enhanced his career.

Jan. 15   American pianist Andre Watts, 16, debuts on television as soloist with conductor Leonard Bernstein on a "Young People's Concert."

Jan. 30   Composer Francis Poulenc, 64, dies in Paris. He studied piano with Ricardo Vines and composition with Charles Koechlin. Poulenc joined the group of young musicians called "Nouveaux Jeunes" at age 18 and later became a member of "Les Six." In addition to composing, he was a professional pianist and often appeared with his close friend, the tenor Pierre Bernac.

His music is noted for its charm, accessibility and vocal grace. It reflects the influence of both Maurice Ravel and Erik Satie. He was not in the least preoccupied with cerebral or novel trends in contemporary music but instead devoted himself to a kind of musical expression that could be termed popular and appealing within the context of serious concert music.

His most famous compositions include various stage works (*Les mamelles de Tiresias*, premiered in 1947; *Les dialogues des Carmelites*, premiered in 1957; and *La voix humaine*, premiered in 1959), instrumental works (*Aubade*, premiered in 1929; *Concerto champetre*, premiered in 1929; Concerto for Organ, String Orchestra and Kettledrums, premiered in 1941) and vocal works (*Gloria*, premiered in 1961). He also wrote many chamber pieces, piano pieces and songs. In 1961 his book on Emmanuel Chabrier was published in Paris. Poulenc is said to have been eccentric. One of his habits was to take a taxicab from his hotel to the concert hall where his latest piece was being premiered — even if the concert hall was less than one city block away.

Feb. 16   Hungarian composer Laszlo Lajtha, 70, dies in Budapest. He is noted primarily for his symphonic music, which is heavily contrapuntal. Those works include nine symphonies. Lajtha was an associate of the Ethnographical Department of the Hungarian National Museum and received the Kossuth Prize for his devotion to Hungarian folk music. He also composed three ballets and much chamber music.

Feb. 20   Hungarian conductor Ferenc Fricsay, 49, dies in Basel. After studying piano with Bela Bartok and composition with Zoltan Kodaly, he began conducting in Szeged. He made his debut at the Budapest Opera in 1945. Two years later, he conducted at the Salzburg Festival and began touring Europe and South America. He made his American debut with the Boston Symphony Orchestra in 1953 and two years later was appointed music director of the Houston Symphony Orchestra. His disagreements with the management led to resignation. He spent his last years in Switzerland.

April 9   Russian pianist Benno Moiseiwitsch, 73, dies in London. After studies in his home town of Odessa, he also studied with Theodor Leschetizky in Vienna. He debuted in England in 1908 and in America in 1919. He concertized all over the world, excelling in the romantic repertoire.

Oct. 11   French writer and designer Jean Cocteau, 74, dies in a Paris suburb. This artist collaborated with Serge Diaghilev's Ballet Russes productions. He wrote scenarios, designed posters and created publicity. He also made films and wrote novels, plays, and many articles and essays on dance. He was elected to the Academie Française in 1955.

Nov. 15   Hungarian conductor Fritz Reiner, 74, dies in New York. Among his important posts were the Court Opera in Dresden (1914–21), the Cincinnati Symphony (1922–31) and the Pittsburgh Symphony (1938–48). He was also a guest conductor at Covent Garden, the San Francisco Opera and the Metropolitan Opera. Perhaps his most important position was director of the Chicago Symphony (1953–62), which he brought to the high degree of

KARL AMADEUS HARTMANN

PAUL CONSTANTINESCU

eminence it still enjoys. He was not liked by many musicians, who resented his autocratic ways and temperament, but most agreed that he was an exceptionally talented conductor. His pupils included Leonard Bernstein and Lukas Foss.

Nov. 26   Italian soprano Amelita Galli-Curci, 81, dies in La Jolla, California. Self-taught in singing, she debuted in Rome in 1909 and sang successfully in Europe until 1915. In 1916 she had a brilliant success in Chicago and later in New York, in the bel canto repertoire. A throat ailment ended her career in 1936, and she retired to California.

Dec. 5   German composer Karl Amadeus Hartmann, 58, dies in Munich. He studied with Hermann Scherchen and later with Anton Webern. He was a "late bloomer," whose first major piece was not composed until he was about 30. His music, which includes pieces for many different kinds of instruments, is largely based on classical forms yet is highly chromatic and sometimes employs complicated rhythmic configurations. Among his works are eight symphonies.

Dec. 17   German conductor-composer Winfried Zillig, 58, dies in Hamburg. After studying composition with Arnold Schoenberg, he conducted in Oldenburg, Dusseldorf and Essen. He was chiefly known as conductor of the

Hesse Radio. He composed four operas, a cello concerto, chamber music, many songs, and piano pieces.

Dec. 20   Rumanian composer Paul Constantinescu, 54, dies in Bucharest. Known principally as a teacher at the Bucharest Conservatory, he wrote music that includes two operas, oratorios, five ballets, and symphonic and chamber music.

Dec. 28   German composer Paul Hindemith, 68, dies in Frankfurt. After early studies on the violin, he entered the Hoch Conservatory in Frankfurt, studying violin and composition. He then conducted at the Frankfurt Opera House, performed as a violist (he was highly proficient on the viola and the viola d'amore as well as on the violin) with the Amar String Quartet and conducted performances of his own works. He frequently participated in new music concerts at Donaueschingen and in Baden-Baden.

His career consisted of four basic activities: composing, performing, teaching and writing about music. His teaching activities took place at the Berlin Hochschule fur Musik and later, after the advent of Nazism, at Ankara Conservatory in Turkey, where he had been invited by the Turkish government to help formulate a program of music education. He also taught at the Berkshire Music Center in Tanglewood and at Yale University. He lectured at Harvard University and at the University of Zurich. His conducting appearances after World War II were mostly in Holland, Italy, England, Germany, Austria and America. His many honors included election to the National Institute of Arts and Letters and the Sibelius Award.

Hindemith's music evolved from an early rebellious style to a series of stages in which he explored, reconciled and transformed various musical styles of past centuries with various compositional trends and innovations in contemporary music theory. These include constructivism, neoclassicism, atonality, romanticism and even baroque tendencies. He synthesized these into a distinctly original style marked by extraordinary craftsmanship. He also concerned himself with a constructive use for music, introducing the concept of "Gebrauchsmusik" (music for use) and advancing the cause of "Hauermusik" (music for amateurs for home performance); he composed works specifically for these purposes.

His most famous compositions include the piano piece *Ludus Tonalis* (premiered in 1943), the opera *Mathis der Maler* (premiered in 1938), *Symphonic Metamorphosis on Themes by Weber* (premiered in 1944) and the song cycle *Das Marienleben* (premiered in 1923 and, after a radical revision, again in 1948). He was exceptionally prolific and wrote works for virtually every medium. These include four ballets as well as chamber, vocal and piano pieces. Hindemith was also a firm believer in the harmonic, or overtone, series as the basis of good harmony. He set down these thoughts in his two-volume treatise *The Craft of Musical Composition*, first published in 1941.

1963 Related Events

The Ballet West is founded this year at the University of Utah in Salt Lake City. It is an outgrowth of the Utah Civic Ballet, and William Christensen is its chief choreographer. The company has approximately 30 dancers and occasionally uses stars as guest performers.

Josef Krips becomes music director of the San Francisco Symphony Orchestra this year, succeeding Enrique Jorda. He holds this post until 1970.

Brazilian conductor Eleazar Carvalho becomes music director of the St. Louis Symphony Orchestra. His tenure, lasting five years, is marked by an interest in contemporary music.

Technological developments in the recording industry this year include the introduction (at the Berlin Radio Exhibition) of Philips' 1/8-inch (3.2 mm), 1 7/8 IPS miniature tape audio cassette. RCA, in an effort to reduce distortion on recordings, introduces its "Dynagroove" method of producing discs. In another development, the Rodgers and Hammerstein Archives of Recorded Sound is established at the New York Public Library.

March 8 Communist Party Chairman Nikita Khrushchev delivers a 2 1/2-hour speech on literature and the arts. Taking place at the Kremlin, it is one of the most oppressive pronouncements on the arts by a Soviet leader and is largely interpreted as guidelines for Soviet composers to follow. Khrushchev states: "It is hard for a normal person to understand what the word 'dodecaphony' means, but apparently it means the same as the word 'cacophony.' Well, we flatly reject this cacophonous music. Our people can't use this garbage as a tool of their ideology." Khrushchev's speech prompts a week-long meeting of the Board of Soviet Composers, which begins on March 23.

March 23 The Board of Soviet Composers holds a week-long plenary meeting as a means of responding to and implementing the dictates propounded in Nikita Khrushchev's speech of March 8. The meeting consists of speeches, discussions and performances of new music by young Soviet composers. One young composer — Rodion Shchedrin (now 30) — delivers the keynote address. He says, in part, "If we are guilty of anything, it is not of backwardness, but because we do not fight avant-garde tendencies with sufficient vigor." Over the next several years, Shchedrin changes course somewhat and begins using aleatoric devices; he then emerges as the "official modernist" composer of the Soviet Union.

May 6 Samuel Barber is awarded the Pulitzer Prize for music for Piano Concerto No. 1.

May 29 Igor Stravinsky is present as *Le Sacre du printemps* is performed by Pierre Monteux and the London Symphony Orchestra at Royal Albert Hall in London. This event marks the 50th anniversary of the work's premiere.

June Le Ballet National Jeunesses Musicales de France is established this month. Its first director is Pierre Lacotte.

Sep. 21 The Place des Arts in Montreal is inaugurated, as Canadian composer Jean Papineau Coutre's *Miroirs* is premiered by Zubin Mehta and the Montreal Symphony Orchestra.

Oct. Soviet musicologist Izrail Nestyev, writing this month in *Sovetskaya Muzyka*, blasts Western music critics for their negative assessments of recent music produced by Soviet composers. Nestyev's article is an outgrowth of recent political events in the Soviet Union affecting music. Last June Nikita Khrushchev urged stricter censorship and advocated centralized control of publishing. Composer Tikhon Khrennikov responds by calling a meeting this month of the directors of the Composers' Union to implement Communist Party guidelines in an effort to resist modernist influences from abroad. Shostakovich speaks at the two-day meeting and proclaims, "The scholastics of serialism, the dry abstractions and monotony of pointillism, the formal tricks of musique concrete have deprived musical art of all that is alive and human, and have destroyed all logic, form, imagery, contrast, and emotion." The participants in the meeting then proceed to collect and collate negative reviews from abroad. Nestyev's article is, in effect, the latest Soviet musical establishment response to the West.

Oct. 11 President John F. Kennedy announces that a new opera company is to be created in Washington, D.C. It will be a company of the Metropolitan Opera associated with the National Cultural Center in Washington.

Oct. 15 Philharmonic Hall in Berlin officially opens today. This building is the new home of the Berlin Philharmonic, conducted by Herbert von Karajan. It was designed by Dr. Ing. E.h. Hans Scharoun, who won the architectural competition for the project in 1956. The hall seats 2,218, and its organ, built by the Berlin firm of Schuke, was planned by Professor Michael Schneider. Karajan conducts today's performance of Beethoven's Ninth Symphony.

Oct. 29 Lukas Foss leads his first concert as the new music director of the Buffalo Philharmonic Symphony Society, conducting music of Charles Ives, Igor Stravinsky and Johannes Brahms at the Kleinhans Music Hall in Buffalo, New York. Foss remains music director of this orchestra for seven years.

HERBERT VON KARAJAN CONDUCTING THE BERLIN PHILHARMONIC ORCHESTRA

Nov. 1   While attempting to enter a Royal Philharmonic Orchestra concert at a segregated theater in Jackson, Mississippi, two black students are arrested for disturbing the peace.

Nov. 22   President John F. Kennedy is assassinated in Dallas, Texas. Erich Leinsdorf, conducting a concert of the Boston Symphony Orchestra, performs a movement from Beethoven's *Eroica* — the *Marcia funebre*. Many in the audience weep openly. Over the next several months, many prominent composers write works in memory of President Kennedy.

Dec. 4   The Second Vatican Council issues its first document. Entitled *Sacrosanctum concilium*, its sixth chapter is de-voted to sacred music. It marks the first time an ecumenical council focuses extensively on music in liturgy and is the culmination of reforms begun by Pope Pius X's *Moto Proprio* of 1903. The two basic reforms embodied in the document are the use of the vernacular in certain parts of the liturgy and the participation of the people through singing. It also permits new styles of sacred music to be performed in church, with instruments, as long as these compositions are appropriate to the occasion. Gregorian chant and poly-phony are retained, to be supplemented with musical styles and traditions of mission lands, largely third-world nations.

1964   Opera

Jan. 9   Dominick Argento's *The Masque of Angels*, with a libretto by John Olon-Scrymgeour, premieres at the Tyrone Guthrie Theater in Minneapolis, Minnesota.

Feb. 17   Hugo Weisgall's opera *Athaliah* is premiered by Thomas Scherman and the Concert Opera Association. The dodecaphonic opera is about a young woman named Jezebel who is fond of murder.

April 19   *Montezuma*, an opera in three acts by Roger Sessions, receives its world premiere in Berlin by the Deutsche Opera Company. The text is by G.A. Borgese. The opera is about the Aztec emperor who was regarded by his people as a god. Borgese died long before the first performance of the work, and Sessions has been shortening the libretto and working on the music for about 30 years. Critical reaction is mixed.

June 3   Humphrey Searle's *The Photo of the Colonel*, based on a play by Eugene Ionesco, premieres in Frankfurt. The three-act dodecaphonic opera is about a murderer. It was premiered in a concert version over radio by the British Broadcasting Corporation last March.

June 16   Ernst Krenek's *The Golden Ram*, with a libretto by the composer, premieres in Hamburg. Krenek conducts. It is about Jason, the argonaut, who travels through time and winds up on Route 66 in 20th-century America. He obtains a golden ram, which is confiscated by Greek customs on his return trip. The opera is a serial work and also uses prerecorded electronic sounds.

July 3   American composer Robert Ward's *The Lady from Colorado* premieres in Hanover, New Hampshire. It is a one-act opera about an Irish immigrant who marries a wealthy Englishman.

July 24   *Don Rodrigo*, by Alberto Ginastera, premieres at the Teatro Colon in Buenos Aires. The music is based on various classical forms, including the rondo and scherzo. The libretto, by Alejandro Casona, is about a warrior who fights the Moors. This piece is Ginastera's first opera. Dodecaphonic, it requires approximately 100 singers, 19 soloists and a large orchestra, including 18 French horns. Harold C. Schonberg of the New York *Times* says, "Mr. Ginastera is professional all the way through." Another writer hails it as "a landmark similar to *Wozzeck*."

Sep. 17   Gottfried von Einem's *Der Zerrissene* premieres in Hamburg. The two-act opera is based on a novel by Johann Nestroy and has a libretto arranged by Boris Blacher. It is a tonal work about a capitalist who discovers his money cannot purchase happiness.

Oct. 8   Lee Hoiby's *Natalie Petrovna*, based on a play by Ivan Turgenev, premieres at the City Center in New York City.

ERNST KRENEK

Nov. 12   Nicholas Maw's chamber opera *One-Man Show* premieres in London. It is about a young art student who is pursued by art dealers. Maw has studied with Lennox Berkeley at London's Royal Academy of Music and with Nadia Boulanger in Paris.

Dec. 1   Ferruccio Busoni's *Doktor Faust* receives its first American performance by the American Opera Society at Carnegie Hall in New York City. The world premiere took place on May 21, 1925.

1964 Dance

Jan. 7   George Balanchine's *Tarantella* — to music by Louis Gottschalk and orchestrated by Hershey Kay, with costumes by Karinska — is performed for the first time by the New York City Ballet in New York. Patricia McBride and Edward Villella dance this pas de deux.

April 2   During the quadricentennial celebrations of Shakespeare's birth, The Royal Ballet premieres Frederick Ashton's *The Dream* set to Felix Mendelssohn's *A Midsummer Night's Dream*. Antoinette Sibley, Anthony Dowell, Keith Martin and Alexander Grant star. The one-act ballet is performed at Covent Garden in London.

April 6   Choreographer Flemming Flindt's *The Lesson* — to music by Georges Delerue, with decor and costumes by

Bernard Dayde — is performed for the first time at the Opera-Comique in Paris. It is based on Ionesco's play.

May 6   Antony Tudor's *Dim Lustre* receives its first performance by the New York City Ballet. It had originally been premiered by the Ballet Theater in 1943. Patricia McBride and Edward Villella star.

June 26   John Butler's ballet *Catulli Carmina* — to music by Carl Orff, with costumes by Jac Venza — premieres at the Caramoor Festival in New York.

July 3   Merce Cunningham's modern dance piece *Cross Currents*, to music by Conlon Nancarrow arranged by John Cage, premieres at the Sadler's Wells Theater in London.

July 7   Hans van Manen's ballet *Opus 12*, to music by Bela Bartok, receives its initial performance at The Hague, Holland by the Nederlands Dans Theatre. The costumes are by Jan van der Wal, and the decor by Co Westerik.

Oct. 27   Maurice Bejart stages his enormous ballet production of Beethoven's Ninth Symphony at the Royal Circus, an outdoor arena in Brussels.

Dec. 31   *The Twelve* is performed for the first time by the Kirov Ballet in Leningrad. Choreography and book are by Leonid Yacobson; music is by Boris Tischenko; designs are by Yevgeny Stengerb.

1964   Instrumental and Vocal Music

Jan. 10   Pierre Boulez's orchestral work *Figures, Doubles and Prismes* premieres in an incomplete version in Basel, the composer conducting. The section called *Doubles* was begun in 1958. Boulez postponed it to work on *Pli selon pli* and returned to it this year, expanding it into a three-section piece.

Jan. 14   Henry Brant's *Voyage Four* receives its initial performance in New Haven, Connecticut. This work features performers placed all around the concert hall to create a stereophonic sensation. It is scored for 1 singer and 83 players.

Jan. 23   Peter Mennin's Symphony No. 7 (*Variation Symphony*) is premiered by George Szell and the Cleveland Orchestra. The piece has five sections in one movement. Mennin was appointed president of the Juilliard School of Music two years ago.

Feb. 7   Symphony No. 5, by Roger Sessions, is performed for the first time by Eugene Ormandy and the Philadelphia Orchestra. It has three movements and is Sessions' shortest symphony.

Feb. 17   *Chamber Concerto for Cello and 10 Players*, by Charles Wuorinen, receives its world premiere by the Group for Contemporary Music in New York City. Robert Martin is soloist, Arthur Bloom conducts. Composed last year, this concerto has five connected movements, each of which casts the soloist in a different light. The work is 12-tone. Wuorinen, now 25, has studied at Columbia University with Otto Luening.

March 12   Benjamin Britten's *Cello Symphony* premieres in Moscow, with Mstislav Rostropovich as soloist.

March 13   Ernst Toch's Symphony No. 5 (*Jeptha's Daughter*) is premiered by Erich Leinsdorf and the Boston Symphony Orchestra. The work, inspired by the biblical story of Jeptha, has one movement and includes such percussion instruments as gong, chimes, xylophone, vibraphone, Chinese temple blocks and anvil.

March 22   Dominick Argento's *Royal Invitation, or Homage to the Queen of Tonga* receives its initial performance by the Saint Paul Philharmonic Society in Saint Paul, Minnesota. The orchestral suite is also adapted as a ballet, with a scenario by John Olon-Scrymgeour.

April 1   Roberto Gerhard's oratorio *The Plague* is premiered by Antal Dorati and the BBC Symphony Orchestra in London. It is scored for orchestra and voices, with the composer calling on the singers to moan, wail, whisper and shout. He also includes a part for an air-raid siren. The music was inspired by Albert Camus' novel of the same name.

April 6   *Elegy for J.F.K.* — by Igor Stravinsky, with text by W.H. Auden — premieres in Santa Monica, California. The 12-tone piece is scored for baritone, two clarinets and corno di bassetto (basset horn).

April 11   Anton Webern's *Schmerz, immer blick nach oben* for voice and string quartet is premiered posthumously by the Juilliard String Quartet and Adele Addison in New York City.

April 22   Ferde Grofe's *World's Fair Suite* premieres at the opening of the New York World's Fair in the midst of rainy weather. The work, scored for orchestra, was composed specifically for the New York World's Fair. Grofe, semiparalyzed from a stroke, listens.

April 24   Rolf Liebermann's *Les echanges* receives its initial performance in Lausanne. This work features various office machines chattering for slightly more than three minutes; the 52 machines include cash registers, teletypes and staplers. The event celebrates the Swiss Exposition of Industry.

May 7   Symphony No. 6, by Carlos Chavez, is premiered by Leonard Bernstein and the New York Philharmonic. Chavez composed the three-movement symphony between 1961 and 1963. The composer states he attempted to write a symphony "within classic limitations," though not in a neoclassical style.

May 10   Roy Harris' symphonic *Epilogue to Profiles in Courage: J.F.K.* premieres in Los Angeles. The piece is a musical tribute to the assassinated president.

May 13   Tikhon Khrennikov's Concerto for Cello and Orchestra premieres in Moscow with Mstislav Rostropovich as soloist.

May 26   Aaron Copland's *Music for a Great City* receives its first performance by the London Symphony Orchestra with the composer conducting. Copland uses musical materials from his film score *Something Wild*. One of the movements of this new piece is called "Subway Jam." A London critic writes in a dispatch to the New York *Times* that Copland's attitude is "one of ironic and exasperated affection. . . ."

June 13   Benjamin Britten's *Curlew River* receives its world premiere at the Aldeburgh Festival, England. The "parable for church performance" was inspired by a Japanese Noh play and is about a woman searching for her son. It is scored for singers and seven players.

July 4   Walter Piston's Concerto for Two Pianos and Orchestra premieres in Hanover, New Hampshire.

Aug. 9   *Chamber Concert for Flute and 10 Players* receives its first performance by the Fromm Players at Tanglewood, Lenox, Massachusetts. The music is composed by Charles Wuorinen. Melvin Strauss conducts, Harvey Sollberger is flute soloist.

Aug. 12   Andrzej Panufnik's *Sinfonia sacra* premieres in Monaco.

Aug. 23   *Abraham and Isaac*, by Igor Stravinsky, receives its world premiere in Jerusalem. Robert Craft conducts and Ephraim Biran is baritone soloist. This sacred ballad for baritone and chamber orchestra was commissioned by the State of Israel. The Hebrew text is taken from the book of Genesis. The serial work is performed near Mount Moriah, where an angel of God is said to have prevented Abraham from sacrificing his son Isaac.

Sep. 10   Georges Enesco's symphonic poem *Vox Maris* premieres posthumously in Bucharest. This is his last work.

Sep. 18   Carlos Chavez's orchestral piece *Resonancias* premieres in Mexico City with the composer conducting. This music involves serial techniques and was composed specifically for the inauguration of Chapultepec's National Archeological Museum.

Oct. 5   Alan Hovhaness' symphonic poem *Meditation on Zeami* is premiered by Leopold Stokowski and the American Symphony Orchestra. The pentatonic piece features heavy brass (trumpets) and bells.

Oct. 7   Symphony No. 5, by Humphrey Searle, premieres in Manchester, England. The Halle Orchestra performs the symphony, which is dedicated to the memory of Anton Webern, Searle's teacher.

Oct. 17   Olivier Messiaen's *Couleurs de la cite celeste* is premiered by Pierre Boulez at the Donaueschingen Festival. It is scored for piano, winds and percussion and is one of Messiaen's most successful works.

Oct. 30   Luigi Dallapiccola's *Parole de San Paolo*, Riccardo Malipiero's *Time of Daffodils* and Giselher Klebe's *Miserere Nobis* are premiered at the Coolidge Auditorium, Library of Congress in Washington, D.C. This event marks the opening concert of the 13th Festival of Chamber Music.

Oct. 31   William Schuman's *Amaryllis*, Darius Milhaud's String Septet, Howard Hanson's *Four Psalms*, Walter Piston's String Sextet and Chilean composer Juan Orrego-Salas' *Sonata a quattro* are premiered at two different concerts today at this year's chamber music festival at the Coolidge Auditorium, Library of Congress in Washington, D.C.

Nov. 1   Virgil Thomson's *The Feast of Love* for baritone and chamber orchestra, and Alberto Ginastera's cantata *Bomarzo* are premiered at today's concert of the chamber music festival at the Coolidge Auditorium, Library of Congress in Washington, D.C.

Dec. 8   *Elytres*, by Lukas Foss, receives its initial performance by Zubin Mehta and the Los Angeles Philharmonic. The music, inspired by wings of insects, is scored for 12 instruments of the middle and upper registral range.

Dec. 18   Henry Cowell's Concerto for Koto and Chamber Orchestra is premiered by Leopold Stokowski and the Philadelphia Orchestra, with Kimio Eto as soloist. The soloist is blind. Cowell's concerto has three movements.

Dec. 28   *The Execution of Stephan Razin* — a cantata by Dmitri Shostakovich, with text by Evgeny Evtushenko — receives its world premiere in Moscow. The piece is scored for solo bass, chorus and orchestra. It celebrates the 50th anniversary of the October Revolution. Razin was a cossack who led the peasants in a revolt and was executed by the tsar's troops. The music scores a major success for Shostakovich.

1964   Births, Deaths and Debuts

Jan. 10   Bass-baritone Donald Gramm makes his Metropolitan Opera debut as Truffaldino in *Ariadne auf Naxos*, by Richard Strauss.

Jan. 22   American composer Marc Blitzstein, 58, dies in Martinique as the result of a bar brawl after a political argument. He studied composition with Nadia Boulanger and Arnold Schoenberg and composed many musical theater works advancing social consciousness. His music is

accessible, and his subjects attract attention. His unfortunate death prevents the completion of an opera about Sacco and Vanzetti, which was scheduled for production at the Metropolitan Opera House in New York.

Feb. 9   Samuel Chotzinoff, 74, dies in New York. A music critic and pianist, he performed with Jascha Heifetz and Efrem Zimbalist. He became a music director of the Na-

PIERRE MONTEUX

phony Orchestra, founded the Orchestre Symphonique de Paris in 1929 and conducted the San Francisco Symphony from 1936 to 1952. One of the century's finest conductors, Monteux excelled as much in the traditional repertoire as he did in the work of Igor Stravinsky and modern French music.

Oct. 1   Composer Ernst Toch, 76, dies in Los Angeles. One of his early string quartets was premiered by the Rose Quartet in Vienna when he was 17 years old. He then studied at the University of Vienna and the Frankfurt Conservatory. He won the Mendelssohn Prize and the Austrian State Prize (four times in succession) and began teaching. He emerged as an important contemporary composer, along with Ernst Krenek and Paul Hindemith, in the early 1920s. After the Nazis came to power, he went to Paris and London before settling in America. He then lived in Hollywood and began composing film music. Toch's music was influenced by the German romantics of the 19th century. His attraction to new techniques of composition is evidenced by his trying though not necessarily adopting, serial techniques. He was extremely prolific and composed works for virtually every combination of instruments and voices. His life was consistently punctuated by honors and awards, including a Pulitzer Prize for music. His pupils include Andre Previn.

tional Broadcasting Company and wrote for the New York *Post* and the New York *World.*

June 9   Russian-American composer Louis Gruenberg, 79, dies in Los Angeles. A pupil of Ferruccio Busoni, he performed with the Berlin Philharmonic as a pianist. He was a contributing force to the League of Composers in America. His music is composed in an accessible style; he was one of the first American composers to include jazz rhythms in his symphonic pieces. His output includes four volumes of Negro spirituals, five symphonies and his opera *The Emperor Jones,* which receives much attention.

July 1   French conductor Pierre Monteux, 89, dies in Hancock, Maine. After starting as a viola player, he was engaged in 1911 to conduct for Serge Diaghilev's Ballets Russes. While at this post, he conducted the premieres of *Petrouchka, Le Sacre du printemps, Le Rossignol, Jeux* and *Daphnis et Chloe.* In 1919 he became conductor of the Boston Sym-

Oct. 4   Swedish tenor Set Svanholm, 50, dies in Saltsjoe-Duvnaes. After beginning his musical career as a church organist, he studied voice and debuted in 1930 as a baritone. By 1936 he was singing tenor roles and had begun an international career. Although he sang roles in the Italian repertoire, he was primarily known for his singing of Wagnerian roles.

Nov. 27   Soviet mezzo-soprano Irina Arkhipova makes her New York debut, performing music of Tchaikovsky, Rachmaninoff, Prokofiev, Mussorgsky, Verdi and Rimsky-Korsakov. Harold C. Schonberg of the New York *Times* describes her as ". . . a musician with brains and temperament. . . ." Louis Biancolli of the *World Telegram* (New York) says, "I didn't find it a voice of great sensuous appeal." Arkhipova made her debut as Carmen at the Bolshoi Theater in 1956.

1964   Related Events

The Harkness Ballet is established this year by the wealthy Rebekah Harkness. Its first director is George Ski-

bine. The company is dedicated to showcasing young American talent. It debuts in Cannes next year. Harkness has studied musical composition with Nadia Boulanger in France and dance with Michel Fokine.

April 19   The Pennsylvania Ballet gives its inaugural concert at the University of Pennsylvania.

April 24   The New York State Theater, the second unit in the Lincoln Center complex, opens in New York, as the New York City Ballet performs George Balanchine's *A Midsummer Night's Dream*. Designed by architect Philip Johnson, the theater will house the New York City Ballet and the New York City Opera. The building cost $19,300,000.

May 12   Dmitri Shostakovich's Symphony No. 3 is revived and performed in Leningrad after 34 years of being ignored for ideological reasons.

May 27   Prague hosts the first International Seminar of Marxist Musicology, the purpose of which is to see musical phenomena in Marxist terms. Delegates arrive from the Soviet Union, East Germany, Hungary, Yugoslavia, Rumania and Bulgaria.

July 23   The first concert of the Meadow Brook Music Festival (at Oakland University in Rochester, Michigan) takes place, as Sixten Ehrling conducts the Detroit Symphony Orchestra in a program of music by Richard Wagner, Johannes Brahms and Jean Sibelius. The concert is at the Baldwin Pavillion, and this festival subsequently becomes internationally known, attracting many famous artists.

Sep. 5   The opera company of La Scala in Milan performs Giacomo Puccini's *Turandot* at the Bolshoi Theater in Moscow. This event marks the first Russian visit by a leading European opera company.

Oct.   The American Dance Theater is organized as a repertory for modern dance. Jose Limon is artistic director.

Oct. 14   The first Festival of American and Spanish Music begins in Madrid and includes performances of music by Ernesto, Rodolfo and Cristobal Halffter; Heitor Villa-Lobos; Aaron Copland; Quincy Porter; Mario Davidosvky; Gerald Strang; Jose Soler; Camargo Guarnieri; Joaquin Turina; Roberto Gerhard; Carlos Chavez; Manual de Falla; Joaquin Rodrigo; and Alberto Ginastera.

Oct. 27   The Bolshoi Opera performs for the first time outside the Soviet Union, presenting Modest Mussorgsky's *Boris Godunov* at La Scala in Milan. This is part of a program of 23 performances of five operas with a company of about 350.

Nov. 6   Carnegie Hall in New York City is designated a National Historic Landmark by the United States Department of the Interior. This action secures the future of the concert hall by protecting it from demolition.

Dec. 6   The Dorothy Chandler Pavilion of the Music Center of Los Angeles County is dedicated today. This concert hall has six levels (seating is on four levels), seats 3,197 people and can accommodate opera as well as symphony concerts. The inner dimensions of the hall, shaped as an almost perfect square, allow 90 percent of the audience to sit within 105 feet of the stage. This building is the new home of the Los Angeles Philharmonic Orchestra.

THE BALDWIN PAVILION OF THE MEADOW BROOK MUSIC FESTIVAL

1965 Opera

Feb. 24   Richard Rodney Bennett's *The Mines of Sulphur* premieres in London. The opera is about gypsies who murder an elderly man. Bennett, whose teachers have included Lennox Berkeley and Pierre Boulez, has taught at the Royal Academy of Music in London. As a composer, he is best known for stage works and film scores.

March 1   *Clitennestra* by Ildebrando Pizzetti, premieres at La Scala in Milan. The opera is based on the Greek tragedy of Clytemnestra.

March 25   Jack Beeson's *Lizzie Borden* receives its initial performance by the New York City Opera. Based on the legend about the young woman who killed her parents, it contains atonal passages and hymnlike melodies. This is Beeson's most successful opera.

April 2   Healey Willan's opera *Deirdre* premieres in a revised version in Toronto. It is based on an Irish legend. An earlier version premiered in 1946.

April 7   Hans Werner Henze's *Der junge Lord* receives its world premiere in Berlin. The two-act opera buffa is about a man who pursues a young woman who turns out to be an ape.

April 11   David Amram's opera *The Final Ingredient* premieres over ABC radio, the composer conducting. This work portrays a Passover celebration in a Nazi concentration camp.

May 22   Australian composer Malcolm Williamson's children's opera *The Happy Prince* premieres in England at the Farnham Festival. The opera is based on a story by Oscar Wilde. It is scored for eight soloists, chorus, semichorus, piano duet and percussion. Williamson had studied with Eugene Goossens and Elisabeth Lutyens.

June 16   Guillaume Landre's opera *Jean Levecq* and Ton de Leeuw's opera *De droom* are premiered at the Holland Festival in Amsterdam. Landre is concerned with reviving the polyphony of the Renaissance Flemish masters. Leeuw explores musical cultures of other countries (particularly Iran and India) and is devoted to ethnomusicology as well as composing. Both are Dutch composers.

Sep. 2   *Herr von Hancken*, by Karl-Birger Blomdahl, premieres in Stockholm. The three-act opera is about a man pursued by God. He flees to a European spa, where he meets the Devil and avoids punishment for his bad deeds.

Sep. 5   Sylvano Bussotti's *La passion selon Sade* receives its first performance in Palermo, Sicily. The theatrical work is for mixed media and combines atonality, polytonality and dodecaphony. It depicts the thoughts of the Marquis de Sade. Bussotti allows the performers to fragment the text and writes in his score, "only when memory is completely extinct can the performance come to a FINE."

Sep. 25   Korean composer Isang Yun's four-part opera *Der Traum des Liu-Tung* premieres in West Berlin. The work is about a philosophical young man who falls asleep and wakes up 16 years later. It is scored for large orchestra and many oriental instruments. This composer, who studied Western music in Korea, settled in Berlin in 1956.

Nov. 4   Ned Rorem's *Miss Julie* premieres in New York City. The opera is based on the Strindberg play.

Dec. 24   The Chinese opera *Ayikuli* receives its world premiere in Peking. This work had been collectively composed by many Communist musicians. Its story relates the life of a slave who becomes a revolutionary.

SCENE FROM *MISS JULIE*

1965 Dance

Jan. 22   The Stuttgart Ballet performs a version of Stravinsky's *Jeu de cartes* choreographed by John Cranko. The designs are by Dorothee Zippel.

Feb. 4   The New York City Ballet performs George Balanchine's *Harlequinade* for the first time in New York. The music is by Riccardo Drigo, with decor, costumes and lighting by Rouben Ter-Arutunian. The principal dancers are Patricia McBride and Edward Villella. This work celebrates commedia dell'arte and is based on an old Marius Petipa ballet called *Les millions d'Arlequin.*

Feb. 9   The Royal Ballet premieres Kenneth MacMillan's version of *Romeo and Juliet*, using the Sergei Prokofiev score. This version, presented at Covent Garden in London, focuses on the two lovers rather than on the society of the period as does the Soviet version. Although originally choreographed for Lynn Seymour and Christopher Gable, the ballet is danced on its opening night by Margot Fonteyn and Rudolf Nureyev, David Blair, Desmond Doyle and Anthony Dowell also star. The work becomes a vehicle for Fonteyn and Nureyev.

Feb. 19   Brian Macdonald's *Time Out of Mind* — to music by Paul Creston, with costumes by Rouben Ter-Arutunian — is premiered by the Harkness Ballet in Cannes, France. The work stars Margaret Mercier and Lawrence Rhodes, dancing emotions of energetic youth. This ballet company, established last year, is now making its debut.

Feb. 21   Choreographer Stuart Hodes' *Abyss* — to music by Marga Richter, with a libretto based on Leonid Andreyev, and costumes and sets by Andre Delfau — is premiered by the Harkness Ballet in Cannes, France. Featured dancers are Erik Bruhn and Lone Isaken.

March 17   Agnes De Mille's *The Wind in the Mountains* — to music by Laurence Rosenthal, with costumes by Stanley Simmons — is performed for the first time by the American Ballet Theater in New York City. Lighting and decor are by Jean Rosenthal. William Glassman is the lead dancer.

March 23   Agnes De Mille's *The Four Marys* — to music by Trude Rittmann, with costumes by Stanley Simmons — is premiered by the American Ballet Theater in New York City. This ballet deals with racism in the South.

March 30   The American Ballet Theater premieres Jerome Robbins' version of Igor Stravinsky's *Les noces.* Leonard Bernstein conducts the choir and orchestra. Erin Martin and William Glassman dance the Bride and Bridegroom.

April 13   John Cranko's *Eugene Onegin* receives its world premiere by the Stuttgart Ballet. Choreographed to music by Tchaikovsky, with costumes and scenery by Jurgen Rose, the work is based on the tale by Alexander Pushkin and the Tchaikovsky opera.

May 28   George Balanchine premieres his evening-length *Don Quixote*, with music by Nicolas Nabokov. It is the first evening-length American work to a commissioned score. The ballet is based on a number of episodes from the Cervantes novel. Richard Rapp, Suzanne Farrell and Deni Lamont star. At a gala preview last night, Balanchine danced the role of Don Quixote.

June 19   Choreographer Rudi van Dantzig's *Monument for a Dead Boy* — to music by Jan Boerman, with costumes and decor by Toer Van Schayk — is premiered by Het Nationale Ballet in Amsterdam. The work is about the childhood and adolescence of a homosexual boy, showing his agony and death.

July 23   Merce Cunningham premieres his new modern dance work *Variations V*, to music by John Cage, in New York City. Video accompaniment is by Stan Vanderbeek.

Oct. 26   Agnes De Mille's *The Rehearsal*, to music by Morton Gould, is premiered at Hunter College in New York City by the Royal Winnipeg Ballet. De Mille, the narrator, speaks her famous line: "Contrary to rumor, choreography is the oldest profession."

Nov. 7   The Stuttgart Ballet performs John Cranko's *Song of the Earth*, set to Gustav Mahler's music of the same name. The semiabstract work in six movements reflects the score. Egon Madsen, Ray Barra, Marcia Haydee and Ana Cardus star. Also premiered today is Cranko's *Opus I*, to music by Anton Webern. Created for Richard Cragun, the work depicts man's vain attempt to reach the state of idealism.

Nov. 24   Merce Cunningham premieres his new modern dance work *How to Pass, Kick, Fall and Run* at the Harper Theater in Chicago. Music is by John Cage, and the work includes readings from Cage's book *Silence, a Year from Monday.*

Dec. 3   *Cede Blue Lake* and *Tank Drive* — two new modern dance works by Twyla Tharp — are performed for the first time in New York City. Tharp, who studied with Martha Graham, Alwin Nikolais and Merce Cunningham, among others, was a member of Paul Taylor's dance company.

1965 Instrumental and Vocal Music

Jan. 20   Paul Dessau's *Requiem for Lumumba* premieres in East Berlin. The 28-movement work is scored for two speakers, speaking chorus, wordless soprano and African percussion instruments. The music is dodecaphonic but ends on a major chord. It glorifies the life of Patrice Lumumba.

Jan. 30   Alan Hovhaness' orchestral ballad *Ukiyo* receives its initial performance in Salt Lake City, Utah. The music was inspired by Buddhist concepts of fate.

Feb. 8   Gunther Schuller's Symphony No. 1 premieres in Dallas. This is one of Schuller's first works in which he attempts to bridge serious concert music and jazz to create a new style known as "third stream." He describes this style as "civilized jazz."

March 4   Gyorgy Ligeti's *Poeme symphonique* for 100 metronomes receives its first American performance in Buffalo, New York. The players are required to wind the metronomes, which are all set at different tempi. Ligeti tells Nicolas Slonimsky in a personal letter that the original premiere in 1963 offended the burgomaster of Hilversum, Holland, and that its scheduled television performance was canceled because the senate of the City of Hilversum saw no point in sharing such music with the public.

March 4   American composer William Flanagan's *Narrative for Orchestra* is premiered by the Detroit Symphony Orchestra.

March 5   Walter Piston's Symphony No. 8 is premiered by Charles Munch and the Boston Symphony Orchestra. The two-movement work is the first in which Piston systematically explores 12-tone procedures.

March 7   Easley Blackwood's Symphony No. 3 premieres in Chicago.

March 9   Gunther Schuller's *American Triptych: Three Studies in Texture* receives its initial performance by the New Orleans Philharmonic Symphony Orchestra with the composer conducting. The 14-minute piece is similar to his earlier work *Seven Studies on Themes of Paul Klee*, in that it attempts to represent visual aspects of paintings (in this case, paintings by Alexander Calder, Jackson Pollock and Stuart Davis) in music. The new work also mixes serialistic writing with jazz elements — Schuller's "third stream" innovation.

March 26   *Eclat*, by Pierre Boulez, receives its world premiere in Los Angeles with the composer conducting. The work, scored for chamber orchestra, is an elaboration of his earlier piece entitled "Don" (a movement from *Pli selon Pli*). Boulez composed up to the moment of performance and adds to the piece after today's premiere. Igor Stravinsky attends and later (unlike his reaction to *Pli selon Pli*) comments in his *Themes and Episodes* that the music is "a

small masterpiece" and that probably no one could conduct the work as well as Boulez.

March 28   Randall Thompson's oratorio *The Passion According to Saint Luke* premieres in Boston.

April 8   Earle Brown's *Calder Piece* receives its initial performance and showing in Paris. This work features four percussion instruments playing music while a mobile by Alexander Calder hangs and moves above them.

April 14   Roy Harris' Symphony No. 10 (*Abraham Lincoln Symphony*) premieres in Long Beach, California. The work is scored for women's chorus, men's chorus, mixed chorus, brass choir, two amplified pianos and percussion. Its five movements commemorate the centennial of Lincoln's assassination.

April 17   Igor Stravinsky's *Variations: Aldous Huxley In Memoriam* and his *Introitus: T.S. Eliot In Memoriam* are premiered by the composer in Chicago. The latter piece is scored for male chorus, solo viola, harp, piano, double bass timpani and tam-tams.

April 25   Roberto Gerhard's Concerto for Orchestra is premiered by the BBC Symphony Orchestra in Boston (this orchestra is now touring America).

April 26   Charles Ives' Symphony No. 4 receives its world premiere by Leopold Stokowski and the American Symphony Orchestra in New York City (the first movement was performed separately on January 29, 1927). The piece is scored for exceptionally large orchestra as well as chorus, large percussion, two pianos and organ. It is Ives' last symphony. It also requires three conductors (besides Stokowski, the other two at today's performance are David Katz and Jose Serebrier). The rhythmic complications are such that an $8,000 Rockefeller Foundation grant was required to finance the rehearsals. The symphony includes quotations from famous tunes, including "The Sweet Bye and Bye," "Nearer My God to Thee," "Marching Through Georgia" and "Columbia, the Gem of the Ocean." Ives, who died almost 11 years ago, stated in his notes that he was concerned with the philosophical question of "What? and Why? which the spirit of man asks of life." The symphony was composed between 1910 and 1916. Critic Alfred J. Frankenstein says the finale "may well be the most original and important movement in any of the symphonies by America's greatest composer."

May 2   William Bolcom's *Oracles* is among the works premiered today by Milton Katims and the Seattle Symphony Orchestra at a festival of contemporary music. *Graffiti*, by Roger Reynolds, is also performed for the first time.

May 7   Olivier Messiaen's *Et exspecto resurrectionem mortuorum* is premiered at a private concert by Serge Baudo at the Saint-Chapelle in Paris. This work is scored for wood-winds, brass and metal percussion.

May 13 David Amram's cantata *A Year in Our Land* is premiered by Harold Aks and the Interracial Chorus and Orchestra at Town Hall in New York City.

June 5 A one-day festival of avant-garde music takes place in Wuppertal, West Germany, and features silent, imagined, verbal and improvisatory works by La Monte Young, Gyorgy Ligeti and others. The festival is called "24 Hours." One composer, Nam June Paik, offers his piece *Creep into the Vagina of a Living Whale*, which he describes as "free improvisation with any animate object."

June 20 Olivier Messiaen's *L'hymne aux morts* premieres at the Cathedral of Chartres. Charles de Gaulle attends the performance.

July 15 The New York Philharmonic premieres Leonard Bernstein's *Chichester Psalms*. Bernstein conducts. It is scored for mixed choir, boy soloist and orchestra and was commissioned by the The Very Reverend Walter Hussey, Dean of Chichester Cathedral. Critic Alfred Frankenstein writes in *High Fidelity* of the finale, "Its idiom recalls the most angelic passages in the Faure *Requiem* — but the wings of these angels are confected of whipped cream."

Aug. 10 William Schuman's *Philharmonic Fanfare* is premiered by William Steinberg and the New York Philharmonic. This event marks the inauguration of summer outdoor park concerts by this orchestra.

Oct. 18 Luigi Nono's oratorio *The Inquest* premieres in Berlin. The text is by Peter Weiss and is based on trials of Nazi criminals. The music includes electronic effects.

Oct. 18 Willis Page and the Nashville, Tennessee Symphony Orchestra premiere Henry Cowell's Symphony No. 19. The five-movement work includes a percussion part for porcelain bowls.

Oct. 24 Benjamin Britten's *Voices for Today* receives its initial performance at the United Nations in New York City. This event marks the United Nations' 20th anniversary. It is scored for two choirs, and its text expresses anti-war sentiments.

Oct. 28 Ned Rorem's symphonic poem *Lions* is premiered by Sixten Ehrling and the Detroit Symphony Orchestra at Carnegie Hall in New York City.

Dec. 2 A two-day program of avant-garde music is featured at the New Music Workshop at the University of California in Los Angeles. It includes performances of unusual works. La Monte Young's *Piano Piece No. 1*, for example, features the following instructions: "Push the piano up to a wall and put the flat side flush against it. Then continue pushing into the wall. If the piano goes through the wall, keep pushing in the same direction regardless of new obstacles." Korean avant-garde composer Nam June Paik presents his *Playable Music No. 4*. His instructions read as follows: "Cut your left arm very slowly with a razor (more than 10 centimeters)." A member of the audience shouts, "Encore! Use your throat!"

Dec. 13 Otto Luening's String Quartet No. 2 receives its initial performance by the Group for Contemporary Music at Columbia University in New York City.

1965 *Births, Deaths and Debuts*

Feb. 6 American soprano Martina Arroyo makes her Metropolitan Opera debut substituting for Birgit Nilsson as Aida.

May 2 Pierre Boulez makes his American debut as a conductor. He conducts the BBC Symphony Orchestra in a performance of his *Doubles* at Carnegie Hall in New York City.

June 8 Scottish composer Erik Chisholm, 61, dies in Rondebosch, South Africa. A pupil of Donald Tovey, he was also a conductor and founded the Singapore Symphony Orchestra. A book he wrote on the operas of Leos Janacek is subsequently published in 1971. His music is characterized by oriental scales and somewhat complicated rhythmic patterns.

Sep. 4 Albert Schweitzer, 90, dies in his hospital in the jungle of Lambarene, Gabon. While studying theology and philosophy in Strasbourg, he was the organist for the Bach Concerts in that city. In 1902 he began teaching at the University of Strasbourg while also taking a medical degree there. He subsequently became a medical missionary in Africa, making occasional concert tours in Europe as an organist to raise money for his cause. In 1952 he was given the Nobel Peace Prize. He published books on philosophy and theology and an important book on the interpretation of the music of Johann Sebastian Bach. He also helped edit the complete organ works of Bach.

Sep. 9 Mexican composer Julian Carrillo, 90, dies in Mexico City. His work involves extensive use of quarter tones, eighth tones and sixteenth tones. He built special instruments that could accommodate these intervals. He was also known as a violin virtuoso and conductor. He termed his fractional-tone theory "sonido 13"; between 1924 and 1925 he expounded his ideas in the magazine *El Sonido 13*, which he edited.

Oct. 1 Georgi Rimsky-Korsakov, 63, dies in Leningrad. Grandson of Nikolai Rimsky-Korsakov and nephew of

Andrei Rimsky-Korsakov, he specialized (both as a composer and as a theorist) in quarter-tone and electronic music. In 1930 he helped invent the emeriton — a musical instrument producing various tone colors and featuring a wide pitch range. He taught for 35 years at the Conservatory of Leningrad.

Oct. 25   German conductor Hans Knappertsbusch, 77, dies in Munich. Famous for his interpretations of Wagner and other German romantic composers, he was a frequent conductor at Bayreuth and in other cities in Germany and Austria. He was known for his dislike of rehearsing, a habit that led to orchestral confusion on several occasions.

Nov. 6   Edgard Varese, 81, dies in New York City. Born in Paris, he wrote an opera (*Martin Paz*) at age 12 and then studied composition with Vincent d'Indy and Albert Roussel, among others. After early encouragement from Claude Debussy, he composed a succession of unique works following his principle of "organized sound," in which musical movement through sonorities replaced thematic development. In 1915 he went to America, where he was active in organizing and promoting performances of new music. Leopold Stokowski was the only major symphonic conductor to program his works, much to the chagrin of Stokowski's audiences. In later life, he also wrote some electronic music. His works — many with mathematical or scientific names like *Hyperprism*, *Integrales* and *Ionisation* are often short, but orchestrally and rhythmically complex. Varese did live to receive recognition of his work late in his life. His influence on young composers was extremely strong. One such composer is Iannis Xenakis, who writes upon Varese's death, "Away with the scale, away

with themes, away with melody, to the devil with so-called 'musical' music!"

Nov. 25   English pianist Dame Myra Hess, 75, dies in London. After studies at the Royal Academy of Music, she made her debut at age 17 in 1907. An international career ensued. She was made a Dame of the British Empire in 1941.

Dec. 10   Henry Dixon Cowell, 68, dies in Shady, New York. The California-born composer studied composition and piano in Germany and spent some time touring as a pianist. He invented the tone cluster — producing a group of tones with the fist or forearm — and was one of the first to produce tones on the piano by plucking the strings directly or striking them with various objects. With Leon Theremin he invented the rhythmicon, which could reproduce various rhythmic patterns. He was on the staff of a number of American universities and conservatories and in 1927 founded the *New Music Quarterly*, which published contemporary scores. His extremely large musical output includes operatic, symphonic, chamber and choral works. His wife, Sidney, is an ethnomusicologist.

Dec. 29   Japanese composer Koscak Yamada, 79, dies in Tokyo. A pupil of Max Bruch, he founded the Tokyo Philharmonic Orchestra and brought Japanese music to New York City in 1918. Much of his music was destroyed during the Second World War, but some has been reconstructed from orchestral parts. In addition to 6 operas and a number of orchestral works, he wrote approximately 1,000 choral works and songs.

1965   Related Events

The Dance Center opens in London this year. It is a complex of dance studios on Floral Street in Covent Garden and was conceived as a London counterpart to the Studio Wacker in Paris, which is now in its final decade of existence.

Dance Horizons begins publication this year. This New York-based publication exists to issue reprints, in paperback, of famous books by people in dance, including Rudolf von Laban, Ted Shawn and Ruth Saint Denis.

Ballett 1965 is published this year. This German ballet annual — subsequently published with the year of its publication as part of its name — focuses on German and international developments in ballet. The publisher is Friedrich Verlag, Velbert-Hannover.

April 18   Contralto Marian Anderson, 63, gives her farewell recital at Carnegie Hall in New York to a standing ovation.

May 7   Washington D.C. hosts the Third Inter-American Festival, beginning today and spanning five days. New works by Alberto Ginastera, Carlos Chavez and Pozzi Escot are among those performed.

May 9   After an absence of 12 years, pianist Vladimir Horowitz gives a recital at Carnegie Hall in New York. The queue for tickets for this concert forms several days in advance. His program includes works by Robert Schumann, Alexander Scriabin, Frederick Chopin and Bach-Busoni. The New York *Times* reports it is "one of the most dramatic events of recent musical history."

Aug. 10   The New York Philharmonic gives its first concert in Central Park, as the inaugural concert of a new annual music festival. Free to the public, the concerts are performed throughout the five boroughs that comprise the greater New York metropolitan area. William Steinberg conducts for an audience of 70,000. The program consists of music by William Schuman (*Philharmonic Fanfare*), Wagner and Beethoven.

Aug. 25   New York City hosts the third annual Avant-Garde Festival, featuring — among other things — cellist Charlotte Moorman. Ms. Moorman is fond of playing topless.

Sep. 29   President Lyndon B. Johnson signs a law creating the National Foundation of the Arts and Humanities to promote a national arts policy for the United States.

Oct. 8   The Musikselskabet Harmonien celebrates its bicentennial. Founded in Bergen, Norway on this date in 1765, this music society gives performances, collects music manuscripts and promotes music in Bergen. It also has its own orchestra and is the oldest music society in existence in the world.

Oct. 11   In Eindhoven, Holland this month Philips announces its new prerecorded tape cassettes. In another recording industry development this year, endless-loop cartridges are marketed for entertainment while driving in automobiles.

Nov. 19   The new National Polish Opera House reopens in Warsaw, after having been destroyed during World War II.

1966 Opera

Jan. 4   Malcolm Williamson's two-act opera *Julius Caesar Jones* premieres in London.

March 21   American composer Peter Westergaard's *Mr. and Mrs. Discobbolos*, based on texts by Edward Lear, is premiered by the Group for Contemporary Music at Columbia University in New York City. The brief opera is scored for two singers and six instrumentalists. Westergaard's teachers have included Walter Piston and Roger Sessions. His music explores aspects of tonal serialization.

March 31   Carlisle Floyd's *Markheim* is performed for the first time in New Orleans. The three-act opera is about a pawnbroker who receives fantastic promises from a stranger. It is based on a tale by Robert Louis Stevenson.

LEONTYNE PRICE IN A SCENE FROM *ANTONY AND CLEOPATRA*

April 28   Douglas Moore's two-act opera *Carrie Nation* premieres at the University of Kansas in Lawrence, Kansas. It is about the famous American woman of the same name who had an aversion to alcoholic beverages.

May 23   Josef Matthias Hauer's *Die schwarze Spinne* premieres posthumously in Vienna. This three-act singspiel was composed in 1935.

June 2   The burlesque opera *17 Tage und 4 Minuten*, by Werner Egk, premieres in Stuttgart. Cast in a style evoking realism, surrealism and mythology, it is about Circe and Ulysses making love.

June 9   Benjamin Britten's church parable *The Burning Fiery Furnace* is premiered by the English Opera Group as part of the Aldeburgh Festival. The text, by William Plomer, is based on the Book of Daniel. London tabloids give the work good reviews.

Aug. 6   Hans Werner Henze's *Die Bassariden* is performed for the first time at the Salzburg Festival. The libretto, by W.H. Auden and Chester Kallman, is based on *The Bacchae*, by Euripides. The one-act opera seria takes 2 1/2 hours to perform. It also contains four orchestral movements. Critic Peter Heyworth writes in the New York *Times*, "Henze has finally made his peace with the whole tradition of German music drama."

Sep. 16   *Antony and Cleopatra* receives its world premiere at the Metropolitan Opera in New York City, performed as the celebration event of the opening of the new Metropolitan Opera House at Lincoln Center. The libretto is by Franco Zeffirelli, based on the play by Shakespeare; Samuel Barber composes the music. The work is a big failure, due, in part, to the failure of stage equipment to move and rotate. Thomas Schippers conducts a cast featuring Leontyne Price (the first black vocalist to play Cleopatra in any opera), Justino Diaz and Jess Thomas. The opera is in 3 acts and 16 scenes. Ticket prices are as high as $250. Barber's music is overshadowed by Zeffirelli's staging. Of that staging, Harold C. Schonberg writes in the New York *Times*, it is "artifice masquerading with a great flourish as art." Of the entire production, Schonberg says, "Almost everything about the evening, artistically speaking, failed in total impact."

Oct. 12   Gunther Schuller's *The Visitation* receives its initial performance by the Hamburg State Opera with the composer conducting. The three-act opera was inspired by Franz Kafka's novel *Der Prozess* and is about a young black male charged with pursuing a young white female.

Nov. 29   Malcolm Williamson's opera *The Violins of Saint Jacques* is premiered by the Sadlers Wells Opera Company in London. The three-act work is his fifth opera. It is about the eruption of Mount Pelee and the stress it puts on the island's inhabitants, which include a lesbian, a homosexual and assorted heterosexual zombies.

Dec. 11   *The Sugar Reapers*, by Alan Bush, receives its initial performance in Leipzig. The two-act opera is about workers on a sugar plantation in British Guyana who oppose British colonial control.

1966 *Dance*

Jan. 25   Choreographer Glen Tetley's *Ricercare* — to music by Mordecai Seter, with decor by Rouben Ter-Arutunian — is performed for the first time by the American Ballet Theater in New York City. The ballet, danced by Mary Hinkson and Scott Douglas, is about a couple's emotional and sensual relationship.

Feb. 10   Choreographer John Cranko's *Brandenburg Nos. 2 and 4* is premiered by The Royal Ballet in London. Among the eight performers dancing to Bach's music are Anthony Dowell and Antoinette Sibley.

March 26   John Cranko's *Mozart Concerto* receives its initial performance by the Stuttgart Ballet in Stuttgart. It is a plotless work danced by 2 couples and 10 men. Ana Cardus and Richard Cragun star.

April 21   George Balanchine's *Brahms-Schoenberg Quartet* — to music by Johannes Brahms, orchestrated by Arnold Schoenberg — is premiered by the New York City Ballet in New York. The lead dancers include Melissa Hayden, Patricia McBride, Edward Villella, Suzanne Farrell and Jacques d'Amboise.

April 25   *Monotones*, choreographed by Frederick Ashton, is performed for the first time by The Royal Ballet in London. The music is by Erik Satie, orchestrated by John Lanchberry. Previously prepared for a one-time gala performance, the ballet proved popular and was expanded for the repertory. The dancers include Antoinette Sibley, Georgina Parkinson, Anthony Dowell, Vyvyan Lorrayne and Robert Mead.

April 28   John Taras' version of *Jeux* receives its first performance by the New York City Ballet in New York. Costumes and decor are by Raoul Pene du Bois. Lead dancers include Edward Villella, Allegra Kent and Melissa Hayden. The ballet uses the libretto by Vaslav Nijinsky.

May 11   Flemming Flindt's *The Three Musketeers* — to music by Georges Delarue, with decor by Bernard Dayde — is premiered by the Royal Danish Ballet in Copenhagen. The ballet retells the famous story by Dumas.

Sep. 13   Choreographer Eugene Loring's *These Three* — to music by David Ward-Steinman, with decor by William Pitkin — is premiered by the City Center Joffrey Ballet in New York City. This work is based on a civil rights conflict in the South during the 1960s.

Nov. 17   Maurice Bejart's *Romeo and Juliet*, to music by Hector Berlioz, is premiered by the Ballet of the 20th Century in Brussels. The decor is by Germinal Casado.

Nov. 23   Choreographer John Butler's *Villon*, to music by Robert Starer, is performed for the first time by the Pennsylvania Ballet in Philadelphia. Ross Parkes dances the lead role in this ballet about the riotous life of the French poet.

Nov. 30   Choreographer Kenneth MacMillan's *Concerto* — to music by Dmitri Shostakovich, with decor by Jurgen Rose — is premiered by the German Opera Ballet in Berlin. The plotless ballet is MacMillan's first new work as ballet director of this company. Didi Carli, Falco Kapuste, Lynn Seymour and Sylvia Kesselheim star.

1966 Instrumental and Vocal Music

Jan. 19   Michael Tippett's cantata *The Vision of Saint Augustine* premieres in London with the composer conducting. The work, set to a Latin text, is scored for baritone, chorus and orchestra. It is considered Tippett's best work for chorus.

Jan. 24   Jean Martinon conducts the Chicago Symphony Orchestra in the American premiere of *Sun-Treader*, by Carl Ruggles. The world premiere took place on January 24, 1926; this performance celebrates the composer's 90th birthday.

Jan. 26   Dominick Argento's *Variations for Orchestra (The Mask of Night)* receives its initial performance by the Minneapolis Civic Orchestra in Minneapolis, Minnesota.

Feb. 8   Symphony on G, by Lou Harrison, receives its first performance in Oakland, California. Gerhard Samuel conducts. This serial work is tonally centered on the pitch class *g*. It has four movements. Harrison composed the work between 1948-54. An earlier version of the piece was performed at the Cabrillo Festival two years ago. He decided to revise the finale for today's performance. The symphony becomes known as one of Harrison's best compositions.

Feb. 10   Richard Rodney Bennett's Symphony No. 1 premieres in London. The three-movement symphony is scored for large orchestra.

March 3   Milton Babbitt's symphonic piece *Relata I* premieres in Cleveland. Last year, Babbitt was elected a member of the National Institute of Arts and Letters.

March 29   Concerto for Orchestra, by William Mathias, receives its first performance in Liverpool.

March 30   Krzysztof Penderecki's oratorio *Saint Luke's Passion* receives its world premiere in Germany at the Cathedral of Munster. The Latin text is set to music combining Gregorian chant and serial techniques.

April 3   *Terretekorth*, by Iannis Xenakis, is premiered by Hermann Scherchen at a contemporary music festival in Royan, France. The orchestral piece has players sitting in and among the audience; they are given little drums and policemen's whistles to produce "sounds similar to flames."

April 5   Sergei Prokofiev's *Cantata* is premiered in Moscow. This event marks the first performance of a 1937 work that had been considered weak by Soviet aestheticians. A section featuring texts by Joseph Stalin is deleted, because that leader's importance is now being downplayed. Prokofiev's work is scored for two choruses, military band, accordions and percussion.

April 28   David Diamond's Symphony No. 5 and Concerto for Piano and Orchestra are premiered by Leonard Bernstein and the New York Philharmonic. The symphony was composed between 1947 and 1964; the concerto, between 1949 and 1950. Diamond conducts the concerto.

May 1   *Sinfonia*, by Nicholas Maw, receives its first performance at Rutherford College of Technology in Newcastle-upon-Tyne, England. The three-movement work is atonal.

May 8   *And on the Seventh Day the Petals Fell in Petaluma*, by Harry Partch, receives its initial performance at the University of California in Los Angeles. This instrumental piece, scored for an assortment of Partch's unusual instruments, is a preparatory work for his *Delusion of the Fury*. It contains 23 one-minute instrumental verses and 11 other instrumental verses that are duets and trios comprising quartets and quintets. It explores more complicated rhythms and polyrhythms than are found in the composer's earlier pieces and also includes, in the latter verses, electronic synthesis of pairs of verses. Partch began the piece in 1963.

May 16   Dominick Argento's *The Revelation of Saint John the Divine* premieres in Minneapolis, Minnesota. This work is a rhapsody for tenor, male chorus, brass ensemble and percussion.

May 16   Heitor Villa-Lobos' Symphony No. 9 and Panamanian composer Roque Cordero's *Sinfonia* are premiered by Eugene Ormandy and the Philadelphia Orchestra as part of the Third Festival of Music in Caracas.

June 1   *Elegy for Orchestra* by John Corigliano Jr., premieres in San Francisco.

June 4   Henri Sauguet's *Symphonie de marches* receives its initial performance in Paris at the International Congress of Railroads. This work was commissioned to publicize train travel.

June 20 Morton Feldman's *The Possibility of a New Work for Electric Guitar* premieres at the Library and Museum of the Performing Arts in New York City.

June 23 French composer Jean Barraque's *Chant apres chant* premieres as part of the 18th International Music Festival in Strasbourg. The piece is scored for six groups of percussion, piano and soprano and reflects the composer's attraction to the permutation of rhythmic cells. Barraque studied with Jean Langlais and Olivier Messiaen. French critic Andre Hodeir states in his book *Music Since Debussy* (1961) that Barraque is the most important composer since Claude Debussy.

June 23 Symphony No. 1, by William Mathias, premieres in Birmingham, England.

June 28 *Akrata*, by Iannis Xenakis, premieres in Oxford. This work is scored for 15 wind instruments and vibraphone and was composed according to the Xenakis theory of "stochastic composition" — music of strict organization based on the occurrence of probable events of pitch, rhythm, melody, dynamics and timbre.

July 22 Anton Webern's *Kinderstuck* for piano (composed in 1924) is premiered posthumously by Caren Glasser in New York City.

Aug. 16 Carlos Surinach's *Melorhythmic Dances* premieres at Oakland University in Rochester, Michigan. The seven-movement work is an orchestral suite.

Aug. 18 *Markings* premieres at Oakland University in Rochester, Michigan. The symphonic essay, by Ulysses Kay, is dedicated to the memory of Dag Hammarskjold, the secretary general of the United Nations who perished in a plane crash five years ago.

Sep. 20 Hans Werner Henze's cantata *Muses of Sicily* receives its first performance in Berlin. It celebrates the 175th anniversary of the Berlin Singakademie.

Sep. 21 Gian Francesco Malipiero's Symphony No. 9, in three movements, premieres in Warsaw.

Sep. 21 Havergal Brian's Symphony No. 6 (*Sinfonia tragica*) premieres in London. The symphony, in three movements, was composed in 1948.

Sep. 25 Dmitri Shostakovich's Violoncello Concerto No. 2 premieres at the Moscow Conservatory, with Mstislav Rostropovich as soloist and Maxim Shostakovich — the composer's son — conducting.

Oct. 8 Igor Stravinsky's *Requiem Canticles* receives its world premiere at Princeton University. Scored for vocal quartet, chorus and orchestra, the piece is conducted by Robert Craft. It contains three instrumental sections and other sections that use the text of the Latin requiem. Critic Bernard Jacobson writes in *High Fidelity*, "The delicacy of Stravinsky's ear and the fertility of his imagination have worked their customary wonders."

Oct. 27 *Janissary Music*, by Charles Wuorinen, receives its initial performance at Swarthmore College (Part 1 only is premiered today; part II is premiered on March 12, 1967). This piece is scored for one percussion player who performs on a variety of percussion instruments.

Oct. 29 Anton Webern's *Four Stefan George Songs* for voice and piano, *Vorfruhling II* for voice and piano, *Wehmut* for voice and piano, and *Hochsommernacht* for soprano, tenor and piano are premiered posthumously at the Third International Webern Festival in Buffalo, New York.

Oct. 30 Anton Webern's *Three Orchestral Songs* (composed in 1913 and 1914) is premiered posthumously by Lukas Foss and the Buffalo Philharmonic Orchestra at the Third International Webern Festival, with Marni Nixon as vocal soloist.

Nov. 19 Roger Sessions' Symphony No. 6 is performed in its complete version in Newark, New Jersey. The three-movement symphony had a partial performance last January.

Dec. 2 *Echoes of Autumn*, by George Crumb, receives its world premiere by the Aeolian Chamber Players at Carnegie Hall in New York City. The piece is scored for violin, alto flute, clarinet and piano. Crumb has studied with Ross Lee Finney and Boris Blacher. Last year, he received a Rockefeller Foundation grant.

1966   Births, Deaths and Debuts

Jan. 9 Noah Greenberg, 46, dies in New York City. He founded the New York Pro Musica Antiqua, which revived liturgical dramas of the medieval period, bringing this rarely performed music before the public. These works included *The Play of Daniel* (1958) and *The Play of Herod* (1963).

Feb. 13 French pianist and teacher Marguerite Long, 91, dies in Paris. Long studied at the Paris Conservatoire and

became a teacher there in 1906. In 1920 she started her own school. She gave many recitals with violinist Jaques Thibaud in the 1940s and founded the Long-Thibaud competitions.

March 30 Violinist Jelly d'Aranyi, 70, dies in Florence. This violinist devoted herself to the performance of modern music. She premiered Maurice Ravel's *Tzigane* and Ralph Vaughan Williams' Violin Concerto. She also claimed to have met Robert Schumann during a seance in which he gave her some secret concerning his unpublished Violin Concerto.

June 12   German conductor Hermann Scherchen, 75, dies in Florence, Italy. A largely self-taught musician, Scherchen was a champion of new music. He conducted many first performances of modern music at the Donaueschingen Festival in Frankfurt, the Collegium Musicum in Switzerland and in Barcelona. In 1918 he founded and directed the Musikgesellschaft in Berlin.

Scherchen was also interested in multitrack recording and engineering. In 1957 he established a laboratory known as *Hexenkuche* in Gravesano, Switzerland. It was created under the auspices of UNESCO and was designed for experimental research in electroacoustics. It issued the journal *Gravesaner Blatter* which featured articles on electroacoustics in relation to recording and broadcasting.

July 3   American composer and writer Deems Taylor, 80, dies in New York City. A noted music critic, he also served as president of ASCAP from 1942 to 1948. Two of his operas, *The King's Henchman* and *Peter Ibbetson*, were very successful in their day but have since vanished from the repertory.

Oct. 13   Composer Arthur Lourie, 74, dies in Princeton, New Jersey. He studied at the Saint Petersburg Conservatory and was influenced by the music of Alexander Scriabin. He remained in the Soviet Union until 1921, when he went to Paris. In 1941 he came to America. His music is derivative of old forms. Lourie composed cantatas, works for orchestra and piano, and one opera (*The Blackamoor of Peter the Great*). He was opposed to expressing nationalism in music.

Oct. 16   Wieland Wagner, 49, dies in Munich. The grandson of Richard Wagner, he came to prominence in 1951 when he took over the staging of Wagner operas at Bayreuth. Discarding the scenic trappings of the 19th century, he conceived productions that relied mainly on sophisticated lighting and simple symbolic scenery. His highly praised production of *Parsifal* in 1951, with its stark simplicity, heavily influenced opera production throughout the next decade.

Nov. 12   American composer Quincy Porter, 69, dies in Bethany, Connecticut. A pupil of Horatio Parker at Yale University and of Vincent d'Indy in Paris, he won many prizes and eventually wound up on the faculties of Vassar College, the New England Conservatory and Yale University. The bulk of his output is orchestral or chamber music. His music is largely polytonal and sometimes combines harmonic dissonance. The style of his work may be described as a blend of French impressionism and German expressionism.

Nov. 28   American composer Vittorio Giannini, 63, dies in New York City. He studied composition with Rubin Goldmark and won a Prix de Rome, after which he joined the faculty at the Juilliard School. He also taught at the Curtis Institute of Music and the Manhattan School of Music. His most famous opera is *The Taming of the Shrew*, which was televised in 1954. His music was tonal and marked by emotional force and bel canto vocal writing. He was appreciated by many opera singers.

1966 Related Events

The third issue of *Ballet Review* is published this year. This is the first issue of this periodical that has a date of publication. The journal, edited by Arlene Croce, has already established itself as an exceptionally brilliant contribution to dance literature. Its publication is later taken over by the Dance Research Foundation.

A major advancement in recording industry technology takes place this year as Dr. Ray Dolby, of Dolby Laboratories Inc. in London, introduces his noise reduction system. Two systems emerge: Dolby A (for professional tape mastering) and Dolby B (for tape recorders). His contribution is later added to film sound tracks as well as music recordings and captivates audiences by suppressing unwanted noise and enhancing crispness of desirable sonorities. Combined with visual special effects in film, his innovation subsequently becomes a tremendous attraction for young audiences. In 'another development, record sales this year (and through next year) reach an all-time high: $1 billion.

April 16   In the evening following the last scheduled performance of *La Boheme*, the old Metropolitan Opera House in New York, opened in 1883, closes with a gala performance featuring excerpts from 25 different operas. Many leading singers perform, and many former stars are on hand for the occasion.

May 2   Leslie Bassett is awarded the Pulitzer Prize for music for *Variations for Orchestra*. No prizes were awarded for 1964 and 1965.

June 26   Soviet tenor Vladimir Atlantov is awarded first prize in the Tchaikovsky International Music Contest in Moscow.

July 8   The inaugural concert of the Saratoga Performing Arts Center takes place in Saratoga, New York, with a performance of the ballet *A Midsummer Night's Dream* (to music by Felix Mendelssohn), danced by the New York City Ballet. The amphitheater, designed by Vollmer Associates of New York City, was begun in 1964 and cost $4 million; it seats 5,103 and features a stage designed specifically for

THE NEW METROPOLITAN OPERA HOUSE AT LINCOLN CENTER FOR THE PERFORMING ARTS

the New York City Ballet to the specifications of George Balanchine.

July 26 Leonard Bernstein conducts the opening concert of New York City's second annual New York Philharmonic concerts in the parks. Attendance is estimated at 75,000 — the largest to date for such an event.

Sep. 16 The new Metropolitan Opera House opens at Lincoln Center in New York with the world premiere of Samuel Barber's opera *Antony and Cleopatra*. The $45,700,000 building is the world's largest opera house, seating 3,788. The main stage is 103 feet wide and 81 feet deep; 7 elevators can vary the stage height and transport scenery to below-stage storage rooms. Decorations include two large murals by Marc Chagall and 32 crystal chandeliers donated by the Austrian government.

Sep. 25 The Soviet government nominates Dmitri Shostakovich as Hero of Socialist Labor. This event also marks the composer's 60th birthday.

Oct. 3 Alan Hovhaness' *Ode to the Temple of Sound* is performed by Sir John Barbirolli and the Houston Symphony Orchestra. This event marks the inauguration of Jesse H. Jones Hall for the Performing Arts in that city. This is also the premiere of the Hovhaness work.

Nov. 4 The Teatro Comunale, Florence's opera house, is damaged by heavy flooding as the Arno River's overflow reaches 15 feet. Many artworks are also damaged or destroyed, including music manuscripts of Alessandro Scarlatti.

Dec. The Ballet de Wallonie is established this month in Charleroi, Belgium. Hanna Vooss is artistic director, and the company incorporates her former Ballet du Hainut. The chief choreographer is Tony Hulbert. The company consists of approximately 50 dancers and focuses on classical dance.

1967 Opera

March 9 Vittorio Giannini's *The Servant of Two Masters*, based on a play by Carlo Goldoni, is premiered posthumously by the New York City Opera Company.

March 17 Marvin David Levy's *Mourning Becomes Electra*, is premiered in New York City by the Metropolitan Opera. The libretto of the three-act opera is based on the play by Eugene O'Neill, which, in turn, is based on the an-cient Greek tale involving Electra, Clytemnestra and Agamemnon but with the setting transferred to New England in 1865. Reviews are mixed, but the opera is performed several times during a few seasons.

April 29 *Geschaftsbericht*, by Paul Dessau, receives its initial performance in Leipzig. The opera's text is, according to the composer, a "business report" in which American soldiers who have died in Vietnam smear President Lyndon B. Johnson. It lasts 10 minutes.

May 19 *Bomarzo*, a two-act opera by Alberto Ginastera, receives its world premiere by the Opera Society of Washington, D.C. The lurid life of Bomarzo, a 16th-century duke, is depicted. Dodecaphony, electronic effects, aleatory and tone clusters are used to represent the duke's immersion in narcissism and lust. A chorus, in the orchestra pit, comments on the action almost in the style of ancient Greek commentary in plays. Unusual instruments, such as a mandolin and Japanese wood chimes, are added to the orchestra. Allen Hughes writes in the New York *Times* that the opera can be experienced "more as a skillful fabrication of effects and sensations than as a sinewy work of art of enduring value." Its Argentine premiere, scheduled for August, is canceled by the mayor and other authorities on the grounds that the piece contains too much sex and violence. *Bomarzo* is the second of three works comprising Ginastera's trilogy of operas based on historical characters. The other two are *Don Rodrigo* and *Beatrix Cenci*.

May 26 Heinrich Sutermeister's opera *Madame Bovary*, based on the novel by Gustave Flaubert, premieres in Zurich. It is in two acts.

June 1 Dominick Argento's ballad-opera *The Shoemaker's Holiday* — based on a play by Thomas Dekker, with additional lyrics by John Olon-Scrymgeour — is premiered by the Minnesota Theater Company at the Tyrone Guthrie Theater in Minneapolis, Minnesota.

June 3 Lennox Berkeley's *Castaway* and William Walton's *The Bear* are performed for the first time at this year's Aldeburgh Festival. The Walton work is based on a play by Anton Chekhov. Both are chamber operas.

Sep. 23 Harry Somers' *Louis Riel* premieres in Toronto. In three acts, the musical drama is about a French-Canadian who, in 1869, defended the rights of mestizos. The libretto is bilingual (English and French), and the music contains 12-tone, electronic and folk song elements.

Oct. 31 Richard Rodney Bennett's comic opera *A Penny for a Song* premieres in London. It is about a crazed Englishman who thinks he is Napoleon.

Nov. 3 *White Nights*, by Tikhon Khrennikov. receives its initial performance in Moscow. The "musical chronicle" satirizes the final years of Tsar Nicholas II and others, including Rasputin.

Nov. 30 Scottish composer Thea Musgrave's *The Decision* premieres in London. The opera is about a miner who is trapped for 23 days and the resultant improvement of conditions for such workers.

Dec. 9 Korean composer Isang Yun's *Die Witwe des Schmetterlings*, with a libretto in German, premieres in Bonn. The opera is about a Chinese man who fancies himself a butterfly. It is finished while the composer is in jail in South Korea on sedition charges and is performed in Germany in his absence.

1967 Dance

Jan. 25 The Royal Ballet presents Antony Tudor's *Shadowplay*, set to music by Charles Koechlin. The jungle is the setting for this allegory about a boy growing to maturity. Anthony Dowell, Derek Rencher and Merle Park star.

Feb. 21 Martha Graham's *Cortege of Eagles* and *Dancing Ground* premiere in New York.

Feb. 23 *Paradise Lost* receives its initial performance by The Royal Ballet in London. The choreography is by Roland Petit, music by Marius Constant and decor by Martial Raysse. Margot Fonteyn and Rudolf Nureyev dance this version of the story of Adam and Eve.

March 31 Eliot Feld's *Harbinger* receives its world premiere by the American Ballet Theater in Miami, Florida. Choreographed to music by Sergei Prokofiev, with costumes by Stanley Simmons, the work is the choreographer's first ballet and is non-narrative. It is subsequently proclaimed as an important work and substantially advances Feld's career. The dancers at today's performance include Cynthia Gregory, Christine Sarry and Feld.

April 3 Maurice Bejart's *Messe pour le temps present* is premiered by the Ballet of the 20th Century in Avignon, France. The music is by Pierre Henry.

April 6 George Balanchine's *Trois Valses Romantiques* — to music by Emmanuel Chabrier, with costumes by Karinska — is performed for the first time by the New York City Ballet in New York. Melissa Hayden and Arthur Mitchell lead the cast.

April 13 George Balanchine's *Jewels* receives its world premiere by the New York City Ballet in New York. The costumes are by Karinska, and the music is a sampler of works by Igor Stravinsky, Tchaikovsky and Gabriel Faure. The decor is by Peter Harvey. This work is the first three-act ballet that is a complete abstraction (sections are titled "Emeralds," "Rubies" and "Diamonds"). The lead dancers are Violette Verdy, Conrad Ludlow, Patricia McBride, Edward Villella, Suzanne Farrell and Jacques d'Amboise.

Sep. 10 Meredith Monk's modern dance piece *Overload* receives its first performance at Expo '67 in Montreal.

Sep. 19 Robert Joffrey's *Astarte* — to music by Crome Syrcus, with costumes by Hugh Sharer and decor by

RUDOLF NUREYEV AND MARGOT FONTEYN IN A SCENE FROM *PARADISE LOST*

Thomas Skelton — is premiered by the City Center Joffrey Ballet in New York City. The principal dancers are Maximilian Zomosa and Trinette Singleton. The mixed-media ballet features film sequences.

Nov. 1   *Night Song*, a ballet choreographed by Norman Walker to music by Alan Hovhaness, is premiered in New York City by the Harkness Ballet.

Nov. 9   Choreographer John Butler's *After Eden*, to music by Lee Hoiby, is premiered by the Harkness Ballet in New York City. The costumes are by Rouben Ter-Arutunian.

Nov. 23   George Balanchine's *Glinkiana* receives its initial performance by the New York City Ballet in New York. Choreographed to music by Mikhail Glinka, with costumes, decor and lighting by Esteban Frances, this work

has no story and is a setting of dances in various national styles. The solo dancers include Violette Verdy, Melissa Hayden, Patricia McBride and Edward Villella.

Dec. 1   Eliot Feld's *At Midnight* — to music by Gustav Mahler, with costumes by Stanley Simmons and decor by Leonard Baskin — is premiered by the American Ballet Theater in New York City. Principal dancers are Bruce Marks, Cynthia Gregory, Terry Orr, Christine Sarry and Feld.

Dec. 17   *Somniloquy*, by Alwin Nikolais, receives its initial performance at the Henry Street Playhouse in New York City. The "sound and vision" piece is about mankind being overwhelmed by the caverns, creatures and forces of life. Murray Louis, Phyllis Lambert, Caroline Carlson and Bill Frank star.

1967   Instrumental and Vocal Music

Jan. 6   Elliott Carter's Concerto for Piano and Orchestra is given its world premiere by Erich Leinsdorf and the Boston Symphony Orchestra, with Jacob Lateiner as soloist. The two-movement piece has themes serially organized in terms of its melodic, harmonic, rhythmic and metric elements.

Jan. 24   George Rochberg's *Music for the Magic Theater*, Mario Davidovsky's *Inflexions* and Easley Blackwood's *Un voyage a Cythere* are premiered at the University of Chicago.

These commissioned works celebrate the 75th anniversary of this university.

March 2   Walter Piston's *Variations for Cello and Orchestra* is given its first performance by Gennady Rozhdestvensky and the London Symphony Orchestra, with Mstislav Rostropovich as soloist. The performance takes place at Carnegie Hall in New York. The music, in one movement, is 12-tone.

March 5 Lukas Foss' Concerto for Violoncello and Orchestra premieres in New York City with the composer conducting. Mstislav Rostropovich is soloist.

March 12 *Janissary Music* (Part II), by Charles Wuorinen, receives its first performance at Carnegie Recital Hall in New York City. The first part was premiered on October 27 of last year. The percussion player Raymond DesRoches performs today.

April 6 Hans Werner Henze's symphonic fantasy *Los caprichos* premieres in Duisberg. This work was inspired by a Francisco de Goya etching depicting a witch on a broom.

April 6 Miklos Rozsa's Concerto for Piano and Orchestra is premiered by Zubin Mehta and the Los Angeles Philharmonic Orchestra, with Leonard Pennario as soloist.

April 6 Paul Creston's orchestral piece *Chthonic Ode* premieres in Detroit. The music is a tribute to the British sculptor Henry Moore.

April 14 Krzysztof Penderecki's *Dies Irae* — to texts by Paul Valery, Louis Aragon and from the Psalms — receives its initial performance in Cracow. The work commemorates the victims of Auschwitz. It is scored for solo voices, chorus and orchestra.

April 19 Gyorgy Ligeti's Cello Concerto premieres in Berlin.

April 27 Lukas Foss' *Phorion* is premiered by Leonard Bernstein and the New York Philharmonic. Scored for orchestra, electronic organ, harpsichord and guitar, the piece was inspired by what Foss said he heard in a dream: "torrents of Baroque 16th-notes washed ashore by ocean waves and sucked in again."

June 2 Alan Hovhaness' tone poem *To Vishnu* is premiered by the New York Philharmonic. The piece is scored for orchestra, with an emphasis on bells and trumpets.

June 18 Gustav Mahler's "Blumine" movement from his Symphony No. 1 is performed as Benjamin Britten conducts at the Aldeburgh Festival. This event marks the movement's first performance this century, although not in the context of a presentation of the full five-movement symphony.

June 28 Gunther Schuller's orchestral piece *Triplum* receives its initial performance in New York City. The concertinolike work has the brass, woodwinds and strings function as distinct, independent groups.

Aug. 10 R. Murray Schafer's *Gita* for chorus, brass ensemble and electronic tape premieres in Lenox, Massachusetts at the Berkshire Festival.

Aug. 31 Humphrey Searle's *Oxus*, based on a poem by Matthew Arnold, premieres in London. This dodecaphonic work is scored for voice and orchestra.

Sep. 13 Aaron Copland's orchestral work *Inscape* receives its world premiere in Ann Arbor at the University of Michigan, as Leonard Bernstein conducts the New York Philharmonic (the piece was commissioned to celebrate the orchestra's 125th anniversary). The music is dodecaphonic and lasts approximately 10 minutes. Copland describes it as a "quasi-mystical illumination." Alan Hughes writes in the New York *Times*, "it has a familar ring despite its dodecaphonic nature."

Oct. 1 Symphony No. 7, by Roger Sessions, is premiered by Jean Martinon and the Chicago Symphony Orchestra in Ann Arbor, Michigan. The three-movement symphony celebrates the sesquicentennial of the University of Michigan.

Oct. 22 Gyorgy Ligeti's orchestral work *Lontano* receives its world premiere at the Donaueschingen festival. This composition becomes a favorite of Ligeti followers and is noted for its orchestral color and almost impressionistic sound. Its rhythmic structure creates a static effect that seems to entrance audiences.

Oct. 29 Vincent Persichetti's Symphony No. 8 is premiered in Berea, Ohio. The symphony has four movements.

Nov. 2 Hans Werner Henze's Concerto for Double Bass and Orchestra is premiered by Jean Martinon and the Chicago Symphony Orchestra, with Gary Karr as soloist.

Nov. 29 Karlheinz Stockhausen's electronic composition *Hymnen* premieres in Cologne. This work is scored for electronic accordion and taped sounds, including shrieks and wheezes.

Dec. 14 Roberto Gerhard's Symphony No. 4 (*New York*) is premiered by William Steinberg and the New York Philharmonic. The one-movement work celebrates the orchestra's 125th anniversary.

1967 Births, Deaths and Debuts

Jan. 3 Soprano Mary Garden, 92, dies in Aberdeen, Scotland. After studies with many teachers, including Mathilde Marchesi, she made a sensational debut in Paris in *Louise* as a last-minute replacement in the middle of a performance. She was selected by Claude Debussy to create the role of Melisande and virtually owned this part as long as she sang. Successes in Chicago and New York followed in such roles as Salome and Thais. In 1921 she became the head of the Chicago Opera Company. After three years under her management, the company was over a million dollars in debt, and she was removed from this position. However, she continued to sing there until 1931. She was one of most glamorous opera stars of the century.

March 6 Hungarian composer Zoltan Kodaly, 84, dies in Budapest. He studied at the University of Budapest and the Budapest Academy of Music. His early work was a combination of sacred pieces and pieces evidencing an interest in folk songs of his native land. He later studied with Charles-Marie Widor in Paris and in 1907 became an instructor at the Budapest Academy of Music. While pursuing his folk song collecting, he also wrote criticism. His work *Psalmus Hungaricus* was composed to celebrate the union of Buda and Pest. His opera *Hary Janos* brought him to international attention. This was followed by *Marosszek Dances* and *Galanta Dances*. During World War II he remained in Budapest and compiled folk songs. Kodaly's music is more conservative than that of Bela Bartok: Its rhythms are more symmetrical; its pitch content almost never embraces atonality. He blended romanticism with impressionism. In addition to many orchestral, choral, chamber and piano pieces, he edited the periodical *Studia Musicologica Academiae Scientiarum Hungaricae*.

March 11   American soprano Geraldine Farrar, 85, dies in Ridgefield, Connecticut. One of the most popular stars of the 20th century, she made a sensational debut in Berlin in 1901. By the time she appeared in the United States in 1906, she was an established European star. Adored by her fans, called "Gerryflappers," she was also admired in more serious critical circles. She was often teamed with Enrico Caruso, to the great delight of the public and the box office. After her operatic retirement in 1922, she continued to give recitals until 1931. Farrar also made a number of silent movies, which helped spread her fame beyond the world of opera. Among her famous roles were Madama Butterfly, Juliet and Carmen.

April 5   Russian violinist Mischa Elman, 76, dies in New York. Having demonstrated huge musical gifts as a young boy, Elman was accepted at the Saint Petersburg Conservatory by Leopold Auer. He made his debut at age 13 in that city to great applause, and subsequent appearances in England and New York were similarly hailed. Known for his romantic playing, he was considered one of this century's greatest virtuosos.

Aug. 8   Czech composer Jaromir Weinberger, 71, commits suicide in Saint Petersburg, Florida by taking a drug overdose. He studied at the Prague Conservatory and with Max Reger in Leipzig. He later taught at the Conservatory of Ithaca in New York and in Bratislava, Prague and Vienna before settling in Saint Petersburg. In 1927 he became internationally famous with his opera *Schwanda, the Bagpiper*. He wrote a number of other operas and orchestral works. He commits suicide after becoming despondent that his recent works were not nearly as successful as his early works.

Dec. 11   Italian conductor Victor de Sabata, 75, dies in Santa Margherita Ligure, Italy. Considered second in Italy only to Arturo Toscanini, he started his professional life as a composer, and an opera of his was produced at La Scala in 1917. He subsequently turned to conducting and was the music director at La Scala for 20 years. He also made guest appearances in America, at the Bayreuth and Salzburg Festivals, and elsewhere. His musical temperament resulted in expansive and romantic interpretations.

1967   Related Events

EDO DE WAART

Edo de Waart becomes associate conductor of the Rotterdam Philharmonic Orchestra this year.

Robert Shaw becomes conductor of the Atlanta Symphony Orchestra this year.

Twentieth Century Music: Its Evolution from the End of the Harmonic Era to the Present Era of Sound, by Peter Yates, is published this year by Minerva Press. The book explores the evolution of contemporary music with a series of brief articles concerning composers, styles and content of music, notation, American music, electronic and computer music, and other aspects of the art.

French conductor Serge Baudo is named music director of the Orchestre de Paris this year.

Feb. 9   American cellist Charlotte Moorman performs topless in New York City and is subsequently charged with indecent exposure.

Feb. 3   The first Concours de Piano "Olivier Messiaen" takes place at Royan, France with Michel Beroff winning first prize.

April 29   Expo '67 opens in Montreal, celebrating Canada's centennial. *Terre des hommes*, an oratorio by Andre Prevost, is performed as a world premiere to accompany the inaugural ceremonies. It is scored for orchestra, chorus and two narrators.

May 1   Leon Kirchner is awarded the Pulitzer Prize for music for Quartet No. 3.

May 9   Cellist Charlotte Moorman receives a suspended jail sentence for her topless performance on February 9.

June 15   Conductor-pianist Daniel Barenboim marries English cellist Jacqueline Du Pre.

June 17   Korean composer Isang Yun and his wife are seized in West Berlin by South Korean agents and taken to Seoul. Later, after Yun is condemned as a North Korean spy and sentenced to life in prison, many internationally known composers (including Igor Stravinsky) protest to the South Korean government. The West German government also hints it will cease economic aid to South Korea. Both Yun and his wife are freed after two years of incarceration.

July 7   The New York Philharmonic celebrates its 125th anniversary by repeating the program of its very first concert in 1842.

July 29   Paul Ben-Haim's *Fanfare to Israel* is performed by William Steinberg and the Israel Philharmonic Orchestra in New York City. This event marks the first concert of this orchestra's American-Canadian tour.

Aug. 10   The Bolshoi Theater Opera Company of Moscow performs Modest Mussorgsky's *Boris Godunov* at Expo '67 in Montreal. This event marks the Bolshoi Opera's first performance in North America.

Aug. 14   Nikolai Rimsky-Korsakov's *The Legend of the Invisible City of Kitezh* is performed in Montreal by the Bolshoi Theater Opera Company of Moscow. This event marks the first Canadian performance of this opera.

Sep. 14   Zubin Mehta and the Los Angeles Philharmonic begin their first world tour. The orchestra will hold concerts from Belgium to India.

Oct. 19   The La Scala Opera Company of Milan, conducted by Herbert von Karajan, performs Giuseppe Verdi's *Requiem* at Carnegie Hall in New York. This event marks this company's first American tour.

1968 Opera

March 5   Humphrey Searle's *Hamlet* premieres in a German version in Hamburg. The dodecaphonic opera is based on the Shakespeare play.

March 17   Henri Posseur's *Votre Faust* premieres in Buffalo, New York. The opera is a contemporary rendition of the Faust legend.

March 24   Carl Orff's *Prometheus* receives its world premiere in Stuttgart. In addition to a host of vocalists, the opera requires an orchestra comprised of 4 pianos, 6 flutes, 6 oboes, 6 trumpets, 6 trombones, 4 banjos, 4 harps, 2 organs, 9 double basses, 5 kettledrums and 70 other percussion instruments.

June 1   *Until the Forests Burn*, an opera by Luigi Nono, receives its initial performance in Florence.

June 8   Harrison Birtwistle's musical puppet show *Punch and Judy* receives its initial performance at the Aldeburgh Festival in England.

Aug. 1   David Amram's *Twelfth Night* premieres at the New York Opera Festival at Lake George, New York.

Aug. 13   Malcolm Williamson's *The Growing Castle*, with a libretto by the composer, premieres in a concert version at

CARL ORFF

Dynevor Castle in Wales. This opera, the composer's sixth, is about a Scandinavian woman who lives in a world of fantasy.

Sep. 29   *Odysseus*, by Luigi Dallapiccola, is performed for the first time at the Deutsche Oper in Berlin. The libretto, by the composer, is a personal interpretation of the character of Ulysses in Homer's Odyssey. Lorin Maazel conducts this dodecaphonic opera.

Oct. 9   Hugo Weisgall's *Nine Rivers from Jordan* receives its initial performance by the New York City Opera. The

three-act opera is about a British soldier during World War II who lets a German prisoner escape.

Dec. 19   *Help! Help! The Globolinks!*, by Gian-Carlo Menotti, receives its world premiere at the Hamburg State Opera. The composer's libretto is about invaders from space who speak a 12-tone language. A school band performs a diatonic march, and they leave. It is somewhat analogous to the science fiction film *War of the Worlds*, where the invaders die at the end from a simple Earth phenomenon — the common cold.

1968 Dance

Jan. 18   *Metastaseis & Pithoprakta* receives its world premiere by the New York City Ballet. The music is by Iannis Xenakis, and the choreography is by George Balanchine. The lead dancers are Suzanne Farrell and Arthur Mitchell.

Jan. 29   John Butler's *Ceremony* — to music by Krzysztof Penderecki, with decor by Rouben Ter-Arutunian — is premiered by the Pennsylvania Ballet in New York City.

Feb. 20   Gerald Arpino's *Secret Places* — to music by Mozart, with decor by Ming Cho Lee and lighting by Thomas Skelton — is performed for the first time by the City Center Joffrey Ballet in New York City.

Feb. 28   Choreographer Gerald Arpino's *The Clowns* — to music by Hershey Kay, with costumes by Edith Lutyens Bel Geddes — is premiered by the City Center Joffrey Ballet in New York City. The principal dancer is Robert Blankshine. The ballet is about man's struggle to choose between self-destruction and survival.

Feb. 29   Rudolf Nureyev's version of *The Nutcracker* receives its initial performance by The Royal Ballet in London. The designs are by Nicholas Georgiadis. The lead dancers are the choreographer, Antoinette Sibley, Anthony Dowell and Merle Park.

April 9   Yuri Grigorovich stages his version of *Spartacus* for the Bolshoi Ballet. Set to Aram Khachaturian's score, it is considered the definitive production of the work. Vladimir Vasiliov, Yekaterina Maximova, Marius Liepa and Nina Timofeyeva star.

April 30   George Balanchine premieres *Slaughter on Tenth Avenue* with the New York City Ballet, in New York. The ballet is taken from the 1936 musical *On Your Toes*, by Richard Rodgers. Suzanne Farrell and Arthur Mitchell star.

May 2   The New York City Ballet presents George Balanchine's *Requiem Canticles* for one performance only. The work is intended as a memorial for Martin Luther King Jr., assassinated a month earlier. Suzanne Farrell and Arthur Mitchell dance to Igor Stravinsky's music.

May 25   Martha Graham's *A Time of Snow*, to music by Norman Dello Joio, premieres in New York City. Designs are by Rouben Ter-Arutunian. Graham's *Lady of the House of Sleep*, to music by Robert Starer, also premieres on the same program.

Oct. 3   Eliot Feld's *Meadowlark* receives its world premiere by the Royal Winnipeg Ballet in Winnipeg, Canada. The music is by Haydn, the costumes by Stanley Simmons and the decor by Robert Prevost. The principal dancers are Richard Rutherford and Sheila Mackinnon. Also premiered today is John Butler's *Labyrinth* — to music by Harry Somers, with decor by Rudi Dorn. Featuring Christine Hennessey, this story of the elements of life is a modern dance work.

Oct. 25   Frederick Ashton's *Enigma Variations* — to music by Edward Elgar, with costumes and decor by Julia Trevelyan Oman — is premiered by The Royal Ballet at Covent Garden, London. Derek Rencher dances the role of Elgar in this biographical ballet about the Edwardian composer.

Nov. 21   Choreographer Glen Tetley's *Embrace Tiger and Return to Mountain* — to music by Morton Subotnick, with decor by Nadine Baylis — is premiered by the Ballet Rambert in London.

Nov. 23   The New York City Ballet premieres George Balanchine's *La Source*, to music by Leo Delibes. The pas de deux, danced by Violette Verdy and John Prinz, is a celebration of 19th-century French dances.

1968 Instrumental and Vocal Music

Jan. 4   Nicolas Nabokov's Symphony No. 3 (*A Prayer*) is premiered by Leonard Bernstein and the New York Philharmonic. The neomedieval symphony is a tribute to Pope John XXIII.

Jan. 12   Isang Yun's *Shav Yang* for cembalo premieres in Freiburg, West Germany.

Jan. 18   Leonard Bernstein and the New York Philharmonic present the initial performance of Richard Rodney Bennett's Symphony No. 2. The 12-tone work is in one movement.

Jan. 31   Bernd Alois Zimmerman's *Musique pour les soupers du Roi Ubu* is premiered by the Berlin Radio Symphony Orchestra in Dusseldorf. This is an orchestral work conceived as a "ballet noir."

Feb. 4   The cantata *Stephen Crane*, by Ulysses Kay, premieres in Chicago. The text consists of four poems by Crane. The piece is scored for chorus and orchestra and celebrates the centennial of the Chicago Musical College.

Feb. 8   Symphony No. 11, by Roy Harris, receives its world premiere by the New York Philharmonic, the composer conducting. Harris states that the music expresses an "emotional rather than intellectual ethos." The symphony celebrates the orchestra's 125th anniversary.

Feb. 29   Howard Hanson's Symphony No. 6 is premiered by the New York Philharmonic. Hanson conducts. The neoromantic work has six movements and features asymmetric rhythms.

March 7   Walter Piston's symphonic work *Ricercare* is premiered by the New York Philharmonic. The piece is neobaroque.

March 11   Cornelius Cardew's *Schooltime Compositions*, Gyorgy Ligeti's *Aventures* and Mauricio Kagel's *Sur scene* receive their first performances in London. Cardew is concerned with music reflecting simplicity and describes this work as having "matrices arranged around vocal sounds, triangles, newspapers, balloons, noises, desire, keyboard, with many people working." The Ligeti work is scored for three singers and seven instruments.

March 13   Havergal Brian's Symphony No. 7 receives its world premiere in London. This work had first been listed as his Sixth Symphony but was later renumbered by the composer.

March 15   Benjamin Lees' Piano Concerto No. 2 is premiered by Erich Leinsdorf and the Boston Symphony Orchestra, with Gary Graffman as soloist.

March 21   Alan Hovhaness' symphonic poem *Fra Angelico*, Op. 220, receives its initial performance by Sixten Ehrling and the Detroit Symphony Orchestra. The music is a tribute to Fra Angelico, the medieval Italian master of fresco.

March 28   Ulysses Kay's Symphony is premiered by Jean Martinon and the Chicago Symphony Orchestra in Macomb, Illinois. The four-movement work celebrates the sesquicentennial of Illinois.

April 4   Jean Barraque's *Le temps restitue* premieres at the Royan Festival, France. Scored for voices and orchestra, the piece was composed in 1957.

April 5   John Corigliano Jr.'s Piano Concerto premieres in San Antonio, Texas. Hilde Somer is the soloist.

April 9   Gustav Mahler's Symphony No. 1 is performed by Frank Brieff and the New Haven Symphony Orchestra. This event marks the work's first full five-movement performance (including the "Blumine" movement) in this century.

May 2   Roger Sessions' Symphony No. 8 is premiered by William Steinberg and the New York Philharmonic. The one-movement symphony is based on a 12-tone row.

May 4   Isang Yun's *Nore fur Violoncello und Klavier* premieres over Radio Bremen.

May 16   Hans Werner Henze's *Concerto fur Klavier und Blasorchester mit Schlagzeug* receives its first performance in Schwetzingen.

May 18   Hans Werner Henze's *Moralities (Drei szenische Kantaten)* premieres in Cincinnati, Ohio.

May 19   *Piece in the Shape of a Square*, by Philip Glass, receives its world premiere in New York. Glass studied at the Peabody Conservatory and the University of Chicago. His teachers included Vincent Persichetti, Nadia Boulanger and Ravi Shankar. He went to India in 1966 to study native music.

May 24   *Invocation and Concerto* for violin and orchestra, by Ralph Shapey, premieres in New York City. This work confines its melodies to a few intervals.

June 10   *The Prodigal Son* by Benjamin Britten, premieres at Orford Church in Aldeburgh, England. This work is one of the composer's church parables.

June 23   Robert Ward's Piano Concerto premieres at today's concert of the Fourth Inter-American Music Festival in Columbia, Maryland.

June 27   Gunther Schuller's Concerto for Double Bass and Orchestra premieres in New York City with the composer conducting.

July 7   *Syzygy*, by David Del Tredici, receives its first performance in New York. This instrumental work is scored for soprano, horn, chimes and chamber ensemble. Del

Tredici studied with Seymour Shifrin at the University of California and with Roger Sessions at Princeton University.

July 9   Reginald Smith Brindle's *Amalgam* premieres at the Cheltenham Festival in England.

July 28   Easley Blackwood's Concerto for Flute and String Orchestra is premiered by Mario di Bonaventura at Dartmouth College in Hanover, New Hampshire, with Robert Willoughby as soloist.

Aug. 1   Ernst Krenek's *Instant Remembered* for soprano and instruments receives its initial performance at the International Webern Festival at Dartmouth College in Hanover, New Hampshire.

Aug. 2   Anton Webern's *Sonatensatz (Rondo) fur Klavier* and his Rondo for String Quartet are premiered posthumously at the fourth International Webern Festival in Hanover, New Hampshire.

Aug. 4   Krzysztof Penderecki's Concerto for Violino Grande and Orchestra premieres at Dartmouth College in Hanover, New Hampshire. Bronislaw Eichenholz is violino grande soloist. This event marks the premiere of a work composed especially for a five-string violin invented by Hans Olot Hanson.

Aug. 17   Lou Harrison's *Peace Pieces* premieres at Cabrillo College in Aptos, California.

Aug. 23   Harrison Birtwistle's *Nomos* receives its first performance by the BBC Symphony Orchestra. This is an orchestral work.

Sep. 19   Richard Rodney Bennett's Piano Concerto premieres at the Birmingham Triennial Festival in England.

Sep. 29   Hans Werner Henze's Piano Concerto No. 2 premieres in Bielefeld, West Germany. The one-movement work is subdivided into three sections and was inspired by existentialist philosophy.

Oct. 10   *Sinfonia*, by Luciano Berio, receives its world premiere in New York City, as the composer conducts the Swingle Singers and the New York Philharmonic. The work consists of four sections and is scored for eight voices and instruments. Berio states that the title of the piece must be understood only in terms of "sounding together" and that the four sections are "united by similar harmonic and articulatory characteristics," including duplication and repetition. The first section consists of texts by Claude Levi-Strauss describing Brazilian myths about the origins of water. The second section is a tribute to Dr. Martin Luther King Jr. in which the text is derived solely from his name. The third section is based on excerpts from *The Unnamable*, by Samuel Beckett, and various other sources, including student slogans of the recent rebellion at the Sorbonne in Paris. It is also a tribute to Gustav Mahler and to Leonard Bernstein, and includes melodic and harmonic references to and quotations from works by Mahler, Bach, Arnold Schoenberg, Claude Debussy, Maurice Ravel, Richard Strauss, Hector Berlioz, Johannes Brahms, Alban Berg, Paul Hindemith, Beethoven, Wagner, Igor Stravinsky, Karlheinz Stockhausen, Pierre Boulez, Charles Ives and others. Berio describes this section both as a documentary and as a "stream-of-consciousness-like flowing" and states, "it is not so much composed as it is assembled. . . ." The fourth section combines elements of the first and third into a coda. The text is set so that it is recognizable only at certain points during the music. Berio states, "The experience of 'not quite hearing,' then, is to be conceived as essential to the nature of the work itself."

The premiere creates a sensation and catapults Berio to international attention. Harold C. Schonberg writes in the New York *Times*: "Gone are the strict constructions and parameters of serialism. It is one of the musics of the future." Critic Winthrop Sargeant, however, subsequently comments in the *New Yorker* magazine on this and other Berio works, questioning the artistic validity of Berio's collage technique and saying, "If the future of music is going to consist of salads tossed together with ingredients from the masterpieces of the past, it does not seem to me to be much of a future."

Oct. 23   Dominick Argento's *Letters from Composers (A Cycle of Seven Songs for Tenor and Guitar)* premieres at Macalester College Concert Hall in Saint Paul, Minnesota.

Oct. 27   *String Trio*, by Charles Wuorinen, receives its initial performance by the Potomac String Trio at the National Gallery in Washington, D.C.

Oct. 28   *The Politics of Harmony: A Masque*, by Charles Wuorinen, receives its world premiere by the Group for Contemporary Music at Columbia University, New York. The composer conducts. The text is by Richard Monaco and the music is scored for mimes, alto, tenor, bass, two flutes, two tubas, two violins, two double basses, three percussion players, two harps and piano. The 12-tone work is based on an ancient Chinese legend.

Harold C. Schonberg reviews a later performance in the New York *Times* and characterizes the work as "one of those academic, post-serial drags, completely amelodic, awkwardly set for three voices."

Nov. 13   *Son of Heldenleben*, by R. Murray Schafer, receives its world premiere in Montreal. This work is an orchestral tribute to and satire on Richard Strauss' tone poem *Ein Heldenleben*. Schafer distorts the melodic themes of the original.

Nov. 17   Leopold Stokowski and the American Symphony Orchestra premiere Andrzej Panufnik's symphonic work *Epitaph for the Victims of Katyn*. It is a tribute to the many Poles slaughtered by the Nazis as they marched into the Soviet Union in 1941. Panufnik is now living in England.

Nov. 18   Paul Creston's Concerto for Two Pianos and Orchestra is premiered by conductor Werner Torkanowsky and the New Orleans Philharmonic Symphony in Montevallo, Alabama.

Nov. 25   Morton Feldman's *Structures* premieres in Scranton, Pennsylvania.

Dec. 16   Gyorgy Ligeti's Quartet for Strings No. 2 premieres in Baden-Baden, West Germany.

Dec. 24   Alexander Tcherepnin's cantata *The Story of Ivan the Fool* premieres over BBC Radio in London, the composer conducting. Scored for narrator, vocalists, chorus, orchestra and electronic effects, it is based on the tale by Tolstoi.

Dec. 31   Morton Feldman's *False Relationships and the Extended Ending* receives its first performance at a contemporary music festival in Palermo, Sicily. The work is scored for two instrumental groups, including piano, violin and trombone; two pianos, cello and chimes. Each group begins together, but they quickly become independent of each other. There is no repetition except for a recurring broken chord in the piano parts. As is characteristic of Feldman's work, the dynamic levels are extremely low throughout the piece.

1968   Births, Deaths and Debuts

Jan. 9   French composer Louis Aubert, 90, dies in Paris. His principal composition teacher was Gabriel Faure, and his opera *The Blue Forest* is his best-known work. He was attracted to the tunes and rhythms of Spanish music, with his music sometimes being compared to that of Maurice Ravel and Claude Debussy.

Jan. 11   Italian baritone Mariano Stabile, 79, dies in Milan. After a debut in 1909, he sang with little acclaim until 1921, when Arturo Toscanini selected him to sing Falstaff at La Scala. His success was pronounced, and he subsequently sang the role more than 1,000 times until he retired in 1960. He was also known for his performances as Scarpia, Don Giovanni, Don Pasquale and Rigoletto.

Feb. 3   Italian conductor Tullio Serafin, 89, dies in Rome. After studies at the Conservatory of Milan, he made his conducting debut in 1900 in Ferrara, and in 1909 he became conductor of La Scala in Milan. From 1924 to 1935 he was at the Metropolitan in New York. In addition to the Italian repertoire, he led many performances of operas by Wagner, Carl Maria von Weber and Mozart. In the 1950s he was often associated with soprano Maria Callas, collaborating on performances and recordings of bel canto operas of Vincenzo Bellini and Gaetano Donizetti.

Feb. 13   Italian composer Ildebrando Pizzetti, 87, dies in Rome. He studied at the Conservatory of Parma and later taught at that conservatory as well as at the Conservatory of Florence, the Conservatory of Milan and the Accademia di Santa Cecilia in Rome. In 1914 he cofounded a periodical entitled *Dissonanza* to advance the cause of new music. Despite Pizzetti's devotion to new music, his own works are largely romantic in style (diatonic melodies, chromatic harmonies). His stage works are, to some degree, a counterpart to the medieval mystery plays. He composed 13 operas (including *Fra Gherardo* — his most famous piece); incidental music; orchestral, choral and chamber works (including two string quartets); and songs (including "I Pastori," composed in 1908). He also transcribed madrigals by Don Carlo Gesualdo and sonatas by Francesco Maria Veracini (1690–1768).

March 12   Italian musicologist Andrea Della Corte, 83, dies in Turin. Also a critic, he wrote many articles and essays on music. He was on the faculty of the Turin Conservatory and the University of Turin. He was known especially for his work in music bibliography.

March 16   Italian-American composer Mario Castelnuovo-Tedesco, 72, dies in Los Angeles. A pupil of Ildebrando Pizzetti at the Cherubini Institute, he emigrated to the United States in 1939. He was popular between World War I and World War II. He was extremely prolific, writing music in all forms. His music, which is noted for its emotional strength, quickly fades, despite its significance during his lifetime.

April 15   Ukrainian composer Boris Liatoshinsky, 73, dies in Kiev. He simultaneously studied jurisprudence at the University of Kiev and musical composition at Kiev Conservatory with Reinhold Gliere. He taught at that conservatory as well as at the Moscow Conservatory. His music is nationalistic and includes folk elements. He composed two operas, five symphonies, four string quartets, many folk song arrangements and other works.

May 15   Australian Wagnerian soprano Florence Austral, 74, dies in Newcastle, New South Wales, Australia. She made her debut as Brunnhilde at Covent Garden in 1922 and specialized in Wagnerian and Italian dramatic roles. She was married to flutist John Amadeo.

June 14   Swedish composer Karl-Birger Blomdahl, 51, dies in Kunsangen. His principal teacher was Hilding Rosenberg. He also studied conducting in Stockholm before teaching at that city's Royal College of Music. He was a music director of the Swedish Radio and, with others, organized the "Monday group" — artists presenting new musical works that departed from Scandinavian romanticism. His music was at first neoclassical; he later became fascinated by electronic music and dodecaphony. He wrote many pieces of varying types and for different combinations of voices and instruments. His best-known work is the opera *Aniara*, composed between 1957 and 1959. *The Saga of the Great Computer*, an unfinished opera, combines synthesized speech and electronic sound.

July 21   American dancer and choreographer Ruth Saint Denis dies in Hollywood at the age of 91. Saint Denis, who was known as the First Lady of American Dance, was a major force in the development of modern dance. She drew her main inspiration from Eastern art, although she did not have a clear understanding of the various styles of oriental dance. Her dances attempted to make music visible and often contained a religious element. As a teacher and choreographer she influenced such important modern choreographers as Martha Graham and Doris Humphrey.

Saint Denis had very little formal dance training. Prior to her career as a concert dancer, she appeared in the music hall productions of David Belasco. She presented her first ballet, *Radha*, in 1906 in a series of New York Sunday Night Smoking Concerts. That same year she choreographed *The Incense* and *The Cobras* for her first recital program. Saint Denis toured Europe from 1906 to 1909 and was enormously successful, particularly in Germany and Austria. In 1914 she married Ted Shawn. Together they founded the Denishawn School which became the first center for modern dance and had its own dance company which toured extensively until 1932. Following her separation from Shawn in 1932 and the disbanding of the Denishawn school, she went into semi-retirement, choreographing religious dances. In 1940 she and Le Meri opened the School of Natya. Saint Denis continued to perform and lecture until her death.

Sep. 3   Argentine composer Juan Jose Castro, 73, dies in Buenos Aires. After studies with Vincent d'Indy in Paris, he established himself as a well-known conductor. He championed the cause of his own music, performing it everywhere he went, often with his own orchestra, the Orquesta de Nacimiento (Buenos Aires). He wrote operas and other works, his big success being his opera *Prosperina e lo straniero* (Milan 1952). His brother Jose Maria Castro was also a composer and conductor.

Nov. 6   Alsatian conductor Charles Munch, 77, dies in Richmond, Virginia. After beginning his career as a violinist, he turned to conducting in 1932. He founded the Orchestre de la Societe Philharmonique in 1935, and in 1949 he was appointed conductor of the Boston Symphony Orchestra, succeeding Serge Koussevitzky. He later organized the Orchestre de Paris, and it was while on tour with this group that he died. He conducted many new works by French composers.

Nov. 6   Dutch composer Guillaume Landre, 63, dies in Amsterdam. He was the son of Willem Landre and studied with Willem Pijper. He held a master's degree in law and even taught economics. As a composer, he was concerned with raising contemporary Dutch music to the status it enjoyed in the Renaissance. He also used serial techniques in some later pieces.

Nov. 11   French organist Jeanne Demessieux, 47, dies in Paris. Considered to be one of the greatest figures in organ improvisation, she taught at the Conservatory of Liege.

Dec. 14   German contralto Margarete Klose, 66, dies in Berlin. After her debut in Ulm in 1927, she became a mainstay of the Berlin State Opera, where she was particularly successful in the Wagnerian repertoire. Her rich contralto voice and her fiery singing won her popular acclaim.

Dec. 20   Czech-Israeli composer, author and critic Max Brod, 84, dies in Tel Aviv. Also a novelist, he went to Tel Aviv in 1939 and decided to stay. His work includes choral, orchestral and other music. Much of his music was inspired by Hebrew themes and Jewish culture.

1968   Related Events

Jan. 24   Powell Symphony Hall in St. Louis, Missouri is inaugurated as Eleazar Carvalho — outgoing music director of the St. Louis Symphony Orchestra — conducts that ensemble in a program of music by Gunther Schuller (*Fanfare for St. Louis* — commissioned especially for this occasion), Benjamin Britten and Igor Stravinsky. American acoustician Cyril Harris was responsible for the acoustics of this new concert hall.

Feb. 24   The Sibelius Museum in Abo, Finland opens today. It is at the Institute of Musicology at Abo Akademi, and its collections consist of music manuscripts, documents, ephemera and an extensive musical instrument collection. Much of its collection concerns the life and work of Jean Sibelius. The museum also has a teaching as well as an exhibition division.

May 6   George Crumb is awarded the Pulitzer Prize for music for *Echoes of Time and the River: Four Processionals for Orchestra.*

July 19   The inaugural concert of the Blossom Music Center takes place north of Akron, Ohio. George Szell conducts music of Beethoven, performed by the Cleveland Orchestra (with its chorus and soloists). The music center is named after the Dudley Blossom family, whose members helped found the center and were major supporters of the Cleveland Orchestra since its founding. The concert pavilion, seating 4,822, is convex with a fan-shaped roof.

July 30   The collectively composed oratorio *Testimonium* — with music by Roman Haubenstock-Ramati, Yitzhak Sadai, Jehoshua Lakner, Sergiu Natra and Zvi Avni — premieres in Jerusalem. This event marks the opening of the Festival of Israel.

Aug. 24   Czech conductor-composer Rafael Kubelik urges musicians to refuse to participate in musical events held in nations that participated in the recent invasion of Czechoslovakia (Poland, East Germany, Hungary, the

THE INTERIOR OF THE SIBELIUS MUSEUM

Soviet Union and Bulgaria). Igor Stravinsky, Otto Klemperer, Bernard Haitink, Claudio Arrau and Artur Rubinstein support Kubelik.

Aug. 9   Conductor Walter Susskind becomes music director of the St. Louis Symphony Orchestra this month. Susskind also brings a young assistant conductor with him — Leonard Slatkin — who becomes music director of this orchestra in 1979.

Oct. 22   Pianist Rudolf Firkusny plays an all-Czechoslovak concert at Carnegie Hall in New York City to celebrate the 50th anniversary of the Czech republic. The program includes works by Leos Janacek, Viteslav Novak, Antonin Dvorak, Bedrich Smetana and others. Harold C. Schonberg writes in the New York *Times*: "He consistently overpedaled. Otherwise the playing was plastic, elegant and songful." The event is emotional due to the Soviet invasion of Czechoslovakia in August.

THE BLOSSOM MUSIC CENTER—SUMMER HOME OF THE CLEVELAND ORCHESTRA

Nov. 9   Hans Werner Henze's oratorio *The Raft of the Medusa*, scheduled to be premiered today in Hamburg, is canceled due to protests by the chorus. The piece was dedicated to Che Guevara, and the musicians were to have performed under a red banner onstage. Although the story of the oratorio dealt with the 1816 wreck of a French frigate, Henze had recently stated his contention that new music premieres are less important than revolution.

Dec. 17   Hungarian conductor Georg Solti, 56, is named music director of the Chicago Symphony. Carlo Maria Giulini is named principal guest conductor.

Dec. 23   English conductor Colin Davis is named music director of the Royal Opera at Covent Garden.

Dec. 29   The new Vittorio Emanuele Theater opens in Messina, Italy, with a performance of Giuseppe Verdi's *Aida*. This event marks the inauguration of a new hall, replacing the one destroyed by the 1908 earthquake.

1969 Opera

March 16   Elie Siegmeister's *The Plough and the Stars* is premiered by conductor Peter Paul Fuchs in Baton Rouge, Louisiana. The three-act opera is based on a play by Sean O'Casey about an Irish rebellion against the British in the early part of the 20th century.

March 29   Richard Rodney Bennett's children's opera *Humpty Dumpty* premieres in Coventry, England.

May 8   British composer Harrison Birtwistle's *Down by the Greenwood Side* receives its initial performance at the Brighton Festival. This work is a dramatic pastorale.

May 29   *Under Western Eyes*, by John Joubert, premieres at the Camden Festival in England. The opera, in three acts, is about Russian exiles in Geneva.

June 20   Krzysztof Penderecki's *The Devils of Loudun*, with a libretto based on Aldous Huxley's novella, receives its world premiere by the Hamburg State Opera. This event marks the opening of this year's International Society for Contemporary Music festival. The three-act opera is about 17th-century nuns confronted by temptation and evil.

Dec. 18   Malcolm Williamson's opera *Lucky Peter's Journey* is premiered by the Sadler's Wells Opera in London.

1969 Dance

Jan. 9   *Delusion of the Fury*, by Harry Partch, receives its world premiere at the University of California in Los Angeles. Choreography is by Storie Crawford, with sets by John Crawford. Danlee Mitchell conducts. The two-act work consists of dance, mime, music and lighting modeled on the Greek concept of a farcical play following a serious play. Act I is based on an 11th-century Japanese Noh play; Act II is based on a farcical African folk tale.

Jan. 23   Choreographer John Clifford's *Fantasies* — set to music by Ralph Vaughan Williams, with costumes by Robert O'Hearn — is premiered by the New York City Ballet in New York. The cast includes Kay Mazzo, Anthony Blum, Sara Leland and Conrad Ludlow.

April 15   Merce Cunningham's modern dance piece *Canfield*, to music by Pauline Oliveros, is performed for the first time at the Brooklyn Academy of Music in New York City.

May 16   John Cranko's *The Taming of the Shrew* — to music by Kurt-Heinz Stolze, based on music by Scarlatti — is premiered by the Stuttgart Ballet. Marcia Haydee and Richard Cragun lead the cast.

May 22   Jerome Robbins' *Dances at a Gathering* receives its world premiere by the New York City Ballet in New York. The work is choreographed to music by Chopin, with costumes by Joe Eula. The principal dancers are Edward Villella, Allegra Kent, Kay Mazzo, Patricia McBride, Sara Leland, Violette Verdy, Anthony Blum, John Clifford, John Prinz and Robert Maiorano. This celebration of dance is Robbins' first ballet for the company in 12 years. It becomes one of his most popular pieces.

May 29   Eliot Feld's *Intermezzo* is premiered by the American Ballet Company in Spoleto, Italy. The costumes are by Stanley Simmons, and the dancers include Christine Sarry, Elizabeth Lee and Christina Stirling. Three couples dance romantically to piano music by Brahms.

June 1   George Balanchine's *Valse Fantaisie* — to music by Mikhail Glinka, with costumes, scenery and lighting by Esteban Frances — is premiered by the New York City Ballet in New York. This work was originally Part II of *Glinkiana* (1967) and is a completely different dance composition from Balanchine's *Valse-fantaisie* premiered in 1953.

June 27   Eliot Feld's *Cortege Burlesque* — to music by Emmanuel Chabrier, orchestrated by Hershey Kay, with scenery by Robert Munford and costumes by Stanley Simmons — is premiered by the American Ballet Company at the Festival of Two Worlds in Spoleto, Italy. Christine Sarry and Feld are the dancers.

Nov. 19   Thea Musgrave's *Beauty and the Beast* is premiered in London by the Scottish Theater Ballet. This work is a ballet for electronic tape and chamber orchestra.

Dec. 4   Choreographer Michael Smuin's *Eternal Idol* — to music by Chopin, with costumes by Marcos Paredes — receives its world premiere by the American Ballet Theater in New York City. The work, inspired by the formal beauty of Auguste Rodin's sculpture, is danced by Cynthia Gregory and Ivan Nagy.

Dec. 4   Choreographer John Clifford's *Reveries* — to music by Tchaikovsky, with costumes by Joe Eula — is performed for the first time by the New York City Ballet in New York. The plotless work features Conrad Ludlow and Gelsey Kirkland.

Dec. 25   Yuri Grigorovich stages a new version of *Swan Lake* for the Bolshoi Ballet.

1969 Instrumental and Vocal Music

Jan. 10   William Schuman's Symphony No. 9 (*Le fosse Ardeatine*) receives its world premiere by Eugene Ormandy and the Philadelphia Orchestra. The work was inspired by the Ardeatine Caves in Rome, where, in 1944, the Nazis murdered 335 Italians in retaliation for acts of violence committed by Italian resistance fighters.

Jan. 13   Anton Webern's *Orchestra Pieces* (1913) is premiered posthumously by Friedrich Cerha and the West German Radio Orchestra in Cologne.

Jan. 14   Toru Takemitsu's *Asterism* for piano and orchestra is premiered by Seiji Ozawa and the Toronto Symphony Orchestra, with Yuji Takahashi as soloist.

Jan. 16   *Relata II* for orchestra, by Milton Babbitt, receives its world premiere by Leonard Bernstein and the New York Philharmonic in New York. This work explores the art of combinatoriality — combining 12-tone sets or segments of sets such that the pitch-class content of the result meets certain criteria predetermined by the composer. Due to an excessive number of mistakes made by music copyists and the scheduling of only six hours of rehearsal time for this complicated piece, the performance is a disaster. At one point during a rehearsal, Bernstein asked Babbitt "Dare we go ahead?" Babbitt is enraged and later comments, "No one is concerned but my interested musical colleagues, those for whom I really offer it."

Jan. 17   Alan Hovhaness' chamber symphony *Mountains and Rivers without End* premieres in Munich.

Jan. 17   Benjamin Lees' Symphony No. 3 receives its initial performance by Sixten Ehrling and the Detroit Symphony Orchestra.

Jan. 20   Gyorgy Ligeti's *Stucke* for wind quintet premieres in Malmo, Sweden.

Jan. 25   Morton Subotnick's orchestral work *The Missions of San Antonio* receives its first performance in San Antonio, Texas.

Jan. 31   *Eonta* for piano and five brass instruments, by Iannis Xenakis, premieres at the Maison de la Culture d'Amiens.

Feb. 6   Chou Wen-chung's *Yun* for winds, brass, 2 pianos and percussion premieres at Wisconsin State University in River Falls, Wisconsin.

Feb. 10   Harrison Birtwistle's *Four Interludes from a Tragedy* for bass clarinet and tape premieres in London.

Feb. 12   Harrison Birtwistle's *Verses for Ensembles* premieres in London.

MORTON SUBOTNICK

Feb. 14   Hans Werner Henze's *Essay on Pigs* receives its initial performance at Queen Elizabeth Hall in London. This cantata — scored for speaker, chamber orchestra and jazz combo — takes its title from derogatory terms used against student protesters in Berlin. Henze conducts.

Feb. 19   Bernd Alois Zimmerman's *Photoptosis — Prelude for Large Orchestra* is premiered by the Gelsenkirchen Symphony Orchestra in Gelsenkirchen, West Germany. This work contains quarter-tone moments.

Feb. 26   Morton Feldman's *Between Categories* receives its first performance at the Kaufman Concert Hall in New York City.

March 2   *Time's Encomium*, by Charles Wuorinen, receives its world premiere (part II only) in Newark, New Jersey. This piece is for synthesized tape and processed sound (tape). The composer describes the title as meaning "the absolute, not the seeming, length of events and sections." It was composed and realized at the Columbia-Princeton Electronic Music Center in New York. The work subsequently receives the Pulitzer Prize for music.

March 2   Jacques Charpentier's Symphony No. 3 (*Shiva Nataraja*) receives its initial performance by l'Orchestre Lyrique de l'O.R.T.F., in Paris. Charpentier, who had lived in India for several years, studied Indian music.

March 3   Roger Sessions' Piano Sonata No. 3 premieres at Occidental College in Los Angeles.

April 3   *Nomos gamma* by Iannis Xenakis, premieres in Royan, France. It is scored for orchestra and percussion.

April 13   Charles Wuorinen's *Making Ends Meet*, for piano duet, premieres in New York City.

April 22   *Eight Songs for a Mad King*, by Peter Maxwell Davies receives its world premiere in London, the composer conducting. The work is scored for voice and instruments. During the last part of the piece, the mad king (George III) grabs a violin from the violinist and smashes it to bits.

April 23   Gyorgy Ligeti's *Ramifications* for string orchestra premieres in Berlin.

May 3   Luciano Berio's *Traces* receives its first performance at the University of Iowa. This work is scored for voices and orchestra.

May 15   Karlheinz Stockhausen's *Klavierstucke IX and VIII* (1955) for piano premieres at Carnegie Recital Hall in New York City.

May 19   Benjamin Britten's *Children's Crusade* receives its initial performance in London. This piece is a ballad based on a work by Bertolt Brecht.

June 3   Norman Dello Joio's orchestral work *Homage to Haydn* premieres in Little Rock, Arkansas.

June 7   Olivier Messiaen's *La transfiguration de Notre Seigneur Jesus-Christ* receives its world premiere in Lisbon, Portugal by conductor Serge Baudo and soloists Yvonne Loriod and Mstislav Rostropovich. This 13-movement piece is scored for voices and orchestra.

June 15   Uruguayan-born composer Jose Serebrier's *Doce por doce* is premiered by the American Wind Symphony in Pittsburgh. Serebrier has studied with Vittorio Giannini at the Curtis Institute in Philadelphia. He also studied conducting with Antal Dorati and Pierre Monteux.

July 3   Dominick Argento's *Bravo Mozart* premieres in Minneapolis. The work is described by the composer as an imaginary biography for oboe, violin, horn and orchestra.

July 27   Alan Hovhaness' *Requiem and Resurrection* receives its first performance by the American Wind Symphony in Pittsburgh.

Aug. 23   Roberto Gerhard's chamber work *Leo* premieres at Dartmouth College.

Oct. 16   Leon Kirchner's *Music for Orchestra* receives its initial performance by the New York Philharmonic in New York City.

Oct. 17   *New People* for mezzo-soprano, violin and piano, by Michael Colgrass, premieres at Alice Tully Hall in New York City.

Oct. 21   *Apokalyptische Fantasie* for orchestra, by Josef Matthias Hauer, premieres posthumously in Graz, Austria.

Oct. 22   Malcolm Williamson's Symphony No. 2 is premiered by the Bournemouth Symphony Orchestra at Colston Hall in Bristol.

Oct. 24   Thea Musgrave's *Night Music* premieres in Cardiff, Wales. This work is scored for chamber orchestra.

Oct. 28   Stefan Wolpe's String Quartet in two movements premieres at Alice Tully Hall in New York City.

Nov. 5   Ned Rorem's *War Scenes*, set to texts by Walt Whitman, premieres at Philharmonic Hall in New York City.

Nov. 5   Luigi Nono's *Y su sangre ya viene cantando* for flute and orchestra premieres in Berlin.

Nov. 19   Hans Werner Henze's Symphony No. 6 receives its initial performance in Havana, Cuba.

Nov. 19   *Contrafactum for Orchestra*, by Charles Wuorinen, receives its initial performance by James Dixon at the University of Iowa.

Dec. 9   Peter Maxwell Davies' *Vesalii icones* premieres in London. Based on 14 anatomical drawing by Vesalius, the piece is scored for solo cello, wind instruments and piano. It has 14 movements.

1969 Births, Deaths and Debuts

Jan. 10   American baritone John Brownlee, 69, dies in New York City. Internationally known as an opera singer, he was also president of the Manhattan School of Music in New York. He made his debut in *La Boheme* at Covent Garden in 1926.

Jan. 16   Russian composer Vladimir Dukelsky, 65, dies in Santa Monica, California. Also known as Vernon Duke, he studied with Reinhold Gliere at the Kiev Conservatory. Serge Diaghilev made him famous by commissioning him to compose the ballet *Zephyr et Flore*, and Serge Koussevitzky performed his works in Boston and Paris. George Gershwin convinced him to anglicize his name. As Vernon Duke he wrote many popular songs, including "April in Paris."

Feb. 2   Italian tenor Giovanni Martinelli, 83, dies in New York. After a debut in Milan, he was chosen by Giacomo Puccini for the European premiere of *The Girl of the Golden West*. Engagements in Europe and America followed, and after Enrico Caruso's death in 1921, he and Beniamino Gigli were considered his successors. He sang at the Metropolitan for a total of 32 years. After his retirement in 1946, he taught singing in New York.

Feb. 20   Swiss conductor Ernest Ansermet, 86, dies in Zurich. Conductor of L'Orchestre de la Suisse Romande, which he founded in 1918, he was also chief conductor of the Geneva Radio Orchestra. As a conductor for Serge Diaghilev's Ballets Russes, he premiered Igor Stravinsky's *L'histoire du soldat* in 1918. He considered 12-tone techniques invalid and explained why in his two-volume book *Les fondements de la musique dans la conscience humaine*. He was an officer in the French Legion of Honor. During his career Ansermet championed much new music, expecially French and Russian.

April 29   American pianist Julius Katchen, 42, dies in Paris. After studies with David Saperton in New York, he made his debut in Philadelphia in 1937. He later settled in Paris and concertized successfully in Europe and the Middle East.

May 17   Music and dance critic Robert Sabin, 57, dies in New York City. He was chief editor of *Musical America* and an editor of *Dance Observer*. He also edited the ninth edition of the *International Cyclopedia of Music and Musicians*.

June 24   American conductor Giuseppe Bamboschek, 79, dies in New York City. He specialized in conducting Italian opera and performed at the Metropolitan Opera.

July 5   German pianist Wilhelm Backhaus, 85, dies in Villach, Austria. He was a student of Eugene d'Albert and began his highly successful career at age 16. Known for his interpretations of Beethoven and Brahms, he continued his concert career until his seventies, still playing with unfailing spirit and constantly deepening eloquence.

July 9   French pianist and composer Pierre Capdevielle, 63, dies in Bordeaux, France. His teachers included Andre Gedalge and Vincent d'Indy. His best-known works were his opera *Les amants captifs* and his three symphonies.

July 25   German musicologist Heinrich Besseler, 69, dies in Leipzig. A contributor to *Die Musik in Geschichte und Gegenwart*, he was a scholar on music in the Renaissance and Middle Ages. He also held an honorary doctorate from the University of Chicago and edited complete editions of music by the Franco-Flemish composers. (Dufay, Okeghem, etc.).

Aug. 6   German musician and philosopher Theodor Wiesengrund Adorno, 65, dies in Visp, Switzerland. He studied composition with Alban Berg and piano with Eduard Steuermann but soon devoted himself to music criticism. He later became involved in radio research at Princeton University. Thomas Mann consulted Adorno on the musical aspects of his novel *Doktor Faustus* (this novel later enraged Arnold Schoenberg, who felt Mann was denigrating him and his 12-tone system of composition). Adorno developed into an essayist and philosopher and used ideas of Karl Marx and Sigmund Freud as a basis for developing his own sociology and philosophy of music. This eventually led to his achieving the status of aesthetician of paramount importance. His writings include *Philosophy of Modern Music* (1949), *Introduction to the Sociology of Music* (1962) and *Negative Dialectics*. Adorno was the 20th century's foremost philosopher of music.

Sep. 16   German composer Heinz Hartig, 62, dies in Berlin. Hartig was relegated to playing minor harpsichord parts during the Nazi regime because he was unsuccessful in maintaining a teaching position. His music embodies different compositional techniques, from conservative neoclassical sounds to dodecaphonic methods. His ballet *Schwarze Sonne* is among his most popular compositions.

Oct. 22   Young conductor Michael Tilson Thomas replaces an ailing William Steinberg in the middle of a concert by the Boston Symphony Orchestra in New York. Harold C. Schonberg writes in the New York *Times*, "Everything sounded clear, propulsive and vital."

Dec. 10   Italian conductor Franco Capuana, 75, dies in Naples. He was director of the San Carlo Opera. His specialty was the music of Richard Wagner and Giuseppe Verdi.

Dec. 30   Cuban-American pianist Jose Echaniz, 64, dies in Pittsford, New York. Also a conductor (he led the Grand Rapids Symphony Orchestra), he taught at the Eastman School of Music and frequently performed as a soloist with American orchestras.

Dec. 31   Bass Salvatore Baccaloni, 69, dies in New York. After his debut in Rome in 1927, he became well known in Europe and America for his interpretations of comic oper-atic parts. He had a huge repertoire of about 150 roles and can be seen in several films.

1969   Related Events

Antal Dorati becomes music director of the National Symphony Orchestra this year, succeeding Howard Mitchell. Dorati holds this position until 1977.

The NAPAC Ballet is established this year in Durban, South Africa. Dudley Davies and Patricia Miller direct this new company, with help from the Natal Performing Arts Council.

Two recording industry firms — Schreiber (America) and Sansui (Japan) — begin developing 40-channel re-cording technology.

Jan. 22   French composer-conductor Pierre Boulez is ap-pointed head of the British Broadcasting Corporation (BBC) Symphony Orchestra, replacing outgoing conduc-tor Colin Davis.

April 27   The documentary film *The World of David Amram* premieres over NET television. The composer's *Three Songs for America* receives its initial performance during the broadcast.

May 5   Karel Husa is awarded the Pulitzer Prize for mu-sic for String Quartet No. 3.

June 1   British housewife Rosemary Brown performs the world premiere of a new Franz Schubert work, *Moment*

PIERRE BOULEZ

Musical, for piano over BBC television. Insisting that the music had been dictated to her by Schubert's spirit, she subsequently takes dictation from the ghosts of Liszt, Chopin, Brahms, Beethoven, Mozart, Bach, Serge Rach-maninoff and Claude Debussy. Music experts remain skeptical.

June 2   The Canadian National Arts Center opens in Ot-tawa with a performance of *Kraanerg,* a new ballet by Ian-nis Xenakis. The music's title means "perfected energy." The new auditorium seats 2,373.

June 10   French composer-conductor Pierre Boulez is appointed music director of the New York Philharmonic, succeeding Leonard Bernstein.

June 25   The first Carinthian Summer Music Festival be-gins in Austria as German pianist and pedagogue Wilhelm Backhaus performs as soloist. The festival, characterized as a "festival of stillness and intensification," includes 16 concerts this summer and quickly expands to become an international festival.

July 31   The Newport Music Festival's inaugural concert takes place at The Breakers (the former Vanderbilt man-sion) in Newport, Rhode Island. Entitled a "Gala Musi-cale," the program features music by Frederick Chopin, Camille Saint-Saens, Niccolo Paganini, Franz Liszt, Gioac-chino Rossini and others. This festival enjoys tremendous success; Harold C. Schonberg of the New York *Times* subsequently calls it "the most unusual music festival in America."

Sep. 11   Alice Tully Hall formally opens tonight at Lin-coln Center for the Performing Arts in New York City. The hall seats 1,096 and was specifically designed to ac-commodate performances of chamber music. It is housed on the main floor of the east side of the Juilliard building and was financed, in part, by Miss Alice Tully. It is the new home of the Chamber Music Society of Lincoln Cen-ter and other professional ensembles. Heinrich Keilholz is responsible for the acoustics.

Oct. 26   The new Juilliard School of Music is officially dedicated in ceremonies at the school's 1,096-seat Alice Tully Hall. The $29,500,000 structure is the last building to be erected in the complex known as Lincoln Center for the Performing Arts.

Nov. 6   L'Orchestre de Lyon gives its first concert. Con-ducted in that city by Louis Fremaux, the program consists of music by Igor Stravinsky, Mozart, Claude Debussy and others.

Dec. 2   The Ballet of Flanders is founded today in Antwerp, with Jeanne Brabants appointed artistic director. This new ballet company has three purposes: training dancers, promoting ballet in Belgium and abroad, and providing divertimenti for the Royal Flemish Opera.

1970 Opera

Jan. 22   Carlisle Floyd's opera *Of Mice and Men* receives its world premiere in Seattle, Washington. The work is based on the novel by John Steinbeck.

Feb. 14   *L'idiota*, by Luciano Chailly, premieres in Rome at the Opera. The libretto is by Alberto Lovesso, based on Fedor Dostoevski's novel *The Idiot*. The work is considered one of the composer's best.

May 8   Gunther Schuller's children's opera *The Fisherman and His Wife* premieres in Boston. The piece is based on a fairy tale by the Grimm brothers.

May 24   Hilding Rosenberg's *House with Two Doors* receives its initial performance in Stockholm.

July 19   *The Rising of the Moon*, an opera by Nicholas Maw, premieres at Glyndebourne.

Aug. 12   *Opera*, a spectacle for mixed media by Luciano Berio, receives its first performance in Santa Fe, New Mexico.

1970 Dance

Jan. 29   *In the Night* is performed for the first time by the New York City Ballet in New York City. Considered to be one of Jerome Robbins' most sensitive works, it was conceived as a companion piece to *Dances at a Gathering*. The music is by Chopin, and the dancers are Violette Verdy, Peter Martins, Kay Mazzo, Anthony Blum, Patricia McBride and Francisco Moncion.

Feb. 5   *Who Cares?*, choreographed by George Balanchine, is performed for the first time by the New York City Ballet. The music is by George Gershwin. Patricia McBride, Jacques d'Amboise, Marnee Morris and Karin von Aroldingen lead the cast.

March 2   Rudi van Dantzig choreographs *The Ropes of Time*, to music by Jan Boerman, for The Royal Ballet at Covent Garden in London. The work, which is a vehicle for Rudolf Nureyev, deals with man's journey through life. Diana Vere and Monica Mason are also in the opening night cast.

March 8   *Brouillards* — a one-act ballet choreographed by John Cranko — receives its world premiere by the Stuttgart Ballet in Stuttgart. The ballet, choreographed to piano preludes by Claude Debussy, explores intimate moods and encounters. It becomes one of Cranko's most famous pieces. Judith Reyn, Susanne Hanke, Birgit Keil, Egon Madsen, Richard Cragun and Heinz Clauss star.

March 24   John Cranko's *Poeme de l'extase* — to music by Alexander Scriabin, with decor by Jurgen Rose — is performed for the first time by the Stuttgart Ballet in Stuttgart. The ballet had been created specifically for Margot Fonteyn. The story is about a mature woman who reflects on lost lovers while being sought after by a young man (danced by Egon Madsen).

April 3   Eliot Feld's *Early Songs* — to music by Richard Strauss — is performed for the first time by the American Ballet Company at the Brooklyn Academy of Music in New York City.

July 30   Jerome Robbins' *The Goldberg Variations* — to music by Johann Sebastian Bach, with costumes by Joe Eula — premieres at a special open rehearsal at Saratoga Springs, New York. Danced by Patricia McBride, Helgi Tomasson, Allegra Kent and others of the New York City Ballet, this work is acclaimed as one of Robbins' most important ballets. The movements of the dance, although rooted in classical forms, step into modern ballet with romance, fun and neatness.

Oct. 21   Eliot Feld's *Cortege parisien* — to music by Emmanuel Chabrier, with lighting by Jules Fisher and costumes by Frank Thompson — is premiered by Eliot Feld's American Ballet Company at the Brooklyn Academy of Music in New York City.

Oct. 24   Eliot Feld's *The Consort* — to music by Dowland and Morley, orchestrated by Christopher Keene, with costumes by Stanley Simmons — is premiered by Eliot Feld's American Ballet Company at the Brooklyn Academy of Music in New York City.

Dec. 12   The Kirov Ballet performs for the first time its version of *Hamlet*. This production features choreography by Konstantin Sergeyev, music by Nikolai Chervinsky and decor by Sofia Yunovich.

1970 Instrumental and Vocal Music

Jan. 9   Georges Auric's *Imaginees II* for cello and piano premieres in Paris.

Jan. 11   Charles Wuorinen's *A Song to the Lute in Musicke* premieres in New York City.

Jan. 11   Norman Dello Joio's *Mass* receives its initial performance in Chicago, Illinois.

Jan. 16   *Music in Fifths*, by Philip Glass, receives its first performance in New York City.

Jan. 26   Jean Francaix' Concerto for Violin and Orchestra receives its initial performance in Quebec.

Jan. 29   *In Praise of Shahn*, subtitled *Canticle for Orchestra*, receives its initial performance by Leonard Bernstein and the New York Philharmonic. The work, composed by William Schuman, was commissioned as a tribute to the memory of artist Ben Shahn.

Feb. 5   Elliott Carter's *Concerto for Orchestra* receives its world premiere in New York City. Performed by Leonard Bernstein and the New York Philharmonic, the music's inspiration was a poem by Saint John Perse that describes changing forces. The four movements of the work interpenetrate each other, and each emerges from dense sound against a background of the other movements. Carter states, "As with all my works, the primary intention is expressive." The piece was commissioned to celebrate the 125th anniversary of this orchestra.

Feb. 7   Bruno Maderna's *Grande Aulodia for Flute, Oboe and Orchestra* premieres in Rome.

Feb. 27   Darius Milhaud's *Musique pour Ars Nova* for 13 instruments premieres in Creteil. This chamber piece includes aleatoric passages.

March 21   *Rhapsody for Orchestra*, by Roger Sessions, is premiered by the Baltimore Symphony Orchestra at Carnegie Hall in New York City.

March 24   Earle Brown's *Corroboree* receives its initial performance at the Whitney Museum in New York City. The piece is scored for three pianos.

April 23   Ross Lee Finney's *Remorseless Rush of Time* premieres at Wisconsin State University in River Falls, Wisconsin.

April 28   *Ringing Changes*, by Charles Wuorinen, receives its world premiere by the New Jersey Percussion Ensemble at Paterson State College in New Jersey. Raymond Des-Roches conducts. The work is scored for percussion ensemble — two vibraphones, anvils, almglocken, cymbals, tamtams, timpani, string drum, and chimes. The single-movement work is in F natural which is also the first pitch element of the twelve-tone set the composer uses.

April 28   Frank Martin's *Ballade for Piano and Orchestra* premieres at Western Illinois University in Macomb.

May 13   Milton Babbitt's *String Quartet No. 4* receives its initial performance in Washington, D.C.

May 30   Cristobal Halffter's *Concerto for Flute and Orchestra* premieres in Lisbon.

June 3   Anton Webern's *Two Pieces* (1899) for violoncello and piano is premiered posthumously by Gregor Piatigorsky and Victor Babin in Cleveland. Also premiered today is his *Cello Sonata*, composed in 1914.

July 8   Michael Tippett's *Shires Suite* for chorus and orchestra premieres in Cheltenham, England.

July 13   Morton Feldman's *Mme. Press died last week at 90* for chamber group premieres in Hawaii.

July 26   Easley Blackwood's Piano Concerto receives its first performance in Highland Park, Illinois.

Aug. 4   Jacques Charpentier's Concerto No. 2 for Guitar and Orchestra premieres in Nice.

Sep. 17   Heinrich Sutermeister's *Serenade for Montreux* for two oboes, two horns and string orchestra premieres in Montreux, Switzerland.

Sep. 25   Dominick Argento's *Tria carmina Paschalia* for women's voices, harp and guitar receives its initial performance at Macalester College in Saint Paul, Minnesota.

Oct. 5   Norman Dello Joio's *Evocations* for orchestra and chorus premieres in Tampa, Florida.

Oct. 6   Gian-Carlo Menotti's *Triple Concerto a Tre* is premiered by the American Symphony Orchestra at Carnegie Hall in New York City.

Oct. 8   Karlheinz Stockhausen's *MANTRA* for two pianos premieres in Donaueschingen.

Oct. 8   David Amram's *Fanfare for 17 Brass and Percussion* premieres in Austin, Texas.

Oct. 12   Michael Tippett's *Songs for Dov* for tenor and large chamber orchestra receives its first performance in Cardiff, Wales.

Oct. 14   Witold Lutoslawski's Cello Concerto premieres at Festival Hall in London.

Oct. 31   George Crumb's *Ancient Voices of Children* receives its world premiere at the Library of Congress in Washington, D.C. Scored for soprano, boy soprano and seven instrumentalists, this work makes Crumb an internationally known composer. The music is set to words by Federico Garcia Lorca. Crumb states, "I have sought musical images that enhance and reinforce the powerful, yet strangely haunting imagery of Lorca's poetry."

EGON WELLESZ

Oct. 31   Cristobal Halffter's String Quartet No. 2 (*Memories, 1970*) premieres in Washington, D.C.

Nov. 10   *Music with Changing Parts*, by Philip Glass, receives its initial performance in New York. Also premiered at today's concert is his *Music for Voices*.

Nov. 20   Egon Wellesz' *Pieces* for string quartet, Op. 109, premieres in London.

Nov. 24   George Rochberg's Symphony No. 3 receives its first performance at the Juilliard School in New York City. This piece is scored for solo voices, chamber chorus, double chorus and orchestra. It employs musical quotations from works by Heinrich Schutz, Bach, Gustav Mahler and Charles Ives. Rochberg has renounced 12-tone music and has returned to tonality.

Nov. 29   Charles Ives' orchestral work *The General Slocum* receives its initial performance by the American Symphony Orchestra at Carnegie Hall in New York City. The piece is named after the steamer that exploded in 1903, killing 1,200 people.

Nov. 29   Gunther Schuller's *Contrasts* for woodwind quintet and orchestra premieres at Carnegie Hall in New York City.

Nov. 30   Bulent Arel's *Stereo Electronic Music No. 2* premieres at Columbia University in New York City.

Dec. 17   Darius Milhaud's *Six danses en trois mouvements* for 2 pianos is performed for the first time in Paris.

Dec. 23   Charles Wuorinen's *A Message to Denmark Hill* (a cantata for baritone, flute, cello and piano) premieres in New York City. Also receiving its first performance today is his Sonata for Piano.

1970   Births, Deaths and Debuts

Jan. 4   Mary Louise Curtis Bok Zimbalist, 93, dies in Philadelphia. The wife of violinist Efrem Zimbalist, she founded the Curtis Institute of Music.

Jan. 8   Greek composer Jani Christou, 44, dies near Athens as the result of an automobile accident. This composer created music that often employed multimedia presentations and visual elements. His philosophy of music involved metaphysics, poetry and choreography; he even studied with Jung.

Jan. 21   French mezzo-soprano Jane Bathori, 93, dies in Paris. A singer who also wrote books on vocal interpretation, she sang in the first performances of many works by modern French composers, including Maurice Ravel, Erik Satie, Darius Milhaud and Claude Debussy.

March 23   Pianist Jascha Spivakovsky, 73, dies near Melbourne, Australia. Brother of violinist Tossy Spivakovsky, he performed under Arthur Nikisch, Richard Strauss and Wilhelm Furtwangler.

April 12   Swedish contralto Kerstin Thorborg, 73, dies in Hedemora, Sweden. She began her career as a member of the Stockholm Opera in 1925 and then sang in Berlin and Vienna. In 1936 she created a sensation at Covent Garden as Fricka and was engaged by the Metropolitan Opera, where she sang until 1950, excelling in Wagnerian roles. In addition to her voice, her intelligence and stage presence were also admired.

June 23   Italian composer Alessandro Bustini, 93, dies in Rome. His music, which includes both operatic and symphonic works, was romantic. He taught at the Santa Cecilia Academy.

July 29   Sir John Barbirolli, 70, famous British conductor, dies in London. After studies at the Royal Academy of Music and a debut at age 11 as a cellist, he decided to become a conductor. He held various British posts and was then awarded the conductorship of the New York Philharmonic and later of the Halle Orchestra in Manchester. He was knighted in 1949.

July 29   Russian soprano Oda Slobodskaya, 81, dies in London. She debuted in Petrograd in 1918. After visiting Paris, she settled in London, where she often sang in music halls under the name Odali Caveno. She later sang at Covent Garden, La Scala and the Teatro Colon in Buenos Aires.

July 30   Hungarian conductor George Szell, 73, dies in Cleveland, Ohio. Having started his career as assistant conductor at the Royal Opera of Berlin in 1915, he was appointed conductor of the Strasbourg Municipal Opera at the recommendation of Richard Strauss. From 1924 to 1929 he was conductor of the Berlin State Opera. During World War II he conducted at the Metropolitan Opera for four years and was then given the post of music director of the Cleveland Orchestra, which he led for 24 years until his death. Under his leadership it became one of the best orchestras in the United States. He was a taskmaster who was not universally loved by all the musicians who worked under him, but his musical results were impressive.

Aug. 7   Swedish-American composer-conductor Ingolf Dahl, 58, dies in Frutigen, Switzerland. After studies at the Conservatory of Cologne and the University of Zurich, he emigrated to America and settled in California. He then taught at the University of Southern California and the Berkshire Music Center at Tanglewood. His music is contrapuntal within the context of harmonic dissonance.

Aug. 18   German musicologist Heinrich Strobel, 72, dies in Baden-Baden. He obtained his doctorate in musicology in 1922 and then wrote music criticism for *Borsenkurier* in Berlin. He settled in Baden-Baden after World War II and became an influential figure in new music circles. He edited the periodical *Melos* until his death. In addition to authoring monographs on Claude Debussy, Paul Hindemith and Igor Stravinsky, he was a major force in launching the career of Pierre Boulez.

Sep. 2   Dutch composer Kees van Baaren, 63, dies in Oegstgeest. He studied at the Berlin Hochschule fur Musik and with Willem Pijper in Rotterdam. He began as a traditional composer but, at age 27, destroyed his early works and adopted serial techniques. His Septet for Concertante Violin, Wind Quintet and Double Bass (composed in 1952) was the first integrally serial work to be written by a Dutch composer. He also composed *Musica for 72 Carillons*, and made another version of the piece for 47 carillons. He was a director of the Amsterdam Music Academy, the Conservatory of Utrecht and the Royal Conservatory of The Hague.

Sep. 25   Soviet composer Jefim (Jef) Golyscheff, 73, dies in Paris. After studies in Odessa (violin) and Berlin (chemistry, music theory and painting), he began to develop procedures of composition that to some degree paralleled those of Arnold Schoenberg. While Schoenberg was developing his 12-tone method and exploring abstract-expressionist ideas of painting in Vienna, Golyscheff was developing a serial method involving 12 different durations for the 12 tones of a 12-tone theme. He called these "Zwolftondauer-Komplexen." He was also painting pictures in the style of Dada and futurism. Golyscheff continued his work until the Nazis came to power. He then went to Paris but was incarcerated after the Nazis invaded that city. Although he was Jewish, he was not murdered, perhaps because he was an expert chemist. In 1956 he relocated to Brazil and gave up musical composition for painting. He remained there for 10 years before returning to Paris.

Oct. 11   Cypriot-American composer and pianist Anis Fuleihan, 70, dies in Palo Alto, California. He studied in Cyprus and in New York and began touring America and the Near East as a concert pianist. Other positions included working for G. Schirmer, Inc., teaching at Indiana University and directing the Beirut Conservatory in Lebanon. He organized the Orchestre classique de Tunis in 1963. He wrote many compositions for different instruments. These include an opera, *Vasco*, premiered in 1960, many concertos, five string quartets, 11 piano sonatas, choral works and songs.

Oct. 22   French pianist Samson Francois, 46, dies in Paris. He studied at the Nice Conservatory and with Alfred Cortot. Touring as a concert pianist he debuted in America in 1947 and toured China in 1964. He was revered for his renditions of Claude Debussy's piano music.

Dec. 5   Austrian composer-conductor Ferdinand Grossmann, 83, dies in Vienna. After studies with Felix Weingartner in Vienna, he founded the Chamber Chorus of the Vienna Academy of Music and toured America and Europe. His *German Mass* (a cappella) was composed in 1952.

1970   *Related Events*

Seiji Ozawa is appointed music director of the San Francisco Symphony Orchestra this year, succeeding Josef Krips, who becomes conductor emeritus. Ozawa continues in this post until 1977 (he is appointed music director of the Boston Symphony Orchestra in 1973 and commutes between Boston and San Francisco for four years to fulfill his contractual obligations).

Quadraphonic discs as well as 4-channel reel and cartridge tapes are introduced in the recording industry for commercial release this year by Columbia (U.S.), Sansui (Japan), and RCA.

Feb. 8   Yuri Simonov, 28, is named first conductor of the Bolshoi Theater, replacing Gennady Rozhdestvensky.

April 3   The Hopkinson Verdi Collection is acquired by the National Library of Scotland in Edinburgh. This collection of approximately 430 items had been purchased from Cecil Hopkinson and consists largely of printed vocal scores and librettos of operas by Giuseppe Verdi. Hopkinson's two-volume bibliography of Verdi (Broude, 1973–76) describes the early editions of the scores.

May 4   Charles Wuorinen is awarded the Pulitzer Prize for music for *Time's Encomium*. This is the first time this prize is given for an electronic composition.

Sep. 4   While on tour in London, Kirov ballerina Natalia Makarova seeks and obtains political asylum in Great Britain.

Sep. 7   An international congress entitled "New Music and Its Criticism" takes place in Rotterdam as a preface to this year's Guadeamus Music Week. Lasting two days, the congress explores the issues of interpretation of new music, music criticism and the public, the function of music criticism and other related topics. The congress is held under the auspices of the International Music Council of UNESCO. It is reviewed in a subsequent issue of *Sonorum Speculum*, published by the Donemus Foundation. The reviewer concludes his criticism by saying that "Much could be improved if critics were to be more organized."

Oct. 25   American pianist Garrick Ohlsson, 22, wins the eighth international Chopin Festival in Warsaw. This festival is an important piano competition.

Dec. 11   What would have been the first U.S. tour of the entire Bolshoi Opera and Ballet companies, which had been arranged by impresario Sol Hurok, is canceled in response to a bomb explosion at the Soviet airline office in New York and a sit-in at the Washington office of the news agency Tass. The incidents were supposedly to protest harassment of Jews in the Soviet Union.

1971 Opera

April 29   *Melusine,* an opera by German composer Aribert Reimann, receives its first performance in Schwetzingen as part of the Schwetzinger Festspiele. Commissioned by the Sueddeutsche Rundfunk in Stuttgart, the work is based on a play by Ivan Goll and has a libretto by Claus H. Henneberg.

May 16   Benjamin Britten's television opera *Owen Wingrave* is premiered by both BBC-TV in London and PBS-TV in New York City. This opera is based on the story by Henry James.

May 23   The first performance of Gottfried von Einem's *Der Besuch der alten Dame* takes place in Vienna at the Statsoper. The libretto is based on the tragicomedy by Friedrich Durrenmatt.

June 19   Lee Hoiby's opera *Summer and Smoke,* based on a play by Tennessee Williams, premieres in Saint Paul, Minnesota.

Aug. 12   Heitor Villa Lobos' *Yerma* premieres posthumously in Santa Fe, New Mexico. The last opera Villa Lobos composed, it is based on a work by Federico Garcia Lorca.

Sep. 10   Alberto Ginastera's *Beatrix Cenci* receives its world premiere at the Kennedy Center in Washington, D.C. This opera is the final work of a trilogy drawn from historic characters.

Oct. 14   Dominick Argento's *Postcard from Morocco*, with a text by John Donahue, is premiered by the Minnesota Opera Company in Minneapolis.

SCENE FROM *MELUSINE*

1971 Dance

March 11   Rudolf Nureyev stars in Maurice Bejart's *Songs of a Wayfarer*, set to Gustav Mahler's *Lieder Eines Fahren-den Gesellen*. The one-act ballet deals with a discontented student soothed by fate. Paolo Bortoluzzi completes the opening night cast. The performance takes place in Brussels.

March 23   *Creation of the World*, choreographed by Natalia Kasatkina and Vladimir Vasilov to music by Andrei Petrov, is performed for the first time in Leningrad. This ballet is based on drawings by Jean Effel.

April 20   Eliot Feld's *Romance*, to music by Brahms, is premiered by Eliot Feld's American Ballet Company in New York City.

April 28   *The Gods Amused*, a ballet choreographed by Eliot Feld to music by Claude Debussy, receives its world premiere by Eliot Feld's American Ballet Company at the Brooklyn Academy of Music in New York City. This pas de trois for two women and one man includes costumes by Frank Thompson and lighting by Jennifer Tipton.

July 1   Choreographer Dennis Nahat's *Mendelssohn Symphony* — to music by Felix Mendelssohn, with costumes by Robert O'Hearn — is performed for the first time by the American Ballet Theater in New York. Cynthia Gregory stars in this abstract work.

July 7   Erik Bruhn's staging of *La Sylphide* is performed for the first time by the American Ballet Theater in New York City. This version subsequently joins the repertories of the National Ballet of Canada and the Royal Swedish Ballet.

July 22   Choreographer Kenneth MacMillan's *Anastasia* — to music by Tchaikovsky and Bohuslav Martinu, with costumes and decor by Barry Kay — is premiered by The Royal Ballet in London. The work, based on the story of Grand Duchess Anastasia, is created for Lynn Seymour.

July 27   *The Ecstasy of Rita Joe* receives its initial performance in Ottawa. Although only a partial presentation of the piece, this event marks the unusual appearance of a multimedia ballet. Choreographed by Norbert Vesak to music by Ann Mortifee, the ballet also includes film, directed by S. Williams. Costumes and lighting are by Vesak. Performed by the Royal Winnipeg Ballet, the story is about an Indian girl and her move into the big bad city. Lead dancers are Ana Maria Gorriz and Salvatore Aiello.

Sep. 21   John Cage's *62 Mesostics re Merce Cunningham* for solo voice and dancer premieres at the Hellenic Festival in Athens. Cage also begins studying the writings of Mao Tse-tung this year.

Oct. 8   Maurice Bejart's *Nijinsky, Clown of God* is premiered by the Ballet of the 20th Century in Brussels. The music is by Pierre Henry and Tchaikovsky, with costumes by Joette Roustan and Roger Bernard. This monumental work is about Vaslav Nijinsky and the progression of his life from choreographic glory to madness. The lead dancers are Jorge Donn and Suzanne Farrell.

Dec. 3   The Museum of Modern Art hosts the first performance of Merce Cunningham's *Loops*, a modern dance piece. The music is by Gordon Mumma.

1971 Instrumental and Vocal Music

Jan. 31   *Juilliard Serenade*, by Bruno Maderna, receives its first performance in New York, the composer conducting. This instrumental piece is scored for chamber orchestra and taped sounds.

Feb. 2   Carl Ruggles' *Evocations* premieres in its orchestral version at Carnegie Hall in New York City. The earlier version was for piano.

Feb. 5   William Sydeman's *Malediction* premieres at Alice Tully Hall in New York City. This work is scored for tenor, speaking actor, string quartet and electronic tape. The text is from *Tristram Shandy*, by Laurence Sterne.

Feb. 11   Hans Werner Henze's *Bars for Self-Centered Questions* premieres in Basel. This work is scored for viola and 22 players.

Feb. 16   R. Murray Schafer's *No Longer than Ten Minutes* premieres in Toronto. The title of this orchestral piece is derived from its maximum length.

Feb. 21   Ulysses Kay's *Aulos* for solo flute and orchestra premieres at Indiana University in Bloomington.

Feb. 25   Morton Subotnick's *Misfortunes of the Immortals: A Concert* premieres at the Hunter College Playhouse in New York City. Subotnick is now Associate Dean and Director of Electronic Music of the School of Music at the California Institute of the Arts in Los Angeles.

March 5   Symphony No. 9, Op. 113 (*Sinfonia: Janiculum*), by Vincent Persichetti, receives its world premiere. Eugene Ormandy conducts the Philadelphia Orchestra. Scored for large orchestra with extensive percussion, the symphony has four contiguous sections. It was composed while Persichetti was at the American Academy in Rome. The music incorporates the sounds of bells from a local church near the academy. It was inspired by questions about the creation and meaning of life. Janiculum refers to the Roman deity Janus and, indirectly, to the month of January and the Janiculum Hill — the highest hill in Rome. The work contains passages of brilliant orchestral color, suggesting creation, and a powerful closing coda. It is, perhaps, Persichetti's masterpiece.

March 7   Otto Luening's Sonata No. 3 for Solo Violin premieres in New York City.

March 12   Luciano Berio's *Memory* for electronic piano and electronic harpsichord receives its initial performance in New York City.

March 22   Lennox Berkeley's *Chinese Songs* premieres at the Purcell Room in London.

April 5   Luciano Berio's *Prayer* for voices and chamber ensemble premieres in New York City, the composer conducting.

April 6   Iannis Xenakis' *Synaphai* for one or two pianos and orchestra premieres at the Festival de Royan.

April 19   George Perle's *Three Movements for Orchestra* receives its initial performance at Carnegie Hall in New York City.

April 27   William Bolcom's *Whisper Moon* is premiered by the Aeolian Chamber Players in New York City.

May 4   Isang Yun's *Namo* for three sopranos and orchestra is premiered by Michael Gielen in West Berlin.

May 18   Richard Rodney Bennett's *Party Piece* for piano and orchestra premieres in Farnham, England.

June 2   Harrison Birtwistle's orchestral work *An Imaginary Landscape* is premiered in London, conducted by Pierre Boulez.

July 21   *Frescoes*, by William Bolcom, receives its initial performance in Toronto. Bruce Mather performs on piano and harmonium, Pierrette Le Page on piano and harpsichord. The work has two parts — "War in Heaven" and "The Caves of Orcus." The piece was inspired by the frescoes at Campo Santo in Pisa, "bits of Virgil and Milton" and other sources, including one of the composer's early piano duets.

Aug. 19   Luigi Dallapiccola's *Tempus Destruendi — Tempus Aedificandi* premieres in Siena.

Aug. 22   Milton Babbitt's electronic piece *Occasional Variations* premieres at Wolf Trap Farm Park in Virginia.

Sep. 8   *Mass, A Theatre Piece for Singers, Players and Dancers,* by Leonard Bernstein, receives its world premiere at the Kennedy Center in Washington, D.C. Maurice Peress conducts. Choreography is by Alvin Ailey, orchestrations by Jonathan Tunick, Hershey Kay and the composer. The text is from the liturgy of the Roman Mass with additional texts by Stephan Schwartz and the composer. This piece is Bernstein's first major work since he became laureate conductor of the New York Philharmonic. The music explores the crisis of faith as the crisis of the 20th century.

Sep. 10   *Fadograph of a Yestern Scene* receives its premiere performance in Pittsburgh. This new work by Samuel Barber is based on James Joyce's *Finnegan's Wake*. It is scored for orchestra.

Sep. 22   Samuel Barber's cantata *The Lovers* receives its initial performance in Philadelphia. It is scored for baritone, chorus and orchestra. The text is excerpted from writings by Pablo Neruda.

Sep. 30   *Holiday Overture*, by William Mathias, is broadcast over BBC radio, marking the work's premiere.

Oct. 11   String Quartet, by Charles Wuorinen, receives its initial performance by the Fine Arts Quartet in Chicago.

Nov. 5   Roger Sessions' Concerto for Violin, Cello and Orchestra premieres at the Juilliard School in New York City.

Nov. 13   Alan Hovhaness' *Saturn*, Op. 243, for clarinet, soprano and piano premieres at Carnegie Recital Hall in New York City.

Nov. 28   Symphony No. 4 (*Quatrieme symphonie du "troisieme age"*), by Henri Sauguet, premieres in Paris.

Dec. 10   Gyorgy Ligeti's orchestral work *Melodien* is premiered by H. Gierster in Nuremburg.

Dec. 14   Marcel Mihalovici's *Symphony for Soprano and Orchestra*, Op. 5, is premiered by the Philarmonique Orchestre de l'ORTF in Paris.

1971   Births, Deaths and Debuts

Jan. 18   New Zealand conductor Warwick Braithwaite, 73, dies in London. A student at the Royal Academy of Music, he went on to conduct many musical organizations of note, including the National Orchestra of Wales, the Sadler's Wells Opera Orchestra in London and the Scottish Orchestra in Glasgow.

Jan. 25   Martha Baird Rockefeller, 75, dies in New York City. She was a generous philanthropist and established a fund for young American composers to advance their careers.

March 6   English musicologist and harpsichordist Thurston Dart, 49, dies in London. After studies at the Royal College of Music, he held teaching positions at Cambridge University and, from 1964, at Kings College at the University of London. His specialty was old English music, and he wrote articles for many music journals on the subject. Also a fine harpsichord player, he appears on many recordings, often contributing to the realizations of these old compositions. He is the author of *The Interpretation of Music*, published in 1954 in London.

March 13   Italian conductor Piero Coppola, 82, dies in Lausanne. A composer of operas (*Sirmione* and *Nikita*), he also wrote symphonic works. He conducted at La Scala and in Paris.

April 3   Israeli violinist Pinchas Zuckerman makes his New York debut.

April 6   Igor Stravinsky, 88, dies in New York City. His father was Feodor Stravinsky, a bass at the Russian Imperial Opera. His parents insisted that he study law and he began those studies at the University of Saint Petersburg but continued studying music and composing as an amateur. At age 19 he showed his work to Nikolai Rimsky-Korsakov. That composer encouraged him and Stravinsky began devoting himself completely to music, studying music theory and harmony with Vassili Kalafati and composition with Rimsky-Korsakov.

Stravinsky's public premiere came on February 5, 1908, when his Symphony in E-flat Major, Op. 1, was performed in Saint Petersburg. This was followed by *Scherzo fantastique* premiered in 1909 in the same city. Serge Diaghilev heard the latter work and, after Anatoly Liadov turned down an opportunity to compose a new ballet for Diaghilev's Paris season, offered the commission to Stravinsky. The new work was to be a ballet on a Russian subject and the result was *The Firebird* (premiered in 1910), the first of his great ballets. Stravinsky was then 28.

In 1911, he relocated to Paris and his professional relationship with Diaghilev blossomed into a revolutionary force in the worlds of dance and music. *Petrouchka* premiered in 1911 and was highly acclaimed. Two years later, Stravinsky stunned the world with *Le Sacre du printemps*, which sparked a riot because of its interacting layers of animated rhythms, its harmonic tension and primitivistic sound. Critics attacked this work which virtually signalled a move away from post-impressionism.

At the beginning of World War I, Stravinsky moved with his wife and children to Switzerland but continued to base his music on Russian subjects. Around 1918 he began to embrace an economy of instrumentation. He and Diaghilev collaborated again on new works. These include the ballet *Pulcinella* and the operas *Mavra* and *Renard*. Stravinsky then moved away from Russian subjects and became preoccupied with an experimental reviving of old musical forms.

In 1920 Stravinsky settled in France (he became a French citizen in 1934). He performed as a conductor during his years in Europe, visiting America twice. With the onset of World War II he moved to the United States, becoming an American citizen in 1945.

Stravinsky's music can be described in terms of four stylistic periods: nationalism, post-impressionism and neo-primitivism; economy of means and a cosmopolitan style with a French orientation; neo-classicism; and serialism.

The first period is characterized by subjects based on Russian folklore and pagan rites, scintillating orchestral colors, bitonality and polytonality, and relentless, but controlled rhythmic drive. Examples of works from this period include the ballets *The Firebird*, *Petrouchka* and *Le Sacre du printemps*.

His second period — which occured roughly during the second decade of the century — was characterized by lean instrumentation and, in addition to Russian subjects, was also based on folklore of other cultures. Works composed during this period include *L'histoire du soldat* for narrator and seven instruments (premiered in 1918); the ballet *Pulcinella* (premiered in 1920); *Renard*, a burlesque for chamber orchestra (premiered in 1922); and the ballet *Les Noces*, scored for chorus, soloists, four pianos and 17 percussion instruments (premiered in 1923).

Stravinsky's third period — neo-classicism — had a dramatic impact on the music of this century. It began at approximately the same time as Arnold Schoenberg's introduction of the 12-tone system, and had a comparable influence on musical life and on young composers. This stylistic period was a logical outgrowth of the economic confusion resulting from World War I that continued to make it difficult to finance large musical productions. In this period Stravinsky looked to the past and revived it within a 20th-century context. His neo-classical music, and the movement in music it spawned, exhibits the following characteristics: Resurrection of the diatonic scale; absence of romantic harmony and programs in titles; revival of Baroque forms, particularly the toccata, passacaglia, scherzo, serenade and sonata; diminished appearance of decorative devices; compaction to one movement of previously larger forms; an emphasis on keyboard instruments, such as the piano and harpsichord; canonic and fugal composition without following the rules of classical voice-leading; and brief development sections coupled with brief recapitulations. Works composed during this period include *Symphonies of Wind Instruments* (premiered in 1921); Concerto for Piano and Wind Orchestra (premiered in 1924); the pantomime *Apollon Musagete* (premiered in 1928); *Capriccio* for Piano and Orchestra (premiered in 1929); the *Serenade in A* for for piano (composed in 1925); the opera-oratorio *Oedipus Rex* (first premiered in concert form, 1927); the *Symphony of Psalms* (premiered in 1930); and the *Dumbarton Oaks Concerto* (premiered in 1938). It was not until 1945 that Stravinsky returned to a musical expression marked by a largeness of gesture and form (*Symphony in Three Movements*, premiered in 1946). This period ended with his opera *The Rake's Progress* (premiered in 1951).

The death of Arnold Schoenberg and Stravinsky's intense attraction to things intellectual turned him suddenly and unexpectedly to using serial techniques. This turn of events was in clear opposition to his youthful, public assault on dodecaphonic music. Stravinsky employed a serial operation known as rotation and combined it with transposition so that a composite form of rotation resulted. In his 12-tone music each strand of pitch elements begins on the same pitch class but is not confined to one stage of a pitch cycle. Works from this period have had a strong influence on young composers both in Europe and in America. Examples of these compositions include *Canticum sacrum ad honorem Sancti Marci nominis* for tenor, baritone, chorus and orchestra (premiered in 1956); the ballet *Agon* (premiered in 1957); *A Sermon, A Narrative and a Prayer* (composed 1960-61); and *Requiem Canticles* for vocal quartet, chorus and orchestra (premiered in 1966). This last work is also performed during the old master's burial in the Russian corner of San Michele Cemetery in Venice.

Stravinsky's ties with his native Russia were severed by the Russian Revolution. He resented Soviet attitudes toward dissonance in music and was himself accused by Soviet critics of Parisian exhibitionism. That Stravinsky enjoyed making money also did not endear him to the Communists. During most of his life his work was not performed in the Soviet Union. Once he began to use serial procedures Soviet critics consistently criticized his music. It was only in 1962, when Stravinsky visited his native land and met Nikita Khrushchev, that his music suddenly began to be performed in the Soviet Union and analyzed from a scholarly perspective.

May 11   Opera administrator David Webster, 67, dies in London. He began staging operas while an undergraduate. After entering the business world, he became chairman of the Liverpool Philharmonic Society. In 1945, he was appointed general administrator of Covent Garden's Royal Opera House. He was known for his financial abilities. He also saw to it that Covent Garden became the permanent home of the Sadler's Wells Ballet as well as the Royal Opera.

May 26   American composer Mark Brunswick, 69, dies in London. He led a cosmopolitan life, in that he began his studies in New York with Rubin Goldmark, then studied with Ernest Bloch in Cleveland and with Nadia Boulanger in Paris. He lived, for a time, in Vienna and eventually returned to New York, the city of his birth, to teach. His best-known works include *Eros and Death* (a choral symphony) and *The Master Builder* (an incomplete opera).

May 30   French organist and composer Marcel Dupre, 85, dies in Meudon, near Paris. The winner of many prizes (including the Prix de Rome), he performed as an organist around the world and toured America 10 times. He wrote two books on organ playing, one of which is a treatise on improvisation. His compositions are, in many cases, the result of improvisation. *Le chemin de la croix* is perhaps his most famous piece.

June 5   James Levine, 28, conducts for the first time at the Metropolitan Opera. The opera is *Tosca*. He is later appointed music director of the company.

Aug. 6   Italian-American conductor Fausto Cleva, 69, dies in Athens while conducting. He was chorusmaster and conductor of the Metropolitan Opera and was later conductor of the San Francisco Opera Company.

Sep. 14   Harald Lander, former ballet master of the Royal Danish Ballet, dies in Copenhagen at the age of 66. Lander was trained at the Royal Danish Ballet School and became one of the company's leading character dancers before being appointed ballet master in 1930. During Lander's tenure, the Company entered a period of great artistic creativity. Among his own ballets are *Etudes* and *Qarrtsiluni*. Lander was also responsible for the beginning of the Bournonville renaissance; under his direction, all the extant ballets of August Bournonville were revived in productions as close to the originals as possible. These have proved the foundation of the Royal Dansih Ballets modern repertory. Lander also revised Hans Beck's staging of *Coppelia*, one of the company's most successful ballets.

Lander was made director of the Royal Danish Ballet School in 1932. Under his direction the school produced some of the most important dancers in Denmark's history, including Borge Ralov, Margot Lander and Erik Bruhn. Lander left the Royal Danish Ballet in 1951 and became ballet master of the Paris Opera in 1953. He also served as director of the Paris Opera School from 1956 to 1957 and from 1959 to 1963.

Oct. 2   German heldentenor Rudolf Laubenthal, 85, dies in Starnbergersee. He made his debut in Berlin and sang both at Covent Garden and with the New York Metropolitan Opera. He also sang in the American premiere of Ernst Krenek's *Jonny Spielt Auf*.

Oct. 16   Michael Tilson Thomas makes his debut as the new music director of the Buffalo Philharmonic Symphony Society. He remains in this post for eight years, when he is succeeded by Julius Rudel. The concert takes place at the Kleinhans Music Hall in Buffalo, New York.

Dec. 6   Mathilda Kschessinska, former prima ballerina assoluta of the Maryinsky Theatre, dies in Paris at the age of 99. One of the most important ballerinas of her generation, she was noted for her clean, precise style, and her strength. She was the first Russian-born ballerina to execute 32 consecutive fouettes. Her technical brilliance made Russian dancers technique-concious.

Kschessinska graduated from the Saint Petersburg Imperial Ballet School in 1890 and was appointed a ballerina in 1892. She was made prima ballerina assoluta in 1895 (the only dancer other than Pierina Legnani to be awarded that title officially). The mistress of Czar Nicholas II, she had tremendous influence in the Imperial Theater. Following the Russian Revolution, she settled in France, where she married the Grand Duke Andre and opened a ballet school. She last appeared on the stage in 1936.

Dec. 7   Australian soprano Marie Collier, 45, dies in London in a fall from her third floor apartment window. Her teachers included Nellie Melba and Gertrude Johnson. She debuted in Melbourne in 1954 and then undertook further studies in Milan with Ugo Benvenuti Giusti. She sang at Covent Garden throughout her career and was especially noted for her performances of operas by Leos Janacek and Giacomo Puccini.

1971 Related Events

Pierre Boulez becomes music director of the New York Philharmonic. He is the first Frenchman to hold this post and strives to place more contemporary music on this orchestra's programs.

Boulez on Music Today is published this year by Faber and Faber. The book is translated from the French by Susan Bradshaw and Richard Rodney Bennett. Boulez analyzes attitudes about musical composition and attacks avant-garde composers he considers intellectually deficient. He writes in depth about aspects of serial composition. The Times Educational Supplement says it may be "the best grammar of advanced musical language so far available to us."

The Classical Style: Haydn, Mozart, Beethoven is published this year in New York. This book, by Charles Rosen, explores the music of these three composers from the perspective of a brilliant writer, pianist and musicologist. The monograph receives the National Book Award next year.

Jan. 13   The Soviet government cancels a scheduled tour to Finland by cellist Mstislav Rostropovich. This was to be his first tour abroad since he publicly defended writer Alexander Solzhenitsyn against attacks in the Soviet press.

May 3   Mario Davidovsky is awarded the Pulitzer Prize for music for *Synchronisms* No. 6.

Sep. 8   Many celebrities are on hand to celebrate the opening of the Kennedy Center in Washington, D.C. Among the works performed in the two-day gala is a new mass by Leonard Bernstein.

Sep. 10   Heinz Hall — the new home of the Pittsburgh Symphony Orchestra in Pittsburgh, Pennsylvania — is inaugurated today with that ensemble performing under the baton of its music director, William Steinberg. The hall seats 2,847 and was a gift to the orchestra from the Howard Heinz Endowment. The lobby features two chandeliers, each weighing more than a ton; the entire building cost $10 million and took 16 months to erect.

Oct. 9   Olivier Messiaen is awarded the Sibelius Prize in Helsinki.

Oct. 28   The Cairo Opera House, built in 1869 to celebrate the opening of the Suez Canal, is destroyed by fire. The theater was famous for having hosted the premiere of Giuseppe Verdi's opera *Aida* in 1871.

1972 Opera

May 11   American composer Tom Johnson's *Four-Note Opera* premieres at the Cubiculo Theater in New York City.

July 12   Peter Maxwell Davies' opera *Taverner* is premiered as Edward Downes conducts at the Royal Opera House in London.

Aug. 15   Rafael Kubelik's *Cornelia Faroli* premieres in Augsburg, the composer conducting. This is one of two operas composed by this famous conductor.

Sep. 7   Sylvano Bussotti's *Lorenzaccio* receives its premiere in Venice at the Teatro la Fenice. The libretto, written by the composer, was inspired by the play of the same title by Alfred de Musset. Bussotti designs 230 costumes for this big grand opera; it opens the Venice Festival of Contemporary Music.

1972 Dance

Jan. 6   Eliot Feld's *Theatre* — to music by Richard Strauss, with costumes by Frank Thompson — is premiered by the American Ballet Theater.

Feb. 3   *Watermill* receives its world premiere by the New York City Ballet in New York. The work is choreographed by Jerome Robbins to music by Teijo Ito, with decor by David Reppa and the choreographer. It is inspired by the

Japanese No theater. Edward Villella dances the lead role in this work about youth and the passage of time.

Feb. 19 Flemming Flindt's *Triumph of Death*, to rock music by Thomas Koppel, is performed live by the Royal Danish Ballet in Copenhagen. The work was originally premiered as a television production. The work disturbs many because of its use of nudity.

April 6 *Tales of Hoffmann*, a three-act ballet, is premiered by the Scottish National Ballet in Edinburgh. The choreography is by Peter Darrell to music by Jacques Offenbach arranged by John Lanchberry, and the principal dancers include Patricia Rianne and Hiday Debden. The work is subsequently danced by the American Ballet Theater in 1973.

June 11 The ballet *Anna Karenina* receives its first performance at the Bolshoi Ballet in Moscow. The choreography is by Maya Plisetskaya, Natalia Ryzhenko and Vladimir Smirnov-Golovanov. The music is by Rodion Shchedrin; costumes by Pierre Cardin. Plisetskaya dances the title role in this work based on the Tolstoy novel.

June 18-25 The Stravinsky Festival begins at the New York State Theater at Lincoln Center in New York City. It spans eight days and features 20 world premieres, with a total of 31 ballet performances. Ballets choreographed by George Balanchine, Jerome Robbins, John Clifford, John Taras, Richard Tanner, Todd Bolender and Leonide Massine are danced to the music of Igor Stravinsky. The festival, one of the first to occur after the death of the old master last year, is also one of the most magnificent.

PETER MARTINS

June 18 George Balanchine's *Violin Concerto* — to music by Igor Stravinsky, with lighting by Ronald Bates — is premiered by the New York City Ballet in New York. Kay Mazzo, Peter Martins, Karin Von Aroldingen and Jean-Pierre Bonnefous lead the cast in this work incorporating visualized rhythms suggested by the music. The event is part of the Lincoln Center Stravinsky Festival. Also premiered on today's program is Balanchine's *Symphony in three Movements* — to music by Stravinsky, with lighting by Ronald Bates. Sara Leland, Marnee Morris, Lynda Yourth, Helgi Tomasson, Edward Villella and Robert Weiss lead the company in this abstract ballet. The final premiere today is Jerome Robbins' *Scherzo fantastique*. Bart Cook and Gelsey Kirkland dance this pas de deux of romance.

June 20 George Balanchine's version of *Danses concertantes* is revived for New York's Stravinsky Festival at Lincoln Center. The work, performed by the New York City Ballet, remains in that company's repertoire.

June 21 George Balanchine's version of the divertissement *Le Baiser de la Fée* is performed by the New York City Ballet at Lincoln Center in New York, celebrating the Stravinsky Festival. *Scherzo a la Russe* also premieres as part of the festival today.

June 22 George Balanchine's *Duo concertante* receives its world premiere at the Stravinsky Festival in New York City. With lighting by Ronald Bates and featuring Kay Mazzo and Peter Martins as lead dancers, this pas de deux is choreographed to Igor Stravinsky's concerto of the same title. Also performed at today's dance concert is *Scenes du ballet*, choreographed by John Taras.

June 23 Jerome Robbins' *Dumbarton Oaks* — to music by Igor Stravinsky, with costumes by Patricia Zipprodt — is premiered by the New York City Ballet as part of the Stravinsky Festival in New York. The lead dancers are Anthony Blum and Allegra Kent. Also danced at today's performance is a production of *Pulcinella*, by Jerome Robbins and George Balanchine. The costumes and decor are by Eugene Berman.

June 25 During the Stravinsky Festival the New York City Ballet premieres Jerome Robbins' *Requiem Canticles*. The work, in six movements, is an abstract setting of Igor Stravinsky's piece by the same name. Merrill Ashley, Susan Hendl, Bruce Wells and Robert Maiorano star. Also premiered is George Balanchine's *Choral Variations* on Bach's tune "Vom Himmel hoch." The music is by Igor Stravinsky, with decor by Rouben Ter-Arutunian.

Sep. 1 Rudolf Nureyev's *The Sleeping Beauty* is performed for the first time by the National Ballet of Canada. The decor for this production is by Nicholas Georgiadis.

Oct. 2 Jose Limon's *Orfeo* is performed for the first time at the American Dance Marathon of the American National Theater Association. On October 5 his new work *Carlotta* also premieres at this festival.

1972 *Instrumental and Vocal Music*

Jan. 16   George Crumb's *Lux Aeternae for 5 Masked Musicians* is premiered by the Philadelphia Composers' Forum in Richmond, Virginia. This work is scored for soprano, bass flute, sitar and two percussion players.

Jan. 20   Seymour Shifrin's *Satires and circumstance* is premiered by Peter Maxwell Davies and The Fires of London in London. The piece is scored for soprano, flute, clarinet, violin, cello, double bass and piano.

Feb. 8   Piano Concerto No. 2, by Tikhon Khrennikov, is premiered by E. Svetlanov in Moscow, with the composer as soloist.

Feb. 23   William Albright's *Marginal Worlds* receives its initial performance by Edwin London and the Contemporary Chamber Players at the University of Illinois Music School in that state. The piece is scored for winds, strings, piano and percussion.

March 3   . . . *Explosante/fixe.* . . receives its world premiere in Stuttgart. Composed by Pierre Boulez, this work employs a computer to make decisions concerning the order of entrances of the instrumental parts. The halaphone, a new electronic device, also alters instrumental "explosions" in progress while the human players perform. The work is scored for halaphone, vibraphone, harp, violin, viola, cello, flute, clarinet and trumpet and is subsequently performed in New York and London. It is dedicated to the memory of Bruno Maderna. One aspect of the halaphone's use is that the duration of the piece varies from performance to performance. Also receiving its premiere today is Boulez' *Domaines encore.*

March 16   Anton Webern's "Rasch," from his *Eight Orchestra Fragments* and his *String Trio Movement* (1927), are premiered posthumously by Friedrich Cerha at the Fifth International Webern Festival in Vienna.

March 20   Olivier Messiaen's *Meditations sur le mystere de la Sainte-Trinite* for organ receives its world premiere by the composer at the National Shrine of the Immaculate Conception in Washington, D.C. The composer is subsequently made doctor honoris causa of Catholic University, Washington, D.C.

March 20   *Grand Bamboula for String Orchestra*, by Charles Wuorinen, receives its first performance at Stonybrook, New York. Paul Zukofsky conducts.

March 28   Olivier Messiaen's *La transfiguration de Notre Seigneur Jesus Christ* receives its first American performance by Antal Dorati and the Washington National Orchestra at the Kennedy Center in Washington, D.C.

April 9   *Rothko Chapel*, by Morton Feldman, receives its world premiere in Houston, Texas. The work — scored for viola, percussion and chorus — was inspired by the chapel of the same name in Houston. Painter Mark Rothko, who painted 14 paintings that are hung throughout the octagonal chapel, conceived of the chapel as a place where people of all faiths could enjoy contemplation and silence. Feldman's music contains four basic sections and includes melodic references to other experiences during the composer's life, including Igor Stravinsky's funeral. Feldman characterizes this music as "an immobile procession not unlike the friezes on Greek temples."

April 26   Iannis Xenakis' *Linaia-Agon* for horn, tenor, trombone and tuba premieres in London.

April 26   Virgil Thomson's *Sneden's Landing with Variations* is premiered by soprano Phyllis Curtin at the Whitney Museum in New York City. Also premiered on this program are Ned Rorem's *For Poulenc* and *I Will Always Love You.*

May 2   Hans Werner Henze's orchestral piece *Heliogabalus Imperator* is premiered by conductor Georg Solti in Chicago.

May 4   Benjamin Lees' Sonata for Violin and Piano is premiered by Rafael Druian and Ilse von Alpenheim at the Coolidge Auditorium in the Library of Congress in Washington, D.C.

May 5   Karlheinz Stockhausen's *Interval* for two pianos four hands premieres in London. Also receiving its first performance at this concert is Stockhausen's *Expo fur 3, ubereinstimmung.*

May 15   Richard Rodney Bennett's *Nightpiece* for soprano and tape premieres in London.

May 29   *Blind Man's Bluff*, by Peter Maxwell Davies, premieres in London. This piece is scored for soprano, dancer, mime and small ensemble.

June 1   Harrison Birtwistle's *A Triumph of Time* receives its first performance by Lawrence Foster and the Royal Philharmonic Orchestra. This work derives its inspiration from a painting of Brueghel.

June 7   *Three Latin-American Sketches*, by Aaron Copland, is premiered by Andre Kostelanetz and the New York Philharmonic in New York City.

June 13   John Cage's *Variations I (Version Welin 1972)* premieres in Nuremberg.

June 20   Ernst Krenek's *Kitharaulos* for harp, oboe and chamber orchestra premieres in The Hague.

June 22   Michael Tippett's Symphony No. 3 receives its world premiere in London. Colin Davis conducts.

July 16   Morton Feldman's *Pianos and Voices* premieres in West Berlin.

Aug. 4   Concerto for Electrified Violin, by Charles Wuorinen, is premiered by Michael Tilson Thomas and the Boston Symphony Orchestra at Tanglewood in Lenox, Massachusetts, with Paul Zukofsky as soloist.

Aug. 8   Gunther Schuller's *Invenzione* premieres at the Festival of Contemporary Music at Tanglewood in Lenox, Massachusetts with the composer conducting. Also premiered is Bruno Maderna's *Giardino religioso*, the composer conducting. This work involves both notated and improvisatory sections that carry the players from delicate moments to crashing sonorities.

Aug. 24   *The Great Learning*, by Cornelius Cardew, receives its world premiere by the Scratch Orchestra at a Promenade Concert in London. This unusual piece features whistling, shrieking, speaking and tapping stones. Its text is a translation of writings of Confucius by Ezra Pound. The work is scored for organ and non-speaking chorus. An earlier version was premiered in 1968. Cardew was dissatisfied with that version and rewrote it. He subtitles today's version "Apply Marxism-Leninism-Mao Tsetung Thought in a living way to the problems of the present." Cardew is devoted to leftist politics.

Aug. 30   John Cage's *Birdcage/Momobird* receives its first performance by David Tudor at the Bavarian Broadcasting Studios in Munich.

Aug. 31   American avant-garde composer Christian Wolff's *Burdocks* for one or more orchestras, for trained and untrained musicians, for conventional, exotic and homemade instruments or found objects is performed at the Bavarian Broadcasting Studios Munich and broadcast over radio. Also premiered is Morton Feldman's *Pianos and Voices II* for five pianos and five sopranos.

Sep. 2   Earle Brown's orchestral piece *Time Spans* premieres in Kiel.

Sep. 2   Krzysztof Penderecki's Concerto for Violoncello and Orchestra receives its initial performance by Alexander Gibson and the Scottish National Orchestra, with S. Palm as cello soloist. The performance takes place in Edinburgh.

Sep. 5   Alexander Tcherepnin's Piano Concerto No. 6 premieres in Lucerne, Switzerland.

Sep. 8   Iain Hamilton's Violin Concerto premieres in Edinburgh, Sir William Walton conducting.

Sep. 16   Concerto for Flute, Oboe and Orchestra, by Gyorgy Ligeti, is premiered by the Berlin Philharmonic in West Berlin.

Sep. 21   R. Murray Schafer's *Enchantress* for soprano, flute and eight cellos is premiered by Mary Morrison, Robert Aitken and members of the Vancouver Cello Club in Vancouver, British Columbia.

Oct. 5   Dominick Argento's *A Ring of Time* (*Preludes and Pageants for Orchestra and Bells*) receives its world premiere by the Minnesota Orchestra at the O'Shaughnessy Auditorium in Saint Paul, Minnesota.

Oct. 10   *Vox Balaenae*, by George Crumb, is premiered by the Aeolian Chamber Players in New York City. This music is based on whale songs. It is scored for flute, cello and piano.

Oct. 13   *Hymn to Saint Magnus* by Peter Maxwell Davies premieres in London. This piece is scored for soprano and chamber ensemble.

Oct. 21   John Cage's *Birdcage — 73', 20.958" for a Composer* premieres in Donaueschingen.

Nov. 1   Ross Lee Finney's Piano Concerto No. 2 premieres in Ann Arbor, Michigan.

Nov. 2   Hans Werner Henze's Violin Concerto No. 2 premieres in Basel.

Nov. 3   *The Last Poems of Wallace Stevens*, by Ned Rorem, premieres at Town Hall in New York City.

Nov. 5   Ross Lee Finney's *Landscape Remembered* for chamber orchestra premieres at Cornell University in Ithaca, New York.

Nov. 7   Olivier Messiaen's *La fauvette des jardins* is premiered by Loriod at the Espace Pierre Cardin in Paris.

Nov. 8   Symphony No. 7 (*Israel*) by Robert Casadesus is premiered by Musica Aeterna and Chorus at Alice Tully Hall in New York City.

Nov. 14   Harry Somer's *Voiceplay* is premiered by vocalist Cathy Berberian at the University of Toronto. This piece is written for a male or female singer/actor.

Nov. 19   Benjamin Lees' *Concerto for Orchestra* is premiered by Antal Dorati and the National Symphony Orchestra at Philharmonic Hall at Lincoln Center in New York City.

Nov. 29   Egon Wellesz' *Vision* is premiered by soprano Christiane Sorell and the ORF Symphony Orchestra in Vienna.

Dec. 16   Andrzej Panufnik's cantata *Winter Solstice* premieres in London.

1972   Births, Deaths and Debuts

Jan. 9   Dancer and choreographer Ted Shawn dies in Orlando, Florida at the age of 80. One of the most important figures in the history of American dance, Shawn began performing in 1911. In 1914 he married Ruth Saint Denis, and together they established Denishawn, a school and company that became one of the foundations of modern dance. In 1933 he founded an All-Male Dancers Group which he toured until it was broken up in World War II. He acquired Jacob's Pillow, a farm near Lee, Massachusetts in 1933 and gradually developed it as the site of one of the most important annual dance festivals. Shawn's contributions to American dance are many: he developed a technique for male dancers that became vitally important in assuring them equal place with women in modern dance; he was a primary force in overcoming prejudice against male dancing in the United States; he helped develop liturgical dance; he introduced ethnic dance forms into dance teaching; and he championed the use of concert music in dance.

Jan. 20   French pianist Jean Casadesus, 44, dies in an automobile accident near Renfrew, Ontario. Son of Robert and Gaby Casadesus, he studied with his parents and at Princeton University. After winning a competition for young pianists organized by the Philadelphia Orchestra, he went on to appear with American and European orchestras.

Feb. 22   Dancer-choreographer Bronislava Nijinska dies in Los Angeles at the age of 81. The sister of Vaslav Nijinsky, she graduated from the Saint Petersburg Imperial Ballet School in 1908 and danced with the Maryinsky Theatre until 1911, when she left in protest of her brother's dismissal. She appeared with Sergei Diaghilev's Ballets Russes in 1909 and, after 1911, was a permanent member of the company. Nijinska returned to Saint Petersburg in 1914. Six years later she left the Soviet Union and returned to Diaghilev's company, eventually becoming its chief choreographer. Among her most famous works are *Les Biches, Les Noces* and *Le Train bleu.* Her modernistic choreography was known for its insightful social comment.

Following the breakup of Diaghilev's company in the late 1920s, she choreographed for a number of European companies including the Paris Opera. In 1938 Nijinska settled in the United States. After 1945 she served primarily as the ballet mistress of the Grand Ballet du Marquis de Cuevas and restaged productions of her most famous works.

March 1   Russian-American pianist Victor Babin, 63, dies in Cleveland. He studied at the Riga Conservatory and later with Artur Schnabel in Berlin. With his wife, Vitya Vronsky, he created a well-known piano duo team.

March 2   German soprano Erna Sack, 74, dies in Wiesbaden. After studies in Prague and Berlin, she debuted at the Municipal Theater in Bielefeld. She then performed a great deal at the Salzburg Festivals. She also sang in America and Australia. She was the possessor of a voice that could reach stratospheric high notes, which she used frequently.

April 29   German conductor-composer Manfred Gurlitt, 81, dies in Tokyo. A grandson of the famous painter Louis Gurlitt, he studied composition with Engelbert Humperdinck and conducting with Karl Muck. He then became a coach at the Berlin Opera and at Bayreuth. After being removed from his posts by the Nazis, he relocated to Japan and founded the Tokyo-based Gurlitt Opera Company. His opera *Wozzeck,* which premiered in 1926, was completely overshadowed by Alban Berg's opera of the same name. He also composed several other operas.

May 29   Hungarian-American musicologist Ernst Ferand, 85, dies in Basel. A colleague of Emile Jaques-Dalcroze, he wrote books on harmony and improvisation and taught at many educational institutions, including the New School for Social Research in New York City.

June 4   Belgian composer Godefroid Devreese, 79, dies in Brussels. He was also a conductor and led the Concertgebouw Orchestra and the Antwerp Opera. He composed much symphonic and chamber music, including four symphonies and seven piano sonatinas.

June 19   Danish tenor Helge Roswaenge, 74, dies in Munich. This dramatic tenor, a member of the Berlin State Opera, excelled in operas of Richard Strauss, Richard Wagner and Carl Maria von Weber but also sang many Italian roles successfully. He was chosen by Arturo Toscanini to sing in his production of *The Magic Flute* at Salzburg.

June 21   American composer, organist, teacher and music director Seth Bingham, 90, dies in New York City. He studied with Horatio Parker, Vincent d'Indy and Charles Marie Widor. His works for organ are performed more often than his other pieces.

June 29   Italian composer, critic and musicologist Giulio Confalonieri, 76, dies in Milan. He authored a detailed two-volume biography of Luigi Cherubini and also edited works by Cherubini and Domenico Cimarosa. Confalonieri's most successful composition is his opera *Rosaspina,* which premiered in 1939.

July 18   Swedish opera director Goeran Gentele, 54, is killed in an automobile accident in Sardinia. His death occurs while on vacation just before he was to begin his first season as manager of the New York Metropolitan Opera.

July 28   American soprano Helen Traubel, 73, dies in Santa Monica, California. She studied voice in her home town, Saint Louis, and debuted there as soloist with the Saint Louis Symphony. In 1926 she was offered a contract with the Metropolitan Opera but turned it down, feeling she needed more study. She finally did sing with that company in the premiere of Walter Damrosch's opera *The Man Without a Country* in 1937. She subsequently appeared there very successfully in Wagnerian roles. She was forced to resign in 1953 because the management objected to her singing in nightclubs. She continued to do so and also appeared on Broadway and in films.

Sep. 19   French pianist and composer Robert Casadesus, 73, dies in Paris. Born into a musical family, he started his concert career after the First World War. He gave many performances — sometimes of his own compositions — with his wife, Gaby, also a pianist, and taught in a number of schools in Europe and the United States. Among Casadesus's many compositions are seven symphonies.

Sep. 25   Austrian music publisher Alfred A. Kalmus, 83, dies in London.

Sep. 29   American tenor Richard Crooks, 72, dies in Portola Valley, California. After his debut in 1922 with the New York Symphony, he gave concerts in Europe, finally making his American operatic debut in 1930. His Metropolitan debut took place on February 25, 1933 in *Manon*, and he sang there until 1943.

Nov. 28   English composer Havergal Brian, 96, dies at Shoreham-by-Sea, Sussex. While a youngster, he studied organ, cello and violin. He was forced to leave school at age 12 to earn a living and help his father. Between 1904 and 1949 he was active as a music journalist. He simultaneously composed symphonies. It was not until age 90 that he began to be noticed. Performances followed with some frequency. He composed seven of his 32 symphonies after the age of 90. The Havergal Brian Society is subsequently established in England and the United States to promote his work.

Brian's music is romantic, with occasional forays into whole-tone fields (his opera *The Tigers*, for example, composed between 1916 and 1918). Despite the attention his work receives during the late 1960s and early 1970s, his symphonies fail to displace those of Ralph Vaughan Williams in terms of their importance in the history of the 20th-century English symphony. He is perhaps somewhat analagous to the prolific Soviet symphonist Nikolai Miaskovsky, who was overshadowed by both Sergei Prokofiev and Dmitri Shostakovich. Brian also wrote four other operas (besides *The Tigers*), concertos, an oratorio and other works.

Nov. 28   Bruno Zirato, 88, dies in New York City. He was a managing director of the New York Philharmonic and Enrico Caruso's private secretary.

Nov. 30   Austrian composer Hans Erich Apostel, 71, dies in Vienna. He studied in Karlsruhe before studying with Arnold Schoenberg and Alban Berg in Vienna. It was not until 30 years later (1951), however, that he adopted the

HANS ERICH APOSTEL

12-tone method of composition. He received many awards and was eventually hired by Universal Edition to prepare for publication Berg's posthumous works. He was a favored figure at contemporary music festivals in Europe, but his work quickly fades after his death. Most of his pieces are scored for chamber ensemble.

Dec. 2   Dancer-choreographer Jose Limon dies in Flemington, New Jersey at the age of 64. One of the outstanding personalities in modern dance, Limon began his career dancing with the Humphrey-Weidman company from 1930 to 1940. Following service in the U.S. Army during World War II, he formed his own troupe with Doris Humphrey, who became his artistic director. For his troupe he choreographed such modern dance classics as *The Moor's Pavane*, *Missa Brevis*, *There Is a Time*, and *La Malinche*. Much of his choreography is influenced by his Mexican background. In 1964 the New York State Council on the Arts made its first attempt to aid the establishment of a permanent modern dance repertory company, and named Limon artistic director of the American Dance Theatre.

Dec. 4   German-British bookseller Heinrich Eisemann, 82, dies in London. He was an expert on literary and musical autographs and was a consultant on Emily Anderson's edition of Beethoven's letters.

Dec. 15   French pianist Monique de la Bruchollerie, 57, dies in Paris. She studied with Isidor Philipp and at the Paris Conservatoire. She then toured as a pianist. In 1964 she proposed that piano keyboards be crescent-shaped to simplify the simultaneous playing of passages registrally distant from each other. She also advocated an electronic keyboard device that would enable the pianist to press a single key to play one full chord (this device is somewhat similar to that invented by Laurens Hammond in 1950 for his "chord organ"). Her innovations were not adopted.

1972 Related Events

Decca (England) and the Musical Heritage Society complete their recording of all of Franz Joseph Haydn's symphonies.

The Ballet du Rhin is established this year in Strasbourg. Jean Babilee is its first director.

April 22   Sir Rudolf Bing — outgoing general manager of the Metropolitan Opera in New York — is honored with a gala performance at the opera house. Performed are solos and ensembles — 35 numbers — from many operas, both in and out of the Met's repertoire. The building is jammed with 4,000 people, and the event was sold out four months ago. Ticket prices range from $10 to $800; 175 standees are selected by lottery. Sir Rudolf presided over the Met for 22 years (1950–72), his tenure in that job being second only to that of Giulio Gatti-Casazza.

May 1   Jacob Druckman is awarded the Pulitzer Prize for music for his orchestral work *Windows*.

Sep. 3   American pianist Murray Perahia wins the Leeds International Pianoforte Competition, marking the first time an American receives this honor.

Sep. 14   The Music Library of Yale University acquires the Quincy Porter papers, presented by the composer's wife, Mrs. Lois Porter.

1973 Opera

March 16   Bruno Maderna's *Satyrikon* receives its world premiere at the Nederlandse Operastichting in Amsterdam. The libretto is based on the first-century novel by Petronius Arbiter.

April 17   Elisabeth Lutyens' opera *Infidelio* premieres at the Sadler's Wells Theater in London.

April 23   American composer John Eaton's television opera *Myshkin*, based on Feodor Dostoeveski's novel *The Idiot*, premieres in Bloomington, Indiana. This music uses quarter-tones. Eaton studied at Princeton University with Milton Babbitt, Edward T. Cone and Roger Sessions.

June 16   Benjamin Britten's *Death in Venice* receives its world premiere at the Maltings in Aldeburgh, England. Myfanwy Piper's libretto is based on the novella by Thomas Mann about an aging writer — Aschenbach — who falls under the spell of a young boy's beauty. Peter Pears creates the role of Aschenbach. John Shirley-Quirk is also in the cast.

Aug. 30   *Apollo contra Marsyas* is premiered by the Finnish National Opera in Helsinki. This opera is by the Finnish composer Einojuhani Rautavaara.

Sep. 15   Boris Blacher's *Yvonne, Prinzessin von Burgund* is premiered by the Wuppertal Opera in Wuppertal.

Oct. 5   Josep Soler's opera *Edio Y Iocasta* is premiered at a music festival in Barcelona.

Nov. 26   Ned Rorem's opera *Bertha* (to a play in 10 scenes by Kenneth Koch) premieres at Alice Tully Hall in New York City.

1973 Dance

Jan. 10   Maya Plisetskaya and Rudy Bryans dance the premiere of *La rose malade*, by Roland Petit. The work is a duet between two lovers, performed to the adagietto from Gustav Mahler's Fifth Symphony. Costumes are by Yves Saint Laurent. The ballet, in three parts, is performed in Paris. The premiere marks the first time that a Soviet ballerina is permitted to dance in a work created for her by a Western company.

Jan. 12   George Balanchine's *Ballet Imperial* is performed in a fully revised version, with costumes and scenery by

Karinska, by the New York City Ballet in New York. The work is later titled *Tchaikovsky Concerto No. 2*.

May 2   Martha Graham premieres two new works, *Mendicants of an Evening* and *Myth of a Voyage*, both performed in New York City. The second features music of Alan Hovhaness.

May 24   Jerome Robbins' *An Evening's Waltzes* — to music by Sergei Prokofiev, with costumes by Rouben Ter-Arutunian — is premiered by the New York City Ballet in New York. The dancers are Helgi Tomasson, Bart Cook,

Patricia McBride, Jean-Pierre Bonnefous, Sara Leland and Christine Redpath.

Oct. 24   Twyla Tharp's *As Time Goes By* — to music by Franz Joseph Haydn, with lighting by Jennifer Tipton and costumes by Chester Weinberg — is premiered by the City Center Joffrey Ballet in New York.

Dec. 22   Glen Tetley's *Voluntaries*, to music by Francis Poulenc, is premiered by the Stuttgart Ballet in Stuttgart. Marcia Haydee and Richard Cragun star in this first ballet the choreographer creates for this company prior to becoming its director.

1973   Instrumental and Vocal Music

Jan. 10   Malcolm Williamson's *Little Carols of the Saints* for organ is premiered by John Rose at Wesminster Abbey in London.

Jan. 14   *Speculum Speculi*, by Charles Wuorinen, receives its initial performance in Grand Forks, North Dakota. Fred Sherry conducts the ensemble known as Speculum Musicae. The piece is scored for flute, bass clarinet, contrabassoon, piano, vibraphone, four drums and three tamtams.

Jan. 16   Alan Hovhaness' Sonata for Cello and Piano premieres at Bellingham, Washington.

Jan. 19   Vittorio Rieti's Trio for Piano, Violin and Cello is premiered by the Beaux Arts Trio at Hunter College in New York City.

Jan. 21   *Cheap Imitation*, by John Cage premieres at Alice Tully Hall in New York City. Scored for piano, the work was inspired by Erik Satie's music.

Jan. 23   String Quartet No. 3, by Elliott Carter, receives its world premiere by the Juilliard String Quartet in New York City. The four players are paired into two duos—violin and cello; violin and viola. Each duo plays continuous fragments in a virtuosic fashion to create "a constant interlacing of moods and materials." The listener must perceive a "separation of sound" in order to follow the musical discourse of the instruments. Carter specifies instructions for the performers in order to facilitate accessibility for the listener. He also says the music can be heard as a play, a debate or a conversation, or even as improvisation (despite the fact that the music is notated). The piece is subsequently awarded the Pulitzer Prize for music.

Jan. 24   Lejaren Hiller's String Quartet No. 6 is premiered by the Concord String Quartet at the New York Cultural Center in New York City. The work was composed in 1972.

Jan. 25   *Lincoln Address*, by Vincent Persichetti, receives its world premiere by the Saint Louis Symphony Orchestra at Carnegie Hall in New York. Its scheduled world premiere at President Richard M. Nixon's inaugural concert on January 19 was cancelled because allusions in the text to war might have been misunderstood in light of the Vietnam conflict.

Jan. 27   Vittorio Rieti's Triple Concerto for Violin, Viola, Piano and Orchestra premieres in New York City.

Feb. 3   Cristobal Halffter's Concerto for Organ and Orchestra receives its initial performance in Madrid.

Feb. 8   *Speech Songs*, by Charles Dodge, is premiered by the Da Capo Chamber Players at Carnegie Hall in New York City. Dodge has studied composition with Darius Milhaud, Gunther Schuller, Arthur Berger, Jack Beeson, Chou Wen-chung, Otto Luening and Vladimir Ussachevsky.

Feb. 8   George Crumb's *Makrokosmos, Vol. I* for piano receives its world premiere by David Burge in Colorado Springs, Colorado. This work, subtitled *Twelve Fantasy-Pieces After the Zodiac for Amplified Piano*, is the first in Crumb's series of *Makrokosmos* pieces. Paul Hume says in the Washington *Post* of this work "With his first large work for solo piano, composer George Crumb has won his right to a place among the instrument's great innovators. . . ."

Feb. 18   Friedrich Cerha's *Curriculum* for 13 wind instruments is premiered by the Chamber Music Society of Lincoln Center at Alice Tully Hall in New York City.

Feb. 27   Andre Jolivet's Violin Concerto receives its initial performance by M. Pommer and the Orchestre de Paris, with L. Yordanoff as soloist. The performance takes place in Paris.

March 3   David Amram's *Elegy* for violin and orchestra is premiered by the Cosmopolitan Young People's Symphony Orchestra at Philharmonic Hall at Lincoln Center in New York City.

March 11   Leon Kirchner's *Lily* is performed in a concert version by Dennis Russell Davies and The Ensemble at Alice Tully Hall in New York City. This performance incorporates materials used in Kirchner's forthcoming opera of the same name, premiered in 1977.

March 15   Henry Brant's *Divinity (Dialogues in the Form of Secret Portraits)* is premiered by the American Brass Quintet at Carnegie Hall in New York City, with Sylvia Marlowe as harpsichord soloist.

March 28   Charles Wuorinen's Trio for Flute, Violoncello and Piano is premiered by the composer, Fred Sherry and Harvey Sollberger at the New York Cultural Center in New York City.

April 4   Isang Yun's *Gagok* for guitar, percussion and voice premieres in Amsterdam.

April 13   *Eridanos* for 8 brasses and 10 string instruments, by Iannis Xenakis, is premiered by the Ensemble Europeen de Musique Contemporaine in La Rochelle, France.

April 16   Milko Kelemen's String Quartet No. 2 is premiered by the Parrenin Quartet in Royan, France.

April 16   Alberto Ginastera's cantata *Milena* for soprano and orchestra receives its initial performance by Brian Priestman and the Denver Symphony Orchestra, with Phyllis Curtin as soloist. The performance takes place in Denver, Colorado.

April 17   Gunther Schuller's String Quartet No. 1 is premiered by the Composers' String Quartet at Carnegie Recital Hall in New York City.

May 1   Nikos Skalkottas' Piano Suite No. 1 premieres at the Bach Festival in London.

May 5   *Early Songs After Li Po*, by Gunther Schuller, premieres at Jordan Hall in Boston.

May 7   George Rochberg's String Quartet No. 2 receives its initial performance by the Concord String Quartet at Carnegie Recital Hall in New York City.

May 15   Mauricio Kagel's orchestral work *Variations Without Fugue* is premiered by Bruno Maderna and the North German Broadcasting Corporation Symphony Orchestra. Maderna also conducts Sylvano Bussotti's *Bergkristall.*

May 21   William Bolcom's String Quartet No. 9 receives its first performance by the Concord String Quartet at Carnegie Recital Hall in New York City.

May 21   *Reflections* for piano, by Andrzej Panufnik, is premiered by John Ogdon at Queen Elizabeth Hall in London.

May 21   Ned Rorem's *Prelude on the Tone Sol* premieres at a festival gala honoring Sol Hurok at the Metropolitan Opera House in New York City.

May 26   Michael Tippett's Piano Sonata No. 3 is premiered by Paul Crossley in Bath, England.

May 31   R. Murray Schafer's *Lustro* trilogy for orchestra receives its initial performance by Marius Constant and the Toronto Symphony Orchestra in Toronto.

June 2   Aaron Copland's *Threnody I: Igor Stravinsky in memoriam* and *Threnody II* (dedicated to Beatrice Cunningham) are premiered by Michael Tilson Thomas and the Ojai Festival Orchestra in Ojai, California. Also premiered posthumously today by the Pacifica Singers is Ingolf Dahl's *A Noiseless, Patient Spider.*

July 3   Richard Rodney Bennett's Viola Concerto receives its initial performance by the Northern Sinfonia Orchestra in York, with Roger Best as soloist.

July 6   Bruno Maderna's Concerto for Oboe, No. 3, premieres at the Holland Festival in Hilversum.

Aug. 3   Lennox Berkeley's *Sinfonia concertante* for oboe and chamber orchestra is premiered by Raymond Leppard and the BBC Northern Symphony Orchestra in London, with Janet Craxton as soloist.

Aug. 13   Thea Musgrave's Viola Concerto receives its first performance by the Scottish National Orchestra in London, the composer conducting.

Sept. 7   Elisabeth Lutyens' cantata *De amore* is premiered by the London Choral Society and the BBC Symphony Orchestra at Albert Hall in London.

Sep. 9   Frank Martin's *Polyptique* is premiered by Edmond de Stoutz and his chamber orchestra at the General Assembly of the International Music Council in Geneva. Scored for violin and two string orchestras, the work is subtitled *Six Images of the Passion of Christ.*

Sep. 22   *Composition for Orchestra* by Luciano Berio, premieres at the Glasgow Festival with the composer conducting.

Oct. 4   Isang Yun's Overture for Orchestra premieres in West Berlin.

Oct. 4   Havergal Brian's Symphony No. 23 is premiered posthumously by Bernard Goodman and the University of Illinois Symphony Orchestra at Knox College in Galesburg, Illinois. This symphony was composed in 1965.

Oct. 15   Gyorgy Ligeti's *Clocks and Clouds* for chorus and orchestra premieres in Graz, Austria.

Oct. 20   Mauricio Kagel's *Two-Man Orchestra* premieres in Donaueschingen.

Nov. 13   Darius Milhaud's *Ani maamir — un chant perdu et retrouve*, with a text by Elie Wiesel, for orchestra, chorus, soprano and four reciters in premiered by Lukas Foss and the Brooklyn Philharmonic at Carnegie Hall in New York City.

Nov. 22   Karlheinz Stockhausen's *Ceylan* (from his collection *Fur kommende Zeiten*) premieres at the Rencontres Internationales de Musique Contemporaine in Metz, France.

Nov. 24   Jacques Charpentier's *Le livre d'orgue* premieres at the Rencontres Internationales de Musique Contemporaine in Metz, France, with the composer as organ soloist.

Dec. 4   Earle Brown's *Centering* for violin and ensemble is premiered by the London Sinfonietta in Manchester, England, with Paul Zukofsky as soloist.

Dec. 6   Elie Siegmeister's Symphony No. 4 receives its first performance by the Cleveland Symphony Orchestra in Cleveland.

Dec. 9   Lucia Dlugoszewski's *Space Is a Diamond* for solo trumpet is premiered by Gerard Schwarz at the O.K. Harris Gallery in New York City.

Dec. 13   Jacob Druckman's *Delizie contente che l'alme beate* is premiered by the Dorian Wind Quintet at Alice Tully Hall in New York City.

1973   Births, Deaths and Debuts

Feb. 19   Hungarian violinist Joseph Szigeti, 80, dies in Lucerne, Switzerland. Having started his career as a teacher, he later turned to performing, very often playing works of 20th-century composers such as Bela Bartok (with whom he performed), Sergei Prokofiev and Ernest Bloch. He was not a virtuoso violinist of the Heifetz school but was much admired by other musicians for his intellectual approach.

March 18   Danish dramatic tenor Lauritz Melchior, 82, dies in Santa Monica, California. After beginning his career as a baritone, he retrained as a tenor and scored enormous success in the Wagnerian repertory. His operatic career lasted some 40 years, and during it he sang the part of Tristan, for example, more than 200 times. He made a number of Hollywood films and was also heard frequently on the radio. His voice, like Enrico Caruso's, had a baritone quality with ringing high notes and, in the long Wagnerian roles, was untiring.

April 5   Herbert Graf, 69, dies in Geneva. He was a stage director with the New York Metropolitan Opera as well as with other famous opera companies around the world.

April 16   Hungarian conductor Istvan Kertesz, 43, is drowned at Kfar Saba, Israel while taking a swim in the Mediterranean. He studied at the Academy of Music in Budapest and in Rome and was the conductor of the London Symphony Orchestra from 1965 to 1968.

May 21   Czech composer and critic Frantisek Bartos, 67, dies in Prague. A writer of books on Mozart, Gustav Mahler and Bedrich Smetana, he was also partly responsible for helping to publish the complete works of Antonin Dvorak. He helped establish the annual Prague Spring Festival as well.

KAREL ANCERL

June 26   Ballet director and choreographer John Cranko, 45, dies during an airplane flight returning from an American tour. The most important figure in the resurgence of German ballet, Cranko studied at the Sadler's Wells School and joined the Sadler's Wells Ballet in 1946. More interested in choreography than in performing, he created a great number of ballets for Sadler's Wells and The Royal Ballet, including *Beauty and the Beast* and *Pineapple Poll.* In 1960 he became ballet director of the Stuttgart Ballet, where, within a few years, he achieved "the Stuttgart ballet miracle." He developed a regional ballet company into one of the greatest in the world by recruiting dancers from around the world and by creating a very large, diversified repertory. Although he choreographed in many styles, he was chiefly known for his full-length dramatic works such as *Romeo and Juliet* and *Eugene Onegin.*

July 1   Laurens Hammond, 78, dies in Cornwall, Connecticut. He invented the Hammond electronic organ as well as the novachord, an instrument simulating the sonorities of other instruments. He also invented the solo-vox, an electronic addition to the piano that generates sounds similar to those of the organ. In 1950 he introduced the "chord organ," which enabled the player to relegate harmony to the pressing of one button for any given chord. Hammond was a pioneer of electronic music in its nascent stage.

July 3   Czech conductor Karel Ancerl, 65, dies in Toronto, Canada. After studies at the Prague Conservatory, he became a conductor specializing in the modern repertory. He survived several years in Nazi concentration camps to become the conductor of the Czech Philharmonic and, later in his life, the Toronto Symphony.

July 6   German conductor Otto Klemperer, 83, dies in Zurich, Switzerland. After studying in Germany, he won his first conducting position in Prague on the recommendation of Gustav Mahler. He was seen in the United States for the first time during the 1925–26 season and later, after fleeing the Nazis, was conductor of the Los Angeles Philharmonic from 1933 to 1939. In 1959 he was appointed principal conductor of the Philharmonia Orchestra in London, with which he made many recordings. He was the composer of six symphonies and other works and was also a champion of contemporary music.

Aug. 17   French composer Jean Barraque, 45, dies in Paris. After studies with Jean Langlais and Olivier Messiaen, he began experimenting with 12-tone procedures and electronics. He was quickly hailed as a brilliant musician, perhaps of genius stature, despite the fact that he composed little. His best-known work is *Sequence* (composed in 1950–55). Other pieces include *Chant apres chant* (composed in 1966).

Sep. 18   German musicologist, writer and teacher Adam Adrio, 72, dies in Renon, Bolzano, Italy. He was noted especially for his work on religious music and as a contributor to *Die Musik in Geschichte und Gegenwart.*

Sep. 18   German modern dancer and choreographer Mary Wigman dies in Berlin at the age of 87. Often described as the originator of modern dance in Europe, Wigman studied with Emile Jaques-Dalcroze and Rudolf von Laban. She made her debut as a dancer in 1914. Wigman's career as a choreographer began after World War I with the premiere of *The Seven Dances of Life* in 1918. In the course of the next three decades, she became known as one of the chief exponents of expressionist dance. Her compositions are characterized by tense, somber introspection. Wigman continued to teach and choreograph well into the 1960s. Her main compositions include *Le Sacre du printemps, Alcestis, Carmina Burana* and *Fruhlingsstimmen.*

Oct. 22   Spanish-born cellist and conductor Pablo Casals, 96, dies in Rio Piedras, Puerto Rico. His debut occurred on November 12, 1899, when he performed as soloist in the Cello Concerto, by Edouard Lalo, conducted by Charles Lamoureux. His tours encompassed the world. He was also a composer of music for the cello.

Nov. 13   Italian composer-conductor Bruno Maderna, 53, dies in Darmstadt. After studying conducting with Hermann Scherchen and composition with Gian Francesco Malipiero, he devoted himself to conducting the most complex scores by contemporary composers. He conducted at Darmstadt and joined the faculty of the Conservatory. He became a West German citizen in 1963. His own music reflects the most intense intellectual currents of the century.

Nov. 23   Russian-American mezzo-soprano Jennie Tourel, 73, dies in New York. Born in Russia, her family later settled in Paris, where she took voice lessons and eventually made her debut at the Opera-Comique in 1933. In 1940 she fled the Nazi occupation of Paris and later settled in the United States. Chosen by Arturo Toscanini to sing with the NBC Symphony, she began to be noticed in America. Tourel sang at the Metropolitan from 1943 to 1947 and appeared many times as a recitalist and as a soloist with various orchestras.

Dec. 30   French composer, organist, conductor and teacher Henri Busser, 101, dies in Paris. He was a director of the Paris Opera. As a youngster he studied with Charles Marie Widor, Cesar Franck and Charles Gounod and was a finalist in the Prix de Rome competition. Also on the faculty of the Paris Conservatoire, he conducted Claude Debussy's *Pelleas et Melisande* at its third performance.

1973 Related Events

The International Dance Council is established this year under the auspices of UNESCO. Based in Paris, the council exists to protect and help professionals in the field to cope with such problems as copyright. It also advances the art of choreography by organizing dance displays.

Finnish composer Joonas Kokkonen is awarded the Sibelius Prize this year.

April 6　"Affine Music," a doctoral dissertation by composer Paul Lansky, is accepted at Princeton University. The dissertation consists of an essay and a string quartet and explains Lansky's system of musical composition, which he began developing in 1969 in collaboration with George Perle (Perle's approach is subsequently presented in his book *Twelve-Tone Tonality*, published in 1977). Lansky extends and develops that approach by constructing a mathematical model for the system and using the algebraic operations known as "affine linear transformations" to extend the logic further. Lansky studied at Queens College of the City University of New York and at Princeton University. He has taught at the Mannes College of Music and at Swarthmore College and is now on the faculty at Princeton. He is also an editor of *Perspectives of New Music* and performed, as a horn player, with the Dorian Wind Quintet.

May 7　Elliott Carter is awarded the Pulitzer Prize for music for his String Quartet No. 3.

June 24　The Santa Fe Chamber Music Festival begins its first season with a concert of chamber music by Mozart, Mendelssohn, Schumann and Schubert. This inaugural concert, which takes place in Santa Fe, New Mexico, is dedicated to Pablo Casals — honorary president of the festival. The festival subsequently travels to La Jolla, California and Seattle, Washington and becomes internationally known.

Sep. 4　The Music Library of Yale University acquires the Carl Ruggles Papers — a collection of music manuscripts, correspondence between Ruggles and other composers and artists, programs, clippings, recordings, transcriptions and other materials. The papers were purchased by the library from the composer's son Micah Ruggles.

Oct. 20　The Sydney Opera House officially opens in that city, as Queen Elizabeth II presides over the event.

THE SYDNEY OPERA HOUSE

The opera house was designed by Danish architect Joern Utzon and consists of four concert halls, two recording halls, restaurants, a library, lounges and offices. At a total cost of $148 million, this building is the most controversial and expensive in Australia's history. It serves a city of slightly more than 3 million people.

1974   Opera

Jan. 18   Claudio Monteverdi's opera *Il ritorno d'Ulisse* is performed by the Opera Society of Washington, D.C., marking the work's American premiere. The production is conducted by Alexander Gibson and directed by Ian Strasfogel; the score is edited by Raymond Leppard. This work received its world premiere in Italy in 1641.

March 4   Hans Werner Henze's *Rachel, la cubana* is premiered over WNET's "Opera Theater" in New York City.

March 16   Iain Hamilton's *The Catiline Conspiracy* is premiered by the Scottish Opera in Stirling, Scotland.

March 26   Alun Hoddinott's *The Beach of Falesa* is premiered by the Welsh National Opera at the New Theater in Cardiff.

Aug. 3   Marc Blitzstein's opera *Idiots First*, completed by Leonard Lehrman, is premiered posthumously in Ithaca, New York.

Aug. 24   Stanley Silverman's opera *Hotel for Criminals*, with a libretto by Richard Foreman, is premiered at the Lenox Arts Center in Wheatleigh, Massachusetts.

Nov. 15   William Grant Still's *A Bayou Legend* is premiered by Opera/South in Jackson, Mississippi. The three-act opera was composed in 1940.

Dec. 21   *Yehu*, a 30-minute opera by Eugen Zador, is performed for the first time by the Municipal Art Department, Bureau of Music, Los Angeles, California. The libretto is by Anna Egyud. The work is a Christmas legend about one of Herod's soldiers called Yehu, who finds he cannot follow Herod's orders to kill.

1974   Dance

Jan. 10   Jerome Robbins' *Four Bagatelles*, to music by Beethoven, is premiered by the New York City Ballet in New York. The dancers are Violette Verdy and Jean-Pierre Bonnefous. This work consists of pas de deux that celebrate the art of the dance.

Jan. 17   George Balanchine's *Variations pour une porte et un soupir* — to music by Pierre Henry, with decor by Rouben Ter-Arutunian — is performed for the first time by the New York City Ballet in New York. John Clifford and Karin Von Aroldingen dance this pas de deux choreographed to musique concrete composed from sounds of a door creaking and human sighs.

April 26   *Don Juan*, a ballet in five scenes choreographed by John Neumeier, receives its first performance by the National Ballet of Canada at the Metropolitan Opera House in New York. The music is by Thomas Luis de Victoria and Christoph Willibald von Gluck. Filippo Sanjust creates the costumes and sets. The ballet is about Don Juan who kills a man in order to have his woman. The dance ends in an orgy at which a coffin appears for Don Juan. Rudolf Nureyev stars.

May 7   Kenneth MacMillan's *Manon* — to music by Jules Massenet arranged and orchestrated by Leighton Lucas, with costumes and scenery by Nicholas Georgiadis — receives its world premiere by the Royal Ballet in London. The ballet is not based on Massenet's opera, even though the music is used; the story is taken from Abbe Prevost's novel *Manon Lescaut*. The lead dancers are Antoinette Sibley, Anthony Dowell, David Wall, Monica Mason, Derek Rencher and David Drew.

May 16   Jerome Robbins' *Dybbuk* — to music by Leonard Bernstein, with scenery by Rouben Ter-Arutunian, costumes by Patricia Zipprodt and lighting by Jennifer Tipton — is premiered by the New York City Ballet in New York. This modern ballet, inspired by Jewish themes and embracing worldly forms of war and love, was performed last night at a gala benefit preview. It stars Patricia McBride and Helgi Tomasson.

May 30   Eliot Feld's *Sephardic Songs*, choreographed to traditional Spanish-Jewish music, is performed for the first time by the Eliot Feld Ballet in New York City. The lighting is by Jennifer Tipton and the decor by Santo Loquasto.

June 2   Eliot Feld's *Tzaddik* — to music by Aaron Copland, with decor by Boris Aronson — is premiered by the Eliot Feld Ballet in New York City. The choreographer leads the cast in this work about the Jewish celebration of the search for knowledge.

July 3   Natalia Makarova's version of the fourth act of *La Bayadere* is performed by the American Ballet Theater at the New York State Theater at Lincoln Center in New York City.

July 17   George Balanchine's version of *Coppelia* receives its world premiere at the Saratoga Performing Arts Center in Saratoga, New York. The dancers include Patricia McBride, Helgi Tomasson and Shaun O'Brien.

1974 Instrumental and Vocal Music

Jan. 18   Alberto Ginastera's *Serenata* is premiered by Aurora Natola-Ginastera, Justino Diaz and the Chamber Music Society of Lincoln Center at Alice Tully Hall in New York City.

Jan. 22   Isang Yun's *Harmonia fur Blasinstruments, Harte, und Schlagzeuge* premieres in Herford, Germany. The piece is scored for 13 or 16 wind instruments, percussion and harp.

Jan. 27   Frederic Rzewski's *Struggle* for baritone and large ensemble premieres at Alice Tully Hall in New York City, with Julius Eastman as soloist.

Feb. 4   Alberto Ginastera's String Quartet No. 3 with soprano is premiered by the Juilliard Quartet in Dallas, Texas, with Benita Valente as soloist.

Feb. 20   Joonas Kokkonen's Quintet for Winds premieres in Helsinki. Kokkonen studied with Selim Palmgren at the Sibelius Institute in Helsinki and became a member of the Finnish Academy in 1963. Two years later he became chairman of the Union of Finnish Composers. His music is highly chromatic, contrapuntal and often dissonant.

Feb. 20   Peter Maxwell Davies' *All Sons of Adam* receives its first performance by the Fires of London in London.

Feb. 25   Mauricio Kagel's String Quartet is premiered by the La Salle Quartet in Hamburg.

Feb. 25   Marvin David Levy's *In Memoriam — W.H. Auden* is premiered by the Saint Paul Chamber Orchestra at Town Hall in New York City, with Paul Sperry as soloist.

Feb. 26   Henri Sauguet's *Cantate sylvestre* for viola, voice and piano receives its initial performance in Paris.

March 9   Dominick Argento's oratorio *Jonah and the Whale* premieres at Plymouth Congregational Church in Minneapolis, Minnesota.

March 9   Peter Maxwell Davies' *Miss Donnithorne's Maggot* premieres in Adelaide, Australia. This work is scored for soprano and six instruments.

March 15   Jean Francaix' *Fantaisie burlesque* premieres in Nuremburg. Also performed for the first time on today's program is his orchestral piece *La ville mysterieuse*.

March 23   Henry Brant's *Solomon's Gardens: A Spatial Cantata* is premiered by Harry Salzman and the Sine Nomine Singers at Alice Tully Hall in New York City.

March 28   Sylvano Bussotti's *Suite de Lorenzaccio*, with a concert arrangement by Gianpiero Taverna, premieres in Royan, France.

April 6   Anton Heiller's *Passionmusik fur Kinderchor und Orgel* premieres in Thalwil, Switzerland. Heiller frequently composes sacred music and sometimes uses serial techniques. He studied at the Vienna Conservatory and received the Austrian Grand Prize for Music in 1969. Two years later he joined the faculty of the Hochschule fur Musik in Vienna.

April 19   Jacques Charpentier's *Une voix pour une autre* for two women's voices, flute, clarinet and percussion premieres in Champigny, France.

April 20   *Lamia*, by Jacob Druckman, is premiered by the Albany Symphony in Albany, New York. This work is scored for soprano and orchestra. Druckman is currently teaching at Brooklyn College of the City University of New York.

April 21   Lucia Dlugoszewski's *Fire fragile flight* is premiered by Dennis Russell Davies and The Ensemble at Alice Tully Hall in New York City.

April 25   *Arie da Capo*, by Milton Babbitt, is premiered by the Da Capo Chamber Players at Alice Tully Hall in New York City.

April 27   *Music for Solo Violin*, by Harry Somers, is premiered by Yehudi Menuhin in Guelph, Canada.

April 28   Jacques Charpentier's Symphony No. 4 (*Brasil*) premieres in Paris.

April 30   Samuel Barber's *Three Songs*, Op. 45, is premiered by the Chamber Music Society of Lincoln Center, with Dietrich Fischer-Dieskau as soloist. The performance takes place in New York City.

May 3   Isang Yun's *Memory for Three Voices* premieres at the Colloquium Musicale in Rome.

May 4   Karlheinz Stockhausen's *Herbstmusik* receives its initial performance by the Pro Musica Nova over Radio Bremen.

May 5   Elisabeth Lutyens' *The Winter of the World*, Op. 98 for cello and chamber orchestra premieres in London.

May 6   Elisabeth Lutyens' *Plenum III*, Op. 88, is premiered by the Chilingirian String Quartet in London.

May 8   Benjamin Lees' *Collage* for string quartet, woodwind quintet and percussion premieres at the University of Wisconsin in Milwaukee.

May 17   A revised version of Kurt Weill's *Ocean Flight* is performed by the New York Choral Society at Avery Fisher Hall in New York City.

May 21   *Erikton (la force de la terre)*, by Iannis Xenakis, a concerto for piano and orchestra, premieres in Paris.

June 1   *Music in 12 parts*, by Philip Glass, receives its premiere at Town Hall in New York City. This marks the work's first full performance.

June 25   Henri Dutilleux' *Preludes pour piano Nos. 1 and 2* premieres in Paris.

July 6   Jacques Charpentier's Concerto No. 5 for Alto Saxophone premieres in Bordeaux.

July 22   Ernst Krenek's *Spatlese*, a song cycle, receives its first performance in Munich.

July 22   Mauricio Kagel's *Mirum fur Tuba* premieres in Darmstadt, Germany.

July 25   Gabriel Faure's *Interlude* for two pianos premieres posthumously in Beziers, France.

July 30   Malcolm Williamson's *Hammarskjold Portraits* premieres at Albert Hall in London. This work is scored for soprano and strings.

Aug. 20   Richard Rodney Bennett's *Tenebrae* for baritone and piano premieres in London.

Aug. 21   Ernst Krenek's *Von vorn herein* premieres in Salzburg.

Sep. 22   *Cendrees* for chorus and orchestra receives its first performance in Bonn. The work is by Iannis Xenakis.

KARLHEINZ STOCKHAUSEN PLAYS ONE OF HIS COMPOSITIONS

Oct. 11   Thea Musgrave's *Space Play*, a concerto for 9 instruments, is premiered by the London Sinfonietta at Queen Elizabeth Hall in London.

Oct. 16   Luciano Berio's *Points on the Curve to Find. . .* for piano and 22 instruments premieres in Donaueschingen, Germany.

Oct. 18   *Vortag uber Hu*, by Karlheinz Stockhausen, premieres in Donaueschingen.

Oct. 19   Iain Hamilton's *Te Deum* receives its initial performance at Duke University in Chapel Hill, North Carolina.

Oct. 20   Dominick Argento's *To Be Sung upon the Water* premieres at Scott Hall in Minneapolis, Minnesota. The piece is scored for high voice, clarinet and piano and was composed two years ago.

Oct. 20   American composer Stanley Silverman's *Crepuscule* for two guitars, clarinet, violin and double bass is premiered by the Chamber Music Society of Lincoln Center at Alice Tully Hall in New York City.

Oct. 20   *Tristan*, preludes for piano, orchestra and electric sound, by Hans Werner Henze, receives its first performance in London.

Nov. 3   Alexander Goehr's *Chaconne*, Op. 19, for 19 wind instruments is premiered by Pierre Boulez at Leeds University, England.

Nov. 3   Isang Yun's *Etudien fur Flote Solo* is performed in its complete version for the first time in Berlin.

Nov. 12   George Crumb's piano piece *Makrokosmos, Vol. II*, receives its first performance by pianist Robert Miller at Alice Tully Hall in New York City.

Nov. 20   *Des canyons aux etoiles*, by Olivier Messiaen, receives its world premiere by the Musica Aeterna Orchestra at Alice Tully Hall in New York City. Yvonne Loriod is the soloist in this work, which is scored for piano.

Nov. 21   Peter Mennin's Symphony No. 8 receives its first performance by the New York Philharmonic at Avery Fisher Hall in New York City.

Dec. 6   Charles Wuorinen's Piano Concerto No 2 receives its world premiere by the New York Philharmonic, with the composer as soloist and Erich Leinsdorf conducting. The score calls for amplified piano. The premiere takes place in New York City.

Dec. 11   Vittorio Rieti's Symphony No. 6 is premiered by Frederic Waldman and the Aeterna Orchestra at Alice Tully Hall in New York City.

Dec. 14   Iain Hamilton's Piano Sonata No. 2 is premiered by Michael Ponti at Hunter College in New York City.

1974   Births, Deaths and Debuts

Jan. 13   Canadian tenor Raoul Jobin, 67, dies in Quebec. After making his debut with the Paris Grand Opera in 1930, he eventually sang with the New York Metropolitan Opera, the San Francisco Opera, the Chicago Opera and the Cincinnati Opera. In a production of *Carmen* (Pittsburgh, 1948), he bled all over the stage after being accidentally slashed by vocalist Gladys Swarthout. He continued singing the performance.

Feb. 2   Belgian composer and teacher Jean Absil, 80, dies in Brussels. Winner of many prizes, he was a prolific composer and a founder of the publication *Revue Internationale de Musique*. He was on the faculty of the Academy of Etterbeek (Brussels) and the Brussels Conservatory. His music is tonal, contrapuntal, and features animated rhythms. He was highly prolific and composed many works for various combinations of voices and instruments.

Feb. 15   Composer Kurt Atterberg, 86, dies in Stockholm. Also a conductor and critic, he was intensely involved in the musical life of Sweden, both as a founding member of the Society of Swedish Composers and as secretary of the Royal Academy of Music. His numerous symphonies are romantic and employ folk melodies. He also composed five operas, two string quartets and many other works for various combinations of voices and instruments.

March 5   Russian-American impresario Sol Hurok, 85, dies in New York. Hurok fled Russia in 1905 and came to the United States. In 1913 he presented a concert series at the New York Hippodrome called "Music for the Masses." Later he became the American manager of many Russian and European stars, such as Feodor Chaliapin, Artur Rubinstein, Anna Pavlova and Gregor Piatigorsky. His first love, however, was the ballet, and after many years of negotiation, he was finally able to bring the Bolshoi Ballet to America in 1959.

May 4   Russian-American composer and piano teacher Israel Citkowitz, 65, dies in London. A pupil of Roger Sessions, Aaron Copland and Nadia Boulanger, he taught at the Dalcroze School of Music in New York City. Most of his work is vocal music.

June 17   Conductor and violinist Arthur B. Lipkin, 67, dies in Princeton, New Jersey. After beginning his career as a violinist with the Philadelphia Orchestra, he went on to become music director of the Birmingham Civic Symphony Orchestra in Alabama.

June 26   Jean Martinon makes his debut as the new music director of The Philharmonic Orchestra, conducting a program of music by Franz Liszt that features Martha Argerich as soloist. The concert takes place at the Congresgebouw in The Hague.

Aug. 2   British pianist Cyril Smith, 65, who made a comeback after being partially paralyzed by a stroke, dies in London. Sir Arthur Bliss and Ralph Vaughan Williams wrote compositions for him.

Sep. 8   Heldentenor Wolfgang Windgassen, 60, dies in Stuttgart, Germany. After singing at the Stuttgart Opera, he was chosen for the 1951 Bayreuth Festival and from then on was in great demand as a Wagnerian tenor. He later worked as an opera director as well.

Sep. 12   Jay S. Harrison, 47, dies in New York City. He was a music editor and critic for the New York *Herald Tribune*, *Music* magazine and *Musical America* (New York). He also possessed many autographed letters from musical celebrities. These are given to the Music Division of the Library of Congress.

Sep. 16   Opera impresario Lawrence Kelly, 46, dies in Kansas City, Missouri. He founded the Dallas Civic Opera.

Oct. 24   Soviet violinist David Oistrakh, 66, dies in Amsterdam. After studies in Odessa, he joined the staff of the Moscow Conservatory in 1934. His international career began after he won first prize at the International Competition in Brussels in 1937, but he didn't play in Paris or London until 1953, nor did he play in America until 1955. He was the teacher of a great many Soviet violinists.

Nov. 9   Austrian composer and musicologist Egon Wellesz, 89, dies in Oxford, England. After studying musicology with Guido Adler and composition with Arnold Schoenberg, he obtained his doctorate and began teaching, first at the Neues Conservatorium in Vienna, then at the University of Vienna until the rise of the Nazis. He then went to England and taught at Oxford University. In 1957 he was made a Commander of the British Empire. As a musicologist, Wellesz was an expert on Byzantine music. His own music was cerebral. He was extremely prolific; his works include six operas, four ballets, nine symphonies, nine string quartets and many other pieces.

FRANK MARTIN

Nov. 21   Swiss composer Frank Martin, 84, dies in Naarden, Holland. After studies in Geneva, Zurich and Paris he performed as a harpsichordist and pianist and began teaching at the Institut Jaques-Dalcroze. He later became president of the Association of Swiss Musicians. In 1946 he moved to Holland and taught composition at the Cologne Hochschule fur Musik. His music underwent three distinct stylistic changes: from French Impressionism to a more Germanic contrapuntal and introspective style to the use of 12-tone procedures, although he never adopted Arnold Schoenberg's 12-tone method completely. He was extraordinarily prolific and composed a long list of vocal and instrumental works. Perhaps his most famous work is the oratorio *In Terra Pax*, composed to celebrate the end of World War II. He also wrote two operas and several ballets.

Dec. 14   Swedish contralto Karin Branzell, 83, dies in Altadena, California. After debuting in Stockholm in 1911, she performed with the Metropolitan Opera, the Berlin State Opera and the Stockholm Royal Opera. She was known for her wide vocal range. King Gustav of Sweden decorated her with the "Litteris et Artibus," a gold medal of honor.

1974   Related Events

The Studio Wacker is demolished this year. This building, at 69 rue de Douai, Paris, was one of the most famous dance studios in Paris and was a meeting place for internationally known and unknown ballet people seeking work and sharing creative ideas. Famous dancers, choreographers and teachers who taught in the building include Olga Preobrajenska, Madame Rousanne, Victor Gsovsky and Nora Kiss.

The Stratification of Musical Rhythm, by Maury Yeston, is published this year by Yale University Press. Yeston's book explores a theory of rhythm in tonal music by analyzing rhythm in terms of pitch levels and abstracting structures that result from the interaction of these levels. He then posits new definitions of accent, syncopation and meter. This original work is based on the theories of Heinrich Schenker. Yeston's final chapter is devoted to the problems of constructing a general theory of rhythm. Yeston is now an assistant professor of music theory at Yale University. He subsequently composes his musical *Nine*, which becomes a tremendous success on Broadway.

Jan. 8 Cellist Mstislav Rostropovich, who had been prevented from appearing outside the Soviet Union for three years because of his support of Alexander Solzhenitsyn, is allowed to leave for Paris.

Feb. 14 Ottorino Respighi's *Pines of Rome* is called one of the "bourgeoisie works of music" by the Chinese news agency Hsinhua. The piece had been conducted by Eugene

Ormandy during a visit to Peking in September 1973. The music of Beethoven and Schubert is also classified as "foreign things."

March 9 The first festival of contemporary music of New Zealand takes place at Victoria University in Wellington. Entitled "Sonic Circus", it is presented by the New Zealand Broadcasting Corporation and features new music by Douglas Lilburn and other native New Zealand composers.

May 7 Donald Martino is awarded the Pulitzer Prize for music for *Notturno*. Roger Sessions is also given a special award and citation for his life's work in musical composition.

June 29 Mikhail Baryshnikov, a leading dancer with the Kirov Ballet, defects to the West while on tour with the Bolshoi Ballet in Toronto, Canada. He cites personal and artistic reasons for his defection.

1975 Opera

Feb. 14 Boris Blacher's opera *Das Geheimnis des entwendeten Briefes* premieres at the West Berlin Hochschule.

April Luigi Nono's *Al Gian Sole Carico d'Amore* is premiered in Milan at La Scala. The composer uses texts by several different revolutionary writers for his libretto, which is a symbolic treatment of various historical revolutionary events.

May 23 *Treemonisha*, an opera by Scott Joplin, is staged by the Houston Opera, bringing this neglected opera to national attention (it was performed at Atlanta Symphony Hall on January 28, 1972 but not in a fully staged production). Frank Corsaro directs and Gunther Schuller conducts. Lead singers include Betty Allen, Carmen Balthorpe and Willard White. The opera takes place in Texarkana on a plantation in 1866 and is about Treemonisha, the adopted daughter of two freed slaves, who becomes educated and grows up to be a leader. Joplin composed this opera in 1911. A 1915 premiere in concert form failed. The New York *Times* says of today's performance, "In Houston, nobody applauded, they just yelled. Some even lost control and dashed onto the stage to join in."

July 17 *Ratsumies*, a new opera by Finnish composer Aulis Sallinen, receives its first performance at the Savonlinna Opera Festival in Finland today. The title of the work means "The Horseman."

Aug. 2 Robert Starer's opera *The Last Lover* premieres at the Caramoor Festival in Katonah, New York.

Sep. 20 Jack Beeson's opera *Captain Jinks of the Horse Marines* premieres in Kansas City, Missouri.

Nov. 4 Boris Blacher's opera *Der Mohr von Venedig* premieres at the Deutsche Opera in Berlin.

Dec. 15 Excerpts from Charles Wuorinen's opera *The W. of Babylon* are premiered by the Group for Contemporary Music at the Manhattan School of Music in New York City. The opera is a satire on French aristocracy of the 1600s. The composer considers this work to be one of his most important.

AULIS SALLINEN·

1975 Dance

Feb. 16   Yuri Grigorovich's *Ivan the Terrible* — to music by Sergei Prokofiev, with costumes and scenery by Simon Virsaladze — is premiered by the Bolshoi Ballet in Moscow. It is based on the life of this infamous and ignoble tsar. The principal dancers are Natalia Bessmertnova, Yuri Vladimirov and Boris Akimov.

March 7   Merce Cunningham's *Rebus*, to music by David Behrman, and his *Changing Steps/Loops*, to music by John Cage, are premiered in Detroit. These are modern dance pieces.

May 14-31   The New York City Ballet opens a Ravel Festival that lasts through May 31. During the festival, 16 new works are premiered by choreographers George Blanchine, Jerome Robbins, John Taras, and Jacques d'Amboise. Today's program includes the premieres of *Sonatine*, choreographed by Balanchine and *Concerto in G*, choreographed by Robbins. The dancers in the former are Violette Verdy and Jean-Pierre Bonnefous; in the latter, Suzanne Farrell and Peter Martins. The program is conducted by Ravel's former pupil, Manuel Rosenthal. Both ballets are plotless works.

May 22   The New York Ballet continues its Ravel Festival. Premiered today are Jerome Robbins' *Introduction and Allegro for Harp*, danced by Patricia McBride and Helgi Tomasson, and his version of *Ma Mere L'Oye*. Also premiered is George Balanchine's *Sheherazade*, danced by Kay Mazzo and Edward Villella. Today's final premiere is John Taras' version of *Daphnis and Chloe*, danced by Peter Martins, Nina Fedorova and Karin von Aroldingen.

May 29   Eight new ballets receive their premieres at the New York City Ballet's Ravel Festival. They are: *Le Tombeau de Couperin*, choreographed by George Balanchine; *Pavane*,

choreographed by Balanchine and danced by Patricia McBride; *Une Barque sur l'ocean*, choreographed by Jerome Robbins; *Tzigane*, choreographed by Balanchine and danced by Suzanne Farrell and Peter Martins; *Gaspard de la Nuit*, choreographed by Balanchine and danced by Colleen Neary, Victor Castelli, Karin von Aroldingen and Sara Leland; *Sarabande and Danse (II)*, choreographed by Jacques d'Amboise; *Chanson Madecasses*, choreographed by Robbins and danced by Patricia McBride and Helgi Tomasson, and, finally, *Rhapsodie Espagnole*, choreographed by Balanchine and danced by Karin von Aroldingen and Peter Schaufuss.

June 29   Choreographer Ronald Hynd's one-act ballet *Orient-Occident* receives its first performance in Venice to celebrate the Festival of Dance 1975. The music is by Iannis Xenakis. The ballet is about the famous journey of Marco Polo. Makato Fukuyama, Lee San Chong, and Hiroshi Sato star in this production by the Tokyo Ballet Company.

July 30   The New York City Ballet premieres George Balanchine's *The Steadfast Soldier* in Saratoga Springs, New York. The music is by Georges Bizet. Patricia McBride and Peter Schaufuss dance the 10-minute pas de deux about the love of a paper doll and a toy soldier.

Dec. 12   *Notre Faust*, a ballet in two parts choreographed by Maurice Bejart, receives its first performance in Brussels. Thierry Bousquet designs the costumes and sets. The music is a combination of South American tangos and works by J. S. Bach. The comic ballet is based on the famous Faust legend. It is praised by critics as a landmark in modern ballet. Yan Le Gac and Bejart are the principal dancers in this production by the Ballet of the 20th Century.

1975 Instrumental and Vocal Music

Jan. 5   Dominick Argento's *From the Diary of Virginia Woolf* is premiered by mezzo-soprano Janet Baker and pianist Martin Isepp at Orchestra Hall in Minneapolis, Minnesota.

Jan. 13   Henry Purcell's *Fantasy on One Note*, arranged for brass by Elliott Carter, is premiered by the American Brass Quintet at Carnegie Recital Hall in New York City.

Jan. 24   Carmen Moore's *Wildfires and Field Songs* is premiered by Pierre Boulez and the New York Philharmonic at Avery Fisher Hall in New York City. Moore's teachers include Stefan Wolpe, Luciano Berio and Vincent Persi-

chetti. He organized the Society of Black Composers in 1968.

Jan. 26   Morton Feldman's *String Quartet and Orchestra* is premiered by the Buffalo Philharmonic and the Cleveland Quartet in Buffalo, New York.

Feb. 12   William Bergsma's *Wishes, Wonders, Portents, Charms* is premiered by Martin Josman and the National Chorale at Avery Fisher Hall, Lincoln Center in New York City. The work is scored for chorus and a combination of instruments.

Feb. 18   George Perle's *Songs of Praise and Lamentation* for choruses and orchestra is premiered by Michael Hammond and the Dessoff and Concordia choirs at Carnegie Hall in New York City.

Feb. 23   Alan Hovhaness' folk oratorio *The Way of Jesus* is premiered by Laszlo Halasz at Saint Patrick's Cathedral in New York City.

Feb. 23   Norman Dello Joio's *Lyric Fantasies* for viola and strings premieres at Alice Tully Hall in New York City.

Feb. 27   *Echoes from an Invisible World*, by Leslie Bassett, receives its world premiere by the Philadelphia Orchestra in Philadelphia. The orchestral work was commissioned by this orchestra and the National Endowment for the Arts specifically for the American Bicentennial.

March 14   Ulysses Kay's *Concerto for Orchestra and Quintet* is premiered by the Juilliard Orchestra at Alice Tully Hall in New York City.

March 21   Elliott Carter's *Duo for Violin and Piano* is premiered by Paul Zukofsky and Gilbert Kalish at the Great Hall, Cooper Union in New York City.

March 23   Heinz Holliger's *Quartet for Strings* premieres at the Royan Festival in France.

March 24   Virgil Thomson's *Family Portrait* is premiered by the American Brass Quintet at Carnegie Recital Hall in New York City.

March 25   Paul Chihara's *Ceremony II (Incantations)* premieres at Carnegie Hall in New York City. This work is scored for flute, two cellos and percussion. Chihara's teachers include Nadia Boulanger. He is currently teaching at the University of California at Los Angeles.

April 2   *Rituel*, by Pierre Boulez, is premiered by the BBC Symphony Orchestra at Festival Hall in London, the composer conducting.

April 3   Leonard Bernstein's *Dybbuk Suite No. 1* is premiered by the New York Philharmonic, the composer conducting. Paul Sperry is tenor soloist, Bruce Fifer bass-baritone soloist. This work is the first of two suites extracted from Bernstein's ballet *Dybbuk*, first performed in 1974.

April 4   George Rochberg's Violin Concerto is premiered by the Pittsburgh Symphony Orchestra in Pittsburgh, Pennsylvania, with Isaac Stern as soloist.

April 7   Paul Lansky's *Mild and Leise* is premiered by the League-ISCM at Carnegie Recital Hall in New York City.

April 8   Anton Heiller's *Meditation uber die Ostersequenz* premieres in Oldenburg, Germany.

April 14   Norman Dello Joio's *Notes from Tom Paine* premieres at Avery Fisher Hall in New York City.

April 17   Leonard Bernstein's *Dybbuk Suite No. 2* is premiered by the New York Philharmonic, the composer conducting.

April 22   Carmen Moore's *Museum Piece* premieres at the Guggenheim Museum in New York City. This is the second of two pieces by this composer to attract considerable attention this year. The other was *Wildfires and Field Songs*.

April 29   Milton Babbitt's *Reflections* for piano and synthesized sound is premiered by pianist Robert Miller at Alice Tully Hall in New York City.

May 6   Philip Glass' *Another Look at Harmony* (Parts 1 and 2) is premiered at Town Hall in New York City.

May 12   Paul Lansky's String Quartet No. 2 is premiered by the American Quartet at Carnegie Recital Hall in New York City.

May 16   Karlheinz Stockhausen's *Atem gibt des Leben* is premiered by the Chor des Norddeutschen Rundfunks in Hamburg, Germany.

June 1   *A Reliquary for Igor Stravinsky*, by Charles Wuorinen, receives its first performance at the Ojai Festival in Ojai, California. Michael Tilson Thomas conducts. The piece is a tribute to Igor Stravinsky, based on his last fragment of music. It is dedicated to Vera Stravinsky and Robert Craft and is scored for a mixture of winds, percussion, harp, piano and strings.

June 18   Richard Franko Goldman's *Seaside Park* is premiered by the Goldman Band at the Guggenheim Memorial Band Shell, Lincoln Center in New York City.

June 24   Cristobal Halffter's Concerto for Violoncello and Orchestra premieres in Granada, Spain.

June 29   Iannis Xenakis' *Empreintes* for orchestra premieres in La Rochelle, France.

Aug. 12   Heinrich Sutermeister's Clarinet Concerto premieres over Radio Suisse Romande.

Sep. 12   Ernst Krenek's *Feiertagskantate*, Op. 221, premieres in Berlin.

Sep. 14   Benjamin Britten's *Sacred and Profane* for five unaccompanied voices is premiered by the Wilbye Consort of Voices at The Maltings, near Aldeburgh, England, Peter Pears conducting. This work is based on medieval poetry.

Sep. 30   Jean Francaix' *Aubade* for 12 solo cellos premieres in Berlin.

Oct. 17   Luciano Berio's *Chemins IV* for oboe and 13 strings is premiered by the London Sinfonietta, with Heinz Holliger as soloist.

Oct. 25   Heinz Holliger's *Studie Uber Mehrklange fur Oboe* premieres in Basel.

Nov. 9   John Corigliano's Concerto for Oboe and Orchestra is premiered by Kazuyoshi Akiyama and the American Symphony Orchestra at Carnegie Hall in New York, with Bert Lucarelli as soloist.

Dec. 4   Mario Davidovsky's *Synchronisms No. 7* is premiered by Pierre Boulez and the New York Philharmonic at Avery Fisher Hall in New York City.

Dec. 5   Ned Rorem's *Air Music* is premiered by the Cincinnati Symphony Orchestra. This work was commissioned for the American bicentennial.

1975   Births, Deaths and Debuts

Jan. 8   American tenor Richard Tucker, 61, dies in Kalamazoo, Michigan. Having begun his musical life in a synagogue choir, he studied voice, debuted at the Metropolitan in 1945 and sang there successfully until the end of his life. In 1949 he was chosen by Arturo Toscanini to sing a radio broadcast of *Aida*.

Jan. 16   Conductor Thor Johnson, 61, dies in Nashville, Tennessee. He studied with Nikolai Malko, Hermann Abendroth, Felix Weingartner, Bruno Walter and Serge Koussevitzky. In addition to touring the United States, Europe and the Orient, he guest-conducted the Philadelphia Orchestra and became principal conductor of the Cincinnati Symphony Orchestra. He was also music director of the Nashville Orchestra in Tennessee.

Jan. 20   Belgian conductor and composer Franz Andre, 81, dies in Brussels. After studying violin with Eugene Ysaye and performing with the Bluthner Orchestra in Berlin, he taught violin at the Brussels Conservatory. He began conducting the Radio Orchestra of Radio Belgique in 1930 and focused on works by contemporary French and Belgian composers. He also conducted many pieces by Arnold Schoenberg.

Jan. 26   Italian soprano Toti Dal Monte, 81, dies in Treviso. After making her debut at La Scala in 1916, she sang at the New York Metropolitan Opera. She also toured Australia and became a well-known teacher. Her real name was Antonietta Mengehelli.

Jan. 30   German composer Boris Blacher, 72, dies in West Berlin. Having switched to music after studying architecture, he became a professor of musical composition at the West Berlin Hochschule fur Musik in 1948. He later became its director. His music is characterized by constant changes of meter — this is evidenced in the fluctuating time signatures used in many of his works. He composed traditional, conservative tonal music as well as modernistic and electronic music with elements of improvisation. He joined the faculty of Technological University in Berlin in 1960 and became director of its Seminar of Electronic Composition. He was extremely prolific and wrote nine operas, including *Incidents at a Forced Landing* — an "operatic reportage" for vocalists, electronic sounds and instruments; six ballets, many orchestral works, including a number of concertos for different instruments with orchestra; chamber music, including four string quartets; various electronic pieces; piano music; and songs.

Jan. 31   Polish opera singer and teacher Elsa Alsen, 94, dies in New York City. She debuted in Germany in 1902 and soon switched from contralto to soprano. She then became known as a Wagnerian soprano and sang with the Manhattan Opera and the Chicago Civic Opera. She also sang in films and gave many recitals.

Feb. 19   Italian composer Luigi Dallapiccola, 71, dies in Florence. He studied at the Cherubini Conservatory and later taught there. He was attracted to atonality while still in his youth and quickly embraced Arnold Schoenberg's 12-tone method. He applied what might be considered an Italian specialty — graceful vocal writing — to his own personal adaptation of the contrapuntal and harmonic complexities of dodecaphonic music. This enabled him to make a contribution to Italian music that separated 20th-century Italian opera and vocal music from that of the 19th century. Two other Italian composers — Luigi Nono and Bruno Maderna — worked along somewhat similar lines. Dallapiccola also taught in America. He was very prolific. Among his works are the opera *Il prigioniero* and the vocal work in three sets *Cori di Michelangelo*.

BORIS BLACHER

Feb. 22   English viola player Lionel Tertis, 98, dies in London. After studies at the Leipzig Conservatory and the Royal Academy of Music in London, he became a string quartet player. Later he chose a solo career and became highly successful both in Europe and in America.

Feb. 24   French-born harpist and composer Marcel Grandjany, 83, dies in New York City. A pupil at the Paris Conservatoire, he debuted in Paris in 1909 and in America in 1924. He taught at the American Conservatory at Fontainebleau and at the Juilliard School of Music. He also composed works for harp with various combinations of other instruments.

Feb. 28   English music writer Sir Neville Cardus, 85, dies in London. He became a writer after studying singing and wrote for the Manchester *Guardian*. In 1963 he was awarded the Wagner Medal given by the City of Bayreuth. He was later knighted. In addition to writing many books on music, he also wrote about and taught cricket.

March 27   Sir Arthur Bliss, 83, dies in London. After studies at Pembroke College, Cambridge he studied with Sir Charles Villiers Stanford, Ralph Vaughan Williams and Gustav Holst at the Royal College of Music in London. While serving in the British army, he was gassed by the Germans. He returned to music after World War I, attracted attention during the early 1920s and traveled to America. He was music director of the BBC during World War II. In 1950 he was knighted; three years later he became Master of the Queen's Musick. He composed two operas, four ballets, many orchestral works, chamber music (including three string quartets) and piano works.

April 17   Hugo von Mendelssohn, 81, dies in Basel. Founder of the International Felix Mendelssohn Society, he was Felix' great-grandson and last surviving relative.

April 19   Danish tenor Aksel Schiotz, 68, dies in Copenhagen. After starting out as a schoolteacher, he did not make his singing debut until he was 33 years old. He specialized in music of Bach and Mozart and also concertized as a lieder singer. Stricken by a disease that resulted in partial paralysis, he later resumed his career as a baritone but had already lost full control of his voice. He was known for his stylistic excellence and consummate taste and was fluent in many languages.

April 26   Godfrey C. Winham, 40, dies of Hodgkin's disease in Princeton, New Jersey. Husband of American vocalist Bethany Beardslee, he was an expert on computer music and music involving synthesized speech and was a member of Princeton University's music faculty. His works include two string quartets and a piece for voice and string quartet entitled *The Habit of Perfection*. The Winham Electronic Music Laboratory at Princeton University is named after him.

June 3   German soprano Frida Leider, 87, dies in Berlin. One of the great Wagnerian sopranos, she made her debut in Halle, Germany and then became a member of the Berlin State Opera. She first appeared in London in 1924 and in America in 1928. After singing at the Metropolitan for two seasons (1933–34), she then returned to Germany. Leider was known for her beautiful voice and impassioned singing.

June 3   German-born cellist Hermann Busch, 77, dies in Bryn Mawr, Pennsylvania. He was a chamber music player and a founder of the Marlboro Festival. He was also the brother of violinist Adolf Busch and conductor Fritz Busch.

June 26   English violinist and conductor Basil Cameron, 90, dies in London. He studied composition with Max Bruch and, upon realizing that German conductors were well respected in England, changed his name to Basil Hindenberg. That lasted until the outbreak of World War II, when he again became known as Basil Cameron. His interest in new music and its degree of abstraction did not endear him to the music public. Orchestras he conducted include the Seattle Symphony Orchestra and the San Francisco Symphony Orchestra.

July 15   Dancer and choreographer Charles Weidman dies in New York at the age of 73. He studied at Denishawn and was a member of that company for eight years. In 1928 Weidman and Doris Humphrey formed a company which continued in various forms until 1945. Weidman choreographed extensively for the group, primarily developing light satirical works such as his famous *And Daddy Was a Fireman*. He also worked on Broadway, staging dances for such shows as *Sing Out Sweet Land, As Thousands Cheer* and *School for Husbands*. During the early 1960s he founded the Expression of Two Arts Theater with sculptor Mikhail Santaro. There, dance shared the emphasis with sculpture, painting and music. Among Weidman's most famous pupils were Jose Limon, Jack Cole and Bob Foss.

Sep. 1   American violinist John Corigliano Sr., 74, dies in Norfolk, Connecticut. Father of American composer John Corigliano Jr., he was concertmaster of the New York Philharmonic and was well-known for his violin recitals.

Sep. 18   Jerzy Semkov makes his debut as the new music director of the Saint Louis Symphony Orchestra, conducting works by Mozart, Beethoven and Gustav Mahler. The concert takes place at Powell Symphony Hall in Saint Louis, Missouri. Critic Frank Peters writes in the Saint Louis *Post-Dispatch* that Semkov's handling of the third movement of Mahler's First Symphony ". . . re-created its dark humor vividly." This orchestra also begins its nationwide broadcasts of concerts this year.

Oct. 8   German opera director Walter Felsenstein, 74, dies in East Berlin. He directed the East Berlin Komische Oper and was known for bringing that house to international attention.

Oct. 29   Music publisher Karl Votterle, 72, dies in Kassel, Germany. In 1924 he founded the Barenreiter-Verlag, which published the important work *Die Musik in Geschichte und Gegenwart*.

Nov. 22   German musicologist Friedrich Blume, 82, dies in Schluchtern, Germany. He studied medicine and philosophy in addition to music. His musicological work includes famous editions of music by Heinrich Schutz, Josquin des Pres, Mozart, Haydn and others. Blume supervised the first edition of *Die Musik in Geschichte und Gegenwart* and established himself as one of the foremost musicologists of the 20th century.

Nov. 30   Dr. Antin Rudnytsky, 73, dies in Toms River, New Jersey. A pianist, conductor and composer, he conducted the Kharkov Opera and the Kiev Opera and taught at many institutions, including the Philadelphia Musical Academy. His own music includes three symphonies and various other pieces.

Dec. 15   Lydia Chaliapin, 74, dies in Stafford Springs, Connecticut. Daughter of the famed Feodor, she coached many singers at New York's Metropolitan Opera.

1975   Related Events

The "soundstream" process of digital recording is developed by Thomas Stockham in America. It is first used to rerecord and enhance the recordings of Enrico Caruso and other early artists.

March 5   Mstislav Rostropovich conducts the National Symphony Orchestra in Washington, D.C. for the first time. He becomes this orchestra's music director in 1977.

April 9   The new organ in Alice Tully Hall at Lincoln Center in New York City is formally dedicated. Built by the Theodore Kuhn Company of Mannedorf, Switzerland, the organ is freestanding and contains 4,192 pipes.

May 5   Dominick Argento is awarded the Pulitzer Prize for music for *From the Diary of Virginia Woolf.*

July 24   A performance of Alexander Scriabin's *Prometheus (The Poem of Fire)*, composed in 1911, takes place at Iowa University, as James Dixon conducts the university's symphony orchestra. This performance features a special laser apparatus designed and built by Lowell Cross, the purpose of which is to render the visualization of color that Scriabin envisaged.

Nov. 12   The MacDowell Colony celebrates Aaron Copland's 75th birthday with a special concert of his music at Alice Tully Hall in New York City.

1976   Opera

Jan. 24   Nino Rota's opera *Torquemada* premieres at the Teatro San Carlo in Naples.

Feb. 11   Alun Hoddinott's opera *Murder, the Magician* premieres over Welsh television.

HANS WERNER HENZE, LEFT, WITH TATJANA GSOOSKY

Feb. 29   Carlisle Floyd's *Bilby's Doll* is premiered by the Houston Grand Opera in Houston. This opera celebrates the American bicentennial.

April 22   Hugo Weisgall's opera *The Hundred Nights* is premiered by the Juilliard American Opera Theater in New York City.

April 24   Dominick Argento's *The Voyage of Edgar Allan Poe*, with a libretto by Charles Nolte, is premiered by the Minnesota Opera Company in Saint Paul, Minnesota.

May 27   *The Hero*, an opera by Gian-Carlo Menotti, is premiered by the Opera Company of Philadelphia at the Academy of Music in Philadelphia, Pennsylvania.

July 12   Hans Werner Henze's opera *We Come to the River* receives its initial performance at the Royal Opera House at Covent Garden in London.

July 25   *Einstein on the Beach*, an opera by Philip Glass and Robert Wilson, receives its world premiere at the Festival of Avignon in France. This opera is later performed in Amsterdam, Belgrade, Brussels, Hamburg, Paris, Rotterdam and at the Metropolitan Opera in New York. The work creates a sensation, largely with younger audiences.

1976 Dance

Jan. 5   *Video Triangle*, choreographed by Merce Cunningham, enjoys its first performance on "Dance in America" over public television in Newark, New Jersey.

Jan. 22   The New York City Ballet premieres George Balanchine's *Chaconne* to music by Christoph Willibald von Gluck. Suzanne Farrell and Peter Martins star.

Feb. 12   *A Month in the Country*, choreographed by Frederick Ashton to music by Frederic Chopin (and arranged by John Lanchberry), receives its first performance by the Royal Ballet at Covent Garden in London. The choreography is loosely based on the play of the same name by Turgenev. Lynn Seymour and Anthony Dowell star.

May 12   *Union Jack*, choreographed by George Balanchine to music by Hershey Kay, is premiered by the New York City Ballet at the New York State Theater, Lincoln Center in New York City.

June 9   Paul Taylor premieres his new modern dance work entitled *Cloven Kingdom* at the Billy Rose Theater in New York City.

Nov. 15   Twyla Tharp premieres her new modern dance work *After All*. It is performed at Superstakes III in New York, to music by Tomaso Albinoni, with costumes by Santo Loquasto.

1976 Instrumental and Vocal Music

Jan. 18   Morton Feldman's *Four Instruments* is premiered by the Cantilena Players at the Jewish Museum in New York City. Also receiving its initial performance at today's concert is David Amram's *Portraits*.

Jan. 27   Roque Cordero's *Soliloquios No. 1 for Flute Solo* receives its first performance by Judith Ross at Illinois State University in Normal, Illinois. His *Three Silly Pieces for Flute Solo* is also premiered.

Jan. 28   Iannis Xenakis' *Phlegra* is premiered by the London Sinfonietta in London. This piece is scored for 11 instruments.

Jan. 29   *Concertmasters* for three solo violins and orchestra, by Michael Colgrass, is premiered by Aldo Ceccato and the Detroit Symphony Orchestra in Detroit.

Jan. 30   Lennox Berkeley's Quintet for Piano and Winds, Op. 90, is premiered by the Chamber Music Society of Lincoln Center at Alice Tully Hall in New York City.

Feb. 2   Roque Cordero's *Variations and Theme for Five* is premiered by the Sonneries Woodwind Quintet at the Gooman Theater Center in Chicago. This piece was composed last year.

Feb. 17   *Wolf*, a work for solo cello by Michael Colgrass, is premiered by Ronald Thomas at the Hunter College Playhouse in New York City.

Feb. 19   Joseph Schwantner's *Canticle of the Evening Bells* is premiered by the Contemporary Chamber Ensemble at Alice Tully Hall in New York City.

Feb. 24   Elliott Carter's *A Mirror on Which to Dwell* for soprano and nine players is premiered by Richard Fitz and Young Concert Artists at Hunter College in New York City. The text consists of six poems by Elizabeth Bishop. The songs are entitled "Anaphora," "Argument," "Sandpiper," "Insomnia," "View of the Capitol from the Library of Congress" and "O Breath."

Feb. 26   *Before the Butterfly*, by Morton Subotnick, receives its world premiere by the Los Angeles Philharmonic in that city. This orchestral work was commissioned by this orchestra and the National Endowment for the Arts specifically for the American bicentennial.

Feb. 29   Ned Rorem's *Book of Hours* for flute and harp is premiered at Alice Tully Hall in New York City.

March 11   Iannis Xenakis' *Mikka "S"* for solo violin is premiered in Orleans, France. The piece was composed in 1972.

March 15   George Rochberg's *Quintet for Piano and String Quartet* is premiered by the Concord String Quartet and Jerome Lowenthal at Alice Tully Hall in New York City.

March 21   *Hyperion*, by Charles Wuorinen, receives its initial performance at the Adelaide Festival of Arts in Adelaide, Australia, as Arthur Weisburg conducts the Contemporary Chamber Ensemble. The piece is scored for a mixture of winds, brass, strings and piano.

March 25   Richard Rodney Bennett's Violin Concerto receives its first performance in Birmingham, England.

March 28   Peter Mennin's *Voices* is premiered by the Chamber Music Society of Lincoln Center at Alice Tully Hall in New York City. This work is scored for voice, percussion, piano, harp and harpsichord. It is based on poetry by Emily Dickinson, Walt Whitman, Herman Melville and Henry David Thoreau.

April 1   Morton Gould's *Symphony of Spirituals* is premiered by Aldo Ceccato and the Detroit Symphony Orchestra in Detroit.

April 13   Andrzej Panufnik's *Symphony of Spheres* is premiered by David Atherton and the London Symphony Orchestra in London.

April 21   *Crossworks*, by Paul Lansky, receives its world premiere by the Da Capo Chamber Players at Carnegie Recital Hall in New York City. This work was composed from a small bit of the harmonic material from the second piece of Arnold Schoenberg's Five Orchestral Pieces, Op. 16. The title refers to this "compositional grafting" and to the formation of melodic lines and harmonies by instruments tumbling over each other's music. The piece was composed in 1974.

April 21   Humphrey Searle's *Contemplations* for mezzo-soprano and orchestra is premiered by Jan De Gaetani and the Clarion Concerts Orchestra at Alice Tully Hall in New York City. Searle is currently teaching at the Royal College of Music in London. This year is his last in that position.

April 24   *Poem on His Birthday* for baritone, chorus and orchestra, by John Corigliano Jr., receives its first performance in Washington, D.C.

May 3   Cristobal Halffter's *Pourquoi?* premieres in Paris. This piece is scored for 12 string instruments.

YEHUDI MENUHIN

May 27   Norman Dello Joio's orchestral piece *Colonial Varianti; 13 Profiles of the Original Colonies, Based on an Ancient Tune* is premiered by Eugene Ormandy and the Philadelphia Orchestra at the Grand Opera House in Wilmington, Delaware.

June 16   Benjamin Britten's *Phaedra* is premiered by the English Chamber Orchestra at Aldeburgh, England, with Janet Baker as vocal soloist.

July 3   Alan Hovhaness' Violin Concerto receives its initial performance by Andre Kostelanetz and the National Symphony Orchestra at Wolf Trap Farm Park, with Yehudi Menuhin as soloist.

July 15   Elisabeth Lutyens' *Plenum IV*, an organ duet, premieres at Westminster Abbey in London.

July 18   *Sirius*, by Karlheinz Stockhausen, receives its world premiere at the Smithsonian Institution in Washington, D.C. This is a multimedia piece scored for vocalists, trumpet, bass clarinet and electronic sound. It was composed as a tribute to American pioneers, particularly American astronauts.

July 19   *Visions of Terror and Wonder*, by Richard Wernick, receives its world premiere at the Aspen Music Festival in Aspen, Colorado. This work is scored for mezzo-soprano and orchestra and has texts from the Koran and the Bible in Greek, Arabic and Hebrew. The piece is later awarded the Pulitzer Prize for music. Wenick has studied with Arthur Berger at Brandeis University, with Boris Blacher at Tanglewood, and with Ernst Toch. He also studied conducting with Leonard Bernstein. He is currently on the music faculty of the University of Pennsylvania in Philadelphia.

Aug. 4   Gian-Carlo Menotti's Symphony No. 1 receives its world premiere at the Saratoga Performing Arts Center in Saratoga, New York. The Philadelphia Orchestra performs the piece, which is the first bicentennial work commissioned by the Saratoga Festival.

Sep. 29   *Renga* with *Apartment House 1776*, by John Cage, receives its world premiere by the Boston Symphony Orchestra in Boston. Seiji Ozawa conducts. It is scored for two synchronized orchestral groups and four vocal soloists and was commissioned by this orchestra and the National Endowment for the Arts specifically for the American bicentennial.

Oct. 2   The Second Sonata for Piano, by Charles Wuorinen, premieres at the Kennedy Center for the Performing Arts in Washington, D.C. The piece was composed for the Bicentennial Piano Series of the Washington Performing Arts Society. Jeffrey Swann is the soloist.

Oct. 7   *The Final Alice*, by David Del Tredici, receives its world premiere in Chicago. This tonal orchestral work is the latest in a series of pieces by Del Tredici inspired by *Alice in Wonderland*. Erich Leinsdorf later says of the music in an interview with New York *Times* critic John Rockwell, "It is in my personal opinion totally without merit — parlaying the major-sixth chord into a 58-minute work...."

Oct. 12   Ulysses Kay's orchestral piece *Western Paradise* is premiered by the National Symphony Orchestra at the Kennedy Center in Washington, D.C.

Oct. 13   *Tashi*, by Charles Wuorinen, receives its first performance by the Cleveland Orchestra in Cleveland, Ohio, the composer conducting. Wuorinen subsequently arranges the work for chamber ensemble. The work is scored for four solos and orchestra.

Dec. 3   *Letter from Mozart*, by Michael Colgrass, is premiered by Frederic Waldman and Jose Serebrier at Alice Tully Hall in New York City. This work is a "collage" for piano and orchestra.

1976   Births, Deaths and Debuts

Jan. 1   American clarinetist Robert E. McGinnis, 65, dies in Syosset, Long Island. He performed as a solo clarinetist under Bruno Walter, Dimitri Mitropoulos, Leonard Bernstein, Josef Krips, George Szell and Arturo Toscanini.

Jan. 5   French composer Georges Migot, 84, dies in Levallois, France. After studies at the Paris Conservatoire with Charles-Marie Widor, Andre Gedalge, Vincent d'Indy and others, he joined the French Army and was wounded in World War I. Although unsuccessful at obtaining a Prix de Rome, he did win the Lily Boulanger Prize in 1918. At about this time he began to paint and had three Paris exhibitions of his work. He continued to compose, most often writing his own texts. His music is characterized by modal melodies and diatonic harmonies. He frequently exploited extreme registers of instruments to create unusual instrumental colors. He was highly prolific and composed symphonic works, including *Hagoromo* for baritone, chorus and orchestra, 13 symphonies, vocal works, including the oratorio *L'Annonciation*, and much chamber music, including many pieces entitled "Dialogues." He also wrote articles and was a curator of old instruments at the Paris Conservatoire. A society devoted to the study of Migot's music is subsequently established. French musicologist Marc Honegger participates in cataloging Migot's works.

Jan. 19   Francis Goodwin II, 80, dies in Wethersfield, Connecticut. He was a founder of the Hartford Symphony Orchestra.

Jan. 22   Thomas F. Pyle, 58, dies in New York City. He was a baritone and was well known for recruiting singers for choral groups, such as the Robert Shaw Chorale, Musica Sacra and the Schola Cantorum.

Jan. 23   American singer-actor Paul Robeson, 77, dies in Philadelphia. After graduating Phi Beta Kappa from Rutgers University and being named to the all-American football team, he got his law degree from Columbia University. He turned to acting and appeared in Eugene O'Neill's *The Emperor Jones* in 1923 and later in *Porgy, The Hairy Ape* and, in London, *Othello*. In 1925 he gave his first recital of spirituals and gospel songs. He sang "Ol' Man River" in the original production of *Showboat* in 1926. He traveled frequently in Europe and the Soviet Union giving recitals. In 1950 his passport was revoked because he refused to deny membership in the Communist Party. His passport having been returned in 1958, he moved shortly afterward to England, where he lived until 1963. His beautiful bass voice and the intensity of his acting made him an extremely effective performer.

Feb. 1   English composer, pianist and editor Maurice Jacobson, 80, dies in Brighton. He wrote vocal, instrumental and dance music and was a president of the British music publishing house J. Curwen & Sons Ltd.

Feb. 3   Heinrich Schalit, 90, dies in Evergreen, Colorado. He was a composer of sacred Jewish music and served as music director of both the Great Synagogue of Rome and the Great Synagogue of Munich.

Feb. 13   French coloratura soprano Lily Pons, 87, dies in Dallas, Texas. After early studies on the piano, she turned to singing, debuting in 1928 as Lakme. She soon came to the Metropolitan, where she became popular in the coloratura repertoire. Her fame spread, and she made appearances in European and South American opera houses. During World War II she toured the Allied fronts giving numerous recitals for the troops. She was married for a time to conductor Andre Kostelanetz. She had a town named after her — Lilypons, Maryland.

Feb. 25   Peter Yates, 66, dies in New York. This Canadian-American writer on music studied at Princeton University and became devoted to helping some composers get their works performed. Although he earned his living as a bureaucrat in the California Department of Employment, he consistently brought composers and musicians together at his important concert series Evenings on the Roof which he established in 1939 (these concerts later became known as the Monday Evening Concerts). He joined the music faculty of the State University of New York (Buffalo) in 1968. He also wrote books and poetry.

Feb. 25   Frank Hubbard, 55, dies in Newton, Massachusetts. He was a prominent harpsichord builder and restorer and authored the book *Three Centuries of Harpsichord Making*.

Feb. 28   Rosalie Joseph Leventritt, 84, dies in New York City. She was a patron of music and a founder of the Leventritt International Competition.

March 1   French conductor and composer Jean Martinon, 66, dies in Paris. After winning first prize at the Paris Conservatoire in violin, he studied composition and conducting with Albert Roussel and Charles Munch. Two years in a German prison camp during World War II inspired several compositions. He was conductor of the Chicago Symphony Orchestra from 1963 to 1968 but was not popular with the audiences or critics there. He returned to France to conduct the Paris Radio National Orchestra.

March 25   Benjamin Franklin Miessner, 85, dies in Miami. He invented electronic musical devices and an electronic piano. His chief accomplishment was the perfection of the Wurlitzer organ.

April 3   Italian soprano Magda Olivero, aged 63, makes her Metropolitan Opera debut as Tosca. Harold C. Schonberg later writes in the New York *Times* of her audience: "They moaned orgiastically."

April 25   Noted Russian pianist Alexander Brailowsky, 80, dies in New York City. He made his debut in Paris after the First World War and debuted in the United States on November 19, 1924 in New York. He was best known for his interpretations of Chopin.

May 15   David Munrow, 33, dies in Buckinghamshire, England. Director of the Early Music Consort, he played bassoon and recorder and was a fluent writer on music. His work in early music constituted an enormous contribution to the music public's appreciation by advancing the cause of unknown works.

May 26   English soprano Maggie Teyte, 88, dies in London. In 1908 she was chosen by Claude Debussy to succeed Mary Garden as Melisande and to appear with him in recitals. She sang with the Beecham Opera Company in London in 1910–11 and with the Chicago Opera in 1911–14. For many years she gave recitals, specializing in French music. In 1958 she became a Dame of the British Empire.

June 6   German soprano Elisabeth Rethberg, 81, dies in Yorktown Heights, New York. After starting at the Dresden Opera at the age of 21, she sang guest appearances in other European cities and then came to the Metropolitan Opera in 1922. She sang there successfully until 1942. She was versatile enough to be at home in the music of Giuseppe Verdi, Richard Wagner, Richard Strauss, Mozart, Giacomo Puccini, Beethoven and others.

June 13   Hungarian pianist Geza Anda, 54, dies in Zurich, Switzerland. A student of Ernst von Dohnanyi, he was famous for his performances of Bela Bartok's music.

June 13   Violinist Isidor Strassner, 80, dies in Miami, Florida. In addition to playing with the New York Philharmonic for 35 years, he conducted the Heckscher Foundation Symphony Orchestra in the 1920s.

June 24   American violinist Samuel Dushkin, 84, dies in New York City. Known primarily for his association with Igor Stravinsky, he helped the composer with his Violin

Concerto, which he premiered, and also gave the first performance of Stravinsky's *Duo concertante*, with the composer at the piano. He published an account of this association in *Working with Stravinsky*.

June 28 Soviet pianist Yakov Zak, 62, dies in Moscow. He won the International Chopin Piano Contest in Warsaw in 1937 and made his debut in New York with the Pittsburgh Symphony Orchestra in 1965. He toured extensively in Europe and America and also taught at the Moscow Conservatory.

June 30 Swiss harpsichordist and composer Marguerite Roesgen-Champion, 82, dies in Paris. After studying with Ernest Bloch and Emile Jaques-Dalcroze, she devoted herself to the harpsichord, performing on and composing for this instrument. Her works, romantic in style, include five concertos for harpsichord and many pieces for flute and harpsichord.

Aug. 6 Russian cellist Gregor Piatigorsky, 73, dies in Los Angeles. After starting his career as an orchestral player, he fled Soviet Russia in 1921 and became the first cellist of the Berlin Philharmonic. He then started a solo career, becoming successful in Europe and America. He commissioned many works for cello by such composers as Paul Hindemith, Mario Castelnuovo-Tedesco and others and also taught at the Curtis Institute and the University of Southern California. Late in life he joined violinist Jascha Heifetz and pianist Leonard Pennario in a series of chamber music recitals and recordings.

Aug. 22 Pianist Gina Bachauer, 63, dies in Athens, Greece. After studies at the Athens Conservatory and with Alfred Cortot and Serge Rachmaninoff, she made her debut in 1935 in Athens with Dimitri Mitropoulos. She was known for her energetic playing and her large repertoire, which included music from Mozart to Igor Stravinsky.

Aug. 26 German soprano Lotte Lehmann, 88, dies in Santa Barbara, California. After studies in Berlin she debuted at the Hamburg Opera in 1910. Following a guest appearance at the Vienna State Opera in 1914, she was engaged as a member of the company. She was a favorite of Richard Strauss, who chose her for the premieres of *Ariadne auf Naxos*, *Die Frau ohne Schatten*, *Intermezzo* and *Arabella*. She was also noted for her interpretation of the roles of the Marschallin in *Der Rosenkavalier*, Leonore in *Fidelio* and Sieglinde in *Die Walkure*. She excelled at lieder singing and gave many recitals. During World War II she settled in the United States and appeared there until her farewell recital in 1951. She wrote four autobiographical books and a novel.

Aug. 30 Helene Berg, 92, dies in Vienna. Widow of Alban Berg, she held up performance of the final act of *Lulu*, claiming that her husband's spirit told her not to allow the music to be performed.

Oct. 7 Janet Daniels Schenck, 93, dies in New York City. Founder of the Manhattan School of Music, she was also a music educator.

Oct. 26 English musicologist Deryck Cooke, 57, dies in London. Although he was basically a writer about music, his arrangement of Gustav Mahler's incomplete Tenth Symphony catapulted him to international attention.

Oct. 27 Conductor Ferdinand Leitner makes his debut as music director of the Hague Philharmonic Orchestra, conducting a program of music by Antonin Dvorak, Beethoven and others at the Congresgebouw in The Hague.

Nov. 9 Russian pianist and teacher Rosina Lhevinne, 96, dies in Glendale, California. She was a gold medal winner at the Kiev Conservatory and in 1899 married the famous pianist Josef Lhevinne, with whom she appeared often in dual recitals. She settled with her husband in the United States after World War I and was a prominent teacher at the Juilliard School.

Nov. 27 Conductor Victor Alessandro, 61, dies in San Antonio, Texas. He was conductor of the San Antonio Symphony.

Dec. 4 English composer Benjamin Britten, 63, dies in Aldeburgh, England. After playing piano as a youth he studied composition with Frank Bridge. He continued to study piano and composition at the Royal College of Music in London (piano with Harold Samuel, composition with John Ireland). With the premiere of his *Fantasy Quartet for Oboe and Strings* (1934) his career began to soar. This was followed by work in film music — mostly for documentaries — which continued until World War II when he became a conscientious objector.

During the years 1947-48, he helped establish both the English Opera Group and the Aldeburgh Festival. Britten then devoted himself principally to composing operas which were performed at English festivals, including the Glyndebourne Festival. Like Igor Stravinsky, his works composed in the middle of his career frequently exhibit a reduced instrumentation to increase the possibility of performance (the orchestral parts in some of his operas are limited to 12).

Britten's music is characterized by tonal, triadic harmonies, vocal melodic lines frequently evolving from a sensitivity to the text, and orchestral interludes which punctuate and enhance the dramatic flow of his operas. His works include the operas *Peter Grimes* (premiered in 1945), *The Rape of Lucretia* (premiered in 1946), *Albert Herring* (premiered in 1947), *Billy Budd* (premiered in 1951), *The Turn of the Screw* (premiered in 1954), and *Death in Venice* (premiered in 1973). His other vocal works include the church parable *Curlew River* (premiered in 1964) and the group of songs, *7 Sonnets of Michaelangelo* (composed in 1940). Other orchestral works include the Serenade for Tenor, Horn and String Orchestra (premiered in 1943). Britten's death brings Michael Tippett into prominence as England's most important living composer.

Dec. 11 Italian tenor Francesco Merli, 89, dies in Milan. He sang at La Scala and taught until he was 84. He was known for his performances at the Teatro Colon in Buenos Aires and at Covent Garden in London.

1976   Related Events

The centennial of recorded sound is celebrated by the recording industry this year on an international scale as conventions and exhibitions are mounted throughout the Western world. This year also marks the first appearance of new discs featuring an enhanced signal-to-noise ratio and processed from digital tape masters by Denon (Japan). BSR (British Sound Reproducers) announces its Accutrac 4000 — a direct-drive turntable featuring remote control, computerized memory bank and electronic track selection.

Jan. 13   Sarah Caldwell becomes the first woman to conduct at the Metropolitan Opera in New York. The opera is *La Traviata*.

Jan. 30   The first "Live from Lincoln Center" radio broadcast takes place with a concert featuring the New York Philharmonic, Andre Previn and Van Cliburn.

April 1   Pianist Arthur Rubinstein is awarded the U.S. Medal of Freedom by President Gerald R. Ford. He is 89 years old.

May 3   Ned Rorem is awarded the Pulitzer Prize for music for *Air Music, 10 etudes for orchestra*. Rorem subsequently comments that now he can "die official." A special award and citation are also given in memory of Scott Joplin as a bicentennial honor bestowed posthumously for contributions to American music.

Queen Elizabeth II makes Benjamin Britten a member of the peerage of Great Britain this month. He is the first composer to receive this honor. Britten dies this December.

June 4   The first concert of the Festival-Institute at Round Top in Texas takes place today as pianist James Dick performs the Tchaikovsky First Piano Concerto with the Dallas Symphony Orchestra, Louis Land conducting. Music by Aaron Copland and Dimitri Shostakovich is also performed. The concert is held on the stage of the Mary Moody Northern Pavilion — the largest transportable stage in the world.

June 7   Organist E. Power Biggs criticizes the management of Carnegie Hall for installing an electronic organ. He says at a public meeting of the New York Chapter of the American Guild of Organists being held at Holy Trinity Church on Central Park West, "The present device cheapens the hall and ruins its image as a place of excellence."

July 4   The United States of America celebrates its bicentennial. Festivals involving music take place all across the nation. The National Endowment for the Arts, in conjunction with six major American symphony orchestras, commissioned six works — all to be performed by each of the six orchestras — for the bicentennial year. The compositions are *Symphony of Three Orchestras*, by Elliott Carter; *Echoes from an Invisible World*, by Leslie Bassett; *The Final Alice*, by David Del Tredici; *Renga* with *Apartment House 1776*, by John Cage; *Before the Butterfly*, by Morton Subotnick; and *Chiaroscuro*, by Jacob Druckman. In a special event held today on the Esplanade in Boston, Arthur Fiedler conducts the Boston Pops Orchestra in a bicentennial concert celebrating American independence. Attendance is estimated at 400,000. Fireworks explode and decorate the night sky.

Sep. 30   The Orchestre Philharmonique de Lorraine gives its first concert in Lorraine, France. Michel Tabachnik conducts a program of music by Franz Schubert, Bela Bartok and Beethoven.

FIREWORKS EXPLODE OVER THE CHARLES RIVER ESPLANADE AS THE BOSTON POPS PLAYS TCHAIKOVSKY'S *1812 OVERTURE*

1977 Opera

Feb. 25 *Kabale und Liebe*, by Gottfried von Einem, is performed for the first time in Vienna at the Staatsoper. The libretto, written by Lotte Ingrisch, is based on the tragedy by Friedrich Schiller.

April 8 John Eaton's opera *Danton et Robespierre* is premiered by conductor Thomas Baldner at the Indiana University Opera Theater in Bloomington, Indiana.

April 14 Leon Kirchner's *Lily* — with a libretto by the composer, based on Saul Bellow's novel *Henderson, the Rain King* — is premiered by the New York City Opera at the New York State Theater, Lincoln Center in New York City. A later work of the same title for violin, viola, cello, woodwind quintet, piano, percussion and voice is based on music from this opera.

June 22 Nino Rota's *Napoli milionaria* receives its first performance in Spoleto at the Teatro Caio Melisso.

1977 Dance

May 12 Twyla Tharp performs two of her new modern dance works at the Brooklyn Academy of Music. They are called *Simon Medley* and *MUD*. *MUD* is choreographed to music by Mozart.

June 4 *Scriabin Etude*, choreographed by George Balanchine to music by Alexander Scriabin, receives its initial performance by the New York City Ballet at the Spoleto Festival USA in Charleston, South Carolina. Patricia McBride and Jean-Pierre Bonnefous star.

June 12 *Soweto*—a one-act ballet choreographed by Mats Ek—receives its initial performance at the Opera House in Stockholm. The Cullberg Ballet performs. Set to a variety of classical and popular music pieces, it is based on the 1976 revolt in Johannesburg to protest apartheid.

June 23 *Vienna Waltzes*, by George Balanchine, is premiered by the New York City Ballet in New York. The music consists of waltzes by Johann Strauss, Franz Lehar and Richard Strauss. The five-part ballet stars Karin von Aroldingen and Jacques d'Amboise.

Nov. 29 A new modern dance work by Paul Taylor, *Aphrodisamania*, receives its first performance at the Brooklyn Academy of Music.

1977 Instrumental and Vocal Music

Jan. 11 American composer Edward T. Cone's *Serenade* for flute, violin, viola and cello premieres at the Guggenheim Museum in New York City.

Jan. 16 John Corigliano Jr.'s *Aria for Oboe and String Orchestra* is premiered by the Connecticut String Orchestra in West Hartford, Connecticut.

Feb. 2 Ned Rorem's *A Quaker Reader* is premiered by Leonard Raver at Alice Tully Hall in New York City. This piece is an organ suite.

Feb. 5 David Diamond's *A Secular Cantata* premieres at Carnegie Recital Hall in New York City. The text is from *Permit Me Voyage*, by James Agee.

Feb. 7 Charles Dodge's *Palinode* for computerized tape and orchestra premieres at Alice Tully Hall in New York City.

Feb. 17 *A Symphony of Three Orchestras*, by Elliott Carter, receives its world premiere by the New York Philharmonic in New York City, as Pierre Boulez conducts. Commissioned for the American bicentennial, the music is divided among three small orchestras, which perform their own movements while overlapping with those of the other smaller groups. The work was inspired by Hart Crane's poem "The Bridge," about the Brooklyn Bridge. The general flow of the music is from high to low registers. It was composed between June and December of last year.

March 7 Kurt Weill's *Two Movements for String Quartet* premieres posthumously at the Library and Museum of the Performing Arts, Lincoln Center in New York City.

March 14 *Chiaroscuro*, by Jacob Druckman, receives its world premiere by the Cleveland Orchestra in Cleveland. Lorin Maazel conducts. This orchestral work was commissioned by this orchestra and the National Endowment for the Arts specifically for the American bicentennial.

March 15   Gian-Carlo Menotti's *Cantilena e scherzo* for harp and string quintet premieres at Alice Tully Hall in New York City.

March 24   Peter Maxwell Davies' *A Mirror of Whitening Light* is premiered by the London Sinfonietta in London.

April 24   Roque Cordero's *Elegy* for string orchestra is premiered by Paul Vermel and the Bloomington National Symphony in Normal, Illinois.

May 4   Symphony No. 29 for baritone horn and orchestra, by Alan Hovhaness, receives its initial performance by the Minnesota Orchestra, with Charles Smith as euphonium soloist.

May 5   *Star-Child*, by George Crumb, receives its world premiere by Pierre Boulez and the New York Philharmonic at Avery Fisher Hall in New York City. It is scored for soprano solo, children's chorus and large orchestra (including much percussion) and requires four conductors to direct performers in different areas of the concert hall. It is one of Crumb's large-scale works.

May 5   Roque Cordero's *Soliloquies No. 3* for solo clarinet is premiered at Illinois State University in Normal Illinois.

Aug. 26   *Song of Remembrance*, a new work by composer Norman Dello Joio, premieres at the Saratoga Performing Arts Center in Saratoga, New York, as Eugene Ormandy conducts the Philadelphia Orchestra.

Sep. 23   Dominick Argento's *In Praise of Music* (*Seven Songs for Orchestra*) receives its initial performance by the Minnesota Orchestra at Orchestra Hall in Minneapolis. The event marks the 75th anniversary of this orchestra.

JACOB DRUCKMAN

Sep. 29   Jacob Druckman's *Animus IV* is premiered by the Ensemble Inter-Contemporain at the Centre de Georges Pompidou in Paris, the composer conducting.

Oct. 6   Michael Tippett's Symphony No. 4 receives its initial performance by Georg Solti and the Chicago Symphony Orchestra in Chicago.

Oct. 9   Alexander Tcherepnin's *Russische Weisen* is premiered by the Blasorchester Sofia in Zurich, Switzerland.

Oct. 11   *Songfest*, by Leonard Bernstein, receives its world premiere by the National Symphony Orchestra at the Kennedy Center in Washington, D.C. with the composer conducting. It is subtitled *A Cycle of American Poems for Six Singers and Orchestra*, and its text features poetry by many American poets. Clamma Dale, Rosalind Elias, Nancy Williams, Neil Rosenshein, John Reardon and Donald Gramm are vocal soloists. The work lasts approximately 40 minutes. Various sections of it were previously performed, including one at the Inaugural Gala of President Jimmy Carter. Also receiving their first performances today are Bernstein's *Three Meditations for Cello and Orchestra*, with Mstislav Rostropovich as cello soloist, and *Slava!* (*Overture for Orchestra*). Rostropovich conducts the final work.

Oct. 20   *Deja Vu* for percussion quartet and orchestra, by Michael Colgrass, receives its world premiere by the New York Philharmonic at Avery Fisher Hall in New York City. The work is subsequently awarded the Pulitzer Prize for music.

Oct. 20   Roque Cordero's String Quartet No. 3 is premiered by the String Quartet of Costa Rica in San Jose, Costa Rica.

Oct. 23   William Bolcom's *Piano Quartet* is premiered by the Chamber Music Society of Lincoln Center at Alice Tully Hall in New York City.

Oct. 24   *Five Pieces for Piano*, by Roger Sessions, is premiered by Robert Miller and the Group for Contemporary Music at the Manhattan School of Music in New York City.

Nov. 1   Richard Wernick's *Contemplation of the Tenth Muse* is premiered by Elsa Charleston at Carnegie Recital Hall in New York City.

Nov. 1   Lukas Foss' *Curriculum Vitae for Accordion* is premiered by William Schimmel at the American Accordionists Association in New York City.

Nov. 4   Jacob Druckman's *Animus III* for clarinet and tape is premiered at a concert of the International Society for Contemporary Music at Carnegie Recital Hall in New York City. Stanley Walden is the clarinet soloist.

Nov. 17   Vincent Persichetti's *Concerto for English Horn and String Orchestra*, Op. 137, is premiered by the New York Philharmonic at Avery Fisher Hall, Lincoln Center in New York City. Thomas Stacy is the soloist.

Nov. 18   George Perle's *Bagatelles for Orchestra* receives its first performance by Seymour Lipkin and the Long Island Symphony Orchestra.

Nov. 19   Iannis Xenakis' *A Colone* for male chorus, French horn, three trombones and three double basses premieres in Metz.

Nov. 20   *Cantico de los marranos*, by Marvin David Levy, is premiered by Philippe Entremont and the San Francisco Symphony Chamber Orchestra in San Francisco, with Phyllis Bryn-Julson as soprano soloist.

Nov. 21   Otto Luening's *Third Short Sonata* premieres at the Manhattan School of Music in New York City. Also receiving its first performance at today's concert is his *Flute Sonata No. 3*.

Nov. 21   John Cage's *49 Waltzes for the Five Boroughs* premieres at Northwestern University in Evanston, Illinois. Cage begins a macrobiotic diet this year after being advised to do so by Yoko Ono.

Dec. 1   *American Cantata*, by Lukas Foss, receives its initial performance by Leonard Bernstein and the New York Philharmonic at Lincoln Center for the Performing Arts in New York City. The piece is scored for tenor, soprano, two speakers, chorus and orchestra.

Dec. 4   Charles Ives' *Christmas Music*, arranged by Lou Harrison, is premiered by Ainslee Cox and the Oklahoma Symphony in Oklahoma City.

Dec. 6   *Clarinet Concerto*, by John Corigliano Jr., is premiered by David Gilbert and the New York Philharmonic, with Stanley Drucker as soloist. The performance takes place in New York City.

Dec. 12   Paul Chihara's *The Beauty of the Rose Is Passing* is premiered by Lawrence Foster and the Los Angeles Philharmonic Chamber Music Society in Los Angeles, California.

Dec. 21   *Jonchaies* for orchestra, by Iannis Xenakis, premieres in Paris.

1977   Births, Deaths and Debuts

March 10   Organist E. Power Biggs, 70, dies in Boston. He made his American debut in 1932 and spent time traveling through Scandinavia and other countries in Europe to hunt for aged church organs. He also performed contemporary music, edited music, loved baroque music and hated electronic organs.

March 15   Greek musicologist Thrasybulos Georgiades, 70, dies in Munich. He was known for his writings on old music (medieval, Byzantine and Greek) and also studied composition with Carl Orff.

April 28   Music bibliographer Cecil Hopkinson, 79, dies in Guildford, England. He devoted much of his life to collecting music scores and materials relating to many famous composers and musicians, including Hector Berlioz. Some of these items were bequeathed to the National Library of Scotland.

May 9   Harold Spivacke, 72, dies in Washington, D.C. He was a chief of the Music Division of the Library of Congress for 35 years and was also a noted musicologist. His efforts led to the successful acquisition by that library of original manuscripts of Arnold Schoenberg.

May 29   Goddard Lieberson, 66, dies in New York City. He was a president of Columbia Records for 13 years. His commitment and diligence as a recording executive led to many new releases of contemporary compositions. He was also a composer himself.

Aug. 17   Composer Pietro Petrides, 85, dies in Athens. After studies in Constantinople and Paris, he fought with the Greek Army (the Balkan War) and again studied music in Paris (with Albert Roussel). In 1917, his songs began to attract attention. In addition to five symphonies, his oratorio *Saint Paul* is well known.

Sep. 13   Conductor Leopold Stokowski, 95, dies in his sleep in Nether Wallop, Hampshire, England. After studies in England, Stokowski came to America in 1905 and was made organist of Saint Bartholomew's Church in New York. In 1909 he was appointed conductor of the Cincinnati Symphony but left after three years to conduct the Philadelphia Orchestra. He led this group for 23 years, introducing many new works to the resistant Philadelphia audience. He experimented with orchestral seating to give him the sound he sought, was very active in the recording studio and made several films. From 1955 to 1962 he led the Houston Symphony, and in 1962 he founded the American Symphony Orchestra in New York. His tampering with orchestration and his orchestral arrangements of Bach caused some criticism, but there was never any doubt about his ability to create orchestral sonority or to follow a musical line. He was one of the most colorful personalities of 20th-century musical life.

Sep. 16   Maria Callas, 53, dies suddenly of a heart attack in Paris. After studying in Athens with Elvira de Hidalgo, she began her career in Italy, where, encouraged by conductor Tullio Serafin, she soon became a star. She excelled in the bel canto operas of Vincenzo Bellini and Gaetano Donizetti as well as those of Giuseppe Verdi. Her on- and off-stage life (including her relationship with Greek shipping magnate Aristotle Onassis) and her fights with various opera managers and other singers were covered assiduously by the international press. Although often criticized for her vocal defects, her fine musicianship and acting won universal praise.

Sep. 21   Czech-born conductor and pianist Kurt Adler, 70, dies in Butler, New Jersey. He fled to the Soviet Union when Adolf Hitler came to power and later settled in America. He founded the Stalingrad Philharmonic Orchestra, was chorus-master and conductor at the Metropolitan Opera and edited a great deal of vocal music.

Nov. 15   English composer Richard Addinsell, 73, dies in London. After law studies at Oxford University and music studies at the Royal College of Music, he studied in Vienna and Berlin. His score to the stage production of *Alice in Wonderland* (1933) was commissioned by actress Eva Le Gallienne. He then moved to Hollywood and devoted himself to film music. His film scores include *Blithe Spirit, A Tale of Two Cities* and *Dangerous Moonlight* (also known as *Suicide Squadron*). One piano and orchestra movement from this last film became known as the *Warsaw Concerto*—that music catapulted Addinsell to international fame. Some critics suggested it was modeled on, if not pilfered from, the Second Piano Concerto by Serge Rachmaninoff.

Dec. 16   Conductor Thomas Schippers, 47, dies of lung cancer in New York. He came to prominence at the age of 20, when he led the first performance of Gian-Carlo Menotti's opera *The Consul*. He was one of the youngest musicians to lead the New York Philharmonic and to appear at the Metropolitan. He also conducted at Bayreuth, La Scala and the Spoleto Festival. In 1970 he became music director of the Cincinnati Orchestra, which he led until 1977, when his illness prevented him from continuing. He left this orchestra $5 million upon his death.

1977   Related Events

Edo de Waart is appointed music director of the San Francisco Symphony Orchestra this year, succeeding Seiji Ozawa. De Waart had conducted the Rotterdam Philharmonic.

The impact of digital recording on the recording industry continues this year as "super-fi" (direct-to-disc) recordings stimulate public interest in purchasing recordings.

THE DOCK STREET THEATER—HOME OF THE SPOLETO FESTIVAL U.S.A. IN CHARLESTON, SOUTH CAROLINA

Twelve-tone Tonality, by George Perle, is published this year by the University of California Press. The book is the culmination both of Perle's earlier book, *Serial Composition and Atonality* (published in four editions), and of his theoretical and compositional work since 1939, in which he combined serial techniques with the hierarchical pitch relationships found in tonal music. He first termed this systematic approach the "12-tone modal system" and, since 1969, "12-tone tonality." The book outlines a huge network of pitch and structural relationships that form the basis of this new approach to musical composition. It also includes a chapter on "Alban Berg's *Master Array of the Interval Cycles*," which Berg tabulated and sent to Arnold Schoenberg in 1920. Much of Perle's work in this area (since 1969) was done in collaboration with Paul Lansky, whose doctoral dissertation entitled *Affine Music* was accepted at Princeton University in 1973.

Jan. 31   The Los Angeles Chamber Music Society is formed by members of the Los Angeles Philharmonic. Its first concerts take place at the Mark Taper Forum of the Los Angeles Music Center.

April 18   Richard Wernick is awarded the Pulitzer Prize for music for his *Visions of Terror and Wonder*.

May   Pierre Boulez leaves his post as music director of the New York Philharmonic to become director of the Institut de Recherche et de Coordination Acoustique/Musique (IRCAM) in Paris — a research and performance center for contemporary music created for him by the government of Georges Pompidou of France.

May 25   The first Spoleto Festival U.S.A., begins today in Charleston, South Carolina. The inaugural production is the opera *The Queen of Spades*, by Tchaikovsky. This festival is founded by Gian-Carlo Menotti as a counterpart to the Festival of Two Worlds, held in Spoleto, Italy, which he founded in 1957.

Oct. 4   Mstislav Rostropovich conducts his first concert as the new music director of the National Symphony Orchestra in Washington, D.C.

Oct. 15   The Metropolitan Opera performs *La Boheme* in New York City, marking the first live telecast by that company. Renata Scotto and Luciano Pavarotti star in this landmark musical event.

1978 Opera

March 17   *Le Grand Macabre*, an opera by Gyorgy Ligeti, with text by the composer and Michael Meschke, receives its world premiere by conductor Elgar Howarth and the Stockholm Royal Opera. The opera is based on the play *La Balade du Grand Macabre* by Michel de Ghelderode. Elisabeth Soderstrom and Kerstin Meyer perform as the young lovers. The opera creates a sensation and is later performed in Hamburg, Saarbrucken, Bologna, Nuremberg, Paris and London (in each case, the performance is given in the language of the country). Andrew Porter subsequently writes in *The New Yorker* magazine that Ligeti commands "force and graphicness of vocal gesture, sureness of timing, variety, contrast, surprise."

April 14   Robert Ward's *Claudia Legare*, with a libretto by Bernard Stambler, is premiered by Phillip Brunelle and the Minnesota Opera Company in Minneapolis, Minnesota.

July 9   *King Lear*, an opera by German composer Aribert Reimann, receives its world premiere at the Bavarian State Opera in Munich.

Nov. 29   Krzysztof Penderecki's *Paradise Lost*, with a libretto based on works by John Milton and Christopher Fry, is premiered at the Lyric Opera of Chicago.

1978 Dance

Jan. 12   *Ballo della Regina*, by George Balanchine, receives its world premiere by the New York City Ballet in New York City. The music is from the third act of Giuseppe Verdi's *Don Carlo*. Merrill Ashley and Robert Weiss are the lead dancers in this plotless work. The ballet was previously performed at a gala performance last November.

Jan. 19   *Calcium Light Night* — a ballet choreographed by Peter Martins to music by Charles Ives, receives its world premiere by the New York City ballet in New York. Daniel Duell and Heather Watts star. Set designs are by Steven Rubin. The work was previously performed at a fund-raising gala last November. This is the second ballet by this company that uses music by Ives (the other is *Ivesiana*, choreographed by George Balanchine in 1954).

Jan. 26   George Balanchine's *Kammermusik No. 2* receives its world premiere by the New York City Ballet in New York City. The music is by Paul Hindemith. Karin von

Aroldingen, Colleen Neary, Adam Luders and Sean Lavery star.

Jan. 27   Maurice Bejart's version of *Gaite Parisienne*, to music by Jacques Offenbach, receives its initial performance in Brussels. The music is adapted and orchestrated by Manuel Rosenthal. Thierry Bosquet designs the costumes and sets. The ballet is about a young dancer who fancies himself in the glorious times of the past. Victor Ullate, Rita Poelvoorde, Jorge Dunn and Catherine Verneuil are in the cast.

Feb. 14   *Mayerling* receives its first performance by the Royal Ballet at Covent Garden, in London. Kenneth MacMillan choreographs music by Franz Liszt which is arranged and orchestrated by John Lanchberry. Nicholas Georgiadis does the stage designs. The story centers around the suicides of Prince Rudolf and his lover, Baroness Marie Vetsera. Stephen Jefferies, Alfreda Thorogood, Denis Dunn, Michael Somes, Monica Mason and Jennifer Penney star.

March 12   Anna Sokolow's *Songs Remembered*, to music by David Diamond, receives its first performance at the Juilliard Concert Hall in New York City.

May 5   *Esoterik Satie* — a ballet in two movements and on an illustrated interval — receives its world premiere at the Teatro Lirico in Milan. Lorca Massine choreographs music by Erik Satie. Raimonda Gaetani designs the costumes and

sets. The ballet depicts through dance the cultural environment of Satie and his life. Lorca Massine, Anna Razzi, Paolo Podini, Bruno Vescovo, Maurizio Bellaza, Oriella Dorella, and Gabriele Tenneriello star.

May 18   *Tricolore* — a three-part ballet conceived by George Balanchine — receives its world premiere by the New York City Ballet in New York. This work celebrates the flag of the French republic and has music by Georges Auric. Peter Martins, Jean-Pierre Bonnefous and Jerome Robbins create the choreography. Rouben Ter-Arutunian designs the costumes and sets. Lead dancers include Colleen Neary, Adam Luders, Merrill Ashley, Peter Martins and Karin von Aroldingen. This ballet is the last of a trilogy, *Entente Cordiale*. The other two are *Stars and Stripes* and *Union Jack*.

June 26   Martha Graham offers new works over the next several days at the Metropolitan Opera House in New York City. Today's premiere is *The Owl and the Pussycat*, to music by Carlos Surinach, with designs by Ming Cho Lee.

June 27   Martha Graham's *Ecuatorial* receives its world premiere at the Metropolitan Opera House in New York City. This choreography is to music of the same title by Edgar Varese.

June 28   Martha Graham closes her run of new premieres at the Metropolitan Opera House in New York with today's first performance of *The Flute of Pan*.

1978 Instrumental and Vocal Music

Jan. 10   Krzysztof Penderecki's Concerto for Violin receives its first performance by the Minnesota Orchestra at Carnegie Hall in New York, with Isaac Stern as soloist.

Jan. 13   Richard Wernick's *Introits and Canons* is premiered by the Penn Contemporary Players at the University of Pennsylvania in Philadelphia.

Jan. 23   Hugo Weisgall's *The Golden Peacock* (*Seven Songs from Yiddish*) is premiered by the International Society for Contemporary Music and Judith Raskin at Carnegie Recital Hall in New York City.

Jan. 26   *Percussion Symphony*, by Charles Wuorinen, receives its first complete performance at Somerset County College in New Jersey, as the composer conducts the New Jersey Percussion Ensemble. The piece is scored for 24 players and a large variety of percussion instruments. The first movement of the work was performed on May 19, 1977.

Jan. 28   Morton Subotnick's *Dance! Cloudless Sulphur* for tape and dancers premieres at the Electronic Music Festival at Virginia Commonwealth University in Richmond, Virginia.

Jan. 29   George Rochberg's *Songs of Inanna and Dumuzi* is premiered by vocalist Katherine Ciesinski at the Museum of Art in Philadelphia, Pennsylvania.

Feb. 2   Joseph Schwantner's *Wild Angels of the Open Hills* is premiered by the Jubal Trio at the Walter Naumburg Foundation in New York City.

Feb. 10   *Syringa* — by Elliott Carter, with a text by John Ashbery and from ancient Greek writings — is premiered by Harvey Sollberger and the Speculum Musicae at Lincoln Center in New York City.

Feb. 16   Anton Webern's String Quartet in A Minor (composed in 1907) is premiered posthumously by the Concord String Quartet in Baton Rouge, Louisiana. This premiere of an early Webern work is the first at this year's International Webern Festival, held in Baton Rouge.

Feb. 17   Anton Webern's *Scherzo and Trio in A Minor* (composed in 1904), his *Trio Movement* for clarinet, trumpet and violin (1920) and his *String Trio Movement* (1925) are premiered posthumously at the sixth International Webern Festival in Baton Rouge, Louisiana.

Feb. 18   *Notations* for piano by Pierre Boulez premieres in Paris.

March 1   Ned Rorem's *Romeo and Juliet* (suite for flute and guitar) premieres at Alice Tully Hall in New York City.

March 2   Frederic Rzewski's *Song and Dance* is premiered by Speculum Musicae at Alice Tully Hall in New York City.

March 2   Dane Rudhyar's *Avent* is premiered by the Kronos String Quartet at the San Francisco Museum of Modern Art in San Francisco.

March 3   Luciano Berio's *Canciones populares espanolas* receives its initial performance by the Rochester Philharmonic Orchestra in Rochester, New York, the composer conducting.

March 11   *Fast Fantasy* for cello and piano, by Charles Wuorinen, receives its initial performance in Chicago. Wuorinen composed this piece as a birthday present for cellist Fred Sherry, who performs today.

March 12   Witold Lutoslawski's *Les espaces de sommeil* is premiered by the Berlin Philharmonic in Berlin. This work is scored for baritone and orchestra.

March 13   Henri Sauguet's *Sonatine en deux chants et un intermede* for clarinet and piano premieres in Paris.

March 17   Elie Siegmeister's *A Set of Houses* premieres at the Contemporary American Composers Festival in Bridgeport, Connecticut. Also receiving its first performance on today's program is his *City Songs*.

CHARLES WUORINEN

April 10   William Bergsma's *Sweet Was the Virgin Sung: Tristan Revisited* receives its first performance by Ranier Miedel and the Seattle Symphony Orchestra in Seattle, Washington.

April 14   Ralph Shapey's *The Covenant* for soprano and 16 players is premiered by the Contemporary Chamber Players at the University of Chicago in Chicago.

April 14   Alexander Tcherepnin's *Duo for Two Flutes* is premiered posthumously in Tokyo by the Swiss Duo Flutists.

April 17   Paul Chihara's *Primavera* is premiered by the Primavera String Quartet at Alice Tully Hall in New York City.

April 28   Theodore Antoniou's *Double Concerto* for percussion and orchestra premieres in Philadelphia, the composer conducting.

April 28   Ned Rorem's *Six Songs for High Voice and Orchestra* is premiered by Lukas Foss and the Brooklyn Philharmonic, with Geanie Faulkner as soloist. The performance takes place in Brooklyn.

April 28   *Freeman Etudes* for violin solo, by John Cage, is premiered by Paul Zukofsky at the Whitney Museum in New York City.

May 11   A novel type of concert — contemporary waltz music — takes place at The Stock Exchange Room of the Art Institute in Chicago. Many waltzes by living American composers are performed. The program includes the following: *Minute Waltz*, by Milton Babbitt; *49 Waltzes for the Five Boroughs — a "guide to 147 locations in New York City arranged in triplets"*, by John Cage; *Modern Love Waltz*, by Philip Glass; *A Waltz for Evelyn Hinrichsen*, by Lou Harrison; *Waltz*, by Roger Sessions; *Valse perpetuelle (The 45 R.P.M.)*, by Ivan Tcherepnin; *Birthday Waltz*, by Virgil Thomson; and *Self-Similar Waltz*, by Charles Wuorinen. Many of the waltzes on the program are repeated at a similar concert held next year at The Kitchen in New York City.

May 20   Luciano Berio's *Pas de quoi* for chamber ensemble premieres in Cologne.

May 20   Gyorgy Ligeti's *Hungarian-Rock* chaconne for cembalo is premiered by Elizabeth Chojnacka and the Westdeutscher Rundfunk.

May 23   Otto Leuning's *Music for Orchestra* receives its first performance by Gunther Schuller and the American Composers Orchestra at Lincoln Center in New York City.

May 24   Pierre Boulez' orchestral version of his *Notations* is premiered by the Orchestre de Paris in Paris.

May 24   Gian-Carlo Menotti's *The Trial of the Gypsy* is premiered by Terence Shook and the Newark Boys Choir at Alice Tully Hall in New York City. This work is scored for treble voices and piano.

June 12   Milko Kelemen's orchestral work *Mageia* is premiered by Gabor Otvos and the Philharmonisches der Stadt Augsburg.

June 18   Jean Francaix' Quintet for Clarinet and Strings premieres in Munich.

July 10   *Auden Variations for Organ*, by Vincent Persichetti, is premiered by Leonard Raver at the International Organists' Convention in Hartford, Connecticut.

Aug. 2   Hans Werner Henze's *Il vitalino raddopiato, ciacona per violino concertante ed orchestra da camera* premieres in Salzburg, with Gidon Kremer as soloist.

Aug. 6   David Amram's *Sonata for Solo Horn*, Op. 101, premieres in Lenox, Massachusetts.

Aug. 25   Eugene Ormandy and the Philadelphia Orchestra give the world premiere of Ned Rorem's orchestral work *Sunday Morning* at the Saratoga Performing Arts Center in Saratoga, New York.

Aug. 26   Ernst Krenek's *Acc-Music*, Op. 225, is premiered by William McGlaughlin, the Kronos String Quartet and the Cabrillo Festival Orchestra in Aptos, California.

Sep. 14   Mauricio Kagel's *Ex-position* for vocal ensemble, percussion, rhythm generators and gymnasts premieres in Oslo, Norway.

Sep. 14   Samuel Barber's *Third Essay for Orchestra* receives its world premiere by Zubin Mehta and the New York Philharmonic at Avery Fisher Hall in New York.

Sep. 28   Gunther Schuller's *Sonata serenata* is premiered by the Aeolian Chamber Players at Carnegie Recital Hall in New York City.

Oct. 22   *New People* for mezzo-soprano, viola and piano, by Michael Colgrass, premieres in Storytowne, New York.

Oct. 29   William Schuman's *In Sweet Music* — a serenade on a setting of Shakespeare for flute, viola, voice and harp — receives its initial performance by Jan De Gaetani, Paula Robison and the Chamber Music Society of Lincoln Center at Alice Tully Hall in New York City.

Nov. 2   Jacob Druckman's Concerto for Viola and Orchestra is premiered by James Levine and the New York Philharmonic, with Sol Greitzer as soloist, at Lincoln Center in New York City.

Nov. 6   Ernst Krenek's *They Knew What They Wanted*, Op. 227, is premiered by the Group for Contemporary Music at the Manhattan School of Music in New York City, the composer conducting. It is scored for vocalists and instruments.

Nov. 9   Isang Yun's *Muak* (*Fantasy for Orchestra*) is premiered by Lothar Zagrosek and the Niederrheinische Sinfoniker in Monchengladbach, Germany.

Dec. 3   Robert Starer's *Transformations* — three songs for mezzo-soprano, violin and piano — is premiered by vocalist Elaine Bonazzi at the Solomon R. Guggenheim Museum in New York City.

Dec. 11   *Two-Part Symphony*, by Charles Wuorinen, receives its world premiere by the American Composers Orchestra at Alice Tully Hall in New York City, as Dennis Russell Davies conducts. It is scored for an orchestra of 85 players with large percussion. Wuorinen describes the work as "a variation squared." Its opening 12-note unordered chord is described as an "ylem" — a "cosmological term derived from the Greek word meaning 'that on which form has not yet been imposed.' " The work lasts approximately 23 minutes.

Dec. 18   Donald Martino's *Triple Concerto* for clarinet, bass clarinet and contrabass clarinet with a chamber orchestra of 16 players is premiered by the Group for Contemporary Music at the Manhattan School of Music in New York City, Harvey Sollberger conducting. Also receiving its first performance on today's program is Charles Wuorinen's *Archangel* for trombone and string quartet.

Dec. 22   Easley Blackwood's Symphony No. 4 is premiered by Georg Solti and the Chicago Symphony Orchestra in Chicago. It was composed between 1972 and 1976.

1978   Births, Deaths and Debuts

Jan. 14   German conductor Robert Heger, 91, dies in Munich. After studying with Max von Schillings he began conducting opera. He was principally known as conductor of the Vienna State Opera, the Berlin State Opera and the Bavarian State Opera in Munich. He composed several operas, three symphonies and other music.

Jan. 18   Soviet composer Ivan Dzerzhinsky, 68, dies in Leningrad. After studies at the Leningrad Conservatory with Boris Asafiev, he began composing operas. His principal aim in life was to create a style of operatic composition that would not only conform to but also glorify Soviet Realism. This resulted in operas featuring melodies akin to folk song and stories steeped in patriotism. His opera *Quiet*

Flows the Don was perhaps the closest he came to achieving this end — Joseph Stalin loved it. Dzerzhinsky's later operas were less successful. He also composed concertos and chamber music.

April 6   Composer Nicolas Nabokov, 74, dies in New York. He studied in Saint Petersburg, Yalta (with Vladimir Rebikov) and Berlin (with Ferruccio Busoni). As with Igor Stravinsky, his early success was due in large part to Serge Diaghilev who commissioned him to compose a new ballet for his Ballets Russes. Unlike Stravinsky, however, Nabokov's career focused mostly on teaching — he did not become a major musical force of the century. His teaching posts included those at the Peabody Conservatory of Music, the State University of New York (Buffalo) and New York University. He also worked for the Congress for Cultural Freedom as secretary-general (1952-1963). His music is largely bitonal and based on Russian folklore. His works include the opera *The Holy Devil*, about Rasputin; the ballet-cantata *Ode, or Meditation at Night on the Majesty of God, as revealed by the Aurora Borealis*; three symphonies and various other works, including songs, piano and chamber music. His first cousin was the writer Vladimir Nabokov.

May 1   Soviet composer Aram Khachaturian, 74, dies in Moscow. As a youngster, he studied mathematics and played the tuba. He later studied cello and composition. After studies with Nikolai Miaskovsky at the Moscow Conservatory, he graduated in 1934. The Soviet musical establishment denigrated his music in 1948 for its non-conformist sound. Still, he travelled abroad, even to America, as a conductor, debuting in 1968. His music is characterized by Russian folk melodies with impressionistic tendencies. The ballet *Gayane* is his most well remembered work — it features the "Sabre Dance". He also composed music for many other different combinations of instruments and vioces.

May 14   Russian-American bass Alexander Kipnis, 87, dies in Westport, Connecticut. After early studies in Warsaw and Berlin, he made his debut in 1916. He sang all over the world, eventually settling in America. Known for his fine bass voice and great interpretive powers, he was one of the few opera stars to also excel in the song repertoire.

May 16   German conductor William Steinberg, 78, dies in New York. Among his many posts were music director of the Frankfurt Opera (1929–33), assistant to Arturo Toscanini with the NBC Symphony Orchestra (1938), conductor of the Pittsburgh Symphony (1952–76) and conductor of the Boston Symphony 1969–72). In 1936 he was forced to leave Nazi Germany, and he eventually settled in the United States, becoming a citizen in 1944.

May 26   Ballerina Tamara Karsavina dies in London at the age of 93. One of the greatest dancers in the history of ballet, she was admired for her performances of the classics and for the many roles she created in important 20th-century works. She graduated from the Saint Petersburg Imperial Ballet School and danced with the Maryinsky Theatre from 1902 to 1918. Karsavina was a member of Sergei Diaghilev's Ballets Russes from its formation in 1909 and became its leading ballerina. A follower and exponent of Michel Fokine's theories, she created the leading roles in many of his ballets, including *Petrouchka, Le Spectre de la rose* and *Firebird*. Following her retirement from performing in the 1920s, she was an important influence on the formation of British ballet. She also served as an adviser and coach for the Royal Ballet.

June 27   Musicologist and critic Karl Laux, 82, dies in Dresden. A former chancellor of the Dresden Academy of Music, he was noted for his scholarly work on Franz Schubert and Carl Maria von Weber.

July 27   Dutch conductor Willem van Otterloo, 70, dies in an automobile accident in Melbourne, Australia. After studies at the Amsterdam Conservatory he began conducting professional orchestras. He was principally known as conductor of the Residente Orchestra (The Hague) and the Dusseldorf Symphony Orchestra.

Aug. 2   Mexican composer Carlos Chavez, 79, dies in Mexico City. After studies with Manuel Ponce and others, he began arranging Mexican songs for piano. His ballet *El fuego Nuevo* brought him to national attention in 1921. During the next few years he went to Europe and discovered Arnold Schoenberg's 12-tone method and Igor Stravinsky's neoclassicism. He later returned to Mexico and conducted works by some of the composers he had learned of while in Europe. These included Schoenberg, Stravinsky, Erik Satie, Darius Milhaud and Edgard Varese. After spending four years in New York City he again returned to Mexico (1928) and established the Orquesta Sinfonica de Mexico. Chavez became an ardent supporter of Silvestre Revueltas. He also taught at prestigious Mexican institutions, and continued conducting in America, South America and Europe. His works were cataloged and the catalog published in three languages in 1971.

Chavez' music was often inspired by Mexican themes without resorting to the quotation of Mexican folk tunes. His music is mostly tonal and includes two operas, five ballets, many orchestral works (seven symphonies, the last unfinished), choral and chamber music and piano music.

Sep. 8   Bulgarian composer Pantcho Vladigerov, 79, dies in Sofia. After studying piano and music theory in Sofia, he studied in Berlin. He then worked at the Max Reinhardt Theater as a conductor and composer. He later taught in Sofia. His music incorporates modernistic harmonies with melodies rooted in Bulgarian folk song. He composed one opera, one ballet, many concertos and other orchestral works as well as vocal and piano music.

Oct. 8   Hungarian composer, violinist, conductor and composer Tibor Serly, 77, dies in London. A pupil of Bela Bartok and Zoltan Kodaly, he performed as a violinist with the NBC Symphony Orchestra, the Philadelphia Orchestra and the Cincinnati Symphony Orchestra. He composed a number of works, including a symphonic suite entitled *Colonial Pageant*. Perhaps his most famous work is *Modus Lascivius* for piano — a series of etudes.

Oct. 26   Carlo Maria Giulini makes his debut as the new music director of the Los Angeles Philharmonic Orchestra, presenting Beethoven's Ninth Symphony at the Los Angeles Music Center. The Los Angeles *Times* calls Giulini an artist who deals "in revelations. . . Los Angeles is very lucky."

Dec. 3   American black composer William Grant Still, 83, dies in Los Angeles. He studied composition with George Whitefield Chadwick and Edgard Varese and received several honorary doctorates. Verna Arvey, his wife, was also his librettist. Still was also devoted to introducing and developing a style of orchestral writing that could be identified as "Negro music." He sometimes incorporated

Negro folksongs. His best-known work of this type is his *Afro-American Symphony*, which premiered in 1931. He also composed many other orchestral works, two ballets, sev-

eral operas, and vocal works. He also composed for symphonic band — a medium that most composers avoid.

1978   Related Events

Feb. 13   Spanish guitarist Andres Segovia, 85, gives a "golden jubilee" concert in New York City.

March   Dr. Donald J. Shelter's article "A Pilot Study of Symphony Orchestra Musicians" is published in *College Music Symposium* this month. The article addresses itself to statistics concerning graduates of music schools. The study reveals that 1 percent of graduates of excellent music schools will succeed in becoming concert artists; 80 percent will become music educators; 13 percent will become orchestral players; and the rest will either leave music as a means of earning a living or enter the field of popular music. Median salary for orchestral players in American symphony orchestras is reported to be $17,200, and the median age of the player, 37. The study also estimates that only 4 percent of the American adult population attends concerts.

March 15   The Presidium of the Supreme Soviet strips Mr. and Mrs. Mstislav Rostropovich of their citizenship for "acts harmful to the prestige of the U.S.S.R." Rostropovich had invited Alexander Solzhenitsyn, the Soviet writer, to stay with him and his wife in their residence near Moscow in the late 1960s and early 1970s. Concert dates and recordings are subsequently canceled by the Soviet authorities, and a news blackout about Rostropovich's work is imposed. Rostropovich had written to President Leonid Brezhnev requesting that these conditions be lifted; American Senator Edward M. Kennedy (D., Mass.) had also spoken with Brezhnev about Rostropovich and his wife. Today's event occurs after they had been issued exit visas by the Soviet government. They subsequently leave the country.

April 14   The Seoul Sejong Cultural Center formally opens in Seoul, South Korea. It is named after King Sejong the Great (1397–1450), who introduced "hangul," the Korean writing system. The center has both a large and small concert hall and is home for the Seoul Philharmonic Orchestra (founded in 1945), the Seoul City Dance Theater (founded in 1974) and several choruses.

April 17   Michael Colgrass is awarded the Pulitzer Prize for music for *Deja Vu* for percussion and orchestra.

May 3   The Music Library of Yale University acquires the Virgil Thomson Collection, containing music manuscripts, correspondence, personal papers, books and other materials. In all, the collection exceeds 50,000 items. Other collections at this library include those relating to Paul Hindemith, Henry F. Gilbert, Lowell Mason, Leo Ornstein, David Stanley Smith and others.

Aug. 4   The San Diego Opera Verdi Festival — "the only annual music festival in the world dedicated to the performance of music by Giuseppe Verdi" — is officially launched today with its first performance of *Aida*. The cast includes Martina Arroyo and bass-baritone Norman Mittelmann and is conducted by Antonio Tauriello. The performance, in Italian, takes place at the Civic Theater in San Diego.

Dec. 4   Soviet conductor Kiril Kondrashin defects to the West after completing a concert engagement in the Netherlands. The winner of two Stalin Prizes and of the USSR's highest cultural award — the title of People's Artist of the USSR — Kondrashin cites restrictions on artistic freedom in the USSR as his reason for defecting.

1979   Opera

Jan. 24   Eric Salzman's opera *Simple Simon*, with a libretto by Michael Saul, is premiered at the QUOG Music Theater in New York City.

Feb. 3   Virgil Thomson's opera *Lord Byron* premieres at the Juilliard School in New York City.

Feb. 24   The complete *Lulu* receives its first performance at the Paris Opera. Pierre Boulez conducts. Teresa Stratas and Yvonne Minton star. Patrice Chereau directs. Helene Berg — the composer's widow — held up performance of

the complete version on the grounds that her husband's spirit told her he did not want the work completed. Upon her death opera companies competed for the privilege of giving this first complete performance. They were the Metropolitan Opera, the Vienna State Opera and the Paris Opera. Completion of the third act was done by Friedrich Cerha, although it is reported that Boulez also contributed finishing touches. The first American performance of the complete opera takes place this July 28. That performance is staged by the Santa Fe Opera.

March 22   Dominick Argento's opera *Miss Havisham's Fire* is premiered by the New York City Opera at Lincoln Center in New York.

June 3   *La Loca*, by Gian-Carlo Menotti, receives its world premiere by the San Diego Opera in that city. It is produced by the New York City Opera this September when Beverly Sills stars and Tito Capobianco directs. Harold C. Schonberg later writes in the New York *Times* that the opera "is almost a caricature of his derivative Puccini style."

July 30   Andre Previn and Tom Stoppard's *Every Good Boy Deserves Favour* opens at the Metropolitan Opera House in New York City. Featuring an on-stage orchestra, the work had previously been shown in London, Philadelphia and Washington, D.C.

Aug. 2   Peter Schat's circus opera *Houdini* premieres at the Aspen Music Festival in Aspen, Colorado.

Oct. 1   John Tavener's opera *Therese* premieres at Covent Garden in London.

Oct. 22   Tchaikovsky's *Maid of Orleans* receives what is thought to be its first American staged performance. Presented by the Michigan Opera Theater in Detroit, the production is given under the title *Joan of Arc* and stars Mignon Dunn. It is conducted by Kurt Klipstatter.

1979 Dance

April 5   *The Tiller in the Fields*, a one-act ballet choreographed by Antony Tudor to music by Antonin Dvorak, premieres by the American Ballet Theater at the Metropolitan Opera House in New York. It is about a gypsy girl who becomes pregnant. Gelsey Kirkland and Patrick Bissell star.

July 13   Peter Martins' *Giardino di Scarlatti* receives its premiere at the Saratoga Performing Arts Center in Saratoga, New York. His choreography is danced by the New York City Ballet.

July 28   Paul Taylor's *Profiles* — to music by Jan Radzynski, with lighting by Mark Litvin and costumes by Gene Moore — is televised live from the Page Auditorium in Durham, North Carolina. This event marks the first live televised dance premiere. The program also includes the choreographer's *Airs, Big Bertha* and *Book of Beasts*.

1979 Instrumental and Vocal Music

Jan. 12   William Bolcom's Second Sonata for Violin and Piano premieres at the Library of Congress in Washington, D.C.

Jan. 18   Peter Mennin's *Reflections of Emily* is premiered by Terence Shook and the Newark Boys Chorus at Alice Tully Hall in New York City.

Jan. 20   George Rochberg's The Concord Quartets (String Quartet No. 4, String Quartet No. 5, String Quartet No. 6), are premiered by the Concord String Quartet in Philadelphia.

Jan. 29   Joseph Schwantner's *Aftertones of Infinity* is premiered by Lukas Foss and the American Composers' Alliance Orchestra at Alice Tully Hall in New York City. The piece is subsequently awarded the Pulitzer Prize for music.

Feb. 10   Milton Babbitt's *A Solo Requiem* is premiered by Continuum at Alice Tully Hall in New York City.

Feb. 11   Henry Brant's *Orbits*, a "symphonic spatial ritual" for 80 trombones and organ, premieres in San Francisco.

Feb. 28   Hans Werner Henze's *L'autunno, musica per 5 suonatori di strumenti a fiato* is premiered by the Konig Ensemble in London. The piece was composed two years ago.

April 22   Gian-Carlo Menotti's *Miracles* is premiered by conductor John Giordano, the Texas Boys Choir and the Fort Worth Symphony Orchestra.

April 26   Henry Brant's *Antiphonal Responses for Improvised Piano and Orchestra* premieres in Oakland, California.

May 15   Milko Kelemen's *Infinity* for orchestra is premiered by the Southwest German Symphony Orchestra of Baden-Baden in Zagreb.

May 18   Norman Dello Joio's *As of a Dream*, based on texts by Walt Whitman — for narrator, mixed chorus, soloists, dancers and orchestra receives its initial performance by the Music Society of the Midland Center for the Arts in Midland, Michigan.

May 18   Rafael Kubelik's *Mass* for soprano and men's chorus is premiered by Ursula Koszut and the chorus of the Bavarian Radio of Munich in Munich.

May 20 Lou Harrison's *String Quartet Set* is premiered by the San Jose String Quartet in San Jose, California.

May 20 String Quartet No. 4, by Michael Tippett, is premiered by the Lindsay Quartet at the Bath Festival in England.

May 23 Hans Werner Henze's *Toccata senze fuga* for organ is premiered by Anton Zapf in Stuttgart.

June 30 Paul Creston's *Suite* for saxophone quartet Op. 111, is premiered by the Swiss Saxophone Quartet during the Sixth World Saxophone Congress at Northwestern University in Evanston, Illinois.

Aug. 1 Charles Wuorinen's Second String Quartet receives its initial performance by the Columbia String Quartet in Jackson, Wyoming.

Oct. 25 Earl Kim's Violin Concerto is premiered by Zubin Mehta and the New York Philharmonic, with Itzhak Perlman as soloist. The premiere takes place in New York.

Nov. 1 A suppressed version of Alban Berg's *Lyric Suite*, featuring a previously unknown vocal part in the last movement, is premiered under the auspices of the American Musicological Society and the International Alban Berg Society. It is performed by the Columbia String Quartet, with Katherine Ciesinski as soloist, at the Abraham Goodman House in New York City. The text of the newly found part is Baudelaire's "De profundis clamavi" from *Fleurs du mal*, translated by Stefan George, and allegedly dramatizes the composer's love affair with Hanna Fuchs-Robettin, a married woman. Composer-theorist George Perle presents the background of the discovery and says that Helene Berg, the composer's deceased widow, donated the manuscript to a Vienna library, where it was subsequently discovered by musicologist Douglass M. Green.

Nov. 2 Gunther Schuller's *Octet* is premiered by the Chamber Music Society of Lincoln Center at Alice Tully Hall, Lincoln Center in New York City.

Nov. 23 Rodolfo Halffter's *Elegie in Memoriam of Carlos Chavez* is premiered by Laszlo Gati and the National Symphony Orchestra of Mexico.

Nov. 25 Alan Mandel premieres Elie Siegmeister's Piano Sonata No. 3 at Carnegie Recital Hall in New York.

Dec. 5 Milton Babbitt's *Images for Saxophone and Synthesized Tape* is premiered by Harvey Pittel at Alice Tully Hall in New York City.

Dec. 6 Frederick Renz and his Ensemble for Early Music give the world premiere of *The Play of Saint Nicholas* at the Cathedral of Saint John the Divine in New York. Directed by Peter Klein, the medieval work is a combination of three plays from the Fleury Playbook.

Dec. 13 American composer Paul Lansky's Serenade is premiered by the League of Composers-International Society for Contemporary Music at Carnegie Recital Hall in New York City.

Lansky is currently synthesizing his latest work — *Six Fantasies on a Poem by Thomas Campion* — which features his wife, actress Hannah MacKay. This new computer piece explores the musical aspects of speech and song. Lansky creates an entire work of music from one reading, by MacKay, of a Campion poem. He employs a technique called "all-pole linear transformation." The reading of the poem is analyzed bit by bit (in bits, or frames as small as 1/112th of a second), and then reconstructed so that the composer has the computer produce desired effects of pitch, rhythm and timbre. The result is music that, through electronic and computer means, plays "with the implicit music within an excellent spoken performance of this explicitly musical poem." The six fantasies are entitled "her voice," "her presence," "her reflection," "her song", "her ritual," "her self."

Dec. 13 Aurora Natola-Ginastera premiers Alberto Ginastera'a Sonata for Cello at Alice Tully Hall in New York City.

1979 Births, Deaths and Debuts

Jan. 10 American banker and composer Avery Claflin, 80, dies in Greenwich, Connecticut. He is best remembered for his *Lament for April 15*, a musical setting of income-tax regulations.

Jan. 13 Australian soprano Marjorie Lawrence, 69, dies in Little Rock, Arkansas. Singing primarily with the New York Metropolitan Opera and the Paris Opera, she made a comeback after being stricken with polio.

March 7 Norwegian composer Klaus Egge, 72, dies in Oslo. After studies in Norway and Berlin, he quickly established himself as a noteworthy composer and eventu-

ally received the rare privilege of being financially supported by the Norwegian government for life. His music is distinctively Scandinavian within the context of modern harmony. He composed five symphonies, three piano concertos and various other works.

March 16 Choreographer and dancer Leonide Massine dies in Cologne, Germany at the age of 83. One of the most important dancers of his generation, he was known as a master of character parts. As a choreographer, he was noted for his contributions to the comedy genre and for his development of symphonic ballets. Massine graduated from the Moscow Bolshoi School in 1912 and danced with the Bolshoi Ballet until joining Sergei Diaghilev's Ballets Russes in 1914. Following the departure of Nijinsky, he became the company's leading male dancer and choreographer. He choreographed such important works as *Parade* and *Le Tricorne* for the company. In 1921 he left Diaghilev to tour with his own company. During the next three decades he choreographed for many ballet companies, including the Ballet Russe de Monte Carlo, and occasionally formed his own touring company. Among his most important works during this period are *Gaite Parisienne* and *Seventh Symphony*. Massine also choreographed for and appeared in films such as *Red Shoes* and *Tales of Hoffmann*.

March 22   Walter Legge, 72, dies in Saint Jean-Cap Ferrat, France. He was a record producer and founder of the Philharmonia Orchestra of London. He was also husband of Elisabeth Schwarzkopf.

March 25   Austrian composer and organist Anton Heiller, 55, dies in Vienna. After studying at the Vienna Conservatory and winning major awards, he joined the faculty of the Vienna Hochschule fur Musik. He was largely a composer of sacred music and used modern counterpoint and 12-tone procedures to evoke a new Renaissance sensibility. An example of this effort is *Kleine Messe uber Zwolftonmodelle*, for a cappella chorus.

April 9   French music librarian and musicologist Vladimir Fedorov, 77, dies in Paris. He was a president of the International Association of Music Librarians and a former president of the International Society of Musicology. He is perhaps best known for his critical biography of Modest Mussorgsky.

April 10   Italian composer Nino Rota, 67, dies in Rome. After studies with Alfredo Casella and Ildebrando Pizzetti, he studied with Rosario Scalero at the Curtis Institute of Music in Philadelphia. He also studied conducting with Fritz Reiner. He later taught in Italy. As a composer, he is best known for his operas and his film scores. The film scores include *La dolce vita* and *Romeo e Giulietta*.

April 25   Austrian conductor Leopold Ludwig, 71, dies in Luneburg. He was principally known as a conductor of the Vienna State Opera and the Hamburg State Opera. He also toured Europe and America.

May 9   American composer Ben Weber, 62, dies in New York. After studying at De Paul University he met Arnold Schoenberg and began composing work that blended 12-tone procedures with tonality. He earned his living principally in the recording industry. Most of his compositions are for orchestra or chamber ensemble.

May 14   Thomas Scherman, 62, dies in New York City. He was founder, benefactor and conductor of the Little Orchestra Society, and his efforts brought neglected classical works as well as some new music to the concert hall. He also established the Book-of-the-Month Club.

June 27   German composer Paul Dessau, 84, dies in East Berlin. After studies at the Klindworth Conservatory (Berlin) he worked as a coach with the Hamburg Opera. He conducted in Cologne, Mainz and Berlin before the advent of Adolf Hitler compelled him to leave Europe. He stayed in New York during the war and then returned to East Germany. He is best known as a composer of stage works but also wrote five string quartets and various pieces dealing with leftist themes.

July 3   Louis Durey, 90, dies near Saint Tropez, France. One of "Les Six," his music was anti-romantic. He was not especially prolific, wrote music criticism and worked against the Nazis during the Nazi occupation of France during World War II. His work includes music for voice, orchestra and chamber ensemble. He also believed in developing a style of composition based on folk song.

July 10   Boston Pops conductor Arthur Fiedler, 84, dies in Brookline, Massachusetts of a heart ailment. After studies with his father and later in Berlin, he joined the Boston Symphony, playing the viola. In 1930 he was appointed conductor of the Boston Pops concerts, a post he held until his death. His grandfatherly appearance, combined with an amusingly cantankerous personality, endeared him to a wide popular audience. He also made the only recording of orchestral music to sell over 1 million copies. Total recording sales of his albums are estimated at 50 million records.

July 16   English countertenor Alfred Deller, 67, dies in Bologna, Italy. After singing as a youth at Canterbury Cathedral and Saint Paul's in London, he established the Deller Consort in 1948, which was devoted to performances of old English music.

July 21   American conductor Karl Krueger, 85, dies in Chicago. A conductor of the Vienna State Opera, he also reorganized the Seattle Symphony Orchestra in 1926 and founded the Kansas City Philharmonic in 1933. In 1958 he published a book entitled *The Way of the Conductor*.

Sep. 29   Composer Ivan Wyschnegradsky, 86, dies in Paris. He studied at the Paris Conservatoire and settled in Paris after the Russian Revolution. This composer wrote micro-tonal and quarter-tone music. He was probably the leading quarter-tone composer of the century. His music was not performed much during his lifetime because special quarter-tone instruments were often needed but unavailable, and because interest in this type of music is not great. He was extremely prolific and composed pieces for many different combinations of voices and instruments. Much of his work is for one or more pianos, such as *Arc-en-ciel* for six pianos, composed in 1956.

Oct. 1   American composer Roy Harris, 81, dies in Santa Monica, California. After studies with Arthur Farwell and others, he went to Paris and studied with Nadia Boulanger. He later returned to America and began to attract attention when Farwell's article on him appeared in the *Musical Quarterly*. Harris became a teacher and held many positions in colleges and universities. These include Westminster Choir College, Colorado College, Indiana University and the University of California at Los Angeles.

Harris was a specialist in instrumental music characterized by fugal and canonic writing, triadic harmonies, asymmetric rhythms and melodies that, while not necessarily derived from folk song, create a sense of what might be termed native American music. He composed many symphonies (of which the third is his most famous piece), concertos, vocal works (but no operas or oratorios), chamber music and piano pieces. Many of his works have titles reflecting their American inspiration, such as *American Creed* for chorus and orchestra, and *Whitman Triptych* for women's voices and piano.

Oct. 4   Edith K. Kanakaole, 65, dies in Hilo, Hawaii. She was considered an expert on Hawaiian chant and hulas.

Oct. 7   Julius Rudel makes his debut as music director of the Buffalo Philharmonic Orchestra Society. The concert, consisting of music by Johannes Brahms and Richard Wagner, takes place at the home of this orchestra — the Kleinhans Music Hall in Buffalo, New York.

Oct. 9   American dancer and choreographer Joyce Trisler, 45, dies in Manhattan. Born in Los Angeles, she had been a member of the Juilliard Dance Theater and had danced with Alvin Ailey. Her choreography has become part of the repertory of both Ailey's company and the Boston Ballet. She was also noted for her authoritative work on Lester Horton.

Oct. 10   French conductor Paul Paray, 93, dies in Monte Carlo. After studies at the Paris Conservatoire he won the Grand Prix de Rome. He fought with the French Army (World War I) and then returned to Paris and in 1923 became conductor of the Concerts Lamoureux. He later conducted orchestras in Monte Carlo, the Colonne Orchestra in Paris and the Detroit Symphony Orchestra.

Oct. 13   Peter Dellheim, 52, dies in New York City. Noted for his expertise in recording technology, he was recording director for many well-known artists, including Van Cliburn, Beverly Sills and Arthur Fiedler. He was an executive producer for RCA Red Seal Records.

Oct. 14   Arthur Mendel, 74, dies in Princeton, New Jersey. A member of the faculty of Princeton University, this scholar was also known as an editor for G. Schirmer, Inc., and for his work on the music of Johann Sebastian Bach. He also wrote music criticism for *The Nation*. He devoted much of his work to the history of pitch and was also one of the first scholars to advocate computer-assisted musical analysis. He was also an editor of *The Bach Reader* (New York, 1945).

Oct. 17   French baritone Pierre Bernac, 80, dies in Villeneuve-les-Avignon, France. Closely associated with Francis Poulenc, Bernac was well known for performances of German lieder as well as French songs. He concertized in Europe and America, usually with Poulenc as his accompanist. He also taught at the American Conservatory in Fontainebleau and authored *The Interpretation of French Song* (New York, 1970).

Oct. 18   Dr. Helmuth von Hase, 88, dies in Wiesbaden. This man became director of the music publishing house Breitkopf & Hartel in 1919. When the Berlin office of this company was destroyed during World War II, he set up business in Wiesbaden and claimed the firm's rights in West Germany.

Oct. 22   Nadia Boulanger, 92, dies in Paris. Sister of composer Lili Boulanger, she studied composition with Gabriel Faure and became, perhaps, the most famous music teacher of the century. Her teaching reputation was carried back to America by such composers as Aaron Copland, Roy Harris, Walter Piston, Elie Siegmeister, Elliott Carter and Virgil Thomson. She is said to have had a photographic memory. Her students — from various parts of the world — often commented unfavorably on her disciplinary style. She was an ardent supporter of Igor Stravinsky and an ardent non-supporter of Arnold Schoenberg.

Oct. 24   Eleanor Robson Belmont, 100, dies in New York City. She was a prominent society figure in the arts and founded the Metropolitan Opera Guild.

Nov. 11   Composer Dimitri Tiomkin, 85, dies in London. After studies with Alexander Glazunov at the Saint Petersburg Conservatory, he also studied piano with Ferruccio Busoni before coming to the United States. He is noted especially for having composed 160 film scores. These include *High Noon* (1952). He also published an autobiography called *Please Don't Hate Me* (New York, 1959).

1979   Related Events

Leonard Slatkin becomes music director of the Saint Louis Symphony Orchestra this year. He is the first American-born conductor to become its music director. Prior to this appointment, he was music director of the New Orleans Philharmonic.

Music publishing house Schott's Sohne in Mainz publishes the *International Electronic Music Discography* — by M. Kondracki, M. Stankiewicz and F.C. Weiland — this year. This massive discography — containing more than 2,400 entries — is the largest of its kind published to date in the field of electronic and concrete, live electronic and computer music. The publication was produced in cooperation with the Institute of Sonology in Utrecht and the University of Utrecht.

April 13   Handel's *Messiah* is performed by Gennady Rozhdestvensky at the Great Hall of the Tchaikovsky Conservatory. The New York *Times* subsequently reports that this event marks the first performance of this work in the Soviet Union since the revolution.

April 16   Joseph Schwantner is awarded the Pulitzer Prize for music for *Aftertones of Infinity*.

May 3   The U.S. House of Representatives releases a study charging the National Endowment for the Arts with conflict of interest and possible mismanagement. The 75-page report suggests that the program may be "without merit" and that the distribution of grant money may have become political.

June 10   American composer, theorist and writer Robert Cogan presents a lecture entitled *"Tone Color: The New Understanding"* at the Zentrum fur Interdisziplinäre Forschung (ZIF), University of Bielefeld, West Germany. Examining tone color through real-time sound spectrum analysis (a recent technological development that dissects acoustical complexities of dense sounds as they occur), Cogan posits that music, acoustics and linguistics are, in these closing years of the century, being studied simultaneously by many musicians and scientists in order to develop an analytic theory of tone color that will illuminate musical and theoretical problems.

June 20   The American Ballet Theater announces the appointment of Mikhail Baryshnikov as its director beginning September 1, 1980.

July 15   A memorial concert in honor of Arthur Fiedler is held in Boston. Attendance is estimated at 100,000, and the audience observes a moment of silence before the Boston Pops plays John Philip Sousa's "The Stars and Stripes Forever."

July 16   The Pierpont Morgan Library in New York City announces it has acquired the holograph manuscript of Mozart's Symphony in D Major, the *Haffner*. Once given to King Ludwig II of Bavaria as a birthday present, it is purchased from the National Orchestral Association at an undisclosed price.

July 20   The Bregenz Floating Stage — a new addition to the annual Bregenz Music Festival in Austria — is inaugurated today with a performance of Giacomo Puccini's *Turandot*. This project began in 1955, when organizers of this festival decided to take advantage of the geographical location of the festival, which is on Lake Constance. The stage can accommodate productions that require as much as 1,800 square meters of space and has seating for 4,323. Officials state that the new stage will enable audiences to imagine that they are in a lagoon, the North Sea or the Atlantic Ocean, depending on the settings of operas that use bodies of water as a backdrop, such as *The Flying Dutchman*, by Richard Wagner.

Aug. 1   The Bolshoi Ballet begins an American tour that is to be marked by political defections of three of its dancers.

Aug. 14   The New York *Times* reports from Moscow that modern music in the Soviet Union is not as underground as it may have been thought to be. The relaxation, including everything from the avant-garde music of John Cage to dodecaphonic music, is reported to have occurred within the last 10 years.

Aug. 22   Soviet ballet dancer Aleksander Godunov, 30, defects to the United States. A member of the Bolshoi Ballet, he states that his motivation is purely for esthetic reasons. Spokesmen for the dancer say he felt "restrained in his artistic life" in the Soviet Union. The dancer's wife, Ludmila Vlasova (also a member of the Bolshoi Ballet) is detained at Kennedy Airport by American officials who state that they believe she is being prevented from returning to the Soviet Union against her will. She is subsequently given clearance to leave and receives a hero's welcome upon her return to the Soviet Union.

Sep. 7   The new Symphony Hall in Salt Lake City, Utah is opened as the home of the Utah Symphony Orchestra. Built at a cost of $10 million, it was designed by the Salt Lake City firm of Fowler, Ferguson, Kingston & Rueben, with acoustician Cyril Harris as sound consultant. The opening program features music by Bela Bartok and Brahms conducted by Stanislas Skrowaczewski.

Sep. 8   The Centennial Celebration concert of the Saint Louis Symphony Orchestra scheduled for today is canceled due to an orchestra strike. The conflict ends October 15, after the federal government mediates a solution and a new salary and benefits package is accepted by orchestra personnel. The season officially begins October 23, when Mstislav Rostropovich agrees to perform in a special concert to celebrate both the orchestra's centennial and the end of its labor dispute.

Sep. 16   In Los Angeles Bolshoi Ballet dancers Leonid and Valentina Koslov defect to the United States. Following the August 22 move of Aleksander Godunov, the husband and wife, both principal dancers, defect on the last day of the Bolshoi tour and are granted political asylum on September 17.

Sep. 17   The first Festival International Hector Berlioz begins today in Lyon, France. Featuring the Orchestra of Lyon, this festival becomes an annual event devoted exclusively to the music of this composer.

Sep. 18   The International Bruckner Festival for this year begins today in Munich and includes what its organizers call a "science fiction" element — "ars electronica" — which is applied to Anton Bruckner's music in the following ways: The music is fed into a computer, which then analyzes its characteristics and composes new music in the style of Bruckner; a "sonoscope" converts the sonorities of the music into form and color; a "sensorium" sensitizes audiences to the music; a "vocoder" transforms the voices of volunteers reading the text of a menu into a choral part in the style of Bruckner, which the organizers call "Bruckner Menu with Choir." The "ars electronica" Grand Prize for the most original and trend-setting new development in electronic sound is presented. Attendance at this event approaches 200,000. The idea was conceived by Dr. Herbert W. Franke, a lecturer in cybernetic aestheticism at the University of Munich.

Sep. 24   The Metropolitan Opera of New York opens its 1979 season with a live telecast of Giuseppe Verdi's *Otello*. Featuring Placido Domingo, Sherrill Milnes, Gilda Cruz-Romo and Kurt Moll, it is the first opening night telecast in 25 years and is seen in 60 American cities reaching between 3 and 10 million viewers.

Sep. 27   The Moscow Symphony cancels its planned American tour due to alleged problems with its conductor, Yevgeny Svetlanov. The U.S. State Department suggests that the cancellation may have been motivated by the recent Bolshoi Ballet political defections.

Sep. 30   The orchestra of the New York City Opera strikes after failing to negotiate a new contract. All operatic performances of the company are canceled pending the settlement.

Oct. 6   American harpsichordist-conductor Jens Nygaard presents a new orchestra — the Jupiter Symphony — at Carnegie Hall in New York City in a program featuring works by Ottorino Respighi, Darius Milhaud, Bach and Mozart. This ensemble was brought together after diligent efforts by Nygaard led to a large Rockefeller Foundation grant.

Oct. 14   The Lyric Opera of Chicago celebrates its 25th anniversary in a gala concert in Chicago featuring Leontyne Price, Luciano Pavarotti, Jon Vickers, Eleanor Steber, Elisabeth Schwarzkopf, John Pritchard, Krzysztof Penderecki and others, performing music of Mozart, Puccini, Donizetti and Penderecki.

Oct. 29   The last of the inaugural concerts celebrating the new music director of the Los Angeles Philharmonic — Carlo Maria Giulini — takes place at the Los Angeles Music Center. It is telecast live nationwide and to Europe by satellite, marking the first live transmission of a concert to Europe from the city of Los Angeles. Between the Los Angeles audience and those watching on television, the number of listeners is estimated at 30 million.

Nov. 2   Soviet All-Union Copyright Agency official Vasily R. Sitnikov asserts that the recently published memoirs of Dmitri Shostakovich are fraudulent.

Nov. 4   Birgit Nilsson gives a recital at the Metropolitan Opera in New York City after some five years' absence and performs music of Richard Wagner and Richard Strauss.

BIRGIT NILSSON

Nov. 18   The Dresden State Orchestra performs a concert at Avery Fisher Hall, Lincoln Center in New York City, featuring music of Beethoven, Mozart and Brahms. This event marks this orchestra's first New York performance. Founded in 1548, it is the oldest orchestra in the world.

Nov. 18   The Sixth All-Union Congress of Composers meets in Moscow to establish creative criteria for Soviet composers. Composer and union official Tikhon Khrennikov denounces seven young Soviet composers for being too abstract and appealing to capitalism. They are Edison Denisov, Viktor Suslin, Dmitri Smirnov, Elena Firsova, Aleksandr Knaifel, Viacheslav Artyomov and Sofia Gubaidulina.

Nov. 24   A festival celebrating the 100th anniversary of the death of Danish choreographer August Bournonville begins in Copenhagen. Attracting critics and dance lovers from around the world, the week-long event features performances of all his extant ballets as well as exhibits and lectures on the life and work of the choreographer.

Bibliography

Adorno, Theodor W. *Introduction to the Sociology of Music.* Translated by E.B. Ashton. New York: Seabury Press, 1962.

Adorno, Theodor W. *Philosophy of Modern Music.* Translated by Anne G. Mitchell and Wesley V. Blomster. New York: Seabury Press, 1973.

Aldous, Donald. "A Selective but Detailed Compilation of the Most Significant Events in the Last Century or So of Recorded Sound." *Hi-fi News & Record Review* 22 (1977): 92-93, 97.

American Society of Composers, Authors and Publishers Biographical Dictionary. 4th ed., edited by Jaques Cattell Press. New York: R.R. Bowker, 1980.

Apel, Willi. *The Harvard Dictionary of Music.* 2d ed. rev. and enl. Cambridge, Mass.: Belknap Press of Harvard University, 1969.

Beaumont, Cyril W. *Complete Book of Ballets.* London: Putnam, 1937.

Beaumont, Cyril W. *Supplement to Complete Book of Ballets.* London: Putnam, 1952.

Bekker, Paul. *Richard Wagner: His Life in His Work.* Translated by M.M. Bozman. London and Toronto: J.M. Dent, 1931. Reprint. New York: Greenwood.

Berger, Kenneth. *The March King and His Band: The Story of John Philip Sousa.* New York: Exposition Press, 1957.

Bernstein, Leonard. *Findings.* New York: Simon and Schuster, 1982.

Boulez, Pierre. *Boulez on Music Today.* Translated by Susan Bradshaw and Richard Rodney Bennett. London: Faber and Faber, 1979.

Boulez, Pierre. *Notes of an Apprenticeship.* Translated by Herbert Weinstock. New York: Alfred A. Knopf, 1968.

Bradley, Carol June. *Music Collections in American Libraries: A Chronology.* Detroit Studies in Music Bibliography, no. 46. Detroit: Information Coordinators, 1981.

Briggs, John. *Requiem for a Yellow Brick Brewery: A History of the Metropolitan Opera.* Boston: Little, Brown, 1969.

Brindle, Reginald Smith. *Serial Composition.* London: Oxford University Press, 1966.

Buckle, Richard. *Nijinsky.* New York: Simon and Schuster, 1971.

Chujoy, Anatole, and Manchester, P.W., eds. *The Dance Encyclopedia.* Rev. and enl. ed. New York: Simon and Schuster, 1967

Clarke, Mary, and Vaughan, David. *The Encyclopedia of Dance and Ballet.* New York: G.P. Putnam's Sons, 1977.

Clynes, Manfred. *Sentics: The Touch of Emotions.* Garden City, N.Y.: Doubleday/Anchor Press, 1978.

Cowell, Henry. *New Musical Resources.* 1930. Reprint. New York: Something Else Press, 1969.

Critchley, Macdonald, and Henson, R.A. *Music and the Brain: Studies in the Neurology of Music.* London: William Heinemann Medical Books, 1977.

Cross, F.L., and Livingstone, Elizabeth A. *The Oxford Dictionary of the Christian Church.* 2d ed. rev. London: Oxford University Press, 1974.

Dolmetsch, Arnold. *The Interpretation of the Music of the Seventeenth and Eighteenth Centuries Revealed by Contemporary Evidence.* Seattle: University of Washington Press, 1969.

Duncan, Irma, and Ross MacDougall, Allan. *Isadora Duncan's Russian Days and Her Last Years in France.* New York: Covici-Friede, 1929.

Eisenstein, Sergei M. *The Film Sense.* Translated and edited by Jay Leyda. New York: Harcourt, Brace & World, 1947.

Ewen, David. *The World of Twentieth Century Music.* Englewood Cliffs, N.J.: Prentice-Hall, 1968.

Franks, A.H. *Twentieth Century Ballet.* London: Burke, 1954.

Gaster, Adrian, ed. *International Who's Who in Music and Musician's Directory.* 9th ed. Detroit: Gale Research Co., 1980.

Gilder, Eric, and Port, June G. *The Dictionary of Composers and Their Music: Every Listener's Companion.* New York: Facts On File, 1978.

Goodwin, Noël, ed. *The Royal Ballet and Sadler's Wells Royal Ballet 1980/81.* London: The Royal Opera House Covent Garden Ltd., 1980.

Hadley, Benjamin, et al., eds. *Britannica Book of Music.* Garden City, N.Y.: Doubleday/Britannica Books, 1980.

Hall, David. *The Talking Machine, Hardware and Software: A Consolidated Chronology.* Unpublished. New York Public Library, Rogers and Hammerstein Archives of Recorded Sound, May, 1978.

Hanslick, Eduard. *The Beautiful in Music: A Contribution to the Revisal of Musical Aesthetics.* Translated by Gustav Cohen and Morris Weitz. Rev. ed. New York: Da Capo Press, 1974. Reprint of 1891 ed.

Haskell, Arnold L., and Nouvel, Walter W. *Diaghileff: His Artistic and Private Life.* New York: Simon and Schuster, 1935. Reprint. New York: Da Capo Press, 1977.

Hayburn, Robert F. *Papal Legislation on Sacred Music 95 A.D. to 1977 A.D.* Collegeville, Minn.: Liturgical Press, 1979.

Hindemith, Paul. *The Craft of Musical Composition.* 4th ed. rev. Translated by Arthur Mendel. 2 vols. Clifton, N.J.: Eur-Am Music, 1945.

Hitchcock, H. Wiley. *Ives*. Oxford Studies of Composers (14). London: Oxford University Press, 1977.

Ives, Charles. *Essays Before a Sonata, The Majority, and Other Writings*. Edited by Howard Boatwright. New York: W.W. Norton, 1970.

Kirstein, Lincoln. *Movement & Metaphor: Four Centuries of Ballet*. New York: Praeger, 1970.

Koegler, Horst. *The Concise Oxford Dictionary of Ballet*. London: Oxford University Press, 1977.

Kolodin, Irving. *The Story of the Metropolitan Opera, 1883-1950: A Candid History*. 4th ed. New York: Alfred A. Knopf, 1966.

Krenek, Ernst. *Horizons Circled: Reflections on My Music*. With Contributions by Will Ogdon and John L. Stewart. Berkeley: University of California Press, 1975.

Kutsch, K.J., and Riemens, Leo. *A Concise Biographical Dictionary of Singers from the Beginning of Recorded Sound to the Present*. Translated by Harry Earl Jones. Philadelphia: Chilton, 1969.

Lansky, Paul. "Affine Music." Ph.D. dissertation, Yale University, 1973.

Lesure, François, ed. *Debussy on Music: The Critical Writings of the Great French Composer Claude Debussy*. Translated by Richard Langham Smith. New York: Alfred A. Knopf, 1977.

Lieven, Petr. *The Birth of Ballets-Russes*. Translated by L. Zarine. Boston and New York: Houghton Mifflin, 1936. Reprint. New York: Dover, 1963.

Lingg, Ann M. *John Philip Sousa*. New York: Henry Holt, 1954.

McDonagh, Don. *Don McDonagh's Complete Guide to Modern Dance*. New York: Popular Library, 1977.

McDonagh, Don. *Martha Graham: A Biography*. New York: Popular Library, 1975.

McDonagh, Don. *Rise and Fall and Rise of Modern Dance*. New York: New American Library, 1971.

Machlis, Joseph. *The Enjoyment of Music: An Introduction to Perceptive Listening*. 4th ed. New York: W.W. Norton, 1977.

Mahler, Alma. *Gustav Mahler: Memories and Letters*. Enl. ed., revised and edited by Donald Mitchell and Knud Martner. Seattle: University of Washington Press, 1974.

Manson, Adele P. *Calendar of Music and Musicians*. Metuchen, N.J.: Scarecrow Press, 1981.

Marsh, Robert C. *The Cleveland Orchestra*. Cleveland and New York: The World Publishing Co., 1967.

Moldenhauer, Hans. *The Death of Anton Webern: A Drama in Documents*. New York: Philosophical Library, 1961.

Moldenhauer, Hans, and Moldenhauer, Rosaleen. *Anton Von Webern: A Chronicle of His Life and Work*. New York: Alfred A. Knopf, 1978.

Monson, Karen. *Alban Berg*. Boston: Houghton Mifflin, 1979.

Mussulman, Joseph A. *Dear People. . . Robert Shaw: A Biography*. Bloomington: Indiana University Press, 1979.

Nichols, Roger. *Messiaen*. Oxford Studies of Composers (13). London: Oxford University Press, 1975.

Partch, Harry. *The Genesis of a Music: An Account of Its Creative Roots and Its Fulfillments*. 2d ed. Reprint. New York: Da Capo Press, 1974.

Perle, George. *Serial Composition and Atonality: An Introduction to the Music of Schoenberg, Berg, and Webern*. 4th ed. rev. Berkeley: University of California Press, 1978.

Perle, George. *Twelve-tone Tonality*. Berkeley: University of California Press, 1978.

Perugini, Mark E. *The Art of Ballet*. Philadelphia: J.B. Lippincott, 1915.

Peyser, Joan. *Boulez, Composer, Conductor, Enigma*. New York: Schirmer Books, 1978.

Rabin, Carol Price. *A Guide to Music Festivals in America*. Stockbridge, Mass.: Berkshire Traveller Press, 1979.

Rauchhaupt, Ursula V., ed. *Schoenberg, Berg, Webern. The String Quartets: A Documentary Study*. Translated by Eugene Hartzell. Hamburg: Deutsche Grammophon Gesellschaft, 1971.

Reich, Willi. *Schoenberg: A Critical Biography*. Translated by Leo Black. New York: Praeger, 1971.

Reynolds, Nancy. *Repertory in Review: 40 Years of the New York City Ballet*. New York: Dial Press, 1977.

Rosenthal, Harold, and Warrack, John, eds. *The Concise Oxford Dictionary of Opera*. 2d ed. London: Oxford University Press, 1979.

Russcol, Herbert. *The Liberation of Sound: An Introduction to Electronic Music*. Englewood Cliffs; N.J.: Prentice-Hall, 1972.

Saleh, Dennis. *Science Fiction Gold: Film Classics of the 50's*. New York: McGraw-Hill, 1979.

Salzman, Eric. *Twentieth-Century Music: An Introduction*. Englewood Cliffs, N.J.: Prentice-Hall, 1967.

Samuel, Claude. *Conversations with Olivier Messiaen*. Translated by Felix Aprahamian. London: Stainer and Bell, 1976.

Schmitt, Francis P. *Church Music Transgressed: Reflections on Reform*. New York: Seabury Press, 1977.

Schneider, Ilya Ilyich. *Isadora Duncan: The Russian Years*. Translated by David Magarshack. New York: Harcourt Brace Jovanovich, 1969.

Scholes, Percy A. *Concise Oxford Dictionary of Music*. 2d ed., edited by John Owen Ward. London: Oxford University Press, 1964.

Schwartz, Elliott, and Childs, Barney, eds. *Contemporary Composers on Contemporary Music*. New York: Holt, Reinhart & Winston, 1967. Reprint. New York: Da Capo Press, 1978.

Schwarz, Boris. *Music and Musical Life in Soviet Russia: 1917-1970*. New York: W.W. Norton, 1973.

Sessions, Roger. *Questions about Music*. New York: W.W. Norton, 1971.

Slonimsky, Nicolas, ed. *Baker's Biographical Dictionary of Musicians*. 6th ed. rev. New York: Schirmer Books, 1978.

Slonimsky, Nicolas. *Lexicon of Musical Invective: Critical Assaults on Composers since Beethoven's Time*. 2d ed. Seattle: University of Washington Press, 1975.

Slonimsky, Nicolas. *Music since 1900*. 4th ed. New York: Charles Scribner's Sons, 1971.

Sokol, Martin L. *The New York City Opera: An American Adventure*. New York: Macmillan, 1981.

Stuckenschmidt, H.H. *Ferruccio Busoni: Chronicle of a European*. Translated by Sandra Morris. New York: St. Martin's Press, 1970.

Stuckenschmidt, H.H. *Twentieth Century Music*. Translated by Richard Deveson. New York: McGraw-Hill, 1969.

Talaske, Richard H., Wetherill, Ewart A., and Cavanaugh, William J., eds. *Halls for Music Performance. Two Decades of Experience: 1962-1982*. New York: American Institute of Physics for the Acoustical Society of America, 1982.

Terry, Walter. *The Ballet Guide*. New York: Popular Library, 1977.

Thompson, Oscar. *The International Cyclopedia of Music and Musicians*. 10th ed., revised and edited by Bruce Bohle. New York: Dodd, Mead, 1975.

Tobias, Matthay. *The Act of Touch in All Its Diversity: An Analysis and Synthesis of Pianoforte Tone-production*. London: Longmans, Green, 1903

Volkov, Solomon, ed. *Testimony: The Memoirs of Dmitri Shostakovich*. Translated by Antonina W. Bouis. New York: Harper & Row, 1979.

Wa-Wan Press, 1901-1911. 5 vols. Edited by Vera Brodsky Lawrence. New York: Arno Press and the New York *Times*, 1970.

Wells, Katherine Gladney. *Symphony and Song. The Saint Louis Symphony Orchestra, The First Hundred Years: 1880-1980*. Woodstock, Vt.: Countryman Press, 1980.

Who's Who in Opera. New York: Arno, 1976.

Wilson, George Buckley Laird. *A Dictionary of the Ballet*. 3d ed. New York: Theatre Arts Books, 1974.

Wooldridge, David. *From the Steeples and Mountains: A Study of Charles Ives*. New York: Alfred A. Knopf, 1974.

Wuorinen, Charles. *Simple Composition*. New York: Longman, 1979.

Yates, Peter B. *Twentieth Century Music: Its Evolution from the End of the Harmonic Era to the Present Era of Sound*. New York: Minerva Press, 1967.

Yeston, Maury. *The Stratification of Musical Rhythm*. New Haven, Conn.: Yale University Press, 1976.

Young, Edgar B. *Lincoln Center: The Building of an Institution*. With a foreword by Frank Stanton. New York and London: New York University Press, 1980.

Alphabetical Index

Note: Index references are given by date and column. In order to save space, the columns have been abbreviated as follows:

A—Opera
B—Dance
C—Instrumental and Vocal Music
D—Births, Deaths and Debuts
E—Related Events

— A —

Abandon d'Ariane, L' — 4/20/28 A
Abbado, Claudio — 6/26/33 D
Abduction of Sita, The — 1/31/21 B
Abendroth, Irene — 9/1/32 D
Aborn, Milton — 11/13/33 D
Abracadabra — 4/23/63 C
Abraham and Isaac — 8/23/64 C
Abravanel, Maurice — 1/6/03 D
Absil, Jean — 5/22/38 E; 2/2/74 D
Abstrakte Oper No. 1 — 6/28/53 A
Abyss — 2/21/65 B
Academic Society for Literature and Music, The — 3/31/13 C
Academie des Beaux-Arts — 6/30/01 E; 6/27/03 E; //62 E
Academy of Choreographic Art — //26 E; 5/5/31 B
Academy of Santa Cecilia (Rome) — 8/22/19 E; 2/2/37 E
Acc-Music — 8/26/78 C
Ackte, Aino — 12/8/10 A
Acoustical and Electromechanical Research Laboratory — 10/4/58 E
Acoustical Society of America — 5/10/29 E
Acres of the Sky — 11/6/51 A
Acrobats of God — 4/27/60 B
Active Society for the Propagation of Contemporary Music — 12/1/30 C
Act of Touch in All Its Diversity, The — 7//03 E
Adam and Eve — 10/4/61 B
Adami, Giuseppe — 3/27/17 A; 12/14/18 A; 4/25/26 A
Adamis — 4/1/22 A
Adamowska, Antoinette Szumowska — 8/18/39 D
Adamowski, Joseph — 5/8/30 D
Adamowski Quartet — 2/3/21 D
Adamowski Trio — 5/8/30 D; 8/18/39 D
Adams, Carolyn — 8/6/43 D
Adams, David — 11/16/43 D; 2/6/48 B; 2/1/55 B
Adams, Diana — 3/29/26 D; 4/10/45 B; 4/22/48 B; 2/25/50 B; 12/4/51 B; 2/19/52 B; 2/28/52 B; 1/6/53 B; 1/19/54 B; 9/14/54 B; 2/27/55 B; 12/19/56 B; 12/1/57 B; 1/17/58 B; 11/16/60 B; 11/22/60 B; 3/22/61 B
Adams, Stanley — 4/28/59 E
Addinsell, Richard — 1/13/04 D; 11/15/77 D
Addison, Adele — 10/20/60 C; 4/11/64 C
Adelaide Festival of Arts — 3/21/76 C
Adelaide, ou le langage des fleurs — 4/22/12 B
Adenauer, Konrad — 11/28/26 B
Adjemova, Sirene — 5/5/46 B

Adler, Guido — 9/30/27 E; 2/15/41 D
Adler, Kurt — 4/2/05 D; 9/21/77 D
Adler, Larry — 2/10/14 D; 5/28/47 C; 5/3/52 C; 8/15/53 C
Adonais — 2/3/00 C
Adorno, Theodor — 9/11/03 D; 4/24/11 C; //48 E; //62 E; 8/6/69 D
Adriana Lecouvreur — 11/26/02 A
Adrio, Adam — 4/4/01 D; 9/18/73 D
Adventures in a Perambulator — 3/19/15 C
AEG — *see* Allgemeine Electricitaets Gesellschaft
Aeolian Chamber Players — 12/2/66 C; 4/27/71 C; 10/10/72 C; 9/28/78 C
Aerophor — 10/19/13 E
AES — *see* Audio Engineering Society (AES)
Aeterna Orchestra — 12/11/74 C
Afro-American Symphony — 10/29/31 C; 12/3/78 D
After All — 11/15/76 B
After Eden — 11/9/67 B
Afternoon of a Faun — 5/14/53 B — *see also Apresmidi d'un faune, L'*
Aftertones of Infinity — 1/29/79 C; 4/16/79 E
Agamemnon — 4/16/27 A; 11/27/27 A
Agee, James — 2/5/77 C
Age of Anxiety, The — 2/26/50 B
Aglavaine et Selisette — 4/3/17 C
AGMA (American Guild of Musical Artists) — 4/9/36 E
Agon (Balanchine) — 12/1/57 B
Agon (Stravinsky) — 6/17/57 C; 4/6/71 D
Agyptische Helena, Die — 6/6/28 A
Ahavah — 11/17/54 C
Ahna, Pauline de — 9/8/49 D
Aida — 1/27/01 D
Aiello, Salvatore — 7/27/71 B
Aiglon, L' — 3/11/37 A
Ailey, Alvin — 1/5/31 D; 1/31/60 B; 9/30/62 B; 9/8/71 C; 10/9/79 D
Air and Dance — 10/12/29 C
Airborne Symphony — 3/23/46 C
Air Music — 12/5/75 C; 5/3/76 E
Air on a Ground Bass — 3/31/29 B
Airs, Big Bertha — 7/28/79 B
Aitken, Robert — 9/21/72 C
Ajanta Frescoes, The — 9/10/23 B
Akimov, Boris — 2/16/75 B
Akiyama, Kazuyoshi — 11/9/75 C
Akoko, Henri — 1/15/41 C
Akrata — 6/28/66 C
Aks, Harold — 5/13/65 C
Aladdin — 2/15/19 C
Albanese, Licia — 7/22/13 D; 12/10/35 D; 2/9/40 D
Albani, Emma — 4/3/30 D

Albany Symphony — 4/20/74 C
Albeniz, Isaac — 1/2/08 C; 5/18/09 D; 10/25/20 B
Albers, Henri — 9/12/26 D
Albert, Eugene d' — 11/15/03 A; 3/5/16 A; 3/10/18 A; 5/16/21 A; 11/14/26 A; 12/1/28 A; 3/3/32 D
Albert Herring — 6/20/47 A; 12/4/76 D
Albinoni, Tomaso — 11/15/76 B
Albright, William — 10/20/44 D; 2/23/72 C
Albuquerque Symphony Orchestra — 11/4/48 C; 3/16/50 C
Alcestis — 4/29/60 B
Alda, Frances — 4/15/04 D; 12/7/08 D; 11/17/09 D; 2/27/13 A; 1/31/20 A; 1/2/25 D; 12/28/29 E; 9/18/52 D
Aldeburgh — *see* Aldeburgh Festival
Aldeburgh Festival — //46 E; 6/14/49 A; 6/17/54 A; 6/13/64 C; 6/9/66 A; 6/3/67 A; 6/18/67 C; 6/8/68 A; 12/4/76 D
Aldrich, Perley Dunn — 11/20/33 D
Aleko — 9/8/42 B
Alessandro, Raffaele d' — 3/17/11 D; 3/17/59 D
Alessandro, Victor — 11/27/76 D
Alexander Nevsky — 5/17/39 C; 3/5/53 D
Alexandrov, Alexander — 1/17/29 E
Alfano, Franco — 11/4/04 A; 12/10/21 A; 4/25/26 A; 3/5/27 A; 12/22/30 C; 1/22/36 A; 10/27/54 D
Alfven, Hugo — 5/10/04 C; 10/25/20 B; 4/30/52 C; 5/8/60 D
Al Gian Sole Carico d'Amore — 4//75 A
Alhambra Ballet — 6/16/02 B; 1/12/03 B
Alhambra Theater — 1/1/01 A; 4/21/02 B; 2/27/05 B; 12/11/05 B
Alice Tully Hall (New York City) — 9/11/69 E; 4/9/75 E
Alkestis — 8/26/22 A
All American Youth Orchestra — //39 E; 5/11/41 C
Allegra brigata, L' — 5/4/50 A
Allegro Brillante — 3/1/56 B
Allen, Betty — 5/23/75 A
Allende, Pedro Humberto — 8/16/59 D
Allen, Maude — 7/15/59 D
Allgemeine Electricitaets Gesellschaft (AEG) — 9/17/31 E; //34 E; //35 E
Allin, Norman — 4/3/25 A
All-Male Dancers Group — 1/9/72 D
Allons Dance — 5/22/00 E
All Souls Carnival — 3/3/57 C
All the Way Around and Back — 1/29/27 C
Alma Mater — 12/6/34 B
Alonso, Alberto — //48 E

Alonso, Alicia — 12/21/21 D; 4/10/45 B;
    9/27/47 B; //48 E; 4/14/48 B; 4/22/48 B;
    5/21/52 B
Alonso, Fernando — //48 E
Alpaert, Flor — 11/22/13 A
Alpenheim, Ilse von — 5/4/72 C
Alpensinfonie, Eine — 10/28/15 C
Alsen, Elsa — 1/31/75 D
Also sprach Zarathustra — 3/21/04 C
Altchevsky, Ivan — 5/19/08 A
Althouse, Paul — 3/23/18 A
Altman, Natan — 12/9/42 B
Altschuler, Modest — 1/28/04 E; 12/20/06 D;
    12/10/08 C; 3/20/15 C
Alvin Ailey Dance Theater — 1/31/60 B
Alvorado na floresta tropical — 1/23/54 C
Alwin, Carl — 10/16/45 D
Amahl and the Night Visitors — 12/24/51 A
Amalgam — 7/9/68 C
Amar String Quartet — 7/19/24 C;
    12/28/63 D
Amaryllis — 10/31/64 C
Amato, Pasquale — 11/20/08 D; 2/6/09 E;
    1/13/10 E; 12/10/10 A; 11/13/11 D;
    2/27/13 A; 1/2/14 A; 1/25/15 A;
    8/12/42 D
Amatore medico, L' — 12/4/13 A
Amaya — 5/22/20 A
Amazing Grace — 1/31/61 A
Amazonas — 5/30/29 C
Amberol cylinders — //08 E
Amboise, Jacques d' — *see* D'Amboise, Jacques
Amboise, Paul d' — *see* D'Amboise, Paul
Amelia al ballo — 4/1/37 A
America — 12/20/28 C
American Academy in Rome — 10/4/21 E
American Accordionists Association —
    11/1/77 C
American Ballet — 12/6/34 B; 3/1/35 B;
    4/27-28/37 B; 5/29/41 B; 10//41 E;
    //48 E
American Ballet Company — 5/29/69 B;
    6/27/69 B; 4/3/70 B; 10/21/70 B;
    10/24/70 B; 4/20/71 B; 4/28/71 B
American Ballet Theater — 4/22/48 B; //57 E;
    4/20/60 B; 10/4/61 B; 3/17/65 B;
    3/23/65 B; 3/30/65 B; 1/25/66 B;
    3/31/67 B; 12/1/67 B; 12/4/69 B;
    7/1/71 B; 7/7/71 B; 1/6/72 B; 4/6/72 B;
    7/3/74 B; 4/5/79 B; 6/20/79 E
American Bicentennial — 2/27/75 C;
    2/26/76 C; 7/4/76 E; 9/29/76 C
American Brass Quintet — 3/15/73 C;
    1/13/75 C; 3/24/75 C
American Cantata — 12/1/77 C
American Composers' Alliance — 12/19/37 E;
    5/9/52 E
American Composers Orchestra — 5/23/78 C;
    12/11/78 C; 1/29/79 C
American Conservatory at Fontainebleau —
    6/27/54 D
American Conservatory of Music — 6/24/21 E;
    11/30/31 D; 8/7/34 D
American Creed — 10/1/79 D
American Dance Festival — 8/4/62 B
American Dance Theater — 10//64 E;
    12/2/72 D
American Document — 8/6/38 B
American Federation of Musicians —
    1/13/42 E; 7/8/42 E; 6/2/58 E
American Festival Overture — 10/6/39 C
American Guild of Musical Artists (AGMA) —
    5/28/52 E
American Guild of Organists — 4/8/37 D;
    6/7/76 E
American in Paris, An — 12/13/28 C
American Jewish Tercentenary Committee —
    12/2/55 C
American Legion — 10/28/19 E

American Musicological Society — 6/3/34 E;
    2/5/59 D; 11/1/79 C
American Opera Society — 12/1/64 A
American Quartet — 5/12/75 C
American Rhapsody — 2/21/54 C
American Society of Composers, Authors, and
    Publishers (ASCAP) — 2/13/14 E;
    12/19/37 E; 10/14/39 E; 4/28/59 E;
    7/3/66 D
American Society of the Ancient Instruments
    — 8/19/46 D
American String Quartet — 2/26/47 D
American Symphony Orchestra — 10/5/64 C;
    4/26/65 C; 11/17/68 C; 10/6/70 C;
    11/29/70 C; 11/9/75 C
American Triptych: Three Studies in Texture —
    3/9/65 C
American Wind Symphony — 6/15/69 C;
    7/27/69 C
Ameriques — 4/9/26 C
Amica — 3/16/05 A
Amor brujo, El — 4/15/15 B
Amore, De — 9/7/73 C
Amore dei tre re, L' — 4/10/13 A; 1/2/14 A
Amores de la Ines, Los — 4/12/02 A
Amour et son amour, L' — 12/13/48 B
Ampex — 1//49 E
Amphion — 6/23/31 A
Amram, David — 11/17/30 D; 2/20/62 C;
    4/11/65 A; 5/13/65 C; 8/1/68 A;
    10/8/70 C; 3/3/73 C; 1/18/76 C;
    8/6/78 C
Amsterdam Ballet — //61 E
Anagram — 6/11/60 C
Anaklasis — 10/16/60 C
Anastasia — 7/22/71 B
Ancerl, Karel — 4/11/08 D; 7/3/73 D
Ancetre, L' — 2/24/06 A
Ancient Voices of Children — 10/31/70 C
Anda, Geza — 11/19/21 D; 6/13/76 D
Anderson, Emily — 12/4/72 D
Anderson, Marian — 2/17/02 D; 8/27/25 E;
    1/2/39 E; 4/9/39 E; 1/6/43 E; 1/26/52 E;
    1/7/55 D; 4/18/65 E
Anderson, Maxwell — 9/26/38 A; 2/4/40 C
Anderson, Stell — 6/25/56 C
Andersson, Gerd — 9/28/63 B
And on the Seventh Day the Petals Fell in Petaluma —
    5/8/66 C
Andrea Chenier — 3/7/20 A
Andre, Franz — 9/13/55 C; 1/20/75 D
Andreyev, Leonid — 2/21/65 B
Andreyev, Vasily — 3/11/06 C
Andromache's Farewell — 4/4/63 C
Andromede ou le plus heureux des trois — 5/15/29 A
And They Lynched Him on a Tree — 6/25/40 C
Angel — //56 E
Angeles, Victoria de Los — 11/1/23 D;
    10/24/50 A; 3/17/51 D
Angelet, Thomas l' — 2/14/24 A
Angelique — 1/28/27 A
Angkor-Vat — 8/12/30 B
Angles, Higini — //31 E
Anglo-American Music Education Conferences
    — 7/31/58 D
Aniara — 5/31/59 A
Ani maamir — un chant perdu et retrouve —
    11/13/73 C
Animated Goblins, The — 4/28/07 B
Animus III — 11/4/72 C
Animus IV — 9/29/77 C
Anisimova, Nina — 11/7/32 B; 12/9/42 B
Ankara Conservatory — 2/14/49 E
Anna Karenina — 6/11/72 B
Annonciation, L' — 1/5/76 D
Annunzio, Gabriele d' — 5/22/11 A;
    12/15/13 A; 3/20/15 A; 11/1/18 A
Another Look at Harmony — 5/6/75 C
Anouilh, Jean — 5/22/48 B

Anrooy, Peter van — 10/31/17 D
Ansermet, Ernest — 4/9/17 C; 11/30/18 E;
    12/6/19 C; 10/30/21 C; 5/18/22 B;
    12/6/29 C; 4/19/36 C; 4/17/40 C;
    10/27/48 C; 2/14/52 B; 6/2/56 E;
    9/1/63 C; 2/20/69 D
Antar — 8/2/14 D
Antheil, George — 7/8/00 D; 6/19/26 C;
    5/25/30 A; 2/28/34 A; 2/13/44 C;
    12/10/44 C; 2/9/47 C; 12/31/48 C;
    2/10/49 C; 1/9/53 A; 7/28/54 A;
    4/2/55 A; 11/27/55 D; 5/24/57 A;
    3/25/58 D; 2/12/59 D
Anthology Sonore — //35 E
Anti-Abolitionist Riots, The — 1/29/27 C
Antic Meet — 8/14/58 B
Antigonae — 8/9/49 A
Antigone — 12/28/27 A
Antiphonal Responses for Improvised Piano and Orchestra — 4/26/79 C
Anti-Symphonie — 4/30/19 C
Antonicelli, F. — 3/10/56 A
Antoniou, Theodore — 4/28/78 C
Antony and Cleopatra — 9/16/66 A
Antwerp Opera — 6/4/72 D
Anush — 8/17/12 A
Aotearoa — 4/16/40 C
Aparebit Repentina Dies — 5/2/47 C
Apartment House 1776 — 7/4/76 E; 9/29/76 C
Aphrodisamania — 11/29/77 B
Aphrodite — 6/4/12 C
Apocalypse — 10/19/51 C
Apokalyptische Fantasie — 10/21/69 C
Apollinaire, Guillaume — 5/18/17 B; 6/3/47 A
Apollon Musagete (Balanchine) — 6/12/28 B;
    4/27-28/37 B
Apollon Musagete (Bolm) — 4/27/28 B
Apollon Musagete (Stravinsky) — 4/6/71 D
Apostel, Hans Erich — 1/22/01 D; 5/17/49 E;
    11/30/72 D
Apostles, The — 10/14/03 C; 3/19/07 D
Apostrophe, L' — 7/1/51 A
Appalachian Spring (Copland) — 5/7/45 E;
    10/4/45 C
Appalachian Spring (Graham) — 10/30/44 B
Apparitions (Ashton) — 2/11/36 B
Apparitions (Ligeti) — 6/19/60 C
Appleyard, Beatrice — 5/5/31 B
Apres-midi d'un faune, L' (Nijinsky) — 1/17/16 B
    — *see also Afternoon of A Faun*
Apres-midi d'un faune, L' (Ravel) — 5/29/12 B
Arabella — 7/1/33 A
Aragon, Louis — 4/14/67 C
Aranyi, Jelly d' — 4/26/24 C; 11/6/25 C;
    4/3/30 C; 3/30/66 D
Arbos, Enrique Fernandez — 4/9/16 C;
    9/11/20 C; 6/2/39 D
Arcana — 4/8/27 C
Arc-en-ciel — 9/29/79 D
Archangel — 12/18/78 C
Archer, Frederick — 1/23/00 E
Archives Internationales de la Danse, Les —
    7/3/32 B
Archiv Production — 1//49 E
Arctic Symphony — 4/5/33 C
Arel, Bulent — 4/23/19 D; 1/8/59 E;
    5/9-10/61 E; 11/30/70 C
Arens, Franz Xavier — 1/28/32 D
Arensky, Anton — 2/25/06 D; 3/21/08 B;
    6/2/09 B; 6/25/10 B
Argentinita, La — //32 E; 5/4/39 B
Argento, Dominick — 10/27/27 D; 5/5/56 C;
    4/20/57 C; 5/6/57 A; 7/14/60 C;
    5/31/63 A; 1/9/64 A; 3/22/64 C;
    1/26/66 C; 5/16/66 C; 6/1/67 A;
    10/23/68 C; 7/3/69 C; 9/25/70 C;
    10/14/71 A; 10/5/72 C; 3/9/74 C;
    10/20/74 C; 1/5/75 C; 5/5/75 E;
    4/24/76 A; 9/23/77 C; 3/22/79 A

Argerich, Martha — 6/26/74 D
Argo (record label) — 6//50 E
Argyle, Pearl — 4/26/31 B; 5/15/34 B;
    10/28/34 B; 11/26/35 B
Ariadne auf Naxos — 10/25/12 A; 10/25/12 C;
    10/4/16 A
Ariadne — 3/2/61 A
Aria for Oboe and String Orchestra — 1/16/77 C
Ariane et Barbe-Bleue — 5/10/07 A
Ariane — 10/31/06 A
Ari, Carina — 10/25/20 B; 6/6/21 B
Arie da Capo — 4/25/74 C
Ariettes oubliees — 3/25/18 D
Arjuna — 2/1/60 C
Arkadische Suite — 7/16/17 D
Arkhipova, Irina — 11/2/25 D; 11/27/64 D
Arlecchino — 5/11/17 A
Armida — 3/25/04 A
Armistead, Horace — 2/2/54 B; 1/8/58 B
Armsby, Mrs. Lenore Wood — //35 E
Armstrong, Edwin H. — 1/5/40 E
Armstrong, John — 4/26/31 B
Arnold, Malcolm — 7/6/51 C; 6/2/53 B;
    1/6/55 B; 6/7/56 B; 11/2/60 C
Aroldingen, Karin von — 9/9/41 D; 2/5/70 B;
    6/18/72 B; 1/17/74 E; 5/22/75 B;
    5/29/75 B; 6/23/77 B; 1/26/78 B;
    5/18/78 B
Aronson, Boris — 1/11/40 B; 2/14/52 B;
    6/2/74 B
Arova, Sonia — 6/20/27 D; 2/6/48 B;
    10/17/51 B; 3/10/62 D; 11/2/62 E
Arpino, Gerald — 1/14/28 D; 2/20/68 B;
    2/28/68 B
Arrau, Claudio — 2/6/03 D
Arroyo, Martina — 2/2/40 D; 4/4/63 C;
    2/6/65 D; 8/4/78 E
Art in the 19th Century (Stasov) — 10/23/06 D
Art of Noises, The — 3/11/13 E
Artyomov, Viacheslav — 11/18/79 E
Arvey, Verna — 12/3/78 D
Asafiev, Boris — 9/25/21 E; 1/1/26 E;
    4/27/27 B; 11/7/32 B; 9/28/34 B;
    12/31/35 B; 4/14/38 B; 1/27/49 D
ASCAP — *see* American Society of Composers,
    Authors and Publishers
Ashbery, John — 2/10/78 C
Ashbridge, Bryan — 3/3/53 B
Ashkenazy, Vladimir — 7/6/37 D; 2/1/53 C
Ashley, Merrill — 6/25/72 B; 1/12/78 B;
    5/18/78 B
Ashmolean Museum (Oxford) — 2/8/39 D
Ashton, Frederick — 9/17/04 D; 2/25/30 B;
    10/19/30 E; 2/6/31 B; 4/26/31 B;
    10/9/32 B; 12/5/33 B; 5/15/34 B; //35 E;
    11/26/35 B; 2/11/36 B; 11/10/36 B;
    2/16/37 B; 4/27/37 B; 10/26/39 B;
    1/23/40 B; 4/6/43 B; 2/20/46 B;
    4/24/46 B; 11/12/46 B; 2/11/48 B;
    11/25/48 B; 12/23/48 B; 3/2/50 B;
    4/5/51 B; 2/28/52 B; 9/3/52 B; 6/2/53 B;
    1/6/55 B; 5/19/55 B; 2/15/56 B;
    5/5/56 B; 2/1/58 B; 10/27/58 B;
    1/28/60 B; 2/14/61 B; 12/12/62 B;
    3/12/63 B; 4/2/64 B; 4/25/66 B;
    10/25/68 B; 2/12/76 B
As of a Dream — 5/18/79 C
Aspen Music Festival — 7/19/76 C; 8/2/79 A
Asrael — 2/3/07 C
Assassinio nella cattedrale — 3/1/58 A
Association of Operatic Dancing —
    12/31/20 E; //36 E
Association of Proletarian Musicians —
    1/1/29 E
Association of Swiss Musicians — 11/21/74 D
Astarte — 9/19/67 B
Asterism — 1/14/69 C
As Time Goes By — 10/24/73 B
Astruc, Gabriel — 5/19/09 B

Astutuli — 10/20/53 A
Asya — 9/28/00 A
Atem gibt des Leben — 5/16/75 C
Athaliah — 2/17/64 A
Atherton, David — 4/13/76 C
Atkins, William — 5/13/57 B
Atlanta Symphony Orchestra — //67 E
Atlantis — 1/31/60 C
Atlantov, Vladimir — 2/19/39 D; 6/26/66 E
Atlas Eclipticalis — 8/3/61 C
At Midnight — 12/1/67 B
At Moscow — 11/28/42 A
Atmospheres — 10/22/61 C
Atonement of Pan, The — 8/10/12 A
Atonement, The — 9/9/03 C
Atterberg, Kurt — 10/15/28 C; 2/14/43 C;
    2/9/45 C; 2/26/57 C; 2/15/74 D
At the Boar's Head — 4/3/25 A
At the Reading of the Psalms — 4/14/15 C
Aubade (Francaix) — 9/30/75 C
Aubade (Nijinska) — 6/19/29 B
Aubade (Poulenc) — 1/30/63 D
Auber, Francois — 12/5/33 B
Aubert, Louis — 1/9/68 D
Aubry, Pierre — 8/31/10 D
Auden Variations for Organ — 7/10/78 C
Auden, W.H. — 5/5/41 A; 9/11/51 A;
    10/20/60 C; 5/20/61 A; 4/6/64 C;
    8/6/66 A
Audio Engineering Society (AES) — //47 E;
    //57 E
Audio Fair — 1//49 E
Audio Fidelity — //57 E
Audiosphere — //54 E
Auer, Leopold — 3/4/05 C; 7/15/30 D
"Auferstanden aus Ruinen und der Zukunft
    zugewandt" — 2/8/50 E; 9/6/62 D
Aufstieg und Fall der Stadt Mahagonny —
    7/17/27 A; 3/9/30 A
Augenlicht, Das — 6/17/38 C
Augusteo Orchestra (Rome) — 12/13/36 C
Aug, Wilma — 11/28/26 B
Aulos — 2/21/71 C
Aureole — 8/4/62 B
Auric, Georges — 1/16/20 E; 6/19/21 B;
    1/19/24 B; 6/17/25 B; 3/4/29 B;
    5/21/29 B; 4/12/32 B; 6/14/50 B;
    10/10/56 E; //62 E; 1/9/70 C; 5/18/78 B
Aurora — 11/5/33 A
Auschwitz — 4/14/67 C
Ausgerechnet und verspielt — 6/27/62 A
Austral, Florence — 5/16/22 D; 5/15/68 D
Australian Ballet — 11/2/62 E
Autori, Franco — 11/9/37 D
Autumn — 8/1/11 C
*Autunno, Musica per 5 Suonatori; di Strumenti a Fiato,
    L'* — 2/28/79 C
Aux Etoiles — 2/26/11 C
Available Forms I — 10/11/63 C
"Avalon" — 1/28/21 E
Ave Maria — 12/3/14 B
Avent — 3/2/78 C
Aventures — 3/11/68 C
Aventures du Roi Pausole, Les — 12/12/30 A
Avery Fisher Hall (New York City) —
    5/14/59 E
Avni, Zvi — 7/30/68 E
Ax, Emanuel — 6/8/49 D
Ayer, Ethan — 10/12/61 A
Ayikuli — 12/24/65 A
Ayres, Lemuel — 10/1/52 B
Azora, Daughter of Montezuma — 12/26/17 A
Azzoni, Italo — 10/1/35 D

— B —

Baal Shem — 10/19/41 C
Baaren, Kees van — 9/2/70 D

Babar the Elephant — 2/21/53 A
Baba Yaga — 3/18/04 C; 8/28/14 D
Babbitt, Milton — 5/10/16 D; 5/2/51 C;
    5/8/52 C; 2//58 E; 1/8/59 E; 4//60 E;
    5/9-10/61 E; 7/9/62 E; 3/3/66 C;
    1/16/69 C; 5/13/70 C; 8/22/71 C;
    4/25/74 C; 4/29/75 C; 5/11/78 C;
    2/10/79 C; 12/5/79 C
Babilee, Jean — 2/2/23 D; 12/13/48 B;
    11/9/49 B; //72 E
Babin, Victor — 12/13/08 D; 11/13/42 C;
    6/3/70 C; 3/1/72 D
Baccaloni, Salvatore — 4/14/00 D; 5/16/28 A;
    2/9/29 A; 12/21/40 D; 12/31/69 D
Bacchanale — 11/9/39 B
Bacchelli, Riccardo — 2/8/60 A
Bacchus and Ariane — 5/22/31 B
Bacchus — 5/5/09 A
Bacewicz, Grazyna — 2/5/09 D
Bach Aria Group — 1/27/48 E
Bachauer, Gina — 5/21/13 D; 1/21/46 D;
    10/29/50 D; 8/22/76 D
Bach Festival — 5/1/73 C
Bachianas Brasileiras No. 3 — 2/19/47 C
Bachianas Brasileiras No. 4 — 6/6/42 C
Bachianas Brasileiras No. 7 — 3/13/44 C
Bachianas Brasileiras No. 8 — 8/6/47 C
Bachianas Brasileiras No. 1 — 9/12/32 C
Bachianas Brasileiras No. 5 — 3/25/39 C
Bach, Johann Sebastian — 5/27/56 C;
    7/30/70 B
Bach Reader, The (book) — 10/14/79 D
Bachrich, Ernst — 2/2/19 C
Backhaus, Wilhelm — 1/5/12 D; 6/25/69 E;
    7/5/69 D
"Badenweiler March" — 2/5/36 D
Badings, Henk — 1/17/07 D; 7/6/30 C;
    10/5/33 C; 5/2/35 C; 5/24/37 E;
    6/12/37 E; 12/7/49 C; 1/11/57 C;
    10/7/58 C; 6/19/59 A; 6/15/60 A;
    12/17/60 C
Badische Analin und Soda Fabrik — //33 E;
    //34 E; //35 E; 11/19/36 E
Badura-Skoda, Paul — 10/6/27 D; 1/10/53 D
Bagarre, La — 11/18/27 C
Bagatelles for Orchestra — 11/18/77 C
Bailey, Sally — 3/10/53 B
Baiser de la fee, Le (Ashton) — 11/26/35 B
Baiser de la fee, Le (Balanchine) — 4/27-38/37 B;
    4/10/40 B; 6/21/72 B
Baiser de la fee, Le (Macmillan) — 4/12/60 B
Baiser de la fee, Le (Nijinska) — 11/27/28 B
Bakawali — 3/11/12 B
Bakchantinnen, Die — 6/20/31 A
Baker, Janet — 8/21/33 D; 1/5/75 C;
    6/16/76 C
Baker, Julius — 9/23/15 D
Baker's Biographical Dictionary of Musicians (book)
    — 10/13/34 D
Baker, Theodore — 10/13/34 D
Bakst, Leon — 6/2/09 B; 5/20/10 B; 6/4/10 B;
    6/18/10 B; 4/19/11 B; 4/26/11 B;
    5/14/12 B; 5/29/12 B; 6/8/12 B;
    5/10/13 B; 5/15/13 B; 2/14/18 E;
    11/2/21 B; 12/28/24 D; 7/16/28 B
Balakirev, Mily — 5/16/07 E; 4/23/09 C;
    5/29/10 D; 5/20/12 B
Balanchine, George — 1/22/04 D; 2/2/20 B;
    3/7/23 B; 6/17/25 B; 12/11/25 B;
    7/3/26 B; 12/3/26 B; 4/30/27 B;
    6/12/28 B; 7/16/28 B; 5/7/29 B; //32 E;
    4/12/32 B; 4/21/32 B; 6/7/33 B; 1/2/34 E;
    6/9/34 B; 12/6/34 B; 3/1/35 B;
    4/27-28/37 B; 12/24/38 E; 4/10/40 B;
    1/22/41 B; 5/29/41 B; 5/29/41 B;
    9/10/44 B; 9/23/44 B; 2/27/46 B;
    7/15/46 B; 11/20/46 B; 11/26/46 B;
    1/13/47 B; 7/28/47 B; 9/27/47 B;
    11/12/47 B; //48 E; 3/22/48 B; 4/28/48 B;

11/27/49 B; 12/1/49 B; 2/18/51 B;
2/20/51 B; 11/14/51 B; 11/20/51 B;
2/19/52 B; 11/11/52 B; 11/25/52 B;
1/1/53 E; 1/6/53 B; 1/19/54 B; 2/2/54 B;
9/14/54 B; 2/27/55 B; 3/1/55 B;
11/9/55 B; 3/1/56 B; 12/19/56 B;
6/17/57 C; 11/21/57 B; 12/1/57 B;
1/8/58 B; 1/17/58 B; 5/14/59 B;
3/29/60 B; 11/16/60 B; 11/22/60 B;
3/22/61 B; 12/7/61 B; 1/17/62 B;
6/14/62 B; 3/20/63 B; 4/9/63 B;
12/10/63 B; 1/7/64 B; 2/4/65 B;
5/28/65 B; 4/21/66 B; 7/8/66 E; 4/6/67 B;
4/13/67 B; 11/23/67 B; 1/18/68 B;
4/30/68 B; 5/2/68 B; 11/23/68 B;
6/1/69 B; 2/5/70 B; 6/18-25/72 B;
6/18/72 B; 6/20/72 B; 6/21/72 B;
6/22/72 B; 6/23/72 B; 1/12/73 B;
1/17/74 B; 7/17/74 B; 5/14-31/75 B;
5/22/75 B; 5/29/75 B; 7/30/75 B;
1/22/76 B; 5/12/76 B; 6/4/77 B;
6/23/77 B; 1/12/78 B; 1/19/78 B;
1/26/78 B; 5/18/78 B

Balanchivadze, Andrei — 6/28/38 B
Balanchivadze, Georgi Melitonovich — *see* Balanchine, George
Balanchivadze, Meliton — 1/22/04 D
Balasz, Bela — 5/12/17 B; 5/24/18 A
Baldina, Alexandra — 5/19/09 B
Baldner, Thomas — 4/8/77 A
Balfour Handel Collection (National Library of Scotland) — 3/9/38 E
Ballade (Faure) — 3/14/19 C
Ballade (Robbins) — 2/14/52 B
Ballade for Piano and Orchestra — 4/28/70 C
Ballad for Americans — 6/25/40 C
Ballad of a Boy Who Remained Unknown — 2/21/44 C
Ballad of a Railroad Man — 2/22/41 C
Ballad of Baby Doe, The — 7/7/56 A
Ballad of Magna Carta, The — 2/4/40 C
Ballard, Lucinda — 1/13/40 B
Ballata delle gnomidi — 4/11/20 C
Bal, Le — 5/7/29 B
Ballet Alicia Alonso — //48 E; 10//48 E; 5/21/52 B
Ballet Annual, The — //47 E
Ballet Caravan — 7/17/36 E; 1/6/38 B; 10/16/38 B; 5/24/39 B; 5/29/41 B; 10//41 E; 1//42 E; //48 E
Ballet Club — 2/25/30 B; 2/6/31 B; 10/9/32 B; 5/15/34 B; 10/28/34 B
Ballet de Cuba — //48 E
Ballet de Madrid — //32 E
Ballet des Champs-Elysees, Les — //51 E; 10/17/51 B
Ballet des Etoiles de Paris — 8/21/53 B
Ballet de Wallonie — 12//66 E
Ballet du Hainut — 12//66 E
Ballet du Rhin — //72 E
Ballet Imperial — 5/29/41 B; 1/12/73 B
Ballet Institute — 2/22/61 D
Ballet International — 10/30/44 E; 2/22/61 D
Ballet International de la Marquese de Cuevas — 2/22/61 D; 6/30/62 E
Ballet mecanique — 6/19/26 C; 2/12/59 D
Ballet Nacional de Cuba — //48 E
Ballet National Jeunesses Musicales de France, Le — 6//63 E
Ballet of Blossoms — 4/21/02 B
Ballet of Flanders — 12/2/69 E
Ballet of the 20th Century (Ballet du XXe Siecle) — //60 E; 11/17/66 B; 4/3/67 B; 10/8/71 B; 12/12/75 B
Ballet Rambert — 1/26/36 B; 2/19/37 B; 2/23/37 B; 5/15/39 B; 11/29/44 B; 6/2/47 B; 11/21/68 B
Ballet Review (periodical) — //66 E

Ballet Russe de Monte Carlo — 4/13/33 B; 4/15/33 B; 10/24/33 B; 4/6/34 B; 3/20/35 B; 7/18/35 B; 7/24/36 B; 10/23/37 B; 1/30/38 E; 2//38 E; 3//38 E; 4/5/38 B; 5/5/38 B; 6/17/38 E; 6/19/38 B; 7/21/38 B; 10//38 E; 10/20/38 B; 5/4/39 B; 5/11/39 B; 10/26/39 B; 10/31/39 B; 11/9/39 B; 4/10/40 B; 10/17/40 B; 10/8/41 B; 10/12/42 B; 10/16/42 B; 9/10/44 B; 9/23/44 B; 2/27/46 B; 1//48 E
Ballets 1933, Les — 6/7/33 B
Ballets 1956 de Paris, Les — 8/21/53 B
Ballets Chiriaeff, Les — //55 E; //57 E
Ballet School — 9/17/62 B
Ballets de l'Etoile, Les — 8/21/53 B; 7/26/55 B; /6/57 E
Ballets de Paris, Les — 5/22/48 B; 5/22/48 B; //51 E
Ballets de Paris de Roland Petit, Les — 4/17/59 B
Ballets des Champs-Elysees, Les — 3//45 E; 3/2/45 B; 6/25/46 B; 5/22/48 B; 12/13/48 B; 11/9/49 B; //51 E; 10/17/51 B
Ballets de Theatre de Monte Carlo, Les — //32 E
Ballets Jooss, Les — 7/3/32 B; 11/21/32 B
Ballet Society — 7/15/46 E; 11/20/46 B; 11/26/46 B; 1/13/47 B; 5/13/47 B; 7/28/47 B; 11/12/47 B; //48 E; 3/22/48 B; 4/28/48 B
Ballets Polonais — 11/20/37 B
Ballet Russe (Colonel de Basil's) — //32 E; 1/30/38 E; 2//38 E; 3//38 E; 6/17/38 E; 6/30/39 B
Ballets Russes de Monte Carlo — 7/27/51 D
Ballets Russes (Diaghilev) — 6/4/10 B; 6/18/10 B; 6/25/10 B; 4/26/11 B; 6/6/11 B; 6/13/11 B; 6/21/11 B; 11/30/11 B; 5/14/12 B; 5/20/12 B; 5/29/12 B; 6/8/12 B; 5/15/13 B; 5/29/13 B; 4/16/14 B; 5/14/14 B; 5/21/14 B; 5/26/14 A; 6/2/14 B; 12/20/15 B; 1/17/16 B; 1/20/16 B; 10/23/16 B; 4/12/17 B; 5/11/17 B; 5/18/17 B; 6/5/19 B; 7/22/19 B; 2/2/20 B; 5/15/20 B; 5/17/21 B; 11/2/21 B; 5/18/22 B; 6/3/22 A; 6/13/23 B; 1/6/24 B; 1/19/24 B; 6/15/24 B; 6/20/24 B; 12/28/24 D; 4/28/25 B; 6/17/25 B; 5/4/26 B; 12/3/26 B; 4/30/27 B; 6/7/27 B; 6/6/28 B; 6/12/28 B; 7/16/28 B; 5/7/29 B; 5/21/29 B; 8/4/29 E; //32 E; *see also* names of offshoots e.g. Ballets Russes de Monte Carlo
Ballets Suedois, Les — 12/10/19 B; //20 E; 10/25/20 B; 6/6/21 B; 6/19/21 B; 1/20/22 B; 10/25/23 B; 11/19/24 B; 12/4/24 B; //53 E
Ballets: U.S.A. — //58 E; 6/6/58 E
Ballett 1965 — //65 E
Ballet Theater — 1/11/40 B; 1/13/40 B; 2/11/41 B; 10/27/41 B; 4/8/42 B; 9/8/42 B; 11/29/42 B; 4/6/43 B; 10/20/43 B; 2/25/44 B; 7/14/44 D; 4/18/44 B; 4/10/45 B; 10/4/45 B; 10/24/46 B; 9/27/47 B; 4/14/48 B; 2/25/50 B; 10/1/52 B; //57 E; 5/13/57 B; 5/6/64 B
Ballet-Theatre de Paris — 8/21/53 B; /6/57 E
Ballet Today (periodical) — /3/46 E
Ballet West — //63 E
Ballo della Regina — 1/12/78 B
Ballo in maschera, Un — 1/27/01 D
Bal martiniquais, La — 12/6/45 C
Balmont, Constantin — 5/29/24 C; 4/19/39 C
Balsam, Artur — 2/8/06 D
Balthorpe, Carmen — 5/23/75 A

Baltimore Symphony Orchestra — 2/11/16 E; 2/17/46 C; 11/25/52 C; 3/21/70 C
Balustrade — 1/22/41 B
Bamboula Rhapsodic Dance — 6/12/10 C
Bampton, Rose — 11/28/08 D
Banffy, Count — 5/12/17 B
Banfield, Rafaello de — 2/24/49 B
Banjuta — 5/29/20 A
Bantock, Granville — 1/18/08 C; 5/24/11 C; 1/17/16 C; 10/16/46 D
Bantock Society — 10/16/46 D
Barabau — 12/11/25 B
Barabeichek, Issay — 12/9/53 D
Barati, George — 4/13/13 D
Bar aux Folies-Bergere — 5/15/34 B
Barbares, Les — 10/23/01 A
Barbe-bleue — 10/10/43 A
Barber, Samuel — 3/9/10 D; 8/30/33 C; 3/23/35 C; 12/13/36 C; 1/21/37 C; 11/5/38 C; 2/7/41 C; 4/16/42 C; 10/29/43 C; 3/3/44 C; 10/8/44 C; 10/24/44 C; 7/3/45 E; 4/5/46 C; 5/10/46 B; 2/27/47 B; 4/9/48 C; 5/6/52 E; 1/29/54 B; 12/3/54 C; 11/15/55 B; 2/2/56 C; 1/15/58 A; 5/5/58 E; 6/17/59 A; 9/30/60 C; 9/24/62 C; 4/4/63 C; 5/6/63 E; 9/16/66 A; 9/10/71 C; 9/22/71 C; 4/30/74 C; 9/14/78 C
Barbirolli, John — 3/13/30 C; //36 E; 11/5/36 D; 4/11/40 C; //41 E; 3/29/41 C; 6/30/48 C; 1/14/53 C; 6/13/54 C; 5/2/56 C; 10/3/66 E; 7/29/70 D
Bardac, Emma — 1/20/08 E
Bardin, Micheline — 7/28/47 B
Barenboim, Daniel — 11/15/42 D; 1/20/57 D; 6/15/67 E
Barenreiter Verlag — 6/30/49 E; 10/29/75 D
Bari, Tania — 4/27/57 E
Barn Dance — 4/23/37 B
Barnet, Samuel and Sons, London — 4/30/03 E; 2//29 E
Barnett, Robert — 3/2/50 B; 3/6/56 B; 1/17/58 B
Baronova, Irina — //32 E; 4/12/32 B; 4/13/33 B; 4/15/33 B; 7/18/35 B; 10/23/37 B; 6/30/39 B; 12/6/40 B; 11/29/42 B
Barque sur l'ocean, Une (Ravel) — 2/3/07 C
Barque sur l'ocean, Une (Robbins) — 5/29/75 B
Barraque, Jean — 1/17/28 D; 10/30/56 C; 6/23/66 C; 4/4/68 C; 8/17/73 D
Barra, Ray — 11/7/65 B
Barraud, Henry — 4/23/00 D; 7/20/61 A
Barrault, Jean-Louis — 1/13/54 E
Barrere Little Symphony — 3/20/27 C
Barrerre, Georges — 11/16/19 C
Barrientos, Maria — 3/6/18 A
Bars for Self-Centered Questions — 2/11/71 C
Barstow — Eight Hitchhiker Inscriptions from a Highway Railing at Barstow, California — 4/22/44 C
Bartered Bride, The — 2/19/09 A
Barth, Hans — 7/21/31 E; 12/9/56 D
Bartlett, Ethel — 11/28/41 C
Bartok, Bela — 1/13/04 C; 2/29/04 C; 11/22/09 C; 2/26/13 C; 5/12/17 B; 5/24/18 A; 1/9/22 C; 11/19/23 C; 10/20/24 C; 11/28/26 B; 4/1/27 C; 7/1/27 C; 5/25/34 C; 4/8/35 C; 1/21/37 C; 5/24/37 E; 1/16/38 C; 1/9/39 C; 4/23/39 C; 6/11/40 C; 10/14/42 C; 12/1/44 C; 9/26/45 D; 2/8/46 C; 12/2/49 C; 1/24/50 B; 10/31/50 B; 10/10/56 E; 4/27/57 B; 5/30/58 C; 7/7/64 B
Bartos, Frantisek — 6/13/05 D; 5/21/73 D
Baryshnikov, Mikhail — 1/27/48 D; 6/29/74 E; 6/20/79 E

Barzin, Leon — 11/27/00 D; 10/28/30 E; 5/13/47 B

BASF — *see* Badische Analin und Soda Fabrik

Basil, Colonel de — 1/30/38 E; 3//38 E; 6/17/38 E; 1//48 E; 7/27/51 D

Baskin, Leonard — 12/1/67 B

Bassariden, Die — 8/6/66 A

Bassett, Leslie — 7/5/62 C; 7/6/63 C; 5/2/66 E; 2/27/75 C; 7/4/76 E

Bates, Ronald — 6/18/72 B; 6/18/72 B; 6/22/72 B

Bath Festival — 5/20/79 C

Bathori, Jane — 1/21/70 D

Battistini, Mattia — 11/7/28 D

"Battle Hymn of the Republic, The" — 7/23/62 E

Bauchant, Andre — 6/12/28 B

Baudo, Serge — 7/16/27 D; 5/7/65 C; //67 E; 6/7/69 C

Bauer, Benjamin — //37 E

Bauer, Harold — 12/18/08 C; 10/6/29 E; 4/1/33 E; 3/12/51 D

Bauermeister, Mary — 6/19/60 C

Bavardes, Les — 1/31/25 C

Bavarian Broadcasting Studios — 8/31/72 C

Bax, Arnold — 10/29/20 C; 12/2/22 C; 12/13/29 C; 3/16/32 C; 1/15/34 C; 6/9/39 C; 2/28/52 B; //53 E; 10/3/53 D

Bayadere, La (Makarova) — 7/3/74 B

Bayadere, La (Nureyev) — 11/27/63 B

Bayadere, La (Gorsky) — 1/31/23 B

Baylis, Lilian — //26 E; 1/6/31 E; 5/5/31 B

Baylis, Nadine — 11/21/68 B

Bayou Legend, A — 11/15/74 A

Bayreuth Festival — 7/2/11 D; 1/5/17 D; 7/22/24 E; 7/23/61 E

BBC Northern Symphony Orchestra — 8/3/73 C

BBC Symphony Orchestra — //30 E; 2/1/33 C; 9/27/34 C; 12/3/34 C; 4/10/35 C; 11/6/35 C; 6/17/38 C; 7/12/46 C; 10/24/48 C; 4/11/53 C; 2/5/58 C; 11/2/60 C; 2/8/61 C; 4/1/64 C; 4/25/65 C; 5/2/65 D; 8/23/68 C; 1/22/69 E; 9/7/73 C; 4/2/75 C

Beach of Falesa, The — 3/26/74 A

Beardslee, Bethany — 12/25/27 D; 8/5/51 C; 3/16/52 C; 4/26/75 D

Bear, The — 6/3/67 A

Beatitudes, The — 5/25/62 C

Beaton, Cecil — 2/11/36 B; 10/1/46 B; 3/2/50 B; 2/28/52 B; 1/15/58 A; 3/12/63 B

Beatrice — 10/23/59 A

Beatrix Cenci — 5/19/67 A; 9/10/71 A

Beatty, Talley — 11/28/59 B

Beau Danube, Le — 4/15/33 B

Beaumont, Count Etienne de — 6/15/24 B

Beautiful in Music, The — 8/6/04 D

Beauty and the Beast — 11/24/38 A; 2/14/46 A; 12/20/49 B; 11/19/69 B

Beauty of the Rose Is Passing, The — 12/12/77 C

Beaux Arts Quartet — 2/20/62 C

Beaux Arts Trio — 1/19/73 C

Becher, Johannes R. — 2/8/50 E

Becker, Gustav — 2/25/59 D

Becker, Hugo — 3/7/06 C

Beckett, Samuel — 10/10/68 C

Beck, Eve — 2/24/55 B

Beck, Hans — 6/10/52 D

Bedells, Phyllis — 12/31/20 E

Beecham Opera Company — 3/1/33 D

Beecham, Sir Thomas — 11/15/07 D; 12/3/08 C; 2/22/09 C; 6/7/09 C; 12/8/10 A; 1/1/16 E; 1/12/28 D; 7/16/28 B; 10/12/29 C; 10/7/32 E; 5//33 E; 1/15/34 C; 11/19/36 E; 11/17/41 C; //47 E; 5/4/53 A; 3/8/61 D

Beer, Richard — 2/25/54 B

Beeson, Jack — 11/22/57 A; 3/25/65 A; 9/20/75 A

Before Dawn — 1/15/50 B

Before the Butterfly — 2/26/76 C; 7/4/76 E

Beggar's Opera, The — 5/24/48 A

Behrman, David — 3/7/75 B

Beijer, Agne — 8/19/22 E

Beinum, Eduard van — 9/3/00 D; //56 E; 4/13/59 D

Bejart, Maurice — 1/1/27 D; 10/31/50 B; 6/14/52 B; 8/21/53 B; 7/26/55 B; /6/57 E; 4/27/57 B; //60 E; 10/27/64 B; 11/17/66 B; 4/3/67 B; 3/11/71 B; 10/8/71 B; 12/12/75 B; 1/27/78 B

Belaiev, Mitrofan — 1/10/04 D

Belar, H. — 1/31/56 E; 10/4/58 E

Belasco, David — 7/21/68 D

Belfagor — 4/26/23 A

Bel Geddes, Edith Lutyens — 2/28/68 B

Belgian Center for Music Documentation — //51 E

Belgian State Radio Orchestra — 4/19/39 C

Belgrade Philharmonic — //23 E

Beliamina, Ira — 6/6/28 B

Bella addormentata nel bosco, La — 4/13/22 A

Bell, Alexander Graham — 2/8/36 D

Bellaza, Maurizio — 5/5/78 C

Belle dame sans merci, La — 10/9/24 C

Bellini, Vincenzo — 2/27/46 B

Bell Laboratories — //19 E; //30 E; //57 E; //58 E

Bell, Marion — 10/10/48 C

Bells of Zlonitz, The — 10/4/36 C

Bells, The — 12/13/13 C

Bell Telephone Laboratories — 5//24 E; 5/10/29 E; 4/9/40 E

Bell-Tower, The — 3/17/57 A

Bellugi, Piero — 4/4/61 C

Belmont, Eleanor Robson — 10/24/79 D

Beloved, The — 11/22/28 B

Belshazzar's Feast — 10/10/31 C

Belsky, Igor — 4/14/61 B

Bembe — 6/11/31 C

Benelli, Sem — 4/10/13 A

Benesh, Joan — 3/24/20 D; //62 E

Benesh, Rudolf — 1/16/16 D; //62 E

Benesh System of Dance Notation — //62 E

Benet, Stephen Vincent — 5/18/39 A

Ben-Haim, Paul — 6/5/41 C; 7/29/67 E

Beni Mora — 5/1/12 C

Benjamin, Arthur — 7/10/14 C; 6/30/48 C; 9/5/50 C; 8/15/53 C

Bennett, Richard Rodney — 3/29/36 D; 2/24/65 A; 2/10/66 C; 10/31/67 A; 1/18/68 C; 9/19/68 C; 3/29/69 A; //71 E; 5/18/71 C; 5/15/72 C; 7/3/73 C; 8/20/74 C; 3/25/76 C

Bennett, Robert Russell — 4/30/32 E; 9/26/43 C

Benois, Alexandre — 4/28/07 B; 11/25/07 B; 5/19/08 A; 5/19/09 B; 6/4/10 B; 6/13/11 B; 11/22/28 B; 11/27/28 B; 1/12/29 B; 2/28/40 B; 10/17/40 B

Benois, Nadia — 2/2/39 B; 5/15/39 B

Benoit, Peter — 3/8/01 D

Bentley, Muriel — 2/25/44 B; 4/14/48 B; 4/22/48 B

Berand, Christian — 5/5/38 B

Berard, Christian — 7/24/36 B

Berberian, Cathy — 7/4/25 D; 11/14/72 C

Berceuse — 11/9/47 C

Berezowsky, Nicolai — 5/17/00 D; 4/30/32 E; 3/24/37 C; 10/22/43 C; 2/21/53 A; 8/27/53 D

Berg, Alban — 4/24/11 C; 3/31/13 C; 12/14/25 A; 11/11/26 A; 11/16/26 E; 1/8/27 C; 2//27 E; 3/20/27 C; 1/21/29 C; 4/14/30 C; 6/4/30 C; 11/30/34 C; 12/24/35 D; 1/14/36 E; 4/19/36 C;

6/2/37 A; 5/22/38 E; 1/13/54 E; 10/10/56 E; 10/10/68 C; 4/29/72 D; 11/30/72 D; 8/30/76 D; //77 E; 11/1/79 C

Bergen Philharmonic — //52 E

Berger, Arthur — 5/15/12 D; 4/11/53 C

Berger, Erna — 10/19/00 D

Berg, Gunnar — 1/11/09 D

Berg, Helene — 1/14/36 E; 4/19/36 C; 6/2/37 A; 8/30/76 D; 2/24/79 A; 11/1/79 C

Bergkristall — 5/15/73 C

Bergonzi, Carlo — 7/13/24 D; 11/13/56 D

Bergsma, William — 5/20/50 C; 9/28/62 C; 2/12/75 C; 4/10/78 C

Berini, Mario — 2/21/44 E

Berio, Luciano — 10/24/25 D; 10/28/52 C; //57 E; 6/13/60 C; 10/22/61 C; 10/10/68 C; 5/3/69 C; 8/12/70 A; 3/12/71 C; 4/5/71 C; 9/22/73 C; 10/16/74 C; 10/17/75 C; 3/3/78 C; 5/20/78 C

Beriosova, Svetlana — 9/24/32 D; 2/6/48 B; 3/3/53 B; 1/6/55 B; 5/5/56 B; 1/1/57 B; 4/12/60 B; 12/12/62 B

Berkeley, Lennox — 5/12/03 D; 7/8/43 C; 6/17/54 A; 9/22/54 A; 2/24/59 C; 6/3/67 A; 3/22/71 C; 8/3/73 C; 1/30/76 C

Berkshire Chamber Music Competition — 10/9/24 C

Berkshire Music Festival — 8/4/38 E; 7/8/40 E; 11/4/53 D; 8/10/67 C

Berkshire Music Center — 9/16/18 E

Berliner, Joseph — 5//00 E

Berliner Phonograph — 5//00 E

Berlin Municipal Opera — 3/11/33 E

Berlin Olympiad — 8/16/36 E

Berlin Philharmonic Orchestra — 11/10/03 E; 12/27/07 C; 1/23/08 D; 10/28/15 C; 8/22/20 E; 1/10/21 C; 3/17/21 C; //22 E; 12/2/28 C; 2/27/30 E; 2/9/31 C; 4/15/32 C; 4/17/32 E; 10/31/32 C; 3/27/33 C; 3/12/34 C; 12/4/34 E; 1//35 E; 4/25/35 E; 8/23/45 D; 2/22/48 C; 2/14/49 E; 2/27/55 E; 10/15/63 E; 9/16/72 C; 3/12/78 C

Berlin Radio Exhibition — //63 E

Berlin Radio Symphony Orchestra — 1/31/68 E

Berlin Royal Opera — 10/15/01 D; 3/31/17 E

Berlin State Opera — 1/15/06 C; 5/7/29 E; 12/4/34 E; 11/24/38 A; 3/19/55 E

Berlin State Opera Orchestra — 11/6/30 C

Berlin, University of — 10/12/10 E

Berlioz, Hector — 7/24/36 B; 11/17/66 B; 10/10/68 C

Berman, Eugene — 7/9/35 B; 6/23/72 B

Berman, Lazar — 2/26/30 D

Bernac, Pierre — 1/30/63 D; 10/17/79 D

Bernard, Roger — 10/8/71 B

Bernauerin, Die — 6/15/47 A

Berners, Lord — 12/3/26 B; 10/9/32 B; 4/27/37 B; 11/12/46 B; 4/19/50 D

Bernhard, August — 3/19/05 E

Bernstein, Elsa — 12/28/10 A

Bernstein, Leonard — 8/25/18 D; 4/21/42 C; 12/17/42 C; 8/25/43 C; 11/14/43 D; 1/28/44 C; 4/18/44 B; 3/23/46 C; 10/24/46 B; 1/23/48 C; 10/10/48 C; 4/8/49 C; 12/2/49 C; 2/26/50 B; //51 E; 2/22/51 C; 6/12/52 A; 10/1/53 C; 9/12/54 C; 10/29/56 A; //57 E; //58 E; 4/16/59 C; 8/25/59 C; 1/15/60 C; 3/20/60 C; 10/20/60 C; 10/26/61 C; 9/23/62 C; 10/4/62 C; 1/15/63 D; 5/16/63 C; 10/3/63 C; 11/15/63 D; 12/10/63 C; 5/7/64 C; 3/30/65 B; 7/15/65 C; 4/28/66 C; 7/26/66 E;

4/27/67 C; 9/13/67 C; 1/4/68 C; 1/18/68 C; 10/10/68 C; 1/16/69 C; 6/10/69 E; 1/29/70 C; 2/5/70 C; 9/8/71 C; 9/8/71 E; 5/16/74 B; 4/3/75 C; 4/17/75 C; 10/11/77 C; 12/1/77 C
Beroff, Michel — 2/3/67 E
Bertha — 11/26/73 A
Bertolami, Viviane — 2/29/52 C
Bertrand, Rene — 4/25/28 E
Besch, Otto — 5/22/38 E
Besseler, Heinrich — 4/2/00 D; 7/25/69 D
Bessmertnova, Natalia — 7/19/41 D; 2/16/75 B
Bessy, Claude — 10/20/32 D
Best, Roger — 7/3/73 C
Besuch der alten Dame, Der — 5/23/71 A
Besuner, Pearl — 1/7/33 A
Betrothal in a Convent — 11/3/46 A
Between Categories — 2/26/69 C
Bewitched, The — 3/26/57 B
Bianca — 10/18/18 A
Bible, Francis — 3/31/49 A
Bibliography of the Book of Common Order and Psalm Book of the Church of Scotland, The (National Library of Scotland) — 5/20/29 E
Bibliotheque Nationale — 2/19/15 D; 3/7/42 E; 6/13/54 D
Biches, Les — 1/6/24 B
Bidmead, Charlotte — 6/15/38 B
Bidule en ut — 3/18/50 C
Biedhy, Demian — 10/29/36 A
Bieling, John H. — 3/30/48 D
Bielrfelder Katalog — //53 E
Bielsky, Vladimir — 11/3/00 A; 2/20/07 A; 10/7/09 A
Biely, Victor — 1/18/29 C
Big Ben — 12/20/34 C
Big City — 11/21/32 B
Bigelow, Lucie — //56 E
Biggs, E. Power — 3/29/06 D; 5/14/30 D; 4/22/38 C; 9/20/42 E; 6/7/76 E; 3/10/77 D
Bilby's Doll — 2/29/76 A
Billy Budd (Britten) — 12/1/51 A; 12/4/76 D
Billy Budd (Ghedini) — 9/7/49 A
Billy the Kid (Copland) — 11/9/40 C
Billy the Kid (Loring) — 10/16/38 B
Bindernagel, Gertrud — 10/23/32 E
Bingham, Seth — 6/21/72 D
Bing, Rudolf — 1/9/02 D; 5//34 E; //47 E; 2/2/50 E; 6/1/50 E; 4/3/52 E; 9/27/53 E; 1/1/56 E; 1/15/58 A; 11/6/58 E; 4/22/72 E
Binyon, Lawrence — 11/24/17 C
Biran, Ephraim — 8/23/64 C
Birdcage — 73', 20.958' for a Composer — 10/21/72 C
Birdcage/Momobird — 8/30/72 C
Birkmeyer, Toni — 5/9/24 B
Birmingham (Ala.) Civic Symphony Orchestra — 6/17/74 D
Birmingham (England) Festival — 10/3/00 C; 10/14/03 C
Birmingham Symphony Orchestra, City of — 11/10/20 E; 10/1/57 C
Birmingham Triennial Festival — 9/19/68 C
Birsh, Patricia — 5/8/55 B
Birthday Offering — 5/5/56 B
Birthday of the Infanta, The — 12/23/19 B
Birthday Waltz — 5/11/78 C
Birth of a Nation, The (film) — 2/8/15 E; 3/12/19 A
Birtwistle, Harrison — 6/8/68 A; 8/23/68 C; 2/10/69 C; 2/12/69 C; 5/8/69 A; 6/2/71 C; 6/1/72 C
Birulki — 8/28/14 D
"Bishop's Love Has Eyes" — 10/26/44 E
Bishop, Will — 3/18/01 B
Bispham, David — 10/2/21 D

Bispham Memorial Award — 10/2/21 D
Bissell, Patrick — 4/5/79 B
Bistolfi, Gian — 4/13/22 A
Bittner, Julius — 1/9/39 D
Bizet, Georges — 5/7/03 B; 3/10/06 A; 2/26/35 C; 7/28/47 B; 2/21/49 B; 10/12/51 A
Bjorling, Jussi — 2/2/11 D; 1/4/38 D; 11/24/38 D; 9/9/60 D
Bjornsson, Fredbjorn — 9/10/26 D; 11/22/57 B
Blacher, Boris — 1/19/03 D; 12/20/46 A; 8/6/47 A; 6/28/53 A; 8/17/53 A; 9/21/60 A; 9/17/64 A; 9/15/73 A; 1/30/75 D; 2/14/75 A; 11/4/75 A
Black Knight, The — 10/3/00 C
Blackwood, Easley — 4/21/33 D; 1/5/61 C; 3/7/65 C; 1/24/67 C; 7/28/68 C; 7/26/70 C; 12/22/78 C
Blair, David — 7/27/32 D; 3/13/51 B; 1/1/57 B; 1/28/60 B; 2/9/65 B
Blake, Delysia — 2/6/48 B
Blankshine, Robert — 2/28/68 B
Blasorchester Sofia — 10/9/77 C
Blass, Robert — 12/24/03 E; 2/19/09 A
Blattnerphon — 2//29 E
Blech, Leo — 4/23/37 E; 8/24/58 D
Blest Pair of Sirens — 10/7/18 D
Blind Man's Bluff — 5/29/72 C
Blinova, Valentina — 4/21/32 B
Bliss, Arthur — 4/27/20 C; 8/7/22 E; 9/7/22 C; 10/22/30 C; 6/15/37 B; 9/3/38 C; 6/10/39 C; 10/26/44 B; 9/29/49 A; //53 E; 5/11/55 C
Bliss, Herbert — 4/28/48 B; 12/1/49 B; 12/4/51 B; 6/2/53 B; 1/19/54 B; 9/14/54 B; 2/27/55 B
Bliss, Robert Woods — 5/8/38 C
Blitz, Paul — 6/21/13 E
Blitzstein, Marc — 3/2/05 D; 4/30/32 E; 6/16/37 A; 1/5/41 A; 9/28/43 C; 3/23/46 C; 1/20/49 B; 10/11/49 A; 6/14/52 A; 5/25/53 A; 1/22/64 D; 8/3/74 A
Bloch, Andre — 8/7/60 D
Bloch, Ernest — 6/23/01 C; 1/27/06 C; 11/30/10 A; 3/23/17 C; 5/3/17 C; 11/5/20 C; 11/11/23 C; 6/1/25 C; 12/20/28 C; 2/18/32 C; 1/12/34 C; 1/21/37 C; 2/11/38 C; 5/22/38 E; 12/15/38 C; 10/19/41 C; 10/26/45 C; 9/3/49 C; 12/2/50 C; 1/1/53 C; 4/11/53 C; 2/15/56 C; 4/4/56 C; 4/15/58 C; 7/15/59 D
Block, Frederick — 6/1/45 D
Blockx, Jan — 1/18/00 A; 5/26/12 D
Blok, Alexander — 11/9/47 C
Blomdahl, Karl-Birger — 12/12/52 C; 5/31/59 A; 6/17/60 C; 9/2/65 A; 6/14/68 D
Blom, Eric — 4/11/59 D
Blonda, Max — 2/1/30 A
Blood Moon — 9/18/61 A
Blood of the People — 1/21/42 A
Bloom, Arthur — 1/17/64 C
Bloomington National Symphony — 4/24/77 C
Blossom Music Center — 7/19/68 E
Bloud — 2/28/36 A
Bluebeard — 10/27/41 B
Blue Flame — 12/15/59 A
Blum, Anthony — 1/23/69 B; 5/22/69 B; 1/29/70 B; 6/23/72 B
Blume, Friedrich — 6/30/49 E; 11/22/75 D
Blumenfeld, F.M. — 5/19/08 A
Blumlein, Alan Dower — 9/17/31 E; //33 E
Blum, Rene — //32 E; 1/30/38 E; 2//38 E; 3//38 E; 6/17/38 E; 10//38 E; 7/27/51 D
Bluthner, Julius Ferdinand — 4/13/10 D

Bluthochzeit, Die — 5/25/57 A
BMI — *see* Broadcast Music Inc.
B Minor Suite — 8/7/31 B
Boam, Monica — 11/26/38 B
Boatswain's Mate, The — 1/28/16 A
Bobyshov, Mikhail — 4/4/35 B
Bodanzky, Artur — 11/18/15 D; 3/8/17 A; 5/3/17 C; 11/19/21 C; 1/19/29 A; 4/1/33 E; 11/23/39 D
Bodrero, James — 3/10/53 B
Boeuf sur le toit, Le — 2/21/20 B
Boerman, Jan — 6/19/65 B; 3/2/70 B
Bogatyri (Borodin) — 10/29/36 A; 11/14/36 E
Bogatyri (Massine) — 10/20/38 B
Boheme, La (Puccini) — 1/14/00 A
Boheme, La (Leoncavallo) — 11/10/00 A; 4/14/13 A
Bohemian String Quartet — 12/24/30 D; 5/29/35 D
Bohm, Karl — 6/24/35 A; 10/15/38 A; 6/30/44 E
Bohnen, Michael — 1/19/29 A
Bohnke, Emil — 5/11/28 D
Boite a joujoux, La — 12/10/19 B
Boito, Arrigo — 6/10/18 D; 5/2/24 A
Bolcom, William — 5/2/65 C; 4/27/71 C; 7/21/71 C; 5/21/73 C; 10/23/77 C; 1/12/79 C
Bolender, Todd — 10/16/38 B; 11/20/46 B; 1/13/47 B; 11/12/47 B; 2/26/50 B; 12/4/51 B; 6/2/53 B; 2/18/54 B; 9/14/54 B; 8/3/55 B; 11/15/55 B; 12/1/57 B; 6/6/58 E; 6/18-25/72 B
Bolender, Yvonne — 3/6/56 B
Bolero — 11/22/28 B
Bolet, Jorge — 11/15/14 D
Bolivar — 5/12/50 A
Bolm, Adolph — 5/19/09 B; 5/20/10 B; 6/21/11 B; 5/20/12 B; 6/8/12 B; 6/2/14 B; 1/17/16 B; 3/6/18 A; 4/27/28 B; 1/13/40 B
Bolshoi Ballet — 1/31/23 B; 2/14/54 B; //59 E; 4/16/59 B; 3/4/60 B; 9/17/62 B; 4/9/68 B; 12/25/69 B; 6/11/72 B; 3/5/74 D; 6/29/74 E; 2/16/75 B; 8/1/79 E; 8/22/79 E; 9/16/79 E; 9/27/79 E
Bolshoi Opera — 5/19/08 A; 10/27/64 E; 8/10/67 E; 8/14/67 E
Bolshoi Theater — 7/14/44 D; 10/8/60 A; 9/5/64 E; 2/8/70 E
Bolt — 4/8/31 B
Bomarzo — 11/1/64 C; 5/19/67 A
Bonaventura, Mario di — 3/29/60 C; 7/28/68 C
Bonazzi, Elaine — 12/3/78 C
Bon-Bon Suite — 1/14/09 C
Bonci, Alessandro — 12/3/06 E; 11/22/07 D; 8/8/40 D
Bonhomme Jadis, Le — *see* Onkel Dazumal
Bonne cuisine, La — 10/10/48 C
Bonnefous, Jean-Pierre — 4/25/43 D; 6/18/72 B; 5/24/73 B; 1/10/74 B; 5/4-31/75 B; 6/4/77 B; 5/18/78 B
Bonsdorff, Edith — 12/4/24 B
Book of Beasts — 7/28/79 B
Book of Hours — 2/29/76 C
Boor, The — 5/6/57 A
Borchard, Leo — 8/23/45 D
Bordes, Charles — 3/29/11 D
Boretz, Benjamin — 10/3/34 D; //62 E
Borgese, G.A. — 4/19/64 A
Borgioli, Dino — 9/12/60 D·
Bori, Lucrezia — 10/31/08 D; 11/11/12 D; 1/2/14 A; 1/21/25 D; 2/7/31 A; 3/29/36 E; 5/14/60 D
Boris Godunov — 5/19/08 A; 6/24/13 A; 2/16/28 A; 10/27/64 E; 8/10/67 E
Borisoff, Alexander — 1/21/37 C
Boris, Ruthanne — 6/12/51 B

Borkor, Margit — 7/1/33 A
Borland, John Ernest — 5/15/37 D
Borlin, Jean — 12/10/19 B; //20 E; 10/25/20 B; 6/6/21 B; 6/19/21 B; 1/20/22 B; 10/25/23 B; 11/19/24 B; 12/4/24 B
Born, Claire — 11/9/26 A
Borodin, Alexander — 5/16/07 E; 5/19/09 B; 6/25/10 B; 10/29/36 A; 11/14/36 E; 10/20/38 B
Borowski, Felix — 3/29/14 E
Bortoluzzi, Paolo — 5/17/38 D; 3/11/71 B
Boruta — 3/15/30 A
Boskovsky, Willi — 6/16/09 D
Bosquet, Thierry — 12/12/75 B; 1/27/78 B
Bossi, Enrico — 2/20/25 D
Boston Chamber Orchestra — 1/10/31 C
Boston Music Company — 7/15/07 D
Boston National Opera — 11/29/32 D
Boston Opera House — 11/8/09 E
Boston Pops — 2/3/21 D; 5/7/30 E; 11/29/32 D; 5/28/43 C; 7/4/76 E
Boston Sinfonietta — 5/7/30 E
Boston Symphony Orchestra — 2/3/00 C; 10/15/00 E; 3/1/07 C; 11/22/07 C; 2/7/08 C; 10/24/08 C; 2/12/09 C; 10/27/11 D; 12/18/14 C; 5/14/15 E; 3/23/17 C; 3/14/18 E; 3/25/18 E; 11/15/19 D; 11/28/19 C; 1/30/20 C; 4/21/22 C; 10/10/24 D; 11/20/25 C; 11/19/26 C; 1/21/27 C; 1/28/27 C; 2/25/27 C; 3/18/27 C; 4/15/27 C; 4/22/27 C; 11/18/27 C; 3/23/28 C; 12/14/28 C; 12/13/29 C; 3/28/30 C; 10/24/30 C; 11/7/30 C; 11/14/30 C; 11/28/30 C; 12/19/30 C; 2/13/31 C; 10/16/31 C; 11/13/31 C; 1/29/32 C; 2/19/32 C; 10/21/32 C; 11/25/32 C; 1/26/34 C; 3/6/34 C; 3/16/34 D; 2/28/36 C; 11/30/36 C; 8/12/37 E; 4/8/38 C; 4/22/38 C; 8/4/38 E; 2/24/39 C; 10/6/39 C; 11/3/39 C; 2/7/41 C; 10/17/41 C; 11/14/41 C; 1/13/42 E; 10/15/42 C; 2/26/43 C; 3/26/43 C; 10/8/43 C; 10/22/43 C; 10/29/43 C; 11/12/43 C; 1/13/44 C; 1/15/44 E; 3/3/44 C; 3/14/44 C; 9/3/44 C; 10/13/44 C; 10/20/44 C; 12/1/44 C; 2/21/45 C; 10/4/45 C; 10/12/45 C; 11/2/45 C; 4/5/46 C; 10/1/46 E; 10/18/46 C; 12/20/46 C; 12/27/46 D; 3/7/47 C; 10/24/47 C; 1/9/48 C; 1/23/48 C; 2/27/48 C; 4/9/48 C; 12/31/48 C; 1/7/49 C; 4/8/49 C; 12/2/49 C; 1/6/50 C; 2/10/50 C; 3/3/50 C; 3/10/50 C; 11/3/50 C; 3/9/51 C; 5/6/52 E; 12/3/54 C; 1/7/55 C; 10/7/55 C; 11/25/55 C; 3/2/56 C; 9/6/56 E; 1/25/57 C; 3/8/57 C; 12/6/57 C; 6/15/58 C; 12/5/58 C; 1/9/59 C; 10/21/60 C; 1/20/61 C; 9/24/62 C; 1/25/63 C; 2/20/63 D; 11/22/63 E; 3/13/64 C; 3/5/65 C; 1/6/67 C; 3/15/68 C; 10/22/69 D; //70 E; 8/4/72 C; 9/29/76 C
Boughton, Rutland — 8/26/14 A; 8/26/22 A
Boulanger, Lili — 7/6/13 E; 3/13/18 D; 10/22/79 D
Boulanger, Nadia — 7/6/13 E; 3/13/18 D; 1/26/24 C; 1/11/25 C; 5/8/38 C; 1/13/54 E; 10/22/79 D
Boulevard Solitude — 2/17/52 A
Boulez on Music Today (book) — //71 E
Boulez, Pierre — 3/26/25 D; 5/2/51 C; 7/13/51 D; 10/6/51 C; 5/26/53 C; 1/13/54 E; 6/18/55 C; 3/16/58 C; 10/19/58 C; 6/13/60 C; 10/21/61 C; 10/3/63 C; 1/10/64 C; 10/17/64 C; 3/26/65 C; 5/2/65 D; 10/10/68 C;

1/22/69 E; 6/10/69 E; 8/18/70 D; //71 E; 6/2/71 C; 3/3/72 C; 11/3/74 C; 1/24/75 C; 4/2/75 C; 12/4/75 C; 2/17/77 C; 5//77 E; 5/5/77 C; 2/18/78 C; 5/24/78 C; 2/24/79 A
Boult, Adrian — 1/26/22 C; 1/30/26 C; //30 E; 2/1/33 C; 4/10/35 C; 6/9/39 C; 6/10/39 C; 10/14/42 C; 4/21/48 C; 11/18/50 C; 2/1/54 C; 2/5/58 C; 4/2/58 C
Bouquetieres, Les — 1/31/25 C
Bourgeois, Denise — 7/28/47 B
Bourgeois Gentilhomme, Le (Balanchine) — 9/23/44 B
Bourgeois Gentilhomme, Le (Strauss, R.) — 10/25/12 C
Bourgogne — 12/15/10 C
Bourmeister, Vladimir — 7/15/04 D
Bournemouth Symphony Orchestra — 10/22/69 C
Bournonville, August — 6/10/52 D; 11/24/79 E
Bourree Fantasque — 12/1/49 B
Boutique fantasque, La — 6/5/19 B; 3/20/35 B
Bovy, Samuel — 11/26/06 D
Boyce, William — 7/4/40 B
Boyt, John — 2/27/55 B
Bozzoni, Max — 7/28/47 B
Brabants, Jeanne — 12/2/69 E
Bracale, Adolfe — 8/27/35 D
Brada, Ede — 5/12/17 B
Bradley, Lisa — 9/30/62 B
Bradshaw, Susan — //71 E
Brae, June — 11/10/36 B; 2/16/37 B; 4/27/37 B; 6/15/37 B
Brahms Briefwechsel (book) — 5/13/00 D
Brahms, Johannes — 2/22/03 D; 4/21/66 B; 10/10/68 C
Brahms-Schoenberg Quartet — 4/21/66 B
Brailey, W.T. — 4/15/12 E
Brailowsky, Alexander — 4/25/76 D
Brain, Aubrey — 5/17/21 D; 9/1/57 D
Brain, Dennis — 5/17/21 D; 9/1/57 D
Braithwaite, Warwick — 1/18/71 D
Brandenberg Concerto — 5/9/59 B
Brandenburg Nos. 2 and 4 — 2/10/66 B
Brandmal, Das — 6/2/38 A
Brannigan, Owen — 6/7/45 A; 6/18/58 A
Brant, Henry — 10/15/13 D; 4/30/32 E; 1/11/40 B; 2/22/41 C; 5/12/45 E; 1/30/48 C; 12/6/53 C; 3/3/57 C; 2/10/58 C; 1/31/60 C; 1/14/64 C; 3/15/73 C; 3/23/74 C; 2/11/79 C; 4/26/79 C
Branzell, Karin — 12/14/74 D
Braque, Georges — 1/19/24 B; 4/28/25 B
Brautwahl, Die — 4/13/12 A
Bravo Mozart — 7/3/69 C
Brazilian Academy of Music — 11/17/59 D
Brecht, Bertolt — 8/3/28 A; 7/28/29 C; 3/9/30 A; 6/30/30 A; 12/13/30 A; 6/7/33 B; 4/18/47 A; 3/17/51 A; 3/1/59 C; 4/13/61 A
Bregenz Music Festival — 7/20/79 E
Breil, Joseph Carl — 3/12/19 A
Breinin, Raymond — 4/10/45 B
Breitkopf & Hartel — 9/30/14 E; 9/25/17 E; 12/4/43 E; 10/18/79 D
Brenaa, Hans — 1/15/48 B
Brendel, Alfred — 1/5/31 D
Breslau, Sophie — 3/23/18 A
Breval, Lucienne — 11/20/01 A; 3/4/13 A; 8/15/35 D
Brezhnev, Leonid — 3/15/78 E
Brian, Havergal — 10/8/07 C; 12/3/08 C; 1/3/13 C; 3/16/22 C; 2/1/54 C; 3/22/58 C; 11/3/58 C; 11/5/59 C; 6/24/61 C; 2/26/62 C; 9/21/66 C; 3/13/68 C; 11/28/72 D; 10/4/73 C

Bricoux, R. — 4/15/12 E
Bride of Dionysus, The — 7/10/40 D
Bride of Messina, The — 3/18/04 C
Bridge, Frank — 9/24/12 C; 3/13/16 C; 1/10/41 D
Brieff, Frank — 4/9/68 C
Brigg Fair — 1/18/08 C
Briggs, Hedley — 1/30/34 B
Bright, Dora — 9/7/08 B
Brighton Festival — 1/14/09 C; 5/8/69 A
Bright Stream, The — 4/4/35 B
Britannia's Realm — 6/16/02 B
British Broadcasting Corporation (BBC) Symphony Orchestra — *see* BBC Symphony Orchestra
British Institute of Recorded Sound — 6/2/51 E
British Music Society — 6/14/21 E
British National Opera — 4/3/25 A; 5//27 E
British Sound Recording Association (BSRA) — //32 E; //33 E; 11/19/36 E; //76 E
Britten, Benjamin — 11/22/13 D; 1/31/33 C; 8/18/38 C; 11/26/38 B; 1/30/40 C; 3/29/41 C; 5/5/41 A; 11/28/41 C; 1/16/42 C; 4/24/42 B; 6/14/42 C; 10/15/43 C; 11/29/44 B; 6/7/45 A; 6/13/45 C; //46 E; 7/12/46 A; 11/29/46 E; 6/20/47 A; 5/24/48 A; 6/5/48 C; 6/14/49 A; 7/14/49 C; 3/2/50 B; 12/1/51 A; 6/2/53 B; 6/8/53 A; 8/20/53 B; 9/14/54 A; 12/3/54 A; 10/10/56 E; 1/1/57 B; 9/1/57 D; 6/18/58 A; 10/16/58 C; 7/22/59 C; 6/11/60 A; 7/1/60 C; 3/3/61 D; 5/30/62 C; 9/1/63 C; 3/12/64 C; 6/13/64 C; 10/24/65 C; 6/9/66 A; 6/18/67 C; 6/10/68 C; 5/19/69 C; 5/16/71 A; 6/16/73 A; 9/14/75 C; /6/76 E; 6/16/76 C; 12/4/76 D
Britton, Donald — 1/18/55 B; 6/7/56 B
Broadcast Music, Inc. (BMI) — 10/14/39 E; 5/9/52 E
Brod, Max — 4/27/27 A; 12/20/68 D
Bronwen, Daughter of Llyr — 2/1/29 A
Bronze Horseman, The — 3/14/49 B
Brooke, Maurice — 2/11/36 B
Brooklyn Academy of Music — 3/19/11 E; 12/11/20 E
Brooklyn Navy Yard — 3/5/07 E
Brooklyn Philharmonic — 11/13/73 C; 4/28/78 C
Brothers, The — 7/28/54 A
Brouillards — 3/8/70 B
Brown, Carolyn — 9/26/27 D; 8/17/58 B
Brown, Earle — 12/26/26 D; 2/10/52 C; 5/24/55 B; 10/11/63 C; 4/8/65 C; 3/24/70 C; 9/2/72 C; 12/4/73 C
Browning, John — 9/24/62 C
Brown, Kelly — 10/1/52 B
Brownlee, John — 1/7/00 D; 1/10/69 D
Brown, Rosemary — 6/1/69 E
Bruch, Max — 10/2/20 D
Bruchollerie, Monique de la — 12/15/72 D
Bruck, Henrik — 1/18/29 C
Bruckner, Anton — 2/11/03 C; 3/18/23 C; 10/12/24 C; 9/18/79 E
Bruckner Festival, International — 9/18/79 E
Bruhn, Erik — 10/3/28 D; 2/6/48 B; 2/25/50 B; 2/22/61 D; 11/2/62 E; 2/21/65 B; 7/7/71 B; 9/14/71 D
Bruneau, Alfred — 6/15/34 D
Brunelle, Phillip — 4/14/78 A
Bruni, Tatiana — 4/8/31 B; 12/9/42 B
Brunswick (corporation) — 3/25/25 E; //26 E; //30 E
Brunswick, Mark — 1/6/02 B; 5/26/71 D
Bryans, Rudy — 1/10/73 B
Bryn-Julson, Phyllis — 11/20/77 C
Buch der Langenden Garten — 7/13/51 D

Buch mit sieben Siegeln — 6/15/38 C
Buchner, Georg — 12/14/25 A
Buck, Dudley — 10/6/09 D
Bucolic Suite — 3/10/02 C
Budapest Opera — 3/15/48 A; 2/20/63 D
Budapest Philharmonic — 3/7/06 C
Budapest Quartet — 4/18/38 E
Buffalo Philharmonic — 2/10/61 C; 1/26/75 C
Buffalo Philharmonic Orchestra — 11/5/36 E;
    11/9/37 D; 11/9/45 E; //54 E; 10/29/63 E;
    11/17/63 C; 10/30/66 C 10/16/71 D;
    10/7/79 D
Bugaku — 3/20/63 B
Buijsero, D. — 7/7/20 A
Bulgakov, Alexis — 5/19/09 B; 5/21/14 B;
    6/14/27 B
Bull, Ole — 9/4/07 D
Bulow, Hans von — 9/8/49 D
Bumbry, Grace — 1/4/37 D; 7/23/61 E
Bunge, Dr. Carl — 1/10/36 D
Burdocks — 8/31/72 C
Burge, David — 2/8/73 C
Burgin, Richard — 12/20/34 C; 2/28/36 C;
    9/3/44 C; 11/2/45 C; 10/24/47 C
Burg, Robert — 11/9/26 A
Burgschaft, Die — 3/10/32 A
Burgstaller, Ludwig — 12/24/03 E
Burkhard, Willy — 4/17/00 D; 6/18/55 D
Burning Fiery Furnace, The — 6/9/66 A
Burra, Edward — 2/2/50 B
Burrian, Karl — 12/9/05 A; 1/22/07 A
Busch, Adolf — //19 E; 3/6/39 E; 7/8/51 E;
    9/14/51 D; 6/9/52 D; 6/3/75 D
Busch, Fritz — //22 E; 11/4/24 A; 5/21/25 A;
    11/9/26 A; 3/10/27 D; 11/25/27 D;
    6/6/28 A; 3/8/33 E; 5//34 E; 9/14/51 D;
    6/3/75 D
Busch, Hermann — 7/8/51 E; 9/14/51 D;
    6/3/75 D
Busch Quartet — //19 E; 6/9/52 D
Busch-Serkin Trio — 7/8/51 E; 6/9/52 D
Bush, Alan — 12/22/00 D; 7/24/42 C;
    6/27/49 C; 11/6/49 C; 11/18/56 A;
    12/11/66 A
Bush, Nancy — 11/18/56 A
Busoni, Ferruccio — 11/10/04 C; 10/21/05 C;
    4/13/12 A; 1/17/16 C; 5/11/17 A;
    1/17/22 E; 8/6/23 C; 7/27/24 D;
    5/21/25 A; 12/1/64 A
Busser, Henri — 6/21/49 A; 12/30/73 D
Bussotti, Sylvano — 6/19/60 C; 9/5/65 A;
    9/7/72 A; 5/15/73 C; 3/28/74 C
Bustini, Alessandro — 6/23/70 D
Butler, John — 9/29/20 D; 11/19/59 B;
    6/26/64 B; 11/23/66 B; 11/9/67 B;
    1/29/68 B; 10/3/68 B
Butler, O'Brien — 12/7/03 A; 5/7/15 D
Butt, Dame Clara — 4/27/31 D; 1/23/36 D
Buzzati, Dino — 10/30/59 A
Byelsky, V. — 10/23/37 B
Byely, Victor — 4/1/25 E
Byng, George — 1/12/03 B; 5/7/03 B;
    2/27/05 B

— C —

Cabrillo Festival — 2/8/66 C
Cabrillo Festival Orchestra — 8/26/78 C
Caccialanza, Gisella — 5/29/41 B; 11/20/46 B;
    11/26/46 B
Cadman, Charles Wakefield — 3/23/18 A;
    12/8/26 A; 12/30/46 D
Cadmus, Paul — 1/6/38 B
Cage, John — 9/5/12 D; 12/9/39 C; 3/1/42 C;
    8/1/42 B; 4/5/44 B; 3/24/46 E; 5/13/47 B;
    12/14/47 B; 8/20/48 B; 5/2/51 C;
    5/2/52 C; 8/29/52 C; 10/17/54 C;
    12/8/54 B; 5/15/58 C; 5/21/58 B;

8/14/58 B; 2/25/60 C; 4/24/61 C;
    8/3/61 C; 7/17/63 B; 7/3/64 B;
    7/23/65 B; 11/24/65 B; 9/21/71 B;
    6/13/72 C; 8/30/72 C; 10/21/72 C;
    1/21/73 C; 3/7/75 B; 7/4/76 E;
    9/29/76 C; 11/21/77 C; 4/28/78 C;
    5/11/78 C; 8/14/79 E
Cage, The — 6/14/51 B
Cagliostro — 11/5/52 A
Cahill, Dr. Thaddeus — 4/12/34 D
Cain, Henri — 1/22/36 A
Cairo Opera House — 10/28/71 E
Cakewalk — 6/12/51 B
Calcium Light Night (Martins) — 1/19/78 B
Calcium Light Night (Ives) — 1/29/27 C;
    5/19/54 D
Calder, Alexander — 3/9/65 C; 4/8/65 C
Calder Piece — 4/8/65 C
Caldwell, Candace — 11/28/59 B
Caldwell, Sarah — 3/6/24 D; 1/13/76 E
Callas, Maria — 12/3/23 D; 8/3/47 D;
    10/29/56 D; 9/3/57 D; 1/2/58 E;
    11/6/58 E; 9/16/77 D
Calve, Emma — 3/2/04 E; 1/6/42 D
Calzare d'argento, Il — 3/23/61 A
Camargo Society — 10/19/30 E; 4/26/31 B;
    7/5/31 B
Cambridge University — 11/22/00 E;
    4/11/02 E; 6/12/07 E
Camden Festival — 5/29/69 A
Cameron, Basil — //30 E; //31 E; //32 E;
    3/16/32 C; 8/15/53 C; 6/26/75 D
Camille — 12/10/30 A; 10/1/46 B
Campanari, Giuseppe — 5/31/27 D
Campanari, Leandro — 4/22/39 D
Campana sommersa, La — 11/18/27 A
Campanini, Cleofonte — 11/26/02 A;
    2/17/04 A; 5/28/04 A; 11/25/07 D;
    11/27/08 A; 12/19/19 D
Campiello, Il — 2/12/36 A
Canadian League of Composers — 2/3/51 E
Canadian National Arts Center — 6/2/69 E
Canciones populares espanolas — 3/3/78 C
Cancunik — 2/15/30 C
Candide — 10/29/56 A
Canfield — 4/15/69 B
Caniglia, Maria — 5/5/06 D
Cannon, Thomas — 4/23/37 B
Canon — 9/20/62 C
Canossa — 1/24/14 A
Cantata academica — 7/1/60 C
Cantata from Proverbs — 5/13/52 C
Cantata Misericordium — 9/1/63 C
Cantata para America magica — 4/30/61 C
Cantata Profana — 5/25/34 C
Cantata (Prokofiev) — 4/5/66 C
Cantata (Stravinsky) — 11/11/52 C
Cantate de Noel, Une — 12/12/53 C
Cantate sylvestre — 2/26/74 C
Cantelli, Guido — 4/27/20 D; 1/15/49 D;
    11/24/56 D
Canterbury Pilgrims, The (De Koven) — 3/8/17 A
Canterbury Pilgrims, The (Dyson) — 3/19/31 C
Canticle for Innocent Comedians — 4/22/52 B
Canticle of the Evening Bells — 2/19/76 C
Canticle of the Sun — 10/28/25 C
Cantico de los marranos — 11/20/77 C
Canticum sacrum ad honorem Sancti Marci nominis —
    9/13/56 C; 9/23/58 C; 4/6/71 D
Canti di Prigionia — 4/10/40 C; 12/11/41 C
Cantilena e scherzo — 3/15/77 C
Cantilena Players — 1/18/76 C
Cantique — 11/7/30 C
Canto sospeso, Il — 10/24/56 C
Canudo, Riciotto — 1/20/22 B
Canyons aux etoiles, Des — 11/20/74 C
Canzoni for Prisoners — 2/6/63 C
Capdevielle, Pierre — 2/1/06 D; 7/9/69 D
Capehart turnover record changer — 9/17/31 E

Capitan Spavento, Il — 3/16/63 A
Capitol (corporation) — 6/21/48 E
Caplet, Andre — 12/10/19 B; 4/22/25 D
Capobianco, Tito — 6/3/79 A
Capricci di Callot, I — 10/24/42 A
Capriccio espagnol — 5/4/39 B
Capriccio (Janacek) — 3/2/28 C
Capriccio (Lieberman) — 3/1/59 C
Capriccio (Strauss, R.) — 10/28/42 A
Capriccio (Stravinsky) — 12/6/29 C; 4/6/71 D
Caprice andalou — 11/13/04 C
Caprichos — 1/24/50 B
Caprichos, Los — 4/6/67 C
Capricorn Concerto — 10/8/44 C
Capriole Suite — 2/25/30 B
Captain Jinks of the Horse Marines — 9/20/75 A
Captain's Daughter, The — 2/27/11 A
Capuana, Franco — 12/10/69 D
Caracole — 2/19/52 B; 12/19/56 B
Caractacus — 10/3/00 C
Caramoor Festival — //56 E; 6/26/64 B;
    8/2/75 A
Cardew, Cornelius — 3/11/68 C; 8/24/72 C
Cardiff Festival — 9/27/07 C; 3/1/62 C
Cardillac — 11/9/26 A; 6/20/52 A
Cardin, Pierre — 6/11/72 B
Cardus, Ana — 11/7/65 B; 3/26/66 B
Cardus, Sir Neville — 2/28/75 D
Carillon — 12/7/14 C
Carinthian Summer Music Festival —
    6/25/69 E
Carl Fischer, Inc. — //41 E
Carli, Didi — 11/30/66 B
Carlo Gesualdo, Prince of Venosa, Musician and Mur-
    derer (book) — 12/17/30 D
Carlo Lesignano, Duke — 7/28/03 D
Carlo, Omar del — 3/17/52 A
Carlson, Caroline — 12/17/67 B
Carmen (Petit) — 2/21/49 B
Carmen (Cormani) — 5/7/03 B
Carmina Burana (Butler) — 11/19/59 B
Carmina Burana (Orff) — 6/8/37 C; 2/13/53 C
Carnaval d'Aix, Le (Milhaud) — 12/9/26 C
Carnaval (Fokine) — 3/5/10 B; 5/20/10 B;
    6/4/10 B; 1/17/16 B; 8/22/42 D
Carnegie, Andrew — //02 E
Carnegie Hall (New York) — 9/9/57 E;
    11/6/64 E; 6/7/76 E
Carnegie Hall Corporation — 9/9/57 E;
    7/1/60 E
Carnival of the Animals — 2/26/22 C
Carolsfeld, Malwine Schnorr von — 2/8/04 D
Caron, Rose — 4/9/30 D
Carosio, Margherita — 1/16/35 A
Carpenter, John Alden — 3/19/15 C;
    3/10/16 C; 12/23/19 B; 11/23/20 C;
    2/19/26 B; 10/21/32 C; 11/30/33 C;
    10/24/40 C; 10/22/42 C; 4/26/51 D
Carre — 10/28/60 C
Carre, Albert — 4/30/02 A; 12/12/38 D
Carreno, Teresa — 1/23/08 D; 6/12/17 D;
    3/3/32 D
Carrie Nation — 4/28/66 A
Carrillo, Julian — 2/15/25 C; 11/30/51 C;
    9/9/65 D
Carter, Bill — 11/22/60 B
Carter, Elliott — 12/11/08 D; 5/24/39 B;
    4/27/44 C; 4/21/56 C; 5/2/60 E;
    9/6/61 C; 1/6/67 C; 2/5/70 C; 1/23/73 C;
    5/7/73 E; 1/13/75 C; 3/21/75 C;
    2/24/76 C; 7/4/76 E; 2/17/77 C;
    2/10/78 C
Carter, Jimmy — 10/11/77 C
Cartieri, Rosanna — 3/17/52 A
Caruso, Enrico — 4/11/02 E; 11/26/02 A;
    11/23/03 D; 2/1/04 E; 10/4/05 E;
    4/17/06 E; 4/18/06 E; 11/16/06 E;
    11/28/06 E; 12/3/06 E; 12/5/06 E;
    11/16/08 D; 12/7/08 D; 2/6/09 E;

4/9/09 E; 1/13/10 E; 12/10/10 A; 11/13/11 D; 12/4/16 D; 11/15/18 D; 9/16/20 E; 12/11/20 E; 12/24/20 E; 8/2/21 D; 6/30/61 D; 3/11/67 D; 11/28/72 D; //75 E
Carvalho, Eleazar — //63 E; 1/24/68 E
Casadesus, Francois Louis — 6/27/54 D
Casadesus, Gaby — 1/20/72 D
Casadesus, Jean — 7/27/27 D; 1/20/72 D
Casadesus, Robert — 9/19/72 D; 11/8/72 C
Casado, Germinal — 11/17/66 B
Casals, Pablo — //05 E; 3/13/30 C; 4/27/31 D; 11/22/34 C; 10/14/51 C; 9/1/53 D; 12/17/60 C; 6/24/73 E; 10/22/73 D
Casari, Gaetano — 10/21/34 C
Casella, Alfredo — 4/23/10 C; 3/29/14 C; 11/19/24 B; 1/22/27 C; 5/7/30 E; 3/17/32 A; 9/6/32 A; 10/30/34 E; 5/6/37 A; 3/27/41 C; 3/5/47 D
Casona, Alejandro — 7/24/64 A
Cassandre, A.M. — 12/15/47 B
Cassa, Pietro — 1/16/35 A
Castaway — 6/3/67 A
Castelli, Victor — 5/29/75 B
Castelnuovo-Tedesco, Mario — 10/28/39 C; 11/18/45 C; 5/25/61 A; 12/4/62 C; 3/16/68 D
Castle Agrazant — 9/3/26 D
Castrato — 4/21/22 D
Castro, Juan Jose — 3/17/52 A; 9/3/68 D
Catalogue d'oiseaux — 4/15/59 C
Catelinet, Philip — 6/13/54 C
Catiline Conspiracy, The — 3/16/74 A
Caton, Edward — 1/13/40 B
Catulli Carmina (Orff) — 6/8/37 C; 11/6/43 C; 2/13/53 C
Catulli Carmina (Butler) — 6/26/64 B
Caturla, Alejandro — 6/11/31 C; 11/12/40 D
Cauldron of Annwyn, The — 2/1/29 A
Cavalieri di Ekebu, I — 3/7/25 A
Cavalieri, Lina — 12/5/06 D; 2/8/44 D
Cavalleria Rusticana (Mascagni) — 1/17/01 A; 8/9/19 D
Caveno, Odali — 7/29/70 D
Cave of the Heart — 5/10/46 B; 2/27/47 B
CBS — 12//38 E
CBS Symphony Orchestra — 5/16/48 C; 5/15/49 C
CeBeDem — see Belgian Center for Music Documentation
Cebotari, Maria — 6/24/35 A; 8/6/47 A
Ceccato, Aldo — 1/29/76 C; 4/1/76 C
Cecchetti, Enrico — 6/4/10 B; 6/13/11 B; 5/21/14 B; 4/12/17 B; 6/5/19 B; 5/15/20 B; 11/13/28 D; 11/5/51 D
Cecchetti Society — 11/26/38 B
Cecilia Society, The — 3/14/00 C; 8/4/38 E
Cede Blue Lake — 12/3/65 B
Celestial Country, The — 4/18/02 C
Cello Concerto (Barber) — 4/5/46 C
Cello Concerto (Hindemith) — 3/8/63 C
Cello Concerto in E Major (Khachaturian) — 10/30/46 C
Cello Concerto (Krenek) — 3/4/54 C
Cello Concerto (Ligeti) — 4/19/67 C
Cello Concerto (Lutoslawski) — 10/14/70 C
Cello Concerto (Thomson) — 3/4/50 C
Cello Concerto (Tovey) — 11/22/34 C
Cello Concerto (Walton) — 1/25/57 C
Cello Sonata (Webern) — 6/3/70 C
Cello Symphony (Britten) — 3/12/64 C
Cendrars, Blaise — 10/25/23 B
Cendrees — 9/22/74 C
Cene delle beffe, La — 12/20/24 A
Cenerentola, La — 2/22/00 A
Centering — 12/4/73 C
Central Archive of Swiss Music — 6/9/57 D
Central Park in the Dark — 1/29/27 C
Century Opera Company — 11/13/33 D

Ceremony — 1/29/68 B
Ceremony II (Incantations) — 3/25/75 C
Ceremony of Carols, A — 6/14/42 C
Cerha, Friedrich — 12/24/35 D; 1/13/69 C; 3/16/72 C; 2/18/73 C; 2/24/79 A
Cerito, Fanny — 5/6/09 D
Cernovich, Nicolas — 8/17/58 B
Ceylan — 11/22/73 C
Chabelska, Maria — 5/18/17 B
Chabrier, Emmanuel — 1/9/13 A; 4/21/32 B; 5/15/34 B; 12/1/49 B; 1/30/63 D; 4/6/67 B; 6/27/69 B; 10/21/70 B
Chabukiani, Vakhtang — 3/12/10 D; 11/7/32 B; 6/28/38 B; 3/22/39 B; 11/29/57 B
Chaconne — 1/22/76 B
Chaconne (Goehr) — 11/3/74 C
Chadwick, George W. — 2/3/00 C; 9/26/01 A; 9/29/05 C; 2/7/08 C; 6/12/10 C; 6/4/12 C; 7/20/21 E; 4/4/31 D
Chagall, Marc — 7/24/33 E; 9/8/42 B; 9/16/66 E
Chailley, Jacques — 3/24/10 D
Chailly, Luciano — 5/22/57 A; 10/30/59 A; 2/14/70 A
Chaliapin, Feodor — 12/4/02 D; 10/27/03 A; 2/2/05 E; 5/16/07 E; 11/20/07 D; 1/6/08 D; 5/19/08 A; 2/19/10 A; 6/24/13 A; 11/7/17 E; 12/9/21 E; 8/24/27 E; 4/12/38 D
Chaliapin, Lydia — 12/15/75 D
Chamber Concert for Flute and 10 Players — 8/9/64 C
Chamber Concerto for Cello and 10 Players — 2/17/64 C
Chamber Music Society of Lincoln Center — 9/11/69 E; 2/18/73 C; 1/18/74 C; 4/30/74 C; 10/20/74 C; 1/30/76 C; 3/28/76 C; 10/23/77 C; 10/29/78 C; 11/2/79 C
Chamber Orchestra of Basel — 1/21/37 C; 5/12/38 C; 2/9/40 C; 3/1/40 C; 6/11/40 C; 1/23/42 C; 5/23/42 C; 5/17/46 C; 1/21/47 C; 1/24/52 C; 12/12/53 C; 1/24/58 C; 2/23/62 C
Chamber Orchestra of Boston — //27 E
Chamber Orchestra of Los Angeles — 12/1/53 C
Chamber Symphony, No. 2 — 12/15/40 C
Chaminade, Cecile — 4/13/44 D
Chaney, Stewart — 4/27-28/37 B
Changing Steps/Loops — 3/7/75 B
Chanler, Theodore — 5/9/55 A; 7/27/61 D
Channie, Tatiana — 12/11/25 B
Chanson Madecasses — 5/29/75 C
Chansons de Bilitis — 2/7/01 C
Chant apres chant — 6/23/66 C; 8/17/73 D
Chant de joie — 5/3/23 C
Chant de la cloche, Le — 12/21/12 A
Chant de liberation — 10/22/44 C; 11/27/55 D
Chant de Nigamon, Le — 1/3/20 C
Chant du rossignol, Le (Balanchine) — 6/17/25 B
Chant du rossignol, Le (Massine) — 2/2/20 B
Chant du rossignol, Le (Stravinsky) — 12/6/19 C
Chants de terre et de ciel — 10/23/50 D
Chapeau de paille d'Italie, Le — 11/30/30 C
Chapelle Musicale Reine Elisabeth — //39 E
Chaplin, Charlie — 9/6/62 D
Chappell & Company — 4/27/33 D
Chappell, Thomas Stanley — 4/27/33 D
Chappell, William — 2/25/30 B; 4/3/34 B; 10/28/34 B
Charbonnier, Pierre — 6/6/28 B
Charles Cros Recording Award — 6/21/48 E
Charleston, Elsa — 11/1/77 C
Charles Weidman Dance Theater Company — 7/11/47 B
Charlip, Remy — 12/8/54 B; 5/24/55 B; 8/17/58 B
Charlton, Loudon — 4/27/31 D

Charpentier, Gustave — 2/2/00 A; 6/4/13 A; 2/18/56 D
Charpentier, Jacques — 3/2/69 C; 8/4/70 C; 11/24/73 C; 4/19/74 C; 4/28/74 C; 7/6/74 C
Charrat, Janine — 7/24/24 D; 3/2/45 B; 2/24/49 B
Char, Rene — 6/18/55 C
Chartreuse de Parme, La — 3/16/39 A
Chase, Lucia — 2/11/41 B; 10/27/41 B; 4/8/42 B; 2/25/44 B
Chasins, Abram — 8/17/03 D; 3/3/33 C
Chateau de la Grande Breteche, Le — 3/28/13 A
Chatfield, Philip — 3/3/53 B
Chatte, Le — 4/30/27 B
Chausson, Ernest — 11/30/03 A; 1/26/36 B
Chauvire, Yvette — 4/22/17 D; 6/19/43 B; 5/5/46 B; 12/15/47 B
Chavez, Carlos — //28 E; 11/4/28 B; 6/11/31 C; 4/30/32 E; 12/15/33 C; 11/23/34 C; 1/23/36 C; 8/27/37 C; 5/16/40 C; 1/1/42 C; 6/26/42 C; 1/23/46 B; 10/31/47 C; 2/29/52 C; 2/11/53 C; 12/1/53 C; 12/11/54 C; 5/9/57 A; 10/28/59 A; 5/7/64 C; 9/18/64 C; 5/7/65 E; 8/2/78 D
Cheap Imitation — 1/21/73 C
Checkmate — 6/15/37 B
Chelsea Symphony Orchestra — 11/23/48 C
Cheltenham Festival — 7/6/51 C; 6/9/53 C; 7/9/68 C
Chemin de la croix, Le — 2/13/31 C; 5/30/71 D
Chemins IV — 10/17/75 C
Chereau, Patrice — 2/24/79 A
Cherubin — 2/14/05 A
Cherubini, Luigi — 6/29/72 D
Chervinsky, Nikolai — 12/12/70 B
Chesnakov, V. — 10/26/30 B
Chevillard, Camille — 12/9/00 C; 10/27/01 C; 10/15/05 C; 12/12/20 C
Chiaroscuro — 7/4/76 E; 3/14/77 C
Chicago Civic Opera — 12/8/26 A; 11/4/29 E; 12/10/30 A
Chicago Lyric Opera Company — 11/6/55 E; 11/25/61 A
Chicago Opera Ballet — 11/6/55 E; 3/10/62 D
Chicago Opera Company — 11/28/13 D; 1/12/16 D; 11/18/16 D; 11/17/17 E; 1/14/19 A; 12/19/19 D; 1/2/20 A; 12/30/21 A
Chicago Symphony Orchestra — 1/4/05 D; 3/19/15 C; 3/10/16 C; 3/5/20 C; 10/29/20 C; 12/16/21 C; 4/7/22 C; 2/18/32 C; 11/30/33 C; 10/10/40 C; 10/17/40 C; 10/24/40 C; 11/7/40 C; 2/6/41 C; 3/6/41 C; 3/27/41 C; 4/3/41 C; 10/22/46 C; 2/7/47 E; 1/13/48 E; 1/19/49 E; 2/2/50 C; 3/20/52 C; 11/20/52 C; 1/1/53 C; 1/24/66 C; 10/1/67 C; 11/2/67 C; 3/28/68 C; 12/17/68 E; 10/6/77 C; 12/22/78 C
Chichester Psalms — 7/15/65 C
Chihara, Paul — 3/25/75 C; 12/12/77 C; 4/17/74 C
Child, Harold — 7/14/24 A
Childhood Miracle, A — 5/10/55 A
Child of Our Time, A — 3/19/44 C
Children's Corner, The — 12/18/08 C
Children's Crusade — 5/19/69 C
Chilingirian String Quartet — 5/6/74 C
Chinese Songs — 3/22/71 C
Chinesische Flote, Die — 6/24/23 C
Chiriaeff, Ludmilla — //55 E
Chirico, Giorgio di — 11/19/24 B; 5/7/29 B; 5/22/31 B
Chisholm, Erik — 6/8/65 D
Choephores, Les — 11/27/27 A; 3/27/35 A
Chojnacka, Elizabeth — 5/20/78 C
Chong, Lee San — 6/29/75 B

Chopin Concerto — 11/20/37 B
Chopin Festival — 10/25/70 E
Chopin, Frederic — 2/12/76 B
Chopiniana — 2/23/07 B; 3/21/08 B — *see also Sylphides, Les*
Choralis Constantinus — 6/20/06 E
Choral Symphony — 10/7/25 C
Choral-Variationen uber das Weihnachtslied — 5/27/56 C
Choral Variations — 6/25/72 B
Choral varie — 5/17/04 C
Chor des Norddeutschen Rundfunks — 5/16/75 C
Chord organ — 7/1/73 D
Choreartium — 10/24/33 B
Choreographie — //26 E
Choreology — //62 E
Choro — 4/20/58 C
Choros Nos. 6 — 7/15/42 C
Choros No. 8 — 10/24/27 C
Choros No. 9 — 7/15/42 C
Choros No. 10 — 12/15/26 C
Choros No. 11 — 7/15/42 C
Choros No. 12 — 2/21/45 C
Chota Roustaveli — 5/5/46 B
Chotzinoff, Samuel — 2/9/64 D
Choudens, Paul — 1/15/10 A
Chout, Le — 5/17/21 B
Chou Wen-chung — 2/6/69 C
Chris and the Wonderful Lamp — 1/1/00 A
Christ-Elflein, Das — 12/11/17 A
Christensen, Lew — 5/9/09 D; 1/6/38 B; 10/16/38 B; 4/24/42 B; 11/20/46 B; 1/13/47 B; 3/10/53 B
Christensen, William — //63 E
Christie, Audrey — //47 E
Christie, John — 5//34 E; 7/4/62 D
Christmas Carol, A — 12/23/54 A
Christmas Music — 12/4/77 C
Christmas Tree, The — 8/4/20 D
Christoff, Boris — 5/18/14 D
Christophe Colomb (Honegger) — 4/17/40 C
Christophe Colomb (Milhaud) — 5/5/30 A
Christopher Sly — 5/31/63 A
Christou, Jani — 1/8/26 D; 1/8/70 D
Chronicle — 4/12/57 C
Chroniques de ma vie — //35 E
Chronochromie — 10/16/60 C
Chrysis — 11/30/12 B
Chthonic Ode — 4/6/67 C
Chujoy, Anatole — //42 E
Chung, Kyung-Wha — 3/26/48 D
Ciccolini, Aldo — 8/15/25 D; 11/2/50 D
Ciesinski, Katherine — 1/29/78 C; 11/1/79 C
Cigale, La — 2/4/04 B
Cilea, Francesco — 11/26/02 A; 11/20/50 D
Cimara, Pietro — 1/13/58 E
Cimarosa, Domenico — 6/29/72 D
Cincinnati College of Music — 1/4/05 D
Cincinnati Musical Festival Association — 5/18/63 C
Cincinnati Opera — 6/27/20 E; 9/3/26 D
Cincinnati Symphony Orchestra — 12/8/17 E; 3/19/37 C; 10/17/41 C; 11/28/41 C; 5/14/42 C; 11/27/42 C; 12/11/42 C; 1/15/43 C; 1/22/43 C; 3/12/43 C; 4/6/45 C; 1/30/48 C; 6/26/50 E; 11/4/55 C; 3/9/62 C; 1/16/75 D; 12/5/75 C
Cincinnati Zoo — 6/27/20 E
Cinderella (Ashton) — 12/23/48 B
Cinderella (Farren) — 1/6/06 B; 8/6/06 B
Cinderella (Fokine) — 6/19/38 B; 11/16/40 B
Cinderella (Zakharov) — 11/21/45 B
Cinerama — 10//52 E
Cininnati Symphony Orchestra — 4/1/27 C
Circe (Egk) — 12/18/48 A
Circe (Graham) — 9/6/63 B
Circus Polka — 1/13/44 C

Cisneros, Eleanora de — 2/3/34 D
Citkowitz, Israel — 5/4/74 D
City Center Joffrey Ballet — 9/13/66 B; 9/19/67 B; 2/20/68 B; 2/28/68 B; 10/24/73 B
City Songs — 3/17/78 C
Civinini, Guelfo — 12/10/10 A
Claflin, Avery — 1/10/79 D
Clair de lune — 3/25/18 D
Clair, Rene — 12/4/24 B
Claretie, Jules — 4/1/12 A
Clarinet Concerto (Corigliano) — 12/6/77 C
Clarinet Concerto (Hindemith) — 12/11/50 C
Clarinet Concerto (Nielsen) — 9/14/28 C
Clarinet Concerto (Sutermeister) — 8/12/75 C
Clarion Concerts Orchestra — 4/21/76 C
Clark, Alfred Corning — 2/16/57 D
Clarke, Cuthbert — 1/14/06 B
Clarke, F. — 4/15/12 E
Clark, Jr., William Andrews — 10/24/19 E
Classical Style: Haydn, Mozart, Beethoven, The (book) — //71 E
Classical Symphony (Prokofiev) — 4/21/18 C; 12/5/38 B
Claudel, Paul — 5/5/30 A; 5/12/38 C; 3/1/40 C
Claudia Legare — 4/14/78 A
Clauss, Heinz — 3/8/70 B
Clave, Antoni — 2/21/49 B; 10/17/51 B
Clavilux — 1/10/22 E
Cleather, Gordon — 9/7/08 B
Clemens, Clara — 10/6/09 E
Clemens, Roman — 6/2/37 A
Cleopatra (Chadwick) — 9/29/05 C
Cleopatra's Night — 1/31/20 A
Cleopatre (Fokine) — *see Nuit d'Egypte, Une*
Cleopatre (Massenet) — 2/23/14 A
Cleva, Fausto — 8/6/71 D
Cleveland Federal Orchestra — 2/20/39 C
Cleveland Institute of Music — //20 E
Cleveland Orchestra — 12/11/18 E; 2/5/31 E; 1/21/37 C; 12/15/38 C; 12/7/39 C; 12/26/40 C; 1/22/42 C; 10/28/43 C; 10/4/45 C; 2/27/47 C; 1/23/58 C; 1/30/58 C; 2/26/59 C; 1/5/61 C; 4/20/61 C; 1/23/64 C; 7/19/68 E; 12/6/73 C; 10/13/76 C; 3/14/77 C
Cleveland Quartet — 1/26/75 C
Cliburn, Van — 7/12/34 D; //58 E; 4/13/58 E; 5/19/58 D; 5/20/58 E; 1/30/76 E
Clifford, John — 6/12/47 D; 1/23/69 B; 5/22/69 B; 12/4/69 B; 6/18-25/72 B; 1/17/74 B
Cliquet-Pleyel, Henri — 6/14/23 E
Clitennestra — 3/1/65 A
Clocks and Clouds — 10/15/73 C
Cloven Kingdom — 6/9/76 B
Clowns, The — 2/28/68 B
Clytemnestra — 4/1/58 B
Coates, Albert — 11/15/20 C; 8/16/32 C; 12/25/34 C; 11/20/36 A; 12/11/53 D
Coates, Eric — 12/21/57 D
Cobbett, Walter Wilson — 10/30/32 E; 1/22/37 D
Cobras, The — 3/26/06 B
Cockaigne Overture — 6/20/01 C
Coco-Cheri — 2/28/13 A
Cocteau, Jean — 5/19/09 B; 5/14/12 B; 5/18/17 B; 2/21/20 B; 6/19/21 B; 6/20/24 B; 5/30/27 C; 12/16/27 A; 12/28/27 A; 6/25/46 B; 6/14/50 B; 2/12/59 D; 10/11/63 D
Coerne, Louis Adolphe — 4/30/05 E; 12/1/05 A; 9/11/22 D
Cogan, Robert — 6/10/79 E
Cohan, Robert — 8/13/48 B; 4/22/52 B
Cohen, Fritz — 7/3/32 B
Cohen, Harriet — 2/1/33 C
Cohen, S.J. — //58 E

Colautti, Arturo — 11/26/02 A
Cole, Jack — 7/15/75 D
Coleridge-Taylor Festival — 11/16/04 E
Coleridge-Taylor, Samuel — 3/14/00 C; 3/22/00 C; 5/5/03 C; 9/9/03 C; 11/16/04 E; 1/14/09 C; 2/3/10 C; 6/12/10 C; 9/1/12 D
Colgrass, Michael — 4/22/32 D; 3/21/62 C; 10/17/69 C; 1/29/76 C; 2/17/76 C; 12/3/76 C; 10/20/77 C; 4/17/78 E; 10/22/78 C
Collage (Cunningham) — 6/14/52 B
Collages (Gerhard) — 2/8/61 C
Collage (Lees) — 5/8/74 C
Collegiate Chorale — 5/15/44 C; 5/14/46 C
Collegium Musicum — 1/25/46 C
Collet, Henri — 1/16/20 E; 11/23/51 D
Collier, Marie — 5/29/62 A; 12/7/71 D
Collins, Georgia — 11/28/59 B
Colloquium Musicale — 5/3/74 C
Colombe de Bouddha, La — 3/21/21 A
Colombia (corporation) — 3/25/25 E
Colone, A — 11/19/77 C
Colonial Pageant — 10/8/78 D
Colonial Varianti — 5/27/76 C
Colonne Concerts — 3/28/10 D
Colonne, Edouard — 3/15/08 C; 3/28/10 D
Colosseum (Rome) — 10/7/51 E
Colour Symphony — 9/7/22 C
Colquhoun, Robert — 12/12/51 B
Colt, Alvin — 10/4/45 B
Columbia (corporation) — 10//01 E; 4/30/03 E; 8//04 E; 7//06 E; //08 E; //12 E; 11/12/22 E; //23 E; 5//24 E; //26 E; 5//27 E; 5//27 E; //28 E; 12/2/28 C; //30 E; 9/17/31 E; 12//38 E; 11/13/40 E; 6/21/48 E; 1//49 E; 6/2/51 E; //70 E; 5/29/77 D
Columbia Broadcasting Symphony Orchestra — 1/23/36 C; 2/19/47 C
Columbia-Princeton Electronic Music Center — 4/12/34 D; 1/8/59 E; 5/9-10/61 E; 3/2/69 C
Columbia Record Club — //55 E
Columbia String Quartet — 8/1/79 C; 11/1/79 C
"Columbia, the Gem of the Ocean" — 2/22/51 C; 4/26/65 C
Columbia University — 1/8/59 E
Columbia University Opera Workshop — 5/17/56 A
Columbus — 10/8/39 A
Combat, Le — 2/24/49 B
Comedians — 4/5/31 B
Comedy on the Bridge — 5/28/51 A
Comes Autumn Time — 1/17/17 C
Commando March — 10/29/43 C
Communist Manifesto (book) — 8/18/42 D
Comoedia de Christi resurrectione — 3/31/56 C
Compassion — 3/31/29 B
Complete Opera Book — 7/27/18 D
Composers' Forum-Laboratory — 10/30/35 E
Composers' Society of Rumania — //21 E
Composers' String Quartet — 4/17/73 C
Composition for Four Instruments — 5/2/51 C
Composition for Orchestra — 9/22/73 C
Composition for Synthesizer — 5/9-10/61 E; 7/9/62 E
Composition for voice and six instruments — 4//60 E
Comus — 1/14/42 B
Con amore — 3/10/53 B
Concertante Variationen uber ein Thema von Beethoven — 2/2/24 C
Concert de bruit — 10/5/48 C
Concerted Piece — 3/20/60 C
Concert for Piano and Orchestra — 5/15/58 C; 5/4/59 E
Concertgebouw Orchestra — 4/23/18 C; 11/2/22 C; 12/15/29 C; 7/6/30 C;

10/11/34 C; 11/14/35 C; 3/17/38 C; 4/23/39 C; 11/23/39 C; 3/14/40 C; 6/15/48 E; 12/7/49 C; 6/16/51 C; //56 E; 6/4/72 D

Concertino (Carpenter) — 3/10/16 C

Concertino for Cello and Orchestra (Prokofiev) — 3/18/60 C

Concertino for Flute, Harp, Celesta and Strings (Luening) — 1/30/35 C

Concertino for Piano and Orchestra (Honegger) — 5/23/25 C

Concertino for Piano and Orchestra (Persichetti) — 10/23/45 C

Concertino (Francaix) — 12/15/34 C

Concertino (Janacek) — 2/12/26 C

Concertmasters — 1/29/76 C

Concerto (MacMillan) — 11/30/66 B

Concerto Accademico in D Minor — 11/6/25 C

Concerto-Ballata — 10/14/33 C

Concerto Barocco — 5/29/41 B

Concerto Champetre — 5/3/29 C; 1/30/63 D

Concerto da camera — 1/23/42 C

Concerto dell'estate — 2/28/29 C

Concerto des ambiguites — 3/18/50 C

Concerto d'Orphee — 7/26/53 C

Concerto for 4 Winds, Harp and Orchestra — 5/15/49 C

Concerto for Cello — 3/27/63 C

Concerto for Cello and Orchestra (Dohnanyi) — 3/7/06 C

Concerto for Cello and Orchestra in E Minor (Prokofiev) — 11/26/38 C

Concerto for Cello and Orchestra in G Minor (Kabalevsky) — 3/15/49 C

Concerto for Cello and Orchestra (Khrennikov) — 5/13/64 C

Concerto for Cello and Orchestra (Prokofiev) — 2/18/52 C

Concerto for Cello and Orchestra (Shostakovich) — 10/4/59 C

Concerto for Clarinet and String Orchestra (Copland) — 11/6/50 C

Concerto for Double Bass and Orchestra (Elgar) — 2/25/05 C

Concerto for Double Bass and Orchestra (Henze) — 11/2/67 C

Concerto for Double Bass and Orchestra (Schuller) — 6/27/68 C

Concerto for Electrified Violin — 8/4/72 C

Concerto for English Horn and String Orchestra (Persichetti) — 11/17/77 C

Concerto for Flute and Orchestra (Halffter) — 5/30/70 C

Concerto for Flute and Orchestra (Nielsen) — 10/21/26 C

Concerto for Flute and String Orchestra — 7/28/68 C

Concerto for Flute, Oboe and Orchestra — 9/16/72 C

Concerto for Flute, Strings, Harp, Celesta and Percussion — 9/18/54 C

Concerto for French Horn and Orchestra — 6/8/50 C

Concerto for Harmonica and Orchestra (Benjamin) — 8/15/53 C

Concerto for Harmonica and Orchestra (Tcherepnin, A.) — 9/11/56 C

Concerto for Harmonica and Orchestra (Villa-Lobos) — 6/5/61 C

Concerto for Harp and Orchestra (Dello Joio) — 10/20/47 C

Concerto for Harp and Orchestra (Villa-Lobos) — 1/14/55 C

Concerto for Harp and Wind Instruments (Salzedo) — 4/17/27 C

Concerto for Harpsichord, Flute, Oboe, Clarinet, Violin and Cello — 11/5/26 C

Concerto for Horn and Orchestra (Gliere) — 1/26/52 C

Concerto for Horn and Orchestra (Schuller) — 4/6/45 C

Concerto for Jazz Band and Symphony Orchestra — 10/17/54 C

Concerto for Koto and Chamber Orchestra (Cowell) — 12/18/64 C

Concerto for Marimba, Vibraphone and Orchestra (Milhaud) — 2/12/49 C

Concerto for Oboe and Chamber Orchestra (Strauss, R.) — 2/26/46 C

Concerto for Oboe and Orchestra — 11/9/75 C

Concerto for Oboe, No. 3 — 7/6/73 C

Concerto for Ondes Martenot and Orchestra (Jolivet) — 4/23/48 C

Concerto for Orchestra (Gerhard) — 4/25/65 C

Concerto for Orchestra (Hovhaness) — 2/20/54 C

Concerto for Orchestra (Lees) — 11/19/72 C

Concerto for Orchestra (Mathias) — 3/29/66 C

Concerto for Orchestra (Tippett) — 8/28/63 C

Concerto for Orchestra and Quintet — 3/14/75 C

Concerto for Orchestra (Bartok) — 12/1/44 C

Concerto for Orchestra (Carter) — 2/5/70 C

Concerto for Orchestra (Kodaly) — 2/6/41 C

Concerto for Orchestra (Lutoslawski) — 11/26/54 C

Concerto for Orchestra (Piston) — 3/6/34 C

Concerto for Orchestra and Quintet — 3/14/75 C

Concerto for Organ and Orchestra (Dupre) — 4/27/38 C

Concerto for Organ and Orchestra (Halffter) — 2/3/73 C

Concerto for Organ and Orchestra (Hindemith) — 4/25/63 C

Concerto for Organ and Orchestra (Sowerby) — 4/22/38 C

Concerto for Organ, String Orchestra and Kettledrums — 1/30/63 D

Concerto for Organ, Tympani and Strings — 6/10/41 C

Concerto for Percussion and Chamber Orchestra — 12/5/30 C

Concerto for Piano and Chamber Orchestra (Piston) — 6/20/37 C

Concerto for Piano and Orchestra (Barber) — 9/24/62 C

Concerto for Piano and Orchestra (Carter) — 1/6/67 C

Concerto for Piano and Orchestra (Diamond) — 4/28/66 C

Concerto for Piano and Orchestra (Hindemith) — 2/27/47 C

Concerto for Piano and Orchestra (La Montaime) — 5/4/59 E

Concerto for Piano and Orchestra in F Minor (Reger) — 12/15/10 C

Concerto for Piano and Orchestra (Khachaturian) — 7/5/37 C

Concerto for Piano and Orchestra (Rozsa) — 4/6/67 C

Concerto for Piano and Orchestra (Scriabin) — 11/24/00 C; 4/27/15 D

Concerto for Piano and Small Orchestra (Schuman) — 1/13/43 C

Concerto for Piano and Wind Octet (McPhee) — 3/11/29 C

Concerto for Piano and Wind Orchestra (Stravinsky) — 4/6/71 D

Concerto for Piano and Winds (Stravinsky) — 5/22/24 C

Concerto for Piano, Flute, Violoncello and String Orchestra (d'Indy) — 4/2/27 C

Concerto for Saxophone in E-flat Major (Glazunov) — 11/25/34 C

Concerto for Soprano and Orchestra (Gliere) — 5/12/43 C

Concerto for String Orchestra — 10/4/61 B

Concerto for the Thereminovox and Orchestra — 2/26/45 C

Concerto for Tuba and Orchestra (Vaughan Williams) — 6/13/54 C

Concerto for Two Guitars and Orchestra (Castelnuovo-Tedesco) — 12/4/62 C

Concerto for Two Pianos and Orchestra (Creston) — 11/18/68 C

Concerto for Two Pianos and Orchestra (Milhaud) — 11/13/42 C

Concerto for Two Pianos and Orchestra (Piston) — 7/4/64 C

Concerto for Two Pianos and Orchestra (Porter) — 3/17/54 C; 5/3/54 E

Concerto for Two Pianos, Percussion and Orchestra (Bartok) — 10/14/42 C

Concerto for Two Pianos (Stravinsky) — 11/21/35 C

Concerto for Viola and Orchestra (Druckman) — 11/2/78 C

Concerto for Viola and Orchestra (Porter) — 5/16/48 C

Concerto for Viola, Strings and Percussion — 7/3/59 C

Concerto for Violin — 1/10/78 C

Concerto for Violin and Orchestra (Elgar) — 11/10/10 C

Concerto for Violin and Orchestra (Francaix) — 1/26/70 C

Concerto for Violin and Orchestra (Hindemith) — 3/14/40 C

Concerto for Violin and Orchestra (Kabalevsky) — 3/15/49 C

Concerto for Violin, Cello and Orchestra (Sessions) — 11/5/71 C

Concerto for Violino Grande and Orchestra — 8/4/68 C

Concerto for Violoncello and Orchestra (Foss) — 3/5/67 C

Concerto for Violoncello and Orchestra (Halffter) — 5/19/62 C; 6/24/75 C

Concerto for Violoncello and Orchestra (Hindemith) — 2/7/41 C

Concerto for Violoncello and Orchestra (Penderecki) — 9/2/72 C

Concerto for Violoncello and Orchestra in C Major — 5/19/62 C

Concerto for Violoncello and Orchestra in E Major (Elgar) — 10/27/19 C

Concerto fur Klavier und Blasorchester mit Schlagzeug (Henze) — 5/16/68 C

Concerto gregoriano (Respighi) — 2/5/22 C

Concerto Grosso (Bloch) — 6/1/25 C

Concerto Grosso (Martinu) — 11/14/41 C

Concerto Grosso No. 2 (Bloch) — 4/11/53 C

Concerto Grosso (Vaughan Williams) — 11/18/50 C

Concerto Grosso (Villa-Lobos) — 7/5/59 C

Concerto (Hindemith) — 7/25/25 C

Concerto in A Minor for Oboe and String Orchestra (Vaughan Williams) — 9/30/44 C

Concerto in A Minor for Violin and Orchestra (Glazunov) — 3/4/05 C

Concerto in A Minor for Violin and Orchestra (Shostakovich) — 10/29/55 C

Concerto in A Minor (Grieg) — 9/4/07 D

Concerto in D for guitar and orchestra (Castelnuovo-Tedesco) — 10/28/39 C

Concerto in D for String Orchestra (Stravinsky) — 1/21/47 C; 6/14/51 C

Concerto in D for Violin and Orchestra (Antheil) — 2/9/47 C

Concerto in D for Violin and Orchestra (Stravinsky) — 10/23/31 C

Concerto in D Major for Violoncello and Orchestra (Hayden) — 5/15/57 E

Concerto in D Major for Piano Left Hand and Orchestra (Ravel) — 1/5/32 C

Concerto in E-flat Major (Stravinsky) — 5/8/38 C

Concerto in F Minor (Gershwin) — 12/3/25 C

Concerto in G — 5/14-31/75 B

Concerto in G Major for Piano and Orchestra (Ravel) — 1/14/32 C

Concerto in modo misolidio (Respighi) — 12/31/25 C

Concerto No. 2 for French Horn and Orchestra (Strauss, R.) — 8/11/43 C

Concerto No. 2 for Guitar and Orchestra — 8/4/70 C

Concerto No. 2 for Orchestra (Petrassi) — 1/24/52 C

Concerto No. 2 for Violoncello and Orchestra (Milhaud) — 11/28/46 C

Concerto No. 2 in C Minor (Rachmaninoff) — 12/15/00 C; 11/9/01 C

Concerto No. 2 in D Minor for Cello and Orchestra (Saint-Saens) — 2/5/05 C

Concerto No. 2 in E Major for Piano and Orchestra (Shostakovich) — 5/10/57 C

Concerto No. 3 for Piano and Orchestra (Martinu) — 11/20/49 C

Concerto No. 3 in D Minor (Rachmaninoff) — 11/28/09 C

Concerto No. 4 for Piano and Orchestra in B-flat Major (Prokofiev) — 9/5/56 C

Concerto No. 5 for Alto Saxophone — 7/6/74 C

Concert Opera Association — 2/17/64 A

Concerto-Rhapsody (Khachaturian) — 11/3/62 C

Concerto symphonique (Bloch) — 9/3/49 C

Concert Overture (Szymanowski) — 2/6/06 C

Concerto (Webern) — 9/4/35 C

Concerts Colonne — 4/17/10 E

Concerts du Petit-Marigny, Les — 1/13/54 E

Concerts Koussevitzky — 4/22/21 E

Concerts Lamoureux — 12/9/00 C; 2/3/01 C; 1/8/05 E; 10/10/79 E

Concert, The — 3/6/56 B; 6/8/58 B

Concert Varieties — 6/1/45 B

Conchita — 10/14/11 A

Concierto argentino — 7/18/41 C

Concierto de Aranjuez — 11/9/40 C

Concierto del sur — 10/4/41 C

Concord Quartets, The — 1/20/79 C

Concord Sonata — 1/20/39 C; 5/19/54 D

Concord String Quartet — 1/24/73 C; 5/7/73 C; 5/21/73 C; 3/15/76 C; 2/16/78 C; 1/20/79 C

Concours de Piano "Olivier Messiaen" — 2/3/67 E

Concours Ysaye — 5/22/38 E

Concurrence, La (Auric) — 4/12/32 B

Cone, Edward T. — 5/4/17 D; 1/11/77 C

Confalonieri, Giulio — 6/29/72 D

Congress for Cultural Freedom — 4/6/78 D

Congress at Composers and Musicologists, International — 5/29/48 E

Congress of Dodecaphonic Music — 5/17/49 E

Connecticut String Orchestra — 1/16/77 C

Connotations for Orchestra — 9/23/62 C

Conquest of the Air — 9/3/38 C

Conrad, Karen — 1/13/40 B

Conreid Opera Company — 4/18/06 E

Conried, Heinrich — 11/16/06 E; 4/27/09 D

Conservatoire, Paris — 10/1/20 E

Conservatorio Nacional de Musica — //28 E

Consolidated Talking Machine Company — 5//00 E

Consort, The — 10/24/70 B

Constantinescu, Paul — 7/13/09 D; 10/26/35 A; 6/27/56 A; 12/20/63 D; 12/28/63 C

Constantino, Florencio — 11/8/09 E

Constantin Palaeologus — 8/12/62 A

Constant linear-speed disc — 11/12/22 E

Constant, Marius — 2/7/25 D; 4/17/59 B; 2/23/67 B; 5/31/73 C

Consul, The — 3/1/50 A; 5/1/50 E

Contemplation of the Tenth Muse — 11/1/77 C

Contemplations — 4/21/76 C

Contemporary Chamber Ensemble — 2/19/76 C; 3/21/76 C

Contemporary Chamber Players — 2/23/72 C

Contrafactum for Orchestra — 11/19/69 C

Contrasts (Bartok) — 1/9/39 C; 1/24/50 B

Contrasts (Schuller) — 10/22/61 C; 11/29/70 C

Converse, Frederick S. — 1/31/06 C; 3/18/10 A; 3/3/11 A; 1/26/12 C; 1/30/20 C; 7/20/21 E; 4/21/22 C; 12/18/23 C; 4/15/27 C; 11/7/40 C

Convertible Counterpoint in the Strict Style (Taneyev) — 6/19/15 D

Cook, Bart — 6/18/72 B; 5/24/73 B

Cooke, Deryck — 10/12/24 C; 12/19/60 C; 10/26/76 D

Coolidge Auditorium (Washington, D.C.) — 10/28/25 E

Coolidge, Elizabeth Sprague — 9/16/18 E; 4/8/35 C; 9/22/38 C; 11/4/53 D

Coolidge, Elizabeth Sprague, Foundation — 10/28/25 C; 4/27/28 B; 10/30/32 E

Coolidge, Elizabeth Sprague, Medal — 10/30/34 E;

Coolidge Quartet — 10/30/41 C

Cooper, Emil — 3/23/12 C

Coopersmith, Jacob Maurice — 11/20/03 D

Copland, Aaron — 11/14/00 D; 1/11/25 C; 11/20/25 C; 1/28/27 C; 1/4/31 C; 2/19/32 C; 4/30/32 E; 11/23/34 C; 4/21/37 A; 7/25/37 C; 8/27/37 C; 12/19/37 E; 10/16/38 B; 12/16/38 C; 2/26/39 C; 11/9/40 C; 1/28/41 C; 10/21/41 C; 1/7/42 C; 5/14/42 C; 10/16/42 B; 12/17/42 C; 3/11/43 B; 3/12/43 C; 5/28/43 C; 10/17/44 C; 10/30/44 B; 5/7/45 E; 10/4/45 C; 2/17/46 C; 10/18/46 C; 2/27/47 C; 5/2/47 C; 12/21/47 B; 10/29/50 C; 11/6/50 C; 12/4/51 B; 4/1/54 A; 10/25/57 C; 3/5/58 C; 3/2/61 C; 9/23/62 C; 12/3/63 C; 5/26/64 C; 9/13/67 C; 6/7/72 C; 6/2/73 C; 6/2/74 B; 11/12/75 E

Coppelia (Balanchine) — 7/17/74 B

Coppelia (Cranko) — 6/10/62 B

Coppelia (Genee) — 5/14/06 B

Coppelia (Saint-Leon) — 2/28/10 B

Coppi, Carlo — 4/21/02 B; 6/16/02 B

Coppola, Piero — 3/13/71 D

Copyright law — 7/1/09 E; 3/20/11 E; 1/22/17 E; //73 E

Coq d'or, Le (Bolm) — 3/6/18 A

Coq d'or, Le (Fokine) — 5/21/14 B; 10/23/37 B

Coq d'or, Le (Rimsky-Korsakov) — 10/7/09 A

Cordero, Roque — 8/16/17 D; 5/16/66 C; 1/27/76 C; 2/2/76 C; 4/24/77 C; 5/5/77 C; 10/20/77 C

Cordon, Norman — 2/20/42 A

Cordovano, Il — 5/12/49 A

Corigliano Jr., John — 2/16/38 D; 12/19/61 C; 6/1/66 C; 4/5/68 C; 11/9/75 C; 4/24/76 C; 1/16/77 C; 12/6/77 C

Corigliano, Sr., John — 8/21/01 D; 9/1/75 D

Cormani, Lucia — 1/12/03 B; 5/7/03 B; 2/27/05 B

Cornelia Faroli — 8/15/72 A

Coronation March — 6/22/11 C

Correck, Joseph — 11/4/24 A

Corregidor, Der — 2/22/03 D

Corroboree — 3/24/70 C

Corsaro, Frank — 5/23/75 A

Corte, Andrea Della — 3/12/68 D

Cortege Burlesque — 6/27/69 B

Cortege funebre, Le — 8/4/40 C

Cortege of Eagles — 2/21/67 B

Cortege parisien — 10/21/70 B

Cortot, Alfred — 5/17/02 E; //05 E; 3/14/19 C; 5/14/19 C; 3/25/25 E; 9/1/53 D; 6/15/62 D

Cortot-Thibaud-Casals Trio — //05 E

Cosmopolitan Young People's Symphony Orchestra — 3/3/73 C

Cosmos — 11/10/45 C; 7/14/60 C

Cossacks of Zaporozh, The — 12/23/25 C

Cossotto, Fiorenza — 1/26/57 A

Cotillion — 4/21/32 B

Cough Music — 1/31/61 A

Couleurs de la cite celeste — 10/17/64 C

Counterpoint: Strict and Free (book) — 12/5/09 D

Cours complet theorique de dictee musicale (book) — 5/28/16 D

Cours de composition musicale (book) — 12/2/31 D

Coutre, Jean Papineau — 9/21/63 E

Covenant, The — 4/14/78 C

Covent Garden — 5/30/01 A; 5/2/04 D; 10/5/07 D; 4/26/09 A; 12/8/10 A; 6/21/11 B; 11/30/11 B; 5/14/23 A; 6/8/26 E; 6/25/29 A; 3/1/33 D; 7/18/35 B; 6/17/38 E; 9/29/49 A; 4/26/51 A; 12/1/51 A; 6/8/53 A; 12/3/54 A; 1/27/55 A; 10/27/58 B; 2/17/59 D; 2/21/62 E; 3/12/63 B; 4/2/64 B; //65 E; 2/9/65 B; 10/25/68 B; 12/23/68 E; 3/2/70 B; 5/11/71 D; 2/12/76 B; 7/12/76 A; 2/14/78 B; 10/1/79 A

Coventry Cathedral Festival — 5/25/62 C

Cowan Collection (National Library of Scotland) — 5/20/29 E

Cowell, Henry — 3/12/12 E; 12/16/23 B; 10/15/27 E; 12/28/30 C; 2/4/31 B; 6/6/31 C; 1/5/32 B; 3/6/33 C; //41 E; 5/11/41 C; 10/24/47 C; 1/5/49 C; 5/9/52 E; 5/30/52 C; 11/25/52 C; 3/1/53 C; 5/29/54 C; 3/3/59 C; 12/11/59 C; 3/28/60 C; 4/27/61 C; 10/7/61 C; 3/21/63 C; 12/18/64 C; 10/18/65 C; 12/10/65 D

Cox, Ainslee — 12/4/77 C

Coy, Judith — 2/24/55 B

Cracow Philharmonic Orchestra — 2/3/45 E; 4/24/61 C

Cradle Will Rock, The — 6/16/37 A

Craft of Musical Composition, The (book) — 12/28/63 D

Craft, Robert — 10/19/53 C; 2/8/54 C; 9/20/54 C; 2/21/55 C; 6/17/57 C; 8/23/64 C; 10/8/66 C; 6/1/75 C

Cragun, Richard — 10/5/44 D; 11/7/65 B; 3/26/66 B; 5/16/69 B; 3/8/70 B; 12/22/73 B

Cramer, Heinz von — 8/17/53 A; 9/23/56 A

Cranko, John — 8/15/27 D; 7/18/49 B; 12/20/49 B; 3/13/51 B; 3/3/53 B; 2/25/54 B; 1/1/57 B; 7/26/58 B; //61 E; 6/10/62 B; 7/15/62 B; 12//62 B; 11/14/63 B; 1/22/65 B; 4/13/65 B; 11/7/65 B; 2/10/66 B; 3/26/66 B; 5/16/69 B; 3/8/70 B; 3/24/70 B; 6/26/73 D

Crawford, John — 1/9/69 B

Crawford, Storie — 1/9/69 B

Craxton, Janet — 8/3/73 C

Creation du monde, La (Borlin) — 10/25/23 B

Creation of the World — 3/23/71 B

Creation-Prologue — 5/9-10/61 E

Creation, The (Gruenberg) — 11/27/26 C

Credendum — 11/4/55 C

Credo in Us — 8/1/42 B

Creep into the Vagina of a Living Whale — 6/5/65 C

Creoles — 1/31/25 C

Crepuscule — 10/20/74 C

Crepusculum — 8/9/19 D

Crespin, Regine — 2/23/27 D; 11/19/62 D
Creston, Paul — 10/10/06 D; 3/6/33 C;
    2/20/39 C; 2/22/41 C; 11/27/42 C;
    2/15/45 C; 10/27/50 C; 1/30/52 C;
    4/4/56 C; 11/17/60 C; 2/19/65 B;
    4/6/67 C; 11/18/68 C; 6/30/79 C
Crimi, Giulio — 12/14/18 A
Critic, or an Open Rehearsal, The — 1/14/16 A
Croce, Arlene — //66 E
Croix sonore — 6/13/54 D
Crooks, Richard — 6/26/00 D; 11/27/30 D;
    9/29/72 D
Cross Currents — 7/3/64 B
Cross, Joan — 6/7/45 A; 7/12/46 A; 6/20/47 A
Crossley, Ada — 4/30/03 E
Crossley, Paul — 5/26/73 C
Crossworks — 4/21/76 C
Crown Imperial — 5/9/37 C; 5/12/37 C
Crown of India — 3/11/12 C
Crozier, Eric — //46 E; 6/20/47 A; 6/5/48 C;
    6/14/49 A; 12/1/51 A
Crucible, The — 10/26/61 A; 5/7/62 E
Crumb, George — 10/24/29 D; 12/2/66 C;
    5/6/68 E; 10/31/70 C; 1/16/72 C;
    10/10/72 C; 2/8/73 C; 11/12/74 C;
    5/5/77 C
Cruz-Romo, Gilda — 9/24/79 E
Cuban Overture — 8/16/32 C; 4/10/33 C
Cubiles, Jose — 4/9/16 C
Cuenod, Hugues-Adhemar — 6/26/02 D
Cuevas, Marquis George de — 10/30/44 E;
    2/22/61 D; 6/30/62 E — see also Ballet In-
    ternational de la Marquese de Cuevas
Cui, Cesar — 11/24/01 A; 1/17/03 A;
    12/27/06 A; 5/16/07 E; 2/27/11 A;
    10/8/13 A; 10/26/17 A; 3/26/18 D
Cullberg Ballet — 6/12/77 B
Cullberg, Birgit — 8/3/08 D; //46 E; 3/1/50 B;
    10/31/50 B; 11/22/57 B; 4/20/60 B;
    10/4/61 B
Cummings, e.e. — 7/14/60 C
Cunningham, Merce — 4/16/19 D;
    12/27/39 B; 8/11/40 B; 8/1/42 B;
    4/5/44 B; 10/30/44 B; 5/13/47 B;
    12/14/47 B; 8/20/48 B; 1/15/50 B; //52 E;
    6/14/52 B; 3/24/53 B; 12/8/54 B;
    5/24/55 B; 5/18/56 B; 7/11/56 B;
    5/21/58 B; 8/14/58 B; 8/17/58 B;
    9/5/58 B; 7/17/63 B; 7/3/64 B;
    7/23/65 B; 11/24/65 B; 4/15/69 B;
    12/3/71 B; 3/7/75 B; 1/5/76 B
Cunning Little Vixen, The — 11/6/24 A
Curlew River — 6/13/64 C; 12/4/76 D
Curriculum — 2/18/73 C
Curriculum Vitae for Accordion — 11/1/77 C
Currier, Ruth — 5/9/59 B
Curwen & Sons Ltd., J. — 2/1/76 C
Curti, Alfredo — 12/11/05 B
Curtin, Phyllis — 4/26/72 C; 4/16/73 C
Curtis Institute of Music — //24 E; 1/4/70 D
Curzon, Clifford — 5/18/07 D; 6/17/51 C
Cutner, Solomon — 8/9/02 D
Cybernetic aestheticism — 9/18/79 E
Cynara — 10/12/29 C
Cyrano de Bergerac (Alfano) — 1/22/36 A
Cyrano de Bergerac (Damrosch) — 2/27/13 A
Cyrano de Bergerac (Petit) — 4/17/59 B
Czaplicki, George — 2/21/44 E
Czech Nonet — 1/17/24 E
Czechoslovak State Radio Orchestra —
    10/4/36 C
Czech Philharmonic Orchestra — 8/12/28 D;
    1/24/34 D; //45 E; //46 E; //48 E
Czerny, Carl — 1/15/48 B
Czinka Panna — 3/15/48 A
Czoble, Lisa — 7/3/32 B

— D —

Da Capo Chamber Players — 2/8/73 C;
    4/25/74 C; 4/21/76 C
Dahl, Anton Luis — 10/31/32 D
Dahlhaus, Carl — //59 E
Dahl, Ingolf — 6/9/12 D; 8/7/70 D; 6/2/73 C
Dalberg, Frederick — 12/1/51 A
Dale, Clamma — 10/11/77 C
Dale, Margaret — 1/14/42 B
Dali, Salvador — 11/9/39 B; 10/8/41 B
Dallapiccola, Luigi — 2/3/04 D; 1/14/36 E;
    4/10/40 C; 5/18/40 A; 12/11/41 C;
    5/17/49 E; 12/4/49 A; 5/20/50 A;
    10/31/50 C; 3/4/52 C; 10/3/54 C;
    10/30/64 C; 9/29/68 A; 8/19/71 C;
    2/19/75 D
Dalla Rizza, Gilda — 2/14/22 A; 7/23/33 A
Dallas Civic Opera — 9/16/74 D
Dallas Symphony Orchestra — 5/22/00 E;
    2/1/47 C; 2/16/47 C; 2/27/49 C;
    11/20/49 C; 6/4/76 E
Dal Monte, Toti — 1/26/75 D
Dalmores, Charles — 12/6/39 D
Dalossy, Ellen — 3/7/20 A
Damase, Jean-Michel — 12/23/52 B
D'Amboise, Jacques — 7/28/34 D; 2/24/52 B;
    2/28/52 B; 6/2/53 B; 2/18/54 B;
    9/14/54 B; 2/27/55 B; 1/8/58 B;
    1/17/58 B; 5/14/59 B; 3/22/61 B;
    12/7/61 B; 4/9/63 B; 12/10/63 B;
    4/21/66 B; 4/13/67 B; 2/5/70 B;
    5/14-31/75 B; 5/29/75 B; 6/23/77 B
D'Amboise, Paul — 11/26/46 B
Dame Kobold — 2/23/16 A
Damrosch, Frank — 4/1/33 E
Damrosch, Leopold — //02 E; 10/15/12 A;
    3/30/28 E
Damrosch Opera Company — 10/15/12 A
Damrosch, Walter — //02 E; //03 E;
    7/24/09 E; 11/28/09 C; 10/15/12 A;
    2/27/13 A; 10/25/17 E; 3/10/23 C;
    1/11/25 C; 12/3/25 C; 11/15/26 C;
    12/26/26 C; 2/12/28 C; 3/30/28 E;
    12/13/28 C; 5/12/37 A; 11/3/42 A;
    5/2/43 C; 12/22/50 D
"Dance Around the Golden Calf" — 7/2/51 C;
    3/12/54 A
Dance Center, The (London) — //65 E
Dance! Cloudless Sulphur — 1/28/78 C
Dance & Dancers (periodical) — 1//50 E
Dance Drama Company — 8/3/55 B
Dance Goes On, The — 11/15/12 C
Dance Horizons (periodical) — //65 E
Dance in America (television series) — 1/5/76 B
Dance Index (periodical) — 1//42 E
Dance in Place Congo, The — 3/23/18 A
Dance Lovers Magazine (periodical) — //26 E
Dance Magazine (periodical) — //26 E
Dance Museum The, (Stockholm) — //53 E
Dance News (periodical) — //42 E
Dance Notation Bureau — //40 E
Dance Observer (periodical) — //33 E
Dance of Sports — 1/5/32 B
Dance of Work — 2/4/31 B
Dance Overture — 8/10/62 C
Dance Panels in Seven Movements — 12/3/63 C
Dance Perspectives (periodical) — //58 E
Dance Players — 4/24/42 B
Dance Research Foundation — //66 E
Dance Rhapsody No. 1 — 9/7/09 C
Dances africanas — 4/5/28 C
Dances at a Gathering — 5/22/69 B; 1/29/70 B
Dances of Galanta — 11/15/46 D
Dances of Marosszek — 11/28/30 C
Dance Sonata — 8/6/38 B
Dance Symphony (Koner) — 8/30/63 B
Dance Symphony, The Greatness of Creation (Lopo-
    kov) — 3/7/23 B

Dancing Ground — 2/21/67 B
Dandre, Victor — 6/17/38 E; 2/6/44 D
Danielian, Leon — 10/31/20 D; 9/10/44 B;
    3/10/53 B
Danieli, Fred — 11/20/46 B; 1/13/47 B
Danielon, Jean — 5/30/27 C
Danilova, Alexandra — 11/20/04 D; 3/7/23 B;
    1/6/24 B; 7/3/26 B; 12/3/26 B; 6/7/27 B;
    7/16/28 B; 5/7/29 B; //32 E; 4/15/33 B;
    10/24/33 B; 3/20/35 B; 2//38 E; 10//38 E;
    10/20/38 B; 5/4/39 B; 10/26/39 B;
    10/31/39 B; 10/12/42 B; 9/10/44 B;
    2/27/46 B
Danse brilliante — 4/22/66 B
Danise, Giuseppe — 3/7/20 A; 1/4/63 D
Danse des morts, La — 3/1/40 C
Danses concertantes (Balanchine) — 9/10/44 B;
    6/20/72 B
Danses concertantes (MacMillan) — 1/18/55 B
Danses concertantes (Stravinsky) — 2/8/42 C
Dante and Beatrice — 5/24/11 C
Dante Sonata — 1/23/40 B
Danton et Robespierre — 4/8/77 A
Dantons Tod — 8/6/47 A
Dantzig, Rudi van — 8/4/33 D; 6/19/65 B;
    3/2/70 B
Danzon cubano — 12/17/42 C; 2/17/46 C
Daphne — 10/15/38 A
Daphnis and Chloe (Ashton) — 4/5/51 B
Daphnis and Chloe (Cranko) — 7/15/62 B
Daphnis and Chloe (Fokine) — 6/8/12 B
Daphnis et Chloe (Ravel) — 4/2/11 C
Daphnis and Chloe (Taras) — 5/22/75 B
Dark Elegies — 2/19/37 B
Dark Meadow — 1/23/46 B
Dark Waters — 5/2/51 A
Darrell, Peter — 9/19/29 D; 4/6/72 B
Darrell, R.D. — 11/19/36 E
Darrieux, Marcel — 10/18/23 C
Darsonval, Lycette — 6/19/43 B; 7/28/47 B
Dart, Thurston — 9/3/21 D; 3/6/71 D
Daughter of Castile, A — 4/5/31 B
Daughter of the Forest, A — 1/5/18 A
Daughters of the American Revolution —
    1/2/38 C; 1/6/43 E
Daunt, Yvonne — 12/16/23 B
Davidenko, Alexander — 4/1/25 E; 1/18/29 C
David — 6/1/54 A
Davidovsky, Mario — 3/4/34 D; 1/8/59 E;
    5/9-10/61 E; 1/24/67 C; 5/3/71 E;
    12/4/75 C
Davies, Dennis Russell — 3/11/73 C;
    4/21/74 C; 12/11/78 C
Davies, Dudley — //69 E
Davies, Peter Maxwell — 9/8/34 D;
    7/13/59 C; 4/22/69 C; 12/9/69 C;
    1/20/72 C; 5/29/72 C; 7/12/72 A;
    10/13/72 C; 3/9/74 C; 3/24/77 C
Davies, Sir Henry Walford — 3/11/41 D;
    10/3/53 D
Davies, T. — 4/3/25 A
Davis, Colin — 9/25/27 D; 12/23/68 E;
    1/22/69 E; 6/22/72 C
Davis, Ellabelle — 3/7/47 C
Davis, Stuart — 3/9/65 C
Dayde, Bernard — 4/6/64 B; 5/11/66 B
Day on Earth — 12/21/47 B
Death and the Maiden — 2/23/37 B
Death in Venice — 6/16/73 A; 12/4/76 D
Death of Minnehaha, The — 3/22/00 C
Death of the Bishop of Brindisi — 5/18/63 C
Deaths and Entrances — 7/18/43 B
Debden, Hiday — 4/6/72 B
Debora e Jaele — 12/16/22 A
Debussy, Claude — 12/9/00 C; 2/7/01 C;
    10/27/01 C; 4/30/02 C; 1/1/03 C;
    1/9/04 C; 10/15/05 C; 3/1/07 C;
    3/21/07 C; 1/2/08 C; 1/20/08 E;
    2/19/08 A; 6/15/08 E; 12/18/08 C;

4/9/09 C; 2/20/10 C; 3/2/10 C;
5/25/10 C; 5/8/11 E; 5/22/11 A;
5/29/12 B; 5/15/13 B; 6/19/13 C;
12/10/13 E; 11/10/15 C; 5/5/17 C;
3/25/18 D; 5/11/19 C; 12/10/19 B;
12/19/19 D; 1/16/20 E; 11/15/24 C;
2/14/52 B; 5/6/52 E; 5/14/53 B; 8/3/55 B;
10/10/68 C; 3/8/70 B; 4/28/71 B
Debutante, The — 1/14/06 B
Decca (record label) — 2//29 E; //34 E; //44 E;
6//50 E; //57 E; //58 E; 9//59 E; //72 E
December 1952 — 10/11/63 C
Decembrists (Shaporin) — 6/23/53 A
Decision, The — 11/30/67 A
Declaration — 1/20/57 C
De Fabritiis, Oliviero — 6/13/04 D
Defauw, Desire — 10/22/46 C
De Forest, Lee — 3/5/07 E; 4/9/09 E
De Gaetani, Jan — 4/21/76 C; 10/29/78 C
Dehn, Paul — 6/17/54 A
Deirdre — 4/20/46 A; 4/2/65 A
Dejanire — 3/14/11 A
Deja Vu — 10/20/77 C; 4/17/78 E
De Koven, Reginald — 3/8/17 A; 1/2/20 A;
1/16/20 D
De Lamarter, Eric — 1/17/17 C
Delannoy, Marcel — 3/4/29 B
Delarova, Eugenia — 4/5/38 B
Delarue, Georges — 5/11/66 B
DeLavallade, Carmen — 11/19/59 B
Delbos, Claire — 12/22/35 E
Delerue, Georges — 4/6/64 B
Delfau, Andre — 2/21/65 B
Delibes, Leo — 12/15/01 B; 1/28/06 B;
3/26/06 B; 8/13/12 D; 3/21/34 B;
9/3/52 B; 11/23/68 B
Delius Festival — 10/12/29 C; 3/8/61 D
Delius, Frederick — 3/30/04 A; 5/24/06 C;
2/21/07 A; 1/18/08 C; 6/4/08 C;
12/11/08 C; 6/7/09 C; 9/7/09 C;
11/15/12 C; 10/2/13 C; 1/11/19 C;
10/21/19 A; 3/23/22 C; //28 E; 3/1/29 E;
10/12/29 C; 9/17/31 C; 5//33 E;
10/3/33 C; 6/10/34 D; 4/24/36 D;
11/10/36 B; 4/6/43 B; 5/4/53 A
Delius Society — 5//33 E
Deliverance de Thesee, La — 4/20/28 A
Delizie contente che l'alme beate — 12/13/73 C
Deller, Alfred — 5/30/12 D; 7/16/79 D
Deller Consort — 7/16/79 D
Dellheim, Peter — 10/13/79 D
Dello Joio, Norman — 1/24/13 D; 10/4/45 B;
12/19/46 E; 10/20/47 C; 8/13/48 B;
5/9/50 A; 12/5/51 B; 5/8/55 B;
5/13/55 A; 4/8/56 A; 4/20/56 B;
5/6/57 E; 9/18/61 A; 3/9/62 C;
5/25/68 B; 6/3/69 C; 1/11/70 C;
10/5/70 C; 2/23/75 C; 4/14/75 C;
5/27/76 C; 8/26/77 C; 5/18/79 C
Del Mar, Norman — 7/31/19 D; 11/23/48 C;
3/22/58 C
Delmas, Marc — 11/30/31 D
Del Monaco, Mario — 7/27/15 D; 1/1/41 D
Delna, Maria — 7/23/32 D
Del Tredici, David — 3/16/37 D; 7/7/68 C;
10/7/76 C
De Luca, Giuseppe — 11/26/02 A; 12/19/03 A;
2/17/04 A; 11/25/15 D; 1/28/16 A;
12/14/18 A; 11/15/18 D; 11/1/26 D;
8/26/50 D
Delusion of the Fury — 5/8/66 C; 1/9/69 B
Delvincourt, Claude — 4/5/54 D
Demessieux, Jeanne — 11/11/68 D
De Mille, Agnes — 10/16/42 B; 4/22/48 B;
10/1/52 B
Demoiselles de la Nuit, Les — 5/22/48 B
Demon, The — 3/13/63 B
Denham, Sergei I. — 1/30/38 E; 1//48 E

Denishawn — 2/22/15 B; 1/31/21 B;
10/28/28 B; 8/6/29 B; //33 E;
12/29/58 D; 7/21/68 D; 1/9/72 D
Denisov, Edison — 11/18/79 E
Denkmaler der Tonkunst in Osterreich — 6/20/06 E
Denon (record company) — //76 E
Denver Symphony Orchestra — 4/16/73 C
Denzler, Robert — 6/2/37 A; 5/28/38 A
Derain, Andre — 7/3/26 B; 4/12/32 B
De Reszke, Edouard — 1/28/03 E; 5/25/17 D
De Reszke, Jean — 3/29/01 E; 4/29/01 E;
2/19/06 E; 4/3/25 D
Dernier sauvage, Le — 10/21/63 A
De Sabata, Victor — 3/21/25 A
Deserto tentato, Il — 5/6/37 A
Deserts — 12/2/54 C
Deshevov, Vladimir — 10/29/24 B; 5/15/30 A
Design for Orchestra — 5/28/55 C
Designs with Strings — 2/6/48 B; 2/25/50 B
Desormiere, Roger — 6/14/23 E; 4/21/45 C;
10/24/48 C
DesRoches, Raymond — 3/12/67 C;
4/28/70 C
Dessau, Paul — 3/17/51 A; 1/20/65 C;
4/29/67 A; 6/27/79 D
Destinn, Emmy — 5/2/04 D; 12/5/06 A;
11/16/08 D; 2/19/09 A; 1/13/10 E;
12/10/10 A; 11/13/11 D; 1/28/30 D
Detroit Symphony Orchestra — 11/21/29 D;
10/23/59 C; 7/23/64 C; 3/4/65 C;
10/28/65 C; 3/21/68 C; 1/17/69 C;
1/29/76 C; 4/1/76 C
Detvan — 8/1/28 A
Deutsche Grammophon — 5//27 E; 2//29 E;
1//49 E; //54 E
Deutsche Oper — //61 E; 4/19/64 A;
9/29/68 A; 11/4/75 A
"Deutschland, Deutschland, uber alles" —
2/5/15 C
Deux images — 2/26/13 C
Devil and Daniel Webster, The — 5/18/39 A
Devilier, Katharina — 5/17/21 B
Devil's Forge, The — 1/12/03 B
Devil's Holiday — 10/26/39 B
Devils of Loudun, The — 6/20/69 A
Devreese, Godefroid — 6/4/72 D
Diaghilev, Serge — 12/26/04 B; 4/15/05 B;
5/16/07 E; 5/19/08 A; 5/19/09 B;
6/4/10 B; 6/18/10 B; 6/25/10 B;
1/26/11 E; 4/26/11 B; 6/6/11 B;
6/13/11 B; 6/21/11 B; 11/30/11 B;
5/14/12 B; 5/20/12 B; 5/29/12 B;
5/10/13 B; 5/15/13 B; 5/29/13 B;
6/8/12 B; 6/12/13 B; 6/24/13 A;
12/3/13 E; 4/16/14 B; 5/14/14 B;
5/21/14 B; 5/26/14 A; 6/2/14 B;
12/20/15 B; 1/17/16 B; 1/20/16 B;
10/23/16 B; 4/9/17 C; 4/12/17 B;
5/11/17 B; 5/18/17 B; 6/5/19 B;
7/22/19 B; 2/2/20 B; 5/15/20 B;
5/17/21 B; 11/2/21 B; 5/18/22 B;
6/3/22 A; 6/13/23 B; 1/6/24 B;
1/19/24 B; 6/15/24 B; 6/20/24 B;
12/28/24 D; 4/28/25 B; 6/17/25 B;
12/11/25 B; 5/4/26 B; 12/3/26 B;
4/30/27 B; 6/7/27 B; 6/6/28 B;
6/12/28 B; 7/16/28 B; 5/7/29 B;
5/21/29 B; 8/4/29 E; 8/19/29 D;
12/15/31 D; //32 E; 3/7/42 E; 4/6/71 D;
4/6/78 D
Dialogues of the Carmelites, The — 1/26/57 A;
1/30/63 D
Diamond, David — 7/9/15 D; 3/24/37 C;
12/21/41 C; 10/13/44 C; 11/24/44 C;
5/12/45 E; 10/20/47 C; 1/23/48 C;
2/1/50 C; 11/3/50 C; 11/17/54 C;
3/8/57 C; 10/26/61 C; 1/26/62 C;
11/17/63 C; 4/28/66 C; 2/5/77 C;
3/12/78 B

Diana — 12/22/23 A
Diary of a Madman, The — 10/3/58 A
Diavolo nel campanile, Il — 4/22/25 A
Diaz, Justino — 9/16/66 A; 1/18/74 C
Dibuc, Il — 3/24/34 A
Dick, James — 6/4/76 E
Dictionary of Music and Musicians (book) —
5/28/00 D
Didur, Adamo — 2/6/09 E; 11/13/11 D;
1/2/14 A; 3/6/18 A
Dieren, Bernard van — 4/24/36 D
Dies Irae — 4/14/67 C
Dieu bleu, Le — 5/14/12 B
Dieux sont morts, Les — 3/19/24 A
Digital recording — //77 E
Digital tape — //76 E
Diktator, Der — 5/6/28 A
Dillon, Enrica C. — 10/9/46 D
Dimensions of Time and Silence — 9/18/60 C
Dim Lustre — 10/20/43 B; 5/6/64 B
Dinner Engagement, A — 6/17/54 A
Dionysion — 1/19/15 B
Dippel, Andreas — 1/22/07 A; 5/12/32 D
Disney, Walt — 11/13/40 E
Dissonanza — 2/13/68 C
Distant Planet, A — 4/12/63 B
Distler, Hugo — 6/24/08 D; 11/1/42 D
Ditson, Charles Healy — 5/14/49 D
Diversion, A — 8/20/48 B
Diversions on a Theme (Britten) — 1/16/42 C
Divertimento (Balanchine) — 1/13/47 B
Divertimento for Chamber Orchestra (Strauss, R.) —
1/31/43 C
Divertiment for String Orchestra (Bartok) —
6/11/40 C
Divertimento No. 15 (Balanchine) — 2/19/52 B;
12/19/56 B
Divertissement (Ibert) — 11/30/30 C
Divertissement (Prokofiev) — 12/22/29 C
Divinity (Dialogues in the Form of Secret Portraits) —
3/15/73 C
Dixon, Dean — 8/10/41 D; 5/16/48 C
Dixon, James — 11/19/69 C
Dix pieces pittoresques — 5/15/34 B
Dlugoszewski, Lucia — 1/19/53 B;
11/24/57 B; 12/9/73 C; 4/21/74 C
Dmitriev, Vladimir — 12/31/35 B
Doboujinsky, Mstislav — 5/10/13 B; 6/2/14 B
Dobrinya Nikititch — 10/27/03 A
Dobrowen, Issay — //30 E; //31 E; //32 E;
12/9/53 D
Doce por doce — 6/15/69 C
Doctor Merryheart — 1/3/13 C
Dodge, Charles — 6/5/42 D; 2/8/73 C;
2/7/77 C
Dohnanyi, Ernst von — 11/29/04 C; 3/7/06 C;
1/22/10 A; 2/21/10 C; 1/20/13 A;
2/17/14 C; 1/9/22 C; 11/19/23 C;
11/17/24 C; 2/9/29 A; 10/25/30 C;
11/28/30 C; 12/14/45 E; 1/22/51 C;
1/26/52 C; 3/3/53 B; 2/21/54 C;
3/15/57 C; 2/9/60 D; 7/27/60 E
Doktor Faust — 5/21/25 A; 12/1/64 A
Dolby, Dr. Ray — //66 E
Dolby Laboratories Inc. — //66 E
Dolce vita, La — 4/10/79 D
Dolin, Anton — 7/24/04 D; 1/19/24 B;
6/20/24 B; 4/28/25 B; 5/7/29 B;
5/5/31 B; 7/5/31 B; 10/27/41 B;
2/25/44 B; 10/1/46 B; 10/24/50 E
Dollar Cacophony — 1/7/51 E
Dollar, William — 3/1/35 B; 1/13/40 B;
5/29/41 B; 11/20/46 B; 11/26/46 B;
2/24/49 B; 2/22/61 D
Dolmetsch, Arnold — //15 E; 2/28/40 D;
8/19/46 D
Dolmetsch, Rudolf — 3/16/43 D
Dolores — 1/4/47 A

Domaine Musicale — 1/13/54 E; 4/15/59 C; 10/3/63 C
Domanda di matrimonio, Una — 5/22/57 A
Domingo, Placido — 1/21/41 D; 9/24/79 E
Donahue, John — 10/14/71 A
Donald McKayle Dance Company — *see* McKayle Dance Company, Donald
Donald of the Burthens — 12/12/51 B
Donaueschingen Festival — 7/20/24 C; 7/25/26 E; 10/6/51 C; 10/7/51 C; 10/11/53 C; 10/17/54 C; 10/19/58 C; 10/17/59 C; 10/15/60 C; 10/16/60 C; 10/21/61 C; 10/22/61 C; 12/28/63 D; 10/17/64 C; 10/22/67 C; 10/8/70 C; 10/20/73 C; 10/16/74 C; 10/18/74 C
Donemus — 5/20/47 E
Donemus Foundation — 9/7/70 E
Donizetti Variations — 11/16/60 B
Don Juan (Ashton) — 11/25/48 B
Don Juan de Manora — 6/24/37 A
Don Juan (Fokine) — 6/25/36 B
Don Juan (Neumeier) — 4/26/74 B
Don Juan (Strauss, R.) — 3/21/04 C; 8/15/14 E
Donna boba, La — 2/1/39 A
Donna serpente, La — 3/17/32 A
Donne curiose, Le — 11/27/03 A
Donn, Jorge — 10/8/71 B
Don Procopio — 3/10/06 A
Don Quichotte a Dulcinee — 12/1/34 C
Don Quichotte (Massenet) — 2/19/10 A
Don Quixote (Balanchine) — 5/28/65 B
Don Quixote (Gorsky) — 2/2/02 B
Don Quixote (Valois) — 2/2/50 B
Don Rodrigo — 7/24/64 A; 5/19/67 A
Dorati, Antal — 4/9/06 D; 2/1/47 C; 2/27/49 C; 12/2/49 C; 3/30/51 C; 3/15/57 C; 11/22/57 C; 11/27/59 C; 1/2/60 C; 4/1/64 C; //69 E; 3/28/72 C; 11/19/72 C
Dorella, Oriella — 5/5/78 B
Dorf ohne Glocke, Das — 4/15/21 A
Dorian Singers — 9/24/60 D
Dorian Wind Quintet — 3/21/62 C; 4/6/73 E; 12/13/73 C
Dornroschens Erwachen — 4/18/31 A
Dorn, Rudi — 10/3/68 B
Dorothy Chandler Pavilion (Los Angeles) — 12/6/64 E
Dorrer, Valery — 4/12/63 B
Dos movimientos — 6/26/57 C
Double Concerto for Harpsichord and Piano with Two Chamber Orchestras (Carter) — 9/6/61 C
Double Concerto for percussion and orchestra — 4/28/78 C
Double Concerto (Holst) — 4/3/30 C
Double Concerto (Krenek) — 10/6/51 C
Double Concerto (Martinu) — 2/9/40 C
Double Counterpoint and Canon (Prout) — 12/5/09 D
Doubles — 1/10/64 C; 5/2/65 D
Doubrovska, Felia — 6/13/23 B; 1/6/24 B; 7/3/26 B; 6/12/28 B; 5/21/29 B
Douglas, Scott — 11/19/59 B; 1/25/66 B
Douze Etudes (Debussy) — 11/10/15 C
Douze, Les — 11/9/47 C
Douze preludes (Debussy) — 5/25/10 C
Dovsky, Beatrice — 9/26/15 A
Dowell, Anthony — 2/16/43 D; 4/2/64 B; 2/9/65 B; 2/10/66 B; 1/25/67 B; 2/29/68 B; 5/7/74 B; 2/12/76 B
Down Among the Dead Men (book) — 4/24/36 D
Down by the Greenwood Side — 5/8/69 A
Downes, Edward — 8/12/11 D; 7/12/72 A
Down in the Valley — 7/15/48 A
Doyle, Desmond — 10/11/60 B; 2/9/65 B
D'Oyly Carte, Richard — 11/22/00 D
Dragon, The — 2/6/58 A
Dramatic Etude — 8/13/48 B
Dramatische Fantasie — 7/16/17 D

Dream of Gerontius, The — 10/3/00 C; 12/3/08 C; 1/15/21 D
Dreams (Prokofiev) — 12/5/10 C
Dream, The (Ashton) — 4/2/64 B
Dreigroschenoper, Die — 8/3/28 A; 5/7/29 E; 6/14/52 A
Drei Klavierstucke (Schoenberg) — 8/7/09 C
Dresden Staatsoper — 5/29/01 A; 1/22/10 A; 9/7/10 E; //22 E; 11/4/24 A; 5/21/25 A; 3/8/33 E; 6/24/35 A; 10/15/38 A
Dresden State Orchestra — 11/18/79 E
Drew, David — 5/7/74 B
Drigo, Riccardo — 2/10/00 B; 2/4/65 B
Dromenon — 12/14/47 B
Droom, De — 6/16/65 A
Drottningholm Court Theater (Sweden) — 8/19/22 E
Drucker, Stanley — 12/6/77 C
Druckman, Jacob — 5/1/72 E; 12/13/73 C; 4/20/74 C; 7/4/76 E; 3/14/77 C; 9/29/77 C; 11/4/77 C; 11/2/78 C
Druian, Rafael — 5/4/72 C
Dryad, The — 9/7/08 B
Du — 5/8/52 C
Dubois, Theodore — 6/26/05 E
Dubost, Mme. Jeanne — 3/4/29 B
Dubrovnik Philharmonic Orchestra — 4/13/25 E
Dubrovnik Symphony Orchestra — *see* Dubrovnik Philharmonic Orchestra
Duckles, Vincent — 9/21/13 D
Dudinskaya, Natalia — 8/21/12 D; 3/22/39 B; 3/14/49 B; 6/28/50 B; 11/5/51 D
Dudko, Mikhail — 9/28/34 B
Dudley, Jane — 8/11/40 B; 7/18/43 B
Dudley, Leon — 12/1/30 C
Duell, Daniel — 1/19/78 B
Duenna, The — 6/27/51 A
Duet Concertino (Strauss, R.) — 4/4/48 C
Dufranne, Hector — 2/19/08 A
Dufy, Raoul — 2/21/20 B
Dugi, Emilio — 4/12/02 A
Dukas, Paul — 5/10/07 A; 4/22/12 B; 2/6/31 B; 5/17/35 D; 2/15/56 B; 9/6/56 E
Duke Bluebeard's Castle — 5/24/18 A
Dukelsky, Vladimir — 10/10/03 D; 4/28/25 B; 1/16/69 D
Dukes, Ashley — 2/25/30 B
Duke, Vernon — *see* Dukelsky, Vladimir
Dumbarton Oaks (Robbins) — 6/23/72 B
Dumbarton Oaks (Stravinsky) — 5/8/38 C; 4/6/71 D
Dunbar, William — 10/6/37 C
Duncan, Isadora — 12/26/04 B; 12/3/14 B; 1/19/15 B; 10/23/22 E; 9/14/27 D
Duncan, Jeff — 2/24/55 B
Duncan, Ronald — 7/12/46 A
Dunham, Katherine — 6/22/12 D
Dunkirk — 5/2/43 C
Dunn, Denis — 2/14/78 B
Dunn, Jorge — 1/27/78 B
Dunn, Mignon — 10/22/79 A
Duo concertante (Balanchine) — 6/22/72 B
Duo for Two Flutes (Tcherepnin) — 4/14/78 C
Duo for Violin and Piano (Carter) — 3/21/75 C
Duparc, Henri — 2/26/11 C; 2/12/33 D
Duplex pianoforte — 10/20/31 D
Dupont, Gabriel — 8/2/14 D
Dupont, Jacques — 2/14/61 A
Du Pre, Jacqueline — 1/26/45 D; 6/15/67 E
Dupre, Marcel — 5/3/01 C; 12/8/21 C; 10/9/24 C; 2/13/31 C; 4/27/38 C; 5/30/71 D
Dupuis, Albert — 3/28/13 A
Durand, Marie-August — 3/2/10 C
Durant, Germaine — 4/20/10 C
Durey, Louis — 1/16/20 E; 6/19/21 B; 7/3/79 D
During the Storm — 10/10/39 A

Durufle, Maurice — 1/11/02 D; 6/10/41 C
Dushkin, Samuel — 10/23/31 C; 6/26/42 C; 6/24/76 D
Dutilleux, Henri — 1/22/16 D; 12/9/59 C; 6/25/74 C
Duval, Denise — 6/3/47 A; 2/6/59 A
Duval, Paul — 8/27/00 A
Dvorak, Antonin — 3/31/01 A; 3/25/04 A; 5/1/04 D; 2/3/07 C; 10/4/36 C; 4/5/79 B
Dybbuk — 5/16/74 B
Dybbuk Suite No. 1 — 4/3/75 C
Dybbuk Suite No. 2 — 4/17/75 C
Dying Swan, The — 12/22/07 B
Dynagroove — //63 E
Dynamophone — 4/25/28 E; 4/12/34 D
Dyson, George — 3/19/31 C
Dzerzhinsky, Ivan — 10/22/35 A; 10/23/37 A; 1/21/42 A; 9/8/43 A; 1/18/78 D

— E —

Eagles — 10/23/59 C
Eames, Emma — 4/18/06 E; 2/15/09 E; 6/13/52 D
Early Music Consort — 5/15/76 D
Early Songs — 4/3/70 B
Early Songs After Li Po — 5/5/73 C
Eash, George — //54 E
East Berlin Komische Oper — 10/8/75 D
East German State Opera House — //55 E
Eastman, George — 3/14/32 D
Eastman, Julius — 1/27/74 C
Eastman School of Music — //21 E; 3/14/32 D
Eastman School of Music Philharmonic — 4/27/61 C
Easton, Florence — 12/14/18 A; 3/12/19 A; 2/17/27 A; 1/19/29 A
Eaton, John — 4/23/73 A; 4/8/77 A
Eau du Nil, L' — 10/10/28 E
Ebert, Carl — 3/11/33 E; 5//34 E
Ebony Concerto (Cranko) — 12/29/70 B
Ebony Concerto (Taras) — 12/7/60 B
Echanges, Les — 4/24/64 C
Echaniz, Jose — 6/4/05 D; 12/30/69 D
Echoes from an Invisible World — 2/27/75 C; 7/4/76 E
Echoes of Autumn — 12/2/66 C
Echoes of Time and the River: Four Processionals for Orchestra — 5/6/68 E
Echoi — 11/11/63 C
Echoing of Trumpets — 9/28/63 B
Eclat — 3/26/65 C
Ecole d'Arcueil — 6/14/23 E
Ecole Normale de Musique — 3/18/50 C; 6/15/62 D
Ecorcheville, Jules — 2/19/15 D
Ecstasy of Rita Joe, The — 7/27/71 B
Ecuatorial — 4/15/34 C; 6/27/78 B
Eddy, Clarence — 1/10/37 D
Edinburgh Festival — //47 E; 9/3/49 c; 6/1/50 E; 8/26/51 C; 9/3/57 D; 7/4/62 D; 8/28/63 C
Edio Y Iocasta — 10/5/73 A
Edipo re — 12/13/20 A
Edison, Thomas A. — 4/30/03 E; 4/11/02 E; //08 E; //12 E; //26 E; 2//29 E
Editio Medicea — 9/5/10 D
Editions Russes de Musique — 3/16/09 E
Editio Vaticana — 9/5/10 D
Eduards, Leslie — 12/12/51 B
Educational Ballets Ltd. — 6/19/38 B; 10//38 E
Education manquee, Une — 1/9/13 A
Edwards, Leslie — 4/6/43 B
Effinger, Cecil — 6/26/55 E
Egdon Heath — 2/12/28 C
Egge, Klaus — 7/19/06 D; 3/4/59 C; 3/7/79 D
Egk, Werner — 5/17/01 D; 5/20/35 A; 8/16/36 E; 11/24/38 A; 7/15/39 E;

12/18/48 A; 6/28/53 A; 8/17/55 A;
5/9/57 A; 11/27/63 A; 6/2/66 A
Eglevsky, Andre — 12/21/17 D; 4/6/34 B;
6/25/36 B; 10//38 E; 10/17/40 B;
10/8/41 B; 11/29/42 B; 2/18/51 B;
11/20/51 B; 2/19/52 B; 11/11/52 B;
2/27/55 B; 3/1/55 B; 11/9/55 B
Egypta — 12/12/10 B
Ehnn, Berta — 3/9/32 D
Ehrling, Sixten — 4/3/18 D; 7/23/64 E;
10/28/65 C; 3/21/68 C; 1/17/69 C
Eichenholz, Bronislaw — 8/4/68 C
Eight Column Line — 5/19/39 B
Eight Early Songs (Webern) — 5/27/62 C
Eight Orchestra Fragments (Webern) — 3/16/72 C
Eight Songs for a Mad King — 4/22/69 C
Eight Songs (Schoenberg) — 7/13/51 D
Eimert, Herbert — 10/1/51 E; //53 E;
10/19/54 C; //55 E; 5/30/56 C
Einem, Gottfried von — 1/24/18 D; 8/6/47 A;
8/17/53 A; 11/16/57 B; 3/1/59 C;
9/17/64 A; 5/23/71 A; 2/25/77 A
Ein-Gev — 10/1/53 C
Einstein, Albert — 1/17/34 E; 2/13/52 D
Einstein, Alfred — //19 E; //22 E; //29 E;
2/13/52 D
Einstein on the Beach — 7/25/76 A
Eisemann, Heinrich — 12/4/72 D
Eisenberg, Maurice — 10/14/33 C
Eisenhower, Dwight D. — 1/20/57 C;
5/14/59 E
Eisenstein, Sergei — 5/17/39 C; 3/5/53 D
Eisler, Hanns — 12/13/30 A; 5/22/38 E;
3/26/48 E; 2/8/50 E; 3/11/53 A; 9/6/62 D
Ek, Mats — 6/12/77 B
El-Dabh, Halim — 4/1/58 B; 1/8/59 E;
5/9-10/61 E
Electrical and Musical Industries (EMI) —
9/17/31 E; 6/2/51 E; 10//52 E; //54 E;
//56 E; //58 E
Electrical Testing Laboratories — 3/20/15 C
Electrola — 3/25/25 E
Electronics — 3/22/61 B
Electronic Study No. 1 — 5/9-10/61 E
Elegie fur junge Liebende — 5/20/61 A
Elegie in Memoriam of Carlos Chavez — 11/23/79 C
Elegy (Amram) — 3/3/73 C
Elegy (Cordero) — 4/24/77 C
Elegy for J.F.K. (Stravinsky) — 4/6/64 C
Elegy for Orchestra (Corigliano) — 6/1/66 C
Elegy for Orchestra (Elgar) — 7/13/09 C
Elegy for Young Lovers — 5/20/61 A
Elektra — 1/25/09 A; 9/7/10 E
Elektrophon — 7/25/26 E
Elfes, Les — 2/26/24 B
Elga — 12/6/16 A
Elgar, Edward — 10/3/00 C; 11/22/00 E;
6/20/01 C; 10/19/01 C; 10/14/03 C;
3/16/04 C; 7/5/04 E; 3/8/05 C;
3/19/07 D; 8/24/07 C; 12/14/07 C;
12/3/08 C; 7/13/09 C; 11/10/10 C;
5/24/11 C; 6/22/11 C; 3/11/12 C;
10/2/13 C; 8/15/14 B; 12/7/14 C;
7/6/15 C; 10/27/19 C; 11/10/20 E;
1/15/21 D; //24 E; 9/20/30 C; 2/23/34 D;
10/25/68 B
Elias, Rosalind — 1/15/58 A; 10/11/77 C
Eliot Feld Ballet — *see* Feld Ballet, Eliot
Elizabeth and Essex — 6/8/53 A
Ellington, Duke — 11/28/59 B
Elman, Mischa — 12/10/08 D; 4/5/67 D
Elmo, Cloe — 3/17/52 A
Elson, Louis Charles — 2/14/20 D
Elson, Louis Charles, Memorial Fund Lectures
— 4/25/46 E
Eluard, Paul — 3/25/45 C; 8/25/54 C
Elvin, Violetta — 5/5/56 B
Elwes, Gervase — 1/15/21 D
Elytres — 12/8/64 C

Embattled Garden — 4/3/58 B
Embrace Tiger and Return to Mountain —
11/21/68 B
Emeriton — 10/1/65 D
EMI — *see* Electrical and Musical Industries
Emperor Jones, The (Gruenberg) — 1/7/33 A
Emperor Jones, The (Limon) — 7/12/56 B
Empire Theater — 3/18/01 B; 1/6/06 B;
1/14/06 B; 5/14/06 B; 8/6/06 B; 9/7/08 B
Empreintres — 6/29/75 C
Empress and the Necromancer, The — 5/12/36 A
Enchanted Lake — 2/21/09 C; 8/28/14 D
Enchanted Pear Tree, The — 2/7/50 A
Enchantements d'Alcine, Les — 5/21/29 B
Enchantress — 9/21/72 C
Encyclopedie de la musique et Dictionnaire du Conser-
vatoire (book) — 5/28/16 D
Ende einer Welt, Das — 12/4/53 A
Endymion's Dream — 2/3/10 C
Energia — 6/11/31 C
Enesco, Georges — 3/8/03 C; 1/21/06 C;
3/28/15 C; 5/25/19 C; //21 E; 5/30/27 C;
2/25/34 C; 3/10/36 A; 1/23/55 C;
5/4/55 D; 10/10/56 E; 9/10/64 C
Enfant prodigue, L' (Debussy) — 3/25/18 D
Enfant prodigue, L' (Prokofiev) — 11/14/30 C
Enfant et les sortileges, L' (Ravel) — 3/21/25 A;
11/26/46 B
Engel, Carl — 5/6/44 D
Engel, Lehman — 4/21/37 A
English Chamber Orchestra — 10/11/60 E;
6/16/76 C
English Folk Song Suite — 7/4/23 C
English Opera Group — //46 E; 6/9/66 A;
12/4/76 D
English Suite No. 3 (Brian) — 3/16/22 C
Enigma Variations (Ashton) — 10/25/68 B
Enlevement, L' — 7/17/27 A
Ensemble Europeen de Musique Contem-
poraine — 4/13/73 C
Ensemble for Early Music — 12/6/79 C
Ensemble Inter-Contemporain — 9/29/77 C
Ensemble, The — 3/11/73 C; 4/21/74 C
Entente Cordiale — 5/18/78 B
Entflieht auf leichten Kahnen — 4/10/27 C
Entremont, Philippe — 11/20/77 C
Eonta — 1/31/69 C
Epic of Gilgamesh, The — 1/24/58 C
Epifanie — 10/22/61 C
Epilogue to Profiles in Courage: J.F.K. — 5/10/64 C
Episodes — 5/14/59 B
Epitaph for the Victims of Katyn — 11/17/68 C
Epitaphium fur das Grabmal des Prinzen Max Egon Fur-
stenberg — 10/17/59 C
Erdman, B. — 3/3/25 B
Erdman, Jean — 8/1/42 B
Erede, Alberto — 11/8/08 D
Eridanos — 4/13/73 C
Erikton (la force de la terre) — 5/21/74 C
Erixon, Sven — 3/1/50 B
Erlanger, Camille — 4/24/19 D
Erlanger, Frederic d' — 7/18/35 B; 6/19/38 B
Ernani — 1/28/03 E; 4/30/03 E
Ernster, Dezso — 6/8/29 A
Eros and Death — 5/26/71 D
Erosion — 11/7/51 C
Errand into the Maze — 2/28/47 B
Erwartung — 6/6/24 A
Escales — 1/6/24 C
Escot, Pozzi — 5/7/65 E
Escurial — 5/4/58 A
Esoterik Satie — 5/5/78 B
Espaces de sommeil, Les — 3/12/78 C
Espinosa, E. — 12/31/20 E
Espinosa, Guillermo — 6/5/61 C
Esplanade Concerts — 5/7/30 E
Essay on Pigs — 2/14/69 C
Essays Before a Sonata (book) — 1/20/39 C
Essen, Viola — 1/13/40 B

Esta — 9/16/20 E
Estampes — 1/9/04 C
Es war einmal — 1/22/00 A
Etait un petit navire, ll — 3/9/51 A
Eternal Idol — 12/4/69 D
Etherophone — 8/5/20 E
Eto, Kimio — 12/18/64 C
Etranger, L' — 1/7/03 A
Etude concrete pour un seul coup de cymbale —
7/9/60 C
Etude Mihalovici — 10/6/51 C
Etudes en forme de scherzo (Wyschnegradsky) —
1/25/37 C
Etudes (Lander) — 1/15/48 B
Etudien fur Flote Solo — 11/3/74 C
Eugene Onegin — 4/13/65 B
Eula, Joe — 5/22/69 B; 12/4/69 B; 7/30/70 B
Eumenides, Les — 11/27/27 A
Eurythmics — 4/15/05 E
Euterpe Society — 9/4/07 D
Evangeline — 5/5/48 A
Evans, Geraint — 2/16/22 D; 12/1/51 A
Evdokimova, Eva — 12/1/48 D
Evenings on the Roof — 10/19/53 C;
2/25/76 D
Evening's Waltzes, An — 5/24/73 B
Eventyr — 1/11/19 C
Everett, Horace — 4/1/54 A
Every Good Boy Deserves Favour — 7/30/79 A
Every Soul Is a Circus — 12/27/39 B
Evocation (Bloch) — 2/11/38 C
Evocation (Loeffler) — 2/5/31 E
Evocations (Dello Joio) — 10/5/70 C
Evocations (Roussel) — 5/18/12 C
Evocations (Ruggles) — 2/2/71 C
Evolution of Modern Orchestration, The (book) —
4/30/05 E
Evtushenko, Evgeny — 12/18/62 C;
12/28/64 C
Ewartung — 7/13/51 D
Excursions of Mr. Broucek — 4/23/20 A
Execution of Stephan Razin, The — 12/28/64 C
Exiles, The — 8/11/50 B
. . . Explosante/fixe. . . 3/3/72 C
Expo '67 — 4/29/67 E
Expo fur 3, ubereinstimmung — 5/5/72 C
Ex-position — 9/14/78 C
Exspecto resurrectionem mortuorum, Et — 5/7/65 C
Extension 3 — 5/2/52 C

— F —

Fables for Our Time — 7/11/47 B
Facade (Ashton) — 4/26/31 B
Facade (Walton) — 1/24/22 C; 6/12/23 C;
9/14/28 C; 3/30/38 C
Facheux, Les — 1/19/24 B
Fachiri, Adila — 4/3/30 C
Facsimile — 10/24/46 B
Fadetta — 3/21/34 B
Fadeyechev, Nicolai — 1/27/33 D; 9/17/62 B
Fadograph of a Yestern Scene — 9/10/71 C
Fair at Sorochinsk, The — 10/8/13 A
Fairfax, Brian — 2/26/62 C
Fair of Sorochinsk, The — 10/26/17 A
Fairyland — 7/1/15 A
Falk, Per — 10/4/61 B
Falla, Manuel de — 4/12/02 A; 4/1/13 A;
2/8/15 E; 4/15/15 B; 4/9/16 C;
7/22/19 B; 3/23/23 A; 6/25/23 A;
11/5/26 C; 10/8/39 E; 11/18/39 C;
11/14/46 D
Fall River Legend — 4/22/48 B; 1/6/49 C
False Relationships and the Extended Ending —
12/31/68 C
Falstaff (Elgar) — 10/2/13 C
Falstaff (Verdi) — 1/27/01 D
Family of Taras, The — 11/7/50 A

Family Portrait — 3/24/75 C
Fanciulla del west, La — 12/10/10 A
Fancy Free — 4/18/44 B
Fanfare — 6/2/53 B
Fanfare de la liberte — 12/11/42 C
Fanfare for 17 Brass and Percussion — 10/8/70 C
Fanfare for Freedom — 1/22/43 C
Fanfare for Orchestra — 1/15/43 C
Fanfare for Paratroopers, A — 11/27/42 C
Fanfare for Saint Louis — 1/24/68 E
Fanfare for the Common Man — 3/12/43 C; 10/18/46 E
Fanfare to Israel — 7/29/67 E
Fantaisie burlesque — 3/15/74 C
Fantaisie portugaise — 3/23/41 C
Fantaisies symphoniques — 9/28/63 B
Fantasia (movie) — 11/13/40 E
Fantasia concertante — 1/31/59 C
Fantasia contrappuntistica — 8/6/23 C
Fantasia dos movimentos mixtos — 12/15/22 C
Fantasia on a Theme by Tallis (Vaughan Williams) — 9/6/10 C; 8/26/58 D
Fantasia on Greensleeves — 9/27/34 C
Fantasia on Sussex — 3/13/30 C
Fantasie (Faure) — 5/14/19 C
Fantasies (Clifford) — 1/23/69 B
Fantasy and Variations (Dello Joio) — 3/9/62 C
Fantasy (Cowell) — 5/30/52 C
Fantasy for Piano and Orchestra — 11/17/54 C
Fantasy for Piano (Copland) — 10/25/57 C
Fantasy in Space — 10/28/52 C
Fantasy on One Note — 1/13/75 C
Fantasy Quartet for Oboe and Strings — 12/4/76 D
Fan, The — 6/8/30 A
Farber, Viola — 8/17/58 B
Farmer and the Fairy, The — 8/13/52 A
Farm Journal — 10/20/47 C
Farnham Festival — 5/22/65 A
Farrally, Betty — //38 E
Farrar, Ernest Bristow — 9/18/18 D
Farrar, Geraldine — 10/15/01 D; 11/26/06 D; 2/6/09 E; 12/28/10 A; 1/25/15 A; 3/31/17 E; 12/14/18 A; 4/22/22 E; 3/11/67 D
Farrell, Eileen — 2/13/20 D; 10/23/50 D; 12/6/60 D
Farrell, Suzanne — 8/16/45 D; 4/9/63 B; 12/10/63 B; 5/28/65 B; 4/21/66 B; 4/13/67 B; 1/18/68 B; 4/30/68 B; 5/2/68 B; 10/8/71 B; 5/14-31/75 B; 5/29/75 B; 1/22/76 B
Farren, Fred — 1/6/06 B; 1/14/06 B
Farron, Julia — 1/6/55 B; 1/1/57 B; 10/27/58 B
Farsa amorosa, La — 2/22/33 A
Farwell, Arthur — 12//01 E; 1/20/52 D
Fast Fantasy — 3/11/78 C
Fauchois, Rene — 3/4/13 A
Fauconnet, Guy-Pierre — 2/21/20 B
Faulkner, Geanie — 4/28/78 C
Faune et la Bergere, Le — 2/29/08 C
Faure, Gabriel — 8/27/00 A; 2/3/01 C; 6/26/05 E; 5/10/07 A; 11/12/10 E; 3/4/13 A; 3/14/19 C; 5/14/19 C; 11/4/24 D; 4/13/67 B; 7/25/74 C
Faust, Reinhold — 11/17/17 E
Fauvette des jardins, La — 11/7/72 C
Favero, Mafalda — 2/9/29 A
Favola del figlio cambiato, La — 1/13/34 A
Favola d'Orfeo, La — 9/6/32 A
Fearis, John S. — 9/2/32 D
Feast in Time of Plague, A — 11/24/01 A
Feast of Ashes — 9/30/62 B
Feast of Love, The — 11/1/64 C
Federal Music Project — 8/1/35 E; 10/30/35 E
Fedorova, Nina — 9/17/62 B; 5/22/75 B
Fedorova, Sophia — 5/19/09 B
Fedorovitch, Sophie — 4/24/46 B
Fedorov, Vladimir — 4/9/79 D

Fedra — 3/20/15 A
Feerique — 12/6/25 C
Feier der neuen Front — 11/30/33 C
Feiertagskantate — 9/12/75 C
Feldbrill, V. — 2/6/63 C
Feld, Eliot — 7/5/42 D; 3/31/67 B; 12/1/67 B; 10/3/68 B; 5/29/69 B; 6/27/69 B; 4/3/70 B; 10/21/70 B; 10/24/70 B; 4/20/71 B; 4/28/71 B; 1/6/72 B; 5/30/74 B; 6/2/74 B
Feld Ballet, Eliot — 5/30/74 B; 6/2/74 B
Feldman, Morton — 5/2/51 C; 2/10/52 C; 5/2/52 C; 10/17/54 C; 8/17/58 B; 10/11/63 C; 6/20/66 C; 11/25/68 C; 12/31/68 C; 2/26/69 C; 7/13/70 C; 4/9/72 C; 7/16/72 C; 8/31/72 C; 1/26/75 C; 1/18/76 C
Felsenstein, Walter — //47 E; 10/8/75 D
Feltzer, Willem — 6/10/18 E
Fenby, Eric — //28 E; 9/17/31 C
Fennimore und Gerda — 10/21/19 A
Fenster, Die — 5/11/17 A
Ferand, Ernst — 5/29/72 D
Feretti, Dom Paolo — 5/25/38 D
Fernandez, Royes — 4/20/60 B
Fernando — 8/18/18 A
Fern Hill — 12/19/61 C
Ferrari, Ermanno Wolf- — 2/1/39 A
Ferrari-Fontana, Edoardo — 1/2/14 A
Ferrier, Kathleen — 4/22/12 D; 10/8/53 D
Ferroud, Pierre Octave — 3/4/29 B; 8/17/36 D
Festa das igrejas — 4/22/42 C
Feste romane — 2/21/29 C
Festin, Le — 5/19/09 B
Festival Ballet (London) — 10/24/50 E
Festival de Royan — 4/6/71 C
Festival Fanfare — 10/10/40 C
Festival-Institute at Round Top — 6/4/76 E
Festival International de Lausanne — 6/2/56 E
Festival International Hector Berlioz — 9/17/79 E
Festival of American and Spanish Music — 10/14/64 E
Festival of Contemporary Music, International — 8/7/22 E
Festival of Israel — 7/30/68 E
Festival of Two Worlds — //58 E; 6/20/58 A; 7/3/59 B; 6/27/69 B; 5/25/77 E — see also Spoleto
Festival Overture — 11/19/23 C
Festival Prelude — 10/19/13 E
Festival Te Deum — 5/12/37 C
Festlicher Hymnus — 6/2/51 C
Festmarsch — 11/21/01 A
Festmusik — 6/11/40 E; 10/27/40 C
Fete Galante — 8/6/06 B
Feuermann, Emanuel — 11/22/02 D; 1/2/35 D; 5/25/42 D
Feuersnot — 11/21/01 A
Fevrier, Henri — 1/14/19 A; 7/6/57 D
Fevrier, Jacques — 1/5/32 C
Fiamma, La — 1/23/34 A
Fiddler's Child — 11/14/17 C
Fiedler, Arthur — 5/7/30 E; 5/28/43 C; 7/4/76 E; 7/10/79 D; 7/15/79 E
Fiedler, Max — 2/12/09 C
Field Dances — 7/17/63 B
Field, John — 4/5/51 B; 11/7/56 E
Fifer, Bruce — 4/3/75 C
Fifield, Elaine — 11/16/48 B; 3/13/51 B; 5/5/56 B
Figlia de Jorio, La — 12/4/54 A
Figoni, Yoland — 1/20/22 B
Figure humaine — 3/25/45 C
Figures, Doubles and Prismes — 1/10/64 C
Figus-Bystry, Viliam — 8/1/28 A
Fille mal gardee, La (Alonso) — 5/21/52 B
Fille mal gardee, La (Ashton) — 1/28/60 B
Filling Station — 1/6/38 B
Filomela e l'Infatuato — 3/31/28 A

Final Alice, The — 7/4/76 E; 10/7/76 C
Final Ingredient, The — 4/11/65 A
Finck, Hermann — //09 E
Finck, Hermine — 3/3/32 D
Fine Arts Quartet — 10/11/71 C
Fine, Vivian — 4/29/60 B
Finials — 3/22/59 B
Finland Awakes — 7/2/00 C
Finlandia — 7/2/00 C; 9/20/57 D
Finney, Ross Lee — 12/23/06 D; 4/23/70 C; 11/1/72 C; 11/5/72 C
Finnish Fantasy — 3/26/10 C
Finto Arlecchino, Il — 12/15/32 A
Finzi, Gerald — 7/14/01 D
Fiocca, Felipe — 4/24/42 B
Fioriture — 6/17/60 C
Firebird (Balanchine) — 11/27/49 B
Firebird, The (Fokine) — 6/25/10 B; 1/17/16 B; 3/20/35 B; 8/22/42 D
Firebird, The (Stravinsky) — 7/27/37 E; 7/29/48 E; 4/6/71 D
Fire fragile flight — 4/21/74 C
Fires of London, The (musical group) — 1/20/72 C
Fireworks — 6/17/08 C
Firkusny, Rudolf — 2/11/12 D; 6/14/20 D; 1/13/38 D; 11/2/45 C; 12/31/48 C; 11/20/49 C; 10/4/56 C; 10/22/68 E
Firsova, Elena — 11/18/79 E
First Cantata (Webern) — 7/12/46 C
First Chamber Symphony (Schoenberg) — 3/31/13 C
First Essay for Orchestra (Barber) — 11/5/38 C
Fischer-Dieskau, Dietrich — 5/28/25 D; 5/2/55 D; 9/1/63 C; 4/30/74 C
Fisher, Avery R. — //37 E
Fisher, Jules — 10/21/70 B
Fisher, Juliet — 8/17/62 B
Fisherman and His Wife, The — 5/8/70 A
Fistoulari, Anatole — 8/20/07 D
Fitelberg, Gregor — 5/20/03 D; 2/6/06 C; 3/26/09 C; 6/3/22 A; 10/9/32 C; 10/6/33 C
Fitelberg, Jerzy — 5/20/03 D
Fitziu, Anna — 1/28/16 A
Fitz, Richard — 2/24/76 C
Five Bagatelles — 10/15/60 C
Five Canons on Latin Texts — 8/5/51 C
Five Concepts for Orchestra — 2/6/63 C
Five Dances (Bartok) — 11/19/23 C
Five Movements — 7/5/62 C
Five Movements for String Quartet (Webern) — 2/8/10 C
Five Orchestral Songs on Picture-Postcard Texts of Peter Altenberg (Berg) — 3/31/13 C
Five Picture Studies — 11/13/31 C
Five Pieces for David Tudor — 6/19/60 C
Five Pieces for Orchestra (Schoenberg) — 9/3/12 C; 10/16/12 C; 1/17/14 D; 12/18/14 C; 7/13/51 D
Five Pieces for Orchestra (Webern) — 6/22/26 C; 11/19/26 C; 1/14/37 E
Five Pieces for Piano (Sessions) — 10/24/77 C
Five Preludes (Scriabin) — 4/15/15 E
Five Sacred Songs (Webern) — 10/9/24 C
Five Songs After Poems by Richard Dehmel — 5/26/62 C
Five Songs from Der siebente Ring — 6/6/19 C
Five Songs on Poems of Stefan George — 2/10/40 C
5 Stucke — 5/30/56 C
Five Tudor Portraits — 9/25/36 C
Five Variants on Dives and Lazarus — 6/10/39 C
Five Variations — 11/10/45 C
Flagstad, Kirsten — 2/2/35 D; 2/14/41 D; 6/9/45 E; 8/1/49 E; 5/22/50 C; 12/7/62 D
Flames of Paris — 11/7/32 B
Flaming Angel, The — 9/14/55 A
Flanagan, William — 3/4/65 C
Fleg, Edmond — 11/30/10 A

Fleischer, Leon — 7/23/28 D; 11/4/44 D
Fleischmann, Julius — 1/30/38 E
Flemish Music School — *see* Royal Flemish Conservatory
Flem, Paul le — 12/22/35 E
Flesch, Carl — 11/14/44 D
Fleta, Miguel — 2/14/22 A; 4/25/26 A; 5/30/38 D
Fletcher, Dr. Harvey — //58 E
"Fleury Playbook" (manuscript) — 12/6/79 C
"Flight of the Bumblebee" — 11/3/00 A
Flindt, Flemming — 6/30/36 D; 4/6/64 B; 5/11/66 B; 2/19/72 B
Flivver 10,000,000, a Joyous Epic: Fantasy for Orchestra — 4/15/27 C
Florentinische Tragodie, Eine — 1/30/17 A
Florida State Symphony Orchestra — 1/22/51 C
Flos Campi — 10/19/25 C
Flothius, Marius — 10/30/14 D
Floyd, Carlisle — 2/24/55 A; 7/16/58 A; 10/11/62 A; 12/2/63 A; 3/31/66 A; 1/22/70 A; 2/29/76 A
Flugel, Gertrude — 1/23/42 C
Flut, Die — 12/20/46 A
Flute of Pan, The — 6/28/78 B
Flute Sonata No. 3 — 11/21/77 C
Foerster, August — 3/18/24 E
Foerster, Josef Bohuslav — 2/28/36 A; 5/29/51 D
Fogg, Eric — 12/19/39 D
Fokine Ballet — 2/26/24 B
Fokine, Michel — 12/26/04 B; 2/23/07 B; 4/28/07 B; 11/25/07 B; 12/22/07 B; 3/21/08 B; 3/21/08 B; 5/19/09 B; 6/2/09 B; 3/5/10 B; 5/20/10 B; 6/4/10 B; 6/18/10 B; 6/25/10 B; 4/19/11 B; 4/26/11 B; 6/6/11 B; 6/13/11 B; 11/30/11 B; 5/14/12 B; 5/20/12 B; 6/8/12 B; 5/10/13 B; 4/16/14 B; 5/14/14 B; 5/21/14 B; 6/2/14 B; 1/17/16 B; 2/26/24 B; 8/19/29 D; 3/20/35 B; 6/25/36 B; 10/23/37 B; 6/19/38 B; 6/30/39 B; 10/31/39 B; 11/16/40 B; 10/27/41 B; 8/22/42 D; 11/29/42 B; 9/20/60 D; 5/26/78 D
Foldes, Andor — 3/16/47 C
Fondements de la musique dans la conscience humaine (book) — 2/20/69 D
Fontana, Edoardo Ferrari — 7/4/36 D
Fonteyn, Margot — 5/18/19 D; 11/26/35 B; 2/11/36 B; 11/10/36 B; 2/16/37 B; 4/27/37 B; 2/2/39 B; 1/23/40 B; 1/14/42 B; 4/6/43 B; 2/20/46 B; 4/24/46 B; 11/12/46 B; 2/11/48 B; 5/22/48 B; 11/25/48 B; 12/23/48 B; 10/9/49 B; 2/2/50 B; 4/5/51 B; 9/3/52 B; 6/2/53 B; 1/1/56 E; 2/15/56 B; 5/5/56 B; 10/27/58 B; 2/21/62 E; 3/12/63 B; 11/27/63 B; 2/9/65 B; 2/23/67 B; 3/24/70 B
Foote, Arthur — 7/20/21 E; 4/8/37 D
Forains, Les — 3/2/45 B
Ford, Gerald R. — 4/1/76 E
Foreman, Richard — 8/24/74 A
Forest, Lee de — 12/1/15 E; 6/30/61 D
Forest of Three — 5/23/53 B
For Piano I — 2/10/52 C
For Poulenc — 4/26/72 C
For Red Petrograd — 4/24/25 A
Forrester, Maureen — 7/25/30 D
Forrest, Hamilton — 12/10/30 A
Forsell, John — 9/26/15 A
Forster, E.M. — 12/1/51 A
Forsyth, Cecil — 3/7/14 E
For the Fallen — 12/16/43 C
For the Hammer and the Sickle — see Life for the Tsar, A
Fortner, Wolfgang — 10/12/07 D; 5/25/57 A; 10/15/60 C; 5/10/62 A

Fort Worth Symphony Orchestra — 4/22/79 C
Forty Nine Waltzes for the Five Boroughs — 11/21/77 B; 5/11/78 C
For Valor — 10/8/07 C
Forzano, Giovacchino — 4/30/17 A; 12/14/18 A; 5/2/21 A
Foss, Bob — 7/15/75 D
Foss, Lukas — 8/15/22 D; 5/15/44 C; 9/3/44 C; 2/4/45 C; 3/7/47 C; 8/19/47 B; 12/31/48 C; 3/10/50 C; 5/18/50 A; 10/7/51 C; 3/11/53 C; 11/6/55 A; 10/24/58 C; 10/20/60 C; 10/29/63 E; 11/11/63 C; 11/15/63 D; 12/8/64 C; 10/30/66 C; 3/5/67 C; 4/27/67 C; 11/13/73 C; 11/1/77 C; 12/1/77 C; 4/28/78 C; 1/29/79 C
Foster, Lawrence — 6/1/72 C; 12/12/77 C
Foulds, John — 9/5/12 C
Foundations of Orchestration (book) — 6/21/08 D
Fountain of Bakhchisaray, The — 9/28/34 B
Fountains of Rome — 3/11/17 C
Four Bagatelles — 1/10/74 B
Four Etudes — 11/7/30 C
Four Freedoms, The — 9/26/43 C
Four Guigno — 6/10/18 D
Four Hungarian Moods — 1/13/44 C
Four Instruments — 1/18/76 C
Four Interludes from a Tragedy — 2/10/69 C
Four Marys, The — 3/23/65 B
Fournier, Pierre — 7/24/06 D
Four-Note Opera — 5/11/72 A
Four Orchestral Pieces — 1/9/22 C
Four Orchestral Songs on Poems of Maeterlinck — 3/31/13 C
Four Pieces for Violin and Piano — 4/24/11 C
Four Psalms — 10/31/64 C
Four Rhapsodies — 11/29/04 C
Four Russian Songs — 2/21/55 C
Four Saints in Three Acts — 2/8/34 A
Four Seasons, The — 12/20/01 C; *see also Saisons, Les*
Four Songs for Voice and Orchestra (Webern) — 2/16/28 C
Four Songs (Schoenberg) — 7/13/51 D
Four Stefan George Songs — 10/29/66 C
Four Temperaments, The (Hindemith) — 11/20/46 B
Four Temperaments, The (Nielsen) — 12/1/02 C
4'33" — 8/29/52 C
Four Tondichtungen Nach Arnold Bocklin — 10/12/13 C
Fowler, Ferguson, Kingston & Rueben — 9/7/79 E
Fox, James — 12/19/11 B
Fox-Strangeways, Arthur Henry — 1/1/20 E; 6/8/34 E; 5/2/48 D
Fox, Virgil — 5/3/12 D
Foyer de danse — 10/9/32 B
Fra Angelico — 3/21/68 C
Fracci, Carla — 8/20/36 D
Frager, Malcolm — 5/25/60 E
Fra Gherardo — 5/16/28 A
Frampton, Eleanor — 10/28/28 B
Franca, Celia — 6/25/21 D; 2/6/48 B; //51 E; 2/1/55 B
Francaix, Jean — 5/23/12 D; 12/15/34 C; 5/22/48 B; 7/1/51 A; 8/7/54 A; 3/31/61 C; 1/26/70 C; 3/15/74 C; 9/30/75 C; 6/18/78 C
Francesca da Rimini (Rachmaninoff) — 1/24/06 A
Francesca da Rimini (Zandonai) — 2/19/14 A
Francescatti, Zino — 8/9/02 D; 11/16/45 C
Frances, Esteban — 11/14/51 B; 11/9/55 B; 11/23/67 B; 6/1/69 B
Franchetti, Aldo — 2/14/48 D
Franck, Cesar — 2/24/46 B; 12/13/48 B
Franck, J.M. — 6/19/29 B
Francois, Samson — 10/22/70 D
Frank, Bill — 12/17/67 B

Franke, Dr. Herbert W. — 9/18/79 E
Frankel, Emily — 8/3/55 B
Frankenstein, Alfred — 10/5/06 D
Frankie and Johnny — 6/19/38 B
Franklin, Frederic — 4/5/38 B; 5/5/38 B; 7/21/38 B; 5/11/39 B; 10/26/39 B; 10/16/42 B
Franzl, Willy — 5/9/24 B
Fraser, Moyra — 1/14/42 B
Frau ohne Schatten, Die — 10/10/19 A
Frederick, Kurt — 11/4/48 C
Freed, Isadore — 5/13/52 C
Freedom Morning — 9/28/43 C
Freedom's Singer — 7/20/50 A
Free Lance, The — 3/27/06 A
Freeman Etudes — 4/28/78 C
Free Song, A — 3/26/43 C
Fremaux, Louis — 11/6/69 E
Fremde Erde — 12/10/30 A
Fremstad, Olive — 11/25/03 D; 4/18/06 E; 1/22/07 A; 4/23/14 E; 4/21/51 D
French, Leslie — 5/5/31 B
Freni, Mirella — 2/27/35 D
Frescoes — 7/21/71 C
Freud, Sigmund — 8/6/69 D
Fricsay, Ferenc — 8/9/14 D; 8/6/47 A; 2/20/63 D
Friedenstag — 7/24/38 A
Friedlander, Dr. Max — 5/2/34 D
Friends and Enemies of Modern Music, Commitee of — 5/19/39 B

Fris, Inger — 11/19/24 B
Frohman, Max — 5/14/12 B
Froissart — 10/3/00 C; 2/23/34 D
Frol Skobeyev — 2/24/50 A
From All Our Hearts — 1/16/51 A; 4/19/51 E; 4/24/51 E; 5/28/58 E
"From Hanover Square North at the End of a Tragic Day the Voice of the People Again Arose" (Ives) — 5/7/15 E
From Here — 10/11/63 C
From Maine to Georgia — 1/22/17 E
Fromm Players — 8/9/64 C
From the Apocalypse — 12/8/12 C
From the Black Belt — 3/20/27 C
From the Diary of Virginia Woolf — 1/5/75 C; 5/5/75 E
From the House of the Dead — 4/12/30 A
From the Middle Ages — 1/3/03 C
From the Northland — 5/27/24 C
Frontier — 4/28/35 B
Fruhlingswogen — 7/16/17 D
Ft. Lauderdale Symphony Orchestra — 3/29/60 C
Fuchs, Joseph — 4/26/00 D; 10/14/60 C
Fuchs, Lukas — *see* Foss, Lukas
Fuchs, Peter Paul — 3/16/69 A
Fuchs-Robettin, Hanna — 11/1/79 C
Fuego nuevo, El — 11/4/28 B; 8/2/78 D
Fuerst, George — 2/5/36 D
Fuge aus der Geographie — 6/17/30 C
Fugere, Lucien — 11/20/01 A
Fugue for Piano — 2/10/52 C
Fugue on a Victory Tune — 10/21/44 C
Fukuyama, Makato — 6/29/75 B
Fuleihan, Anis — 2/26/45 C; 10/11/70 D
Fundamentals of the Classic Dance (book) — //34 E
Funeral Music (Hindemith) — 1/22/36 C
Furse, Roger — 7/4/40 B
Furtwangler, Wilhelm — //22 E; //26 E; 7/1/27 C; 12/2/28 C; 2/9/31 C; 4/15/32 C; 4/17/32 E; 10/31/32 C; 3/27/33 C; 4/10/33 E; 11/15/33 E; 3/12/34 C; 12/4/34 E; 1//35 E; 4/25/35 E; 3/14/36 E; 12/17/46 E; 11/28/47 E; 2/22/48 C; 1/19/49 E; 5/22/50 C; 11/30/54 D; 2/27/55 E

— G —

Gable, Christopher — 10/11/60 B; 2/14/61 B; 2/9/65 B
Gabo, Naum — 4/30/27 B
Gabor, Arnold — 2/10/34 A
Gabovich, Mikhail — 11/21/45 B
Gabrilowitsch, Ossip — 11/12/00 D; 11/16/00 E; 10/6/09 E; //31 E; 4/1/33 E; 10/30/35 D; 9/14/36 D
Gac, Yan Le — 12/12/75 B
Gadski, Johanna — 2/22/32 D; 12/22/50 D
Gaetani, Raimonda — 5/5/78 B
Gageure imprevue, La — 7/4/44 A
Gagok — 4/4/73 C
Gain, Richard — 8/17/62 B; 9/6/63 B
Gaite Parisienne — 4/5/38 B; 1/27/78 B
Galanta Dances — 3/6/67 D
Gala Performance — 12/5/38 B
Galaxy — 5/18/56 B
Galjow, Warren — 10/28/52 C
Gallantry — 3/19/58 A
Galli-Curci, Amelita — 11/18/16 D; 1/28/18 D; 11/14/21 D; 11/26/63 D
Galway, James — 12/8/39 D
Gamelan — 9/30/62 B
Ganne, Louis — 4/21/02 B
Gantvoort, Arnold — 5/18/37 D
Ganz, Rudolph — 11/11/21 E
Garbousova, Raya — 4/5/46 C
Garcia-Lorca, Federico — //32 E
Garcia, Manuel Patricio — 7/1/06 D
Garden, Mary — 4/10/00 D; 2/18/02 A; 4/30/02 A; 11/25/07 D; 2/19/08 A; 11/27/08 A; 1/14/19 A; 12/10/30 A; 1/3/67 D
Garden of Death, The — 5/4/08 C
Garden of Fand, The — 10/29/20 C
Garden of Kama, The — 2/22/15 B
Gardner, John — 3/2/17 D
Gargoyles for Violin Solo and Synthesized Sound — 5/9-10/61 E
Garrard Engineering — //15 E; 9//59 E
Gaskell, Sonia — //61 E
Gaspard de la Nuit — 5/29/75 B
Gassamann, Remi — 3/22/61 B
Gati, Laszlo — 11/23/79 C
Gatti-Casazza, Giulio — 11/16/08 D; 2/15/09 E; 3/18/10 A; 3/8/17 A; 3/12/19 A; 5/10/35 D; 9/2/40 D; 4/22/72 E
Gatty, Nicholas Comyn — 3/1/06 A; 5/21/21 A
Gaubert, Phillippe — 11/22/08 D
Gaudeamus — 3/18/19 A
Gaudeamus Music Week — 8/31/57 E
Gauk, Alexander — 1/21/30 C
Gaulle, Charles de — 6/20/65 C
Gavazzeni, Gianandrea — 7/25/09 D
Gayane (Anisimova) — 12/9/42 B
Gayane (Khachaturian) — 5/1/78 D
Gaziel — 10/27/06 A
"Gebrauchsmusik" — 12/28/63 D
Gedalge, Andre — 2/5/26 D
Gedda, Nicolai — 7/11/25 D; 1/15/58 A
Geheime Konigreich, Das (Krenek) — 5/6/28 A
Geheimuis des entwendelen Briefes, Das — 2/14/75 A
Geigy and Company, J. R. — 6/6/58 C
Geigy Festival Concerto — 6/6/58 C
Geissler, Louis — 11/14/36 D
Gelsenkirchen Symphony Orchestra — 2/19/69 C
Geltzer, Yekaterina — 6/14/27 B
Gencer, Leila — 1/26/57 A
Genee, Adeline — 3/18/01 B; 1/6/06 B; 5/14/06 B; 9/7/08 B; 12/31/20 E; 10/19/30 E; //36 E
Genee, Alexandre — 9/7/08 B
General Phonograph Company — //26 E

General Slocum, The — 11/29/70 C
Genese — 10/7/58 C
Genesis — 11/18/45 C
Genesis of a Music (book) — //49 E
Gennett Records — //18 E
Gentele, Goeran — 9/20/17 D; 7/18/72 D
George V, King (G. Br.) — 6/22/11 C; 3/11/12 C
George, Carolyn — 11/15/55 B
George, Stefan — 12/21/08 C; 4/10/27 C; 6/4/30 C; 11/1/79 C
Georgiades, Thrasybulos — 1/4/07 D; 3/15/77 D
Georgiadis, Nicholas — 10/11/60 B; 7/15/62 B; 7/13/63 B; 2/29/68 B; 9/1/72 B; 5/7/74 B; 2/14/78 B
Gerdt, Pavel — 12/15/01 B; 11/25/07 B; 3/21/08 B; 8/11/17 D; 10/29/24 B
Gerelli, Ennio — 2/12/07 D
Gerhard, Roberto — 2/2/50 B; 6/27/51 A; 10/28/59 C; 2/8/61 C; 4/1/64 C; 4/25/65 C; 12/14/67 C; 8/23/69 C
Gerlach, Horst — 10/23/33 E
German Opera Ballet — 11/30/66 B
German Tonkunstler Verein — 6/12/37 E
Gernsback, Hugo — 11/1/23 E
Gerryflappers — 3/11/67 D
Gershwin, George — 2/12/24 C; 12/3/25 C; 12/13/28 C; 1/29/32 C; 8/16/32 C; 4/10/33 C; 1/14/34 C; 9/30/35 A; 2/2/37 E; 7/11/37 D; //41 E; 7/3/45 E; 12/26/55 E; 2/5/70 B
Gerster, Etelka — 8/20/20 D
Gerville-Reache, Jeanne — 2/19/08 A
Gesang der Junglinge, Der — 5/30/56 C
Geschaftsbericht — 4/29/67 A
Gesellschaft der Musikfreunde — 9/18/13 E; 2/6/46 D
Gesicht Jesajas, Das — 6/18/55 D
"Gesprochene Musik" — 6/17/30 C
Gewandhaus Orchestra of Leipzig — 10/13/08 C; 12/15/10 C
Gezeichneten, Die — 4/25/18 A
Ghedini, Giorgio Federico — 9/9/37 A; 1/26/39 A; 2/15/40 A; 9/7/49 A; 3/10/56 A
Gheusi, P.B. — 10/23/01 A
Ghiaurov, Nicolai — 9/13/29 D
Ghisalberti, Mario — 3/5/31 A; 2/12/36 A
Giacosa, Giuseppe — 1/14/00 A; 2/17/04 A
Giannini, Dusolina — 12/19/02 D; 5/26/37 C
Giannini, Vittorio — 10/19/03 D; 10/20/34 A; 1/19/36 C; 5/26/37 C; 6/2/38 A; 11/24/38 A; 2/14/46 A; 1/31/53 A; 3/13/54 E; 5/27/60 C; 11/25/61 A; 2/15/62 A; 11/28/66 D; 3/9/67 A
Gianni Schicchi — 12/14/18 A
Giants in the Earth — 3/28/51 A; 5/7/51 E
Giara, La — 11/19/24 B
Giardino di Scarlatti — 7/13/79 B
Giardino religioso — 8/8/72 C
Gibson, Alexander — 9/2/72 C; 1/18/74 A
Gide, Andre — 4/30/34 B
Gielen, Michael — 5/4/71 C
Gierster, H. — 12/10/71 C
Gieseking, Walter — 2/22/26 D; 10/8/26 C; 1/25/49 E; 10/26/56 D

Gigli, Beniamino — 11/26/20 D; 1/2/25 D
Gigue — 3/31/29 B
Gilbert, David — 12/6/77 C
Gilbert, Henry F. — 12//01 E; 6/5/13 C; 3/23/18 A; 7/20/21 E; 5/19/28 D; 5/3/78 E
Gilbert, Sir William Schwenck — 11/22/00 D; 5/29/11 D
Gilels, Emil — 10/19/16 D; 5/22/38 E
Gilfond, Edythe — 5/10/46 B; 2/28/47 B
Gilgamesh — 8/27/53 D

Gilmour, Sally — 11/29/44 B; 6/2/47 B
Gilpin, John — 6/2/47 B; 10/24/50 E

Ginastera, Alberto — 4/11/16 D; 11/27/37 C; 7/18/41 C; 5/12/42 C; 5/12/44 C; 5/31/46 C; 10/29/49 C; 6/2/53 C; 10/20/54 C; 4/30/61 C; 4/13/63 C; 10/3/63 C; 7/24/64 A; 11/1/64 C; 5/7/65 E; 5/19/67 A; 9/10/71 A; 4/16/73 C; 1/18/74 C; 2/4/74 C; 12/13/79 C
Gioielli della Madonna, I — 12/23/11 A
Giordano, John — 4/22/79 C
Giordano, Umberto — 12/19/03 A; 3/17/10 A; 1/25/15 A; 3/7/20 A; 12/20/24 A; 11/12/48 D
"Giovinezza" — 5/14/31 E
Giraud, Albert — 10/16/12 C
Giselle — 6/18/10 B
Gismonda — 1/14/19 A
Gita — 8/10/67 C
Giulietta e Romeo — 2/14/22 A
Giulini, Carlo Maria — 5/9/14 D; 12/17/68 E; 10/26/78 D; 10/29/79 E
Giulio Cesare — 2/8/36 A
Give Me the Splendid Silent Sun — 4/27/61 C
Gladke, Peter — 4/22/48 B
Gladkovsky, Arseny — 4/24/25 A
Glagolitic Mass — 12/5/27 C
Glanville-Hicks, Peggy — 12/29/12 D; 4/4/54 A
Glaser, G.J.M. — 1/14/06 B
Glasgow Festival — 9/22/73 C
Glasser, Caren — 7/22/66 C
Glass, Frank — 1/24/50 B
Glassman, William — 3/17/65 B; 3/30/65 B
Glass, Philip — 5/19/68 C; 1/16/70 C; 11/10/70 C; 6/1/74 C; 5/6/75 C; 7/25/76 A; 5/11/78 C
Glazunov, Alexander — 1/17/00 B; 1/3/03 C; 2/20/00 B; 3/4/05 C; 3/19/05 E; 12/5/05 E; 3/11/06 C; 12/22/06 C; 5/16/07 E; 6/12/07 E; 6/18/07 E; 6/2/09 B; 3/26/10 C; 5/20/10 B; 6/25/10 B; 10/27/11 D; 3/15/15 C; 11/11/17 C; 7/29/18 E; 9/23/18 E; 6/15/28 E; 11/21/29 D; 10/14/33 C; 11/25/34 C; 3/21/36 D; 11/9/55 B; 5/5/56 B; 12/7/61 B; 9/17/62 B
Glebov, Igor — 1/27/49 D
Gli Amanti sposi — 2/19/25 A
Gli Dei a Tebe — 7/5/48 A
Gliere, Reinhold — 1/16/03 C; 2/2/05 E; 1/23/08 C; 3/23/12 C; 11/30/12 B; 12/23/25 C; 6/14/27 B; 4/5/31 B; 5/12/43 C; 10/30/45 C; 4/19/47 A; 3/14/49 B; 1/26/52 C; 6/23/56 D
Glinka, Mikhail — 5/16/07 E; 6/2/09 B; 12/3/24 C; 2/37/39 A; 1/6/53 B; 3/1/55 B; 11/23/67 B; 6/1/69 B
Glinka Prize — 12/10/04 E; 3/23/12 C; 12/5/58 C
Glinkiana — 11/23/67 B; 6/1/69 B
"Glitter, and Be Gay" — 10/29/56 A
Glockenspiel, Etude uber Tongemische — 10/19/54 C
Gloire, La — 2/26/52 B
Gloriana — 6/8/53 A
Gloria — 1/20/61 C; 1/30/63 D
Gloucester Music Festival — 9/7/04 C
Gluck, Alma — 11/16/09 D; 7/15/14 E
Gluck, Christoph Willibald — 2/25/44 B; 4/26/74 B
Gluckliche Hand, Die — 10/14/24 A; 4/11/30 B
Glyndebourne Festival — 5//34 E; //35 E; 6/20/47 A; 7/4/62 B; 7/19/70 A; 12/4/76 D
Glyndebourne Opera — 6/1/50 E
Glyndebourne Society Ltd. — //47 E
Gnessin, Mikhail — 5/6/57 D

Gobbi, Tito — 10/24/13 D; 3/10/56 A
Godard, Benjamin — 3/1/35 B
Godfrey, Sir Dan — 7/20/39 D
Godowsky, Leopold — 11/21/38 D
Gods Amused, The — 4/28/71 D
Gods Go A-Begging, The — 7/16/28 B
Godunov, Aleksander — 8/22/79 E; 9/16/79 E
Goebbels, Joseph — 4/10/33 E; 11/15/33 E;
   6/11/34 E; 12/6/34 E; 11/27/36 E;
   6/8/48 E; 2/14/49 E
Goehr, Alexander — 11/3/74 C
Goehr, Walter — 5/28/03 D; 3/19/44 C
Goergi, Yvonne — 7/1/50 D
Goetschius, Percy — 10/29/43 D
Goetz, Anselm — 10/9/16 E
Goldberg Variations, The — 7/30/70 B
Golden Age, The — 10/26/30 B
Golden Gate Park — 4/18/06 E
Golden Legend, The — 11/22/00 D
Golden Peacock, The — 1/23/78 C
Golden Ram, The — 6/16/64 A
Goldman Band — 11/15/26 E; 6/18/75 C
Goldman, Edwin Franko — 12/7/10 D;
   11/15/26 E
Goldman, Richard Franko — 12/7/10 D;
   6/18/75 C
Goldmark, Karl — 1/2/15 D
Goldmark, Peter Carl — 12/2/06 D; 6/21/48 E
Goldmark, Rubin — 12//01 E; 1/2/15 D;
   1/30/19 C; 1/18/23 C; 4/1/33 E; 3/6/36 D
Goldovsky, Boris — 6/7/08 D
Goldsand, Robert — 3/17/11 D
Goldsborough, Arnold — 10/11/60 E
Goldsborough Orchestra — 10/11/60 E
Goldschmidt, Berthold — 12/19/60 C
Goleizovsky, Kasian — 3/3/25 B
Golem, Der — 11/14/26 A
Golgotha — 4/29/49 C
Golisciani, Enrico — 12/4/09 A; 12/23/11 A
Gollner, Nana — 4/14/48 B
Golovine, Alexander — 5/19/08 A; 6/25/10 B;
   4/27/27 B
Golovine, Serge — 12/23/52 B
Golschmann, Vladimir — 6/19/26 C;
   1/28/27 A; //31 E; 12/10/44 C;
   12/16/44 C; 12/22/49 C; //58 E
Golyscheff, Jefim (Jef) — 4/30/19 C;
   5/24/19 C; 9/25/70 D
Gontcharova, Nathalie — 5/21/14 B;
   6/13/23 B; 3/20/35 B; 10/23/37 B;
   6/19/38 B; 10/20/38 B; 10/31/39 B;
   12/6/40 B
Goodall, Reginald — 6/7/45 A
Good-Humored Ladies, The (Massine) — 4/12/17 B
Goodman, Benny — 1/9/39 C; 11/6/50 C;
   12/11/50 C
Goodman, Bernard — 10/4/73 C
Goodwin II, Francis — 1/19/76 D
Goossens, Eugene — 6/20/12 C; 10/13/14 C;
   1/14/16 A; 1/29/27 C; 5//27 E;
   6/25/29 A; //31 E; 6/24/37 A; 3/19/37 C;
   6/9/39 C; 4/12/40 C; 10/17/41 C;
   11/28/41 C; 11/27/42 C; 12/11/42 C;
   9/5/50 C; 3/9/56 E; 6/13/62 D
Goossens, Leon — 9/30/44 C
Gordon, Gavin — 5/20/35 B
Gordon, Jacques — 8/22/30 E
Gordon, Nicholas — 9/15/48 D
Gordon Quartet — 8/22/30 E
Gore, Walter — 5/20/35 B; 11/29/44 B;
   6/2/47 B; 11/11/52 B
Gorin, Igor — 10/26/08 D
Goritz, Otto — 12/28/10 A; 12/9/13 A
Gorodnitzki, Sascha — 5/24/05 D
Gorriz, Maria — 7/27/71 B
Gorshykov, G. — 4/8/31 B
Gorsky, Alexander — 2/2/02 B; 1/31/23 B
Gotham Symphony Orchestra — 10/21/36 C
Gottschalk, Louis — 6/12/51 B; 1/7/64 B

"Gott strafe England" — 7/15/16 E
Gould, Diana — 2/25/30 B; 5/15/34 B;
   10/28/34 B
Gould, Glenn — 9/25/32 D; 10/20/60 C
Gould, Morton — 12/10/13 D; 7/31/38 C;
   2/9/41 C; 2/22/41 C; 1/22/43 C;
   3/5/43 C; 8/25/43 C; 6/1/45 B;
   2/16/47 C; 4/22/48 B; 1/6/49 C;
   4/13/52 C; 2/10/57 C; 2/2/57 C;
   10/26/65 B; 4/1/76 C
Gounod, Charles — 1/8/58 B
Gounod Symphony — 1/8/58 B
Govrin, Gloria — 12/7/61 B
Goyescas — 3/11/11 C; 1/28/16 A
Gradmann-Luscher, Marguerite — 2/10/40 C;
   12/5/43 C
Graduation Ball — 2/28/40 B
Graener, Paul — 11/15/33 E; 5/24/37 E;
   11/13/44 D
Graeser, Wolfgang — 6/13/28 D
Graffiti — 5/2/65 C
Graffman, Gary — 3/15/68 C
Graf, Herbert — 4/10/03 D; 4/5/73 D
Graham-Lujan, James — 3/10/53 B
Graham, Martha — 4/11/30 B; 2/2/31 B;
   4/28/35 B; 8/6/38 B; //39 E; 12/27/39 B;
   8/11/40 B; 7/18/43 B; 12/26/43 B;
   10/30/44 B; 1/23/46 B; 5/10/46 B;
   2/27/47 B; 2/28/47 B; 5/3/47 B;
   1/4/50 B; 12/5/51 B; 5/8/55 B;
   4/12/57 C; 4/1/58 B; 5/14/59 B;
   4/27/60 B; 4/29/60 B; 4/16/61 B;
   3/4/62 B; 3/6/62 B; 9/6/63 B; 2/21/67 B;
   5/25/68 B; 7/21/68 B; 5/2/73 B;
   6/26/78 B; 6/27/78 B; 6/28/78 B
Grahn, Lucile — 4/4/07 D
Grainger, Percy — 2/11/15 D; 3/10/16 C;
   2/20/61 D
Gramm, Donald — 2/26/27 D; 1/10/64 D;
   10/11/77 C E
Gramophone Company — 5//00 E; 4/11/02 E;
   4/30/03 E; 11/10/03 E; 8//04 E; //09 E;
   9/17/31 E; //32 E
Gramophone Shop Encyclopedia of Recorded Music
   (book) — 11/19/36 E
Gramophone, The (periodical) — //23 E
Granados, Enrique — 10/27/06 A; 3/11/11 C;
   2/8/15 E; 1/28/16 A; 3/24/16 D
Grand Ballet de Monte Carlo — 2/22/61 D
Grand Ballet du Marquis de Cuevas —
   2/22/61 D
Grand Bamboula for String Orchestra — 3/20/72 C
Grand Canyon Suite — 11/22/31 C
Grande Aulodia fur Flute, Oboe and Orchestra —
   2/7/70 C
Grandes Ballets Canadiens, Les — //57 E
Grandjany, Marcel — 2/24/75 D
Grand Macabre, Le — 3/17/78 A
Grand Opera Company (Chicago) —
   1/30/35 C
Grand Opera House (San Francisco) —
   4/18/06 E
Grant, Alexander — 2/2/50 B; 4/5/51 B;
   12/12/51 B; 10/27/58 B; 1/28/60 B;
   12/12/62 B; 4/2/64 B
Gray-Lhevinne, Estelle — 5/23/33 D
Grazina — 11/26/55 C
Great American Goof, The — 1/11/40 B
Great Friendship — 9/28/47 A
Great Learning, The — 8/24/72 C
Great-Russian Orchestra — 3/11/06 C
Greek Passion, The — 6/9/61 C
Greenberg, Noah — 4/9/19 D; //52 E;
   1/9/66 D
Green, Douglass M. — 1/8/27 C; 11/1/79 C
Green Mansions — 10/17/37 A
Green, Ray — 8/6/38 B
Green Table, The — 7/3/32 B
Greenwich Orchestra — 5/25/38 C

Gregorian chant — 5/17/01 E; 11/22/03 E;
   1/18/30 D; 12/4/63 E; 3/30/66 C
Gregor, Josef — 7/24/38 A; 10/15/38 A;
   9/8/49 D; 8/14/52 A
Gregorovich, Yuri — 3/23/61 B
Gregory, Cynthia — 7/8/46 D; 3/31/67 B;
   12/1/67 B; 12/4/69 B; 7/1/71 B
Gregory Fistoulari — 8/20/07 D
Greig, Edvard — 4/27/27 B
Greitzer, Sol — 11/2/78 C
Gretchaninoff, Alexander — 10/27/03 A;
   2/2/05 E; 3/3/11 C; 10/25/12 A;
   5/29/24 C; 1/3/56 D
Grew, Joseph Clark — 12/7/41 E
Grey, Beryl — 11/12/46 B; 12/12/51 B;
   5/5/56 B
Greysteel — 3/1/06 A
Gribov, Alexander — 4/27/57 B; 3/23/61 B
Grieg, Edvard — 5/29/06 E; 9/4/07 D;
   10/8/08 A; 6/25/10 B
Griffelkin — 11/6/55 A
Griffes, Charles Tomlinson — 11/16/19 C;
   11/28/19 C; 12/19/19 C; 4/8/20 D
Griffith, D.W. — 2/8/15 E; 3/12/19 A
Grigorieva, Tamara — 6/30/39 B
Grigoriev, Serge — 6/5/19 B; 6/17/38 E
Grigorovich, Yuri — 1/2/27 D; 4/27/57 B;
   4/9/68 B; 12/25/69 B; 2/16/75 B
Grillo del focolare, Il — 11/28/08 A
Grindin, Anatoli — 4/27/57 B
Gris du monde — 6/2/31 C
Griselidis — 11/20/01 A
Grisi, Giulia — 9/27/19 D
Gris, Juan — 7/16/28 B
Grofe, Ferde — 11/22/31 C; 4/23/60 C;
   2/10/61 C; 4/22/64 C
Grogan, Walter — 11/11/09 A
Gropius, Manon — 4/19/36 C
Gropius, Walter — 4/19/36 C
"Grossdeutschland zum 10 April" — 3/24/38 E
Grossmann, Ferdinand — 12/5/70 D
Group for Contemporary Music — //62 E;
   2/17/64 C; 12/13/65 C; 3/21/66 A;
   10/28/68 C; 12/15/75 C; 10/24/77 C;
   11/6/78 C; 12/18/78 C
Groves, Charles — 3/10/15 D
Grove's Dictionary of Music and Musicians (book) —
   4/11/59 D
Grove, Sir George — 5/28/00 D
Growing Castre, The — 8/13/68 A
Gruenberg, Louis — 11/27/26 C; 4/30/32 E;
   1/7/33 A; 10/17/37 A; 6/9/64 D
Grumiaux, Arthur — 3/21/21 D
Grummer, Elisabeth — 3/31/11 D
Gruppen — 3/24/59 C
Gsovsky, Victor — //74 E
Guarnieri, Camargo — 4/20/58 C
Guastalla, Claudio — 4/26/23 A; 11/18/27 A;
   7/23/33 A; 1/23/34 A
Gubaidulina, Sofia — 11/18/79 E
Guerin, Jules — 11/4/29 E
Guerra, La — 2/25/56 A
Guerro, Rosario — 5/7/03 B
Guests, The — 1/20/49 B
Guevara, Che — 11/9/68 E
Guilmant, Alexandre — 3/29/11 D
Guiterman, Arthur — 5/12/37 A
Guntram — 10/22/40 A
Guridi, Jesus — 5/22/20 A
Gurlitt, Louis — 4/29/72 D
Gurlitt, Manfred — 4/29/72 D
Gurlitt Opera Company — 4/29/72 D
Gurlitt, Wilibald — //59 E
Gurre-Lieder — 2/23/13 C; 7/13/51 D
Gusey, Pytor — 4/27/27 B
Gutheil-Schroder, Marie — 12/21/08 C
Guttoveggio, Joseph — *see* Creston, Paul
Gylfond, E. — 8/11/40 B

— H —

Haas, Joseph — 3/30/60 D
Haba, Alois — 7/31/21 C; 5/17/31 A; 10/15/60 C
Haberl, Franz Xaver — 9/5/10 D
Habit of Perfection, The — 4/26/75 D
Hacquart, Carolus — 7/7/20 A
Haddy, Arthur — //44 E
Hadley, Henry — 12/20/01 C; 12/27/07 C; 4/4/09 A; 6/6/11 C; 12/8/11 E; 8/10/12 A; //13 E; 12/26/17 A; 10/18/18 A; 1/31/20 A; 11/17/21 C; 8/6/26 E; 9/24/30 C; 6/2/35 C; 9/6/37 D
Hadzic, Nuri — 6/2/37 A
Haefliger, Ernest — 7/6/19 D
Hafner, Herbert — 6/23/50 C
Hageman, Richard — 5/2/26 E
Hagith — 5/13/22 A
Hagoromo — 1/5/76 D
Hague Philharmonic Orchestra — 11/20/04 E; 10/31/17 D; 11/11/38 D; 6/15/48 E; 4/2/49 D; 10/27/76 D
Hahn, Reynaldo — 5/14/12 B; 3/21/21 A; 1/28/47 D; 6/21/49 A
Haieff, Alexei — 1/13/47 B
Hail, California! — 6/19/15 C
Haitink, Bernard — 3/4/29 D
Halaphone — 3/3/72 C
Halasz, Laszlo — 2/21/44 E; 5/28/52 E; 2/23/75 C
Hale, Philip — 11/30/34 D
Halffter, Cristobal — 3/13/54 C; 6/26/57 C; 5/30/70 C; 10/31/70 C; 2/3/73 C; 6/24/75 C; 5/3/76 C
Halffter, Ernesto — 1/16/05 D; 3/23/41 C
Halffter, Rodolfo — 6/26/42 C; 11/23/79 C
Halir, Varl — 10/19/05 C
Halle, Charles — 3/16/04 C
Halle Orchestra of Manchester — 3/16/04 C; 12/3/08 C; 1/14/53 C; 10/7/64 C
Hall, Olive — 11/30/37 A
Hamburg State Opera — 10/17/55 A; 10/12/66 A; 12/19/68 A; 6/20/69 A; 4/25/79 D
Hamerik, Asger — 7/13/23 D
Hamilton, Gordon — 5/22/48 B
Hamilton, Iain — 6/9/53 C; 9/8/72 C; 3/16/74 A; 10/19/74 C; 12/14/74 C
Hamlet (Helpmann) — 5/19/42 B
Hamlet (Searle) — 3/5/68 A
Hamlet (Sergeyev) — 12/12/70 B
Hamlin, George — 1/20/23 D
Hammarskjold, Dag — 8/18/66 C
Hammarskjold Portraits — 7/30/74 C
Hammerstein, Oscar — 11/16/06 E; 12/3/06 E; 8/1/19 D
Hammond, Laurens — //33 E; 2/2/39 E; 9/4/39 E; 12/15/72 D; 7/1/73 D
Hammond, Michael — 2/18/75 C
Hammond organ — //33 E; 4/12/34 D; 2/2/39 E; 9/4/39 E; 7/1/73 D
Hanau, Cesare — 11/4/04 A
Handbook of Conducting (book) — 6/1/29 E
Hand of Bridge, A — 6/17/59 A
Hanka, Erika — 11/16/57 B
Hanke, Susanne — 3/8/70 B
Hanon, Charles-Louis — 3/19/00 D
Hanslick, Eduard — 8/6/04 D
Hanson, Hans Olot — 8/4/68 C
Hanson, Howard — 5/30/23 C; 5/27/24 C; 2/20/30 C; 11/28/30 C; 10/29/31 C; 3/24/32 C; 5/20/33 A; 2/10/34 A; 9/19/37 C; 3/26/38 C; 11/3/39 C; 4/25/40 C; 12/3/43 C; 4/27/44 C; 5/1/44 E; 5/12/45 E; 10/23/45 C; 10/21/47 C; 12/31/48 C; 5/2/51 C; 2/18/55 C; 4/9/57 C; 1/23/58 C;

3/10/59 C; 4/27/61 C; 12/10/63 C; 10/31/64 C; 2/29/68 C
Happy Prince, The — 5/22/65 A
Harbinger — 3/31/67 B
Harcourt, Lewis V. — 7/23/12 E
Harkarvy, Benjamin — //59 E
Harker, Joseph — 3/18/01 B
Harkness Ballet — //64 E; 2/19/65 B; 2/21/65 B; 11/1/67 B; 11/9/67 B
Harkness, Rebekah — //64 E
Harlequinade — 2/4/65 B
Harmonia fur Blasinstruments, Harte, und Schlagzeuge — 1/22/74 C
Harmonie der Welt, Die (instrumental work) — 1/24/52 C;
Harmonie der West, Die (opera) — 8/11/57 A
Harmonielehre — 7/1/11 E
Harmony: Its Theory and Practice (book) — 12/5/09 D
Harnaise — 5/11/35 B
Har no Umi — 12/31/55 C
Harper, Heather — 5/8/30 D
Harpies, The — 5/25/53 A
Harris, Cyril — 1/24/68 E; 9/7/79 E
Harris, Leslie — 1/24/50 B
Harrison, Henry C. — //19 E; 5//24 E
Harrison, Jay S. — 9/12/74 D
Harrison, Lou — 5/14/17 D; 4/5/46 C; 12/14/47 B; 2/10/52 C; 5/14/59 A; 10/18/61 C; 9/30/62 B; 2/8/66 C; 8/17/68 C; 12/4/77 C; 5/11/78 C; 5/20/79 C
Harris, Roy — 4/30/32 E; 1/26/34 C; 1/13/35 C; 10/30/35 E; 2/28/36 C; 2/28/36 C; 2/24/39 C; 4/25/40 C; 6/25/40 C; 12/26/40 C; 2/22/41 C; 2/26/43 C; 3/14/44 C; 7/3/45 E; 4/5/49 C; 5/30/52 C; 11/20/52 C; 11/17/54 C; 9/15/55 C; 4/27/61 C; 1/17/62 C; 1/18/63 C; 5/10/64 C; 4/14/65 C; 2/8/68 C; 10/1/79 D
Harrold, Orville — 1/31/20 A
Harsanyi, Tibor — 5/5/46 B; 10/7/51 C
Harsanyi, Zsolt — 10/16/26 A
Hartford Symphony Orchestra — 1/19/76 D
Hartig, Heinz — 9/16/69 D
Hart, John — 1/14/42 B
Hartleben, Otto Erich — 10/16/12 C
Hartley, W. — 4/15/12 E
Hartmann, Karl Amadeus — 4/2/48 C; 4/21/51 C; 3/15/59 C; 12/5/63 D
Harty, Sir Hamilton — 12/3/34 C; 11/6/35 C; 2/19/41 D
Harvard University — 5/1/47 C
Harvest According, The — 10/1/52 B
Harvest, The — 11/25/61 A
Harvey, Peter — 4/9/63 B; 4/13/67 B
Harvey, Thomas F. — 1/15/44 E
Hary Janos — 10/16/26 A; 3/6/67 D
Hase, Dr. Helmuth von — 10/18/79 D
Hashish — 3/11/14 C
Haskell, Arnold — //47 E
Haskil, Clara — 12/7/60 D
Hassall, Christopher — 12/3/54 A
Hastings, Baird — 1//42 E
Hatch Memorial Shell — 5/7/30 E
Hattstaedt, John J. — 11/30/31 D
Haubenstock-Ramati, Roman — 7/30/68 E
Hauer, Josef Matthias — 6/7/13 C; 4/30/19 C; 11/12/29 C; 5/22/38 E; 5/17/49 E; 5/19/52 E; 9/22/59 D; 5/23/66 A; 10/21/69 C
"Hauermusik" — 12/28/63 D
Haunted Ballroom, The — 4/3/34 B
Havana Philharmonic — 12/28/30 C
Havemann, Gustav — 11/15/33 E
Hawaiian chant — 10/4/79 D
Hawkins, Erick — //09 D; 12/27/39 B; 8/11/40 B; 10/30/44 B; 1/23/46 B;

5/10/46 B; 2/27/47 B; 5/3/47 B; 8/13/48 B; 1/19/53 B; 11/24/57 B
Haydee, Marcia — 4/18/39 D; 11/7/65 B; 5/16/69 B; 12/22/73 B
Hayden, Melissa — 3/2/50 B; 12/4/51 B; 2/19/52 B; 1/6/53 B; 3/1/55 B; 12/19/56 B; 12/1/57 B; 1/17/58 B; 5/14/59 B; 11/16/60 B; 11/22/60 B; 1/17/62 B; 4/21/66 B; 4/28/66 B; 4/6/67 B; 11/23/67 B
Haydn, Franz Joseph — 5/19/62 C; //72 E; 10/24/73 B
Hayes, Roland — 9/28/43 C
Hays, David — 1/17/58 B; 5/14/59 B; 11/22/60 B; 12/7/60 B; 4/9/63 B
Headless Horseman, The — 3/5/37 A
Heart of the Hills, The — 6/28/38 B
Heaton, Anne — 10/11/60 B
Hebridean Symphony — 1/17/16 C
Heckelphone — //04 E
Heckel, Wilhelm — //04 E
Heckroth, Hein — 7/3/32 B
Heckscher Foundation Symphony Orchestra — 6/13/76 D
Hedeby, Kerstin — 4/20/60 B
Hedley, Arthur — 11/12/05 D
Heeley, Desmond — 1/1/57 B
Heger, Robert — 1/14/78 D
Heifetz, Benar — 1/16/28 C
Heifetz, Jascha — 2/2/01 D; 10/28/12 D; 9/10/17 E; 10/27/17 D; //31 E; 2/24/39 C; 12/7/39 C
Heiller, Anton — 9/15/23 D; 4/6/74 C; 4/8/75 C; 3/25/79 D
Heinz Hall (Pittsburg) — 9/10/71 E
Heirat wider Willen, Die — 4/14/05 A
Heldenleben, Ein — 11/13/68 C
Helene — 2/18/04 A
Helen of Troy — 11/29/42 B
Helen Retires — 2/28/34 A
Heliogabalus Imperator — 5/2/72 C
Helios — 10/8/03 C
Helle, Andre — 12/10/19 B
Hellman, Lillian — 10/29/56 A
Help! Help! The Globolinks! — 12/19/68 A
Helpmann, Robert — 4/9/09 D; 12/5/33 B; 4/3/34 B; 11/20/34 B; 2/11/36 B; 11/10/36 B; 4/27/37 B; 6/15/37 B; 2/2/39 B; 1/23/40 B; 1/14/42 B; 5/19/42 B; 4/6/43 B; 10/26/44 B; 2/20/46 B; 11/12/46 B; 11/25/48 B; 12/23/48 B; 10/9/49 B; 2/2/50 B
Helsinki Philharmonic — 7/2/00 C
Helvetia, the Land of Mountains, and Its People — 2/18/32 C
Hemming, Percy — 1/14/16 A
Hempel, Frieda — 12/27/12 D; 12/9/13 A; 10/7/55 D
Henderson, William James — 6/5/37 D
Hendl, Susan — 6/25/72 B
Hendl, Walter — 1/12/17 D; 2/27/47 C; 11/20/49 C
Henneberg, Claus H. — 4/29/71 A
Hennessey, Christine — 10/3/68 B
Henry, Pierre — 3/18/50 C; 6/14/52 B; 7/26/55 B; 4/3/67 B; 10/8/71 B; 1/17/74 B
Henschel, George — 3/25/18 E
Henze, Hans Werner — 7/1/26 D; 8/25/48 C; 12/12/48 C; 5/7/49 A; 12/1/49 C; 10/7/51 C; 11/29/51 C; 2/17/52 A; 12/4/53 A; 5/6/54 C; 9/23/56 A; 10/27/58 B; 5/22/60 A; 5/20/61 A; 4/24/63 C; 5/16/63 C; 10/9/63 C; 4/7/65 A; 8/6/66 A; 9/20/66 C; 4/6/67 C; 11/2/67 C; 5/16/68 C; 5/18/68 C; 9/29/68 C; 11/9/68 E; 2/14/69 C; 11/19/69 C; 2/11/71 C; 5/2/72 C; 11/2/72 C; 3/4/74 A; 10/20/74 C;

7/12/76 A; 8/2/78 C; 2/28/79 C;
5/23/79 C
Herbert, Victor — 1/23/00 E; 3/14/12 A;
2/13/14 E; 5/26/24 D
Herbstmusik — 5/4/74 C
Here and Now with Watchers — 11/24/57 B
Hereford (England) Festival — 9/9/03 C
Hermanas, Las — 7/13/63 B
Hermann, Bernard — 6/29/11 D; 12/16/43 C
"Hermann Goring March" — 10/23/33 E
Hermanns, Heida — 1/26/35 C
Herman, Woody — 3/25/46 C
Hernant, Abel — 5/22/31 B
Hero and Leander — 12/3/08 C
Herold, Francois Joseph — 1/28/60 B
Hero, The — 5/27/76 A
Herrmann, Bernard — 4/11/40 C; 12/23/54 A
Herr von Hancken — 9/2/65 A
Hertz, Alfred — 12/24/03 E; 1/22/07 A;
12/28/10 A; 3/14/12 A; 2/27/13 A;
12/9/13 A; 10/12/15 E; 7/11/22 E; //30 E;
4/1/33 E
Herz, Das — 11/12/31 A
Heseltine, Philip — 12/17/30 D
Hess, Myra — 11/15/07 D; 6/12/41 E;
11/25/65 D
Heuberger, Richard — 10/27/14 D
Heure espagnole, L' — 5/19/11 A
Hiawatha's Departure — 3/22/00 C; 3/22/00 C
Hiawatha's Wedding Feast — 3/14/00 C;
3/22/00 C
Hiden, Georgia — 11/20/46 B; 11/26/46 B
Hieroglyphs — 12/15/18 C
Higgins, Dick — 1/31/61 A
Higginson, Henry — 3/25/18 E; 11/15/19 D
High Fidelity (periodical) — 6/2/51 E
High fidelity — //34 E
High Noon — 11/11/79 D
Hightower, Loren — 5/13/57 B
Hightower, Rosella — 1/30/20 D; 12/23/52 B;
2/22/61 D
Highway No. 1, U.S.A. — 5/13/63 A
Hill, Alfred — 2/16/03 A; 10/30/60 D
Hill, Arthur F. — 2/8/39 D
Hill, Dorothy — 1/24/50 B
Hill, Edward Burlingame — 7/20/21 E;
7/9/60 D
Hiller, Lejaren — //57 E; 1/24/73 C
Hill, Margaret — 6/7/56 B
Himmlische Vagant, Der — 10/6/51 C
Hindemith, Paul — 9/25/17 E; 6/4/21 A;
8/1/21 C; 3/26/22 A; 7/31/22 C;
6/17/23 C; 7/25/25 C; 11/9/26 A;
2//27 E; 7/17/27 A; 6/8/29 A; 7/28/29 C;
10/3/29 C; 12/15/29 C; //30 E;
3/28/30 C; 6/21/30 A; 4/3/31 C;
11/21/31 C; 4/15/32 C; 3/12/34 C;
12/4/34 E; 12/6/34 E; 1//35 E; 4/25/35 E;
11/14/35 C; 1/22/36 C; 5/22/38 E;
5/28/38 A; 7/21/38 B; 3/14/40 C;
2/7/41 C; 11/21/41 C; 1/20/44 C;
2/15/44 C; 9/3/44 C; 5/14/46 C;
11/20/46 B; 2/1/47 C; 2/27/47 C;
5/2/47 C; 2/14/49 E; 5/15/49 C;
3/1/50 C; 6/8/50 C; 12/11/50 C;
1/24/52 C; 6/20/52 A; 11/25/52 B;
//54 E; 8/11/57 A; 1/30/59 C; 3/1/60 C;
12/17/61 A; 3/8/63 C; 3/13/63 B;
4/25/63 C; 11/12/63 C; 12/28/63 D;
10/10/68 C; 1/26/78 B; 5/3/78 E
Hindenberg, Basil — 6/26/75 D
Hinkson, Mary — 4/22/52 B; 5/8/55 B;
5/10/59 B; 4/27/60 B; 9/6/63 B;
1/25/66 B
Hintze, Wilhelm — 10/23/32 E
Hin und Zuruck — 7/17/27 A
Hircus Nocturnus — 2/3/09 C
Hirzel, Max — 11/9/26 A
His Master's Voice (record label) — 5//24 E

Histoire du soldat, L' — 9/28/18 B; 4/6/71 D
Histoires naturelles — 1/12/07 C
Historiettes au crepuscule — 7/15/59 D
History of Jewish Music (book) — 8/14/38 D
Hitler, Adolf — 3/11/28 E; 4/1/33 E;
9/22/33 E; 11/30/33 C; 6/11/34 E;
2/5/36 D; 7/6/37 E; 3/24/38 E; 5/6/38 E;
11/24/38 A; 6/2/39 D; 7/15/39 E;
3/26/48 E; 6/8/48 E; 2/14/49 E
Hiver-Printemps — 1/27/06 C
H.M.S. Pinafore — 11/22/00 D; 5/29/11 D
Hobi, Frank — 6/12/51 B; 11/11/52 B;
6/2/53 B
Hochsommernacht — 10/29/66 C
Hochzeit der Sobeide, Die — 3/17/33 A
Hoddinott, Alun — 3/26/74 A; 2/11/76 A
Hodeir, Andre — 6/23/66 C
Hodes, Stuart — 4/22/52 B; 2/21/65 B
Hodie — 9/8/54 C
Hoeffer, Paul — 8/16/36 E
Hoffman, Gertrude — 1/20/16 B
Hoffmann, E.T.A. — 11/5/33 A
Hofmann, Josef — 11/28/37 E; 2/16/57 D
Hofmannsthal, Hugo von — 1/25/09 A;
1/26/11 A; 8/22/20 E; 10/25/12 A;
10/10/19 A; 6/6/28 A; 7/1/33 A;
9/8/49 D
Hogan, Michael — 7/18/49 B
Hoiby, Lee — 6/20/58 A; 10/23/59 A;
10/8/64 A; 11/9/67 B; 6/19/71 A
Holbrooke, Josef — 11/11/09 A; 2/1/29 A;
8/5/58 D
Holden, Stanley — 11/16/48 B; 1/28/60 B
Holiday Overture — 9/30/71 C
Hollander, Lorin — 3/9/62 C
Holland Festival — 6/15/48 E; 6/16/65 A;
7/6/73 C
Holliger, Heinz — 5/21/39 D; 3/23/75 C;
10/17/75 C; 10/25/75 C
Hollmann, Otakar — 3/2/28 C
Hollywood Bowl — 7/11/22 E
Holm, Hanya — 8/13/48 B; 7/1/50 D
Holms, Berenice — 4/27/28 B
Holofernes — 10/27/23 A
Holst, Gustav — 4/6/10 C; 5/1/12 C;
12/5/16 A; 9/29/18 C; 11/15/20 C;
5/14/23 A; 4/3/25 A; 10/7/25 C;
2/12/28 C; 4/3/30 C; 5/25/34 D;
10/28/34 B
Holt, Alton Gilbert — 8/7/34 D
Holy Devil, The — 4/6/78 D
"Homage a Pickwick, Esq." — 6/19/13 C
Homage to Haydn — 6/3/69 C
Homage to the Queen — 6/2/53 B
Homenajes — 11/18/39 C
Homer, Louise — 11/14/00 D; 4/18/06 E;
11/16/08 D; 11/8/09 E; 12/28/10 A;
3/14/12 A; 5/6/47 D
Hommage a Chopin — 8/21/53 B
Homme et son desir, L' — 6/6/21 B
Honegger, Arthur — 4/3/17 C; 1/15/18 E;
1/3/20 C; 1/16/20 E; 4/22/21 E;
6/11/21 A; 6/19/21 B; 10/30/21 C;
1/20/22 B; 5/3/23 C; 5/8/24 C;
6/11/25 C; 2/13/26 A; 12/28/27 A;
10/19/28 C; 12/31/28 E; 8/6/29 B;
12/12/30 A; 2/13/31 C; 6/2/31 C;
12/16/32 C; 3/27/33 C; 5/11/34 B;
10/19/35 C; 3/11/37 A; 5/12/38 C;
5/15/39 B; 3/1/40 C; 4/17/40 C;
3/7/42 E; 5/23/42 C; 10/22/44 C;
5/5/46 B; 8/17/46 C; 12/11/46 C;
1/21/47 C; 2/28/51 C; 3/9/51 C;
6/12/51 C; 10/7/51 C; 5/6/52 E;
12/12/53 C; 11/27/55 D; 6/2/56 E;
10/10/56 E; 10/21/60 A
Honegger, Marc — 1/5/76 D
Honer, Mary — 2/16/37 B; 4/27/37 B
Hongen, Elisabeth — 12/7/06 D

Honolulu Ad Club — 9/18/17 E
Honolulu — 12/11/17 C
Hooke, Emelie — 7/12/46 C
Hopkins, Kenyon — 2/24/55 B
Hopkinson, Cecil — 4/3/70 E; 4/28/77 D
Hoppenot, Henri — 4/20/28 A
Horace Victorieux — 10/30/21 C
Hora Novissima — 12/18/19 D
Horizontes — 11/30/51 C
Horloge de flore, L' — 3/31/61 C
Hormat, Boriska — 5/12/17 B
Hornblit Prize — 4/8/49 C
Horn Concerto in C Minor — 5/31/05 D
Horne, Marilyn — 1/16/34 D; 5/7/47 A
Horowitz, Vladimir — 10/1/04 D; 1/12/28 D;
//31 E; 5/9/65 E
Horst, Louis — 11/3/19 B; 1/31/21 B;
2/2/31 B; //33 E; 4/28/35 B
Horton, Lester — 10/9/79 D
Hotel for Criminals — 8/24/74 A
Hotter, Hans — 1/19/09 D; 10/28/42 A
Houdini — 8/2/79 A
Housman, A.E. — 10/20/60 C
House with Two Doors — 5/24/70 A
Houston Grand Opera — 5/23/75 A;
2/29/76 A
Houston Symphony Orchestra — 6/21/13 E;
3/28/60 C; 2/20/63 D; 10/3/66 E
Hovhaness, Alan — 3/8/11 D; 3/6/49 C;
2/20/54 C; 12/15/59 A; 2/1/60 C;
3/28/63 C; 9/6/63 B; 10/23/63 C;
10/5/64 C; 1/30/65 C; 10/3/66 E;
6/2/67 C; 11/1/67 B; 3/21/68 C;
1/17/69 C; 7/27/69 C; 11/13/71 C;
1/16/73 C; 5/2/73 B; 2/23/75 C;
7/3/76 C; 5/4/77 C
Hoving, Lucas — 3/31/49 B; 8/17/49 B;
8/20/53 B; 8/19/54 B
Howard, Andree — 2/25/30 B; 2/23/37 B;
5/15/39 B; 6/2/47 B; 11/16/48 B
Howard, Holly — 3/1/35 B
Howard, Kathleen — 3/7/20 A
Howarth, Elgar — 3/17/78 A
Howe, Hubert S. — //58 E
Howell, Herman — 11/28/59 B
Howells, Herbert — 7/10/14 C
How to Pass — 11/24/65 B
Hristic, Stevan — //23 E
Hubbard, Frank — 2/25/76 D
Huber, Hans — 12/25/21 D
Huber, Kurt — 7/13/43 D; 6/15/47 A
Huberman, Bronislaw — 6/15/47 D
Hudson Valley Chorale — 1/31/60 C
Hudson Valley Philharmonic Orchestra —
1/31/60 C
Huelgas Codex, The — //31 E
Hughes, Langston — 3/31/49 A
Hugh the Drover — 7/14/24 A
Hugo, Jean — 7/18/35 B
Hugo, John Adam — 3/12/19 A
Huguenots, Les — 12/27/12 D
Hulbert, Tony — 12//66 E
Hume, J. — 4/15/12 E
Humpbacked Horse, The — 3/4/60 B
Humperdinck, Engelbert — 4/14/05 A;
12/28/10 A; 12/23/11 C; 5/10/14 A;
3/18/19 A; 9/27/21 D
Humphrey, Doris — 10/28/28 B; 3/31/29 B;
4/11/30 B; 11/12/30 B; 2/23/35 B;
3/11/43 B; 12/21/47 B; 4/15/53 B;
8/20/53 B; 4/20/56 B; 12/29/58 D;
5/9/59 B; 7/21/68 D; 12/2/72 D;
7/15/75 D
Humphrey-Weidman Concert Group —
10/28/28 B
Humpty Dumpty — 3/29/69 A
Hundred Kisses, The — 7/18/35 B
Hundred Nights, The — 4/22/76 A
Huneker, James Gibbons — 2/9/21 D

Hungarian Commission of Fine Arts — 5/24/18 A
Hungarian Ministry of Justice — 12/14/45 E
Hungarian People's Ensemble — 4/4/51 C
Hungarian-Rock — 5/20/78 C
Huni-Mihacsek, Felicie — 10/9/24 C
Hurok, Sol — //32 E; 2//38 E; 10//38 E; 12/11/70 E; 5/21/73 C; 3/5/74 D
Hurry, Leslie — 5/19/42 B
Husa, Karel — 5/5/69 E
Hussey, Walter — 7/15/65 C
Huygens, Christian — 9/8/50 E
Hyde, Edwin Francis — 3/19/01 D
Hyman, Charles — 1/4/50 B
Hymne aux morts, L' — 6/20/65 C
Hymnen — 11/29/67 C
"Hymn of Free Russia" — 1/3/56 D
Hymns and Responses for the Church Year — 10/24/59 C
Hymn to Art — 3/29/01 C
Hymn to Bolivar — 12/22/30 C
Hymn to Saint Magnus — 10/13/72 C
Hymnus — 3/31/01 A; 5/1/04 D
Hynd, Ronald — 1/6/55 B; 6/29/75 B
Hyperion — 3/21/76 C
Hyperprism — 3/4/23 C; 11/6/65 D

— I —

Iberia (Albeniz) — 1/2/08 C
Iberia (Borlin) — 10/25/20 B
Iberia (Debussy) — 2/20/10 C
Ibert, Jacques — 1/6/24 C; 1/31/25 C; 12/6/25 C; 1/28/27 A; 3/4/29 B; 5/15/29 A; 11/30/30 C; 3/11/37 A; 10/10/43 A; 2/23/51 C; 11/11/52 B; 2/5/62 D; 1/25/63 C; 10/6/63 C
Icare — 7/9/35 B
Ice and Steel — 5/15/30 A
Ice Maiden, The — 4/27/27 B
Ideas of Order — 4/11/53 C
Ide, Letitia — 12/21/47 B
Idelsohn, Abraham Zevi — 8/14/38 D
Idiota, L' — 2/14/70 A
Idiots First — 8/3/74 A
Idyll — 10/3/33 C
Idyll of Theocritus — 1/14/56 C
Idzikowski, Stanislas — 4/12/17 B; 5/11/17 B; 6/5/19 B; 7/22/19 B; 2/2/20 B; 5/15/20 B; 11/2/21 B; 5/18/22 B; 7/3/26 B; 12/5/33 B
Ifigenia — 5/4/51 A
I.G. Farben — 9/17/31 E
Igrak — 4/29/29 A
Igrouchka — 10/31/39 B
I Hate Music (Five Kid Songs) — 8/25/43 C
Ihlert, Heinz — 11/15/33 E
Illiac Suite — //57 E
Illica, Luigi — 1/14/00 A; 1/17/01 A; 12/19/03 A; 6/2/11 A
Illuminations (Ashton) — 3/2/50 B
Illuminations, Les (Britten) — 1/30/40 C
Ilustracion musical hispano-americana (Pedrell) — 8/19/22 D
Il vitalino raddopiato, ciacona per violino concertante ed orchestra da camera — 8/2/78 C
Ilya Murometz — 3/23/12 C
Image in the Snow — 11/13/52 C
Images — 2/20/10 C; 3/2/10 C; 3/25/18 D
Images for Saxophone and Synthesized Tape — 12/5/79 C
Imaginary Landscape, An — 6/2/71 C
Imaginary Landscape No. 1 — 12/9/39 C
Imaginary Landscape No. 3 — 3/1/42 C
Imaginary Landscape No. 4 — 5/2/51 C
Imaginees II — 1/9/70 C
Imbrie, Andrew — 4/22/58 C
Immortal Hour, The — 8/26/14 A

Imperio, Pastora — 4/15/15 B
Impressioni brasiliane — 6/16/28 C
Impressioni dal vero — 5/15/13 C; 3/11/17 C
Impromptu, The — 7/12/13 B
In a Persian Garden — 9/19/18 D
In a Summer Garden — 12/11/08 C
In a Vodka Shop — 10/3/53 D
Incense, The — 3/26/06 B
Incidents at a Forced Landing — 1/30/75 D
Incognita — 12/5/51 A
Incontri for 24 instruments — 5/30/55 C
Incredible Flutist, The — 5/30/38 B
Indianapolis Symphony Orchestra — 11/2/30 E; 11/7/40 C; 1/15/55 C
Indiana University Opera Theater — 4/8/77 A
Indianische Fantasie — 1/17/16 C
Indy, Vincent d' — 1/7/03 A; 2/28/04 C; 5/17/04 C; 2/18/06 C; 4/20/07 C; 6/15/08 E; 3/29/11 D; 12/21/12 A; 12/14/19 C; 6/9/20 A; 12/1/21 C; 4/2/27 C; 6/10/27 A; 12/2/31 D
Infidelio — 4/17/73 A
Infinity — 5/15/79 C
Inflexions — 1/24/67 C
Inghelbrecht, Desire — 10/25/20 B
Inglis Collection (National Library of Scotland) — 5/13/29 E
Ingrisch, Lotte — 2/25/77 A
In Honour of the City of London — 10/6/37 C
In Japan — 4/21/02 B
In Memoriam Dylan Thomas — 9/20/54 C
In Memoriam: The Colored Soldiers Who Died for Democracy — 1/5/44 C
In Memoriam: Theodore Roosevelt — 1/19/36 C
In Memoriam — W.H. Auden — 2/25/74 C
Innate, The — 1/29/27 C
Innocente, L' — 9/5/28 A
In Praise of Music — 9/23/77 C
In Praise of Shahn — 1/29/70 C
Inquest, The — 10/18/65 C
Inscape — 9/13/67 C
In seinem Garten liebt Don Perlimpin Belison — 5/10/62 A
Instant Remembered — 8/1/68 C
Institut de Recherche et de Coordination Acoustique/Musique (IRCAM) — 5//77 E
Institute for Eurhythmics — 10/3/10 E; 10/12/15 E
Institute for Jewish Music — 8/14/38 D
Institute of Choreology — //62 E
Institute of Electrical Engineers — 1/31/56 E
Institute of Sonology — 6/12/61 E; //79 E
Instrumentation — 12/5/09 D
Instruments of the Orchestra — 11/29/46 E
In Sweet Music — 10/29/78 C
Integrales — 3/1/25 C; 11/6/65 D
Inter-American Music Festival — 4/18/58 C; 5/7/65 E
Interlude — 7/25/74 C
Intermezzo (Feld) — 5/29/69 B
Intermezzo (Strauss, R.) — 11/4/24 A
Intermissions — 2/10/52 C
International Alban Berg Society — 11/1/79 C
International Ballet of the Marquis de Cuevas — see Ballet International de la Marquese de Cuevas
International Composers' Guild — 5/3/21 E; 3/4/23 C; 4/11/23 E
International Dance Council — //73 E
International Electronic Music Discography (book) — //79 E
International Musical Society — 6/1/14 E; 9/30/14 E
International Music Council — 9/7/70 E; 9/9/73 C
International Musicological Society — 9/30/27 E
International Society for Contemporary Music — 8/6/23 C; 6/22/26 C; 6/22/26 C;

7/1/27 C; 9/14/28 C; 4/2/34 C; 4/19/36 C; 6/17/38 C
International Society for Promoting Cooperation Among Composers — 5/24/37 E
International Standards Organization — 6/17/55 E
International Summer Academy of Dance — //57 E
International Talking Machine Company (Odeon/Parlophone) — 4/30/03 E
International Women's League — 10/30/35 D
International Zonophone Company — 10//01 E
Interplay — 8/25/43 C; 6/1/45 B
Interpretation of French Song, The (book) — 10/17/79 D
Interpretation of Music, The (book) — 3/6/71 D
Interpretation of the Music of the XVIIth and XVIIIth Centuries, The (book) — //15 E
Interracial Chorus and Orchestra — 5/13/65 C
In Terra Pax — 11/21/74 C
Intersection for Magnetic Tape — 10/17/54 C
Interval — 5/5/72 C
In the Beginning — 5/2/47 C
In the Fen Country — 2/22/09 C
In the Night — 1/29/70 B
In the South — 3/16/04 C
Intolerance — 3/12/19 A
Intoleranza 1971 — 4/13/61 A
Intoleranza 1960 — 4/13/61 A
Introduction and Allegro (Elgar) — 3/8/05 C
Introduction and Allegro for Harp — 5/22/75 B
Introduction and Allegro (Ravel) — 2/22/07 C
Introduction and Allegro (Robbins) — 5/22/75 B
Introduction to the Sociology of Music (book) — //62 E; 8/6/69 D
Introits and Canons — 1/13/78 C
Introitus: T.S. Eliot In Memoriam — 4/17/65 C
Intruder, The — 12/4/56 A
Invention — 10/28/52 C
Invenzione — 8/8/72 C
Invitation, The — 10/11/60 B
Invocation and Concerto — 5/24/68 C
Invocation and Dance — 3/1/62 C
Iolanthe — 11/22/00 D; 5/29/11 D
Ionisation — 3/6/33 C; 11/6/65 D
Iphigenia in Aulis — 2/23/35 B
Ipocrita felice, L' — 3/10/56 A
Ippolitov-Ivanov, Mikhail — 9/28/00 A; 12/16/02 A; 12/25/02 A; 9//05 E; 11/21/16 A; 3/20/34 C; 1/28/35 D
Iracema-Brugelmann, Hedy — 9/26/15 A
Ireland, John — 8/17/37 C; 6/12/62 D
Irische Legende — 8/17/55 A
Irish Washerwoman, The — 1/17/17 C
Irmelin — 5/4/53 A
Iron Curtain, The (movie) — 4/11/48 E
Ironside, Christopher — 9/3/52 B
Isaac, Heinrich — 6/20/06 E
Isaacson, Charles David — 2/15/36 D
Isaacson, Leonard M. — //57 E
Isabeau — 6/2/11 A
Isaken, Lone — 2/21/65 B
Isepp, Martin — 1/5/75 C
Island God, The — 2/20/42 A
Isle of Death, The — 3/29/28 A
Isle of the Dead, The — 5/1/09 C
Israeli State Prize — 10/1/53 C
Israel Philharmonic Orchestra — 10/1/53 C; 7/29/67 E
Israel Symphony — 5/3/17 C
Istituzioni e monumenti dell'antica musica italiana (collection) — 10/21/34 D
Istomin, Eugene — 11/26/25 D; 11/21/43 E
Italia — 4/23/10 C
Ito, Teijo — 2/3/72 B
Iturbi, Jose — 8/25/43 C
Ivanhoe — 11/22/00 D
Ivan le Terrible (Bizet) — 10/12/51 A

Ivanov, Lev — 12/11/01 D; 12/15/01 B
Ivan Susanin — 2/37/39 A
Ivan the Terrible (Grigorovich) — 2/16/75 B
Ivan the Terrible (Prokofiev) — 3/5/53 D
Ives, Charles — 4/18/02 C; 1/1/09 E; 5/7/15 E;
    6/8/20 E; 1/29/27 C; 1/10/31 C;
    4/30/32 E; 1/20/39 C; 4/5/46 C;
    5/5/47 E; 2/22/51 C; 5/19/54 D;
    9/14/54 B; 8/25/59 C; 4/26/65 C;
    10/10/68 C; 11/24/70 C; 11/29/70 C;
    12/4/77 C; 1/19/78 B
Ives, Harmony — 2/22/56 E
Ivesiana — 9/14/54 B; 1/19/78 B
Ives & Myrick — 1/1/09 E; 5/19/54 D
Iwaskiewicz, Jaroslaw — 6/19/26 A
I Will Always Love You — 4/26/72 C

— J —

Jacchia, Agide — 11/29/32 D
Jack-in-the-Box — 7/3/26 B
Jackson, Rowena — 5/5/56 B
Jacob chez Laban — 5/19/25 A
Jacobi, Frederick — 10/28/25 C
Jacob, Maxim — 6/14/23 E
Jacobsen, Jen Peter — 2/23/13 C
Jacobson, Leonid — 1/15/04 D
Jacobson, Maurice — 2/1/76 D
Jacob's Pillow — //33 E; //41 E; 7/11/47 B;
    8/27/48 B; 8/3/55 B; 7/11/56 B; 1/9/72 D
Jadlowker, Hermann — 12/28/10 A;
    10/25/12 A
Jakobsleiter, Die — 6/16/61 C
Jalowetz, Heinrich — 9/4/35 C
James, Lewis Cairns — 1/14/16 A
Janacek, Leos — 1/21/04 A; 11/14/17 C;
    4/23/20 A; 10/9/21 C; 11/23/21 A;
    11/6/24 A; 11/11/25 A; 2/12/26 C;
    6/29/26 C; 11/16/26 E; 12/18/26 A;
    12/5/27 C; 3/2/28 C; 8/12/28 D;
    4/12/30 A; 9/18/34 A; 10/25/58 A;
    6/8/65 D
Janigro, Antonio — 1/21/18 D
Janis, Byron — 3/24/28 D; 2/20/44 D
Janissary Music — 10/27/66 C; 3/12/67 C
Jankelvitch, Ida — 7/1/37 C
Janssen Symphony Orchestra — 2/8/42 C;
    11/18/45 C
Janssen, Werner — 2/28/36 C; 11/18/45 C
Jaques-Dalcroze, Emile — 4/15/05 E;
    5/25/05 A; 3/30/08 A; 10/3/10 E;
    10/12/15 E; 7/1/50 D; 5/29/72 D
Jardin de Marguerite, Au — 4/18/13 C
Jardins sous la pluie — 1/9/04 C
Jarnach, Philipp — 5/21/25 A
Jarnefelt, Armas — 6/23/58 D
Jarvis, Lillian — 2/1/55 B
Jasager, Der — 6/30/30 A
Jasinski, Roman — 10/24/33 B; 1/22/41 B
Jean Levecq — 6/16/65 A
Jeanmaire, Renee — 2/21/49 B; 4/17/59 B
Jeanne d'Arc au Bucher — 5/12/38 C
Jeanne, Marie — 10/16/38 B
Jeanne's Fan — 3/4/29 B
Jefferies, Stephan — 2/14/78 B
Jehin, Leon — 3/4/13 A
Jeji pastorkyna — see Jenufa
Jekyll and Hyde Variations — 2/2/57 C
Jealous Old Man, The — 5/12/49 A
Jenkins, Florence Foster — 11/4/43 E;
    10/26/44 E; 11/26/44 D
Jensen, Svend Erik — 1/15/48 B
Jenufa — 1/21/04 A; 8/12/28 D
Jeremiah Symphony — 1/28/44 C
Jerger, Alfred — 10/14/24 A; 7/1/33 A
Jeritza, Maria — 10/25/12 A; 10/4/16 A;
    10/10/19 A; 11/19/21 A; 11/19/21 D
Jesse H. Jones Hall (Houston) — 10/3/66 E

Jeu de cartes (Balanchine) — 4/27-28/37 B
Jeu de cartes (Cranko) — 1/22/65 B
Jeux d'eau — 4/5/02 C
Jeux (Debussy) — 3/25/18 D
Jeux (Nijinsky) — 5/15/13 B
Jeux (Taras) — 4/28/66 B
Jeux venitiens — 4/24/61 C
Jewels — 4/13/67 B
Jewish War Veterans — 2/27/55 E
Jillana — 12/4/51 B; 6/2/53 B; 2/18/54 B;
    11/22/60 B
Jinx — 4/24/42 B
Jirak, Karel — //22 E; 8/26/51 C
Joachim, Joseph — 5/16/04 E; 8/15/07 D
Job (Dallapiccola) — 10/31/50 C
Jobin, Raoul — 4/8/06 D; 2/20/42 A;
    1/13/74 D
Job (Valois) — 7/5/31 B
Jochum, Eugen — 11/1/02 D
Joffrey, Robert — 12/24/30 D; 9/19/67 B
Johannesburg Festival Overture — 9/25/56 C
Johannesburg Symphony Orchestra —
    12/11/53 D
Johannesen, Grant — 7/30/21 D
Johannes Faustus — 3/11/53 A
Johansen, Gunnar — 1/21/06 D
Johansson, Christian — 12/12/03 D
Johnny Johnson — 11/19/36 A
Johns, Jasper — 12/8/54 B
Johnson, Albert — 4/6/34 B
Johnson, Edward — 2/17/27 A; 2/7/31 A;
    6/1/50 E
Johnson, Eldridge — 5//00 E; 10//01 E; //26 E
Johnson, Hunter — 8/11/40 B; 7/18/43 B
Johnson, James Weldon — 11/27/26 C
Johnson, Nancy — 3/10/53 B
Johnson, Philip — 4/24/64 E
Johnson, Lyndon B. — 9/29/65 E; 4/29/67 A
Johnson, Ray — 5/24/55 B
Johnson, Thor — 1/30/48 C; 5/15/49 C;
    6/26/50 E; 8/14/54 C; 11/4/55 C;
    1/16/75 D
Johnson, Tom — 5/11/72 A
Johnson, Tommy — 11/28/59 B
Jolivet, Andre — 8/8/05 D; 12/22/35 E;
    10/28/42 C; 1/4/47 A; 4/23/48 C;
    10/22/48 C; 6/19/51 C; 9/24/55 C;
    10/3/59 C; 2/27/73 C
Jonah and the Whale — 3/9/74 C
Jonchaies — 12/21/77 C
Jone, Hildegard — 6/17/38 C; 7/12/46 C;
    6/23/50 C
Jones, Betty — 8/17/49 B
Jones, Robert Edmond — 10/23/16 B;
    4/11/30 B
Jones, Sidney — 1/6/06 B
Jones, W.B. — //28 E
Jongen, Leon — 2/14/24 A; 11/21/35 C
Jongleur de Notre Dame, Le — 2/18/02 A;
    11/27/08 A
Jonny spielt auf — 2/10/27 A; 3/21/28 E;
    1/19/29 A
Jonson, David — 1/31/61 A
Jooss, Kurt — 7/3/32 B; 11/21/32 B;
    4/30/34 B; //40 E
Joplin, Scott — 4/1/17 D; 5/23/75 A; 5/3/76 E
Jorda, Enrique — //54 E; 4/22/58 C;
    1/17/62 C; 2/16/62 C; //63 E
Jordan, Olga — 11/7/32 B
Joseffy, Rafael — 6/25/15 D
Jose Limon Dance Company — 3/11/43 B;
    12/21/47 B; 3/31/49 B; 8/17/49 B;
    8/11/50 B; 8/20/53 B; 8/19/54 B;
    4/20/56 B
Joseph and His Brethren — 3/23/48 C
Joseph the Beautiful — 3/3/25 B
Josman, Martin — 2/12/75 C
Jota, La — 4/26/11 A
Joubert, John — 3/20/27 D; 5/29/69 A

Joueur de viole, Le — 12/24/25 A
Jour d'ete à la montagne — 2/18/06 C
Journet, Marcel — 9/5/33 D
Joyce, James — 2/12/59 D
Jubal Trio — 2/2/78 C
Judgment of Paris, The — 6/15/38 B
Judith (Chadwick) — 9/26/01 A
Judith (Goosens, E.) — 6/25/29 A
Judith (Graham) — 1/4/50 B
Judith (Honegger) — 6/11/25 C; 2/13/26 A
Judson, Stanley — 5/5/31 B
Juilliard American Opera Theater — 4/22/76 A
Juilliard, Augustus D. — 4/25/19 D
Juilliard Dance Theater — 4/11/58 B; 5/9/59 B
Juilliard School of Music — 4/25/19 D;
    10/26/69 E
Juilliard Serenade — 1/31/71 C
Juilliard String Quartet — 4/18/38 E;
    4/11/64 C; 1/23/73 C; 2/4/74 C
Juinar of the Sea — 11/3/19 B
Julien — 6/4/13 A
Julietta — 3/16/38 A
Julius Caesar Jones — 1/4/66 A
Jumeaux de Bergame, Les — 3/30/08 A
Jumping Frog of Calaveras County, The — 5/18/50 A
Junge Lord, Der — 4/7/65 A
Jupiter Symphony — 10/6/79 E
Jurgenson, Peter — 1/2/04 D
Jurinac, Sena — 10/24/21 D

— K —

Kabale und Liebe — 2/25/77 A
Kabalevsky, Dmitri — 12/30/04 D;
    12/11/31 C; 11/9/32 C; 1/21/34 C;
    12/25/34 C; 5/12/36 C; 11/28/42 A;
    10/29/48 C; 3/15/49 C; 11/7/50 A;
    2/1/53 C; 3/5/53 D; 10/17/56 C;
    2/6/62 C; 2/9/63 C
Kabasta, Oswald — 1/10/34 C; 2/6/46 D
Kabos, Ilona — 10/14/42 C
Kadosa, Pal — 9/6/03 D
Kafka, Franz — 10/20/60 C
Kagel, Mauricio — 6/11/60 C; 3/11/68 C;
    5/15/73 C; 10/20/73 C; 2/25/74 C;
    7/22/74 C; 9/14/78 C
Kain und Abel — 5/17/14 A
Kairn of Koridwen, The — 4/8/20 D
Kaiser, Georg — 3/27/26 A; 2/18/28 A
Kajanus, Robert — 7/2/00 C
Kaleidoscope (Cui) — 3/26/18 D
Kaleidoscope (Nikolais) — 5/23/53 B
Kalinnikov, Vassili — 1/11/01 D
Kalioujny, Alexandre — 5/5/46 B; 7/28/47 B
Kalish, Gilbert — 3/21/75 C
Kallman, Chester — 9/11/51 A; 5/20/61 A;
    8/6/66 A
Kallo Double — 4/4/51 C
Kalmus, Alfred A. — 9/25/72 D
Kalnins, Alfreds — 5/29/20 A
Kalomiris, Manolis — 3/24/16 A; 4/3/62 D;
    8/12/62 A
Kalter, Sabine — 6/8/29 A
Kammerkonzert — 3/20/27 C
Kammermusik No. 1 — 7/31/22 C
Kammermusik No. 2 — 1/26/78 B
Kammersymphonie — 2/8/07 C
Kanakaole, Edith K. — 10/4/79 D
Kanda, Akiko — 4/16/61 B
Kansas City Philharmonic — 11/2/30 E;
    2/24/48 C; 7/21/79 D
Kantorei (record label) — 9/17/31 E
Kapell, William — 9/20/22 D; 10/28/41 D;
    10/29/53 D
Kapp, Eugen — 6/21/45 A; 7/20/50 A
Kapp, Jack — //34 E
Kapuste, Falco — 11/30/66 B

Karajan, Herbert von — 4/5/08 D;
  12/17/28 D; 2/27/55 E; //56 E;
  10/15/63 E; 10/19/67 E
Karalli, Vera — 5/19/09 B
Karayev, Kara — 1/4/58 B
Karel, Rudolf — 3/6/45 D; 10/28/48 A
Kares, Milos — 4/27/27 A
Karinska — 2/18/51 B; 2/20/51 B; 11/25/52 B;
  1/6/53 B; 2/2/54 B; 2/27/55 B; 3/1/55 B;
  12/19/56 B; 1/8/58 B; 1/17/58 B;
  5/14/59 B; 11/22/60 B; 12/10/63 B;
  1/7/64 B; 4/6/67 B; 4/13/67 B; 1/12/73 B
Karlin, Rita — 11/20/46 B
Karl V — 4/19/36 C; 6/15/38 A
Karr, Gary — 11/2/67 C
Karsavina, Jean — 5/18/50 A
Karsavina, Tamara — 3/21/08 B; 5/19/09 B;
  6/2/09 B; 3/5/10 B; 6/18/10 B;
  6/25/10 B; 6/25/10 B; 4/19/11 B;
  4/26/11 B; 6/13/11 B; 6/21/11 B;
  5/14/12 B; 5/20/12 B; 6/8/12 B;
  5/10/13 B; 5/15/13 B; 6/12/13 B;
  5/21/14 B; 6/2/14 B; 7/22/19 B;
  2/2/20 B; 5/15/20 B; 12/31/20 E;
  5/26/78 D
Kasatkina, Natalia — 3/23/71 B
Kashchei the Immortal — 12/25/02 A; 3/27/05 E
Kassern, Tadeusz — 5/2/57 D
Kassya — 8/13/12 D
Kastorsky, Vladimir — 5/19/08 A
Katcharoff, Michel — 2/27/46 B
Katcharov, Michel — 9/23/44 B
Katchen, Julius — 8/15/26 D; 10/21/37 D;
  4/29/69 D
Katerina Ismailova — see Lady Macbeth of the District of
  Mtinsk
Kathrin, Die — 10/7/39 A
Katims, Milton — 6/24/09 D; 5/2/65 C
Katya Kabanova — 11/23/21 A
Katz, David — 4/26/65 C
Kauffer, E. McKnight — 6/15/37 B
Kay, Barry — 7/22/71 B
Kaye, Danny — 1/23/41 A
Kaye, Nora — 1/17/20 D; 10/27/41 B;
  4/8/42 B; 10/20/43 B; 10/24/46 B;
  4/22/48 B; 2/18/51 B; 6/14/51 B;
  2/14/52 B; 2/26/52 B
Kay, Hershey — 2/27/55 B; 3/6/56 B;
  1/17/58 B; 1/7/64 B; 2/28/68 B;
  6/27/69 B; 9/8/71 C; 5/12/76 B
Kay, Ulysses — 1/7/17 D; 5/2/51 C;
  8/18/66 C; 2/4/68 C; 3/28/68 C;
  2/21/71 C; 3/14/75 C; 10/12/76 C
Kazantzakis, Nikos — 6/9/61 C
Keats, John — 2/3/10 C; 10/7/25 C
Keene, Christopher — 10/24/70 B
Kehlet, Niels — 9/6/38 A
Keil, Birgit — 3/8/70 B
Keilholz, Heinrich — 9/11/69 E
Keilland, Olav — //52 E
Kelberine, Alexander — 1/27/40 D
Kelemen, Milko — 4/16/73 C; 6/12/78 C;
  5/15/79 C
Kelly, Lawrence — 9/16/74 D
Kempe, Rudolf — 6/14/10 D
Kenilworth — 11/22/00 D
Kenin, Herman D. — 6/2/58 E
Kennedy Center for the Performing Arts
  (Washington, D.C.) — 9/8/71 E
Kennedy, John F. — 10/11/63 E; 11/22/63 E
Kennedy, Edward M. — 3/15/78 E
Kent, Allegra — 9/14/54 B; 1/17/58 B;
  3/20/63 B; 4/28/66 B; 5/22/69 B;
  7/30/70 B; 6/23/72 B
Kentner, Louis — 10/14/42 C
Kenton, Stan — 2/1/53 B
Kentucky Spring — 4/5/49 C
Keogh, Tom — 11/9/49 B
Kerensky, Alexander — 5/8/17 E

Kertesz, Istvan — 8/28/29 D; 4/16/73 D
Kesselheim, Sylvia — 11/30/66 B
Ketschendorf, Ernest — 7/28/03 D
Kette, Kreis und Spiegel — 1/24/58 C
Keuchmaneuver (Cough Music) — 5/24/19 C
Khachaturian, Aram — 6/6/03 D; 7/5/37 C;
  11/29/38 C; 11/16/40 C; 12/9/42 B;
  12/30/43 C; 10/30/46 C; 2/11/48 E;
  2/21/48 E; 4/11/48 E; 10/10/56 E;
  12/27/56 B; 5/28/58 E; 11/3/62 C;
  4/9/68 B; 7/7/74 C; 5/1/78 D
Khaikin, Boris — 10/26/04 D; 12/30/43 C
Khamma — 11/15/24 C
Khan, Ali Akbar — 4/14/22 D
Kharkov Opera — 11/30/75 D
Khikmet, Nazim — 3/23/61 B
Khodasevich, Valentina — 4/14/38 B
Khrennikov, Tikhon — 6/10/13 D;
  10/10/35 C; 10/10/39 A; 1/10/43 C;
  6/9/44 C; 2/24/50 A; 10/26/57 A;
  10/21/59 C; 10//63 E; 5/13/64 C;
  11/3/67 A; 2/8/72 C; 11/18/79 E
Khrushchev, Nikita — 9/26/62 C; 12/18/62 C;
  3/8/63 E; 3/23/63 E; 10//63 E; 4/6/71 D
Kick, Fall and Run — 11/24/65 B
Kidd, Michael — 10/4/45 B
Kielland, Olav — 8/16/01 D
Kiepura, Jan — 2/9/29 A
Kiev Opera — 11/30/75 D
Kikimora — 12/12/09 C; 8/28/14 D
Kilinski, Zbigniew — 11/20/37 B
Kimball, Renee — 8/4/62 B
Kim, Earl — 10/25/79 C
Kim, Willa — 9/30/62 B
Kinderstuck — 7/22/66 C
Kindertotenlieder — 3/31/13 C; 2/19/37 B
Kindler, Hans — 11/2/31 E; 3/5/44 C;
  1/25/48 C; //49 E
Kinetographie — //26 E; //62 E
King Jr., Dr. Martin Luther — 10/10/68 C
King Lear — 7/9/78 A
King Priam — 5/29/62 A
King's Henchman, The — 2/17/27 A
Kingston, Morgan — 3/12/19 A
Kinkeldey, Otto — 4/25/46 E
Kinney, Sharon — 8/4/62 B
Kipnis, Alexander — 2/12/23 D; 1/5/40 D;
  5/14/78 D
Kirchenmusikalisches Jahrbuch (periodical) —
  9/5/10 D
Kirchhoff, Walter — 1/19/29 A
Kirchner, Leon — 1/24/19 D; 2/23/56 C;
  5/1/67 E; 10/16/69 C; 3/11/73 C;
  4/14/77 A
Kirkland, Gelsey — 12/4/69 B; 6/18/72 B;
  4/5/79 B
Kirkpatrick, John — 3/18/05 D; 1/20/39 C
Kirkpatrick, Ralph — 6/10/11 D; 9/6/61 C
Kirov Ballet — 4/27/27 B; 10/26/30 B;
  4/8/31 B; 12/31/35 B; 6/28/38 B;
  3/22/39 B; 12/9/42 B; 3/14/49 B;
  6/28/50 B; 12/27/56 B; 4/27/57 B;
  3/23/61 B; 6/16/61 B; 4/12/63 B;
  12/31/64 B; 12/12/70 B; 6/29/74 E
Kirov Theatre of Opera and Ballet — //35 E
Kirsova Ballet — 7//41 E
Kirstein, Lincoln — 1/2/34 E; 12/6/34 B;
  7/17/36 E; 1/6/38 B; //40 E; 1//42 E;
  7/15/46 E; //48 E
Kirsten, Dorothy — 7/6/18 D
Kiss, Nora — //74 E
Kitharaulos — 6/20/72 C
Klafsky, Katharina — 12/22/50 D
Klagende Lied, Das — 2/17/01 C
Klangfiguren II — 5/30/56 C
Klavierstucke IX and VIII — 5/15/69 C
Klavierstuck — 2/8/63 C
Klebe, Giselher — 10/30/64 C
Kleiber, Carlos — 7/3/30 D

Kleiber, Erich — 12/14/25 A; 1/7/33 A;
  11/30/34 C; 3/19/55 E; 1/27/56 D
Kleider machen Leute — 12/2/10 A
Kleine Messe uber Zwolftonmodelle — 3/25/79 D
Kleine Theater-Suite — 2/9/31 C
Klein, Peter — 12/6/79 C
Klemperer, Otto — 12/4/20 A; 1/22/27 C;
  6/8/29 A; 11/6/30 C; //33 E; 4/10/33 E;
  5/18/35 C; 3/1/36 E; 12/10/36 C;
  1/21/37 C; //39 E; 7/6/73 D
Klenau, Paul von — 11/4/33 A
Klenovsky, Paul — 8/19/44 D
Kletzki, Paul — 3/21/00 D
Klindworth, Karl — 7/27/16 D
Klingsor, Tristan — 5/17/04 C
Klipstatter, Kurt — 10/22/79 A
Klose, Margarete — 8/6/02 D; 12/14/68 D
Kluge, Die — 2/20/43 A
Knaifel, Aleksandr — 11/18/79 E
Knappertsbusch, Hans — 10/25/65 D
Knauss, Charles E. — 5/5/03 C
Kneisel, Franz — 3/26/26 D; 5/7/30 E
Kneisel Quartet — 3/26/26 D; 4/8/37 D
Knickerbocker Holiday — 9/26/38 A
Knipper, Lev — 11/13/26 C
Knoxville: Summer of 1915 — 4/9/48 C
Knudsen, Paul — 5/12/22 B
Knusheitzky, Sviatoslav — 3/15/49 C
Koanga — 3/30/04 A
Kobbe, Gustav — 7/27/18 D
Kobbe's Complete Opera Book (book) — 7/27/18 D
Kochanski, Paul — 10/6/33 C
Kochel, Ludwig von — 2/13/52 D
Kochno, Boris — 6/3/22 A; 1/19/24 B;
  4/28/25 B; 6/17/25 B; 6/6/28 B;
  5/7/29 B; 3/2/45 B
Kodaly, Zoltan — 11/19/23 C; 10/16/26 A;
  4/3/30 C; 11/28/30 C; 4/24/32 A;
  9/11/36 C; 11/23/39 C; 2/6/41 C;
  11/15/46 D; 3/15/48 A; 4/4/51 C;
  4/11/58 B; 8/16/61 C; 3/6/67 D
Koechlin, Charles — 11/15/24 C; 5/19/25 A;
  12/31/50 D; 1/25/67 B
Koesun, Ruth Ann — 10/1/52 B
Kogan, Leonid — 11/14/24 D; 11/3/62 C
Kokitch, Casimir — 10/16/42 B
Kokkonen, Joonas — //73 E; 2/20/74 C
Kolisch Quartet — 1/8/27 C; 9/19/27 C;
  9/22/38 C
Kolisch, Rudolf — 1/16/28 C; 4/13/31 C
Kolish, Gertrud — 2/1/30 A
Kol Nidre (Bruch) — 10/2/20 D
Kol Nidre (Schoenberg) — 7/13/51 D
Kolodin, Irving — 2/22/08 D
Kolpakova, Irina — 5/22/33 D; 11/5/51 D;
  4/27/57 B; 3/23/61 B
Komarova, Natalie — 1/6/24 B
Kondracki, M. — //79 E
Kondrashin, Kiril — 3/6/14 D; 5/19/58 D;
  12/4/78 E
Koner, Pauline — 3/31/49 B; 8/20/53 B
Konig Ensemble — 2/28/79 C
Konig, Gottfried Michael — 5/30/56 C
Konig Hirsch — 9/23/56 A; 10/9/63 C
Konigin von Saba, Die — 1/2/15 D
Konigsberg University — 7/1/06 D
Konigskinder, Die — 12/28/10 A
Kontakte — 6/11/60 C
Kontra-Punkte — 5/26/53 C
Konzert-Haus (Vienna) — 10/19/13 E
Konzert in alten Stil — 10/4/12 C
Konzertmusik — 3/28/30 C; 4/3/31 C
Koppel, Thomas — 2/19/72 B
Koren, Sergei — 1/11/40 B
Korngold, Erich Wolfgang — 10/4/10 A;
  11/17/10 C; 12/14/11 C; 3/28/16 A;
  12/4/20 A; 11/19/21 A; 10/7/27 A;
  10/7/39 A; 11/29/57 D; 3/3/61 D
Korovin, Konstantin — 1/31/23 B

Koshetz, Nina — 12/30/21 A
Koslov, Valentina — 9/16/79 E
Kossuth — 1/13/04 C
Kostelanetz, Andre — 12/22/01 D; 5/14/42 C; 12/31/55 C; 6/7/72 C; 2/13/76 D; 7/3/76 C
Koszut, Ursula — 5/18/79 C
Kotonski, Wlodzimierz — 8/23/25 D; 7/9/60 C
Koussevitzky, Serge — 2/25/05 C; 9/8/05 E; 8/23/06 C; 1/23/08 C; 1/23/08 D; 3/16/09 E; 3/15/11 C; 12/10/13 E; 4/14/15 C; 12/12/16 E; 5/8/17 E; 9/16/18 E; 4/22/21 E; 6/10/21 C; 10/19/22 C; 5/3/23 C; 10/18/23 C; 5/8/24 C; 5/22/24 C; 5/29/24 C; 10/10/24 D; 5/23/25 C; 5/30/25 C; 6/6/25 C; 11/20/25 C; 11/19/26 C; 1/21/27 C; 1/28/27 C; 2/25/27 C; 3/18/27 C; 4/15/27 C; 4/22/27 C; 11/18/27 C; 12/14/28 C; 12/13/29 C; 10/24/30 C; 11/7/30 C; 11/14/30 C; 11/28/30 C; 12/19/30 C; 2/13/31 C; 4/3/31 C; 10/16/31 C; 11/13/31 C; 1/29/32 C; 2/19/32 C; 10/21/32 C; 11/25/32 C; 4/1/33 E; 1/26/34 C; 11/30/36 C; 8/12/37 E; 4/22/38 C; 8/4/38 E; 2/24/39 C; 10/6/39 C; 7/8/40 E; //41 E; 2/7/41 C; 10/17/41 C; 11/14/41 C; 10/15/42 C; 2/26/43 C; 3/26/43 C; 10/8/43 C; 10/29/43 C; 11/12/43 C; 3/3/44 C; 3/14/44 C; 10/13/44 C; 10/20/44 C; 12/1/44 C; 10/12/45 C; 4/5/46 C; 10/1/46 E; 10/18/46 C; 3/7/47 C; 1/9/48 C; 2/27/48 C; 4/9/48 C; 1/7/49 C; 4/8/49 C; 6/4/51 D; 9/14/55 A
Koval, Marian — 1/18/29 C
Kovarovic, Karel — 12/6/20 D
Kraanerg — 6/2/69 E
Kraft, Anton — 5/15/57 E
Krasa, Hans — 10/16/44 D
Krasner, Louis — 4/19/36 C; 12/6/40 C
Krasova, Marta — 3/16/01 D
Krassovska, Nathalie — 5/11/39 B; 10/12/42 B; 9/23/44 B; 10/24/50 E
Kraul, Earl — 2/1/55 B
Kraus, Lili — 4/3/05 D
Kraus, Otakar — 12/10/09 D; 9/11/51 A
Krauss, Clemens — 7/1/33 A; 7/24/38 A; 2/5/39 A; 10/28/42 A; 5/16/54 D
Kreidekreis, Der — 10/14/33 A
Krein, Alexander — 3/22/39 B; 4/21/51 D
Kreisler, Fritz — 11/10/12 C; 11/11/21 E; 1/29/62 D
Kremer, Gidon — 8/2/78 C
Kremnev, Nicolas — 5/11/17 B
Krenek, Ernst — 8/23/00 D; 7/31/21 C; 7/30/22 C; 6/9/24 A; 10/12/24 C; 10/16/24 C; 11/27/26 A; 2//27 E; 2/10/27 A; 5/21/27 A; 3/21/28 E; 5/6/28 A; 1/19/29 A; 1/19/30 A; 4/19/36 C; 3/17/38 C; 5/22/38 E; 6/15/38 A; 5/19/39 B; 5/13/41 A; 1/24/45 E; 11/22/46 C; 4/11/47 C; 11/27/47 C; 5/17/49 E; //50 E; 3/16/50 C; 7/16/50 A; 5/2/51 A; 10/6/51 C; 3/13/53 C; 3/4/54 C; 10/17/55 A; 5/30/56 C; 3/17/57 A; 1/24/58 C; 9/30/60 C; 6/27/62 A; 6/16/64 A; 8/1/68 C; 6/20/72 C; 7/22/74 C; 8/21/74 C; 9/12/75 C; 8/26/78 C; 11/6/78 C
Krenn, Fritz — 6/8/29 A
Kreutz, Arthur — 7/25/06 D; 11/6/51 A
Kreuzspiel — 5/2/51 C
Kriessig, Hans — 5/22/00 E
Krins, G. — 4/15/12 E

Krips, Josef — 4/8/02 D; 10/14/45 E; 11/9/45 E; 7/18/50 E; //54 E; //63 E; //70 E
Kriza, John — 4/18/44 B; 6/1/45 B; 10/24/46 B; 4/22/48 B
Kroller, Heinrich — 5/9/24 B
Krol Roger — 6/19/26 A
Kronos String Quartet — 3/2/78 C; 8/26/78 C
Kronstam, Henning — 6/29/34 D; 5/19/55 B; 11/22/57 B
Krueger, Karl — 7/21/79 D
Krull, Anny — 1/25/09 A
Kschessinska, Mathilda — 2/10/00 B; 2/20/00 B; 11/30/11 B; 12/6/71 D
Kubelik, Jan — 4/2/06 E; 6/29/14 D; 10/30/35 D; 12/5/40 D
Kubelik, Rafael — 6/29/14 D; 1/24/34 D; 5/27/47 C; 6/16/51 C; 3/20/52 C; 11/20/52 C; 1/1/53 C; 8/24/68 E; 8/15/72 A; 5/18/79 C
Kubik, Gail — 9/5/14 D; 1/7/52 C; 5/5/52 E
Kubrick, Stanley — 10/22/61 C
Kuch, Richard — 8/17/62 B
Kudisch, Alexis — 2/26/47 D
Kuhn Children's Choir — //45 E
Ku Klux Klan — 2/8/15 E
Kukusche — 10/24/48 D
Kunneke, Eduard — 4/15/21 A
Kunwald, Ernst — 12/8/17 E
Kunz, Erich — 5/20/09 D
Kurtz, Edmund — 11/28/46 C
Kurtz, Efrem — 11/7/00 D
Kurz, Selma — 10/4/16 A; 5/10/33 D
Kvapil, Jaroslav — 3/31/01 A
Kwartin, Clara — 7/20/24 C
Kwast-Hodapp, Frieda — 12/15/10 C
Kylian, Jiri — 3/21/47 D

— L —

Labanotation — //26 E; //62 E
Laban, Rudolf von — //26 E; //40 E; //62 E; //65 E
Labisse, Felix — 12/23/52 B
Labyrinth (Butler) — 10/3/68 B
Labyrinth (Massine) — 10/8/41 B
Labyrinth (Menotti) — 3/3/63 A
Lacotte, Pierre — 6//63 B
Lady and the Fool, The — 2/25/54 B
Lady from Colorado, The — 7/3/64 A
Lady from the Sea — 4/20/60 B
Lady in the Dark — 1/23/41 A
Lady into Fox — 5/15/39 B
Lady Macbeth of the District of Mtsensk — 1/22/34 A; 1/28/36 E; 11/21/37 C; 12/30/62 A
Lady of the House of Sleep — 5/25/68 B
Lafon, Madeleine — 7/28/47 B
Lagerborg, Anne-Marie — 10/31/50 B
Lagut, Irene — 6/19/21 B
Laing, Hugh — 10/28/34 B; 1/26/36 B; 2/19/37 B; 6/15/38 B; 11/26/38 B; 4/8/42 B; 9/8/42 B; 4/6/43 B; 10/20/43 B; 2/25/44 B; 4/10/45 B; 4/14/48 B; 2/26/52 B
Lajtha, Laszlo — 11/26/32 C; 2/16/63 D
Lakner, Jehoshua — 7/30/68 E
Lalay, Louis — 6/1/23 A
Lalo, Edouard — 6/19/43 B
Lamarr, Hedi — 2/12/59 D
Lambert, Constant — 8/23/05 D; 5/4/26 B; 12/12/29 C; 5/5/31 B; 7/4/40 B; 8/21/51 D
Lambert, Phyllis — 12/17/67 B
Lambert, Thomas B. — 5//00 E
Lamentatio Jeremiae Prophetae — 5/13/41 A
Lament for April 15 — 1/10/79 D
Lamia — 10/24/08 C; 4/20/74 C
Laminated-stock discs — 11/12/22 E

La Montaine, John — 5/4/59 E
Lamont, Deni — 5/28/65 B
Lamoureux Orchestra — 10/27/01 C; 2/28/04 C; 10/15/05 C; 12/12/20 C
Lanchbery, John — 1/28/60 B; 4/25/66 B; 4/6/72 B; 2/12/76 B; 2/14/78 B
Lancie, John de — 3/31/61 C
Landarzt, Eine — 11/29/51 C
"Land der Berge, Land am Strome" — 10/22/46 E
Lander, Harald — 2/25/05 D; //32 E; 1/15/48 B; 9/14/71 D
Lander, Margot — 8/2/10 D; 1/15/48 B; 7/19/61 D; 9/14/71 D
Land, Louis — 6/4/76 E
Landowska, Wanda — 11/5/26 C; 5/3/29 C; 8/16/59 D
Landre, Guillaume — 6/12/37 E; 3/6/46 C; 6/16/51 C; 6/16/65 A; 11/6/68 D
Landscape Remembered — 11/5/72 C
Lane, Maryon — 2/1/53 B; 1/18/55 B
Lanese, Lillian — 2/25/50 B
Lang, B.J. — 3/14/00 C
Lange, Francisco Curt — 12/12/03 D
Lange, Hans — 4/11/36 C
Langfield, Therese — 6/15/38 B
Lang, Harold — 4/18/44 B
Langlais, Jean — 2/15/07 D
Lang, Pearl — 8/13/48 B; 4/22/52 B
Langsamer Satz — 5/27/62 C
Lanner, Katti — 3/18/01 B
Lansky, Paul — 4/6/73 E; 4/7/75 C; 5/12/75 C; 4/21/76 C; //77 E; 12/13/79 C
Laparra, Raoul — 6/27/03 E; 4/26/11 A; 12/24/25 A; 4/4/43 D
Lappe, Gemze de — 10/1/52 B
Larionov, Mikhail — 5/11/17 B; 5/17/21 B; 5/18/22 B
Larrocha, Alicia de — 5/23/23 D
Larsen, Gerd — 11/26/38 B; 12/5/38 B; 12/12/62 B
Larsen, Niels Bjorn — 10/5/13 D; //51 E; 5/19/55 B
Larsson, Irene — 6/2/53 B; 11/15/55 B
Larsson, Lars-Erik — 5/15/08 D
Laryngoscope — 7/1/06 D
La Salle Quartet — 2/25/74 C
La Scala — 12/19/03 A; 2/17/04 A; 11/9/07 A; 4/10/13 A; 12/15/13 A; 3/20/15 A; 11/1/18 A; 12/26/21 E; 12/16/22 A; 4/26/23 A; 5/2/24 A; 12/20/24 A; 3/7/25 A; 4/22/25 A; 4/25/26 A; 12/29/27 A; 2/9/29 A; 3/24/34 A; 1/16/35 A; 2/12/36 A; 1/1/38 A; 2/1/39 A; 5/11/46 E; 12/26/46 E; 1/2/47 A; 5/10/47 E; 5/12/49 E; 5/4/50 A; 3/17/52 A; 3/19/55 E; 12/26/55 E; 1/26/57 A; 3/1/58 A; 3/23/61 A; 9/5/64 E; 10/27/64 E; 3/1/65 A; 10/19/67 E; 12/11/67 D; 4//75 A
La Scala Opera Ballet — 2/1/58 B; 7/26/58 B
Laschilin, Lev — 6/14/27 B
Lassus, L. Auge de — 2/24/06 A
Last Lover, The — 8/2/75 A
Last Poems of Wallace Stevens, The — 11/3/72 C
Lateiner, Jacob — 1/6/67 C
Late Lark, A — 10/12/29 C
Latin-American Symphonette — 2/22/41 C
Latouche, John — 7/7/56 A; 10/29/56 A
Lattini, Carol — 1/2/58 E
Lattuada, Felice — 2/9/29 A
Latvian National Opera House — 12/2/19 E; 5/29/20 A
Laubenthal, Rudolf — 10/2/71 D
Laurencia — 3/22/39 B
Laurencie, Lionel de la — 3/17/17 E
Laurencin, Marie — 1/6/24 B
Laurent, Jean — 8/21/53 B; /6/57 E

Lauret, Jeannette — 6/25/36 B; 5/5/38 B; 7/21/38 B
Lauri-Volpi, Giacomo — 11/1/26 D
Lauterer, Arch — 8/11/40 B
Laux, Karl — 6/27/78 D
Lavery, Emmet — 1/26/57 A
Lavery, Sean — 1/26/78 B
Lavignac, Albert — 5/28/16 D
Lavinia — 7/20/61 A
Lavish Escapade — 5/18/56 B
Lavrovsky, Leonid — 6/18/05 D; 3/7/23 B; 3/21/34 B; 4/14/38 B; 1/11/40 B; 2/12/54 B; 4/7/60 B
Lavrovsky, Mikhail — 9/17/62 B
Lawrence, Gertrude — 1/23/41 A
Lawrence, Marjorie — 2/17/09 D; 1/13/79 D
Lawrence, Pauline — 10/28/28 B; 11/12/30 B; 3/31/49 B; 8/17/49 B; 8/11/50 B; 8/19/54 B; 4/20/56 B
Lawrence, Robert — 5/5/46 C
League of Composers — 4/11/23 E; 2/25/24 E; 11/27/26 C; 12/18/29 C; 4/11/30 B; 1/4/31 C; 4/1/54 A
Leben des Orest — 1/19/30 A
Lebenstanz — 11/15/12 C
Leblanc, Georgette — 4/30/02 A
Le Boulaire, Jean — 1/15/41 C
LeClerq, Tanaquil — 10/2/29 D; 11/20/46 B; 5/13/47 B; 11/12/47 B; 3/22/48 B; 12/1/49 B; 2/26/50 B; 3/2/50 B; 2/20/51 B; 6/12/51 B; 12/4/51 B; 2/14/52 B; 2/19/52 B; 11/25/52 B; 1/6/53 B; 5/14/53 B; 1/1/53 E; 1/19/54 B; 2/2/54 B; 9/14/54 B; 2/27/55 B; 3/6/56 B
Leeder, Sigurd — 11/21/32 B
Leeds Festival — 10/12/10 C; 10/2/13 C; 10/7/25 C; 10/10/31 C
Leeds Music Company — 7/29/48 E; 3/9/49 E
Lee, Elizabeth — 5/29/69 B
Lee, Ming Cho — 4/11/58 B; 2/20/68 B; 6/26/78 B
Lees, Benjamin — 3/15/68 C; 1/17/69 C; 5/4/72 C; 11/19/72 C; 5/8/74 C
Leeuw, Ton de — 6/16/65 A
Lefebvre, Jules — 12/22/35 E
Le Gallienne, Eva — 11/15/77 D
Legende de Joseph, La — 5/14/14 B
Legende de Saint-Christophe, La — 6/9/20 A
Legende vom vertauschten Sohn, Die — 1/13/34 A
Legend of Love — 3/23/61 B
Legend of the Great City of Kitezh and the Calm Lake Svetoyar, The — 3/1/02 C; 3/3/03 A
Legend of the Invisible City of Kitezh, The — 2/20/07 A; 8/14/67 E
Legend, The — 3/12/19 A
Leger, Fernand — 1/20/22 B; 10/25/23 B; 6/19/26 C
Leggenda di Sakuntala, La — 12/10/21 A
Legge, Walter — 3/22/79 D
Legnani, Pierina — 1/17/00 B; //23 D
Lehar, Franz — 12/28/05 A; 10/24/48 D; 6/23/77 B
Lehmann, Lilli — 5/16/29 D
Lehmann, Liza — 9/19/18 D
Lehmann, Lotte — 10/4/16 A; 10/10/19 A; 11/4/24 A; 1/11/34 D; 2/16/51 E; 8/26/76 D
Lehner, Eugen — 1/16/28 C
Lehrbuch des Dirigierens — 6/1/29 E
Lehrman, Leonard — 8/3/74 A
Leibowitz, Rene — 2/17/13 D; //47 E
Leichner, Emil — 1/17/24 E
Leichtentritt, Hugo — 11/13/51 D
Leider, Frida — 1/16/33 D; 6/3/75 D
Leifs, Jon — 5/24/37 E
Leigh, Angela — 2/1/55 B
Leigh, Walter — 6/12/42 D
Leinsdorf, Erich — 2/4/12 D; 1/21/38 D; 10/28/43 C; 4/27/53 C; 9/24/62 C; 11/22/63 E; 3/13/64 C; 1/6/67 C; 3/15/68 C; 12/6/74 C

Leipzig Opera — 2/10/27 A
Leitner, Ferdinand — 10/27/76 D
Leiyla and the Poet — 5/9-10/61 E
Leland, Sara — 1/23/69 B; 5/22/69 B; 6/18/72 B; 5/24/73 B; 5/29/75 B
Lena, Maurice — 2/18/02 A
Lendvai, Erwin — 12/6/16 A
Lenepveu, Charles — 6/11/55 D
Lengyel, Menyhert — 11/28/26 B
Leningrad Association for Contemporary Music — 1/1/26 E; 2//27 E
Leningrad Choreographic School — 3/21/34 B
Leningrad Conservatory — 9/6/56 E
Leningrad Opera — 1/21/42 A; 9/8/43 A
Leningrad Palace of Culture — 12/26/55 E
Leningrad Philharmonic — 5/12/26 C; 1/21/30 C; 11/21/37 C; 11/3/45 C
Leningrad — 10/15/42 C
Lenin — 1/21/34 C
Lenin, Vladimir — 7/12/18 E; 9/23/18 E
Lenox Avenue — 5/23/37 C
Lenya, Lotte — 8/3/28 A; 3/21/33 E; 6/7/33 B
Leo — 8/23/69 C
Leoncavallo, Ruggero — 11/10/00 A; 2/1/04 E; 12/13/04 A; 1/15/10 A; 1/19/10 A; 6/24/12 A; 9/16/12 A; 4/14/13 A; 8/9/19 D; 12/13/20 A; 3/10/40 E
Leonore 40/45 — 3/25/52 A; 3/1/59 C
Leontiev, Leonide — 5/20/10 B
Leo XIII, Pope — 5/17/01 E
Le Page, Pierrette — 7/21/71 C
Leppard, Raymond — 10/11/60 E; 8/3/73 C; 1/18/74 A
Leroux, Xavier — 2/2/19 D
Leschetizky, Theodor — 11/14/15 D
Lessing, Florence — 3/11/43 B
Lesson, The — 4/6/64 B
Lesur, Daniel — 12/22/35 E
Leterrier, Eugene — 1/9/13 A
Let's Make an Opera — 6/14/49 A
Letter — A Depression Message from a Hobo Friend, The — 4/22/44 C
Letter form Mozart — 12/3/76 C
Letter from Home — 10/17/44 C; 2/27/47 C
Letters from Composers (A Cycle of Seven Songs for Tenor and Guitar) — 10/23/68 C
Letter to the World — 8/11/40 B
Leuning, Otto — 5/23/78 C
Levasseur, Andre — 12/23/52 B; 2/15/56 B
Leventritt International Competition — 11/21/43 E; 2/28/76 D
Leventritt, Rosalie Joseph — 2/28/76 D
Levidis, Dimitri — 5/30/51 D
Levi, Hermann — 5/13/00 D
Levina, Zara — 1/18/29 C
Levine, James — 6/23/43 D; 6/5/71 D; 11/2/78 C
Levi-Strauss, Claude — 10/10/68 C
Levitzki, Mischa — 10/17/16 D
Levy, Marvin David — 8/2/32 D; 8/2/57 A; 5/4/58 A; 3/17/67 A; 2/25/74 C; 11/20/77 C
Lewisohn, Adolph — 5/29/15 E; 1/17/34 E
Lewisohn Stadium — 5/29/15 E; 6/23/18 E; 8/27/25 E
Lewis, Richard — 5/29/62 A
Lexicon of Musical Invective (book) — //53 E
Lhevinne, Josef — 1/27/06 D; 12/3/44 D; 11/9/76 D
Lhevinne, Rosina — 11/9/76 D
Liadov, Anatoly — 11/24/00 C; 1/25/02 C; 3/18/04 C; 3/19/05 E; 2/21/09 C; 12/12/09 C; 5/20/10 B; 12/8/12 C; 8/28/14 D; 5/11/17 B; 9/17/62 B; 4/6/71 D
Liapunov, Sergei — 4/23/09 C; 3/11/14 C; 11/8/24 D; 9/17/62 B

Liatoshinsky, Boris — 11/26/55 C; 4/15/68 D
Library of Congress — 1/1/15 E; 2/14/20 D; 10/28/25 C; 10/28/25 E; 4/27/28 B; 12/11/28 E; 10/6/29 E; 10/30/32 E; 10/30/34 E; 12/16/35 E; 4/18/38 E; 3/6/39 E; 4/25/46 E; //50 E; 2/8/52 C; 11/4/53 D; 1/29/62 D; 10/30/64 C; 10/31/64 C; 11/1/64 C; 10/31/70 C; 5/4/72 C; 9/12/74 D; 5/9/77 D
Lichine, David — 10/25/10 D; 4/21/32 B; 4/13/33 B; 4/15/33 B; 10/24/33 B; 4/6/34 B; 7/18/35 B; 12/1/39 B; 2/28/40 B; 11/29/42 B; 10/24/50 E
Lidolt, Mascha — 11/21/32 B
Lidova, Irene — 8/21/53 B
Liebe der Danae, Die — 8/16/44 E; 8/14/52 A
Liebermann, Rolf — 10/6/51 C; 3/25/52 A; 8/17/54 A; 10/17/54 C; 8/17/57 A; 6/6/58 C; 3/1/59 C; 4/24/64 C
Lieberson, Goddard — 4/5/11 D; 5/29/77 D
Liebeslieder Walzer — 11/22/60 B
Liebhaber als Arzt, Der — 12/4/13 A
Lieder Eines Fahrenden Gesellen — 3/11/71 B
Lied von der Erde, Das (Schoenberg) — 11/20/11 C
Lied von der Erde, Das (Tudor) — 4/14/48 B
Liepa, Marius — 7/27/36 D; 4/9/68 B
Lieutenant Kije — 2/20/37 C
Lifar, Serge — 4/2/05 D; 4/28/25 E; 6/17/25 B; 12/11/25 B; 12/3/26 B; 4/30/27 B; 6/7/27 B; 6/6/28 B; 6/12/28 B; //29 E; 5/7/29 B; 5/21/29 B; 5/22/31 B; 12/16/32 B; 7/9/35 B; 1/5/37 E; 1/7/38 B; 2//38 E; 10//38 E; 3/7/42 E; 6/19/43 E; 5/5/46 B; 12/15/47 B; 6/14/50 B
Life and Afterlife in Egypt, Greece and India — 7/29/16 B
Life for the Tsar, A — 12/3/24 A; 2/37/39 A
Life of a Bee — 3/31/29 B
Ligeti, Gyorgy — 6/19/60 C; 10/22/61 C; 3/4/65 C; 6/5/65 C; 4/19/67 C; 10/22/67 C; 3/11/68 C; 12/16/68 C; 1/20/69 C; 4/23/69 C; 12/10/71 C; 9/16/72 C; 10/15/73 C; 3/17/78 A; 5/20/78 C
Light of the World, The — 11/22/00 D
Ligue Nationale pour la Defense de la Musique Francaise — 6/7/16 E
Lilac Garden — 1/26/36 B
Lilburn, Douglas — 4/16/40 C; 3/9/74 E
Lily — 3/11/73 C; 4/14/77 A
Limon, Jose — 1/12/08 D; 8/7/31 B; 3/11/43 B; 8/19/47 B; 3/31/49 B; 8/11/50 B; 8/20/53 B; 1/29/54 B; 8/19/54 B; 4/20/56 B; 7/12/56 B; 4/11/58 B; 3/13/63 B; 10//64 E; 10/2/72 B; 12/2/72 D; 7/15/75 D
Linaia-Agon — 4/26/72 C
Lincoln Address — 1/25/73 C
Lincoln Center Festival Overture — 9/25/62 C
Lincoln Center for the Performing Arts — 9/9/57 E; 5/14/59 E; 9/23/62 C; 9/11/69 E; 10/26/69 E
Lincoln Portrait — 5/14/42 C
Lincoln Symphony, The — 10/17/41 C
Lindberghflug — 7/28/29 C
Lindbergh, Charles — 11/18/27 C; 7/28/29 C
Lindberg, Svante — 9/28/63 B
Lind, Jenny — 7/1/06 D; 10/7/55 D
Lindsay Quartet — 5/20/79 C
Lindsay, Rosemary — 3/3/53 B
Lindstrom, Carl — 4/30/03 E
Linnite — 11/10/45 C
Lion, Ferdinand — 11/9/26 A
Lions — 10/28/65 C
Lipatti, Dinu — 4/1/17 D; 12/2/50 D
Lipkin, Arthur B. — 6/17/74 D
Lipkin, Seymour — 11/18/77 C
Lis de Saron, Le — 10/24/57 C

Lissenko, Nikolai — 12/20/03 A; 11/6/12 D
List, Eugene — 7/6/18 D; 1/1/42 C
Liszt, Franz — 11/22/28 B; 2/11/36 B;
    6/12/37 E; 1/23/40 B; 3/12/63 B;
    2/18/78 B
Litchfield Choral Union — 6/12/10 C;
    6/4/14 C
Lithuanian National Opera — 12/31/20 E
Little Carols of the Saints — 1/10/73 C
Little Fantasy — 5/3/59 C
Littlefield Ballet Company — 4/23/37 B
Littlefield, Catherine — 2/11/37 B; 4/23/37 B
Littlefield, Dorothie — 4/23/37 B
Little Group, The — 8/7/31 B
Little Masonic Cantata — 10/22/46 E
Little Orchestra Society — 10/20/47 C;
    2/21/53 A; 3/3/59 C; 5/14/79 D
Little Shop, The — 6/14/49 A
Little Symphony of New York — 4/5/46 C
Little Symphony Orchestra — 5/3/52 C
Liturgy of Saint John Chrysostom — 11/25/10 C
Litvin, Mark — 7/28/79 B
Litvinne, Felia — 2/14/18 E
Live from Lincoln Center (television program) —
    1/30/76 E
Liverpool Philharmonic Orchestra —
    9/30/44 C; 9/2/60 C
Liviabella, Lino — 8/16/36 E
Livre de vie, Le — 6/13/54 D
Livre d'orgue, Le (Charpentier) — 11/24/73 C
Livre d'orgue (Messiaen) — 3/21/55 C
Lizzie Borden — 3/25/65 A
Lland, Michael — 2/25/50 B
Lloyd, Gweneth — //38 E
Lloyd, Maude — 10/28/34 B; 1/26/36 B;
    2/19/37 B; 11/26/38 B; 12/5/38 B
Lloyd, Norman — 11/8/09 D; 3/31/49 B
Llubera, Lina — 3/5/53 D
Loca, La — 6/3/79 A
Lodivici, Cesare — 3/17/32 A
Lodoletta — 4/30/17 A
Loeffler, Charles Martin — 11/22/07 C;
    10/28/25 C; 2/5/31 E; 4/1/33 E;
    5/19/35 D
Loewe, Ferdinand — 2/11/03 C
Loew's Inc. — 9/11/54 E
Lomonov, Mikhail — 6/6/28 B
London Ballet — 12/5/38 B
London Choral Society — 9/7/73 C
London, Edwin — 2/23/72 C
London, George — 5/30/19 D; 4/20/41 D
London Overture, A — 8/17/37 C
London Palace Orchestra — //09 E
London Philharmonic — 6/20/01 C;
    12/11/08 C; 11/10/10 C; 10/7/32 E;
    1/15/34 C; 11/19/36 E; 7/24/42 C;
    2/1/54 C; 4/2/58 C; 3/8/63 C
London Royal Academy of Dancing — //62 E
London Sinfonietta — 12/4/73 C; 10/11/74 C;
    10/17/75 C; 1/28/76 C; 3/24/77 C
London Symphony, A — 3/27/14 C; 5/14/20 C
London Symphony Orchestra — 6/9/04 E;
    3/8/05 C; 6/14/12 E; 10/12/29 C;
    11/4/29 D; 9/28/43 C; 5/6/51 C;
    6/17/51 C; 8/15/53 C; 6/13/54 C;
    3/22/58 C; 7/13/59 C; 5/29/63 E;
    5/26/64 C; 3/2/67 C; 4/13/76 C
Long Christmas Dinner, The — 12/17/61 A
Long Island Symphony Orchestra —
    11/18/77 C
Longmans, Green and Co. — 7//03 E
Long, Marguerite — 11/10/15 C; 1/14/32 C;
    11/23/34 C; 2/13/66 D
Long-Thibaud competitions — 2/13/66 D
Longy School of Music — //15 E
Lontano — 10/22/67 C
Loomis, Harvey Worthington — 3/26/06 B
Loops — 12/3/71 B
Loos, Adolf — 4/13/31 C

L'Opera Russe a Paris — //32 E
Lopokhova, Lydia — 5/20/10 B
Lopokov, Andrei — 1/11/40 B
Lopokova, Lydia — 5/20/10 B; 4/12/17 B;
    5/18/17 B; 6/5/19 B; 11/2/21 B;
    4/26/31 B; 3/21/33 B
Lopokov, Feodor — 3/7/23 B; 10/29/24 B;
    4/27/27 B; 4/8/31 B; 4/4/35 B
Lopukhov, Andrei — 1/11/40 B
Loquasto, Santo — 5/30/74 B; 11/15/76 B
Lorca, Federico Garcia — 10/31/70 C
Lord Byron — 2/3/79 A
Lorenzaccio — 9/7/72 A
Lorenz, Max — 5/17/01 D
Loring, Eugene — 10/16/38 B; 1/11/40 B;
    1/13/40 B; 2/11/41 B; 9/13/66 B
Loriod, Yvonne — 5/10/43 C; 4/15/59 C;
    10/21/61 C; 6/7/69 C; 11/20/74 C
Los Angeles Chamber Music Society —
    1/31/77 E
Los Angeles Philharmonic — 10/24/19 E;
    //27 E; //29 E; //33 E; 5/18/35 C;
    12/10/36 C; 1/21/37 C; //39 E; //43 E;
    //56 E; 11/17/60 C; 12//61 E; 12/6/64 E;
    12/8/64 C; 4/6/67 C; 9/14/67 E;
    2/26/76 C; 1/31/77 E; 10/26/78 D;
    10/29/79 E
Los Angeles Philharmonic Chamber Music So-
    ciety — 12/12/77 C
Losch, Tilly — 5/9/24 B; 6/7/33 B
"Lost Chord, The" — 11/22/00 D
Lost Flute, The — 8/14/54 C
Lost Illusions — 12/31/35 B
Lost in the Stars — 10/30/49 A
Lothar, Rudolf — 11/15/03 A
Louise — 2/2/00 A
Louisiana Story — 11/26/48 C; 5/2/49 E
Louis, Murray — 12/17/67 B
Louis Riel — 9/23/67 A
Louisville Orchestra — 11/2/37 E; 12/7/48 C;
    4/5/49 C; 2/1/50 C; 3/1/50 C; 2/28/51 C;
    11/7/51 C; 2/11/53 C; 11/18/53 C;
    2/13/54 C; 3/17/54 C; 8/28/54 C;
    5/28/55 C; 9/24/55 C; 4/21/56 C;
    3/5/58 C; 3/1/60 C; 10/7/61 C;
    10/18/61 C
Lourie, Arthur — 10/13/66 D
Louw, Allan — 3/14/52 B
Love for Three Oranges, The — 12/30/21 A
Love of Peace, The — 10/15/12 A
Lovers, The — 9/22/71 C
Lovesso, Alberto — 2/14/70 A
Love's Triumph — 7/7/20 A
Love that Casteth Out Fear, The — 9/7/04 C
Lowenthal, Jerome — 3/15/76 C
Low, Johann — 4/13/31 C
Low Speed — 10/28/52 C
Lualdi, Adriano — 4/22/25 A
Lubell, Roberta — 12/1/57 B
Lucarelli, Bert — 11/9/75 C
Lucas, Leighton — 5/7/74 B
Lucedia — 10/20/34 A
Lucevan le stelle, E — 1/28/21 E
Lucifer — 3/8/01 D
Lucky Peter's Journey — 12/18/69 A
Lucrezia — 2/24/37 A
Luders, Adam — 1/26/78 B; 5/18/78 B
Ludlow, Conrad — 3/29/60 B; 11/16/60 B;
    11/22/60 B; 4/13/67 B; 1/23/69 B;
    12/4/69 B
Ludus de nato infante mirificus — 12/11/60 A
Ludus Tonalis — 2/15/44 C; 12/28/63 D
Ludwig, Christa — 3/16/28 D
Ludwig, Leopold — 1/12/08 D; 4/25/79 D
Luening, Otto — 6/15/00 D; 1/30/35 C;
    4/11/36 C; 5/5/48 A; 10/28/52 C;
    3/20/54 C; 12/2/54 C; 4/20/56 B;
    1/8/59 E; 3/20/60 C; 5/9-10/61 E;
    5/15/62 C; 10/22/63 C; 12/13/65 C;
    3/7/71 C; 11/21/77 C

Lulu — 11/30/34 C; 1/14/36 E; 6/2/37 A;
    8/30/76 D; 2/24/79 A
Lumumba, Patrice — 1/20/65 C
Lunacharsky, Anatol — 11/8/17 E; 12/1/17 E;
    7/12/18 E; 9/23/18 E; 9/25/21 E;
    5/5/23 E; 5/21/27 A
Lundborg, Arne — 2/11/41 B
Lunel, Armand — 5/7/26 A; 6/1/54 A
Lustige Witwe, Die — 12/28/05 A; 10/24/48 D
Lustro — 5/31/73 C
Lutge, Mme. Norma K. — 10/30/35 D
Lutoslawski, Witold — 1/25/13 D; 6/17/39 C;
    4/1/48 C; 4/20/51 C; 11/26/54 C;
    4/24/61 C; 10/14/70 C; 3/12/78 C
Lutyens, Elisabeth — 7/9/06 D; 4/17/73 A;
    9/7/73 C; 5/5/74 C; 5/6/74 C; 7/15/76 C
Lux Aeternae — 1/16/72 C
Lyford, Ralph — 6/27/20 E; 9/3/26 D
Lyon, Annabelle — 2/11/41 B; 4/8/42 B
Lyric Fantasies — 2/23/75 C
Lyric Opera of Chicago — 11/29/78 A;
    10/14/79 E
Lyric Suite — 1/8/27 C; 1/21/29 C; 11/1/79 C

— M —

Maag, Peter — 5/10/19 D
Maazel, Lorin — 3/6/30 D; 8/14/39 D;
    9/29/68 A; 3/14/77 C
Macbeth — 11/30/10 A; 7/15/59 D
MacBryde, Robert — 12/12/51 B
Macdonald, Brian — 2/19/65 B
MacDonough, Glen — 1/1/00 A
MacDowell Colony (Peterborough, N.H.) —
    1/23/08 D; 11/12/75 E
MacDowell, Edward — 1/23/08 D; 10/24/08 C
MacDowell Memorial Association —
    1/23/08 D
MacGregor, Willard — 2/15/44 C
Machavariani, Alexei — 11/29/57 B
MacKaye, Percy — 3/8/17 A
MacKay, Hannah — 12/13/79 C
Mackerras, Charles — 2/25/54 B; 6/18/58 A
MacKervas, Charles — 3/13/51 B
Mackinnon, Sheila — 10/3/68 B
MacLeary, Donald — 4/12/60 B
Macleod, Fiona — 8/26/14 A
Maclezova, Xenia — 1/17/16 B
MacMillan, Kenneth — 12/11/29 D; 2/1/53 B;
    2/25/54 B; 1/18/55 B; 6/7/56 B;
    4/12/60 B; 10/11/60 B; 5/8/62 B;
    7/13/63 B; 2/9/65 B; 11/30/66 B;
    7/22/71 B; 5/7/74 B; 2/14/78 B
MacNeil, Cornell — 9/24/22 D; 3/15/50 D
Madama Butterfly — 2/17/04 A; 5/28/04 A;
    10/15/06 A; 2/11/49 D
Madame Bovary — 5/26/67 A
Madame Sans-Gene — 3/17/10 A; 1/25/15 A
Madeira, Jean — 11/14/18 D
Maderna, Bruno — 4/21/20 D; //57 E;
    2/7/70 C; 1/31/71 C; 3/3/72 C; 8/8/72 C;
    3/16/73 A; 5/15/73 C; 7/6/73 C;
    11/13/73 D
Madonna Imperia — 3/5/27 A
Madrid — 11/7/30 C
Madsen, Egon — 8/24/42 D; 11/7/65 B;
    3/8/70 B; 3/24/70 B
Maeterlinck, Maurice — 2/3/01 C; 4/30/02 A;
    10/25/12 A
Magallanes, Nicholas — 9/23/44 B; 2/27/46 B;
    3/22/48 B; 4/28/48 B; 1/20/49 B;
    12/1/49 B; 3/2/50 B; 2/20/51 B;
    6/14/51 B; 12/4/51 B; 2/19/52 B;
    11/25/52 B; 1/6/53 B; 1/19/54 B;
    2/2/54 B; 2/27/55 B; 3/1/56 B;
    11/21/57 B; 11/22/60 B
Magdelena — 7/26/40 A
Mageia — 6/12/78 C

Mager, Jorg — 7/25/26 E
Magic Mirror, The — 7/14/10 D
Magister Choralis — 9/5/10 D
Magnard, Alberic — 9/3/14 D
Magnecord — 1//49 E
Magnetic tape — 9/17/31 E; 12//38 E
Magnetophon — //35 E
Magriel, Paul — 1//42 E
Mahler, Alma — 10/12/24 C; 4/19/36 C; 12/19/60 C
Mahler, Fritz — 7/16/01 D; 2/22/41 C
Mahler, Gustav — 1/22/00 A; 2/17/01 C; 7/16/01 D; 11/25/01 C; 3/10/02 E; 6/9/02 C; 2/22/03 D; 10/18/04 C; 5/27/06 C; 10/15/07 E; 1/1/08 D; 9/19/08 C; //09 E; 2/19/09 A; 4/17/10 E; 9/12/10 C; 3/19/11 E; 4/24/11 C; 5/17/11 E; 5/18/11 D; 11/20/11 C; 6/26/12 C; 3/31/13 C; 10/12/24 C; 10/16/31 C; 3/1/36 E; 2/19/37 B; 11/28/47 E; 4/14/48 B; 12/19/60 C; 11/7/65 B; 6/18/67 C; 12/1/67 B; 4/9/68 C; 10/10/68 C; 11/24/70 C; 3/11/71 B; 1/10/73 B; 10/26/76 D
Maia — 1/15/10 A
"Maiden Sang in a Church Choir, A" (Vassilenko) — 3/11/56 D
Maid of Orleans — 10/22/79 A
Maid of Pskov, The — 6/21/08 D
Maids, The — 5/13/57 B
Mainardi, Enrico — 5/15/57 E
Maiorano, Robert — 5/22/69 B; 6/25/72 B
Maitland, Robert — 6/27/20 E
Maizel, B.S. — 4/12/63 B
Major, Ervin — 1/26/01 D
Makarova, Natalia — 10/21/40 D; 9/4/70 E; 7/3/74 B
Makarov, Askold — 12/27/56 B
Making Ends Meet — 4/13/69 C
Makrokosmos, Vol. I — 2/8/73 C
Makrokosmos, Vol. II — 11/12/74 C
Makropulos Affair, The — 12/18/26 A
Malaise — 11/21/35 C
Malbruk — 1/19/10 A
Malcolm, George — 2/28/17 D
Malediction — 2/5/71 C
Malibran, Maria — 7/1/06 D
Malinche, La — 3/31/49 B
Malipiero, Gian Francesco — 5/15/13 C; 1/24/14 A; 1/27/18 C; 3/11/17 C; 11/5/25 A; 3/24/26 A; 3/31/28 A; 5/15/31 A; 9/6/32 A; 12/15/32 A; 1/13/34 A; 4/2/34 C; 2/8/36 A; 10/24/42 A; 6/30/43 A; 5/2/47 C; 2/27/48 C; 2/11/49 C; 11/3/49 C; 5/4/50 A; 3/21/51 C; 3/16/63 A; 4/23/63 C; 9/21/66 C
Malipiero, Riccardo — 10/30/64 C
Maliszewski, Witold — 3/15/30 A
Malkin Conservatory — 7/13/51 D
Malkin, Joseph — 7/13/51 D
Malko, Nikolai — 5/12/26 C

Maltheurs d'Orphee, Les — 5/7/26 A
Mamelles de Tiresias, Les — 6/3/47 A; 1/30/63 D
Ma mere l'Oye (Robbins) — 5/22/75 B
Ma Mere l'Oye (Ravel) — 4/20/10 C
Mam'zelle Fifi — 1/17/03 A
Manaieff, Michel — 5/11/39 B
Manchester, P.W. — 3/13/46 E
Mandel, Alan — 11/25/79 C
Mandelberg, Yevgeny — 3/22/39 B
Mandia, John — 3/6/56 B
Mandu-Carara — 1/23/48 C
Manen, Hans van — 7/11/32 D; 7/7/64 B
Man from Midian, The — 11/1/51 C

Manhattan Opera — 11/25/07 D; 1/15/08 D; 2/19/08 A; 11/10/09 D; 8/1/19 D; 12/19/19 D
Manhattan School of Music — //17 E; 10/7/76 D
Manlove, John — 5/31/63 A
Manner von Blackmoor, Die — 11/18/56 A
Mannes College of Music — //16 E
Mann, Thomas — 12/17/46 E; //48 E; 4/4/54 A; 8/6/69 D
Manon — 5/7/74 B
Manon Lescaut — 1/14/00 A
Manru — 5/29/01 A
MANTRA — 10/8/70 C
Manual of Harmony (book) — 2/25/06 D
Man Without a Country, The — 5/12/37 A
"Maple Leaf Rag" — 4/1/17 D
Mapleson's Opera Company, Colonel Henry — 8/20/20 D
Marcella — 11/9/07 A
Marchesi de Castrone, Salvatore — 11/17/13 D
Marchesi, Mathilde — 11/17/13 D
Marche solennelle — 3/26/18 D
Marconi, Guglielmo — 12/11/01 E; 7//06 E
Marconi Velvetone disc — //30 E
Marco Takes a Walk — 11/14/42 C
Mardones, Jose — 11/15/18 D
Mare, Rolf de — //20 E; 10/25/20 B; //53 E
Margherita da Cortona — 1/1/38 A
Marginal Worlds — 2/23/72 C
Margolies, Linda — 5/8/55 B
Margot — 10/10/14 A
Marguerite and Armand — 3/12/63 B
Margulies Trio — 11/17/10 C
Maria d'Alessandria — 9/9/37 A
Maria del Carmen — 10/27/06 A
Maria Egiziaca — 3/16/32 A; 7/23/33 A
Maria Golovin — 8/20/58 A
Marie Jeanne — 5/29/41 B
Marienleben, Das — 6/17/23 C; 12/28/63 D
Maries de la Tour Eiffel, Les — 6/19/21 B
Marinetti, Filippo — 2/4/47 D
Marinuzzi, Giuseppe — 7/23/33 A; 5/6/38 E; 8/17/45 D
Marketenderin, Die — 5/10/14 A
Markevitch, Igor — 7/27/12 D; 12/15/31 D; 6/2/53 C
Markheim — 3/31/66 A
Mark II RCA Synthesizer — 1/8/59 E
Markings — 8/18/66 C
Markova, Alicia — 12/1/10 D; 6/17/25 B; 2/6/31 B; 4/26/31 B; 10/9/32 B; 12/5/33 B; 1/30/34 B; 4/3/34 B; 5/15/34 B; 11/20/34 B; 5/20/35 B; 2//38 E; 5/5/38 B; 10//38 E; 5/11/39 B; 10/17/40 B; 10/7/41 B; 9/8/42 B; 4/6/43 B; 10/1/46 B; 10/24/50 E; 11/6/55 E; 2/22/61 D
Marks, Bruce — 12/1/67 B
Marks, Lillian Alicia — *see* Markova, Alicia
Marlboro Festival — 6/3/75 D
Marlboro Music School — 7/8/51 E
Marlowe, Sylvia — 9/26/08 B; 3/15/73 C
Marosszek Dances — 3/6/67 D
Marouf, Savetier du Caire — 5/15/14 A
Marquis de Cuevas Ballet — 12/23/52 B
Marriage, The (Martinu) — 2/7/53 A
Marriage, The (Mussorgsky) — 10/26/17 A; 9/14/37 A
"Marseillaise, La" — 7/14/15 E; 8/24/44 E
Marteau, Henri — 10/13/08 C
Marteau sans Maitre, Le — 6/18/55 C; 6/13/60 C
Martenot, Maurice — 4/20/28 E; 1/13/38 E
Martha Graham Dance Company — 8/13/48 B; 4/22/52 B; 5/8/55 B; 4/3/58 B; 8/17/62 B
Martin, Easthope — 6/14/12 E

Martinelli, Giovanni — 12/29/10 D; 11/20/13 D; 1/25/15 A; 1/28/16 A; 2/2/69 D
Martin, Erin — 3/30/65 B
Martinet, Francoise — 9/30/62 B
Martinez, G. — 4/15/15 B
Martinez, Jose — 11/20/46 B
Martin, Frank — 3/26/42 C; 5/17/46 C; 4/29/49 C; 1/24/52 C; 6/17/56 A; 12/24/59 C; 4/23/63 A; 7/13/63 B; 4/28/70 C; 9/9/73 C; 11/21/74 D
Martin, Grace-Lynne — 2/8/54 C
Martin, Keith — 4/2/64 B
Martin Korda, D.P. — 6/15/60 A
Martin, Mary — 10/7/43 A
Martino, Donald — 5/7/74 E; 12/18/78 C
Martinon, Jean — 1/10/10 D; 10/24/57 C; 1/24/66 C; 10/1/67 C; 11/2/67 C; 3/28/68 C; 6/26/74 D; 3/1/76 D
Martin Paz (Varese) — 11/6/65 D
Martin, Riccardo — 1/13/10 E
Martin, Robert — 2/17/64 C
Martins, Peter — 10/27/46 D; 1/29/70 B; 6/18/72 B; 6/22/72 B; 5/4-31/75 B; 5/22/75 B; 5/29/75 B; 1/22/76 B; 1/19/78 B; 5/18/78 B; 5/18/78 B; 7/13/79 B
Martinu, Bohuslav — 11/18/27 C; 12/14/28 C; 9/19/33 B; 3/18/37 A; 3/16/38 A; 2/9/40 C; 11/14/41 C; 1/23/42 C; 10/15/42 C; 10/28/43 C; 10/12/45 C; 11/30/45 C; 12/19/45 C; 1/21/47 C; 5/1/47 C; 5/27/47 C; 11/20/49 C; 12/8/50 C; 5/28/51 A; 2/7/53 A; 1/7/55 C; 5/20/55 A; 10/4/56 C; 1/24/58 C; 1/31/59 C; 5/17/59 A; 8/28/59 D; 6/23/60 C; 10/15/60 C; 3/2/61 A; 6/9/61 C; 4/2/63 C; 9/28/63 B; 7/22/71 B
Martucci, Giuseppe — 6/1/09 D
Martucci, Vicente — 6/24/30 E
Martyre de Saint-Sebastien, Le — 5/8/11 E; 5/22/11 A
Marx, Karl — 8/6/69 D
Mary Moody Northern Pavilion (transportable stage) — 6/4/76 E
Mascagni, Pietro — 1/17/01 A; 3/16/05 A; 1/15/10 A; 6/2/11 A; 12/15/13 A; 4/30/17 A; 7/2/17 C; 5/2/21 A; 3/23/32 A; 1/16/35 A; 8/2/45 D
Maschere, Le — 1/17/01 A
Maskarade — 11/11/06 A
Masks, Props and Mobiles — 1/26/53 B
Maslow, Sophie — 7/18/43 B
Mason, Daniel Gregory — 12/4/53 D
Mason, Edith — 3/8/17 A
Mason & Hamlin — 12/4/53 D
Mason, Henry — 12/4/53 D
Mason, Lowell — 12/4/53 D; 5/3/78 E
Mason, Monica — 5/8/62 B; 3/2/70 B; 5/7/74 B; 2/14/78 B
Mason, William — 12/4/53 D
Masque of Angels, The — 1/9/64 A
Masque of the Red Death, The — 1/29/16 C
Mass (Bernstein) — 9/8/71 C
Mass (Dello Joio) — 1/11/70 C
Mass (Hindemith) — 11/12/63 C
Mass (Kubelik) — 5/18/79 C
Mass (Smyth) — 4/9/02 A
Mass (Stravinsky) — 10/27/48 C
Masselos, William — 8/11/20 D; 10/25/57 C
Massenet, Jules — 11/20/01 A; 2/18/02 A; 2/4/04 A; 2/14/05 A; 10/31/06 A; 2/7/07 A; 11/25/07 D; 11/27/08 A; 5/5/09 A; 2/19/10 A; 2/17/12 A; 8/13/12 D; 4/25/13 A; 2/23/14 A; 4/1/22 A; 3/21/34 B; 3/7/42 E; 5/7/74 B
Massey, Guy — 11/26/38 B

Massine, Leonide — 5/14/14 B; 12/20/15 B;
   1/17/16 B; 4/12/17 B; 5/11/17 B;
   5/18/17 B; 6/5/19 B; 7/22/19 B;
   2/2/20 B; 5/15/20 B; 1/19/24 B;
   6/15/24 B; 4/28/25 B; 6/17/25 B;
   6/7/27 B; 6/6/28 B; 4/11/30 B; //32 E;
   4/13/33 B; 4/15/33 B; 4/15/33 B;
   10/24/33 B; 4/6/34 B; 3/20/35 B;
   7/24/36 B; 1/30/38 B; 2//38 E; 3//38 E;
   4/5/38 B; 5/5/38 B; 6/17/38 E; 7/21/38 B;
   10//38 E; 10/20/38 B; 5/4/39 B;
   5/11/39 B; 11/9/39 B; 10/8/41 B;
   9/8/42 B; 1//48 E; 10/24/50 E;
   12/12/51 B; 2/22/61 D; 6/18-25/72 B;
   3/16/79 D
Massine, Lorca — 5/5/78 B
Mass in G Minor (Vaughan Williams) —
   8/26/58 D
Mass of Life, A — 6/4/08 C; 6/7/09 C
Master Array of the Interval Cycles — //77 E
Master-Builder (Kalomiris) — 3/24/16 A
Master Builder, The (Brunswick) — 5/26/71 D
Matelots, Les — 6/17/25 B
Mathematical Basis of the Arts, The (book) —
   3/23/43 D
Mather, Bruce — 7/21/71 C
Mathews, Max — //58 E
Mathias, William — 11/1/34 D; 3/1/62 C;
   8/10/62 C; 3/29/66 C; 6/23/66 C;
   9/30/71 C
Mathis der Maler — 3/12/34 C; 5/28/38 A;
   3/8/63 C; 12/28/63 D
Matisse, Henri — 2/2/20 B
Matsudaira, Yoritsune — 5/5/07 D; 6/3/54 C;
   10/16/60 C
Matteo Falcone — 12/27/06 A
Mattfeld, Marie — 2/19/09 A
Matthay, Tobias — 7//03 E; 12/14/45 D
Matzenauer, Margarete — 11/13/11 D;
   11/1/26 D
Maule, Michael — 6/14/51 B; 11/11/52 B
Maurel, Victor — 10/22/23 D
Mavra (Stravinsky) — 6/3/22 A; 4/6/71 D
Maw, Nicholas — 11/5/35 D; 11/12/64 A;
   5/1/66 C; 7/19/70 A
Max, Burle — 9/12/32 C
Maxfield, Joseph P. — //19 E; 5//24 E
Maximilien — 1/4/32 A
Maximova, Yekaterina — 2/1/39 D;
   9/17/62 B; 4/9/68 B
Maxixe — 12/10/17 E
Mayakovsky, Vladimir — 1/21/34 C
Mayerling — 2/14/78 B
May, Pamela — 2/16/37 B; 6/15/37 B;
   1/23/40 B; 12/23/48 B
Mayr, Richard — 10/10/19 A
Mayuzumi, Toshiro — 3/20/63 B
Mazzo, Kay — 1/23/69 B; 5/22/69 B;
   1/29/70 B; 6/18/72 B; 6/22/72 B;
   5/22/75 B
McBride, Patricia — 11/27/49 B; 1/7/64 B;
   5/6/64 B; 2/4/65 B; 4/21/66 B;
   4/13/67 B; 11/23/67 B; 5/22/69 B;
   1/29/70 B; 2/5/70 B; 7/30/70 B;
   5/24/73 B; 5/16/74 B; 7/17/74 B;
   5/22/75 B; 5/29/75 B; 7/30/75 B;
   6/4/77 B
McCarran Act — 11/20/50 E
McCarthy, Sheila — 5/5/31 B
McCoon, Cosme — 10/26/44 E
McCormack, John — 10/5/07 D; 11/10/09 D;
   11/29/10 D; 9/16/45 D
McDonald, Gene — 9/6/63 B
McGehee, Helen — 8/13/48 B; 4/22/52 B;
   4/27/60 B; 3/4/62 B; 8/17/62 B
McGinnis, Robert E. — 1/1/76 D
McGlaughlin, William — 8/26/78 C
McKayle, Donald — 2/24/55 B

McKayle Dance Company, Donald —
   5/10/59 B
McPhee, Colin — 3/15/01 D; 3/11/29 C
Mead, George — 4/1/37 A
Meadow Brook Music Festival — 7/23/64 E
Meadowlark — 10/3/68 B
Measures Taken, The — 12/13/30 A
Meck, Mme. Nadezhda von — 3/25/18 D
Medea (Cullberg) — 10/31/50 B
Medea (Krenek) — 3/13/53 C
Medea (Tommasini) — 4/8/06 A
Medee (Milhaud) — 10/7/39 A
Mediator Dei — 11/20/47 E
Meditation at Night on the Majesty of God as Revealed
   by the Aurora Borealis — 6/6/28 B
Meditation — 12/10/63 B
Meditation on Zeami — 10/5/64 C
Meditations of Ecclesiastes — 5/6/57 E
Meditations sur le mystere de la Sainte-Trinite —
   3/20/72 C
Meditation uber die Ostersequenz — 4/8/75 C
Medium, The — 5/8/46 A
Medtner, Nikolai — 11/13/51 D
Medusa — 11/16/57 B
Meeker, Jess — 1/28/06 B
Meeting of the Volga with the Don River, The —
   2/22/52 C
Mefistofele — 6/10/18 D
Mehta, Zubin — 4/29/36 D; 12//61 E;
   9/21/63 E; 12/8/64 C; 4/6/67 C;
   9/14/67 E; 9/14/78 C; 10/25/79 C
Meier, Gustave — 9/6/61 C
Meistersinger, Die — 5/31/05 D; 7/22/24 E
Mela and Fair — 12/11/59 C
Melba, Nellie — 4/11/02 E; 2/18/04 A;
   11/29/10 D; 6/8/26 E; 2/23/31 D;
   4/27/31 D
Melbourne Conservatory — 6/8/26 E
Melchior, Lauritz — 4/2/13 D; 10/9/18 D;
   2/17/26 D; 2/2/50 E; 3/18/73 D
Melenis — 11/13/12 A
Melikov, Arif — 3/23/61 B
Melik-Pashayev, Alexander — 10/23/05 D
Melodien — 12/10/71 C
Melorhythmic Dances — 8/16/66 C
Melos (periodical) — 2/1/20 E; 1/17/22 E;
   8/18/70 D
Melos-Verlag — 2/1/20 E
Melusine — 4/29/71 A
Memoirs d'un amnesique — 7/1/25 D
Memorial to Lidice — 10/28/43 C
Memory — 3/12/71 C
Memory for Three Voices — 5/3/74 C
Men and Mountains — 12/7/24 C; 10/15/27 E
Mendel, Arthur — 6/6/05 D; 10/14/79 D
Mendelson, Myra — 3/5/53 D
Mendelssohn, Felix — 2/26/24 B; 3/1/36 E;
   11/11/52 B; 4/2/64 B; 7/1/71 B
Mendelssohn, Hugo von — 4/17/75 D
Mendelssohn, Mira — 6/12/46 A; 11/3/46 A
Mendelssohn Society, International Felix —
   4/17/75 D
Mendelssohn Symphony — 7/1/71 B
Mendes, Catulle — 10/31/06 A
Mendicants of an Evening — 5/2/73 B
Meneo, Cesare — 9/9/37 A
Mengarelli, Mario — 9/28/63 B
Mengehelli, Antonietta — 1/26/75 D
Mengelberg, Willem — //03 E; 10/4/12 C;
   4/23/18 C; 4/11/22 E; 11/2/22 C;
   12/9/26 C; 3/30/28 E; 7/6/30 C;
   11/14/35 C; 4/23/39 C; 11/23/39 C;
   3/14/40 C; 3/21/51 D
Mennini, Peter — see Mennin, Peter
Mennin, Peter — 5/17/23 D; 2/27/47 C;
   11/18/53 C; 1/23/64 C; 11/21/74 C;
   3/28/76 C; 1/18/79 C
Men of Blackmoor, The — 11/18/56 A

Menotti, Gian-Carlo — 7/7/11 D; 4/1/37 A;
   4/22/39 A; 2/11/41 A; 2/20/42 A;
   11/2/45 C; 5/8/46 A; 2/18/47 A;
   2/28/47 B; 3/1/50A; 5/1/50 E;
   12/24/51 A; 10/19/51 C; 12/27/54 A;
   5/2/55 E; 1/15/58 A; 8/20/58 A; //58 E;
   6/17/59 A; 3/3/63 A; 10/21/63 A;
   5/18/63 C; 12/19/68 A; 10/6/70 C;
   5/27/76 A; 8/4/76 C; 3/15/77 C;
   5/25/77 E; 5/24/78 C; 6/3/79 A;
   4/22/79 C
Mentchinova, Vera — 5/15/20 B
Menuhin, Yehudi — 4/22/16 D; 11/25/27 D;
   11/4/29 D; //31 E; 5/4/55 D; 4/27/74 C;
   7/3/76 C
Merante, Louis — 2/14/61 B
Mercante di Venezia, Il — 5/25/61 A
Mercier, Margaret — 2/19/65 B
Mercure — 6/15/24 B
Mercury (record label) — 6/21/48 E
Meri, Le — 7/21/68 D
Mer, La (Debussy) — 10/15/05 C; 3/1/07 C;
   3/21/07 C; 3/25/18 D
Merli, Francesco — 12/11/76 D
Merram-Nikisch, Grete — 11/9/26 A
Merrill, Robert — 6/4/17 D; 12/15/45 D
Merry Mount — 5/20/33 A; 2/10/34 A
Meschke, Michael — 3/17/78 A
Mese mariano — 3/17/10 A
Messager, Andre — 2/2/00 A; 11/20/01 A;
   4/30/02 A; 4/7/19 A; 2/24/29 D;
   2/14/61 B
Message to Denmark Hill, A — 12/23/70 C
Messel, Oliver — 2/20/46 B; 6/2/53 B
Messe pour le temps present — 4/3/67 B
Messerer, Asaf — 11/6/03 D; 9/17/62 B
Messiaen, Olivier — 12/10/08 D; 2/19/31 C;
   2/12/33 C; 12/22/35 E; 1/15/41 C;
   5/10/43 C; 4/21/45 C; 12/2/49 C;
   5/2/51 C; 10/11/53 C; 3/21/55 C;
   10/10/56 E; 4/15/59 C; 10/16/60 C;
   10/3/63 C; 10/17/64 C; 5/7/65 C;
   6/20/65 C; 6/7/69 C; 10/9/71 E;
   3/20/72 C; 3/28/72 C; 11/7/72 C;
   11/20/74 C
Messiah — 4/13/79 E
Metamorphosen (Strauss, R.) — 1/25/46 C
Metamorphosen, Modi XII (Respighi) — 11/7/30 C
Metamorphoses (Balanchine) — 11/25/52 B
Metamorphoses on Saibara — 6/3/54 C
Metastaseis & Pithoprakta — 1/18/68 B
Methode complete de flute — 11/22/08 D
Metropolitan Ballet — 2/6/48 B
Metropolitan Day — 8/6/38 B
Metropolitan Opera — 11/14/00 D; 1/28/03 E;
   11/23/03 D; 11/25/03 D; 12/24/03 E;
   3/2/04 E; 4/17/06 E; 4/18/06 E;
   11/16/06 E; 11/26/06 D; 12/3/06 E;
   12/5/06 D; 1/22/07 A; 1/27/07 E;
   11/20/07 D; 11/22/07 D; 1/1/08 D;
   1/6/08 D; 11/4/08 D; 11/16/08 D;
   11/20/08 D; 11/26/08 D; 11/27/08 A;
   12/7/08 D; 2/6/09 E; 2/15/09 E;
   2/19/09 A; 4/9/09 E; 4/27/09 D;
   11/16/09 D; 11/17/09 D; 1/13/10 E;
   2/28/10 B; 3/18/10 A; 11/29/10 D;
   12/10/10 A; 12/28/10 A; 5/18/11 D;
   11/13/11 D; 12/28/11 D; 3/14/12 A;
   12/27/12 D; 2/27/13 A; 10/23/13 D;
   12/9/13 A; 1/2/14 A; 4/23/14 E;
   8/12/14 D; 11/20/14 D; 1/25/15 A;
   10/12/15 E; 11/18/15 D; 11/25/15 D;
   1/28/16 A; 10/23/16 B; 12/4/16 D;
   3/8/17 A; 3/6/18 A; 3/23/18 A;
   11/15/18 D; 12/14/18 A; 3/12/19 A;
   12/19/19 D; 1/31/20 A; 3/7/20 A;
   11/26/20 D; 12/24/20 E; 11/14/21 D;
   11/19/21 A; 11/19/21 D; 12/9/21 E;
   1/19/22 D; 4/22/22 E; 11/22/22 D;

2/23/24 D; 2/26/24 B; 11/3/24 D;
1/2/25 D; 2/17/26 D; 2/19/26 B;
11/1/26 D; 2/17/27 A; 2/7/28 D;
1/19/29 A; 12/28/29 E; 1/3/31 D;
2/7/31 A; 3/11/32 E; 1/7/33 A;
1/16/33 D; 1/20/33 E; 5/20/33 A;
1/11/34 D; 2/10/34 A; 2/2/35 D;
5/10/35 D; 3/29/36 E; 12/21/36 D;
2/13/37 D; 5/12/37 A; 5/15/37 D;
12/17/37 D; 1/21/38 D; 11/24/38 D;
1/13/39 D; 1/5/40 D; 2/9/40 D;
3/10/40 E; 12/21/40 D; 11/29/41 D;
2/20/42 A; 1/25/45 D; 12/15/45 D;
2/4/49 D; 2/2/50 E; 6/1/50 E;
11/17/50 D; 3/17/51 D; 12/11/52 E;
9/27/53 E; 1/7/55 D; 1/1/56 E;
10/29/56 D; 11/13/56 D; 1/13/58 E;
1/15/58 A; 11/6/58 E; 3/4/60 D;
5/14/60 D; 12/6/60 D; 1/27/61 D;
3/8/61 D; 11/19/62 D; 1/10/64 D;
2/6/65 D; 4/16/66 E; 9/16/66 A;
9/16/66 E; 3/17/67 A; 6/5/71 D;
4/22/72 E; 7/18/72 D; 4/5/73 D;
1/13/76 E; 4/3/76 D; 10/15/77 E;
2/24/79 A; 9/24/79 E

Metropolitan Opera Guild — 10/24/79 D
Metropolitan Opera Prize — 3/14/12 A
Meurte d'Abel, Le — 3/8/01 D
Mexican Opera Nacional — 10/16/45 D
Meyerbeer, Giacomo — 12/27/12 D; 3/1/36 E;
    10/29/36 A; 2/16/37 B
Meyer, Kerstin — 3/17/78 A
Meyer, Marcelle — 7/1/37 C
MGM — 6/21/48 E
Miaskovsky, Nikolai — 6/13/11 C; 6/2/14 C;
    2/27/15 C; 7/18/20 C; 5/4/24 C;
    2/8/25 C; 5/23/26 C; 4/7/28 C;
    4/29/28 C; 6/1/32 C; 1/16/33 C;
    10/16/34 C; 2/24/35 C; 10/28/35 C;
    10/24/36 C; 10/1/37 C; 2/15/39 C;
    11/16/40 C; 11/28/40 C; 1/12/42 C;
    7/20/42 C; 12/8/43 C; 3/6/47 C;
    4/11/48 E; 2/12/48 C; 8/8/50 D;
    12/5/50 C; 5/28/58 E; 11/28/72 D
Michael Kohlhaas — 11/4/33 A
Michaux, Henri — 10/19/58 C
Michelangeli, Arturo Benedetti — 1/5/20 D
Michigan Opera Theater — 10/22/79 A
Midas — 6/2/14 B
Midsommarvaka — 5/10/04 C
Midsummer Marriage, The — 1/27/55 A
Midsummer Night's Dream, A (Balanchine) —
    1/17/62 B; 4/24/64 E
Midsummer Night's Dream, A (Britten) —
    6/11/60 A
Miedel, Ranier — 4/10/78 C
Mielziner, Jo — 4/8/42 B
Miessner, Benjamin Franklin — 3/25/76 D
Mighty Casey, The — 5/4/53 A
Mighty Five of Russian Music, The —
    10/23/06 D
Mignone, Francisco — 9/5/28 A; 4/22/42 C
Migot, Georges — 12/22/35 E; 3/7/42 E;
    1/5/76 D
Mihalovici, Marcel — 10/6/51 C; 12/14/71 C
Mikado, The — 11/22/00 D
Mikka "S" — 3/11/76 C
Mikrokosmos — 9/26/45 D; 10/31/50 B
Milanov, Zinka — 5/17/06 D; 12/17/37 D
Milberg, Barbara — 12/1/57 B
Mild and Leise — 4/7/75 C
Mildmay, Audrey — 12/19/00 D; 5//34 E
Milena — 4/16/73 C
Milhaud, Darius — 1/16/20 E; 2/21/20 B;
    6/6/21 B; 6/19/21 B; 8/7/22 E;
    10/25/23 B; 6/20/24 B; 5/7/26 A;
    12/9/26 C; 4/16/27 A; 7/17/27 A;
    11/27/27 A; 12/16/27 A; 4/20/28 A;
    3/4/29 B; 12/15/29 C; 5/5/30 A;

12/5/30 C; 1/4/32 A; 11/23/34 C;
    3/27/35 A; 7/1/37 C; 9/12/37 C;
    12/2/38 C; 10/7/39 A; 8/4/40 C;
    10/17/40 C; 11/13/42 C; 12/11/42 C;
    12/6/43 C; 11/16/45 C; 11/18/45 C;
    12/6/45 C; 5/26/46 C; 11/28/46 C;
    12/20/46 C; 5/28/47 C; 10/30/47 C;
    5/20/48 C; 2/12/49 C; 5/18/49 C;
    8/10/49 C; 3/3/50 C; 5/12/50 A;
    5/13/52 C; 5/30/52 C; 10/16/53 C;
    6/1/54 A; 9/13/55 C; 10/7/55 C;
    6/25/56 C; 10/10/56 E; 5/13/57 B;
    4/22/58 C; 3/29/60 C; 4/4/61 C;
    2/16/62 C; 12/3/63 C; 12/20/63 C;
    10/31/64 C; 2/27/70 C; 12/17/70 C;
    11/13/73 C
Millar, Patricia — 12/20/49 B
Millay, Edna Saint Vincent — 2/17/27 A
Mille, Agnes de — //09 D; 2/19/37 B;
    6/15/38 B; 2/11/41 B; 2/25/44 B;
    3/17/65 B; 3/23/65 B; 10/26/65 B
Miller, Elizabeth — 2/16/37 B
Miller, Patricia — 2/25/54 B; //69 E
Miller, Robert — 11/12/74 C; 4/29/75 C;
    10/24/77 C
Millions d'Arlequin, Les — 2/10/00 B
Milnes, Sherrill — 9/24/79 E
Milstein, Nathan — 12/31/04 D; 10/28/29 D
Mimi Pinson — 4/14/13 A
Mines of Sulphur, The — 2/24/65 A
Ming, Hsien — 8/14/54 C
Mingled Chime, A — 3/8/61 D
Minkus, Alois — 2/2/02 B; 12/7/17 D;
    1/31/23 B; 2/18/51 B
Minneapolis Symphony Orchestra —
    11/5/03 B; 5/22/33 D; 1/13/35 D;
    12/2/38 C; 11/21/41 C; 11/11/44 C;
    11/24/44 C; 11/22/46 C; 3/30/51 C;
    3/15/57 C; 11/22/57 C; 11/27/59 C;
    1/2/60 C
Minnesota Opera Company — 10/14/71 A;
    4/24/76 A; 4/14/78 A
Minnesota Orchestra — 5/4/77 C; 9/23/77 C;
    1/10/78 C
Minnesota Theater Company — 6/1/67 A
Minton, Yvonne — 2/24/79 A
Minuet for Drums — 8/27/48 B
Minute Waltz — 5/11/78 C
Minutiae — 12/8/54 B
Miracle in the Gorbals — 10/26/44 B
Miracles (Menotti) — 4/22/79 C
Miracle, The (play) — 12/23/11 C
Miraculous Mandarin, The (Bartok) — 4/1/27 C
Miraculous Mandarin, The (Strobach) —
    11/28/26 B
Mirages, Les — 12/15/47 B
Mirandoline — 5/17/59 A
Mir Iskusstva (The World of Art) (periodical) —
    8/19/29 D
Miroirs — 9/21/63 E
Mirror of Whitening Light, A — 3/24/77 C
Mirror on Which to Dwell, A — 2/24/76 C
Mirum fur Tuba — 7/22/74 C
Miserere Nobis — 10/30/64 C
Miserly Knight, The — 1/24/06 A
Misfortunes of the Immortals: A Concert — 2/25/71 C
Miskovitch, Milorad — 8/21/53 B
Missa Brevis (Britten) — 7/22/59 C
Missa Brevis (Limon) — 4/11/58 B
Missa in Dedicatione Ecclesiae — 10/25/30 C
Missa oecumenica — 1/3/56 D
Missa pro Defunctis — 5/14/60 C
Miss Donnithorne's Maggot — 3/9/74 C
Miss Havisham's Fire — 3/22/79 A
Missions of San Antonio, The — 1/25/69 C
Miss Julie (Cullberg) — 3/1/50 B
Miss Julie (MacMillan) — 3/8/70 B
Miss Julie (Rorem) — 4/4/65

Mistero di Venezia, Il — 12/15/32 A
Mitchell, Arthur — 12/1/57 B; 1/17/62 B;
    4/6/67 B; 1/18/68 B; 4/30/68 B; 5/2/68 B
Mitchell, Danlee — 1/9/69 B
Mitchell, Howard — 3/11/11 D; //49 E;
    1/30/52 C; 4/4/56 C; 1/20/57 C; //69 E
Mitropoulos, Dimitri — 5/20/19 A; 2/27/30 E;
    12/2/38 C; 12/15/38 C; 11/21/41 C;
    12/21/41 C; 1/1/42 C; 1/7/42 C;
    11/11/44 C; 11/24/44 C; 11/22/46 C;
    11/27/47 C; //49 E; //50 E; //51 E;
    11/1/51 C; 4/11/53 C; 2/2/56 C;
    2/23/56 C; //57 E; 2/2/57 C; 1/15/58 A;
    11/2/60 D
Mittelmann, Norman — 8/4/78 E
Mitusov, Stephan — 5/26/14 A
Miyagi, Michio — 12/31/55 C
Mladova, Milada — 10/16/42 B
Mlaker, Veronika — 11/19/59 B
Mlynarski, Emil — 4/5/35 D
Mme. Press died last week at 90 — 7/13/70 C
Mobley, Lusschanya — 5/21/37 D
Moby Dick — 4/11/40 C
Mocquereau, Dom Andre — 7/1/01 E;
    1/18/30 D
Mode de valeurs et d'intensites — 5/2/51 C
"Modern Love Waltz" — 5/11/78 C
Modern Music (periodical) — 2/25/24 E
Modus Lascivius — 10/8/78 D
Mohr von Venedig, Der — 11/4/75 A
Moiseiwitsch, Benno — 10/1/08 D;
    11/29/19 D; 4/9/63 D
Moiseyev, Igor — 1/21/06 D
Mokranjac, Stevan — 9/19/14 D
Moldenhauer, Hans — 9/15/45 D; 5/25/62 C
Molinari, Bernardino — 4/11/20 C;
    12/14/24 C; //31 E; 12/13/36 C;
    12/25/52 D
Moll, Kurt — 9/24/79 E
Moloch — 12/8/06 A
Mona — 3/14/12 A
Monaco, Richard — 10/28/68 C
Mona Lisa — 9/26/15 A
Moncion, Francisco — 11/20/46 B; 1/13/47 B;
    4/28/48 B; 1/20/49 B; 11/27/49 B;
    2/26/50 B; 2/20/51 B; 2/26/52 B;
    5/14/53 B; 1/19/54 B; 9/14/54 B;
    1/29/70 B
Monday Evening Concerts — 2/25/76 D
Mond, Der — 2/5/39 A
Monkey-house scandal — 11/16/06 E;
    11/28/06 E
Monk, Meredith — 11/20/43 D; 9/10/67 B
Monod, Jacques — 8/5/51 C; 3/16/52 C
Monopartita — 6/12/51 C
Monotones — 4/25/66 B
Monsieur Beaucaire — 4/7/19 A
Monsieur de Pourceaugnac — 4/23/63 A
Monte Cristo — 3/18/01 B
Montemezzi, Italo — 4/10/13 A; 1/2/14 A;
    11/1/18 A; 5/15/52 D
Montesanto, Luigi — 12/14/18 A
Monteux, Claude — 1/31/60 C
Monteux, Pierre — 6/13/11 B; 6/8/12 B;
    5/15/13 B; 5/29/13 B; 4/5/14 C;
    5/26/14 A; 10/9/16 E; 3/6/18 A;
    11/28/19 C; 4/21/22 C; 10/28/26 C;
    5/3/29 C; 12/15/29 C; 2/10/30 C; //35 E;
    12/6/43 C; 11/4/44 D; 10/26/45 C;
    1/9/47 C; 1/6/49 C; 2/10/49 C; 5/8/52 E;
    //54 E; 6/25/56 C; 5/29/63 E; 7/1/64 D
Monteverdi, Claudio — 1/18/74 A
Montezuma — 4/19/64 A
Month in the Country, A — 2/12/76 B
Montreal Opera — 11/29/32 D
Montreal Symphony Orchestra — 2/6/63 C;
    9/21/63 E
Monument for a Dead Boy — 6/19/65 B

Monumentum pro Gesualdo (Balanchine) — 11/16/60 B; 4/9/63 B
Monumentum pro Gesualdo di Venosa ad CD Annum — 9/27/60 C
Moog synthesizer — 4/12/34 D
Moon Reindeer, The — 11/22/57 B
Moore, Carmen — 1/24/75 C; 4/22/75 C
Moore, Douglas — 3/5/37 A; 5/18/39 A; 5/5/46 C; 10/20/47 C; 2/9/49 A; 3/28/51 A; 5/7/51 E; 7/7/56 A; 3/19/58 A; 10/12/61 A; 4/28/66 A
Moore, Gene — 7/28/79 B
Moore, Grace — 2/7/28 D; 1/26/47 D
Moore, Henry — 4/6/67 C
Moore, Jack — 2/24/55 B
Moor, Emanuel — 10/20/31 D
Moorman, Charlotte — 8/25/65 E; 2/9/67 E; 5/9/67 E
Moor's Pavane, The — 8/17/49 B
Moralities (Drei szenische Kantaten) — 5/18/68 C
Morand, Eugene — 11/20/01 A
Moranzoni, Roberto — 3/23/18 A; 12/14/18 A; 3/7/20 A
Moravian Music Festival — 6/26/50 E
Morax, Rene — 6/11/21 A; 2/13/26 A
Morcom, James Stewart — 11/12/47 B
Morder, Hoffnung der Frauen — 6/4/21 A
Mordkin Ballet — 7/14/44 D
Mordkin, Mikhail — 5/19/09 B; 2/28/10 B; 12/19/11 B; 7/14/44 D
Mordkin Russian Ballet — 10/10/38 B
Moreau, Jacqueline — 7/28/47 B; 10/17/51 B
Morel, Jean — 1/10/03 D
Moreschi, Alessandro — 4/21/22 D
Moreton, Ursula — 5/5/31 B; 5/20/35 B
Morley, Ruth — 11/19/59 B
Mormon Tabernacle Choir — 7/23/62 E
Morning Heroes — 10/22/30 C
Moross, Jerome — 6/19/38 B
Morrice, Norman — 9/10/31 D
Morris, Marnee — 2/5/70 B; 6/18/72 B
Morrison, Mary — 9/21/72 C
Morte dell'aria, La — 10/24/50 A
Mortifee, Ann — 7/27/71 B
Mosaics — 1/23/58 C
Mosaval, Johaar — 2/25/54 B
Moscow Conservatory — 9//05 E
Moscow Imperial School of Ballet — 7/14/44 D
Moscow Institute of Musical Science — 12/12/16 E
Moscow Opera — //31 E; 11/21/40 E
Moscow Philharmonic — 11/9/01 C; 2/8/08 C; 5/2/36 C
Moscow Prison Philanthropic Committee — 12/15/00 C
Moscow Radio Orchestra — 10/28/35 C
Moscow (Shebalin) — 12/14/46 C
Moscow Symphony — 9/27/79 E
Moses und Aron (Schoenberg) — 7/2/51 C; 3/12/54 A; 6/6/57 A
Moszkowski, Moritz — 3/4/25 D
Mother Goose Suite — 12/20/49 B
Mother — 10/26/57 A
Mother of Us All, The — 5/7/47 A
Mottl, Felix — 10/8/05 C; 7/2/11 D; 11/28/47 E
Mounsey, Yvonne — 6/12/51 B; 6/14/51 B; 6/2/53 B
Mountains and Rivers without End — 1/17/69 C
Mountain Village, A — 3/8/01 D
Mourning Becomes Electra — 3/17/67 A
Mouvement symphonique (Bostoniana) (Ibert) — 1/25/63 C
Mouvement symphonique No. 3 (Honegger) — 3/27/33 C
Movements for Piano and Orchestra (Balanchine) — 4/9/63 B

Movements for Piano and Orchestra (Stravinsky) — 1/10/60 C
Moves — 7/3/59 B
Moylan, Mary Ellen — 11/20/46 B; 1/13/47 B
Mozart Concerto — 3/26/66 B
Mozart, Wolfgang Amadeus — 10/22/46 E
Mr. and Mrs. Discobbolos — 3/21/66 A
Mravinsky, Evgheny — 6/4/03 D; 11/4/43 C; 11/3/45 C; 10/29/55 C
Mr. Bloom and the Cyclops — 2/12/59 D
Mr. Broucek's Flight to the Moon — 4/23/20 A
Mr. Broucek's Trip to the 15th Century — 4/23/20 A
Muak — 11/9/78 C
Mucci, Emidio — 1/1/38 A
Much Ado About Nothing — 5/30/01 A
Muck, Karl — 10/15/01 D; 4/9/02 A; 11/10/04 C; 3/1/07 C; 3/21/07 C; 11/22/07 C; 2/7/08 C; 12/18/14 C; 5/14/15 E; 3/31/17 E; 3/14/18 E; 3/25/18 E; 11/15/19 D; 5/7/30 E; 3/3/40 D; 11/28/47 E
MUD — 5/12/77 B
Mugone, Leopoldo — 1/14/00 A
Muhlmann, Adolph — 2/19/09 A
Muirgheis — 12/7/03 A
Mullings, Frank — 1/14/16 A
Mumma, Gordon — 12/3/71 B
Munch, Charles — 11/1/32 D; 4/17/40 C; 6/10/41 C; 8/17/46 C; 12/27/46 D; 10/14/48 E; 1/6/50 C; 2/10/50 C; 3/3/50 C; 11/3/50 C; 3/9/51 C; 5/6/52 E; 12/3/54 C; 1/7/55 C; 11/25/55 C; 9/6/56 E; 1/25/57 C; 3/8/57 C; 12/6/57 C; 6/15/58 C; 12/5/58 C; 12/9/59 C; 10/21/60 C; 1/20/61 C; 1/25/63 C; 12/20/63 C; 3/5/65 C; 11/6/68 D
Munchen Walzer — 5/24/39 C; 3/31/51 C
Munich, University of — 9/18/79 E
Munford, Robert — 6/27/69 B
Mungalova, Olga — 4/27/27 B
Munich Philharmonic — 2/6/46 D
Munrow, David — 5/15/76 D
Muradelli, Vano — 9/28/47 A
Murai, Ilona — 1/24/50 B
Murder of a Great Chief of State. In Memory of John F. Kennedy — 12/3/63 C
Murder, the Magician — 2/11/76 A
Muses of Sicily — 9/20/66 C
Museum of Modern Art (New York City) — //40 E; 10/28/52 C
Museum Piece — 4/22/75 C
Musgrave, Thea — 11/30/67 A; 10/24/69 C; 11/19/69 B; 8/13/73 C; 10/11/74 C
Musica Aeterna — 11/8/72 C; 11/20/74 C
Musica divina — 9/5/10 D
Musica for 72 Carillons — 9/2/70 D
Musical Accompaniment to a Motion Picture Scene — 1/19/54 B
Musical Circular Guillotine — 4/30/19 C
Musical Contemporary (Musikalny Sovremennik), The (periodical) — 5/23/40 D
Musical Heritage Society — //72 E
Musical Quarterly, The (periodical) — 1/1/15 E
Music and Letters — 1/1/20 E; 6/8/34 E
Musica religiosa (periodical) — 8/19/22 D
Musica sacra (periodical) — 9/5/10 D
Musica Sacra (Chorus) — 1/22/76 D
Musica Sacra (record label) — //32 E
Music Center of Los Angeles County — 12/6/64 E
Music for a Film — 11/6/30 C
Music for a Great City — 5/26/64 C
Music for Amplified Toy Pianos — 2/25/60 C
Music for an Orchestra — 3/23/28 C
Music for a Scene from Shelley — 3/23/35 C
Music for Orchestra (Kirchner) — 10/16/69 C
Music for Orchestra (Luening) — 5/23/78 C
Music for Radio — 7/25/37 C

Music for Solo Violin — 4/27/74 C
Music for Strings, Percussion and Celesta — 1/21/37 C
Music for the Magic Theater — 1/24/67 C
Music for the Masses — 3/5/74 D
Music for the Theater — 11/20/25 C
Music for Voices — 11/10/70 C
Music in 12 parts — 6/1/74 C
Music in Fifths — 1/16/'70 C
Music Librarians, International Association of — 4/9/79 D
Music Mountain — 8/22/30 E
Music of Changes — 5/2/51 C
Music of the Church Hymnary, The (National Library of Scotland) — 5/20/29 E
Musicology, International Society of — 4/9/79 D
Music Pictures — 9/5/12 C
Music Review, The (periodical) — 2/1/40 E
Music Since 1900 (book) — 11/4/37 E
Music Since Debussy (book) — 6/23/66 C
Music Supervisors National Conference — 3/29/30 E
Music to a Child's Play — 12/14/07 C
Music typewriter — 9/14/36 E
Music with Changing Parts — 11/10/70 C
Musicwriter — 6/26/55 E
Musik, Die (periodical) — 9/20/01 E; 11/1/34 E; 1//35 E; 3/1/36 E
Musik in Geschichte und Gegenwart, Die (book) — 6/30/49 E; 7/25/69 D; 9/18/73 D; 10/29/75 D; 11/22/75 D
Musik-Lexikon (book) — //19 E; 7/10/19 D; //22 E; //29 E; 2/13/52 D; //59 E
Musikselskabet Harmonien — 10/8/65 E
Musiktage fur die zeitgenossische Tonkunst — 10/15/60 C
Musique d'ameublement — 3/8/20 C
Musique pour Ars Nova — 2/27/70 C
Musique pour les soupers du Roi Ubu — 1/31/68 C
Mussolini, Benito — 1/13/34 A; 5/21/37 D
Mussorgsky, Modest — 5/16/07 E; 5/19/08 A; 6/24/13 A; 10/8/13 A; 10/26/17 A; 10/19/22 C; 2/16/28 A; 9/14/37 A; 10/27/64 E; 4/9/79 D
Muti, Riccardo — 7/28/41 D
Mutter, Die — 5/17/31 A
Mutual Broadcasting System — 10/1/34 E; 12/29/36 E
Muzio, Claudia — 2/7/12 D; 12/4/16 D; 3/7/20 A; 5/24/36 D
My Lady Nicotine — 2/27/05 B
Myrick, Julian — 4/18/02 C; 1/1/09 E
Myshkin — 4/23/73 A
Mystere de la nativite, Le — 12/24/59 C
Mysterium — 5/19/54 D
Mythical Beasts — 2/10/58 C
Myth of a Voyage — 5/2/73 B

— N —

Nabokov, Nicolas — 4/17/03 D; 6/6/28 B; 2/16/30 C; 4/6/34 B; 11/27/59 A; 5/28/65 B; 1/4/68 C; 4/6/78 D
Nabokov, Vladimir — 4/17/03 D; 4/6/78 D
Nabucco — 1/27/01 D
Nadezhda Svetlova — 9/8/43 A
Naginski, Charles — 8/4/40 D
Nagy, Ivan — 4/28/43 D; 12/4/69 B
Nahat, Dennis — 7/1/71 B
Nahowski, Helene — 4/24/11 C
Naissance de la Lyre, La — 7/1/25 A
Namo — 5/4/71 C
Nancarrow, Conlon — 10/27/12 D; 7/3/64 B
NAPAC Ballet — //69 E
Napoli milionaria — 6/22/77 A
Napravnik, Eduard — 11/23/16 D
Narcisse — 4/26/11 B

Narrative for Orchestra — 3/4/65 C
Nashville Orchestra — 1/16/75 D
Nast, Minnie — 1/26/11 A
Natalie Petrovna — 10/8/64 A
Natal Performing Arts Council — //69 E
National Ballet of Canada — //51 E; 2/1/55 B;
7/7/71 B; 9/1/72 B; 4/26/74 B
National Book Award — //71 E
National Broadcasting Company — 11/15/26 E
National Bureau of Standards — 8/29/36 E
National Chorale — 2/12/75 C
Nationale Ballet — //61 E; 6/19/65 B
National Education Association of America —
4/9/57 C
National Endowment for the Arts —
2/27/75 C; 2/26/76 C; 7/4/76 E;
9/29/76 C; 3/14/77 C; 5/3/79 E
National Federation of Women's Clubs —
7/1/15 A
National Foundation of the Arts and Humanities — 9/29/65 E
National Gramophone Company — 10//01 E
National Gramophone Society — 5//24 E
National Harp Festival — 3/29/28 E
National Institute of Arts and Letters —
3/3/66 C
National Library of Scotland — 5/13/29 E;
5/20/29 E; 3/9/38 E; 4/3/70 E
National Opera House, Tashkent — 11/1/28 E
National Opera of Colombia — 8/27/35 D
National Orchestral Association — 10/28/30 E;
7/16/79 E
National Polish Opera House — 11/19/65 E
National-Socialist Kulturgemeinde —
11/1/34 E
National Socialist Symphony Orchestra —
1/10/32 E
National Symphony Orchestra — 11/2/30 E;
11/2/31 E; 2/2/43 C; 3/5/44 C;
1/25/48 C; //49 E; 1/30/52 C; 4/4/56 C;
1/20/57 C; //69 E; 11/19/72 C; 3/5/75 C;
7/3/76 C; 10/12/76 C; 10/4/77 E;
10/11/77 C; 11/23/79 C
National Youth Administration Symphony
Orchestra — 2/22/41 C
Natola-Ginastera, Aurora — 1/18/74 C;
12/13/79 C
Natra, Sergiu — 7/30/68 E
Natzka, Oscar — 3/31/49 A
Nauko o hudebních formách (book) — //22 E
Nave, La — 11/1/18 A
NBC Symphony Orchestra — 12/25/37 E;
3/26/38 C; 11/5/38 C; 4/22/42 C;
5/2/43 C; 9/26/43 C; 2/6/44 C;
2/13/44 C; 11/24/45 C; 1/15/49 D;
11/6/50 C; 4/4/54 E; 10/27/54 E;
5/19/58 D
"Nearer My God to Thee" — 4/26/65 C
Neary, Colleen — 5/29/75 B; 1/26/78 B;
5/18/78 B
Neary, Patricia — 12/7/61 B
Nedbal, Oscar — 12/24/30 D
Nederlands Ballet — //61 E
Nederlandsche Opera — 6/15/48 E
Nederlands Dans Theater — 7/7/64 B
Nederlandse Operastichting — 3/16/73 A
Negative Dialectics (book) — 8/6/69 D
Negro Rhapsody (Gilbert) — 6/5/13 C
Negro Rhapsody (Goldmark, R.) — 1/18/23 C
Neil, Sara — 6/7/56 B
Nelidova, Lydia — 5/14/12 B
Nelson — 9/22/54 A
Nemchinova, Vera — 6/5/19 B; 1/6/24 B;
6/17/25 B
Neophone Company — 8//04 E
Nerina, Nadia — 5/5/56 B; 1/28/60 B
Nero Film Company — 10/20/30 E
Nerone (Boito) — 6/10/18 D; 5/2/24 A
Nerone (Mascagni) — 1/16/35 A

Neruda, Pablo — 9/22/71 C
Nestiev, I — *see* Nestyev, Izrail
Nestyev, Izrail — 4/17/11 D; 11/3/45 C;
1/7/51 E; 10/63 E
Netherlands Ballet, Het — //59 E
Netherlands Dance Theater — //59 E
Networks of Noises — 4/21/14 C
Neue Musikalische Theorien und Fantasien —
1/14/35 D
Neues vom Tage — 6/8/29 A; 12/6/34 E
Neumann, Frantisek — 11/11/25 A;
12/18/26 A
Neumann, Vaclav — //45 E; //48 E
Neumeier, John — 2/24/42 D; 4/26/74 B
Neveu, Ginette — 10/28/49 D
Nevin, Arthur Finley — 1/15/06 C; 4/23/07 A;
4/23/10 A; 1/5/18 A
Newark Boys Choir — 5/24/78 C; 1/18/79 C
New Ballet Company — 11/11/52 B
Newbolt, Henry — 4/30/25 A
New Dance — 12/29/58 D
New England Episodes — 4/18/58 C
New England Watch and Ward Society —
1/28/07 E
New Friends of Music — 12/15/40 C
New Haven Symphony Orchestra — 4/9/68 C
New Jersey Percussion Ensemble — 4/28/70 C;
1/26/78 C
New London Orchestra — 1/21/46 D
Newman, Cardinal — 10/3/00 C
Newman, Ernest — //15 E; 7/7/59 D
New Music (periodical) — 10/15/27 E
New Music Quarterly (periodical) — 12/10/65 D
New Orleans Philharmonic Symphony Orchestra — 3/10/59 C; 3/9/65 C;
11/18/68 C
New People — 10/17/69 C; 10/22/78 C
Newport Music Festival — 7/31/69 E
New School for Social Research — 5/29/72 D
New South Wales Conservatorium of Music —
3/9/56 E
Newsreel — 7/14/42 C
New Symphony Orchestra of London —
10/29/05 E; 4/11/19 E
Newton, Joy — 5/5/31 B; 5/20/35 B
New York Academy of Music — 3/7/20 A
New York Chamber Symphony — 5/3/59 C
New York Choral Society — 5/17/74 C
New York City Ballet — //48 E; 10/11/48 E;
1/20/49 B; 11/27/49 B; 12/1/49 B;
2/26/50 B; 3/2/50 B; 2/18/51 B;
2/20/51 B; 6/12/51 B; 11/14/51 B;
11/20/51 B; 12/4/51 B; 2/14/52 B;
2/19/52 B; 2/26/52 B; 2/28/52 B;
11/11/52 B; 11/25/52 B; 1/6/53 B;
5/14/53 B; 6/2/53 B; 1/19/54 B;
2/2/54 B; 2/18/54 B; 9/14/54 B;
2/27/55 B; 3/1/55 B; 8/3/55 B;
11/9/55 B; 11/15/55 B; 3/1/56 B;
3/6/56 B; 12/19/56 B; 11/21/57 B;
12/1/57 B; 1/8/58 B; 1/17/58 B;
5/14/59 B; 3/29/60 B; 11/16/60 B;
11/22/60 B; 12/7/60 B; 3/22/61 B;
12/7/61 B; 1/17/62 B; 3/20/63 B;
4/9/63 B; 12/10/63 B; 1/7/64 B;
4/24/64 E; 5/6/64 B; 2/4/65 B; 4/21/66 B;
4/28/66 B; 7/8/66 B; 4/6/67 B; 4/13/67 B;
11/23/67 B; 1/18/68 B; 4/30/68 B;
5/2/68 B; 11/23/68 B; 1/23/69 B;
5/22/69 B; 6/1/69 B; 12/4/69 B;
1/29/70 B; 2/5/70 B; 7/30/70 B;
2/3/72 B; 6/18/72 B; 6/21/72 B;
6/23/72 B; 6/25/72 B; 1/12/73 B;
5/24/73 B; 1/10/74 B; 1/17/74 B;
5/16/74 B; 5/14-31/75 B; 5/29/75 B;
7/30/75 B; 1/22/76 B; 5/12/76 B;
6/4/77 B; 6/23/77 B; 1/12/78 B;
1/19/78 B; 1/26/78 B; 5/18/78 B;
7/13/79 B

New York City Opera — 2/21/44 E; 5/28/52 E;
11/19/53 E; 4/1/54 A; 4/26/59 A;
10/12/61 A; 10/11/62 A; 4/24/64 E;
3/25/65 A; 3/9/67 A; 10/9/68 A;
3/22/79 A; 6/3/79 A; 9/30/79 E
New York City Symphony Orchestra —
3/23/46 C
New York Days and Nights — 7/30/26 C
New York Music Critics Circle Award —
1/7/55 C
New York Opera Festival — 8/1/68 A
New York People's Symphony Concerts —
1/28/32 D
New York Philharmonic — 12/20/01 C;
//02 E; //03 E; 1/4/05 D; 2/10/05 D;
9//05 E; //06 E; 10/15/07 E; //09 E;
3/19/11 E; 5/17/11 E; 5/18/11 D;
6/5/13 C; 1/21/18 E; 6/23/18 E;
1/30/19 E; 8/22/20 E; 11/17/21 C;
4/11/22 E; 12/7/22 C; 1/18/23 C;
1/8/25 D; 8/27/25 E; 12/31/25 C;
8/6/26 E; 12/9/26 C; 1/22/27 C;
12/20/28 C; //29 E; 2/21/29 C;
2/28/29 C; 12/29/29 D; 4/3/30 C;
1/2/35 D; 3/23/35 C; //36 E; 3/14/36 E;
4/11/36 C; 11/5/36 D; 4/2/38 C;
7/31/38 C; 6/9/39 C; 6/10/39 C;
4/11/40 C; 6/25/40 C; 7/5/40 C; //41 E;
8/10/41 D; 12/21/41 C; 1/1/42 C;
1/7/42 C; 4/16/42 C; 10/22/42 C; //43 E;
10/28/43 C; 12/16/43 C; 1/5/44 C;
1/20/44 C; 2/17/44 C; 10/21/44 C;
11/4/44 D; 11/23/44 C; 2/3/45 C;
2/15/45 C; 2/22/45 C; 10/4/45 C;
12/6/45 C; 1/24/46 C; 11/28/46 C;
12/19/46 C; 12/29/46 C; 1/18/47 C;
2/3/47 C; 2/7/47 E; 2/27/47 C;
10/30/47 C; 11/27/47 C; //49 E;
11/24/49 C; //50 E; //51 E; 2/22/51 C;
11/1/51 C; 4/11/53 C; 3/26/55 D;
12/31/55 C; 2/2/56 C; 2/23/56 C; //57 E;
2/2/57 C; 9/9/57 E; //58 E; 4/16/59 C;
5/14/59 E; 8/25/59 C; 1/15/60 C;
3/20/60 C; 10/20/60 C; 4/14/61 D;
10/26/61 C; 9/23/62 C; 10/4/62 C;
4/4/63 C; 4/25/63 C; 5/16/63 C;
10/3/63 C; 5/7/64 C; 7/15/65 C;
8/10/65 C; 8/10/65 E; 4/28/66 C;
7/26/66 E; 4/27/67 C; 6/27/67 C;
7/7/67 E; 9/13/67 C; 12/14/67 C;
1/4/68 C; 1/18/68 C; 2/8/68 C;
2/29/68 C; 3/7/68 C; 5/2/68 C;
10/10/68 C; 1/16/69 C; 6/10/69 E;
10/16/69 C; 1/29/70 C; 2/5/70 C; //71 E;
6/7/72 C; 11/21/74 C; 12/6/74 C;
1/24/75 C; 4/3/75 C; 4/17/75 C;
12/4/75 C; 1/30/76 C; 2/17/77 C;
5//77 E; 5/5/77 C; 10/20/77 C;
12/1/77 C; 12/6/77 C; 9/14/78 C;
11/2/78 C; 10/25/79 C
New York Polyphonic Symphony Orchestra —
2/26/47 D
New York Pro Musica Antiqua — //52 E;
1/9/66 D
New York Skyline — 4/7/40 C
New York Society of the Friends of Music —
5/3/17 C
New York State Theater — 4/24/64 E
New York Sunday Night Smoking Concerts —
7/21/68 D
New York Symphony Orchestra — 1/17/06 D;
7/24/09 E; 11/28/09 C; 11/21/72 D;
12/1/21 C; 12/3/25 D; 11/15/26 E;
11/25/27 D; 2/12/28 C; 2/26/45 C
New York Symphony Society Orchestra —
3/10/23 C; 12/26/26 C; 3/10/27 D;
3/30/28 E — *see also* New York Philharmonic
New York Telharmonic Hall — 3/5/07 E

New York University Opera Workshop — 2/6/58 A
New York World's Fair — 9/23/38 E; 8/14/39 D
New Zealand Broadcasting Corporation — 3/9/74 E
New Zealand Symphony Orchestra — 10/26/46 E; 3/6/47 E
Niagara Falls Suite — 2/10/61 C
Nibelungen-Marsch — 12/8/36 E; 7/6/37 E
Nicholaides, Melisa — 12/21/47 B
Nicholas II, Tsar — 3/26/18 D
Niederrheinische Sinfoniker — 11/9/78 C
Nielsen, Carl — 11/28/02 A; 12/1/02 C; 10/8/03 C; 11/11/06 A; 2/28/12 C; 2/1/16 C; 2/11/18 C; 2/15/19 C; 1/24/22 C; 12/11/25 C; 10/21/26 C; 9/14/28 C; 10/3/31 D; 5/24/37 E
Nielsen, Lavina — 8/20/53 B
Niemann, Albert — 1/13/17 D
Nightingale, The — 5/10/55 A
Night Journey — 5/3/47 B
Night Music — 10/24/69 C
Nightpiece — 5/15/72 C
Night Shadow — 2/27/46 B
Night Song — 11/1/67 B
Night Wandering — 9/5/58 B
Nigrin, Ada — 5/9/24 B
Nijinska, Bronislava — 11/2/21 B; 5/18/22 B; 6/13/23 B; 1/6/24 B; 1/6/24 B; 1/19/24 B; 6/20/24 B; 11/22/28 B; 11/27/28 B; 1/12/29 B; 6/19/29 B; 7/18/35 B; 4/27-28/37 B; 11/20/37 B; 10/12/42 B; 5/21/52 B; 2/22/72 D
Nijinsky, Clown of God — 10/8/71 B
Nijinsky, Vaslav — 11/25/07 B; 3/21/08 B; 3/21/08 B; 5/19/09 B; 6/2/09 B; 3/5/10 B; 6/4/10 B; 6/18/10 B; 1/26/11 E; 4/19/11 B; 4/26/11 B; 6/13/11 B; 6/21/11 B; 11/30/11 B; 5/14/12 B; 5/29/12 B; 6/8/12 B; 5/15/13 B; 5/29/13 B; 9/10/13 E; 12/3/13 E; 1/17/16 B; 10/23/16 B; 4/8/50 D; 4/28/66 B; 10/8/71 B
Nikiforov, N. — 3/21/34 B
Nikisch, Arthur — 11/10/03 E; 5/29/05 C; 5/16/07 E; 10/13/08 C; 12/15/10 C; 12/14/11 C; 6/14/12 E; 10/28/12 D; 1/10/21 C; 6/16/21 E; //22 E; 1/23/22 D; 11/28/47 E
Nikitina, Alice — 1/6/24 B; 4/28/25 B; 6/12/28 B; 5/7/29 B
Nikolais, Alwin — 11/25/12 D; 5/19/39 B; 8/13/48 B; 3/18/50 B; 1/26/53 B; 5/23/53 B; 3/26/57 B; 3/22/59 B; 1/29/60 B; 12/17/67 B
Nikola Subric Zrinski — 12/16/14 D
Nikolska, J. — 5/11/35 B
Nikonov, Vladimir — 9/17/62 B
Nilsson, Birgit — 5/17/18 D; 2/6/65 D; 11/4/79 E
Nilsson, Bo — 10/15/60 C
Nilsson, Kristina — 11/22/21 D
Nine Rivers from Jordan — 10/9/68 A
19 February 1861 — 3/3/11 C
1940 — 6/25/40 C
1941 — 1/21/43 C
Ninth Symphony — 10/27/64 B
Nippon Polydor — 5//27 E
NIR Chamber Orchestra and Chorus — 6/23/50 C
Nirschy, Emilia — 5/12/17 B
Nixa (record label) — 6//50 E
Nixon, Marni — 10/30/66 C
Nixon, Richard M. — 1/25/73 C
Noah and the Flood — 6/14/62 B
Noapte furtunoasa, O — 10/26/35 A
Nobel Peace Prize — 9/4/65 D
Noble, T. Tertius — 3/3/19 E

Nobilissima visione — 7/21/38 B
Noces, Les (Nijinska) — 6/13/23 B
Noces, Les (Robbins) — 3/30/65 B
Noces, Les (Stravinsky) — 4/6/71 D
Noches en los jardines de Espana (Falla) — 4/9/16 C
Nocturne (Antheil) — 12/10/44 C
Nocturne (Ashton) — 11/10/36 B
Nocturne (Britten) — 10/16/58 C
Nocturnes (Cunningham) — 7/11/56 B
Nocturnes (Debussy) — 12/9/00 C
No for An Answer — 1/5/41 A
Noguchi, Isamu — 4/28/35 B; 10/30/44 B; 5/10/46 B; 2/28/47 B; 5/13/47 B; 4/29/60 B
Noiseless, Patient Spider, A — 6/2/73 C
Nolan, Mary E. — 2/8/36 D
Nolan, Sidney — 5/8/62 B
No Longer than Ten Minutes — 2/16/71 C
Nolte, Charles — 4/24/76 A
Nombre musical gregorien ou rythmique gregorienne, Le (book) — 1/18/30 D
Nomoi — 9/22/59 D
Nomos (Birtwistle) — 8/23/68 C
Nomos gamma — 4/3/69 C
Nomos (Hauer) — 6/7/13 C; 4/30/19 C
Nonet for Strings (Copland) — 3/2/61 C
Nono, Luigi — 1/13/54 E; 8/25/54 C; 5/30/55 C; 10/24/56 C; 4/13/61 A; 8/22/62 C; 10/18/65 C; 6/1/68 A; 11/5/69 C; 4//75 A
Nordica, Lillian — 11/8/09 E; 5/10/14 D
Nordic Symphony — 5/30/23 C
Nordoff, Paul — 12/27/39 B; 12/26/43 B; 2/25/44 B
Nore fur Violoncello und Klavier — 5/4/68 C
Norfolk Rhapsody No. 1 in E Minor (Vaughan Williams) — 8/23/06 C
Norfolk Rhapsody No. 2 (Vaughan Williams) — 9/27/07 C
Norfolk Rhapsody No. 3 (Vaughan Williams) — 9/27/07 C
Noring, Inga — 10/31/50 B
North American Phonograph Company — 10//01 E
Northern Sinfonia Orchestra in York, with — 7/3/74 C
North German Broadcasting Corporation Symphony Orchestra — 5/15/73 C
Nose, The — 1/12/30 A
Nossig, Alfred — 5/29/01 A
Notations — 2/18/78 C; 5/24/78 C
Notes from Tom Paine — 4/14/75 C
Nototyp Rundslater — 9/14/36 E
Notre Dame (Schmidt, F.) — 4/1/14 A
Notre Faust — 12/12/75 B
Notte de un nevrastenico, La — 2/8/60 A
Notte di Maggio — 3/29/14 C
Notturno — 5/7/74 E
Notturno romantico, Il — 4/25/36 A
Noumenon Mobilius — 1/26/53 B
Nouveau Ballet de Monte Carlo — 5/5/46 B; 2/22/61 D
Nouveaux Jeunes — 1/15/18 E; 1/30/63 D
Novacek, Victor — 2/8/04 C
Novachord — 2/2/39 E; 7/1/73 D
Novae de infinito laudes — 4/24/63 C
Novaes, Guiomar — 11/11/15 D
Novak, Sigmund — 5/15/20 B
Novello & Company — //15 E
Noye's Fludde — 6/18/58 A
Nuit de Saint Jean, La — 10/25/20 B
Null, Eduard van der — 3/12/45 E
Nureyev, Rudolf — 3/17/38 D; 6/16/61 E; 2/21/62 E; 3/10/62 D; 3/12/63 B; 11/27/63 B; 2/9/65 B; 2/23/67 B; 2/29/68 B; 3/2/70 B; 3/11/71 B; 9/1/72 B; 4/26/74 B
Nusch-Nuschi, Das — 6/4/21 A
Nussbaumer, Otto — 6/15/04 E

Nutcracker, The (Balanchine) — 2/2/54 B
Nutcracker, The (Cranko) — 12/4/66 B
Nutcracker, The (Nureyev) — 2/29/68 B
Nutcracker, The (Sergeyev) — 1/30/34 B
Nygaard, Jens — 10/6/79 E
Nyiregyhazi, Erwin — 1/19/03 D; 10/14/15 D

— O —

Oakland Symphony — 12/3/63 C
Oberhoffer, Emil — 11/5/03 E; 5/22/33 D
Ober, Margarete — 12/9/13 A; 3/8/17 A
Oberto, conte di San Bonifacio — 1/27/01 D
Obertura para el Faust criollo — 5/12/44 C
Obouhov, Nicolas — 6/3/26 C; 6/13/54 D
Oboussier, Robert — 7/9/00 D; 6/9/57 D
Obraztsova, Elena — 7/7/37 D
O'Brien, Shaun — 7/17/74 B
Obrist, Aloys — 6/29/10 D
Obukhov, Mikhail — 2/23/07 B
Occasional Variations — 8/22/71 C
Ocean Flight — 5/17/74 C
Oceanides — 6/4/14 C
Ocean, The — 11/17/21 C
Octandre — 1/13/24 C
Octet (Schuller) — 11/2/79 C
Octet (Stravinsky) — 10/18/23 C
Ode an den Westwind — 5/6/54 C
Ode (Massine) — 6/6/28 B
Odeon — 4/30/03 E; 8//04 E; //09 E
Ode, or Meditation at Night on the Majesty of God, as revealed by the Aurora Borealis — 4/6/78 D
Ode (Stravinsky) — 10/8/43 C
Ode to Napoleon Bonaparte — 11/23/44 C; 7/13/51 D
Ode to the Dance — 1/29/54 B
Ode to the End of War — 11/10/45 C
Ode to the Temple of Sound — 10/3/66 E
Ode to the West Wind — 4/20/57 C
Odisseia de uma raca — 5/30/54 C
O'Donnell, May — 10/30/44 B; 1/23/46 B; 5/10/46 B; 2/27/47 B; 8/13/48 B
Odysseus — 9/29/68 A
Oedipe — 3/10/36 A
Oedipus der Tyrann — 12/11/59 A
Oedipus (Partch) — 3/14/52 B
Oedipus Rex — 5/30/27 C; 4/6/71 D
Oestvig, Karl — 10/10/19 A
Offenbach in the Underworld — 2/1/55 B
Offenbach, Jacques — 3/1/36 E; 10/29/36 A; 4/5/38 B; 10/27/41 B; 11/29/42 B; 4/6/72 B; 1/27/78 B
Offrandes oubliees, Les — 2/19/31 C
Offset head pickup — //37 E
Of Mice and Men — 1/22/70 A
O Frabulous Day! (The Jabberwock) — 2/13/54 C
Ogdon, John — 5/21/73 C
O'Hearn, Robert — 1/23/69 B; 7/1/71 B
Ohlsson, Garrick — 10/25/70 E
Ohn, Gerard — 10/17/51 B
Oiseaux exotiques — 10/11/53 C
Oistrakh, David — 9/30/08 D; 10/29/55 C; 10/24/74 D
Ojai Festival — 6/1/75 C
Ojai Festival Orchestra — 6/2/73 C
Okeh — //30 E
Oklahoma Symphony — 12/4/77 C
Olav Trygvason — 10/8/08 A
Olczewska, Maria — 12/4/20 A
Oldham, Arthur — 6/2/47 B
Old King Cole — 6/5/23 B
Old Maid and the Thief, The — 4/22/39 A; 2/11/41 A
Ole from Nordland — 11/21/16 A
Olefsky, Paul — 3/4/50 C
Olivero, Magda — 3/25/12 D; 2/25/56 A; 4/3/76 D
Oliveros, Pauline — 4/15/69 B

Olivieri, Elsa — 2/24/37 A
Ollantay — 10/29/49 C
Ol-Ol — 1/31/28 A
Olon-Scrymgeour, John — 5/6/57 A; 1/9/64 A; 3/22/64 C; 6/1/67 A
Olsen, Paul — 5/13/57 B
Olson, H.F. — 1/31/56 E; 10/4/58 E
Olympians, The — 9/29/49 A
Oman, Julia Trevelyan — 10/25/68 B
O-Mika — 3/11/12 B
Ommaggio a Cage — 11/13/59 C
Ondes Martenot — 4/20/28 E; 5/11/34 B; 1/13/38 E; 12/2/49 C
Ondine (Ashton) — 10/27/58 B
114 Songs (Ives) — 5/19/54 D
One-Man Show — 11/12/64 A
One Touch of Venus — 10/7/43 A
On Guard for Peace — 12/19/50 C
On Hearing the First Cuckoo in Spring — 10/2/13 C
Onkel Dazumal — 5/25/05 A
On ne badine pas avec l'amour — 5/30/10 A
On Stage! — 10/4/45 B
On Wenlock Edge — 11/15/09 C
On Your Toes — 4/30/68 B
Opening of the Eye — 1/19/53 B
Opening Suite — 3/18/50 B
Open Road, The — 12/14/47 B
Opera (mixed media spectical) — 8/12/70 A
Opera Cloak, The — 11/3/42 A
Opera-Comique — 2/2/00 A; 11/20/01 A; 4/30/02 A; 4/15/04 D; 12/26/05 A; 5/10/07 A; 5/30/10 A; 11/30/10 A; 4/26/11 A; 5/19/11 A; 6/4/13 A; 5/15/14 A; 12/24/25 A; 12/16/27 A; 7/4/44 A; 6/3/47 A; 6/21/49 A; 3/9/51 A; 2/6/59 A; //62 E; 10/21/63 A; 4/6/64 B
Opera Society of Washington — 5/19/67 A; 1/18/74 A
Opera/South — 11/15/74 A
"O Promise Me" — 1/16/20 D
Opus 12 — 7/7/64 B
Opus 34 — 1/19/54 B
Opus Americanum — 12/6/43 C
Opus Clavicembalisticum — 12/1/30 C
Opus I — 11/7/65 B
Opus (Weidman) — 8/6/38 B
Oracles — 5/2/65 C
Oratorio Society of New York — 3/19/07 D; 11/15/26 E
Orbits — 2/11/79 C
Orchestral Set No. 1 (Haba) — 1/10/31 C
Orchestral Variations (Copland) — 3/5/58 C
Orchestra of Lyon — 9/17/79 E
Orchestra of the Belgian Institute National de Radiodiffusion — 9/13/55 C
Orchestra Pieces — 1/13/69 C
Orchestration — 3/7/14 E
Orchestre classique de Tunis — 10/11/70 D
Orchestre de la Societe Philharmonique — 11/6/68 D
Orchestre de la Suisse Romande, L' — 11/30/18 E; 2/6/19 C; 6/2/56 E; 9/1/63 C; 2/20/69 C
Orchestre de Lyon, L' — 11/6/69 E
Orchestre de Paris — //67 E; 11/6/68 D; 2/27/73 C; 5/24/78 C
Orchestre Lyrique de l'O.R.T.F., l' — 3/2/69 C; 12/14/71 C
Orchestre National de France — 10/14/48 E
Orchestre Philharmonique de Lorraine — 9/30/76 E
Orchestre Symphonique de Paris — 10/19/28 C; 5/3/29 C; 12/6/29 C; 2/16/30 C; 2/25/32 C; 7/1/64 D
O'Reilly, Sheila — 7/18/49 B
Orestea (Milhaud) — 4/16/27 A; 11/27/27 A; 3/27/35 A
Oresteia (Taneyev) — 6/19/15 D
Orfeide, L' (Malipiero) — 11/5/25 A

Orff, Carl — 6/8/37 C; 2/5/39 A; 2/20/43 A; 11/6/43 C; 6/15/47 A; 8/9/49 A; 2/13/53 C; 10/20/53 A; 3/31/56 C; 11/19/59 B; 12/11/59 A; 12/11/60 A; 6/26/64 B; 3/24/68 A
ORF Symphony Orchestra — 11/29/72 C
Organum — 11/24/49 C
Oriane et le Prince d'Amour — 1/7/38 B
Oriane et le prince — 5/11/34 B
Oriane — 5/11/34 B
Orientale (Cui) — 3/26/18 D
Orientales, Les (Nijinsky) — 6/25/10 B
Orient-Occident — 6/29/75 B
Original Ballet Russe — 10//38 E; 12/1/39 B; 2/28/40 B; 11/16/40 B; 12/6/40 B; 1/22/41 B; 10/1/46 B; 1//48 E; 7/27/51 D
Orlov, Alexandre — 6/13/11 B
Orlov, Nicholas — 4/6/43 B
Ormandy, Eugene — 10/30/31 D; 1/13/35 C; 1/3/41 C; 2/7/41 C; 1/16/42 C; 11/16/45 C; 11/30/45 C; 2/8/46 C; 11/21/47 C; 3/20/48 E; 11/26/48 C; 12/31/48 C; 3/4/50 C; 10/27/50 C; 12/11/50 C; 12/17/54 C; 2/18/55 C; 9/15/55 C; 9/30/60 C; 2/10/61 C; 3/31/61 C; 1/26/62 C; 9/25/62 C; 1/18/63 C; 2/7/64 C; 5/16/66 C; 1/10/69 C; 3/5/71 C; 2/14/74 E; 5/27/76 C; 8/26/77 C; 8/25/78 C
Ormazd — 1/26/12 C
Ornstein, Leo — 1/13/25 C; 5/3/78 E
Oro, L' — 1/2/47 A
Orpheus and Eurydike — 11/27/26 A
Orpheus — 4/28/48 B
Orpheus Dionysos — 6/22/30 B
Orpheus Oratorio Society — 5/5/03 C
Orquesta de Conciertos de Caibarien — 11/12/40 D
Orquesta de Nacimiento — 9/3/68 D
Orquesta Filarmonica of Madrid — 4/9/16 C
Orquesta Sinfonica de Mexico — //28 E; 12/15/33 C; 8/27/37 C; 6/26/42 C; 8/2/78 D
Orquesta Sinfonica Venezuela — 6/24/30 E
Orrego-Salas, Juan — 10/31/64 C
Orr, Terry — 12/1/67 B
Orseolo — 5/5/35 A
Orthophonic Victrola — 5//24 E; 3/25/25 E
Osgood, Betty — 7/11/47 B
Osipenko, Alla — 4/27/57 B
Oslo Philharmonic Orchestra — //52 E
Osten, Eva von der — 1/26/11 A
Ostmark-Overture — 5/22/38 E
Ostrcil, Otakar — 11/11/26 A; 4/27/27 A
Osud — 9/18/34 A; 10/25/58 A
Otello (Verdi) — 1/27/01 D; 9/24/79 E
Othello (Chaboukiani) — 11/29/57 C
Otterloo, Willem van — 12/27/00 D; 4/2/49 D; 7/27/78 D
Otvos, Gabor — 6/12/78 C
Oui des jeunes filles, Le — 6/21/49 A
Outdoor Overture, An — 12/16/38 C
Overload — 9/10/67 B
Overton, Hal — 2/7/50 A
Overture for Orchestra — 10/4/73 C
Overture in C — 5/24/78 C
Overture on Hebrew Themes — 1/26/20 C
Overture to the School for Scandal — 8/30/33 C
Owen, Wilfred — 5/30/62 C
Owen Wingrave — 5/16/71 A
Owl and the Pussycat, The — 6/26/78 B
Oxford Companion to Music, The (book) — 7/31/58 D
Oxford University — 5/29/06 E; 6/18/07 E; 6/26/07 E
Oxus — 8/31/67 C
Ozawa, Seiji — 9/1/35 D; 4/14/61 D; 1/14/69 C; //70 E; 9/29/76 C; //77 E

— P —

Pacem in terris — 12/20/63 C
Pachmann, Vladimir de — 1/6/33 D
Pacific 231 (Honegger) — 5/8/24 C; 11/27/55 D
Pacific 231 (Shawn) — 8/6/29 B
Pacifica Singers — 6/2/73 C
Paderewski, Ignace — 5/15/00 E; 5/29/01 A; 2/12/09 C; 1/17/19 E; 11/27/19 E; 5/8/30 D; 8/12/36 E; 2/26/39 E; 8/18/39 D; 11/6/40 E; 6/29/41 D
Paderewski Prize — 5/15/00 E; 12/20/01 C
Padmavati — 6/1/23 A
Paganini (Fokine) — 6/30/39 B
Paganini (Lavrovsky) — 4/7/60 B
Pagan Poem, A — 11/22/07 C
Pagava, Ethery — 3/2/45 B
Page, Ruth — 3/22/05 D; 4/27/28 B; 6/19/38 B; 10/17/51 B; 11/6/55 E
Page-Stone Ballet — 6/19/38 B
Page, Willis — 10/18/65 C
Pagliacci — 11/10/00 A; 2/1/04 E; 8/9/19 D
Paik, Nam June — 7/20/32 D; 11/13/59 C; 6/5/65 C; 12/2/65 C
Paine, John Knowles — 4/25/06 D
Paladilhe, Emile — 1/6/26 D
Palais de cristal — 7/28/47 B
Palais hante, Le — 1/8/05 C
Paleographie musicale (book) — 1/18/30 D
Palestine Symphony Orchestra — 12/26/36 E; 6/15/47 D; 4/4/48 C
Palestrina — 6/12/17 A
Palestrina Society — 9/5/10 D
Paliashvili Theater of Opera and Ballet — 11/29/57 B
Palinode — 2/7/77 C
Pallas Athene weint — 10/17/55 A
Palley, Anna — 5/12/17 B
Palmgren, Selim — 12/13/51 D
Palm, S. — 9/2/72 C
Paltenghi, David — 1/14/42 B; 10/26/44 B
Paltrinieri, Giordano — 2/10/34 A
Pampeana No. 3 — 10/20/54 C
Panaieff, Michel — 5/4/39 B
Pana Lesnea Rusalim — 6/27/56 A
Panama-Pacific International Exposition — 5/14/15 E; 6/19/15 C
Panambi — 11/27/37 C
Pan-American Association of Composers — 6/6/31 C; 3/6/33 C
Pan American Union — 4/18/58 C
Pan and Syrinx — 2/11/18 C
Pandor, Miriam — 12/21/47 B
Panfilo and Lauretta — 5/9/57 A; 10/28/59 A
Panotrope — 3/25/25 E
Pantaloon — 5/17/56 A
Pantea — 9/6/32 A
Panufnik, Andrzej — 9/24/14 D; 11/9/47 C; 3/24/49 C; 5/13/49 C; 5/25/51 C; 10/1/57 C; 8/12/64 C; 11/17/68 C; 12/16/72 C; 5/21/73 C; 4/13/76 C
Panurge — 4/25/13 A
Pan Voyevoda — 10/16/04 A
Papi, Gennaro — 1/31/20 A
Papillon (Fokine) — 5/10/13 B; 4/16/14 B
Papillons, Les — 3/18/01 B
Papillons, Les (Fokine) — 4/16/14 B
Papko, Tatiana — 9/17/62 B
Pappenheim, Marie — 6/6/24 A
Paque, Desire — 11/20/39 D
Parable of Death, A — 3/11/53 C
Parade — 5/18/17 B
Paradise Lost — 2/23/67 B; 11/29/78 A
Paraphrases of the National Anthems of the Allied Nations (Glazunov) — 3/15/15 C
Paray, Paul — 10/23/59 C; 10/10/79 D
Paredes, Marcos — 12/4/69 B
Parergon zur Symphonia Domestica — 10/16/25 C
Paris a nous deux — 8/7/54 A

Paris Broadcasting Orchestra — 5/5/46 C
Paris Conservatoire — 6/26/05 E
Paris — 11/10/36 B
Paris Exhibition — 5/1/25 E
Parisiana (Curti) — 12/11/05 B
Parisina (Mascagni) — 12/15/13 A
Paris Opera — 10/23/01 A; 7/28/03 D;
    10/31/06 A; 5/5/09 A; 6/4/10 B;
    5/21/14 B; 3/24/18 E; 6/9/20 A;
    6/3/22 A; 6/1/23 A; 3/19/24 A; 7/1/25 A;
    3/4/29 B; 5/15/29 A; 5/21/29 B;
    6/23/31 A; 1/4/32 A; 4/30/34 B;
    8/15/35 D; 3/10/36 A; 3/16/39 A;
    7/28/47 B; 10/21/63 A; 2/24/79 A
Paris Opera Ballet — //29 E; 7/9/35 B;
    6/19/43 B; 12/15/47 B; 3/22/48 B;
    6/14/50 B; //58 E
Parker, Dorothy — 10/29/56 A
Parker, Horatio — 4/11/02 E; 6/12/10 C;
    3/14/12 A; 7/1/15 A; 12/18/19 D
Parkes, Ross — 11/23/66 B
Parkinson, Georgina — 4/25/66 B
Park, Merle — 10/6/37 D; 1/25/67 B;
    2/29/68 B
Parlaphone Company — 3/25/25 E
Parole de San Paolo — 10/30/64 C
Parr, Andree — 6/6/21 B
Parrenin Quartet — 4/16/73 C
Parr, Gladys — 6/18/58 A
Parry, Sir Hubert — 9/7/04 C; 12/5/12 C;
    10/7/18 D
Parsifal — 5/13/00 D; 12/24/03 E; 5/31/05 D
Partch, Harry — 6/24/01 D; 6/8/34 E;
    4/22/44 C; //49 E; 3/14/52 B;
    11/19/53 B; 2/13/54 C; 3/26/57 B;
    5/8/66 C; 1/9/69 B
Partita for Orchestra — 1/30/58 C
Partiturophon — 7/25/26 E
Partos, Oedoen — 10/1/53 C
Party Piece — 5/18/71 C
Parysatis — 8/17/02 C
Pas d'acier, Le — 6/7/27 B
Pas de dix — 11/9/55 B
Pasdeloup Orchestra — 2/28/20 C; 10/19/35 C
Pas de quoi — 5/20/78 C
Pas de Trois (Balanchine) — 2/18/51 B; 3/1/55 B
Pashchenko, Andrei — 5/2/24 C
Pasquier, Etienne — 1/15/41 C
Passacaglia for Orchestra (Debussy) — 2/2/19 C
Passacaglia for Orchestra (Webern) — 11/4/08 C
Passacaglia (Humphrey) — 12/29/58 D
Passion According to Saint Luke, The — 3/28/65 C
Passionmusik fur Kinderchor und Orgel — 4/6/74 C
Passion of Jonathan Wade, The — 10/11/62 A
Passion selon Sade, La — 9/5/65 A
Passmore, Melvena — 6/27/20 E
Pastoral Symphony — 1/26/22 C
Pathe Freres — //28 E
Path of October, The — 1/18/29 C
Path of Thunder, The — 1/4/58 B
Patience — 11/22/00 D
Patineurs, Les — 2/16/37 B
Patterns — 10/21/32 C
Patti, Adelina — 12/1/06 E; 9/27/19 D
Patzak, Julius — 2/5/39 A; 8/6/47 A
Pauer, Ernst — 5/9/05 D
Paul Bunyan — 5/5/41 A
Paulini, Bela — 10/16/26 A
Paul Taylor Company — 8/4/62 B
Paur, Emil — 12/20/01 C; //02 E
Pause del silenzio — 1/27/18 C
Pauvre matelot, Le — 12/16/27 A
Pavane — 5/29/75 B
Pavane pour une Infante defunte — 4/5/02 C
Pavarotti, Luciano — 10/12/35 D; 10/15/77 E;
    10/14/79 E
Pavillon d'armide, Le — 4/28/07 B; 11/25/07 B;
    5/19/09 B

Pavlova, Anna — 2/23/07 B; 11/25/07 B;
    12/22/07 B; 3/21/08 B; 3/21/08 B;
    6/2/09 B; 2/28/10 B; 9/10/23 B;
    1/23/31 D; 8/22/42 D; 7/14/44 D
Peaceable Kingdom, The — 1/31/61 A
Peace Pieces — 8/17/68 C
Peacock Variations — 11/23/39 C
Pears, Peter — 6/22/10 D; 6/7/45 A;
    7/12/46 A; 6/20/47 A; 12/1/51 A;
    6/11/60 A; 9/1/63 C; 6/16/73 A;
    9/14/75 C
Pecheurs de Saint-Jean, Les — 12/26/05 A
Pedrell, Felipe — 5/18/09 D; 8/19/22 D
Peerce, Jan — 6/3/04 D; 11/29/41 D
Peer Gynt (Grieg) — 9/4/07 D
Peer Gynt (Egk) — 11/24/38 A; 7/15/39 E
Peeters, Flor — 7/4/03 D
Pelleas et Melisande (Debussy) — 4/30/02 A;
    2/19/08 A; 3/25/18 D; 12/19/19 D
Pelleas et Melisande (Faure) — 2/3/01 C
Pelleas et Melisande (Schoenberg) — 7/13/51 D
Pelleas und Melisande (Schoenberg) — 1/26/05 C;
    12/21/12 E
Pemberton-Billing, Noel — 11/12/22 E
Penderecki, Krzysztof — 11/23/33 D;
    9/17/59 C; 9/18/60 C; 10/16/60 C;
    5/31/61 C; 4/16/62 C; 6/26/62 C;
    9/20/62 C; 3/30/66 C; 4/14/67 C;
    1/29/68 C; 8/4/68 C; 6/20/69 A;
    9/2/72 C; 1/10/78 C; 11/29/78 A;
    10/14/79 E
Pene du Bois, Raoul — 4/28/66 B
Penelope — 3/4/13 A; 8/17/54 A; 3/1/59 C
Pennario, Leonard — 4/6/67 C
Penn Contemporary Players — 1/13/78 C
Penney, Jennifer — 2/14/78 B
Pennsylvania Ballet — 4/19/64 E; 11/23/66 B;
    1/29/68 B
Penny for a Song, A — 10/31/67 A
Pentathis — 10/11/63 C
People's Philharmonic Choral Society —
    7/5/40 C
Perahia, Murray — 4/19/47 D; 9/3/72 E
Percussion Symphony — 1/26/78 C
Peress, Maurice — 9/8/71 C
Peretti, Serge — 5/22/31 B
Perfect Fool, The — 5/14/23 A
Pergolesi, Giovanni Battista — 12/23/37 E
Perier, Jean — 2/19/08 A
Peri, La (Ashton) — 2/15/56 B
Peri, La (Dukas) — 4/22/12 B; 2/6/31 B
Perini, Flora — 12/14/18 A
Perle, George — 5/6/15 D; 1/8/27 C;
    5/6/49 C; //62 E; 4/19/71 C; 4/6/73 E;
    2/18/75 C; //77 E; 11/18/77 C; 11/1/79 C
Perlman, Itzhak — 8/31/45 D; 10/25/79 C
Peron, Juan — 1/10/50 E
Perosi, Don Lorenzo — 10/12/56 D
Perrault, Serge — 2/21/49 B
Perron, Carl — 12/9/05 A; 1/26/11 A
Persephone (Ashton) — 12/12/62 B
Persephone (Jooss) — 4/30/34 B
Perseus — 10/13/14 C
Persichetti, Vincent — 6/6/15 D; 10/23/45 C;
    10/21/47 C; 11/21/47 C; 8/28/54 C;
    12/17/54 C; 4/16/56 C; 10/24/59 C;
    10/29/67 C; 3/5/71 C; 1/25/73 C;
    11/17/77 C; 7/10/78 C
Persinger, Louis — 11/15/28 D
Perspectives of New Music (periodical) — //62 E;
    7/9/62 E; 4/6/73 E
Pertile, Aureliano — 1/16/35 A; 1/11/52 D
Pervyi Symphonichesky Ensemble —
    2/13/22 E
Pesebre, El — 12/17/60 C
Pessard, Emile-Louis-Fortune — 2/10/17 D
Peter and the Wolf (Prokofiev) — 5/2/36 C
Peter and the Wolf (Bolm) — 1/13/40 B

Peter Grimes — 6/7/45 A; 6/13/45 C; 12/3/54 A;
    12/4/76 D
Peter Ibbetson — 2/7/31 A
Peters, C.F. — 9/3/12 C
Peters, Roberta — 11/17/50 D
Petina, Irra — 2/10/34 A
Petipa, Lubov — 1/17/00 B
Petipa, Marie — 1/17/00 B
Petipa, Marius — 1/17/00 B; 2/10/00 B;
    2/20/00 B; 2/2/02 B; 5/19/09 B;
    7/14/10 D; 11/30/11 B; 11/2/21 B;
    1/31/23 B; 12/7/61 B; 2/4/65 B
Petipa, Nadejda — 1/17/00 B
Petit Elfe Ferme-l'oeil, Le — 12/1/23 C
Petite Suite — 4/20/51 C
Petite symphonie concertante — 5/17/46 C
Petit, Roland — 1/13/24 D; 3//45 E; 3/2/45 B;
    6/25/46 B; 5/22/48 B; 2/21/49 B; //51 E;
    2/23/67 B; 1/10/73 B
Petrassi, Goffredo — 7/16/04 D; 5/12/49 A;
    10/24/50 A; 1/24/52 C
Petrides, Pietro — 8/17/77 D
Petri, Egon — 2/27/30 E
Petrillo, James — 1/13/42 E; 7/8/42 E;
    6/2/58 E
Petroff, Paul — 10/24/33 B; 6/19/38 B;
    6/30/39 B; 1/22/41 B
Petrouchka (Fokine) — 6/13/11 B; 8/22/42 D
Petrouchka (Lczowsky) — 3/12/70 B
Petrouchka (Stravinsky) — 1/17/16 B; 4/6/71 D
Petrov, Andrei — 3/23/71 B
Pet Shop, The — 4/14/58 A
Pevsner, Antoine — 4/30/27 B
Pfitzner, Hans — 11/9/01 A; 6/12/17 A;
    12/11/17 A; 11/12/31 A; 5/22/49 D
Pfundmayr, Hedy — 5/9/24 B; 10/14/24 A
Phaedra (Britten) — 6/16/76 C
Phaedra (Graham) — 3/4/62 B
Phedre (Lifar) — 6/14/50 B
Philadelphia Ballet — 2/11/37 B
Philadelphia Composers' Forum — 1/16/72 C
Philadelphia Opera Company — 11/27/30 D;
    4/5/35 D; 2/11/41 A
Philadelphia Orchestra — 11/16/00 E;
    10/11/12 D; 9/10/17 E; 11/9/17 E;
    12/19/19 C; 11/23/20 C; 2/13/25 C;
    4/9/26 C; 3/18/27 C; 4/8/27 C;
    10/28/29 D; 10/30/31 D; //32 E;
    8/28/32 E; 3/3/33 C; 8/30/33 C;
    11/7/34 C; 2/28/36 C; 11/6/36 C;
    10/21/37 D; 11/13/40 E; 12/6/40 C;
    1/3/41 C; 2/7/41 C; 1/16/42 C;
    10/26/45 C; 11/16/45 C; 11/30/45 C;
    2/8/46 C; 5/28/47 C; 11/21/47 C;
    3/20/48 E; 11/26/48 C; 12/31/48 C;
    3/4/50 C; 10/27/50 C; 12/11/50 C;
    3/13/53 C; 12/17/54 C; 1/14/55 C;
    2/18/55 C; 3/18/55 C; 9/15/55 C;
    10/23/59 C; 9/30/60 C; 2/10/61 C;
    3/31/61 C; 1/26/62 C; 9/25/62 C;
    1/18/63 C; 2/7/64 C; 12/18/64 C;
    5/16/66 C; 1/10/69 C; 3/5/71 C;
    2/27/75 C; 5/27/76 C; 8/4/76 C;
    8/26/77 C; 8/25/78 C
Philco — 6/21/48 E
Philco Radio Orchestra — 10/17/44 C
Philharmonia Hungarica — 5/28/57 E
Philharmonia Orchestra of London —
    3/22/79 D
Philharmonic Fanfare — 8/10/65 C
Philharmonic Hall (New York City) —
    9/9/57 E; 5/14/59 E; — see also Avery
    Fisher Hall
Philharmonic Orchestra of London —
    12/19/60 C
Philharmonic Orchestra of Rio de Janeiro —
    9/12/32 C
Philharmonic Orchestra, The — 6/26/74 D
Philharmonic Radio of New York — //37 E

Philharmonic Society of Budapest — 1/9/22 C

Philharmonic-Symphony Society of New York, Inc. — 3/19/01 D; 3/30/28 E; 12/13/28 C; — see also New York Philharmonic

Philharmonisches der Stadt Augsburg — 6/12/78 C

Philharmonisches Konzert — 4/15/32 C

Philipp, Isidor — 2/20/58 D

Philips (record label) — 6//50 E; //63 E; 10/11/65 E

Phillippart, Nathalie — 12/13/48 B

Phillips, Ailne — 5/20/35 B

Philosophy of Modern Music (book) — //48 E; 8/6/69 D

Phlegra — 1/28/76 C

Phonographische Zeitschrift — 5//00 E

Phonycord Company — //30 E

Phorion — 4/27/67 C

Photo of the Colonel, The — 6/3/64 A

Photoptosis — Prelude for Large Orchestra — 2/19/69 C

Pianiste-virtuose, Le — 3/19/00 D

Piano Concerto (Benjamin) — 9/5/50 C

Piano Concerto (Bennett) — 9/19/68 C

Piano Concerto (Blackwood) — 7/26/70 C

Piano Concerto (Bliss) — 6/10/39 C

Piano Concerto (Britten) — 8/18/38 C

Piano Concerto (Busoni) — 11/10/04 C

Piano Concerto (Chavez) — 1/1/42 C

Piano Concerto (Copland) — 1/28/27 C

Piano Concerto (Corigliano) — 4/5/68 C

Piano Concerto (Cowell) — 12/28/30 C

Piano Concerto (Delius) — 10/12/29 C

Piano Concerto (*Equatoriales*)(Jolivet) — 6/19/51 C

Piano Concerto (Halffter) — 3/13/54 C

Piano Concerto (Hanson) — 12/31/48 C

Piano Concerto (Kirchner) — 2/23/56 C

Piano Concerto in C Major (Vaughan Williams) — 2/1/33 C

Piano Concerto in C Minor (Howells) — 7/10/14 C

Piano Concerto in F Major (Menotti) — 11/2/45 C

Piano Concerto No. 1 (Barber) — 5/6/63 E

Piano Concerto No. 1 (Bartok) — 7/1/27 C

Piano Concerto No. 1 in A Minor (Kabalevsky) — 12/11/31 C

Piano Concerto No. 1 in D-flat Major (Prokofiev) — 8/7/12 C; 5/24/14 E

Piano Concerto No. 1 (Milhaud) — 11/23/34 C; 12/2/38 C

Piano Concerto No. 1 (Shostakovich) — 10/15/33 C

Piano Concerto No. 1 (Toch) — 10/8/26 C

Piano Concerto No. 1 (Vladigerov) — 3/17/21 C

Piano Concerto No. 2 (Finney) — 11/1/72 C

Piano Concerto No. 2 (Lees) — 3/15/68 C

Piano Concerto No. 2 (Wuorinen) — 12/6/74 C

Piano Concerto No. 2 (Chasins) — 3/3/33 C

Piano Concerto No. 2 (Dohnanyi) — 1/22/51 C

Piano Concerto No. 2 (Foss) — 10/7/51 C

Piano Concerto No. 2 (Henze) — 9/29/68 C

Piano Concerto No. 2 in B Major (Glazunov) — 11/11/17 C

Piano Concerto No. 2 in G Minor (Kabalevsky) — 5/12/36 C

Piano Concerto No. 2 in G Minor (Prokofiev) — 9/5/13 C; 5/8/24 C

Piano Concerto No. 2 (Khrennikov) — 2/8/72 C

Piano Concerto No. 2 (Krenek) — 3/17/38 C

Piano Concerto No. 2 (Ornstein) — 2/13/25 C

Piano Concerto No. 2 (Rawsthorne) — 6/17/51 C

Piano Concerto No. 2 (Sowerby) — 11/30/36 C

Piano Concerto No. 2 (Tcherepnin, A.) — 1/26/24 C

Piano Concerto No. 2 (Toch) — 1/26/35 C

Piano Concerto No. 3 in C Major (Prokofiev) — 12/16/21 C

Piano Concerto No. 3 in D Major (Kabalevsky) — 3/15/49 C; 2/1/53 C

Piano Concerto No. 3 (Krenek) — 11/22/46 C

Piano Concerto No. 3 (Milhaud) — 5/26/46 C

Piano Concerto No. 3 (Tcherepnin, A.) — 2/5/33 C

Piano Concerto No. 4 in G Minor (Rachmaninoff) — 3/18/27 C

Piano Concerto No. 4 (Martinu) — 10/4/56 C

Piano Concerto No. 4 (Milhaud) — 3/3/50 C

Piano Concerto No. 5 in G Major (Prokofiev) — 10/31/32 C

Piano Concerto No. 5 (Milhaud) — 6/25/56 C

Piano Concerto No. 6 (Tcherepnin, A.) — 9/5/72 C

Piano Concerto (Poulenc) — 1/6/50 C

Piano Concerto (Schoenberg) — 2/6/44 C

Piano Concerto (Sowerby) — 3/5/20 C

Piano Concerto (Tailleferre) — 5/30/25 C

Piano Concerto (Ward) — 6/23/68 C

Pianoforte Competition, International — 9/3/72 C

Pianola — 6/14/12 E

Piano Piece No. 1 — 12/2/65 C

Piano Quartet — 10/23/77 C

Pianos and Voices — 7/16/72 C

Pianos and Voices II — 8/31/72 C

Piano Sonata (Copland) — 10/21/41 C

Piano Sonata (Liebermann) — 10/6/51 C

Piano Sonata in F Minor (Prokofiev) — 12/5/10 C

Piano Sonata No. 1 (Ives) — 1/29/27 C

Piano Sonata No. 2 (Hamilton) — 12/14/74 C

Piano Sonata No. 2 (Sessions) — 3/16/47 C

Piano Sonata No. 3 (Sessions) — 3/3/69 C

Piano Sonata No. 3 (Siegmeister) — 11/25/79 C

Piano Sonata No. 3 (Tippett) — 5/26/74 C

Piano Suite No. 1 (Skalkottas) — 5/1/73 C

Piano Trio in D Major (Korngold) — 11/17/10 C

Piano Variations (Copland) — 1/4/31 C; 3/5/58 C

Piatigorsky, Gregor — 4/17/03 D; 12/29/29 D; 2/7/41 C; 1/25/57 C; 6/3/70 C; 8/6/76 D

Piatti, Ugo — 6/2/13 E

Picabia, F. — 12/4/24 B

Picasso, Pablo — 5/18/17 B; 7/22/19 B; 5/15/20 B; 6/15/24 B; 6/20/24 B; 8/25/54 C

Piccola Scala, La — 12/26/55 E; 3/10/56 A; 5/22/57 A; 2/8/60 A

Piccolo Marat, Il — 5/2/21 A

Pichler, Gusti — 5/9/24 B

Pick-Mangiagalli, Riccardo — 12/17/32 E; 4/25/36 A; 7/8/49 D

Pickwick — 11/20/36 A

Picnic at Tintagel — 2/28/52 B

Pictures at an Exhibition — 10/19/22 C

Piece in the Shape of a Square — 5/19/68 C

Piece Period — 12/27/62 B

Pieces — 11/20/70 C

Pied Piper, The — 12/4/51 B

Piege de lumiere — 12/23/52 B

Pierce, J.R. — //57 E; //58 E

Pierne, Gabriel — 2/3/07 C; 5/30/10 A; 4/2/11 C; 6/16/21 E; 10/29/21 C; 2/26/22 C; 12/6/25 C; 7/17/37 D

Pierpont Morgan Library — 7/16/79 E

Pierrot and Pierrette — 11/11/09 A

Pierrot Lunaire (Schoenberg) — 10/16/12 C; 7/13/51 D

Pierrot Lunaire (Tetley) — 5/5/62 B

Pijper, Willem — 4/23/18 C; 11/2/22 C; 10/28/26 C; 3/18/47 D

Pilgrim's Progress, The — 4/26/51 A

Pilgrim Vision, A — 11/23/20 C

Pillar of Fire — 4/8/42 B

Pineapple Poll — 3/13/51 B

Pinelli, Tullio — 2/15/40 A

Pine, Sandra — 2/24/55 B

Pines of Rome, The — 3/11/17 C; 12/14/24 C; 2/14/74 E

Pinocchio — 12/10/36 C

Pinotta — 3/23/32 A

Pinza, Ezio — 11/1/26 D; 5/9/57 D

Pipe of Desire, The — 1/31/06 A; 3/18/10 A

Piper, John — //46 E; 1/1/57 B

Piper, Myfanwy — 9/14/54 A; 6/16/73 A

Pirandello, Luigi — 11/19/24 B; 1/13/34 A

Pirates of Penzance, The — 11/22/00 D; 5/29/11 D

Pirinoes, Los — 8/19/22 D

Pisk, Paul A. — 2/2/19 C

Piston, Walter — 3/23/28 C; 3/28/30 C; 4/30/32 E; 3/6/34 C; 6/20/37 C; 4/8/38 C; 5/30/38 B; 3/18/40 C; 3/5/44 C; 10/21/44 C; 5/12/45 E; 5/1/47 C; 1/9/48 C; 4/3/48 E; 3/30/51 C; 5/6/52 E; 11/25/55 C; 2/24/56 C; 9/6/56 E; 10/23/59 C; 10/14/60 C; 2/10/61 C; 4/20/61 C; 5/1/61 E; 9/25/62 C; 7/4/64 C; 10/31/64 C; 3/5/65 C; 3/2/67 C; 3/7/68 C

Piteov, Ludmilla — 9/28/18 B

Pitkin, William — 9/13/66 B

Pittel, Harvey — 12/5/79 C

Pittsburgh Orchestra Association — 11/9/17 E

Pittsburgh Symphony — 1/30/59 C

Pittsburgh Symphony Orchestra — 1/23/00 E; 1/15/06 E; //13 E; 5/2/26 E; 11/13/42 C; 3/5/43 C; 1/28/44 C; 2/20/44 D; 2/4/45 C; 11/15/46 D; 2/6/47 E; 11/30/51 C; 12/2/55 C; 10/24/58 C; 1/30/59 C; 10/14/60 C; 9/10/71 E; 4/4/75 C

Pius XII, Pope — 9/4/39 E; 11/20/47 E

Pius X, Pope — 11/22/03 E; 7/10/14 E; 12/4/63 E

Pius X School of Liturgical Music — 5/25/38 D

Pizzetti, Ildebrando — 3/20/15 A; 12/16/22 A; 5/16/28 A; 2/28/29 C; 4/29/30 A; 12/17/32 E; 5/5/35 A; 1/2/47 A; 5/4/51 A; 11/5/52 A; 12/4/54 A; 3/1/58 A; 3/23/61 A; 3/1/65 A; 2/13/68 D

Pizzolato, Giuseppe — 3/19/06 A

Place des Arts (Montreal) — 9/21/63 E

Plague, The — 4/1/64 C

Plancon, Pol — 11/26/06 D; 8/12/14 D

Planets, The (Holst) — 9/29/18 C; 11/15/20 C

Planets, The (Tudor) — 10/28/34 B

Plante, Francis — 12/19/34 D

Plaschke, Friedrich — 6/24/35 A

Platoff, Marc — 5/11/39 B; 10/26/39 B

Playable Music No. 4 — 12/2/65 C

Play of Daniel, The — 1/9/66 D

Play of Herod, The — 1/9/66 D

Play of Saint Nicholas, The — 12/6/79 C

Please Don't Hate Me (book) — 11/11/79 D

Pleasure Dome of Kubla Khan, The — 11/28/19 C; 4/8/20 D

Plectra and Percussion Dances — 11/19/53 B

Plenum III — 5/6/74 C

Plenum IV — 7/15/76 C

Pli selon pli — 6/13/60 C; 1/10/64 C; 3/26/65 C

Plisetskaya, Maya — 11/20/25 D; 2/12/54 B; 3/4/60 B; 9/17/62 B; 6/11/72 B; 1/10/73 B

Plomer, William — 6/8/53 A; 6/9/66 A

Plough and the Stars, The — 3/16/69 A

Pocahontas — 5/24/39 B

Podini, Paolo — 5/5/78 B
Podrecca, Vittorio — 4/13/22 A
Poelvoorde, Rita — 1/27/78 B
Poem About Stalin, A — 11/29/38 C
Poeme de l'Extase (Cranko) — 3/24/70 B
Poeme de l'Extase, Le (Scribin) — 12/10/08 C
Poeme des rivages — 12/1/21 C
Poeme mecanique — 9/3/27 E
Poeme symphonique — 3/4/65 C
Poem for Flute and Orchestra — 11/16/19 C
Poem for Tables, Chairs and Benches — 1/5/60 C
Poem on His Birthday — 4/24/76 C
Poesie pour pouvoir — 10/19/58 C
Pohjola's Daughter — 12/29/06 C; 9/20/57 D
Poia — 1/15/06 C; 4/23/07 A; 4/23/10 A
Points on the Curve to Find... 10/16/74 C
Poisoned Kiss, The — 5/12/36 A
Polacco, Giorgio — 11/4/29 E
Polevetsian Dances — 5/19/09 B
Polignac, Armande de — 1/2/08 C
Polikoff, Max — 5/9-10/61 E
Polish Relief Fund — 7/6/15 C
Politics of Harmony: A Masque, The — 10/28/68 C
Polka in C (Strauss, R.) — 9/8/49 D
Pollack, Egon — 12/4/20 A
Pollock, Jackson — 3/9/65 C
Pollini, Maurizio — 1/5/42 D
Polonia — 7/6/15 C
Polydor (record label) — 2//29 E
Polymorphie — 4/16/62 C
Polyphonia Symphony Orchestra — 2/26/62 C
Polyphonie X — 10/6/51 C
Polyptique — 9/9/73 C
Pommer, M. — 2/27/73 C
Pomp and Circumstance (Elgar) — 10/19/01 C; 9/20/30 C
Pomp and Circumstance No. 3 — 3/8/05 C
Pomp and Circumstance No. 4 — 8/24/07 C
Pompidou, Georges — 5//77 E
Ponce, Manuel — 10/4/41 C; 4/24/48 D
Pond, The — 1/29/27 C; 5/19/54 D
Ponselle, Rosa — 11/15/18 D; 3/12/19 A; 11/1/26 D
Pons, Lily — 1/3/31 D; 2/13/76 D
Pontifical Institute of Sacred Music — 7/10/14 E; 5/25/38 D
Ponti, Michael — 12/14/74 C
Poole, David — 12/20/49 B; 3/13/51 B; 2/1/53 B; 1/18/55 B
Pool of Darkness — 1/15/50 B
Poot, Marcel — 5/7/01 D; 10/22/46 C; 5/25/60 E
Popper, David — 8/7/13 D
Porgy and Bess — 9/30/35 A; 12/26/55 E
Porter, Mrs. Lois — 9/14/72 E
Porter, Quincy — 4/2/38 C; 5/16/48 C; 3/17/54 C; 5/3/54 E; 4/18/58 C; 11/12/66 D; 9/14/72 E
Portland Symphony Orchestra — 4/4/61 C
Portraits — 1/18/76 C
Portsmouth Point — 6/22/26 C; 11/19/26 C
Posselt, Ruth — 3/18/40 C
Posseur, Henri — 10/19/54 C; 3/17/68 A
Possibility of a New Work for Electric Guitar, The — 6/20/66 C
Postcard from Morocco — 10/14/71 A
Potemkin Holiday — 12/16/02 A
Pothier, Dom Joseph — 12/8/23 D; 1/18/30 D
Pot of Fat, The — 5/9/55 A
Potomac String Trio — 10/27/68 C
Pougin, Arthur — 8/8/21 D
Poulenc, Francis — 12/11/17 C; 1/16/20 E; 6/19/21 B; 1/6/24 B; 3/4/29 B; 5/3/29 C; 6/19/29 B; 6/10/41 C; 3/25/45 C; 6/3/47 A; 10/24/48 C; 1/6/50 C; 6/13/51 C; 1/26/57 A; 2/6/59 A; 1/20/61 C; 1/30/63 D; 12/22/73 B; 10/17/79 D
Poulet, Gaston — 5/5/17 C

Pound, Ezra — 2/12/59 D; 8/24/72 C
Pourquoi? — 5/3/76 C
Pour une fete de printemps — 10/29/21 C
Powell, John — 3/23/18 C
Powell, Robert — 8/17/62 B; 9/6/63 B
Powell Symphony Hall (St. Louis, Mo.) — 1/24/68 E
Powers, Marie — 3/31/49 A
Praagh, Peggy van — 9/1/10 D; 1/26/36 B; 2/19/37 B; 11/26/38 B; 12/5/38 B; 11/2/62 E
Praeludium — 10/19/53 C
Prague Philharmonic Choir — //45 E
Prague Philharmonic Orchestra — 6/14/20 D
Prague Spring International Music Festival — //46 E; 5/21/74 D
Prairie Legend — 12/29/46 C; 1/18/47 C
Prairie, The — 5/15/44 C
Pratella, Francesco Balilla — 12/4/09 A; 7/18/12 E; 5/18/55 D
Prayer — 4/5/71 C
Prayer in Time of War — 2/13/43 C
Prayers of Kierkegaard — 12/3/54 C
Preface au Livre de Vie — 6/3/26 C
Preis, A. — 1/12/30 A; 1/22/34 A
Prelude a l'Apres-midi d'un faune — 3/25/18 D
Prelude and Fugue for String Orchestra (Harris) — 2/28/36 C
Prelude from Pre-first Sonata — 1/29/27 C
Prelude on the Tone Sol — 5/21/73 C
Preludes pour piano (Debussy) — 6/19/13 C
Preludes pour piano (Dutilleux) — 6/25/74 C
Preludes (Wyschnegradsky) — 1/25/37 C
Preludio a Cristobal Colon — 2/15/25 C
Preobrajenska, Olga — 2/10/00 D; 12/15/01 B; 3/21/08 B; 11/5/51 D; //74 E
Preobrazhensky, Vladimir — 2/12/54 B
Preradovic, Paul — 10/22/46 E
Presages, Les — 4/13/33 B
Pre-Second String Quartet — 1/29/27 C
Press, The — 3/18/01 B
Previn, Andre — 4/6/29 D; 10/1/64 D; 1/30/76 E; 7/30/79 A
Prevost, Andre — 4/29/67 E
Prevost, Robert — 10/3/68 B
Prey, Hermann — 7/11/29 D
Preziose ridicole, Le — 2/9/29 A
Price, Leontyne — 2/10/27 C; 12/3/54 C; 1/27/61 D; 9/16/66 A; 10/14/79 E
Priestley, J.B. — 9/29/49 A
Priestman, Brian — 4/16/73 C
Prigioniero, Il — 12/4/49 A; 5/20/50 A
Primavera (Chihara) — 4/17/78 C
Prima vera, La (Respighi) — 3/4/23 C
Primavera String Quartet — 4/17/78 C
Primitive Mysteries — 2/2/31 B
Primrose, William — 8/23/03 D; 12/2/49 C
Prince Ferelon — 5/21/21 A
Prince of the Pagodas, The — 1/1/57 B
Princeton University — 1/8/59 E
Prinzessin auf der Erbse, Die — 7/17/27 A
Prinzessin Girnara, Die — 5/15/21 A; 9/2/28 A
Prinz, John — 11/23/68 B; 5/22/69 B
Prinz von Homburg, Der — 5/22/60 A
Prisoner of the Caucasus, The — 4/14/38 B
Pritchard, John — 1/27/55 A; 9/2/60 C; 5/29/62 A; 10/14/79 E
Prix de Rome — 10/20/28 E
Procedura penale — 10/30/59 A
Procesion del rocio, La — 3/30/13 C
Prodigal Son, The (Balanchine) — 5/21/29 B
Prodigal Son, The (Britten) — 6/10/68 C
Prodigal Son, The (Lichine) — 12/1/39 B
Profiles — 7/28/79 B
Prohaska, Felix — 5/16/12 D
Projections I — 5/2/51 C
Projections II — 5/2/51 C
Prokofiev, Sergei — 12/31/08 D; 9/14/09 E; 12/5/10 C; 8/1/11 C; 8/7/12 C; 9/5/13 C;

5/24/14 E; 1/29/16 C; 12/10/16 C; 12/12/16 E; 1/30/17 E; 4/21/18 C; 11/20/18 D; 1/26/20 C; 4/22/21 E; 5/17/21 B; 12/16/21 C; 12/30/21 A; 10/18/23 C; 5/8/24 C; 5/29/24 C; 6/6/25 C; 6/7/27 B; 4/29/29 A; 5/21/29 B; 12/22/29 C; 2/27/30 E; 11/14/30 C; //31 E; 10/31/32 C; 12/16/32 B; //33 E; 3/11/34 C; 4/14/34 C; 12/1/35 C; 5/2/36 C; 10/29/36 C; 11/24/36 C; 1/5/37 E; 2/20/37 C; 4/15/37 C; 1/5/38 C; 11/26/38 C; 12/5/38 B; 5/17/39 C; 12/21/39 C; 1/11/40 B; 1/13/40 B; 6/23/40 A; 11/16/40 B; 1/21/43 C; 2/21/44 C; 1/13/45 C; 11/10/45 C; 11/21/45 B; 3/8/46 C; 6/12/46 A; 10/1/46 E; 11/3/46 A; 10/11/47 C; 2/11/48 E; 2/21/48 E; 4/11/48 E; 12/3/48 A; 12/23/48 B; 12/19/50 C; 2/18/52 C; 2/22/52 C; 10/11/52 C; 3/5/53 D; 2/12/54 B; 2/18/54 B; 4/1/55 A; 5/19/55 B; 9/14/55 A; 9/5/56 C; 10/10/56 E; 4/27/57 B; 5/28/58 E; 7/26/58 B; 3/18/60 C; 10/8/60 A; 12//62 B; 2/9/65 B; 4/5/66 C; 3/31/67 B; 11/28/72 D; 5/24/73 B; 2/16/75 B
Proletarian Musician, The — 1/1/29 E
Prologue to a Tragedy — 3/9/09 C
Promenade Concerts — 8/15/14 E; 7/28/44 E
Promethee — 8/27/00 A
Prometheus (Orff) — 3/24/68 A
Prometheus (The Poem of Fire) (Scriabin) — 3/15/11 C; 3/20/15 C; 7/24/75 E
Pro Musica Nova — 5/4/74 C
Prophecy of Isaiah — 4/2/63 C
Proserpina e lo straniero — 3/17/52 A
Prospect Before Us, The — 7/4/40 B
Prosperos Beschworung — 2/19/38 C
Protagonist, Der — 3/27/26 A
Prout, Ebenezer — 12/5/09 D
Prozess, Der — 8/17/53 A
Pruna, Pedro — 6/17/25 B
Prussak, Eugene — 4/24/25 A
Prussian Academy of Arts — 5/30/33 E
Psalm 67 (Ives) — 5/19/54 D
Psalm 90 (Ives) — 5/19/54 D
Psalm 100 (Reger) — 2/23/10 C
Psalmus Hungaricus — 11/19/23 C; 3/6/67 D
Psalm XLVII — 12/27/06 C
Psalmy Dawida — 6/26/62 C
Puccini, Giacomo — 1/14/00 A; 2/17/04 A; 5/28/04 A; 10/15/06 A; 12/10/10 A; 3/27/17 A; 12/14/18 A; 1/28/21 E; 9/19/24 A; 11/29/24 E; 4/25/26 A; 9/5/64 E; 7/20/79 E
Pugni, Cesare — 3/4/60 B
Pulce d'oro, La — 2/15/40 A
Pulcinella (Balanchine) — 6/23/72 B
Pulcinella (Massine) — 5/15/20 B
Pulcinella (Stravinsky) — 6/10/21 C; 4/6/71 D
Pulitzer Prize for music — 5/3/43 E; 5/1/44 E; 5/7/45 E; 5/6/46 E; 5/5/47 E; 4/3/48 E; 5/2/49 E; 5/1/50 E; 5/7/51 E; 5/5/52 E; 5/3/54 E; 5/2/55 E; 5/7/56 E; 5/6/57 E; 5/5/58 E; 5/4/59 E; 5/2/60 E; 5/1/61 E; 5/7/62 E; 5/6/63 E; 5/2/66 E; 5/1/67 E; 5/6/68 E; 5/5/69 E; 5/4/70 E; 5/3/71 E; 5/1/72 E; 5/7/73 E; 5/5/75 E; 5/3/76 E; 4/18/77 E; 4/17/78 E; 4/16/79 E
Pulszky, Romola de — 9/10/13 E
Punch and Judy — 6/8/68 A
Punch Opera, The — 5/10/55 A
Purcell, Henry — 1/14/42 B; 11/29/46 E; 8/17/49 B; 1/13/75 C
Purgatory — 2/17/61 A
Pyle, Thomas F. — 1/22/76 D

— Q —

Quaderni — 6/13/60 C
Quadraphonic discs — //70 E
Quaestio Temporis — 9/30/60 C
Quaker Reader, A — 2/2/77 C
Quarr Abbey — 1/18/30 D
Quartet — 2/18/54 B
Quarter-tone piano — 3/18/24 E; 7/21/31 E
Quartet for Piano and Strings (Copland) — 10/29/50 C
Quartet for Strings (Holliger) — 3/23/75 C
Quartet for Strings No. 2 (Ligeti) — 12/16/68 C
Quartet for the End of Time — 1/15/41 C
Quartet No. 3 (Kirchner) — 5/1/67 E
Quartet (Webern) — 4/13/31 C
Quattro rusteghi, I — 3/19/06 A
Queen Elisabeth International Music Competition — 5/25/60 E
Queen of Spades, The — 5/25/77 E
Queen's Hall (London) — 5/10/41 E
Queen's Hall Orchestra — 3/8/61 D
Quest, The — 4/6/43 B
Quiet City — 1/28/41 C
Quiet Flows the Don — 10/22/35 A; 10/23/37 A; 1/18/78 D
Quintana, Paolo — 6/27/20 E
Quintete — 11/11/23 C
Quintet for Clarinet and Strings (Francaix) — 6/18/78 C
Quintet for Flute, Oboe, Clarinet, Bassoon and Horn (Schoenberg) — 7/13/51 D
Quintet for Piano and String Quartet (Rochberg) — 3/15/76 C
Quintet for Piano and Strings (Ginastera) — 4/13/63 C
Quintet for Piano and Strings (Shostakovich) — 11/23/40 C
Quintet for Piano and Winds (Berkeley) — 1/30/76 C
Quintet for Winds (Colgrass) — 3/21/62 C
Quintet for Winds (Kokkonen) — 2/20/74 C
Quintet (Grieg) — 11/7/07 C
Quintet No. 2 for Piano and Strings (Bloch) — 4/15/58 C
Quodlibet, eine Unterhaltungsmusik — 2/6/26 C

— R —

Raabe, Peter — 4/12/45 D
Rabaud, Henri — 5/15/14 A; 10/1/20 E; 9/11/49 D
Rabin, Michael — 11/17/60 C
Rabinovich, Nikolai — 10/7/08 D
Rachel — 4/19/47 A
Rachel, la cubana — 3/4/74 A
Rachmaninoff, Serge — 12/15/00 C; 11/9/01 C; 12/10/04 E; 2/2/05 E; 1/24/06 A; 5/16/07 E; 2/8/08 C; 5/1/09 C; 11/4/09 D; 11/28/09 C; 11/25/10 C; 12/13/13 C; 3/10/15 C; 1/5/18 E; 3/18/27 C; //31 E; 11/7/34 C; 11/6/36 C; 6/30/39 B; 1/3/41 C; 2/1/43 E; 3/28/43 D; 4/7/60 B; 11/15/77 D
Radford, Robert — 3/1/33 D
Radha — 1/28/06 B
Radio — 1/13/10 E; 1/4/23 E; //26 E; //33 E; 4/4/33 E; 6/30/61 D
Radio Corporation of America (RCA) — see Victor, R.C.A.
Radio Orchestra of Rome (RAI) — 7/6/63 C
Radio-Panoramique — 10/19/35 C
Radunsky, Alexander — 3/4/60 B
Radzynski, Jan — 7/28/79 B
Raft of the Medusa, The — 11/9/68 E
Ragtime — 4/27/20 C

Rainbow Round My Shoulder — 5/10/59 B
Raisa, Rosa — 11/28/13 D; 4/25/26 A; 11/4/29 E
Rake's Progress, The (Stravinsky) — 9/11/51 A; 4/6/71 D
Rake's Progress, The (Valois) — 5/20/35 B
Ralf, Torsten — 10/15/38 A
Ralov, Borge — 9/14/71 D
Rambert, Marie Dancers — 2/25/30 B
Rambert, Marie — 2/25/30 B; 7/1/50 D
Ramifications — 4/23/69 C
Rampal, Jean-Pierre — 1/7/22 D
Ramuntcho — 2/10/42 A
Ranalow, Frederick — 1/14/16 A
Randazzo, Petero — 8/17/62 B; 9/6/63 B
Rangstrom, Ture — 3/1/50 B
Rankl, Karl — 7/12/46 C
Rape of Lucretia, The — 7/12/46 A; 12/4/76 D
Rapp, Richard — 5/28/65 B
Rapp, Siegfried — 9/5/56 C
Rapsodia satanica — 7/2/17 C
Rapsodie Espagnole — 5/29/75 B
Rapsodie negre (Poulenc) — 12/11/17 C
Rapsodie negre (Powell) — 3/23/18 C
Rapunzel — 5/14/59 A
Rasa, Lina Bruna — 1/16/35 A
Rascher, Sigurd — 11/25/34 C
Raskin, Judith — 1/23/78 C
Raskolnikoff — 10/14/48 A
Rassine, Alexis — 10/26/44 B
Rathaus, Karol — 12/10/30 A; 4/4/48 C; 11/21/54 D
Ratsumies — 7/17/75 A
Rauschenberg, Robert — 12/8/54 B; 5/24/55 B; 7/11/56 B; 8/17/58 B; 7/17/63 B
Rautavaara, Einojuhani — 8/30/73 A
Ravel, Maurice — 6/30/01 E; 4/5/02 C; 6/27/03 E; 3/5/04 C; 5/17/04 C; 1/12/07 C; 2/3/07 C; 2/22/07 C; 3/15/08 C; 5/19/09 B; 4/20/10 C; 4/2/11 C; 5/19/11 A; 1/21/12 C; 4/22/12 B; 6/8/12 B; 6/7/16 E; 2/28/20 C; 12/12/20 C; 4/22/21 E; 10/19/22 C; 4/26/24 C; 3/21/25 A; 5/30/27 C; 11/22/28 B; 1/12/29 B; 3/4/29 B; 1/5/32 C; 1/14/32 C; 12/1/34 C; 11/26/46 B; 12/20/49 B; 2/20/51 B; 5/6/52 B; 9/6/56 E; 10/10/56 E; 2/1/58 B; 3/3/61 D; 7/15/62 B; 10/10/68 C
Raverat, Gwendolen — 7/5/31 B
Raver, Leonard — 2/2/77 C; 7/10/78 C
Rawsthorne, Alan — 5/2/05 D; 7/1/48 C; 6/17/51 C
Raymonda (Petipa) — 12/7/61 B
Raymonda (Glazunov) — 12/7/61 B
Raymonda Variations (Balanchine) — 12/7/61 B
Raysse, Martial — 2/23/67 B
Razzi, Anna — 5/5/78 B
RCA — see Victor, R.C.A.
RCA electronic music synthesizer — 4/12/34 D; 1/31/56 E; 10/4/58 E
RCA Victor — see Victor, R.C.A.
Reallexikon der Musikinstrumente (book) — 2/5/59 D
Reardon, John — 10/11/77 C
Rebikov, Vladimir — 8/4/20 D
Rebus — 12/15/31 D; 3/7/75 B
Recording industry — 5/00 E; 10//01 E; 4/11/02 E; 4/30/03 E; 8//04 E; //05 E; 7//06 E; //08 E; //09 E; //12 E; //15 E; //19 E; 9/16/20 E; 11/12/22 E; //23 E; 5//24 E; 3/25/25 E; //26 E; 5//27 E; //28 E; 2//29 E; //30 E; 9/17/31 E; //32 E; //33 E; //34 E; //35 E; 11/19/36 E; 12//38 E; 11/13/40 E; //44 E; //47 E; 6/21/48 E; 1//49 E; 6//50 E; 6/2/51 E; 10//52 E; //53 E; //54 E; //55 E; //58 E;

//63 E; 10/11/65 E; //66 E; //69 E; //70 E; //76 E; //77 E
Recording Industry Association — //53 E
Red Army Ensemble — 1/17/29 E
Red Flower, The — 6/14/27 B
Redpath, Christine — 5/24/73 B
Red Poppy, The — 6/14/27 B
Red Whirlwind, The — 10/29/24 B
Reed, Janet — 6/1/45 B; 12/1/49 B; 6/12/51 B; 6/12/51 B; 12/4/51 B; 9/14/54 B; 2/27/55 B
Reed, Ramon — 2/11/41 B
Re Enzo — 3/12/05 A
Refice, Licinio — 1/1/38 A
Reflections — 5/21/73 C; 4/29/75 C
Reflections of Emily — 1/18/79 C
Reger, Max — 10/8/05 C; 7/1/08 E; 10/13/08 C; 3/9/09 C; 2/23/10 C; 10/12/10 E; 12/15/10 C; 10/4/12 C; 10/11/12 C; 10/12/13 C; 2/5/15 C; 5/11/16 D
Regina — 10/11/49 A
Reginetta delle rose, La — 6/24/12 A
Regio Conservatorio Musicale di Santa Cecilia — 8/22/19 E
Re Hassan — 1/26/39 A
Rehearsal Call — 2/15/62 A
Rehearsal, The — 10/26/65 B
Reich, George — 4/17/59 B
Reichsmusikkammer — 9/22/33 E; 11/15/33 E; 12/4/34 E; 7/13/35 E; 8/30/35 E; 4/3/36 E; 5/1/38 E; 6/8/48 E; 9/8/49 D
Reichwein, Leopold — 4/8/45 D
Reid, Alastair — 11/6/55 A
Reid Symphony Orchestra — 11/22/34 C
Reihe, Die (periodical) — //55 E
Reiman, Elise — 4/27/28 B; 3/1/35 B; 11/20/46 B; 11/26/46 B
Reimann, Aribert — 3/4/36 D; 4/29/71 A; 7/9/78 A
Reiner, Fritz — 4/1/27 C; 4/1/33 E; 4/1/37 A; //41 E; 11/13/42 C; 2/6/47 E; 2/4/49 D; 11/6/50 C; 11/15/63 D
Reinhardt, Max — 12/23/11 C; 8/22/20 E; 4/10/33 E
Reisenberg, Nadia — 7/14/05 D
Reisman Orchestra, Leo — 1/14/34 C
Reiter, Josef — 6/2/39 D
Relache — 12/4/24 B
Relata I — 3/3/66 C
Relata II — 1/16/69 C
Reliquary for Igor Stravinsky, A — 6/1/75 C
Remick & Company, J.H. — 1/28/21 E
Reminiscence — 3/1/35 B
Remisoff, Nicholas — 4/27/28 B
Remoortel, Edouard van — //58 E; 3/2/59 E; 10/24/59 C
Remorseless Rush of Time — 4/23/70 C
Renard, Le (Lifar) — 5/21/29 B
Renard, Le (Nijinska) — 5/18/22 B
Renard, Le (Stravinsky) — 1/13/47 B; 4/6/71 D
Renault, Michel — 7/28/47 B
Rencher, Derek — 12/12/62 B; 1/25/67 B; 10/25/68 B; 5/7/74 B
Rencontres Internationales de Musique Contemporaine — 11/22/73 C; 11/24/73 C
Rendezvous, Le — 12/5/33 B
Renga — 7/4/76 E; 9/29/76 C
Rennert, Gunther — 4/1/11 D
Renz, Frederick — 12/6/79 C
Reppa, David — 2/3/72 B
Republican National Convention — 6/8/20 E
Requiem and Resurrection — 7/27/69 C
Requiem Canticles (Balanchine) — 5/2/68 B
Requiem Canticles (Robbins) — 6/25/72 B
Requiem Canticles (Stravinsky) — 10/8/66 C; 4/6/71 D
Requiem (Delius) — 3/23/22 C

Requiem for Lumumba — 1/20/65 C
Requiem (Giannini) — 5/26/37 C
Requiem (Goldmark, R.) — 1/30/19 C
Requiem (Kabalevsky) — 2/9/63 C
Requiem (Thompson) — 5/22/58 C
Resonancias — 9/18/64 C
Respighi, Ottorino — 3/12/05 A; 11/20/10 A;
   1/24/15 C; 3/11/17 C; 6/5/19 B;
   4/11/20 C; 2/5/22 C; 4/13/22 A;
   3/4/23 C; 4/26/23 A; 12/14/24 C;
   12/31/25 C; 2/25/27 C; 11/18/27 A;
   6/16/28 C; 2/21/29 C; 11/7/30 C;
   11/13/31 C; 3/16/32 A; 12/17/32 E;
   7/23/33 A; 1/23/34 A; 4/18/36 D;
   2/24/37 A; 2/11/41 B; 2/14/74 E
Resurrection of Don Juan, The — 5/5/56 C
Resurrection — 5/17/04 C
Retablo de Maese Pedro, El — 3/23/23 A;
   6/25/23 A
Rethberg, Elisabeth — 11/22/22 D; 6/6/28 A;
   6/6/76 D
Reutter, Hermann — 6/17/00 D; 10/6/51 C
Reve de Cyniras, Le — 6/10/27 A
Reveil des oiseaux, Le — 10/11/53 C
Revelation of Saint John the Divine, The — 5/16/66 C
Revelations — 1/31/60 C
Revenge — 10/17/51 B
Reveries — 12/4/69 B
Revisor, Der — 5/9/57 A
Revolutionary Episode — 11/13/26 C
Revue Internationale de Musique (periodical) —
   2/2/74 D
Revueltas, Silvestre — 4/30/32 E; 10/5/40 D;
   8/2/78 D
Reyer, Louis-Etienne-Ernest — 1/15/09 D
Reyn, Judith — 3/8/70 B
Reynolds, Oliver — 5/15/34 B
Reynolds, Roger — 5/2/65 C
Reznicek, Emil Nikolaus von — 10/27/23 A;
   8/2/45 D
Rhapsodic Fantasy — 10/28/25 C
Rhapsodic Variations — 3/20/54 C
Rhapsodie espagnole — 3/15/08 C
Rhapsody for Orchestra (Sessions) — 3/21/70 C
Rhapsody for Saxophone (Debussy) — 5/11/19 C
Rhapsody in Blue — 2/12/24 C
Rhapsody No. 2 for Piano and Orchestra (Gershwin)
   — 1/29/32 C
Rhapsody on a Theme by Paganini in A Minor (Rach-
   maninoff) — 11/7/34 C; 4/7/60 B
Rheinberger, Josef Gabriel — 11/25/01 D
Rhodes, Lawrence — 2/19/65 B
Rhythmicon — 12/10/65 D
Riabouchinska, Tatiana — 5/23/17 D; //32 E;
   4/13/33 B; 4/15/33 B; 10/24/33 B;
   10/23/37 B; 6/19/38 B; 6/30/39 B;
   10/24/50 E
Rianne, Patricia — 4/6/72 B
Riausov, Sergei — 1/18/29 C
Ribbink, Thomas — 4/22/52 B
Ricci, Ruggiero — 7/24/18 D; 11/15/28 D;
   10/3/63 C
Rice, Elmer — 1/9/47 A
Ricercare (Piston) — 3/7/68 C
Ricercare (Tetley) — 1/25/66 B
Ricercari (Dello Joio) — 12/19/46 C
Ricercari (Tansman) — 12/22/49 C
Richardson, Philip John Sampney —
   12/31/20 E
Richter, Hans — 10/3/00 C; 6/9/04 E;
   12/3/08 C; 12/5/16 D; 11/28/47 E
Richter, Marga — 2/21/65 B
Richter, Sviatoslav — 3/20/15 D
Ricordi & Company, G. — 1/28/21 E
Ricordi, Tito — 2/19/14 A
Ride of the Valkyries, The — 2/8/15 E
Riders to the Sea — 11/30/37 A

Riegger, Wallingford — 10/9/24 C; 4/30/32 E;
   7/3/45 E; 5/16/48 C; 5/17/49 E;
   2/13/54 C; 4/12/57 C; 4/2/61 D
Riemann, Hugo — 7/10/19 D; //19 E; //22 E;
   //29 E; 2/13/52 D; //59 E
Rieti, Vittorio — 12/11/25 B; 5/7/29 B;
   12/16/44 C; 2/27/46 B; 10/1/46 B;
   4/14/58 A; 1/19/73 C; 1/27/73 C;
   12/11/74 C
Rigoletto — 1/27/01 D
Riisager, Knudage — 7/17/26 C; 3/5/27 C;
   9/3/27 C; 11/21/35 C; 10/24/40 C;
   1/15/48 B; 11/21/50 C; 10/11/51 C;
   11/22/57 B; 4/20/60 B
Rilke, Rainer Maria — 5/6/49 C
Rimbaud, Arthur — 1/30/40 C
Rimsky-Korsakov, Andrei — 5/23/40 D
Rimsky-Korsakov, Georgi — 12/26/01 D;
   5/5/23 E; 10/1/65 D
Rimsky-Korsakov, Nikolai — 11/3/00 A;
   12/26/01 D; 10/14/02 A; 12/25/02 A;
   10/16/04 A; 3/19/05 E; 3/27/05 E;
   12/5/05 E; 2/20/07 A; 4/27/07 C;
   5/16/07 E; 5/19/08 A; 6/21/08 D;
   6/2/09 B; 10/7/09 A; 5/20/10 B;
   6/4/10 B; 6/6/11 B; 5/21/14 B; 5/5/23 E;
   2/16/28 A; 10/23/37 B; 5/4/39 D;
   10/31/39 B; 8/14/67 E
Rinaldo and Armida — 1/6/55 B
Rinelli, Tullio — 1/26/39 A
Ring des Polykrates, Der — 3/28/16 A
Ringing Changes — 4/28/70 C
Ringling Brothers Barnum and Bailey Circus —
   1/13/44 C
Ring of Time, A — 10/5/72 C
Rio Grande — 12/12/29 C
Rioton, Marthe — 4/10/00 D
Rip van Winkle (Chadwick) — 4/4/31 D
Rip Van Winkle (De Koven) — 1/2/20 A
Rise of Music in the Ancient World, The (book) —
   2/5/59 D
Rising of the Moon, The — 7/19/70 A
Risurrezione — 11/4/04 A
Rite of Spring, The — see *Sacre du printemps*
Ritmo jondo — 4/15/53 B
Ritorno d'Ulisse, Il — 1/18/74 A
Ritter, Alexander — 9/8/49 D
Rittmann, Trude — 3/23/65 B
Rituel — 4/2/75 C
Ritz, Roger — 7/28/47 B
Road of the Phoebe Snow — 11/28/59 B
Robbers, The — 4/14/58 A
Robbins, Jerome — 10/11/18 D; 2/11/41 B;
   10/27/41 B; 11/29/42 B; 4/18/44 B;
   6/1/45 B; 10/24/46 B; //48 E; 1/20/49 B;
   12/1/49 B; 2/26/50 B; 6/14/51 B;
   12/4/51 B; 2/14/52 B; 2/19/52 B;
   5/14/53 B; 6/2/53 B; 2/2/54 B;
   2/18/54 B; 3/6/56 B; 6/6/58 B; 7/3/59 B;
   3/30/65 B; 5/22/69 B; 1/29/70 B;
   7/30/70 B; 2/3/72 B; 6/18-25/72 B;
   6/18/72 B; 6/23/72 B; 6/23/72 B;
   6/25/72 B; 5/24/73 B; 1/10/74 B;
   5/16/74 B; 5/14-31/75 B; 5/29/75 B;
   5/18/78 B
Robert Shaw Chorale — //48 E; 1/22/76 D
Robertson, Rae — 11/28/41 C
Robeson, Paul — 5/9/47 E; 1/23/76 D
Robin Hood — 1/16/20 D
Robin, Jean — //51 E
Robinson, Earl — 6/25/40 C
Robison, Paula — 10/29/78 C
Rocca, Lodovico — 3/24/34 A
Rochberg, George — 7/5/18 D; 3/28/58 C;
   2/26/59 C; 10/22/60 C; 1/24/67 C;
   11/24/70 C; 5/7/73 C; 4/4/75 C;
   3/15/76 C; 1/29/78 C; 1/20/79 C

Rochester Philharmonic — 2/20/30 C;
   11/2/30 E; 10/29/31 C; 3/24/32 C;
   3/3/78 C
Rockefeller Foundation — 1/8/59 E; 4/26/65 C
Rockefeller, Martha Baird — 1/25/71 D
Rockmore, Clara — 2/26/45 C
Rodeo (Copland) — 5/28/43 C
Rodeo: The Courting at Burnt Ranch (De Mille) —
   10/16/42 B
Rodgers and Hammerstein Archives of Re-
   corded Sound — //63 E
Rodgers, Richard — 4/30/68 B
Rodin, Auguste — 5/19/09 B; 12/4/69 B
Rodrigo, Joaquin — 11/9/40 C
Rodrigo, Juan — 11/9/40 C
Rodzinski, Artur — 4/17/27 C; //29 E; //33 E;
   1/21/37 C; 12/7/39 C; 6/25/40 C;
   7/5/40 C; 1/22/42 C; //43 E; 10/28/43 C;
   1/5/44 C; 1/20/44 C; 2/17/44 C;
   10/21/44 C; 11/23/44 C; 2/15/45 C;
   11/28/46 C; 2/3/47 E; 2/7/47 E;
   1/13/48 E; 11/27/58 D
Roerich, Nicholas — 5/19/09 B; 5/29/13 B
Roesgen-Champion, Marguerite — 6/30/76 D
Roger, Bernard — 5/10/55 A
Roger-Ducasse, Jean-Jules — 8/27/00 A;
   4/18/13 C; 5/11/19 C; 7/19/54 D
Rogowski, Ludomir — 3/14/54 D
Roi Arthur, Le — 11/30/03 A
Roi David, Le — 6/11/21 A; 10/21/60 A
Roi des etoiles, Le — 4/19/39 C
Roland-Manuel, Alexis — 3/4/29 B
Roland Petit's Ballets de Paris — 2/21/49 B;
   2/24/49 B
Roland von Berlin, Der — 12/13/04 A
Roldan, Amadeo — 3/2/39 D
Rolland, Romain — 12/30/44 D
Roma — 2/17/12 A
Romance — 4/20/71 B
Romance in D-flat (Vaughan Williams) —
   5/3/52 C
Romanoff, Dimitri — 10/27/41 B
Romanov, Boris — 6/12/13 B
Romantische Suite (Reger) — 10/11/12 C
Romeo and Juliet (Ashton) — 5/19/55 B
Romeo and Juliet (Bejart) — 11/17/66 B
Romeo and Juliet (Cranko) — 12//62 B
Romeo and Juliet (Diamond) — 10/20/47 C
Romeo and Juliet (Lambert) — 5/4/26 B
Romeo and Juliet (Lavrovsky) — 1/11/40 B
Romeo and Juliet (MacMillan) — 2/9/65 B
Romeo and Juliet (Prokofiev) — 11/24/36 C;
   4/15/37 C; 3/8/46 C
Romeo and Juliet (Rorem) — 3/1/78 C
Romeo and Juliet (Tudor) — 4/6/43 B
Romeo e Giulietta (Rota) — 4/10/79 D
Rome Opera — 10/7/51 E; 1/2/58 E
Romeo und Julia auf dem Dorfe — 2/21/07 A
Ronald, Landon — 6/16/02 D
Rondes de Printemps — 3/2/10 C
Rondine, La — 3/27/17 A
Rondo capriccioso — 9/20/08 D
Rondo for String Quartet (Webern) —
   8/2/68 C
Rooms — 2/24/55 B
Roosevelt, Eleanor — 1/2/39 E
Roosevelt, Theodore — 4/23/07 A
Rootham, Cyril — 3/18/38 D
Ropartz, Guy — 11/22/55 D
Ropes of Time, The — 3/2/70 B
Rorem, Ned — 5/7/49 C; 5/10/55 A;
   5/28/55 C; 8/5/56 C; 4/14/58 A;
   4/16/59 C; 10/23/59 C; 10/28/65 C;
   11/4/65 A; 11/5/69 C; 4/26/72 C;
   11/3/72 C; 5/21/73 C; 11/26/73 A;
   12/5/75 C; 2/29/76 C; 5/3/76 E;
   2/2/77 C; 3/1/78 C; 4/28/78 C;
   8/25/78 C
Rosamunde — 11/22/00 D

Rosamunde Floris — 9/21/60 A
Rosaspina — 6/29/72 D
Rosbaud, Hans — 1/13/54 E; 3/12/54 A; 10/19/58 C; 10/16/60 C; 12/29/62 D
Rose, Billy — 2/3/45 C; 6/1/45 B; 2/11/48 B
Rose, John — 1/10/73 C
Rose, Jurgen — 11/14/63 B; 4/13/65 B; 11/30/66 B; 3/24/70 B
Rose, Leonard — 7/27/18 D
Rose malade, La — 1/10/73 C
Rosenberg, Alfred — 1//35 E
Rosenberg, Hilding — 3/23/48 C; 10/4/61 B; 5/24/70 A
Rosen, Charles — 9/6/61 C; //71 E
Rosenkavalier, Der — 9/7/10 E; 1/26/11 A; 12/9/13 A
Rosenshein, Neil — 10/11/77 C
Rosenstock, Joseph — 12/7/41 E; 5/28/52 E
Rosenthal, Jean — 3/17/65 B
Rosenthal, Laurence — 3/17/65 B
Rosenthal, Manuel — 10/25/51 E; 5/14-31/75 B; 1/27/78 B
Rosenthal, Moriz — 9/3/46 D
Rosen, Walter Tower — //56 E
Rose String Quartet — 3/18/02 C; 12/21/08 C; 4/24/11 C; 10/1/64 D
Rose vom Liebesgarten, Die — 11/9/01 A
Roslavetz, Nikolai — 8/23/44 D
Rossato, Arturo — 2/14/22 A; 3/7/25 A; 2/9/29 A; 4/25/36 A
Ross, Bertram — 4/22/52 B; 5/8/55 B; 4/1/58 B; 4/3/58 B; 4/27/60 B; 4/29/60 B; 4/16/61 B; 3/4/62 B; 9/6/63 B
Rossellini, Renzo — 2/2/08 D; 2/25/56 A; 3/11/61 A
Ross, Herbert — 1/24/50 B; 1/24/50 B; 5/13/57 B
Rossignol, Le — 5/26/14 A
Rossi, Mario — 3/29/02 D
Ross, Judith — 1/27/76 C
Rosson, Keith — 12/12/62 B
Rostoff, Dmitri — 6/30/39 B
Rostova, Lubov — 4/21/32 B; 7/21/38 B
Rostropovich, Mstislav — 3/27/27 D; 11/26/33 C; 2/18/52 C; 10/4/59 C; 3/18/60 C; 2/6/62 C; 3/12/64 C; 5/13/64 C; 9/25/66 C; 3/2/67 C; 3/5/67 C; 6/7/69 C; 1/13/71 E; 1/8/74 E; 3/5/75 E; 10/4/77 E; 10/11/77 C; 3/15/78 E; 9/8/79 E
Roswaenge, Helge — 6/19/72 D
Rosza, Miklos — 4/18/07 D
Rota, Nino — 12/3/11 D; 2/8/60 A; 1/24/76 A; 6/22/77 A; 4/10/79 D
Rothier, Leon — 12/6/51 D
Rothko Chapel — 4/9/72 C
Rothko, Mark — 4/9/72 C
Rothwell, Joan — *see* Benesh, Joan
Rothwell, Walter Henry — 10/24/19 E; //27 E
Rotterdam City Centre — 5/14/40 E
Rotterdam Philharmonic Orchestra — 6/10/18 E; 5/14/40 E; 6/15/48 E; //67 E
Rouault, Georges — 5/21/29 B
Roudenko, Lubov — 4/5/38 B
Rouge et noir — 5/11/39 B
Rouget de Lisle, Amedee — 7/14/15 E
Rouget de Lisle, Claude-Joseph — 7/14/15 E
Rounds for String Orchestra — 11/24/44 C
Rounseville, Robert — 9/11/51 A
Rousanne, Madame — //74 E
Roussel, Albert — 5/17/04 C; 3/22/08 C; 6/15/08 B; 5/18/12 C; 4/22/21 E; 10/29/21 C; 3/4/22 C; 6/1/23 A; 7/1/25 A; 1/21/27 C; 3/4/29 B; 10/24/30 C; 5/22/31 B; 12/16/32 C; 10/19/35 C; 11/14/36 A; 8/23/37 D
Rousseliere, Charles — 11/26/06 D; 3/4/13 A
Roustan, Joette — 10/8/71 B
Rowicki, Witold — 2/26/14 D

Royal Academy of Dancing — //36 E
Royal Ballet, The — //26 E; 11/13/28 D; 10/31/56 E; 1/1/57 B; 10/27/58 B; 1/28/60 B; 10/11/60 B; 2/14/61 B; 5/8/62 B; 12/12/62 B; 3/12/63 B; 11/27/63 B; 4/2/64 B; 2/9/65 B; 4/25/66 B; 1/25/67 B; 2/23/67 B; 2/29/68 B; 10/25/68 B; 3/2/70 B; 7/22/71 B; 6/26/73 D; 5/7/74 B; 2/12/76 B; 2/14/78 B
Royal Ballet School, The — //62 E
Royal Choral Society — 3/22/00 C
Royal Covent Garden Ballet Russe — 6/17/38 E; 10//38 E
Royal Danish Ballet, The — 5/12/22 B; 1/15/48 B; //51 E; 5/19/55 B; 11/22/57 B; 5/11/66 B; 2/19/72 B
Royal Danish Ballet School — //32 E
Royal Danish Theatre — 6/10/52 D
Royal Festival Hall (London) — //51 E
Royal Flemish Conservatory — 3/8/01 D
Royal Flemish Opera — 12/2/69 E
Royal Invitation, or Homage to the Queen of Tonga — 3/22/64 C
Royal National Institute for the Blind and Saint Dunstans — //54 E
Royal Opera (London) — 12/23/68 E
Royal Palace — 3/2/27 A
Royal Philharmonic Orchestra — 3/13/30 C; 10/14/42 C; //47 E; 4/21/48 C; 11/1/63 E; 6/1/72 C
Royal Philharmonic Society — 3/3/09 D
Royal Swedish Ballet — 9/28/63 B; 7/7/71 B
Royal Winnipeg Ballet — //38 E; //51 E; 10/26/65 B; 10/3/68 B; 7/27/71 B
Rozhdestvensky, Gennady — 3/2/67 C; 2/8/70 E; 4/13/79 E
Rozsa, Miklos — 11/14/43 D; 4/6/67 C
Rozsnyai, Zoltan — 5/28/57 E
Rubbra, Edmund — 5/23/01 D; 4/30/37 C; 12/16/38 C; 12/15/40 C; 8/14/42 C; 1/26/49 C; 1/17/54 C; 11/17/54 C; 10/1/57 C
Rubinstein, Arthur — 1/8/06 D; 1/28/30 C; 4/1/76 E
Rubinstein Company, Ida — 11/22/28 B; 11/27/28 B; 1/12/29 B
Rubinstein, Ida — 6/2/09 B; 6/4/10 B; 5/8/11 E; 2/14/18 E; 11/22/28 B; 11/27/28 B; 1/12/29 B; 5/21/29 B; 6/23/31 A; 4/30/34 B; 5/11/34 B; 9/20/60 D
Rubinstein Prize — 5/24/14 E
Rubin, Steven — 1/19/78 B
Ruby, The — 5/13/55 A
Rudel, Julius — 10/16/71 D; 10/7/79 D
Rudhyar, Dane — 3/2/78 C
Rudnytsky, Antin — 11/30/75 D
Rudolf, Max — 6/15/02 D; 3/9/62 C; 5/18/63 C
Ruffo, Titta — 1/19/22 D; 7/5/53 D
Rugby — 10/19/28 C; 12/31/28 E
Ruggles, Carl — 12/7/24 C; 10/15/27 E; 2/25/32 C; 11/24/49 C; 1/24/66 C; 2/2/71 C
Ruggles, Micah — 9/4/73 E
Ruins and Visions — 8/20/53 B
Rumanian Rhapsodies — 3/8/03 C
Rumi, Jalal al-Din — 1/20/17 C
Rural Antiphonies — 12/6/53 C
Ruralia Hungarica — 11/17/24 C
Rusalka — 3/31/01 A
Ruses d'amour, Les — 1/17/00 B
Russell, Francia — 12/1/57 B
Russell, Henry — 11/8/09 E
Russian Fantasy — 3/11/06 C
Russian Musical Society — 3/23/12 C; 7/29/18 E

Russian Music During the Last 25 Years (book) — 10/23/06 D
Russian Overture — 10/29/36 C
Russian Revolution — 11/7/17 E; 9/23/18 E
Russian Symphony Concerts — 11/24/00 C; 1/25/02 C; 1/3/03 C
Russian Symphony Orchestra — 1/28/04 E; 1/27/06 D; 12/20/06 D; 2/29/08 C; 12/10/08 C; 12/10/08 D; 3/20/15 C; 3/23/18 C
Russische Weisen — 10/9/77 C
Russolo, Luigi — 3/11/13 E; 6/2/13 E; 4/21/14 C; 2/4/47 D; 5/18/55 D
Russolophone — 2/4/47 D
Rutherford, Richard — 10/3/68 B
Ruyeman, Daniel — 12/15/18 C
Ryder, Mark — 2/28/47 B; 5/3/47 B; 8/3/55 B
Rysanek, Leonie — 11/14/26 D
Rysdael, Basil — 3/8/17 A
Ryzhenko, Natalia — 6/11/72 B
Rzewski, Frederic — 1/27/74 C; 3/2/78 C

— S —

Saarinen, Eliel — 8/4/38 E
Sabaneyev, Leonid — 12/12/16 E; 1/30/17 E
Sabata, Victor de — 12/11/67 D
Sabbath Morning Service — 5/18/49 C
Sabin, Robert — 5/17/69 D
Sacher, Paul — 1/21/37 C; 5/12/38 C; 2/9/40 C; 3/1/40 C; 6/11/40 C; 1/23/42 C; 5/23/42 C; 1/25/46 C; 5/17/46 C; 7/12/46 C; 1/21/47 C; 2/11/49 C; 1/24/52 C; 12/12/53 C; 1/24/58 C; 6/9/61 C; 2/23/62 C
Sachs, Curt — //35 E; 2/5/59 D
Sack, Erna — 6/24/35 A; 3/2/72 D
Sacred and Profane — 9/14/75 C
Sacred Ground, The — 11/17/63 C
Sacred Service — 1/12/34 C
Sacre du printemps, Le (Kasatinka, Vasilion) — 6/29/54 B
Sacre du printemps, Le (MacMillan) — 5/8/62 B
Sacre du printemps, Le (Massine) — 4/11/30 B
Sacre du printemps, Le (Nijinsky) — 5/29/13 B
Sacre du printemps, Le (Stravinsky) — 4/5/14 C; 5/8/52 E; 8/25/59 C; 5/29/63 E; 4/6/71 D
Sacrifice, The — 3/3/11 A
Sacrosanctum concilium (papal document) — 12/4/63 E
Sadai, Yitzhak — 7/30/68 E
Sadko — 6/6/11 B
Sadler's Wells Ballet — 12/5/33 B; 1/30/34 B; 11/20/34 B; 11/26/35 B; 6/15/37 B; 2/2/39 B; 1/23/40 B; 7/4/40 B; 1/14/42 B; 5/19/42 B; 4/6/43 B; 10/26/44 B; //46 E; 2/20/46 B; 4/24/46 B; 11/12/46 B; 11/16/48 B; 11/25/48 B; 12/23/48 B; 7/18/49 B; 10/9/49 B; 12/20/49 B; 2/2/50 B; 3/13/51 B; 4/5/51 B; 12/12/51 B; 9/3/52 B; 3/3/53 B; 6/2/53 B; 2/25/54 B; 1/6/55 B; 1/18/55 B; 2/15/56 B; 5/5/56 B; 6/7/56 B; //56 E; 10/31/56 B; 5/11/71 D; 4/17/73 A; 6/26/73 D
Sadler's Wells Choreographic Group — 2/1/53 B
Sadlers Wells Opera Company — 11/29/66 A; 12/13/69 A
Sadoff, Simon — 8/17/49 B
Saeverud, Harald — 5/27/43 C
Safie — 4/4/09 A
Safonov, Vassily — 3/29/01 C; //03 E; 9//05 E; //06 E; 1/27/06 D; //09 E
Saga, En — 9/20/57 D
Saga of the Great Computer, The — 6/14/68 D
Saidenberg Little Symphony — 1/28/41 C
Sailor's Return, The — 6/2/47 B

Saint Just, Emy — 1/24/50 B
Saint-Leon, Arthur — 2/28/10 B; 3/4/60 B
Saint Luke's Passion — 3/30/66 C
Saint Michael — 7/13/59 C
Saint Nicolas — 6/5/48 C
Saint of Bleecker Street, The — 12/27/54 A;
   5/2/55 E
Saint Paul — 8/17/77 D
Saint Paul Chamber Orchestra — 2/25/74 C
Saint Paul Philharmonic Society — 3/22/64 C
Saint Petersburg Conservatory — 3/19/05 E;
   3/27/05 E; 12/5/05 E; 9/14/09 E;
   12/5/10 C; 5/24/14 E
Saint-Saens, Camille — 10/23/01 A;
   8/17/02 C; 2/18/04 A; 11/13/04 C;
   2/5/05 C; 2/24/06 A; 6/26/07 E;
   12/22/07 B; 4/26/09 A; 3/14/11 A;
   1/11/13 E; 9/19/14 E; 6/19/15 C;
   5/20/20 E; 12/16/21 D; 2/26/22 C;
   2/24/29 D; 3/7/42 E
Saint Thomas Choir School (New York City) —
   3/3/19 E
Saisons, Les — 2/20/00 B
Sakuntala — 1/2/15 D
Salade (Cranko) — 6/1/68 B
Salade (Milhaud) — 12/9/26 C
Salem Shore — 12/26/43 B
Sallinen, Aulis — 7/17/75 A
Salmond, Felix — 10/27/19 C
Salome (Strauss, R.) — 12/9/05 A; 12/5/06 A;
   1/22/07 A; 1/27/07 E; 1/28/07 E;
   9/7/10 E; 12/8/10 A; 5/3/17 C
Salon Mexico, El (Copland) — 8/27/37 C
Salon Mexico, El (Humphrey) — 3/11/43 B
Salto mortale — 6/19/59 A
Salzburg Festival — 8/22/20 E; 8/1/46 E;
   8/6/47 E; 8/17/53 A; //56 E; 1/15/58 A;
   2/20/63 D; 8/6/66 A; 12/11/67 D;
   3/2/72 D
Salzedo, Carlos — 4/17/27 C; 3/29/28 E;
   3/6/33 C
Salzman, Eric — 1/24/79 A
Salzman, Harry — 3/23/74 C
Saminsky, Lazare — 4/29/58 C
Sammelbande der Internationalen Musikgesellschaft (International Musical Society) — 9/30/14 E
Samokhvalova, Maya — 9/17/62 B
Samson Agonistes — 3/6/62 B
Samson et Dalila — 4/26/09 A
Samuel, Bernard — 12/3/63 C
Samuel, Gerhard — 2/8/66 C
Samuel-Rousseau, Marcel — 6/11/55 D
Samuels, Bernard — 10/19/13 E
San Antonio Symphony — 11/27/76 D
Sanasardo, Paul — 2/24/55 B
San Carlo Opera — 12/10/69 D
San Carlo Opera House — 11/15/43 E
Sancta Civitas — 5/7/26 C
Sancta Susanna — 3/26/22 A
Sandberg, Herbert — 10/31/50 B
Sanderson, Sibyl — 5/15/03 D
San Diego Opera — 6/3/79 A
Sandor, Gyorgy — 9/21/12 D; 2/8/46 C
*San Francisco — A Setting of the Cries of Two Newsboys
   on a Foggy Night in the Twenties* — 4/22/44 C
San Francisco Ballet — 3/10/53 B
San Francisco (Calif.) — 4/17/06 E; 4/29/06 E
San Francisco Conservatory — //17 E
San Francisco Opera Company — 9/13/53 D;
   8/6/71 D
San Francisco Orchestra — 3/16/32 C
San Francisco Suite — 4/23/60 C
San Francisco Symphony Chamber Orchestra
   — 11/20/77 C
San Francisco Symphony Orchestra —
   12/8/11 E; //13 E; 10/12/15 E; //30 E;
   //31 E; //32 E; //35 E; 2/11/38 E;
   12/6/43 E; 3/22/46 C; 1/9/47 C;
   1/6/49 C; 2/10/49 C; //54 E; 4/22/58 C;

4/23/60 C; 1/17/62 C; 2/16/62 C; //63 E;
   //70 E; //77 E
San Jose String Quartet — 5/20/79 C
Sanjust, Filippo — 4/26/74 B
Sanroma, Jesus Maria — 2/27/47 C
Sansui (record company) — //69 E; //70 E
Santa Fe Chamber Music Festival — 6/24/73 E
Santa Fe Opera — 8/2/57 A; 7/16/58 A;
   2/24/79 A
Santa Fe Time Table, The — 4/11/47 C
Santaro, Mikhail — 7/15/75 D
Santini, Gabriele — 2/9/29 A
Santley, Charles — 9/22/22 D
Sanzogno, Nino — 1/26/57 A
Sarabande and Danse (II) — 5/29/75 B
Sarasate, Pablo — 9/20/08 D
Saratoga Performing Arts Center — 7/8/66 E;
   7/17/74 B; 8/4/76 C; 8/25/78 C
Sardana, La — 10/14/51 C
Sardou, V. — 10/23/01 A
Sargent, Malcolm — 4/3/25 A; 3/21/29 A;
   10/10/31 C; 11/30/37 A; 9/30/44 C;
   6/17/51 C; 4/11/53 C
Sarka — 11/11/25 A
Sarnoff, General David — 1/31/56 E
Saroyan, William — 11/11/40 B
Sarry, Christine — 3/31/67 C; 12/1/67 B;
   5/29/69 B; 6/27/69 B
Sartre, Jean-Paul — 4/13/61 A
Satie, Erik — 6/15/08 E; 2/28/13 A; 5/18/17 B;
   2/14/20 C; 3/8/20 C; 6/7/20 C;
   6/14/23 E; 6/15/24 B; 12/4/24 B;
   7/1/25 D; 7/3/26 B; 7/11/56 B;
   4/25/66 B; 1/21/73 C; 5/5/78 B
Satires and circumstance — 1/20/72 C
Sato, Hiroshi — 6/29/75 B
Saturday's Child — 3/13/26 C
Saturn — 11/13/71 C
Satyrikon — 3/16/73 A
Satz fur Klavier — 12/2/58 C
Satz fur Streichtrio — 2/8/63 C
Sauer, Emil von — 4/27/42 D
Sauguet, Henri — 5/18/01 D; 6/14/23 E;
   4/30/27 B; 3/16/39 A; 7/4/44 A;
   3/2/45 B; 12/15/47 B; 2/8/48 C;
   7/26/53 C; 6/4/66 C; 11/28/71 C;
   2/26/74 C; 3/13/78 C
Saul, Michael — 1/24/79 A
Saul og David — 11/28/02 A
Sauvage, Cecile — 12/10/08 D
Savage Opera Company, Henry W. —
   10/15/06 A
Savitri — 12/5/16 A
Savonlinna Opera Festival — 7/17/75 A
Sayao, Bidu — 5/11/02 D; 2/13/37 D;
   1/4/63 D
Sayers, Dido — 12/1/57 B
Scancarella, John — 11/26/46 B
Scapino — 4/3/41 C
Scaramouche (Milhaud) — 7/1/37 C
Scaramouche (Walbom) — 5/12/22 B
Scarecrow Sketches — 12/18/23 C
Scarf, The — 6/20/58 A
Scarlatti, Alessandro — 11/4/66 E
Scarlattiana — 1/22/27 C
Scarlatti, Domenico — 4/12/17 B
Scarlet Letter, The — 6/2/38 A
Scenes de ballet (Ashton) — 2/11/48 B
Scenes de ballet (Stravinsky) — 2/3/45 C;
   2/11/48 B
Scenes du ballet (Taras) — 6/22/72 B
Scenes from the Saga of King Olaf — 10/3/00 C;
   2/23/34 D
Schaefer, Ferdinand — 11/2/30 E
Schaeffer, Pierre — 8/14/10 D; 8/24/44 E;
   4/15/48 E; 10/5/48 C; 3/18/50 C;
   6/14/52 B; 7/26/55 B

Schafer, R. Murray — 7/18/33 D; 2/6/63 C;
   8/10/67 C; 11/13/68 C; 2/16/71 C;
   9/21/72 C; 5/31/73 C
Schalit, Heinrich — 2/3/76 D
Schalk, Franz — 10/4/16 A; 10/10/19 A;
   10/12/24 C
Scharoun, Dr. Ing. E.h. Hans — 10/15/63 E
Scharwenka Conservatory — 7/27/16 D;
   12/8/24 D
Scharwenka, Franz Xaver — 12/8/24 D
Scharwenka, Philipp — 7/16/17 D
Schat, Peter — 8/2/79 A
Schaufuss, Frank — 5/19/55 B
Schaufuss, Peter — 5/29/75 B; 7/30/75 B
Schauspiel-Ouverture — 12/14/11 C
Schayk, Toer Van — 6/19/65 B
Schechter, Boris — 4/1/25 E
Scheel, Fritz — 11/16/00 E
Scheherazade (Fokine) — 6/4/10 B; 8/22/42 D
Schekhter, Boris — 1/18/29 C
Schelling, Ernst — 12/8/39 D
Schelomo — 5/3/17 C; 7/15/59 D
Schenck, Janet Daniels — 10/7/76 D
Schenker, Heinrich — 1/14/35 D; 3/18/47 D;
   //74 E
Scherchen, Hermann — 2/1/20 E; 3/20/27 C;
   2/16/28 C; 1/27/29 C; 6/1/29 E;
   10/16/34 C; 4/19/36 C; 6/17/38 C;
   3/3/43 C; 5/20/50 A; 1/13/54 E;
   12/2/54 C; 10/3/58 A; 4/3/66 C
Scherman, Thomas — 2/12/17 D; 2/21/53 A;
   3/3/59 C; 2/17/64 A; 5/14/79 D
Scherzo a la Russe (Stravinsky) — 3/22/46 C
Scherzo a la Russe (Balanchine) — 6/21/72 B
Scherzo and Trio in A Minor (Webern) —
   2/17/78 C
Scherzo (Bartok) — 2/29/04 C
Scherzo fantastique (Bloch) — 12/2/50 C
Scherzo fantastique (Robbins) — 6/18/72 B
Scherzo fantastique (Stravinsky) — 2/6/09 C;
   4/6/71 D
Schiffer, Marcellus — 6/8/29 A
Schillinger, Joseph — //41 E; 3/23/43 D
Schillinger System of Musical Composition, The (book)
   — //41 E; 3/23/43 D
Schillings, Max von — 12/8/06 A; 9/26/15 A;
   7/24/33 D
Schimmel, William — 11/1/77 C
Schindler, Alma Maria — 3/10/02 E
Schiotz, Aksel — 9/1/06 D; 4/19/75 D
Schippers, Thomas — 3/9/30 D; 3/26/55 D;
   4/4/63 C; 9/16/66 A; 12/16/77 D
Schirach, Baldur von — 11/30/33 C
Schirmer, Gustav — 7/15/07 D
Schirmer, G. (publisher) — 7/15/07 D; //12 E;
   1/1/15 E
Schjelderup, Gerhard — 7/29/33 D
Schlagobers — 5/9/24 B
Schleier der Pierrette, Der — 1/22/10 A
Schlesinger, B.W. — 2/17/62 D
Schloezer, Tatiana — 5/29/05 C; 12/20/06 D
Schlossberg, Lois — 8/17/62 B
Schlusnus, Heinrich — 6/18/52 D
Schmerz, immer blick nach oben — 4/11/64 C
Schmid, Erich — 2/10/40 C
Schmidt-Bloss, Karl — 6/2/37 A
Schmidt, Franz — 1/25/02 C; 12/3/13 C;
   4/1/14 A; 2/2/24 C; 12/2/28 C;
   1/10/34 C; 6/15/38 C; 2/11/39 D
Schmidt-Isserstedt, Hans — 5/5/00 D
Schmied von Gent, Der — 10/29/32 A
Schmied von Marienburg, Der — 12/16/23 A
Schmitt, Florent — 1/8/05 C; 12/27/06 C;
   11/9/07 C; 6/12/13 B; 1/23 C;
   3/4/29 B; 2/15/30 C; 11/25/32 C;
   5/11/34 B; 1/7/38 B; 6/15/58 C;
   8/17/58 D
Schnabel, Artur — 8/6/09 D; //32 E;
   8/15/51 D

Schnabel, Karl Ulrich — 8/6/09 D
Schneemann, Der — 10/4/10 A
Schneevoight, Georg — 10/24/19 E; //27 E; //29 E
Schneider, Alexander — 10/21/08 D
Schneider, Professor Michael — 10/15/63 E
Schoeck, Othmar — 6/2/51 C; 3/8/57 D
Schoeffler, Paul — 8/6/47 A
Schoenberg, Arnold — 3/18/02 C; 1/26/05 C; 2/5/07 C; 2/8/07 C; 11/7/07 C; 12/21/08 C; 8/7/09 C; 4/24/11 C; 7/1/11 E; 9/3/12 C; 10/16/12 C; 12/21/12 E; 2/23/13 C; 3/31/13 C; 1/17/14 D; 12/18/14 C; 11/1/18 E; 4/30/19 C; 12/7/22 C; 6/6/24 A; 7/20/24 C; 10/14/24 A; 4/10/27 C; 9/19/27 C; 12/2/28 C; 2/1/30 A; 4/11/30 B; 11/6/30 C; 5/30/33 E; 7/24/33 E; 10/31/33 E; 3/16/34 D; 5/18/35 C; 1/14/36 E; 5/22/38 E; 12/6/40 C; 12/15/40 C; 4/11/41 E; 4/8/42 B; 2/6/44 C; 10/20/44 C; 11/23/44 C; 11/18/45 C; 5/1/47 C; //48 E; 11/4/48 C; 12/19/48 E; 5/17/49 E; 8/11/50 B; 7/2/51 C; 7/13/51 D; 2/8/52 C; 1/13/54 E; 1/19/54 B; 3/12/54 A; 10/10/56 E; 6/6/57 A; 9/22/59 D; 6/16/61 C; 5/5/62 B; 4/21/66 B; 10/10/68 C; 4/21/76 C; //77 E; 10/22/79 D
Schoenberg et son ecole — //47 E
Schola Cantorum — 6/15/08 E; 3/29/11 D; 1/22/76 D
Scholes, Percy — 7/31/58 D
Schollar, Ludmilla — 5/15/13 B; 11/27/28 B
Schonberg, Harold — 11/29/15 D
School of American Ballet — 1/2/34 E; 6/9/34 B; //48 E
School of Natya — 7/21/68 D
Schooltime Compositions — 3/11/68 C
Schorer, Suki — 12/7/61 B
Schorr, Friedrich — 2/23/24 D; 8/14/53 D
Schott, Paul — 12/4/20 A
Schott's Sohne — //79 E
Schreiber (record company) — //69 E
Schreker, Franz — 2/23/13 C; 4/25/18 A; 10/29/32 C; 5/30/33 E; 3/21/34 D
Schubert, Franz — 11/22/00 D; 12/3/14 B; 8/18/18 A; 11/22/28 B; 2/23/37 B; 10/8/41 B; 10/1/46 B; 6/1/69 E
Schubert Memorial Prize — 12/2/28 C; 10/15/28 C
Schubert, Richard — 12/4/20 A
Schuch, Ernst von — 11/21/01 A; 12/9/05 A; 1/25/09 A; 1/22/10 A; 1/26/11 A; 5/10/14 D
Schule der Frauen — 8/17/57 A
Schulhoff, Erwin — 8/18/42 D
Schuller, Gunther — 4/6/45 C; 8/19/54 B; 5/3/59 C; 11/27/59 C; 1/15/60 C; 10/22/61 C; 2/8/65 C; 3/9/65 C; 10/12/66 A; 6/28/67 C; 1/24/68 E; 6/27/68 C; 5/8/70 A; 11/29/70 C; 8/8/72 C; 4/17/73 C; 5/5/73 C; 5/23/75 A; 5/23/78 C; 9/28/78 C; 11/2/79 C
Schumann, Elisabeth — 11/20/14 D; 4/23/52 D
Schumann-Heink, Ernestine — 1/25/09 A; 3/11/32 E; 11/16/36 D
Schumann, Robert — 3/5/10 B; 5/20/10 B; 5/10/13 B; 9/11/54 E; 3/30/66 D
Schuman, William — 8/4/10 D; 3/6/33 C; 10/21/36 C; 5/25/38 C; 10/6/39 C; 7/5/40 C; 10/17/41 C; 1/22/42 C; 7/14/42 C; 1/13/43 C; 2/13/43 C; 3/26/43 C; 5/3/43 C; 11/12/43 C; 2/17/44 C; 4/10/45 B; 5/3/47 B; 2/27/49 C; 1/4/50 B; 2/10/50 C;

5/4/53 A; 11/4/55 C; 10/21/60 C; 9/28/62 C; 10/4/62 C; 10/31/64 C; 8/10/65 C; 8/10/65 E; 1/10/69 C; 1/29/70 C; 10/29/78 C
Schutzendorf, Leo — 12/14/25 A
Schutz, Heinrich — 11/24/70 C
Schuurman, Frits — 11/11/38 D
Schwanendreher, Die — 11/14/35 C
Schwann Long Playing Record Catalog (periodical) — 1//49 E
Schwantner, Joseph — 2/19/76 C; 2/2/78 C; 1/29/79 C; 4/16/79 E
Schwartzkopf, Elisabeth — 9/11/51 A
Schwartz, Stephan — 9/8/71 C
Schwarze Orchidee, Die — 12/1/28 A
Schwarze Spinne, Die — 10/15/36 A; 3/2/49 A; 5/23/66 A
Schwarz, Gerard — 12/9/73 C
Schwarzkopf, Elisabeth — 12/9/15 D; 9/11/51 A; 3/22/79 D; 10/14/79 E
Schwarz, Solange — 6/19/43 B
Schwarzwald School — 6/20/06 B
Schweigsame Frau, Die — 6/24/35 A
Schweitzer, Albert — 3/12/37 D; 9/4/65 D
Schwergewicht, oder die Ehre der Nation — 5/6/28 A
Schwetzinger Festspiele — 4/29/71 A
Scialojas, T. — 10/24/50 A
Sciarretti, Salvatore — 6/27/20 E
Scie musicale — 5/1/25 E
Sciortino, Edouard — 12/22/35 E
Sciutti, Graziella — 3/10/56 A
Scotch Symphony — 11/11/52 B
Scott, Dorothy — 2/25/50 B
Scotti, Antonio — 1/28/03 E; 11/16/08 D; 2/6/09 E; 11/17/09 D; 12/4/16 D; 1/2/25 D; 1/20/33 E; 2/26/36 D
Scottish Ballad — 11/28/41 C
Scottish National Ballet — 4/6/72 B
Scottish National Orchestra — 4/5/35 D; 9/2/72 C; 8/13/73 C
Scottish Opera — 3/16/74 A
Scottish Theater Ballet — 11/19/69 B
Scott of the Antarctic — 11/29/48 E; 1/14/53 C
Scotto, Renata — 2/24/34 D; 5/30/57 D; 9/3/57 D; 10/15/77 E
Scratch Orchestra — 8/24/72 C
Scriabin, Alexander — 11/24/00 C; 3/29/01 C; 1/25/02 C; 12/10/04 E; 5/29/05 C; 12/20/06 D; 5/16/07 E; 12/10/08 C; 3/16/09 E; 3/15/11 C; 3/20/15 C; 4/15/15 E; 4/27/15 D; 5/19/54 D; 3/24/70 B; 7/24/75 E; 6/4/77 B
Scriabin Etude — 6/4/77 B
Scythian Suite — 1/29/16 C; 12/12/16 E; 1/30/17 E
Sea Change — 7/18/49 B
Sea Drift — 5/24/06 C; 11/30/33 C
Seaglia, Ferruccio — 7/6/63 C
Searle, Humphrey — 8/26/15 D; 10/3/58 A; 9/3/60 C; 11/8/62 C; 3/12/63 B; 6/3/64 A; 10/7/64 C; 8/31/67 C; 3/5/68 A; 4/21/76 C
Seaside Park — 6/18/75 C
Seasons, The (Cranko) — 6/15/62 B
Seasons, The (Cunningham) — 5/13/47 B
Sea, The — 9/24/12 C
Seattle Symphony Orchestra — 12/29/03 E; 12/8/11 E; 11/17/41 C; 10/25/51 E; 3/8/61 D; 5/2/65 C; 4/10/78 C; 7/21/79 D
Sebastian, John — 6/5/61 C
Sechste Tag, Der — 10/7/58 C
Seckler, Beatrice — 2/24/55 B
Second American Symphonette — 7/31/38 C
Second Cantata — 6/23/50 C
Second Essay for Orchestra (Barber) — 4/16/42 C
Second Festival of Swiss Music — 6/23/01 C
Second Hurricane, The — 4/21/37 A

Second Sonata for Piano (Wuorinen) — 10/2/76 C
Second Sonata for Violin and Piano (Bolcom) — 1/12/79 C
Second String Quartet (Wuorinen) — 8/1/79 C
Second Suite (Bartok) — 11/22/09 C
Second Vatican Council — 12/4/63 E
Secret Places — 2/20/68 B
Secular Cantata, A (Diamond) — 2/5/77 C
Secular Cantata No. 2, A Free Song (Schuman) — 5/3/43 E
Secular Games — 8/17/62 B
Seeds of Brightness — 8/1/42 B
Seefried, Irmgard — 10/9/19 D; 5/2/43 D
Seeger, Ruth Crawford — 7/3/01 D
Segovia, Andres — 4/7/24 D; 10/28/39 C; 10/4/41 C; 2/13/78 E
Segreto di Susanna, Il — 12/4/09 A
Seiber, Matyas — 5/4/05 D; 9/24/60 D
Seigneuret, Michele — 7/26/55 B; 4/27/57 B
Seine at Night, The — 2/24/48 C
Seinemeyer, Meta — 5/21/25 A
Seismogramme — 10/19/54 C
Sekh, Yaroslav — 4/7/60 B
Self-Similar Waltz — 5/11/78 C
Selina — 11/16/48 B
Sellem, Elaine de — 6/27/20 E
Sellner, Gustav — //61 E
Selva, Blanche — 1/2/08 C
Sembach, Johannes — 3/8/17 A
Sembrich, Marcella — 1/28/03 E; 4/18/06 E; 2/6/09 E; 1/11/35 D
Semenov, Simon — 7/21/38 B; 10/26/39 B
Semenov, Victor — 10/29/24 B
Semirama (Respighi) — 11/20/10 A
Semiramis (Rubinstein, I.) — 5/11/34 B
Semkov, Jerzy — 9/18/75 D
Seoul City Dance Theater — 4/14/78 E
Seoul Philharmonic Orchestra — 4/14/78 E
Seoul Sejong Cultural Center — 4/14/78 E
Sephardic Songs — 5/30/74 B
"September Song" — 9/26/38 A
Septet for Concertante Violin, Wind Quintet and Double Bass — 9/2/70 D
Septet (Stravinsky) — 1/23/54 C
Sept Haikai — 10/3/63 C
Sequence — 3/10/56 C
Serafin, Tullio — 4/10/13 A; 12/10/21 A; 11/3/24 D; 1/2/25 D; 11/1/26 D; 2/17/27 A; 2/7/31 A; 1/7/33 A; 5/20/33 A; 2/10/34 A; 12/26/46 E; 5/10/47 E; 2/3/68 D
Seraphic Dialogue — 5/8/55 B
Serebrier, Jose — 12/3/38 D; 4/26/65 C; 6/15/69 C; 12/3/76 C
Serenade a Angelique — 12/11/46 C
Serenade (Balanchine) — 6/9/34 B; 12/6/34 B
Serenade (Bernstein) — 9/12/54 C
Serenade (Cone) — 1/11/77 C
Serenade for Montreux — 9/17/70 C
Serenade for Tenor, Horn and Strings (Britten) — 10/15/43 C; 9/1/57 D; 12/4/76 D
Serenade in A (Stravinsky) — 4/6/71 D
Serenade (Krenek) — 7/31/21 C
Serenade (Lansky) — 12/13/79 C
Serenade No. 2 (Subotnick) — 4/16/63 C
Serenade (Schoenberg) — 7/20/24 C
Serenade to Music (Vaughan Williams) — 10/5/38 C
Serenata (Ginastera) — 1/18/74 C
Sergeyev, Konstantin — 2/20/10 D; 1/11/40 B; 3/14/49 B; 6/28/50 B; 1/4/58 B; 4/12/63 B; 12/12/70 B
Sergeyev, Nicholas — 11/2/21 B; 1/30/34 B; 11/20/34 B; 2/2/39 B
Serial Composition and Atonality (book) — //62 E; //77 E
Serkin, Peter — 7/24/47 D

Serkin, Rudolf — 3/28/03 D; 3/6/39 E;
    7/24/47 D; 7/8/51 E
Serly, Tibor — 11/25/00 D; 12/2/49 C;
    10/8/78 D
Sermon, a Narrative and a Prayer, A — 2/23/62 C;
    4/6/71 D
Serov, Alexander — 10/29/36 A
Serpent Heart, The (Barber) — 2/2/56 C
Serpent's Heart (Graham) — 5/10/46 B
Serrano, Lupe — 4/20/60 B
Servant of Two Masters, The — 3/9/67 A
Serva padrona, La — 12/23/37 E
Servilia — 10/14/02 A
Sessions, Roger — 4/22/27 C; 4/30/32 E;
    1/8/40 C; 1/9/47 C; 3/16/47 C;
    4/18/47 A; 1/14/56 C; 12/6/57 C;
    1/8/59 E; 1/2/60 C; 2/7/64 C; 4/19/64 A;
    11/19/66 C; 10/1/67 C; 5/2/68 C;
    3/3/69 C; 3/21/70 C; 11/5/71 C;
    5/7/74 E; 10/24/77 C; 5/11/78 C
Seter, Mordecai — 1/25/66 B
Set of Houses, A — 3/17/78 C
Setti, Giulio — 10/2/38 D
Sevarac, Deodat de — 3/24/21 D
Sevastianov, German — 6/17/38 E
Sevcik, Otakar — 1/18/34 D
Seven Deadly Sins — 6/7/33 B
Seven Lively Arts, The (review) — 2/3/45 C;
    2/11/48 B
Seven Sonnets of Michaelangelo — 12/4/76 D
Seven Studies on Themes of Paul Klee — 11/27/59 C;
    3/9/65 C
17 Tage und 4 minuten — 6/2/66 A
Seven, They Are Seven — 5/29/24 C
Seventh Symphony (Belsky) — 4/14/61 B
Seventh Symphony (Massine) — 5/5/38 B
Severance Hall (Cleveland) — 2/5/31 E
Sevilla — 9/11/20 C
Sevitzky, Fabien — 11/7/40 C; 1/15/55 C
Sextet (Copland) — 2/26/39 C
Seymour, Lynn — 4/12/60 B; 10/11/60 B;
    2/14/61 B; 2/9/65 B; 11/30/66 B;
    7/22/71 B; 2/12/76 B
Sgambati, Giovanni — 12/14/14 D
Sguardo del Ponte, Uno — 3/11/61 A
Shabelevski, Yurek — 10/24/33 B
Shadow of the Wind — 4/14/48 B
Shadowplay — 1/25/67 B
Shadow, The — 3/3/53 B
Shakers, The (Humphrey) — 11/12/30 B;
    12/29/58 D
Shanewis — 3/23/18 A
Shannon, M.E. — //57 E
Shapey, Ralph — 3/12/21 D; 5/24/68 C;
    4/14/78 C
Shaporin, Yuri — 11/16/40 C; 6/23/53 A
Sharaff, Irene — 4/6/34 B; 4/27-28/37 B;
    10/24/46 B; 2/25/50 B; 2/26/50 B
Sharer, Hugh — 9/19/67 B
Sharp, Evelyn — 5/12/36 A
Sharp, Geoffrey — 2/1/40 E
Shav Yang — 1/12/68 C
Shaw, Carlos Fernandez — 4/1/13 A
Shawn, Ted — 2/22/15 B; 7/29/16 B;
    11/3/19 B; 1/31/21 B; 6/8/29 B;
    6/22/30 B; //33 E; //41 E; 8/27/48 B;
    //65 E; 7/21/68 D; 1/9/72 D
Shaw, Robert — 4/30/16 D; 5/15/44 C;
    5/14/46 C; //67 E
Shchedrin, Rodion — 12/16/32 D; 3/4/60 B;
    3/23/63 E; 6/11/72 B
Shea, Mary Jane — 5/29/41 B
Shearer, Moira — 10/26/44 B; 11/25/48 B;
    12/23/48 B
Shebalin, Vissarion — 10/8/13 A; 11/13/26 C;
    1/21/34 C; 12/9/41 E; 12/14/46 C;
    5/25/57 A; 12/22/69 A
Sheherazade (Balanchine) — 5/22/75 B
Sheherazade (Ravel) — 5/17/04 C

Shelest, Alla — 12/27/56 B
Shelter, Dr. Donald J. — 3//78 E
Shepherd, Arthur — 2/20/39 C
Shepherds of the Delectable Mountains, The —
    7/11/22 A
Sherman, Alec — 1/21/46 D
Sherman, William — 1/4/50 B
Sherry, Fred — 1/14/73 C; 3/28/73 C;
    3/11/78 C
Shervashidze, Prince A. — 12/3/26 B
Shifrin, Seymour — 1/20/72 C
Shilkret, Nathaniel — 11/18/45 C
Shires Suite — 7/8/70 C
Shirley-Quirk, John — 8/2/31 D; 6/16/73 A
Shoemaker's Holiday, The — 6/1/67 A
Sho-Jo — 4/8/20 D
Shook, Terence — 5/24/78 C; 1/18/79 C
Shore, Jane — 7/18/49 B
Short Symphony (Copland) — 11/23/34 C
Short Symphony (Cowell) — 10/24/47 C
Shostakovich, Dmitri — 9/25/06 D;
    1/21/30 C; 10/26/30 B; 4/8/31 B;
    10/15/33 C; 1/22/34 A; 4/4/35 B;
    1/28/36 E; 11/21/37 C; 5/11/39 B;
    11/5/39 C; 11/23/40 C; 3/1/42 C;
    10/15/42 C; 11/4/43 C; 11/3/45 C;
    10/1/46 E; 2/11/48 E; 2/21/48 E;
    4/11/48 E; 11/15/49 C; 3/8/50 E;
    12/17/53 C; 10/29/55 C; 10/10/56 E;
    5/10/57 C; 10/30/57 C; 5/28/58 E;
    10/4/59 C; 4/14/61 B; 1/20/62 C;
    9/17/62 B; 12/18/62 C; 12/30/62 A;
    12/28/64 C; 5/12/64 E; 9/25/66 C;
    9/25/66 E; 11/30/66 B; 11/28/72 D;
    11/2/79 E
Shostakovich, Maxim — 5/10/57 C; 9/25/66 C
Shuk, Lajos — 11/5/36 E
Shurale — 6/28/50 B
Shylock — 11/22/13 A
Sibelius, Jean — 7/2/00 C; 3/8/02 C; 2/8/04 C;
    4/25/04 C; 10/19/05 C; 12/29/06 C;
    9/25/07 C; 4/3/11 C; 6/4/14 C;
    6/17/14 E; 12/8/15 C; 5/12/22 B;
    2/19/23 C; 3/24/24 C; 12/26/26 C;
    9/23/38 E; 9/1/44 E; 7/18/49 B;
    9/20/57 D; 8/26/58 D; 2/24/68 E
Sibelius Museum (Abo, Finland) — 2/24/68 E
Sibelius Prize — //54 E; 10/9/71 E; //73 E
Siberia — 12/19/03 A
Sibley, Antoinette — 2/27/39 D; 4/2/64 B;
    2/10/66 B; 4/25/66 B; 2/29/68 B;
    5/7/74 B
Siccard von Siccardsburg, August — 3/12/45 E
Sieber, Matyas — 10/11/60 B
Siegmeister, Elie — 1/15/09 D; 11/11/44 C;
    11/24/45 C; 7/3/45 E; 12/29/46 C;
    1/18/47 C; 10/30/47 C; 3/16/69 A;
    12/6/73 C; 3/17/78 C; 11/25/79 C
Siems, Margarethe — 1/25/09 A; 1/26/11 A;
    10/25/12 A
Siepi, Cesare — 2/10/23 D
Sigurd — 1/15/09 D
Silence — 6/13/11 C
Silence, a Year from Monday — 11/24/65 C
Sills, Beverly — 5/25/29 D; 6/3/79 A
Siloti, Alexander — 11/9/01 C; 2/6/09 C;
    12/12/09 C; 12/8/12 C; 1/20/17 C;
    12/8/45 D
Silverman, Stanley — 8/24/74 A; 10/20/74 C
Silvestre, Armand — 11/20/01 A
Simeon Kotko — 6/23/40 A
Simionato, Giulietta — 12/15/10 D; 3/17/52 A
Simmons, Stanley — 3/17/65 B; 3/23/65 B;
    3/31/67 B; 12/1/67 B; 10/3/68 B;
    5/29/69 B; 6/27/69 B; 10/24/70 B
Simon Boccanegra — 1/13/39 D
Simoneau, Leopold — 5/3/18 D

Simoni, Renato — 1/25/15 A; 4/25/26 A;
    3/24/34 A
Simon Medley — 5/12/77 B
Simonov, Yuri — 2/8/70 E
Simon, Victoria — 12/7/61 B
Simple Simon — 1/24/79 A
Simple Symphony — 11/29/44 B
Sina d'Vargoun, La — 12/4/09 A
Sinding, Christian — 6/25/10 B; 1/10/21 C;
    12/3/41 D
Sine Nomine Singers — 3/23/74 C
Sinfonia (Beno) — 10/10/68 C
Sinfonia (Cordero) — 5/16/66 C
Sinfonia antartica (Vaughan Williams) —
    11/29/48 E
Sinfonia breve — 4/11/53 C
Sinfonia brevis de Bello Gallico — 12/14/19 C
Sinfonia concertante (Berkeley) — 8/3/73 C
Sinfonia concertante (Martinu) — 12/8/50 C
Sinfonia da Requiem (Britten) — 3/29/41 C
Sinfonia de Antigona — 12/15/33 C
Sinfonia drammatica (Respighi) — 1/24/15 C
Sinfonia elegiaca (Ginastera) — 5/31/46 C
Sinfonia funebre — 1/6/23 C
Sinfonia India — 1/23/36 C
Sinfonia (Maw) — 5/1/66 C
Sinfonia portena — 5/12/42 C
Sinfonia rustica (Panufnik) — 5/13/49 C
Sinfonia sacra (Panufnik) — 8/12/64 C
Sinfonia sevillana — see *Sevilla*
Sinfonia tripartita — 12/16/44 C
Sinfonia visionaria (Atterberg) — 2/26/57 C
Sinfonietta (Britten) — 1/31/33 C
Sinfonietta flamenca — 1/9/54 C
Sinfonietta in A Major (Reger) — 10/8/05 C
Sinfonietta in E (Hindemith) — 3/1/50 C;
    3/1/60 C
Sinfonietta (Janacek) — 6/29/26 C
Sinfonietta (Poot) — 10/22/46 C
Sinfonietta (Poulenc) — 10/24/48 C
Singapore Symphony Orchestra — 6/8/65 D
Singleton, Trinette — 9/19/67 B
Sirenes — 12/9/00 C
Sirenes (Debussy) — 10/27/01 C
Sirenes, Les (Ashton) — 11/12/46 B
Sirius — 7/18/76 C
Sir John in Love — 3/21/29 A; 9/27/34 C
Sirocco — 5/16/21 A
Sistine Chapel, Vatican City — 8//04 E;
    10/12/56 D
Sitnikov, Vasily R. — 11/2/79 E
Sitwell, Edith — 1/24/22 C; 6/12/23 C;
    4/26/31 B
Sitwell, Osbert — 10/10/31 C
Six Bagatelles for String Quartet (Webern) —
    7/19/24 C
Six Characters in Search of an Author — 4/26/59 A
Six danses en trois mouvements — 12/17/70 C
Six epigraphes antiques — 2/7/01 C
Six Fantasies on a Poem by Thomas Campion —
    12/13/79 C
Six, Les — 1/16/20 E; 6/19/21 B; 5/30/25 C;
    11/23/51 D
Six Pieces for Large Orchestra (Webern) —
    1/27/29 C
Six Pieces for Orchestra (Webern) — 3/31/13 C
Six Songs for High Voice and Orchestra — 4/28/78 C
Six Songs on Poems of Georg Trakl (Webern) —
    7/20/24 C
Sixth All-Union Congress of Composers —
    11/18/79 E
62 Mesostics re Merce Cunningham — 9/21/71 B
Sizova, Alla — 4/14/61 B
Skalkottas, Nikos — 3/8/04 D; 9/19/49 D;
    5/1/73 C
Skating Rink (Borlin) — 1/20/22 B
Skelton, John — 9/25/36 C
Skelton, Thomas — 9/19/67 B; 2/20/68 B

Skibine, George — 9/8/42 B; //58 E; 2/22/61 D; //64 E
Skilton, Charles Stanford — 10/29/16 C; 4/17/30 A
Skolovsky, Zadel — 3/3/50 C
Skouratoff, Vladimir — 2/24/49 B; 10/17/51 B; 12/23/52 B
Skyscrapers — 2/19/26 B
Slater, Montagu — 6/7/45 A
Slatkin, Leonard — //79 E
Slaughter on Tenth Avenue — 4/30/68 B
Slava! (Overture for Orchestra) — 10/11/77 C
Slavinsky, Tadeo — 5/17/21 B; 6/17/25 B
Slawska, Olga — 11/20/37 B
Sleeping Beauty (Petipa) — 1/17/00 B
Sleeping Beauty, The (Ashton) — 2/20/46 B
Sleeping Beauty, The (Littlefield) — 2/11/37 B
Sleeping Beauty, The (Messerer) — 4/9/52 B
Sleeping Beauty, The (Nureyev) — 9/1/72 B
Sleeping Beauty, The (Sergeyev) — 11/2/21 B; 2/2/39 B; 10/9/49 B
Slezak, Leo — 11/17/09 D; 6/1/46 D
Slobodskaya, Oda — 6/3/22 A; 7/29/70 D
Slonimsky, Nicolas — 6/3/26 C; //27 E; 1/10/31 C; 6/6/31 C; 11/11/31 C; 2/25/32 C; 3/6/33 C; 4/10/33 C; 4/15/34 C; 1/14/37 C; 5/6/37 A; 11/4/37 E; 5/2/52 C; //53 E; 11/3/62 C; 3/4/65 C
Sly — 12/29/27 A
Smallens, Alexander — 12/18/29 C; 9/30/35 A
Smernov, Dimitri — 5/19/08 A
Smetana, Bedrich — 2/19/09 A
Smetana Quartet — //45 E; //45 E; //48 E
Smirnova, Helen — 5/19/09 B
Smirnova, Margarita — 9/17/62 B
Smirnov, Dmitri — 11/18/79 E
Smirnov-Golovanov, Vladimir — 6/11/72 B
Smirnov, V. — 4/8/31 B
Smith-Brindle, Reginald — 1/5/17 D; 7/14/60 C; 7/9/68 C
Smith, Carleton Sprague — 6/3/34 E
Smith, Cecil — 7/12/06 D
Smith, Charles — 5/4/77 C
Smith, Cyril — 8/2/74 D
Smith, David Stanley — 5/3/78 E
Smith, Kay — 1/20/22 B
Smith, Oliver — 10/4/45 B; 10/24/46 B; 4/22/48 B; 2/26/50 B
Smuin, Michael — 12/4/69 B
Smyth, Ethel Mary — 4/9/02 A; 11/11/06 A; 7/23/12 E; 1/28/16 A; 5/8/44 D
Sneden's Landing with Variations — 4/26/72 C
Snow Maiden, The (Bourmeister) — 7/17/61 B
Snow Maiden, The (Nijinska) — 10/12/42 B
Sobotka, Ruth — 12/1/57 B
Sociedad Nacional de Musica — 2/8/15 E
Societa Italiana di Fonotipia — 8//04 E
Societe des Grandes Auditions Musicales de France — 5/16/07 E
Societe Francaise de Musicologie, La — 3/17/17 E
Societe Musicale Independante — 4/20/10 C; 5/25/10 C
Societe Nationale de Musique — 4/5/02 C; 1/9/04 C; 3/5/04 C; 5/17/04 C; 1/12/07 C; 4/20/10 C; 11/10/15 C; 5/11/19 C; 5/14/19 C; 12/14/19 C; 2/14/20 C; 12/16/21 D; 1/26/24 C
Society for Art and Culture — 4/24/11 C
Society for Private Musical Performances — 11/1/18 E; 2/2/19 C; 4/30/19 C; 7/13/51 D
Society for the Prevention of Cruelty to Children — 2/16/57 D
Society of Black Composers — 1/24/75 C
Society of Friends and Enemies of Modern Music — 2/8/34 A

Society of Friends of Music — 12/11/28 E
Society of Quarter-Tone Music — 5/5/23 E
Society of Rumanian Composers — 10/20/24 C
Society of Swedish Composers — 2/15/74 D
Socrate (Satie) — 2/14/20 C; 6/7/20 C
Soderstrom, Elisabeth — 3/17/78 A
Soeur Beatrice — 10/25/12 A; 5/20/19 A
Soil Upturned — 10/23/37 A
Soiree musicale — 11/26/38 B
Sojourner and Mollie Sinclair, The — 12/2/63 A
Sojo, Vicente Emilio — 6/24/30 E
Sokoloff, Nikolai — 12/11/18 E
Sokolova, Evgenia — 12/3/26 B
Sokolova, Lydia — 5/11/17 B; 6/5/19 B; 2/2/20 B; 6/17/25 B; 5/7/29 B
Sokolov, Vladislav — 2/9/63 C
Sokolow, Anna — 2/9/15 D; //39 E; 2/24/55 B; 3/12/78 B
Soldiers of the Queen — 1/1/01 B
Soleil de nuit, La — 12/20/15 B
Soler, Josep — 5/5/73 A
Solesmes, Benedictine monks of — 5/17/01 E; 7/1/01 E; 9/5/10 D; 4/1/22 E
Soliloquies No. 3 — 5/5/77 C
Soliloquios No. 1 for Flute Solo — 1/27/76 C
Solitaire — 6/7/56 B
Sollberger, Harvey — //62 E; 8/9/64 C; 3/28/73 C; 2/10/78 C; 12/18/78 C
Solomon (Cutner, Solomon) — 8/9/02 D; 6/30/11 D
Solomon and Balkis — 3/29/42 A
Solomon's Gardens — 3/23/74 C
Solo Requiem, A — 2/10/79 C
Soloviev, Yuri — 8/10/40 D
Solovox — 2/2/39 E; 7/1/73 D
Solovyov, Yuri — 4/14/61 B
Solti, Georg — 10/21/12 D; 9/13/53 D; 12/17/68 E; 5/2/72 C; 10/6/77 C; 12/22/78 C
Solzhenitsyn, Alexander — 1/13/71 E; 1/8/74 E; 3/15/78 E
Somer, Harry — 11/14/72 C
Somer, Hilde — 4/5/68 C
Somerset Rhapsody, A — 4/6/10 C
Somers, Harry — 9/11/25 D; 2/6/63 C; 3/19/63 C; 9/23/67 A; 10/3/68 B; 4/27/74 C
Somes, Michael — 9/28/17 D; 1/23/40 B; 4/24/46 B; 11/12/46 B; 2/11/48 B; 12/23/48 B; 4/5/51 B; 9/3/52 B; 6/2/53 B; 1/6/55 B; 2/15/56 B; 10/27/58 B; 3/12/63 B; 2/14/78 B
Some Southpaw Pitching — 1/29/27 C
Something Wild — 5/26/64 C
Sommerwind, Im — 5/25/62 C
Somnambulism — 2/1/53 B
Somniloquy — 12/17/67 B
Sonata a quattro — 10/31/64 C
Sonata for 2 Pianos and Percussion (Bartok) — 4/27/57 B
Sonata for Cello and Piano (Hovhaness) — 1/16/73 C
Sonata for Cello (Ginastera) — 12/13/79 C
Sonata for Cello in B-flat Major (Kabalevsky) — 2/6/62 C
Sonata for Clarinet and Piano (Bernstein) — 4/21/42 C
Sonata for Cello and Piano (Hovhaness) — 1/16/73 C
Sonata for Piano (Wuorinen) — 12/23/70 C
Sonata for Solo Horn — 8/6/78 C
Sonata for Two Pianos and Percussion (Bartok) — 1/16/38 C
Sonata for Violin and Piano (Lees) — 5/4/72 C
Sonata for Violin and Piano (Ravel) — 5/30/27 C
Sonata No. 2 for Piano (Prokofiev) — 11/20/18 D

Sonata No. 3 for Solo Violin (Luening) — 3/7/71 C
Sonata serenata — 9/28/78 C
Sonate a frois — 4/27/57 B
Sonatensatz (Rondo) fur Klavier (Webern) — 8/2/68 C
Sonatina No. 1 (Strauss, R.) — 6/18/44 C
Sonatina No. 2 (Strauss, R.) — 3/25/46 C
Sonatine (Balanchine) — 5/14-31/75 B
Sonatine en deux chants et un intermede — 3/13/78 C
Sonatine (Honegger) — 12/16/32 C
Song and Dance — 3/2/78 C
Songfest — 10/11/77 C
Song of Anguish — 3/10/50 C
Song of Democracy — 4/9/57 C
Song of Friendship — 11/6/49 C
Song of Hiawatha, The — 3/22/00 C; 5/5/03 C; 11/16/04 E
Song of Human Rights — 12/10/63 C
Song of Orpheus — 9/28/62 C
Song of Remembrance — 8/26/77 C
Song of Songs (Limon) — 8/19/47 B
Song of Songs, The (Foss) — 3/7/47 C
Song of Summer, A — 9/17/31 C
Song of the Earth — 11/7/65 B
Song of the Forests — 11/15/49 C
Song of the Night — 1/20/17 C
Songs About Spring — 7/14/60 C
Songs for Dov — 10/12/70 C
Songs of a Wayfarer — 3/11/71 B
Songs of Inanna and Dumuzi — 1/29/78 C
Songs of Our Day — 1/5/38 C
Songs of Praise and Lamentation — 2/18/75 C
Songs of the West (Holst) — 4/6/10 C
Songs Remembered — 3/12/78 C
Song to the Lute in Musicke, A — 1/11/70 C
Sonic Contours — 10/28/52 C
Sonido 13, El (periodical) — 9/9/65 D
Sonneck Memorial Fund — 10/6/29 E
Sonneck, Oscar G. — 1/1/15 E; 10/6/29 E
Sonneries Woodwind Quintet — 2/2/76 C
Sonntag, Gottfried — 12/8/36 E; 7/6/37 E
Son of Heldenleben — 11/13/68 C
Son of the Sun — 5/23/29 A
Sonority Canon for Four Solo Flutes Accompanied by 33 Flutes on Tape — 5/15/62 C
Sons of Light, The — 5/6/51 C
Soot, Fritz — 12/14/25 A
Sorabji, Kaikhosru — 12/1/30 C
Sorell, Christiane — 11/29/72 C
Sorelle d'Italia, Le — 6/10/18 D
Sosi — 3/6/49 C
Sospiri — 8/15/14 E
Soudeikine, Serge — 6/12/13 B
Soulima-Stravinsky, Sviatoslav — 11/21/35 C
Sounds and Words — 2//58 E
Source, La — 11/23/68 B
Sousa, John Philip — 1/1/00 A; 3/27/06 A; 3/6/32 D; 10/8/46 E; 1/17/58 B; 7/15/79 E
Southwest German Symphony Orchestra — 5/15/79 C
Souvenirs (Bolender) — 11/15/55 B
Souvenirs (d'Indy) — 4/20/07 C
Souzay, Gerard — 11/26/50 D
Soviet All-Union Arts Committee — 4/24/51 E
Soviet All-Union Copyright Agency — 11/2/79 E
Soviet Communist Party's Central Committee — 4/24/51 E
Sovietskaya Musica (periodical) — 2/23/33 E
Soviet Society for Promotion of Proletarian Music, Production Collective — 4/1/25 E
Soviet Union — 11/8/17 E; 1/5/18 E; //33 E; 7/3/45 E; 9/6/56 E; 3/23/63 E; 10//63 E; 8/14/79 E
Sowerby, Leo — 1/17/17 C; 3/5/20 C; 7/20/21 E; 10/4/21 E; 4/7/22 C; 5/27/24 C; 3/29/29 C; 11/30/36 C;

4/22/38 C; 3/6/41 C; 5/6/46 E; 1/7/49 C;
11/18/57 C
Soweto — 6/12/77 B
Space and Duration — 1/29/27 C; 5/19/54 D
Space Is a Diamond — 12/9/73 C
Space Play — 10/11/74 C
Spalding, Albert — 2/7/41 C
Spalicek — 9/19/33 B
Spartacus (Grigorovich) — 4/9/68 B
Spartacus (Moiseyev) — 3/11/58 B
Spatlese — 7/22/74 C
Spectra — 1/15/60 C
Spectre de la Rose, Le — 4/19/11 B; 8/22/42 D
Speculum Musicae — 1/14/73 C; 2/10/78 C;
3/2/78 C
Speculum Speculi — 1/14/73 C
Speech Songs — 2/8/73 C
Speed — 3/31/29 B
Spellbound Child, The — 11/26/46 B
Sperry, Paul — 2/25/74 C; 4/3/75 C
Spessivtzeva, Olga — 11/2/21 B; 4/30/27 B;
5/22/31 B
Spharophon — 7/25/26 E
Spirale, La — 12/22/35 E
Spirit of England, The — 11/24/17 C
Spirituals for String Choir and Orchestra — 2/9/41 C
Spiritus Intelligentiae Sanctus — 5/30/56 C
Spivacke, Harold — 7/18/04 D; 5/9/77 D
Spivakovsky, Jascha — 3/23/70 D
Spivakovsky, Tossy — 3/23/70 D
Spoleto — //58 E; 7/13/59 B
Spoleto Festival U.S.A. — 5/25/77 E; 6/4/77 B
Spontaneous Earth — 4/5/44 B
Sprechstimme — 10/16/12 C; 11/4/33 A;
7/13/51 D; 3/12/54 A
Spring Symphony — 7/14/49 C
Springweather and People — 5/24/55 B
Sprung uber den Schatten, Der — 6/9/24 A;
5/21/27 A
Square Dance — 11/21/57 B
Stabat Mater (Poulenc) — 6/13/51 C
Stabile, Mariano — 12/26/21 E; 1/11/68 D
Staccatophone — 11/1/23 E
Stacy, Thomas — 11/17/77 C
Stad, Ben — 8/19/46 D
Stadium Symphony Orchestra — 6/25/56 C
Stadlen, Peter — 10/26/37 C
Stadtische Oper (Berlin) — //61 E
Staff, Frank — 6/2/47 B
Stainer, Sir John — 3/31/01 D
Stalin, Joseph — 12/5/50 C; 3/5/53 D;
12/17/53 C; 4/5/66 C; 1/18/78 D
Stalin Prize — 1/27/49 D; 3/8/50 E
Stambler, Bernard — 10/26/61 A; 4/14/78 A
Stanford, Charles Villiers — 5/30/01 A;
1/14/16 A; 3/29/24 D; 4/30/25 A
Stanhope, Mrs. Hannah — 11/16/06 E
Stankiewicz, M. — //79 E
Star-Child — 5/5/77 C
Starer, Robert — 4/27/53 C; 12/4/56 A;
7/3/59 C; 4/16/61 B; 3/4/62 B; 3/6/62 B;
8/17/62 B; 11/23/66 B; 5/25/68 B;
8/2/75 A; 12/3/78 C
Star Opera Company of New York City —
10/28/19 E
Starr Piano Company — //18 E
Stars and Stripes — 1/17/58 B; 5/18/78 B
"Stars and Stripes Forever, The" — 10/8/46 E;
7/15/79 E
"Star-Spangled Banner, The" — 3/29/30 E;
3/3/31 E; 5/18/37 D; 1/13/44 C;
1/15/44 E
Stasov, Vladimir — 10/23/06 D
Statements for Orchestra — 1/7/42 C
Steadfast Soldier, The — 7/30/75 B
Steber, Eleanor — 7/17/16 D; 4/9/48 C;
1/15/58 A; 10/14/79 E
Steel and Stone — 2/4/31 B
Steffy, Geyer — 5/30/58 C

Steinberg, Maximilian — 6/2/14 B
Steinberg, William — 2/1/30 A; 1/26/35 C;
11/9/37 D; 11/9/40 C; 11/9/45 E;
12/2/55 C; 10/14/60 C; 8/10/65 C;
8/10/65 E; 7/29/67 E; 12/14/67 C;
5/2/68 C; 10/22/69 D; 9/10/71 E;
5/16/78 D
Stein, Erwin — 1/14/36 E
Stein, Fritz — 11/15/33 E
Stein, Gertrude — 4/27/37 B; 5/7/47 A
Steingruber, Ilona — 6/23/50 C
Stein, Richard H. — 5/22/09 E; 8/11/42 D
Steinway & Sons — 4/18/06 E
Steinweg, Gertrud — 5/17/21 B
Stember, Joseph — 1/24/50 B
Stengerb, Yevgeny — 12/31/64 B
Stephen Crane — 2/4/68 C
Stereo Electronic Music No. 1 — 5/9-10/61 E
Stereo Electronic Music No. 2 — 11/30/70 C
Stereophony for Orchestra — 3/19/63 C
Sterling, Louis — 11/12/22 E
Sterne, Laurence — 2/5/71 C
Stern, Isaac — 7/21/20 D; 10/11/37 D;
2/10/50 C; 9/12/54 C; 5/3/56 E;
9/9/57 E; 7/1/60 E; 4/4/75 C; 1/10/78 C
Steuermann, Eduard — 2/2/19 C; 4/13/31 C;
2/6/44 C; 8/6/69 D
Stevens, Halsey — 3/7/46 C
Stevens, Larry — 1/24/50 B
Stevenson, Hugh — 11/20/34 B; 1/26/36 B
Stevens, Rise — 6/11/13 D
Stevnsborg, Alfred Bernhardt — 2/25/05 D
Stewart Morcom, James — 4/24/42 B
Stewart, Reginald — 2/17/46 C; 11/25/52 C
Stiedry, Fritz — 10/14/24 A; 3/11/33 E;
12/15/40 C
Stier von Olivera, Der — 3/10/18 A
Stignani, Ebe — 5/16/28 A; 2/9/29 A
Still Point, The — 8/3/55 B
Still, William Grant — 3/20/27 C; 10/29/31 C;
5/23/37 C; 6/25/40 C; 1/5/44 C;
3/31/49 A; 5/13/63 A; 11/15/74 A;
12/3/78 D
Stirling, Christina — 5/29/69 B
St. Denis, Ruth — 1/28/06 B; 3/26/06 B;
2/9/08 B; 12/12/10 B; 3/11/12 B;
7/12/13 B; 2/22/15 B; 7/29/16 B;
8/12/30 B; 12/29/58 B; //65 E;
7/21/68 D; 1/9/72 D
St. Laurent, Yves — 1/10/73 B
St. Louis Institute of Music — //24 E
St. Louis Symphony Orchestra — 1/26/12 C;
2/3/21 D; 11/11/21 E; //31 E;
12/10/44 C; 12/16/44 C; 2/12/49 C;
12/22/49 C; //58 E; 3/2/59 E;
10/24/59 C; 10/22/60 C; //63 E;
1/24/68 E; 8/9/68 E; 1/25/73 C;
9/18/75 D; //79 E; 9/8/79 E
Stock, Frederick — 4/7/22 C; 10/28/25 C;
2/18/32 C; 11/30/33 C; 10/10/40 C;
2/6/41 C; 3/6/41 C; 3/27/41 C; 4/3/41 C
Stockham, Thomas — //75 E
Stockhausen, Karlheinz — 8/22/28 D;
5/2/51 C; //53 E; 5/26/53 C; 1/13/54 E;
10/19/54 C; //55 E; 5/30/56 C;
3/24/59 C; 6/11/60 C; 10/28/60 C;
11/29/67 C; 10/10/68 C; 5/15/69 C;
10/8/70 C; 5/5/72 C; 11/22/73 C;
5/4/74 C; 10/18/74 C; 5/16/75 C;
7/18/76 C
Stockholm Concert Hall — 4/7/26 E
Stockholm Philharmonic Orchestra —
4/7/26 E
Stockholm Royal Opera — 3/17/78 A
Stock-Hug, Else — 12/2/58 C
Stoeckel, Carl — 6/12/10 C
Stoessel, Albert — 11/15/26 E; 5/12/43 D
Stokowski, Leopold — 10/11/12 D; 9/10/17 E;
12/19/19 C; 2/13/25 C; 4/9/26 C;

3/18/27 C; 4/8/27 C; //32 E; 3/3/33 C;
11/7/34 C; 11/6/36 C; //39 E;
11/13/40 E; 12/6/40 C; 5/11/41 C;
2/6/44 C; 2/13/44 C; 2/26/45 C;
12/29/46 C; 1/18/47 C; 10/30/47 C;
//49 E; 11/24/49 C; 11/30/51 C;
5/9/52 E; 10/28/52 C; 10/4/56 C;
1/20/57 D; 3/28/60 C; 10/5/64 C;
12/18/64 C; 4/26/65 C; 11/6/65 D;
11/17/68 C; 9/13/77 D
Stoltz, Rosine — 7/28/03 D
Stolze, Kurt-Heinz — 5/16/69 B
Stolz, Teresa — 8/23/02 D
Stone, Bentley — 6/19/38 B
Stone, Cynthia — 8/17/58 B
Stone Flower, The (Lavrovsky) — 2/12/54 B
Stone Flower, The (Prokofiev) — 4/27/57 B
Stoppard, Tom — 7/30/79 A
Stopwatch and an Ordnance Map, A — 10/24/44 C
Storchio, Rosina — 11/10/00 A; 12/19/03 A;
2/17/04 A; 7/24/45 D
Story of a Flemish Farm, The — 7/31/45 C
Story of a Real Man, A (Prokofiev) — 12/3/48 A;
10/8/60 A
Story of Ivan the Fool, The — 12/24/68 C
Stoutz, Edmond de — 9/9/73 C
Stradivari (violins) — 9/20/08 D; 12/16/35 E;
4/18/38 E; 2/8/39 D; 9/30/48 E
Straits of Magellan — 10/11/63 C
Stramm, August — 5/8/52 C
Strandin, Ebon — 10/25/23 B
Strandrecht — 11/11/06 A
Strang, Dr. Walter — 11/1/34 E
Straniero, Lo — 4/29/30 A
Stransky, Josef — 12/15/10 C; 5/17/11 E;
12/7/22 C; 1/18/23 C
Straram Orchestra — 11/1/32 D
Strarem, Walter — 2/19/31 C
Strasfogel, Ian — 1/18/74 A
Strassner, Isidor — 6/13/76 D
Stratas, Teresa — 5/26/38 D; 10/16/58 D;
2/24/79 A
Strategie — 4/23/63 C
Stratification of Musical Rhythm, The (book) —
//74 E
Strauss, Franz — 5/31/05 D
Strauss, Johann — 4/15/33 B; 7/24/39 E;
2/28/40 B; 6/23/77 B
Strauss, Melvin — 8/9/64 C
Strauss, Richard — 11/21/01 A; //03 E;
3/21/04 C; 12/9/05 A; 12/5/06 A;
1/22/07 A; 1/27/07 E; 1/28/07 E;
1/25/09 A; 9/7/10 E; 1/26/11 A;
10/25/12 A; 10/25/12 C; 10/19/13 E;
12/9/13 A; 5/14/14 B; 6/14/14 E;
8/15/14 E; 10/28/15 C; 10/4/16 A;
10/9/16 E; 10/23/16 B; 5/3/17 C;
10/10/19 A; 5/9/24 B; 11/4/24 A;
10/16/25 C; 6/6/28 A; //30 E; 7/1/33 A;
11/15/33 B; 6/11/34 E; 6/24/35 A;
7/13/35 E; 8/16/36 E; 7/24/38 A;
10/15/38 A; 5/24/39 C; 6/11/40 E;
10/22/40 A; 10/27/40 C; 10/28/42 A;
1/31/43 C; 8/11/43 C; 10/20/43 B;
6/11/44 E; 6/18/44 C; 8/16/44 E;
9/23/44 B; 4/12/45 D; 1/25/46 C;
2/26/46 C; 3/25/46 C; 4/4/48 C;
6/8/48 E; 9/8/49 D; 11/9/49 B;
5/22/50 C; 3/31/51 C; 11/14/51 B;
8/14/52 A; 3/3/61 D; 10/10/68 C;
11/13/68 C; 4/3/70 B; 1/6/72 B;
6/23/77 B
Strauss, Feodor Ignatievich — 12/4/02 D
Stravinsky Festival (New York City) —
6/18-25/72 B; 6/18/72 B; 6/20/72 B;
6/21/72 B; 6/22/72 B; 6/23/72 B;
6/25/72 B
Stravinsky, Igor — 4/27/07 C; 2/29/08 C;
6/17/08 C; 2/6/09 C; 6/25/10 B;

6/13/11 B; 5/29/13 B; 4/5/14 C;
5/26/14 A; 12/2/14 C; 1/17/16 B;
4/9/17 C; 2/14/18 E; 9/28/18 B;
12/6/19 C; 2/2/20 B; 4/27/20 C;
5/15/20 B; 4/22/21 E; 6/10/21 C;
5/18/22 B; 6/3/22 A; 6/13/23 B;
10/18/23 C; 5/22/24 C; 1/8/25 D;
6/17/25 B; 5/30/27 C; 4/27/28 B;
6/12/28 B; 11/27/28 B; 5/21/29 B;
12/6/29 C; 11/7/30 C; 12/13/30 C;
12/19/30 C; 10/23/31 C; 4/30/34 B;
6/10/34 E; //35 E; 11/21/35 C;
11/26/35 B; 1/14/36 E; 7/27/37 E;
5/8/38 C; 5/22/38 E; 4/19/39 C;
11/7/40 C; 11/13/40 E; 1/22/41 B;
2/8/42 C; 10/8/43 C; 1/13/44 C;
1/15/44 E; 9/10/44 B; 2/3/45 C;
11/18/45 C; 12/28/45 E; 1/24/46 C;
3/22/46 C; 3/25/46 C; 1/13/47 B;
1/21/47 C; //48 E; 2/11/48 B; 4/28/48 B;
7/29/48 E; 10/27/48 C; 3/9/49 E;
11/27/49 B; 1/7/51 E; 3/17/51 A;
6/14/51 B; 9/11/51 A; 5/8/52 E;
11/11/52 C; 10/19/53 C; 1/13/54 E;
1/23/54 C; 9/20/54 C; 1/18/55 B;
2/21/55 C; 5/27/56 C; 9/13/56 C;
6/17/57 C; 12/1/57 B; 9/23/58 C;
8/25/59 C; 10/17/59 C; 1/10/60 C;
4/12/60 B; 6/13/60 C; 9/27/60 C;
11/16/60 B; 12/7/60 B; 2/23/62 C;
6/14/62 B; 9/26/62 E; 12/12/62 B;
4/9/63 B; 5/29/63 E; 4/6/64 C; 7/1/64 D;
8/23/64 C; 3/26/65 C; 3/30/65 B;
4/17/65 C; 10/8/66 C; 4/13/67 B;
6/17/67 E; 5/2/68 B; 10/10/68 C;
4/6/71 D; 4/9/72 C; 6/18-25/72 B;
6/18/72 B; 6/22/72 B; 6/23/72 B;
6/25/72 B; 6/1/75 C; 6/24/76 D;
10/22/79 D
Stravinsky, Vera — 6/1/75 C
Strayhorn, Billy — 11/28/59 B
Street Games — 11/11/52 B
Street Scene — 1/9/47 A
Streets of Peking — 9/24/30 C
String Octet (Milhaud) — 8/10/49 C
String Quartet (Amram) — 2/20/62 C
String Quartet and Orchestra (Feldman) —
1/26/75 C
String Quartet (Berg) — 4/24/11 C
String Quartet (Britten) — 8/20/53 B
String Quartet (Debussy) — 5/12/31 D;
8/3/55 B
String Quartet (Kagel) — 2/25/74 C
String Quartet (Wolpe) — 10/28/69 C
String Quartet (Wuorinen) — 10/11/71 C
String Quartet in A Minor (Webern) —
2/16/78 C
String Quartet in D Major (Schoenberg) —
2/8/52 C
String Quartet in D Minor (Schoenberg) —
7/13/51 D
String Quartet No. 1 in D Minor (Schoenberg)
— 2/5/07 C; 7/13/51 D
String Quartet No. 1 in D Minor (Thompson)
— 10/30/41 C
String Quartet No. 1 (Schuller) — 4/17/73 C
String Quartet No. 2 (Halffter) — 10/31/70 C
String Quartet No. 2 (Kelemen) — 4/16/73 C
String Quartet No. 2 (Carter) — 5/2/60 E
String Quartet No. 2 in F-sharp Minor (Scho-
enberg) — 12/21/08 C; 7/13/51 D
String Quartet No. 2 (Lansky) — 5/12/75 C;
String Quartet No. 2 (Luening) — 12/13/65 C
String Quartet No. 2 (Rochberg) — 5/7/73 C
String Quartet No. 3 (Cordero) — 10/20/77 C
String Quartet No. 3 (Husa) — 5/5/69 E
String Quartet No. 3 (Carter) — 1/23/73 C;
5/7/73 E
String Quartet No. 3 (Ginastera) — 2/4/74 C

String Quartet No. 3 (Hindemith) — 8/1/21 C
String Quartet No. 3 (Piston) — 5/1/47 C
String Quartet No. 3 (Roussel) — 12/16/32 C
String Quartet No. 3 (Schoenberg) —
9/19/27 C
String Quartet No. 4 (Babbitt) — 5/13/70 C
String Quartet No. 4 (Rochberg) — 1/20/79 C
String Quartet No. 4 (Tippett) — 5/20/79 C
String Quartet No. 4 (Haba) — 7/31/21 C
String Quartet No. 4 (Martinu) — 10/15/60 C
String Quartet No. 4 (Schoenberg) —
7/13/51 D
String Quartet No. 5 (Bartok) — 4/8/35 C
String Quartet No. 5 (Rochberg) — 1/20/79 C
String Quartet No. 6 (Hiller) — 1/24/73 C;
1/20/79 C
String Quartet No. 6 (Martinu) — 5/1/47 C
String Quartet No. 9 (Bolcom) — 5/21/73 C
String Quartet No. 12 (Haba) — 10/15/60 C
String Quartet of Costa Rica — 10/20/77 C
String Quartet (Ravel) — 3/5/04 C
String Quartet (Roussel) — 12/16/32 C
String Quartet Set — 5/20/79 C
String Quartet (Webern) — 9/22/38 C
String Septet (Milhaud) — 10/31/64 C
String Sextet (Piston) — 10/31/64 C
String Trio Movement (Webern) — 3/16/72 C;
2/17/78 C
String Trio (Schoenberg) — 5/1/47 C;
7/13/51 D
String Trio (Webern) — 1/16/28 C
String Trio (Wuorinen) — 10/27/68 C
Strobel, Heinrich — 3/25/52 A; 8/17/54 A;
8/18/70 D
Stroganova, Nina — 1/13/40 B
Strohbach, Hans — 11/28/26 B
Stronger, The — 8/9/52 A
Strong, George Templeton — 6/27/48 D
Strophes — 9/17/59 C
Strube, Gustav — 2/11/16 E
Structures (Feldman) — 11/25/68 C
Structures, Book II — 10/21/61 C
Structures I — 5/2/51 C
Struggle — 1/27/74 C
Strunk, William Oliver — 3/22/01 D;
10/30/34 E
Stucke — 1/20/69 C
Stuckenschmidt, Hans Heinz — 11/1/01 D
Studia Musicologica Academiae Scientiarum Hungaricae
(periodical) — 3/6/67 D
Studie I — 10/19/54 C
Studie II — 10/19/54 C
Studie Uber Mehrklange fur Oboe — 10/25/75 C
Studio di Fonologia Musicale — 10/28/52 C;
//57 E
Studio Wacker — //65 E; //74 E
Study for Pianola — 11/7/30 C
Stumpf, Karl — 5//00 E
Stundenlied, Das — 3/1/59 C
Sturm, Der — 6/17/56 A
Stuttgart Ballet — 6/10/62 B; 7/15/62 B;
7/13/63 B; 11/14/63 B; 1/22/65 B;
4/13/65 B; 11/7/65 B; 3/26/66 B;
5/16/69 B; 3/8/70 B; 3/24/70 B;
6/26/73 D; 12/22/73 B
Subotnick, Morton — 4/16/63 C; 11/21/68 B;
1/25/69 C; 2/25/71 C; 2/26/76 C;
7/4/76 E; 1/28/78 C
Sugar Reapers, The — 12/11/66 A
Suite Archaique — 2/28/51 C
Suite bergamasque — 3/25/18 D
Suite by Chance — 3/24/53 B
Suite (Creston) — 6/30/79 C
Suite de Lorenzaccio — 3/28/74 C
Suite delphique — 10/22/48 C
Suite en blanc — 6/19/43 B
Suite for Five in Space and Time — 5/18/56 B
Suite for Harmonica and Orchestra (Milhaud)
— 5/28/47 C

Suite for Orchestra in F-sharp Minor (Doh-
nanyi) — 2/21/10 C; 3/3/53 B
Suite for Orchestra (Piston) — 3/28/30 C
Suite for Orchestra (Thomson) — 11/26/48 C
Suite for String Orchestra (Schoenberg) —
5/18/35 C
Suite for Symphonic Strings — 10/18/61 C
Suite for Two — 5/21/58 B
Suite for Viola and Chamber Orchestra (Vaug-
han Williams) — 11/12/34 C
Suite for Viola and Orchestra (Bloch) —
11/5/20 C
Suite for Viola and Piano (Bloch) — 11/5/20 C
Suite for Violin and Orchestra (Milhaud) —
11/16/45 C
Suite Georgienne — 4/17/40 C
Suite hebraique — 1/1/53 C
Suite in C Major (Casella) — 4/23/10 C
Suite in F (Roussel) — 1/21/27 C
Suite of Dances — 10/16/60 C
Suite on the Frescoes of Piero della Francesca —
6/23/60 C
Suite Provencal — 9/12/37 C
Suite symphonique (Bloch) — 10/26/45 C
Suite transoceane (Jolivet) — 9/24/55 C
Suk, Josef — 2/3/07 C; 5/29/35 D
Sullivan, Arthur — 3/13/51 B
Sullivan, Thomas F. — 1/15/44 E
Sullivan, Sir Arthur — 11/22/00 D
Summer and Smoke — 6/19/71 A
Summer — 3/13/16 C
Summer Evening — 4/3/30 C
Summer Night on the River — 10/2/13 C
Summer Seascape (Hanson) — 3/10/59 C
Summerspace — 8/17/58 B
Sumner, Carol — 12/7/61 B
Sun Bride, The — 4/17/30 A
Sunday Morning — 8/25/78 C
Sundelius, Marie — 3/23/18 A
Sun over the Steppe, The — 12/22/59 A
Sun-Treader — 2/25/32 C; 1/24/66 C
Suor Angelica — 12/14/18 A
Supervia, Conchita — 1/12/16 D; 2/7/32 D;
3/30/36 D
Surinach, Carlos — 3/4/15 D; 4/15/53 B;
1/9/54 C; 4/3/58 B; 9/30/62 B;
8/16/66 C; 6/26/78 B
Sur le Borysthene — 12/16/32 B; 3/11/34 C;
1/5/37 E
Sur scene — 3/11/68 C
Survivor from Warsaw, A — 7/13/51 D
Survivor of Warsaw — 11/4/48 C
Susannah — 2/24/55 A
Suslin, Viktor — 11/18/79 E
Susskind, Walter — 5/1/13 D; 8/9/68 E
Sutermeister, Heinrich — 10/15/36 A;
10/14/48 A; 3/2/49 A; 5/26/67 A;
9/17/70 C; 8/12/75 C
Sutherland, Joan — 11/7/26 D; 1/27/55 A;
2/17/59 D; 11/26/61 D
Sutherland, Paul — 9/30/62 B
Sutter, Anna — 6/29/10 D
Suvorov — 2/21/42 A
Svanda dudak — 4/27/27 A
Svanholm, Set — 9/2/04 D; 10/4/64 D
Svetlanov, Evgeny — 9/6/28 D; 2/8/72 C;
9/27/79 E
Swados, Kim — 7/12/56 B
Swaezey, Marjorie — 3/14/52 B
Swallows of Salangan, The — 10/11/63 C
"Swanee" — 7/11/37 D
Swan Lake (Balanchine) — 11/20/51 B
Swan Lake (Blair) — 2/16/67 B
Swan Lake (Bruhn) — 3/27/67 B
Swan Lake (Cranko) — 11/14/63 B
Swan Lake (Flindt) — 5/10/69 B
Swan Lake (Fokine) — 11/30/11 B
Swan Lake (Grigorovich) — 12/25/69 B
Swan Lake (MacMillan) — 5/14/69 B

Swan Lake (Mordkin) — 12/19/11 B
Swan Lake (Nureyev) — 10/15/64 B
Swan Lake (Sergeyev) — 11/20/34 B
Swann, Jeffrey — 10/2/76 C
Swan of Tuonela, The — 9/20/57 D
Swarthout, Gladys — 12/25/00 D; 1/13/74 D
Swedish Ballet — 3/1/50 B
Swedish Dance Theatre — //46 E
"Sweet Bye and Bye, The" — 11/22/57 A;
    4/26/65 C
Sweet Was the Virgin Sung: Tristan Revisited —
    4/10/78 C
Swingle Singers — 10/10/68 C
Swiss Duo Flutists — 4/14/78 C
Swiss Exposition of Industry — 4/24/64 C
Swiss Saxophone Quartet — 6/30/79 C
Sydeman, William — 2/5/71 C
Sydney Opera House — //57 E; 10/20/73 E
Sydney Symphony Orchestra — 9/5/50 C;
    3/9/56 E
Sygietynski, Tadeusz — 4/13/25 E
Sylbert, Paul — 11/19/59 B
Sylphide, La — 7/7/71 B
Sylphides, Les — 2/23/07 B; 6/2/09 B; 1/20/16 B
Sylvia (Ashton) — 9/3/52 B
Sylvia (Ivanov) — 12/15/01 B
Sylwan, Kari — 9/28/63 B
Symphonia domestica — 3/21/04 C; 10/16/25 C
Symphonia sacra — 5/9-10/61 E
Symphonia serena (Hindemith) — 2/1/47 C
Symphonic Dances (Rachmaninoff) — 1/3/41 C
Symphonic Fragments (Wyschnegradsky) —
    1/25/37 C
Symphonic Metamorphosis on Themes by Weber (Hin-
    demith) — 1/20/44 C; 12/28/63 D
Symphonic Music for Nine Solo Instruments (Krenek)
    — 7/30/22 C
Symphonic Mystery (Pashchenko) — 5/2/24 C
Symphonic Ode (Copland) — 2/19/32 C
Symphonic Prelude (Piston) — 4/20/61 C
Symphonic Sketches (Chadwick) — 2/7/08 C
Symphonic Song (Prokofiev) — 4/14/34 C
Symphonic Suite (Berg) — 11/30/34 C
Symphonic Variations (Ashton) — 4/24/46 B
Symphonie antique — 3/22/11 C
Symphonie concertante (Balanchine) — 11/12/47 B
Symphonie concertante (Ibert) — 2/23/51 C
Symphonie-Concertante (Kubik) — 5/5/52 E
Symphonie concertante (Schmitt, F.) — 11/25/32 C
Symphonie concertante (Szymanowski) —
    10/9/32 C
Symphonie de chambre (Enesco) — 1/23/55 C
Symphonie de marches — 6/4/66 C
Symphonie expiatoire — 2/8/48 C
Symphonie fantastique (Massine) — 7/24/36 B
Symphonie, La — 12/14/28 C
Symphonie liturgique (Honegger) — 8/17/46 C
Symphonie lyrique (Nabokov) — 2/16/30 C
Symphonie marine (Ibert) — 10/6/63 C
Symphonie-Passion (Dupre) — 12/8/21 C;
    10/9/24 C
Symphonie pour un homme seul — 3/18/50 C;
    6/14/52 B; 7/26/55 B
Symphonies of Wind Instruments (Stravinsky) —
    6/10/21 C; 4/6/71 D
Symphony — 3/28/68 C
Symphony Concertante — 1/7/52 C; 5/5/52 E
Symphony-Concerto in E Minor for Violon-
    cello and Orchestra (Prokofiev) —
    2/18/52 C
Symphony-Fantasy in B Minor — 12/5/12 C
Symphony for Organ and Orchestra (Copland)
    — 1/11/25 C
Symphony for Piano and Orchestra (Toch) —
    8/20/34 C
Symphony for Soprano and Orchestra
    (Mihalovici) — 12/14/71 C
Symphony for Trombone and Orchestra
    (Bloch) — 4/4/56 C

Symphony Hall (Boston) — 10/15/00 E
Symphony Hall (Salt Lake City) — 9/7/79 E
Symphony in B Minor (Paderewski) —
    2/12/09 C
Symphony in C (Balanchine) — 3/22/48 B
Symphony in C (Carpenter) — 10/24/40 C
Symphony in C Major (Atterberg) —
    10/15/28 C
Symphony in C (Stravinsky) — 11/7/40 C
Symphony in D Minor (Bruckner) —
    3/18/23 C; 10/12/24 C
Symphony in D Minor (Enesco) — 2/25/34 C
Symphony in D Minor (Strauss, R.) —
    9/8/49 D
Symphony in E-flat (Bloch) — 2/15/56 C
Symphony in E-flat (Hindemith) —
    11/21/41 C
Symphony in E-flat Major (Stravinsky) —
    4/6/71 D
Symphony in E (Kay) — 5/2/51 C
Symphony in E Minor (Dvorak) — 5/1/04 D
Symphony in F (Antheil) — 6/19/26 C
Symphony in F Minor (Bruckner) —
    3/18/23 C; 10/12/24 C
Symphony in F Minor (Shebalin) —
    11/13/26 C
Symphony in F Minor (Strauss, R.) —
    9/8/49 D
Symphony in G (Foss) — 2/4/45 C
Symphony in G (Harrison) — 2/8/66 C
Symphony in One Movement (Barber) —
    12/13/36 C
Symphony in One Movement (Harris) —
    5/30/52 C
Symphony in three Movements (Balanchine) —
    6/18/72 B
Symphony in Three Movements (Stravinsky)
    — 1/24/46 C
Symphony in Three Movements (Stravinsky) —
    4/6/71 D
Symphony No. 1 (Arnold) — 7/6/51 C
Symphony No. 1 (Badings) — 7/6/30 C
Symphony No. 1 (Barber) — 1/21/37 C
Symphony No. 1 (Ben-Haim) — 6/5/41 C
Symphony No. 1 (Benjamin) — 6/30/48 C
Symphony No. 1 (Bennett) — 2/10/66 C
Symphony No. 1 (Bergsma) — 5/20/50 C
Symphony No. 1 (Berkeley) — 7/8/43 C
Symphony No. 1 (Brant) — 1/30/48 C
Symphony No. 1 (Bush) — 7/24/42 C
Symphony No. 1 (Carter) — 4/27/44 C
Symphony No. 1 (Converse) — 1/30/20 C
Symphony No. 1 (Creston) — 2/22/41 C
Symphony No. 1 (Diamond) — 12/21/41 C
Symphony No. 1 (Goosens, E.) — 4/12/40 C
Symphony No. 1 (Brian) — 6/24/61 C
Symphony No. 1 (Gould) — 3/5/43 C
Symphony No. 1 (Harris) — 1/26/34 C
Symphony No. 1 (Hauer) — 6/7/13 C
Symphony No. 1 (Henze) — 8/25/48 C
Symphony No. 1 (Honegger) — 2/13/31 C
Symphony No. 1 in A-flat Major (Elgar) —
    12/3/08 C
Symphony No. 1 in A Minor (Tansman) —
    3/18/27 C
Symphony No. 1 in B-flat Minor (Khrennikov)
    — 10/10/35 C
Symphony No. 1 in C Major (Bizet) —
    2/26/35 C
Symphony No. 1 in C Minor (Miaskovsky) —
    6/2/14 C
Symphony No. 1 in C-sharp Minor (Kaba-
    levsky) — 11/9/32 C
Symphony No. 1 in D Minor (Willan) —
    10/8/36 C
Symphony No. 1 in E-flat Major (Bax) —
    12/2/22 C
Symphony No. 1 in E-flat Major (Enesco) —
    1/21/06 C

Symphony No. 1 in E-flat Major (Gliere) —
    1/16/03 C
Symphony No. 1 in E-flat Major (Stravinsky)
    — 4/27/07 C
Symphony No. 1 in E Major (Schmidt, F.) —
    1/25/02 C
Symphony No. 1 in E Minor (Hanson) —
    5/30/23 C
Symphony No. 1 in E Minor (Scriabin) —
    11/24/00 C; 3/29/01 C
Symphony No. 1 in E Minor (Sessions) —
    4/22/27 C
Symphony No. 1 in F Minor (Shostakovich) —
    5/12/26 C
Symphony No. 1 in F Minor (Szymanowski) —
    3/26/09 C
Symphony No. 1 (Lutoslawski) — 4/1/48 C
Symphony No. 1 (Mahler) — 6/18/67 C;
    4/9/68 C
Symphony No. 1 (Malipiero) — 4/2/34 C
Symphony No. 1 (Martinu) — 10/15/42 C
Symphony No. 1 (Menotti) — 8/4/76 C
Symphony No. 1 (Milhaud) — 10/17/40 C
Symphony No. 1 (Persichetti) — 10/21/47 C
Symphony No. 1 (Pijper) — 4/23/18 C
Symphony No. 1 (Piston) — 4/8/38 C
Symphony No. 1 (Porter) — 4/2/38 C
Symphony No. 1 (Riisager) — 7/17/26 C
Symphony No. 1 (Rochberg) — 3/28/58 C
Symphony No. 1 (Roussel) — 3/22/08 C
Symphony No. 1 (Rubbra) — 4/30/37 C
Symphony No. 1 (Schuller) — 2/8/65 C
Symphony No. 1 (Schuman) — 10/21/36 C
Symphony No. 1 (Siegmeister) — 10/30/47 C
Symphony No. 1 (Sowerby) — 4/7/22 C
Symphony No. 1 (Stevens) — 3/7/46 C
Symphony No. 1 (Tcherepnin, A.) —
    10/29/27 C
Symphony No. 1 (Thompson) — 2/20/30 C
Symphony No. 1 (Toch) — 12/20/50 C
Symphony No. 1 (Uribe-Holguin) —
    7/20/19 C
Symphony No. 1 (Vaughan Williams) —
    10/12/10 C; 2/4/13 C
Symphony No. 1 (Walton) — 12/3/34 C;
    11/6/35 C
Symphony No. 1 (Ward) — 5/10/41 C
Symphony No. 2 (Badings) — 10/5/33 C
Symphony No. 2 (Barber) — 3/3/44 C
Symphony No. 2 (Bax) — 12/13/29 C
Symphony No. 2 (Bennett) — 1/18/68 C
Symphony No. 2 (Berkeley) — 2/24/59 C
Symphony No. 2 (Blackwood) — 1/5/61 C
Symphony No. 2 (Blomdahl) — 12/12/52 C
Symphony No. 2 (Bush) — 6/27/49 C
Symphony No. 2 (Carpenter) — 10/22/42 C
Symphony No. 2 (Chavez) — 1/23/36 C
Symphony No. 2 (Converse) — 4/21/22 C
Symphony No. 2 (Creston) — 2/15/45 C
Symphony No. 2 (Diamond) — 10/13/44 C
Symphony No. 2 (Dutilleux) — 12/9/59 C
Symphony No. 2 (Forsyth) — 3/5/27 C
Symphony No. 2 (Furtwangler) — 2/22/48 C
Symphony No. 2 (Gerhard) — 10/28/59 C
Symphony No. 2 (Gliere) — 1/23/08 C
Symphony No. 2 (Hadley) — 12/20/01 C
Symphony No. 2 (Hamilton) — 6/9/53 C
Symphony No. 2 (Harris) — 2/28/36 C
Symphony No. 2 (Henze) — 12/1/49 C
Symphony No. 2 (Honegger) — 5/23/42 C
Symphony No. 2 in A Major (Enesco) —
    3/28/15 C
Symphony No. 2 in B-flat Major (d'Indy) —
    2/28/04 C
Symphony No. 2 in B-flat Major (Szymanow-
    ski) — 4/7/11 C
Symphony No. 2 in B Major (Roussel) —
    3/4/22 C

Symphony No. 2 in B Minor (Sowerby) — 3/29/29 C
Symphony No. 2 in C Major (Khrennikov) — 1/10/43 C; 6/9/44 C
Symphony No. 2 in C Minor (Casella) — 4/23/10 C
Symphony No. 2 in C Minor (Scriabin) — 1/25/02 C
Symphony No. 2 in C Minor (Suk) — 2/3/07 C
Symphony No. 2 in C Minor (Willan) — 5/18/50 C
Symphony No. 2 in C-sharp Minor (Miaskovsky) — 7/24/12 C
Symphony No. 2 in D Minor (Balakirev) — 4/23/09 C
Symphony No. 2 in D Minor (Prokofiev) — 6/6/25 C
Symphony No. 2 in D Minor (Sibelius) — 3/8/02 C
Symphony No. 2 in E-flat Major (Elgar) — 5/24/11 C
Symphony No. 2 in E Major (Dohnanyi) — 11/23/48 C; 3/15/57 C
Symphony No. 2 in E Minor (Rachmaninoff) — 2/8/08 C
Symphony No. 2 (Ives) — 2/22/51 C
Symphony No. 2 (Jolivet) — 10/3/59 C
Symphony No. 2 (Kabalevsky) — 12/25/34 C
Symphony No. 2 (Landre) — 3/6/46 C
Symphony No. 2 (Martinu) — 10/28/43 C
Symphony No. 2 (Milhaud) — 12/20/46 C
Symphony No. 2 (Moore) — 5/5/46 C
Symphony No. 2 (Nielsen) — 12/1/02 C
Symphony No. 2 (Pijper) — 11/2/22 C
Symphony No. 2 (Piston) — 3/5/44 C
Symphony No. 2 (Hanson) — 11/28/30 C
Symphony No. 2 (Rochberg) — 2/26/59 C
Symphony No. 2 (Rorem) — 8/5/56 C
Symphony No. 2 (Rubbra) — 12/16/38 C
Symphony No. 2 (Schmidt, F.) — 12/3/13 C
Symphony No. 2 (Schmitt, F.) — 6/15/58 C
Symphony No. 2 (Schuman) — 5/25/38 C
Symphony No. 2 (Sessions) — 1/9/47 C
Symphony No. 2 (Shostakovich) — 11/6/27 C; 4/14/61 B
Symphony No. 2 (Starer) — 4/27/53 C
Symphony No. 2 (Khachaturian) — 12/30/43 C
Symphony No. 2 (Tcherepnin, A.) — 3/20/52 C
Symphony No. 2 (Bernstein) — 4/8/49 C
Symphony No. 2 (Thompson) — 3/24/32 C
Symphony No. 2 (Thomson) — 11/17/41 C
Symphony No. 2 (Tippett) — 2/5/58 C
Symphony No. 2 (Toch) — 1/11/52 C
Symphony No. 2 (Vaughan Williams) — 3/27/14 C; 5/14/20 C
Symphony No. 2 (Walton) — 9/2/60 C
Symphony No. 2 (Ward) — 1/25/48 C
Symphony No. 2 (Weill) — 10/11/34 C
Symphony No. 2 (Whithorne) — 3/19/37 C
Symphony No. 2 (Williamson) — 10/22/69 C
Symphony No. 3 (Nabokov) — 1/4/68 C
Symphony No. 3 (Badings) — 5/2/35 C
Symphony No. 3 (Blackwood) — 3/7/65 C
Symphony No. 3 (Casella) — 3/27/41 C
Symphony No. 3 (Charpentier) — 3/2/69 C
Symphony No. 3 (Chavez) — 12/11/54 C
Symphony No. 3 (Copland) — 10/18/46 C
Symphony No. 3 (Diamond) — 11/3/50 C
Symphony No. 3 (d'Indy) — 12/14/19 C
Symphony No. 3 (Egge) — 3/4/59 C
Symphony No. 3 (Gould) — 2/16/47 C
Symphony No. 3 (Hanson) — 9/19/37 C; 3/26/38 C; 11/3/39 C
Symphony No. 3 (Harris) — 2/24/39 C
Symphony No. 3 (Henze) — 10/7/51 C
Symphony No. 3 (Milhaud) — 10/30/47 C

Symphony No. 3 in A Major (Schmidt, F.) — 12/2/28 C
Symphony No. 3 in A Minor (Miaskovsky) — 2/27/15 C
Symphony No. 3 in A Minor (Rachmaninoff) — 11/6/36 C
Symphony No. 3 in A Minor (Thompson) — 5/15/49 C
Symphony No. 3 in B Minor (Gliere) — 3/23/12 C
Symphony No. 3 in B Minor (Hadley) — 12/27/07 C
Symphony No. 3 in C Major (Enesco) — 5/25/19 C
Symphony No. 3 in C Major (Scriabin) The 5/29/05 C
Symphony No. 3 in C Major (Sibelius) — 9/25/07 C
Symphony No. 3 in D Minor (Mahler) — 6/9/02 C
Symphony No. 3 in E Major (Gretchaninoff) — 5/29/24 C
Symphony No. 3 in E (Piston) — 1/9/48 C
Symphony No. 3 in F-sharp (Tcherepnin, A.) — 1/15/55 C
Symphony No. 3 in G Minor (Roussel) — 10/24/30 C
Symphony No. 3 (Ives) — 4/5/46 C
Symphony No. 3 (Kabalevsky) — 1/21/34 C
Symphony No. 3 (Bernstein) — 12/10/63 C
Symphony No. 3 (Landre) — 6/16/51 C
Symphony No. 3 (Lees) — 1/17/69 C
Symphony No. 3 (Martinu) — 10/12/45 C
Symphony No. 3 (Mennin) — 2/27/47 C
Symphony No. 3 (Nielsen) — 2/28/12 C
Symphony No. 3 (Persichetti) — 11/21/47 C
Symphony No. 3 (Pijper) — 10/28/26 C
Symphony No. 3 (Piston) — 4/3/48 E
Symphony No. 3 (Riegger) — 5/16/48 C
Symphony No. 3 (Riisager) — 11/21/35 C
Symphony No. 3 (Rochberg) — 11/24/70 C
Symphony No. 3 (Rorem) — 4/16/59 C
Symphony No. 3 (Rubbra) — 12/15/40 C
Symphony No. 3 (Schuman) — 10/17/41 C
Symphony No. 3 (Seale) — 9/3/60 C
Symphony No. 3 (Sessions) — 12/6/57 C
Symphony No. 3 — 3/2/69 C
Symphony No. 3 (Shostakovich) — 1/21/30 C; 5/12/64 E
Symphony No. 3 (Sinding) — 1/10/21 C
Symphony No. 3 (Sowerby) — 3/6/41 C
Symphony No. 3 (Szymanowski) — 1/20/17 C
Symphony No. 3 (Creston) — 10/27/50 C
Symphony No. 3 (Tippett) — 6/22/72 C
Symphony No. 3 (Toch) — 12/2/55 C; 5/7/56 E
Symphony No. 3 (Vaughan Williams) — 1/26/22 C
Symphony No. 4 (Antheil) — 2/13/44 C
Symphony No. 4 (Arnold) — 11/2/60 C
Symphony No. 4 (Bax) — 3/16/32 C
Symphony No. 4 (Berezowsky) — 10/22/43 C
Symphony No. 4 (Blackwood) — 12/22/78 C
Symphony No. 4 (Charpentier) — 4/28/74 C
Symphony No. 4 (Creston) — 1/30/52 C
Symphony No. 4 (Diamond) — 1/23/48 C
Symphony No. 4 (Gerhard) — 12/14/67 C
Symphony No. 4 (Harris) — 4/25/40 C; 12/26/40 C
Symphony No. 4 (Giannini) — 5/27/60 C
Symphony No. 4 (Gould) — 4/13/52 C
Symphony No. 4 (Hadley) — 6/6/11 C
Symphony No. 4 (Hanson) — 12/3/43 C; 5/1/44 E
Symphony No. 4 (Hartmann) — 4/2/48 C
Symphony No. 4 (Henze) — 10/9/63 C
Symphony No. 4 (Honegger) — 1/21/47 C
Symphony No. 4 in A Major (Roussel) — 10/19/35 C

Symphony No. 4 in A Minor (Sibelius) — 4/3/11 C
Symphony No. 4 in C Major (Prokofiev) — 11/14/30 C
Symphony No. 4 in C Major (Schmidt, F.) — 1/10/34 C
Symphony No. 4 in E Minor (Miaskovsky) — 2/8/25 C
Symphony No. 4 in E (Tcherepnin, A.) — 12/5/58 C
Symphony No. 4 in F Minor (Vaughan Williams) — 4/10/35 C; 8/26/58 D
Symphony No. 4 in G Major (Mahler) — 11/25/01 C
Symphony No. 4 (Gerhard) — 12/14/67 C
Symphony No. 4 (Ives) — 1/29/27 C; 4/26/65 C
Symphony No. 4 (Kabalevsky) — 10/17/56 C
Symphony No. 4 (Krenek) — 11/27/47 C
Symphony No. 4 (Malipiero) — 2/27/48 C
Symphony No. 4 (Martinu) — 11/30/45 C
Symphony No. 4 (Milhaud) — 5/20/48 C
Symphony No. 4 (Persichetti) — 12/17/54 C
Symphony No. 4 (Piston) — 3/30/51 C
Symphony No. 4 (Riegger) — 4/12/57 C
Symphony No. 4 (Riisager) — 10/24/40 C
Symphony No. 4 (Rubbra) — 8/14/42 C
Symphony No. 4 (Sauguet) — 11/28/71 C
Symphony No. 4 (Schuman) — 1/22/42 C
Symphony No. 4 (Scriabin) — 12/10/08 C
Symphony No. 4 (Searle) — 11/8/62 C
Symphony No. 4 (Sessions) — 1/2/60 C
Symphony No. 4 (Shostakovich) — 1/20/62 C
Symphony No. 4 (Siegmeister) — 12/6/73 C
Symphony No. 4 (Sinfonia romantica)(Chavez) — 2/11/53 C
Symphony No. 4 (Sowerby) — 1/7/49 C
Symphony No. 4 (The Inextinguishable)(Nielsen) — 2/1/16 C
Symphony No. 4 (Tippett) — 10/6/77 C
Symphony No. 4 (Toch) — 11/22/57 C
Symphony No. 5 (Alfven) — 4/30/52 C
Symphony No. 5 (Antheil) — 12/31/48 C
Symphony No. 5 (Atterberg) — 1/6/23 C
Symphony No. 5 (Badings) — 12/7/49 C
Symphony No. 5 (Bax) — 1/15/34 C
Symphony No. 5 (Chavez) — 12/1/53 C
Symphony No. 5 (Cowell) — 1/5/49 C
Symphony No. 5 (Creston) — 4/4/56 C
Symphony No. 5 (Diamond) — 4/28/66 C
Symphony No. 5 (Hadley) — 6/2/35 C
Symphony No. 5 (Harris) — 2/26/43 C
Symphony No. 5 (Henze) — 5/16/63 C
Symphony No. 5 (Honegger) — 3/9/51 C
Symphony No. 5 in B-flat Minor (Rubbra) — 1/26/49 C
Symphony No. 5 in C-sharp Minor (Mahler) — 10/18/04 C
Symphony No. 5 in D Major (Miaskovsky) — 7/18/20 C
Symphony No. 5 in D Major (Vaughan Williams) — 6/24/43 C; 8/26/58 D
Symphony No. 5 in D Minor (Tansman) — 2/2/43 C
Symphony No. 5 in E-flat Major (Sibelius) — 12/8/15 C
Symphony No. 5 (Toch) — 3/13/64 C
Symphony No. 5 (Jirak) — 8/26/51 C
Symphony No. 5 (Krenek) — 3/16/50 C
Symphony No. 5 (Martinu) — 5/27/47 C
Symphony No. 5 (Milhaud) — 10/16/53 C
Symphony No. 5 (Nielsen) — 1/24/22 C
Symphony No. 5 (Piston) — 2/24/56 C
Symphony No. 5 (Prokofiev) — 1/13/45 C
Symphony No. 5 (Riisager) — 11/21/50 C
Symphony No. 5 (Saminsky) — 4/29/58 C
Symphony No. 5 (Scriabin) — 3/15/11 C
Symphony No. 5 (Searle) — 10/7/64 C
Symphony No. 5 (Sessions) — 2/7/64 C

Symphony No. 5 (Shostakovich) — 11/21/37 C
Symphony No. 5 (*Sinfonia sacra*)(Hanson) — 2/18/55 C
Symphony No. 5 (*Symphonie concertante*) (Hartmann) — 4/21/51 C
Symphony No. 5 (*Symphony of Strings*) (Persichetti) — 8/28/54 C
Symphony No. 5 (*Symphony for Strings*) (Schuman) — 11/12/43 C
Symphony No. 6 (Antheil) — 2/10/49 C
Symphony No. 6 (Chavez) — 5/7/64 C
Symphony No. 6 (Converse) — 11/7/40 C
Symphony No. 6 (Diamond) — 3/8/57 C
Symphony No. 6 (Hanson) — 2/29/68 C
Symphony No. 6 (Harris) — 3/14/44 C; 10/7/55 C
Symphony No. 6 (Henze) — 11/19/69 C
Symphony No. 6 in A Minor (Mahler) — 5/27/06 C
Symphony No. 6 (*Fantaisies symphoniques*) (Martinu) — 1/7/55 C
Symphony No. 6 in D Minor (Sibelius) — 2/19/23 C
Symphony No. 6 in E-flat minor (Miaskovsky) — 5/4/24 C
Symphony No. 6 in E-flat Minor (Prokofiev) — 10/11/47 C
Symphony No. 6 in E Minor (Vaughan Williams) — 4/21/48 C
Symphony No. 6 (Malipiero) — 2/11/49 C
Symphony No. 6 (Mennin) — 11/18/53 C
Symphony No. 6 (Nielsen) — 12/11/25 C
Symphony No. 6 (Piston) — 11/25/55 C
Symphony No. 6 (Ricti) — 12/11/74 C
Symphony No. 6 (Rubbra) — 1/17/54 C; 11/17/54 C
Symphony No. 6 (Schuman) — 2/27/49 C
Symphony No. 6 (Sessions) — 11/19/66 C
Symphony No. 6 (Shostakovich) — 11/5/39 C
Symphony No. 6 (Brian) — 9/21/66 C
Symphony No. 6 (Persichetti) — 4/16/56 C
Symphony No. 6 (Saeverud) — 5/27/43 C
Symphony No. 7 (Atterberg) — 2/14/43 C
Symphony No. 7 (Brian) — 3/13/68 C
Symphony No. 7 (Casadesus) — 11/8/72 C
Symphony No. 7 (Cowell) — 11/25/52 C
Symphony No. 7 (Diamond) — 1/26/62 C
Symphony No. 7 (Harris) — 11/20/52 C; 9/15/55 C
Symphony No. 7 (Hartmann) — 3/15/59 C
Symphony No. 7 in A-flat Major (Bax) — 6/9/39 C
Symphony No. 7 in B Minor (Miaskovsky) — 2/8/25 C
Symphony No. 7 in C Major (Sibelius) — 3/24/24 C
Symphony No. 7 in C-sharp Minor (Prokofiev) — 10/11/52 C
Symphony No. 7 in E Minor (Mahler) — 9/19/08 C
Symphony No. 7 in F Major (Glazunov) — 1/3/03 C
Symphony No. 7 (Malipiero) — 11/3/49 C
Symphony No. 7 (Mennin) — 1/23/64 C
Symphony No. 7 (Milhaud) — 9/13/55 C
Symphony No. 7 (Persichetti) — 10/24/59 C
Symphony No. 7 (Piston) — 2/10/61 C; 5/1/61 E
Symphony No. 7 (Rubbra) — 10/1/57 C
Symphony No. 7 (Schuman) — 10/21/60 C
Symphony No. 7 (Sessions) — 10/1/67 C
Symphony No. 7 (Shostakovich) — 3/1/42 C
Symphony No. 7 (Vaughan Williams) — 11/29/48 E;1/14/53 C
Symphony No. 8 (Atterberg) — 2/9/45 C
Symphony No. 8 (Badings) — 1/11/57 C
Symphony No. 8 (Brian) — 2/1/54 C
Symphony No. 8 (Cowell) — 3/1/53 C

Symphony No. 8 (Diamond) — 10/26/61 C
Symphony No. 8 (Harris) — 1/17/62 C
Symphony No. 8 in A Major (Miaskovsky) — 5/23/26 C
Symphony No. 8 in D Minor (Vaughan Williams) — 5/2/56 C
Symphony No. 8 in E-flat (Mahler) — 9/12/10 C
Symphony No. 8 in E-flat Major (Glazunov) — 12/22/06 C
Symphony No. 8 (Malipiero) — 3/21/51 C
Symphony No. 8 (Mennin) — 11/21/74 C
Symphony No. 8 (Milhaud) — 4/22/58 C
Symphony No. 8 (Persichetti) — 10/29/67 C
Symphony No. 8 (Piston) — 3/5/65 C
Symphony No. 8 (Schuman) — 10/4/62 C
Symphony No. 8 (Sessions) — 5/2/68 C
Symphony No. 8 (Shostakovich) — 11/4/43 C
Symphony No. 8 (Villa-Lobos) — 1/14/55 C
Symphony No. 9 (Badings) — 12/17/60 C
Symphony No. 9 (Brian) — 3/22/58 C
Symphony No. 9 (Harris) — 1/18/63 C
Symphony No. 9 in D (Mahler) — 6/26/12 C; 10/16/31 C
Symphony No. 9 in D Minor (Bruckner) — 2/11/03 C
Symphony No. 9 in E Minor (Miaskovsky) — 4/29/28 C
Symphony No. 9 in E Minor (Vaughan Williams) — 4/2/58 C
Symphony No. 9 (Malipiero) — 9/21/66 C
Symphony No. 9 (Milhaud) — 3/29/60 C
Symphony No. 9 (Persichetti) — 3/5/71 C
Symphony No. 9 (Schuman) — 1/10/69 C
Symphony No. 9 (Shostakovich) — 11/3/45 C
Symphony No. 9 (Villa-Lobos) — 5/16/66 C
Symphony No. 10 (Brian) — 11/3/58 C
Symphony No. 10 (Harris) — 4/14/65 C
Symphony No. 10 in F Minor (Miaskovsky) — 4/7/28 C
Symphony No. 10 (Mahler) — 10/12/24 C; 12/19/60 C
Symphony No. 10 (Milhaud) — 4/4/61 C
Symphony No. 10 (Shostakovich) — 12/17/53 C
Symphony No. 10 (Villa-Lobos) — 4/4/57 C
Symphony No. 11 (Brian) — 11/5/59 C
Symphony No. 11 (Cowell) — 5/29/54 C
Symphony No. 11 (Harris) — 2/8/68 C
Symphony No. 11 in E Minor (Miaskovsky) — 1/16/33 C
Symphony No. 11, in G Minor (1905) (Shostakovich) — 10/30/57 C
Symphony No. 11 (Villa-Lobos) — 3/2/56 C
Symphony No. 12 (Brian) — 11/5/59 C
Symphony No. 12 (Cowell) — 3/28/60 C
Symphony No. 12 in G Minor (Miaskovsky) — 6/1/32 C
Symphony No. 12 (Milhaud) — 2/16/62 C
Symphony No. 12 (Shostakovich) — 10/1/61 C
Symphony No. 12 (Villa-Lobos) — 4/20/58 C
Symphony No. 13 (Cowell) — 3/3/59 C
Symphony No. 13 in B-flat Minor (Miaskovsky) — 10/16/34 C
Symphony No. 13 (Shostakovich) — 12/18/62 C
Symphony No. 14 (Cowell) — 4/27/61 C
Symphony No. 14 in C Major (Miaskovsky) — 2/24/35 C
Symphony No. 15 (Hovhaness) — 3/28/63 C
Symphony No. 15 in D Minor (Miaskovsky) — 10/28/35 C
Symphony No. 15 (*Silver Pilgrimage*)3/28/63 C
Symphony No. 15 (*Thesis*)(Cowell) — 10/7/61 C
Symphony No. 16 (Icelandic) (Cowell) — 3/21/63 C

Symphony No. 16 in F Major (Miaskovsky) — 10/24/36 C
Symphony No. 17 (Hovhaness) — 10/23/63 C
Symphony No. 18 (Brian) — 2/26/62 C
Symphony No. 18 in C Major (Miaskovsky) — 10/1/37 C
Symphony No. 19 (Cowell) — 10/18/65 C
Symphony No. 19 in E-flat Major (Miaskovsky) — 2/15/39 C
Symphony No. 20 in E Major (Miaskovsky) — 11/28/40 C
Symphony No. 21 in F-sharp Minor (Miaskovsky) — 11/16/40 C
Symphony No. 22 in B Minor (Miaskovsky) — 1/12/42 C
Symphony No. 23 (Brian) — 10/4/73 C
Symphony No. 23 in A Minor (Miaskovsky) — 7/20/42 C
Symphony No. 24 in F Minor (Miaskovsky) — 12/8/43 C
Symphony No. 25 in D-flat Major (Miaskovsky) — 3/6/47 C
Symphony No. 26 (Miaskovsky) — 12/28/48 C
Symphony No. 27 in C Minor (Miaskovsky) — 12/5/50 C
Symphony No. 29 (Hovhaness) — 5/4/77 C
Symphony of Chorales for Orchestra (Foss) — 10/24/58 C
Symphony of Peace — 5/25/51 C
Symphony of Psalms (Stravinsky) — 12/13/30 C; 12/19/30 C; 4/6/71 D
Symphony of Spheres — 4/13/76 C
Symphony of Spirituals — 4/1/76 C
Symphony of the Air — 10/27/54 E; 10/4/56 C
Symphony of Three Orchestras (Carter) — 2/17/77 C; 7/4/76 E
Symphony on a Hymn Tune (Thomson) — 2/22/45 C
Symphony on G (Harrison) — 2/8/66 C
Symphony on Poems of William Blake — 10/28/52 C
Symphony Piece (Piston) — 3/23/28 C
Symphony (Webern) — 12/18/29 C
Synaphai — 4/6/71 C
Synchronisms No. 6 — 5/3/71 E
Synchronisms No. 7 — 12/4/75 C
Synchrony — 6/6/31 C
Synder, Gina — 1/24/50 B
Synthesis for Orchestra and Electronic Sound — 10/22/63 C
Syrcus, Crome — 9/19/67 B
Syringa — 2/10/78 C
Syzygy — 7/7/68 C
Szbolisi, Bence — 4/24/32 A
Szekely fono — 4/24/32 A
Szekely, Zoltan — 4/23/39 C
Szell, George — //31 E; 12/19/46 C; 2/27/47 C; 8/17/54 A; 1/23/58 C; 1/30/58 C; 2/26/59 C; 1/5/61 C; 4/20/61 C; 1/23/64 C; 7/19/68 E; 7/30/70 D
Szene I — 10/15/60 C
Szigeti, Joseph — 12/15/38 C; 1/9/39 C; 10/19/41 C; 11/20/50 E; 2/19/73 D
Szimfonia (Kodaly) — 8/16/61 C
Szumowska, Antoinette — 5/8/30 D
Szyfer, J.E. — 7/9/35 B
Szymanowski, Karol — 2/6/06 C; 3/26/09 C; 4/7/11 C; 1/20/17 C; 5/13/22 A; 6/19/26 A; 10/9/32 C; 10/6/33 C; 5/11/35 B; 3/28/37 D; 10/10/56 E

— T —

Tabachnik, Michel — 9/30/76 E
Tabarro, Il — 12/14/18 A
Tabor Opera House — 7/7/56 A
Taffanel, Paul — 11/22/08 D

Taft, William Howard — 6/8/20 E
Tagliavini, Feruccio — 8/14/13 D
Tailleferre, Germaine — 1/16/20 E; 4/22/21 E;
    6/19/21 B; 5/30/25 C; 3/9/51 A
Takahashi, Yuji — 1/14/69 C
Takemitsu, Toru — 1/14/69 C
Tale of Tsar Saltan, The — 11/3/00 A
Tales of Hoffmann — 4/6/72 B
Tales of the Countryside — 5/11/41 C
Tal, Josef — 6/3/54 C
Tallchief, Maria — 1/24/25 D; 2/27/46 B;
    11/12/47 B; 3/22/48 B; 4/28/48 B;
    1/20/49 B; 11/27/49 B; 12/1/49 B;
    2/18/51 B; 11/20/51 B; 2/19/52 B;
    11/11/52 B; 2/2/54 B; 11/9/55 B;
    3/1/56 B; 1/8/58 B
Tallchief, Marjorie — 2/22/61 D
Tally-Ho! — 2/25/44 B
Tamagno, Francesco — 8/31/05 D
Taming of the Shrew, The (Cranko) — 5/16/69 B
Taming of the Shrew, The (Giannini) — 1/31/53 A;
    3/13/54 E
Taming of the Shrew (Shebalin) — 5/25/57 A
Taneyev, Sergei — 12/10/04 E; 2/2/05 E;
    9//05 E; 6/2/09 B; 4/14/15 C; 6/19/15 D
Tanglewood — 9/16/18 B; 8/12/37 E; 8/4/38 E
Tango (dance) — 12/10/17 E
Tango, Igisto — 5/24/18 A
Tango (Stravinsky) — 10/19/53 C
Tank Drive — 12/3/65 B
Tanner, Richard — 6/18-25/72 B
Tansman, Alexandre — 3/18/27 C;
    11/21/32 B; 2/2/43 C; 11/18/45 C;
    12/22/49 C
Tante Simona — 1/20/13 A
Tapiola — 12/26/26 C
Tapu — 2/16/03 A
Tarakanova, Nina — 4/5/38 B
Tarantella (Balanchine) — 1/7/64 B
Taras Bulba (Janacek) — 10/9/21 C
Taras Bulba (Lissenko) — 12/20/03 A
Taras, John — 4/18/19 D; 10/1/46 B;
    1/13/47 B; 2/6/48 B; 2/25/50 B;
    12/23/52 B; 12/7/60 B; 4/28/66 B;
    6/18-25/72 B; 6/22/72 B; 5/14-31/75 B;
    5/22/75 B
Targioni-Tozzetti, Giovanni — 5/2/21 A;
    1/16/35 A
Tarkington, Newton Booth — 4/7/19 A
Tarnopolsky, Vladimir — 1/18/29 C
Tarquin — 5/13/41 A; 7/16/50 A
Tarrega, Francisco — 12/15/09 D
Tartiniana — 3/4/52 C
Tashi — 10/13/76 C
Tass (news agency) — 12/11/70 E
Tauber, Richard — 3/2/13 D; 1/8/48 D
Tauriello, Antonio — 8/4/78 E
Tavener, John — 10/1/79 A
Taverna, Gianpiero — 3/28/74 C
Taverner — 7/12/72 A
Taylor, Deems — 2/18/19 C; 3/10/23 C;
    2/17/27 A; 2/7/31 A; 2/10/42 A;
    11/14/42 C; 2/6/58 A; 7/3/66 D
Taylor, Paul — 7/29/30 D; 4/1/58 B;
    5/14/59 B; 4/27/60 B; 4/29/60 B;
    4/16/61 B; 3/4/62 B; 12/27/62 B;
    6/9/76 B; 11/29/77 B; 7/28/79 B
Taylor, P.C. — 4/15/12 E
Taylor & Company, J. — 12/15/18 C
Tchaikovsky — 1/17/00 B; 5/16/07 E;
    11/2/21 B; 5/19/42 B; 9/8/42 B;
    4/13/65 B; 4/13/67 B; 12/4/69 B;
    5/25/77 E; 10/22/79 A
Tchaikovsky Concerto No. 2 (Balanchine) —
    1/12/73 B
Tchaikovsky Conservatory — 4/13/79 E
Tchaikovsky, Modest — 1/15/16 D
Tchaikovsky Musem (Klin, U.S.S.R.) —
    12/15/41 E

Tchaikovsky Pas de Deux — 3/29/60 B
Tchaikovsky Suite No. 2 — 1/9/69 B
Tchelitchev, Pavel — 6/6/28 B
Tchemberdzhi, Nicolai — 1/18/29 C
Tcherepnin, Alexander — 10/26/17 A;
    9/10/23 B; 1/26/24 C; 10/29/27 C;
    1/31/28 A; 2/5/33 C; 3/17/33 A;
    9/14/37 A; 10/10/38 B; 4/17/40 C;
    5/5/46 B; 11/9/47 C; 3/20/52 C;
    8/13/52 A; 8/14/54 C; 1/15/55 C;
    9/11/56 C; 12/5/58 C; 12/24/68 C;
    9/5/72 C; 10/9/77 C; 4/14/78 C
Tcherepnin, Ivan — 5/11/78 C
Tcherepnin, Nicolas — 4/28/07 B; 11/25/07 B;
    2/21/09 C; 5/19/09 B; 5/20/10 B;
    4/26/11 B; 1/29/16 C; 10/26/17 A;
    6/26/45 D
Tchernicheva, Lubov — 4/12/17 B; 6/5/19 B;
    5/15/20 B; 1/6/24 B; 1/19/24 B;
    7/3/26 B; 12/3/26 B; 6/12/28 B
T-DOXC — 9/3/27 C
Teatro alla Scala — *see* La Scala
Teatro Augusteo — 5/13/36 E
Teatro Colon — 5/5/28 E; 7/24/64 A
Teatro Comunale — 11/4/66 E; 9/7/72 A
Teatro la Fenice — 11/4/66 E; 9/7/72 A
Teatro Nacional in Caracas — 6/24/30 E
Tebaldi, Renata — 2/1/22 D
Te Deum (Hamilton) — 10/19/74 C
Te Deum (Bruckner) — 2/11/03 C
Te Deum of Budavar — 9/11/36 C
Teibler, H. — 11/27/03 A
Teldec — 6//50 E
Telefunken (record label) — //32 E
Telephone, The — 2/18/47 A
Telharmonium — 4/12/34 D
Telmanyi, Emil — 2/28/12 C
Telstar — 7/23/62 E
Temkin, Alice — 1/24/50 B
Temple Dancer, The — 3/12/19 A
Temps restitute, Le — 4/4/68 C
Tempus Destruendi — Tempus Aedificandi —
    8/19/71 C
Tender Land, The — 4/1/54 A
Tenebrae — 8/20/74 C
Tengbom, Ivar — 4/7/26 E
Tenneriello, Gabriele — 5/5/78 B
Tennstedt, Klaus — 6/6/26 D
Tenor, Der (Dohnanyi) — 2/9/29 A
Tenor, The (Weisgall) — 2/11/52 A
Tentation derniere, La — 10/28/42 C
Ter-Arutunian, Rouben — 3/6/62 B; 5/5/62 B;
    2/4/65 B; 2/19/65 B; 1/25/66 B;
    11/9/67 B; 1/29/68 B; 5/25/68 B;
    6/25/72 B; 5/24/73 B; 1/17/74 B;
    5/16/74 B; 5/18/78 B
Ternina, Milka — 12/24/03 E; 12/22/50 D
Terra, La — 5/2/47 C
Terre des hommes — 4/29/67 E
Terretekorth — 4/3/66 C
Tertis, Lionel — 11/12/34 C; 2/22/75 D
Terzi, Suzanne — 9/30/48 E
Teschemacher, Marguerite — 10/15/38 A
Testament de la tante Caroline, Le — 11/14/36 A
Testimonium — 7/30/68 E
Tetley, Glen — 2/3/26 D; 4/3/58 B;
    11/19/59 B; 4/20/60 B; 5/5/62 B;
    1/25/66 B; 11/21/68 B; 12/22/73 B
Tetrazzini, Luisa — 1/15/08 D; 11/10/09 D;
    12/28/11 D; 4/28/40 D
Texas Boys Choir — 4/22/79 C
Texier, Rosalie — 10/27/01 C; 1/20/08 E
Teyte, Maggie — 5/26/76 D
Tezenas, Suzanne — 1/13/54 E
Thamar — 5/20/12 B
Thanksgiving and/or Forefather's Day — 1/29/27 C
Thanksgiving for Victory — 5/8/45 C
Tharp, Twyla — 7/1/42 D; 12/3/65 B;
    10/24/73 B; 11/15/76 B; 5/12/77 B
Theater des Westens (Berlin) — //61 E

Theatre — 1/6/72 B
Theatre Piece # 2 (Humphrey) — 4/20/56 B
Theatre Piece (Humphrey) — 12/29/58 D
Thebom, Blanche — 9/19/18 D
Theilade, Nini — 5/5/38 B; 7/21/38 B
Theme and Variations According to the Four Tempera-
    ments — 9/3/44 C
Theme and Variations (Balanchine) — 9/27/47 B
Theme and Variations for Orchestra (Schoenberg) —
    10/20/44 C; 12/19/48 E; 7/13/51 D
Themes and Episodes (Stravinsky) — 3/26/65 C
Theme, Variations and Finale (Rozsa) —
    11/14/43 D
Theodore Kuhn Company — 4/9/75 E
Theory of Evolving Tonality, A (book) — //32 E
Theory of Harmony (book) — *see* Harmonielehre
Theremin — *see* Thereminovox
Theremin, Leon — 8/5/20 E; 2/26/45 C;
    12/10/65 D
Thereminovox — 8/5/20 E; 5/2/24 C;
    4/15/34 C
Therese — 2/7/07 A; 10/1/79 A
Thesaurus of Hebrew-Oriental Melodies (book) —
    8/14/38 D
These Three — 9/13/66 B
They Knew What They Wanted — 11/6/78 C
Thibaud, Jacques — //05 E; 9/1/53 D
Third Concerto for Piano and Orchestra (Bar-
    tok) — 2/8/46 C
Third Essay for Orchestra (Barber) — 9/14/78 C
Third International Webern Festival —
    10/30/66 C
Third Short Sonata (Luening) — 11/21/77 C
34'46.776" — 10/17/54 C
This Is Our Time — 7/5/40 C
13 Profiles of the Original Colonies, Based on an Ancient
    Tune — 5/27/76 C
Thomas, Dylan — 12/19/61 C
Thomas, Jess — 9/16/66 A
Thomas K. Scherman — 10/20/47 C
Thomas, Kurt — 5/25/04 D; 8/16/36 E
Thomas, Michael Tilson — 12/21/44 D;
    10/22/69 D; 10/16/71 D; 8/4/72 C;
    6/2/73 C; 6/1/75 C
Thomas, Richard — 3/6/56 B
Thomas, Ronald — 2/17/76 C
Thomas, Theodore — 1/4/05 D
Thompson, Clive — 8/17/62 B; 9/6/63 B
Thompson, Frank — 10/21/70 B; 4/28/71 B;
    1/6/72 B
Thompson, Randall — 2/20/30 C; 3/24/32 C;
    10/30/41 C; 3/29/42 A; 5/15/49 C;
    3/18/55 C; 5/22/58 C; 3/28/65 C
Thompson, Woodman — 9/27/47 B
Thomson, Virgil — 4/30/32 E; 2/8/34 A;
    1/6/38 B; 11/17/41 C; 1/15/43 C;
    2/22/45 C; 5/7/47 A; 2/24/48 C;
    11/26/48 C; 12/7/48 C; 5/2/49 E;
    3/4/50 C; 10/1/52 B; 9/18/54 C;
    5/14/60 C; 11/1/64 C; 4/26/72 C;
    3/24/75 C; 5/3/78 E; 5/11/78 C; 2/3/79 A
Thorborg, Kerstin — 12/21/36 D; 4/12/70 D
Thorogood, Alfreda — 2/14/78 B
Three Compositions for Piano — 5/2/51 C
Three-Cornered Hat, The — 7/22/19 B
Three Hairs of the Old Wise Man — 10/28/48 A
Three Jewish Poems — *see* Trois poemes juifs
Three Latin-American Sketches — 6/7/72 C
Three Little Pieces for Violoncello and Piano —
    12/2/24 C
Three Meditations for Cello and Orchestra —
    10/11/77 C
Three Movements for Orchestra (Perle) — 4/19/71 C
Three Musketeers, The — 5/11/66 B
Three New England Sketches — 10/23/59 C
Three Orchestral Songs (Webern) — 10/30/66 C
Threepenny Opera — 10/20/30 E
3-Page Sonata — 1/29/27 C
Three Piano Pieces (Schoenberg) — 7/13/51 D

Three Pieces for Cello and Piano (Hindemith) — 9/25/17 E
Three Pieces for String Quartet (Stravinsky) — 11/7/30 C
Three Places in New England (Ives) — 1/10/31 C
Three Poems for Voice and Piano (Webern) — 5/26/62 C
Three Poems from the Japanese — 12/2/14 C
Three Psalms (Bloch) — 5/3/17 C
Three Quartertone Piano Pieces (Ives) — 5/19/54 D
Three Silly Pieces for Flute Solo — 1/27/76 C
Three Songs After Poems by Ferdinand Avenarius — 5/26/62 C
Three Songs for America — 4/27/69 E
Three Songs from Viae inviae (Webern) — 12/5/43 C
Three Songs of Life and Love — 8/22/62 C
Three Songs on Poems of Hildegard Jone — 3/16/52 C
Three Songs (Webern) — 2/8/54 C
Three Tales for Children — 2/21/55 C
Three Traditional Rhymes — 3/16/52 C
Three Virgins and a Devil — 2/11/41 B
Threni — 9/23/58 C
Threnody for the Victims of Hiroshima — 5/31/61 C
Threnody I: Igor Stravinsky in memoriam — 6/2/73 C
Throne of God, The — 11/18/57 C
Through the Looking Glass — 2/18/19 C; 3/10/23 C
Thunderbolt P-47 — 12/19/45 C
Thus Spake Zarathustra (Wyschnegradsky) — 1/25/37 C
Thyl Uylenspiegel — 1/18/00 A
Tibbett, Lawrence — 1/2/25 D; 2/17/27 A; 2/7/31 A; 1/7/33 A; 7/15/60 D
Tiefland — 11/15/03 A
Tigers, The — 11/28/72 D
Tigranian, Armen — 8/17/12 A
Tikhomirov, Vasili — 1/31/23 B; 6/14/27 B
Til Eulenspiegel (Babilee) — 11/9/49 B
Til Eulenspiegel (Nijinsky) — 10/23/16 B
Til Eulenspiegel — see also Tyl Ulenspiegel
Tiller in the Fields, The — 4/5/79 B
Till Eulenspiegel — 10/9/16 E
Time Cycle — 10/20/60 C
Time of Daffodils — 10/30/64 C
Time of Snow, A — 5/25/68 B
Time Out of Mind — 2/19/65 B
Times — 6/18/00 E
Time's Encomium — 3/2/69 C; 5/4/70 E
Time-Span (Rochberg) — 10/22/60 C
Time Spans (Brown) — 9/2/72 C
Timofeyeva, Nina — 4/9/68 B
Timon of Athens — 2/1/50 C
Tiomkin, Dimitri — 11/11/79 D
Tippett, Michael — 1/2/05 D; 6/21/43 E; 3/19/44 C; 1/27/55 A; 2/5/58 C; 5/29/62 A; 8/28/63 C; 1/19/66 C; 7/8/70 C; 10/12/70 C; 6/22/72 C; 5/26/73 C; 12/4/76 D; 10/6/77 C; 5/20/79 C
Tipton, Jennifer — 4/28/71 B; 10/24/73 B; 5/16/74 B; 5/30/74 B
Tischenko, Boris — 12/31/64 B
Titanic, S. S. — 4/15/12 E
To Be Sung upon the Water — 10/20/74 C
Tobias and the Angel — 5/19/60 A
Tobias, Roy — 12/4/51 B; 12/1/57 B
Toccata festiva — 9/30/60 C
Toccata for Percussion Instruments (Chavez) — 10/31/47 C
Toccata for the Sixth Day — 9/28/62 C
Toccata senze fuga — 5/23/79 C
Toch, Ernst — 6/24/23 C; 10/8/26 C; 7/17/27 A; 6/8/30 A; 6/17/30 C; 2/9/31 C; 8/20/34 C; 12/20/34 C; 1/26/35 C; 12/10/36 C; 5/22/38 E; 11/18/45 C; 12/20/50 C; 1/11/52 C; 12/2/55 C; 5/7/56 E; 11/22/57 C; 3/13/64 C; 10/1/64 D

Tod des Grigori Rasputin, Der — 11/27/59 A
Tokyo Ballet Company — 6/29/75 B
Tokyo Philharmonic Orchestra — 12/29/65 D
Tomasi, Henri — 8/17/01 D
Tomasson, Helgi — 7/30/70 B; 6/18/72 B; 5/24/73 B; 5/16/74 B; 7/17/74 B; 5/22/75 B; 5/29/75 B
Tombeau de Couperin, Le (Balanchine) — 5/29/75 B
Tombeau de Couperin, Le (Ravel) — 2/28/20 C
Tombeau resplendissant, Le — 2/12/33 C
Tommasini, Vincenzo — 4/8/06 A; 2/20/13 A; 4/12/17 B; 10/26/39 B; 12/23/50 D
Tompkins, Beatrice — 11/20/46 B; 11/26/46 B; 5/13/47 B; 6/12/51 B
Tone-Roads — 5/19/54 D
Tonhalle-Orchester — 6/16/21 E; 6/22/26 C
Tonkunstlervein Orchestra — 11/4/08 C
To October — 11/6/27 C
Torkanowsky, Werner — 11/18/68 C
Torneo notturno — 5/15/31 A
Toronto Opera — 10/16/58 D
Toronto Symphony Orchestra — 3/19/63 C; 1/14/69 C; 5/31/73 C
Torquemada — 1/24/76 A
Toscanini, Arturo — 1/17/01 A; 11/16/08 D; 11/17/09 D; 12/10/10 A; 11/13/11 D; 1/2/14 A; 1/25/15 A; 11/19/16 E; 12/28/20 E; 12/26/21 E; 2/13/22 E; 12/16/22 A; 5/2/24 A; 12/20/24 A; 3/7/25 A; 4/25/26 A; 3/30/28 E; 5/16/28 A; //29 E; 2/21/29 C; 2/28/29 C; 4/3/30 C; 4/27/31 D; 5/14/31 E; 4/1/33 E; 6/5/33 E; //36 E; 11/5/36 D; 12/26/36 E; 12/25/37 E; 11/5/38 C; 5/31/40 E; //41 E; 11/24/45 C; 5/11/46 E; 3/20/48 E; 1/21/49 D; 4/4/54 E; 10/27/54 E; 1/16/57 D; 8/16/61 C
Tosca — 1/14/00 A; 1/28/21 E; 9/19/24 A
Totem — 1/29/60 B
Toten Augen, Die — 3/5/16 A
Totenmal, Das — 6/24/30 B
Tote Stadt, Die — 12/4/20 A; 11/19/21 A
Toumanova, Tamara — //32 E; 4/12/32 B; 4/21/32 B; 4/6/34 B; 7/24/36 B; 2//38 E; 10//38 E; 1/22/41 B; 10/8/41 B; 7/28/47 B; 6/14/50 B
Tourel, Jennie — 6/22/00 D; 5/15/37 D; 8/25/43 C; 1/28/44 C; 9/11/51 A; 11/23/73 D
Tournemire, Charles — 3/19/24 A
Tovey, Sir Donald Francis — 11/22/34 C; 7/10/40 D
To Vishnu — 6/2/67 C
Tower, The — 8/2/57 A
Toyama, Muchiko — 1/8/59 E
Toye, Geoffrey — 3/27/14 C; 4/3/34 B
Traces — 5/3/69 C
Tragedie de Salome, La (Diaghilev) — 6/12/13 B
Tragedie de Salome, La (Schmitt, F.) — 11/9/07 C
Tragic Overture — 3/24/49 C
Train bleu, Le — 6/20/24 B
Traite de fugue (book) — 2/5/26 D
Traite d'harmonie tonale, atonale et totale (book) — 6/13/54 C
Traitor, The — 8/19/54 B
Tra le sollicitudini (papal document) — 11/22/03 E
Trampler, Walter — 8/25/15 D
Transatlantique — 5/25/30 A; 2/12/59 D
Transfiguration de Notre Seigneur Jesus-Christ, La — 6/7/69 C; 3/28/72 C
Transformations — 12/3/78 C
Transposed Heads, The — 4/4/54 A
Trantoul, Antonin — 5/16/28 A
Trapeze — 12/22/29 C
Traubel, Helen — 5/12/37 A; 9/27/53 E; 7/28/72 D
Traum des Liu-Tung, Der — 9/25/65 A

Trautonium — //30 E
Trautvetter, Paul — 8/19/54 B
Trautwein, Friedrich — //30 E
Travelling Companion, The — 4/30/25 A
Traviata, La — 1/27/01 D
Treatise on Musical Forms (book) — //22 E
Tre commedie goldoniane (Malipiero) — 3/24/26 A
Trecu, Pirmin — 11/16/48 B
Tredici, David Del — 7/4/76 E
Treemonisha — 4/1/17 D; 5/23/75 A
Trefilova, Vera — 5/18/22 B
Trepak — 10/10/38 B
Tria carmina Paschalia — 9/25/70 C
Trial at Rouen, The — 4/8/56 A
Trial of Damis, The — see Ruses d'Amour, Les
Trial of Lucullus, The — 4/18/47 A
Trial of the Gypsy, The — 5/24/78 C
Tricolore — 5/18/78 B
Trio for Flute, Violoncello and Piano (Wuorinen) — 3/28/73 C
Trio for Piano, Violin and Cello (Rieti) — 1/19/73 C
Trio for violin, clarinet and piano (Ives) — 1/29/27 C
Trio Movement (Webern) — 2/17/78 C
Trionfo di Afrodite — 6/8/37 C; 2/13/53 C
Triple Concerto a Tre (Menotti) — 10/6/70 C
Triple Concerto for Violin, Piano, Cello and Orchestra — 12/28/63 C
Triple Concerto for Violin, Viola, Piano and Orchestra — 1/27/73 C
Triple Concerto (Martino) — 12/18/78 C
Triple Paced — 4/5/44 B
Triplum — 6/28/67 C
Trip to Nahant, A — 3/18/55 C
Triskaidekaphobia — 7/13/51 D
Trisler, Joyce — 10/9/79 D
Tristan — 10/20/74 C
Tristan und Isolde — 5/31/05 D; 1/1/08 D; 6/1/09 D
Tristram Shandy — 2/5/71 C
Trittico, Il — 12/14/18 A
Triumph of Death — 2/19/72 B
Triumph of Neptune, The — 12/3/26 B
Triumph of Saint Joan, The (Dello Joio) — 5/9/50 A
Triumph of Saint Joan, The (Graham) — 12/5/51 B
Triumph of Time, A — 6/1/72 C
Troilus and Cressida — 12/3/54 A
Trois chansons de Charles d'Orleans — 4/9/09 C
Trois morceaux en forme de poire — 7/1/25 D
Trois Nocturnes (Debussy) — 12/9/00 C; 10/27/01 C; 3/25/18 D
Trois petites liturgies de la Presence Divine — 4/21/45 C
Trois poemes juifs — 3/23/17 C; 7/15/59 D
Trois Valses Romantiques — 4/6/67 B
Troubled Island, The — 3/31/49 A
Trouble in Tahiti — 6/12/52 A
Trouhanova, Natacha — 4/22/12 B
Trovatore, Il — 1/27/01 D
Truman, Margaret — 12/20/49 E
Trunk, Richard — 11/30/33 C
Tsar Kaloyan — 4/20/36 A
Tshupiatov, L. — 10/29/24 B
Tucker, Richard — 8/28/13 D; 1/25/45 D; 1/8/75 D
Tudor, Antony — 4/4/08 D; 10/28/34 B; 1/26/36 B; 2/19/37 B; 6/15/38 B; 11/26/38 B; 12/5/38 B; 10/27/41 B; 4/8/42 B; 4/8/42 B; 9/8/42 B; 4/6/43 B; 10/20/43 B; 4/10/45 B; 4/14/48 B; 2/26/52 B; 2/1/55 B; 9/28/63 B; 5/6/64 B; 1/25/67 B; 4/5/79 B
Tudor, David — 1/20/26 D; 2/10/52 C; 5/2/52 C; 8/29/52 C; 2/25/60 C
Tuleelegid — 6/21/45 A
Tully, Miss Alice — 9/11/69 E
Tunick, Jonathan — 9/8/71 C
Turandot (Busoni) — 5/11/17 A

Turandot (Puccini) — 4/25/26 A; 9/5/64 E; 7/20/79 E
Turandot Suite (Busoni) — 10/21/05 C
Turangalila-symphonie — 12/2/49 C
Tureck, Rosalyn — 12/14/14 D
Turina, Joaquin — 3/30/13 C; 10/10/14 A; 2/8/15 E; 9/11/20 C; 1/14/49 D
Turner, Godfrey — 3/27/13 D; 12/7/48 D
Turner, Harold — 2/25/30 B; 1/30/34 B; 5/2/35 B; 11/26/35 B; 2/11/36 B; 2/16/37 B; 6/15/37 B
Turney, Matt — 5/8/55 B; 4/3/58 B; 4/16/61 B
Turn of the Screw, The — 9/14/54 A; 12/4/76 D
Twain, Mark — 10/6/09 E
Twelfth Night — 8/1/68 A
Twelve, The — 12/31/64 B
12 Tonadas de Character popular chileno — 8/16/59 D
Twelve-Tone Tonality (book) — //77 E
20th Century Fox — 4/11/48 E
Twentieth Century Music: Its Evolution from the End of the Harmonic Era to the Present Era of Sound (book) — //67 E
Twitchell, Harmony — 5/19/54 D
Two Assyrian Prayers — 10/28/25 C
Two Chorale Preludes (Schoenberg) — 12/7/22 C
Two Choric Dances — 2/20/39 C
Two Indian Dances — 10/29/16 C
Two-Man Orchestra — 10/20/73 C
Two Movements for String Quartet (Weill) — 3/7/77 C
Two-Part Symphony — 12/11/78 C
Two Pieces (Webern) — 6/3/70 C
Two Pigeons — 2/14/61 B
Two Songs in German — 5/6/49 C
Two Sounds — 1/31/61 A
Two Symphonic Interludes — 4/11/36 C
2001 — 10/22/61 C
Tyl Ulenspiegel (Balanchine) — 11/14/51 B
Tyrer, Andersen — 10/26/46 E; 3/6/47 E
Tyrwhitt-Wilson, Gerald Hugh — 4/19/50 D
Tzaddik — 6/2/74 B
Tzigane (Ravel) — 4/26/24 C; 3/30/66 D
Tzigane (Balanchine) — 5/29/75 B

— U —

Ugale fortuna — 2/20/13 A
"Ugly Duckling, The" — 12/10/16 C
Uirapuru — 5/25/35 C
Ukelele — 9/18/17 E
Ukiyo — 1/30/65 C
Ulanova, Galina — 1/8/10 D; 11/7/32 B; 9/28/34 B; 1/11/40 B; 11/5/51 D; 2/12/54 B; //59 E; 4/16/59 B
Ullate, Victor — 1/27/78 B
Ultimo Abencerraje, El — 8/19/22 D
Ultraphon — 9/16/20 E; 3/25/25 E; //32 E
Ulysses at the Edge — 4/22/44 C
Unanswered Question, The — 1/29/27 C; 8/25/59 C
Unaufhorliche, Das — 11/21/31 C
Undertow — 4/10/45 B
Under Western Eyes — 5/29/69 A
UNESCO — 11/4/55 C; 9/7/70 E; //73 E
Unesco Prize — 10/1/53 C
Union Carbide Company — //32 E
Union Jack — 5/12/76 B; 5/18/78 B
Union of Polish Composers — 9/3/45 E
Union of Rumanian Composers — //21 E
Union of Soviet Composers — 12/29/48 E
Union Pacific — 4/6/34 B
United Independent Broadcasters (CBS) — 5//27 E
United Temple Chorus — 5/13/52 C
Universal Art Inc. — 1/30/38 E; 3//38 E; 6/17/38 E

Universal Edition — 6/1/01 E; 12/14/25 A; 1/14/36 E; 6/2/39 D; 11/30/72 D
Universe Symphony — 5/19/54 D
University of Illinois Symphony Orchestra — 10/4/73 C
Until the Forests Burn — 6/1/68 A
Uppman, Theodor — 12/1/51 A
Uribe-Holguin, Guillermo — 7/20/19 C
Ursuleac, Viorica — 7/1/33 A; 10/28/42 A
U.S. Highball, a Musical Account of a Transcontinental Hobo Trip — 4/22/44 C
Ushkov, Natalie — 9/8/05 E
Ussachevsky, Vladimir — 11/3/11 D; 5/9/52 E; 10/28/52 C; 3/20/54 C; 12/2/54 C; 1/8/59 E; 3/20/60 C; 5/9-10/61 E
Utah Civic Ballet — //63 E
Utah Symphony Orchestra — 9/7/79 E
Uthoff, Ernst — 7/3/32 B; 11/21/32 B
Utrecht, University of — 6/12/61 E; //79 E
Utrillo, Maurice — 12/11/25 B
Utzon, Joern — 10/20/73 E
Uzbekistan — 3/20/34 C
Uzbek Symphony Orchestra — 3/20/34 C

— V —

Vaganova, Agrippina — //34 E; 11/5/51 D
Vainonen, Vasily — 10/26/30 B; 11/7/32 B
Valen, Fartein — 12/14/52 D
Valen Society — 12/14/52 D
Valente, Benita — 2/4/74 C
Valery, Paul — 6/23/31 A; 4/14/67 C
Valois, Ninette de — 1/6/24 B; //26 E; 10/19/30 E; 5/5/31 B; 7/5/31 B; 12/5/33 B; 4/3/34 B; 5/15/34 B; 5/20/35 B; 6/15/37 B; 7/4/40 B; 2/20/46 B; 2/2/50 B
Valse-fantaisie — 1/6/53 B; 6/1/69 B
Valse, La (Ashton) — 2/1/58 B
Valse, La (Balanchine) — 2/20/51 B
Valse, La (Nijinska) — 1/12/29 B
Valse, La (Ravel) — 12/12/20 C
Valse perpetuelle (The 45 R.P.M.) — 5/11/78 C
Valse Triste — 4/25/04 C
Vance, Norma — 2/25/50 B
Vancouver Cello Club — 9/21/72 C
Vanderbeek, Stan — 7/23/65 B
Vandoyev, Jean-Louis — 4/19/11 B
Vanessa — 1/15/58 A; 5/5/58 E
Vangsaa, Mona — 5/19/55 B; 11/22/57 B
Van, Guillaume de — 3/7/42 E
Van Hamel, Martine — 11/16/45 D
Van Lier, Bertus — 6/12/37 E
Vanloo, Albert — 1/9/13 A
Van Rooy, Anton — 12/24/03 E; 1/22/07 A; 11/28/32 D
Vardar — 3/25/28 C
Varese, Edgard — 12/15/10 C; 4/11/19 E; 5/3/21 E; 3/4/23 C; 1/13/24 C; 3/1/25 C; 4/9/26 C; 4/8/27 C; 3/6/33 C; 4/15/34 C; 12/2/54 C; 11/6/65 D; 6/27/78 B
Variaciones concertantes — 6/2/53 C
Variationen und Fuge uber ein Thema von Mozart — 2/5/15 C
Variations: Aldous Huxley In Memoriam — 4/17/65 C
Variations and Theme for Five — 2/2/76 C
Variations for Cello and Orchestra (Piston) — 3/2/67 C
Variations for Orchestra (Argento) — 5/2/66 C
Variations for Orchestra (Bassett) — 7/6/63 C
Variations for Orchestra (Carter) — 4/21/56 C
Variations for Orchestra (Schoenberg) — 12/2/28 C; 7/13/51 D
Variations for Orchestra (The Mask of Night) — 1/26/66 C
Variations for Orchestra (Webern) — 3/3/43 C

Variations for Piano and Orchestra (Riegger) — 2/13/54 C
Variations for Piano (Webern) — 10/26/37 C
Variations I (Version Welin 1972) — 6/13/72 C
Variations on a Chinese Theme — 6/20/12 C
Variations on America (Ives) — 5/19/54 D
Variations on a Nursery Song (Dohnanyi) — 2/17/14 C
Variations on a Theme by Hindemith (Walton) — 3/8/63 C
Variations on "I Got Rhythm" — 1/14/34 C
Variations pour une porte et un soupir — 1/17/74 B
Variations Symphoniques (Lutoslawski) — 6/17/39 C
Variations V (Cunningham) — 7/23/65 B
Variations Without Fugue — 5/15/73 C
Variazioni per orchestra — 10/3/54 C
Varnay, Astrid — 4/25/18 D; 12/6/41 D; 2/20/42 A
Vasco — 10/11/70 D
Vasiliov, Vladimir — 4/18/40 D; 9/17/62 B; 4/9/68 B; 3/23/71 B
Vassilenko, Sergei — 3/1/02 C; 3/3/03 A; 5/4/08 C; 2/3/09 C; 3/3/25 B; 5/23/29 A; 4/5/33 C; 2/21/42 A; 3/11/56 D
Vaterlandische Ouverture, Eine — 2/5/15 C
Vaucaire, Maurizio — 10/14/11 A
Vaudeville — 12/29/19 E
Vaughan Williams, Ralph — 3/10/02 C; 8/23/06 C; 9/27/07 C; 2/22/09 C; 11/15/09 C; 11/26/09 C; 9/6/10 C; 10/12/10 C; 7/23/12 C; 2/4/13 C; 3/27/14 C; 5/14/20 C; 1/26/22 C; 7/11/22 A; 6/5/23 B; 7/4/23 C; 7/14/24 A; 10/19/25 C; 11/6/25 C; 5/7/26 C; 3/21/29 A; 3/13/30 C; 7/5/31 B; 2/1/33 C; 9/27/34 C; 11/12/34 C; 4/10/35 C; 5/12/36 A; 9/25/36 C; 5/12/37 C; 11/30/37 A; 10/5/38 C; 6/10/39 C; 6/24/43 C; 9/30/44 C; 5/8/45 C; 7/31/45 C; 4/21/48 C; 11/29/48 E; 11/18/50 C; 4/26/51 A; 5/6/51 C; 5/3/52 C; 1/14/53 C; 6/13/54 C; 9/8/54 C; 5/2/56 C; 6/4/56 C; 4/2/58 C; 8/26/58 D; 1/23/69 B; 11/28/72 D
Vaurabourg, Andree — 5/23/25 C
Veasey, Josephine — 5/29/62 A
Vedova scaltra, La — 3/5/31 A
Veen, Jan — 5/30/38 B
Velitchkova, Ljuba — see Welitsch, Ljuba
Venice Festival of Contemporary Music — 9/7/72 A
Venus in Africa — 5/24/57 A
Venza, Jac — 6/26/64 B
Veracini, Francesco Maria — 2/13/68 D
Verchinina, Nina — 4/13/33 B; 10/24/33 B
Verdi, Giuseppe — 1/27/01 D; 1/28/03 E; 4/30/03 E; 10/29/36 A; 10/17/51 B; 2/25/54 B; 1/12/78 B; 8/4/78 E; 9/24/79 E
Verdy, Violette — 3/29/60 B; 11/22/60 B; 3/22/61 B; 4/13/67 B; 11/23/67 B; 11/23/68 B; 5/22/69 B; 1/29/70 B; 1/10/74 B; 5/14-31/75 B
Vere, Diana — 3/2/70 B
Veress, Sandor — 2/1/07 D
Verger, Christine — 4/20/10 C
Verhor des Lukullus, Das — 3/17/51 A
Verklarte Nacht — 3/18/02 C; 4/8/42 B; 7/13/51 D
Verlobung von San Domingo, Die — 11/27/63 A
Vermel, Paul — 4/24/77 C
Verneuil, Catherine — 1/27/78 B
Verneuil, Claudine Pillard — 10/25/51 E
Verses for Ensembles — 2/12/69 C
Vertes, Marcel — 10/27/41 B; 11/29/42 B
Vertical Thoughts — 10/11/63 C

Vesak, Norbert — 7/27/71 B
Vesalii icones — 12/9/69 C
Vescovo, Bruno — 5/5/78 B
Veselohra na moste — 3/18/37 A; 5/28/51 A
Vesper Mass (Rachmaninoff) — 3/10/15 C
Veste di cielo — 4/21/27 A
Vetrate di chiesa (Respighi) — 2/25/27 C
Vetschlova, Tatiana — 9/28/34 B
Vetter aus Dingsda, Der — 4/15/21 A
Via della finestra, La (Zandonai) — 7/29/19 A
Vianesi, August — 11/4/08 D
Viardot-Garcia, Pauline — 7/1/06 D;
    5/18/10 D
Viardot, Louis — 5/18/10 D
Viber, Eric — 11/19/24 B
Vickers, Jon — 10/14/79 E
Victoire de Guernica, La — 8/25/54 C
Victor R.C.A. — 10//01 E; 4/30/03 E;
    2/1/04 E; //05 E; 7//06 E; //08 E;
    9/10/17 E; //18 E; //19 E; 9/16/20 E;
    4/11/22 E; 5//24 E; 3/25/25 E; //26 E;
    5//27 E; //28 E; 9/17/31 E; 2/18/32 C;
    //34 E; 11/14/36 D;
    11/13/40 E;10/8/46 E; //47 E; 1//49 E;
    6//50 E; //58 E; //63 E; //70 E;
    10/13/79 D
Victor Book of the Opera — //12 E
Victor Concert Orchestra — 9/17/31 E
Victor Herbert v. The Shanley Company — 1/22/17 E
Victoria, S.S — 7/20/20 E
Victoria, Thomas Luis de — 4/26/74 B
Victory — 10/30/45 C
Victrola — 7//06 E
Vic-Wells Ballet — 5/5/31 B; 3/21/33 B;
    4/3/34 B; //35 E; 5/20/35 B; 2/11/36 B;
    11/10/36 B; 2/16/37 B; 4/27/37 B
Vida breve, La — 4/1/13 A
Video Triangle — 1/5/76 B
Vienna Chamber Chorus — 11/12/63 C
Vienna Konzertverein — 6/9/52 D
Vienna Music Academy — 12/17/28 D
Vienna Opera — 1/22/00 A; 2/22/03 D;
    10/15/07 E; 10/4/10 A; 10/10/19 A;
    5/2/43 D 3/12/45 B; 9/20/47 D; //56 E;
    2/24/79 A; 4/25/79 D
Vienna Philharmonic — 2/17/01 C; 6/26/12 C;
    2/19/38 C; 11/28/47 E
Vienna Phonogram Archiv — 11/12/22 E
Vienna Radio Orchestra — 2/6/46 D
Vienna State Opera — *see* Vienna Opera
Vienna State Opera House — 6/30/44 E;
    11/5/55 E
Vienna, University of — 6/20/06 E; 7/1/08 E
Vienna Waltzes — 6/23/77 B
Vier Grobiane, Die — 3/19/06 A
Vier Letzte Lieder — 5/22/50 C
Vieru, Anatol — 3/27/63 C
Villa-Lobos, Heitor — 11/13/15 D;
    12/15/22 C; 12/15/26 C; 10/24/27 C;
    4/5/28 C; 5/30/29 C; 9/12/32 C;
    5/25/35 C; 2/2/37 E; 3/25/39 C;
    4/7/40 C; 7/26/40 A; 6/6/42 C;
    7/15/42 C; 3/13/44 C; 2/21/45 C;
    2/19/47 C; 8/6/47 C; 1/23/48 C;
    11/7/51 C; 1/23/54 C; 5/30/54 C;
    1/14/55 C; 3/2/56 C; 7/12/56 B;
    4/4/57 C; 4/20/58 C; 7/5/59 C;
    11/17/59 D; 6/5/61 C; 5/16/66 C;
    8/12/71 A
Villella, Edward — 1/10/37 D; 3/22/61 B;
    1/17/62 B; 3/20/63 B; 1/7/64 B;
    5/6/64 B; 2/4/65 B; 4/21/66 B;
    4/28/66 B; 4/13/67 B; 11/23/67 B;
    5/22/69 B; 2/3/72 B; 6/18/72 B;
    5/22/75 B
Ville mysterieuse, La — 3/15/74 C
Villon — 11/23/66 B
Vilna Symphony Orchestra — 3/14/54 D

Vilzak, Anatole — 1/6/24 B; 1/19/24 B;
    11/22/28 B; 11/22/28 B; 11/27/28 B;
    1/12/29 B; 6/25/36 B
Vinay, Ramon — 8/31/12 D
Vines, Ricardo — 4/5/02 C; 1/9/04 C
Vinogradov, Nikolai — 9/19/24 A
Viola Concerto — 6/3/54 C
Viola Concerto (Bartok) — 12/2/49 C
Viola Concerto (Bennett) — 7/3/73 C
Viola Concerto (Milhaud) — 12/15/29 C
Viola Concerto (Walton) — 10/3/29 C
Violanta — 3/28/16 A
Violin Concerto (Balanchine) — 6/18/72 B
Violin Concerto (Barber) — 2/7/41 C
Violin Concerto (Bartok) — 4/23/39 C
Violin Concerto (Bennett) — 3/25/76 C
Violin Concerto (Berg) — 4/19/36 C
Violin Concerto (Bliss) — 5/11/55 C
Violin Concerto (Bloch) — 12/15/38 C
Violin Concerto (Brant) — 2/22/41 C
Violin Concerto (Chavez) — 2/29/52 C
Violin Concerto (Diamond) — 3/24/37 C
Violin Concerto (Ginastera) — 10/3/63 C
Violin Concerto (Halffter) — 6/26/42 C
Violin Concerto (Hamilton) — 9/8/72 C
Violin Concerto (Hauer) — 11/12/29 C
Violin Concerto (Hovhaness) — 7/3/76 C
Violin Concerto in A Major (Reger) —
    10/13/08 C
Violin Concerto in D Minor (Sibelius) —
    2/8/04 C; 10/19/05 C
Violin Concerto in G Minor (Bruch) —
    10/2/20 D
Violin Concerto (Jolivet) — 2/27/73 C
Violin Concerto (Kabalevsky) — 10/29/48 C
Violin Concerto (Khachaturian) — 11/16/40 C
Violin Concerto (Khrennikov) — 10/21/59 C
Violin Concerto (Kim) — 10/25/79 C
Violin Concerto (Martin) — 1/24/52 C
Violin Concerto (Nielsen) — 2/28/12 C
Violin Concerto No. 1 (Bartok) — 5/30/58 C
Violin Concerto No. 1 (Imbrie) — 4/22/58 C
Violin Concerto No. 1 in D Major (Prokofiev)
    — 10/18/23 C
Violin Concerto No. 2 — 11/2/72 C
Violin Concerto No. 2 (Creston) — 11/17/60 C
Violin Concerto No. 2 (Dohnanyi) —
    1/26/52 C
Violin Concerto No. 2 in G Minor (Prokofiev)
    — 12/1/35 C
Violin Concerto No. 2 (Piston) — 10/14/60 C
Violin Concerto No. 2 (Szymanowski) —
    10/6/33 C
Violin Concerto (Piston) — 3/18/40 C
Violin Concerto (Rawsthorne) — 7/1/48 C
Violin Concerto (Riisager) — 10/11/51 C
Violin Concerto (Rochberg) — 4/4/75 C
Violin Concerto (Schoenberg) — 12/6/40 C
Violin Concerto (Schuman) — 2/10/50 C
Violin Concerto (Sessions) — 1/8/40 C
Violin Concerto (Strauss, R.) — 9/8/49 D
Violin Concerto (Walton) — 12/7/39 C
Violin Concerto (Wellesz) — 1/19/62 C
Violins of Saint Jacques, The — 11/29/66 A
Violin Sonata (Debussy) — 5/5/17 C
Violin Sonata No. 1 (Ives) — 1/29/27 C
Violin Sonata No. 2 (Bartok) — 10/20/24 C
Violoncello Concerto No. 2 (Shostakovich) —
    9/25/66 C
Viotta, Henri — 11/20/04 E
Virsaladze, Simon — 6/28/38 B; 3/22/39 B;
    3/23/61 B; 2/16/75 B
Vishnevskaya, Galina — 10/25/26 D
Vision — 11/29/72 C
Vision and Prayer — 7/9/62 E
Visionary Recital — 4/16/61 B; 3/6/62 B
Vision de Jacob, La — 5/3/01 C
Vision dramatique — 4/4/48 C

Vision of Aeroplanes, A — 6/4/56 C
Vision of Saint Augustine, The — 1/19/66 C
Visions de l'amen — 5/10/43 C
Visions of Terror and Wonder — 7/19/76 C;
    4/18/77 E
Visitation, The — 10/12/66 A
Vita e sogno, La — 6/30/43 A
Vita Nuova, La — 3/21/03 C
Vitaphone Company — 8/6/26 E
Vittorio Emanuele Theater (Messina, Italy) —
    12/29/68 E
Vives, Amadeo — 4/12/02 A
Vivre Aimer — 6/23/01 C
Vladigerov, Pantcho — 3/17/21 C; 3/25/28 C;
    4/20/36 A; 5/24/37 E; 9/8/78 D
Vladimiroff, Pierre — 11/2/21 B
Vladimirov, Yuri — 5/18/22 B; 2/16/75 B
Vlad, Roman — 12/29/19 D
Vlasova, Ludmila — 8/22/79 E
Vocalion — //26 E
Vo-coder — *see* Voder
Voder — 1/5/39 E; 9/18/79 E
Voice in the Wilderness — 1/21/37 C
Voice of the Victor — 7//06 E
Voiceplay — 11/14/72 C
Voices — 3/28/76 C
Voices for Today — 10/24/65 C
Voix humaine, La — 2/6/59 A; 1/30/63 D
Voix pour une autre, Une — 4/19/74 C
Volga Boatman's Song, The (Stravinsky) —
    4/9/17 C
Volkov, Nikolai — 4/14/38 B
Vollmer Associates — 7/8/66 E
Volo di notte — 5/18/40 A
Volpone — 1/9/53 A
Voluntaries — 12/22/73 B
Von Heute auf Morgen — 2/1/30 A
Von vorn herein — 8/21/74 C
Vooss, Hanna — 12//66 E
Vorfruhling II (Webern) — 10/29/66 C
Vortag uber Hu — 10/18/74 C
Votre Faust — 3/17/68 A
Votterle, Karl — 10/29/75 D
Vox Balaenae — 10/10/72 C
Vox Maris — 9/10/64 C
Voyage a Cythere, Un — 1/24/67 C
Voyage Four — 1/14/64 C
Voyage of Edgar Allan Poe, The — 4/24/76 A
Vronsky, Vitya — 8/22/09 D; 11/13/42 C;
    3/1/72 D
Vuckovic, Vojislav — 12/25/42 D
Vuillermoz, Emile — 6/19/13 C

— W —

Waart, Edo de — 6/1/41 D; //67 E; //77 E
Wagenaar, Johan — 6/12/37 E
Waggoner, Dan — 8/4/62 B
Wagner, Cosima — 4/1/30 D
Wagner Museum (Tribschen, Switz.) —
    7/30/33 E
Wagner-Regeny, Rudolf — 11/1/34 E
Wagner, Richard — 5/13/00 D; 2/22/03 D;
    12/24/03 D; //04 E; 5/31/05 D; 9/19/14 E;
    2/8/15 E; 11/8/19 E; 7/22/74 E;
    11/9/39 B; 11/21/40 E; 10/7/79 D
Wagner, Siegfried — 12/24/03 E; 12/16/23 A;
    8/4/30 D
Wagner, Wieland — 1/5/17 D; 10/16/66 D
Wagoner, Dan — 4/16/61 B
Wakhevitch, Georges — 6/25/46 B
Walbom, Emilie — 5/12/22 B
Walcha, Helmut — 10/27/07 D
Walczak, Barbara — 12/1/57 B
Wald, Der — 4/9/02 A; 5/25/57 A
Walden, Stanley — 11/4/77 C
Waldman, Frederic — 12/11/74 C; 12/3/76 C
Waldteufel, Emil — 2/16/15 D

Wal, Jan van der — 7/7/64 B
Walker, Norman — 11/1/67 B
Walkure, Die — 11/21/40 E
Wall, David — 5/7/74 B
Wall, Edmund — 12/4/51 B
Wallenstein, Alfred — //39 E; //43 E; //56 E
Wallerstein, Edward — 12//38 E
Wallman, Margarete — 6/22/30 B
Walter, Bruno — 3/3/09 D; 11/20/11 C;
    6/26/12 C; 6/12/17 A; 6/16/21 E;
    3/16/33 E; 4/10/33 E; 10/11/34 C;
    2/19/38 E; 3/17/38 C; //41 E; 2/14/41 D;
    1/13/42 E; 4/16/42 C; 10/22/42 C;
    11/14/43 D; 2/3/47 E; //49 E; 2/17/52 D;
    2/17/62 D
Walton, Elizabeth — 8/4/62 B
Walton, William — 3/29/02 D; 1/24/22 C;
    6/12/23 C; 6/22/26 C; 11/19/26 C;
    9/14/28 C; 10/3/29 C; 4/26/31 B;
    10/10/31 C; 12/3/34 C; 11/6/35 C;
    5/9/37 C; 5/12/37 C; 10/6/37 C;
    3/30/38 C; 12/7/39 C; 4/3/41 C;
    4/6/43 B; 12/3/54 A; 9/25/56 C;
    1/25/57 C; 1/30/58 C; 9/2/60 C;
    3/8/63 C; 6/3/67 A; 9/8/72 C
Waltz (sessions) — 5/11/78 C
"Waltz for Evelyn Hinrichsen, A" —
    5/11/78 C
Wand of Youth, The — 12/14/07 C
War and Peace — 6/12/46 A; 3/5/53 D;
    4/1/55 A
Warburg, Edward — 1/2/34 E; 12/6/34 B
Ward, Robert — 9/13/17 D; 5/10/41 C;
    1/25/48 C; 5/17/56 A; 10/26/61 A;
    5/7/62 E; 7/3/64 A; 6/23/68 C; 4/14/78 A
Ward-Steinman, David — 9/13/66 B
Warfield, William — 1/22/20 D; 3/19/50 D
Warlock, Peter — 2/25/30 B; 12/17/30 D
War Memorial Opera House (San Francisco) —
    5/24/36 D; 8/1/49 E
Warner Brothers — //30 E; 7/27/37 E
War of the Worlds — 12/19/68 A
Warren, Leonard — 4/21/11 D; 1/13/39 D;
    2/20/42 A; 3/4/60 D
War Requiem — 5/30/62 C
Warsaw Autumn Festival — 10/10/56 E
Warsaw Concerto — 11/15/77 D
Warsaw Conservatory — 4/5/35 D
Warsaw Philharmonic Orchestra — 3/26/09 C;
    10/6/33 C
War Scenes — 11/5/69 C
Washington National Orchestra — 3/28/72 C
Wasps, The — 11/26/09 C; 7/23/12 C
Watanabe, Akeo — //56 E
Watermill — 2/3/72 B
Water Music (Cage) — 5/2/52 C
Water Study (Humphrey) — 10/28/28 B
Watts, Andre — 6/20/46 D; 1/15/63 D
Watts, Heather — 1/19/78 B
Watts, Jonathan — 12/1/57 B; 11/16/60 B;
    11/22/60 B
Wa-Wan Press, The — 12//01 E; //12 E
Way of Jesus, The — 2/23/75 C
Way of the Conductor, The (book) — 7/21/79 D
Wayward, The — 4/22/44 C
Weber, Ben — 7/23/16 D; 1/15/50 B;
    10/28/52 C; 11/13/52 C; 5/9/79 D
Weber, Carl Maria von — 4/19/11 B
Weber, Margrit — 1/31/59 C; 1/10/60 C
Webern, Anton — 6/20/06 E; 11/7/07 C;
    11/4/08 C; 2/8/10 C; 4/24/11 C;
    3/31/13 C; 2/2/19 C; 6/6/19 C;
    7/19/24 C; 7/20/24 C; 10/9/24 C;
    12/2/24 C; 6/22/26 C; 11/19/26 C;
    4/10/27 C; 1/16/28 C; 2/16/28 C;
    1/27/29 C; 12/18/29 C; 4/13/31 C;
    9/4/35 C; 1/14/36 E; 4/19/36 C;
    1/14/37 E; 10/26/37 C; 6/17/38 C;
    9/22/38 C; 2/10/40 C; 3/3/43 C;

12/5/43 C; 9/15/45 D; 7/12/46 C;
    6/23/50 C; 8/5/51 C; 3/16/52 C;
    1/13/54 E; 2/8/54 C; 12/2/58 C;
    5/14/59 B; 5/25/62 C; 5/26/62 C;
    5/27/62 C; 2/8/63 C; 4/11/64 C;
    11/7/65 B; 7/22/66 C; 10/29/66 C;
    10/30/66 C; 8/2/68 C; 1/13/69 C;
    6/3/70 C; 3/16/72 C; 2/16/78 C;
    2/17/78 C
Webern, Anton von — *see* Webern, Anton
Webern Festival, International — 5/25/62 C;
    5/26/62 C; 5/27/62 C; 10/29/66 C;
    8/1/68 C; 8/2/68 C
Webster, Beveridge — 5/30/08 D
Webster, David — 7/3/03 D; 5/11/71 D
We Come to the River — 7/12/76 A
Wedding Bouquet, A — 4/27/37 B
Weede, Robert — 3/31/49 A
Weed, Marion — 1/22/07 A
Wehmut — 10/29/66 C
Weidman, Charles — 3/31/29 B; 2/4/31 B;
    1/5/32 B; 2/23/35 B; 8/6/38 B;
    7/11/47 B; 7/15/75 D
Weidt, Lucie — 10/10/19 A
Weiland, F.C. — //79 E
Weil, Greta — 2/17/52 A
Weill, Hermann — 12/9/13 A
Weill, Kurt — 3/2/00 D; 2/6/26 C; 3/27/26 A;
    3/2/27 A; 7/17/27 A; 2/18/28 A;
    8/3/28 A; 5/7/29 E; 7/28/29 C; 3/9/30 A;
    6/30/30 A; 10/20/30 E; 3/10/32 A;
    3/21/33 E; 10/11/34 C; 3/1/36 E;
    11/19/36 A; 6/15/38 B; 2/4/40 C;
    1/23/41 A; 10/7/43 A; 1/9/47 A;
    7/15/48 A; 10/30/49 A; 4/3/50 D;
    6/14/52 A; 5/17/74 C; 3/7/77 C
Wein, Der — 6/4/30 C
Weinberg, Chester — 10/24/73 B
Weinberger, Jaromir — 4/27/27 A;
    10/17/41 C; 8/8/67 D
Weingartner, Felix — //03 E; 2/10/05 D;
    1/17/06 D; 5/17/14 A; 2/23/16 A;
    2/26/35 C; 5/7/42 D; 11/28/47 E
Weisburg, Arthur — 3/21/76 C
Weisgall, Hugo — 10/13/12 D; 2/11/52 A;
    8/9/52 A; 4/26/59 A; 2/17/61 A;
    2/17/64 A; 10/9/68 A; 4/22/76 A;
    1/23/78 C
Weismann, Julius — 11/1/34 E
Weiss, Peter — 10/18/65 C
Weiss, Robert — 6/18/72 B; 1/12/78 B
Weitz, George L. — 12/9/56 D
Welitsch, Ljuba — 7/10/13 D; 6/11/44 E;
    9/20/47 D; 2/4/49 D
Wellesz, Egon — 5/15/21 A; 9/2/28 A;
    6/20/31 A; 2/19/38 C; 12/5/51 A;
    1/19/62 C; 11/20/70 C; 11/29/72 C;
    11/9/74 D
Wells, Bruce — 6/25/72 B
Welsh National Opera — 4//46 E; 3/26/74 A
Wenzel, Leopold — 3/18/01 B
Werfel, Franz — 11/16/26 E
Wernick, Richard — 7/19/76 C; 4/18/77 E;
    11/1/77 C; 1/13/78 C
Weschler, Anita — 8/11/50 B
Westdeutscher Rundfunk — 5/30/56 C;
    5/20/78 C
Westergaard, Peter — 5/28/31 D; 3/21/66 A
Westerik, Co — 7/7/64 B
Western Electric — //28 E
Western Paradise — 10/12/76 C
Western Suite — 11/24/45 C
Western Symphony — 2/27/55 B
West German Radio Orchestra — 1/13/69 C
West, Harry — 12/29/03 E
Westhreen, P.A. von — 7/7/20 A
Westminster Records — 1//49 E
West Point Suite — 5/30/52 C
Westrex — //57 E

Wetzler Symphony Orchestra — 3/21/04 C
What Men Live By — 5/20/55 A
Wheat Field at Noon — 12/7/48 C
When Johnny Comes Marching Home — 1/13/35 C
When Lilacs Last in the Dooryard Bloom'd —
    5/14/46 C
Whisper Moon — 4/27/71 C
Whitehall, Clarence — 12/8/10 A; 12/19/32 D
Whiteman, Paul — 2/12/24 C; 11/22/31 C;
    10/17/44 C
White, Miles — 4/22/48 B
White Nights — 11/3/67 A
White Peacock, The — 12/19/19 C; 4/8/20 D
White, Willard — 5/23/75 A
White Wings — 2/9/49 A
Whithorne, Emerson — 1/30/26 C; 3/13/26 C;
    7/30/26 C; 3/19/37 C; 3/25/58 D
Whitman Triptych — 10/1/79 D
Whitman, Walt — 10/12/10 C; 3/26/43 C;
    5/14/46 C; 4/9/57 C; 11/5/69 C
Whitney, Robert — 7/9/04 D; 11/2/37 E;
    3/11/53 C; 3/20/54 C; 4/21/56 C;
    3/5/58 C; 3/1/60 C; 10/7/61 C
Whittall Foundation — 12/16/35 E
Whittall, Gertrude Clarke — 12/16/35 E;
    4/18/38 E
Whittall Pavilion (Washington, D.C.) —
    4/18/38 E; 3/6/39 E
Who Cares? — 2/5/70 B
Whyte, Ian — 12/12/51 B
Widor, Charles-Marie — 12/26/05 A;
    3/22/11 C; 3/12/37 D
Wiedersheim-Paul, Annette — 9/28/63 B
Wiener, Otto — 6/23/50 C
Wiesel, Elie — 11/13/73 C
Wiesengrund, Theodor — *see* Adorno, Theodor
Wigman, Mary — 6/24/30 B; 8/6/38 B;
    7/1/50 D; 9/18/73 D
Wihtol, Joseph — 4/24/48 D
Wilbur, Richard — 10/29/56 A
Wilbye Consort of Voices — 9/14/75 C
Wild Angels of the Open Hills — 2/2/78 C
Wild, Earl — 11/26/15 D
Wilde, Patricia — 7/16/28 D; 6/12/51 B;
    2/19/52 B; 11/11/52 B; 1/19/54 B;
    2/18/54 B; 9/14/54 B; 2/27/55 B;
    3/1/55 B; 12/19/56 B; 11/21/57 B;
    12/7/61 B
Wildfires and Field Songs — 1/24/75 C
Wilfred, Thomas — 1/10/22 E
Wilhelm II, Emperor — 12/13/04 A
Wilhelm, C. — 3/18/01 B; 1/6/06 B;
    1/14/06 B
Wilkenson, Peter — 9/1/63 C
Willan, Healey — 10/8/36 C; 4/20/46 A;
    5/18/50 C; 4/2/65 A
Willcocks, David — 12/30/19 D
William Billings Overture — 2/17/44 C
Williams, Alberto — 6/17/52 D
Williams, Dudley — 8/17/62 B
Williams Mix — 10/17/54 C
Williams, Nancy — 10/11/77 C
Williamson, J.C. — 2/16/03 A
Williamson, Malcolm — 11/21/31 D;
    5/22/65 A; 1/4/66 A; 11/29/66 A;
    8/13/68 A; 10/22/69 C; 12/18/69 A;
    1/10/73 C; 7/30/74 C
Williams, Peter — 1//50 E
Williams, Pyotr — 11/21/45 B
Williams, S. — 7/27/71 B
Williams, Vera — 5/24/55 B
William Tell Variations — 3/12/69 B
Willis, Constance — 4/3/25 A
Willoughby, Robert — 7/28/68 C
Wilson, Charles — 6/16/02 B
Wilson, Robert — 7/25/76 A
Wilson, Ronald — 11/11/52 B
Windgassen, Wolfgang — 6/26/14 D;
    9/8/74 D

Windheim, Marek — 1/7/33 A
Wind in the Mountains, The — 3/17/65 B
Windows — 5/1/72 E
Winfield, Hemsley — 1/7/33 A
Wings of the Dove, The — 10/12/61 A
Winham Electronic Music Laboratory — 4/26/75 E
Winham, Godfrey — 12/11/34 D; //58 E; 4/26/75 D
Winnipeg Ballet — //38 E
Winter, Ethel — 3/4/62 B
Winter of the World, The — 5/5/74 C
Winter, Paul — 3/24/38 E
Winter Solstice — 12/16/72 C
Wir bauen eine Stadt — 6/21/30 A
Wirz-Wyss, Clara — 2/16/28 C
Wishes, Wonders, Portents, Charms — 2/12/75 C
Wish, The — 4/2/55 A
Witch of Salem, A — 12/8/26 A
Witherspoon, Herbert — 11/26/08 D; 3/14/12 A; 5/10/35 D
With My Red Fires — 12/29/58 D
Wittgenstein, Paul — 2/2/24 C; 10/16/25 C; 1/5/32 C; 1/16/42 C; 9/5/56 C; 3/3/61 D
Wittich, Marie — 12/9/05 A
Witwe des Schmetterlings, Die — 12/9/67 A
Wlach, Leopold — 4/13/31 C

W. of Babylon, The — 12/15/75 A
Woizikovsky, Leon — 4/12/17 B; 5/18/17 B; 6/5/19 B; 7/22/19 B; 6/13/23 B; 1/6/24 B; 6/20/24 B; 6/17/25 B; 12/11/25 B; 6/7/27 B; 7/16/28 B; 4/12/32 B; 4/21/32 B
Wolf — 2/17/76 C
Wolf, Albert — 10/19/35 C
Wolfe, James — 2/10/34 A
Wolff, Albert — 6/3/47 A
Wolff, Christian — 2/10/52 C; 8/31/72 C
Wolf-Ferrari, Ermanno — 2/22/00 A; 3/21/03 C; 11/27/03 A; 3/19/06 A; 12/4/09 A; 12/23/11 A; 12/4/13 A; 2/19/25 A; 4/21/27 A; 12/29/27 A; 3/5/31 A; 2/12/36 A; 7/5/43 A; 1/21/48 D
Wolf, Hugo — 2/22/03 D; 3/24/53 B
Wolpe, Stefan — 8/25/02 D; 11/1/51 C; 10/28/69 C
Wolzogen, Ernst von — 11/21/01 A
Wolzogen, Hans von — 6/2/38 D
Wood, David — 8/17/62 B
Wooden Prince, The — 5/12/17 B
Wood, George — 1/24/50 B
Wood, Henry — 10/8/07 C
Wood, Marilyn — 8/17/58 B
Wood, Sir Henry — 3/15/12 C; 9/24/12 C; 1/11/19 C; 6/16/21 E; 8/17/37 C; 8/18/38 C; 10/5/38 C; 7/28/44 E; 8/19/44 D
Woodward, J.W. — 4/15/12 E
Worcester (Massachusetts) Music Festival — 9/26/01 A; 9/29/05 C
Workers' Music Association — 11/6/49 C
Workman, Jenny — 10/1/52 B
World Art Inc. — 1/30/38 E; 2//38 E; 3//38 E
World of David Amram, The — 4/27/69 E
World's Fair Suite — 4/22/64 C
World War I — 8/1/14 E; 9/30/14 E; 2/5/15 C; 3/15/15 C; 10/23/16 B; 3/8/17 A; 3/31/17 E; 11/11/18 E; 12/26/21 E
World War II — 9/1/39 E; 5/8/45 E; 2/14/49 E
Wozzeck (Berg) — 12/14/25 A; 11/11/26 A; 11/16/26 E
Wozzeck (Gurlitt) — 4/29/72 D
WPA Orchestra — 10/19/41 C
Wullner, Franz — 9/7/02 D
Wulstan, David — 1/18/37 D
Wunder der Heliane, Das — 10/7/27 A
Wundertheater, Das — 5/7/49 A

Wuorinen, Charles — 6/9/38 D; 1/8/59 E; 5/9-10/61 E; //62 E; 2/17/64 C; 8/9/64 C; 10/27/66 C; 3/12/67 C; 10/27/68 C; 10/28/68 C; 3/2/69 C; 4/13/69 C; 11/19/69 C; 1/11/70 C; 4/28/70 C; 5/4/70 E; 12/23/70 C; 10/11/71 C; 3/20/72 C; 8/4/72 C; 1/14/73 C; 3/28/73 C; 12/6/74 C; 6/1/75 C; 12/15/75 A; 3/21/76 C; 10/2/76 C; 10/13/76 C; 1/26/78 C; 3/11/78 C; 5/11/78 C; 12/11/78 C; 12/18/78 C; 8/1/79 C
Wuppertal Opera — 9/15/73 A
Wurlitzer organ — 3/25/76 D
Wurtemburg State Opera — //61 E
Wuthering Heights — 7/16/58 A
Wyschnegradsky, Ivan — 1/25/37 C; 11/10/45 C; 9/29/79 D

— X —

Xenakis, Iannis — 5/29/22 D; 4/23/63 C; 11/6/65 D; 4/3/66 C; 6/28/66 C; 1/18/68 B; 3/13/69 C; 4/3/69 C; 6/2/69 E; 4/6/71 C; 4/26/72 C; 4/13/73 C; 5/21/74 C; 9/22/74 C; 6/29/75 B; 6/29/75 C; 1/28/76 C; 3/11/76 C; 11/19/77 C; 12/21/77 C
X-mal Rembrandt — 5/24/30 A
Xochipilli — 8/13/48 B
Xochipilli Macuilxochitl — 5/16/40 C

— Y —

Yacobson, Leonid — 10/26/30 B; 6/28/50 B; 12/27/56 B; 12/31/64 B
Yaddo Festival — 1/4/31 C; 2/19/32 C; 4/30/32 E
Yale University — 6/17/14 E; 2/22/56 E; 9/14/72 E; 9/4/73 E; 5/3/78 E
Yamada, Koscak — 5/25/45 E; 12/29/65 D
Yankee Doodle Fantasy — 4/22/44 C
Yarullin, Farid — 6/28/50 B
Yasser, Joseph — //32 E; 1/3/56 D
Yates, Peter — 10/19/53 C; //67 E; 2/25/76 D
Year in Our Land, A — 5/13/65 C
Yehu — 12/21/74 C
Yeomen of the Guard, The — 11/22/00 D
Yerma — 8/12/71 A
Yermolaev, Alexei — 2/12/54 B
Yeston, Maury — //74 E
Yogi, The — 2/9/08 B
Yordanoff, L. — 2/27/73 C
Young Concert Artists — 2/24/76 C
Young, La Monte — 10/14/35 D; 1/5/60 C; 6/5/65 C; 12/2/65 C
Young Man and Death, The — 6/25/46 B
Young People's Concerts — //58 E; 1/15/63 D
Young Person's Guide to the Orchestra (Britten) — 11/29/46 E; 6/2/53 B
Yourth, Lynda — 6/18/72 B
Youskevitch, Igor — 3/13/12 D; 2//38 E; 4/5/38 B; 5/5/38 B; 10//38 E; 5/11/39 B; 10/12/42 B; 9/27/47 B; 4/14/48 B
Ysaye, Eugene — 5/12/31 D
Y su sangre ya viene cantando — 11/5/69 C
Yuize, Shinichi — 12/31/55 C
Yun — 2/6/69 C
Yun, Isang — 9/17/17 D; 12/27/62 B; 9/25/65 A; 6/17/67 E; 12/9/67 A; 1/12/68 C; 5/4/68 C; 5/4/71 C; 4/4/73 C; 10/4/73 C; 1/22/74 C; 5/3/74 C; 11/3/74 C; 11/9/78 C
Yunovich, Sofia — 12/12/70 B
Yuriko — 5/10/46 B; 2/27/47 B; 4/22/52 B; 4/1/58 B; 4/3/58 B
Yuszkiewicz, Nina — 11/20/37 B
Yuzhina, Natalia — 5/19/08 A

Yvonne, Prinzessin von Burgund — 9/15/73 A

— Z —

Zabaleta, Nicanor — 1/7/07 D; 1/14/55 C
Zach, Max — 1/26/12 C; 2/3/21 D; 5/7/30 E
Zador, Eugen — 12/22/23 A; 3/29/28 A; 5/24/30 A; 4/18/31 A; 10/8/39 A; 12/21/74 A
Zagrosek, Lothar — 11/9/78 C
Zakharov, Rostislav — 9/28/34 B; 12/31/35 B; 11/21/45 B; 3/14/49 B
Zak, Yakov — 6/28/76 D
Zamboni, Maria — 4/25/26 A
Zandonai, Riccardo — 11/28/08 A; 10/14/11 A; 11/13/12 A; 2/19/14 A; 6/9/15 E; 7/29/19 A; 2/14/22 A; 3/7/25 A; 12/17/32 E; 2/22/33 A
Zangarini, Carlo — 12/10/10 A; 10/14/11 A; 12/23/11 A
Zapf, Anton — 5/23/79 C
Zar lasst sich Photographieren, Der — 2/18/28 A
Zaubergeige, Die — 5/20/35 A
Zaytz, Giovanni von — 12/16/14 D
Zaza — 11/10/00 A
Zdravitza — 12/21/39 C
Zeani, Virginia — 1/26/57 A
Zeffirelli, Franco — 9/16/66 A
Zehme, Albertine — 10/16/12 C
Zeiller, Ernst — 11/28/26 B
Zeisler, Fannie Bloomfield — 8/20/27 D
Zeitschrift der Internationalen Musikgesellschaft (International Musical Society) — 9/30/14 E
Zemlinsky, Alexander von — 1/22/00 A; 10/4/10 A; 12/2/10 A; 3/31/13 C; 1/30/17 A; 5/28/22 A; 10/14/33 A; 1/14/36 E; 3/15/42 D
Zenatello, Giovanni — 12/19/03 A; 2/17/04 A; //13 E; 2/11/49 D
Zenobia — 12/1/05 A
Zentrum fur Interdisziplinäre Forschung (ZIF) — 6/10/79 E
Zephyr et Flore — 4/28/25 B
Zeretelli, Prince — //32 E; 7/27/51 D
Zerrissene, Der — 9/17/64 A
Zhdanov, Yuri — 4/16/59 B
Zhukovsky, Herman — 1/16/51 A; 4/19/51 E; 4/24/51 E; 5/28/58 E
Zichy, Count Geza — 1/14/24 D
Zilbershtein, I. — 4/14/38 B
Zillig, Winfried — 6/16/61 C; 12/17/63 D
Zimbalist, Efrem — 10/27/11 D; 7/15/14 E; 1/4/70 D
Zimbalist, Mary Louise Curtis Bok — 9/30/60 C; 1/4/70 D
Zimmerl, Christl — 11/16/57 B
Zimmerman, Bernd Alois — 3/20/18 D; 1/31/68 C; 2/19/69 C
Zingari — 9/16/12 A
Zippel, Dorothee — 1/22/65 B
Zipprodt, Patricia — 6/23/72 B; 5/16/74 B
Zirato, Bruno — 11/28/72 D
Zobisch, Otto — 5/12/17 B
Zomosa, Maximilian — 9/19/67 B
Zonophone — 4/30/03 E; 7//06 E
Zorina, Vera — 10/24/33 B; 12/24/38 E; 3/11/53 C
Zoritch, George — 10/26/39 B
Zubkovskaya, Inna — 12/27/56 B; 3/23/61 B
Zuckerman, Pinchas — 7/16/48 D; 4/3/71 D
Zukofsky, Paul — 3/20/72 C; 8/4/72 C; 12/4/73 C; 3/21/75 C; 4/28/78 C
Zullig, Hans — 11/16/48 B; 7/18/49 B
Zurich International June Festival — 6/16/21 E
Zurich Opera — 6/9/61 C
Zverev, Nicholas — 5/18/17 B; 6/5/19 B; 5/15/20 B; 1/6/24 B
Zvezdoliki — 4/19/39 C

Zweig, Stefan — 6/24/35 A; 7/13/35 E;
    9/8/49 D
Zwerg, Der — 5/28/22 A
Zwingburg — 10/16/24 C
Zwolftonmusik for Orchestra with a Solo Instrument
    (Hauer) — 11/12/29 C
Zwolftonspiel-Manifest (book) — 5/19/52 E;
    9/22/59 D

ACKNOWLEDGMENTS

The New York Public Library
Picture Collection
Page: 80, 99, 113, 146, 148, 195, 204, 210, 226, 242, 273, 280, 293, 297

Music Division
The New York Public Library at Lincoln Center
Astor, Lenox, Tilden Foundations
Page: 320, 321, 344

Billy Rose Theatre Collection
The New York Public Library at Lincoln Center
Astor, Lenox, Tilden Foundations
Page: 63, 87, 104, 354

Dance Collection
The New York Public Library at Lincoln Center
Astor, Lenox, Tilden Foundations
Page: 29, 58, 76, 94 (left), 122, 141, 174, 197, 228, 229, 252, 356

Opera News
Page: 1 (bottom), 10, 11 (right), 40, 47 (bottom), 52, 67, 71, 110, 156, 170, 259, 324, 349

CTK Praha
Page: 21, 28, 41, 100, 117, 127, 171, 188 (bottom), 200, 249, 254, 389

French Cultural Services
Page: 24, 86, 153, 159, 183, 187, 233, 316, 330, 370

Austrian Press and Information Service New York
Page: 59, 163, 290, 312 (bottom), 339, 373, 385

Swedish Information Service
Page: 94 (right), 107, 133, 188 (top), 308, 424

Inter Nationes e. V., Bonn
Page: 131, 206, 214, 263, 267, 288, 332, 335, 338, 359, 375, 394, 400, 402, 404

Danish Information Office in the United States
Page: 149 (bottom), 331, 381

Consulate General of Finland, New York
Page: 265, 299, 397

Page 20: Uppsala Universitetsbibliotek

Page 22: Het Residentie-Orkest

Page 45: New York Philharmonic

Page 66, 149 (top), 391: Australian Information Service

Page 79: Baltimore Symphony Orchestra

Page 90: Konrad Cramer, Maverick Concerts

Page 167: George and Ira Gershwin Collection, Music Division, Library of Congress

Page 173, 336: Editura stiintifica si enciclopedica, Bucharest

Page 266: Marlboro Music

Page 306: Italian Government Travel Office

Page 312 (top), 396: Swiss Music Archives, Zurich

Page 318: Editio Musica Budapest

Page 321: Photo by Tony Perry, Courtesy of The Santa Fe Opera

Page 325: Institute of Sonology

Page 342: Carnegie Hall Archives

Page 343: Meadow Brook Music Festival, Oakland University

Page 358: Photo by Mike Evans, Courtesy Columbia Artists Management, Inc., New York

Page 365 (top): Sibeliusmuseum

Page 365 (bottom): Cleveland Orchestra

Page 367, 410: Sheldon Soffer Management, Inc., New York

Page 408: Boston Pops

Page 412: Spoleto Festival, U.S.A.

Page 415: Charles Wuorinen

Picture research: Judith Linn

Picture research assistant: Anita Jacobson

Photographic reproduction: Bill Lichtman, Universal Photo

Every effort has been made to locate the copyright owners of material reproduced in this book. Omissions brought to our attention will be corrected in subsequent editions.